The Handbook of Language
and Sexuality

Blackwell Handbooks in Linguistics

This outstanding multi-volume series covers all the major subdisciplines within linguistics today to offer a comprehensive survey of linguistics as a whole.
To see the full list of titles available in the series please visit www.wiley.com/go/linguistics-handbooks

The Handbook of Language, Gender, and Sexuality

Second Edition

Edited by

Susan Ehrlich, Miriam Meyerhoff, and Janet Holmes

WILEY Blackwell

Registered Offices
John Wiley & Sons, Inc., 111 River Street, Hoboken, NJ 07030, USA

Editorial Office
9600 Garsington Road, Oxford, OX4 2DQ, UK

For details of our global editorial offices, customer services, and more information about Wiley products visit us at www.wiley.com.

Wiley also publishes its books in a variety of electronic formats and by print-on-demand. Some content that appears in standard print versions of this book may not be available in other formats.

Library of Congress Catalog Number: 2013042749

Paperback: 9781119384205

Cover Image: *Under the Pergola in Naples or Under the Pergola*, 1914 (oil on canvas), Boccioni, Umberto (1882–1916) / Galleria Civica d'Arte Moderna, Milan, Italy / Bridgeman Images

Set in 10/12pt PalatinoLTStd by SPi Global, Chennai, India

10 9 8 7 6 5 4 3 2 1

For our mothers,
Bernice "Bunny" Ehrlich, Mary Meyerhoff Cresswell, and Muriel Quirk

Contents

List of Figures

List of Tables

Notes on Contributors

Enam Al-Wer is Senior Lecturer in Linguistics at the University of Essex. Her research and publications focus on variation and change, and dialect contact in modern Arabic dialects. She co-edited *Arabic in the City* (2007) and *Arabic Dialectology* (2009). She is the co-editor (with Abbas Benmamoun) of the Routledge Arabic Linguistics Series.

Frederick Attenborough is a Lecturer in Communication and Media Studies in the Department of Social Sciences at Loughborough University. His current research interests are in discourse analysis, textual ethnomethodology, and membership categorization analysis.

Bethan Benwell is Senior Lecturer in Language and Linguistics at the University of Stirling. She has published on discourses of masculinity in popular culture, and discursive approaches to reception. She is editor of *Masculinity and Men's Lifestyle Magazines* (2003) and co-author (with Elizabeth Stokoe) of *Discourse and Identity* (2006).

Niko Besnier is Professor of Cultural Anthropology at the University of Amsterdam. His last books are *Gossip and the Everyday Production of Politics* (2009), *On the Edge of the Global: Modern Anxieties in a Pacific Island Nation* (2011), and *Gender on the Edge: Transgender, Gay, and Other Pacific Islanders* (co-edited, 2013).

Mary Bucholtz is Professor of Linguistics at the University of California, Santa Barbara, where she specializes in language and identity. She is the author of *White Kids* (2011) and has edited several volumes on language, gender, and sexuality, including *Gender Articulated* (1995), *Reinventing Identities* (1999), and *Language and Woman's Place: Text and Commentaries* (1994).

Deborah Cameron is Professor of Language and Communication at the University of Oxford. Her publications on language, gender, and sexuality include *Feminism* *and Linguistic Theory* (1992), *Language and Sexuality* (with Don Kulick, 2003) *On Language and Sexual Politics* (2006), and *The Myth of Mars and Venus* (2007).

Penelope Eckert is Professor of Linguistics at Stanford University. Her ethnographic work in schools examines the role of variation in the emergence of adolescent social structure. Her work on gender has led her to focus particularly on the social meaning of variation and its role in the construction of personae.

Susan Ehrlich is Professor of Linguistics at York University, Toronto, Canada. She is the author of *Representing Rape: Language and Sexual Consent* (2001), and co-editor of *"Why Do You Ask?": The Function of Questions in Institutional Discourse* (with Alice Freed, 2010) and *Discursive Constructions of Consent in the Legal Process* (with Diana Eades and Janet Ainsworth, 2016).

Alice F. Freed is Professor Emeritus of Linguistics at Montclair State University, New Jersey. Her research interests include language and gender, discourse analysis, and sociolinguistics. She is author of *The Semantics of English Aspectual Complementation* (1979) and co-editor of *Rethinking Language and Gender Research: Theory and Practice* (with Victoria Bergvall and Janet Bing, 1996) and *"Why Do You Ask?" The Function of Questions in Institutional Discourse* (with Susan Ehrlich, 2010). She has published works in journals such as *Language in Society* and the *Journal of Pragmatics*.

Marjorie Harness Goodwin is Professor of Anthropology at the University of California, Los Angeles. Her work investigates how talk is used to build social organization within face-to-face interaction in the social worlds of children and families. Her monographs include *He-Said-She Said: Talk as Social Organization among Black Children* (1990) and *The Hidden Life of Girls: Games of Stance, Status, and Exclusion* (2006), studies that combine the methodologies of long-term ethnography with conversation analysis.

Kira Hall is a linguistic anthropologist at the University of Colorado. Her publications focus on issues of language and identity, particularly as they emerge within hierarchies of gender, sexuality, and socioeconomic class in a globalizing India. Significant texts include *Gender Articulated* (with Mary Bucholtz, 1995), *Queerly Phrased* (with Anna Livia, 1997), and a set of articles with Mary Bucholtz on the theorization of identity in sociocultural linguistics.

Susan C. Herring is Professor of Information Science and Linguistics at Indiana University Bloomington. She was one of the first scholars to apply linguistic methods of analysis to computer-mediated communication (CMC), beginning with a focus on gender issues. She later consolidated those methods into the computer-mediated discourse analysis approach, which she has applied to analyze structural, pragmatic, interactional, and social phenomena in digital discourse. Her current interests include multilingual and multimodal (especially, convergent media) CMC and telepresence robotics.

Janet Holmes is Emeritus Professor in Linguistics at Victoria University of Wellington, New Zealand and Associate Director of the Wellington Language in the Workplace project. She is the author of *Gendered Talk at Work* (Blackwell, 2006), *An Introduction to Sociolinguistics*, Fourth edition (Pearson, 2013) and co-editor (with Kirk Hazen) of *Research Methods in Sociolinguistics* (Wiley Blackwell, 2014).

Sakiko Kajino is a PhD candidate at the Linguistics Department of Georgetown University. Her dissertation focuses on sociophonetics and regional variation in female Japanese speech across Tokyo, Kyoto, and Osaka in the domains of fricatives, intonation, and voice quality.

Agnieszka Kiełkiewicz-Janowiak is Associate Professor at the Faculty of English, Adam Mickiewicz University in Poznań, Poland. She has published and lectured on social dialectology, historical sociolinguistics, discourse analysis, as well as language and gender issues. Her current research interests focus on age as a social construct and a sociolinguistic variable.

Celia Kitzinger is Professor of Conversation Analysis, Gender and Sexuality in the Department of Sociology at the University of York, UK. Her current research focuses on interactions around childbirth and end-of-life decision-making.

Don Kulick is the author of *Travesti: Sex, Gender and Culture among Brazilian Transgendered Prostitutes* (1998), and the co-author, with Deborah Cameron, of *Language and Sexuality* (2003). His latest book, with Jens Rydström, is *Excessibility Guidelines: Sex, Disability and the Ethics of Engagement* (forthcoming).

Amy Kyratzis is Professor of Education at the Gevirtz Graduate School of Education, University of California, Santa Barbara. She uses ethnography and talk-in-interaction to study children's peer language socialization. Her current research examines preschoolers' bilingual practices in play negotiations. She guest-edited "Children Socializing Children: Practices for Organizing the Social and Moral Order among Peers" (*Research on Language and Social Interaction*, 2007, with M. H. Goodwin), and "Heteroglossia and Language Ideologies in Children's Peer Play Interactions" (*Pragmatics*, 2010, with J. F. Reynolds and A.-C. Evaldsson).

Michelle M. Lazar is Associate Professor, Assistant Dean for Research, and Coordinator of the Gender Studies Minor Programme in the Faculty of Arts and Social Sciences, National University of Singapore. She is founding editor of the Routledge Critical Studies in Discourse book series, and is presently the Vice-President/President-Elect of the International Gender and Language Association. Her research includes critical feminist analyses of discourses of gender relations and identities and postfeminism.

Anna Livia (1955–2007), linguist of French literature and lesbian feminist writer, is best known in the field of language and gender for her pioneering work in queer linguistics. She produced a number of significant publications on language and sexuality over the course of her career, among them *Queerly Phrased* (with Kira Hall, 1997) and *Pronoun Envy: Literary Uses of Linguistic Gender* (2001).

Sally McConnell-Ginet is Professor Emerita of Linguistics at Cornell University, where she also directed Women's Studies (now Feminist, Gender, and Sexuality Studies). She came to linguistics from mathematics and philosophy and continues research on meaning as connected to language structure and as integral to social life and conflict.

Bonnie McElhinny is Director of the Women and Gender Studies Institute, and Associate Professor of Anthropology and Women and Gender Studies at the University of Toronto. She is founding co-editor of *Gender and Language*. Recent publications include *Words, Worlds, Material Girls: Language and Gender in a Global Economy* and *Filipinos in Canada* (2008), as well as articles in *American Anthropologist*, *Philippine Studies*, and the *Annual Review of Anthropology*.

Barbra A. Meek is Associate Professor of Anthropology and Linguistics at the University of Michigan. Her current research and teaching focus on representations and performances of linguistic "otherness," in addition to ongoing work on language endangerment and revitalization.

Julia Menard-Warwick is Associate Professor of Linguistics at University of California, Davis. She is interested in second-language learning, multilingual development, and narrative analysis. Her book *Gendered Identities and Immigrant Language Learning* was published in 2009, and she is working on another book about English teaching in California and Chile.

Miriam Meyerhoff is Professor of Linguistics at Victoria University of Wellington, New Zealand. She is co-editor of *Social Lives in Language: Sociolinguistics and multilingual speech communities* (with Naomi Nagy, 2008), *Doing Sociolinguistics* (with Erik Schleef and Laurel Mackenzie, 2015), *Bequia Talk* (with James A. Walker, 2013), *The Sociolinguistics Reader* (with Erik Schleef, 2010) and is the author of *Introducing Sociolinguistics, Second Edition* (2011).

Tommaso M. Milani is Associate Professor of Linguistics at the University of the Witwatersrand, Johannesburg, His areas of research encompass language politics, media discourse, multimodality, and language gender and sexuality. His publications include articles in *Gender and Language*, *Journal of Sociolinguistics*, *Journal of Language and Politics*, and *Language in Society*.

Luiz Paulo Moita-Lopes is Full Professor of Applied Linguistics at the Universidade Federal do Rio de Janeiro and a Researcher of the Brazilian Research Council.

He holds a PhD from the University of London. His most recent book is *Português no Século XXI: Cenário Geopolítico e Sociolinguístico* (Portuguese in the 21st Century: Geopolitical and Sociolinguistic Scenario, 2013).

Miki Mori is a PhD candidate in linguistics at the University of California, Davis. Her research focuses on second-language academic writing development as it relates to Bakhtinian theory of dialogic voicing, intertextuality, plagiarism, and patchwriting. She has taught English as a second language for several years at university and college level.

Momoko Nakamura is Professor at Kanto Gakuin University. Her recent work in English is "Women's and Men's Languages As Heterosexual Resource" in *Femininity, Feminism and Gendered Discourse* (2010). Her recent books are *Jendaa de manabu gengogaku* (Linguistics and Gender, 2010) and *Onna kotoba to Nihongo* (Women's Language and Japanese, 2012).

Ana Cristina Ostermann is Full Professor of Applied Linguistics at the Universidade do Vale do Rio dos Sinos and a Researcher of the Brazilian Research Council. She holds a PhD from the University of Michigan. Her most recent book is *Humanização, Gênero, Poder: Contribuições dos Estudos de Fala-em-Interação para a Atenção à Saúde* (Humanization, Gender, Power: Contributions of Interactional Studies to Healthcare, 2013).

Joanna Pawelczyk is Associate Professor of sociolinguistics at the Faculty of English at Adam Mickiewicz University in Poznań, Poland. Her research interests include language and gender, discourses of psychotherapy and loss, and computer-mediated communication. She has published in a range of international journals and in edited collections on gender and therapeutic discourse.

Susan U. Philips is Professor Emerita of Anthropology at the University of Arizona. She is a linguistic anthropologist and is the author of *The Invisible Culture* (1983) and *Ideology in the Language of Judges* (1998), and the co-editor of *Language, Gender and Sex in Comparative Perspective* (1987). Her current research is on Tongan lexical honorifics and honorification.

Robert J. Podesva is Assistant Professor of Linguistics at Stanford University. His research examines the social and interactional significance of phonetic variation, particularly in the domain of voice quality. He has co-edited *Research Methods in Linguistics* (2013), *Language and Sexuality* (2002), and a special issue of *American Speech* on "Sociophonetics and Sexuality" (2011).

Robin Queen is Associate Professor of Linguistics, Germanic Languages and Literatures, and English Language and Literatures and an Arthur F. Thurnau Professor at the University of Michigan. Her research focuses on language and sexuality, language contact, language in the mass media, and general sociolinguistics.

Sharon Stoerger is Director of the Information, Technology, and Informatics program at Rutgers University. Her research interests lie at the intersection of communication, gender, and emerging technologies. This includes the ways in which technology impacts the educational experience. Much of this work is viewed through a social informatics lens.

Elizabeth Stokoe is Professor of Social Interaction in the Department of Social Sciences at Loughborough University. Her current research interests are in conversation analysis, membership categorization, and social interaction in various ordinary and institutional settings. She is currently co-editor of *Gender and Language*.

Mary Talbot has published widely on language and gender, particularly in relation to media, consumerism, and popular culture. Recent books include *Language and Gender* (2010) and her first graphic novel, *Dotter of Her Father's Eyes* (with Bryan Talbot, 2012). She is now a freelance writer and consultant.

Deborah Tannen is University Professor and Professor of Linguistics at Georgetown University. Her books include *Talking Voices* (1989), *Conversational Style* (1984), *You Just Don't Understand* (1990), *Talking from 9 to 5* (1972), *You're Wearing That?* (2006), and *You were Always Mom's Favorite!* (2009). Her website is at www.deborahtannen.com.

Sara Trechter is a Professor of Linguistics at California State University, Chico. Her work on language, gender, and ethnicity has focused on gender in Siouan languages and the discourse construction of whiteness. She currently works with the last fluent speaker of the Nu'eta language to produce accessible, culturally relevant linguistic description.

Sue Wilkinson is Professor of Feminist and Health Studies in the Department of Social Sciences at Loughborough University. Her current research focuses on interactions on telephone helplines, and she is writing a textbook on conversation analysis.

Serena Williams is a PhD candidate in linguistics at the University of California, Davis, with research interests in language and gender, and the analysis of interaction and discourse in Spanish and English. She has taught Spanish and English as a second language at university level.

Acknowledgments

We have benefited greatly from the practical and moral support of many people at various stages in the production of this book. We would like to thank the following people: Chie Adachi, Paul Baker, Andrew Beach, Debbie Cameron, Agata Daleszynska, Margaret Field, Atiqa Hachimi, Kira Hall, Helga Kotthoff, Don Kulick, Ronald Beline Mendes, Sam Meyerhoff, Tommaso Milani, Liz Morrish, Louise Mullany, Amy Paugh, Robin Queen, Lauren Squires, Jane Stuart-Smith, Jane Sunderland, Shonna Trinch, and Ann Weatherall.

We are grateful to Julia Kirk and Danielle Descoteaux, from Wiley-Blackwell, for their help and support throughout the lengthy process of producing this *Handbook*. And we thank our careful and meticulous copy-editor, Jacqueline Harvey, and our outstanding freelance project manager, Nik Prowse. Special thanks go to our amazing editorial assistant, Anna Romanov.

Introduction
Language, Gender, and Sexuality

SUSAN EHRLICH AND MIRIAM MEYERHOFF

1. Introduction

The opportunity to publish a second edition of any book is always a welcome one. In this case, it is perhaps particularly so, because the 10 years between the appearance of the first edition of *The Handbook of Language and Gender* (HLG) and this second edition have seen significant shifts in the study of gender and language, including increased attention to the relationship between gender and sexuality. Thus, the most obvious difference between this edition and the first is its title, *The Handbook of Language, Gender, and Sexuality* (HLGS), through which we have attempted to highlight the ongoing importance of sexuality to the field and the close connections between gender and sexuality. A concern with questions of sexuality is, of course, not the only change the field has witnessed in the last 10 years; the field has also been enriched by, among other things, connections forged with research on globalization and on masculinities, topics that both receive greater prominence in this edition of the *Handbook*.

Another key difference between the two editions of this *Handbook* lies in our better understanding of how readers want to use *HLG* as a resource. The purpose of a handbook in any field is to outline the key topics, themes, debates, and methods that give life to that field of study. When we elicited feedback on the first edition we found, somewhat to our surprise, that the first edition of *HLG* had been adopted quite widely as a teaching text. This was not the primary purpose we had imagined a handbook might serve when we commissioned chapters for the first edition, and understanding this has informed some of our decisions as we revised the book for a second edition. In particular, we felt that a number of the chapters in the first edition read a lot like independent research articles – they offered tremendous analytical depth, but often presupposed a degree of familiarity with language and gender research (and with some of the debates that animated the field at that time) that students might not have. For this reason, not every chapter from the first

The Handbook of Language, Gender, and Sexuality, Second Edition.
Edited by Susan Ehrlich, Miriam Meyerhoff, and Janet Holmes.
© 2014 John Wiley & Sons, Inc. Published 2017 by John Wiley & Sons, Inc.

edition seemed to directly serve the central purpose of the second edition. For the *HLGS*, we have encouraged authors to emphasize comprehensive coverage of their topics rather than develop complex, in-depth arguments about very specific sets of data. We have commissioned new chapters with these goals in mind and have also asked many of the authors from the first edition to update their chapters in ways that address a broader readership, one that includes not only mature scholars but also students.

The field of language and gender is much better served by textbooks now than in 2003 when *HLG* was published. Anyone teaching a course on language and gender today can choose from introductory works suited to beginning students or a general readership (e.g., Cameron 2007; Julé 2008), to more advanced texts (e.g., Cameron and Kulick 2003; 2006; J. Coates 2004; J. Coates and Pichler 2011; Eckert and McConnell-Ginet 2003; 2013; Lakoff 2004; Litosseliti 2006; Mills and Mullany 2011; Sunderland 2004; 2006; Talbot 2010; Weatherall 2002). Other books focus more explicitly on methods used when studying language and gender (e.g., Lazar 2005; Speer 2005; Harrington et al. 2008; Pichler and Eppler 2009; Speer and Stokoe 2011). In light of this, one might ask what a new edition of *HLG* has to offer. We believe there is also a need for a comprehensive, authoritative, and multivocal perspective on the state of the art, and that this version of the *Handbook* offers readers a uniquely broad experience of developments in the field of language, gender, and sexuality. Its breadth lies not only in the diverse list of contributing authors, but also in the approaches they draw on in the service of each chapter.

Knowing the *Handbook* might be used for teaching purposes led us to make other changes as well. There were some specific topics that we felt ought to be covered if someone were relying on the *HLGS* as the primary text in an undergraduate or graduate course on language and gender. The main change in this respect was the addition of a section on research methods used in language, gender, and sexuality studies. We are confident that these chapters, written by some of the leading scholars and teachers of these methods (Besnier and Philips (6), Lazar (9), Meyerhoff (4), Podesva and Kajino (5), Stokoe and Attenborough (8), Wilkinson and Kitzinger (7)) will be of value for several different kinds of readers. Naturally, we had in mind our own students who are often looking for ideas on what kinds of data to use, what kinds of questions can be explored most readily with different kinds of data, and what those explorations might look like. However, in addition to novices looking for guidance and practical advice, we hope readers who already have a clear idea about the method(s) they would like to use with a given data set will find reading across these chapters rewarding. Our sense is that it affords the reader an excellent comparative perspective on the kinds of questions asked (and answered) by different methods.

In sum, in attempting to respond to new developments in the field and to the fact that the *Handbook* could be useful for teaching, we have commissioned new chapters and asked some authors to revise and update their chapters from the first edition (and many have done so in a substantial way).[1] Thus, not only have we introduced a new section on methods, but we have also, in the area of language and sexuality, included a chapter devoted exclusively to language and sexual

African American men. (See Tannen, Chapter 25, for a different view on the separate worlds hypothesis.)

Investigations of the intersection of gender and ethnicity have also raised important theoretical and methodological questions. Trechter (Chapter 17) considers research that examines the way gender and ethnicity/race are mutually constituted in linguistic practice, although cautioning readers about the circularity that can plague such investigations: they may define the linguistic practices of a particular, predefined, community while also maintaining that the community is defined by its linguistic practice. At the same time, Trechter cites scholars who see a risk in focusing on the "performance" of identities, arguing that such a focus prematurely erases the racial and ethnic categories (i.e., identity categories) necessary for political mobilization, what McElhinny and Holmes have called strategic essentialism (Holmes 2007; McElhinny 1996). Trechter's comments regarding the tensions that have accompanied the "performative turn" in language and gender studies are echoed in other chapters in this volume.

Milani (Chapter 13) argues that in spite of the major epistemological shift in the field of language and gender triggered by Butler and other poststructuralist theorists, "the largest portion of scholarship on language and masculinities has focused on male participants (and, not unsurprisingly, research on femininities on females)." Stokoe and Attenborough (Chapter 8) and Benwell (Chapter 12) make a similar point: they argue that much work claiming to adopt an anti-essentialist, constructivist understanding of gender tends to precategorize groups of people as women and men and then investigates how women "do femininity" and how men "do masculinity." For Stokoe and Attenborough, then, such research raises methodological questions as how best to study gender in nonessentialist ways, that is, without assuming that masculinity and femininity are directly linked (Ochs 1992) to male and female subjects, respectively. (We return to this issue below.) Milani makes a somewhat different argument in the context of his chapter on the queering of masculinities: he maintains that we must engage in a more careful mapping of how "women … as well as transgendered and intersex individuals also do masculinities in their daily lives," that is, what he terms, the queering of "epistemological normality."

2.2   Queer linguistics

As Bucholtz (Chapter 1) notes, a crucial dimension of Butler's notion of performativity lies in the possibility of "disrupting the normative alignment of sex assignment, gender identity, and sexual identity" through practices that make visible its constructed nature. Within sociolinguistics and linguistic anthropology, this possibility provided the impetus for a series of studies in the 1990s that focused on what McElhinny (Chapter 2) calls sex/gender "transgressions" – a focus on language users who fell outside of hegemonic norms of sex, gender, and sexuality (e.g., Barrett 1999; Gaudio 1997; Hall 1997; Hall and O'Donovan 1996; Kulick 1998; Livia and Hall 1997). Indeed, Hall (Chapter 11) argues that the study of non-normative gender identity (what she refers to as "exceptional speakers"), while having a marginal status in the field in its early stages, is foundational to current thinking about language, gender, and sexuality. More recently, researchers have looked at linguistic performances of heterosexuality (Cameron 2005a; Eckert, Chapter 27 in this volume; Kiesling 2002) as a way of understanding how heterosexuality is normalized. That is, in the same way that hegemonic masculinity has been interrogated within the field of language and gender (Kiesling 2002; 2005; 2011; Milani 2011; Benwell, Chapter 12 in this volume), so heterosexuality has become the object of critical investigations that attempt to deconstruct the processes through which it is rendered unmarked (Kitzinger 2005; Milani, Chapter 13 in this volume). In fact, much of this work is devoted to both projects simultaneously given the close connections between hegemonic masculinity and heterosexuality. (See Trechter, Chapter 17, for a similar unpacking of whiteness as the unmarked racial category.)

This critical engagement with heterosexuality and heteronormativity is, of course, a hallmark of queer theory, a theory which "interrogates heterosexuality by dismissing its claims to naturalness" (Cameron and Kulick 2003, 55). Milani (Chapter 13) uses queer theory to cast a critical light on heterosexual masculinities, but in the process notes that queer theory cannot be restricted to critiquing the production and perpetuation of heteronormativity but should also make visible "the ways in which certain forms of same-sex desire can *themselves* become normalized and legitimized over time." Here, Milani, like other queer theorists, expresses skepticism about a politics that relies on sexual identities as a mechanism for social change.

The tension Milani describes between a politics reliant on identity categories and one suspicious of such categories as the basis for social change has also played out, in a sometimes heated way, in the academic arena of queer linguistics. Indeed, Queen (Chapter 10) remarks that one of the central debates in queer linguistics has concerned the issue of identity. Kulick (Chapter 3), who initiated this debate with the publication of the 2000 article, "Gay and Lesbian Language," critiques early work on language and sexuality, arguing that much of it confused symbolic resources with actual linguistic practices in much the same way that early work in language and gender did. As Kulick (this volume) says, this confounding of the symbolic and the actual fails to recognize that the linguistic resources "understood to compose a phenomenon like 'women's language' (or 'gay language') are available to any speaker to use (and any hearer to interpret) regardless of whatever the speaker may think about her or his sexuality, gender or anything else." Kulick goes on to propose that language and sexuality scholars move beyond the study of sexual identities in order to examine the relationship between language and desire.

Queen (Chapter 10) provides a detailed and insightful discussion of Kulick's proposals, and the desire–identity debate more generally. According to Queen, critics of Kulick's proposal, and of the more extended proposal put forward in Cameron and Kulick (2003), maintain that an exclusive focus on desire downplays the fact that sexuality is socially mediated and, consequently, that sexual desires and practices are often linked to subject positions (and object positions) that are expressed as social categories. In spite of such critiques, recent work has investigated both the linguistic details of desire (as does Kulick's chapter (3) in this volume) and of sexual identities and identifications, and Queen ultimately concludes that "our understandings of language and sexualities are more likely to advance by taking seriously a focus on both social identification and eroticism." Bucholtz (Chapter 1) also reviews research from a queer perspective that focuses both on lesbian, gay, bisexual, and transgender (LGBT) identities and on the linguistic dimensions of erotic practices.

2.3   Agency and constraints

As noted above, the theorizing of gender as performative has encouraged language and gender researchers (since the 1990s) to focus on the agency and creativity of social actors in the constitution of gender. At the same time, some scholars have argued that there has been much less emphasis placed on another aspect of Butler's framework – the "highly rigid regulatory frame" (Butler 1990, 32) within which gendered identities are produced (see McElhinny, Chapter 2, for discussion). This emphasis on the performative aspect of Butler's work, rather than on her discussions of the regulatory norms that define and police normative constructions of gender, may arise because, as Cameron (1997) suggests, philosophical accounts of Butler's "rigid regulatory frame" have often been very abstract. (See, however, Mills and Mullany 2011 for a more specific articulation of the "rigid regulatory frame" from Butler's later work.) Nonetheless, regulatory norms make certain performances of gender "a 'natural' kind of being" (Butler 1990, 32) while others are rendered inappropriate or unintelligible and, as Holmes and Meyerhoff (2003) and McElhinny (Chapter 2) point out, subject to social and physical sanctions and penalties, such as gay bashing, the "fixing" of intersexed infants, and so on. In other words, the challenging of dominant gender norms, although useful in making visible the constructed nature of such norms, can have devastating social costs for those who transgress; as Cameron (Chapter 14) says, "the price of non-normality can be high." Cameron makes these comments in the context of her discussion of linguistic ideologies that endow certain speech styles with gendered meanings. Such ideologies, she argues, "shape our understanding of what is 'normal'" and in this sense have a kind of regulatory force. Cameron provides evidence that individuals draw upon these cultural notions of "women's language" and "men's language" in producing themselves as gendered subjects because to do otherwise would be to risk the social costs associated with nonconformity. In a similar way, Nakamura (Chapter 19) suggests that Japanese women's language, while an ideological-historical category constructed by metalinguistic discourses such as etiquette books and fictional conversations, nevertheless restricts the speech of contemporary Japanese women. (See Inoue 2006 for a somewhat different perspective.) In fact, Nakamura believes that one of the advantages of her "historical discourse approach" is that it allows researchers to ask how language ideologies "simultaneously enable and restrict" actual linguistic practices.

The constraints that ideological representations can impose on gendered performances is also a theme taken up in McConnell-Ginet's chapter (16) for this volume.

According to McConnell-Ginet, ideologies of gender and sexuality load linguistic expressions with "conceptual baggage" in ways that can limit communicative and semantic effectiveness. For example, gendered ideologies can be important to speakers' success in performing certain kinds of illocutionary acts: A woman may say "no" to a man's sexual advances, but ideologies about women's passive, acquiescing sexualities or women "playing hard to get" can result in explicit refusals being understood, perhaps strategically on the part of many men, as illocutionary acts of permission. And, when such disputes over meaning enter courtrooms, as they sometimes do, Ehrlich's chapter (23) shows that similar ideologies circulate in the public discourse of rape trials, transforming women's denials into expressions of consent.

The role of ideologies in policing and constraining gendered practices and identities is also evident in institutions, as the preceding reference to courtrooms indicates. Gal (1991) argues that gender is an organizing principle of institutions such that gendered ideologies and norms can form the lens through which practices and behavior are evaluated and allocated resources (see also McElhinny and Philips, Chapters 2 and 15, respectively). As Holmes and Meyerhoff (2003) put it, "No matter what we [as researchers] say about the inadequacy and invidiousness of essentialized, dichotomous conceptions of gender … in everyday life it really is often the case that gender is 'essential' … that gender as a social category *matters*" (2003, 9; emphasis original). Holmes (Chapter 22), for example, discusses the masculine conception of leadership that characterizes many workplaces. While Holmes reports that effective leaders, both men and women, are generally flexible in their use of discursive styles, female managers are more likely than male managers to be negatively evaluated for this flexibility, in particular, for deploying ways of speaking that are symbolically associated with masculinity. Talbot's chapter (31) on popular culture also considers the fate of women who enter masculine domains. As Talbot points out, women have made major advances in professional media environments, yet her analysis of a female sportscaster "routinely positioned as the butt of humor" shows that the discursive spaces women can "legitimately" occupy on air are restricted. Holmes' and Talbot's chapters, then, remind us of the double bind experienced by many women who occupy powerful positions in traditionally masculine domains (e.g., politics) and are a further illustration of the potential costs associated with the performance of non-normative gendered identities.

Menard-Warwick, Mori, and Williams (Chapter 24) also elucidate the extent to which an institution's norms of evaluation and assessment can be gendered. Women may be positioned as female subjects in classrooms or in learning situations outside of the classroom, yet the standards used to evaluate their learning outcomes are based on the experiences of boys and men. In a similar way, Ehrlich's chapter (23) shows how masculine norms operate in the evaluation of women's attempts to resist perpetrators of sexual assault. Specifically, the unequal power relations that often characterize situations of sexual violence are sidelined in rape trials when women survivors are sanctioned for not expressing their resistance in ways that male norms consider sufficiently forceful and aggressive. As L. Coates,

Bavelas, and Gibson (1994, 195) have pointed out, the conception of resistance in play here is based on male-to-male combat, where continued fighting may be appropriate, rather than on a context of asymmetry, where women's physical resistance may only intensify the violence of their perpetrators. Within the family, another social institution, Tannen (Chapter 25) points to the complex relationship between power (negotiations along the hierarchy–equality axis) and connection (negotiations along the closeness–distance axis), focusing in particular on the important contribution of the mother in negotiating gender identities and roles within the family.

The ways in which women may be disadvantaged by the gendered ideologies of institutions is no doubt connected to another theme taken up by a number of chapters in this volume – the historical barriers faced by women in gaining access to public domains (see Al-Wer, Meek, Philips, Chapters 20, 28, and 15, respectively, and also Baxter 2006). As Philips (Chapter 15) points out, a common pattern in cultures of the world has been one in which highly valued public speech genres are symbolically and materially associated with masculinity or certain versions of masculinity. Meek (Chapter 28) argues that women tend to be the primary vector for the transmission of endangered languages and are actively involved in language revitalization. Yet, because this transmission occurs primarily in the private sphere (e.g., homes and preschool immersion programs), women are not positioned as "the predominant authorities on the processes of language revitalization." Rather, it is men, associated with highly visible public institutions and bureaucratic attempts to revive endangered languages, who are granted this authority.

That the regulatory force of institutions – or of ideologies embedded in institutions – can be resisted in at least some contexts is a theme developed by Talbot in her chapter (31) on language, gender, and popular culture. As she points out, a Gramscian perspective on popular culture and gender holds that mediated popular cultural forms are involved in securing consent to dominant conceptualizations of gender and sexuality. In contrast to face-to-face interaction, media communication is relatively one-sided and thus has the power to unilaterally construct implied readers or viewers – imaginary addressees who have particular beliefs, values, and interests, that is, particular identities. So, for instance, Talbot's analysis of a feature article in a young women's magazine reveals that the kind of feminine identity constructed for readers is one based on consumption and relationships with men – an identity that Talbot characterizes as "unsisterly" (Talbot 1995). But what is it that determines whether readers will use these kinds of subject positions in constructing their own identities? Reception studies have shown that readers and viewers do not necessarily consume texts in straightforward or predictable ways. Thus, while Talbot shows that young women's magazines reinforce conventional norms of femininity in order to encourage the consumption of commodities (e.g., cosmetics), she also cites research from Benwell (2005; see also Benwell, Chapter 12 in this volume) and from her own study (Chapter 31 in this volume) of women watching talk shows that attests to the complexity of consumers' practices with respect to media "texts."

2.4   *Determining when gender is relevant*

Central to an ongoing methodological debate within discourse analysis is the question of whose categories – analysts' or participants' – should come to inform the analysis of data. Gender has figured prominently in these debates as a result of a 1997 *Discourse & Society* article (that provoked a series of other articles, rebuttals, and counter-rebuttals) in which Emmanuel Schegloff used the construct of gender to claim that what counts as an explanatory category in a given interaction is that which *participants* understand to be relevant. In making this argument, Schegloff (1997, 167) seemed to be targeting proponents of critical discourse analysis (CDA) whom he claims display a kind of "theoretical imperialism" because they allow their own political preoccupations to dominate their analyses. Since there are a multitude of contextual factors potentially relevant to a particular interaction, how does a researcher determine which should be privileged? For a conversational analyst such as Schegloff, without evidence that conversational participants are themselves demonstrably orienting to a feature of the context (such as gender), investigators risk imposing their own a priori analytic and cultural constructs upon interactions.

Stokoe and Attenborough (Chapter 8) believe it is precisely this feature of ethnomethodological approaches like conversation analysis (CA) and membership categorization analysis (MCA) that makes them useful for the study of language and gender. Claims about gender are grounded in participants' orientations rather than in analysts' own assumptions and categories and, for Stokoe and Attenborough, this avoids the a priori theorizing about gender that they suggest is evident in some constructivist work when the (gendered) categories supposedly under investigation are assumed from the outset. Wilkinson and Kitzinger (Chapter 7) make a similar argument about CA: "it is able to discover how the social world actually works, rather than reinforcing presuppositions about it." (See also Benwell, Chapter 12.)

It perhaps goes without saying that this ethnomethodological perspective has its critics. As Stokoe and Attenborough (Chapter 8) point out, the question of when gender is relevant or, put differently, how researchers "warrant" claims about gender is "one of the most controversial debates" in the field in recent years. Weatherall (2000, 287–288), for example, in a rebuttal to the Schegloff article cited above, argues that gender is "a pervasive social category" and, as such, "is an omnipresent feature of all interactions" (see also Wetherell 1998). In a somewhat similar way, Lazar (Chapter 9) suggests gender is always "*potentially* relevant" to an interaction, and Herring and Stoerger (Chapter 29) show us that this potential is realized in mediated online communication in ways starkly reminiscent of the issues arising from the study of gender in face-to-face interaction. That is, even if, as Lazar says "an individual's … professional or religious or racial identity is foregrounded in a particular context," the *gendering* of this professional or religious or racial identity is always a possibility. In contrast to Schegloff who seems to assume that the various dimensions of individuals' identities are discrete, Lazar's view is that such dimensions can be "in play" simultaneously.

Weatherall's and Lazar's claims about the "global" relevance of gender find empirical substance in the work of McConnell-Ginet (2011; Chapter 16). Specifically, McConnell-Ginet demonstrates how hearers routinely go beyond the surface forms of utterances in the process of meaning-making, drawing inferences that are often informed by ideologies of gender and sexuality. That is, interlocutors may "orient to" gender and sexuality even though gender and sexuality are not explicitly encoded in their – or their interlocutors' – talk (see also Cameron 2005b). Interestingly, Wilkinson and Kitzinger (Chapter 7) voice a similar critique of work in CA that considers "only explicit orientations to gender (or sexuality, or ethnicity) as valid objects of study" given the naturalized and often inexplicit quality of sexist, racist, and heterosexist assumptions in talk. They advocate the development of a clearer specification of what constitutes an "orientation" to social categories such as gender, presumably so as to include those orientations that may be inexplicit and indirect (Ochs 1992).

The chapter by Stokoe and Attenborough (8) goes some way in illustrating precisely this kind of orientation to gender: membership categorization devices that are "inference-rich" and can convey participants' implicit and taken-for-granted understandings of gender. Benwell's chapter (12) also addresses the issue of how to warrant claims about gender, specifically masculinity, when masculinity is not explicitly indexed in talk. Benwell's solution combines a close analysis of the naturally occurring talk with "a more ethnographically inflected … attention to the intertexts circulating and informing such talk." Meyerhoff's chapter (4) notes that in variationist studies, it has become common for researchers to explore emergent and indirect orientations to gender by interrogating the relationship between particular uses of a variant and ideologies about larger social categories such as gender.

Like the methods of CA and MCA, ethnographic approaches to language and gender also focus on the social categories that have significance to "participants" or members of a given community. As Besnier and Philips (Chapter 6) point out, "ethnography's approach is from the ground up, in the sense that analytic categories and explanations emerge in the fieldwork situation as opposed to being imported from a predetermined model." Of course, fieldwork for an ethnographer typically involves extended immersion in a community through the technique of participant observation. One of the features, then, that distinguishes ethnography from more "textual" methods such as CA and MCA is the ethnographer's ability to move beyond the locality of the "text" to other kinds of contextual data, for example, the temporal and spatial surroundings in which texts are produced, the activities that accompany the production of texts, and interviews and debriefing sessions, where research participants can reflect on their "texts," be they conversations, political speeches, or meetings. This means that in determining how linguistic and interactional practices may index gender and sexuality (and their intersectionality with other social categories), ethnographers have a rich and "thick" (Geertz 1973) description of a situation. Indeed, for a linguistic anthropologist such as Duranti (1997, 272), ethnographic methods provide a compelling solution to the problem of relevance: if analysts are to determine which dimensions of context are relevant to talk, then they need a way of "retrieving the contextual information that may not be available in the talk itself." This retrieval is possible, according to Duranti, only with the kind of documentation that ethnography provides. Another way of putting this could be to say that the mission of ethnography is to enable ethnographers to align their perceptions of what is significant with the participants' perceptions of what is relevant in a given context.

The challenge of aligning an analysis with what is locally relevant is not restricted to qualitative research methods. One of the fundamental questions a variationist sociolinguist has to address when undertaking an analysis of a variable is "Which categories will the study focus on?" One school of thought holds that the social categories the researcher analyzes ought to have relevance to the speakers themselves and there ought to be evidence that they are orienting to and have some metalinguistic awareness of those categories. A somewhat different school of thought holds that the task of the analyst is to provide a more critical perspective on what kinds of social categories underpin or run counter to those that the speakers have labeled themselves. The chapters by Meyerhoff (4) and Podesva and Kajino (5) deal with this most directly and give some idea of how this question has shaped the directions of quantitative variationist research.

Finally, the problem of alignment of the participants relative to that of the third-party researcher takes on a particular twist when we look at data through the lens of language that is in some way mediated. Freed (Chapter 32) highlights the gap in alignment between scholarly research on language, gender, and sexuality and the way this research is amplified in the mass media. Freed's chapter (and those by Cameron and Talbot, Chapters 14 and 31, respectively) show that while researchers in the field of gender, language, and sexuality have been developing nuanced views of gender and ways of substantiating when gender is relevant to linguistic practices, the mass media consistently transform scholarly research into simplistic terms that support essentialized and dichotomous views of gender and gender differences. Indeed, both Freed and Cameron speculate that the persistence of such popular stereotypes about gender may be a reaction to the social changes that have taken place in the last half century in the West. That is, ideas about the immutability of gender and gender differences need to be reasserted in a climate where significant social upheaval has resulted in "a steady erosion of traditional gender distinctions" (Cameron, Chapter 14). The chapters by Livia (30) and Herring and Stoerger (29) also provide indications of such anxieties in instances where language users try to destabilize the traditionally accepted gender order through the medium of literature, translation, or online communication.

2.5   *Globalization of gender*

The movement away from monolithic and essentialist understandings of gender and sexuality has meant that scholars, in addition to examining how these categories intersect with race, ethnicity, class, and age, have begun to explore language and gender in a range of different global contexts (McElhinny, Besnier and Philips, Lazar, Cameron, Holmes, Meek, all in this volume.) (See also McElhinny's important 2007 collection on language, gender, and globalization.)

While globalization can be defined in various ways, we mean it here as a set of historical contingencies which have a potentially profound impact on individuals' relationships to ideas and opportunities across time and space (Besnier 2007), where the mass media and travel expose us to multiple life choices (Dewey and Brison 2012). One of the paradoxes of globalization is that while it enables people to participate directly, indirectly, or even imaginatively with supra-local ideas, trends, and ideologies, it nevertheless leaves them struggling with the task of giving a local meaning to the supra-local (see Meyerhoff and Niedzielski 2003). Dewey and Brison (2012) argue that this challenge is particularly acute for young people and that it inevitably requires reconciling traditional, local gender and ethnic identities with transnational images of youth identity. These of course involve language – how speakers talk and how they discursively express their ideas about traditional and newer identities (Besnier 2003; Meyerhoff 2003).

It is useful to remember that people have been resolving tensions such as these for a long time. The gendering of transnational contact and exchange is hardly new: we like to think that the globalization we live with today, facilitated by the mass media, the Internet, international trade, and inexpensive air travel, is unique and that therefore the reinterpretation of gendered identities prompted by these new technologies is similarly unique. But at other times in history, there have been other "new" technologies, and these enabled a similar compression of space and time through changes in global economic flows to the ones we now think about under the rubric of globalization. What is important for our purposes here is that the historical record shows how, just as new technologies today motivate new ways of thinking about gendered identities, the impact of other technologies in the past also created a context in which gender was central to social and interactional change. To give but one example, the widespread adoption of new navigational aids such as the chronometer in the nineteenth century suddenly made long-distance sea travel a much less precarious undertaking. Global trade routes connecting Europe, China, Africa, and India via the Caribbean and the Pacific created opportunities for transnational contact with a comparable impact to today's digital communication routes. But, while the primary purpose of these global networks was economic, social change followed closely behind. Globalization in the nineteenth and early twentieth centuries transported and expanded supra-local ideologies of mother-hood, changing the ways in which women and men talk, and were talked about in some of the smaller communities caught up in the global reach of religious missions and economic trade (e.g., Dureau 1998; Jolly 1993). Jolly and Dureau demonstrate that, as gendered ideologies expanded, they were localized (we might say today, they were "rebranded") in ways that simultaneously made sense in traditional and indigenous terms.

In current scholarship on language, gender, and sexuality, the tension between the local and the supra-local has been especially productive, and we can see a great deal of work that plays off an agent's groundedness in a specific place or commu-nity with their engagement with (and attempts to participate in) trends beyond that place and community. Besnier (2003) shows how multilingualism (even when speakers can draw on only an impoverished and broken form of an international language like English) reframe gender identities in the face of social change in

Tonga, and Meyerhoff (2003) argues that Ni-Vanuatu women, having moved to new homes upon marriage, draw on the national language, Bislama, and specific empathetic speech routines to claim a "place" for themselves in the families and villages they have married into.

But finally, the impact of having a more global sense of the pluralities of gender is about more than descriptive adequacy; it has also served to reinvigorate the political basis of earlier work on language and gender. New modes of communication and new kinds of social and political alignments associated with the fundamental paradoxes of globalization have for many researchers reinspired a concern with power. Researchers are asking questions like: What are the different and gendered effects that globalization has on individuals and groups? How is the tension between the local and the supra-local made material in individuals' aspirations? How do tensions between the local and the transnational limit individual agency despite globalization being intimately associated with neoliberal discourses of individual agency? The act of asking and answering these questions throws into focus the mechanisms by which power is claimed, contested, enforced, and submitted to (Cameron 2000; McElhinny 2007; Piller and Takahashi 2010; Dewey and Brison 2012).

Within the academy, the influence of globalization has led to questions about how to insure that scholarly work is circulated widely and to diverse audiences, and how such "new forms of intellectual exchange" may have an impact on the creation of disciplinary canons (McElhinny, Chapter 2). With respect to language and gender scholarship, one could ask how knowledge production has been influenced by the hegemony of research conducted on English and/or in accordance with the scholarly paradigms adopted in anglophone or Western European locations. In keeping with such questions, the "global" chapters in this volume are meant, in part, to "decenter" (McElhinny, Chapter 2) dominant perspectives on language and gender scholarship, which have emerged primarily in anglophone contexts. These chapters provide overviews of language and gender in the context of Brazil (Chapter 21), Poland (Chapter 18), Japan (Chapter 19), and the Arabic-speaking world (Al-Wer, Chapter 20).[2] While the topics and approaches covered necessarily reflect the authors' own interests and expertise, they are also an indication of what issues are most vital within the broader academic, cultural and linguistic context in each location.

The focus on language-planning issues in Kiełkiewicz-Janiowak and Pawelczyk's chapter on Poland (18), for example, serves as a timely reminder in a field dominated by research into English (and other Western European languages) that, in some areas, discussion about the role of language in enforcing and creating power differentials starts with the (not so) simple choices people make about how to make women visible in mundane, everyday discourse. In Japan, the notion of "women's language" is an ideological-historical construct and, as such, Nakamura's chapter (19) does not investigate the actual linguistic practices of women, but rather tracks the emergence of this construct over time. Within the Arabic-speaking world, Al-Wer (Chapter 20) notes that variationist investigations of women's speech in relation to standard varieties have yielded anomalous results because they have adopted a notion of the standard based on anglophone contexts. As Al-Wer remarks, the transnational Arabic standard is "simply irrelevant in the processes of variation and change in vernacular Arabic" (Chapter 20). In the context of Brazil, Ostermann and Moita-Lopes (Chapter 21) note that studies of gender and sexuality have been slow to emerge because, across the academy, Marxist theory and a focus on social class have been viewed as essential theoretical tools in opposing the right-wing dictatorial regime in power from 1964 to 1985.

3. Conclusion

The theoretical and methodological themes discussed above do not, of course, exhaust those covered in the *Handbook*; they do, however, point to some of the debates and controversies that are likely to shape future developments in the field. For example, the issues of how best to study gender as an interactionally emergent phenomenon and how best to warrant claims about gender relevance will no doubt continue to raise questions about research design and methods. As indicated above, attempts to determine gender relevance seem increasingly to be informed both by ethnography and by pragmatic principles, given the indirect means by which gender can be encoded and retrieved in talk. From our point of view, then, the blending of different kinds of analytic and disciplinary methods is a productive way of addressing some of the problems and tensions that accompany social constructionist approaches to gender.

We also note the important role that mixed methods research – the practice of drawing on both qualitative and quantitative methods in analysis – has had in the field over the last decade or so. As Holmes and Meyerhoff (2003, 15) argued in the first edition of the *Handbook,* there are clear advantages in bringing together quantitative and qualitative approaches to the extent that "macro-level quantitative research identifies the gendered norms on which speakers are drawing, the ground against which individual choices must be interpreted." Holmes (1997) represents an early effort to mix qualitative approaches and the quantitative methods of variation theory, but more recently, mixed methods research in language, gender, and sexuality has become closely associated with Penelope Eckert's work. Her 2000 book made a significant contribution both to the quantitative analysis of sound change in American English and to the qualitative analysis of gender as an emergent social category, grounded in local interactional practices. Mendoza-Denton (2008), Bucholtz (2011), and work summarized by Podesva and Kajino and by Meyerhoff (Chapters 5 and 4, respectively) testify to the profound influence Eckert's work continues to have on the field. A slightly different model for mixing methods can be discerned in work that uses corpus linguistics in combination with discourse analysis. Examples of such work are evident in this volume (e.g., Freed and Stokoe and Attenborough, Chapters 32 and 8, respectively) and in Baker (2008; 2010).

In addition to forces internal to a given discipline, Cameron (2008) has made the point that the wider social, political, and material culture can have a significant impact on the kinds of questions that preoccupy scholars at particular points in time. She argues, for example, that sexuality and sexual diversity have become pressing concerns for scholars of language and gender because they are increasingly important in the cultures researchers are investigating. Work such as Zimman and Hall's (2010) on "the third sex" are good examples of how changing cultural practices can have an impact on scholarship and, in turn, on the kinds of questions researchers might ask (see also chapters in Herdt 1993). For example, Zimman and Hall argue that studies of "the third sex" necessitate a *refocusing* on the body in language and sexuality studies. The economic and social phenomenon of globalization (while not entirely new) has also produced new kinds of research inquiries (see above and McElhinny, Chapter 2) in addition to methodological challenges. Besnier and Philips (Chapter 6), for instance, point to the ways that ethnographic methods have been reconfigured in response to "the fact that people, ideas, and resources are today fundamentally mobile."

Other developments in the field of language, gender, and sexuality can be seen as influenced by broader social and cultural forces as well. For example, we foresee that from the point of view of material culture, innovations in technology and fresh forms of social media will allow researchers to access new kinds of data and to explore potentially new ways of constructing gendered and sexual identities. Technical advances in research tools have already made it possible to undertake more nuanced investigations of gender and sexuality. As Podesva and Kajino (Chapter 5) demonstrate, linguistic software for tracking pitch and mapping tone contours (for example, Praat; see Boersma and Weenink 2013) has greatly facilitated the study of how phonation, pitch, and other suprasegmentals can be deployed as resources in the production of gender and sexuality. In a similar way, Bucholtz (Chapter 1) suggests that the use of video analysis will greatly enhance research into gendered or sexual identities since, through video, researchers are able to consider the embodied aspects of communication. And, as other chapters demonstrate, there is a growing need for multimodal analyses in the field, given the fact that individuals increasingly communicate across modalities other than face-to-face speech and paper-based writing.

Ten years ago, in the introduction to the first edition of the *Handbook*, Holmes and Meyerhoff (2003, 14) commented that there seems little point to our academic pursuits if they do not at some point "travel out of the academy" in order to question and challenge social inequities. There is no doubt that our research has traveled outside of the academy, yet, as several chapters in this volume demonstrate (e.g., Cameron and Freed, Chapters 14 and 32, respectively), popular representations of language and gender may serve only to reinforce understandings of gender that our research is attempting to counter. This is perhaps not surprising since we know that transplanting texts into new contexts typically involves recontextualization and, correspondingly, transformations in meaning (Bauman and Briggs 1990; Blommaert 2005). But this propensity for movement and transformation must also give us some cause for optimism. The field of language, gender, and sexuality is virtually unique in academic linguistics for the immediate relevance of its questions and its data to everyday life. On the one hand, this makes it relatively straightforward to transplant our work; on the other hand, it raises the stakes in the sense that we must remain vigilant about how our work can be appropriated by conservative forces. In conclusion, then, we hope that this volume, with its wide range of theoretical models, methodological approaches, and applications to real-world issues, will inform – in productive ways – the movement of our work from the academy into the fields of social policy and political action.

Acknowledgments

We are grateful to Andrew Beach, Alice Freed, and Janet Holmes who all provided valuable feedback on previous versions of this introduction. We are, of course, responsible for any remaining shortcomings.

NOTES

1   Anna Livia's chapter on gender in literary texts (Chapter 30) is republished unchanged from the first edition, following her unfortunate early death.
2   The regionally focused chapters will enable readers to seek out further research on gender, sexuality, and language from these areas. Adachi (2012), Inoue (2006), and Okamoto and Shibamoto-Smith (2004) provide further investigations of gender and Japanese; Zilles and King (2005) combine qualitative and quantitative approaches in Brazil; and Badran, Sadiqi, and Rashidi (2002), Bassiouney (2009), Eid (2002), and Hachimi (2013) all expand on gender and language in North Africa.

REFERENCES

Adachi, Chie. 2012. *Compliments and Compliment Responses among Young Japanese: A Sociolinguistic Investigation.* Cologne: Lambert Academic.

Badran, Margot, Fatima Sadiqi, and Linda Stumpf Rashidi, eds. 2002. "Language and Gender in the Arab World" (special issue). *Langues et Linguistiques*, 9.

Baker, Paul. 2008. *Sexed Texts: Language, Gender and Sexuality.* London: Equinox.

Baker, Paul. 2010. *Corpus Linguistics and Sociolinguistics.* Edinburgh: Edinburgh University Press.

Barrett, Rusty. 1999. "Indexing Polyphonous Identity in the Speech of African American Drag Queens." In Mary Bucholtz, A. C. Liang, and Laurel A. Sutton (eds.), *Reinventing Identities: The Gendered Self in Discourse*, 313–331. New York: Oxford University Press.

Bassiouney, Reem. 2009. *Arabic Sociolinguistics.* Edinburgh: Edinburgh University Press.

Bauman, Richard, and Charles L. Briggs. 1990. "Poetics and Performance as Critical Perspectives on Language and Social Life." *Annual Review of Anthropology*, 19: 59–88.

Baxter, Judith, ed. 2006. *Speaking Out: The Female Voice in Public Contexts.* Basingstoke: Palgrave Macmillan.

Benwell, Bethan. 2005. "'Lucky This is Anonymous': Ethnographies of Reception in Men's Magazines: A 'Textual Culture' Approach." *Discourse & Society*, 16: 147–172.

Besnier, Niko. 2003. "Crossing Gender, Mixing Languages: The Linguistic

Construction of Trangenderism in Tonga."
In Janet Holmes and Miriam Meyerhoff
(eds.), *The Handbook of Language and
Gender*, 279–301. Oxford: Blackwell.

Besnier, Niko. 2007. "Language and Gender
Research at the Intersection of the Global
and the Local." *Gender and Language*, 1:
67–78.

Blommaert, 2005. *Discourse*. Cambridge:
Cambridge University Press.

Boersma, Paul, and David Weenink. 2013.
"Praat: Doing Phonetics by Computer
[Computer program]. Version 5.3.53." At
http://www.praat.org/, accessed October
8, 2013.

Bucholtz, Mary. 2011. *White Kids: Language,
Race, and Styles of Youth Identity*.
Cambridge: Cambridge University Press.

Butler, Judith. 1990. *Gender Trouble: Feminism
and the Subversion of Identity*. New York:
Routledge.

Cameron, Deborah. 1997. "Theoretical
Debates in Feminist Linguistics: Questions
of Sex and Gender." In Ruth Wodak (ed.),
Gender and Discourse, 21–36. London: Sage.

Cameron, Deborah. 2000. *Good to Talk? Living
and Working in a Communication Culture*.
London: Sage.

Cameron, Deborah. 2005a. "Language,
Gender and Sexuality: Current Issues and
New Directions." *Applied Linguistics*, 26(4):
482–502.

Cameron, Deborah. 2005b. "Reality and Its
Discontents: Language, Gender and
Pragmatics." *Intercultural Pragmatics*, 2–3:
321–334.

Cameron, Deborah. 2007. *The Myth of Mars
and Venus: Do Men and Women Really Speak
Different Languages?* Oxford: Oxford
University Press.

Cameron, Deborah. 2008. "Theoretical Issues
for the Study of Gender and Spoken
Interaction." In Pia Pichler and Eva Eppler
(eds.), *Gender and Spoken Interaction*, 1–17.
Basingstoke: Palgrave Macmillan.

Cameron, Deborah, and Don Kulick. 2003.
Language and Sexuality. Cambridge:
Cambridge University Press.

Cameron, Deborah, and Don Kulick, eds.
2006. *The Language and Sexuality Reader*.
London: Routledge.

Coates, Jennifer. 2004. *Women, Men and
Language: A Sociolinguistic Account of
Gender Differences in Language*, 3rd edn.
London: Pearson Longman.

Coates, Jennifer, and Pia Pichler, eds. 2011.
Language and Gender: A Reader, 2nd edn.
Oxford: Wiley-Blackwell.

Coates, Linda, Janet Beavin Bavelas, and
James Gibson. 1994. "Anomalous
Language in Sexual Assault Trial
Judgments." *Discourse & Society*, 5:
189–206.

Dewey, Susan, and Karen J. Brison, eds. 2012.
*Supergirls, Ganstas, Freeters, and
Xenomaniacs: Gender and Modernity in
Global Youth Cultures*. Syracuse, NY:
Syracuse University Press.

Duranti, Alessandro. 1997. *Linguistic
Anthropology*. Cambridge: Cambridge
University Press.

Dureau, Christine. 1998. "From Sisters to
Wives: Changing Contexts of Maternity on
Simbo, Western Solomon Islands." In
Kalpana Ram and Margaret Jolly (eds.),
*Maternities and Modernities: Colonial and
Postcolonial Experiences in Asia and the
Pacific*, 239–274. Oxford: Oxford University
Press.

Eckert, Penelope. 2000. *Linguistic Variation as
Social Practice: The Linguistic Construction of
Identity at Belten High*. Oxford: Blackwell.

Eckert, Penelope, and Sally McConnell-Ginet.
1992. "Think Practically and Look Locally:
Language and Gender as
Community-Based Practice." *Annual
Review of Anthropology*, 21: 461–490.

Eckert, Penelope, and Sally McConnell-Ginet.
2003. *Language and Gender*. Cambridge:
Cambridge University Press.

Eckert, Penelope, and Sally McConnell-Ginet.
2013. *Language and Gender*, 2nd edn.
Cambridge: Cambridge University Press.

Eid, Mushira. 2002. *The World of Obituaries:
Gender across Cultures and over Time*.
Detroit: Wayne State University Press.

Gal, Susan. 1991. "Between Speech and
Silence: The Problematics of Research on
Language and Gender." In Micaela di
Leonardo (ed.), *Gender at the Crossroads of
Knowledge: Feminist Anthropology in the
Postmodern Era*, 175–203. Berkeley:
University of California Press.

Gaudio, Rudolph. 1997. "Not Talking Straight in Hausa." In Anna Livia and Kira Hall (eds.), *Queerly Phrased: Language, Gender, and Sexuality*, 416–429. New York: Oxford University Press.

Geertz, Clifford. 1973. *The Interpretation of Cultures: Selected Essays*. New York: Basic Books.

Hachimi, Atiqa. 2013. "The Maghreb–Mashreq Language Ideology and the Politics of Identity in a Globalized Arab World." *Journal of Sociolinguistics*, 17(3): 269–296.

Hall, Kira. 1997. "Go Suck Your Husband's Sugarcane! Hijras and the Use of Sexual Insult." In Anna Livia and Kira Hall (eds.), *Queerly Phrased: Language, Gender, and Sexuality*, 430–460. New York: Oxford University Press.

Hall, Kira, and Veronica O'Dononvan. 1996. "Shifting Gender Positions among Hindi-Speaking Hijras." In Victoria L. Bergvall, Janet M. Bing, and Alice F. Freed (eds.), *Rethinking Language and Gender Research: Theory and Practice*, 228–266. London: Longman.

Harrington, Kate, Lia Litoselliti, Helen Sauntson, and Jane Sunderland, eds. 2008. *Gender and Language Research Methodologies*. Basingstoke: Palgrave Macmillan.

Herdt, Gilbert H., ed. 1993. *Third Sex, Third Gender: Beyond Sexual Dimorphism in Culture and History*. New York: Zone Books.

Holmes, Janet. 1997. "Women, Language and Identity." *Journal of Sociolinguistics*, 2: 195–223.

Holmes, Janet. 2007. "Social Constructionism, Postmodernism and Feminist Sociolinguistics." *Gender and Language*, 1: 51–65.

Holmes, Janet, and Miriam Meyerhoff. 2003. "Different Voices, Different Views: An Introduction to Current Research in Language and Gender." In Janet Holmes and Miriam Meyerhoff (eds.), *The Handbook of Language and Gender*, 1–17. Oxford: Blackwell.

Inoue, Miyako. 2006. *Vicarious Language: Gender and Linguistic Modernity in Japan*. Berkeley: University of California Press.

Jolly, Margaret. 1993. "Colonizing Women: The Maternal Body and Empire." In Sneja Gunew and Anna Yeatman (eds.), *Feminism and the Politics of Difference*, 103–127. St Leonard's, NSW: Allen & Unwin.

Julé, Allyson. 2008. *A Beginner's Guide to Gender and Language*. Clevedon: Multilingual Matters.

Kiesling, Scott F. 2002. "Playing the Straight Man: Displaying and Maintaining Male Heterosexuality in Discourse." In Kathryn Campbell-Kibler, Robert Podesva, Sarah Roberts, and Andrew Wong (eds.), *Language and Sexuality: Contesting Meaning in Theory and Practice*, 249–266. Stanford: CSLI Publications.

Kiesling, Scott F. 2005. "Homosocial Desire in Men's Talk: Balancing and Recreating Cultural Discourses of Masculinity." *Language in Society*, 34(5): 695–727.

Kiesling, Scott F. 2011. "Masculinities, Desire, and Discourse." *Gender and Language*, 5: 213–239.

Kitzinger, Celia. 2005. "Heteronormativity in Action: Reproducing the Heterosexual Nuclear Family in After-Hours Medical Calls." *Social Problems*, 52: 477–498.

Kulick, Don. 1998. *Travesti: Sex, Gender and Culture among Brazilian Transgendered Prostitutes*. Chicago: University of Chicago Press.

Kulick, Don. 2000. "Gay and Lesbian Language." *Annual Review of Anthropology*, 29: 243–285.

Lakoff, Robin T. 2004. *Language and Woman's Place*, rev. and expanded edn, ed. Mary Bucholtz. Oxford: Oxford University Press.

Lazar, Michelle M., ed. 2005. *Feminist Critical Discourse Analysis: Gender, Power and Ideology in Discourse*. Basingstoke: Palgrave Macmillan.

Litosseliti, Lia. 2006. *Gender and Language: Theory and Practice*. London: Hodder Education.

Livia, Anna, and Kira Hall, eds. 1997. *Queerly Phrased: Language, Gender and Sexuality*. Oxford: Oxford University Press.

Maltz, Daniel N., and Ruth A. Borker. 1982. "A Cultural Approach to Male–Female Miscommunication." In John J. Gumperz

(ed.), *Language and Social Identity*, 196–216.
Cambridge: Cambridge University Press

McConnell-Ginet, Sally. 2011. *Gender,
Sexuality, and Meaning: Linguistic Practice
and Politics*. Oxford: Oxford University
Press.

McElhinny, Bonnie. 1996. "Strategic
Essentialism in Sociolinguistic Studies of
Gender." In Natasha Warner, Jocelyn
Ahlers, Leela Bilmes, Monica Oliver,
Suzanne Wertheim, and Melinda Chen
(eds.), *Gender and Belief Systems: Proceedings
of the Fourth Berkeley Women and Language
Conference*, 469–480. Berkeley: Berkeley
Women and Language Group.

McElhinny, Bonnie S., ed. 2007. *Words,
Worlds, and Material Girls: Language, Gender,
Globalization*. Berlin: Mouton de Gruyter.

Mendoza-Denton, Norma. 2008. *Homegirls:
Language and Cultural Practice among Latina
Youth Gangs*. Oxford: Blackwell.

Meyerhoff, Miriam. 2003. "Claiming a Place:
Gender, Knowledge, and Authority as
Emergent Properties." In Janet Holmes
and Miriam Meyerhoff (eds.), *The
Handbook of Language and Gender*, 302–326.
Malden, MA: Blackwell.

Meyerhoff, Miriam, and Nancy Niedzielski.
2003. "The Globalisation of Vernacular
Variation." *Journal of Sociolinguistics*, 7(4):
534–555.

Milani, Tommaso M. 2011. "Introduction:
Re-casting Language and Masculinities."
Gender and Language, 5(2): 175–186.

Mills, Sara, and Louise Mullany. 2011.
*Language, Gender and Feminism: Theory,
Methodology and Practice*. London:
Routledge.

Ochs, Elinor. 1992. "Indexing Gender." In
Alessandro Duranti and Charles Goodwin
(eds.), *Rethinking Context: Language as an
Interactive Phenomenon*, 335–358.
Cambridge: Cambridge University Press.

Okamoto, Shigeko, and Janet S.
Shibamoto-Smith, eds. 2004. *Japanese
Language, Gender, and Ideology: Cultural
Models and Real People*. Oxford: Oxford
University Press.

Pichler, Pia, and Eva Eppler, eds. 2009.
Gender and Spoken Interaction. Basingstoke:
Palgrave Macmillan.

Piller, Ingrid, and Kimie Takahashi. 2010.
"At the Intersection of Gender, Language
and Transnationalism." In Nikolas
Coupland (ed.), *The Handbook of Language
and Globalization*, 540–554. Oxford:
Blackwell.

Schegloff, Emmanuel. 1997. "Whose Text?
Whose Context?" *Discourse & Society*, 8(2):
165–187.

Speer, Susan A. 2005. *Gender Talk: Feminism,
Discourse and Conversation Analysis*.
London: Routledge.

Speer, Susan A., and Elizabeth Stokoe, eds.
2011. *Conversation and Gender*. Cambridge:
Cambridge University Press.

Sunderland, Jane. 2004. *Gendered Discourses*.
Basingstoke: Palgrave Macmillan.

Sunderland, Jane. 2006. *Language and Gender:
An Advanced Resource Book*. London:
Routledge.

Talbot, Mary. 1995. "Synthetic Sisterhood:
False Friends in a Teenage Magazine." In
Kira Hall and Mary Bucholtz (eds.), *Gender
Articulated: Language and the Socially
Constructed Self*, 143–165. New York:
Routledge.

Talbot, Mary. 2010. *Language and Gender*, 2nd
edn. Cambridge: Polity.

Tannen, Deborah. 1990. *You Just Don't
Understand: Women and Men in
Conversation*. New York: HarperCollins.

Weatherall, Ann. 2000. "Gender Relevance in
Talk-in-Interaction and Discourse."
Discourse & Society, 11: 290–292.

Weatherall, Ann. 2002. *Gender, Language and
Discourse*. London: Routledge.

Wetherell, Margaret. 1998. "Positioning and
Interpretive Repertoires: Conversation
Analysis and Poststructuralism in
Dialogue." *Discourse & Society*, 9: 387–412.

Zilles, Ana M. S., and Kendall King. 2005.
"Self-Presentation in Sociolinguistic
Interviews: Identities and Language
Variation in Panambi, Brazil." *Journal of
Sociolinguistics*, 9(1): 74–94.

Zimman, Lal, and Kira Hall. 2010.
"Language, Embodiment and the 'Third
Sex.'" In Dominic Watt and Carmen
Llamas (eds.), *Language and Identities*,
166–178. Edinburgh: Edinburgh University
Press.

Part I Theory and History

1 The Feminist Foundations of Language, Gender, and Sexuality Research

MARY BUCHOLTZ

1. Introduction: Linguistics and Feminism

Feminist linguists have been in dialogue with feminists in other disciplines since the field's formation, yet this historical relationship and its implications for current work are only occasionally highlighted in scholarship. This chapter reaffirms the feminist foundations of a wide range of research on language, gender, and sexuality by highlighting and illustrating the numerous, sometimes clashing, and often not fully articulated feminist positionings taken up within various studies over the course of the field's development.

Because the term "feminism" is often misunderstood, I offer the following definition:

> *Feminism*: a diverse and sometimes conflicting set of theoretical, methodological, and political perspectives that have in common a commitment to understanding and challenging social inequalities related to gender and sexuality.

Although "feminism" often appears in the singular, its reference is always plural; there is no unified feminist theoretical, methodological, or political perspective. Yet, despite the often vigorous and heated debates between different versions of feminism, they share a commitment to addressing social inequality. Furthermore, the field of language, gender, and sexuality is both unified and divided in precisely the same way as is feminism itself: more or less unified in its general political goals, divided in the perspectives it takes toward achieving those goals. But despite this broad scope, not all scholarship on the intersection of language with gender and sexuality is part of the field, because not all of it shares a political commitment to social justice. Indeed, a sizable body of traditional social science research seeks

The Handbook of Language, Gender, and Sexuality, Second Edition.
Edited by Susan Ehrlich, Miriam Meyerhoff, and Janet Holmes.
© 2014 John Wiley & Sons, Inc. Published 2017 by John Wiley & Sons, Inc.

simply to correlate language patterns with categories of gender and/or sexuality and does not engage meaningfully either with feminist theory or with feminist linguistics.[1]

The chapter is organized according to three significant bodies of feminist thought that emerged in the late twentieth and early twenty-first centuries: *difference feminisms*, which take gender difference as their starting point and focus on the position of women within structures of gender; *critical feminisms*, or critiques or extensions of difference perspectives that nevertheless share certain commonalities with them; and *queer feminisms*, which refocus the field on the problematization of gender and its relationship to sexual identities and practices. Although a rough chronology could be imposed on these frameworks, the following discussion is not primarily a historical account, since all of the feminist theories considered here remain in active use and development by feminist academics and activists of various stripes. Feminist studies is an extremely dynamic field, and inevitably all of these theories have come in for a great deal of critique by those that have come later (as well as by their predecessors). Nevertheless, all of them have value for current feminist linguistic scholarship and activism. For this reason, researchers must be wary of unreflexively privileging certain forms of feminism over others in our study of language, gender, and sexuality.

The following discussion focuses on linguistic scholarship and feminist theory in the English-speaking world, and particularly in the United States, the tradition with which I am most familiar. It is hoped that this preliminary sketch will inaugurate a larger discussion of the relationship between feminist theories and empirical research on language, gender, and sexuality in diverse intellectual traditions around the globe. For the most part, I have set aside approaches that have been influential in feminist theory but have had relatively little impact on the empirical linguistic study of gender and sexuality. Most prominent among these are the poststructuralist theories of language advanced by French feminist literary theorists and philosophers influenced by the psychoanalytic work of Jacques Lacan (Marks and de Courtivron 1980; for some empirical linguistic perspectives on this general approach, see, e.g., Hass 2000; Livia 2000; Livia, Chapter 30 in this volume).

The brief descriptions of each theory presented below are intended to give a sense of the varied concerns of different branches of feminist thinking rather than to provide absolute criteria for one approach versus another. The discussion foregrounds individuals whose work has become iconic of particular theoretical perspectives; more detailed overviews of feminist theory offer a fuller account of the issues explored here (e.g., Beasley 1999; Jackson and Jones 1998; Tong 2009). Likewise, my discussion of specific linguistic studies in relation to specific brands of feminism necessarily highlights some aspects over others and focuses on only a small subset of the scholarship of the researchers under discussion. The reader should consult these scholars' full body of work for a more complete picture.

The following discussion is in some ways a continuation and extension of a conversation between feminist theory and theories of language that Deborah Cameron launched over 25 years ago. Her pathbreaking book *Feminism and Linguistic Theory*

(1985) articulated the theoretical and political grounds for linking language and gender in both scholarship and activism and demonstrated the deep linguistic roots of feminist questions. Cameron's work was an important early step in what became a revolution in feminist linguistics. Thanks to developments in feminist theory that are further discussed later in the chapter, by the 1990s language had become central to feminist theorizing not only in France, where the issue had long been explored, but also in the English-speaking world. In the same period, feminist theory became more explicitly central to empirical linguistic investigations than ever before. Before examining this turn of events, however, it is necessary to consider the feminist foundations of language, gender, and sexuality studies from the very beginning of the field.

2. Difference Feminisms

Many Anglo-American feminist theories of the 1960s through the 1980s grew out of the political movement that has been dubbed *second-wave feminism*, which built on the advances of the first-wave feminist movement of the nineteenth and early twentieth centuries. Although primarily fueled, like all feminist thought and action, by real-world political goals, second-wave feminism had intellectual underpinnings in a range of feminist theories that responded both to the political changes of the time and to developments within the academy. These theories include liberal feminism, cultural feminism, and radical feminism. What unifies these forms of second-wave feminism is a focus on gender difference as the foundation of feminist thinking. Where they diverge, however, is in their understanding of this difference and how it should be addressed by feminists.

2.1 *Liberal feminism and women's language*

The form of feminism that is currently most widely advocated by nonfeminists – albeit generally not under this label – is liberal feminism. The primary goal of liberal feminism is to establish equality between women and men in all aspects of society by eradicating barriers to women's full participation; thus, it does not seek to change the structure of society but rather to provide equal opportunities for women within existing social structures. Unlike many of the other feminist theories discussed in this chapter, liberal feminism has taken its primary inspiration from public advocates and popular commentators rather than from the academy (e.g., Friedan 1963). At the same time, much of the mainstream – as opposed to overtly feminist – scholarly research on gender continues to be directly or indirectly informed by broadly liberal feminist goals.

Indeed, the success of liberal feminism in integrating feminist viewpoints into public discourse and policy during the latter half of the twentieth century is evident in the fact that it is often no longer recognized as feminism at all. For example, as many feminist linguists know only too well from our experiences of teaching undergraduate classes, many younger women – and men – reject the label "feminism" for themselves while embracing its goals (Houvouras and Carter 2008). And even a number of conservative political figures in the United States espouse liberal feminist principles of gender equality, although they do not generally support policies designed to uphold these principles.

While liberal feminism has made important strides in establishing equality for all women through its focus on such fundamental issues as equal pay, abortion rights, and domestic violence, its impact has been particularly significant for middle-class women, who have benefited from liberal feminist efforts to expand women's access to traditionally male institutions of influence and power such as politics, the law, and professional workplaces. Given its concern to bring women into men's spheres, liberal feminism has generally aimed to eradicate gender inequality by eradicating or at least reducing gender difference. Beginning in the 1970s and 1980s, some attempts to advance this notion, particularly in middle-class workplaces, had the unintended consequence of encouraging women to look, act, and speak more like men, producing a widely circulating stereotype of "ball-busting bitches" dressed in broad-shouldered power suits. Thus, despite some liberal feminists' early advocacy of androgyny for both women and men as an escape from the constraints of gender roles, in practice, efforts to eliminate gender differences have sometimes resulted in societal expectations that women must adapt to male norms.

Liberal feminism was also extremely influential in the early foundations of language, gender, and sexuality research, an impact that continues to the present day. Perhaps the most widely discussed aspect of liberal feminist linguistics has been the controversial – yet at least partly successful – effort to eradicate the most overt forms of sexism in the English language. These include the use of the masculine as a generic form and gendered agent nouns like *fireman*, as well as status asymmetries in the semantics of gendered pairs like *master/mistress* and *major/majorette* (e.g., Frank and Treichler 1989; Lakoff 2004 [1975]; Miller and Swift 1977; Pauwels 1998). However, within the field the concern with women's ways of using language eventually overshadowed this issue.

The primary figure associated with liberal feminist linguistics is Robin Lakoff, whose text *Language and Woman's Place* (2004 [1975]) played a crucial role in establishing the study of language, gender, and sexuality as a linguistic subfield.[2] This pioneering book has been nevertheless widely criticized by both feminist and nonfeminist linguists on a number of theoretical, political, and methodological grounds (for discussions, see, e.g., Bucholtz 2004; Bucholtz and Hall 1995), and it has especially been targeted for what critics have viewed as a privileging of male linguistic norms and a devaluing of women's linguistic practices. In fact, however, Lakoff is not endorsing but simply describing a culture-wide ideology that scorns and trivializes both women and women's ways of speaking. Her work has served as a touchstone for the field for over 30 years thanks to its cogent characterization of "women's language" as a set of ideologically saturated linguistic practices constraining women's ability to participate in male domains. As she puts it, "women are systematically denied access to power, on the grounds that they are not capable of holding it as demonstrated by their linguistic behavior" (2004 [1975], 42). Scholars continue to debate the concept of "women's language" as well as the empirical evidence for and against the claims Lakoff made about its specific features, from the use of hedges and tag questions to women's perceived inability to tell jokes. Nevertheless, her broader concern with the ideological effects of language in disempowering women remains an important liberal feminist contribution.

More recent work that shares some aspects of this general perspective is Judith Baxter's (2010) research on the speech of women who hold leadership positions within the business world. While importantly informed by other feminist theories in addition to liberal feminism, Baxter's analysis aligns with this approach in calling attention to the way that gender ideologies in male-dominated workplaces limit women's access to corporate power. Her finding that women in such workplaces must constantly monitor their language is reminiscent of Lakoff's double bind, whereby "a woman is damned if she does [speak in accordance with gender ideologies] and damned if she doesn't" (2004 [1975], 85). Thus liberal feminist issues have continued relevance in research on language, gender, and sexuality even as contemporary scholars expand their theoretical toolkit to include other perspectives as well.

2.2 *Cultural feminism and gendered interactional styles*

While liberal feminism concentrates on the downplaying of gender difference in order to achieve gender equality, another second-wave theory, sometimes termed "cultural feminism" (though generally not by those to whom it is applied), instead views women's ways of thinking, acting, and speaking as distinctive and inherent qualities that should be valorized by scholars and society (e.g., Belenky et al. 1986; Gilligan 1982). These practices have often been attributed to a distinct women's culture, said to be rooted in early socialization experiences as well as in women's biological potential to be mothers and hence nurturers.

Because cultural feminism takes somewhat different forms, it is useful to distinguish between *liberal cultural feminism* and *radical cultural feminism*. Liberal cultural feminism, like liberal feminism more generally, advocates equality between the genders; however, where other forms of liberal feminism promote gender equality via the reduction of gender differences, liberal cultural feminism seeks acknowledgment of the equal value of what are seen as women's distinctive practices.

Within linguistics, the most prominent representative of a liberal cultural feminist approach is Deborah Tannen, whose bestselling book *You Just Don't Understand* (1990) catapulted the study of language and gender to international awareness. Tannen's basic claim both in this popular text and in her scholarly writings on gender (e.g., Tannen 1994) is that women and men in intimate heterosexual relationships often miscommunicate because of different gendered interactional styles. In particular, she proposes that women have a cultural preference for cooperative, egalitarian interaction and for "rapport talk," or emotion-based, connection-oriented communication, while men have a preference for competitive, hierarchical interaction and "report talk," or fact-based, information-oriented communication. (See Tannen, Chapter 25 in this volume.)

Tannen's analysis of heterosexual interaction is deeply influenced by earlier work that proposed that gender differences stem from early childhood cultures, in girls' and boys' gender-segregated play groups (e.g., Maltz and Borker 1982). Critics have argued that girls' interaction may be characterized by both cooperation and competition. Such varied practices complicate but do not entirely refute cultural feminist linguistic analysis, which is often more nuanced than its representations in popular and secondhand recirculations would suggest. Indeed, some liberal cultural feminists have argued that the often Machiavellian politics of girls' social worlds may work hand in hand with an ethos of cooperation and egalitarianism among ingroup members (Simmons 2002; for an alternative perspective, see Goodwin 2006; Goodwin and Kyratzis, Chapter 26 in this volume).

As with Lakoff's work, which has also reached a wide audience, Tannen's research has been more warmly received outside of the academy than within it, and once again feminist linguists in particular have been highly critical of the book's theory, methodology, and politics as well as skeptical of its author's feminist credentials (e.g., Davis 1996; 1997; Freed 1992; Troemel-Ploetz 1991; Uchida 1992; for a defense of Tannen, see Yerian 1997).[3] Because her primary goal has been to help individual women and men address difficulties in their personal relationships by becoming more aware of gendered interactional differences, some feminist critics perceive Tannen's approach as apolitical, and they charge her with encouraging women, who are more likely to read her book and follow her advice, to accommodate to male norms. Nevertheless, Tannen certainly had feminist goals in writing the book and made clear that she viewed women's interactional style as just as legitimate as men's. In this regard, her perspective is closely aligned with that of liberal cultural feminists in other disciplines.

The second form of cultural feminism, radical cultural feminism, shares with its liberal counterpart a view of women's ways of thinking, speaking, and acting as distinctive from men's. However, rather than treating the two genders as equal, the radical version of cultural feminism elevates women's practices over men's, often grounding this position in women's reproductive capacity. Focusing on what they view as women's superior cognitive, affective, and experiential relationship to the world, radical cultural feminists have argued that a women-led, or even a women-only, society would be far preferable to male domination (e.g., Daly 1978). As part of imagining this new utopia, some radical cultural feminists even created a new lexicon that placed women's concerns at the center of language (e.g., Daly and Caputi 1987).

Within linguistic research, however, the focus of radical cultural feminist analysis has been more concerned with interaction than lexis, and most scholars who have taken up this perspective in their work, while extolling women's interactional abilities, do not align themselves with the more provocative utopian politics of some strands of radical cultural feminism (but see Penelope 1990). For example, Janet Holmes offers what she describes as a "tongue-in-cheek" counterpoint to Chomsky by proposing that "New Zealand women constitute ideal speaker-hearers," or at least "attractive conversational partners" (1993, 111). Through a quantitative comparison of women's and men's interactional practices based on data collected in New Zealand, Holmes finds that women are more attentive to their interlocutors' face needs, producing more positive-politeness hedges, more facilitative tag questions, and fewer interruptions, among other practices. While a Lakoffian liberal feminist perspective would argue that such practices are indexical of powerlessness, Holmes rejects this view, although she acknowledges that women's interactional dexterity may work to men's advantage in conversation due to a general male "lack of interactive sensitivity" (1993, 112; see also Fishman 1983). By inverting the liberal feminist understanding of women's linguistic practices as the interactional apparatus of gender subordination, Holmes offers a valuable counterpoint that positions women as skilled and agentive language users.

A second linguistic study that draws on radical cultural feminist principles is Jennifer Coates's (1996) work on talk in women's friendship groups. Her book *Women Talk* ends with a powerful statement of the value and significance of women's talk: "It is the radical potential of women's friendships that makes them worthy of close investigation. They can be seen as a model of the way relationships should be, of the way relationships might be in the future" (Coates 1996, 286). Coates's celebratory tone echoes Holmes's positive assessment of women's special interactional abilities as well as the utopian vision articulated by radical cultural feminist theory. Such work once again provides an important alternative to the more pessimistic view of women's interactional practices found in liberal feminism.

At the same time, given the vast variety of women's speaking styles, numerous individual women and even entire cultural groups do not conform to the characterizations presented by these scholars, and it is unclear whether theories of female linguistic superiority can accommodate such speakers (Bucholtz 1999). Such claims are better seen as political strategies to enhance awareness and appreciation of (some) women's interactional practices. While idealizing women's interaction can lead to the establishment of an intragender hierarchy in which some women are problematized and marginalized, this move also calls attention to women's skills. Radical cultural feminists within linguistics have therefore made an important theoretical and political contribution by celebrating the often undervalued interactional practices associated with many women. The ongoing influence of this perspective is evident in the growing effort among feminist linguists to highlight women's and girls' linguistic abilities.

2.3 Radical feminism and linguistic violence

The final second-wave feminist theory I consider here is radical feminism, of which radical cultural feminism is a special case. Where radical cultural feminism focuses on the unique situation of women, sometimes even to the exclusion of any consideration of men, the more general form of radical feminism keeps its focus squarely on the relation between women and men. Radical feminism is what most members of the public think of when they hear the term "feminism" and is presumably part of the reason that many people do not identify as feminists; in part this situation is due to the fact that "radical feminist" has become an epithet hurled by hostile right-wing commentators. Yet the principles and goals of radical feminism are quite different from those ascribed to it in highly distorted popular representations. What makes radical feminism radical is not its goals but its founding principles; here radical means not "extreme" but "root." For radical feminists, the root cause of social inequality is gender inequality, which is based in men's systematic and structural subordination of women, or patriarchy. It is crucial to recognize that in radical feminist thought, patriarchy is not simply the power of individual men over individual women but a system of oppression from which every man benefits in countless ways, even without recognizing or intentionally participating in this system. Thus individual men sympathetic to feminist aims cannot simply renounce their patriarchal privilege.

The leading theorists of radical feminism are many, but I focus here on two influential figures, Susan Brownmiller (1975) and Andrea Dworkin (1974), who argue that male sexualized violence against women is the very cornerstone of patriarchy, allowing men to maintain their dominant position over women. Although Brownmiller distinguishes rape, as an act of power, from sex, as an act of eroticism, Dworkin (1987) takes a stronger position, arguing that all heterosexual intercourse under patriarchy is necessarily coercive. Dworkin's perspective has not been widely embraced in feminist circles, but Brownmiller's characterization of rape as rooted in power rather than desire has not only shaped feminist thinking but also helped to transform the understanding of rape within the law, the media, and the culture at large. At the same time, sexist and misogynistic misperceptions about rape and its victims continue to circulate widely, an issue in which language is paramount.

The linguistic dimensions of rape as a radical feminist issue are investigated in Susan Ehrlich's scholarship on language and sexual violence (e.g., Ehrlich 2001; Chapter 23 in this volume). Ehrlich's work demonstrates the payoff for feminist linguists in engaging directly with feminist theory and research in other fields. Building on insights from Susan Estrich (1987) and other feminist researchers, Ehrlich convincingly shows how the discourse of rape culture permeates the legal system in ways that structurally disadvantage female rape survivors.[4]

In the view of radical feminism, the threat of such violence is evident not only in acts of rape and sexual assault but also through mundane linguistic practices discussed by a number of scholars, like street remarks (e.g., Gardner 1980; Kissling 1991) and sexual harassment in workplace settings (e.g., Ragan et al. 1996) and online (e.g., Herring 1999; Herring and Stoerger, Chapter 29 in this volume). At the same time, influential feminist linguistic research has argued that men also engage in acts of conversational domination over women such as interruption, lack of uptake of women's topics, and problematizing of women (Fishman 1983; Ochs and Taylor 1995; Spender 1985). Although radical feminism has been critiqued for its emphasis on the subjugation of women under patriarchy to the exclusion of other issues, its insights into the mechanisms of gendered power remain directly relevant to feminist linguists' efforts to combat linguistic and physical violence (e.g., Kitzinger and Frith 1999; Trinch 2003).

3. From Gender Difference to Gendered Experiences

Within linguistics, second-wave feminist approaches are widely classified according to a broad three-way taxonomy of *deficit* (liberal feminism), *difference* (cultural feminism), and *dominance* (radical feminism) (Cameron 1995). While this tripartite categorization highlights some of the important distinctions among these perspectives, it obscures what they share: All three of these forms of second-wave feminism are in fact "difference" approaches, in that they take gender difference as their starting point. Relatedly, all three theories position women's experiences both as universally shared and as central to feminist inquiry. This perspective is often criticized as *essentialism*, which in the case of gender posits a shared cultural "essence" that unites all women and differentiates them from men. Such an approach was necessary in the early years of second-wave feminism in order to establish gender as a relevant topic for scholarship and to bring women into focus across the academy, and this form of analysis remains a valuable tool of feminist research if its limitations are recognized. Yet in foregrounding the category of women, the second-wave perspective underplays other important aspects of gender. I now turn to alternative frameworks that broaden the scope of feminist critique both to include issues of race and class as well as gender and to encompass the analysis of masculinity and men's experiences alongside the traditional focus on women. Unlike second-wave feminist linguistics, which is often associated with a few iconic figures, these new approaches have been pursued by many different scholars from a number of angles. For the most part I therefore identify key trends in each area rather than focusing in detail on the work of individual scholars.

3.1   *Material feminism and linguistic capital*

While radical feminists posit gender oppression as the root or fundamental form of inequality, other feminist theorists argue that women's subordination is a consequence of class oppression, which they take to be primary. This perspective is found within Marxist and socialist branches of material feminism. However, material feminist approaches range well beyond these viewpoints, while sharing a general concern with the physical conditions of gender. Material feminisms examine such diverse issues as the situation of women in the domestic sphere, both as unpaid labor and, in some contexts, as male property; the role of gender in the labor market and the class system; feminized aspects of economic production; gendered dimensions of consumption under capitalism; the linguistic commodification of gender and sexuality; and the relationship of gender and sexuality to bodies and embodied experience, biological and genetic discourses, and the natural and built environment (e.g., Alaimo and Hekman 2008; Hennessy and Ingraham 1997; see also Cameron 2006 on radical materialist feminism). This general perspective thus overlaps with the second-wave feminist theories already discussed, sharing with liberal feminism, for example, a commitment to workplace rights for women, and sharing with radical feminism a concern with sexual violence.

Linguistic research that engages material feminist concerns is equally broad in its scope, spanning studies of the relationship between gender, class, and variation (Eckert 1989); the ideologies and realities of women's linguistic labor in the home as mothers and wives within the traditional nuclear family (Kendall 2008; Sunderland 2006); the role of language in marketing to female and male consumers of various kinds (Benwell 2004; Lazar 2006); and the links between language and gendered embodied practices (Speer and Green 2007). In addition, examinations of gendered language in work contexts ranging from beauty salons (Toerien and Kitzinger 2007) to call centers (Cameron 2000) to factory floors (Holmes 2006) to phone sex (Hall 1995) demonstrate the enduring role of gender ideologies in the workplace as well as the growing commodification of feminized ways of speaking. (See also Holmes, Chapter 22 in this volume.) Perhaps the most widespread materialist approach within feminist linguistics is critical discourse analysis, which emerged from neo-Marxist theories of language and examines how ideological power is enacted, especially through institutional discourses such as the media, politics, and education. An explicitly feminist version of critical discourse analysis has been extremely influential (Lazar 2005; Chapter 9 in this volume); in addition, some of the most current work on sexist and homophobic language takes a critical discourse analytic standpoint (e.g., Mills 2008).

Given the vast range of theoretical, methodological, and political concerns represented by such work, it is unsurprising that material feminist approaches within linguistics have not consolidated into a single recognizable perspective as have the second-wave approaches discussed above. Rather, researchers studying one aspect of the gendered materiality of language typically do not interact closely with scholars pursuing other aspects. Yet, as I discuss further at the end of this chapter, this broad approach holds significant potential to influence the field as a whole, as well as feminism more generally, for materialist and discursive views of gender, often conceptualized as antithetical within feminist theory, are effectively combined in material feminist linguistics in all its forms.

3.2 Critical race feminisms and linguistic intersectionalities

While material feminisms often call attention to socioeconomic class, they do not necessarily focus on race and ethnicity, despite the fact that racialization is rooted in sociopolitical interpretations of the body and is hence a fundamentally material issue. The investigation of the intersection of race and ethnicity with class, gender, sexuality, and other dimensions of subjectivity in relation to historical and present-day workings of power is the concern of what is sometimes called multiracial feminism (Thompson 2002) and the closely related approach of postcolonial feminism (e.g., Mohanty, Russo, and Torres 1991). This long-standing political and intellectual movement, which goes by a number of names, has been an important counterpoint to white-dominated versions of feminism (e.g., Collins 1990; Moraga and Anzaldúa 1981; Smith 1983), and some theorists set aside the label "feminism" altogether in favor of terms that place women of color at the center of political thought and action (as seen, e.g., in Walker's 1983 concept of "womanism"). Such feminist theories may focus on the experiences of particular groups of women as well as commonalities of experience of women across politically subordinated communities; they may additionally consider the sometimes shared and sometimes divergent experiences of men of color. Some forms of multiracial feminism have been criticized as similar to cultural feminism in their focus on the cultural situatedness of gendered experience, which is often read as a form of essentialism. It is important to understand, however, that the primary concern of feminist theories of alterity based on race, ethnicity, and colonial status is not a depoliticized notion of culture; instead, such theories conceptualize the cultures of politically subordinated groups as a set of historically specific practices – including linguistic practices – that function as agentive responses to shared experiences of oppression based on inequities of race, gender, class, and nation.

Within linguistics, one of the most important contributions of multiracial feminist research has been to challenge the field's tendency to marginalize the distinctive experiences of women of color. The goal of much of this work is explicitly noncomparative, in contrast to most second-wave feminist linguistics as well as nonfeminist sociolinguistic research on gender. Multiracial feminist linguistic scholarship is committed to understanding the linguistic experiences and practices of women of color on their own terms, often with little if any comparison either to white women or to men of color. In the US context, the largest body of linguistic scholarship from this general perspective focuses on African American girls and women (Jacobs-Huey 2006; Lanehart 2009; Morgan 1999; Troutman 2001), although language and gender researchers have increasingly attended to Native Americans, Asian Americans, and Latinas as well (Ahlers 2012; Chun 2004; Mendoza-Denton 2008; Meek, Chapter 28 in this volume), as well as to whiteness as an often overlooked racialized and gendered category that merits greater scholarly scrutiny (Bucholtz 2011).

Linguistic research from a specifically postcolonial feminist standpoint remains less common. However, feminist linguistic scholarship in postcolonial settings is growing, offering the possibility of dialogue and theoretical convergence as the field continues to develop. Relevant studies include work on gender and creole languages (Escure 2001; Meyerhoff 2004), gender and multilingualism in postcolonial societies (Sadiqi 2008; Walters 1999); gendered representations of the colonized Other (Irvine 2001; Mills 1991); and clashing Western and local discourses of sexuality and gender in public health and development efforts (Clark 2006; Pigg 2001). Some of this work also makes common cause with material feminist linguistic scholarship concerned with gendered processes of globalization (McElhinny 2007; Piller and Takahashi 2006). These and other studies of gendered language ideologies and linguistic practices in contexts of racialized inequity around the world work to undo the long-standing pattern of erasure, marginalization, and exoticism of politically subordinated women and girls within linguistic scholarship, while demonstrating the intersectionality (Crenshaw 1991) of power-saturated social categories of race, class, nation, gender, and sexuality within language use.

3.3   *Theorizing masculinities in language*

A third general approach that critiques and expands the inclusiveness of feminist theory vis-à-vis difference-based frameworks is the set of feminist perspectives on masculinity. For many years, men's experience of gender remained largely unexplored in comparison to the extensive study of women's gendered lives. To be sure, masculinity is a key issue in second-wave feminist theories focused on cross-gender difference, but in such frameworks it is often treated as relatively fixed and monolithic and is rarely a sustained object of study. The field of masculinity studies aims to incorporate men more fully into the study of gender by taking masculinity as the starting point of inquiry rather than as the explanation for gender inequality (Connell 1995; Kimmel 1987).

Masculinity studies is sometimes seen as synonymous with and sometimes as distinct from men's studies, a field grounded in radical feminism that seeks to dismantle patriarchy through the rejection of dominant forms of masculinity (Stoltenberg 1989). Masculinity studies is also starkly different from so-called male studies, a deliberately antifeminist and academically marginal field informed by a politically conservative form of cultural and biological essentialism (Epstein 2010). Intellectually, masculinity studies is primarily concerned with investigating masculinity as a sociocultural construct that takes diverse forms. Politically, its goals are both to challenge masculinity as a warrant for male dominance and to undo the constraining effects of masculinity on men's subjectivities. Because of the racialized and politicized dimensions of masculinity, hegemonic and subaltern masculinities have also figured centrally in multicultural and postcolonial scholarship as well as in materialist approaches.

The general perspective on masculinity taken by masculinity studies has been influential in linguistic research, which has documented the variability of masculinities as they are constructed through language (Benwell, Chapter 12 in this volume; Johnson and Meinhof 1997; Kiesling 2001). In this theoretical approach, what unifies diverse forms of masculinity is power, which is conceptualized as fundamental to how masculinity works. More recent linguistic scholarship complicates the link between masculinity and power, noting in particular the growing ideological destabilization of hegemonic forms of masculinity and the constant identity work required to sustain this construct (Bucholtz and Lopez 2011; Korobov 2009; Milani 2011; Chapter 13 in this volume; Sunderland 2000). Such research points to the insecure status of masculine hegemony at this cultural moment as well as the critical role of language in both delinking and relinking masculinity and power. As discussed further below, following recent trends in gender theory (e.g., Halberstam 1998) scholars are also beginning to conceptually separate masculinity from men by examining the role of masculinity among women as well as those with fluid or nonbinary gender identifications.

All of the critical approaches discussed above open up feminist theory – and feminist linguistics – to the possibility of more complex conceptualizations of gender than a simple matter of women and men. The final set of feminist frameworks considered in this chapter addresses this issue from a variety of perspectives.

4. Queering Feminism: From Gender to Sexuality and Back Again

Whereas both second-wave feminist scholarship and the critical forms of feminism that respond to it often take gender as a given, other feminist theories have sought to interrogate gender itself, frequently by examining the close relationship between gender and sexuality. Sexuality in these theoretical approaches is generally understood both as a form of identity (especially with respect to sexual orientation) and as a set of embodied practices (especially with respect to sexual activity) (Bucholtz and Hall 2004). Such feminist theories come from a broadly queer perspective in that they challenge binary and normative categories based on gender, sexuality, or both. Of course, many of the theories discussed above contribute to this endeavor as well. For example, the critical writings of lesbians of color foreground sexual identity alongside race and ethnicity as a crucial component of intersectionality (e.g., Anzaldúa 1987; Lorde 1984; Moraga 1983), and masculinity studies shares some important conceptual connections with feminist theories of gender and transgender (e.g., Connell 1987; Halberstam 1998). At the same time, there are considerable disagreements within and among all of these overarching approaches.

4.1 Theorizing lesbian, gay, and bisexual identities in language

Like many of the theoretical perspectives on gender discussed above, the focus on lesbian, gay, bisexual, and transgender (LGBT) issues began as a series of political movements and developed a scholarly arm as LGBT research began to gain ground in academia. Despite the shared discourse of rights and inequality found in both liberal feminism and the gay liberation movement, the relationship between feminism and the gay rights movement was historically fraught with tension (see, e.g., Frye 1983). More intimate links existed between radical feminism and lesbian feminism (e.g., Hoagland and Penelope 1992), and between New Age-influenced versions of men's studies and certain gay subcultures (see discussion in Barrett, in press). More recently, feminist and LGBT efforts have become more closely allied in political coalitions as well as in scholarly discourse, the latter in part owing to their shared reliance on Butler's gender theory, as discussed below. These two areas continue to develop separately as well as in tandem.

In all its manifestations, LGBT studies aims both to challenge the sociopolitical marginalization of those who do not conform to heteronormative regimes of sexuality and gender and to investigate the experiences and practices associated with these identities (Abelove, Barale, and Halperin 1993). Such work sometimes focuses on individual categories of non-normative sexuality and/or gender and sometimes on two or more of these together. This political and intellectual coalition, however, has been uneasy at times. Despite ongoing efforts to be maximally inclusive of the identities represented, as reflected by its increasingly unwieldy acronym, within this approach bisexual and transgender identities in particular have often remained marginalized (but see Thorne 2013 as well as the discussion below for new feminist linguistic research on these topics).

Linguistic approaches to LGBT issues generally investigate three types of questions: linguistic aspects of the social and political struggle of LGBT groups and individuals (VanderStouwe 2013), the linguistic practices of particular LGBT-identified groups (Jones 2012; Leap 1996; R. Queen 2005), and discursive representations of LGBT identities by both ingroup and outgroup members (Baker 2005; Koller 2008). Although some of the earliest work from this perspective has come in for attack for what has been characterized as an essentialized understanding of sexual identity (Kulick 2000; Chapter 3 in this volume), the vast majority of recent research is grounded in contemporary theories of gender and sexuality that view identities as highly variable sociocultural constructs produced in large part through language. And even the earlier scholarship, which sometimes elides distinctions between groups in a strategic essentialist move to advance the political goal of social equality, resembles radical cultural feminism in its efforts to validate the language of sexual (and sometimes, gender) minorities (cf. McElhinny 1996).

4.2   Sex-positive feminism and the language of sexual practice

In addition to examining sexuality as identity, particularly with regard to sexual minorities, feminist perspectives have also been taken toward sexuality as practice. This undertaking has both activist and academic dimensions, as sex workers, sex educators, and pro-sex advocates have made common cause with scholars around the issue of women's sexual pleasure (e.g., Califia 1994; C. Queen 1997; Vance 1984). This topic has long been fraught with controversy within feminist politics, due to the early radical feminist theorizing of heterosexual sex and pornography as inherently violent and oppressive, a viewpoint that has also often been extended to lesbian pornography and to lesbian sexual activities that explore and eroticize ritual dominance and submission (including bondage/discipline and sadism/masochism, often referred to by the acronym BDSM). By legitimating women's sexual pleasure in all its forms, including these politically and culturally taboo sexual practices, sex-positive feminists emphasize that acknowledging the diversity of sexual experiences and desires for all sexual actors is not only consistent with but central to feminist goals. Sex-positive feminism has also produced an extensive body of feminist erotica (e.g., Bright 1988), which linguistically produces women as sexual subjects with complex desires, in contrast to traditional representations in bodice-ripper supermarket romances aimed at heterosexual women (Talbot 1997).

As the example of erotica suggests, language is an important dimension of sexual activities and practices. Yet, as in other arenas of gender and sexuality that centrally involve embodiment and physicality, material feminist concerns have often been privileged in feminist thinking about these matters to the exclusion of linguistic issues; thus, feminist linguistic research is well positioned to unify materialist and discursive perspectives. Indeed, scholars of language, gender, and sexuality have used linguistic insights to examine a variety of sexual practices (Harvey and Shalom 1997), from the use of safewords in BDSM (Cameron and Kulick 2003) to the linguistic management of physicality in gay men's online sexual encounters (Jones 2005; 2008) to discussions of sexual knowledge among teenage girls (Skapoulli 2009). Despite the considerable ethical and practical challenges in documenting language use in sexual contexts, such work, when responsibly conducted, is invaluable for shedding light on the pivotal role of language in sexual situations.

4.3 Poststructuralist feminism and the linguistic challenge to gender

The final theoretical framework considered in this chapter, which sometimes goes by the label *poststructuralist* (or *postmodern*) *feminism* (cf. Nicholson 1990), scrutinizes binary models of sex, gender, and sexuality for what they reveal about the social organization of these categories and how they are challenged by complex identities and practices, including not only lesbian, gay, and bisexual identities, but also transgender, transsexual, intersex, genderqueer, and other identities that are increasingly moving to the center of feminist theory. This general perspective takes as its starting point Judith Butler's (1990) revolutionary notion of performativity, or the idea that gender and sexuality are brought into being through the repeated discursive enactment of cultural norms. Crucial to this concept is the possibility of disrupting the normative alignment of sex assignment, gender identity, and sexual identity through such practices as drag performances, in which gay men appropriate femininity in order to challenge heteronormativity. For this reason, queer theory, especially in its more feminist forms, draws heavily on Butler's work (Marinucci 2010). Approaches that interrogate gender also encompass the study of everyday rather than staged practices that decouple gender from assigned sex and sexuality, as with some transgender and transsexual identities, or practices that refuse gender categorization altogether, as with some trans and intersex identities (e.g., Bornstein 1994; Kessler 1998; Stryker and Whittle 2006).

Performativity derives from a concept within the philosophy of language, the performative speech act (Austin 1962), or speech that changes the world through language. Performativity is therefore a fundamentally linguistic – or, more generally, semiotic – act. Not surprisingly, then, Butler's theory precipitated an outpouring of feminist linguistic research examining the linguistic resources that bring gender into being (e.g., Bergvall, Bing, and Freed 1996; Bucholtz, Liang, and Sutton 1999; Hall and Bucholtz 1995; McIlvenny 2002), as well as the development of an explicitly poststructuralist feminist discourse analytic framework (Baxter 2003). Within feminist linguistics, a queer perspective has also been engaged by a number of researchers, beginning with the foundation of queer linguistics (Livia and Hall 1997) and continuing with the work of a new generation of scholars (e.g., Milani, Chapter 13 in this volume; Zimman, Davis, and Raclaw, in press). These authors aim not simply to dismantle binaries but to examine their productive potential for nonhegemonic gender and sexual subjectivities (Zimman and Hall 2010), not only via investigations of the sorts of drag performances that inspired Butler (e.g., Barrett 1999) but also through an ongoing focus on gender categories around the world that challenge Western binaries (e.g., Besnier 2003; Boellstorff 2004; Borba and Ostermann 2007; Gaudio 2009; Hall 2005; Hall and O'Donovan 1996). This latter body of research intersects with postcolonial feminism in its attention to how non-normative gender identities are mapped onto binaries like modern/traditional. Recently, feminist linguistic scholarship has likewise begun to examine how categories of gender, sex, and sexuality are put to work in more-than-binary identities in the late modern West (e.g., Speer and Green 2007; Speer and Parsons 2006; Zimman 2009).

Linguistic research from a queer perspective thus ranges from a concern with sexual alterity to the linguistic dimensions of sexual activity to the nuanced con-figurations of gender, sex, and sexuality that transgender and other nonbinary identities make possible. And once again, in its focus on these issues as simul-taneously discursive and embodied, such research offers a much needed bridge between discourse-centered poststructuralist perspectives and material feminist concerns with the body.

5. A New Linguistic Turn?

As I hope to have demonstrated in this brief survey, feminist linguistics is richly informed by feminist theory. And in the past 20 years there has been a noticeable trend toward embracing theory more explicitly than in previous decades – particularly the version of feminist theory articulated by Butler (1990). Such a turn of events is no accident, for Butler was instrumental in popularizing the so-called linguistic turn in Anglo-American feminist theory (e.g., Fraser 1995), parallel to similar developments in French feminism and in critical theory and philosophy more generally. It is no wonder, then, that researchers who had long recognized the intimate connection between language, gender, and sexuality would welcome this newfound feminist interest in the workings of language. Although the linguistic turn did not result in a raised profile for language, gender, and sexuality studies among feminists in other fields, it did lead Butler's work to enter the theoretical canon of feminist linguistics, where it has frequently been used with insight and sophistication. Yet there is much more to the field of language, gender, and sexuality than can be captured by any single theory, no matter how brilliant and groundbreaking. While Butler's work has provided one of the most productive theories the field has encountered, it is important to expand recognition of the many theoretical perspectives that inform feminist linguistic work, both explicitly and implicitly.

Moreover, feminist linguistics is uniquely positioned to play a leading role in shaping new developments in feminist theory, and particularly in forging a rapprochement between discursive and materialist perspectives, which have too often been at odds in feminist theoretical debates (e.g., Ahmed 2008; Barad 2003). Feminist linguistics bridges this artificial divide, thanks in part to the growing use of new methodologies, especially video analysis, that require recognition of the fundamental materiality of language. But more generally, the field has long been concerned with the simultaneously discursive and material character of gender and sexuality, as seen in a wide range of phenomena, including embodied communicative action that indexes gendered or sexual subjectivities; linguistic and bodily engagements with the environment and technology; the gendered and sexualized voice; the global commodification of gendered language; language in sexual practice; and the material effects of discourses of gender and sexuality (cf. Shankar and Cavanaugh 2012). One example of what a linguistically informed feminist theory might look like is Mel Chen's (2012) rich and highly innovative work bringing cognitive linguistics into dialogue with queer theory, animal studies, and understandings of the body. But of course many other sorts of theoretical engagements are both possible and necessary. It may be time, then, for a new linguistic turn in feminist theory, one that is equally concerned with discourse and materiality as consequential for the workings of gender and sexuality.

6. Conclusion

In this chapter I have sought both to reaffirm and to revisit the feminist foundations of language, gender, and sexuality studies, at least as I understand them from my vantage point as a US-trained scholar who came of age as a feminist and a linguist in the 1990s. As I have discussed, the theoretical roots of feminist linguistics lie in the difference-based theories that emerged during feminism's second wave, which placed women's concerns at the center of scholarly analysis for the first time in history. The field has gone on to expand its remit from its original focus on white straight middle-class women to a more inclusive perspective, thanks to the influence of critical feminisms concerned with materiality, race and colonialism, and masculinity. And in response to feminist interrogations of the relationship of gender to sexuality on the one hand and to sex on the other under the general banner of queer feminism, growing numbers of language-oriented scholars address questions of sexual identity and practice as well as of gender and sexual alterity. I have also argued for the continuing value of poststructuralist feminism even as the field moves toward an approach to discourse grounded in the materialities of the body, the natural and built environment, and the global political economy.

A continuing engagement with feminist theory will lead feminist linguistics in many fruitful directions by creatively combining insights from multiple perspectives, by introducing new theoretical approaches, and by tying scholarship more closely to activism and advocacy work. Throughout this process, feminist linguists must also develop our own endogenous theoretical perspectives in dialogue with feminists in other fields.

Acknowledgments

My deepest thanks to the editors of this volume for their patience and forbearance during the slow development of this chapter. Some of the material in these pages was presented, in a rather different form, to the 7th International Gender and Language Association Conference in São Leopoldo, Brazil, in 2012; thanks are due to audience members for their feedback. The ideas presented here have also benefited from the invaluable comments of an anonymous reviewer; from the insights of my graduate and undergraduate students in language, gender, and sexuality; and from ongoing discussions of feminist theory with Kira Hall. I owe special thanks to Kira for her careful and astute reading of an earlier version of the chapter. I alone am responsible for any problems of representation, interpretation, or omission in these pages.

NOTES

1   Henceforth, the term "feminist linguistics" is used interchangeably with "language, gender, and sexuality," but it is important to recognize that many of the researchers within the field are affiliated with disciplines other than linguistics.
2   Although I argue here that Lakoff's earliest work is generally aligned with liberal feminism, her later writings include elements of radical feminism as well. See McElhinny (2004) for Lakoff's radical feminist orientation beginning with *Language and Woman's Place*, and Cameron (1990, 23) for a discussion of Lakoff's concern with male dominance.
3   It is worth noting that Tannen earned her PhD under Lakoff's supervision; Lakoff was also my own graduate adviser.
4   I focus here on Ehrlich's contributions to a radical feminist critique of gendered violence, but her work is also informed by material feminism (Ehrlich 2004) and poststructuralist feminism (Ehrlich 2007), among others.

REFERENCES

Abelove, Henry, Michèle Aina Barale, and David M. Halperin, eds. 1993. *The Lesbian and Gay Studies Reader*. New York: Routledge.

Ahlers, Jocelyn C. 2012. "Language Revitalization and the (Re)Constituting of Gender: Silence and Women in Native California Language Revitalization." *Gender and Language*, 6(2): 309–337.

Ahmed, Sara. 2008. "Imaginary Prohibitions: Some Preliminary Remarks on the Founding Gestures of the 'New Materialism.'" *European Journal of Women's Studies*, 15(1): 23–39.

Alaimo, Stacy, and Susan Hekman, eds. 2008. *Material Feminisms*. Bloomington: Indiana University Press.

Anzaldúa, Gloria. 1987. *Borderlands/La Frontera: The New Mestiza*. San Francisco: Spinsters/Aunt Lute.

Austin, J. L. 1962. *How to Do Things with Words*. Cambridge, MA: Harvard University Press.

Baker, Paul. 2005. *Public Discourses of Gay Men*. London: Routledge.

Barad, Karen. 2003. "Posthumanist Performativity: Toward an Understanding of How Matter Comes to Matter." *Signs*, 28(3): 801–831.

Barrett, Rusty. 1999. "Indexing Polyphonous Identity in the Speech of African American Drag Queens." In Mary Bucholtz, A. C. Liang, and Laurel A. Sutton (eds.), *Reinventing Identities: The Gendered Self in Discourse*, 313–331. New York: Oxford University Press.

Barrett, Rusty. In press. *From Drag Queens to Leathermen: Language, Gender, and Gay Male Subcultures*. New York: Oxford University Press.

Baxter, Judith. 2003. *Positioning Gender in Discourse: A Feminist Methodology*. Basingstoke: Palgrave Macmillan.

Baxter, Judith. 2010. *The Language of Female Leadership*. Basingstoke: Palgrave Macmillan.

Beasley, Chris. 1999. *What Is Feminism? An Introduction to Feminist Theory*. Thousand Oaks, CA: Sage.

Belenky, Mary, Blythe McVicker Clinchy, Nancy Rule Goldberger, and Jill Mattuck Tarule. 1986. *Women's Ways of Knowing*. New York: Basic Books.

Benwell, Bethan. 2004. "Ironic Discourse: Evasive Masculinity in Men's Lifestyle Magazines." *Men and Masculinities*, 7(1): 3–21.

Bergvall, Victoria L., Janet M. Bing, and Alice F. Freed, eds. 1996. *Rethinking Language and Gender Research: Theory and Practice*. London: Longman.

Besnier, Niko. 2003. "Crossing Gender, Mixing Languages: The Linguistic Construction of Transgenderism in Tonga." In Janet Holmes and Miriam Meyerhoff (eds.), *The Handbook of Language and Gender*, 279–301. Oxford: Blackwell.

Boellstorff, Tom. 2004. "*Gay* Language in Indonesia." *Journal of Linguistic Anthropology*, 14(2): 248–268.

Borba, Rodrigo, and Ana C. Ostermann. 2007. "Do Bodies Matter? Travestis' Embodment of (Trans)Gender Identity through the Manipulation of the Brazilian Portuguese Grammatical Gender System." *Gender and Language*, 1(1): 131–147.

Bornstein, Kate. 1994. *On Men, Women, and the Rest of Us*. New York: Routledge.

Bright, Susie, ed. 1988. *Herotica: A Collection of Women's Erotic Fiction*. San Francisco: Down There Press.

Brownmiller, Susan. 1975. *Against Our Will: Men, Women, and Rape*. New York: Simon & Schuster.

Bucholtz, Mary. 1999. "Review of *Women Talk* by Jennifer Coates." *American Speech*, 74(4): 433–436.

Bucholtz, Mary. 2004. "Changing Places: *Language and Woman's Place* in Context." In Robin Tolmach Lakoff, *Language and Woman's Place: Text and Commentaries*, rev. and expanded edn, ed. Mary Bucholtz, 121–128. New York: Oxford University Press.

Bucholtz, Mary. 2011. *White Kids: Language, Race, and Styles of Youth Identity*. Cambridge. Cambridge University Press.

Bucholtz, Mary, and Kira Hall. 1995. "Introduction: Twenty Years after *Language and Woman's Place*." In Kira Hall and Mary Bucholtz (eds.), *Gender Articulated: Language and the Socially Constructed Self*, 1–22. New York: Routledge.

Bucholtz, Mary, and Kira Hall. 2004. "Theorizing Identity in Language and Sexuality Research." *Language in Society*, 33(4): 501–547.

Bucholtz, Mary, A. C. Liang, and Laurel A. Sutton, eds. 1999. *Reinventing Identities: The Gendered Self in Discourse*. New York: Oxford University Press.

Bucholtz, Mary, and Qiuana Lopez. 2011. "Performing Blackness, Forming Whiteness: Linguistic Minstrelsy in Hollywood Film." *Journal of Sociolinguistics*, 15(5): 680–706.

Butler, Judith. 1990. *Gender Trouble: Feminism and the Subversion of Identity*. New York: Routledge.

Califia, Pat. 1994. *Public Sex: The Culture of Radical Sex*. San Francisco: Cleis Press.

Cameron, Deborah. 1985. *Feminism and Linguistic Theory*. Basingstoke: Macmillan.

Cameron, Deborah, ed. 1990. *The Feminist Critique of Language*. London: Routledge.

Cameron, Deborah. 1995. "Rethinking Language and Gender Studies: Some Issues for the 1990s." In Sara Mills (ed.), *Language and Gender: Interdisciplinary Perspectives*, 31–44. Harlow: Longman.

Cameron, Deborah. 2000. "Styling the Worker: Gender and the Commodification of Language in the Globalized Service Economy." *Journal of Sociolinguistics*, 4(3): 323–347.

Cameron, Deborah. 2006. *On Language and Sexual Politics*. London: Routledge.

Cameron, Deborah, and Don Kulick. 2003. *Language and Sexuality*. Cambridge: Cambridge University Press.

Chen, Mel Y. 2012. *Animacies: Biopolitics, Racial Mattering, and Queer Affect*. Durham, NC: Duke University Press.

Chun, Elaine W. 2004. "Ideologies of Legitimate Mockery: Margaret Cho's Revoicings of Mock Asian." *Pragmatics*, 14(2–3): 263–289.

Clark, Jude. 2006. "The Role of Language and Gender in the Naming and Framing of HIV/AIDS in the South African Context." *Southern African Linguistics and Applied Language Studies*, 24(4): 461–471.

Coates, Jennifer. 1996. *Women Talk*. Oxford: Blackwell.

Collins, Patricia Hill. 1990. *Black Feminist Thought: Knowledge, Consciousness, and the Politics of Empowerment*. Boston: Unwin Hyman.

Connell, R. W. 1987. *Gender and Power*. Stanford: Stanford University Press.

Connell, R. W. 1995. *Masculinities*. Berkeley: University of California Press.

Crenshaw, Kimberlé W. 1991. "Mapping the Margins: Intersectionality, Identity Politics, and Violence against Women of Color." *Stanford Law Review*, 43(6): 1241–1299.

Daly, Mary. 1978. *Gyn/Ecology: The Metaethics of Radical Feminism*. Boston: Beacon.

Daly, Mary, and Jane Caputi. 1987. *Websters' First New Intergalactic Wickedary of the English Language*. Boston: Beacon.

Davis, Hayley. 1996. "Review Article: Theorizing Women's and Men's Language." *Language and Communication*, 16(1): 71–79.

Davis, Hayley. 1997. "Gender, Discourse and *Gender and Discourse*." *Language and Communication*, 17(4): 353–357.

Dworkin, Andrea. 1974. *Woman Hating: A Radical Look at Sexuality*. New York: Dutton.

Dworkin, Andrea. 1987. *Intercourse*. New York: Free Press.

Eckert, Penelope. 1989. "The Whole Woman: Sex and Gender Differences in Variation." *Language Variation and Change*, 1: 245–267.

Ehrlich, Susan. 2001. *Representing Rape: Language and Sexual Consent*. New York: Routledge.

Ehrlich, Susan. 2004. "Linguistic Discrimination and Violence against Women: Discursive Practices and Material Effects." In Robin Tolmach Lakoff, *Language and Woman's Place: Text and Commentaries*, rev. and expanded edn, ed. Mary Bucholtz, 223–228. New York: Oxford University Press.

Ehrlich, Susan. 2007. "Legal Discourse and the Cultural Intelligibility of Gendered Meanings." *Journal of Sociolinguistics*, 11(4): 452–477.

Epstein, Jennifer. 2010. "Male Studies vs. Men's Studies." *Inside Higher Ed* (April 8). At http://www.insidehighered.com/news/2010/04/08/males, accessed October 8, 2013.

Escure, Geneviève. 2001. "Belizean Creole: Gender, Creole, and the Role of Women in Language Change." In Marlis Hellinger and Hadumod Bussmann (eds.), *Gender across Languages: The Linguistic Representation of Women and Men*, vol. 1, 53–84. Amsterdam: Benjamins.

Estrich, Susan. 1987. *Real Rape*. Cambridge, MA: Harvard University Press.

Fishman, Pamela. 1983. "Interaction: The Work Women Do." In Barrie Thorne, Cheris Kramarae, and Nancy Henley (eds.), *Language, Gender, and Society*, 89–101. Cambridge, MA: Newbury House.

Frank, Francine Wattman, and Paula A. Treichler. 1989. *Language, Gender, and Professional Writing*. New York: Modern Language Association.

Fraser, Nancy. 1995. "Pragmatism, Feminism, and the Linguistic Turn." In Seyla Benhabib, Judith Butler, Drucilla Cornell, and Nancy Fraser (eds.), *Feminist Contentions: A Philosophical Exchange*, 157–171. New York: Routledge.

Freed, Alice. 1992. "We Understand Perfectly: A Critique of Tannen's View of Cross-Sex Communication." In Kira Hall, Mary Bucholtz, and Birch Moonwomon (eds.), *Locating Power: Proceedings of the Second Berkeley Women and Language Conference*, vol. 2, 144–152. Berkeley: Berkeley Women and Language Group.

Friedan, Betty. 1963. *The Feminine Mystique*. New York: Norton.

Frye, Marilyn. 1983. *The Politics of Reality: Essays in Feminist Theory*. Freedom, CA: Crossing Press.

Gardner, Carol Brooks. 1980. "Passing By: Street Remarks, Address Rights, and the Urban Female." *Sociological Inquiry*, 50(3–4): 328–356.

Gaudio, Rudolf Pell. 2009. *Allah Made Us: Sexual Outlaws in an Islamic African City*. Oxford: Blackwell.

Gilligan, Carol. 1982. *In a Different Voice: Psychological Theory and Women's Development*. Cambridge, MA: Harvard University Press.

Goodwin, Marjorie Harness. 2006. *The Hidden Life of Girls: Games of Stance, Status, and Exclusion*. Malden, MA: Blackwell.

Halberstam, Judith. 1998. *Female Masculinity*. Durham, NC: Duke University Press.

Hall, Kira. 1995. "Lip Service on the Fantasy Lines." In Kira Hall and Mary Bucholtz (eds.), *Gender Articulated: Language and the Socially Constructed Self*, 183–216. New York: Routledge.

Hall, Kira. 2005. "Intertextual Sexuality: Parodies of Class, Identity, and Desire in Delhi." *Journal of Linguistic Anthropology*, 15(1): 125–144.

Hall, Kira, and Mary Bucholtz, eds. 1995. *Gender Articulated: Language and the Socially Constructed Self*. New York: Routledge.

Hall, Kira, and Veronica O'Donovan. 1996. "Shifting Gender Positions among Hindi-Speaking Hijras." In Victoria L. Bergvall, Janet M. Bing, and Alice F. Freed (eds.), *Rethinking Language and Gender Research: Theory and Practice*, 228–266. London: Longman.

Harvey, Keith, and Celia Shalom, eds. 1997. *Language and Desire: Encoding Sex, Romance and Intimacy*. London: Routledge.

Hass, Mary. 2000. "The Style of the Speaking Subject: Irigaray's Empirical Studies of Language Production." *Hypatia*, 15(1): 64–89.

Hennessy, Rosemary, and Chrys Ingraham, eds. 1997. *Materialist Feminism: A Reader in Class, Difference, and Women's Lives*. New York: Routledge.

Herring, Susan C. 1999. "The Rhetorical Dynamics of Gender Harassment On-line." *Information Society*, 15(3): 151–167.

Hoagland, Sarah Lucia, and Julia Penelope, eds. 1992. *For Lesbians Only: A Separatist Anthology*. London: Onlywomen Press.

Holmes, Janet. 1993. "New Zealand Women Are Good to Talk to: An Analysis of Politeness Strategies in Interaction." *Journal of Pragmatics*, 20(2): 91–116.

Holmes, Janet. 2006. *Gendered Talk at Work: Constructing Gender Identity through Workplace Discourse*. Oxford: Blackwell.

Houvouras, Shannon, and J. Scott Carter. 2008. "The F Word: College Students' Definitions of a Feminist." *Sociological Forum*, 23(2): 234–256.

Irvine, Judith T. 2001. "The Family Romance of Colonial Linguistics: Gender and Family in Nineteenth-Century Representations of African Languages." In Susan Gal and Kathryn A. Woolard (eds.), *Languages and Publics: The Making of Authority*, 13–29. Manchester: St. Jerome.

Jackson, Stevi, and Jackie Jones, eds. 1998. *Contemporary Feminist Theories*. Edinburgh: Edinburgh University Press.

Jacobs-Huey, Lanita. 2006. *From the Kitchen to the Parlor: Language and Becoming in African American Women's Hair Care*. New York: Oxford University Press.

Johnson, Sally, and Ulrike Meinhof, eds. 1997. *Language and Masculinity*. Oxford: Blackwell.

Jones, Lucy. 2012. *Dyke/Girl: Language and Identities in a Lesbian Group*. Basingstoke: Palgrave Macmillan.

Jones, Rodney H. 2005. "'You Show Me Yours, I'll Show You Mine': The Negotiation of Shifts from Textual to Visual Modes in Computer-Mediated Interaction among Gay Men." *Visual Communication*, 4(1): 69–92.

Jones, Rodney H. 2008. "The Role of Text in Televideo Cybersex." *Text and Talk*, 28(4): 453–473.

Kendall, Shari. 2008. "The Balancing Act: Framing Gendered Parental Identities at Dinnertime." *Language in Society*, 37(4): 539–568.

Kessler, Suzanne J. 1998. *Lessons from the Intersexed*. New Brunswick, NJ: Rutgers University Press.

Kiesling, Scott Fabius. 2001. "'Now I Gotta Watch What I Say': Shifting Constructions of Masculinity in Discourse." *Journal of Linguistic Anthropology*, 11(2): 250–273.

Kimmel, Michael. 1987. *Changing Men: New Directions in the Study of Men and Masculinity*. Newbury Park, CA: Sage.

Kissling, Elizabeth Arveda. 1991. "Street Harassment: The Language of Sexual Terrorism." *Discourse and Society*, 2(4): 451–460.

Kitzinger, Celia, and Hannah Frith 1999. "Just Say No? The Use of Conversation Analysis in Developing a Feminist Perspective on Sexual Refusal." *Discourse and Society*, 10(3): 293–316.

Koller, Veronika. 2008. *Lesbian Discourses: Images of a Community*. London: Routledge.

Korobov, Neill. 2009. "'He's Got No Game': Young Men's Stories about Failed Romantic and Sexual Experiences." *Journal of Gender Studies*, 18(2): 99–114.

Kulick, Don. 2000. "Gay and Lesbian Language." *Annual Review of Anthropology*, 29: 243–285.

Lakoff, Robin Tolmach. 2004 [1975]. *Language and Woman's Place: Text and Commentaries*, rev. and expanded edn, ed. Mary Bucholtz. New York: Oxford University Press. (First published New York: Harper & Row.)

Lanehart, Sonja L., ed. 2009. *African American Women's Language: Discourse, Education, and Identity*. Newcastle upon Tyne: Cambridge Scholars Publishing.

Lazar, Michelle M., ed. 2005. *Feminist Critical Discourse Analysis: Gender, Power and Ideology in Discourse*. Basingstoke: Palgrave Macmillan.

Lazar, Michelle M. 2006. "'Discover the Power of Femininity!' Analyzing Global 'Power Femininity' in Local Advertising." *Feminist Media Studies*, 6(4): 505–517.

Leap, William L. 1996. *Word's Out: Gay Men's English*. Minneapolis: University of Minnesota Press.

Livia, Anna. 2000. *Pronoun Envy: Literary Uses of Linguistic Gender*. Oxford: Oxford University Press.

Livia, Anna, and Kira Hall, eds. 1997. *Queerly Phrased: Language, Gender, and Sexuality*. New York: Oxford University Press.

Lorde, Audre. 1984. *Sister Outsider: Essays and Speeches*. Berkeley, CA: Crossing Press.

Maltz, Daniel N., and Ruth A. Borker. 1982. "A Cultural Approach to Male–Female Miscommunication." In John J. Gumperz (ed.), *Language and Social Identity*, 196–216. Cambridge: Cambridge University Press.

Marinucci, Mimi. 2010. *Feminism Is Queer: The Intimate Connection between Queer and Feminist Theory*. London: Zed.

Marks, Elaine, and Isabelle de Courtivron. 1980. *New French Feminisms: An Anthology*. New York: Schocken.

McElhinny, Bonnie. 1996. "Strategic Essentialism in Sociolinguistic Studies of Gender." In Natasha Warner, Jocelyn Ahlers, Leela Bilmes, Monica Oliver, Suzanne Wertheim, and Melinda Chen (eds.), *Gender and Belief Systems: Proceedings of the Fourth Berkeley Women and Language Conference*, 469–480. Berkeley: Berkeley Women and Language Group.

McElhinny, Bonnie. 2004. "'Radical Feminist' as Label, Libel, and Laudatory Chant: The Politics of Theoretical Taxonomies in Feminist Linguistics." In Robin Tolmach Lakoff, *Language and Woman's Place: Text and Commentaries*, rev. and expanded edn, ed. Mary Bucholtz, 129–135. New York: Oxford University Press.

McElhinny, Bonnie, ed. 2007. *Words, Worlds, and Material Girls: Language, Gender, Globalized Economy.* Berlin: Mouton de Gruyter.

McIlvenny, Paul, ed. 2002. *Talking Gender and Sexuality.* Amsterdam: Benjamins.

Mendoza-Denton, Norma. 2008. *Homegirls: Language and Cultural Practice among Latina Youth Gangs.* Oxford: Blackwell.

Meyerhoff, Miriam. 2004. "Attitudes to Gender and Creoles: A Case Study on Mokes and Titas." *Te Reo*, 47: 63–82.

Milani, Tommaso M., ed. 2011. "Re-casting Language and Masculinities" (special issue). *Gender and Language*, 5(2).

Miller, Casey, and Kate Swift. 1977. *Words and Women.* New York: Knopf.

Mills, Sara. 1991. *Discourses of Difference: Analysis of Women's Travel Writing and Colonialism.* London: Routledge.

Mills, Sara. 2008. *Language and Sexism.* Cambridge: Cambridge University Press.

Mohanty, Chandra Talpade, Ann Russo, and Lourdes Torres, eds. 1991. *Third World Women and the Politics of Feminism.* Bloomington: Indiana University Press.

Moraga, Cherríe. 1983. *Loving in the War Years: Lo que Nunca Pasó por sus Labios.* Boston: South End Press.

Moraga, Cherríe, and Gloria Anzaldúa, eds. 1981. *This Bridge Called My Back: Writings by Radical Women of Color.* New York: Kitchen Table: Women of Color Press.

Morgan, Marcyliena. 1999. "No Woman No Cry: Claiming African American Women's Place." In Mary Bucholtz, A. C. Liang, and Laurel A. Sutton (eds.), *Reinventing Identities: The Gendered Self in Discourse*, 27–45. New York: Oxford University Press.

Nicholson, Linda J., ed. 1990. *Feminism/Postmodernism.* New York: Routledge.

Ochs, Elinor, and Carolyn Taylor. 1995. "The 'Father Knows Best' Dynamic in Dinnertime Narratives." In Kira Hall and Mary Bucholtz (eds.), *Gender Articulated: Language and the Socially Constructed Self*, 97–120. New York: Routledge.

Pauwels, Anne. 1998. *Women Changing Language.* London: Longman.

Penelope, Julia. 1990. *Speaking Freely: Unlearning the Lies of the Fathers' Tongues.* New York: Pergamon Press.

Pigg, Stacy Leigh. 2001. "Languages of Sex and AIDS in Nepal: Notes on the Social Production of Commensurability." *Cultural Anthropology*, 16(4): 481–541.

Piller, Ingrid, and Kimie Takahashi. 2006. "A Passion for English: Desire and the Language Market." In Aneta Pavlenko (ed.), *Bilingual Minds: Emotional Experience, Expression and Representation*, 59–83. Clevedon: Multilingual Matters.

Queen, Carol. 1997. *Real Live Nude Girl: Chronicles of Sex-Positive Culture.* San Francisco: Cleis Press.

Queen, Robin. 2005. "'How Many Lesbians Does it Take…': Jokes, Teasing, and the Negotiation of Stereotypes about Lesbians." *Journal of Linguistic Anthropology*, 15(2): 239–257.

Ragan, Sandra L., Dianne G. Bystrom, Lynda Lee Kaid, and Christina S. Beck, eds. 1996. *The Lynching of Language: Gender, Politics, and Power in the Hill-Thomas Hearings.* Urbana: University of Illinois Press.

Sadiqi, Fatima. 2008. "Language and Gender in Moroccan Urban Areas." *International Journal of the Sociology of Language*, 190: 145–165.

Shankar, Shalini, and Jillian R. Cavanaugh. 2012. "Language and Materiality in Global Capitalism." *Annual Review of Anthropology*, 41: 355–369.

Simmons, Rachel. 2002. *Odd Girl Out: The Hidden Culture of Aggression in Girls.* San Diego: Harcourt.

Skapoulli, Elena. 2009. "Transforming the Label of 'Whore': Teenage Girls' Negotiation of Local and Global Gender Ideologies in Cyprus." *Pragmatics*, 19(1): 85–101.

Smith, Barbara, ed. 1983. *Home Girls: A Black Feminist Anthology.* New York: Kitchen Table: Women of Color Press.

Speer, Susan A., and Richard Green. 2007. "On Passing: The Interactional Organization of Appearance Attributions in the Psychiatric Assessment of Transsexual Patients." In Victoria Clark and Elizabeth Peel (eds.), *Out in Psychology: Lesbian, Gay, Bisexual, Trans and Queer Perspectives*, 335–368. Chichester: Wiley.

Speer, Susan A., and Ceri Parsons. 2006. "Gatekeeping Gender: Some Features of the Use of Hypothetical Questions in the Psychiatric Assessment of Transsexual Patients." *Discourse and Society*, 18(1): 785–812.

Spender, Dale. 1985. *Man Made Language*, 2nd edn. London: Routledge & Kegan Paul.

Stoltenberg, John. 1989. *Refusing to Be a Man: Essays on Sex and Justice*. Portland, OR: Breitenbush Books.

Stryker, Susan, and Stephen Whittle, eds. 2006. *The Transgender Studies Reader*. New York: Routledge.

Sunderland, Jane. 2000. "Baby Entertainer, Bumbling Assistant and Line Manager: Discourses of Fatherhood in Parentcraft Texts." *Discourse and Society*, 11(2): 249–274.

Sunderland, Jane. 2006. "'Parenting' or 'Mothering'? The Case of Modern Childcare Magazines." *Discourse and Society*, 17(4): 503–528.

Talbot, Mary. 1997. "'An Explosion Deep Inside Her': Women's Desire and Popular Romance Fiction." In Keith Harvey and Celia Shalom (eds.), *Language and Desire: Encoding Sex, Romance and Intimacy*, 222–244. London: Routledge.

Tannen, Deborah. 1990. *You Just Don't Understand: Women and Men in Conversation*. New York: William Morrow.

Tannen, Deborah. 1994. *Gender and Discourse*. New York: Oxford University Press.

Thompson, Becky. 2002. "Multiracial Feminism: Recasting the Chronology of Second Wave Feminism." *Feminist Studies*, 28(2): 337–360.

Thorne, Lisa. 2013. "'But I'm Attracted to Women': Sexuality and Sexual Identity Performance in Interactional Discourse among Bisexual Students." *Journal of Language and Sexuality*, 2(1): 70–100.

Toerien, Merran, and Celia Kitzinger. 2007. "Emotional Labour in Action: Navigating Multiple Involvements in the Beauty Salon." *Sociology*, 41(4): 645–662.

Tong, Rosemarie. 2009. *Feminist Thought: A More Comprehensive Introduction*, 3rd edn. Boulder, CO: Westview Press.

Trinch, Shonna. 2003. *Latinas' Narratives of Domestic Abuse: Discrepant Versions of Violence*. Amsterdam: Benjamins.

Troemel-Ploetz, Senta. 1991. "Review Essay: Selling the Apolitical." *Discourse & Society*, 2(4): 489–502.

Troutman, Denise. 2001. "African American Women: Talking That Talk." In Sonja L. Lanehart (ed.), *Sociocultural and Historical Contexts of African American English*, 211–237. Amsterdam: Benjamins.

Uchida, Aki. 1992. "When 'Difference' is 'Dominance': A Critique of the 'Anti-Power-Based' Cultural Approach to Sex Differences." *Language in Society*, 21: 547–568.

Vance, Carol, ed. 1984. *Pleasure and Danger: Exploring Female Sexuality*. London: Routledge & Kegan Paul.

VanderStouwe, Chris. 2013. "Religious Victimization as Social Empowerment in Discrimination Narratives from California's Proposition 8 Campaign." *Journal of Language and Sexuality*, 2(2): 235–261.

Walker, Alice. 1983. *In Search of Our Mothers' Gardens: Womanist Prose*. San Diego: Harcourt Brace Jovanovich.

Walters, Keith. 1999. "'Opening the Door of Paradise a Cubit': Educated Tunisian Women, Embodied Linguistic Practice, and Theories of Language and Gender." In Mary Bucholtz, A. C. Liang, and Laurel A. Sutton (eds.), *Reinventing Identities: From Category to Practice in Language and Gender Research*, 200–217. New York: Oxford University Press.

Yerian, Keli. 1997. "From Stereotypes of Gender Difference to Stereotypes of Theory: A Response to Hayley Davis' Review of Deborah Tannen's *Gender and*

Discourse." Language & Communication, 17(2): 165–176.

Zimman, Lal. 2009. "'The Other Kind of Coming Out': Transgender People and the Coming Out Narrative Genre." *Gender and Language,* 3(1): 53–80.

Zimman, Lal, Jenny L. Davis, and Joshua Raclaw, eds. In press. *Queer Excursions:*

Retheorizing Binaries in Language, Gender, and Sexuality. New York: Oxford University Press.

Zimman, Lal, and Kira Hall. 2010. "Language, Embodiment, and the 'Third Sex.'" In Carmen Llamas and Dominic Watt (eds.), *Language and Identities,* 166–178. Edinburgh: Edinburgh University Press.

2 Theorizing Gender in Sociolinguistics and Linguistic Anthropology

Toward Effective Interventions in Gender Inequity

BONNIE MCELHINNY

1. Introduction

Increasingly, feminist scholars in linguistics and in other fields have realized that we need to ask how empirical gaps come to be created given "that existing paradigms systematically ignore or erase the significance of women's experiences and the organization of gender" (Thorne and Stacey 1993, 168). The task of feminist scholarship thus goes beyond simply adding discussions of women and women's experiences into our disciplines, to encompass the broader task of interrogating and transforming existing conceptual schemes. In history, for instance, feminist and other radical scholars challenged the assumption that history is primarily about politics, public policy, and famous individuals. The inclusion of women led to a rethinking of the notion of historical periodization itself (Kelly-Gadol 1977). In literature, feminist scholars extended their project from the critique of texts by male authors and the recovery of texts written by female authors to asking questions about how literary periods and notions of dominant aesthetic modes are established, and thus how certain writers, texts, and genres become valued as central or canonical (see, e.g., Feldman and Kelley 1995). Feminist anthropologists have also asked questions about how the canon of anthropological thought gets constructed (Behar and Gordan 1995).

In the 1980s and 1990s, feminist sociolinguists and linguistic anthropologists also increasingly asked questions about fundamental analytic concepts. The definition of hypercorrection (Cameron and Coates 1988), standard and vernacular

The Handbook of Language, Gender, and Sexuality, Second Edition.
Edited by Susan Ehrlich, Miriam Meyerhoff, and Janet Holmes.
© 2014 John Wiley & Sons, Inc. Published 2017 by John Wiley & Sons, Inc.

language (Morgan 1994; 2002), definitions of speech community (Eckert and McConnell-Ginet 1992; Holmes and Meyerhoff 1999), and even theories about the way language constructs social identity (Ochs 1992) were all examined by feminist sociolinguists. It is not only, however, analytic concepts which are distinctively sociolinguistic that require feminist re-examination. I argue here that the fundamental feminist category of "gender," as implemented in sociolinguistics, has often included certain political and social assumptions which prematurely narrowed our area of inquiry.

Early sociolinguistic studies of gender often assumed that gender should be studied where it was most salient, and that gender was most salient "in cross-sex interaction between potentially sexually accessible interlocutors, or same-sex interaction in gender-specific tasks" (Brown and Levinson 1983, 53). At its best, work based on this assumption led to a series of insightful studies of the linguistic styles of men and women in romantic heterosexual relationships or in experimental settings designed to simulate such relationships (e.g. Fishman 1983; Gleason 1987; Tannen 1990; West and Zimmerman 1983; Zimmerman and West 1975). There are, however, a number of problematic, theoretical assumptions about gender embedded in this recommendation: (1) gender is closely wedded to sex, and the study of gender is closely wedded to the study of heterosexuality; (2) gender is an attribute; and (3) the study of gender is the study of individuals rather than institutions and larger systems.[1] In this chapter I explore each of these in turn. Cameron (2006, 16) argues that one central goal of language and gender scholarship has to be political, and that such research must contribute to the wider struggle against unjust and oppressive gender relations. Deciding between different theories of gender is thus no mere theoretical exercise; it is directly linked to deciding upon political strategies for effective feminist activism (see also Jaggar 1983).

2. The Relationship of Gender to Sex and Sexuality

When feminist linguists are studying social inequalities as manifest in language are they, or should they be, studying sex or gender? The distinction between sex and gender has been one of the foundations of Western feminist thought. The following pairs of definitions are typical.

> [Sex and gender] serve a useful analytic purpose in contrasting a set of biological facts with a set of cultural facts. Were I to be scrupulous in my use of terms, I would use the term "sex" only when I was speaking of biological differences between males and females and use "gender" whenever I was referring to the social, cultural, psychological constructs that are imposed upon these biological differences … [G]ender designates a set of categories to which we can give the same label crosslinguistically or crossculturally because they have some connection to sex differences. (Shapiro 1981, cited in Yanagisako and Collier 1990, 139)

The distinction between sex and gender attempts to counter views which attribute differences and inequalities between women and men to sex or biology, as in opinions like the following:

> In all primate societies the division of labor by gender creates a highly stable social system, the dominant males controlling territorial boundaries and maintaining order among lesser males by containing and preventing their aggression, the females tending the young and forming alliances with other females. Human primates follow this same pattern so remarkably that it is not difficult to argue for biological bases for the type of social order that channels aggression to guard the territory which in turn maintains an equable environment for the young. (McGuinness and Pribam, cited in Sperling 1991, 208)

In this sociobiological view there is no gender, for there are no cultural determinants of human life. All is "sex." This view of sex as naturally dictating behavior and roles supports a functionalist model of human social organization. Feminists who make a distinction between sex and gender do not necessarily abandon the idea that there are some biological differences between women and men, but most attempt to sharply circumscribe that which can be attributed to such differences. Often implicit in such distinctions is the idea that what is socially constructed (gender) can be more easily transformed than what is biological (sex).

An increasing number of feminists argue that sex–gender models like Shapiro's are problematic, both in their conception of gender and in their assumptions about sex (see also Cameron 1997b). To say that "gender" refers "to the social, cultural, psychological constructs that are imposed upon these biological differences" implies that there are *two* genders, based upon two sexes. Linda Nicholson (1994) calls this the "coat-rack" model of sex and gender. This dichotomous picture of gender is problematic because it overstates similarity within each of the categories so designated, and understates similarities across these categories. Further, underlying the assumption that the sex–gender distinction is dualistic is an assumption that these differences are necessary for reproduction, which is often linked to heterosexuality (see, e.g., Kapchan 1996, 19). The methodological recommendation to study gender "in cross-sex interaction between potentially sexually accessible interlocutors" illustrates how the idea of just two genders can be conflated with a presumption of heterosexuality. Assumptions about heterosexuality as normative thus directly inform notions of sex and gender and vice versa (for more on language, gender, and sexuality see Cameron and Kulick 2003; Campbell-Kibler et al. 2002; Livia and Hall 1997; and in this volume Kulick, Chapter 3; Milani, Chapter 13; Queen, Chapter 10).

Feminist scholars have taken two different paths to redressing problems with the sex–gender distinction. One path, often followed by physical anthropologists and biologists, is to offer a more nuanced picture of the biological, and how it interacts with the social (Sperling 1991; Worthman 1995). This approach challenges the notion of biology as more fixed and less amenable to change than culture. For instance, Worthman (1995) considers the ways that gender as a principle for social organization affects biological development in terms of risk factors for breast cancer. Much recent work in sociolinguistics adopts a second approach, one which in effect subsumes what was traditionally placed under the domain of sex into the domain of gender. Scholars with this view look at the social construction of "sex" and "gender." Indeed, Cameron (2006) argues that feminist sociolinguistics now assumes radical social constructedness to such a degree that scholars no longer engage sufficiently with powerful, and widely held, notions about biological difference (like the notion that women's verbal abilities are superior to men's), in ways that risk marginalizing the field, and leaving such notions intact.

Proponents of radical social constructionist approaches argue that, in addition to recognizing cultural differences in understanding the body (Nicholson 1994), we need to look at how certain definitions of sex and gender become hegemonic and are contested within a given society. Philosopher Judith Butler argues that:

> Gender ought not to be conceived merely as the cultural inscription of meaning on a pregiven sex … gender must also designate the very apparatus of production whereby the sexes themselves are established. As a result, gender is not to culture as sex is to nature; gender is also the discursive/cultural means by which "sexed nature" or "a natural sex" is produced and established as "prediscursive" prior to culture, a politically neutral surface on which culture acts. (1990, 7)

Instead of asking "What are the gender differences?" this approach (an approach which has been called poststructuralist or deconstructive feminist) leads one to ask "What difference does gender make?" and "How did gender come to make a difference?" To argue that differences found in people's behavior, including their speech behavior, can simply be explained by invoking gender is to fail to question how gender is constructed. Instead, one needs to ask how and why gender differences are constructed in particular ways and what political interests are served by such constructions. This question is often linked to an intersectional approach to the construction of identity, where gender is understood as imbricated with sexuality, race/ethnicity, class, nation, and so on. Where certain behaviors or certain people do not conform to dominant norms of how sex, gender, and sexuality should be aligned, they may not be recognized as socially appropriate or even legitimately human; they may also be subject to repercussions and sanctions which vary according to local context. Some are economic, with people being confined to certain kinds of work and expelled from others. In the United States, women working as police officers often find themselves addressed as "sir" and occasionally find that others assume they are lesbians, regardless of any other information about sexual identity, simply because of the work that they do. Other sanctions are physical interventions, in the form of violence ("gay-bashing") or medical procedures (in North America, intersexed infants are operated on in order to be easily categorizable as male or female). Yet other sanctions are emotional: witness the expulsion from biological families of many Indian *hijras*, Nigerian *'yan daudu*, and American gays and lesbians.

Challenges to norms of sex and gender can cast a particularly illuminating light on the construction of sex and gender because they make visible norms and counternorms of gender. Indeed, the study of such challenges has become one methodological corollary of a poststructuralist theoretical approach. Although one argument against a deconstructive feminist approach has been that it focuses on marginal cases of gender construction, cases of deviance, in ways that do not explain gender construction in the majority of people's lives, this argument fails to recognize the principal point being made by this approach, a point that is more familiar perhaps in the study of other marginalized groups. From the perspective of Marxism, the ideas held by elite groups about why and how social stratification and conflict comes about are suspect because they are more likely to reify the status quo than to question it. For instance, a bourgeois perspective might see each worker as a free agent, constrained only by free will in how s/he contracts out labor power, while workers see domination, exploitation, and the accumulation of wealth among a few. Similarly, gender "outliers" bear the costs of hegemonic views about gender in ways that may cause them to question why such views are so powerful and so widely held (on feminist standpoint theory see Collins 1990; Harding 1991; Jaggar 1983).

In linguistics and elsewhere, a poststructuralist approach led to a series of studies in the 1990s and 2000s which focused on various kinds of sex/gender "transgression," in part for what they reveal about dominant norms of sex, gender, and/or sexual identity. The term "transgression" implies these norms are accepted, though the studies contest precisely that. For instance, Hall's work with Indian *hijras* (ritual specialists, mostly men, who describe themselves as hermaphrodites but have often undergone a castration operation) highlights the process of socialization into gender: femaleness and femininity must be learned by *hijras*, in a way similar to how others acquire a second language. Hall's work also interrogates the assumption that highly visible and culturally central gender ambiguity suggests higher cultural tolerance for gender variation, pointing out the range of exclusion and abuse experienced by *hijras* in India (Hall 1997; 2005; 2009). By looking at the ways that '*yan daudu*' (Nigerian men who talk like women, and often have men as sexual partners) transgress norms of gender and sexuality, Gaudio (2009) suggests how, even in a patriarchal Islamic society that in principle accords all men potential access to masculine power, this access is not equally distributed, nor unconditional. Cameron's (1997a) study of men who are college students watching a basketball game, and gossiping about other men whom they label "gay," shows how some men continually construct themselves as heterosexual by denigrating other men, labeling them as "gay" in the absence of any information or even any indicators about their sexuality because their clothes or behavior or speech are perceived as "insufficiently masculine." Kulick's (1998) work on Brazilian *travestis* addresses how hegemonic definitions of sexuality and gender in Brazil make it logical and meaningful for males who desire other males to radically modify their bodies, while Borba and Ostermann (2006) argue that Brazilian trans identities are not only tied to transgression of biological limits, but also to social performances. Koller's (2009) essay on "butch camp" shows how certain butch/femme practices associated especially with working-class women can be read not simply as reinforcing stereotypical binary gender roles, but rather as destabilizing essentialist discourses.

Studying discourse from or about groups or individuals who are deemed sexual "minorities" (the term is problematic because it reifies rather than challenges the notion of what counts as normative practice) is not, however, the only strategy for highlighting how gender is learned and performed. Indeed, to study gender in this way may suggest or assume that there is a closer relationship between sexuality and gender than between either of these and any other aspect of social identity, a question which itself deserves investigation (Sedgwick 1990). It may also suggest that the construction of hegemonic gender norms is most closely linked to procreational needs (Hawkesworth 1997). The ways in which certain notions of gender can reinforce or challenge certain notions about class and ethnicity is part of what scholars of language and gender can investigate more closely. By looking at men and women's crossover into spheres and spaces often predominantly associated with others – where these others are also always imbricated in class, race, sexual, and national understandings of what is appropriate – we are beginning to get a sense of how the boundaries between those spheres are actively maintained, how gender in interaction with other axes of social identity is policed, how people resist these boundaries, and perhaps what transformation requires.

Barrett's (1994) study of the linguistic strategies used by African American drag queens shows how they appropriate stereotypes of white women's speech in order to parody and critique certain white stereotypes about black men, including the myth of the black male rapist. My work on women working in a traditionally masculine, working-class workplace highlights some prevailing notions of what it means to be a woman, what it means to be a man, and what it means to be a police officer, as it examines how those notions are critiqued and changed by black and white female police officers (McElhinny 1995; 2003a). (See also Holmes 2006 and Chapter 22 in this volume on language, gender, and work.)

Moments of significantly changing expectations linked to imperial occupation, national remaking, attempts to "modernize" and "develop," and/or neoliberal transformations can also help highlight contesting hegemonic ideas about gender, and various challenges to them. Inoue's (2006b) genealogical approach to Japanese women's language (JWL) highlights the co-construction of gender, class, and national identity. Although some linguists have described JWL as a speech variety spoken by all Japanese women, traceable back to feudal Japan, Inoue shows how JWL was actively constructed during the late nineteenth century as part of the construction and consolidation of a modern nation-state meant to withstand the Western colonial inroads visible elsewhere in Asia. (See also Nakamura, Chapter 19 in this volume, for a perspective on JWL.) Weidman (2006) notes that in postcolonial south India, Karnatic classical music is now valued as a sign of uncolonized Indian distinctiveness. Her geneaological work considers how the revaluing of music as a sign of bourgeois respectability for upper-caste family women in the colonial period was linked to the interiorization of music and expression within the body, an interiority inflected by gender and race in that Indian womanhood was thus constructed as pure and untouched by Western influence. My work on attempts to transform Filipino child-rearing practices during the American colonial occupation offers another example of colonial and national elite attempts to intervene in local interactional practices, in the name of public health and modernity (McElhinny 2005; 2007b; 2009). In the midst of concern about high infant mortality in the early twentieth century during the American colonial occupation, Filipino child-rearing strategies were stigmatized as overly indulgent in ways that can be linked to metropolitan concerns about production of the "new industrial man," as they were used to develop a racialized critique of the cultural practices of America's "little brown brothers" and, in particular, of the child-rearing practices of Filipinas. Education in English was also about education in hygienic and appropriate forms of gendered comportment and interaction. For other examples of work on language and gender attentive to history and social change, see Ahearn (2001) on modernizing discourses in Nepal, Gal (1997) on transformations after 1989 in east and east central Europe, Inoue (2006a) on neoliberal transformations in Japanese workplaces, Kuipers (1998) on transformations of masculinity and ritual speech after the arrival of Dutch colonial administrators in Sumba, Kulick (1992) on language shift and modernization in Papua New Guinea, and Yang (2007a; 2007b) on neoliberal restructuring of gender in socialist China. McElhinny (2010) provides a further overview of these and other works.

3. Gender as Activity and Relation

To suggest that gender is something one continually does is to challenge the idea that gender is something one has. A variety of metaphors have arisen to capture this idea: gender as activity, gender as performance, gender as accomplishment. As a group they can be understood as embodying a practice-based approach to gender, and as such they participate in a wider move within linguistic and sociocultural anthropology since the mid-1970s to use practice-based models (Abu-Lughod 1991; Hanks 1990; Ochs 1996; Ortner 1996). Practice theory reacts against structural-determinist social theories (e.g., British and American structural functionalism, determinist strands of Marxism and French structuralism) that did not incorporate a sufficient sense of how human actions make structure (see Klassen 2008 for a helpful overview). Although Ortner (1996) argues that key practice theorists often make little attempt to engage with work by feminist, subaltern, postcolonial, and minority scholars, her argument ignores feminist linguistic anthropological work (see McElhinny 1998). Before exploring these works, however, it is useful to consider the roots of the notion of gender as an attribute, and the problems with that notion that a practice-based approach tries to address.

Judith Butler argues that:

> A humanist feminist position might understand gender as an attribute of a person who is characterized essentially as a pregendered substance or "core" called the person, denoting a universal capacity for reason, moral deliberation or language. (1990, 10)

Although Butler does not make this point, others have pointed out that the model of personhood she describes is a form of abstract individualism. Liberal philosophy argued for the inherent equality of men (I use the masculine noun advisedly), based on each man's inherent rationality. Each was supposed to be able to identify his own interests, and to be enabled to pursue them. Ensuring the conditions for each man's autonomy and fulfillment has been linked to preserving the right to private property (Jaggar 1983, 34). The focus on rationality as the essence of human nature has led to an ahistoricism and universalism in liberal theory (Jaggar 1983).

Significantly, one of the best-developed scholarly accounts in the sociolinguistic tradition of gender as an activity, rather than an attribute or possession, draws on a Marxist psychological tradition: Soviet activity theory. The roots of activity theory are in the work of Vygotsky, with its emphasis on the social origins of consciousness (drawing upon Marx's sixth thesis on Feuerbach). The concept of activity was further developed by Leontyev, who elaborated upon Marx's first thesis on Feuerbach. Goodwin (1990) draws on the Vygotskyan tradition to argue that activities, rather than cultures, groups, individuals, or gender, should be the basic unit of analysis for the study of interactive phenomena.

A focus on activities suggests that individuals have access to different activities, and thus to different cultures and different social identities, including a range of different genders. We discover that

> stereotypes about women's speech … fall apart when talk in a range of activities is examined; in order to construct social personae appropriate to the events of the moment, the same individuals [will] articulate talk and gender differently as they move from one activity to another. (Goodwin 1990, 9)

It is crucial to note here that it is not just talk which varies across context, a point long familiar in sociolinguistics. Language and gender co-vary.

Eckert and McConnell-Ginet (1992) have also argued that studying how gender is constructed in communities of practice challenges existing approaches to the study of gender in sociolinguistics. A community of practice "is an aggregate of people who come together around mutual engagement in an endeavor. Ways of doing things, ways of talking, beliefs, values, power relations – in short, practices – emerge in the course of this mutual endeavor" (1992, 464). Communities of practice articulate between macro-sociological structures such as class and everyday interactional practices by considering the groups in which individuals participate and how these shape their interactions. The groups in which they participate are in turn determined and constituted by their place within larger social structures. Studying communities of practice also allows us to investigate how gender interacts with other aspects of identity because "people's access and exposure to, need for, and interest in different communities of practice are related to such things as their class, age, and ethnicity as well as to their sex" (Eckert and McConnell-Ginet 1992, 472).[2]

To focus on activities and practices does not lead us in precisely the same direction. Practice, in particular, allows one to retain some sense of the sedimentation of actions that occurs in certain institutional or cultural contexts. Still, both approaches critique essentializing analytic categories. This may not require us to abandon such notions as "gender," as Goodwin recommends. "Gender" retains significance for people living their lives, not just people analyzing how people live their lives. This, too, is part of what we must capture in our analysis (compare Ortner 1996 on culture).

The study of gender in institutional settings in ways attentive to political and economic contexts also suggests some need to modify the strong claim that "the relevant unit for the analysis of cultural phenomena, including gender, is thus not the group as a whole, or the individual, but rather situated activities" (Goodwin 1990, 9). Gender is used as a way of allocating access to different forms of work and other resources. To focus on gender in activities alone may be to focus on the gender of individuals, but to lose sight of the gender of institutions, and thus how gender is linked to systemic and structural inequities. Many activity theorists, drawing on Marxist social theory, have remained cognizant of the importance of situating activities within larger social systems (cf. Leontyev 1981, 47). Nevertheless, in Soviet psychology, and in American practices influenced by it, the move beyond small-group interactions to the analysis of "the system of social relations," the study of "collectivities, institutions and historical processes" (Connell 1987, 139) is often endlessly deferred. The use of activities as a unit of analysis can be readily reconciled with a systemic focus, if it is adopted as a methodological tool rather than a theoretical approach.

The study of gender in institutions also highlights some problems with a notion related to "activity" and "practice" which currently enjoys significant popularity in gender theory, that of performativity (see Butler 1990; Parker and Sedgwick 1995). A focus on the construction of gender in activities seems to accord speakers a great deal of agency in their language choice, and in their construction of social identity. Indeed, Ortner (1996) points out that the practice-based approach moves beyond a view of social behavior as ordered by rules and norms, but that it also grants actors a great deal of agency, thus perhaps reproducing the hegemonic model of personhood of Western capitalism.

And yet, gender is perhaps only so malleable in a limited range of activities, including play activities, movies, masquerades. To focus on the malleable diverts focus from continuing patterns of exclusion, subordination, normalization, and discrimination (see Cameron 1997b; Holmes 2006). Critiques such as this have led Butler to develop a revised notion of performativity, going under the name of citationality (1993), that in its very name seems to focus less on agency and more on institutional constraints. Livia and Hall (1997) make a strong case that Butler's use of speech act theory attends closely to institutional constraints, while Butler herself has repeatedly argued against an approach to agency that does not take political conditions underlying its possibility into account (Butler 1992). However, this later version of her work may have swung too far in the opposite direction, with too great a focus on construction in ways which make agency invisible. In addition, "institutional constraints," as described by Butler, remain abstract rather than historically or socially precise. One of the critiques of constructivist approaches that has been widely elaborated in recent years is that it is a "weak" form of description and explanation (see Hacking 1999; Smith 1999). Constructivism is not, Trouillot argues, fully attentive to sociohistorical processes, and "tracking power requires a richer view of historical production" (1995, 25; see also Grewal and Kaplan 1994; McElhinny 2007a; 2010; 2011). Strikingly, feminist indigenous scholars have argued that the language of social construction is too strong; in colonial contexts like those in the United States and Canada (and other settler colonial countries) where indigenous people are often asked to demonstrate "primordial" practices in order to make claims for rights and recognition, arguments that Native identities are constructed conspire with a range of other practices to weaken Native claims (Lawrence 2004). However, despite this seeming disagreement, there is no contradiction: whether critics see the notion of social construction as too strong or too weak, they agree that more detailed attention to history, politics, and economy is needed. Rose (1999) argues that history helps us to think about where and when objects emerge, which authorities can pronounce on them, the concepts and explanatory regimes through which they are specified, and how certain constructions acquire the status of truth.

In an exhaustive account of the ways celebratory notions of flexibility play into neoliberal visions of bodies and corporate culture, Martin (1994) asks whether the embrace of practice-based theory allows scholars to resist older systems, but not see emerging systems with new forms of repression. It is worth asking when and how representing the self as performed in sociolinguistic accounts may contribute to the formation of an ideology of a flexible subject in a flexible workforce more adequate to a globally dispersed, multinational corporate culture (Hennessy 1993, 6), and when it may be used to challenge reified notions of identity and social relations in ways that envision alternatives to these forms of capitalism (see McElhinny 2011).

If one agrees that feminist scholarship has as its primary goal the identification of inequitable social formations, with an aim to redressing them, we need to ask whether, when, and how our current analytic concepts enable such critique. Such a materialist feminist critique aims to understand "why representations of identity are changing … and how these changes in identity are connected to historical shifts in the production of life under late capitalism" (Hennessy and Ingraham 1997, 9). It is striking to note that a focus on elaborating these discourses of flexibility in feminist sociolinguistics emerges in the late 1980s and early 1990s, in such critical and influential books as *Gender Articulated: Language and the Socially Constructed Self* (Hall and Bucholtz 1995). Many of us – and I decidedly include myself (see McElhinny 1995; 1998) – were implicated in the elaboration of these ideas. To the extent that we saw such ideas as a scientific advance – a better way of understanding gender – we may not have been fully attending to the conditions that were leading to changes in the way identity was produced, and therefore not fully attentive to whether the elaboration of these new ways of thinking about gender were describing, or prescribing, the same forms of personhood prescribed in other settings. The focus on the development of a variety of new ways of conceptualizing gender in sociolinguistics and elsewhere – on gender as performance, activity, practice – could be seen as sometimes complicit in spelling out what ideologies of personhood should be in these new economies. A crucial question for further consideration is when and how this has been true.

4. Gender and Political Economy

A final problem with a focus on studying gender in heterosexual dyads is that it suggests that "gendered talk is mainly a personal characteristic or limited to the institution of the family" (Gal 1991, 185). This is then accompanied by a preference for studying gender in "informal conversations, often in one-to-one or small-group relationships in the family or neighborhood" (Gal 1991, 185). A focus on interactions between romantic partners in sociolinguistics can draw attention away from the importance of studying the ways that "gender is a structural principle [organizing] other social institutions: workplaces, schools, courts, political assemblies and the state" and the patterns they display in "the recruitment, allocation, treatment, and mobility of men as opposed to women" (Gal 1991, 185). Because certain linguistic strategies are indirectly and indexically linked with certain groups, institutions need only be organized to define, demonstrate, and enforce the legitimacy and authority of linguistic strategies associated with a particular gender while denying the power of others to exclude one group without needing to make that exclusion explicit. In the case of policing, for example, the downplaying of the importance of talk for effectively doing the job, and the overplaying of the importance of physical strength, can be seen as one strategy for excluding women from the job.

Gender differences are created in bureaucratic interactions in legal, medical, psychiatric, work and welfare settings (McElhinny 1997). Gender is a principle for allocating access to resources, and a defense for systematic inequalities. It is, like class and racialized ethnicity, not an attribute or even merely an activity, but an axis for the organization of inequality (Scott 1986, 1054, 1069). Institutional definitions of gender have been influential in history (Scott 1986), sociology (Connell 1987, 139), and sociocultural anthropology (Ortner 1996; Silverblatt 1991), but the focus on dyads has been much more significant in sociolinguistics than in other fields. For some trenchant examples of studies of gender and sexuality in institutions, see Gal 1997; Inoue 2006a; 2006b; Kuipers 1998; Leap 2010; McElhinny 1995; 2010; 2011; Philips 2000; Chapter 15 in this volume, as well as chapters in this volume by Ehrlich (23), Holmes (22), Tannen (25), Menard-Warwick, Mori, and Williams (24), and Herring and Stoerger (29) on law, work, the family, education, and computer-mediated communication.

Several key questions still remain to be addressed in studies of institutions. First, we need to ask which institutions have been ignored, and why. Studies of work still focus overwhelmingly on professional jobs and some service industries; such emphases reflect gender, class, and Western biases. Sociolinguists have undertaken relatively few studies of religious settings, nongovernmental organizations, cooperatives, factories, or other working-class jobs. Second, institutions may, in their own conceptions of themselves, see themselves as distinct from the state or other institutions; social analysts need to critique this. As Philips notes:

> state institutions [are] articulated with civil society in such a way that the boundaries between government and not-government are not clear. Political party ideologies and interests, economic interests, religious interests, and regional interests could be mutually constituted and could unite or fragment in efforts to control the state or particular institutions. (1998, 214)

Third, studies of institutions and other practices need to pay more attention to transnational processes (Besnier 2006; Briggs 2004; Briggs and Mantini-Briggs 2003; Philips 1998). In much recent scholarship, globalization has been offered as an explanation for the changing ways that people understand interactions and social relations. Harvey (2005) conceptualizes globalization as changing experiences of space and time, shaped by the periodic crises of capitalist overaccumulation. He argues that the Fordist regime of mass production of standardized products in Western economies became so successful and efficient that it began to overproduce, leading to the layoff of workers and a reduced demand for products. A post-Fordist regime of flexible accumulation has emerged in its place, with a focus on flexible labor processes, production arrangements, and consumption focused on niche markets versus mass production, all of which have transnational implications (see McElhinny 2007a for further discussion). Studies of language and gender have begun to adopt a number of approaches to questions of transnationalism and globalization, from considering what hegemony looks like if one goes beyond a national focus (Leap and Boellstorff 2004; Philips 2007; Yang 2007a; 2007b) to considering the role that language and gender play in debates over modernity, nationalism, colonialism, and development (Ahearn 2001; Gaudio 2009; Inoue 2006a; McElhinny 2007b; 2010; Mendoza-Denton 2008; Mitchell 2009; Nair 2002; Ramaswamy 1997; Weidman 2006), from investigating the changing meanings of language and nationalism during moments of industrial restructuring, heightened migration (or heightened attention to migration), and war (Heller 2007; Machin and van Leeuwen 2003; Nguyen 2007; Pujolar 2007; Tetreault 2008) to investigating whether globalization means homogenization by thinking about the meanings of global commodities and practices in a range of settings (Besnier 2007; Bucholtz 2007; Zhang 2007). Some studies also investigate the changing meanings of gender, work, and welfare in ways attentive to global dynamics in times of (attempted) neoliberal restructuring (Cameron 2000; 2001; Gaudio 2003; Inoue 2006a; 2007; Kingfisher 2007; Lorente 2007; Pitt 2002; Salonga 2010; Yang 2007a; 2007b; 2010). This is also evident in this volume in the addition of chapters on the Middle East and North Africa (Al-Wer, Chapter 20), the former Eastern Bloc (Kiełkiewicz-Janowiak and Pawelczyk, Chapter 18), Brazil (Ostermann and Moita-Lopes, Chapter 21), and Japan (Nakamura, Chapter 19).

Globalization does not, however, have its impact only on other institutions but on the academy as well. This is evident in changing ideas about appropriate topics and changes in what our organizations and journals look like. The establishment, or new importance, of such organizations as the International Gender and Language Association, the World Council of Anthropological Associations, and the International Union for Anthropological and Ethnological Sciences, are raising questions about how to insure wider circulation of scholarly work to ever more diverse audiences; what "international" and "multilingual" mean; what canons are, should, and will be created by new forms of intellectual exchange, access to scholarship and publication; what counts as appropriate peer review; what scholarly work to hold people responsible to and for; and even what constitutes appropriate subjects for scholarly investigation. These developments could create new centers and new forms of inequity; they could also decenter the role of Anglo-dominated North American and European perspectives on knowledge production in international fora (see Chen 2010 for a thoughtful account of what this might require), with important and ongoing implications for what we think the central questions are in the study of language and gender.

5. Conclusion

This chapter has suggested that certain theoretical assumptions about gender can lead to a focus on certain kinds of studies in sociolinguistics to the neglect of others. Indeed, "theoretical assumptions" is too general a description. Instead, it is possible to speak of these presuppositions as ideologies linked to some dominant ways of conceptualizing gender in Western capitalist contexts. Some are linked to long-standing understandings of abstract individualism elaborated in liberal thought to undergird early and continuing capitalist development; others are linked with more emergent, but not necessarily less hegemonic, understandings of individuals and society linked to neoliberalism. Razack, Smith, and Thobani (2010) note that neoliberalism depoliticizes structural inequalities. Certain assumptions about gender do the same, and thus may be unwittingly complicit with rationalizing or even deepening existing inequalities in ways that feminist scholars need to continue to interrogate. To assume that gender is attached only to individuals is to adopt uncritically the hegemonic ideology of gender in Western capitalism. An elegant exposition of this is given by Ortner (1991), who points out that one analytic puzzle for anthropologists studying the United States is how to talk about class when Americans rarely use this analytic category themselves. She argues that class must be understood in terms of its displacement onto other categories: because hegemonic American culture takes both the ideology of social mobility and the ideology of individualism seriously, explanations for nonmobility not only focus on the failure of individuals (because they are said to be inherently lazy or stupid or whatever), but shift the domain of discourse to arenas that are taken to be "locked into" individuals – gender, race, ethnic origin, and so forth (Ortner 1991, 171). Such an account becomes a serious critique of definitions of gender that uncritically adopt this hegemonic notion of gender as attached to individuals since they will fail to allow the theorizing of gender as a structural principle or the interaction of gender with systems of inequity (see also Comaroff and Comaroff 2001; Klein 2000). If studies of gender proceed without assuming a close association between gender, sex, and (hetero)sexuality, if gender is understood as an activity rather than a relation, if we consider gender as an axis for allocating access to resources, if we understanding gender in its local and global dimensions (as we interrogate how those scales are invoked), then it becomes possible to study gender and language in communities, contexts, cultures, and times where alternative assumptions prevail, and to challenge dominant ideologies where they help to perpetuate inequities.

NOTES

1 A fourth assumption is that gender is best studied where most salient or relevant, which raises the question of what salient and relevant mean. I addressed this question in detail in the first edition of this handbook (McElhinny 2003b); in this edition, these issues are addressed in other chapters, especially those reviewing feminism and conversational analysis (see Benwell, Chapter 12, Wilkinson and Kitzinger, Chapter 7, and Stokoe and Attenborough, Chapter 8, in this volume).
2 For ongoing debates on practice theory see Barton and Tusting 2005; Bergvall 1999; Bucholtz 1999; Davies 2005; Eckert 2000; Eckert and McConnell-Ginet 2006; Eckert and Wenger 2005; Holmes and Meyerhoff 1999; Mallinson and Childs 2007; and Meyerhoff 2002.

REFERENCES

Abu-Lughod, Lila. 1991. "Writing against Culture." In Richard Fox (ed.), *Recapturing Anthropology: Working in the Present*, 137–162. Santa Fe, NM: School of American Research Press.

Ahearn, Laura. 2001. *Invitations to Love: Literacy, Love Letters and Social Change in Nepal*. Ann Arbor: University of Michigan Press.

Barrett, Rusty. 1994. " 'She is Not White Woman': Appropriation of White Women's Language by African American Drag Queens." In Mary Bucholtz, Anita C. Liang, Laurel A. Sutton, and Caitlin Hines (eds.), *Cultural Performances: Proceedings of the Third Berkeley Women and Language Conference*, 1–14. Berkeley: Berkeley Women and Language Group.

Barton, David, and Karin Tusting, eds. 2005. *Beyond Communities of Practice: Language,* *Power and Social Context*. Cambridge: Cambridge University Press.

Behar, Ruth, and Deborah Gordan, eds. 1995. *Women Writing Culture*. Berkeley: University of California Press.

Bergvall, Victoria. 1999. "Toward a Comprehensive Theory of Language and Gender." *Language in Society*, 28(2): 273–293.

Besnier, Niko. 2006. "Language and Gender Research at the Intersection of the Global and the Local." *Gender and Language*, 1(1): 67–78.

Besnier, Niko. 2007. "Gender and Interaction in a Globalizing World: Negotiating the Gendered Self in Tonga." In Bonnie McElhinny (ed.), *Words, Worlds, and Material Girls: Language, Gender, Globalization*, 423–446. Berlin: Mouton de Gruyter.

Borba, Rodrigo, and Ana Cristina Ostermann. 2006. " 'Do Bodies Matter'? Travestis' Embodiment of (Trans)Gender Identity through the Manipulation of the Brazilian Portuguese Grammatical Gender System." *Gender and Language*, 1(1): 131–148.

Briggs, Charles. 2004. "Theorizing Modernity Conspiratorially: Science, Scale, and the Political Economy of Public Discourse in Explanations of a Cholera Epidemic." *American Ethnologist*, 31(2): 163–186.

Briggs, Charles L., and Clara Mantini-Briggs. 2003. *Stories in the Time of Cholera: Racial Profiling during a Medical Nightmare.* Berkeley: University of California Press.

Brown, Penelope, and Stephen Levinson. 1983. *Politeness: Some Universals in Language Usage.* Cambridge: Cambridge University Press.

Bucholtz, Mary. 1999. "Why be Normal? Language and Identity Practices in a Community of Nerd Girls." *Language in Society*, 28(2): 203–224.

Bucholtz, Mary. 2007. "Shop Talk: Branding, Consumption and Gender in American Middle-Class Youth Interaction." In Bonnie McElhinny (ed.), *Words, Worlds, and Material Girls: Language, Gender, Globalization*, 371–402. Berlin: Mouton de Gruyter.

Butler, Judith. 1990. *Gender Trouble: Feminism and the Subversion of Identity.* New York: Routledge.

Butler, Judith. 1992. "Contingent Foundations: Feminism and the Question of 'Postmodernism.' " In Judith Butler and Joan Scott (eds.), *Feminists Theorize the Political*, 3–21. New York: Routledge.

Butler, Judith. 1993. *Bodies that Matter.* New York: Routledge.

Cameron, Deborah. 1997a. "Performing Gender Identity: Young Men's Talk and the Construction of Heterosexual Masculinity." In Sally Johnson and Ulrike Hanna Meinhof (eds.), *Language and Masculinity*, 47–64. Oxford: Blackwell.

Cameron, Deborah. 1997b. "Theoretical Debates in Feminist Linguistics: Questions of Sex and Gender." In Ruth Wodak (ed.), *Gender and Discourse*, 21–36. London: Sage.

Cameron, Deborah. 2000. "Styling the Worker: Gender and the Commodification of Language in the Globalized Service Economy." *Journal of Sociolinguistics*, 4(3): 323–347.

Cameron, Deborah. 2001. *Good to Talk?* London: Sage.

Cameron, Deborah. 2006. "Unanswered Questions and Unquestioned Assumptions in the Study of Language and Gender: Female Verbal Superiority." *Gender and Language*, 1(1): 15–26.

Cameron, Deborah, and Jennifer Coates. 1988. "Some Problems in the Sociolinguistic Explanation of Sex Differences." In Deborah Cameron and Jennifer Coates (eds.), *Women in Their Speech Communities*, 13–26. London: Longman.

Cameron, Deborah, and Don Kulick. 2003. *Language and Sexuality.* Cambridge: Cambridge University Press.

Campbell-Kibler, Kathryn, Robert Podesva, Sarah Roberts, and Andrew Wong. 2002. *Language and Sexuality: Contesting Meaning in Theory and Practice.* Stanford: CSLI Publications.

Chen, Kuan-Hsing. 2010. *Asia as Method: Toward Deimperialization.* Durham, NC: Duke University Press.

Collins, Patricia Hill. 1990. *Black Feminist Thought.* New York: Routledge.

Comaroff, Jean, and John Comaroff. 2001. "Millennial Capitalism: First Thoughts on a Second Coming." In Jean Comaroff and John Comaroff (eds.), *Millennial Capitalism and the Culture of Neoliberalism*, 1–56. Durham, NC: Duke University Press.

Connell, Robert W. 1987. *Gender and Power: Society, the Person, and Sexual Politics.* Stanford: Stanford University Press.

Davies, Bethan. 2005. "Communities of Practice: Legitimacy not Choice." *Journal of Sociolinguistics*, 9(4): 557–581.

Eckert, Penelope. 2000. *Linguistic Variation as Social Practice.* Oxford: Blackwell.

Eckert, Penelope, and Sally McConnell-Ginet. 1992. "Think Practically and Look Locally: Language and Gender as Community-Based Practice." *Annual Review of Anthropology*, 21: 461–490.

Eckert, Penelope, and Sally McConnell-Ginet. 2006. "Putting Communities of Practice in Their Place." *Gender and Language*, 1(1): 27–38.

Eckert, Penelope, and Etienne Wenger. 2005. "Dialogue: Communities of Practice in Sociolingustics: What is the Role of Power in Sociolinguistic Variation?" *Journal of Sociolinguistics*, 9(4): 582–589.

Feldman, Paula, and Theresa Kelley, eds. 1995. *Romantic Women Writers: Voices/Countervoices*. Hanover, NH: University Press of New England.

Fishman, Pamela. 1983. "Interaction: The Work Women Do." In Barrie Thorne, Cheris Kramarae, and Nancy Henley (eds.), *Language, Gender, and Society*, 89–101. Cambridge, MA: Newbury House.

Gal, Susan. 1991. "Between Speech and Silence: The Problematics of Research on Language and Gender." In Micaela di Leonardo (ed.), *Gender at the Crossroads of Knowledge: Feminist Anthropology in the Postmodern Era*, 175–203. Berkeley: University of California Press.

Gal, Susan. 1997. "Gender in the Post-Socialist Transition: The Abortion Debate in Hungary." In Roger Lancaster and Micaela di Leonardo (eds.), *The Gender/Sexuality Reader*, 122–133. New York: Routledge.

Gaudio, Rudolf. 2003. "Coffeetalk: Starbucks™ and the Commercialization of Casual Conversation." *Language in Society*, 32(5): 659–692.

Gaudio, Rudolf P. 2009. *Allah Made Us: Sexual Outlaws in an Islamic African City*. Oxford: Wiley-Blackwell.

Gleason, Jean Berko. 1987. "Sex Differences in Parent–Child Interaction." In Susan Philips, Susan Steele, and Christine Tanz (eds.), *Language, Gender and Sex in Comparative Perspective*, 189–199. Cambridge: Cambridge University Press.

Goodwin, Marjorie Harness. 1990. *He-Said-She-Said: Talk as Social Organization among Black Children*. Bloomington: Indiana University Press.

Grewal, Inderpal, and Caren Kaplan. 1994. "Transnational Feminist Practices and Questions of Postmodernity." In Inderpal Grewal and Caren Kaplan (eds.), *Scattered Hegemonies: Postmodernity and Transnational Feminist Practices*, 1–36. Minneapolis: University of Minnesota Press.

Hacking, Ian. 1999. *The Social Construction of What?* Cambridge, MA: Harvard University Press.

Hall, Kira. 1997. " 'Go Suck Your Husband's Sugarcane': Hijras and the Use of Sexual Insult." In Anna Livia and Kira Hall (eds.), *Queerly Phrased: Language, Gender and Sexuality*, 430–460. New York: Oxford University Press.

Hall, Kira. 2005. "Intertextual Sexuality: Parodies of Class, Identity and Desire in Liminal Delhi." *Journal of Linguistic Anthropology*, 15(1): 125–144.

Hall, Kira. 2009. "Boys' Talk: Hindi, Moustaches, and Masculinity in New Delhi." In Pia Pichler and Eva Eppler (eds.), *Gender and Spoken Interaction*, 139–162. Basingstoke: Palgrave Macmillan.

Hall, Kira, and Mary Bucholtz, eds. 1995. *Gender Articulated: Language and the Socially Constructed Self*. New York: Routledge.

Hanks, William. 1990. *Referential Practices: Language and Lived Space among the Maya*. Chicago: University of Chicago Press.

Harding, Sandra. 1991. *Whose Science? Whose Knowledge?* Ithaca, NY: Cornell University Press.

Harvey, David. 2005. *A Brief History of Neoliberalism*. Oxford: Oxford University Press.

Hawkesworth, Mary. 1997. "Confounding Gender." *Signs*, 22(1): 649–686.

Heller, Monica. 2007. "Gender and Bilingualism in the New Economy." In Bonnie McElhinny (ed.), *Words, Worlds, and Material Girls: Language, Gender, Globalization*, 287–304. Berlin: Mouton de Gruyter.

Hennessy, Rosemary. 1993. *Materialist Feminism and the Politics of Discourse*. New York: Routledge.

Hennessy, Rosemary, and Chrys Ingraham, eds. 1997. *Materialist Feminism: A Reader in Class, Difference, and Women's Lives*. New York: Routledge.

Holmes, Janet. 2006. "Social Constructionism, Postmodernism and Feminist Sociolinguistics." *Gender and Language*, 1(1): 51–66.

Holmes, Janet, and Miriam Meyerhoff. 1999. "The Community of Practice: Theories and Methodologies in Language and Gender Research." *Language in Society*, 28(2): 173–184.

Inoue, Miyako. 2006a. "Language and Gender in an Age of Neoliberalism." *Gender and Language*, 1(1): 79–92.

Inoue, Miyako. 2006b. *Vicarious Language: Gender and Linguistic Modernity in Japan*. Berkeley: University of California Press.

Inoue, Miyako. 2007. "Echoes of Modernity: Nationalism and the Enigma of 'Women's Language in Late Nineteenth Century Japan.' " In Bonnie McElhinny (ed.), *Words, Worlds, and Material Girls: Language, Gender, Globalization*, 157–204. Berlin: Mouton de Gruyter.

Jaggar, Alison. 1983. *Feminist Politics and Human Nature*. Totowa, NJ: Rowman & Allanheld.

Kapchan, Deborah. 1996. *Gender on the Market: Moroccan Women and the Revoicing of Tradition*. Philadelphia: University of Pennsylvania Press.

Kelly-Gadol, Joan. 1977. "Did Women have a Renaissance?" In Renate Bridenthal and Clandia Koonz (eds.), *Becoming Visible: Women in European History*, 139–163. Boston: Houghton Mifflin.

Kingfisher, Catherine. 2007. "What D/discourse Analysis Can Tell us about Neoliberal Constructions of (Gendered) Personhood: Some Notes on Commonsense and Temporality." *Gender and Language*, 1(1): 93–106.

Klassen, Pamela. 2008. "Practice." In David Morgan (ed.), *Key Words in Religion, Media and Culture*, 136–147. New York: Routledge.

Klein, Naomi. 2000. *No Logo: Taking Aim at the Brand Bullies*. Toronto: Vintage.

Koller, Veronika. 2009. "Butch Camp: On the Discursive Construction of a Queer Identity Position." *Gender and Language*, 3(2): 249–274.

Kuipers, Joel. 1998. *Language, Identity and Marginality in Indonesia: The Changing Nature of Ritual Speech on the Island of Sumba*. Cambridge: Cambridge University Press, 42–66.

Kulick, Don. 1992. *Language Shift and Cultural Reproduction: Socialization, Self and Syncretism in a Papua New Guinean Village*. Cambridge: Cambridge UniversityPress.

Kulick, Don. 1998. *Travesti: Sex, Gender and Culture among Brazilian Transgendered Prostitutes*. Chicago: University of Chicago Press.

Lawrence, Bonita. 2004. *"Real" Indians and Others: Mixed-Blood Urban Native Peoples and Indigenous Nationhood*. Vancouver: UBC Press.

Leap, William, ed. 2010. "Language and Homophobia" (special issue). *Gender and Language*, 4(2).

Leap, William, and Tom Boellstorff, eds. 2004. *Speaking in Queer Tongues: Gay Language and Globalization*. Urbana: University of Illinois Press.

Leontyev, Aleksei N. 1981. *Problems of the Development of the Mind*. Moscow: Progress Publishers.

Livia, Anna, and Kira Hall. 1997. " 'It's a girl!' Bringing Performativity Back to Linguistics." In Anna Livia and Kira Hall (eds.), *Queerly Phrased: Language, Gender, and Sexuality*, 1–18. New York: Oxford University Press.

Lorente, Beatriz. 2007. "Mapping English Linguistic Capital: The Case of Filipino Domestic Workers in Singapore." Unpublished PhD dissertation, National University of Singapore.

Machin, David, and Theo van Leeuwen. 2003. "Global Schemas and Local Discourses in Cosmopolitan." *Journal of Sociolinguistics*, 7(4): 493–512.

Mallinson, Christine, and Becky Childs. 2007. "Communities of Practice in Sociolinguistic Description: Analyzing Language and Identity Practices among Black Women in Appalachia." *Gender and Language*, 1(2): 173–206.

Martin, Emily. 1994. *Flexible Bodies: Tracking Immunity in American Culture from the Days of Polio to the Age of Aids*. Boston: Beacon.

McElhinny, Bonnie. 1995. "Challenging Hegemonic Masculinities: Female and Male Police Officers Handling Domestic Violence." In Kira Hall and Mary Bucholtz (eds.), *Gender Articulated: Language and the*

Socially Constructed Self, 217–243. New York: Routledge.

McElhinny, Bonnie. 1997. "Ideologies of Public and Private Language in Sociolinguistics." In Ruth Wodak (ed.), *Gender and Discourse*, 106–139. London: Sage.

McElhinny, Bonnie. 1998. "Genealogies of Gender Theory: Practice Theory and Feminism in Sociocultural and Linguistic Anthropology." *Social Analysis*, 42(3): 164–189.

McElhinny, Bonnie. 2003a. "Fearful, Forceful Agents of the Law: Ideologies about Language and Gender in Police Officers' Narratives about the Use of Physical Force." *Pragmatics*, 13(2): 253–284.

McElhinny, Bonnie. 2003b. "Theorizing Gender in Sociolinguistics and Linguistic Anthropology." In Janet Holmes and Miriam Meyerhoff (eds.), *The Language and Gender Handbook*, 21–42. Oxford: Blackwell.

McElhinny, Bonnie. 2005. " 'Kissing a Baby is Not at All Good for Him': Infant Mortality, Medicine and Colonial Modernity in the U.S.-Occupied Philippines." *American Anthropologist*, 107(2): 183–194.

McElhinny, Bonnie. 2007a. "Language, Gender and Economies in Global Transitions: Provocative and Provoking Questions about How Gender is Articulated." In Bonnie McElhinny (ed.), *Words, Worlds, and Material Girls: Language, Gender, Globalization*, 1–38. Berlin: Mouton de Gruyter.

McElhinny, Bonnie. 2007b. "Recontextualizing the American Occupation of the Philippines: Erasure and Ventriloquism in Colonial Discourse around Men, Medicine and Infant Mortality." In Bonnie McElhinny (ed.), *Words, Worlds, and Material Girls: Language, Gender, Globalization*, 205–236. Berlin: Mouton de Gruyter.

McElhinny, Bonnie. 2009. "Producing the A-1 Baby: Puericulture Centres and the Birth of the Clinic in the U.S. Occupied Philippines 1906–1946." *Philippine Studies*, 57(2): 219–260.

McElhinny, Bonnie. 2010. "The Audacity of Affect: Gender, Race and History in Linguistic Accounts of Legitimacy and Belonging." *Annual Review of Anthropology*, 39: 309–328.

McElhinny, Bonnie. 2011. "Silicon Valley Sociolinguistics? Analyzing Language, Gender and Communities of Practice in the New Knowledge Economy." In Alexandre Duchêne and Monica Heller (eds.), *Language in Late Capitalism: Pride and Profit*, 230–261. New York: Routledge.

Mendoza-Denton, Norma. 2008. *Homegirls: Language and Cultural Practice among Latina Youth Gangs*. Oxford: Blackwell.

Meyerhoff, Miriam. 2002. "Communities of Practice." In J. K. Chambers, Peter Trudgill, and Natalie Schilling-Estes (eds.), *The Handbook of Language Variation and Change*, 526–548. Hoboken, NJ: Wiley.

Mitchell, Lisa. 2009. *Language, Emotion, and Politics in South India: The Making of a Mother Tongue*. Bloomington: Indiana University Press.

Morgan, Marcyliena. 1994. "No Woman, No Cry: The Linguistic Representation of African American Women." In Mary Bucholtz, Anita C. Liang, Laurel Sutton, and Caitlin Hines (eds.), *Cultural Performances: Proceedings of the Third Berkeley Women and Language Conference*, 525–541. Berkeley: Berkeley Women and Language Group.

Morgan, Marcyliena. 2002. *Language, Discourse and Power in African American Culture*. Cambridge: Cambridge University Press.

Nair, Rukmini Bhaya. 2002. *Lying on the Postcolonial Couch: The Idea of Indifference*. Minneapolis: University of Minnesota Press.

Nguyen, Binh. 2007. "Gender, Multilingualism and the American War in Vietnam." In Bonnie McElhinny (ed.), *Words, Worlds, and Material Girls: Language, Gender, Globalization*, 349–370. Berlin: Mouton de Gruyter.

Nicholson, Linda. 1994. "Interpreting Gender." *Signs*, 20(1): 79–105.

Ochs, Elinor. 1992. "Indexing Gender." In Alessandro Duranti and Charles Goodwin (eds.), *Rethinking Context: Language as an Interactive Phenomenon*, 335–358. Cambridge: Cambridge University Press.

Ochs, Elinor. 1996. "Linguistic Resources for Socializing Humanity." In John J. Gumperz and Stephen Levinson (eds.), *Rethinking Linguistic Relativity*, 407–437. Cambridge: Cambridge University Press.

Ortner, Sherry. 1991. "Reading America: Preliminary Notes on Class and Culture." In Richard Fox (ed.), *Recapturing Anthropology: Working in the Present*, 163–190. Santa Fe, NM: School of American Research Press.

Ortner, Sherry. 1996. *Making Gender: The Politics and Erotics of Gender*. Boston: Beacon.

Parker, Andrew, and Eve Kosofsky Sedgwick, eds. 1995. *Performativity and Performance*. New York: Routledge.

Philips, Susan. 1998. "Language Ideologies in Institutions of Power: A Commentary." In Bambi Schiefelin, Kathryn Woolard, and Paul Kroskrity (eds.), *Language Ideologies: Practice and Theory*, 211–228. Oxford: Oxford University Press.

Philips, Susan. 2000. "Constructing a Tongan Nation-State through Language Ideology in the Courtroom." In Paul Kroskrity (ed.), *Regimes of Language: Ideologies, Polities and Identities*, 229–258. Santa Fe, NM: School of American Research Press.

Philips, Susan. 2007. "Symbolically Central and Materially Marginal: Women's Talk in a Tongan Work Group." In Bonnie S. McElhinny (ed.), *Words, Worlds, and Material Girls: Language, Gender, Globalization*, 41–76. Berlin: Mouton de Gruyter.

Pitt, Kathy. 2002. "Being a New Capitalist Mother." *Discourse and Society*, 13: 251–267.

Pujolar, Joan. 2007. "African Women in Catalan Language Courses: Struggles over Class, Gender and Ethnicity in Advanced Liberalism." In Bonnie McElhinny (ed.), *Words, Worlds, and Material Girls: Language, Gender, Globalization*, 305–349. Berlin: Mouton de Gruyter.

Ramaswamy Sumathi. 1997. *Passions of the Tongue: Language Devotion in Tamil India*

1891 –1970. Berkeley: University of California Press.

Razack, Sherene, Malinda Smith, and Sunera Thobani. 2010. "States of Race: Critical Race Feminism for the 21st Century." In Sherene Razack, Malinda Smith, and Sunera Thobani (eds.), *States of Race: Critical Race Feminism for the 21st Century*, 1–22. Toronto: Between the Lines.

Rose, Nikolas. 1999. *Governing the Soul: The Shaping of the Private Self*, 2nd edn. London: Free Association Books.

Salonga, Aileen. 2010. "Language and Situated Agency: An Exploration of the Dominant Linguistic and Communication Practices in the Philippine Offshore Call Centers." Unpublished PhD dissertation, National University of Singapore.

Scott, Joan. 1986. "Gender: A Useful Category of Historical Analysis." *American Historical Review*, 91(5): 1053–1075.

Sedgwick, Eve Kosofsky. 1990. *Epistemology of the Closet*. Berkeley: University of California Press.

Shapiro, Judith. 1981. "Anthropology and the Study of Gender." *Soundings: An Interdisciplinary Journal*, 64: 446–465.

Silverblatt, Irene. 1991. " 'Interpreting Women in States': New Feminist Ethnohistories." In Micaela di Leonardo (ed.), *Gender at the Crossroads of Knowledge: Feminist Anthropology in the Postmodern Era*, 140–174. Berkeley: University of California Press.

Smith, Gavin. 1999. *Confronting the Present: Towards a Politically Engaged Anthropology*. Oxford: Berg.

Sperling, Susan. 1991. "Baboons with Briefcases vs. Langurs in Lipstick: Feminism and Functionalism in Primate Studies." In Micaela di Leonardo (ed.), *Gender at the Crossroads of Knowledge: Feminist Anthropology in the Postmodern Era*, 204–234. Berkeley: University of California Press.

Tannen, Deborah. 1990. *You Just Don't Understand: Women and Men in Conversation*. New York: William Morrow.

Tetreault, Chantal. 2008. "La Racaille: Figuring Gender, Generation, and Stigmatized Space in a French Cité." *Gender and Language*, 2(2): 141–170.

Thorne, Barrie, and Judith Stacey. 1993. "The Missing Feminist Revolution in Sociology." In Linda Kauffman (ed.), *American Feminist Thought at Century's End*, 167–188. Oxford: Blackwell.

Trouillot, Michel-Rolph. 1995. *Silencing the Past: Power and the Production of History*. Boston: Beacon.

Weidman, Amanda. 2006. *Singing the Classical, Voicing the Modern: The Postcolonial Politics of Music in South India*. Durham, NC: Duke University Press.

West, Candace, and Don Zimmerman. 1983. "Small Insults: A Study of Interruptions in Cross-Sex Conversations between Unacquainted Persons." In Barrie Thorne, Cheris Kramarae, and Nancy Henley (ed.), *Language, Gender and Society*, 102–117. Cambridge, MA: Newbury House.

Worthman, Carol. 1995. "Hormones, Sex and Gender." *Annual Review of Anthropology*, 24: 593–616.

Yanagisako, Sylvia, and Jane F. Collier. 1990. "The Mode of Reproduction in Anthropology." In Deborah Rhode (ed.), *Theoretical Perspectives on Sexual Difference*, 131–144. New Haven: Yale University Press.

Yang, Jie. 2007a. "Re-employment Stars: Language, Gender and Neoliberal Restructuring in China." In Bonnie McElhinny (ed.), *Words, Worlds, and Material Girls: Language, Gender, Globalization*, 77–105. Berlin: Mouton de Gruyter.

Yang, Jie. 2007b. "Zuiqian 'Deficient Mouth': Language, Gender and Domestic Violence in Urban China." *Gender and Language*, 1(1): 105–116.

Yang, Jie. 2010. "The Crisis of Masculinity: Class, Gender, and Kindly Power in Post-Mao China." *American Ethnologist*, 37(3): 550–562.

Zhang, Qing. 2007. "Cosmopolitanism and Linguistic Capital in China: Language, Gender and the Transition to a Globalized Market Economy in Beijing." In Bonnie McElhinny (ed.), *Words, Worlds, and Material Girls: Language, Gender, Globalization*, 403–420. Berlin: Mouton de Gruyter.

Zimmerman, Don, and Candace West. 1975. "Sex Roles, Interruptions, and Silences in Conversation." In Barrie Thorne and Nancy Henley (eds.), *Language and Sex: Difference and Dominance*, 105–129. Rowley, MA: Newbury House.

3 Language and Desire

DON KULICK

The relationship between language and different kinds of desire is a frequent topic in texts directed at psychoanalytic practitioners, even though therapists "tend to look *through* language rather than *at* its forms" (Capps and Ochs 1995, 186; emphasis original; for an example of this kind of text, see Fink 1997). Language and desire has also occasionally been discussed in literary criticism and philosophical texts (e.g., Barthes 1978; Kristeva 1980). However, research based on empirical material – material that examines how desire is actually conveyed through language in social life – is rare. The closest type of study that investigates desire in language is work that examines how sexuality is signaled through words, innuendo, or particular linguistic registers. This kind of research has been conducted since the 1940s in a number of disciplinary fields, such as philology, linguistics, women's studies, anthropology, and speech communication. Most of the early work on this topic is not well known, largely because there isn't very much of it, and what was written often appeared in obscure or esoteric publications. Beginning in the 1980s, research on lexicon was supplemented by work that examined other dimensions of language, such as pronoun usage, camp sensibility, and coming out narratives. And since then, work on gay and lesbian language has mushroomed, producing studies on everything from intonational patterns to the semiotic means by which gay men create private spaces in ostensibly public domains.

This past research on gay and lesbian language from the 1920s through the 1990s has been reviewed extensively in Kulick 2000 and Cameron and Kulick 2003. Those reviews identified three consequential shortcomings in much of that work.

The first concerns the fact that even though past research on gay and lesbian language ostensibly was concerned with understanding the relationship between sexual orientation and language, *it had no theory of sexuality*. That is to say, it had no real understanding of what sexuality is, how it is acquired, and what the relationship is between what Butler would call its "literal performance" and the unconscious foreclosures and prohibitions that structure and limit that performance. Instead, from its inception as a topic of research, the literature on language and sexuality has conceptualized sexuality exclusively in terms of

The Handbook of Language, Gender, and Sexuality, Second Edition.
Edited by Susan Ehrlich, Miriam Meyerhoff, and Janet Holmes.
© 2014 John Wiley & Sons, Inc. Published 2017 by John Wiley & Sons, Inc.

identity categories. The dimensions of sexuality that define it in disciplines like psychoanalysis – dimensions like fantasy, pleasure, repression, disavowal, and desire – all of these were nowhere considered. This means that research did not in fact focus on how language conveys sexuality. It focused, instead, on how language conveys identity.

This has had consequences for the kind of language behavior that was studied, which is the second problem. Because the concern was to show how people with particular identities signal those identities to others, the only people whose language behavior was examined were people who were assumed to have those identities, that is, men and women who openly identify as homosexual, or who researchers for some reason suspected were homosexual. The assumption was that if there is a gay or lesbian language, then that language must be grounded in gay and lesbian identities, and instantiated in the speech of gays and lesbians. That nonhomosexuals (imposters, actors, fag hags, hip or unwary heterosexuals) can and do use language that signals queerness was largely ignored, and on the few occasions it was considered, such usage was dismissed by researchers as "inauthentic" (Leap 1995; 1996). The lack of attention to the inherent *appropriability* of language meant that research conflated the symbolic position of queerness with the concrete social practices of men and women who self-define as gay and lesbian. In other words, ways of speaking that invoked or performed queerness were not considered separately from the linguistic behavior of people who claimed to be queer. The two can and do overlap, but they are not exactly the same thing.

For example, when a man who identifies as gay uses gender inversion to refer another male – let's say, "What's wrong with her?" – the inversion can be understood to signal perhaps both the speaker's disdain for the target of his question and also his own facility with a particular kind of gay ingroup linguistic convention. It indexes gayness, and in this sense, previous researchers would all agree, is "gay language." But what about a high school baseball coach's shout of "What's wrong with her?" hollered toward the boy in left field who just dropped the ball? Like the first example, the coach's utterance indexes femininity, disdain, and, arguably, homosexuality as well. So is it, too, an example of "gay language"? If it is, then is it the same as the gay man's "gay language"? If it is different, then is the difference between the two uses of "gay language" really to be comprehended on the grounds of "authenticity," as a scholar like Leap would have it? Authentic of what, one might ask? Decided by whom? And if the coach's taunt isn't "gay language" because the person who utters it doesn't identify as gay, then we are left with a concept of "gay language" that is restricted to language used by self-identified gay men. This is equivalent to saying that the only people who can use or do use or are allowed to use "women's language" are (self-identified?) women – a standpoint that was abandoned a very long time ago in gender and language studies (to the extent that anybody ever really held it in the first place). The idea that "women's language" only applied to language used by women was discarded precisely because it was understood that such a view of language misrecognizes gender as a position in language as being the same as gender as an actually occurring kind of social identity. Such a misrecognition blocks an exploration of how the phonological, prosodic, lexical, and discursive elements of what are understood to compose a phenomenon like "women's language" (or "gay language") are available to any speaker to use (and any hearer to interpret) regardless of whatever the speaker may think about her or his sexuality, gender, or anything else.

The third problem follows from this. Because attention focused solely on whether or not gay-identified people reveal or conceal their sexual orientation, what was foregrounded in the study of language and sexuality was speaker intention. So the criterion for deciding if something constitutes gay or lesbian language has been to find out whether the speaker intended for his or her language to be understood in that way. Until recently, this was a structuring principle of all work on gay and lesbian language, but it has only been made explicit in some of the most recent work on queer language. Livia and Hall, for example, assert that "[a]n utterance becomes typically lesbian or gay only if the hearer/reader understands that it was the speaker's intent that it should be taken up that way. Queerspeak should thus be considered an essentially intentional phenomenon" (1997, 14; see also Leap 1996, 21–23; Livia 2001, 200–202).

What is theoretically untenable about the idea that "queerspeak should … be considered an essentially intentional phenomenon" is that *no* language can be considered "an essentially intentional phenomenon." Meaning is always structured by more than will or intent – this was one of Freud's most fundamental insights, and was expressed in his articulation of the unconscious as that structure or dynamic which thwarts and subverts any attempt to fully know what we mean. It was recognized by Saussure, who in the opening pages of *Course in General Linguistics* observed that "the sign always to some extent eludes control by the will" (1983, 16). It is insisted on by Bakthin, who analyzed at length how meaning is always divided, both in the sense of "not whole" and "shared" (e.g., Voloshinov 1973). And that meaning must always exceed intent is also the principle point of Derrida's (1995 [1972]) criticism of Austin's concept of the performative. Derrida argues that performatives work not because they depend on the intention of the speaker, but because they embody conventional forms of language that are already in existence before the speaker utters them. Performatives work, and language generally works, because they are quotable. This is the meaning of Derrida's example of the signature, with which he concluded his article "Signature Event Context." In order for a mark to count as a signature, he observed, it has to be repeatable; it has to enter into a structure of what he calls *iterability*, which means both "to repeat" and "to change" (Derrida 1995 [1972], 7). Signatures are particularly good examples of iterability, partly because even though one repeats them every time one signs one's name, no two signatures are ever exactly the same. But the main point is that in order to signify, in order to be authentic, one's mark *has* to be repeatable – if I sign my name "XCFRD" one time and "W4H7V" the next time, and "LQYGMP" the next time, and so on, it won't mean anything; it will not be recognized as a signature, as a meaningful mark. To be so recognized, the mark has to be repeated.

The rub here is that if something is repeatable, it also, therefore, necessarily, is forever at risk of failure. For example, if I am drunk and sign my name fuzzily, my signature may not be recognized in relation to the one I have on my driver's license:

in this context, my mark will fail and my check will not be cashed. If something is repeatable, it also becomes available for misuse and forgery. This availability for quotation without my permission, untethered to any intention I may have, is what Derrida means when he says that failure and fraud are not parasitical to language, exceptions, distortions (as Austin (1997 [1962], 22) maintains). On the contrary, quotability is the very foundational condition that allows language to exist and work at all. The fact that all signs are quotable (and hence, subject to failure and available for misrepresentation) means that signification cannot be located in the intention of speakers, but rather in the economy of difference that characterizes language itself. In this sense, failure and misuse are not accidental; they are structural: a signature succeeds not in spite of the possibility of forgery, but because of it. Derrida's point, one that Butler relies on extensively in her own work (see especially Butler 1997) is that a speaker's intention is never enough to anchor meaning and exhaustively determine context. This is not the same as saying that speaker intention is completely irrelevant. Derrida notes that if one recognizes the iterable structure of language, "the category of intention will not disappear; it will have its place." But "from this place it will no longer be able to govern the entire scene and system of utterances" (1995 [1972], 18). Why? Because language necessarily and always evokes meanings that exceed, contradict, undermine, and disrupt the language user's intentions. If this is acknowledged, it follows that any attempt to define a queer linguistics through appeals to intentionality is fatally flawed from the start because it depends on an understanding about the relationship between intention and language that Derrida definitively dispensed with 40 years ago.

Because of these three fundamental problems with the kind of research that until recently has investigated the relationship between language and sexuality, Deborah Cameron and I have advocated that scholars of language interested in this area might want to reframe the questions they ask at least partly in terms of the relationship between language and desire (Cameron and Kulick 2003; 2005; Kulick 2000). There are three immediate advantages to be gained by beginning to think about desire.

First, an exploration of "desire" would compel research to decisively shift the ground of inquiry from identity categories to culturally grounded semiotic practices. The desire for recognition, for intimacy, for erotic fulfillment – none of this, in itself, is specific to any particular kind of person. What is specific to different kinds of people are the precise things they desire and the manner in which particular desires are signaled in culturally codified ways. For example, the sexual desire of a man for a woman is conveyed through a range of semiotic codes that may or may not be conscious, but that are recognizable as conveying desire because they are iterable signs that continually get recirculated in social life. The iterability of codes is what allows us to recognize desire *as* desire. This means that all the codes are resources available for anyone to use – be they straight, gay, bisexual, shoe fetishists, or anything else. It also means that desire cannot best be thought of in terms of individual intentionality. Because it relies on structures of iterability for its expression, desire is available for appropriation and forgery; as we know from cases where men invoke the desire of the other to claim – ingenuously or not – that they thought the woman they raped desired them, or that they thought the man they killed was coming on to them. Researchers interested in language and desire need to be able to explain this too – they need to explain not only intentional desire, but appropriated or forged desire.

Second, a focus on desire would move inquiry to engage with theoretical debates about what desire is, how it is structured, and how it is communicated. One of the many problems with the concept of sexuality, especially when it is linked to identity, tends to be conceptualized as intransitive (one *has* a sexuality, *is* a sexuality); hence research comes to concentrate on how subjects reveal or conceal their sexuality (and hence, once again, the centrality of intentional subjects in this literature). An advantage with the concept of desire is that it is definitionally transitive – one can certainly be said to *have* desire, but that desire is always *for* something, directed toward something. This means that research is impelled to problematize both the subject and the object of desire, and investigate how those *relationships* are materialized through language. Because desire, in any theoretical framework, both encompasses and exceeds sexuality, research will, furthermore, be directed toward investigating the ways in which different kinds of desires, for different things, become bound up with or detached from erotic desire.

Third, thinking about desire widens the range and scope of phenomena that might be considered when thinking about different kinds of interactions. Desire provides a framework for thinking about the roles that fantasy, repression, and disavowals play in linguistic interactions. Desire directs us to look at how language is precisely *not* an essentially intentional phenomenon. It encourages scholars to develop theories and techniques for analyzing not only what is said, but also how what is said is in many senses dependent on what remains unsaid, or unsayable.

1. Theories of Desire

What is desire? In most discussions, that question will be answered with reference to psychoanalysis, since psychoanalysis posits desire as the force that both enables and limits human subjectivity and action.

The distinguishing feature of desire in much psychoanalysis is that it is always, definitionally, bound up with sexuality. Sexual desire is a constitutive dimension of human existence. For Freud, "the germs of the sexual impulses are already present in the new-born child" (1975, 42). Ontogenetic development consists of learning to restrict those impulses in particular ways, managing them (or not) in relation to socially sanctioned objects and relationships. This learning occurs largely beyond conscious reflection, and is the outcome of specific prohibitions and repressions which children internalize and come to embody.

Although Freud was more inclined to speak of "sexual impulses" or "libido" than "desire" (note, though, that "libido" is a Latin word meaning "wish" or "desire"), he would undoubtedly have agreed with Lacan's Spinozan epigraph that "desire is the essence of man" (Lacan 1998, 275). Freud would probably not have agreed, however, with the specific attributions that Lacan attaches to desire. In Lacan's work, desire has a very particular meaning. Unlike libido, which for Freud was a kind of energy or force that continually sought its own satisfaction, desire, for Lacan, is associated with absence, loss, and lack.

A starting point in Lacanian psychoanalysis is the assumption that infants come into the world with no sense of division or separation from anything. Because they sense no separation, and because their physical needs are met by others, infants do not perceive themselves to lack anything; instead, they imagine themselves to be complete and whole. This imagined wholeness is the source of the term *Imaginary*, which is one of the three registers of subjectivity identified by Lacan. Lacan argues that this psychic state must be superseded (by the *Symbolic*, which means language and culture), because to remain in it or to return to it for any length of time would be the equivalent of psychosis.

Exit from the Imaginary occurs as infants develop and come to perceive the difference between themselves and their caregiver(s). Lacan believes that this awareness is registered as traumatic, because at this point, the infant realizes that caregivers are not just *there*. Nourishment, protection, and love are not simply or always just given, or given satisfyingly; instead, they are given (always temporarily) as a result of particular signifying acts, like crying, squirming, or vocalizing. Sensing this, infants begin to signify. That is, they begin to formulate their needs as what Lacan calls "demands." In other words, whereas previously, bodily movements and vocalizations had no purpose or goal, they now come to be directed at prompting or controlling (m)others.

Once needs are formulated as demands, they are lost to us, because needs exist in a different order (Lacan's *Real*, which is his name *not* for "reality," but for that which remains beyond or outside signification). In a similar way as Kant argued that language both gives us our world of experience, and also keeps us from perceiving the world in an unmediated form, Lacan asserts that signification can substitute for needs, but it cannot fulfill them. This gap between the need and its expression – between a hope and its fulfillment – is where Lacan locates the origins and workings of desire.

The idea that desire arises when an infant registers loss of (imagined) wholeness means that the real object of desire (to regain that original plenitude) will forever remain out of reach. But because we do not know that this is what we want (in an important sense, we *cannot* know this, since this dynamic is what structures the unconscious), we displace this desire onto other things, and we desire those things, hoping – always in vain – that they will satisfy our needs. The displacement of desire onto other things means that the demands through which desire is symbolized actually has not one, but two objects: one spoken (the object demanded), and one unspoken (the maintenance of a relationship to the other to whom the demand is addressed). So the thing demanded is a rationalization for maintaining a relation to the other: the demand for food is also a demand for recognition, for the other's desire. The catch is that even if this recognition is granted, we can't assume that it will always be granted ("Will you still love me tomorrow … "); hence, we repeat the demand, endlessly.

The relationship of all this to sexuality lies in the linkage that psychoanalysis articulates between sexual difference and desire. There is a purposeful conflation in Lacan's writing between sexuality and sex, that is, between erotics and being a man or a woman. (In English, the terms "masculine" and "feminine" express a similar conflation, since those terms denote both "ways of being" and "sexual positions"). Lacan's interest is to explain how infants, who are born unaware of sex and sexuality, come to assume particular positions in language and culture, which is where sex and sexuality are produced and sustained. Because becoming a man or a woman occurs largely through the adoption or refusal of particular sexual roles in relation to one's parents (roles that supposedly get worked out in the course of the Oedipal process), sexuality is the primary channel through which we arrive at our identities as sexed beings. In other words, *gender is achieved through sexuality.* Furthermore, the fact that our demands are always in some sense a demand for the desire of an other means that our sense of who we are is continually formed through libidinal relations.

This relationship between sexuality and sex is central to Judith Butler's claims about the workings and power of what she has termed the heterosexual matrix. Her argument is that men and women are produced as such through the refusals we are required by culture to make in relation to our parents. Culture, Butler says, has come to be constituted in such a way that what she calls heterosexual cathexis (that is, the desire for his mother of a person culturally designated as a boy, or the desire for her father of a person culturally designated as a girl) is displaced, so that a boy's mother is forbidden to him, but women in general are not. In the case of girls, something similar happens: her father is forbidden to her, but men in general are not. In other words, the object of the desire is tabooed, but the modality of desire is not – indeed, that modality of desire is culturally incited, encouraged, and even demanded. Not so with homosexual cathexis (the desire for his father of a person culturally designated as a boy, or the desire for her mother of a person culturally designated as a girl). Not only is the object of that desire forbidden; in this case, the modality of desire itself is tabooed.

These prohibitions produce homosexual cathexis as something that *cannot be.* And since its very existence is not recognized, the loss we experience (of the father for the boy and of the mother for the girl) cannot be acknowledged. Drawing on Freud's writings on the psychic structure of melancholia (Freud 1957; 1960), Butler (1990) argues that when the loss of a loved one cannot be acknowledged, the desire that was directed at that loved one cannot be transferred to other objects. In effect, desire gets stuck, it stays put, it bogs down, it cannot move on. Instead, it moves *in.* It becomes incorporated into the psyche in such a way that we *become* what we cannot acknowledge losing. Hence persons culturally designated as boys come to inhabit the position of that which they cannot acknowledge losing (i.e., males), and persons culturally designated as girls become females, for the same reason. Once again, gender is accomplished through the disavowal of particular desires and the achievement of others.

Unlike Lacan, who equivocates on whether the psychic structures he describes are universal or culturally and historically specific, Butler is at pains to stress that the melancholic structures she postulates are the effects of particular cultural conventions. However, because she does not historicize her explanation, pinpointing when the conventions that form its backdrop are supposed to have arisen and entrenched themselves in people's psychic lives, and also because the only material she analyzes to make her points about melancholy is drawn from contemporary Western societies, it is hard to see what Butler sees as actually (rather than just theoretically) variable. Gender is a fact of social life everywhere, not just in the contemporary West. Do Butler's arguments about gender identity and melancholia apply in Andean villages, Papua New Guinean rainforests, or the Mongolian steppe? This isn't clear. And since Butler does not indicate where she sees the limits of her approach to the assumption of gendered identities, it is difficult to resist the conclusion that her model, despite her assertions to the contrary, is universalistic in scope.

However one wishes to read Butler here, the point is that this explanation of why certain human beings come to be men and certain others come to be women lies at the heart of performativity theory. This fundamental reliance on psychoanalysis is downplayed or ignored in some summaries of Butler's work (e.g., Hall 1999; Jagose 1996), and my own suspicion is that many readers of *Gender Trouble* simply skip over chapter 2, which is where she develops her claim that "gender identity is a melancholic structure" (Butler 1990, 68). But performativity theory, as Butler has elaborated it, is inseparable from psychoanalytic assumptions about the relationship between desire, sexuality, and sex. If you remove the psychoanalysis, what remains is simply a kind of performance theory à la Goffman – the kind of theory that inattentive readers mistakenly accused Butler of promoting in *Gender Trouble* (e.g., Jeffreys 1994; Weston 1993).

A dramatic contrast to psychoanalytic theories of desire is found in the work of Gilles Deleuze and Félix Guattari. Deleuze and Guattari (1996) take great pleasure in criticizing and mocking psychoanalysis (chapter 2 of *A Thousand Plateaus*, about Freud's patient the Wolf-Man, reads like a stand-up comedy routine, with psychoanalysis as the butt of all the jokes). They insist that psychoanalysis has fundamentally misconstrued the nature of desire because it sees desire as always linked to sexuality. This is to misrepresent it: "Sleeping is a desire," Deleuze observes, "Walking is a desire. Listening to music, or making music, or writing, are desires. A spring, a winter, are desires. Old age is also a desire. Even death" (Deleuze and Parnet 1987, 95). In a recent article, sociolinguist Scott Kiesling has remarked that such an expansive view of desire "doesn't really help an analyst with finding desire, because it is everywhere" (2012, 217). He goes on to say that this omnipresence makes the Deleuzian concept "useless," but this seems an unnecessary conclusion. After all, language, in its broadest sense as a system of signs, is also arguably "everywhere." And power, Foucault famously proclaimed, also "is everywhere; not because it embraces everything, but because it comes from everywhere" (1980, 93). The perception that phenomena like language and power are "everywhere" has not rendered them useless: on the contrary, it has spurred a dazzling range of theories and methods for trying to understand how they manifest and how they work.

The dimension of Deleuze and Guattari's understanding of desire that makes it especially inviting for thinking about language is that it is not necessarily linked to sexuality, even though sexuality may well be one dimension (one "flux") that, together with other fluxes, creates desire. That psychoanalysis distills sexuality out of every desire is symptomatic of its relentless reductionism: "For [Freud] there will always be a reduction to the One: … it all leads back to daddy" (Deleuze and Guattari 1996, 31, 35). Lacan's insistence that desire is related to absence and lack is also a reflex of the same reductionist impulse, and it is unable to conceptualize how voids are "fully" part of desire, not evidence of a lack (Deleuze and Parnet 1987, 90). Deleuze exemplifies this with courtly love:

> it is well known that courtly love implies tests which postpone pleasure, or at least postpone the ending of coitus. This is certainly not a method of deprivation. It is the constitution of a field of immanence, where desire constructs its own plane and lacks nothing. (Deleuze and Parnet 1987, 101)

In contrast to psychoanalysts like Freud and Lacan (and Butler), who understand desire in terms of developmental history, Deleuze and Guattari see it in terms of geography. That is to say, they see their tasks as analysts as mapping the ways desire is made possible and charting the ways it moves, acts, and forms connections. They have no need to theorize the ontogenetic origins of desire, since desire is an immanent feature of all relations. For linguists and anthropologists, an advantage with this conceptualization of desire, regardless of whether or not one elects to adopt Deleuze and Guattari's entire analytical edifice, is that it foregrounds desire as continually being (dis/re)assembled. Thus, attention can focus on whether and how different kinds of relations emit desire, fabricate it and/or block it, exhaust it.

Deleuze and Guattari's framework is not abstract psychoanalysis, even though its formidable philosophical erudition, deliberately contorted presentational style, and highly idiosyncratic lexicon (hecceities, rhizomes, machines, bodies without organs, etc.) make it just as daunting as even Lacan's writing. Despite these difficulties, Deleuze and Guattari direct attention to desire without requiring that we derive all its formations from a particular source or a specific constellation of psychosocial relations (" … it all leads back to daddy").

This interest in mapping desire as a geographer would map a landscape links Deleuze and Guattari to Foucault. Perhaps the most productive way of thinking about desire would be to see it in more or less the same terms as how Foucault conceptualized power. Although he highlighted power in all his work, Foucault was explicit about not wanting to erect a coherent theory of power. "If one tries to erect a theory of power," he argued,

> one will always be obliged to view it as emerging at a given place and time and hence to deduce it, to reconstruct its genesis. But if power is in reality a open, more or less coordinated (in the event, no doubt, ill-coordinated) cluster of relations, then the only problem is to provide oneself with a grid of analysis which makes possible an analytic of relations of power. (Foucault 1980, 199)

Following Foucault's lead, it should be possible to study desire without having to decide in advance what it is and why it emerges; that is, without having to become a psychoanalyst. Instead of a theory of desire, the point would be to develop a means of delineating, examining, and elucidating those domains and those relations that are created through desire, not forgetting for a second to highlight the ways in which those domains and relations will always be bound up with power.

2. Investigating Desire in Language

Desire in relation to sociolinguistics was first raised explicitly only relatively recently, in 1997, by Keith Harvey and Celia Shalom in their anthology titled *Language and Desire: Encoding Sex, Romance and Intimacy*. Harvey and Shalom argued that "the encoding of desire results in distinct and describable linguistic features and patterns" (1997, 3), and the contributions to the book analyzed data ranging from personal ads to intimate conversations between lovers in order to show that erotic desire was something produced through language and particular structures of interaction. *Language and Desire* is an important and pioneering book, but it made little impact. The next texts to foreground desire, my own review article titled "Gay and Lesbian Language" (Kulick 2000) and the book titled *Language and Sexuality* (2003), which Deborah Cameron and I wrote soon after that, met with an entirely different kind of reception. That article and book critiqued past work on gay and lesbian language and more recent work on "queer" language along the lines summarized in the first section of this chapter, and both the article and the book concluded with the suggestion that research on language and sexuality develop methods and theories that allow an investigation of desire in language. (See Milani, Chapter 13 in this volume, for a discussion of research that draws upon Cameron and Kulick's (2003) proposals.)

"Gay and Lesbian Language" and *Language and Sexuality* turned out to be polarizing works. The criticism they developed of research on gay and lesbian language angered a number of the scholars who had been working on those topics, and as a result, storm clouds gathered and battle lines became drawn. A field of language and sexuality, different from the previous field of "gay and lesbian language" emerged, but it was a field portrayed by some as sundered by and oriented around a fundamental division. That division was declared to be between "identity" on the one hand, and "desire" on the other. (See Queen, Chapter 10 in this volume, for a discussion of the identity–desire debate.) Our critique of the role that identity had played in the research on gay and lesbian language became interpreted by some as an attack on the very idea of identity in general and of sexual identity in particular. Morrish and Leap, for example, suggested that "one of the outcomes of a desire-centered approach is the erasure of 'lesbian/gay' from academic inquiry" (2007, 37). More melodramatically, Bucholtz and Hall accused "Gay and Lesbian Language" and *Language and Sexuality* of waging a "crusade against sexual identity" (2004, 507). By misleadingly portraying those works as insisting that speaker identities were somehow either nonexistent, unimportant, or irrelevant to the study of language, scholars like Morrish and Leap and Bucholtz and Hall were able to characterize attention to desire as a research concern that was *opposed* to attention to identity. This supposed antithesis allowed those writers to depict themselves as rescuing identity from the war that Cameron and I apparently were busy mobilizing against it. It also allowed them to portray themselves as offering a synthesis to the polarization that they had announced, one that conceded that desire might be considered, but only as a kind of appendage or afterthought to identity, and only as long as any talk of psychoanalysis or repression was left out of the picture altogether. (Our response to some of this is in Cameron and Kulick 2005.)

Other researchers have found the call to explore desire in language to be a productive one. Ingrid Piller and Kimie Takahashi employ the concept of desire to discuss the attraction that the English language has for Japanese women (2006; 2010; see also Piller 2002, 2008; Takahashi 2010). They argue that "desire" is preferable to "motivation," which is the concept usually invoked in the literature on second-language learning in reference to something that learners either do or do not "have." Piller and Takahashi, instead, highlight desire, which they suggest "is a complex and multifaceted construction that is both internal and external to language learners, and is not linked to success in any straightforward fashion ... the link may even be negative" (2006, 59).

Piller and Takahashi show how desire for English is both incited and enacted. They discuss Japanese women's magazines that portray the West as glamorous, nonpatriarchal and full of handsome, gentlemanly white men. Private language schools try to attract students by displaying smiling portraits of male teachers, along with promises that a female student's English will improve faster because she "will be anxious to see her good-looking white teacher again soon" (2006, 65). Teaching material is often explicitly sexualized: one English-study magazine is actually titled *Virgin English*. It instructs women how to "learn love and sex through movies," through the repetition of lines like "You know what's going to happen? I'm gonna fall in love with you. Because I always, always do" (Marilyn Monroe in *The Prince and the Showgirl*), and "Oh yeah, right there" (Meg Ryan in *When Harry Met Sally*).

Japanese women who go to English-speaking countries to improve their English are unavoidably influenced by these discourses. The erotic connection stoked between the English language and white men encourages Japanese women to actively pursue relationships with white men and to reject partners who are not white. One woman recounted in an interview that:

> Listen, I told you that my friend told me that there would be many Australians at the BBQ party? So I was really looking forward to it. Well, there were a lot of people, mostly my friend's flatmate's friends, but they were all Asian-Australian! They were all native speakers or spoke English really well. But I felt, "they aren't my type of men" ... I am not here to waste my time mixing with men like these guys. Once again I had this self-confirmation that what I want is a white boyfriend. (Piller and Takahashi 2006, 74)

This kind of enactment of desire has a range of positive consequences – it often helps improve the women's English and, as Piller and Takahashi show, the Japanese women they interviewed are not shy about playing up their own sexual charms to get white men to talk to them. But the "bundle of desires" (2006, 80) that animate many of these women's dreams and interactions also set the women up for failure: many do not end up with a white Prince Charming boyfriend, and no matter how hard they try they will never become a white native speaker of English. In the end, the researchers note, desire can easily give way to depression.

Desire as an analytic concept also figures prominently in Scott Kiesling's (2005; 2012) analyses of talk among men in a fraternity. Fraternities are a kind of social men's club that exist in many US universities (their female equivalents are called "sororities"). They are composed of male undergraduate students who are invited to join by already active fraternity members. These fraternity "brothers" often live together in a large house, which is also the site of social activities and parties. Fraternities perform different kinds of public service, but they are widely known mostly for the excessive drinking that occurs in many of them, the baroque and demeaning rituals of hazing to which some of them subject potential members, and the expressions of sexism and homophobia that structure some of what many fraternity brothers say and do.

Kiesling uses the concept of desire to understand the structure and content of talk in a fraternity. He explains that fraternity brothers are in a tricky position in relation to one another. Much of what they do together is oriented toward engendering male bonding and male homosociality. But the line between homosociality and homo*sexuality* is a fine one, especially in contexts in which the young men express their feelings about the importance of being together with other men, or in which they attempt to attract nonmembers to join their fraternity (Kiesling coyly labels this latter, relatively ritualized, activity as "homosocial flirting" (2005, 711)).

Kiesling understands desire as a lack, but not a Lacanian lack that only relates to sexuality. He invokes masculinity studies scholar Stephen Whitehead's (2002) notion of "ontological desire" to argue that the interactions he observed in the fraternity where he did fieldwork act to encourage and sustain desire to inhabit and embody a particular kind of subjectivity – that of being a man. Given that the interactions that Kiesling describes occur together with others and are clearly incited, scaffolded, and narrated by those others, one wonders whether a more promising perspective on desire here might be framed less as a question of ontology and more as one of Levinasian ethics (e.g., Levinas 1969), where the ego emerges as a result of a susceptibility to specific others, or in terms of what Adriana Cavarero (2000) discusses as a "narratable self." But no matter how one might analyze it philosophically, an important dimension of Kiesling's argument is that this desire is not only articulated as interdictions on what men cannot or must not do. Desire, like Foucault's concept of power, is not just prohibitive, it is also generative and creative: discursive practices among fraternity brothers "motivate the men's desires as something the men actively seek. They organize the men's perceptions of what is lacking in their identity, and how the men wish to achieve masculine identity" (Kiesling 2005, 702).

   Like Piller and Takahashi, who argue that it is not enough to simply proclaim that individuals either do or do not have the motivation to perform particular activities or to invest in particular identities, Kiesling shows how language performatively enacts, invites, and directs desire. This enactment is sometimes cathected to the institution of the fraternity. Thus, men can announce to a group of fraternity brothers, "I love you all," or they can tell the group how being in their company entails "the best feelings ever." But they can do this only as long as the addressee of these declarations is a group or the institution of the fraternity, not individual men (Kiesling 2005, 711). In interactions, Kiesling shows how conversational alignment can be analyzed as the "doing" of desire. He argues that thinking about desire allows us to see more clearly how identities are not so much personal possessions as they are dispersed, relational, and contingent *achievements* that are created and sustained (or unmade and undermined) through interactional moves of alignment and nonalignment (Kiesling 2012, 234).
   A final example of recent scholarly work that uses desire to understand interactional data is Bethan Benwell's (2011) analysis of how young men talk about men's magazines. An important observation made in psychoanalytic texts about desire is that desire is not, and, as I discussed above, in some senses *cannot* be fully conscious. Nor is it structurally coherent. One way that Freud and other psychoanalysts explored the fractured nature of desire was through the distinction they made between "identity" and "identification." Stuart Hall has discussed this distinction, and his definition of "identity" is as good as any: identities, he writes, are "points of temporary attachment to the subject positions which discursive practices construct for us" (Hall 1996, 6). Identification is something different. Feminist scholar Diana Fuss, who has written a book on the topic, defines identification as "a process that keeps identity at a distance, that prevents identity from ever approximating the status of an ontological given." Identifications are "mobile, elastic and volatile," Fuss explains, and she argues that approaches to identity need to come to terms with the way that identity "is continually compromised, imperiled, one might even say *embarrassed* by identification" (1995, 2, 8, 10, emphasis original; see also Kulick 2003; Levon 2010; Milani 2012).
   Any analysis of desire in language will want to at least keep in mind this distinction between "identity" and "identification" because the structurally antagonistic relationship between the two processes will direct attention to the ways in which language always necessarily both constructs and simultaneously undermines the positions and roles that speakers materialize in their interactions and narratives. Benwell's analysis of young men talking about men's magazines focuses on how both these antagonistic processes are evident in talk. Her concern is to show how ethnomethodological approaches such as conversation analysis (CA) are just as appropriate for tracking anxieties and disavowals in language as they are for identifying affirmations. This is a point made repeatedly by Michael Billig in his important work on discursive psychology (Billig 1997; 1999; Billig and Schegloff 1999). But Billig's discussions focus on the tacit epistemological assumptions made in CA, not on an analysis of actual extracts of conversations. Therefore, it is helpful

to see concrete examples of how an interpretive methodology like CA can identify features in language that can plausibly be analyzed as identifications – that is, as features of discourse that compromise (or threaten to compromise) the identity claims made by speakers, even as speakers make them. Here is an extended example of how Benwell analyzes a stretch of talk in terms of identifications. Two young men (D and M) are responding to the interviewer's questions about why a feature on grooming for men is framed by humor in the magazine (transcription conventions modified):

D: I think humour is a good way of getting around touchy subjects, like y' know … if you asked a normal kind of lad who'd be like "oh I'm not going to go and have a facial" or something

I: having read it, would any of you be interested in those kinds of product?

M: great! If I had the money I'd have a go at it.

This exchange reveals what the assumptions, values and anxieties of a "normal lad" are. It also implies that the two speakers do not identify with this heteronormative construction, and with the mention of "normal," an opposite construction ("abnormal," "alternative," "subversive," "feminine" or "gay") is invoked. This disavowal is done in a number ways: firstly speaker D employs third-person, distancing strategies ("a normal kind of lad"), where the prosodic emphasis on "normal" and the hedge, "kind of," create a generic identity … but which is not explicitly aligned to by the speaker. The generic identity is also attributed a certain predictability by his stereotypical response: "who'd be like "oh I'm not going to go and have a facial" or something," where the general extender (Cheshire 2007) "or something" indexes something formulaic. Similarly, the use of the colloquial quotative "like" has a curious dual function here of introducing (imagined) reported speech whilst simultaneously indexing something stereotypical … The speaker deliberately distances himself from this kind of generic or predictable masculine response and construct. Secondly [speaker M] provides an explicit, positive, non-ironic alignment to the grooming feature, "Great! If I had the money I'd have a go at it." (Benwell 2012, 195)

The point of Benwell's examination of this short stretch of speech is to highlight how the speakers both invoke normative masculinity, and, even as they do so, almost simultaneously disavow it. This subtle and complex choreography of invocation, recognition, alignment, and disavowal is characteristic of the "new lad": an identity that Benwell says "occupies an ironic space somewhere between traditional, hegemonic realisations of masculinity and a humorous, anti-heroic, self-deprecating masculinity" (2012, 196–197). But it is also characteristic in a broader analytical sense of the way in which desires – to be, not to be, to recognize, to distance, to see, not to see – materialize in language. Benwell shows us that while ethnomethodological approaches like CA cannot exactly give us access to speakers' unconscious thoughts or desires, they can nevertheless be used to show how speakers both stake explicit claims to particular subject positions, even as they also equivocate, disavow, repress, and undermine those claims in their talk.

3. Conclusion

Paraphrasing Roland Barthes, who was writing about love, we could say that to write about desire is "to confront the *muck* of language: that region of hysteria where language is *too much* and *too little*, excessive … and impoverished (Barthes 1978, 99; emphasis original). The theoretical project discussed in this chapter is undoubtedly mucky. But what dimension of language and life isn't? I have suggested some of the advantages that sociolinguists, linguistic anthropologists, and other scholars who work with language in context might gain by thinking about both psychoanalytic and nonpsychoanalytic or even antipsychoanalytic understandings of desire. A concept like desire can help us see how different positions, identities, identifications, and relations are materialized and co-constructed in language. Desire as a frame of analysis is opening up new lines of inquiry, establishing new theoretical and methodological linkages, and encouraging new connections to be made across disciplines. Those connections promise to strengthen cooperation between linguists, anthropologists, literary theorists, and scholars interested in psychoanalysis, and they have the potential to enrich the study of language in exciting and highly desirable ways.

REFERENCES

Austin, J. L. 1997 [1962]. *How to Do Things with Words*, 2nd edn. Cambridge, MA: Harvard University Press.

Barthes, Roland. 1978. *A Lover's Discourse*. New York: Farrar, Straus and Giroux.

Benwell, Bethan. 2012. "Masculine Identity and Identification as Ethnomethodological Phenomena: Revisiting Cameron and Kulick." *Gender and Language*, 5(2): 187–210.

Billig, Michael. 1997. "The Dialogic Unconscious: Psychoanalysis, Discursive Psychology and the Nature of Repression." *British Journal of Social Psychology*, 36: 139–159.

Billig, Michael. 1999. *Freudian Repression: Conversation Creating the Unconscious*. Cambridge: Cambridge University Press.

Billig, Michael, and Emanuel A. Schegloff. 1999. "Critical Discourse Analysis and Conversation Analysis: An Exchange between Michael Billig and Emanuel A. Schegloff." *Discourse & Society*, 10(4): 543–582.

Bucholtz, Mary, and Kira Hall. 2004. "Theorizing Identity in Language and Sexuality Research." *Language in Society*, 33(4): 501–547.

Butler, Judith. 1990. *Gender Trouble: Feminism and the Subversion of Identity*. New York: Routledge.

Butler, Judith. 1997. *Excitable Speech: A Politics of the Performative*. New York: Routledge.

Cameron, Deborah, and Don Kulick. 2003. *Language and Sexuality*. Cambridge: Cambridge University Press.

Cameron, Deborah, and Don Kulick. 2005. "Identity Crisis?" *Language & Communication*, 25: 107–125.

Capps, Lisa, and Elinor Ochs. 1995. *Constructing Panic: The Discourse of Agoraphobia*. Cambridge, MA: Harvard University Press.

Cavarero, Adriana. 2000. *Relating Narratives: Storytelling and Selfhood*. London: Routledge.

Cheshire, Jenny. 2007. "Discourse Variation, Grammaticalisation and Stuff Like

That." *Journal of Sociolinguistics*, 11(2): 155–193.

Deleuze, Gilles, and Félix Guattari. 1996. *A Thousand Plateaus: Capitalism and Schizophrenia*. London: Althone Press.

Deleuze, Gilles, and Claire Parnet. 1987. *Dialogues*. New York: Columbia University Press.

Derrida, Jacques. 1995 [1972]. "Signature Event Context." In *Limited Inc.*, 1–23. Evanston, IL: Northwestern University Press.

Fink, Bruce. 1997. *A Clinical Introduction to Lacanian Psychoanalysis: Theory and Technique*. Cambridge, MA: Harvard University Press.

Foucault, Michel. 1980. *Power/Knowledge: Selected Interviews and Other Writings, 1972–1977*, ed. Colin Gordon. New York: Pantheon.

Freud, Sigmund. 1957. "Mourning and Melancholia." In *The Standard Edition of the Complete Psychological Works of Sigmund Freud* (24 vols.), ed. James Strachey, vol. 14, 239–258. London: Hogarth Press.

Freud, Sigmund. 1960. *The Ego and the Id*. New York: W. W. Norton.

Freud, Sigmund. 1975. *Three Essays on the Theory of Sexuality*. New York: Basic Books.

Fuss, Diana. 1995. *Identification Papers*. London: Routledge.

Hall, Kira. 1999. "Performativity." *Journal of Linguistic Anthropology*, 9(1–2): 184–187.

Hall, Stuart. 1996. "Introduction: Who Needs 'Identity'?" In Stuart Hall and Paul du Gay (eds.), *Questions of Cultural Identity*, 1–17. London: Sage.

Harvey, Keith, and Celia Shalom. 1997. *Language and Desire: Encoding Sex, Romance and Intimacy*. London: Routledge.

Jagose, Annamarie. 1996. *Queer Theory*. Melbourne: Melbourne University Press.

Jeffreys, Sheila. 1994. "The Queer Disappearance of Lesbians: Sexuality in the Academy." *Women's Studies International Forum*, 17(5): 459–472.

Kiesling, Scott. 2005. "Homosocial Desire in Men's Talk: Balancing and Re-creating Cultural Discourses of Masculinity." *Language in Society*, 34(5): 695–726.

Kiesling, Scott. 2012. "The Interactional Construction of Desire as Gender." *Gender and Language*, 5(2): 213–239.

Kristeva, Julia. 1980. *Desire in Language: A Semiotic Approach to Literature and Art*. Oxford: Blackwell.

Kulick, Don. 2000. "Gay and Lesbian Language." *Annual Review of Anthropology*, 29: 243–285.

Kulick, Don. 2003. "No." *Language and Communication*, 23: 139–151.

Lacan, Jacques. 1998. *The Four Fundamental Concepts of Psychoanalysis*. New York: W. W. Norton.

Leap, William. 1995. "Introduction." In William L. Leap (ed.), *Beyond the Lavender Lexicon: Authenticity, Imagination and Appropriation in Lesbian and Gay Languages*, vii–xix. Buffalo, NY: Gordon & Breach.

Leap, William. 1996. *Word's Out: Gay Men's English*. Minneapolis: University of Minnesota Press.

Levinas, Emmanuel. 1969. *Totality and Infinity*. Pittsburgh: Duquesne University Press.

Levon, Erez. 2010. *Language and the Politics of Sexuality: Lesbians and Gays in Israel*. Basingstoke: Palgrave Macmillan.

Livia, Anna. 2001. *Pronoun Envy: Literary Uses of Linguistic Gender*. Oxford: Oxford University Press.

Livia, Anna, and Kira Hall. 1997. " 'It's a Girl!': Bringing Performativity Back to Linguistics." In Anna Livia and Kira Hall (eds.), *Queerly Phrased: Language, Gender and Sexuality*, 3–20. Oxford: Oxford University Press.

Milani, Tommaso. 2012. "Introduction: Re-casting Language and Masculinities." *Gender and Language*, 5(2): 175–186.

Morrish, Liz, and William Leap. 2007. "Sex Talk: Language, Desire, Identity and Beyond." In Helen Sauntson and Sakis Kyratzis (eds.), *Language, Sexualities and Desires: Cross-Cultural Perspectives*, 17–40. Basingstoke: Palgrave Macmillan.

Piller, Ingrid. 2002. *Bilingual Couples Talk: The Discursive Construction of Hybridity*. Amsterdam: Benjamins.

Piller, Ingrid. 2008. " 'I Always Wanted to Marry a Cowboy': Bilingual Couples, Language, and Desire." In Terri A. Karis and Kyle D. Killian (eds.), *Intercultural Couples: Exploring Diversity in Intimate Relationships*, 53–70. London: Routledge.

Piller, Ingrid, and Kimie Takahashi. 2006. "A Passion for English: Desire and the Language Market." In Aneta Pavlenko (ed.), *Bilingual Minds: Emotional Experience, Expression, and Representation*, 59–83. Clevedon: Multilingual Matters.

Piller, Ingrid, and Kimie Takahashi. 2010. "At the Intersection of Gender, Language and Transnationalism." In Nikolas Coupland (ed.), *The Handbook of Language and Globalization*, 540–554. Malden, MA: Blackwell.

Saussure, Ferdinand de. 1983. *Course in General Linguistics*. La Salle, IL: Open Court.

Takahashi, Kimie. 2010. "Multilingual Couple Talk: Romance, Identity and the Political Economy of Language." In David Nunan and Julie Choi (eds.), *Language and Culture: Reflective Narratives and the Emergence of Identity*, 199–207. London: Routledge.

Voloshinov, V. N. 1973. *Marxism and the Philosophy of Language*, trans. Ladislav Matejka and I. R. Titunik. Cambridge, MA: Harvard University Press.

Weston, Kath. 1993. "'Do Clothes Make the Woman?' Gender, Performance Theory and Lesbian Eroticism." *Genders*, 17: 1–21.

Whitehead, Stephen M. 2002. *Men and Masculinities*. Cambridge: Polity.

Part II   Methods

4 Variation and Gender

MIRIAM MEYERHOFF

1. Introduction

In some ways, the history of language and gender research can be told through the history of how gender has been handled in variationist sociolinguistics. This chapter will trace the changing approaches to gender and language, from a focus on identifying and describing differences between the sexes' use of language, to a focus on hidden power through the relativistic norms of postmodernism, and back to a concern with feminist scholarship as the purpose of research on language and gender.

The idea that there might be distinct patterns that differentiate the language of female and male speakers in society has been present since the earliest stages of descriptive field linguistics. Early reports from the Caribbean suggested that in some parts of the Caribbean men and women spoke different languages. In fact, the lengthiest fieldwork done at that time made a more modest claim: "it often seems as if the women [have] another language than the men" (Rochefort 1665, cited in Jespersen 1998 [1922]). The approximately 10 percent difference in core vocabulary between men and women is attributed to a point in prehistory when Carib-speaking males invaded an Arawak-speaking community, killing off the men and settling with the autochthonous women. One of the hazards associated with talking about "women's language" and "men's language" is that it may suggest that the gender differences within a community are as different as French and Italian, but in fact, many of the differences were more subtle. In the case Rochefort documented, the core vocabulary differed but the inflectional morphology was the same for "women's" and "men's" words. Conversely, it was the inflectional prefixes used by adult men in the Yanyuwa community (Australia) that were different from the prefixes used by everyone else (Kirton 1988). What's interesting for us is that such subtle differences were characterized as different gender "languages" – as opposed to, say, gender "dialects." Classifying differences between varieties as dialectal variation emphasizes underlying similarity and often the standardness of one variety over the other(s). By contrast,

The Handbook of Language, Gender, and Sexuality, Second Edition.
Edited by Susan Ehrlich, Miriam Meyerhoff, and Janet Holmes.
© 2014 John Wiley & Sons, Inc. Published 2017 by John Wiley & Sons, Inc.

classifying difference as language variation constructs a much more fundamental divergence between both the varieties and the speakers. Perhaps the only reliably attested case of women and men speaking distinct languages in one community is the longhouse tradition in the Vaupés where people seek a husband or wife from an outgroup, and outgroup membership is defined as speaking another language. Once married the women continue to speak their own first language to their children, so each longhouse is multilingual. Aikhenvald (2002) reviews the early ethnographic work in the Vaupés and updates it with data on more recent sociolinguistic changes that have taken place.

2. First and Second Waves of Variation Studies: Production of Gender Differences

Penelope Eckert (2012) has argued that the study of variation and gender falls roughly into three waves (there is an intended analogy with the three waves of feminism). The "first wave" – what Eckert calls the "survey era" – reflects the dialectological interests of sociolinguistics; differences between the way speakers talk within a large, usually urban, speech community were shown to be stratified according to social class and style (using the methods of Labov 2006 [1966]). Gender was often also implicated, and there was a repeated convergence between careful style, middle-class speech, and women's speech (see Figure 4.1). What made these studies first wave is that research stopped when it had described

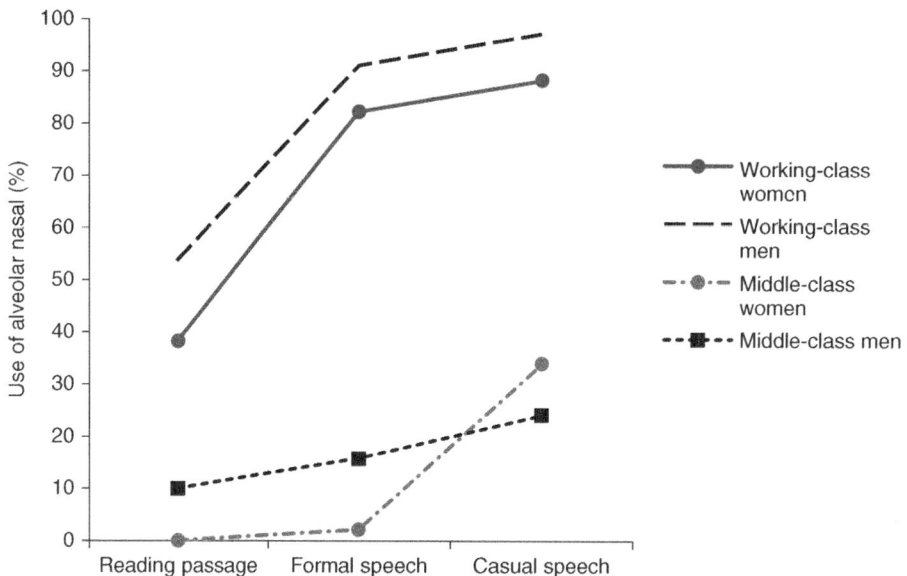

Figure 4.1.   Men's and women's use of the alveolar nasal in unstressed (ing) in three styles and in two social classes, in Norwich (based on Trudgill 1972)

these differences and when it had used them to shed light on the dynamics of language change. There was little attempt to interrogate why these social factors might pattern together in urban speech communities and what their convergence signified about the societies concerned. Issues relating to power and social order were not part of the analysis.

An attempt to go beyond the survey in order to explore the social meaning of the variables characterizes what Eckert calls the "second wave" of language and gender research. Research in the second wave is typified by asking questions about the local context of language variation at the time the research is conducted. Usually associated with studies of small communities of speakers, the research draws on more detailed knowledge of the way the community is organized and what drives social action in the community. While the first wave shows the close links between variationist studies (on the one hand) and dialectology and historical linguistics (on the other), second-wave research highlights the close connections between early sociolinguistics and anthropology.

Labov's (1972 [1963]) study of Martha's Vineyard in Massachusetts is a good example of research that did both. The study examined how the use of raised onsets in two key diphthongs (the (aw) and (ay) diphthongs in *mouth* and *price*) had become more than a marker of localness; it had become a strong indicator of how speakers on Martha's Vineyard felt about the island and their place on it. The clearest distinction was between people who liked or felt neutral about living there (and had higher rates of centralized onsets) and people who didn't like living there and who had lower onsets (more like speakers from the mainland United States). Labov observed that centralized onsets also correlated with people who lived in the least tourist-dominated part of the island, with speakers who worked in the traditional Vineyard trade of fishing, and with middle-aged men (who were more likely to actively participate in the fishing lifestyle) – in this way, he built up a much larger picture of gender as one component in the expression and iconicization of what it means to be a "real" Vineyarder.

David Sankoff and Suzanne Laberge (1978) also considered in more depth what certain convergences of gender, style, and social class in early social dialect surveys might mean. Drawing on work by the sociologist Pierre Bourdieu (who was accessible to francophone sociolinguists like Sankoff and Laberge long before he was available in translation to anglophone ones), they noted that not all women were associated with the use of the middle-class speech variants; rather there seemed to be an effect for how much a woman was integrated into the standard language marketplace. Bourdieu's economic metaphor makes an analogy between the trading of money for markers of status (e.g., a new car) with the conversion (trading) of certain ways of talking into status. For example, women whose jobs placed them in professions where language was a crucial resource (e.g., receptionists, teachers) were more likely to use middle-class variants than women working in professions where standard language was not a key marker of success (e.g., cleaner, home-maker). The fact that even lower-class women were more often directed into professions that are part of the linguistic marketplace than men is about how society is organized rather than about women per se.

The notion that linguistic variants might serve as social capital also appears in work by Peter Trudgill (1972), where he combines production and perception. Trudgill noted two things in his social dialect survey of Norwich, in England. First, women often used more of the supralocal Standard Southern British English (SSBE) variants and men often used more of the local Norwich variants in their speech. Second, when he presented people with two possible pronunciations of words like *tune* (locally [tun]; SSBE [tjun]), and asked speakers to say which variant they thought they used most often, women and men typically displayed different patterns of reporting *errors*. Men's errors favored the local variant; that is, if they reported their own norms incorrectly, they were more likely to say that they said [tun] (when, in fact, they used the SSBE [tjun] more). Women's errors favored SSBE, that is, they claimed they used SSBE [tjun] (when, in fact, they used the local [tun] more).

Trudgill suggested the Norwich women's self-report errors indicated they oriented to *overt prestige* norms (what's standard is best) and the men's self-report errors indicated they oriented to *covert prestige* norms (what's local or nonstandard is best). He suggested that the difference in which norms men and women oriented to might stem from women's and men's differential access to markers of prestige in society more generally. Norwich women might be orienting to language as a marker of social status (both in production – what they say – and in perception – what they believe they say) more than men because men had many other ways of marking status, for example, through their job or the material comforts afforded by their job).

The idea that women may draw on linguistic symbols of social status more than men recurs in Eckert's later work (2000) where she was studying teenagers in the United States. Eckert suggests that high school girls made use of a broader linguistic repertoire (collectively and as individuals) than high school boys did for a number of reasons, including the fact that the boys had access to a more varied repertoire of social markers that enabled them to position themselves in the high school community, for example, leadership in school council, sports activities. This more socially situated analysis of gender patterns in speech set the ground for the "third wave" of language and gender research, in which researchers conceptualize variables as components of styles, an approach I return to shortly.

As Eckert points out, some of the second-wave work actually predates some of the survey studies of the first wave. That is, the successive waves reflect research sensibilities (analogous to the notions of first-, second-, and third-wave feminism) and are not a chronological history of the field.

3. Perceived Association and Meanings

The question of how speakers perceive the social meaning of certain variables (discussed not only by Trudgill, but also by Labov 2006 [1966]) was elaborated by the social psychologist Howard Giles, who argued that in order to fully understand the alignment between male speakers and nonstandard or local variants, and between women and middle-class or Standard English variants, it is important to take into consideration how people "hear" the variants in question. In one experiment, Elyan et al. (1978) showed that middle-class accents, and in particular the higher-status accent known as RP (Received Pronunciation) in Britain, had multiple social meanings, some of which men might want to distance themselves from. Although RP was perceived as authoritative, this effect was stronger for women users; RP also had connotations of weakness and this effect was marked for male users. Hence, it may not simply be that male speakers are aligning with local variants, but rather that they are distancing themselves from some of the social meanings associated with RP.

A corollary of this was proposed by Elizabeth Gordon (1997). She found that listeners were more likely to associate a broad New Zealand accent with negative social attributes for girls, for example, smoking and being sexually promiscuous. Gordon discusses historical data that suggest the identification of lower-class women with sexually proscribed behavior is not new. She suggests, therefore, that some women may avoid linguistic features associated with working-class accents in order to distance themselves from negative evaluations about their character. In other words, women are not using standard variants because they want to talk themselves "up"; rather, they are avoiding the social costs associated with using local variants. An obvious question arising from this is whether negative evaluations are also made about men with strong working-class or nonstandard features in their speech. Research by social psychologists suggests not: on the contrary – as Trudgill found – men may aspire to, and produce, highly local and nonstandard forms; in some cases, this may be related to the widespread association between vernacular speech styles and some forms of "toughness." However, most of the social psychology research does not focus on linguistic detail, so there remains a lot for linguists to contribute to this area.

4. Relativising the Generalisations about Gender and Variation

Starting in the 1980s, several studies of urban speech communities in the Middle East produced findings that seemed to challenge the first-wave association between gender, style, and social class. Whereas Western surveys had found that women used more of the standard variants than men when a variable was above the level of social awareness, in the Middle Eastern studies women seemed to reverse this pattern. There, they were more typically users of the local colloquial Arabic variants, and men were associated with more frequent use of the "standard" Classical Arabic forms in careful speech. The alternation between Classical Arabic and colloquial Arabic forms was something that people were very aware of; hence, it seemed to run counter to the findings of, for example, Labov and Trudgill.

However, building on the work of Abdel-Jawad (1981), Niloofar Haeri (1994) noted that awareness alone was not sufficient for women to orient to the prestige norms of Classical Arabic. Because familiarity with Classical Arabic depends on formal instruction, men's greater opportunities for formal education meant that they had better access to Classical Arabic norms than women did in most Arab-speaking communities (see Al Wer, Chapter 20 in this volume).

Interestingly, the same argument had been made for creole speech communities in the Caribbean by Robert Le Page and André Tabouret-Keller (1985) in arguing for variation as "acts of identity." Le Page and Tabouret-Keller argued that (among other things) it was crucial for speakers to have access to adequate models of a speech style (or particular variants) for them to use that style or variant.

Haeri's work on variation in Cairene Arabic highlighted the importance of analyzing variation in its social context. The ecology of variation (and hence the generalizations that could be made about gender and language variation) in the Arab-speaking world was different from the ecology of language variation in the Western world. Gendered patterns in language variation emerge as a direct function of what gender means as a social category that is assigned to individuals in a society. Gender is about individuals' life choices, their opportunities (such as access to formal education), and how those choices and opportunities are evaluated by the community at large.

5. Form versus Function

The connection between women's and men's life choices and how gendered roles position women and men in society was the subject of Robin Lakoff's (1975) influential work exploring the nature of women's language in middle-class Western society. Whereas the work reviewed above largely focused on phonetic or phonological variables, Lakoff was interested in variation at all levels of linguistic structure. She highlighted normative differences in the kinds of words women and men use (whether swear words, color terms, or evaluative adjectives) and the kinds of structures they use (e.g., tag questions on declarative statements, or declaratives with a rising intonation pattern). She also considered asymmetries in the ways terms referring to women and men were used.

Lakoff's work drew a connection between the gender differences she believed existed and the social place of women in middle-class white American society at the time she was writing. Noting that some of the features she identified as "women's language" were also prototypically associated with gay men and academics, she points out that in some respects what she was calling "women's language" was really a collection of markers used by and associated with groups that are not part of the hegemonic masculinity valorized by society (see Hall, Chapter 11, and Trechter, Chapter 17, both in this volume).

Lakoff's work spurred a large number of empirical responses in the ensuing decade. Her work overtly invited reappraisal because (1) her caveat on the scope of what she was calling "women's language" highlighted the social embeddedness of the use of these features, and (2) because most of her claims were based on her introspections of what she knew about middle-class American society.

Independently, Janet Holmes and Deborah Cameron made the point that Lakoff's generalizations suggested a one-to-one match between form and function that was not supported empirically. Tag questions or overlapping talk, for instance, can have the function of supportive feedback to the interlocutor, or a challenge to take control of the floor. With many pragmatic particles (e.g., *you know*, *I think*, *sort of*) there are multiple functions and, in addition, any given use of a form may be ambiguous between some of these multiple meanings (Cameron, McAlinden, and O'Leary 1989; Holmes 1984).

Thus, in an extensive research program (summarized in Holmes 1995), Holmes demonstrated that generalizations to the effect that women (or men) use more (or less) of any given linguistic form are not very informative, unless the analyst carefully separates out the functions that those forms are used for. Moreover, such careful focus on form and function provides a more illuminating picture of precisely the kinds of dynamics Lakoff was interested in (cf. Holmes 2004), what power relations are in society and what is normatively expected of women and men and why they may avoid or even be sanctioned for transgressions on what is considered normative. A careful attention to distinguishing form and function was pioneered in gender and language studies, and is influential now in corpus linguistics.

6. Apparent Gender Paradox in Variation

The 1980s were a fertile period for variationist research on language and gender. However, they ended at a crossroads. In a 1990 paper, Labov summarized the generalizations to have emerged about gender and language variation from the first- and second-wave research on speech communities over the previous 20 or more years. In this paper, he drew attention to what he called the "gender paradox," namely that there were two very different patterns associated with women and language change.

On the one hand, for a change that is above the level of conscious awareness (variation which speakers can identify and express opinions about, such as the [tun~ tjun] alternation in Norwich or the (ing) variable in most varieties of English), women tend to use more of the standard variant and fewer of the nonstandard or local variant(s) than men – we saw this in Figure 4.1. (This is true of variation where there is no change in progress, that is, an alternation, to which a lot of social evaluation is attached, has been stably present in the speech community for some time and shows no signs of being likely to disappear, for example, the use of negative concord, as in *She didn't know nobody there*.)

On the other hand, where variation is part of a change that is taking place below the level of conscious awareness, women tend to use more of the innovative (and in some cases, by definition, less "standard"-like) variants than men. Figure 4.2 shows the deletion of /r/ in Garifuna (Ravindranath 2009), an innovation below the level of conscious awareness that women are leading. The results in alternations such as *barana* "sea" [baɹana] ~ [baːna], *wurinouga* "yesterday" [wʊɹinouga]

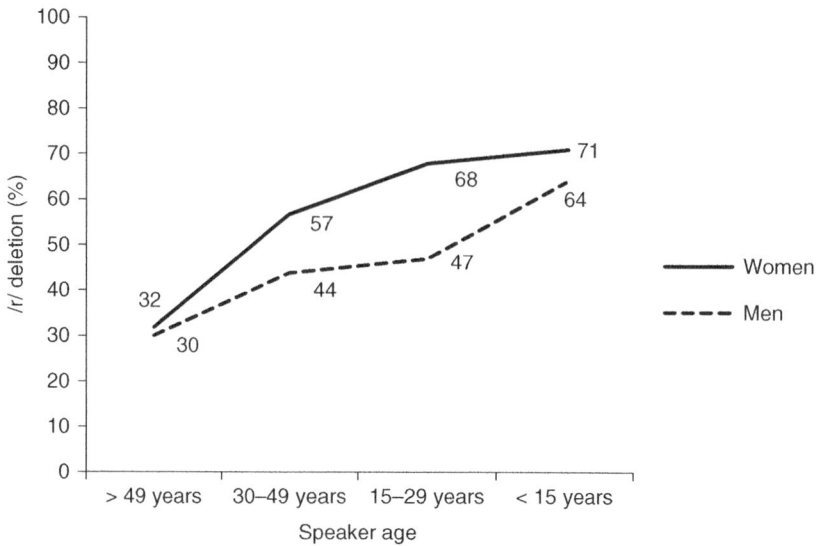

Figure 4.2.   Percentage of /r/ deletion in women's and men's speech in Garifuna (based on Ravindranath 2009)

[~wuinouga]. In other words, the gender paradox was that, when seen globally, women's linguistic behavior was both more conservative (and standard-like) *and* more innovative (and less standard-like) than men's.

Eckert's response (1989; 2000) was to observe that this is a paradox only if we assume it is the same women in each case, but this is not necessarily so. Her extensive ethnographic work in schools has shown how different girls use the variants available to different social effect. In doing so, she urged sociolinguists to pay much closer attention to the place language variation plays alongside other social practices in constructing and projecting different styles and personas.

Eckert's (2000) study of teenagers in suburban Detroit showed that it was true that some of the teenage girls were more conservative and some more innovative than the teenage boys in their school, but gender was not the most salient social division. Much more important to the teenagers concerned was the division between what they called *Jocks* and *Burnouts* (roughly speaking, the kids who were "into" school and those who weren't), a division so important that even the (majority of) kids who did not fall neatly into those two groups, identified themselves in relation to the groups, describing themselves to Eckert as *In-between(s)*. This is not to say that gender was not salient; however, it means that gender was embedded in even more salient local social categories. Eckert showed that for what we can call the "urban" sound changes, that is, the ones that seemed to be emanating from urban Detroit, such as the backing of the STRUT vowel /ʌ/, the most innovative speakers were the Burnout girls. Conversely, for the innovations that were not associated with Detroit city, Jock girls were leading. I will return to Eckert's work shortly when we discuss the turn to communities of practice and the analysis of language variation as a socially situated practice that contributes to the formation of personal and group styles.

The pattern of women generally leading changes from below seems to have been a characteristic of Anglo-Saxon society for some time. Terttu Nevalainen and her associates at the University of Helsinki have undertaken the detailed study of a number of changes taking place in English from around the fifteenth to the seventeenth centuries (Nevalainen and Raumolin-Brunberg 2003; Nevalainen, Raumolin-Brunberg, and Mannila 2011). They have often found remarkably similar patterns for gender (and social class) to those observed in the twentieth and twenty-first centuries in the large-scale studies of urban sound change. Nevalainen and her associates have been careful to relativize their generalizations about gender and language change by differentiating between women and men with different social profiles. Queen Elizabeth I (who had very high social status and considerably more education than the average woman in her time) was particularly innovative in her adoption of changes in progress, while an upwardly mobile man, such as Thomas Cromwell (who was born a blacksmith's son but ended up ennobled as the Earl of Essex), was notably conservative in his language use, apparently avoiding new changes until their social value had been well established by being adopted among the gentry. Their work thus highlights the socially situated nature of gender patterns in language (a point we will return to shortly).

7. The "Cultural" Turn

Also during the 1980s and early 1990s, the field of language and gender saw a parallel stream of research emerge. Unlike the studies reviewed above, the emphasis here was not so much on understanding whether gendered patterns of variation were implicated in language change (and if so, how). Instead, the emphasis shifted to a more descriptive mode in which the seeds of cultural relativism can be found. This work, which is sometimes referred to as the "two cultures" model of language variation, adopted a stance in which women and men were portrayed as representatives of different cultures with all the communication difficulties attendant on that. So, for example, we know that there may be communicative difficulties between someone from Western European society who has been acculturated to see avoidance of eye contact as a sign of "shiftiness" and someone from Pacific society where it is rude to look a more senior person directly in the eye and for whom avoidance of eye contact is a sign of respect. It was proposed that women and men similarly experience miscommunication on account of having been acculturated in different communities. The approach to language variation taken under this paradigm was different from core variationist work, and it is well discussed in other chapters in this volume (e.g., Goodwin and Kyratzis, Chapter 26, and Tannen, Chapter 25), so I will not go into detail here.

The loss of a social and political perspective to language and gender research that accompanied the two cultures approach was not welcome to some researchers (see Freed 1992; Philips, Chapter 15 in this volume; and Trömel-Plötz 1992). While earlier work on language and gender (e.g., first-wave research) had not necessarily been political, there had always been some researchers drawing on feminism to explore the patterns and motivations for gender-based language variation (cf. Cameron 1985; Lakoff 1975). The two cultures model, however, presented variation as a social fact detached from the larger social matrix. For example, it is all very well to say that a rising contour on an utterance invites active or implicit collaboration with the interlocutor because it is canonically associated with question-and-answer pairs, and that this conventional meaning of rising intonation is used by women in declarative sentences because their acculturation trains them to valorize routines that emphasize interpersonal connection. But this fails to address the issue that the use of rising intonation on declaratives is routinely interpreted as a signal not of affiliation and connection, but rather as a marker of uncertainty or indecision, thus feeding broader social stereotypes of women as weak and unsuitable for strong leadership roles.

Other problems with the two cultures model were also expressed: Eckert and McConnell-Ginet (2003) point out that the cultural separation of women and men in Western society is embedded in a vast number of activities and practices that bring them together and means that they interact with each other on a daily basis. They argue that Western society likes to focus on minor differences even if there are overarching similarities in the way men and women undertake these activities.

8. Social Constructionist Accounts of Variation

The two cultures analysis of gender differences in language did not come out of nowhere. In some ways, it is clearly situated in the intellectual trends of the time. The philosophical movement of postmodernism had existed for some time, but in the 1970s and 1980s its influence began to be felt in the social sciences and humanities. Postmodernism rejected or queried the modernist notions of objective and absolute truths; instead it focused on the potential for multiplicities of meaning and subjective notions of truth. If meaning and truth are subjective, then it is easy to see why analysts might refrain from judgmental positions – my subjective truth cannot be inherently better than your subjective truth. Postmodernism has come to be associated with social constructionism, a movement that became important at about the same time, because social constructionism held that many of the social facts we take for granted are products of how our society, and our individual histories, shape and construct our understanding of them.

The two cultures approach to variation was weakly in accord with a social constructionist view of the world because it claimed that women's and men's use of language differed, and that those differences were constructed by the different norms and gendered subcultures they grew up with. It also fitted in well with a reluctance to make value judgments associated with postmodernism – differences are simply differences, no one person's way of talking is better or worse than any other's.

But the turn to social constructionism in research on variation and gender gained its fullest expression in the late 1980s and early 1990s, when Penelope Eckert and Sally McConnell-Ginet introduced the concept of the "community of practice" to the field. Eckert and McConnell-Ginet (1992) argued against an overly simplistic dichotomy between "men" and "women," characteristic of not only the first-wave, survey-style research on variation and language, but also the two cultures model. They argued that gender is realized and experienced through the practices of the many communities that we are members of. That is, one is not simply a woman; one is a woman who is a member of a family (sister, mother, grandmother), a woman who is a member of a workplace (teacher, police officer, or train conductor), a woman who is a member of social groups (a tennis player, a yachtie, a member of the film society), and so forth. How gender is enacted in all those spheres of our lives makes us "women" or "men," and provides us with a repertoire – partly shared with others – that creates not only gendered styles that have meaning across individuals, but also personal styles that may be more or less gendered (see Podesva and Kajino, Chapter 5 in this volume).

This led to a methodological shift in how variation was analyzed. Instead of aggregating large groups of speakers according to predetermined, macro-social categories such as sex, social class, or age, the analyst was looking for and working with social categories that were locally meaningful. By "local" we mean distinctions that the participants themselves can and often do orient to explicitly (like the Jocks and Burnouts mentioned above, or the social "roles" identified in the last paragraph). Ideally, close and lengthy ethnographic work with a community is conducted to understand what is locally meaningful and what the salient communities of practice are. At this level of analysis it is possible that new variants will raise their heads, variants which may or may not become amplified and gain meaning within the larger community.

Indeed, the relationship between the individual and the group and the society becomes the object of a study of communities of practice. By looking closely at how meaning emerges and is associated with the use of different variants in interactions, the analyst is able to explore in more detail the kinds of interpersonal and social structures that support larger categories such as gender and social class which in turn shape individuals' social lives and life chances. The communities of practice framework need not be inherently antistructuralist, since analysts acknowledge the existence of power differences between different groups in society. However, by looking very locally, the researcher hopes to shed light on how such large-scale categories are sustained, contested, or created and how they are related to each other and more local categories (see Stokoe and Atkinson, Chapter 8 in this volume).

Since about 2005, it has been less common for the community of practice to be explicitly invoked as a framework for research in language and gender (perhaps partly because of criticisms about the lack of agency in the framework: cf. Meyerhoff and Strycharz 2013 and references there); however, its influence has been immense. Research on variation and gender now must either position itself as part of the shift to more local notions of gender and identity, or explicitly position itself outside such analyses of gender identities and justify this stance, perhaps for methodological or ontological reasons, such as a desire to focus on the dynamics of language change across groups and over longer periods of time.

9. Situating Variation in Its Social Context

The communities of practice approach obliges researchers to explore variation in terms of its local significance and to contextualize gendered patterns of linguistic behavior in terms of very local social dynamics. These local dynamics afford meanings which in turn are related to larger social categories like social class, or masculinity/femininity in ways that allow researchers to interrogate what those larger categories mean and represent socially. In this respect, the communities of practice approach stood in contrast principally to the tradition of social dialect surveys, and it had a good deal of sympathy with some of the work already being done on the gendering of speech acts and conversational routines (as we noted earlier, the three waves of sociolinguistic approaches to variation are not purely chronological).

In an influential study, Fishman (1983) looked at a range of features of conversational interaction between husbands and wives who were recorded talking casually at home. She looked at, among other things, who introduced conversational topics, who developed and supported their partner's topics (and how), and silences. The analysis of her observations was socially situated from the start; she notes that in every couple that she asked to make recordings for her, it was the man who took control of when the recorder was turned on and off. Her conclusion was that in intimate couples, much of the language variation she observed was due to women being responsible for what she called the conversational "shitwork," somewhat analogous to the household scut work that women typically undertake (Cameron 1992).

Similarly, work on the distribution of speech acts, such as compliments and apologies (Holmes 1995), considered not only the structural patterns associated with compliments delivered by men and women but also what those patterns reflected or signaled about what was valued in women and men in the communities where the data were collected. Holmes notes that the preponderance of compliments to women about their appearance, rather than their qualities and skills, constructs a restricted view of what it is to be womanly in New Zealand society. In Meyerhoff (2003), I note that saying "sorry" in Bislama in Vanuatu is a routine that has a strongly gendered dimension: only women (not men) in my corpus use the routine to express empathy (cf. Dureau 2012 on the gendering of "love" in the Solomon Islands). I interpreted this distributional difference by relating it to larger ideologies of what constitutes model womanly and manly behavior in the communities where my data was collected, and I argued that routines for showing empathy and alignment with others are more likely to be seen as appropriate for women than for men. I suggested that social approval of demonstrations of empathy may be used instrumentally by women in order to align themselves with others and thereby establish a degree of authority and a sense of belonging to a particular "place" – something that can otherwise be problematic since in Vanuatu women have to adapt their identity to align with a new sense of family "place" after they get married.

Silence, too, can be a speech act that reveals much about gender. Norma Mendoza-Denton (1995) considered the distribution of pauses following the testimony of Clarence Thomas and Anita Hill in the Congressional hearings on his nomination as Supreme Court Justice in 1991. She observed that the absence of long pauses after Hill's testimony (which characterized Thomas' testimony) served to construct Hill as less authoritative than Thomas.

It is also clear that adopting a very local analysis of variation need not preclude the researcher situating their findings in the larger historical context. Scott Kiesling's (2004) analysis of the use of *dude* as an address term (increasingly to refer to women as well as men) argues that the word expresses the speaker's attitude, specifically a stance of nonchalance, and he attributes this meaning to the origins of the word *dude* in subcultures, such as surfers and stoners, where adopting a nonchalant stance to life in general is highly valued.

10. Conclusion

The shift to analyzing gender as a socially constructed and socially situated identity makes it somewhat easier to reconcile what otherwise appear to be very different branches of research into language variation. In this conclusion, I will attempt to explain why this might be.

The social dialect surveys starting in the 1960s operated with an understanding of the sociolinguistic variable as being an abstract representation of two or more ways of saying "the same thing." While this is easily satisfied in studies of sound change (whether you use a centralized or lower onset for PRICE or a glottal or oral stop for intervocalic /t/ in *water* makes no difference to the sense or reference of the word uttered), it is less straightforward when you move to variables that have some inherent semantics, such as the final [-t] in a regular past tense verb like *jumped*, or the choice between lexical items such as *great* and *lovely* in a compliment, or the use of *sorry* to express empathy. In general, variationists are content if functional or distributional equivalence can be satisfied between variants (Torres Cacoullos and Walker 2009). This is important because without an acceptance of functional equivalence it is hard to see the connection between the different kinds of studies of language variation that have focused on gender in the past.

On the one hand, social dialectologists and historical linguists have drawn attention to the role women typically play in leading language change. On the other hand, research on epistemological hedges and boosters (e.g., the use of *sort of* or *really*) and speech acts such as compliments and apologies have had little to say about language change, but instead have drawn attention to the division of linguistic and social labor associated with these pragmatic features. In doing so, they suggest what these differences might signify about how women and men are perceived in society.

The turn to a more socially situated analysis of gender and variation (e.g., with communities of practice) demonstrates the potential for unifying these distinct branches of variationist inquiry, some aspects of which are progressing faster than others. There are two points at which this unification is possible: methodology and analysis.

If we assume that the imperative is to understand what variation means locally, even down to the level of a single interaction between individuals, and then to understand how variation at this level of interaction may be reinscribed in terms of larger social identities, then this means that researchers will be inclined to adopt methodologies that move between the quantificational approach (associated with aggregated data in social dialect surveys), and a more qualitative analysis of specific instances of a variant (typical of discourse analysis). In this way, the methodological differences of social dialectology and discourse analysis are realigned as complementary, rather than incompatible, approaches.

There are flow-on effects of this in how we analyze variation as well. As noted in this chapter, top-down analysis (working from the significance of broad social categories in society at large) and bottom-up analysis (working from the locally meaningful variation found in communities of practice) address fundamentally different questions and posit fundamentally different ideas about the relationship between variation and social meaning. However, in drawing on both broader ideologies of gender (or other social group) difference and the close analysis of interaction, we are beginning to see new approaches to the analysis of variation. These include analyses that look qualitatively at how interlocutors might be deploying a number of variables that are of interest in a short stretch of text, and analyses that relate the use of a single token of a specific variable to the way that more than one variable cluster within and across the speech of different individuals. These kinds of analyses require the researcher to situate variation in the widest possible context(s) – sometimes it helps to not only know what use of a variant means today, but what it might have meant in the past (a point that Mugglestone (2003) makes well) – and in relating variables across different levels of linguistic structure, studies of language variation provide a distinctive perspective on what constitutes a linguistic *system*.

There is no sign of a reduced fascination in the ways language and gender interact – in the formal research of the academy or in the popular media (a search for "gender differences" on YouTube testifies to this) – and this of course speaks to the significance of gender in society at large (see the chapters by Holmes (22), Philips (15), Cameron (14), and Freed (32) in this volume). However, studies of gender and variation are increasingly well equipped to take this fascination beyond the sterile description of who does how much of what, into more rewarding inquiry, such as: how subtle and systematic variation in language gives form to social meaning, what linguists actually mean when they talk about language as a cognitive system, and how these systems of meaning and cognition interact with the social dynamics that afford different opportunities to different people in our society and limits on how we imagine each other.

REFERENCES

Abdel-Jawad, Hassan. 1981. "Lexical and Phonological Variation in Spoken Arabic in Amman." Unpublished PhD dissertation, University of Pennsylvania.

Aikhenvald, Alexandra Y. 2002. *Language Contact in Amazonia*. Cambridge: Cambridge University Press.

Cameron, Deborah. 1985. *Feminism and Linguistic Theory*. London: Macmillan.

Cameron, Deborah. 1992. *Feminism and Linguistic Theory*, 2nd edn. London: Macmillan.

Cameron, Deborah, Fiona McAlinden, and Kathy O'Leary. 1989. "Lakoff in Context: The Social and Linguistic Functions of Tag Questions." In Jennifer Coates and Deborah Cameron (eds.), *Women and Men in Their Speech Communities*, 74–93. London: Longman.

Dureau, Christine. 2012. "Translating Love." *Ethos*, 40: 142–163.

Eckert, Penelope. 1989. "The Whole Woman." *Language Variation and Change*, 1: 245–267.

Eckert, Penelope. 2000. *Linguistic Variation as Social Practice*. Oxford: Blackwell.

Eckert, Penelope. 2012. "Three Waves of Variation Study: The Emergence of Meaning in the Study of Sociolinguistic Variation." *Annual Review of Anthropology*, 41: 87–100.

Eckert, Penelope, and Sally McConnell-Ginet. 1992. "Think Practically and Look Locally: Language and Gender as Community-Based Practice." *Annual Review of Anthropology*, 21: 461–490.

Eckert, Penelope, and Sally McConnell-Ginet. 2003. *Language and Gender*. Cambridge: Cambridge University Press.

Elyan, Olwen, Philip Smith, Howard Giles, and Richard Bourhis. 1978. "R.P.-Accented Female Speech: The Voice of Perceived Androgyny?" In Peter Trudgill (ed.), *Sociolinguistic Patterns in British English*, 122–131. London: Edward Arnold.

Fishman, Pamela. 1983. "Interaction: The Work Women Do." In Barrie Thorne, Cheris Kramarae, and Nancy Henley (eds.), *Language, Gender, and Society*, 89–101. Rowley, MA: Newbury House.

Freed, Alice T. 1992. "We Understand Perfectly: A Critique of Tannen's View of Cross-Sex Communication." In Kira Hall, Mary Bucholtz, and Birch Moonwomon (eds.), *Locating Power: Proceedings of the Second Berkeley Women and Language Conference*, vol. 1, 144–152. Berkeley: Berkeley Women and Language Group.

Gordon, Elizabeth. 1997. "Sex, Speech, and Stereotypes: Why Women Use Prestige Speech Forms More than Men." *Language in Society*, 26: 47–63.

Haeri, Niloofar. 1994. "A Linguistic Innovation of Women in Cairo." *Language Variation and Change*, 6: 87–112.

Holmes, Janet. 1984. "'Women's Language': A Functional Approach." *General Linguistics*, 24: 149–178.

Holmes, Janet. 1995. *Women, Men and Politeness*. London: Longman.

Holmes, Janet 2004. "Power, *Lady*, and Linguistic Politeness in *Language and Woman's Place*." In Robin Tolmach Lakoff, *Language and Woman's Place: Text and Commentaries*, rev. and expanded edn, ed. Mary Bucholtz, 151–157. Oxford: Oxford University Press.

Jespersen, Otto. 1998 [1922]. "The Woman." In *Language: Its Nature, Development, and Origin*. New York: Reinhart, Holt. Repr. in Deborah Cameron (ed.), *The Feminist Critique of Language: A Reader*, 2nd edn, 225–241. London: Routledge.

Kiesling, Scott F. 2004. "Dude." *American Speech*, 79: 281–305.

Kirton, Jean F. 1988. "Men's and Women's Dialects." *Aboriginal Linguistics*, 1: 111–125.

Labov, William. 1972 [1963]. "The Social Motivation of a Sound Change." In *Sociolinguistic Patterns*, 1–42. Philadelphia: University of Pennsylvania Press.

Labov, William. 1990. "The Intersection of Sex and Social Class in the Course of Linguistic Change." *Language Variation and Change*, 2: 205–251.

Labov, William. 2006 [1966]. *The Social Stratification of English in New York City*, Washington DC: Center for Applied Linguistics.

Lakoff, Robin Tolmach. 1975. *Language and Woman's Place*. New York: Harper & Row.

Le Page, Robert B., and André Tabouret-Keller. 1985. *Acts of Identity: Creole-Based Approaches to Language and Ethnicity*. Cambridge: Cambridge University Press.

Mendoza-Denton, Norma. 1995. "Pregnant Pauses: Silence and Authority in the Hill-Thomas Hearings." In Mary Bucholtz and Kira Hall (eds.), *Gender Articulated: Language and the Culturally Constructed Self*, 51–66. Routledge: New York.

Meyerhoff, Miriam. 2003. "Claiming a Place: Gender, Knowledge and Authority as Emergent Properties." In Janet Holmes and Miriam Meyerhoff (eds.), *The Handbook of Language and Gender*, 302–326. Oxford: Blackwell.

Meyerhoff, Miriam, and Anna Strycharz. 2013. "Communities of Practice." In J. K. Chambers and Natalie Schilling (eds.), *The Handbook of Language Variation and Change*, 2nd edn, 428–447. Oxford: Wiley-Blackwell.

Mugglestone, Lynda. 2003. *Talking Proper: The Rise of Accent as Social Symbol*. Oxford: Clarendon Press.

Nevalainen, Terttu, and Helena Raumolin-Brunberg. 2003. *Historical Sociolinguistics: Language Change in Tudor and Stuart England*. London: Pearson Education.

Nevalainen, Terttu, Helena Raumolin-Brunberg, and Heikki Mannila. 2011. "The Diffusion of Language Change in Real Time: Progressive and Conservative Individuals and the Time Depth of Change." *Language Variation and Change*, 23: 1–43.

Ravindranath, Maya. 2009. "Language Shift and the Speech Community: Sociolinguistic Change in a Garifuna Community in Belize." Unpublished PhD dissertation, University of Pennsylvania.

Rochefort, Charles de. 1665. *Histoire naturelle et morale des iles Antilles de l'Amerique*, 2nd edn. Rotterdam.

Sankoff, David, and Suzanne Laberge. 1978. "The Linguistic Market and the Statistical Explanation of Variability." In David Sankoff (ed.), *Linguistic Variation: Models and Methods*, 239–250. New York: Academic Press.

Torres Cacoullos, Rena, and James A. Walker. 2009. "The Present of the English Future: Grammatical Variation and Collocations in Discourse." *Language*, 85: 321–354.

Trömel-Plötz, Senta. 1992. "Selling the Apolitical." *Discourse and Society*, 2: 489–502.

Trudgill, Peter. 1972. "Sex, Covert Prestige and Linguistic Change in the Urban British English of Norwich." *Language in Society*, 1: 179–195.

5 Sociophonetics, Gender, and Sexuality

ROBERT J. PODESVA AND SAKIKO KAJINO

1. Introduction

The field of sociophonetics is concerned with the phonetic aspects of sociolinguistic variation, as well as the social significance of phonetic variation. Sociophonetics can be considered a branch of variationist sociolinguistics, differentiated from its parent field primarily by its methodological approach to data analysis. (See Meyerhoff, Chapter 4 in this volume, for a description of a variationist sociolinguistic approach to gender.) While variationists have historically sought to determine the linguistic and social factors affecting the use of one variable form over another (i.e., variation between categories of variant), sociophoneticians typically seek to uncover how similar factors influence the scalar realization of a variable. So while a variationist might investigate the realization of the vowel in (ing) by categorizing variants as either [ɪ] or [i], a sociophonetician might instead employ instrumental techniques to measure the first and second formant frequencies and thereby determine where in the range between a speaker's average [ɪ] and [i] any given token of (ing) falls. Sociophoneticians have also drawn on perceptual methodologies, popular in phonetics and psycholinguistics, to examine not only how social factors affect how listeners perceive speech (e.g., Strand and Johnson 1996, in which the phoneme boundary between /s/ and /ʃ/ depends on the speaker's perceived gender), but also how listeners subjectively evaluate speech (e.g., Campbell-Kibler 2011, in which listeners rated speech samples containing fronted variants of /s/ as sounding gayer and less masculine).

While the connections between phonetics on the one hand and gender/sexuality on the other have not always been a central area of investigation for researchers in either field, some of the earliest work on language and gender (Lakoff 1975) drew attention to the gendering of phonetic features. For example, the predominance of the high phrase-final boundary tone – the High Rising Terminal (HRT), known more informally as "uptalk" – in the speech of English-speaking young women

The Handbook of Language, Gender, and Sexuality, Second Edition.
Edited by Susan Ehrlich, Miriam Meyerhoff, and Janet Holmes.
© 2014 John Wiley & Sons, Inc. Published 2017 by John Wiley & Sons, Inc.

the world over (Britain 1992; Guy et al. 1986; McLemore 1991; Warren 2005) has steadily held the attention of linguists and the media for decades. In the field of sociophonetics, gender has been one of the field's central foci from its inception. In one of the earliest studies that might be labeled sociophonetics, Henton and Bladon (1988) found that creaky voice was much more prevalent in the speech of men compared to women, irrespective of their dialect area (Received Pronunciation versus Modified Northern English).

Gender has played a significant role in the evolution of sociophonetics because, for some analysts, much of the phonetic material that speakers produce is believed to be an automatic consequence of physiology – and sexual dimorphism among humans extends to vocal tract anatomy. As reported by Ohala (1984), the male larynx is, on average, 50 percent larger than the female larynx, the acoustic consequence of which is a slower rate of vocal fold vibration, hence lower pitch. Ohala further points out that male larynges sit lower in the throat than female larynges, yielding vocal tracts that are 15–20 percent longer, which produce lower resonant frequencies in vowels and sonorant consonants.

While it cannot be denied that phonetic output is heavily influenced by physiology, the roles of culture, social convention, and gender ideology cannot be discounted. Sociolinguists have long observed that pitch differences between boys and girls can arise even before puberty, when sex-based physiological differences emerge (Graddol and Swann 1983). Significant cross-linguistic differences have also been observed, as reported in Johnson's (2006) comparison of the difference between women and men in the first three formants in 16 languages. His study reveals, among other things, that the sex difference in F2 is slightly higher than 0.2 Bark in Danish and nearly 1.4 Bark in Norwegian. Perhaps even more striking is the difference in the same measure between New Zealand (0.45 Bark) and California (1.3 Bark) varieties of the same language, English. It appears, then, that physiology merely determines the range of phonetic possibilities, while sociocultural factors set conventions for the phonetic practices actually employed. (For a comprehensive overview of sex-based phonetic difference, see Simpson 2009.)

Although the strong connection between sociophonetics and gender did not develop until some years after the field of language and gender emerged as a discipline unto itself, the connection between sociophonetics and sexuality has been strong nearly from the inception of language and sexuality as an area of inquiry. This has stemmed, in part, from overwhelming interest in ascertaining the phonetic correlates of "sounding gay." Gaudio's (1994) study on pitch as one of the potential correlates provided the impetus for a host of subsequent studies investigating the potential roles of pitch (Smyth, Jacobs, and Rogers 2003), the duration (Levon 2006; 2007; Linville 1998) and spectral properties (Munson 2007; Munson et al. 2006) of sibilants, and vowel quality (Munson et al. 2006; Pierrehumbert et al. 2004). This line of research has given rise to both methodological and theoretical advances in the sociophonetics–sexuality interface. From a theoretical perspective, researchers have stopped "looking for the linguistic features or habits of speech that uniquely and unambiguously proclaim the speaker's sexual identity as this or that" (Cameron 2011), having recognized that readings of sexuality come from both how linguistic features are packaged with others and how they are employed in an interactional context. On the methodological side, the expansion of the set of phonetic features examined has necessitated the use of increasingly sophisticated acoustic measures and digital manipulation techniques, both of which have been facilitated in part by the increased participation and interest on the part of phoneticians.

The increased use of phonetic methodologies in sociophonetics has produced a number of positive outcomes for the study of language, gender, and sexuality. For example, treating linguistic features as scalar rather than discrete variables allows for speakers to be placed on gender continua, enabling analysts to avoid conceiving of one variable as marking femininity or masculinity, with nothing in between. A danger inherent in this approach, however, is the potential overemphasis on a single dimension of language, or a single notion of gender. Perceptual methodologies have gone a long way toward preventing analysts from relying too heavily on underanalyzed, monolithic notions of gender. For example, it is rare that a study will ask listeners to evaluate how masculine or how feminine a speaker sounds without also asking them to rate the speaker on a number of other scales, such as neat, lazy, or prudish (as used in Levon 2006; 2007). These attributes are themselves gendered, and their patterning with respect to particular linguistic features provides us with a window into what kind of masculinity and what kind of femininity we are tapping into during the course of an experiment. In spite of inroads such as these, considerable work remains with regard to operationalizing gender in an experimental context. Methods are needed for determining how a given study participant conceptualizes terms like "masculine," "feminine," "gay," and "lesbian" – since rather different notions of each term are likely to emerge across a subject population. Otherwise, it is unclear what precisely we have found when we discover, for example, that a given variant of a feature is judged to make a speaker sound gayer than a competing variant.

Our goals for the remainder of the chapter are to introduce the most commonly studied phonetic features that can index gender, sexuality, and the meanings that constitute them; selectively review classic and current literature on the sociophonetics of gender and sexuality; and highlight important theoretical issues relating to the enterprise of studying gender and sexuality from a sociophonetic perspective. We discuss each major domain of linguistic sound in turn, and conclude with a discussion of what we believe to be exciting new horizons in the study of the sociophonetics of gender and sexuality.

2. Pitch and Intonation

In sociophonetic research on gender, no feature has been studied as comprehensively as pitch, particularly mean pitch levels. Gross anatomical differences between men and women in vocal fold physiology unsurprisingly yield cross-linguistic differences in pitch levels. While these differences can be quite similar cross-linguistically, the magnitude of the difference can vary substantially across languages due to differing cross-cultural gender norms. To test the hypothesis that fundamental frequency (F0) differences between Japanese and Dutch women stemmed from culture-specific ideology, Van Bezooijen (1995) asked listeners to evaluate speech in both languages that was artificially raised or lowered in pitch. Japanese listeners evaluated samples with higher F0 more positively, while Dutch listeners preferred lower F0 levels. Both patterns reflect the norms of production in the respective languages.

While some studies have focused on average speaking F0, others consider pitch range. Henton (1989) re-evaluates published data on pitch range differences between women and men, and shows that once the linear Hz scale is converted to a semitone scale that adjusts for the logarithmic perception of pitch, women no longer exhibit wider pitch ranges than men.

Systematic pitch properties can be also observed in the domain of intonation, where the concern is not merely the pitch level, but the shape of pitch contours and how these shapes are distributed over the course of utterances. Easily the most widely studied intonational variant in English is the HRT, sometimes referred to more informally as "uptalk" in the media. One of the earliest discussions of this feature appeared in Lakoff (1975), who suggested that the feature is more prevalent in the speech of women because women are more likely to (and are encouraged to) take stances of uncertainty or tentativeness. Others have since argued that HRTs can be used in more powerful ways, such as when politely challenging an interlocutor, to grab an interlocutor's attention, or to maintain control of the floor (McConnell-Ginet 1983). Empirical support for these proposals is evident in McLemore's (1991) work on intonational patterns among sorority members. She reports that officers in the sorority use the HRT most often, especially to signal the continuation of their turn, but also to establish common ground. Similar patterns have been reported in other varieties of English (e.g., Fletcher, Grabe, and Warren's 2005 study on New Zealand English). In spite of the wealth of work complicating the range of pragmatic functions HRTs serve, the beliefs that they convey uncertainty, and that they are a feature of women's but not men's speech, continue to be promulgated by the media. This is perhaps due to the fact that the rise in pitch resembles (but is not necessarily equivalent to) that of a yes-no question.

While rising intonational contours on statements are commonly associated with the speech of women, this relationship does not hold universally, even across the varieties of English. Lowry (2002) shows that in Belfast English, a rise plateau contour dominates in statements, and that women use a falling contour more than men. In a study examining the interpretation of the falling contour in Belfast English, Lowry (2011) finds that the fall strongly correlates with ratings of "enthusiastic" and "emotionally engaged," and crucially not "neutral" (as it is evaluated in varieties of English in which the HRT is marked). It is worth noting that, across the varieties of English, the pattern exhibited by women (or believed to be exhibited by women) is evaluated as marked, regardless of the shape of the contour. This raises questions about whether the interpretation of intonational contours stems from their linguistic properties (i.e., whether they rise or fall, and how quickly they do so) or ideologies about who most commonly uses them.

The discussion above has focused on the relationship between pitch (and intonation) and gender. Pitch has played an equally important role in the study of sociophonetics and sexuality, particularly with regard to the phonetic correlates of "sounding gay," which has invariably been used to refer to sounding like a gay man. Most studies examining speakers' mean fundamental frequency have found no difference between gay(-sounding) and straight(-sounding) voices (Gaudio 1994; Smyth, Jacobs, and Rogers 2003). Although one study does report that gay speakers have higher F0 levels than straight speakers (Baeck, Corthals, and Van Borsel 2011), the magnitude of this difference is very small. Levon (2007) examines this issue from the perspective of perception, by acoustically modifying the pitch ranges of stimuli and asking listeners to evaluate the manipulated samples on a number of scales. He reports that expanded pitch ranges are sufficient on their own to increase how gay a speaker is rated as sounding. While pitch can, in some contexts, mark speakers as belonging to a gay male identity category, it can also be drawn on to construct specific gay personas. Podesva (2011b) investigates intraspeaker variation in the speech of gay professionals and shows that pitch levels, pitch ranges, and intonational contours are combined in unique ways from one situation to the next. Two of the speakers in particular, Heath and Regan, exhibit higher pitch levels and wider ranges when speaking with groups. Podesva argues that Heath and Regan are on the one hand engaged in similar practices – by being "animated" – but that they are channeling their animatedness into constructing distinct kinds of gay personas – a diva and a partier, respectively.

Although a great deal of attention has been paid to the phenomenon of "sounding gay," few studies have endeavored to investigate the phenomenon of "sounding lesbian." In the earliest study investigating this matter, Moonwomon-Baird (1997) examined the pitch properties of four women (two lesbian, two heterosexual) and found suggestive evidence of higher, more dynamic pitch patterns in the speech of the straight women, while no clear pitch characteristics united the speech of the two lesbians. Lutzross (2010) systematically manipulated the pitch range in otherwise identical speech samples and found that clips exhibiting lower pitch and smaller ranges were judged as more "lesbian-sounding." Production data analyzed in the same study show, as might be expected, that lesbians in the sample (four lesbians, as compared to four heterosexual women and four who identify as "other") do not actually produce such pitch patterns.

The divergence between production and perception patterns in Lutzross (2010) serves as a reminder not to essentialize linguistic practice on the basis of identity category membership and begs the question: How might lesbians draw on pitch and other phonetic resources to construct lesbian identity? Levon (2011) argues that two groups of Israeli lesbians draw on mean pitch to construct sexuality, but that the two groups orient to different ideologies about the connection between pitch and gender/sexuality. The group of "mainstream" lesbians produce higher pitch levels when talking about gay-themed topics than when talking other topics. These lesbians maintain the stance that lesbians and straight women are, in essence, the same; they therefore orient to traditional norms for their gender when discussing gay issues. A second group of lesbians – the "radical" lesbians – also produce higher pitch levels when talking about gay topics, but the same explanation does not apply in this case; members of this group reject the mainstream women's notion of feminism, which they argue is overly traditional.

While these studies suggest that pitch may play some role in constructing lesbian identities, the indexical link between low pitch (or narrow pitch ranges) and lesbian identity is clearly not as strong as that between high pitch (and wide pitch ranges) and gay male identity. Cameron (2011, 100) addresses this issue in some detail, pointing out that "although [lesbians] are associated with a rich repertoire of general cultural stereotypes, these do not seem to have any clear linguistic correlate, either in the folklinguistic imagination or in the empirical reality described by linguists." One proposal for why "sounding lesbian" was not as recognized a concept as "sounding gay" was proposed by Zwicky (1997), who argued that gay-stereotyped speech represents gay men's rejection of traditional masculinity, while lesbians on the whole still very much identify with their gender identities. Cameron adds the important point that lesbians may have available to them fewer resources from which to construct a distinctive lesbian linguistic style. For example, the use of feminine pronouns to refer to gay men can be considered an element of a gay linguistic style, but it is legible as referring to sexuality rather than gender only because of the pre-existence of a gay male identity as gender inversion. The same discourses are not available in the case of lesbians, so the use of masculine pronouns to refer to lesbians can therefore not emerge as easily as a component of a lesbian speech style. Cameron (2011, 103) concludes that persona construction is "constrained by the resources available to do it, which in turn are shaped by material conditions – those of the past as well as the present," and suggests that distinctively lesbian styles might be observed in places where richer resources might be available – such as "total female institutions like women's prisons, girls' boarding schools, and the relevant parts of the military services." As sociophonetic investigations of such institutions are few and far between, further work in this vein has great potential to shed light on the extent to which phonetic resources might be drawn on to index lesbian identity.

The sociophonetic work relating pitch to gender and sexuality provides overwhelmingly broader coverage of cisgender individuals, though in the last decade a body of work on trans individuals has grown. Gorham-Rowan and Morris (2006) report that F0 levels among trans women are significantly higher than those among cis men, and that listeners were likely to rate F0 levels of 180 Hz or greater as feminine-sounding. While some degree of longitudinal change in F0 over the course of gender transitions can be attributed to speakers' laryngeal control, medical interventions such as hormone therapy also play a significant role. Zimman (2012) documents longitudinal changes in F0 among trans men taking testosterone, who typically exhibit an unambiguously male-sounding pitch range within a year. While all participants in Zimman's study experienced a significant lowering of F0 over time, there was significant variation in the magnitude of the change, as well as the trajectory and time course over which the change transpired.

The studies above indicate that pitch is a rich resource for the construction of both gender and sexuality, and that it figures prominently in both their performance and their legibility. While there are long-standing and robust ideologies linking high pitch to femininity and low pitch to masculinity, ideologies that work recursively within gender groups (e.g., high-pitched male voices may be deemed as sounding less masculine than low-pitched male voices), observed patterns of use are not as straightforward. Pitch and intonation are recruited to do much more than gender and sexuality (e.g., age, affect, size), so any analysis examining pitch practices should situate gender and sexuality in relation to these other potential indexical values.

3. Vowels

Variation in vowel quality in many respects constitutes the bread and butter of variation analysis and dialectology. As discussed in Meyerhoff (Chapter 4 in this volume), the connection between gender and regional variation is well-charted territory, due to the ubiquitous if not exceptionless finding that women lead language change as it sweeps through geographic space. In the current chapter, we will not be addressing the connection between gender and regional variation. We will, however, discuss nonregional gender-based variation in vowel quality, as well as the potential for vowel quality to index sexuality.

In addition to carrying information about vowel quality, resonant frequencies (or formants) provide cues regarding vocal tract (and body) size, which (as discussed above) varies as a function of speaker sex. As Van Dommelen and Moxness (1995) point out, listeners use formant frequencies as a phonetic cue to predict speaker size (in terms of height and weight), with lower values predicting larger bodies. Size can in turn be gendered, for example, if speakers produce high formant frequencies when performing stylized affect (Geenberg 2010).

Formant frequencies can also index the clarity of speakers' voices, under the rationale that larger vowel spaces are indicative of greater articulatory precision, maximal vowel dispersion, and minimal overlap between different vowel phonemes. Clarity, as achieved through expanded vowel spaces, can serve any number of functions. It can, for instance, be used to facilitate comprehension of speech directed toward small children (Kuhl et al. 1997) in the "motherese" (or child-directed speech) register, though this is not a universal pattern (Wassink, Wright, and Franklin 2007). Clarity may also, if sufficiently extreme, index prissiness, which has been noted as a resource for constructing flamboyantly gay personas (Podesva 2006).

This connection may be what underlies Pierrehumbert et al. (2004) finding that the gay men in their study had a significantly larger vowel space than straight men, though this finding was not replicated in Munson et al. (2006). Munson et al. (2006) did, however, find differences between gay and straight men in the vowels /ɛ/ and /æ/, both lower for gay men. While Pierrehumbert et al. (2004) and Munson et al. (2006) make acoustic comparisons based on speakers' reported sexual orientations,

Zimman (2013) instead compares the speech of those perceived to sound gay to those perceived to sound straight and finds no significant difference in terms of vowel dispersion. A number of vowel patterns also differentiate the speech of lesbian and bisexual women from that of straight women (Munson et al. 2006; Pierrehumbert et al. 2004), though the forces driving these patterns is unclear.

Although it has not always been the practice, studies examining the potential connection between vowel quality and sexuality should interpret trends with respect to the range of possibilities defined by regional variation. As Podesva (2011a) notes, a backed /u/ may constitute a clear vowel in a variety that does not exhibit fronting of the back vowels, but a fronted /u/ may be interpreted similarly in a fronting variety. In the only study to report a significant influence of sexual orientation on regional sound change, Conn (2005) shows that in Philadelphia lesbians lead in the backing of (aw) and raising of (eyC), and that gay men resist these changes. Podesva (2011a) demonstrates that the degree to which a gay man from California shifts his vowels in the direction of the California vowel shift varies from one situation to another. He argues that California vowels index not only geographic region, but also the traits associated with California stereotypes – being fun and laid-back. These traits can participate in the construction of certain personas (e.g., gay partier) that have more to do with ideologies about California than the geographic space occupied by the state, and simultaneously evoke sexuality. These two studies notwithstanding, there is a dire need for embedding research on the phonetic correlates of sounding gay in larger-scale community studies. It may be the case that regional variants – well represented in the domain of vowels – are poor indices of sexuality because sexuality cuts across region, but it could also be the case that the number of observed correlations between vowel variation and sexuality are few only because so few studies have entertained the possibility.

4. Consonants

This section focuses on the roles that fricatives and stops play in the construction of gender and sexuality. Sonorant consonants (i.e., glides, liquids, nasals) are not discussed here, since their phonetic realizations are rarely discussed as an index of gender or sexuality.

4.1   *Fricatives*

Gender effects on the realization of fricatives have been investigated most extensively for the voiceless anterior sibilant of English, /s/. Given gross differences in the size of the vocal tract between women and men, as well as men's disproportionately larger lips relative to the vocal tract, it is perhaps no surprise that fricative energy is generally concentrated at higher frequencies for women. However, the acoustic consequences of anatomical difference do not define or determine speakers' production patterns. In Glaswegian English, for example,

Stuart-Smith, Timmins, and Tweedie (2007) report that not only do males exhibit lower peak frequencies and centers of gravity, but they produce *retracted* variants of /s/, in effect augmenting the physiologically rooted difference between women and men. While speakers can, on the one hand, enhance physiological difference, so too can they counteract it. In other work on the same community in Glasgow, Stuart-Smith (2007) provides acoustic evidence that young working-class women exhibit patterns that more closely resemble men's patterns than those of the other women in their community. This study brings to the fore the important point that the construction of gender may have every bit as much to do with constructing orthogonal dimensions of identity (e.g., class) as it does with producing male–female difference.

There is strong evidence that listeners are aware of gender differences in the production of /s/, and that they categorize speech according to their awareness. In their classic studies on the interaction between speaker gender and phoneme categorization, Strand and Johnson (1996) investigated whether speaker gender influenced where listeners drew the boundary between /s/ and /ʃ/ on a synthesized fricative continuum. The synthesized fricatives were used as the initial sound in monosyllabic stimuli ending in /ad/. Importantly, /ad/ was recorded in the voice of both male and female speakers, independently rated in terms of gender prototypicality. At each step in the fricative continuum, and for each of the speakers, listeners were asked to categorize whether they heard "sod" or "shod." The results indicate that stimuli containing /ad/ produced by males were heard as /s/ at lower frequencies than those produced by females. Perhaps more strikingly, gender affected the categorization of sounds gradiently, as nonprototypically gendered voices fell in between prototypically male and prototypically female voices. Listeners do not simply make a binary distinction between males and females and normalize accordingly to that categorization. Rather, they perceive speech gradiently according to more nuanced cognitive representations of gender. This study issues a reminder that the cognitive and the social are more intertwined than scholars working in either tradition typically grant.

Sociophonetic studies of sibilant production among trans men and women provide additional evidence that speakers orient to an ideology that associates high frequency energy with femininity and low frequency energy with masculinity. In his analysis of the spectral properties of /s/ in discourse marker *so* among speakers in Ottawa, Hazenberg (2012) reports that straight women have the highest mean of center of gravity followed by queer women and trans women, while the straight men have the lowest, and queer men and trans men fall between cis women and straight men. The fact that trans women and men pattern with members of their own gender, rather than with members of their biological sex, indicates that the frequency of /s/ is a sufficiently salient feature that trans men and women develop new norms during the transition process. In Zimman's (2012) longitudinal study, trans men recorded for a year-long period showed an overall negative relationship between center of gravity for /s/ and weeks on testosterone. At the same time, Zimman stresses that the entire population exhibited a wide range of variation, one that encompasses the entire ranges for women and men reported in other studies.

He argues that interspeaker variation can best be understood by attending to the specific kinds of masculinity and sexualities to which individuals are orienting.

Given how strongly fricative frequencies implicate gender, it is unsurprising that they figure prominently in the construction of sexuality as well. While studies investigating the phonetic correlates of sounding gay eventually came to focus on the spectral properties of /s/, the focus was initially placed on the duration of /s/. Not only do gay(-sounding) men produce longer /s/ than straight(-sounding) men (Linville 1998), but listeners rely on this durational cue, under some circumstances, when assessing how gay speech samples sound (Levon 2006; 2007).

While sibilant duration shows some potential to influence listeners as they categorize speakers' sexual orientations, the spectral properties of sibilants exert an even stronger influence. Munson, Jefferson, and McDonald (2006) investigated the extent to which the way fricatives are categorized depends on whether the speaker sounds gay or straight. They constructed a continuum of sounds ranging from [s] to [ʃ] and asked listeners to categorize each of the sounds on the continuum. Listener categorizations depended on whether female speakers sounded gay or straight, which had been established previously; the same was not true for the male speakers. In another study, Munson et al. (2006) found that /s/ produced by gay men exhibited a more negatively skewed spectrum; regression analysis revealed that listeners likely drew on this feature in their categorizations. Campbell-Kibler (2011) systematically varied the spectral properties of /s/ along with (ing) to investigate the interplay between features and examine the effect that the interplay has on the perceived sexuality of speakers. Results indicate that fronted /s/ robustly increased perceptions of gayness and lowered perceptions of masculinity. When interpreted in conjunction with velar variants of (ing), the meaning of fronted /s/ transforms into something that is not simply the union of the style's component features' meanings: the "sassy gay friend" stereotype, which according to Campbell-Kibler is characterized in part by gayness and intelligence, but many other traits as well. Campbell-Kibler (2011) (as well as Levon 2007 and Podesva 2011b) emphasizes that linguistic styles do not simply index disembodied identity categories like gay, straight, woman, or man. Listeners orient to fleshed-out people, or figures of personhood.

4.2   Stops

Stop consonants can be characterized as comprising three main phases (Foulkes, Docherty, and Jones 2010), each of which can exhibit variation with respect to gender and/or sexuality.

First, during the onset, the articulators move into position for the closure. The primary parameter of interest is whether secondary glottal activity accompanies formant transitions leading into the stop. Glottal reinforcement, or the addition of glottalization to the oral articulation of a stop, has been discussed in several varieties of British English, and is often contrasted with glottal replacement, whereby an oral stop is debuccalized, losing its oral articulation altogether (Docherty and Foulkes 2005; Foulkes, Docherty, and Watt 2005; Milroy et al. 1994).

Foulkes, Docherty, and Watt's (2005) study has strong implications for the role of caregivers in shaping the emergence of gender-based variation in speech. They find that women living in Tyneside show a great preference for glottal variants of (t), yet when they speak to children, released variants predominate. More strikingly, their patterns in child-directed speech vary according to whether they are talking to boys or girls; in the former case, glottals are better represented. The authors conclude that these women are modeling normatively gendered speech. While glottal and glottalized variants of voiceless stops, particularly /t/, are well studied in a British context, far fewer studies have endeavored to investigate glottalized /t/ in American English. Eddington and Taylor (2009) report a higher incidence of glottalized /t/ in intervocalic, word-final position in the speech of young women, suggesting a change in progress. It is unclear whether this tendency toward greater glottalization is related to the tendency for young women to employ creaky voice more than their male counterparts, discussed below.

In the second phase, the closure, the articulators have reached their target and are held in place for some time. The closure can vary in terms of its duration, as well as whether it exhibits any voicing during the closure. Jacewicz, Fox, and O'Neill (2009) examine the extent of closure voicing in [b], comparing the speech of women from Wisconsin to that of women from North Carolina. They report that women from North Carolina fully voice stop closures much more frequently than women from Wisconsin. Thus, even low-level phonetic features like stop voicing can exhibit systematic intragender differences.

Finally, the stop closure is let go in the release phase. The transient characterizing the release may be either present (i.e., visible in the acoustic record and perceivable in the auditory record) or absent (i.e., obscured by neighboring articulatory gestures). In their study on Tyneside, Docherty and Foulkes (2005) find that older men have a higher incidence of release bursts, indicating that the coordination of articulatory gestures is socially conditioned. A relatively long list of scholars have hypothesized about the social meanings of released stops, leading Eckert (2008) to theorize about the ways in which these meanings relate to one another. Many of these meanings are associated with gender and sexuality. Benor (2004) observes high rates of released /t/ among Orthodox Jewish men. She argues that stop releases index learnedness, and that in this particular cultural context, learnedness indirectly indexes masculinity. Released /t/ is most common in the speech of those who have attended yeshiva, the majority of whom are men. Stop releases have also been linked to sounding gay. Podesva, Roberts, and Campbell-Kibler (2002) compare the speech of two opponents in a radio debate on the issue of whether the Boy Scouts of America should be allowed to discriminate on the basis of sexual orientation. They find that a lawyer representing Lambda Legal produces higher rates of released word-final stops than his opponent, who does not publicly identify as gay, and argue that stop releases enable the attorney to put forth a public image that is gay but not flamboyant, drawing on the "learned" meaning potential of released stops to construct a persona that is professional and competent in addition to gay. Sclafani (2007) further expands the range of indexical meanings associated with released /t/ in her work on parodies of Martha Stewart. She finds that actors portraying the popular television personality typically produce hyperstandard speech while engaged in violent, often aggressive acts. In the face of such undeniably bad behavior – the kind of behavior that led the real Martha Stewart to prison for insider trading – categorically released /t/s enable the actor playing her to portray a "good woman" image on the surface.

While stop releases can serve to distinguish between speakers on the basis of gender or sexuality, they can also be used to draw distinctions within groups on the basis of the same factors. Drager (2009), for example, examines the realization of /k/ in the word *like* among girls attending Selwyn Girls' High, a high school in Christchurch. Her year-long ethnography revealed a meaningful distinction between girls who ate lunch in the common room and those who did not. Whether any given girl released /k/ depended on the intersection between the grammatical function of *like* and to which group's norms the girl ascribed. That is, non-common-room girls were more likely to release /k/ in quotative *like*, while common-room girls did so more often in discourse particle *like*. Here we see that the phonetic realization of /k/ enables girls in Selwyn to linguistically perform intragender differences germane to the community.

If a release burst is present, it can also exhibit scalar phonetic variation in terms of the strength of the release. Podesva (2006) reports that even though the gay professionals participating in his intraspeaker variation study released coronal stops more often in professional speaking situations, one particular speaker produces phonetically stronger releases at an informal barbecue with friends. In this situation, released stops – though less frequent – are longer and exhibit greater intensity. Podesva argues that the amplified phonetic content, achieved through longer duration and higher intensity, serves to amplify the meanings of clarity and precision traditionally associated with the variable, yielding an exaggerated version of these characteristics – prissiness – which partly constitutes the speaker's diva persona. This study draws our attention to the fact that the social meanings that participate in the construction of gender and sexuality are indexed not only through the categorical choice of a linguistic variant, but in the continuous phonetic dimensions that shape each variant's unique acoustics.

5. Voice Quality

Since the great majority of sociophonetic work on voice quality focuses on phonation, the discussion here deals primarily with differences in the mode of vocal fold vibration.

The tendency for women to use breathier phonation than men is sometimes attributed to incomplete vocal fold closure, resulting from females' relatively thinner vocal folds (Södersten and Lindestad 1990). However, the common finding that H1-H2 (an acoustic measure often used to quantify breathiness) is higher for women than men (e.g., Henton and Bladon 1985) stems largely from the fact that

H1 is falsely amplified by a nasal formant in the same frequency vicinity (Simpson 2012). Breathy voice can nevertheless be strategically manipulated in performances of gender. Transgender women, for example, exhibit higher peak airflow rates than biological women (Gorham-Rowan and Morris 2006). Starr (2010) discusses a more overtly performative behavior in Japanese anime, arguing that voice actresses use "sweet voice," characterized in part by syllables ending in breathy voice, to convey an inner, true femininity. Breathy voice can also be used to construct stances that, although they do not directly index gender, may nevertheless be inseparable from it – for instance, to convey sexual arousal in American English (Hall 1995) and Japanese (Kajino and Moon 2011).

On the other extreme of glottal aperture from breathy voice lies creaky voice, which unsurprisingly has been frequently noted as a feature of men's speech, particularly in varieties of English spoken in the United Kingdom (e.g., Henton and Bladon 1988; Stuart-Smith 1999). The association between creaky voice and masculinity is iconic, in the sense that the low pitch acoustically characterizing creaky voice is interpreted as resembling masculinity (due to sex-based pitch differences, as discussed above). This iconic association can be reworked at higher orders of indexicality (Silverstein 2003) and forges a connection to stances associated with masculinity, such as toughness. Consistent with this interpretation is Mendoza-Denton's (2007; 2011) finding that girls in Latina gangs use high rates of creaky voice when telling fight stories. Of course, even the most iconic connections between linguistic form and meaning are mediated by ideology. Creaky voice could, in principle, be associated with femininity, which is in fact what has happened, at least in the United States. Yuasa (2010) reports that young women in California use creaky voice more than their male peers, and Podesva (2013) reports the same finding for both African American and white women in Washington, DC. Based on a language attitudes survey, Yuasa (2010, 332) suggests that creaky voice is perceived as a marker of a professional, upwardly mobile, woman "capable of competing with their male counterparts." In spite of the rather positive indexical values that Yuasa proposes, creaky voice – characterized as a feature of women's voices exclusively – has been pathologized in its media portrayals, where it has been labeled "vocal fry." Zimman (2013) further observes that creaky voice is more prevalent in the speech of gay men and trans men, compared to straight men. It is unclear whether the forces underlying this pattern bear any connection to the greater incidence of creaky voice in the speech of women that has recently been observed.

If creaky voice can be said to be iconic of masculinity, falsetto – with its characteristically high F0 – can be considered an icon of femininity. And indeed, it has been observed more frequently in the speech of African American women compared to men (Podesva 2013) in Washington, DC. Podesva (2013) argues that falsetto serves not as an index of gender, but as a linguistic means of taking an oppositional stance toward gentrification, a discursive move made more frequently by African American women in the data analyzed. Podesva (2007) suggests that, at its core, falsetto indexes expressiveness, and that expressiveness can be marshaled in constructing a variety of character types, including a gay diva persona. Because falsetto's connection to gender and sexuality is mediated by stances that may not be explicitly gendered, it can be used in discursive practices that have little to do with femininity, such as "battlin," as discussed in Alim's (2004) work on the hip hop community in Sunnyside.

The work on the range of meanings, gendered and otherwise, of nonmodal phonation types indicates that phonation is rich terrain for unpacking the ideologies undergirding the voice–gender connection. It is important to take note of the iconic connections that forge this connection, and perhaps more important still to uncover and understand the culturally specific ways in which iconization takes place.

6. New Horizons

From the above discussion, it is evident that scholars of phonetics and language and gender alike have demonstrated a healthy and ever growing interest in the intersection of their fields. We conclude with a brief discussion of some lines of inquiry that, in our opinion, represent promising and important directions for the field to pursue.

In spite of significant inroads in the study of segmental phonetics and suprasegmentals like intonation and voice quality, scholars have yet to grasp the full potential of rhythm as an index of gender and sexuality. Nevertheless, a handful of studies collectively indicate that gendered patterns surface in a variety of rhythmical domains, such as timing (Callier 2011), phrase-final lengthening (Kajino 2010), and pausing (Mendoza-Denton 1995).

While the speech of gay and straight women and men (i.e., cisgender individuals) has received significant attention within sociophonetics, considerable less work has taken the speech of transgender individuals as its focus. This is to the detriment of our understanding of phonetic social constructionism, as the phonetic practices of transgender people give us more direct insight into how identities are constructed, as well as which dominant ideologies of gender are attended to as members of the transgender community fashion their linguistic selves. The extant work on the phonetics of transgender voices (Gorham-Rowan and Morris 2006; Hazenberg 2012; Zimman 2010; 2012) has provided a rich springboard from which other work could depart. An important direction, in our view, is the consideration of transgender language in more conversational contexts. The majority of previous work has necessarily examined speech collected in controlled contexts (i.e., reading passages), though it remains to be seen how trans men and women strategically draw on phonetic speech features as resources in everyday contexts. While linguistic practice is arguably most strategic for transgender individuals in highly self-conscious speaking contexts, such as when reading texts, it remains to be determined how much of the behavior observed in such contexts can be attributed to stylistic skill versus medical interventions like hormone therapy. By examining intraspeaker variation patterns, we are able to better observe the range of variation possible at a single point in time, which presumably is produced with a fairly stable physiology. Disentangling these sources of vocal change, by comparing individuals' magnitude of longitudinal change to their ranges of intraspeaker variation, could provide transitioning individuals with data that would help them make more informed choices about their transitioning process – for example, whether to undergo medical interventions – depending on individual goals. On a more theoretical level, this issue raises questions about how theories of style might factor in the role of technology in shaping stylistic practice – an issue that will likely only become more important as time progresses, within and outside of the transgender community. Research that utilizes conversational speech must be embedded in studies that also draw on long-term participant observation. As Zimman (2012, 195) notes, transgender individuals could be orienting to any number of masculinities, and it is only by examining speakers' "gender assignments, gender roles, gender identities, gender presentations, and sexualities' that these orientations can be ascertained.

Sociophonetic research on transgender speech encourages us to take the body as an important locus of investigation. At the start of the article, we warned against taking a deterministic view on the relationship between the body and phonetic substance; even though physiology strongly influences the phonetic manifestation of speech, it merely sets the stage for what is phonetically possible for a given individual's vocal tract. At the same time, the body needs to be taken more seriously as a resource for linguistic expression. Currently, sociophoneticians nearly without exception use audio-only recordings in their research. While language is a rich resource in its own right, it is not contextually divorced from other modalities of expression. The body provides a context for language, so to analyze speech independently of embodiment is at best to only partially represent the circumstances under which language is produced. Since sociolinguists, pragmaticists, and semanticists would all grant that much of linguistic meaning is derived from context, it would be worth considering how much of the social meaning saturating language we miss out on by failing to incorporate gesture and other forms of embodiment into sociophonetic analysis.

Understanding social meaning is central to the study of language and gender/sexuality, because social meaning is in many regards constitutive of gender and sexuality. Ochs's (1992) foundational work on indexing gender encourages us to think about gender not as an atomic category, but rather as comprising a number of stances, acts, and activities that are themselves indices of gender. Affective stances, in particular, play a crucial role in the construction of gender and sexuality. Phonetic features (or sets of phonetic features, i.e., styles) that might be read as "gay" or "feminine" may, in moments of interaction, have more to do with the expression of affect (Eckert 2011; Podesva 2007). Eckert (2011) posits a specific relationship between the second formant and affect, in her discussion of Rachel, a preadolescent girl who employs fronted variants of (ow) (higher F2) to express a cool teenage persona and backed variants of the same feature (lower F2) to elicit sympathy. While drawing an indexical link between phonetic features and affect is less inherently problematic than drawing similar connections between phonetic features and categories of gender or sexuality, much work remains to be done to better understand how affect is indexed through phonetic behavior. Also crucial to this enterprise will be unpacking the indexicality of sound symbolism and greater theorizing about the culturally specific, ideological processes that naturalize the connections between phonetic features and emotion.

A focus on affect enables the sociophonetician and the gender theorist to zero in on how gender and sexuality are constituted, to avoid assuming an essentialized connection between linguistic behavior and identity categories. The body of work on the phonetic correlates of sounding gay has, over the last decade, avoided essentializing phonetic practices in this way. Studies therefore commonly compare the voices of people judged to sound gay to those judged not to. Yet, when it comes to the study of the sociophonetics of gender (in contrast to sexuality), studies are typically designed to compare the speech of women to that of men, rather than the speech of those who are judged to sound female, feminine, or feminine in a particular way to those who are judged to sound male, masculine, or masculine in a particular way. Another way to avoid essentializing gender in sociophonetics would be to deconstruct the concepts of masculinity and femininity. Returning to affect, what might be gained by comparing the speech of those judged to sound excited to those judged to sound bored, and how might this comparison and others like it shed light on the construction of gender? Asking questions like this will help us avoid the pitfall (and common practice) of assuming that people who are categorized as belonging to the same gender category exhibit similar phonetic patterns. Stuart-Smith's (2007) study of the realization of /s/ in Glasgow importantly reminds us that a wider range of phonetic patterns may be evident within gender groups than across them. Since intragender similarity is often assumed in studies that seek to uncover intergender patterns, further research aimed specifically at intragender difference, and the reasons underlying its emergence, is necessary.

Scholars interested in the sociophonetics of gender and sexuality approach the topic from a variety of disciplines, including sociolinguistics, laboratory phonology, and speech and hearing sciences. As Eckert and Podesva (2011) point out, researchers from such disparate fields bring to the research enterprise a broad range of methodologies and often differing fundamental assumptions. It is important that future work continues to utilize the collective strengths of the entire research community. Laboratory phonologists have added an increasingly sophisticated array of phonetic analytical techniques – including acoustic measures, methods of data collection, and statistical approaches – to the methodological toolkit, thereby improving our ability to characterize and quantify phonetic practice and to identify what phonetic practices need to be interpreted. Likewise, sociolinguists and linguistic anthropologists have pushed the field to refrain from underestimating the complexity of gender and sexuality and of how language comes to index them. In a rather short period of time, scholars interested in the sociophonetics of gender and sexuality have learned a great deal about the role of sound in indexing, constructing, and perceiving gender and sexuality. Cross-disciplinary dialogue and collaboration have facilitated this growth and are crucial to the continued advancement of this trend.

REFERENCES

Alim, H. Samy. 2004. *You Know My Steez: An Ethnographic and Sociolinguistic Study of Styleshifting in a Black American Speech Community*. Durham, NC: Duke University Press.

Baeck, Heidi, Paul Corthals, and John Van Borsel. 2011. "Pitch Characteristics of Homosexual Males." *Journal of Voice*, 25(5): 211–214.

Benor, Sarah. 2004. "Second Style Acquisition: Language and Newly Orthodox Jews." Unpublished PhD dissertation, Stanford University.

Britain, David. 1992. "Linguistic Change in Intonation: The Use of High Rising Intonation in New Zealand English." *Language Variation and Change*, 4(1): 77–104.

Callier, Patrick. 2011. "Social Meaning in Prosodic Variability." *University of Pennsylvania Working Papers in Linguistics*, 17(1). At http://repository.upenn.edu/pwpl/vol17/iss1/6/, accessed October 14, 2013.

Cameron, Deborah. 2011. "Sociophonetics and Sexuality: Discussion." *American Speech*, 86(1): 98–103.

Campbell-Kibler, Kathryn. 2011. "Intersecting Variables and Perceived Sexual Orientation in Men." *American Speech*, 86(1): 52–68.

Conn, Jeffrey C. 2005. "Of 'Moice' and Men: The Evolution of Male-Led Sound Change." Unpublished PhD dissertation, University of Pennsylvania.

Docherty, Gerry, and Paul Foulkes. 2005. "Glottal Variants of /t/ in the Tyneside Variety of English." In William J. Hardcastle and Janet Mackenzie Beck (eds.), *A Figure of Speech: A Festschrift for John Laver*, 173–197. London: Lawrence Erlbaum.

Drager, Katie 2009. "A Sociophonetic Ethnography of Selwyn Girls' High." Unpublished PhD dissertation, University of Canterbury, New Zealand.

Eddington, David, and Michael Taylor. 2009. "T-Glottalization in American English." *American Speech*, 84(3): 298–314.

Eckert, Penelope. 2008. "Variation and the Indexical Field." *Journal of Sociolinguistics*, 12: 453–476.

Eckert, Penelope. 2011. "Language and Power in the Preadolescent Heterosexual Market." *American Speech*, 86(1): 85–97.

Eckert, Penelope, and Robert J. Podesva. 2011. "Sociophonetics and Sexuality: Toward a Symbiosis of Sociolingusitics and Laboratory Phonology." *American Speech*, 86(1): 6–13.

Fletcher, Janet, Esther Grabe, and Paul Warren. 2005. "Intonational Variation in Four Dialects of English: The High Rising Tune." In Sun-Ah Jun (ed.), *Prosodic Typology: The Phonology of Intonation and Phrasing*, 390–409. Oxford: Oxford University Press.

Foulkes, Paul, Gerard Docherty, and Mark Jones. 2010. "Analysing Stops." In Marianna Di Paolo and Malcah Yaeger-Dror (eds.), *Sociophonetics: A Student's Guide*, 172–202. London: Routledge.

Foulkes, Paul, Gerard Docherty, and Dominic Watt. 2005. "Phonological Variation in Child-Directed Speech." *Language*, 81(1): 177–206.

Gaudio, Rudolf P. 1994. "Sounding Gay: Pitch Properties in the Speech of Gay and Straight Men." *American Speech*, 69(1): 30–57.

Geenberg, Katherine. 2010. "'Poor baby, you got a boo-boo!' Sound Symbolism in Adult Baby Talk." Paper presented at the New Ways of Analyzing Variation (NWAV) 39 Conference, University of Texas at San Antonio.

Gorham-Rowan, Mary, and Richard Morris. 2006. "Aerodynamic Analysis of Male-to-Female Transgender Voice." *Journal of Voice*, 20(2): 251–262.

Graddol, David, and Joan Swann. 1983. "Speaking Fundamental Frequency: Some Physical and Social Correlates." *Language and Speech*, 26(4): 351–366.

Guy, Gregory, Barbara Horvath, Julia Vonwiller, Elaine Daisley, and Inge Rogers. 1986. "An Intonational Change in Progress in Australian English." *Language in Society*, 15: 23–52.

Hall, Kira. 1995. "Lip Service on the Fantasy Lines." In Kira Hall and Mary Bucholtz (eds.), *Gender Articulated: Language and the Socially Constructed Self*, 321–343. New York: Routledge.

Hazenberg, Evan. 2012. "Language and Identity Practice: A Sociolinguistic Study of Gender in Ottawa, Ontario." Unpublished MA thesis, Memorial University of Newfoundland.

Henton, Caroline. 1989. "Fact and Fiction in the Description of Female and Male Pitch." *Language & Communication*, 9(4): 299–311.

Henton, Caroline, and Anthony Bladon. 1985. "Breathiness in Normal Female Speech: Inefficiency versus Desirability." *Language and Communication*, 5: 221–227.

Henton, Caroline, and Anthony Bladon. 1988. "Creak as a Sociophonetic Marker." In Larry Hyman and Charles N. Li (eds.), *Language, Speech, and Mind*, 3–29. London: Routledge.

Jacewicz, Ewa, Robert A. Fox, and Caitlin O'Neill. 2009. "Articulation Rate across Dialect, Age, and Gender." *Language Variation and Change*, 21: 233–256.

Johnson, Keith. 2006. "Resonance in an Exemplar-Based Lexicon: The Emergence of Social Identity and Phonology." *Journal of Phonetics*, 34: 485–499.

Kajino, Sakiko. 2010. "Coexistence of Contradictory Meanings of a Variable: Phrasal Final Lengthening in Speech of a Japanese Pop Star Ayumi Hamasaki." Paper presented at the New Ways of Analyzing Variation (NWAV) 39 Conference, University of Texas at San Antonio.

Kajino, Sakiko, and Kyuwon Moon. 2011. "The Stylistic Construction of Sexual Sweetness: Voice Quality Variation of Japanese Porn Actresses." Paper presented at the New Ways of Analyzing Variation (NWAV) 40 Conference, Georgetown University.

Kuhl, Patricia K., Jean E. Andruski, Inna A. Chistovich, Ludmilla A. Chistovich, Elena V. Kozhevnikova, et al. 1997. "Cross-Language Analysis of Phonetic Units in Language Addressed to Infants." *Science*, 277: 684–686.

Lakoff, Robin. 1975. *Language and Woman's Place*. New York: Harper & Row.

Levon, Erez. 2006. "Hearing 'Gay': Prosody, Interpretation, and the Affective Judgments of Men's Speech." *American Speech*, 81: 56–78.

Levon, Erez. 2007. "Sexuality in Context: Variation and the Sociolinguistic Perception of Identity." *Language in Society*, 36(4): 533–554.

Levon, Erez. 2011. "Teasing Apart to Bring Together: Gender and Sexuality in Variationist Research." *American Speech*, 86(1): 69–84.

Linville, Sue E. 1998. "Acoustic Correlates of Perceived versus Actual Sexual Orientation in Men's Speech." *Folia Phoniatrica et Logopaedica*, 50(1): 35–48.

Lowry, Orla. 2002. "The Stylistic Variation of Nuclear Patterns in Belfast English." *Journal of the International Phonetic Association*, 32(1): 33–42.

Lowry, Orla. 2011. "Belfast Intonation and Speaker Gender." *Journal of English Linguistics*, 39(3): 209–232.

Lutzross, Auburn. 2010. "You Sound Like a Lesbian: Sociophonetic Stereotypes of Lesbian Speech." Unpublished BA thesis, Hampshire College, Amhurst, MA.

McConnell-Ginet, Sally. 1983. "Intonation in a Man's World." In Barrie Thorne, Cheris Kramarae, and Nancy Henley (eds.), *Language, Gender, and Society*, 69–88. Boston: Heinle & Heinle.

McLemore, Cynthia A. 1991. "The Pragmatic Interpretation of English Intonation: Sorority Speech." Unpublished PhD dissertation, University of Texas at Austin.

Mendoza-Denton, Norma. 1995. "Pregnant Pauses: Silence and Authority in the Anita Hill–Clarence Thomas Hearings." In Kira Hall and Mary Bucholtz (eds.), *Gender Articulated: Language and the Culturally Constructed Self*, 51–66. Routledge: New York.

Mendoza-Denton, Norma. 2007. "Creaky Voice in Gang Girl Narratives." Paper presented at the Annual Meeting of the

American Anthropological Association, Washington, DC.

Mendoza-Denton, Norma. 2011. "The Semiotic Hitchhiker's Guide to Creaky Voice: Circulation and Gendered Hardcore in a Chicana/o Gang Persona." *Journal of Linguistic Anthropology*, 21(2): 261–280

Milroy, James, Lesley Milroy, Sue Hartley, and David Walshaw. 1994. "Glottal Stops and Tyneside Glottalization: Competing Patterns of Variation and Change in British English." *Language Variation and Change*, 6(3): 327–357.

Moonwomon-Baird, Birch. 1997. "Toward the Study of Lesbian Speech." In Anna Livia and Kira Hall (eds.), *Queerly Phrased: Language, Gender, and Sexuality*, 202–213. New York: Oxford University Press.

Munson, Benjamin. 2007. "The Acoustic Correlates of Perceived Masculinity, Perceived Femininity, and Perceived Sexual Orientation." *Language and Speech*, 50(1): 125–142.

Munson, Benjamin, and Molly Babel. 2007. "Loose Lips and Silver Tongues, or, Projecting Sexual Orientation through Speech." *Language and Linguistics Compass*, 1: 416–449.

Munson, Benjamin, Sarah V. Jefferson, and Elizabeth C. McDonald. 2006. "The Influence of Perceived Sexual Orientation on Fricative Perception." *Journal of the Acoustical Society of America*, 119(4): 2427–2437.

Munson, Benjamin, Elizabeth C. McDonald, Nancy L. DeBoe, and Aubrey R. White. 2006. "The Acoustic and Perceptual Bases of Judgments of Women and Men's Sexual Orientation from Read Speech." *Journal of Phonetics*, 34(2): 202–240.

Ochs, Elinor. 1992. "Indexing Gender." In Alessandro Duranti and Charles Goodwin (eds.), *Rethinking Context: Language as an Interactive Phenomenon*, 335–358. Cambridge: Cambridge University Press.

Ohala, John J. 1984. "An Ethnological Perspective on Common Cross-Language Utilization of F_0 of Voice." *Phonetica*, 41: 1–16.

Pierrehumbert, Janet B., Tessa Bent, Benjamin Munson, Ann R. Bradlow, and Michael J.

Bailey. 2004. "The Influence of Sexual Orientation on Vowel Production (L)." *Journal of the Acoustical Society of America*, 116(4): 1905–1908.

Podesva, Robert J. 2006. "Phonetic Detail in Sociolinguistic Variation: Its Linguistic Significance and Role in the Construction of Social Meaning." Unpublished PhD dissertation, Stanford University.

Podesva, Robert J. 2007. "Phonation Type as a Stylistic Variable: The Use of Falsetto in Constructing a Persona." *Journal of Sociolinguistics*, 11: 478–504.

Podesva, Robert J. 2011a. "The California Vowel Shift and Gay Identity." *American Speech*, 86(1): 32–51.

Podesva, Robert J. 2011b. "Salience and the Social Meaning of Declarative Contours: Three Case Studies of Gay Professionals." *Journal of English Linguistics*, 39(3): 233–264.

Podesva, Robert J. 2013. "Gender and the Social Meaning of Non-modal Phonation Types." *Proceedings of the Berkeley Linguistics Society*, 37: 427–448.

Podesva, Robert J., Sara J. Roberts, and Kathryn Campbell-Kibler. 2002. "Sharing Resources and Indexing Meanings in the Production of Gay Styles." In Kathryn Campbell-Kibler, Robert J. Podesva, Sarah J. Roberts, and Andrew Wong (eds.), *Language and Sexuality: Contesting Meaning in Theory and Practice*, 175–189. Stanford: Center for the Study of Language and Information, Stanford University.

Sclafani, Jennifer. 2007. "Martha Stewart Style: Using Parody to Uncover the Symbolic Meaning of Linguistic Style." Paper presented at the New Ways of Analyzing Variation (NWAV) 36 Conference, Philadelphia.

Silverstein, Michael. 2003. "Indexical Order and the Dialectics of Sociolinguistic Life." *Language and Communication*, 23: 193–229.

Simpson, Adrian. 2009. "Phonetic Differences between Male and Female Speech." *Language and Linguistics Compass*, 3(2): 621–640.

Simpson, Adrian. 2012. "The First and Second Harmonics Should Not Be Used to Measure Breathiness in Male and Female Voices." *Journal of Phonetics*, 40: 477–490.

Smyth, Ron, Greg Jacobs, and Henry Rogers. 2003. "Male Voices and Perceived Sexual Orientation: An Experimental and Theoretical Approach." *Language in Society*, 32(3): 329–350.

Södersten, Maria, and Per-Åke Lindestad. 1990. "Glottal Closure and Perceived Breathiness during Phonation in Normally Speaking Subjects." *Journal of Speech and Hearing Research*, 33: 601–611.

Starr, Rebecca L. 2010. "Sweet Voice: The Role of Voice Quality in a Japanese Feminine Style." Unpublished paper.

Strand, Elizabeth A., and Keith Johnson. 1996. "Gradient and Visual Speaker Normalization in the Perception of Fricatives." In Dafydd Gibbon (ed.), *Natural Language Processing and Speech Technology: Results of the 3rd KOVENS Conference, Bielefeld, October, 1996*, 14–26. Berlin: Mouton de Gruyter.

Stuart-Smith, Jane. 1999. "Glasgow: Accent and Voice Quality." In Paul Foulkes and Gerry Docherty (eds.), *Urban Voices: Variation and Change in British Accents*, 203–222. London: Arnold.

Stuart-Smith, Jane. 2007. "Empirical Evidence for Gendered Speech Production: /s/ in Glaswegian." In Jennifer Cole, and José Ignacio Hualde (ed.), *Laboratory Phonology 9*, 65–86. New York: Mouton de Gruyter.

Stuart-Smith, Jane, Claire Timmins, and Fiona Tweedie. 2007. "'Talkin' Jockney'? Variation and Change in Glaswegian Accent." *Journal of Sociolinguistics*, 11: 221–260.

Van Bezooijen, Renée. 1995. "Sociocultural Aspects of Pitch Differences between Japanese and Dutch Women." *Language and Speech*, 38: 253–265.

Van Dommelen, Wim A., and Bente H. Moxness. 1995. "Acoustic Parameters in Speaker Height and Weight Identification: Sex-Specific Behavior." *Language and Speech*, 38(3): 267–287.

Warren, Paul. 2005. "Patterns of Late Rising in New Zealand English: Intonational Variation or Intonation Change?" *Language Variation and Change*, 17: 209–230.

Wassink, Alicia Beckford, Richard A. Wright, and Amber D. Franklin. 2007. "Intraspeaker Variability in Vowel Production: An Investigation of Motherese, Hyperspeech, and Lombard Speech in Jamaican Speakers." *Journal of Phonetics*, 35(3): 363–379.

Yuasa, Ikuko Patricia. 2010. "Creaky Voice: A New Feminine Voice Quality for Young Urban-Oriented Upwardly Mobile American Women?" *American Speech*, 85(3): 315–337.

Zimman, Lal. 2010. "Female-to-Male Transsexuals and Gay-Sounding Voices: A Pilot Study." *Colorado Research in Linguistics* 22(1). At http://www.colorado.edu/ling/CRIL/Volume22_Issue1/paper_ZIMMAN.pdf, accessed October 14, 2013.

Zimman, Lal. 2012. "Voice in Transition: Testoserone, Transmasculinity, and the Gendered Voice among Female-to-Male Transgender People." Unpublished PhD dissertation, University of Colorado, Boulder.

Zimman, Lal. 2013. "Hegemonic Masculinity and the Variability of Gay-Sounding Speech: The Perceived Sexuality of Transgender Men." *Journal of Language and Sexuality*, 2(1): 1–39.

Zwicky, Arnold. 1997. "Two Lavender Issues for Linguists." In Anna Livia and Kira Hall (eds.), *Queerly Phrased: Language, Gender, and Sexuality*, 21–34. New York: Oxford University Press.

6 Ethnographic Methods for Language and Gender Research

NIKO BESNIER AND SUSAN U. PHILIPS

1. The Historical Emergence of Ethnography as Method

Ethnography emerged at the beginning of the twentieth century as the central method for anthropological research, and its emergence can be thought of as having taken two parallel but independent courses, which were somewhat mutually hostile. One, based in the United States, was associated with Franz Boas, widely recognized as the father of American anthropology. In contrast to previous approaches to anthropological research, Boas laid the foundation of a historically oriented, fieldwork-based anthropology grounded on the collection of data by the anthropologist during extended sojourns among the people whose lives he or she sought to document. Boas and many of his students were particularly interested in the lifeways of indigenous groups in the United States that were seriously disenfranchised and threatened, collecting data on every aspect of the lives of peoples, from body measurements to folklore to the structure of their languages. As a result, their work came to be known as *salvage ethnography*. They conceptualized written ethnographies as descriptions of cultures, while *ethnology* was defined as the comparison of these descriptions in theoretical inquiries into similarities and differences in human societies. Ethnography at the time was often not embedded in a critical perspective on the forces that threatened the cultural worlds in question, although Boas did mobilize this critical perspective in other respects, as in his political activism against racially based immigration policies in the United States in the 1920s.

During the same time period, another approach emerged on the other side of the Atlantic.[1] In Britain, the first significant endeavor that was recognizably ethnographic was the 1898 Cambridge Anthropological Expedition to the Torres Straits,

The Handbook of Language, Gender, and Sexuality, Second Edition.
Edited by Susan Ehrlich, Miriam Meyerhoff, and Janet Holmes.
© 2014 John Wiley & Sons, Inc. Published 2017 by John Wiley & Sons, Inc.

a vast project conducted under the leadership of zoologist A. C. Haddon. Over the course of a year, members of the expedition collected a vast quantity of facts and artifacts from a group of islands stretching from northern Queensland in Australia to the southern coast of New Guinea. The expedition generated an encyclopedic account of every thinkable aspect of islanders' lives, including language, but the account said little about the manner in which the data had been collected. It was two decades later that a systematic foundation of ethnographic fieldwork was laid out by Bronisław Malinowski, notably in the celebrated introduction to his magnum opus *Argonauts of the Western Pacific* (1922). Rather than assuming the task of data collection as a self-evident enterprise, Malinowski identified the cornerstones of a classic ethnographic method: based on a long-term intimate engagement with the people whose lives are recorded, which includes language-learning, ethnography involves both participating and observing and aims to collect a vast array of materials out of which anthropological analysis emerges. Studiously sidelining the Torres Straits expedition's accomplishments, Malinowski positioned ethnography against an earlier tradition in which data-collecting and data analysis were conducted by different agents: as interest in the lifeworlds of "primitive peoples" had grown in the course of the nineteenth-century (alongside the colonization of the rest of the world by European powers), the task of collecting ethnographic materials had been entrusted to missionaries, traders, travelers, and colonial officials, which were then analyzed and systematized by scholars. These scholars later came to be known, somewhat disparagingly, as "armchair anthropologists." In contrast, Malinowski insisted that first-hand participation in the activities one seeks to understand involved learning and that this learning was essential to understanding these activities.

While Malinowski's program was later subjected to a variety of criticisms, for example for the nebulously "magical" quality of the transition from data to analysis that it advocated (Stocking 1983) and for its reliance on an "I was there" trope of legitimization (Pratt 1986), it has nevertheless left an enduring imprint worldwide on what ethnography consists of. The nature of this imprint, however, has varied in different theoretical traditions. In North America, Malinowski's insistence on first-hand fieldwork was congruent with the Boasian model, although the two scholars differed in other respects (such as Boas's insistence on history, which Malinowski deemed speculative and useless). In Britain, Malinowski's contemporary and rival A. R. Radcliffe-Brown developed an anthropological theory that came to be known as *structural functionalism* and was the dominant paradigm in Britain for several decades. Its goal was to compare social structures across societies and to develop formal models based on this comparison, sidelining matters of "culture" as not amenable to scientific inquiry. British and North American anthropologists at the time disagreed on the nature of the proper object of anthropological inquiry: in Britain it was social relations while in North America it was culture, although of course what *culture* actually meant could differ from one context to another. Because of their insistence on science and comparison, structural functionalists produced works in which the actual workings of ethnography were more obscure than in works inspired by either Malinowski or Boas.

Language played a central role in both Boasian and Malinowskian anthropology, as both object of inquiry and method. For Boas and many of his students (particularly Edward Sapir), grammatical systems, vocabularies, and texts were part of the vast array of information that it behooved an anthropologist to gather in the field, from which emerged a conceptualization of linguistic anthropology as one of the four subfields of the discipline. Although Sapir developed an enduring body of theoretical works about language, the Boasian approach to language differed significantly from what we identify today as the ethnographic analysis of language, in that it consisted in the collection of materials laboriously elicited from informants, rather than the analysis of communicative practices in their context (Darnell 2000). The fact that recording technologies were still in their infancy posed serious limitations on the kinds of materials the ethnographer could collect. Malinowski, in contrast, approached the relation of language to society and culture as a theoretical problem. Distancing himself from philosophical views that dominated at the time of language as a simple mirror of reality, he argued for an ethnographically based analysis of language, which provided a perspective on language as constitutive of social and cultural reality and meaning as dependent on the activity in which communication takes place (Malinowski 1923). The attention to language that both Boas and Malinowski insisted on contrasted sharply with the lack of it in other approaches to anthropology. Radcliffe-Brown, for one, was reputed to be a poor language learner; since he did not consider language to be part of social structure in the first place (except for kinship terms and similar lexical categories), he deemed it not worthy of investigation.

Subsequently, ethnography came to be claimed as a method by disciplines other than anthropology. The first was sociology. In particular, ethnography as a sociological method was championed by members of the Chicago School of Sociology in the 1920s and 1930s, which foregrounded as an object of research the everyday lives and face-to-face interactions of ordinary people in modern urban contexts and favored the methodological immersion of the researcher in the research context. Trained in the Chicago School, sociologist Erving Goffman was particularly instrumental in bringing about a rapprochement between sociology and anthropology through an emphasis on ethnography. In *Asylums* (1961), for example, he defined the context of his investigation, the mental hospital, as a total institution, that is, an autonomous institution with its own social structure and organization, separate from the world around it. As a residential community whose members maintained daily face-to-face contact, it resembled in important ways the (seemingly) bounded communities that anthropologists had traditionally studied, thus enabling the use of methodologies that anthropologists had employed in these other contexts. In the process of gathering data, the sociologist was structurally positioned in a similar fashion to the anthropologist, namely as a temporary member of the community. Of course, when sociologists studied contexts that were not total institutions, and when anthropologists began realizing that the communities they had traditionally studied were not as bounded as they had thought, the replication of these methods was no longer straightforward. Fieldworkers from both disciplines were able to adapt, through invention and bricolage, traditional ethnography to more complex situations.

During the first half of the twentieth century, North American anthropologists had viewed the complete description of a language as consisting of a grammar, a dictionary, and a collection of texts elicited from bilingual consultants, recognizing that all of these representations of language were also representations of culture. In the 1960s the research program laid out by John Gumperz and Dell Hymes, which they referred to as the "ethnography of communication" (Hymes 1964), coupled with improvements in recording technologies, brought about an important methodological shift, with ethnography now focusing on speech as it occurred in face-to-face interactions that were part of people's ongoing lives. Gumperz and Hymes conceptualized language as a set of resources drawn upon selectively to accomplish various social actions, or what Hymes referred to as different "functions" of language. The way to document and analyze functional diversity was to actually record speech in different kinds of social activities and to compare the resulting data. The "speech genre," or "form of talk," became an important unit of analysis. Interactional units have continued to the present to be treated as units of analysis in linguistic ethnography (Philips 2013).

Ethnography today is widely recognized as the key method of both sociocultural and linguistic anthropology, but also as what anthropology can contribute to other disciplines, including sociolinguistics. In sociology, ethnography is viewed as one of several methods, which distinguishes in particular qualitative from quantitative sociology (although it is not the only method in qualitative sociology, as Wilkinson and Kitzinger's chapter on conversation analysis (7) demonstrates). Heralded in the 1960s by the humanities-inflected and politically engaged work of the Centre for Contemporary Cultural Studies at the University of Birmingham, cultural studies in its various guises shares with both anthropology and the subfields of sociology an interest in culture as an everyday production that is embedded in the realm of the political. Some cultural studies scholars implement this focus through fieldwork practices that closely resemble the practices of ethnography. However, one has also witnessed in the last few years the tendency to label as *ethnography* any activity in which the researcher engages with human subjects, no matter how superficial, short-term, or limited in scope. For example, interviews of research participants with whom the researcher is unlikely to interact before or after the interview do not constitute ethnography, despite increasingly frequent claims to the contrary.

2. The Tools of Ethnography

Ethnography has a number of characteristic features that distinguishes it from other methodological practices and that constitute its distinctive contribution to research on language and gender. First and foremost, it is a naturalistic endeavor that involves no attempt to interfere with the normal course of events and rarely involves experimentation. Researchers disagree, however, about whether it is possible to avoid interference, and about whether it is desirable to aspire to passivity. Ethnography's approach is from the ground up, in the sense that analytic categories and explanations emerge in the fieldwork situation as opposed to being imported from a predetermined model. It presumes a direct, (preferably) empathetic, and long-term interaction between the researcher and the social actors whose lives the former seeks to understand, during which the boundary between research and friendship often becomes blurred. It is opportunity-driven, in the sense that the ethnographer is willing to pursue unpredicted avenues of investigation as they emerge in the course of fieldwork. The aim of the ethnographer is to arrive at what anthropologist Clifford Geertz (1973) famously called "thick description" (a concept he borrowed from philosopher Gilbert Ryle), that is, an understanding of an ethnographic situation that derives from exploring it under multiple guises and acknowledging that human action is subject to a multiplicity of interpretations and perspectives. Since the investigation of language and gender involves an understanding of both language as a system and gender as a sociocultural category, ethnography provides a particularly important window in the workings of the latter in relation to the former.

Ethnographers mobilize a broad variety of techniques, of which the most important is participant observation, but which also typically include interviews of different kinds, censuses, questionnaires, inventories and catalogues, the collection of texts, the recording of still and moving images, sound recordings, and so on. Data collection using these various techniques takes the form of notes (fieldnotes and diaries), transcripts, and of course collections of visual and audio materials, all of which occupy the interstices between "raw data" and "preliminary analysis."

Like all methodologies, ethnography has both advantages and disadvantages. Among its advantages figures the contextual richness of research based on ethnography; its emphasis on a multiplicity of perspectives; the diversity of what constitutes "data," which enables the researcher to arrive at an analysis from different angles; its ability to generate materials that are not accessible with other methods; and a focus on the complex relationship between people's actions and their explanations for their actions. These characteristics are important for an investigation of language and gender that approaches gender as a complex category at once cultural, social, and political, and which can be transformed by many other dimensions of human difference, such as social class, ethnicity and race, citizenship, and religion. An ethnographic approach will make the mutual interaction of these dimensions its primary analytic focus.

Among the disadvantages of ethnography, whether for language and gender research or other purposes, is its time-consuming nature, which Marcus and Okely (2008) refer to, tongue in cheek, as "the unbearable slowness of fieldwork." In addition, ethnography can be an emotionally draining activity for the researcher, particularly when it takes place in an unfamiliar society, where lack of experience can reduce the researcher to the status of an inept child. Ethnographic research has also been criticized for rendering opaque the relationship between data collection and its final textual account, prompting some to insist that good ethnography must enable readers of articles and books to be able to reconstruct from the text how the ethnographer arrived at his or her analysis. In some circumstances, ethnographic fieldwork is simply not possible; such is the case of, for example, situations of extreme danger (e.g., war zones) or marked hostility (e.g., indigenous groups with a long history of exploitation or marginalization), despite the fact that the questions raised in these situations can be intellectually important and politically urgent. Last but not least, as the time and other resources that institutions allocate to doctoral and postdoctoral research continue to decrease in many national contexts, long-term ethnographic fieldwork is in danger of becoming a luxury of the past.

In contrast to methodologies in the social sciences in which the researcher is shielded from the object of study by a literal or metaphorical one-way mirror, ethnography requires the researcher to be physically and socially present in the research. This presence engenders complexities that have both enabling and limiting effects. On the one hand, the researcher must learn the activities that he or she seeks to understand, and this first-hand learning process provides particularly rich insights. The fact of *being there*, which pioneers like Malinowski insisted on, also means that the ethnographer experiences immersion in the context of the data he or she will subsequently analyze, an experience that is crucial to an understanding of the material. On the other hand, the ethnographer's own identity, including gender, may determine the kinds of people and the types of materials to which he or she has access.

Thus the lack of attention paid to women and children in classical ethnography, which was largely the consequence of a male-biased approach to "what matters" in society, also reflected the restrictions on whom male ethnographers were allowed to socialize or were interested in socializing with in the contexts in which they conducted ethnography. This is why early efforts to making gender a legitimate topic of ethnographic inquiry were heralded by women anthropologists, often the wife of a husband-and-wife team, who wrote the monograph on "women" while the husband wrote the work on "the society" (e.g., Fernea 1969; Shostak 1981; Wolf 1960). (These early works on gender, however, paid no attention to language as constitutive of gender.)

In a similar vein, the ethnographer's presence in the ethnographic context is often made possible by the sponsorship of a legitimate member of the host community, and the ethnographer inherits the characteristics of the positionality of the sponsor. If the sponsor is a high-status person, for example, the ethnographer may have difficulties accessing low-status members. Since the turn to reflexivity in anthropology in the 1980s (Clifford and Marcus 1986), ethnographers have dealt with these complexities by turning their own positionality into an object of critical inquiry and embracing the fundamentally intersubjective nature of ethnographic fieldwork.

The importance of being there has implications for the ethnographer's relationship to the data. The person best qualified to analyze ethnographic materials is the person who gathered these materials in the first place, as early twentieth-century anthropologists on both sides of the Atlantic argued convincingly. Analyzing someone else's data (including interactional data that form the basis of linguistic anthropological research) is at best difficult because the analyst lacks the feel for the context in which the materials were gathered. These dynamics pose particularly thorny problems for trends heralded by funding foundations and other institutions that require researchers across disciplines to make their data public to prevent scientific fraud as well as to enable other researchers to reanalyze the data, a practice that is referred to by some institutions as "repurposing." While these practices make sense for some kinds of data (e.g., quantifiable answers to surveys), they are poorly suited to ethnographic data, the interpretation of which is difficult without access to the original context in which they were collected.

At the same time, the rise in analytic interest in processes of deterritorialization that are referred to as "globalization" since the 1980s have called for a reconfiguration of ethnographic methods. Ethnographers must contend with the fact that people, ideas, and resources are today fundamentally mobile, and that even people who stay in place are exposed to images, technologies, political ideals, and so on that are not produced in the local context (Appadurai 1996; Hannerz 1996). In other words, the relationship between place and culture is no longer straightforward (Gupta and Ferguson 1997). These dynamics call for what Marcus (1995) famously called "multi-sited ethnography," in which the ethnographer "follows" people, things, resources, metaphors, and ideas across space (including cyberspace). The canonical case of multisited ethnography is transnational, whereby the fieldworker conducts research in different national contexts. Multisited ethnography also takes place within a nation-state so that multiple residential units, regions, and institutional loci can be compared. But then ethnographers have always studied multiple contexts, so perhaps multisitedness understood in this fashion may not be that innovative after all.

Multisited ethnography has important implications for the traditional conceptualization of ethnography (Faubion and Marcus 2009). It has the obvious advantage of engaging seriously with the increased importance of connections and flows in the contemporary world. It has the disadvantage of potentially eroding the very features that gave conventional ethnography its power as a method, namely the intimate knowledge of, in particular, fieldwork contexts with all their layers of complexity and different perspectives. Time and other constraints may prevent the fieldworker researching several locations from learning languages, seeking different interpretations, and maintaining the long-term rapport that was so important to traditional fieldwork. At its best, multisited ethnography draws ethnographers' attention to the implications of the choices that they make in their research – whom they record, and whom they talk to. It also highlights the fact that fieldwork in one location is necessarily influenced by ethnographers' understanding of other fieldwork contexts, a point that has been clear all along to ethnographers who had worked in several independent field sites but is now brought to the fore in the pursuit of a single ethnographic project.

Ethics is of utmost importance in ethnographic research and has become the focus of increased attention since the end of the last millennium, with ambiguous consequences. Above all, ethnography is based on the long-term interpersonal involvement of the researcher, the development and maintenance of trust, and the researcher's personal commitment to research participants (in contrast to most research in psychology, political science, or economics). More than any other social scientific method, ethnography engages with the complexities of ethics, for example, with the fact that ethical responsibilities cannot be expediently spirited away by asking research participants to sign informed consent forms, as commonly prescribed by institutional codes of ethics. While institutional regulations in many countries today require the use of such documents of all social science research, they often hinder ethnographic research, as when ethnographers are required to use them when simply observing daily life as it unfolds. This renders the task of obtaining approval for ethnographic research from ethical review boards particularly difficult, as their procedures were developed primarily for medical research in the aftermaths of historical scandals (Lederman 2006). The requirements imposed by these boards have a potentially negative effect on ethnographic research, leading some researchers to limit their methods to activities like interviews that are clearly bounded in time, space, and purpose. These resemble the research practices for which ethical regulations were originally designed, but provide considerably more impoverished materials than ethnographic work (Lederman 2013; Tope et al. 2005).

Despite the deeply personal nature of the rapport that ethnographers seek to cultivate with research participants, they must remember that they do not cease to be, in the eyes of the latter, representatives of particular social types: in the case of "traditional" field research by an ethnographer from the global North in relatively underprivileged communities in the global South, he or she will continue to have access to considerably more substantial resources (e.g., money, travel opportunities, education) than members of the host community, even though the latter can also find the researcher inferior to themselves in one way or another (e.g., in terms of morality or status). These inequalities are not necessarily suspended if the researcher is an "insider," in one way or another, in the community.

3. Ethnography, Context, and Indexicality

Some ethnographic materials, and thus the ethnographic techniques designed to generate them, occupy a more central role in linguistic anthropology, and by implication in ethnographic approaches to language and gender, than in social and cultural anthropology as a whole. Since the 1970s, linguistic anthropologists have given particular prominence to the recording of audio and video material and the gathering of other interactional materials, particularly of a naturalistic kind, since their research focuses specifically on the analysis of these materials. However, audio and video recording does not in and of itself constitute ethnography, since a particularly important task of linguistic anthropological research is to understand how the meaning of "texts" (conversations, political speeches, meetings, ritual performances, letters, publications, etc.) derives from their articulation with their "contexts." This analytic stance contrasts with that of conversation analysis, for which the analysis is located in the sequential organization of the text, independent of context (see Wilkinson and Kitzinger, Chapter 7 in this volume). For ethnographers, the claim that meaning can be retrieved solely from the text betrays a lack of self-consciousness of the fact that the interpretation often derives from the analyst's own life experience. This opacity is common when working in one's own cultural context, but is impossible to overlook when working in a different cultural context from the researcher's home turf.

These dynamics explain the importance that ethnographers attach to understanding linguistic practices in their context and their insistence on supplementing the collection and transcription of interactional data with the collection of other forms of data, particularly detailed information about the social structuring of interactions (e.g., location, seating arrangements, temporal organization) and the concurrent activities in which research participants engage (e.g., body hexis, movements, gaze). Traditionally, ethnographers did their best to capture contextual details by taking detailed notes, but the imprecise nature of this method has motivated fieldworkers to gravitate toward video recordings whenever possible, since they greatly facilitate the recording of precise contextual data, particularly as technological advancements have made the capturing and handling of visual data increasingly easy. Video recording, however, is not possible in all situations, and has a serious disadvantage of being considerably more intrusive than audio recording. In some situations, neither audio nor video recording is practically possible or welcomed by research participants.

When the gathering of video and audio materials is possible, some linguistic anthropologists engage in the ingenious practice of "debriefing," which consists in showing or playing the recordings to the research participants themselves and inviting them to reflect on the recorded interactions and other activities. This technique was developed by linguistic anthropologists and education theorists Frederick Erickson and Jeffrey Shultz in their classic study of interactions between counselors and clients (1982). Ochs's research on child language acquisition in Samoa and Schieffelin's among the Kaluli of Papua New Guinea involved such "debriefing" practices, eliciting caregivers' own local interpretations of children's utterances (Schieffelin and Ochs 1987). A comparable technique consists in asking several local research assistants to code the same data separately and talking about the differences in the results. These practices have been known to yield an interpretive richness that the ethnographer alone cannot hope for. Of course, they do not substitute for analysis, in that local interpretations are generally laden with an ideology that the ethnographer must unpack. In addition, they may not work in all cultural contexts: in some societies, people abide by a "doctrine of the opacity of other minds" (Robbins and Rumsey 2008), according to which it is impossible or unwise to try to interpret what motivates other people (or perhaps certain other people, like high-status individuals) to say something or act in a particular fashion.

For ethnographers working on interactional materials, agents involved in the task of meaning-making in interaction rely on indexical relationships, and consequently indexicality figures centrally in the ethnographer's analysis. In the foundational work of nineteenth-century pragmatist philosopher Charles Sanders

Peirce, indexicality is one of three types of semiotic relationships, alongside symbolism and iconicity. An index is a sign that is linked to an object by pointing or being contiguous to it, and whose capability to mean is contingent on being anchored in a context. In language structure, canonical examples of indexes are personal pronouns and tenses, since *I* and the marking of verbs for the present tense are intelligible only if one knows who is speaking and when. Linguist Otto Jespersen (1965 [1924]) called these linguistic categories "shifters." Roman Jakobson (1971 [1957]) further developed the notion, arguing that they represent a conduit between what he called the "narrated event" (what speakers talk about) and the "speech event" (the context in which speakers are interacting). Another linguist, Charles Fillmore (1997 [1971]), distinguished shifters that are associated with social categories from other kinds of shifters, calling them "social deixis," a category that Silverstein (1976) further elaborated.

This history represents a gradual expansion of our understanding of the working of indexicality in language, to the point where, today, linguistic anthropologists consider that any aspect of language and interaction is potentially related to context indexically, and is thus potentially involved in meaning-making. At the same time, there are constraints on what can serve as an index and what an index can index, and thus on the kinds of interpretations one can draw from interactional data: meaning in interaction, for example, is enabled by the way in which meaning was constructed in prior interactions and, more generally, through general "typifications" based on the knowledge that one derives from one's life history, forming what Silverstein (2005) terms "interdiscursivity" and Butler (1990) "citationality" (the latter in reference to gender but not to language). Several characteristics of indexes make them a particularly powerful tool for the construction of meaning in interaction: their context dependence and thus potentially variable meaning; their location in nonsegmentable aspects of linguistic structure (e.g., prosody); the fact that they work in groups (e.g., gender is indexed in multiple aspects of language); and the fact that one index can provide information about multiple aspects of the context (e.g., a single index can evoke at the same time gender, social class, age, and power). These various characteristics are the reasons for which meaning in interaction is interpretable only when the context is analyzed.

Indexes can work in "chains," as it were: features of language use and interaction (e.g., dialect choices, lexicon, phonology) can index one aspect of context, such as stances, practices, and acts, which in turn index aspects of agents' identity. This "indirect indexicality" is particularly important in understanding how gender is constructed through interaction (Ochs 1993): the relationship between linguistic practices and gender categories are mediated by other characteristics of sociocultural contexts, which are in turn in a constitutive relationship with gender. Furthermore, the mediating sociocultural context may operate on multiple scales at once, not just local ones: agents may be gendered through images and practices that transcend the local but that agents make interactionally relevant (Besnier 2007).

This approach to the relationship between language and gender has a number of implications. One is that gender is not a predetermined category, but rather the emergent production of social practices, including interactional practices. Gender is not a property of individuals, but a characteristic of relationships, in which power and inequality figure prominently, not only between men and women, but also among men and among women, with multiple parameters of difference that variously inform, reinforce, or defy gender differences (race, ethnicity, age, nationality, religious affiliation, sexuality, etc.).[2] One immediate consequence is that language and gender research must not confine its focus to the study of women and marginal men, as has often been the case to date, but must also problematize what has come to be known as "hegemonic masculinities" (see Benwell, Chapter 12 in this volume), although ethnographically informed works on the relationship between language and these forms of masculinity are still relatively sparse. Finally, dynamics that shape gender are multiscalar, from macroscopic ones like the state, globalization, and colonialism, to the microscopic unfolding of interaction, involving language but also the semiotics of the body and the way in which bodies move in space and time, all of which articulate with language in what Pierre Bourdieu, alluding to Aristotle, called "hexis" (Brownell and Besnier 2013). All these factors require that the ethnographic analysis of language and gender be attentive to not only the way in which language indexes context, but also the way in which gender is constructed through social practices and cultural dynamics.

4. Ethnographic Research on Language and Gender

The ethnographic study of gender and the ethnographic study of language and interaction began to converge in the 1970s. The former was spurred on by the awakening of feminist consciousness in public and intellectual life in the 1960s, gradually shedding its original exclusive focus on women to take on gender as an object of analysis that recognized its power-laden nature and the fact that it permeates all aspects of society and culture (Brownell and Besnier 2013; di Leonardo 1991). Early ethnographic works on language and gender recognized interaction as a prime site for testing, with materials from non-Western societies, hypotheses about the nature and the universality of gendered inequality, such as those advanced by linguist Robin Lakoff (1975). For example, Keenan (Ochs) (1974) demonstrated that women in Madagascar were far from the accommodating and self-effacing "shrinking violets" that Western accounts in those days depicted women to be, but confrontational women who needed to get their commodities sold in the marketplace, leaving to men the niceties of oblique, metaphorical, and allusive interaction. In Andalusia, Susan Harding (1975) found that gender oppression was strongly mitigated by women's potentially devastating gossip behind closed doors. Susan Gal's (1979) research on the Austrian–Hungarian border, which combined ethnography with sociolinguistics, analyzed ways in which rural Hungarian women's desire for upward and geographical mobility was encoded in their linguistic practices. Penelope Brown's (1980) ethnographic work in Central America showed that the relationship between politeness and gender was complicated by a host of other factors. While these pioneering works assumed a view of gender as a somewhat unproblematic category, they provided a solid foundation for subsequent scholarship.

Since then, issues of universality versus local specificity have somewhat receded into the background, and contemporary ethnographically based works explore the way in which gender is indexically constructed through interaction, alongside other dimensions of human difference. We conclude this chapter with summaries of selected works on language and gender that have employed ethnographic methods in exemplary fashion. Our choices, which are avowedly subjective, reflect a range of approaches, from works that are primarily focused on language and interaction but utilize ethnographic methods to bring in the sociocultural context, to works that are embedded primarily in an anthropological tradition but utilize linguistic and interactional materials to good effect. They also provide examples of a range of topics that have proven particularly useful in ethnographic approaches to language and gender.

4.1 Veiled sentiments: honor and poetry in a Bedouin society

Highly regarded in cultural and linguistic anthropology, Leila Abu-Lughod's (1986) *Veiled Sentiments* is a classic example of an ethnographic study of gender and language. Abu-Lughod's ethnography of women's lives among Bedouins of the Western Desert of Egypt focuses on a genre of oral poetry that is composed and sometimes recited or sung by women in relatively private settings. Through this genre, Bedouin women project a view of life that is quite different from the public rhetoric about Bedouin identity projected by men, which emphasizes honor, bravery, and emotional restraint in their projections about what is worth valuing in life. Through their poetry, women express the value of love and the sorrow over loss of love. This book played an important role in showing how discourse genres can be gendered in point of view and performance, an important theme at the time. It also demonstrates how ideological diversity is organized through discourse structure.

4.2 Vicarious language: gender and linguistic modernity in Japan

Miyako Inoue's (2006) *Vicarious Language* focuses on Japanese women's language, a robust topic in comparative sociolinguistic research on gender and language, but about which she asks us to think differently from previous scholarship on the topic. She is politely critical of the "productionist ideology" of analyses of Japanese women's language (and of women's language generally), which envisions women as constituting themselves as gendered through their frequent use of certain grammatical features of Japanese, including certain pronoun forms, sentence-final particles, and a "beautifying" nominal prefix. Rather than searching for these features in speech behavior, Inoue focuses on how women talk about ideas of Japanese women's speech and how these ideas relate to their actual use of these stereotypical features. This focus on metapragmatics allows Inoue to both reflect on and contribute to the two-decade-long fascination with language ideologies in linguistic anthropology. Japanese women's speech does not reflect Japanese women's timeless aesthetic sensibilities, as Japanese language ideology would have it, but rather a Foucauldian discourse that emerged and was transformed as part of Japan's internal dialogue over its own development into a modern industrial nation-state in the course of the twentieth century.

Methodologically, Inoue combines ethnographic research in a Japanese pharmaceutical company with an analysis of historical transformations in the discourse about women's language in written genres, such as novels and magazines. This approach returns linguistic anthropology to the study of historical processes, but in a very different way than Boas imagined. The women in the company offices had diverse "takes" on women's language depending on their position within the company, which in turn related to their age and employment seniority. More often than not, the use of linguistic features marked as "women's language" was a matter of avoidance or ironic mockery rather than sincerity, attesting to Japanese women's alienation from the experientially empty but ideologically powerful concept of women's language. (See also Nakamura, Chapter 19 in this volume, for a discussion of Japanese "women's language.")

4.3   Homegirls in suburban ethnic America

Norma Mendoza-Denton's (2008) *Homegirls* analyzes the touchingly elaborate and creative semiotic opposition between two Mexican American girl gangs in a suburban high school in the San Francisco Bay Area in the United States. Mendoza-Denton first spent time in the high school as a volunteer and then increasingly devoted her time to the girls over lunch, eventually going out with them outside of school and recording them in naturalistic settings (e.g., as they drove around) and in sociolinguistic interviews. Mendoza-Denton was trained in a variationist sociolinguistic tradition but, as a student of Penelope Eckert, she took seriously Eckert's theoretical urging that works on language variation be contextualized in the study of communities of practice (Eckert and McConnell-Ginet 1992).

The girls belonged to rival Norteño or Sureño gangs. The former identified with the United States and aspects of culture they associated with the United States, particularly musical styles, while the latter identified with Mexico and its cultural associations. To some extent, members of the two gangs were drawn from different backgrounds. Piporras, associated with Sureños, were recent rural Mexican migrants and usually spoke Spanish, while the cosmopolitan Fresas, associated with Norteños, had no background in Mexico and spoke English.

Over the course of her research, Mendoza-Denton came to an increasingly better understanding of the lived reality of oppositional social categories and the meaning of choices between Spanish and English, clothing colors, art and poetry, makeup and hair styles, and numbers with symbolic significance indexing the different historical origins of the gangs. This ethnographic knowledge enabled her to develop the social categories that she then used in a variationist analysis of the Chicano English vowel /ɪ/. The leaders of both gangs showed higher frequencies than other girls of the high-front variant [i] of this phoneme, a feature associated with Chicano English. The core members of the gangs showed the next highest frequencies, followed by the social category Mendoza-Denton called "gang Wannabes" who were loyal to, identified with, and wore the colors of one gang or the other, but were not part of the gangs. But all the young women showed higher frequencies of the variant [i] than young Mexican American women who were not gang-identified, and thus the phonological characteristics of the speech of members of two gang groups were similar relative to the other young women in their social sphere, despite their constant efforts to elaborate their opposition to one other. They claimed a more pronouncedly Chicano variety of English than other Mexican American girls, and thus a more ethnically marked identity.

The multimodal approach that Mendoza-Denton takes is consistent with a growing interest in linguistic and cultural anthropology in analyzing sign systems within a broadly semiotic perspective, asking how language is related to a wider range of semiotic systems, such as those that are inscribed on and through the body. Rather than approaching the material with a predetermined notion of what gender is, *Homegirls* derives its understanding of gender and of the dynamics of social difference that transect it from the specifics of the ethnographic context, thereby demonstrating how the sociolinguistic study of language variation can become ethnographic to good effect.

4.4   Youth, morality, and modernity in rural Tonga

As *Homegirls* illustrates, gender and interaction in youth culture has emerged as a particularly productive topic in research on gender and language (e.g., Bucholtz 2011; Eckert 1989; Pujolar 2000; Rampton 1995). Mary Good's (2012) "Modern Moralities, Moral Modernities" approaches youth culture from the perspective of cultural anthropology, particularly the anthropology of morality and global modernity. The author conducted fieldwork on the rural island of 'Eua, part of the Polynesian nation of Tonga. She lived with a family, volunteered in a local high school, where she also took some teaching responsibilities, was involved in an island-wide youth congress, took part in the youth group of a local church, and recorded open-ended interviews with youth. Situating her work in the broad context of anthropological questions about the changing moral terrain in which youth operate worldwide, Good asks how Tongan teenagers, particularly girls, experience the co-presence of local cultural frameworks with new ones emerging from abroad, particularly through the very active transnational mobility of members of this society. Youth experience the resulting conflicts most acutely in terms of morality, particularly the morality of relations between the sexes.

Good focuses on three areas of cultural contact between dynamics that are identified as local and what she refers to as "global modernity": the use of mobile telephones; HIV prevention education classes; and soap operas imported from the Philippines, which feature moral dilemmas in the lives of the characters. Each of these three areas introduces Tongan youth to new ways of thinking and to new genres of interaction. For example, in the "traditional" order, teenage boys and girls are not supposed to interact with each other on a one-to-one basis, particularly when alone and if they harbor a romantic interest in each other. Mobile telephones have radically altered these dynamics, in a way that is reminiscent, in other parts of the world, of the emergence of letter-writing with the increase in literacy (Ahearn 2001). Mobile phone calls between young women and their boyfriends constitute a new interactional situation: the two are not physically together, and yet they are in a sense alone together to the degree that only they have access to the entire interaction between them. Is this morally acceptable in traditional Tongan terms? This is a key question that young Tongan women, as well as the adults that supervise them, have to grapple with.

Good wants us to realize that the experience of modernity in local settings that are somewhat removed from the supposed sources of the modern is not just about capitalism, communication, and consumption, but it is also felt on an emotional and a moral level. She demonstrates this in a way that allows us to momentarily step inside the lives of the young people she worked with and be moved by their struggles with competing moralities as they incorporate new ideas and technologies into their lives.

5. Approaching Language and Gender Ethnographically

Ethnographic approaches to language and gender in the contemporary world tackle both the complexities of language as an index of social identity and the complexities of these identities. Ethnographic methods can provide particularly powerful insights into the way in which humans can mobilize language to create and contest structures of power and difference. Ethnography can be fruitfully married with other kinds of approaches and methods, and offers the tools to bridge the traditional divide between microscopic and macroscopic analyses, as it encourages researchers to explore the way in which large-scale dynamics and the moment of interaction are mutually constructed. While ethnographic methods are vulnerable to new institutional ways of circumscribing what counts as legitimate research, they will continue to provide powerful tools for the investigation of interactional dynamics and social processes.

NOTES

1   In fact, several scholars had produced works that closely resembled modern-day ethnography in the course of the nineteenth century. These included the Russian Nikolai Miklukho-Maklay (1846–1888) and the Polish Jan Stanilaw Kubary (1846–1896), who documented the lives of Pacific Island peoples among whom they spent considerable time. They had the misfortune

of writing in less well-known languages and of dying young, and as a result their works were largely ignored.
2   This is what has come to be known in sociology, somewhat problematically, as "intersectionality" (Crenshaw 1991). See Choo and Marx Ferree (2010), among others, for a critique of the uses of this particular notion in sociology.

REFERENCES

Abu-Lughod, Leila. 1986. *Veiled Sentiments: Honor and Poetry in a Bedouin Society.* Berkeley: University of California Press.

Ahearn, Laura M. 2001. *Invitations to Love: Literacy, Love Letters, and Social Change in Nepal.* Ann Arbor: University of Michigan Press.

Appadurai, Arjun. 1996. *Modernity at Large: Cultural Dimensions of Globalization.* Minneapolis: University of Minnesota Press.

Besnier, Niko. 2007. "Gender and Interaction in a Globalizing World: Negotiating the Gendered Self in Tonga." In Bonnie McElhinny (ed.), *Words, Worlds, and Material Girls: Language, Gender, Globalization,* 423–446. Berlin: Mouton de Gruyter.

Brown, Penelope. 1980. "How and Why are Women More Polite: Some Evidence from a Mayan Community." In Sally McConnell-Ginet, Ruth Borker, and Nelly Furman (eds.), *Women and Language in Literature and Society,* 111–136. New York: Praeger.

Brownell, Susan, and Niko Besnier. 2013. "Gender and Sexuality." In James G. Carrier and Deborah B. Gewertz (eds.), *The Handbook of Sociocultural Anthropology,* 239–258. London: Bloomsbury.

Bucholtz, Mary. 2011. *White Kids: Language, Race, and Styles of Youth Identity.* Cambridge: Cambridge University Press.

Butler, Judith. 1990. *Gender Trouble: Feminism and the Subversion of Identity.* London: Routledge.

Choo, Hae Yeon, and Myra Marx Ferree. 2010. "Practicing Intersectionality in Sociological Research: A Critical Analysis of Inclusions, Interactions, and Institutions in the Study of Inequalities." *Sociological Theory,* 28: 129–149.

Clifford, James, and George E. Marcus, eds. 1986. *Writing Culture: The Politics and Poetics of Ethnography.* Berkeley: University of California Press.

Crenshaw, Kimberlé W. 1991. "Mapping the Margins: Intersectionality, Identity Politics, and Violence against Women of Color." *Stanford Law Review,* 43: 1241–1299.

Darnell, Regna. 2000. *And Along Came Boas: Continuity and Revolution in Americanist Anthropology.* Amsterdam: Benjamins.

di Leonardo, Micaela. 1991. "Gender, Culture, and Political Economy: Feminist Anthropology in Historical Perspective." In Micaela di Leonardo (ed.), *Gender at the Crossroads of Knowledge: Feminist Anthropology in the Postmodern Era,* 1–48. Berkeley: University of California Press.

Eckert, Penelope. 1989. *Jocks and Burnouts: Social Categories and Identity in the High School.* New York: Teachers College Press.

Eckert, Penelope, and Sally McConnell-Ginet. 1992. "Think Practically and Look Locally: Language and Gender as Community-Based Practice." *Annual Review of Anthropology,* 21: 461–490.

Erickson, Frederick, and Jeffrey Shultz. 1982. *The Counselor as Gatekeeper: Social Interaction in Interviews.* New York: Academic Press.

Faubion, James D., and George E. Marcus, eds. 2009. *Fieldwork is Not What It Used to Be: Learning Anthropology's Method in a Time of Transition.* Ithaca, NY: Cornell University Press.

Fernea, Elizabeth Warnock. 1969. *Guests of the Sheik: An Ethnography of an Iraqi Village.* New York: Doubleday.

Fillmore, Charles. 1997 [1971]. *Lectures on Deixis.* Stanford: CSLI Publications.

Gal, Susan. 1979. *Language Shift: Social Determinants of Linguistic Change in Bilingual Austria*. New York: Academic Press.

Geertz, Clifford. 1973. "Thick Description: Toward an Interpretive Theory of Culture." In *The Interpretation of Cultures: Selected Essays*, 3–30. New York: Basic Books.

Goffman, Erving. 1961. *Asylums: Essays on the Social Situation of Mental Patients and Other Inmates*. New York: Doubleday.

Good, Mary. 2012. "Modern Moralities, Moral Modernities: Ambivalence and Change among Youth in Tonga." Unpublished PhD dissertation, University of Arizona.

Gupta, Akhil, and James Ferguson, eds. 1997. *Anthropological Locations: Boundaries and Ground in a Field Science*. Berkeley: University of California Press.

Hannerz, Ulf. 1996. *Transnational Connections: Culture, People, Places*. London: Routledge.

Harding, Susan. 1975. "Women and Words in a Spanish Village." In Rayna R. Reiter (ed.), *Toward an Anthropology of Women*, 283–308. New York: Monthly Review Press.

Hymes, Dell. 1964. "Introduction: Toward Ethnographies of Communication." *American Anthropologist*, 66(2): 1–34.

Inoue, Miyako. 2006. *Vicarious Language. Gender and Linguistic Modernity in Japan*. Berkeley: University of California Press.

Jakobson, Roman. 1971 [1957]. "Shifters, Verbal Categories, and the Russian Verb." In *Selected Writings*, vol. 2, 130–147. The Hague: Mouton.

Jespersen, Otto. 1965 [1924]. *The Philosophy of Grammar*. New York: W. W. Norton.

Keenan (Ochs), Elinor. 1974. "Norm-Makers, Norm-Breakers: Use of Speech by Men and Women in a Malagasy Community." In Richard Bauman, and Joel Sherzer (eds.), *Explorations in the Ethnography of Speaking*, 125–143. Cambridge: Cambridge University Press.

Lakoff, Robin T. 1975. *Language and Woman's Place*. New York: Harper & Row.

Lederman, Rena. 2006. "Anxious Borders between Work and Life in a Time of Bureaucratic Ethics Regulation." *American Ethnologist*, 33: 477–481.

Lederman, Rena. 2013. "Ethics: Practices, Principles, and Comparative Perspectives." In James G. Carrier and Deborah B. Gewertz (eds.), *The Handbook of Sociocultural Anthropology*, 588–611. London: Bloomsbury.

Malinowski, Bronisław. 1922. *Argonauts of the Western Pacific: An Account of Native Enterprise and Adventure in the Archipelagoes of Melanesian New Guinea*. London: Routledge & Kegan Paul.

Malinowski, Bronisław. 1923. "The Problem of Meaning in Primitive Languages." In Charles K. Ogden and Ivor A. Richards (eds.), *The Meaning of Meaning*, 451–510. New York: Routledge & Kegan Paul.

Marcus, George. 1995. "Ethnography in/of the World System: The Emergence of Multi-sited Ethnography." *Annual Review of Anthropology*, 24: 95–117.

Marcus, George E., and Judith Okely. 2008. "How Short Can Fieldwork Be?" *Social Anthropology*, 15: 353–367.

Mendoza-Denton, Norma. 2008. *Homegirls: Language and Cultural Practice among Latina Youth Gangs*. Oxford: Blackwell.

Ochs, Elinor. 1993. "Indexing Gender." In Barbara Diane Miller (ed.), *Gender and Sex Hierarchies*, 146–169. Cambridge: Cambridge University Press.

Philips, Susan U. 2013. "Method in Anthropological Discourse Analysis: The Comparison of Units of Discourse." *Journal of Linguistic Anthropology*, 23: 83–96.

Pratt, Mary Louise. 1986. "Fieldwork in Common Places." In James Clifford and George E. Marcus (eds.), *Writing Culture: The Poetics and Politics of Ethnography*, 27–50. Berkeley: University of California Press.

Pujolar, Joan. 2000. *Gender, Heteroglossia and Power: A Sociolinguistic Ethnography of Youth Culture*. Berlin: Mouton de Gruyter.

Rampton, Ben. 1995. *Crossing: Language and Ethnicity among Adolescents*. London: Longman.

Robbins, Joel, and Alan Rumsey. 2008. "Cultural and Linguistic Anthropology and the Opacity of Other Minds." *Anthropological Quarterly*, 81: 407–420.

Schieffelin, Bambi B., and Elinor Ochs, eds. 1987. *Language Socialization across Cultures.* Cambridge: Cambridge University Press.

Shostak, Marjorie. 1981. *Nisa: The Life and Words of a !Kung Woman.* Cambridge, MA: Harvard University Press.

Silverstein, Michael. 1976. "Shifters, Linguistic Categories, and Cultural Description." In Keith Basso and Henry Selby (eds.), *Meaning in Anthropology*, 1–55. Albuquerque: University of New Mexico Press.

Silverstein, Michael. 2005. "Axes of Evals: Token versus Type Interdiscursivity." *Journal of Linguistic Anthropology*, 15: 6–22.

Stocking, George W., Jr. 1983. "The Ethnographer's Magic: Fieldwork in British Anthropology from Tylor to Malinowski." In *Observers Observed: Essays on Ethnographic Fieldwork*, 70–120. Madison: University of Wisconsin Press.

Tope, Daniel, Lindsey Joyce Chamberlain, Martha Crowley, and Randy Hodson. 2005. "The Benefits of Being There: Evidence from the Literature on Work." *Journal of Contemporary Ethnography*, 34: 470–493.

Wolf, Marjorie. 1960. *The House of Lim: A Study of a Chinese Family.* Englewood Cliffs, NJ: Prentice Hall.

7 Conversation Analysis in Language and Gender Studies

SUE WILKINSON AND CELIA KITZINGER

Gender and language scholars have drawn on conversation analysis (CA) since its inception in the late 1960s. "Classic" studies include West's and Zimmerman's explorations of interruptions in cross-sex conversations (e.g., West 1979; Zimmerman and West 1975) and Goodwin's analyses of girls' talk (e.g., M. H. Goodwin 1990). In the last 15 years or so there has been a dramatic increase in CA and CA-influenced research on gender and language, establishing the field of "feminist conversation analysis" (Kitzinger 2000; 2008a), generating edited collections (e.g., Speer and Stokoe 2011; Stokoe and Weatherall 2002), and addressing topics such as refusing sex (Kitzinger and Frith 1999); violence against women (Guimaraes 2007; Stokoe 2010a); transgender issues (Speer and Green 2007); "coming out" as lesbian or gay (Land and Kitzinger 2005); heteronormativity (Kitzinger 2005a; 2005b); ethnicity (Wilkinson 2011a; 2011b); woman-to-woman helpline interaction (Kitzinger 2011; Shaw and Kitzinger 2007a; 2007b; 2012; Wilkinson 2011c; Wilkinson and Kitzinger 2013); and gender categories in interaction (Kitzinger 2007; Kitzinger and Rickford 2007; Speer 2005; Stokoe 2003; 2006; 2010b; Stokoe and Attenborough, Chapter 8 in this volume).

Conversation analysis – the study of talk-in-interaction – originated though the work of Harvey Sacks (see Sacks 1992), in collaboration with Emanuel Schegloff and Gail Jefferson (e.g., Sacks, Schegloff, and Jefferson 1974). Sacks was influenced by the developing tradition of ethnomethodology, concerned with social members' ways of making sense of the everyday social world. CA examines talk not as *language*, but as *action* – what people *do* with talk (and associated body behaviors), for example, actions such as inviting, apologizing, disagreeing, telling news, or giving advice. It relies on *actual instances* of talk-in-interaction (rather than self-report or experimental data, or the hypothetical and idealized instances often used in language studies); and it spans both ordinary, everyday interactions – such as family mealtimes – and institutional interactions – such as calls to telephone helplines, medical consultations, or TV news interviews (see Heritage and Clayman 2010 for a review).

The Handbook of Language, Gender, and Sexuality, Second Edition.
Edited by Susan Ehrlich, Miriam Meyerhoff, and Janet Holmes.
© 2014 John Wiley & Sons, Inc. Published 2017 by John Wiley & Sons, Inc.

The invention of the (audio) tape recorder enabled Sacks to capture and repeatedly inspect talk-in-interaction; and the subsequent development of video technology has enabled CA researchers to capture not just the talk, but also nonverbal features of face-to-face interaction, such as gesture, body deployment, and gaze (e.g., C. Goodwin 1981). Transcription of data for CA analysis uses a detailed notation system – originally invented by Gail Jefferson (e.g., Jefferson 2004) and subsequently developed by other CA researchers (e.g., Hepburn and Bolden 2013) – which enables representation of various features of the timing and delivery of talk. For example, in extract 1, at lines 1–2, overlapping talk between speakers is marked by square brackets; at line 3, in the word "PO:SSibly," increased volume (relative to surrounding talk) is indicated by capital letters, increased emphasis by underlining, and a sound stretch (on the immediately preceding sound) by a colon; and a within-turn silence of eight-tenths of a second (at the end of the line) is represented by (0.8) – that is, the length of the silence in round brackets. We need these fine-grained details because interactional participants are demonstrably oriented to them, and they are consequential for how an interaction develops. However, it is the recordings (not the transcripts) that constitute the primary data for analysis, and best practice in contemporary CA – subject to appropriate permissions – is to make the recordings of data extracts displayed in published articles available on the web. CA is unusual in that data sets are often shared across the CA community, frequently reanalyzed for new phenomena, and extracts from them appear in publications by several different authors.

Each episode of talk-in-interaction has unique characteristics; but each is also made up of some recurrent features: the "building blocks" of social life. CA aims to identify these features and understand how they are used in action. Data analysis, then, focuses on the organized, recurrent, *structural* features of talk-in-interaction, features which – importantly for the study of gender and language – stand independently of the characteristics of individual speakers, or the relationship between them (we will return to this point later). CA develops *technical specifications* of the recurrent patterns, structures, and practices that constitute the basic characteristics of talk-in-interaction. These include, centrally, turn-taking, action formation, sequence organization, repair, word selection, and the overall structural organization of talk (Schegloff 2007, xiv). This reliance on, and contribution to, a set of cumulative, empirically derived, technical specifications of interactional phenomena is an important part of what differentiates CA from other methods of analyzing talk, including discourse analysis and discursive psychology (see also Kitzinger 2006).

We focus here on the domain of turn-taking, showing how it can inform gender and language research on interruption and on cooperative talk. In the final section of the chapter, we briefly review some gender and language studies which draw on other interactional phenomena (e.g., sequence organization and repair), and evaluate CA as a method for gender and language research, considering how it has shaped the field, the kinds of questions it is well suited to answer, and those it is not.

1. Turn-Taking, Interruption, and Cooperative Talk

For scholars of gender and language, ever since Zimmerman and West (1975) claimed that women are disproportionately interrupted by men and that these interruptions are displays of dominance and control, interruption has been a recurrent concern – with contradictory and, ultimately, inconclusive findings. On reading the literature on interruption, it is apparent that few gender-related studies have used the insights of CA – yet the CA domain of turn-taking is centrally relevant to understanding interactions in which the talk of two different speakers overlaps (or does not overlap).

There is a range of situations in which someone begins to talk before the prior speaker has completed her turn. Here are three examples:

Fragment (a)

```
A:   I think if you had to pay for
       yo[ur  (lo-)]
B:       [You're ex]a:ggera[:tin' (it.) ]
```

Fragment (b)

```
A:   Uh you been down here before [havenche.
B:                                [Yeh.
```

Fragment (c)

```
A:   I: would hesitate to: uhm
B:   recomm[en]d her.
```

In each, as we will show, A has not completed her turn at talk at the point at which B starts up (although only fragments (a) and (b) include overlapping talk) – and each represents a very different kind of social action. We will look at each of these data fragments in context, and in more detail, below.

The first of the three instances above is a clear case of interruption. From an overview of existing data sets, it is apparent that interrupting (as defined by CA) is surprisingly rare. Fragment (a) is taken from an argument between a mother ("Mom") and her teenage daughter, Virginia ("Vir"), over a family meal. Looking at it in context (extract 1 below), we can see that Virginia is making an impassioned plea for an increase in her weekly allowance (from $5 to $10 – these data were recorded in the early 1970s) and that, resisting this, her mother is questioning Virginia's expenditure. Here, the argument turns to the cost of Virginia's phone calls:

Extract 1

Virginia 10 (SW retrans)

```
01  MOM:  [.hh Well- if] you got ten dollars a wee:k, (0.2)=
02  WES:  [ huh huh hm ]
03  MOM:  =.hh do you think that you could PO:SSibly (0.8)
```

```
04          pay for your t- long distance telephone calls.
05          (0.2)
06   VIR:   .hh hh I don't m[ake that ma]:ny.
07   MOM:              [ Ohh  I th-]
08          (0.8) ((Mom opens and closes mouth))
09   MOM:   We:ll u- last month it was twenny dollars.
10   VIR:   Woo-  ((shakes head))
11   MOM:   I think if you had to pay for
12          yo[ur (lo-) ]
13   VIR:     [You're ex]a:ggera[:tin' (it.) ]
14   MOM:                       [pay for your] long distance
15          telephone calls you wouldn't make so ma:ny.
```

Virginia's turn at line 13 (in overlap with Mom's talk at line 12) is clearly inter-ruptive in that Mom cannot possibly have finished her utterance-in-progress: she is only just beginning to produce the object of the verb "to pay for" (highly pro-jectable, from her turn at line 4, as "your long distance telephone calls"); and she is part-way through the *if* component of an *if–then* construction, with the *then* yet to come.[1] We can identify Virginia's utterance as interruptive from these features alone. However, there is additional evidence at lines 14–15, in that Mom treats her-self as having been interrupted. When she continues speaking, she completes the utterance that was in progress when Virginia intervened, rather than producing a new turn. She repeats her last three words ("pay for your") – a classic way of show-ing yourself to have been interrupted (Schegloff 2000a); then produces the object projectably missing from line 12 ("long distance telephone calls"); and follows this with the *then* component, which was yet to come ("you wouldn't make so many"), completing the *if–then* construction.

What makes this an interruption (independently of Mum's treatment of it as such) is that it violates normative turn-taking practices, as first laid out in the classic, foundational CA article by Sacks, Schegloff, and Jefferson (1974). Over-whelmingly, people speak one at a time. Co-interactants track their own talk and that of their co-conversationalist(s) in the course of its production, using syntax, prosody, and pragmatics as resources to project when a turn is coming to possible completion. A next speaker may legitimately start to speak at a place where a turn at talk is possibly complete (a "transition relevance place"). This is typically at the end of any one of the units (sentences, clauses, phrases, lexical items) out of which a turn can (in any given context) be constructed – these are known as "turn con-structional units," or TCUs (see Sacks, Schegloff, and Jefferson (1974) for a detailed exposition). A current speaker is entitled to complete their TCU-in-progress before the next speaker starts up.

A key finding of CA research – indeed, one of those that underpins the turn-taking organization – is that a great deal of overlapping talk is caused by next speaker start-up at a place where a turn could, indeed, have been possibly complete but – as it turns out – is not, because the first speaker goes on talking past a transition relevance place. In CA terms, this is not interruption, merely overlap that is, in effect "accidental," because it is caused by misprojection of the ending of the turn: as in fragment (b), reproduced as extract 2 below.

Extract 2

[NB:III:3:5, from Sacks, Schegloff, and Jefferson 1974, 707]

```
01   A:   Uh you been down here before [havenche.
02   B:                                [Yeh.
```

Here, speaker B (quite legitimately) figures that A will be done at the end of the word "before" (grammatically, a declarative; pragmatically, a question), and comes in at that point with a confirmatory "yeh." However, it turns out that A isn't actually done there, but adds what Sacks, Schegloff, and Jefferson term an "optional element": the tag question[2] "haven't you." This means that, although B starts up at a point at which it was projectable that the prior turn would be complete and that her turn would be launched in the clear without either a gap or an overlap, this turns out to be a misprojection, and she finds herself in overlap with the final (optional) element of the prior turn. We can see a similar thing in extract 3, where the second speaker misprojects the ending of the prior turn because the first speaker adds the address term "sir" as a final optional element.

Extract 3

[FD:IV:35, from Sacks, Schegloff, and Jefferson 1974, 708]

```
01   A:   What's yer name again please [sir,
02   B:                                [F.T. Galloway.
```

Brief and unproblematic instances of overlap like these are very common in conversation and they are characteristically resolved by one speaker stopping talking a few syllables (or beats) into the overlap (Schegloff 2000a). They are not exercises of power or attempts to dominate the conversation, but a by-product of the operation of the turn taking system. As one of the authors of the classic turn-taking paper subsequently noted: "Looking at talk which might well be characterized as someone starting up 'interruptively,' i.e. in the midst of another's utterance, I found again and again that the places at which such talk started were perfectly reasonable 'completion' points" (Jefferson 1986, 153). In confronting the contradictory findings of research on gender differences in interruption, questions of definition and coding are of central concern. Although some researchers do make a distinction between (accidental) "overlap" (an error in projecting where a speaker is planning to end their turn, as in extracts 2 and 3 above) and "interruption" (a start-up at a point in a speaker's talk where it cannot possibly be complete, as in extract 1), it is apparent that in practice these two concepts are confusingly and inconsistently applied. In particular, much of the "interruption" literature in gender and language studies codes as interruptive many instances of overlapping talk which conversation analysts would see as simple misprojection. CA knowledge about turn-taking rules – and, in particular, about the projectability of turn constructional units – enables us to differentiate clearly between the onset of overlapping talk as interruptive (i.e., violative of turn-taking rules) and the onset of overlapping talk as a (rule-governed) misprojection. Coding of overlapping talk informed by CA allows researchers more accurately to address the question as to whether men (or some men, or particular types of men in particular types of setting) disproportionately interrupt women (see Kitzinger 2008b for a fuller discussion).

There is another problem with much of the "interruption" literature in gender and language studies. Not only does it code as interruptive many instances of overlapping talk which conversation analysts would see as simple misprojection; it also fails to capture much of the interactional import of overlapping talk. The common assumption that interruptions are displays of conversational dominance and control turns out to be much too stark.

For example, extract 4 involves a man (Earl) interrupting a woman (Emma) – but he does so in order to implement a *cooperative* action. Emma has phoned to speak to her friend Lottie, but it is Lottie's husband, Earl, who has answered and it is apparent to Emma – as she later says – that Lottie and Earl "have company" (i.e., people visiting them). When Earl offers to call his wife to the phone ("you want to talk to Lottie?," line 2), Emma – who clearly *does* want to talk to Lottie – demurs. After a short silence (line 3) and turn-initial delay ("uh," line 4) she confirms that she *did* want to talk to Lottie, but immediately follows this with a display of her realization that Lottie is "busy" (i.e., occupied with the couple's guests) and launches a counter-offer – she will call back later (line 4). This is the turn that is interrupted by Earl when he says "here" (line 5) – this seems to be addressed to Emma, but may also constitute a first move to hand the phone over to his wife.

Extract 4

[NBIV:12]

```
01   Emm:   How'r you:.
02   Ear:   Fine'ow'r you Emma yih wan'talk tih Lottie
03          (0.2)
04   Emm:   Uh ya:h WELL ↑LI[:STEN sh]e's busy I'll [call'er]
05   Ear:                   [ He:re. ]              [No: she]'s
06          right he:re waitaminit.
07          (0.3)
08   Ear:   Wayamin' hol' it.
09          (1.0)
10          ((receiver down))
11          (5.0)
12          ((receiver up))
13   Lot:   Ye:ah.
```

Earl first overlaps Emma after she has confirmed that she wants to talk to Lottie, but has also indicated her awareness of some problem with this (with "WELL," line 4). Finding himself to have interrupted, he waits until after Emma's next unit ("Well listen she's busy," line 4) and then – at this possible transition relevance place – he rejects Emma's implication that Lottie might not be available to speak to her (with "No," line 5). However, he has misprojected the end of Emma's turn, and he finds himself again in overlap with Emma, who is now offering to call back later. Emma abandons her unit (after "I'll call her" where presumably what was projectable was something like "I'll call her back later/tomorrow/some other time") and Earl persists, countering Emma's "she's busy" with his offer "she's right here" (lines 5–6). He directs her to "wait a minute" (lines 6 and 8) and to "hold it" (line 8). Seven seconds later, Lottie comes to the phone. Emma and Lottie get to talk to each other in part because Earl interrupted Emma, who was proposing to abandon the current attempt at conversation, thereby preventing her from putting down the phone. In this extract, then, a man interrupts a woman at a point where she cannot possibly have finished speaking. However, this is not a display of male dominance and control – rather, from Emma's point of view this interruption was implementing a helpful action, keeping her on the phone, so that he can then enable her to speak to her friend right away.

So far, we have shown how knowledge and understanding of the CA domain of turn-taking is valuable for researchers studying interruption, both in allowing them more accurately to code instances of overlapping talk (as either "interruption" or "misprojection"), and in facilitating a more nuanced understanding of the interactional import of interruption. CA provides key resources for examining this central topic in language and gender research, and, more broadly, for understanding interaction between (and within) the genders across a wide range of situations. It enables researchers to look beyond the characteristics of individual speakers to focus on the recurrent, *structural* features of talk-in-interaction – such as the organization of turn-taking – and how these are used to achieve particular interactional goals.

We turn now to the third data fragment we showed in which a second speaker starts up before a first speaker is done. The person who speaks second in fragment (c) is doing something very special: she is not producing a new turn of her own – as in fragments (a) and (b) – rather, she is completing the turn her co-conversationalist was in the course of producing. In CA terms, a single turn constructional unit (TCU) is jointly constructed by two different speakers: the first speaker begins the TCU and the second speaker ends it.

This phenomenon – referred to in the CA literature as "collaborative completion" – has been extensively studied by Gene Lerner (1991; 1994; 1996a; 1996b; 2002; 2004; 2013). Lerner's work explores how it is possible for people to do collaborative talk of this type, the constraints on how it is done, and what kinds of interactional purposes it serves. The instance shown in fragment (c) constitutes a "relaxation" of the turn-taking rules, because, generally speaking, a current speaker is entitled to complete their TCU-in-progress before next speaker start-up. Extract 5 below – an expansion of fragment (c) – involves a negative assessment of a third party. As in many of the cases analyzed by Lerner, collaborative completion is used as a way of getting *another person* to articulate a negative or critical assessment, thereby co-implicating them in that assessment. A speaker brings a TCU to just the point at which a co-conversationalist is able to discern (using projectability) the sort of thing they mean to say about the person, and then leaves it to *them* to say it. Lerner (2013) refers to this co-construction of an interactionally delicate formulation as "collaborative indiscretion."

Extract 5 is taken from a telephone conversation between two nurses. They are discussing a third nurse (the "she" of lines 1 and 5) whom Bee is suggesting as a possible relief nurse – someone whom Amy feels unable to "recommend" for the job. At lines 5–7 (previously shown as fragment (c)), a single TCU is jointly constructed: it is started by Amy and ended by Bee.

Extract 5

[SBL]

```
01  Bee:  Well do you think she would fit i:n¿
02        (.)
03  Amy:  Uh:m .hh (.) uh I don't kno:w=What I'm:
04        hesitating abou:t is uhm .hh uhm (.) maybe
05        she wou:ld .hh (0.8) uh but I: would
06        hesitate to: uhm
07  Bee:  recomm[en]d her.
08  Amy:        [I-]
09  Amy:  Ye:s.
```

Although Amy starts the negative assessment ("I would hesitate to," lines 5–6), she doesn't complete it. Instead, after the word "to" she produces a filled pause ("uhm") and it is Bee who completes the TCU that Amy began, adding the words "recommend her" (line 7), which Amy accepts as correct ("Yes," line 9). An important interactional effect of the collaborative construction is that both parties are implicated in the negative assessment.

Notice that the *only* thing the second speaker does is complete the first speaker's TCU. She does not, for example, produce additional talk of her own, or respond in any way to the TCU she has completed (which would be a violation of the turn-taking rules). In other words, the second speaker treats herself as having only what Lerner refers to as "conditional entry" into the first speaker's turn space: it is conditional in the sense that all a second speaker should properly do in that slot is complete the first speaker's TCU on their behalf (in this sense the turn-taking rules are merely "relaxed," not violated). Both participants treat the TCU as still "belonging" to the first speaker: the second speaker does this by restricting what she says to completing the TCU; the first speaker does it by assessing the "correctness" of the second speaker's completion as a more or less adequate version of what they meant to say (Amy's "Yes," line 9). In ratifying (as in extract 5) or – as is also possible – repudiating (Lerner 2004) a TCU completion, the first speaker treats the TCU as, by right, her own.

The capacity to complete a TCU started by a co-conversationalist is a kind of "mind-reading." It demonstrates an understanding of what another speaker might be about to say, thereby offering a powerful resource for one party to an interaction to display affiliation and empathy with another. Empathy – showing someone that you understand their feelings or situation – is an important construct in counseling, therapeutic and medical practice (e.g., Dekeyser, Elliott, and Leijssen 2011; Neumann et al. 2009; Rogers 1975). It is particularly central to the provision of feminist or woman-centered counseling services – those run by women for women – which typically list among their goals "active listening," "empathic understanding," and "validating women's experience" (Kitzinger 2011). We can use the CA domain of turn-taking – specifically the phenomenon of collaborative completion – to help us both understand how helpline call-takers display empathy and also to capture the interactional import of such empathic displays (see Wilkinson and Kitzinger forthcoming for a more elaborated account).

Extracts 6 and 7 are taken from calls to a helpline for women in crisis after giving birth (see Kitzinger and Kitzinger 2007). In both cases – as with extract 5 above – the first speaker (the caller to the helpline) begins the interactionally delicate business of giving a negative assessment of a third party, here medical professionals. And in both cases, it is the second speaker (the helpline call-taker) who actually completes the assessment, thereby co-implicating herself in it.

In extract 6, the caller, Hannah, is describing what happened after her emergency hysterectomy. She is cautiously building a case for the possibility that her healthcare team may be to blame for her hysterectomy. On the very brink of producing this negative assessment of their behavior, Hannah slows down her talk mid-TCU (with the silence after "were" and the increasingly protracted sound stretches, line 9), thereby creating an opportunity for the call-taker to come in prior to completion and to complete the TCU on her behalf (line 10):

Extract 6

[BCC205; "Hannah"]

```
01  Han:  If things had just naturally gone wro:ng
02        .hh[hh] they'd've been looking at the file=
03  Clt:     [Mm]
04  Han:  'n: sayin' "Oh this woman was just damned
05        unlucky[:".]
06  Clt:         [Y e]ah. hh
07  Han:  Uhm (0.2) But I almost felt that these::
08        (1.0) looking ba:ck: (0.2) that (.) these
09        people we:re (.) coming i::n to:::
10  Clt:  cover their ba:ck[s.]
11  Han:                   [c ]over themse:lves.
12        In [some] wa:y.
13  Clt:     [Yes:]
14  Clt:  .hhh Y- Yours is a very: intelligent and
15        reasonable response to all this:.
```

By speaking before Hannah's turn is possibly complete (still in the middle of a sentential TCU and part-way through a verb clause), and by speaking so as to voice the unspoken part of Hannah's turn, the call-taker is engaged in an affiliative action. She is showing both that she understands Hannah's position, and – by co-implicating herself in its articulation – that she is treating it as a reasonable position to take. Hannah's subsequent delayed completion of her own talk with a near-repeat of what the call-taker has said (line 11) ratifies the call-taker's completion while also reasserting authority over her turn's talk and making relevant a next turn responsive to it. The call-taker's next turn receipts Hannah's claim and positively assesses it – as "a very intelligent and reasonable response" (lines 14–15).

In extract 7, Melanie is calling the Birth Crisis helpline to report a positive birth experience, culminating in the safe delivery of her son. She had been overdue, but managed to resist pressure to have her labor induced. At lines 1–2, she describes the pressure she experienced – including being threatened with a caesarean section – as a "circumstance" in which "you don't know who to trust," and (at line 6) as "a downward slope." At line 8, and again at line 10, the call-taker explicitly agrees. At lines 10–13, she shows *how* it is she is able to agree: by drawing on her generic knowledge – as a childbirth expert and experienced call-taker – of what happens to women in that circumstance. She treats Melanie as one case of what any woman would have experienced in that kind of situation – and Melanie agrees (at lines 16–17) that, despite her strength, she found the situation "really challenging." So, the collaborative completion – at lines 21–23 – occurs in a context in which there is already considerable alignment between caller and call-taker.

Extract 7

[BCC320; "Melanie"]

```
01  Mel:  Then you kind'v: (.) you don't know
02        who to trust in that circumstance so
03        you kind'v accept it'n >I think once=
04  Clt:  [ N o : . ]
05  Mel:  =[the< mind's] accepted that it's: (.)
06        it's on a downward slo:pe reall[y: i]sn't [it.]
07  Clt:                                 [Mm:.]       [Mm.]
08        I agree.
09        (0.2)
10  Clt:  I agree. You-you jus:t take away a woman's
11        self-confidence [.hhhh] and she becomes=
12  Mel:                  [Yea:h]
13  Clt:  =dependant.
14  Mel:  That's right.  I mean it's really is: you
15        know you don't realise how well I didn't
16        realise how .hhh I mean I'm a pretty strong
17        pe:rson but that was really challenging.
18  Clt:  mYea:h.
19  Mel:  You know [not just- The] b↑irth itself was=
20  Clt:          [ Y e a :h (s)]
21  Mel:  =easy: compared to: (.) it was the dealing
22        with  thu:h
23  Clt:  thu(h)h ↑peo(h)ple [huh!huh!]
24  Mel:                     [peo:ple!]
25  Clt:  ↑HAH-HAH-HAH! YE:s:!
26  Mel:  £You kno:w¿£
27  Clt:  £Ye:s£
28  Mel:  They we:re [in( .)      [(But) uh:m]
29  Clt:             [£I kno:w.£ [. hh(h)h  ]
```

```
30   Mel:   An' I thought to myself y'know "well
31          .hhhh try 'n see it from their point'v
32          view" 'n I did- did you know 'n I (.) said
33          but they were saying things to me like...
```

In establishing alignment between caller and call-taker in the first part of this extract (up to line 18), the focus has been firmly on the birthing woman herself. At lines 19–22, Melanie makes three attempts ("not just-"/"compared to:"/"it was the dealing with thu:h") to shift the focus back to what she experienced as the main problem: the behavior of the health professionals. Her manifest difficulty in articulating this is strongly suggestive of its interactional delicacy. She sets up a contrast between the physiological event of "the birth itself" (as "easy") and what she was "dealing with," leaving her TCU unfinished (at line 22) with a stretched "thu:h," creating the opportunity for the call-taker to come in and complete it on her behalf. When the call-taker does so, offering "thuh people"[3] (accompanied and followed by laughter, which – according to Jefferson, Sacks, and Schegloff (1987) – often marks a reported behavioral transgression), Melanie enthusiastically repeats the word "people" (line 24), assimilating it into her unfinished sentence, and thereby making it her own.[4] The two have brought off – in Lerner's (2013) terms a "collaborative indiscretion"; and the call-taker has shown that she understands what Melanie was trying to say sufficiently well to be able (appropriately) to complete her utterance for her. Displays of empathetic understanding of this kind are an important component of helpline work in "woman-to-woman" organizations seeking to "empower" women, such as the Birth Crisis helpline, and the CA domain of turn-taking offers valuable resources for understanding how such displays are accomplished, and what they can achieve, interactionally.

In this section, then, we have shown the value of a CA approach for understanding interruptive and cooperative talk. The CA domain of turn-taking, in particular, enables the scholar of gender and language more accurately to code instances of overlapping talk (differentiating between interruption and misprojection) and more fully to capture their interactional import. Knowledge of how turn-taking normatively works facilitates a focus on non-normative practices, such as the joint construction by two speakers of a single TCU. We have shown how, in the context of the woman-to-woman helpline, this practice can be used as an interactional resource to bring off displays of empathy.

2. Reviewing CA as a Method for Gender and Language Research

We have focused on the contribution of (some aspects of) just one key domain of CA (turn-taking) to just one area of gender and language research (interruptive and cooperative talk). CA also spans the domains of sequence organization, repair, word selection, action formation, and the overall structural organization of talk

(Schegloff 2007, xiv). Research drawing on these other domains – separately and in combination – has also contributed to the field. We will give just two examples (both again from studies of woman-to-woman helplines), and will then evaluate a CA approach overall.

First, sequence organization refers to the recurrent patterns which describe how courses of action get implemented through talk (Schegloff 2007). In general, a first (sequence-initiating) action makes relevant another (responsive) action, from a limited range of "types": for example, a greeting makes relevant a return greeting; inviting makes relevant acceptance, or rejection (Drew 1984); requesting makes relevant granting, or refusal (Curl and Drew 2008). Some of these responsive actions (e.g., accepting an invitation, granting a request) stand in a "preferred" relationship to the first action; others (e.g., rejecting an invitation, refusing a request) are relatively "dispreferred." It is not always readily apparent what the "most preferred" responsive action might be: for example, the most preferred response to an apology is not acceptance of the apology, but mitigating or undermining the apology's claim to have caused offense (Robinson 2004).

Our example concerns responses to the action of complimenting. Previous CA work (e.g., Pomerantz 1978) suggests that in ordinary, everyday conversation the most preferred response to a compliment is not acceptance – because accepting praise is dispreferred – but, rather, deflecting or downgrading the compliment in some way. Shaw and Kitzinger (2012) examined 112 compliments made by a single call-taker in a corpus of 80 calls[5] to the Home Birth helpline (a UK-based organization which offers support and information for women planning a home birth): for example, "you are brilliant," "I admire what you're doing," "oh you clever woman!," "you do sound very clued-up," "what a sensible woman you are." They found that, unlike in everyday conversation, compliments on the helpline were often accepted (around a third of them); and that compliment recipients were *not* primarily oriented to avoiding self-praise: rather, they were concerned with other actions being implemented by the call-taker's turn (e.g., supporting their plans for giving birth at home). The authors suggest that complimenting is an important resource for the call-taker. For example, in extract 8 below, her compliment (at lines 3–4) transforms what the caller presents as a negative (feeling "totally stressed out") into a positive (sounding as if she's "handling it well"). This clearly has the desired effect of encouraging the caller to "get onto the hospital" (lines 5–6), since this is what she next undertakes to do.

Extract 8

[HB42; "Shelley"]

```
01  She:  I feel £totally stressed out at the
02        [minute.£ [huh huh]
03  Clt:  [.h h h   [W e l l] you s-sound as
04        if you're handling it well.
05  She:  Huh huh huh Okay well I'll get onto the
06        hospit[al    [an'[(see what they say)]
07  Clt:       [.hhh [O k[ ay do let me know ]
08        how things go:!
```

The authors suggest that one way of understanding such compliments in their data is as an attempt by the call-taker to implement and embody in her own practice the theoretical construct of "empowerment" – which she believes to be crucial to her work, and which is central to the helpline's feminist goal of "empowering" callers. This insight would not have been possible without a general understanding of the principles of sequence organization, and a more specialized knowledge of normative practices of responding to compliments.

Second, the CA domain of repair (e.g., Schegloff 2000b; Schegloff, Jefferson, and Sacks 1997) addresses problems in speaking, hearing, or understanding, and how these are resolved by co-interactants. Our example here also intersects with the CA domain of word selection: it is concerned with what happens when one person fails to understand a word used by another, or when the speaker thinks that her recipient might not understand a particular word (Kitzinger and Mandelbaum 2013). In a helpline context, an examination of practices of repair and word selection can shed valuable light on participants' orientations to expertise (e.g., to what extent the call-taker is taken to be the legitimate expert; what expertise she supposes any given caller to have), and how this displays – and helps to constitute – the relationship between them.

The following data extract is taken from a call to the Birth Crisis helpline, in which the call-taker is attempting to reassure the caller – who is nearing her expected date of delivery and has a worrying vaginal discharge – that she may not yet be going into labor. In formulating possible sources of the discharge (other than urine), the call-taker uses circumlocutions or vernacular rather than specialist terms (line 12: "waters from up above the baby's bottom"; lines 14–15: "water from down in front of the baby's head"; line 16: "it comes from the bit above the baby's bottom"). This becomes particularly apparent when the caller responds with a report of having speculated about the same possibility, but uses the specialist term "hind waters" (line 20), in place of the call-taker's circumlocution. Notice, also, how she tactfully defers to the expertise of the call-taker by ostensibly providing the term with a display of uncertainty as to its correctness ("is it hind waters").

Extract 9

[BCC379; "Belinda"]

```
10  Clt:  ...   .h[hh But you see it could b    ]e: .hhh=
11  Bel:        [(It doesn't smell) like urine.]
12  Clt:  =waters from up abov::e the baby's bottom
13  Bel:  mm [hm ]
14  Clt:     [.hh] Or it could be water from down in
15        front of the baby's head. .hhhh Sometimes when
16        it comes from .hh the bit above the baby's bottom
17        [.hhh ] it leaks and then seals itself up again.
18  Bel:  [mm hm]
19        (.)
20  Bel:  Yes. I did wonder whethe:r is it hind waters,
21        [(                              )]
22  Clt:  [Yes, that's right. Yes I'm sorry] I should be
23        £ using the correct termino(h)logy. Ye(h)s.
```

Here, then, the call-taker has designed her talk for a less knowledgeable recipient than Belinda turns out to be. In producing the circumlocution, she has apparently underassumed her recipient's familiarity with the specialist term "hind waters," thereby implying that she does not have (professional) expertise in the domain of childbirth. The caller, in subsequently using the specialist term "hind waters" (line 20), demonstrates that she does, in fact, have expertise in this domain; she also reveals her understanding that the call-taker may have "hearably" avoided using the specialist term. The call-taker apparently hears Belinda's turn using the specialist term (rather than the circumlocution) as a rebuke, and responds to this – substantially delaying the progressivity of the sequence (line 21) – with an acknowledgment that Belinda has used the proper term (line 22) and a (laughing) apology for not using "the correct terminology" (lines 23–24).

These kinds of lexical choices can have profound interactional reverberations. A speaker's use of a circumlocution or vernacular term provides evidence of a supposition that her recipient is less educated, knowledgeable, or competent than she displays herself to be. And, of course, a recipient may not respond as graciously as does Belinda above – rather, an erroneous supposition that a recipient does not know the meaning of a word could be treated as insulting, patronizing, or offensive, and serious interactional trouble could consequentially ensue. Further, in the context of a woman-to-woman helpline, exposing asymmetries of expertise and understanding may run counter to feminist ideals of mutuality, equality, and the valuing of experiential knowledge.

Finally, we turn to an evaluation of CA as a method for gender and language research. We identify several important advantages of using a CA approach, and then some problems and limitations. First, CA moves the study of gender and language away from the idealized or intuitive data typical of laboratory or self-report studies to focus instead on naturally occurring data. Rather than studying – and, sometimes, reproducing – stereotypes of men's and women's talk, CA focuses on the structural features of language which stand independently of the characteristics of individual speakers, including their categorical memberships. In this way, it is able to discover how the social world actually works, rather than reinforcing presuppositions about it. For feminists and other critical scholars who want to change the world for the better, an essential prerequisite is an accurate understanding of how the world is now.

Second, CA offers some concrete, practical resources for actually effecting such change. For example, analyses of how helpline interaction works can be used to help service providers to improve their services, and to train helpline call-takers (Kitzinger and Kitzinger 2007; Wilkinson 2011b).[6]

Third, a CA approach allows us both to develop precise operational definitions of conversational practices (e.g., using the turn-taking rules to define when speaking in overlap constitutes an interruption, rather than a simple misprojection) and to examine in a relatively sophisticated way what such conversational practices may be used to achieve in interaction (e.g., implementing helpful or cooperative actions, as well as hostile ones). This not only improves the accuracy of studies which attempt to code such conversational practices; it also expands our understanding of the subtleties and complexities of human interaction.

CA also offers the possibility of operationally defining broader, harder-to-specify practices in specific conversational terms (e.g., "displaying empathy" through the practice of successfully completing another's utterance; "displaying expertise" through selecting specialist rather than vernacular terms; or "empowerment" as enacted – at least in part – through the practice of complimenting). Again, such understandings can be harnessed to understand interactional inequalities and to devise communication skills training to improve services.

For many researchers, the biggest *dis*advantage of CA as an approach to studying social life is that it does not purport to tell us what is going on inside people's heads: only what they *do* in the course of any given interaction.[7] In fact, although some conversation analysts eschew any mention of "feelings" or "intentions" as entirely unwarranted, others are more ambivalent or agnostic about importing cognitive concepts (see Te Molder and Potter 2005 for a review). Either way, CA would probably not be the approach of choice for addressing a determinedly psychological or psychoanalytically designed research question.

Others have deemed CA too narrow and restrictive in scope, claiming that it relies simply on snippets of decontextualized talk. One critic, reviewing theories of language and gender, avows that CA severely "limits admissible context" (Bucholtz 2003, 52). In fact, CA's notion of context is extremely broad: spanning sequential, structural, institutional, and cultural notions of context. It is sequential context that tells us whether a short utterance (e.g., someone saying their name, as in extract 3, line 2 above) is or isn't a possible complete turn (here, we see it is – as responsive to a request for repetition). The location of an utterance within an interaction's overall structural organization is another way of looking at its context: whether a request for antibiotics comes in the opening or diagnosis phase of a medical interaction, for example, and the consequences of its structural location, in terms of whether antibiotics are prescribed (Stivers 2007). CA also examines the ways in which particular institutional contexts – for example, educational, legal, medical – are "talked into being": how the talk constitutes the context as a classroom, courtroom, or consulting room interaction, for example. And, at the broadest level, CA understands the cultural contexts in which we live as constituted by – and constitutive of – our interactions. The words we are able to select and the inferences associated with them (e.g., "wife" and "husband" normatively refer to opposite-sex, co-resident partners: Kitzinger 2005a), the grammatical, phonetic, and other resources we have available to build our talk – all of these rely on, and reproduce, culture.

A third (and related) perceived limitation of CA is its focus on participant orientations, and the dilemmas this poses for the researcher who wants to study something to which participants are *not* demonstrably oriented.[8] It is a commonplace that we reproduce cultural patterns and practices (e.g., heteronormativity: see Kitzinger 2005a; 2005b) without being oriented to them – indeed, their very "invisibility" is part of their power. How can we study these phenomena when, for the most part, they do not even ruffle the surface of the conversation? One answer is that we can't, as a legitimate part of the CA enterprise (and within the CA orthodoxy, there is some resistance to even attempting this endeavor). But accepting only explicit orientations to gender (or sexuality, or ethnicity) as valid objects of study has led some researchers to focus only on the most egregious instances (e.g., "speaking as a woman … ") – and we know that gendering (etc.) is much more subtle than that. For example, cultural members can invoke categories without naming them (see Wilkinson and Kitzinger 2003); and linguistically gendered terms (e.g., "husband," "girlfriend") are not always gendered interactionally – that is, they may not be *relevantly* gendered on any given occasion of use (Kitzinger 2007; Wilkinson and Kitzinger 2003). (Also – conversely – linguistically nongendered terms (e.g., "partners," "people") may sometimes be gendered interactionally: Stockill and Kitzinger 2007.) The challenge for those working in this area is to develop a technical language to specify more clearly and comprehensively what constitutes an "orientation" (and what does not).

In sum, then, CA offers the gender and language researcher a theoretical framework (social life as constituted through talk-in-interaction); a methodology (repeated inspection of recorded, naturally occurring interaction); and a cumulative set of empirical findings (the patterns, structures, and practices that constitute the basic characteristics of talk-in-interaction). Taken together, these constitute a powerful set of tools for understanding the everyday social world, including the operation of social phenomena such as power and oppression. For conversation analysts, conversation is never "just" conversation – rather, it is profoundly constitutive of social action.

NOTES

1   Indeed, CA work has shown that, overwhelmingly, incoming speakers do not start up even after completion of the *if* component of an *if–then* construction – rather, they wait for the *then* component to be completed (Kitzinger 2008a).
2   See also Hepburn and Potter (2011) for an analysis of tag questions in relation to gender.
3   Note that the word selected by the call-taker to complete the utterance – "thuh people" – is a general enough construction to embrace anyone and everyone who may have contributed to the "really challenging" circumstances surrounding the birth (and Melanie has already identified half a dozen individuals).
4   Also note that although the call-taker receipts Melanie's endorsement of her completion ("Yes," line 25); and – in response to Melanie's check – claims to understand the situation ("Yes," line 27; "I know," line 29), this is apparently not enough for Melanie – who continues to build her turn in pursuit of a more robust *display* of understanding that the challenges of her birth experience were not her fault, but the fault of the health professionals.
5   For more information about the corpus, see Shaw and Kitzinger (2005; 2007a; 2007b).
6   Although see also Kitzinger (2011) for a discussion of some of the limitations of CA in this regard.
7   Probably for this reason, a number of discourse and conversation analysts, including scholars of gender and language, have begun to incorporate elements of psychoanalysis into their work (e.g., Wetherell 2012).
8   See Kitzinger (2008a) for further discussion of this.

REFERENCES

Bucholtz, Mary. 2003. "Theories of Discourse as Theories of Gender." In Janet Holmes and Miriam Meyerhoff (eds.), *The Handbook of Language and Gender*, 43–68. Oxford: Blackwell.

Curl, Tracey S., and Paul Drew. 2008. "Contingency and Action: A Comparison of Two Forms of Requesting." *Research on Language and Social Interaction*, 41: 129–153.

Dekeyser, Mathias, Robert Elliott, and Mia Leijssen. 2011. "Empathy in Psychotherapy: Dialogue and Embodied Understanding." In Jean Decety and William Ickes (eds.), *The Social Neuroscience of Empathy*, 113–124. Cambridge, MA: MIT Press.

Drew, Paul. 1984. "Speakers' Reportings in Invitation Sequences." In J. Maxwell Atkinson and John Heritage (eds.), *Structures of Social Action*, 129–151. Cambridge: Cambridge University Press.

Goodwin, Charles. 1981. *Conversational Organization: Interaction between Speakers and Hearers*. New York: Academic Press.

Goodwin, Marjorie H. 1990. *He-Said-She-Said: Talk as Social Organization among Black Children*. Bloomington: Indiana University Press.

Guimaraes, Estefania. 2007. "Feminist Research Practice: Using Conversation Analysis to Explore the Researcher's Interaction with Participants." *Feminism & Psychology*, 17: 149–161.

Hepburn, Alexa, and Galina B. Bolden. 2013. "The Conversation Analytic Approach to Transcription." In Tanya Stivers and Jack Sidnell (eds.), *The Handbook of Conversation Analysis*, 57–76. Oxford: Blackwell.

Hepburn, Alexa, and Jonathan Potter. 2011. "Recipients Designed: Tag Questions and Gender." In Susan A. Speer and Elizabeth Stokoe (eds.), *Conversation and Gender*, 135–152. Cambridge: Cambridge University Press.

Heritage, John, and Steven Clayman. 2010. *Talk in Action: Interaction, Identities and Institutions*. Oxford: Wiley-Blackwell.

Jefferson, Gail. 1986. "Notes on 'Latency' in Overlap Onset." *Human Studies*, 9: 153–183.

Jefferson, Gail. 2004. "Glossary of Transcript Symbols with an Introduction." In Gene H. Lerner (ed.), *Conversation Analysis: Studies from the First Generation*, 13–31. Amsterdam: Benjamins.

Jefferson, Gail, Harvey Sacks, and Emanuel A. Schegloff. 1987. "Notes on Laughter in the Pursuit of Intimacy." In Graham Button and John R. E. Lee (eds.), *Talk and Social Organisation*, 152–205. Clevedon: Multilingual Matters.

Kitzinger, Celia. 2000. "Doing Feminist Conversation Analysis." *Feminism & Psychology*, 10: 163–193.

Kitzinger, Celia. 2005a. "Heteronormativity in Action: Reproducing the Heterosexual Nuclear Family in After-Hours Medical Calls." *Social Problems*, 52(4): 477–498.

Kitzinger, Celia. 2005b. "Speaking as a Heterosexual: (How) Does Sexuality Matter for Talk-in-Interaction?" *Research on Language and Social Interaction*, 38(3): 221–265.

Kitzinger, Celia. 2006. "After Post-cognitivism." *Discourse Studies*, 8(1): 67–83.

Kitzinger, Celia. 2007. "Is 'Woman' Always Relevantly Gendered?" *Gender and Language*, 1(1): 39–50.

Kitzinger, Celia. 2008a. "Developing Feminist Conversation Analysis: A Response to Wowk." *Human Studies*, 31: 179–208

Kitzinger, Celia. 2008b. "Conversation Analysis: Technical Matters for Gender Research." In Kate Harrington, Lia Litosseliti, Helen Sauntson, and Jane Sunderland (eds.), *Gender and Language Research Methodologies*, 119–138. Basingstoke: Palgrave Macmillan.

Kitzinger, Celia. 2011. "Working with Childbirth Helplines: The Contributions and Limitations of Conversation

Analysis." In Charles Antaki (ed.), *Applied Conversation Analysis: Intervention and Change in Institutional Talk*, 98–118. Basingstoke: Palgrave Macmillan.

Kitzinger, Celia, and Hannah Frith. 1999. "Just Say No? The Use of Conversation Analysis in Developing a Feminist Perspective on Sexual Refusal." *Discourse & Society*, 10(3): 293–316.

Kitzinger, Celia, and Sheila Kitzinger. 2007. "Birth Trauma: Talking with Women and the Value of Conversation Analysis." *British Journal of Midwifery*, 15(5): 256–264.

Kitzinger, Celia, and Jenny Mandelbaum. 2013. "Word Selection and Social Identities in Talk-in-Interaction." *Communication Monographs* 80(2). doi: 10.1080/03637751.2013.776171

Kitzinger, Celia, and Rose Rickford. 2007. "Becoming a 'Bloke': The Construction of Gender in Interaction." *Feminism & Psychology*, 17: 214–223.

Land, Victoria, and Celia Kitzinger. 2005. "Speaking as a Lesbian: Correcting the Heterosexist Presumption." *Research on Language and Social Interaction*, 38(4): 371–416.

Lerner, Gene H. 1991. "On the Syntax of Sentences-in-Progress." *Language in Society*, 20: 441–458.

Lerner, Gene H. 1994. "Responsive List Construction: A Conversational Resource for Accomplishing Multifaceted Social Action." *Journal of Language and Social Psychology*, 13(1): 20–33.

Lerner, Gene H. 1996a. "Finding 'Face' in the Preference Structures of Talk in Interaction." *Social Psychology Quarterly*, 59: 303–321.

Lerner, Gene H. 1996b. "On the 'Semi-permeable' Character of Grammatical Units in Conversation: Conditional Entry into the Turn Space of Another Speaker." In Elinor Ochs, Emanuel A. Schegloff, and Sandra A. Thompson (eds.), *Interaction and Grammar*, 238–276. Cambridge: Cambridge University Press.

Lerner, Gene H. 2002. "Turn-Sharing: The Choral Co-Production of Talk-in-Interaction." In Cecilia Ford, Barbara Fox, and Sandra Thompson (eds.), *The Language of Turn and Sequence*, 225–256. Oxford: Oxford University Press.

Lerner, Gene H. 2004. "Collaborative Turn Sequences." In Gene H. Lerner (ed.), *Conversation Analysis: Studies from the First Generation*, 225–256. Amsterdam: Benjamins.

Lerner, Gene H. 2013. "On the Place of Hesitating in Delicate Formulations: A Turn-Constructional Infrastructure for Collaborative Indiscretion." In Makoto Hayashi, Geoffrey Raymond and Jack Sidnell (eds.), *Conversational Repair and Human Understanding*, 95–134. Cambridge: Cambridge University Press.

Neumann, Melanie, Jozien Bensing, Stewart Mercer, Nicole Ernstmann, Oliver Ommen, and Holger Pfaff. 2009. "Analyzing the 'Nature' and 'Specific Effectiveness' of Clinical Empathy." *Patient Education and Counseling*, 74(3): 339–346.

Pomerantz, Anita. 1978. "Compliment Responses: Notes on the Co-option of Multiple Constraints." In Jim Schenkein (ed.), *Studies in the Organization of Conversational Interaction*, 79–112. New York: Academic Press.

Robinson, Jeffrey D. 2004. "The Sequential Organization of 'Explicit' Apologies in Naturally Occurring English." *Research on Language and Social Interaction*, 37(3): 291–330.

Rogers, Carl R. 1975. "Empathetic: An Unappreciated Way of Being." *Counseling Psychologist*, 5: 2–10.

Sacks, Harvey. 1992. *Lectures on Conversation*. Oxford: Blackwell.

Sacks, Harvey, Emanuel A. Schegloff, and Gail Jefferson. 1974. "A Simplest Systematics for the Organization of Turn-Taking for Conversation." *Language*, 50: 696–735.

Schegloff, Emanuel A. 2000a. "Overlapping Talk and the Organization of Turn Taking for Conversation." *Language in Society*, 29: 1–63.

Schegloff, Emanuel A. 2000b. "When 'Others' Initiate Repair." *Applied Linguistics*, 21(2): 205–243.

Schegloff, Emanuel A. 2007. *Sequence Organization in Interaction: A Primer in Conversation Analysis*, vol. 1. Cambridge: Cambridge University Press.

Schegloff, Emanuel A., Gail Jefferson, and Harvey Sacks. 1977. "The Preference for Self-Correction in the Organization of Repair in Conversation." *Language*, 53: 361–382.

Shaw, Rebecca, and Celia Kitzinger. 2005. "Calls to a Home Birth Helpline: Empowerment in Childbirth." *Social Science & Medicine*, 61: 2374–2383.

Shaw, Rebecca, and Celia Kitzinger. 2007a. "Problem Presentation and Advice-Giving on a Home Birth Helpline." *Feminism & Psychology*, 17: 203–213.

Shaw, Rebecca, and Celia Kitzinger. 2007b. "Memory in Interaction: An Analysis of Repeat Calls to a Home Birth Helpline." *Research on Language and Social Interaction*, 40: 117–144.

Shaw, Rebecca, and Celia Kitzinger. 2012. "Compliments on a Home Birth Helpline." *Research on Language and Social Interaction*, 45(3): 1–32.

Speer, Susan A. 2005. *Gender Talk: Feminism, Discourse and Conversation Analysis*. London: Routledge.

Speer, Susan A., and Richard Green. 2007. "On Passing: The Interactional Organization of Appearance Attributions in the Psychiatric Assessment of Transsexual Patients." In Victoria Clarke and Elizabeth Peel (eds.), *Out in Psychology*, 335–368. Chichester: Wiley.

Speer, Susan A., and Elizabeth Stokoe, eds. 2011. *Conversation and Gender*. Cambridge: Cambridge University Press.

Stivers, Tanya. 2007. *Prescribing under Pressure: Parent–Physician Conversations and Antibiotics*. Oxford: Oxford University Press.

Stockill, Clare, and Celia Kitzinger. 2007. "Gendered 'People': How Linguistically Non-gendered Terms Can Have Gendered Interactional Relevance." *Feminism & Psychology*, 17: 224–236.

Stokoe, Elizabeth. 2003. "Mothers, Single Women and Sluts: Gender, Morality and Membership Categorization in Neighbor Disputes." *Feminism & Psychology*, 13(3): 317–344.

Stokoe, Elizabeth. 2006. "On Ethno-methodology, Feminism, and the Analysis of Categorical Reference to Gender in Talk-in-Interaction." *Sociological Review*, 54(3): 467–494.

Stokoe, Elizabeth. 2010a. "'I'm Not Gonna Hit a Lady': Conversation Analysis, Membership Categorization and Men's Denials of Violence towards Women." *Discourse & Society*, 21(1): 1–24.

Stokoe, Elizabeth. 2010b. "Gender, Conversation Analysis, and the Anatomy of Membership Categorization Practices." *Social and Personality Psychology Compass*, 4(7): 428–438.

Stokoe, Elizabeth, and Ann Weatherall, eds. 2002. "Gender, Language, Conversation Analysis and Feminism" (special issue). *Discourse & Society*, 13(6).

Te Molder, Hedwig, and Jonathan A. Potter, eds. 2005. *Conversation and Cognition*. Cambridge: Cambridge University Press.

West, Candace. 1979. "Against Our Will: Male Interruptions of Females in Cross-Sex Conversations." *Annals of the New York Academy of Sciences*, 327: 81–97.

Wetherell, Margaret. 2012. *Affect and Emotion: A New Social Science Understanding*. London: Sage.

Wilkinson, Sue. 2011a. "Constructing Ethnicity Statistics in Talk-in-Interaction: Producing the 'White European'." *Discourse & Society*, 22(3): 343–361.

Wilkinson, Sue. 2011b. "Improving Ethnic Monitoring on a Telephone Helpline." In Charles Antaki (ed.), *Applied Conversation Analysis: Intervention and Change in Institutional Talk*, 75–97. Basingstoke: Palgrave Macmillan.

Wilkinson, Sue. 2011c. "Gender, Routinization and Recipient Design." In Susan A. Speer and Elizabeth Stokoe (eds.), *Conversation and Gender*, 112–134. Cambridge: Cambridge University Press.

Wilkinson, Sue, and Celia Kitzinger. 2003. "Constructing Identities: A Feminist Conversation Analytic Approach to Positioning in Action." In Rom Harre and Fathali Moghaddam (eds.), *The Self and Others*, 157–180. Westport, CT: Praeger.

Wilkinson, Sue, and Celia Kitzinger. Forthcoming. "Empathy as an Interactional Achievement: The Use of 'Collaborative Completion' in Telephone Helpline Talk."

Zimmerman, Don, and Candace West. 1975. "Sex Roles, Interruptions, and Silences in Conversation." In Barrie Thorne and Nancy Henley (eds.), *Language and Sex: Difference and Dominance*, 105–129. Rowley, MA: Newbury House.

8 Gender and Categorial Systematics

ELIZABETH STOKOE AND FREDERICK ATTENBOROUGH

1. Introduction

Membership categorization analysis (MCA) represents an ethnomethodological approach to data analysis, and, more or less explicitly, to the theorization of gender. At such an abstract level of philosophical principles, it is not difficult to see the family resemblances shared between MCA and conversation analysis (CA; see Wilkinson and Kitzinger, Chapter 7 in this volume). When we descend to the level of empirical practicalities, however, the two approaches are often framed differently. Whereas CA is understood as a systematic method for studying structural features of talk and interaction across large conversational data corpora, MCA tends to be viewed as a method solely for the study of specific categorial features of talk and interaction within particular case studies of distinct settings. In this chapter, however, we explore MCA as a method for interrogating the systematic ways in which gender, as an everyday members' category, is invoked, given meaning, and sustained in various spoken and textual forms of social interaction. To this end, the chapter begins with a discussion of recent developments within MCA and how they allow for the possibility not just of a *categorial systematics*, but of a categorial systematics that can contribute to the project of language and gender studies. A practical, step-by-step explanation of how to do categorial systematics is then followed by three case studies that exemplify the method in use. In this way, the chapter shows that and how MCA works as a corpus-based approach which, like CA, can use collections of naturally occurring data to reveal people's discourse practices for accomplishing social action.

2. Membership Categorization, Conversation Analysis, and Gender

One of the most controversial debates in the field of gender and language studies over recent years has centered on a question of epistemology: how can we, as

The Handbook of Language, Gender, and Sexuality, Second Edition.
Edited by Susan Ehrlich, Miriam Meyerhoff, and Janet Holmes.
© 2014 John Wiley & Sons, Inc. Published 2017 by John Wiley & Sons, Inc.

analysts, know when gender becomes relevant in and through language, text, talk, or whatever? Any answer to this question will depend largely upon whether one takes the word "relevant" to mean relevant *to us, as analysts* or relevant *to them, as participants*. Both MCA and CA have made significant contributions to the field by adopting the latter position. For ethnomethodologists, any analysis of a social category like "gender" has to be grounded in what participants themselves do and say; that is, in the categories that they deploy, rather than in what analysts take to be relevant as a function of their research questions, politics, or theory (Schegloff 1991). The analytic task for MCA and CA, in other words, is to analyze the workings of categories like gender, "not to merely use them as they are used in the world" (Jefferson 2004, 118). Interpretation is thus achieved not from *without* – by analysts deciding what is, and what is not, "relevant" – but rather, from *within* – by participants themselves who, in and as their own interaction(s), reveal to each other and to the analyst, what is, and what is not, relevant. (See also Benwell, Chapter 12, and Wilkinson and Kitzinger, Chapter 7, both in this volume, for discussion.)

This is in stark contrast to two of the main trajectories of language and gender research: studies of *gender difference* – which attempt to map sociolinguistic and interactional variables onto gender – and studies of *gender construction* – which collect the talk of women or men in interviews or natural settings, and then look at how women perform femininities and men perform masculinities. To be sure, there is much that could be written about these studies qua empirical case studies. But here, in the context of a chapter advocating an ethnomethodological position, the most relevant point is that, for both, gender stands as an analyst's, and not a participant's, category. As a consequence, categories do not get analyzed "in the activities in which they're employed" (Sacks 1992, 27), but rather, get treated as pre-theorized analysts' tools, to be mapped onto particular features of discourse data. Empirical translations of "gender as construction," for instance, tend to collect the talk of women in interviews or natural settings, before then looking at how women perform what the analyst has already defined, a priori, as "femininity" or "femininities" (Stokoe 2008). Put another way, irrespective of whether "femininities," "gender," or whatever other category, are actually getting invoked, defined, or oriented to by the participants themselves, it is the analyst, and the analyst alone, with the power to decide when "femininities," "gender," and so on are, or are not, becoming relevant in and through language. And this is problematic, allowing for analysis to slide toward reproducing, rather than actually studying, gendered "facts," stereotypes, and presumed asymmetries (see Velody and Williams 1998).

Ethnomethodological studies, however, manage to avoid this problem precisely by focusing on what it is that becomes relevant to participants qua participants. In that such studies remain indifferent to gendered explanations for patterns in particular interactional phenomena, they reveal the methodological flaws in language and gender studies that start with a priori assumptions about, for example, gender difference, gender and interruption (Kitzinger 2008; Wilkinson and Kitzinger, Chapter 7 in this volume) and tag questions (Hepburn and Potter 2011). CA, for instance, has shown how gender becomes consequentially relevant to interaction, in different sequential environments, and is invoked *by participants* in the accomplishment of particular actions, while MCA has shown how gendered "common sense" is constructed, challenged, and maintained, and how gender is realized, and made morally accountable (e.g., Eglin and Hester 1999; Stokoe 2010a; Wowk 1984). Across all of this ethnomethodological work, there is a focus on understanding members' reality analysis (Hester and Francis 1997) with regard to gender and how people constitute themselves as recognizably, take-for-grantedly, gendered, and how they resist such categorizations, or hold each other accountable for membership of that category (Stokoe 2008).

While MCA and CA are both rooted in Sacks's (1992) groundbreaking *Lectures on Conversation*, their somewhat separate trajectories have been much discussed (see Stokoe 2012a). Table 8.1 glosses the differences between the approaches. As Table 8.1 suggests, in terms of general focus and analytic approach, MCA seems to lend itself more readily than CA to the study of language and gender. Indeed, as Stokoe (e.g., 2012a) has argued, MCA gives researchers with a primary

Table 8.1. Membership categorization analysis (MCA) and conversation analysis (CA)

	Membership categorization analysis	*Conversation analysis*
General focus	Focuses on "members' methodical practices in describing *the world*, and displaying their understanding of *the world* and of the *common-sense* routine workings of *society*" (Fitzgerald, Housley, and Butler 2009, 47; emphases added)	Focuses on specifying "the normative *structuring* and *logics* of particular courses of social action and their *organization* into *systems* through which participants manage turn-taking, repair, and other *systemic* dimensions of interaction" (Heritage 2005, 104; emphases added)
Analytic approach	Focuses on the way "category work," including turn-generated "identities-for-interaction," work logically to produce moral and cultural knowledge	Focuses on systematic structural organizations in talk such as turn-taking, turn design, repair, word selection, sequence organization, action formation
Procedural issues	Works principally with case studies of distinct interactional and textual settings	Works principally and *cumulatively* across large conversational data corpora in domestic and institutional settings

interest in categorial or "topical" issues (e.g., gender, sexuality, ethnicity, identity), rather than (or alongside) sequential issues, an empirically tractable method for studying both issues in ways that solve the methodological problems of *gender difference* and *gender construction* studies. But as the procedural issues shown in Table 8.1 also suggest, MCA's contribution to the field – its potential to capture categorial issues "in flight" – has been hampered by the fact that, unlike CA, it is often treated as a *specific*, rather than a *systematic*, method of analysis. What can be said with some certainty, however, is that this treatment is rarely dictated by *epistemological*, but often by *pragmatic* concerns. To explain, we might note that in opposition to Chomskian assumptions about the "disorderliness of real talk" (e.g., Chomsky 1957), CA has long since revealed "order at all points" (Sacks 1992, 484), establishing the idea that social interaction comprises systematic practices of turn, sequence, and action. Given this, it seems safe to assume that categorization practices too will not just happen as, and in, one-off instances, and that social interaction will *also* involve the doing of systematic, consequential things with categories and categorizations, across myriad settings. The real problem, then, the reason why we are still waiting for a categorial systematics, has to do with MCA's perceived methodological inability to "capture" categorial phenomena in and as social interaction (Stokoe 2009; 2010a).

> [We cannot] simply go into the field and observe how, when, where, and with whom people talk with others about [identity] groups ... Finding data ... would amount to a search for the proverbial needle in the haystack. (van Dijk 1987, 18, 119)

> Because we cannot know in advance when a person will explicitly invoke a ... category, there is no way to plan data collection of them ... collections ... in all likelihood, would not be instances of the same interactional phenomenon. (Pomerantz and Mandelbaum 2005, 154)

What we want to suggest, however, is that these methodological problems are not irresolvable. Stokoe, for instance, has shown that by adopting a corpus-based approach to MCA, and working with collections of phenomena like CA does, the hitherto "uncapturable" is, in fact, systematically capturable (see Stokoe 2012a for an overview). The rest of this chapter explains and illustrates MCA as a method, like CA, for building a cumulative evidential basis for making claims about gender and categorial systematics.

3. Doing Membership Categorization Analysis

MCA studies work with collections of instances of categorial phenomena gathered from *different discourse contexts*, and aim to show how one may identify categories as central to *systematic discourse practices*. They may, but do not have to, start with a specific, and specifically gendered, category like, for example, "lady," "slut," "husband," and so on. In this sense, MCA shares some basic methodological steps and assumptions with corpus linguistics and collocation analysis. As with corpus linguistics, MCA rejects the Chomskian notion that real language is too messy to study, and uses naturally occurring data to pursue patterns across collections of phenomena. Both approaches can also work with large corpora of transcribed, naturally occurring talk – which may be shared across research groups and, as they are "machine-readable," are easy to search – and written texts – which may be aided by keyword or phrase-based searches of other databases such as the newspaper database *Lexus Nexus* (see Attenborough 2010). But MCA also has something in common with corpus linguistics – in that corpus linguistics examines the co-occurrence of words and phrases such that they acquire a kind of cultural and ontological solidity (e.g., "woman driver"), it is an approach that shares MCA's interest in the mundane workings of ideology (see Baker 2000), or what we might also call "culture in action" (Hester and Eglin 1997).

But if this is what it *is*, then how does one actually do it? There is an absence of "how to" guides in the research methods literature (see Stokoe 2012a). Although a number of publications include descriptions of categorization methodology (e.g., Baker 2000; Hester and Eglin 1997; Schegloff 2007a; Silverman 1998), only one textbook exists (Lepper 2000). In contrast, many CA textbooks provide step-by-step guidance. Sidnell (2010), for example, lists a number of analytic steps, and provides a number of "keys" that analysts can use to track through and define instances of CA phenomena (e.g., self-repair, transition relevance places, silence, etc.). In Table 8.2, we offer up a similarly structured "how to" guide for MCA, comprising five steps for a corpus-based approach, while Table 8.3 provides 10 keys into any data analysis (see Stokoe 2012a).

Table 8.2.   Steps in membership categorization analysis (MCA)

1   *Collect* data across different sorts of domestic and institutional settings; collect both interactional and written textual materials depending on the focus of the study. Data collection may be *purposive* (gathering together instances of particular categories because of an existing interest in that category) or *unmotivated* (noticing a category's use and pursuing it within and across multiple discourse sites).

2   *Build* collections of explicit mentions of categories (e.g., man, human, boy-racer, anarchist, teacher, etc.); membership categorization devices (e.g., "occupation," "parties to a crime," "stage of life," etc.); and category-resonant descriptions (e.g., the descriptions "she's 89 years old" and "don't be so testosterony" do not mention categories explicitly but are attributes that "convey the sense … of being deployed as categories": Schegloff 2007a, 480).

3   *Locate* the sequential position of each categorial instance with in the ongoing interaction, or within the text.

4   *Analyze* the design and action orientation of the turn or text in which the category, device, or resonant description appears.

5   *Look* for evidence that and how recipients orient to the category, device, or resonant description; for the interactional consequences of a category's use; for co-occurring component features of categorial formulations; and for the way speakers within and between turns build and resist categorizations.

Table 8.3. Keys to membership categorization analysis (MCA)

1 *Membership categorization device (MCD)* refers to the apparatus through which categories are understood to "belong" to a collective category (e.g., the categories "mommy" and "baby" are heard to belong to the MCD "family"). Categories may belong to myriad MCDs (e.g., "baby" can belong to the MCDs "stage of life" or "terms of endearment"), via various rules of application.

2 *Category-bound activities* are activities that are, in situ, linked to categories such as "Why are *men* [category] so *reluctant to go to the doctor* [activity]?" That activities and predicates are category-bound can become a resource for action. Thus people can complain about "absent activities" (e.g., if a *neighbor* [category] *plays loud music at night* [activity]; or about a *lecturer* not fulfilling obligations to a *student* [two categories in a standardized relational pair]).

3 *Standardized relational pairs* are pairs of categories that carry duties and moral obligations in relation to one another, such as "parent–child," "teacher–pupil," "neighbor–neighbor."

4 *Category-tied predicates*: A category's characteristics, such as "this *mother* [category] *cares* [predicate] tremendously for her baby." Categories, activities, and predicates do not "go together" in a decontextualized way. In other words, their "going together" "cannot simply be asserted on the analyst's authority" (Schegloff 1992, xlii), but "is achieved and is to be found in the local specifics of categorization as an activity" (Hester and Eglin 1997, 46).

   (a) Categories are "inference-rich," storing "a great deal of the knowledge that members of a society have about the society" (Sacks 1992, 40–41). For example, a particular "woman" may also be correctly categorized as a "mother," "lady," "wife," or "daughter," but each category carries a different set of category-bound activities, predicates, or rights and obligations that are expectable for an incumbent of that category to perform or possess. Categories and their inferential upshots can be implied, but not overtly stated, by mentioning some category-incumbent features.

5 *Duplicative organization* refers to categories that work in a unit or "team-like" way, having specific obligations to each other, for example, "center-forward," "goalkeeper," and "defender" in a "football team."

6 *Positioned categories* occupy a hierarchical relationship (e.g., "baby," "teenager," "adult"), such that an "adult" can be accused of behaving like a "teenager," and so on.

7 *Category-activity "puzzles"* are the result of people putting together (un)expected combinations such as "Killer Nuns!" Jokes are often built this way (e.g., "women drivers"); gendering is often marked this way (e.g., "male nurse"); and social change becomes visible as such associations diminish or are replaced or deleted (Sacks 1979).

8 *The economy rule*: A single category may be sufficient to describe a person, such as in Silverman's (2001) example of the newspaper headline "*Father* and *Daughter* in Snow Ordeal."

Table 8.3.   (*continued*)

9   *The consistency rule*: If two or more categories are used next to each other, like "father" and "daughter" in "*Father* and *Daughter* in Snow Ordeal," and both belong to a standard collection or MCD (e.g., family), then hear the people referred to as members of the same family, as each other's father and daughter (Silverman 2001).

10   *Categorization "maxims"*: As a consequence of these *rules of application*, Sacks (1992, 221, 259) derived the *hearer's maxim* for duplicatively organized categories ("if two or more categories are used to categorize two or more members of some population, and those categories can be heard as categories from the same collection, then: hear them that way") and the *viewer's maxim* for category-bound activities ("if a Member sees a category-bound activity being done, then, if one sees it being done by a member of a category to which the activity is bound, see it that way").

Having set out some key steps and concepts for doing MCA, we now move on to provide three illustrations of it in use. In each case, we worked in a similar way: one extract provided an initial "noticing" of a potential phenomenon of interest. Next, we searched our data corpora for more potential instances, analyzing each to rule it "in" or "out" of the collection. Finally, we analyzed each instance for turn design, sequential location, and action orientation. In the first example, we show how categories regularly co-occur with other component features of talk, and that the combination of these features constitutes practices for accomplishing a particular action: *accounting*. In the second section, we examine the sequential format of question–answer "adjacency pairs" and how speakers "go categorial" therein. Finally, we examine how categories can be formulated from people's names, and how such practices package and infer gendered meanings in ways that vary in their explicitness. These examples will lead into a concluding discussion about the analytic problem of relevance and the empirical warrants for making analytic, rather than analyst-driven, claims about data.

4. Example 1: Finding Patterns in Categorial Formulations

A key observation about the following collection of extracts is that Sacks's (1992) notion of the "inference-rich" nature of categories is built into categorial formulations: people treat categories *as* carrying inferential resources in the design of their turns in which categorial formulations appear. Category selection is important not only for insuring that the "right" resonances and inferences are made relevant for the object of description, but also for the "subject-side" inferences that can be made about the speaker (Edwards 2005). In the data below, participants include a "common knowledge component" (e.g., *you know?*) alongside categories, which proffers them as known-in-common. Categorial phrases function as short-cutting devices that delete the need for further unpacking. If a category-feature formulation "works" – that is, it does not become the object of repair – then it works on the basis that speakers share category knowledge and unspecified inferences enough to progress the sequence underway.

Extract 1 comes from a radio broadcast in which the presenter (I) is interviewing a pharmacist (Ph) about a scheme to sell Viagra directly to customers in high street chemists. Extract 2 comes toward the end of a telephone call between a member of the public (C) and a local council antisocial behavior officer (A). C has complained about noise and aggressive behavior from a neighbor and here she is providing an account of why it is that she cannot speak to him. Extract 3 comes from an online advice forum, in which the current poster is formulating a possible account for another poster's problematic boyfriend.

Extract 1: *Case Notes*, BBC Radio 4, September 2007

```
1   P:  A lot of men when we ta:lk to them have said I've been
2       meaning to do something about this for a:ges an' I've just
3       never got round to it, (0.2) ↑typical guy response.=re(h)ally
4       y'know.=.hh an' eventually they think w'll I really do need to
5       do something about it now.=
```

Extract 2: AC-8

```
1   C:  ='E- 'e's: it's because I won't speak to him.=*you see,*
2       it all goes back t'five years 'e offered me a lift an'
3       I wouldn't go in: you know how men [are:]=an' 'e=
4   A:                                     [Mmm.]
5   C:  =(drinks) a lot.
```

Extract 3: "Grrrrr so angry at my ex … ," *Yahoo! Answers*[1]

```
1   P:  He just needs to cool off. By the morning he will be fine and
2       will probably act as though nothing ever happened—you know
3       what men are like!
```

In extract 1, the pharmacist is midway through answering a question about the sort of person that has been coming to her for Viagra. She describes an instance of the accounts given by "a lot of men" when they ask for Viagra, using the direct reported speech of individual men ("I've been meaning to do something about this," "I've just never got round to it"). The pharmacist then formulates a categorial upshot of her description: "↑typical guy response." (line 3). In so doing, it is she – and not the analyst – that proposes that the described activities of the individual men she encounters are typical of "guys" in general. The notion that men are reluctant to go to the doctor, as a function of "hegemonic masculinity," is well documented (e.g., Seymour-Smith, Wetherell, and Phoenix 2002). However, using MCA allows us to nail down precisely phenomena that might otherwise be glossed as "discourses," and then overladen with theoretical baggage in a "what the researcher knows first," rather than a "what the participants show us" approach to analysis (see Stokoe 2010a; 2012c; Wooffitt 2005).

Returning to extract 1, "↑typical guy response." ends the turn constructional unit (TCU) that the pharmacist is currently formulating – note the falling pitch contour at the end of "response." At this point, the turn is possibly complete and, as such, is at a transition relevance place (TRP), the point at which the next speaker may legitimately start talking. However, the pharmacist rushes past the TRP to add a turn increment ("re(h)ally y'know."), keeping hold of the floor, and the interviewer does not make any response (she might have produced a "continuer" such as "Mhm"). The turn increment comprises two words, the first of which is embedded with a laughter particle "re(h)ally" and the second is the *common knowledge component* in our categorial practice ("y'know."). By using these words, the pharmacist proposes to the recipient that her description and categorial upshot are recognizable and mutually shared, as part of the ongoing maintenance of a commonly shared, objectively existing world. The "re(h)ally" component, with its little laugh, also makes relevant the speakers' shared membership of the category "women," who, by virtue of that membership also share cultural knowledge of a category's features (here, with an tongue-in-cheek stance, what men are typically like).

It is well established that radio presenters and news interviewers generally display a neutral stance toward much of what their interviewees say (cf. Clayman and Heritage 2002). This may account for why the presenter does not display shared category knowledge at the point at which it might be relevant for her to do so. In extract 2, however, there is some co-construction between speakers. At lines 1–3, C describes how she rejected an invitation from her neighbor and he responded badly ("it's because I won't speak to him.=*you see,* =it all goes back t'five years 'e offered me a lift an' I wouldn't go in:"). C then moves from a *description* of the individual man's activities, to their formulation as *categorial* and *common sense* ("you know how men are:"). At line 4, in the midst of C's account, A produces a continuer, "Mmm" (see Gardner 2002). Note its placement as C formulates the common knowledge component "you know." Here, then, is collaboration between speakers in terms of establishing some aspect of a man's behavior as typical of men in general. While this collaboration is fairly minimal (A's continuer *aligns* with C's general project of providing an account for her dispute, but does not *affiliate* or take a stance on it – for example, "oh yes, I know!": see Stivers 2008), what is important is that A does not initiate repair ("Huh?"); the continuer is located precisely to display understanding of the particular category-based point C is making. Mutual category knowledge is foundational to the smooth progress of the activities underway.

In extract 2, "you know how men are:" has an idiomatic quality, packaging and short-cutting common sense knowledge that the speakers, as members of the identity category "women," will share. What is this shared knowledge? There are infinite, defeasible, versions. It is something like the notion that men initiate and are the agents of romantic encounters, with women being in the position of saying "no" and establishing the boundaries of such encounters (see Kitzinger and Frith 1999; Wowk 1984). But the inferences of the category are not further specified, or, to be more ethnomethodologically precise, *are not further specified such that an analyst could assert them*: the categorial formulation short-cuts any further explanation as common ground is proffered and accepted. For the *participants*, however, there is enough shared category knowledge about "how men are" for the conversation to continue.

In extract 3, the same component features can be observed in written text. The online poster *describes* the possible activities of a particular man ("cooling off," "acting fine in the morning"), accounts for them as typical of the *category* "men" in general, and constructs this categorial knowledge as shared ("*you know* what men are like!"). In this online environment, there are limited possibilities for producing the sorts of "continuer" turns we observed in extract 2, and subsequent responses from original posters tend to orient to the action of the posts ("thanks for all your advice!"). Nevertheless, such materials provide further evidence for the robustness of this categorial practice, in which three coalescing components work together to formulate an idiom or idiomatic-sounding phrase (e.g., "typical guy response really, you know," "you know how men are," "you know what men are like!").

The coalescing features that comprise our target phenomena range across many other examples in many other settings (see Stokoe 2010b; 2012a; 2012b; 2012c). We have seen how categorial formulations follow descriptions of individual activities or events; that speakers treat their own or each other's descriptions as category-resonant or category-bound and, via a common knowledge component, propose that knowledge of such categories is shared, or pursued as shared. This categorial practice occurred within a particular action-oriented environment: account-giving. So, we are already starting to see how categorial phenomena fall out into patterns more readily than one might intuit.

5. Example 2: "Going Categorial" in Sequential Environments

This section addresses a fundamental CA phenomenon which has been researched extensively across numerous domestic and institutional contexts: the question–answer adjacency pair (Schegloff 2007b; for a recent review and collection of studies, see Freed and Ehrlich 2010). Within this extensive body of work, however, little, if any, attention has been paid to categorial responses to questions and their function. Yet generalizing, or "going categorial," is precisely an activity that people can seek to do when answering a question about a specific thing.

In extract 4, we return to the radio interview with the pharmacist we encountered earlier. This question–answer pair occurs just before extract 1.

Extract 4: *Case Notes*, BBC Radio 4, September 2007

```
1  I:   What sort'v people (.) have been co:ming
2       t'you.
3       (0.2)
4  Ph:  .hh we've had a: wi:de variety of ↓gentlemen
5       coming to see us:. to access the Viagra
6       thro:ugh our programme
```

The interviewer's question makes relevant a categorial answer, asking about the "sort'v people" that have visited the pharmacist. Thus the first-pair part of this question–answer adjacency pair generates a category-relevant environment and, indeed, the pharmacist responds in categorial terms: "a: wi:de variety of ↓gentlemen" have visited her pharmacy. In this way, the pharmacist's preferred response is fitted to the *wh-* question that initiates the sequence. However, in extract 5, a categorial answer is produced in response to a *wh-* question that makes relevant an account, but not necessarily a category-based account. It comes from a police interview with a suspect arrested for assault of another man.

Extract 5: PN-48

```
1  P: Why didn't you: walk off: after 'e'd 'it yuh.
2     (1.3)
3  S: .pffff uh heh i- it's a ma:le thing I s'(h)po(h)se
4     innit.
```

The question that initiates the sequence prefers a descriptive, but not necessarily categorial, account. However, S supplies a category-based response: that he did not "walk off" when his neighbor hit him because "it's a ma:le thing." S's answer treats the activity of "walking off" from a fight as problematic for a member of the category "male." In so doing, S implies that his actions were justified by virtue of "male" category incumbency.

In extracts 6–8, a particular sequential pattern can be observed in the way suspects in police interrogations supply category-based accounts after type-conforming answers to questions. In each case, the suspect has been arrested on an assault charge (for an extended treatment of these and similar extracts, see Stokoe 2010a).

Extract 6: PN-63

```
1  P: You threaten 'er at all.
2     (0.4)
3  S: No I didn't threaten 'er.
4     (1.1)
5  S: .hh I've got no reason to threaten 'e:r, I've never 'it a
6     woman in my life.=an' I never will 'it a woman in my life.
7     (0.8)
8  P: ( ) heard the front door. ((reading from statement))
```

Extract 7: PN-111b

```
1  P:  D'you think [your husband hit her¿]
2  S:              [ N- my husband ] would n:ever hit
3      a woman,
```

Extract 8: PN-61

```
1   P1:  D'y'member 'er falling down to the gro:und,
2   S:   .hhhhhhhh
3        (0.3)
4   S:   ↑M:ye:ah. >See I wer-< I was pullin' 'er u- (0.2)
5        ar- ar pullin' 'er arm t'kee- keep 'er awa:y from
6        me like.<an' I swung 'er a:rm like that.=An' don't
7        forget I'm still this ra:ge, an- (0.4) an: uh she fell
8        t- fell t- fell to the la:wn.
9        (1.1)
10  S:   But the way's not to kick a ↑wo↓man as you
11       might say.
12       (.)
13  S:   I wouldn't do that.'.shih
14       (0.8)
15  S:   Wouldn't be ri:ght (0.2) tuh- f'me to do ↓that.
16       ((papers rustl[ing))
17  P2:  [But you'd kick a bloke in the 'ead three
18       ti:mes.
```

In each instance, suspects are *denying* the actions they are accused of, or, in the case of extract 7, that their partner is accused of. The questions are formatted grammatically as yes-no interrogatives about a specific person or incident. Suspects respond with a type-conforming response ("yes" or "no") but then follow up with an account in which they supply a category-based denial (Stokoe 2009) in a "post-expansion" slot. That is, they *expand* the basic first and second pair part adjacency pair of turns in order to "go categorial." In extract 6, P asks S whether or not he "threatened" the alleged assault victim. S answers the question with a denial (line 3) before then providing an account (lines 5–6). While P's question is about a *particular* person, S's response moves from the particular to the *general* via categorization. S's account is built as three items in a list: the first attends to the police-relevant issue of "motive" and addresses the woman in question ("I've got *no reason* to threaten 'e:r,"); the second – "I've never "it a woman in my life." – addresses a generalized category ("a woman"); and the third – "I never will 'it a woman" – includes the modal term "will" (of which "would" is a past tense form). Edwards (2006, 475) has shown how, when denying a charge put to them, suspects may use such modalized declaratives to "claim a disposition to act in ways inconsistent with whatever offence they are accused of." Here, then, because S would not in general do the action he is charged with, he did not do it this time. Taken together, items 2 and 3 in the list categorize S as the kind of man who, as a part of his disposition or character, does not "hit women" *in general*. In this sense the "I" is an instance of what Jackson (2011, 31) calls a "gendered I," a self-referential pronoun which "can be rendered hearably gendered in the context of its production."

Note also, that we, as analysts, are making no inferences or claims as to what is, and is not, gender relevant. To be sure, P does not respond to S's self-categorization as the type of man who does not hit women (line 7); that is, he neither accepts nor rejects it as a piece of evidence but instead launches a new sequence about further witness testimony. But neither does P display, *to us or to S*, any trouble in recognizing the account by, say, initiating repair. The recognizability of his account rests on shared knowledge of S's pairing of a *category* with an *activity*: that "men" may "hit women." So S simultaneously recruits the culturally familiar notion that men perpetrate violence toward women (that is, there are gender-specific slots that map onto the categories "perpetrator" and "victim": see Lee 1984), and uses it to deny that he is such a man, taking up a moral stance against "men who hit women."

The same pattern can be observed in extracts 7 and 8. In extract 7, P asks S about the possible involvement of S's husband in the assault of another woman. S's account, like the suspect's account in extract 6, constructs a recognizable category–activity combination (that of "men" + "hitting" + "women"), but uses it to deny that her husband hit their neighbor because he is the kind of man who "would n:ever hit a woman,." Similarly, in extract 8, the suspect produces an account for his type-confirming denial: "But the way's not to kick a ↑wo↓man as you might say. (.) I wouldn't ↑do th:at.." S moves away from a general, scripted claim ("the way's … ,": cf. Edwards 1994) to a specific one ("I wouldn't … "), pairing "wouldn't" with a generalized formulation of the gender category "a ↑wo↓man," rather than the particular woman he is accused of kicking. S then reiterates his denial: "Wouldn't be ri:ght. (0.2) to: f'me to do ↓that." In his follow-up question, P2 invokes S's denial: "But you'd kick a bloke in the 'ead three ti:mes," which S does not challenge. Note that P also uses a generalized gender category "a bloke" here, that orients to "a woman" as a member of a contrastive relational pair: as participants, both S and P are therefore oriented to the same MCD. Here, then, S admits assaulting another "man," but denies assaulting a "woman," making his own gender identity relevant. Such a denial works on the basis that assaulting members of *equivalent* categories – with regards to power, physical strength, and vulnerability – is a more morally acceptable action than assaulting members of relatively "weaker" categories (see Stokoe 2009, on "young" suspects' denials of assaulting "old" people). In other words, S constructs "man" and "woman" as positioned categories. Note the way S's denial is built: it starts with "But the way's" and ends with "as you might say." These parts of the turn work to formulate the middle bit, "not to kick a↑wo↓man" as common sense and idiomatic, and, as such, reality-constructing with regards to the asymmetrical organization of a culture's categories: there are "hittable men and unhittable women," "men who do and do not hit women." In this sense, MCA offers not just a commentary on the sequential structures of, here, police interrogation, but also, and in addition, an insight into "culture in action" (Hester and Eglin 1997).

6. Example 3: Names as Categories

The first two examples summarized published research that showed systematic ways of working with categories. In the final section, we show explicitly how initial noticings about potential phenomena may be built by considering a third type of categorial phenomena that we are currently pursuing across different datasets including the newspaper archive *Lexus Nexus*. This work started with two data extracts from different sources, and a noticing about the way people's names may be used to do categorial work. The first example comes from a mediation meeting between three disputing neighbours – C1, C2 and C3 – and a mediator – M1 – who is attempting to help resolve matters. C1 and C3 have been involved in a long dispute about communal garden space. C1 maintains that the plants C3 has added are "spiky" and, as such, "dangerous." However, we join the meeting at a point where C3 is introducing a potentially new element to the dispute.

Extract 9: NM:RT

```
1   C3:   But uh: can I say this[:: uh: when we[:: moved-]=
2   M1:                         [Yeh?
3   C1:                                      [ Um: it's]=
4   C3:   =[first move]d i:n, and uh: (1.2) I:: remember (0.3)=
5   C1:   =[dangerous Joe.]
6   C3:   =~uh:~ having a word with Gary about something he accu:sed me
7         of being uh- (0.5) like a Barbra <Strei:sand.>
```

At line 7, C3 describes C1's alleged "accusation" of her being like "a Barbra <Strei:sand.>." Note the use of the indefinite article "a," which formulates the name as a category. At this point, we know from the formulation "accu:sed" that C3 is intending her description to be hearable, by C1 – and no doubt by M1 too – as a description of an insult. As analysts we do not have to intuit this; on the contrary, C1 is displaying this, in and through her talk, to us, herself, and to her co-interactants. That much is obvious. But what is less obvious is what it is about being "a Barbra <Strei:sand.>" that C3 is attempting to treat as an insult. Again, as analysts, we might note that, in any other context, getting described as "a Barbra <Strei:sand.>" might be something reportable as a compliment: Barbra Streisand is, after all, "famous," a "singer," an "actor," and so on. Thus the features that are being associated with the category "Barbra <Strei:sand.>," such that it is treatable as an insult, need further unpacking. But – and this is crucial – it is not us, as analysts, who need to perform this task. The extract continues as follows:

```
8   C3:   ... which meant I must be aggressive: (0.5) Jewish, (0.3)
9         which I am neither,
```

As we can see, C3 goes on to display her own understanding in and through her own talk, formulating the categorial features she takes C1 to have implied through the use of "Barbra <Strei:sand.>" as a category that carries specific inferences.

The first point to note here is this: a name, an "I," is being used as a peg upon which participants are able to hang their own understandings of what that someone does, in their opinion, stand for. Indeed, where Goffman (1959) once wrote of "the body" as a peg upon which an identity of collaborative manufacture may be hung, here we are claiming that same function for "the proper noun." Second, and relatedly, there is the methodological issue of relevance. It is not us, as analysts, seeking to interpret what might have been meant by C3. On the contrary, we simply follow the interactants: "Barbra <Strei:sand.>" is given meaning reflexively and indexically, in and through their action-accomplishing practices. The speakers' categorial reasoning is made explicit for, and to, us: it does not mean what we might infer it to mean, but rather, what C3 meant, and then showed us that she meant.

So far we have dealt with naming as a categorial phenomenon that can be achieved in and as the actions of participants qua participants. But what, now, of the systematic capturability of such phenomena? While one of us (Stokoe) was analyzing mediation materials drawn from a large data corpus, the other (Attenborough) was using *Lexus Nexus* to analyze the various objectifying ways in which physicist Laura Grant was represented as a *"celebrity physicist"* across the British print press (see Attenborough 2011). While conducting this work, Attenborough noticed one particular newspaper headline.

Extract 10: *Sunday Times*, March 2, 2008

```
1  The Nigella of science
```

As with extract 9, we find a name, "Nigella," getting used as a category, that is, as a peg upon which a host of as yet unspecified meanings may be being hung as a component part of a newspaper headline that readers are presumed to be able to unpack. So what, then, is the name-as-category "Nigella" intended to achieve? In one sense, its comprehensibility depends on the reader knowing that "Nigella" refers to a person, not the small spicy seed, and that it also refers to "Nigella Lawson," the British television chef. The precise category-bound meanings are unspecified here, at least in the headline. And yet, in another sense, the journalist-as-participant-in-this-categorizing-work, is demonstrating to us, herself, and to her readership, that "Nigella" *does* have a particular set of meanings. For once we get beyond the headline, we find that the text unpacks what it means for Grant to be a "Nigella": Grant is described as wearing "white lab coats, safety goggles – and killer heels," as being "the femme fatale of physics" and "a 28 year-old beauty with a brain," and as "getting teenagers all steamed up over science." If we wish to understand who Grant really is, this name-as-category leaves us in little doubt: she is, metaphorically, the category "Nigella," and the category "Nigella" has been manufactured such that it represents a body, and, most importantly, a *gendered* body.

But note: this is not a one-off instance. It is not, in other words, an example of Van Dijk's "proverbial needle in the haystack" (1987, 119). Although, as Pomerantz and Mandelbaum rightly suggest, "we cannot know in advance when a person will explicitly invoke a category," it does not necessarily follow that "there is no way to plan data collection of them" (2005, 154). The trick is in the initial noticing. In this case, noticing "the Nigella of Science" allowed us to pursue an unmotivated form of data collection (step 1 of our Steps in MCA: Table 8.2). The classificatory power of a search engine like *Lexus Nexus* subsequently allowed us to build collections of explicit mentions of this particular name-as-category (step 2). Here, then, are two further examples from these collections in which "Nigella" gets used as a category with which to describe some other in an article's headline, before the intended categorial inferences are unpacked in the main body of the text.

Extract 11: *Daily Mail*, August 12, 2007

```
1   The Indian Nigella who has outsold Harry Potter
2   Her cut-glass accent and flirtatious on-camera manner
3   have led to her being dubbed the "Indian Nigella"
```

Extract 12: *Express*, September 17, 2007

```
1   Ramsay's Tana wants to be a dish like Nigella
2   ..."I'll never have that 'Nigella' quality. She is a star.
3   I love her. She manages to look ravishing in just about anything.
4   She could turn up in a pair of jeans and old shirt and still look
5   sexy..."
```

"Being a dish," "cut-glass accent," "flirtatious manner," "looking ravishing": if gender is being made relevant here, then in extracts 11 and 12 it is never quite the same kind of relevance that becomes relevant: each category-bound feature is slightly different, not quite synonymous. What we see here is the power of categories to imply things that may or may not be evidenced empirically: categories work on the basis that meanings can be implied, but the producer of the text is not accountable for any specific meaning. But this is where MCA finds its métier. If a name as category is akin to a peg upon which people can hang their own understanding(s) of what that named person does, is, or stands for, then there are potentially limitless facets to, and uses for, such a category. It is both the potential and the promise of a systematic, rather than merely specific, MCA to understand that and how this can happen in ways that invoke, orient to, define, manipulate, and so on, gender.

7. Gender and Categorial Systematics

In this chapter, we have described and illustrated MCA as a method for interrogating "gender." Our empirical examples have demonstrated two things: first, how order can be found in the intuitively "messy" discourse phenomenon of membership categories; and second, how it is possible to approach their analysis systematically such that they may be studied as robust features of particular action-oriented environments. Crucially, gender categories did not start out as (our) analysts' categories: we did not use "gender" to explain the presence of particular actions, or make tenuous assertions about the relevant activities and predicates that are bound to it. Across the different analytic sections, we have seen how speakers invoke, produce, sustain, and/or resist a category's situated meanings. We can see "what counts," in our examples, as gendered attributes and actions. As categories hove interactionally and textually into view, they are given a taken-for-granted and enduring veracity. Our suggestion, therefore, is that it is possible to study the gendered topics of social science, such as health, violence, dating, and so on, as tenacious everyday practices, rather than as analysts' topics. In so doing, we offer a robust view of the gendered world and its maintenance in discourse.

MCA can, therefore, give analysts a warrantable method for making claims about "the world" and its categorial arrangements. Our suggestion is that, not "by their nature," but in their empirical use, categories short-cut and package common sense knowledge about category members and their actions. That is, by building into categorial formulations devices for saying "there is more to this category than I need to describe here" (a common knowledge component; an idiomatic quality), and by observing that such formulations are often collaboratively built between parties, the inference-rich nature of categories is, in fact, an endogenous orientation of those parties. Building large, multimodal, and multisetting data sets enables this kind of systematic, corpus-based MCA. Furthermore, juxtaposing data extracts from disparate settings that nevertheless contain the component and sequential features, builds our understanding of the social world, social order, and social categories. Overall, then, we hope that this chapter provides a framework of procedures for, and examples of, MCA that will stimulate further, and systematic, studies of the gendered categories that exist within everyday domestic, institutional, and virtual lives.

NOTE

1 At http://uk.answers.yahoo.com/question/index?qid=20100409150215AATGftd, accessed November 6, 2013.

REFERENCES

Attenborough, Frederick. 2010. "'A Novel Coronavirus was Isolated from Patients': Recovering the Intricacies of Practice from Textual Accounts of the 2003 Severe Acute Respiratory Syndrome (SARS) Outbreak." *Medical Sociology Online*, 5(1): 2–15.

Attenborough, Frederick. 2011. "Complicating the Sexualisation Thesis: The Media, Gender and 'Sci-candy.'" *Discourse & Society*, 22(6): 659–676.

Baker, Carolyn D. 2000. "Locating Culture in Action: Membership Categorization in Texts and Talk." In Alison Lee and Cate Poynton (eds.), *Culture and Text: Discourse and Methodology in Social Research and Cultural Studies*, 99–113. London: Routledge.

Chomsky, Noam. 1957. *Syntactic Structures*. The Hague: Mouton de Gruyter.

Clayman, Steve, and John Heritage. 2002. *The News Interview: Journalists and Public*

Figures on the Air. Cambridge: Cambridge University Press.

Edwards, Derek. 1994. "Script Formulations: A Study of Event Descriptions in Conversation." *Journal of Language and Social Psychology*, 13(3): 211–247.

Edwards, Derek. 2005. "Moaning, Whinging and Laughing: The Subjective Side of Complaints." *Discourse Studies*, 7(1): 5–29.

Edwards, Derek. 2006. "Facts, Norms and Dispositions: Practical Uses of the Modal Would in Police Interrogations." *Discourse Studies*, 8(4): 475–501.

Eglin, Peter, and Stephen Hester. 1999. " 'You're All a Bunch of Feminists!': Categorization and the Politics of Terror in the Montreal Massacre." *Human Studies*, 22: 253–272.

Fitzgerald, Richard, William Housley, and Carly Butler. 2009. "Omnirelevance and Interactional Context." *Australian Journal of Communication*, 36(3): 45–64.

Freed, Alice F., and Susan Ehrlich, eds. 2010. *"Why do You Ask?" The Function of Questions in Institutional Discourse*. Oxford: Oxford University Press.

Gardner, Rod. 2002. *When Listeners Talk: Response Tokens and Recipient Stance with Special Reference to "Mm."* Amsterdam: Benjamins.

Goffman, Erving. 1959. *The Presentation of Self in Everyday Life*. New York: Doubleday Anchor.

Hepburn, Alexa, and Jonathan Potter. 2011. "Recipients Designed: Tag Questions and Gender." In Susan Speer and Elizabeth Stokoe (eds.), *Conversation and Gender*, 135–152. Cambridge: Cambridge University Press.

Heritage, John. 2005. "Conversation Analysis and Institutional Talk." In Kristine L. Fitch and Robert E. Sanders (eds.), *Handbook of Language and Social Interaction*, 103–147. Mahwah, NJ: Lawrence Erlbaum.

Hester, Stephen, and Peter Eglin, eds. 1997. *Culture in Action: Studies in Membership Categorization Analysis*. Boston: International Institute for Ethnomethodology and University Press of America.

Hester, Stephen, and David Francis. 1997. "Reality Analysis in a Classroom Storytelling." *British Journal of Sociology*, 48(1): 95–112.

Jackson, Clare. 2011. "The Gendered 'I.' " In Susan Speer and Elizabeth Stokoe (eds.), *Conversation and Gender*, 31–47. Cambridge: Cambridge University Press.

Jefferson, Gail. 2004. "A Note on Laughter in 'Male–Female' Interaction." *Discourse Studies*, 6: 117–133.

Kitzinger, Celia. 2008. "Conversation Analysis: Technical Matters for Gender Research." In Kate Harrington, Lia Litosseliti, Helen Saunston, and Jane Sunderland (eds.), *Gender and Language Research Methodologies*, 119–138. Basingstoke: Palgrave Macmillan.

Kitzinger, Celia, and Hannah Frith. 1999. "Just Say No? The Use of Conversation Analysis in Developing a Feminist Perspective on Sexual Refusal." *Discourse & Society*, 10(3): 293–316.

Lee, John. 1984. "Innocent Victims and Evil-Doers." *Women's Studies International Forum*, 7(1): 69–73.

Lepper, Georgia. 2000. *Categories in Text and Talk*. London: Sage.

Pomerantz, Anita, and Jenny Mandelbaum. 2005. "Conversation Analytic Approaches to the Relevance and Uses of Relationship Categories in Interaction." In Kristine L. Fitch and Robert E. Sanders (eds.), *Handbook of Language and Social Interaction*, 149–171. Mahwah, NJ: Lawrence Erlbaum.

Sacks, Harvey. 1979. "A Revolutionary Category: Hotrodder." In George Psathas (ed.), *Everyday Language: Studies in Ethnomethodology*, 7–14. New York: Irvington.

Sacks, Harvey. 1992. *Lectures on Conversation*, vols. 1 and 2, ed. Gail Jefferson. Oxford: Blackwell.

Schegloff, Emanuel A. 1991. "Reflections on Talk and Social Structure." In Deirdre Boden and Don Zimmerman (eds.), *Talk and Social Structure*, 44–70. Berkeley: University of California Press.

Schegloff, Emanuel A. 1992. "Introduction." In Harvey Sacks, *Lectures on Conversation*, ed. Gail Jefferson, ix–lxii. Oxford: Blackwell.

Schegloff, Emanuel A. 2007a. "A Tutorial on Membership Categorization." *Journal of Pragmatics*, 39: 462–482.

Schegloff, Emanuel A. 2007b. *Sequence Organization in Interaction: A Primer in Conversation Analysis*. Cambridge: Cambridge University Press.

Seymour-Smith, Sarah, Margaret Wetherell, and Ann Phoenix. 2002. " 'My Wife Ordered Me to Come!' A Discursive Analysis of Doctors' and Nurses' Accounts of Men's Use of General Practitioners." *Journal of Health Psychology*, 7(3): 253–267.

Sidnell, Jack. 2010. *Conversation Analysis: An Introduction*. Oxford: Wiley-Blackwell.

Silverman, David. 1998. *Harvey Sacks: Social Science and Conversation Analysis*. Cambridge: Polity.

Silverman, David. 2001. *Interpreting Qualitative Data: Methods for Analysing Talk, Text and Interaction*. London: Sage.

Stivers, Tanya. 2008. "Stance, Alignment, and Affiliation during Storytelling: When Nodding is a Token of Affiliation." *Research on Language and Social Interaction*, 41(1): 31–57.

Stokoe, Elizabeth. 2008. "Categories and Sequences: Formulating Gender in Talk-in-Interaction." In Kate Harrington, Lia Litosseliti, Helen Saunston, and Jane Sunderland (eds.), *Gender and Language Research Methodologies*, 139–157. Basingstoke: Palgrave Macmillan.

Stokoe, Elizabeth. 2009. "Doing Actions with Identity Categories: Complaints and Denials in Neighbour Disputes." *Text and Talk*, 29(1): 75–97.

Stokoe, Elizabeth. 2010a. " 'I'm not Gonna Nit a Lady': Conversation Analysis, Membership Categorization and Men's Denials of Violence towards Women." *Discourse & Society*, 21(1): 1–24.

Stokoe, Elizabeth. 2010b. "Gender, Conversation Analysis, and the Anatomy of Membership Categorization Practices." *Social and Personality Psychology Compass*, 4(7): 428–438.

Stokoe, Elizabeth. 2012a. "Moving Forward with Membership Categorization Analysis: Methods for Systematic Analysis." *Discourse Studies*, 14(3): 277–303.

Stokoe, Elizabeth. 2012b. "Categorial Systematics." *Discourse Studies*, 14(3): 345–354

Stokoe, Elizabeth. 2012c. " 'You Know How Men Are': Description, Categorization and the Anatomy of a Categorial Practice." *Gender and Language*, 6(1): 231–253.

van Dijk, Teun. 1987. *Communicating Racism: Ethnic Prejudice in Thought and Talk*. London: Sage.

Velody, Irving, and Robin Williams, eds. 1998. *The Politics of Constructionism*. London: Sage.

Wooffitt, Robin. 2005. *Conversation Analysis and Discourse Analysis: A Comparative and Critical Introduction*. London: Sage.

Wowk, Maria T. 1984. "Blame Allocation, Sex and Gender in a Murder Interrogation." *Women's Studies International Forum*, 7: 75–82.

9 Feminist Critical Discourse Analysis

Relevance for Current Gender and Language Research

MICHELLE M. LAZAR

1. Introduction

Relations of power have been changing over the last decades in various countries and communities, arising from important social changes. In some societies, some women can now make greater decisions about sexual reproduction, and have access to education and paid employment; a few have broken through the metaphoric glass ceiling. Blatant gender discrimination is not as widespread in some educational settings, workplaces, and the media, and more women have achieved legal rights (Lazar and Kramarae 2011).

Yet most women throughout the world are still bunched together in the same types of occupations, receive lower wages than men for the same jobs, encounter more difficulty obtaining promotion and leadership positions, and do most of the housework and care for children and the elderly. Even in societies where there is legislation against overt forms of sexism, gender-based discrimination, sexual harassment, and physical violence against women are commonplace. Where cyberspace was once considered a potentially democratic, "neutral" platform for women with access to participation on an equal footing with men, studies have shown that gender asymmetries in face-to-face interactions have carried over and that women, particularly, have been targets for cyber-bullying (Herring and Stoerger, Chapter 29 in this volume; Herring, Johnson, and DiBeneditto 2011; Taylor, Kramarae, and Ebben 1993).

Gender asymmetries are materially as well as symbolically enacted, explicitly in some contexts, implicitly in others. The fact remains that women (and men), globally, continue to "live with patriarchy" (cf. Majstorovic and Lassen 2011), albeit enacted and experienced, in various forms and extents across different social

The Handbook of Language, Gender, and Sexuality, Second Edition.
Edited by Susan Ehrlich, Miriam Meyerhoff, and Janet Holmes.
© 2014 John Wiley & Sons, Inc. Published 2017 by John Wiley & Sons, Inc.

contexts. Some scholars, in fact, have commented on increasing inequality in this time of "neoliberal free-for-all" (Williams 2006, 457), while others have noted the emergence of indirect but no less grievous forms of sexism (S. Mills 2008). At the same time, in many industrialized societies today, there appears a general inability or reluctance to recognize and identify "patriarchy" – the systemic gendering of privilege and inequality – as existing in one's community or as personally relevant.

Several kinds of disavowal are evident. The first kind is generational, and particularly prevalent in contemporary popular culture and media discourses, which suggests that we are now living in a "postfeminist" era in which sexism (and feminism) is passé. Postfeminist media representations are purportedly gender-equal or pro-women in depicting young women as visible and active in the public sphere, and as powerful in all kinds of situations (Gill 2003; Lazar 2006), and so question the relevance of a feminist critique of sexism today.

Where sexism and patriarchy are acknowledged, these are seen to apply in contexts elsewhere and not one's own. Along with generational distancing, this is a second kind of disavowal based on geographical or cultural "othering." For instance, the view that "patriarchy" as a construct is applicable insofar as it describes gender inequalities in the so-called "third world," but not in "first-world" societies, including Singapore, is commonly held by my students in Singapore. Cultural othering of patriarchy is observed in the West, too, regarding gender relations among non-Western migrant communities.

Forsberg (2010) noted a third kind of disavowal among some white, middle-class men in the West, for whom "hegemonic masculinity" was a notion that referred to "other" men, and not themselves. Forsberg commented that there was a lack of connection in such men's individual biographies to public issues, which allowed them to "feel sufficiently comfortable, appear as progressive and gender-equal, but without facing their own participation in maintaining patriarchy" (2010, 4).

Finally, even among feminists in academia, some "third-wave" feminists have rejected the terms "patriarchy" and "sexism" as outdated analytical categories (see S. Mills 2008). In language and gender studies, too, some have begun to question the legitimacy of a focus on gender (and gender inequality) in feminist research: Is gender relevant? (Holmes 2005; Swann 2002; Wodak 2008). Although the motivation for asking this varies from study to study, the raising of such a question is telling of the times. Whereas feminists had earlier lamented on the "gender undersensitivity" in mainstream research (see Alvesson and Billing 2009; Spender 1981), there is now a cautiousness about "gender oversensitivity," that is reading "gender" into every situation, even where other identities might be more relevant in given contexts. Notwithstanding that this invites important theoretical and methodological self-reflection, read against the wider climate of disavowing the relevance of gender issues, we feminists might inadvertently contribute toward the emergence of a new gender undersensitivity.

In sum, although on the one hand major power imbalances in terms of gender continue to exist in systematic and predictable ways, on the other hand there appears a tendency to disclaim "sexism" and "patriarchy" as antiquated, or as not directly or personally relevant to individuals. Kelan (2007), for instance, noticed that people may be less willing or able to articulate the reasons for these imbalances, and often suggest that gender is irrelevant to them, and that reasons other than sexism account for injustices and continued gender inequality.

It is against this backdrop of the remarkable persistence of gender inequality (albeit taking different and newer forms), yet at the same time a tendency toward critical inertia that a feminist critical discourse analysis (FCDA) has much work to do. In what follows, I present FCDA as a critical feminist perspective for contemporary language and gender research, and develop the key principles of FCDA that I outlined earlier (Lazar 2005a; 2007).

2. Feminist Critical Discourse Analysis

FCDA is a perspective that seeks to examine the complex, subtle, and sometimes not so subtle ways in which frequently taken-for-granted gendered assumptions and power asymmetries get discursively produced, sustained, negotiated, and contested in specific communities and discourse contexts. With a focus on social justice and transformation, the aim is to challenge discourses that entrench gendered social arrangements that work toward a closure of possibilities for women and men as human persons.

FCDA as a critical perspective has developed at the intersection of critical discourse analysis (CDA) and feminist studies, both of which are guided by goals of social emancipation and transformation. Unlike feminist approaches that work with descriptive discourse analytic methods, FCDA has the advantage of operating, at the outset, within a politically invested, socially explanatory program of discourse analysis. CDA has developed a variety of theoretical frameworks for the study of the relationships between social practices and discourse structures (see Wodak and Meyer 2009), and offers a wide range of analytical "tools" for detailed analysis of contextualized texts and talk. Further, there is much to gain from CDA research that documents a variety of discursive strategies employed in the enactment of diverse forms of social inequality. Drawing on CDA for feminist purposes, therefore, has the potential for producing rich and insightful analyses.

FCDA, however, cannot simply be the application of existing CDA frameworks in a cookie-cutter fashion for the study of gender. There is a difference, I suggest, between using CDA to study gender and a *feminist* critical discourse analysis. Whereas the study of gender using CDA suggests that the theories and methods of a CDA approach remain unchanged, except that the object of study happens to be "gender," FCDA is fundamentally driven by developments in critical feminist theory and practice, and shaped by a "feminist political imagination" (Bell 1999).

The notion of a "feminist imagination" derives from Charles Wright Mills' classical concept of the "sociological imagination," which aims to connect individual experiences with societal relations and "translate private troubles into public issues" (C. W. Mills 2000 [1959], 187, quoted in Forsberg 2010). Not only does this resonate with the famous feminist maxim "the personal is political"; central to a feminist imagination (unlike Mills' conceptualization) is a political struggle for social change. In the feminist political imagination, "gender" becomes a radical issue and relies on feminist theory to continue its radical critique of dominant discourses on gender (de Lauretis 1987). Studying gender, therefore, is a political choice (Majstorovic and Lassen 2011, 4).

This has implications for the interdisciplinarity of FCDA. In terms of its theoretical inspirations, FCDA not only inherits, historically, its critical impetus from the Frankfurt School via CDA, but it draws upon contemporary feminist theorization, which includes feminist poststructuralism and postcolonialism. The theoretical interdisciplinarity of FCDA, therefore, places it in a position to undertake analyses of discursive enactments of structural domination (the type CDA is well known for), as much as analyses of discursive strategies of negotiation, resistance, solidarity, and social empowerment of disenfranchised women (a type of analysis that remains underdeveloped within CDA). FCDA's theoretical eclecticism also makes it possible to draw upon feminists' uptake on Foucault's theories, as well as take on board feminist intersectionality theories that call attention both to individuals' multiple identities and the diversity among "women" (and "men").

The interdisciplinary character of FCDA is inevitable. Even as we critique discourses of gender inequality, there is a need to recognize and analyze the conditions that enable these asymmetrical relations to prevail, and why patriarchy is so resilient. As Acker (2006) notes, there is still no convincing explanation for the remarkable persistence and stability of gender inequality. Collaboration, therefore, is necessary among discourse analysts and social researchers from many other disciplines, such as sociology, economics, anthropology, political science, and law. Only by working together can parts of the complex problem be understood and considered interventions proposed (Lazar and Kramarae 2011).

Although FCDA (or for that matter CDA) has received relatively marginal attention in language and gender studies, since the publication of the volume explicitly titled *Feminist Critical Discourse Analysis* (2005a), there has been a growing recognition of a *feminist* CDA perspective. Over the past few years, I have received a good number of correspondences, reviewed articles for journals, and read published works (e.g., Makoni 2013; Marling 2010; Nguyen 2011) which refer explicitly to a FCDA perspective. It is noteworthy, also, that debate *within* FCDA has surfaced (see Wodak 2008), indicating that it is a perspective that takes itself (as it is being taken) seriously.

3. Key Principles of FCDA

In this section, key (interrelated) principles of a feminist perspective of CDA are discussed. The discussion develops my earlier articulations of FCDA as theory and practice.

3.1   Feminist analytical activism

A central concern for FCDA is a critical analysis of discourses which sustain a gendered social order in which some people, by virtue of being "men," are accorded
privileges systemically, and others, by virtue of being "women" are routinely
disadvantaged, excluded, and not taken seriously. FCDA, like CDA, takes the view
that social practices are reflected in as well as constituted by discourse (Fairclough
1992, *passim*), but also takes it a step further by arguing that many social practices,
far from being "neutral," are in fact deeply gendered. Studies on organizational
and workplace cultures, for instance, have documented how naturalized and
deep-seated androcentric assumptions are in these institutional practices (Holmes
2005; Chapter 22 in this volume; Martin-Rojo and Esteban 2005). The accepted
communicative style of power and authority in the public sphere is decidedly
masculine (e.g., in terms of tone of voice, intonation in giving orders, and use
of direct speech acts), which makes it difficult for women (especially in senior
management positions) to get their communicative styles "right" and to be taken
seriously. The challenge lies in the fact that androcentrism frequently assumes
the status of universality, rationality, and impartiality, all of which contribute
to conventionally understood notions of "professionalism" and authority in the
public sphere.

Although feminist political critique of gendered social practices and relations is aimed at effecting social emancipation and transformation, these are
not once-and-for-all accomplishments. Rather, they are a continuous striving,
guided by a feminist humanist vision of a just society, in which gender does not
predetermine or mediate our relationships with others, and our sense of who we
are or might become (Grant 1993; Hill Collins 1990). The goal is toward constantly
imagining and opening up ways of "doing" and "becoming" that are more socially
inclusive and respectful of all persons.

The ongoing struggle against patriarchal modes of thought and discrimination
might be better understood and confronted by maintaining what hooks describes
as "an openness of conviction, a 'radical openness,' in voicing critique and in forming communities of resistance" (hooks 1984, 149). FCDA offers an openness of
conviction in voicing critique through the analysis of discourse that shows up the
workings of power and ideology that sustain hierarchical gender relations. Insofar
as feminist discourse scholars are engaged in critique of this sort, we are forming
communities of analytical resistance and activism.

The radical emancipatory agenda of FCDA makes it a praxis-oriented research
that is based on a dialectical relationship between theory and practice (Lather 1986),
which mobilizes theory in order to create critical awareness and develop feminist
strategies for resistance and change. The imbrication of power and ideology in
discourse is sometimes not apparent to participants involved in particular social
practices as it is from the vantage point of critical theorization of their interrelations
(Fairclough, Mulderrig, and Wodak 2011; Kress 1990). To speak from the position of
a "woman" then is not the same as speaking from the political perspective of a feminist subject. To know as a "woman" *means* to know from the ideological perspective

of gender. However, a feminist subject is one who has a "doubled vision" in that she is at the same time both inside and outside the ideology of gender, and is conscious of the twofold pull, which allows her to have a critical distance on gender and on herself (de Lauretis 1987; Grant 1993).

The critical praxis orientation not only informs the approach to social justice; it also shapes the theory itself. In relation to FCDA, like CDA in general, such an orientation would entail making "linguistics itself more accountable, more responsible, and more responsive to questions of social equity" (Kress 1990, 88). Moreover, critical praxis research also dissolves the theory/practice dichotomy among feminists, in which "theory" gets associated with academic feminists and "practice" with grassroots feminist activists. Instead, the work of critical academic feminists can be viewed as "academic activism," of which FCDA constitutes one form. FCDA's theorization and analysis of gendered discourse practices raises critical awareness through research and teaching. Where awareness-raising is itself a form of activism, the political critique of discourse can be viewed not only for action, but *as* action. Critical awareness-raising is an action that enables one to begin to see things differently than before, with regard to not only other people's situations "out there," but our own attitudes and dispositions.

Below is an example of analytical activism in the context of teaching and learning FCDA, where it is evident from a student's statement on how she became critically aware of the relevance of gender inequality personally, and the realization that she herself has been complicit in perpetuating patriarchal ideologies. (The extract was written by Priscilla, a 21-year-old female undergraduate in my spring 2012 class, as part of a written assignment in which students were asked to reflect critically on our class discussions.[1])

> This week was the first time I saw so clearly how entrenched patriarchal discourses are in our society. Previously it seemed a nebulous concept, one that applied mainly to the oppressed women of religiously devout nations in the Middle East and intensely cultural societies like the caste system of India. It didn't occur to me that when I watched the "Final Question" section of Miss Universe pageants half in disdain and half in intrigue, being surprised when I heard "insightful" answers instead of formulaic ones, that I myself was perpetuating patriarchal discourses against my own gender. Even as a woman, the "sexy–smart" dichotomy is still very much present.

"Doing" FCDA is clearly not just an academic exercise in deconstruction of texts and talk for its own sake. It starts from a position of knowing that the issues dealt with have material consequences for groups of women and men in specific communities and contexts, and is driven by a conviction in effecting social change. A critical praxis-oriented research, therefore, does not pretend to adopt a neutral stance, but makes its political stance part of its argument (Lather 1986). To critics who scoff at such research as lacking in "objectivity" and "scientificity," one could argue that, apart from the fact that these notions are tenuous in themselves, studies which include social variables (such as group identities, power relations, and ideologies) that typically get excluded as "irrelevant" from other academic enterprises, in fact, make for *more* "objective," holistic research.

3.2   *"Gender" as ideological structure and practice*

A critical view of ideologies is that they are group-based sociocognitive representations of practices in the service of power, that is, they are perspectival representations developed in the interest of maintaining unequal power relations and
dominance (Fairclough 1992; van Dijk 1998). For feminists, "gender" is considered
an ideological structure that divides people hierarchically into two classes, "men"
and "women." Based upon sexual difference, the gender structure imposes a social
dichotomy of labor and human attributes for women and men, the substance of
which varies across time and place. Feminists have criticized the simple mapping
of biological sex onto social gender, as well as the naturalness of "sex" categories,
arguing that the latter, too, are socially constructed (Butler 1993). While it is true
that the structure of gender acts through and is inscribed on sexed bodies, Grant
(1993, 185) contends that "the whole idea of two sexes only has meaning because
those meanings are required by the gender structure in the first place." Although
the meanings vary with each culture, the "sex–gender" system is always intertwined with political and economic factors in each society. The mapping of sex onto
gender, and the asymmetry that characterizes the gender structure cross-culturally,
therefore, are understood as "systematically linked to the organization of social
inequality" (de Lauretis 1987, 5).

Gender ideology is hegemonic in that it often does not appear as dominance
at all, but as consensual and acceptable to most in a community. The winning
of consent and the perpetuation of the otherwise tenuous relation of dominance
(Gramsci 1971) are largely accomplished through discursive means, especially
in the ways ideological assumptions are constantly re-enacted and circulated
through discourse as commonsensical and natural. The taken-for-grantedness and
normalcy of such knowledge is what mystifies or obscures the power differential
and inequality at work. In a study on domestic violence against women in
Colombia, Tolton (2011), for instance, noted that the discourse on violence is
normalized in heterosexual relationships through an ideology that links authority
with masculinity, suffering with femininity, and abuse with love. Or in a study
on parenting discourses in Singapore, it was found that mothers are "naturally"
assumed to be the primary caregivers, and even where they also work outside the
home, they are required to prioritize the needs of the family, whereas fathers may
be optionally involved in childcare, as the public sphere is considered primarily
men's domain (Lazar 2000).

To claim that patriarchal gender ideology is structural is to say that it is enacted
and renewed in a society's institutions and social practices, which mediate between
the individual and the social order. As earlier mentioned, institutions are substan-
tively structured in terms of gender ideology (Connell 1987), so that even though
gender may not always be the most salient identity in particular interactions, it
remains potentially relevant. Holmes' (2005; Chapter 22 in this volume) study of
New Zealand workplace discourses found that even where gender was not the
primary focus, it remained below the surface in social interactions, and was ready
to emerge and reinstate the limits of acceptable behavior for women at work, in

a way that was absent for male workers. The pervasiveness of tacit androcentrism in many institutional cultures and discourse is such that not only men but women also are complicit in its reproduction. This in itself is unsurprising as patriarchy is a system which influences the attitudes and behaviors of men as well as women. Another study on workplace cultures, Martin-Rojo and Esteban's (2005) research in Spain, revealed that even in organizations with management models that ostensibly seem to favor women, deep-seated androcentrism socially isolated and excluded women managers. Female workers who were subordinates were as unsupportive of female bosses as were male co-workers and subordinates.

However, the existing gender ideology is not absolute in its influence nor uniform in its uptake. The material practices of individuals in any given context, as well as the availability of access to alternative discourses, can and do pose challenges to the gender structure. If it did not, historical changes in gender relations would not have been possible, and it would make futile the continued imagination of a feminist future. Understanding discursively enacted challenges to and transgressions of the status quo needs to be an important analytical concern for FCDA, a point to which I will return below.

3.3   Complexity of gender and power relations

Power relations are a struggle over interests, which are maintained, and resisted, through a variety of modalities, extents, and degrees of explicitness from context to context. Overt forms of gender asymmetry include exclusionary gatekeeping social practices, physical violence against women and girls, and sexual harassment and denigration of them. Such overt manifestations of power (or the threat of it) remain a reality for women in many societies, even where legal recourse is available. In an online news report of a story about how a woman was abducted from the car park of a popular shopping mall in Kuala Lumpur, Malaysia, and was nearly raped by two men, her account of the ordeal on Facebook was published in the news report in which she made this plea:

> Girls, be so very careful. Be vigilant, and please try not to go anywhere alone. If you need to walk to the car park, and you're alone, get a [security] guard to go with you ... Guys, watch out for your girlfriends, wives, mothers, sisters and friends. Walk with them, don't take their paranoia or fear lightly. Watch out for them. (Lourdes 2012)

The survivor's appeal is indicative of the psychological control ("paranoia," "fear") patriarchal systems have over women, sending the message that public spaces do not belong equally to women as to men. Women are required to constantly exercise self-surveillance and to rely on men for protection against other predatory men. Even though the discourse of female victimhood, as found above, has become unpopular in postfeminist circles (Wolf 1993), for its positioning of women as powerless, the material circumstances and lived experiences of women in patriarchal systems is evidently a real concern for some women.[2]

In contemporary times, sexism is also taking complex, covert, and indirect forms, so that at first glance something may not seem sexist, and may in fact appear to subscribe to progressive egalitarian values. Only upon closer scrutiny does the gender asymmetry become apparent. In a study of a pair of government advertisements in Singapore that were addressed to single professional women and men, encouraging them to find partners in a pro-family national campaign, Lazar (1993) found the coexistence of two discourses. On the surface, there was a discourse of egalitarianism, which seemed to address gender biases by encouraging men to reassess their sexist attitudes toward women, and by representing women (like men) as busy professionals in their own right. However, on closer analysis, a covert sexist discourse was at work, which maintained gender disparity, and required women to change their behavior to accommodate men's expectations. Similarly, in a study of a commercial dating advertisement in the United Kingdom, Sara Mills (1998) found gender-neutral references that seemed to stress gender equality. Yet, further analysis revealed the implicit presence of gendered "discursive frameworks" that would lead women to assume that they were the primary targets of the message, while the text codified information that was largely in the interest of men.

In dealing with the complex and subtle relations of power, Foucault (1977) has been instructive, especially in showing how modern power is substantially discursive in nature. This form of power, which is pervasive, is embedded and dispersed throughout networks of relations, is self-regulating, and produces subjects. However, even though power may be "everywhere," feminists have argued that gendered subjects are affected in different ways (Ramazanoglu 1993).

For critical discourse analysts, it has been useful to complement the concept of modern power with dominance and hegemonic power relations. The effectiveness of modern power and hegemony is that these are mostly cognitive, based on an internalization of gendered norms, and acted out routinely in the texts and talk of everyday life. This makes it an invisible power, "misrecognized" as such, and viewed instead as quite legitimate and natural (Bourdieu 1991).

Relations of power and dominance (see Foucault, Bourdieu, and Gramsci), however, can be discursively resisted as well as counter-resisted in a dynamic struggle over securing and challenging the interests at stake. In CDA scholarship, studies on how discourse is used by historically disadvantaged groups to resist and challenge the social status quo remain largely undeveloped, even though the potential exists. In my view, FCDA needs to engage more broadly with the various aspects of power relations – in terms of top-down institutional power, and also how individuals as members of social groups contend with and resist social structures and strictures. Also of relevance is access to forms of discourse, such as particular communicative events and culturally valued genres (see van Dijk 1996) which can be empowering for women's participation in public domains. The discursive analysis of individual or collective contestations, however, must be situated within the constraints and possibilities afforded by social structures and practices historically. The extent to which, and for whom, an interaction can be genuinely contestive, depends on particular social structures and contexts (Chouliaraki and Fairclough 1999).

Power struggles, however, work dynamically both ways. Just as members of disadvantaged groups may resist, interactionally, the exercise of power by dominant groups, so too dominant groups may engage in discourses of counter-resistance. Hegemonic structures are resilient in that they mutate and adapt to conditions of social change and contestation. Lazar (2005b) showed how the pragmatically driven Singapore government was involved in the "remaking of hegemonic gender relations" in a national campaign, which while purporting to encourage active fatherhood, did little to support a radical redistribution of parental responsibilities. In a study on "retrosexism," Williamson (2003) explained how objections by feminist critics to sexist representations in the media have sometimes led to the recycling of these same images dressed up in seemingly inoffensive parodic ways. Drawing on British media discourse, she showed how blatantly sexist content framed in a period style is presented to a contemporary audience in a light-hearted, nostalgic manner. For FCDA, the task then is to examine how power and dominance are discursively produced, resisted, and counter-resisted in a variety of ways through textual representations of gendered social practices, and through interactional strategies of talk.

Not only are the mechanisms of power varied and complex, but relations of asymmetry are also produced and experienced in different ways for and by different groups of women. Contemporary feminist theory has shown that, in order to avoid making simplistic and universalizing claims, "gender" needs to be viewed as interconnected with other socially stratified identities based on, for instance, race/ethnicity, social class and position, sexuality, (dis)ability, age, culture, nationality, and professional contexts. According to intersectionality theory, gender identity is not homogeneous or singular; rather, femininities and masculinities are heterogeneous and plural.

While for FCDA, gender remains a radical political focus, that does not mean that other potentially relevant dimensions of social identity are overlooked and that gender is studied as an isolated category, as suggested by Wodak (2008). Even though women as a social category are structurally disadvantaged in the patriarchal gender order, the intersection of gender with other systems of power based on race, social class, sexuality, and so on means that gender oppression is neither materially experienced nor discursively enacted in the same way for women everywhere. Women (and men) are positioned differently in these sets of social relations, and are affected differently in different sets (de Lauretis 1987). For example, heterosexuality and gender combine to produce normative gender identities that are implicitly heterosexist, which affords more privilege to "straight" women than to lesbians. Lesbians, in fact, may experience greater discrimination in that not only are they marginalized by heteropatriarchy, but they are made further invisible as "women" even within the discourse of the gay community (see Gouveia 2005). Wodak's (2008) study of migrants in Austria also shows that an analysis of the discourse topics pertaining to general aspects of migrants' experiences revealed a gendered pattern of discrimination. It was found that the migrant status amplified the gender discrimination faced by these women compared to nonmigrant women.

Acknowledging the multiplicity and diversity of identities among women and the forms of sexism to which they are differentially subject does not eschew the broader feminist political project of emancipation and social justice for "women."

Rather, feminist political action must be inflected by the specificity of cultural, historical, and institutional frameworks, and contextualized in terms of women's complexly constructed social identities and multiple levels of overlapping oppression. FCDA then would suggest a perspective that is implicitly comparative rather than universalizing, attentive to the discursive aspects of the forms of oppression and interests which divide as well as unite women.

3.4   *Discourse in the (de)construction of gender*

Poststructuralist conceptions of discourse as socially constitutive signifying practices have been fruitfully combined with linguistic approaches in CDA and gender and language studies (e.g., Baxter 2003). Like CDA, FCDA takes the view of discourse as one (among several) element of social practices; of particular interest to discourse analysts are those aspects of social practices that are discursive in character, and which are discursively represented in particular ideological ways (Chouliariaki and Fairclough 1999). The relationship between discourse and the social is a dialectical one, in which discourse constitutes (and is constituted by) social situations, institutions, and structures (Fairclough 1992, *passim*). Every act of meaning-making through language and other forms of semiosis contributes to the reproduction and maintenance of the social order, as well as to resisting and transforming that order.

The discursive constitution of the social can be analyzed broadly in terms of representations, interactions, and identities (Fairclough 1992). For FCDA, the interest lies in how gender ideology and gendered relations of power get (re)produced, negotiated, and contested in representations of social practices, in social relationships between people, and in people's social and personal identities in texts and talk. The analysis of gender in discourse includes the co-constructedness of gender relations. Ways of doing and being a woman vis-à-vis a man in particular communities of practice, in the public as well as private spheres of life, show up the power asymmetries between women and men in particular gender orders.

A critical discursive analysis of gender also entails an analytic focus on relationships among men and among women. The diversity that exists among women and men means that one cannot assume the uniformity of either category nor make sweeping dichotomized generalizations. For FCDA, a focus on forms of masculinity is of interest in terms of how these entrench or challenge particular gender orders that restrict the potentialities for men as well as women. There also needs to be a critical awareness of relations among (groups of) women. For example, how women may rally together in solidarity to oppose discrimination or propose changes, or how women themselves operating within androcentric cultures may perpetuate sexist attitudes and practices against other women. Where the aim of praxis-oriented analysis is concerned with social transformation of the existing gender order, awareness and attitudinal change by both men and women are necessary.

Although for FCDA gender is of political analytical focus, does that mean that gender is always relevant in every context and interaction, given that individuals subscribe to multiple identities? Wodak has proposed that "there are many situations where other identities *override* gender identities" (2008, 194; emphasis original). In my view, it is useful to think, as de Lauretis (1987) suggests, in terms of "sets of identities" at play simultaneously, rather than as multiple discrete identities. Therefore, although gender may not be the most salient in the matrix of other relevant identities in a given moment or context, it remains *potentially* relevant. It may well be that an individual's, say, professional or religious or racial identity is foregrounded in a particular context, and attention is not given to gender. Yet the gendering of the professional, religious, or racial identity potentially exists. In fact, in arguing that in the extreme example of the overtly racist categorization and exclusion of people by the Nazis, Wodak (2008, 194) herself notes that the experiences of the victims after deportation, nonetheless, were gendered. For feminist discourse analysts, then, of interest is the gendering of these other identities – to notice those points when (and how) gender does become relevant. This is notwithstanding the fact that individuals may not even be consciously attending to, or disclaim, the relevance of gender in particular situations (Kelan 2007).

Moving beyond the question of whether gender is relevant or not, we might ask another important question when analyzing gender in discourse: What other social categories are relevant for understanding the situatedness of gender in any given context? In analyzing excerpts from *Sex and the City: The Movie* transcripts, for example, Lazar and Kramarae (2011) found that the postfeminist feminine identity in the data was a product of the interaction of multiple axes of relevant social categories, namely, gender, class, regionalism, heterosexuality, ethnicity (whiteness), and age.

Social constructionist approaches emphasize the ongoing, iterative, and active accomplishment of gender (along with other social identities) in and through discourse. "Accomplishment" suggests that rather than assume identities to be immanent, through their linguistic (and nonlinguistic) practices, people "do" or "perform" identities as "women" and "men" in particular historical and cultural locations. Although the categories of gender are socially constructed and variable, in the worlds we live in, however, those categories, with their attendant asymmetry, are often treated as fixed and self-evident.

The interdisciplinary character of FCDA – in fact, it is more aptly "postdisciplinary" in that it is not constitutive of a single "discipline" interacting with others, but is a hybridized critical perspective at the outset – means that it accommodates a variety of analytical approaches and methods. In terms of methodology, some FCDA studies collect and contextualize their linguistic data based on ethnographic methods (see Besnier and Philips, Chapter 6 in this volume), which include interviews and participant observation, while others undertake close textual analysis of written and spoken discourse with a view to interpreting and explaining societal structures. In terms of analytical approaches, a variety of linguistic and discourse analytic frameworks and categories may be used, for example, from stylistics, pragmatics (see McConnell-Ginet, Chapter 16 in this volume), semantics, social semiotics and systemic-functional linguistics, corpus linguistics, narrative analysis, discursive psychology, ethnomethodology and conversation analysis (see Stokoe and Attenborough, Chapter 8, and Wilkinson and Kitzinger, Chapter 7, respectively, in this volume). A variety of frameworks also exist within CDA that can be drawn upon.

Based on close empirical analysis, the data in FCDA includes contextualized instances of spoken and written language as well as multimodal communication in a variety of genres and settings. The analysis includes overtly expressed meanings in communication, as well as less obvious, nuanced, and implicit meanings to get at the subtle, contradictory, or ambivalent renderings of ideological assumptions and power relations in contemporary modern societies. Analysis of the relationship between semiotic resources (say, between language and images) in the data is worth attention, for instance, in the way gender-neutral language may be used, even while stereotypical notions continue to get recycled in the images of the text.

Levels and foci of analysis in FCDA are also wide-ranging, including choices in lexis, clauses, utterances, conversational turns, structures of argument and genre, and interactions among discourses. The latter, known as "interdiscursivity" (Fairclough 1992), which is derived from Bakhtinian notions of heteroglossia and dialogism (Bakhtin 1981), is concerned with the interaction between different discourses within texts and talk. I have found it to be a particularly productive analytical category for the study of changing social relations, contradictions, and ambivalences in my work – for instance, the co-presence of competing discourses of gender relations in the same texts (Lazar 1993; 2000) or the threading together of "second-" and "third- wave" feminist voices along with traditional discourses of femininity and consumerism to constitute an overarching postfeminist discourse (Lazar 2006). The plurivocality of discourses within texts indexes social and cultural changes within a society, and recognizes the complexity of audience positions in regard to views of gender relations, as well as contributes to the form(ul)ation of complex hybrid gender identities.

3.5   *Critical reflexivity as praxis*

"Reflexivity," following Giddens (1991), is the generally pronounced characteristic of late modern societies, in which people increasingly utilize ("expert") knowledge about social processes and practices in a way that shapes their subsequent practices. Fairclough, Mulderrig, and Wodak (2011, 360) refer to reflexivity as a "critical awareness" which has become a "normal" feature of people's everyday life. It is true that nowadays, given mainstream awareness of feminism, it is often not possible for a blatantly sexist remark made in public to go unnoticed. For example, Asus, an electronics company recently tweeted a photo of a woman photographed from the back demonstrating one of its products at a major exhibition, with the caption "The rear looks pretty nice. So does the new Transformer AIO" (Zap 2012). Immediately there was an outcry of sexism by netizens and the company was forced to remove the post and make a public apology. Noteworthy was the widespread reaction of the public to the post, demonstrating people's reflexivity in everyday life. As the news article reporting the case wrote:

> on the Internet, the world is your stage – and the world was not happy with Asus ... a roundup of Twitter responses to the photo noted the general sense of outrage. From Leigh Honeywell, "Hey, Asus, do you not want women as customers or something? Not cool." Pwang added, "Wow, ASUS poignantly shows why tech is an uphill battle for women." And Anil Dash posed, "How sexist is tech?" How sexist, indeed? The photo brought attention to the controversial use of the "booth babe" and the broader issue of sexism in the high-tech industry.

Attention to reflexive practices of this kind must constitute an important part of FCDA practice, as it is an indicator of levels of social awareness and possibility for change. At the same time, however, as critical feminist analysts, we need to be alert to how hegemonic processes may co-opt reflexivity so that, while an impression of progressivism is evident in rhetoric, in fact very little gets established structurally and in practice. In this regard, I will highlight how reflexivity may be manifested as well as co-opted in institutional practices. This has implications for creating or impeding change in the personal attitudes and practices of individuals.

Reflexivity by institutions is of interest to FCDA both in terms of progressive institutional practices that aid individuals' capacity for critical (self-)awareness, as well as in terms of strategic appropriation of feminism to further nonfeminist goals. Awareness of feminist concerns for the inclusion of women's knowledge(s) and practices in the public sphere has resulted in the implementation of women-friendly programs in some organizations. In academia, for example, a growing number of universities around the world now include gender-related modules – such as "gender and language" in linguistic programs – in their curricula. When taught from a feminist perspective, such studies afford a space for discussion and reflection on, for instance, gender and language issues, and have the potential for raising critical language awareness among students. The example of Priscilla, the 21-year-old undergraduate, mentioned earlier, is a case in point. Gender mainstreaming and the adoption of "female management models" are also recognized by some organizations as beneficial, to some extent (Martin-Rojo and Esteban 2005). At the same time, there are also reflexive institutional practices that recuperate feminist values of egalitarianism and empowerment only to undermine them. The advertising industry is a notable example, where it is not simply about the strategic use of feminism for commercial gain, but that such appropriation entails a subversion of feminism as a political force, rendering it merely the value of a "look" or a style (Goldman 1992).

FCDA also needs to maintain a critical focus on self-reflexivity within feminist theory and practice as well, lest we inadvertently contribute to the perpetuation, rather than the elimination, of hierarchically different and exclusionary treatment of some women. An issue worth clarifying is what we mean and expect by the term "emancipation." For feminist critical discourse analysts, as mentioned, the ultimate goal is a radical social transformation based on social justice that opens up unrestricted possibilities for women and men as human beings. Discursive critique of the prevailing restrictive structures is a step in that direction.

From this view, liberal reformist positions are inadequate and can be co-opted by the dominant structures. Classical liberal notions of "equality" and "freedom" are problematic in that they are premised upon an abstract universalism and "sameness." On the one hand, "equality" implies "same as men" – a yardstick already set by men, and so women are required to fit into the prevailing androcentric structures. On the other hand, the dominant liberal ideology assumes the sameness of all women, which has allowed middle-class, heterosexual, Western, white women to represent their partial experiences as universally shared by all women, thereby ignoring the material conditions and needs of non-Western, nonwhite, lesbian, disabled, and poor women around the globe (hooks 1984; Moghadam 1994; Mohanty, Russo, and Lourdes 1991).

Although liberalism has limitations, the ideals of freedom and equality remain important for politically disadvantaged groups of women who have been systematically denied equality under the law, and freedom to control their lives, make choices, and act as agents in the world. For a pragmatic feminist politics, feminists have, therefore, proposed reconceptualizing universality in "concrete" rather than in abstract terms, based on acknowledgment of specific differences in the material conditions, contexts, and situations of women's lives. Only by attending to, instead of negating, "difference" can feminists identify and theorize more accurately the commonalities of gender oppression, and build alliances among women in tackling specific issues and achieving concrete political goals (Benhabib 1987; Hirschmann 1999). Feminist critical discourse analysis based on close analysis of contextualized instances of texts and talk in a variety of local situations aims to contribute to feminist politics in this way.

Even while acknowledging the usefulness of certain liberal ideals reconceptualized in critical feminist terms, care is needed to not slip into neoliberalism popular in late modern societies today. Of particular concern to FCDA is the global neoliberal discourse of postfeminism, which suggests that once certain equality indicators (such as rights of educational access, labor force participation, property ownership, and abortion and fertility) have been achieved by some women, sexism and feminism cease to be relevant. Unlike overtly sexist discourse like the example of the Asus tweet above, the discourse of popular postfeminism creates a climate of post-critique, lulling one into thinking that struggles over the social transformation of the gender order have become defunct. Not only is such a discourse promoted by the popular media, some third-wave feminists have also contributed to it, claiming this to be a moment of "power feminism," a time to celebrate women's newfound power and achievements (e.g., Walter 1999; Wolf 1993). While it is important to acknowledge the social, economic, and political achievements of a growing number of (young) women in some societies today, there is a need to be critically circumspect as well. One of the problematic assumptions of a postfeminist discourse is that women can "have it all" if only they put their minds to it or try hard enough, which reframes women's struggles and accomplishments as a purely personal choice, thus obscuring actual social and material constraints faced by different women in different contexts.

Ironically, this represents a backsliding on (second-wave) feminists' efforts to put the "personal as political" on the social agenda. Concomitantly, there seems to be an inward-looking focus and contentment only in the achievement of individual freedoms and fulfillment. A self-focused "me-feminism" of this sort shifts attention away from a collective "we-feminism" needed for a transformational political program. In the current sway of postfeminism in late modernity, Segal pointedly argues for the continued relevance of feminism: "Why feminism? Because its most radical goal, both personal and collective, has yet to be realized: a world which is a better place not just for some women, but for all women" (1999, 232).

Finally, feminist self-reflexivity must extend beyond a position of theoretical critique to include our own practices as well. Here, I provide an example that highlights the need for ongoing feminist self-reflection in academic practice (see Lazar 2008). In 2005 there was an email thread on a gender and language list, which began as a critique of the bias toward "white, Anglophone (or European) male academics" in the entries of a newly released sociolinguistics dictionary. The person who initiated the thread requested list members to recommend names of female sociolinguists who ought to have been included. The subsequent nomination exercise was then critiqued by a small minority of women on the discussion forum, who rightly pointed out that neither the criteria for the nominations nor the definition(s) of "sociolinguistics" were spelled out by the respondents. The list of nominations was profoundly exclusionary: as one of the women remarked, "now we know who happens to be in some people's radar today, and the more names that pile up the more glaring the omissions." For what had emerged from the list were names of female sociolinguists from the English-speaking North. Consequently, a few posts requested the inclusion of scholars working on languages other than English and one appealed that female sociolinguists from the South not be overlooked. Signaling a discourse of critical reflexivity, therefore, the critics called the exercise of feminist naming itself "a nice object lesson in academic politics," and as indicative of the "operative disciplinary hegemony." In fact, one of the critics likened the name request to the "old boys" network, pointing out the ironically masculinist and elitist practice that underlay this particular exercise. The critical reflexivity demonstrated in these posts highlight the deeply exclusionary practices in the academic public sphere, misrecognized as normal and self-evident professional activities. As feminists struggle to break hierarchical gender relations of power, critical self-reflexivity of this kind is necessary to safeguard against inadvertently reproducing relations that privilege and exclude some groups of women in the public sphere.

4. Conclusion

At a time when patriarchy and sexism are, paradoxically, stable as well as changing, assuming newer, and sometimes not so clearly recognizable, forms, FCDA scholars have their work cut out for them. This was discussed around five organizing principles in the chapter, which I shall summarize by way of conclusion. FCDA is an analytical mode of activism, whereby critical analyses in research and teaching are not simply preparing the way for action, but constitute action itself; raising critical awareness is activism. In FCDA, "gender" has a radical political status. Ideologically, "gender" is a hierarchical dualistic structure which both underlies and organizes social practices, as well as gets drawn upon by individuals in commonsensical ways in everyday interaction to enact identities as "women" and as "men." Although asymmetrical power relations of gender may be overt and blatant, power is increasingly exercised in subtle and covert forms in contemporary "modern" societies. Power relations are dynamic in that relations of dominance may be resisted and challenged; yet at the same time, hegemony works through counter-resistance. Although patriarchal power relations are crystallized along gender lines, because gender identity exists in a set of multiple social identities for individuals, where it may be more or less salient depending on context, gender remains potentially relevant in any context. A critical analysis of gender in FCDA needs to be nuanced and contingent, that is, mindful of the complexity of social identities and context-sensitive, yet alert to the workings of gendered power. Gender (along with other social identities) is viewed as iteratively and continually formed in and through discourse, and can be deconstructed using a wide variety of analytical frameworks to analyze the language and multimodal aspects of texts and talk. Related to the analytical activism of FCDA is the practice of critical reflexivity. Attention to practices of self-reflexivity highlights growing social awareness and possible social transformation. However, a critical focus on institutional co-optation of reflexivity, as well as critical attention to feminist activity itself (both in theory and in practice), is necessary. At a time when "gender" as an analytical focus is itself being questioned from all sides, the FCDA position is that gender clearly continues to be relevant.

NOTES

1   My thanks to Priscilla Samuel for granting me permission to quote from her class assignment.
2   The fatal gang rape of a 23-year-old Indian student in New Delhi in December 2012, which received worldwide media coverage, is another example of gender-based violence endemic in patriarchal cultures.

REFERENCES

Acker, Joan. 2006. "Introduction: The Missing Feminist Revolution Symposium." *Social Problems*, 53: 444–447.

Alvesson, Mats, and Yvonna D. Billing. 2009. *Understanding Gender and Organisations*, 2nd edn. London: Sage.

Bakhtin, Mikhail. 1981. *The Dialogic Imagination: Four Essays*, trans.

H. Holoquist, C. Emerson, and M. Holoquist. Austin: Texas University Press.

Baxter, Judith. 2003. *Positioning Gender in Discourse*. Basingstoke: Palgrave Macmillan.

Bell, Vikki. 1999. *Feminist Imagination*. London: Sage.

Benhabib, Seyla. 1987. "The Generalised and the Concrete Other: The Kohlberg-Gilligan Controversy and Feminist Theory." In Seyla Benhabib and Drucilla Cornell (eds.), *Feminism as Critique*, 68–79. Minneapolis: University of Minnesota Press.

Bourdieu, Pierre. 1991. *Language and Symbolic Power*. Cambridge: Polity.

Butler, Judith. 1993. *Bodies that Matter: On the Discursive Limits of "Sex."* New York: Routledge.

Chouliaraki, Lilie, and Norman Fairclough. 1999. *Discourse in Late Modernity: Rethinking Critical Discourse Analysis*. Edinburgh: Edinburgh University Press.

Connell, Robert W. 1987. *Gender and Power: Society, the Person, and Sexual Politics*. Stanford: Stanford University Press.

de Lauretis, Teresa. 1987. *Technologies of Gender: Essays on Theory, Film, and Fiction*. Bloomington: Indiana University Press.

Fairclough, Norman. 1992. *Discourse and Social Change*. Cambridge: Polity.

Fairclough, Norman, Jane Mulderrig, and Ruth Wodak. 2011. *Critical Discourse Analysis*. In Teun A. van Dijk (ed.), *Discourse Studies*, 2nd edn, 357–378. London: Sage.

Forsberg, Lucas. 2010. "Masculinity Studies as Fetish and the Need of a Feminist Imagination." *Norma : Nordic Journal for Masculinity Studies*, 1(2010): 1–4. At http://www.idunn.no/ts/norma/2010/01/art01, accessed October 16, 2013.

Foucault, Michel. 1977. *Discipline and Punish*. London: Allen Lane.

Giddens, Anthony. 1991. *Modernity and Self-Identity*. Cambridge: Polity.

Gill, Rosalind. 2003. "From Sexual Objectification to Sexual Subjectification: The Re-sexualisation of Women's Bodies in the Media." *Feminist Media Studies*, 3: 100–106.

Goldman, Robert. 1992. *Reading Ads Socially*. New York: Routledge.

Gouveia, Carlos. 2005. "Assumptions about Gender, Power and Opportunity: Gays and Lesbians as Discursive Subjects in a Portuguese Newspaper." In Michelle M. Lazar (ed.), *Feminist Critical Discourse Analysis*, 229–250. Basingstoke: Palgrave Macmillan.

Gramsci, Antonio. 1971. *Selections from the Prison Notebooks*. London: Lawrence & Wishart.

Grant, Judith. 1993. *Fundamental Feminism: Contesting the Core Concepts of Feminist Theory*. New York: Routledge.

Herring, Susan, Deborah Johnson, and Tamara DiBeneditto. 2011. "Participation in Electronic Discourse in a 'Feminist' Field." In Jennifer Coates and Pia Pichler (eds.), *Language and Gender: A Reader*, 2nd edn, 197–210. Oxford: Wiley-Blackwell.

Hill Collins, Patricia. 1990. *Black Feminist Thought*. New York: Routledge.

Hirschmann, Nancy J. 1999. "Difference as an Occasion for Rights: A Feminist Rethinking of Rights, Liberalism, and Difference." In Susan Hekman (ed.), *Feminism, Identity and Difference*, 27–55. London: Frank Cass.

Holmes, Janet. 2005. "Power and Discourse at Work: Is Gender Relevant?" In Michelle M. Lazar (ed.), *Feminist Critical Discourse Analysis: Gender, Power and Ideology in Discourse*, 31–60. Basingstoke: Palgrave Macmillan.

hooks, bell. 1984. *Feminist Theory: From Margin to Center*. Boston: South End Press.

Kelan, Elizabeth. 2007. " 'I Don't Know Why': Accounting for the Scarcity of Women in ICT Work." *Women's Studies International Forum*, 30: 499–511.

Kress, Gunther. 1990. "Critical Discourse Analysis." *Annual Review of Applied Linguistics*, 11: 84–99.

Lather, Patti. 1986. "Research as Praxis." *Harvard Educational Review*, 56: 257–277.

Lazar, Michelle M. 1993. "Equalizing Gender Relations: A Case of Double-Talk." *Discourse & Society*, 4: 443–465.

Lazar, Michelle M. 2000. "Gender, Discourse and Semiotics: The Politics of Parenthood Representations." *Discourse & Society*, 11: 373–400.

Lazar, Michelle M., ed. 2005a. *Feminist Critical Discourse Analysis: Gender, Power and Ideology in Discourse*. Basingstoke: Palgrave Macmillan.

Lazar, Michelle M. 2005b. "Performing State Fatherhood: The Remaking of Hegemony." In Michelle M. Lazar (ed.), *Feminist Critical Discourse Analysis: Gender, Power and Ideology in Discourse*, 139–163. Basingstoke: Palgrave Macmillan.

Lazar, Michelle M. 2006. " 'Discover the Power of Femininity!' Analysing Global 'Power Femininity' in Local Advertising." *Feminist Media Studies*, 6: 505–517.

Lazar, Michelle M. 2007. "Feminist Critical Discourse Analysis: Articulating a Feminist Discourse Praxis." *Critical Discourse Studies*, 4(2): 141–164.

Lazar, Michelle M. 2008. "Language, Communication and the Public Sphere: A Perspective from Feminist Critical Discourse Analysis." In Ruth Wodak and Veronika Koller (eds.), *Handbook of Communication in the Public Sphere*, 89–110. Berlin: Mouton de Gruyter.

Lazar, Michelle M., and Cheris Kramarae. 2011. "Gender and Power in Discourse." In Teun van Dijk (ed.), *Discourse Studies*, 217–240. London: Sage.

Lourdes, Marc. 2012. "Woman Abducted, Almost Raped at The Curve." *Yahoo! News*, May 30. At http://sg.news.yahoo.com/woman-abducted--almost-raped-at-the-curve.html, accessed October 23, 2013.

Majstorovic, Danijela, and Inger Lassen. 2011. *Living with Patriarchy: Discursive Constructions of Gendered Subjects across Cultures*. Amsterdam: Benjamins.

Makoni, Busi. 2013. " 'Women of the Diaspora': A Feminist Critical Discourse Analysis of Migration Narratives of Dual Career Zimbabwean Migrants." *Gender and Language*, 7(2): 201–229.

Marling, Raili. 2010. "The Intimidating Other: Feminist Critical Discourse Analysis of the Representation of Feminism in Estonian Media." *Nordic Journal of Feminist and Gender Research*, 18(1): 7–19.

Martin-Rojo, Luisa, and Concepción Esteban. 2005. "The Gender of Power: The Female Style in Labour Organisations." In Michelle M. Lazar (ed.), *Feminist Critical Discourse Analysis*, 61–89. Basingstoke: Palgrave Macmillan.

Mills, Charles Wright. 2000 [1959]. *The Sociological Imagination*. Oxford: Oxford University Press.

Mills, Sara. 1998. "Post-feminist Text Analysis." *Language and Literature*, 7(3): 235–253.

Mills, Sara. 2008. *Language and Sexism*. Cambridge: Cambridge University Press.

Moghadam, Valentine M. 1994. "Introduction: Women and Identity Politics in Theoretical and Comparative Perspective." In Valentine M. Moghadam (ed.), *Identity Politics and Women: Cultural Reassertions and Feminisms in International Perspective*, 3–26. Boulder, CO: Westview Press.

Mohanty, Chandra T., Ann Russo, and Torres Lourdes, eds. 1991. *Third World Women and the Politics of Feminism*. Bloomington: Indiana University Press.

Nguyen, Thi Thu Ha. 2011. "Gender Ideologies in the Vietnamese Printed Media." In Danijela Majstorovic and Inger Lassen (eds.), *Living with Patriarchy*, 195–217. Amsterdam: Benjamins.

Ramazanoglu, Caroline. 1993. *Up against Foucault*. New York: Routledge

Segal, Lynne. 1999. *Why Feminism? Gender, Psychology, Politics*. New York: Columbia University Press.

Spender, Dale. 1981. *Men's Studies Modified: The Impact of Feminism on the Academic Disciplines*. Oxford: Pergamon Press.

Swann, Joan. 2002. "Yes, but Is It Gender?" In Lia Litosseliti and Jane Sunderland (eds.), *Gender Identity and Discourse Analysis*, 43–68. Amsterdam: Benjamins.

Taylor, H. Jeanie, Cheris Kramarae, and Maureen Ebben. 1993. "Women and Men on Electronic Networks: A Conversation or a Monologue?" In *Women, Information Technology, and Scholarship*, 52–60. Urbana, IL: Women, Information Technology, and Scholarship Colloquium, Center for Advanced Study.

Tolton, Laura. 2011 " 'He Beat Her So Hard She Fell Head over Heels': Normalising Wife Abuse in Colombia." In Danijela Majstorovic and Inger Lassen (eds.), *Living with Patriarchy*, 17–48. Amsterdam: Benjamins.

van Dijk, Teun A. 1996. "Discourse, Power and Access." In Carmen Rosa, Caldas-Coulthard, and Malcolm Coulthard (eds.), *Texts and Practices: Readings in Critical Discourse Analysis*, 84–104. London: Routledge.

van Dijk, Teun A. 1998. *Ideology: A Multidisciplinary Approach*. London: Sage.

Walter, Natasha. 1999. *The New Feminism*. London: Virago.

Williams, Christine. 2006. "Still Missing? Comments on the Twentieth Anniversary of 'The Missing Feminist Revolution in Sociology.'" *Social Problems*, 53(4): 454–458.

Williamson, Judith. 2003. "Sexism with an Alibi." *Guardian*, May 31. At http://www.theguardian.com/media/2003/may/31/advertising.comment, accessed October 16, 2013.

Wodak, Ruth. 2008. "Controversial Issues in Feminist Critical Discourse Analysis." In Kate Harrington, Lia Litosseliti, Helen Saunston, and Jane Sunderland (eds.), *Gender and Language Research Methodologies*, 193–210. Basingstoke: Palgrave Macmillan.

Wodak, Ruth, and Michael Meyer, eds. 2009. *Methods of Critical Discourse Analysis*, 2nd edn. London: Sage.

Wolf, Naomi. 1993. *Fire with Fire: The New Female Power and How to Use It*. New York: Fawcett Columbine.

Zap, Claudine. 2012. "Asus Tweet Stirs Controversy." *Yahoo! Singapore Finance*, June 5. At http://sg.finance.yahoo.com/news/asus-tweet-stirs-controversy.html, accessed October 16, 2013.

Part III   Identities

10 Language and Sexual Identities

ROBIN QUEEN

1. Introduction

As I write this chapter, a child sex abuse scandal at Pennsylvania State University is unfolding. This scandal involves allegations that a former football coach was involved in various acts of criminal sexual activity with young boys. The scandal also includes allegations of various degrees of cover-up on the part of university officials. It is safe to say that the scandal has roiled the Penn State campus and left many institutions (of higher education and others) examining their own practices for the possibility that anything similar could occur there. Among the components of this story to emerge has been the question of how the behaviors that have been alleged are named by the various players involved. Terms such as "horsing around," "sexual misconduct," "rape," "something of a sexual nature," and "sexual assault" have been used, and each has also been contested in various ways in public discussions and news accounts of the scandal.

While fully recognizing the delicacy of beginning an essay on language and sexual identities with a discussion of sexual crimes involving children, I find that this story reveals many of the central elements involved in theorizing how language and sexual identities can and do intersect. Most commonly, of course, those intersections do not involve criminal acts and it is most especially uncomfortable to discuss such acts when they involve children. At the same time, that discomfort is perhaps on the extreme edge of a more general concern with how cultures incorporate sexualities into the broader realms of the social landscape. With respect to language, this incorporation involves not only how we go about naming particular behaviors and those who engage in them but also the role of language in the social policing of sexual conduct, in the emergence of power and other social relations as they relate to sexualities and sexual activity, in the constitution of normativity and taboo, and in presenting the self (or in positioning others) as a particular kind of person in a particular kind of socially informed time and space. As I hope

The Handbook of Language, Gender, and Sexuality, Second Edition.
Edited by Susan Ehrlich, Miriam Meyerhoff, and Janet Holmes.
© 2014 John Wiley & Sons, Inc. Published 2017 by John Wiley & Sons, Inc.

to show in the rest of this chapter (and using less problematic examples than the one with which I began), these have been and remain the central questions for the bulk of research that has queried sexual identities in connection with language. Indeed, the fundamental question underlying this area of research is how research can scientifically and rigorously explain and perhaps predict the interrelationships of language, in particular language variation (either within or across individuals), with sexuality, where sexuality refers simultaneously to practices, identities, beliefs, and ideologies that are tied in one way or another to the eroticized body (see Bucholtz and Hall 2004). Far more specific kinds of questions can unfold from this very broad one, and answering any such questions ultimately serves to increase our understandings of both language and sexuality as human cognitive, historical, social, and biological phenomena.

Before proceeding too far with this survey, I want to be explicit about the meanings of some of the terms I will be using as many of them are often poorly defined or not defined at all, a situation that can lead to misinterpretation and misunderstanding. In this review, I distinguish *sex* as a descriptor used for the biological body (e.g., "male," "female"); *gender* as a descriptor for the social and cultural expression of the sexed body (e.g., "masculine," "feminine," "man," "woman"); and *sexual orientation* as a descriptor for the sex and gender of sexual object choices (e.g., "heterosexual," "lesbian"). Further, I distinguish sexual identity from eroticism. *Sexual identity* is a descriptor for the social framings through which individuals and groups are socially categorized (by themselves or others) based on their sexual orientation, beliefs about their sexuality, and/or their sexual practices. *Eroticism*, on the other hand, references the description or indexing of specifically erotic desires and erotic practices. I use the terms *sexuality* and *sexualities* as umbrella terms encompassing both sexual identity and eroticism, recognizing, of course, that "sexual identity" and "eroticism" as I use them here are not and cannot be categorically distinct from one another (any more than can "sex," "gender," and "sexual orientation"), nor are they necessarily used as such in the studies and approaches I will be discussing.

The inextricability of sex, gender, sexual identity, and eroticism points toward another intersection that is pivotal for research on language and sexual identities. While in many ways distinctive, language and sexuality research has both historical and contemporary ties to research on language and gender. Indeed, much of the work on language and sexuality is subsumed under the scholarly umbrella of the field of language and gender (as evidenced, for instance, by the inclusion of this chapter in this particular *Handbook*). Initially this relationship provided a kind of protection to scholarship on language and sexual identities as homophobia both within and outside the community of scholars made working on sexualities a potentially risky endeavor (see Queen 2002). However, as the scholarly exoticism of the so-called sexual minorities has declined, and as scholarship that questions the degree to which performances of gender may be better conceptualized as performances of sexuality (and vice versa) has grown, any clear distinction between the two areas that might have once existed has largely disappeared. As Cameron writes, "gender and sexuality are not only inseparable from one another, they are also inseparable from the social facts of power" (2011, 101). This is of course also true of scholarship on both of them.

My own interest in language and sexuality emerged when I ran into a comic zine called *Hothead Paisan: Homicidal Lesbian Terrorist* (DiMassa 1999). By far most striking for me was the variation in the representations of prosodies as well as the phonological, lexical, and morphosyntactic features in the representation of the characters' speech (Queen 1997). The particular ways in which the author/artist stylized language use among her characters simultaneously drew on stereotypical characteristics of various social actors while also creating unique personae among the characters. Further, the nature of the stereotypes on which the artist, Diane DiMassa, drew involved both broad cultural stereotypes concerning gender, sexual identity, and erotic behavior as well as stereotypes that are widely known among lesbians but otherwise not widespread.

When I requested permission to reprint some of the cartoon frames from the original fanzines, DiMassa responded with surprise, writing back to me that she'd never thought of the language as something worthy of exploration. Her reaction is not uncommon, as many aspects of language variation frequently operate below the level of metapragmatic awareness and the reaction itself forms a part of what is fundamentally curious about the intersections of language and sexualities. For instance, while it is exceedingly easy to elicit stereotypes about how gay men purportedly speak, it is quite difficult to elicit the same about lesbians' speech patterns. (See Podesva and Kajino, Chapter 5 in this volume, for discussion.) Regardless, lesbians, like all social actors, can and do use language to index themselves as lesbians when they choose to. We also use language to make assessments about who might be a lesbian.

It is specifically in the realm of perception and representation that the question of stereotype is most central for language and sexuality, despite the fact that the bulk of existing research has focused on exploring production and performativity on the part of speaking subjects. Language is surely a powerful mechanism for speakers in the service of their own personae and identifications, and a broad question that runs throughout several areas of linguistics, most especially sociolinguistics, is how language serves as a more general semiotic resource in the alignment of self and other into positions associated with particular identities, stances, and personae. However, that semiotic power lies at least as critically in the realm of interpretation as in the realm of production since it is in the realm of interpretation (and interaction) that the raw input becomes linked to a sociocognitive schema.

It is this more general linkage that has animated recent research in and theorizing about language and sexual identities precisely because of the ways in which sexuality lies at the nexus of essentialist and social constructivist ideas about the nature of social life. In this chapter, newly commissioned for the second edition of this *Handbook*, I lay out the historical dimensions of this field of inquiry as it has unfolded since approximately the mid-1970s and present some of the key findings and theoretical issues that have emerged. The chapter focuses primarily on work that has appeared since the first edition of the *Handbook* was published (Holmes and Meyerhoff 2003). I generally avoid re-reviewing work that has been widely reviewed already. The bulk of that work can be found in some or all of the following: Baker 2008; Bucholtz and Hall 2004; Cameron and Kulick 2003; Kulick 2000 (see also Chapter 3 in this volume); Morrish and Sauntson 2007; Queen 2007. Cameron and Kulick (2006) provide a unified collection of much of the original scholarship relevant to the development of the field.

2. Situating the Study of Language and Sexual Identity

The majority of nonliterary studies of language and sexuality that were produced prior to the early 1970s focused on issues related to the lexicon, particularly in terms of lexical items with covert or culturally specific meanings, such as "queen" to indicate a particular kind of gay man. Much of this work has a dictionary-like quality, with very little analysis, and constructs the language use of gay men and lesbians (primarily) as something particularly exotic and unusual. Within the field of communication studies, work focusing on the connection between sexual identities and language use beyond the lexicon began to emerge as early as the late 1970s. In that work, broader discourse structures were linked to gay and lesbian subject positions; however, the nature of the analysis is primarily rhetorical rather than specifically linguistic.

Beginning in the early 1990s, research on language and sexual identities began to emerge from within linguistic anthropology and sociolinguistics, with particularly strong connections to the broad field of language and gender research. Following the emerging field of queer theory, though, scholars argued that it would be fruitful to uncouple sexuality from gender theoretically and analytically. William Leap's publication of *Beyond the Lavender Lexicon* (1995) and Anna Livia and Kira Hall's publication of *Queerly Phrased* (1997) mark two of the earliest interventions in what quickly became known as "queer linguistics." (See Bucholtz, Chapter 1, and Milani, Chapter 13, in this volume for more recent developments in queer linguistics.)

Much as with the difference and dominance debates of the 1980s and 1990s within the field of language and gender research, one of the central debates to emerge within this area of research has concerned the place of identity within studies linking sexuality and language variation. Kulick (2000; see also Chapter 3 in this volume) initiated this conversation with his review of work on "gay and lesbian language." In the review, Kulick argued that examining the language practices of any particular social group did not necessarily tell you anything useful about that social group; thus, studying the linguistic practices of gay men and lesbians revealed little about gay men and lesbians per se. His theoretical solution to this problem was a turn to theories of language from fields other than linguistics, such as cultural studies and psychoanalytic theory, and to argue that a focus on voicing desires would be a more promising avenue. Some answered this critique with the argument that excluding identity and focusing on something like desire potentially ignores the salience of socially constructed subject (and to some degree object) positions that are tied to sexual desire and practice and thus runs the risk of mystifying desire and ignoring altogether matters of power and other fundamentally social phenomena (Barrett 2003; Bucholtz and Hall 2004; Eckert 2002; Queen 2002). The critique was explicitly challenged in an influential paper by Mary Bucholtz and Kira Hall (2004), which focused on the place of identities and particularly the place of social and material power as manifest in identities for sociolinguistic models seeking to link language variation to social dynamics like gender, sex, and sexuality. They called their model a tactics of intersubjectivity and focused it on conceptualizing affiliation/disaffiliation, authentication, and authority.

Until recently, both approaches relied almost exclusively on ethnography, conversational analysis, and discourse analysis as their methods of data collection and analysis. While these approaches continue to underlie the bulk of research of language and sexualities, recent research has expanded to include sociophonetic experimentation (Campbell-Kibler 2011; Levon 2006; Mack and Munson 2012; Munson, Jefferson, and McDonald 2006; Munson et al. 2006; Pierrehumbert et al. 2004) and corpus-based work (Baker 2008; Myketiak 2011). (See Podesva and Kajino, Chapter 5 in this volume, for a review of work investigating language and sexuality from the perspective of sociophonetics.) An additional area of influence has come from scholars working within the "third-wave" model of sociolinguistics proposed by Penelope Eckert (n.d.). In this model, as with the other two, the central question concerns how linguistic variation becomes socially meaningful for speakers and listeners. Within this model, the theoretical position of identity has been replaced by the more fluid concepts of stance, style, and personae. These concepts are meant to capture the inherent instability in any presentation of a social self and to capture more robustly the nature of intraspeaker variability rather than focusing centrally on interspeaker variability. Within the sociophonetic literature, there has also been a growing interest in questions of listener perception (Levon 2006; Munson 2011).

The ultimate conclusion embraced by most scholars in this area has necessarily been that our understandings of language and sexualities are more likely to advance by taking seriously a focus on both social identification and eroticism. Further, while a decline in publications focusing on language and sexualities followed the initial debate, the number of publications in peer-reviewed journals of linguistics or linguistic anthropology that deal with language and sexuality has recently risen significantly, more than doubling in the period 2006–2012 relative to the period 2000–2005. More critically, it is specifically work that queries language variation as connected to sexuality that has brought the question of social meaning into much more central focus within sociolinguistics and related areas.

3. Language, Eroticism, and Identity

One of the fundamental criticisms of language and sexuality research from the 1980s and 1990s was that very little of it focused on one of the central components of sexuality, namely "fantasy, desire, repression, pleasure, fear and the unconscious"

(Kulick 2000, 270). Much of the recent scholarship on language and sexualities has heeded this critique and there has been a significant increase in the number of publications that focus specifically on the linguistic details of expressions of desire.

Despite the theoretical interest in exploring eroticism, however, one of the more significant problems in focusing on its linguistic expression is that it can be difficult to find an appropriate method for collecting and analyzing expressions of erotic desire. This is partly tied to the somewhat limited role that language may play in expressions of desire and sexual activity. More centrally, though, it is also tied to the ideological delicacy involved with recording expressions of desire and sexual activity and presumed privacy associated with such expression. One of the very interesting consequences of the ideological orientation toward privacy in matters of sexual activity and desire is that silence on matters of sexual activity is one powerful mechanism through which hegemonic sexualities, particularly heteronormative sexualities, can retain dominant positions within the hierarchy of forms of sexual expression.

For instance, Stokoe's (2010) discussion of speed-dating encounters illustrates some of the promise of a focus on erotic desire, particularly when taken in tandem with questions related to interaction. In her study, Stokoe shows that participants in speed-dating encounters frame their interest in erotic and romantic potential through the interactional dynamics of everyday encounters. For the participants in her study, however, erotic possibility was fully linked to heteronormativity in which those participants, especially the men, who had never been married, were asked to account for this fact more so than those who had been divorced or in otherwise complicated relationships.

One of the motivations behind the call for a linguistics of desire is exploring the structuring relationship that holds between that which can be said and that which can't (Cameron and Kulick 2003, 139). In terms of language production, and to some degree interpretation, empirical research on the unsaid and unsayable presents a formidable challenge. As a consequence, much of the work that does attempt such an exploration uses introspective data, such as in Kulick's (2003) discussion of the use of "no" in a variety of different contexts, or relies primarily on written expressions of desire. (But, see Kulick, Chapter 3 in this volume, for a discussion of work that investigates desire in spoken language.) Thorne and Coupland (1998) explore how dating advertisements can be a site for the construction of desire tied to specific identity positions. Ahearn (2003) similarly shows how an emerging genre of love letters among villagers in Nepal interweaves discourses of modernity with discourses of desire and how written conventions can be used to analyze aspects of desire that are not or cannot be articulated. In her study, writers used strategies such as ellipses as a means of indicating desires that can't be written down (Ahearn 2003, 113).

Ritual and the supernatural present further avenues through which to pursue questions related to sexual desires that are and aren't articulable. Kang (2003), for instance, discusses how the ritual use of magic spells highlights linguistic expressions of erotic desire as a means for Petalangan women to insure fidelity by their husbands. Thompson (2011) presents a fascinating study of how Zanzabari women use discussions about supernatural sexual encounters to transgress existing cultural taboos concerning the revelation of desire and explicit description of particular sexual acts. Finally, Smith (2010) explores how playing marbles allows Aymara boys to engage in metapragmatic expressions of masculinity that are culturally linked to expressions of hetero- and homosexuality.

Likewise, a subgenre of research on language and sexualities examines specific articulations of desire through various channels on the Internet (del Teso-Craviotto 2005; 2008; Thorne and Coupland 1998). As Myketiak (2011, 109) points out, most of the work focusing on expressions of desire on the Internet are linked to situations in which the researchers went to places (such as dating sites) that are specifically framed in terms of sex and sexualities, something which circumscribes how research can investigate language as connected to erotic desire and behavior. As an alternative, Myketiak investigates sexuality within an online community that was not otherwise oriented specifically around sexual desire and in which she was otherwise not a participant. In so doing, she discovered a wide range of practices that ultimately reinforced the hegemony of heterosexual, indeed heteronomative, behaviors and ideologies specifically in the face of the potential transgression made possible through an online venue. Many of these practices did involve same-sex participants; however, they were primarily linked to homosocial bonding, much like the discussions of sexuality among fraternity men discussed by Kiesling (2005). For example, Myketiak found that sexual commands such as "snog" and "shag" were typically used by participants in the MUD (multi-user dimension) as a way of initiating competitive game-playing and joking but were not typically involved in initiating actual sexual encounters between participants.

The textual representation of those encounters relied on a wholly different set of mechanisms linked largely to the discontinuity between being online and offline. All the examples of cybersex proved to be heteronormative and dyadic, involving complex co-narration and intimate revelation. Of particular interest was the fact that once someone initiated a cybersex encounter, he or she frequently shifted from first-person self-reference to third-person self-reference, while maintaining the second-person reference for the interlocutor. In this way, the encounter takes on a heightened narrative quality relative to nonsexual interactions. Additionally, one of the hallmarks of cybersexual activity in this space involved the marking of intimacy, which was constituted by bringing offline knowledge about the individuals involved and activities in which they jointly participated into the online space of the sexual encounter.

As the examples above have shown, our understanding of eroticism can be enhanced through an examination of its linguistic expression. At the same time, these examples also illustrate that the paths through which erotic desire become recognizable social (and erotic) practice do not inhere in the desires themselves but rather in the semiotics that organize, relativize, and order those desires. Those semiotics are what allow our understanding of language to be enhanced through an examination of its role in the erotic. For instance, Penny Eckert's groundbreaking work on the emergence of the heterosexual market in preadolescence is among the most important studies to illustrate how erotic desire and desire for identity are inextricable (2002; 2003; 2011; Chapter 27 in this volume). The intersectionality of erotic desire (and behavior) with identities, particularly heteronormative ones, also explains a variety of cases in which adolescents talk about and evaluate sexual practices (Archakis and Lampropoulou 2009; Pichler 2007; Skapoulli 2010). In a similar vein, Hoppe (2011) illustrates how gay men who identify themselves as "bottoms" (i.e., the "receptive" sexual partner) locate that identity specifically in terms of the erotic desire to produce pleasure in, and to submit sexually to, their partner. In Hoppe's analysis, these desires, and the identity linked to them by the men who adopt them, are wholly constrained by the existing social discourses concerning sexual pleasure and often come into semiotically meaningful conflict with other discourses, for instance those concerning safer sex practices. Thus, we can see in the emergence of a sociolinguistics of eroticism a useful interrelationship between individual fantasy and desire with the identifications, stances, and personae that help give the erotic some of its social form.

4. Sexual Identity and Identification

Despite the growing number of publications that attend to Kulick's call for a linguistics of desire, the bulk of the research on language and sexualities has continued to focus in some way or other on sexual identities and identifications. Much of the work on language and sexualities that was published in the 1990s and early 2000s focused directly on language use within communities of queer speakers which McElhinny (2002) has labeled the "queer peers" approach. McElhinny's primary point was to call attention to the fact that much of this work focuses on local interactions among groups of friends without a clear focus on broader questions of power, hegemony, and political economies. McElhinny argues that the queer peers approach represented primarily a methodological convenience for researchers; however, Baker (2008, 58) goes further to highlight the more general desire among many of these researchers to make visible (or audible as the case may be) groups of people who had largely been erased or ignored in prior linguistic scholarship. Baker points out that one unintended consequence of the queer peers approach was that work on language and sexuality in this period mirrored work on language and gender in setting up a juxtaposition to a heterosexual male norm which thereby reinscribed the normativity of both heterosexuality and maleness.

As a result of this normativity, many scholars began focusing specifically on exploring heterosexuality and heteronormativity. For instance, in a wide-ranging body of work exploring the discursive construction of masculinity, Kiesling (2002; 2005; 2011) has argued that exploring the mechanisms by which men engage in homosocial bonding provides an important lens on how hegemonic positions of power are attained and maintained. Kiesling (2005) notes that these discourses include essentialized gender difference, heterosexism, dominance, and male solidarity. One of his important points is that the men in his studies go to great lengths to constrain the possibilities that they be perceived as gay, something which they feel would undermine their claims to particular kinds of power. In this way, gender and sexuality become indirectly implicated in the ways the men use language to achieve power. Approaching the question of power from a somewhat different kind of data, Zimman and Hall (2010) illustrate something similar in their discussion of how transgender men index sex and gender indirectly via the discursive construction of their bodies. For instance, transgender men frame their own genitalia using the same lexical referents regardless of whether they are speaking of an anatomical penis or clitoris. They also refer to their and others' bodies in complex ways that serve to undermine their connection to femaleness and assert their essentialized similarity to other men.

Further, in a pair of articles about speaking as a heterosexual and speaking as a lesbian, Kitzinger (2005) and Land and Kitzinger (2005) show how the dynamics of sexuality play themselves out in places where sexuality doesn't overtly matter, for instance in telephone calls about other topics. As Land and Kitzinger (2005, 387) point out, "heteronormativity enables heterosexuals to take for granted their right to refer to their heterosexual relationships without this being treated as conveying information about who they go to bed with or as stating that they are heterosexual." They illustrate how, in intimate phone conversations where their interlocutors know their sexual identities, lesbians are not significantly different from people of other sexual orientations in the ways they make their sexuality relevant in a conversational context. In institutional contexts, however, where the presumption is of heterosexuality but the discourse may be about any number of topics, lesbians employ several strategies for challenging the presumption of heterosexuality, including both implicit and explicit correction and repair.

For the most part, studies of heteronormative identifications engage directly questions of social power and power dynamics. For example, Archakis and Lampropoulou (2009) illustrate how adolescents who affiliate with different personae (such as "Christian" or "university-bound") use different discursive strategies and mechanisms for presenting heterosexual identities. Interestingly, they construct those identities as normative primarily through an ordering of certain erotic desires as deviant or not. The nature of the deviance is linked in many ways to the adolescents' understanding of adult norms and behaviors and ultimately to adult power dynamics. Similarly, Hall (2009) points out how Western-style discourses of queer civil rights became incorporated in the context of middle-class Hindi LGBT activists working on HIV/AIDS education. In this case, the global discourse of queerness was used locally to distinguish the middle-class activists from groups such as "boys," that is, women who orient toward models of female masculinity long associated more with rural India. Likewise, Barrett (2003) illustrates how travel guides aimed at English-speaking gay male tourists engage in the ideological work of positioning American gay men as either culturally unique as gay men or as culturally no different from straight men save for their particular sexual desires (see also Leap and Boellstorff (2004) for similar points). In this case, local ideas of desire become anchored in global tourism. Piller and Takahashi (2006) also engage the issue of globalized desire. They illustrate that the bilinguals in their study turn language itself into an object of desire in their hopes to attract a partner who speaks a particular language and then to raise children who are bilingual with that partner. In their analysis, romantic and sexual desires become wholly enmeshed with linguistic desire.

Labeling conventions for different kinds of social identities and practices represent another area in which identification and desire frequently intersect linguistically. For example, research has explored kinship terms being reconfigured away from biogenetic ties and toward other kinds of social and erotic relationships (Queen 2006), sexual practices and preferences being captured with terms like "top" and "bottom" (Barrett 2003) or discussions of the boundaries of terms like "queer" and "gay" (McConnell-Ginet 2002). More recent work that focuses on questions related to the lexicon has addressed the questions more centrally in terms of social meaning. For instance, both Wong (2002; 2005) and Murray (2003) deal with the shifting meanings of particular terms (*tongzhi* in Chinese and *takatāpui* in te reo Maori) from general meanings dealing with close friendships (roughly "comrade" for *tongzhi* and "intimate same-sex companion" for *takatāpui*) to specific meanings tied to same-sex sexualities and their social manifestations.

There is also a relatively sizable body of research that uses the tools of narrative analysis to understand particular genres that have been associated with sexual identities such as coming out stories (Chirrey 2003), fuck stories (Kiesling 2002), and various other narrative genres. Peebles (2004), for instance, explores ex-gay and ex-ex-gay narratives as a strategy for highlighting the tensions around questions of desire and identity as well as those around constructivism and essentialism. A similar tension emerges in Zimman's (2009) discussion of coming out narratives told by transgender speakers. In Zimman's analysis, the coherence of identity that is often a hallmark of coming out narratives as told by lesbian, gay, and bisexual people often differs for transgendered people depending on their gender presentation at the time of telling the narrative. For transgendered people, the nature of coming out may be more centrally linked to individual gender histories than specifically to identity.

4.1   Sociophonetics and sexual identities

Finally, among studies that orient more around questions of sexual identifications than eroticism, there is a large and expanding body of work linked to sociophonetics. (See Podesva and Kajino, Chapter 5 in this volume.) The bulk of this strand of research has been focused on the one hand on the types of phonetic parameters that lead to linguistic percepts of homosexuality and on the other to the ways in which speakers make indexical use of phonetic variability. In both cases, the vast majority of the work has focused on the perception of speakers as gay males or on the phonetic production of gay males.

In general, most perception-based studies find that listeners are reasonably successful at labeling speakers' sexual identities in ways that correspond to the speaker's own self-assessments (Gaudio 1994; Smyth, Jacobs, and Rogers 2003). Paradoxically, however, few studies have shown significant differences in the acoustic signals produced by speakers of differing sexual orientations. In particular, differences in the fundamental frequency, which have been widely theorized as indexical of sexual orientation (with gay men assumed to have greater pitch range than straight men and lesbians assumed to have narrower pitch ranges than straight women), have been inconclusive and few significant differences in pitch range have been found (Gaudio 1994; Levon 2006; Moonwomon 1997; Smyth, Jacobs, and Rogers 2003; Waksler 2001). Pierrehumbert et al. (2004) found, however, that there were specific differences in the vowel spaces of speakers who identified themselves with different sexual orientations, and concluded that those differences provided evidence that gay men's and lesbians' manipulations of the vocal tract are learned behavior rather than somehow biological in nature. This finding is based on the lack of any crossover effect between sex and sexual orientation (e.g., it was not the case that gay men's vowel spaces were similar to straight women's or that lesbians' were similar to straight men's).

Additional evidence that phonetic variation can be linked to sexual identity can be found in a series of studies conducted by Benjamin Munson and his colleagues. Generally, Munson and his colleagues are concerned with how sexual identity as an independent or fixed variable can inform theories of phonetic variation. For instance, Munson, Jefferson, and McDonald (2006) show that perceptions of masculinity, femininity, and perceived sexual identification are correlated with one another. However, it was not the case that speakers who were perceived to be gay were also perceived to be less masculine based on the same set of acoustic and perceptual criteria. Indeed, the criteria listeners used to label a speaker as gay or lesbian differed from those used to label a speaker as more or less masculine or feminine. Munson et al. (2006) find that listeners are sensitive to the degree of retraction of /ae/ in gay and straight men's speech and categorize speakers with retracted /ae/ as more gay-sounding than those without. Later studies of the same phenomena found a much more complicated picture of this variable. Smith, Hall, and Munson (2010) argue that the differences across these studies illustrate the challenge of pinpointing the sociophonetic characteristics listeners rely on when making assessments about who speakers are.

The articulation of /s/ has also received serious attention from sociophoneticians. Like the motivation behind the comparison of gay men's and straight men's pitch, the motivation for the study of /s/ derives from a lay perception, or stereotype, that gay men "lisp." Researchers have used this perception to study whether or not gay male speakers actually produce /s/ with characteristics that differ from nongay male speakers and have found that, while there are differences, they are not consistent with a lisp. Perhaps more interestingly, researchers have used this perception to ask whether or not changing the acoustic characteristics of /s/ results in stronger perceptions concerning the sexual orientation of the speaker. Two recent studies suggest that they do. In an explicit labeling task, Mack and Munson (2012) found that changing the acoustic characteristics of initial /s/ in male speakers was enough to change listener perceptions concerning the assumed sexual orientation of the speaker. A second experiment involving an implicit priming task revealed independent main effects for /s/ quality and previously established perceptions of sexual orientation but no interactions between the two. In a similarly oriented perception experiment, Campbell-Kibler (2011) found that a fronted /s/

was associated with judgments of speakers sounding less masculine, more gay, and less competent. On the other hand, /s/ backing was associated with a much more complex set of social evaluations.

Finally, in a series of papers concerning gay speech styles, Robert Podesva has shown that context is central to understanding intraspeaker variation (2006; 2007; 2011a; 2011b). By studying individual speakers in a range of contexts, Podesva shows that speakers actively construct different personae that may or may not directly involve gayness. Further, in contexts in which speakers highlight their gayness, they may do so using a range of gay personae including the "diva," "partier," and "professional" personae. Following Eckert (2008), who proposed that social meanings are organized in terms of indexical fields, Podesva argues that the indexicality of linguistic features is multivaried and arises at least in part via contexts of situated co-occurrence.

4.2   *The special case of the lesbian*

As Cameron (2011, 100) notes, the case of the lesbian presents some challenges for models based on stance, style, and persona because of the lack of an "essentialized linguistic construct" upon which to build lesbian performances. This lack of an ideologically grounded linguistic stereotype has had consequences for scholarship on language use among lesbians, and lesbians have been erased from the bulk of scholarship on language and gender and on language and sexuality. This erasure points to an important fact about those scholarships, which is the degree to which they were fundamentally positioned in relation to heteronormative masculinity (see also Kulick (2010) for a similar discussion). Rather than positioning the lesbian as the perfect test case for many of the theoretical claims concerning the connection of language to matters of gender and sexuality, much of the research in these areas moved instead to deconstruct heteronormative masculinity, showing that maleness, masculinity, and heterosexuality are also the result of ideological, indexical, semiotic, and social processes.

Despite the lack of broadly circulating stereotypes about lesbians, research continues to emerge that examines the connection of language variation to the expression of lesbian subjectivities and stances. One intriguing example of such work is Veronika Koller's book *Lesbian Discourses: Images of a Community* (2008). Koller explores the ways in which images of lesbian communities in the United States and Great Britain have been created in nonfictional texts and seeks to understand how these images have and haven't changed over time. Deborah Chirrey (2007) explores similar ideas within the context of advice pamphlets written for lesbians considering coming out as lesbian. Her analysis shows that, at least for lesbians themselves, there are indeed powerful semiotic processes linked specifically to ideologies of invisibility.

Such ideologies are also under discussion in Lucy Jones's (2011) examination of discourses of authenticity among lesbians who are part of a hiking community. Jones shows that ideologies concerning gender binarism remain a powerful component of the ideological construction of authentic lesbian identities among her participants. Her participants questioned the authenticity of feminine lesbians, for instance, and articulated an understanding of the biological roots of their authentic lesbianism as tied to increased testosterone. Jones's analysis illustrates how broad cultural notions concerning identity iterate through local contexts, providing exactly the kind of ideological grounding Cameron notes as lacking for lesbians. In my work on lesbian joking behavior (Queen 2005), I have found something quite similar. Formulaic jokes about lesbians frequently present a lesbian identity simultaneously based in masculinity and femininity and yet independent of them as well. For the participants in my and Jones's studies, it is not necessarily the case that there is no stereotype upon which to draw for a lesbian stance or persona; it's more that the specifics of that stereotype do not lend themselves as robustly to broader circulation. Wagner (2010) shows a startlingly similar case in her examinations of dinnertime conversations in families with lesbian parents. While many of the dynamics found in dinnertime conversations involving lesbian parents are quite similar to those involving heterosexual parents, the power dynamics were much more diffused relative to masculine and feminine positionality across the two lesbian partners.

It is exactly this analytic puzzle that Kulick (2010) and Levon (2011) explore. Kulick illustrates that the stereotype of the "humorless" lesbian is a reflection of her structural position as a masculine woman in a culture in which masculinity itself is not a matter of humor because it is ideologically nonperformative. This is an intriguing proposal; however, it does not adequately account for the equally widespread stereotype of the humorless (heterosexual) feminist. One area for further inquiry opened up by Kulick's proposal is the degree to which the humorless lesbian is a stereotype rooted in the social politics of masculinity and the degree to which it is rooted in its unclear relationship to both masculinity and femininity.

Whereas Kulick's analysis is primarily introspective, Levon (2011) relies on ethnography and sociophonetic analysis to explore the linguistic production of two groups of lesbian activists. He finds that the two groups both use higher mean pitch when discussing gay topics despite having fundamentally oppositional beliefs about key social factors and argues that his findings illustrate the indeterminacy of indexical meaning when considered independently of context. At the same time, his findings exemplify the difficulties inherent in a strict focus on the local context of linguistic production since the two groups share an ambiguous position relative to gender binarism and the power relations embedded therein.

5. Conclusion

My own perspective with respect to this area of research, including my own contributions to it, is that the new insights developed from theories and methods coming primarily out of cultural studies and queer theory seem to have largely run their course and that the emergence of new directions with respect to language and sexualities (and by extension to sociolinguistics) will depend on the development of theories, and especially methods, that meld the understandings thus far gained with standard social scientific and experimental approaches, such as are emerging from work in sociophonetics and corpus linguistics.

In the end, the study of language and sexualities, like the study of sociolinguistics more generally, has to be tied to the desire for an accurate model of language variation and its ties to cognitive, social, and historical landscapes. Such a model has to take seriously the emergent properties of social meaning and the idiosyncrasies of local experience and individual particularity while at the same time recognizing that humans live in a world that shapes and constrains the contours of those idiosyncrasies through institutions, political economies, norms of social engagement, histories, cultures, and even biology, thus making at least some aspects of those contours generalizable and predictable. Finding ways to blend our theory-building more concretely with scientific methods would thus go far toward reconciling one of the inherent problems of trying to study language, namely that it is at once a property of individuals and a property of groups of individuals.

REFERENCES

Ahearn, Laura M. 2003. "Writing Desire in Nepali Love Letters." *Language and Communication*, 23: 107–122.

Archakis, Argiris, and Sofia Lampropoulou. 2009. "Talking Different Heterosexualities: The Permissive, the Normative and the Moralistic Perspective – Evidence from Greek Youth Storytelling." *Discourse & Society*, 20(3): 307–326.

Baker, Paul. 2008. *Sexed Texts: Language, Gender and Sexuality*. London: Equinox.

Barrett, Rusty. 2003. "Models of Gay Male Identity and the Marketing of 'Gay Language' in Foreign-Language Phrasebooks for Gay Men." *Estudios de Sociolingüística*, 4(2): 533–562.

Bucholtz, Mary, and Kira Hall. 2004. "Theorizing Identity in Language and Sexuality." *Language in Society*, 34(4): 501–547.

Cameron, Deborah. 2011. "Sociophonetics and Sexuality: Discussion." *American Speech*, 86(1): 98–103.

Cameron, Deborah, and Don Kulick. 2003. *Language and Sexuality*. Cambridge: Cambridge University Press.

Cameron, Deborah, and Don Kulick. 2006. *The Language and Sexuality Reader*. New York: Routledge.

Campbell-Kibler, Kathryn. 2011. "Intersecting Variables and Perceived Sexual Orientation in Men." *American Speech*, 86(1): 52–68.

Chirrey, Deborah. 2003. "I Hereby Come Out: What Sort of Speech Act is Coming Out?" *Journal of Sociolinguistics*, 7(1): 24–37.

Chirrey, Deborah. 2007. "Women Like Us: Mediating and Contesting Identity in Lesbian Advice Literature." In Sakis Kyratsis and Helen Sauntson (eds.), *Language, Sexualities and Desires*, 223–243. Basingstoke: Palgrave Macmillan.

del Teso-Craviotto, Marisol. 2005. "Language and Sexuality in Spanish and English Dating Chats." *Journal of Sociolinguistics*, 10(4): 460–480.

del Teso-Craviotto, Marisol. 2008. "Gender and Sexual Identity Authentication in Language Use: The Case of Chat Room." *Discourse Studies*, 10(2): 251–270.

DiMassa, Diane. 1999. *The Complete Hothead Paisan: Homicidal Lesbian Terrorist*. New York: Cleis Press.

Eckert, Penelope. n.d. "Third Wave Variation Studies." At http://www.stanford.edu/~eckert/thirdwave.html, accessed October 17, 2013.

Eckert, Penelope. 2002. "Demystifying Sexuality and Desire." In Kathryn Campbell-Kibler, Robert J. Podesva, Sarah

J. Roberts, and Andrew Wong (eds.), *Language and Sexuality: Contesting Meaning in Theory and Practice*, 99–110. Stanford: CSLI Publications.

Eckert, Penelope. 2003. "Sociolinguistics and Authenticity: An Elephant in the Room." *Journal of Sociolinguistics*, 7(3): 392–431.

Eckert, Penelope. 2008. "Variation and the Indexical Field." *Journal of Sociolinguistics*, 12(4): 453–476.

Eckert, Penelope. 2011. "Language and Power in the Preadolescent Heterosexual Market." *American Speech*, 86(1): 85–97.

Gaudio, Rudolf. 1994. "Sounding Gay: Pitch Properties in the Speech of Gay and Straight Men." *American Speech*, 69(1): 30–37.

Hall, Kira. 2009. "Boy's Talk: Hindi, Moustaches, and Masculinity in New Delhi." In Pia Pichler and Eva M. Eppler (eds.), *Gender and Spoken Interaction*, 139–162. Basingstoke: Palgrave Macmillan.

Holmes, Janet, and Miriam Meyerhoff, eds. 2003. *The Handbook of Language and Gender*. Oxford: Blackwell.

Hoppe, Trevor. 2011. "Circuits of Power, Circuits of Pleasure: Sexual Scripting in Gay Men's Bottom Narratives." *Sexualities*, 14(2): 193–217.

Jones, Lucy. 2011. " 'The Only Dykey One': Constructions of (In)Authenticity in a Lesbian Community of Practice." *Journal of Homosexuality*, 58(6–7): 719–741.

Kang, Yoonhee. 2003. "The Desire to be Desired: Magic Spells, Agency, and the Politics of Desire among Petalangan People in Indonesia." *Language and Communication*, 23: 153–167.

Kiesling, Scott Fabius. 2002. "Playing the Straight Man: Displaying and Maintaining Male Heterosexuality in Discourse." In Kathryn Campbell-Kibler, Robert J. Podesva, Sarah J. Roberts, and Andrew Wong (eds.), *Language and Sexuality: Contesting Meaning in Theory and Practice*, 249–266. Stanford: CSLI Publications.

Kiesling, Scott Fabius. 2005. "Homosocial Desire in Men's Talk: Balancing and Re-creating Cultural Discourses of Masculinity." *Language in Society*, 34: 695–726.

Kiesling, Scott Fabius. 2011. "Masculinities, Desire, and Discourse." *Gender and Language*, 5(2): 213–239.

Kitzinger, Celia. 2005. " 'Speaking as a Heterosexual': (How) Does Sexuality Matter for Talk-in-Interaction?" *Research on Language and Social Interaction*, 38(3): 221–265.

Koller, Veronika. 2008. *Lesbian Discourses: Images of a Community*. New York: Routledge.

Kulick, Don. 2000. "Gay and Lesbian Language." *Annual Review of Anthropology*, 29: 243–285.

Kulick, Don. 2003. "No." *Language and Communication*, 23: 139–151.

Kulick, Don. 2010. "Humorless Lesbians." In Janet Holmes and Meredith Marra (eds.), *Femininity, Feminism and Gendered Discourse*, 59–82. Newcastle upon Tyne: Cambridge Scholars Publishing.

Land, Victoria, and Celia Kitzinger. 2005. "Speaking as a Lesbian: Correcting Heterosexist Presumption." *Research on Language and Social Interaction*, 38(4): 371–416.

Leap, William. 1995. *Beyond the Lavender Lexicon*. New York: Gordon & Breach.

Leap, William, and Thomas Boellstorff. 2004. *Speaking in Queer Tongues: Globalization and Gay Language*. Urbana: University of Illinois Press.

Levon, Erez. 2006. "Hearing 'Gay': Prosody, Interpretation, and the Affective Judgments of Men's Speech." *American Speech*, 81(1): 56–78.

Levon, Erez. 2011. "Teasing Apart to Bring Together: Gender and Sexuality in Variationist Research." *American Speech*, 86(1): 69–84.

Livia, Anna, and Kira Hall. 1997. *Queerly Phrased: Language, Gender and Sexuality*. Oxford: Oxford University Press.

Mack, Sarah, and Benjamin Munson. 2012. "The Influence of /s/ Quality on Ratings of Men's Sexual Orientation: Explicit and Implicit Measures of the 'Gay Lisp' Stereotype." *Journal of Phonetics*, 40: 198–212.

McConnell-Ginet, Sally. 2002. "Queering Semantics: Definitional Struggles." In Kathryn Campbell-Kibler, Robert J. Podesva, Sarah J. Roberts, and Andrew Wong (eds.), *Language and Sexuality: Contesting Meaning in Theory and Practice*, 137–160. Stanford: CSLI Publications.

McElhinny, Bonnie. 2002. "Language, Sexuality and Political Economy." In Kathryn Campbell-Kibler, Robert J. Podesva, Sarah J. Roberts, and Andrew Wong (eds.), *Language and Sexuality: Contesting Meaning in Theory and Practice*, 111–134. Stanford: CSLI Publications.

Moonwomon, Birch. 1997. "Toward the Study of Lesbian Speech." In Anna Livia and Kira Hall (eds.), *Queerly Phrased: Language, Gender, and Sexuality*, 202–213. Oxford: Oxford University Press.

Morrish, Liz, and Helen Sauntson. 2007. *New Perspectives on Language and Sexual Identity*. Basingstoke: Palgrave Macmillan.

Munson, Benjamin. 2011. "Lavender Lessons Learned; or, What Sexuality Can Teach Us about Phonetic Variation." *American Speech*, 86(1): 14–31.

Munson, Benjamin, Sarah Jefferson, and Elizabeth McDonald. 2006. "The Influence of Perceived Sexual Orientation on Fricative Identification." *Journal of the Acoustical Society of America*, 119: 2427–2437.

Munson, Benjamin, Elizabeth McDonald, Nancy DeBoe, and Aubrey White. 2006. "The Acoustic and Perceptual Bases of Judgments of Women and Men's Sexual Orientation from Read Speech." *Journal of Phonetics*, 34(2): 202–240.

Murray, David A. B. 2003. "Who is Takatāpui? Maori Language, Sexuality and Identity in Aotearoa/New Zealand." *Anthropologica*, 45: 233–244.

Myketiak, Chrystie. 2011. "Discourses of Desire: The Normative in Online Sex Talk." Unpublished PhD dissertation, Queen Mary, University of London.

Peebles, Amy E. 2004. "Sexual and Spiritual Identity Transformation among Ex-Gays and Ex-Ex-Gays: Narrating a New Self." Unpublished PhD dissertation, University of Texas.

Pichler, Pia. 2007. " 'This Sex Thing is Such a Big Issue Now': Sex Talk and Identities in Three Groups of Adolescent Girls." In Sakis Kyratzis and Helen Sauntson (eds.), *Language, Sexualities and Desires*, 68–95. Basingstoke: Palgrave Macmillan.

Pierrehumbert, Janet, Tessa Bent, Benjamin Munson, Ann R. Bradlow, and Michael J. Bailey. 2004. "The Influence of Sexual Orientation on Vowel Production." *Journal of the Acoustical Society of America*, 116(4): 1905–1908.

Piller, Ingrid, and Kimie Takahashi. 2006. "A Passion for English: Desire and the Language Market." In Aneta Pavlenko (ed.), *Bilingual Minds: Emotional Experience, Expression and Representation*, 59–83. Clevedon: Multilingual Matters.

Podesva, Robert. 2006. "Intonational Variation and Social Meaning: Categorical and Phonetic Aspects." *University of Pennsylvania Working Papers in Linguistics*, 12(2): 189–202.

Podesva, Robert. 2007. "Phonation Type as a Stylistic Variable: The Use of Falsetto in Constructing a Persona." *Journal of Sociolinguistics*, 11(4): 478–504.

Podesva, Robert. 2011a. "The California Vowel Shift and Gay Identity." *American Speech*, 86(1): 32–51.

Podesva, Robert. 2011b. "Salience and the Social Meaning of Declarative Contours: Three Case Studies of Gay Professionals." *Journal of English Linguistics*, 39(3): 233–264.

Queen, Robin. 1997. " 'I Don't Speak Spritch': Locating Lesbian Language." In Anna Livia and Kira Hall (eds.), *Queerly Phrased: Language, Gender, and Sexuality*, 233–256. New York: Oxford University Press.

Queen, Robin. 2002. "A Matter of Interpretation: The 'Future' of 'Queer Linguistics.' " In Kathryn Campbell-Kibler, Robert J. Podesva, Sarah J. Roberts, and Andrew Wong (eds.), *Language and Sexuality: Contesting Meaning in Theory and Practice*, 69–86. Stanford: CSLI Publications.

Queen, Robin. 2005. " 'How Many Lesbians Does it Take … ': Jokes, Teasing, and the Negotiation of Stereotypes about

Lesbians." *Journal of Linguistic Anthropology*, 15(2): 239–257.

Queen, Robin. 2006. *Heterosexism and/in Language: Encyclopedia of Language and Lingusitics*. Amsterdam: Elsevier.

Queen, Robin. 2007. "Sociolinguistic Horizons: Language and Sexuality." *Language and Linguistic Compass*, 1(4): 314–330.

Skapoulli, Elena. 2010. "Transforming the Label of 'Whore': Teenage Girls' Negotiation of Local and Global Gender Ideologies in Cyprus." *Pragmatics*, 19(1): 85–101.

Smith, Allyn E., Kathleen Currie Hall, and Benjamin Munson. 2010. "Bringing Semantics to Sociophonetics: Social Variables and Secondary Entailments." *Journal of Laboratory Phonology*, 1: 121–155.

Smith, Benjamin. 2010. "Of Marbles and (Little) Men: Bad Luck and Masculine Identification in Aymara Boyhood." *Journal of Linguistic Anthropology*, 20(1): 225–239.

Smyth, Ron, Greg Jacobs, and Henry Rogers. 2003. "Male Voices and Perceived Sexual Orientation: An Experimental and Theoretical Approach." *Language in Society*, 32: 329–350.

Stokoe, Elizabeth. 2010. " 'Have You Been Married, or … ?': Eliciting and Accounting for Relationship Histories in Speed-Dating Interaction." *Research on Language and Social Interaction*, 43(3): 260–282.

Thompson, Katrina. 2011. "Zanzibari Women's Discursive and Sexual Agency: Violating Gendered Speech Prohibitions through Talk about Supernatural Sex." *Discourse & Society*, 22(3): 3–20.

Thorne, Adrian, and Justine Coupland. 1998. "Articulations of Same-Sex Desire: Lesbian and Gay Male Dating Advertisements." *Journal of Sociolinguistics*, 2(2): 233–257.

Wagner, Sarah. 2010. "Bringing Sexuality to the Table: Language, Gender and Power in Seven Lesbian Families." *Gender and Language*, 4(1): 33–72.

Waksler, Rachelle. 2001. "Pitch Range and Women's Sexual Orientation." *Word*, 52(1): 69–77.

Wong, Andrew. 2002. "The Semantic Derogation of Tongzhi: A Synchronic Perspective." In Kathryn Campbell-Kibler, Robert J. Podesva, Sarah J. Roberts, and Andrew Wong (eds.), *Language and Sexuality: Contesting Meaning in Theory and Practice*, 161–174. Stanford: CSLI Publications.

Wong, Andrew. 2005. "The Reappropriation of *Tongzhi*." *Language in Society*, 34: 763–793.

Zimman, Lal. 2009. " 'The Other Kind of Coming Out': Transgender People and the Coming Out Narrative Genre." *Gender and Language*, 3(1): 53–80.

Zimman, Lal, and Kira Hall. 2010. "Language, Embodiment, and the 'Third Sex.' " In Dominic Watt and Carmen Llamas (eds.), *Language and Identities*, 166–178. Edinburgh: University of Edinburgh Press.

11 Exceptional Speakers
Contested and Problematized Gender Identities

KIRA HALL

1. Introduction

The field of language and gender has witnessed several pivotal shifts in its interpretation of normative and non-normative gender identity. This review aims to expose these shifts in an examination of the ways in which scholars have supported theoretical claims by referencing the speech patterns of "the linguistic deviant" – the speaker who fails to follow normative expectations of how men and women should speak. What becomes apparent in an overview of the literature is that linguistic deviance takes as many forms as the field has theories. In foundational discussions of language and gender in the early 1900s (e.g., Jespersen 1990 [1922]) the linguistic deviant is the "woman" herself, whose speaking patterns are peculiarly divergent from more normative (in this era of scholarship, male) ways of speaking. In early feminist work by those arguing for what has been termed a *dominance model* of language and gender (e.g., Lakoff 1975), which theorizes women's speech patterns as a by-product of male dominance, the linguistic deviant is multiplied in some texts to include all speakers who are in some way disenfranchised from institutionalized male power – women, hippies, homosexuals, and even academic men. When the field shifted in the 1980s to a *difference* or *two-cultures model* of language and gender, which works on the assumption that children are socialized into divergent interactional patterns within single-sex playgroups (e.g., Maltz and Borker 1982), the linguistic deviant resurfaced as tomboy and sissy, whose preference for other-sex playmates was discussed as proving the more normative, two-cultures rule. This latter use of the linguistic deviant could be said to parallel early discussions of non-Indo-European "women's languages" and "men's languages" in the first half of the twentieth century (e.g., Chamberlain 1912; Flannery 1946), where the "effeminate man" or "mannish woman" appeared in the footnotes as strange and deviant exceptions to an otherwise unshakable linguistic dichotomy.

The Handbook of Language, Gender, and Sexuality, Second Edition.
Edited by Susan Ehrlich, Miriam Meyerhoff, and Janet Holmes.
© 2014 John Wiley & Sons, Inc. Published 2017 by John Wiley & Sons, Inc.

Because the overwhelming majority of our field's theories have been based not just on the speech patterns of heterosexuals, but also on those of white middle-class English speakers, the deviant "ethnic" is also a common character, particularly in discussions that seek to make universal claims about how women and men speak. Most notable in this respect are studies supporting a two-cultures model of language and gender, where women whose speech styles do not conform to those identified for the unmarked middle-class white woman become problematic for the theory. When scholars began to diversify the canon by studying the speech patterns of men and women in a variety of communities, societies, and cultures, a new theory of language and gender was born that had as its focus organizations of language and gender in *communities of practice* (Eckert and McConnell-Ginet 1992). It is only when the field shifts to this perspective that we begin to see the purported linguistic deviant on her or his own terms, as a member of a community whose speaking styles are influenced by more localized norms of language and gender. Because what is "normative" becomes potentially infinite within this theoretical paradigm, the research canon becomes diversified as well, enabling not only more sophisticated research on language, gender, and ethnicity, but also the development of a field that has the sexual and gender deviance of previous generations at its center: *queer linguistics*.

This chapter serves as what we might call an "underbelly" review of major works in language and gender research. It is not my intention to criticize earlier studies for their exclusions of certain communities of speakers, as all theories are limited by the intellect of the time in which they were developed. Rather, I offer this review as an exposition of the historical shifts governing our field's understanding of normativity on the one hand and deviance on the other. What I illustrate here is that the concept of non-normative gender identity, while addressed in the gender and language literature in a peripheral manner until quite recently, is nevertheless foundational to the major theoretical perspectives that have developed within the field.

2. Footnote Effeminates and Feminists

The field's first exceptional speakers surface in a flurry of anthropological discussions on sex-based "languages" that appeared at the turn of the twentieth century. Early anthropologists and ethnographers, in their explorations of non-European languages and cultures, developed the twin concepts of "women's language" and "men's language" as a means of explaining the morphological and phonological differences they observed between the speech of women and of men. It is appropriate to begin our discussion here, not only because the work of these anthropologists ushered in a long trajectory of intertextual discussion regarding the social origins of gendered ways of speaking, but also because their representations of non-Indo-European languages initiated a dichotomous understanding of normative linguistic behavior that remains surprisingly influential in the field today.

What many of these texts have in common is what I identify here as "foot-note deviance" – the casual and cursory mention of speakers who, simply put, do not play by the linguistic rules. Because so many of these scholars were, in pre-Whorfian mode, discussing divergent patterns of speaking for women and men in "primitive" societies as reflecting and reinforcing a social configuration of gender unknown to more "civilized" European cultures, the unyielding nature of the dichotomy between women's speech and men's speech was repetitively emphasized, so much so that scholars regularly spoke of these gender-influenced varieties as "separate languages" (e.g., Lasch 1907). What results is the kind of rep-resentation aptly identified by Sara Trechter (1999) as linguistic exoticism, where non-European languages, and the cultures carried through them, are portrayed as having rigidly defined gender roles, even to the point of restricting the way peo-ple talk on the basis of sex. Early portraits of languages like English are hardly parallel, for even when divergent patterns of speaking for women and men are acknowledged, as in Otto Jespersen's (1990 [1922]) piece on "The Woman," they are discussed more as a matter of individual choice, if not taste. And so we arrive at the long-standing distinction in the literature between "sex-exclusive languages" and "sex-preferential languages," with the first designation giving the impression of rigidity and coercion and the second of fluidity and choice.

Even as scholars are presenting the "women's languages" and "men's lan-guages" of various non-European cultures as rigidly dichotomized and mutually exclusive, they also make mention of the speakers who buck the system. The most popular of these deviants is the effeminate man, the cross-talker whose nonconformity to a sex-exclusive language model makes him not just a linguistic anomaly, but a social weirdo, an outcast. The fact that he is labeled as "effeminate" or "womanly" by the rest of society for using women's language is then held up as evidence for the extreme and unforgiving nature of the model. An early example of this approach comes to us from Alexander Chamberlain's (1912) review of "Women's Languages" which appeared in *American Anthropologist*. Chamberlain quotes a Caraya speaker as declaring that one of the researchers "was a woman" because "he pronounced the Brazilian word *jacuba* (a kind of drink), not *šăúbă*, as a man would have done, but *šăkúbă* after the fashion of the women" (1912, 580). The anecdote underscores the separateness of the two varieties, since a male speaker who crosses the linguistic divide will not just be seen as womanly or effeminate; he will actually *be* a woman. The resulting portrait of women's and men's language use is rigidly dichotomous, so much so that a speaker's use of the "other" variety changes his sex altogether in public perception.

A more modern example of this same approach is found 30 years later in Paul Furfey's (1944) review entitled "Men's and Women's Language," which includes the following footnote as a quick aside: "Particularly interesting was Dr. Herz-field's observation that a man using a woman's expression would be considered effeminate" (1944, 223 n.). As the author offers no further explanation in the foot-notes as to why this observation is "particularly interesting," the import of the com-ment is clear only when read alongside the larger argument developed within the text. Furfey repeatedly suggests that the sex-based linguistic differences evident in many non-European languages point to a "consciousness of men and women as different categories of human beings" – one that is, in his own words, "bound up with a masculine assertion of superiority" (1944, 222). The implication is that the same sort of hierarchical consciousness does not exist in European cultures, a point behind Furfey's stated goals for writing the article: "The present paper will discuss divergencies in the language usages of men and women, a phenomenon which is barely discernible in the familiar languages of Europe, but which is not at all uncommon among primitive peoples," for which it "serves as a tool of sex dominance" (1944, 218). By avoiding any in-depth discussion of gender in European languages, Furfey's review works to exoticize the oppressive nature of gender in non-European cultures. The most exotic proof of this oppression is the linguistic effeminate, whose use of women's language emasculates him to a position of powerlessness.

The significance of this emasculation potential is also articulated in Regina Flannery's (1946) article on "Men's and Women's Speech in Gros Ventre," albeit for a rather different reason. We find a slight shift of tone in this article, as Flannery appears to move away from previous representations of sex-based speaking styles as distinct "languages" with her use of the term "speech differences." Yet Flannery also emphasizes the mutually exclusive nature of these gendered styles by detailing the place of the "mannish" woman and "effeminate" man in the community, who serve as a source of "mortification" and "shame" for their families. We later learn that it is this very mortification and shame that is accelerating language loss in the more general population. Because children are afraid that they will be laughed at by older generations for being "bisexual" if they use the wrong gendered forms – knowing, as they do, "the connotations in the minds of older generations" (Flannery 1946, 135) – they choose to avoid using Gros Ventre altogether by speaking only English. Flannery's argument is a historical one, and our footnote effeminate wins the dubious distinction of promoting language shift.

The kind of evolutionary logic reflected in Flannery's discussion of language shift is evident in the majority of these early descriptions of men's and women's languages, which regularly contrast the "archaic" and "primitive" nature of sex-exclusive language systems with the modernity carried by sex-preferential systems such as English. A case in point is Otto Jespersen's (1990 [1922]) early discussion entitled "The Woman," in which he outlines the many different kinds of sex differentiation evident in the world's languages. An important fact that has gone unnoticed about Jespersen's article – now infamous in language and gender studies for its representation of "the woman" as the linguistic other – is the evolutionary logic betrayed by its organization. Extreme phonetic differences existing in non-European languages give way to "very few traces of sex dialects in our Aryan languages" (206) followed by only "a few differences in pronunciation between the two sexes" (209) in contemporary English. The vocabulary and word-choice differences evident for the sexes in English, in contrast to the phonetic differences evident for the sexes in non-European languages, hold a more advanced position on the evolutionary linguistic continuum. This representation hinges on Jespersen's sociological explanations for phonetic divergence, with primitive tribes and early civilized peoples sharing a sex-based division of labor that resulted in different phonological systems for men and women. Modern-day languages like English do not have distinctive grammars for the two sexes since the age-old division of labor has, in Jespersen's understanding, only "lingering effects" (219) in the twentieth century.

This teleological logic is also betrayed by the kinds of exceptional speakers Jespersen chooses for three of his four "time periods" in language and gender relations. We move from the young Carib-speaking man who is not "allowed" to pronounce the war words of men's language until passing certain tests of bravery and patriotism, to the sixteenth-century French-speaking effeminate who imitates women in his reduction of the trilled *r*, to the modern-day English-speaking feminist who imitates the slang of men. The gendered rigidity evident in the non-European languages mentioned at the beginning of the article gives way to a certain fluency in the European languages discussed later, with the crucial turning point being sixteenth-century France. It is at this juncture, suggests Jespersen, that the sex-based division of labor, with its rigid linguistic reflexes, is replaced by a sex-based public/private dichotomy – a sociological shift that leads not to separate languages, but to the possibility of cross-sex appropriation. Jespersen's exceptional speakers thus enter the text in order to illuminate how our present-day linguistic and cultural situation differs from that of the less civilized world that precedes us. The height of this linguistic evolution is captured by the educated feminist of the final time period. Her use of the "new and fresh expressions" of men, precipitated by "the rise of the feminist movement" (1990 [1922], 212), points to an equality between the sexes that was heretofore nonexistent. The divergent uses of vocabulary and syntax that Jespersen subsequently identifies are then theorized not as sociological, but as cognitive, psychological, and personal.

3. The Woman

Given the care with which many of these early anthropologists describe both "men's language" and "women's language" as normative aspects of a particular linguistic and cultural system, Jespersen's more concentrated focus on "the woman" marks an important theoretical shift in the literature. Jespersen ushered in a new understanding of linguistic deviance, with English-speaking women and their speech peculiarities usurping the cross-talking effeminates of non-European cultures. For Jespersen, men's speech is the norm and women's speech the deviation. This is a new form of linguistic exoticism, one that has "women's speech" in modern-day English as its target instead of the women's and men's languages of non-European cultures. The scholars who followed Jespersen, also observing differences between women's conversational patterns and the more socially accepted or dominant patterns of men, tended to represent women's speech as abnormal, as the marked case, as norm-breaking. In this segment of our field's early history, then, the most contested and problematized gender identity becomes "the woman" herself.

Literature that addressed the historical development of women's and men's languages contributed to this perspective (see Haas 1964 [1944] for a review), as it tended to position women's forms as derivational, even in cases where they were thought to be more archaic. For example, Gatschet (1884, 79–81) discusses the existence of an "ancient female dialect" in Hitchiti, still spoken by women and elders in the community. But even though he claims that this dialect was formerly the language of men as well as women, he chooses to provide a grammar only of the newer "common form (or male language)." Although the women's variety is older and apparently basic, Gatschet's prose positions it as both "uncommon" and marked. Similarly, Edward Sapir (1949 [1929]) is careful to argue for two different directions of derivation in Yana, with male forms fundamental in some cases and female forms fundamental in others. Yet in his conclusion, when theorizing why these sex forms might have come to exist in the first place, he ignores the latter of these directions and discusses women's forms as purely reductive (a decision that seems to rest on an earlier observation that the male form in both cases "is longer than the female form"): "Possibly the reduced female forms constitute a conventionalized symbolism of the less considered or ceremonious status of women in the community. Men, in dealing with men, speak fully and deliberately; where women are concerned, one prefers a clipped style of utterance!" (1949 [1929], 212). Women cannot win in these early texts: when their language forms are discussed as fundamental or older, they are theorized as conservative and archaic in comparison to their more innovative and youthful male counterparts; when their language forms are discussed as derived or newer, they are theorized as psychologically deviant or otherwise abnormal. The simple fact that so many of the early articles on sex differentiation in language carry the title "Women's Speech" or "Women's Language" points to an understanding of male speech as *the* language and women's speech as a kind of oddity.

The term "peculiar" becomes the most common descriptor for women's speech in the literature of this period. Jespersen (1990 [1922]) himself is a big fan of this buzzword, using it to describe women's divergent uses of vocabulary (e.g., citing Greenough and Kittredge 1901, 210, "The use of *common* in the sense of 'vulgar' is distinctly a feminine peculiarity"), as well as to theorize women's divergent uses of syntax ("These sentences are the linguistic symptoms of a peculiarity of feminine psychology": 216). His prose parallels that of Bogoras (1922, 665–666) in his article on Chukchee published during the same year, who also discusses certain facets of women's pronunciation as sounding "quite peculiar" and "not easily understood by an inexperienced ear" (665). Bogoras's discussion is an especially clear case of the male linguistic gaze that characterizes much of this literature, with the author assuming a male readership that would identify with male uses of the language as opposed to female ones (certainly these phonetic forms do not sound so peculiar to the women who use them).

4. Hippies, Historians, and Homos

We find reflexes of this early trend even in the ethnographically informed discussions of women's and men's speech patterns that surfaced with the rise of speech act theory in the 1960s and 1970s. Elinor Keenan (Ochs)'s (1996 [1974]) influential study of Malagasy speakers in Madagascar, entitled "Norm-Makers, Norm-Breakers: Uses of Speech by Men and Women in a Malagasy Community," is a case in point. Keenan (Ochs) spends the first three-quarters of her article outlining the linguistic repertoire of "the people of Namoizamanga" (1996 [1974], 100), describing in great detail their varied discursive strategies for avoiding direct affront. It is only in the last few pages of the article that we come to realize that women are not included in this description because of their preference for a more direct and confrontational speaking style. Although Keenan (Ochs) presents Malagasy-speaking men as "norm-makers" and Malagasy-speaking women as "norm-breakers," the women of her study are certainly adhering to "a norm" just as much as the men are: their expected participation in more direct forms of information-finding, bargaining, and child-scolding speaks to the strength and persistence of that very norm. But since it is a norm deemed inferior by the more dominant male-speaking population, Keenan (Ochs) chooses to portray the speech of these Madagascar women as deviant, or even (as the title of her article might imply) subversive. The representation of women as a problematized gender identity, then, becomes central to feminists working within the *dominance model* of language and gender, which focuses on how women's speech patterns are trivialized, or otherwise marginalized, in male-dominant societies. Norms in such studies are viewed as singular, and women become the non-normative exception.

But the women of these texts rarely stand as the lone exception to an oppressive discursive regime. As with Sapir's (1949 [1915]) work on deviant speech in Nootka, early researchers frequently discussed the speech patterns of women with reference to other marginalized identities in order to emphasize their abnormality, or as in the case of Robin Lakoff (1975), to highlight their disenfranchisement from the powers that be. Most scholars have read Lakoff's work as exclusively concerned with women's patterns of speaking, ignoring her rather extensive discussions of a variety of other identities, among them the effeminate homosexual, the anticapitalist hippie, and the asocial male professor. For Lakoff, such men have much in common with women: specifically, they share a marginality determined by their exclusion from institutionalized male power. Central to Lakoff's explanation for this shared marginality is the gendered division of labor, and, more specifically, the differential orientations to politeness brought about by this division. Women, excluded from a male workplace built on "present-day reflexes of male bonding" (1975, 77), tend to orient themselves to politeness forms that discourage bonding, gravitating toward the first two rules of Lakoff's politeness paradigm: *formality* (keep aloof) and *deference* (give options). Men, on the other hand, as a result of their socialization within workplace situations that require them to develop techniques of working together as a group, are more likely to embrace Lakoff's third rule of politeness: *camaraderie*. The latter rule would be essential in, for example, a male-dominated corporate workplace, as group members must develop interactive measures to gloss over emotional reactions and disagreements that might hinder progress toward a common goal. These are measures women have generally not needed to develop, Lakoff suggests, since they have historically been excluded from these group-oriented work environments. Her remark that women's use of terms like *divine* is "not a mark of feelings of inferiority but rather a mere badge of class" (1975, 52) is telling in this respect. Consistent with radical feminist discussions of the time that identified women as a *fourth world* (Burris 1973) or *separate caste* (Dunbar 1970), Lakoff situates women within a powerless "female class" that exists outside of the institutionalized power structure and employs a non-work-related vocabulary deemed irrelevant by this very power structure. To borrow from the title of Lakoff's book, "woman's place" is a place excluded from the public sphere of men's work, and the language patterns that have developed as a result of this exclusion are devalued as "women's language."

The notion of a masculine workplace, then, is fundamental to Lakoff's theoretical explanation for men's and women's differential use of linguistic phenomena. This explains why academic males, hippies, and homosexuals occupy the margins of Lakoff's text as problematized gender identities. Like women, these groups are in some way excluded from a social history of male bonding in the labor force, and as with women, this exclusion leads to language patterns dissociated from what Lakoff terms "real-world power." The following excerpts from Lakoff's text underscore the fact that her work is not so much about gender as it is about power:

Hippies

I think it is significant that this word ["groovy"] was introduced by the hippies, and, when used seriously rather than sarcastically, used principally by people who have accepted the hippies' values. Principal among these is the denial of the Protestant work ethic: to a hippie, something can be worth thinking about even if it isn't influential in the power structure, or moneymaking. Hippies are separated from the activities of the real world just as women are – though in the former case it is due to a decision on their parts, while this is not uncontroversially true in the case of women. (Lakoff 1975, 13)

Academic men

Another group that has, ostensibly at least, taken itself out of the search for power and money is that of academic men. They are frequently viewed by other groups as analogous in some ways to women ... what they do doesn't really count in the real world ... The suburban home finds its counterpart in the ivory tower: one is supposedly shielded from harsh realities in both. Therefore it is not too surprising that many academic men ... often use "women's language." (Lakoff 1975, 14)

Homosexuals

It is of interest, by the way, to note that men's language is increasingly being used by women, but women's language is not being adopted by men, apart from those who reject the American masculine image [for example, homosexuals]. This is analogous to the fact that men's jobs are being sought by women, but few men are rushing to become housewives or secretaries. The language of the favored group, the group that holds the power, along with its nonlinguistic behavior, is generally adopted by the other group, not vice versa. (Lakoff 1975, 10)

For Lakoff, male hippies, academics, and homosexuals are all in some sense gender deviants – identities who have forsaken a capitalistic power structure built on masculine ideals for pursuits considered trivial in the "real world." This would explain, suggests Lakoff, why the language patterns of hippie, academic, or homosexual so often appear to resemble that of the American middle-class housewife. That these disenfranchised groups are likely to use some of the same specialized lexical items as American middle-class women, she argues, points to a more general conclusion: "These words aren't, basically, 'feminine'; rather they signal 'uninvolved' or 'out of power'" (Lakoff 1975, 14). While certain patterns of speech may be considered feminine because women are, in her own terms, the "'uninvolved' 'out of power' group *par excellence*," Lakoff is careful to note that any group in society may use patterns associated with "women's language" (an observation that best explains her consistent use of scare quotes around the term). For Lakoff, it is the feminine-sounding male, marginal to the world of institutionalized masculinity, who ultimately enables her to formulate the crux of her argument: "The decisive factor is less purely gender than power in the real world" (1975, 57).

In spite of their centrality to Lakoff's theory, these marginal figures are frequently overlooked in subsequent discussions of her work. The majority of her critics, swept up in an imperative to test her argument empirically, interpreted Lakoff as suggesting that only women speak "women's language," developing study upon study to determine whether or not female speakers actually use this register more than their male interlocutors. What is amusing, in retrospect, is that a great number of these studies analyze the speech patterns of the very academics that Lakoff identifies as linguistically divergent in order to "disprove" her hypothesis, such as Dubois and Crouch's (1975) study of men's use of tag questions at an academic conference. But the mission of critics to distinguish the female register from the female speaker (see also Crosby and Nyquist 1977; O'Barr and Atkins 1980) is nevertheless admirable. It is this distinction that in many ways enabled the development of *queer linguistics* – a field that explicitly questions the assumption that gendered ways of talking are indexically derived from the sex of the speaker.

5. Sissies and Tomboys

The 1980s ushered in an alternative flavor of language and gender research, marked in part by Daniel Maltz and Ruth Borker's (1982) proposal of a new framework for examining differences in the language use of American women and men. Their approach, sometimes identified as a two-cultures or difference model of language and gender, holds that American women and men come from two different sociolinguistic subcultures, in which they learn different rules for interacting with one another and interpreting conversational contributions. In an extension of John Gumperz's (1982) cultural explanation for interethnic (mis)communication, Maltz and Borker argue that boys and girls orient to their own sex as preschoolers and thus develop divergent cultures of talk. (See

Goodwin and Kyratzis, Chapter 26 in this volume, for discussion.) The singular norm of studies in the dominance approach becomes dual again, with male and female speakers traveling on different (and frequently oppositional) tracks of normativity. Interesting in Maltz and Borker's platform is a short aside in their concluding notes, where they give us the "tomboy," together with "lesbians and gay men," as one of "a number of specific problems that appear to be highly promising for future research" (1982, 94). Why these marginal identities might be "potential research problems" for a two-cultures approach to language and gender is fairly clear. Because the argument is based on the assumption that boys and girls are socialized into interaction differently in their single-sex playgroups, what happens to the theory when we find children who appear to shun this very socialization? Do they grow up to be lesbians and gay men who share conversational patterns with the other sex? The sissy and the tomboy, then, as apparent exceptions to a socialization rule presented as having few if any defectors, become oddly important to a two-cultures perspective.

The most overtly theorized discussion of sissies and tomboys appears in Eleanor Maccoby's (1998) *The Two Sexes: Growing Up Apart, Coming Together*, a comprehensive review of previous research that supports a two-cultures approach to the subject of gender. Maccoby is interested in how biological, social, and cognitive forces come together to constitute what she calls gender's "explanatory web," creating divergent patterns of behavior for the two sexes that begin in the womb, materialize in early childhood, remain through adulthood, and are ultimately transferred to the next generation. In contrast to much of the two-cultures research that has as a main goal a description of "what boys do" as opposed to "what girls do" (offering linguistic evidence, for instance, to support the claim that boys' interaction is more "hierarchical" while girls' is more "collaborative"), Maccoby seeks to determine *why* these interactional differences arise in the first place. As her focus is on gender conformity in same-sex childhood playgroups, not dissension, tomboys and sissies appear in the text not so much as trouble-shooters for a two-cultures approach (or as identities whose interaction is interesting in their own right), but as exceptions that prove the more normative rule. And because this normative rule is produced biologically as well as socially for Maccoby, our tomboy and sissy come to play an interesting role in her theorizing of each of these influences.

Maccoby's primary sociological argument for why divergent patterns of interaction exist between the two sexes has to do with the "greater strength" (1998, 41) of boys' playgroups as opposed to girls'. The forces binding groups of boys together, she argues, are much stronger than those binding girls together, leading to a much more exclusionary kind of play in which peer group acceptance becomes the overriding concern. Boys therefore have a much greater need for recognition from other boys, and this drives them to engage in the status-oriented discursive behaviors identified by many linguists for all-boys' groups. The fact that girls do not enact sanctions against tomboy behavior in the same way that boys enact sanctions against sissy behavior illustrates that boys' groups are more cohesive, more conforming, more gender-exclusionary: "Clearly, an essential element in becoming masculine is becoming not-feminine, while girls can be feminine without having to prove that they are not masculine" (Maccoby 1998, 52). It is worth noting that Maccoby's use of the tomboy is diametrically opposed to Lakoff's (1975), who points to the "little girl [who] talks rough like a boy" as evidence for the strength of female socialization. For Lakoff, the fact that the tomboy is "ostracized, scolded, or made fun of" by parents and friends is suggestive of how society "keeps her in line, in her place" (1975, 5).

The disparity between Lakoff's and Maccoby's sociological analysis of the tomboy could be a result of the 20-year time differential between the two texts. But to say that boys' groups are more cohesive because the label *sissy* operates as an insult whereas *tomboy* does not, as Maccoby does, ignores the import of age on peer acceptance of gender deviance. Certainly, Penelope Eckert's (2002; Chapter 27 in this volume) research on adolescent girls' management of the "heterosexual marketplace" suggests that it would be quite difficult, if not socially detrimental, for a girl to continue her tomboy leanings into the teen years. The differences of perspective voiced here undoubtedly have much to do with the fact that there is very little ethnographic, much less linguistic, research on so-called "deviant" gender identities in either childhood or adolescence. The tomboy's unwritten nature, then, makes her ripe for all sorts of scholarly pickings. In fact, Barrie Thorne (1993), in her ethnographic study of gender in American elementary schools, discusses tomboys and sissies as part of a larger critique of the very two-cultures approach espoused by scholars like Maccoby, arguing that the variation we find within genders is greater than the variation we find between boys and girls taken as groups. For Thorne, the tomboy is just one aspect of a "complicated continuum of crossing" (1993, 112) – a continuum that is, in her opinion, obscured by research that operates on the assumption of gender as separation and difference.

Maccoby argues that gendered behavior in childhood is a function of biology as well as of socialization, so it is not surprising that we find extended discussions of prenatal deviants as well. We learn about the male play patterns of girls who were exposed to excess amounts of adrenal androgen while in the womb (identified in the scientific literature as females with adrenogenital syndrome, or AGS), along with the rough-and-tumble play of female rhesus monkeys whose mothers had been injected with testosterone when pregnant. Maccoby is careful to avoid drawing links between this scientific research and sociological discussions of actual tomboys, but here again we see deviance embraced as evidence for normativity. The argument goes something like this. "Normal" boys and girls, as a result of prenatal hormonal priming, have different rates of maturation when it comes to particular kinds of behavior. Girls appear to self-regulate their behavior much earlier than boys do, having earlier success at potty-training, for example, and showing faster progress in language development. A boy's lack of self-control earns him more hierarchical, disciplinary commands from his parents as well as more rough-and-tumble play; a girl's more advanced language capacity invites more relational and nurturant talk about feelings. These same children eventually come to self-select playmates who behave as they do. The resulting single-sex playgroups begin to accentuate the behaviors encouraged earlier by parents, until definitively divergent patterns of interaction emerge for the two groups. The AGS girl stands on the sidelines of this discussion, stepping in at critical junctures as evidence for the biological component of Maccoby's explanatory web. The fact that AGS girls prefer male play partners and high levels of rough-and-tumble play gives Maccoby the evidence she needs to argue for biology's role in the construction of dichotomous gendered behaviors. And it is the biological aspect of Maccoby's argument that is particularly powerful, as it enables her to make a universal claim about how gender operates. Our bio-tom, then, in her conjoined biological and social deviance, provides evidence not only for a two-cultures gender normativity, but also for its cross-cultural persistence.

One last remark is called for regarding the way in which Maccoby suggests that the phenomenon of early same-sex attraction might have an additional evolutionary purpose. She references anthropologist Arthur Wolf's (1995) study of boys and girls in southern China who, because they had been affianced by their parents at an early age, lived together in the same household for several years in preparation for marriage. Wolf found that such children come to lack sexual interest in each other when they reach adolescence, offering as evidence the fact that their subsequent marriages have exceptionally low rates of fertility. Maccoby's interest in Wolf's research again has to do with the biological aspect of the explanatory web, as his findings provide yet another biologically oriented reason for why same-sex segregation might occur: "Children's spontaneous avoidance of cross-sex others who are not kin serves the biological function of keeping these others within the pool of potential mates" (Maccoby 1998, 94). Yet this claim forces a connection between gender identity and sexual orientation. If tomboys and sissies spend much of their childhood with "the other sex" instead of their own, do they then, as Wolf's theory implies, grow up to lack sexual interest in the opposite sex? Is this where lesbians and gay men come from? Certainly, Maltz and Borker's (1982) juxtaposition of "tomboys" and "lesbians and gay men" as potential problems in their early research platform implies some connection between early deviant gender identities and the sexual orientation of adults. Indeed, the conflation of gender and sexual identity appears through much of the language and gender literature, where, until quite recently, the conversational practices of lesbians and gay men are discussed not as indexing community membership, but as instancing gender deviance.

A telling example of this conflation surfaces in Burrell and Fitzpatrick (1989), where we find the heterosexualization of a conversational excerpt that takes place between two gay men in Deborah Tannen's *That's Not What I Meant! How Conversational Style Makes or Breaks Relationships* (1986). In her bestseller, which includes a chapter on the cross-cultural nature of male–female communication, Tannen gives us one of the field's first gay couples in the form of Mike and Ken, whom she describes, refreshingly, as "two people who lived together and loved each other" (1986, 126). The excerpt at issue regards a fight over salad dressing, where, according to Tannen, each partner misunderstands the conversational frame used by the other. But while Tannen discusses this exchange in gender-free terms in order to demonstrate the kinds of misunderstandings that can occur in close relationships, Burrell and Fitzpatrick reinterpret virtually the same exchange entirely along gendered lines; Mike and Ken even surface as "Bob" and

"Joanne." The two excerpts – Tannen's followed by Burrell and Fitzpatrick's – are reproduced below:

Mike:	What kind of salad dressing should I make?
Ken:	Oil and vinegar, what else?
Mike:	What do you mean, "what else?"
Ken:	Well, I always make oil and vinegar, but if you want, we could try something else.
Mike:	Does that mean you don't like it when I make other dressings?
Ken:	No, I like it. Go ahead. Make something else.
Mike:	Not if you want oil and vinegar.
Ken:	I don't. Make a yogurt dressing.
	(Mike makes a yogurt dressing, tastes it, and makes a face.)
Ken:	Isn't it good?
Mike:	I don't know how to make a yogurt dressing.
Ken:	Well, if you don't like it, throw it out.
Mike:	Never mind.
Ken:	What never mind? It's just a little yogurt.
Mike:	You're making a big deal about nothing.
Ken:	*You* are!

(Tannen 1986, 119)

Bob:	What kind of salad dressing should I make?
Joanne:	Vinaigrette, what else?
Bob:	What do you mean, "what else?"
Joanne:	Well, I always make vinaigrette, but if you want make something else.
Bob:	Does that mean, you don't like it when I make other dressings?
Joanne:	No, I like it. Go ahead. Make something else.
Bob:	Not if you want vinaigrette.
Joanne:	I don't. Make a yogurt dressing.
	(Bob makes a yogurt dressing, tastes it, and makes a face.)
Joanne:	Isn't it good?
Bob:	I don't know how to make a yogurt dressing.
Joanne:	Well, if you don't like it, throw it out.
Bob:	Never mind.
Joanne:	What never mind? It's just a little yogurt.
Bob:	You're making a big deal about nothing.
Joanne:	You are!

(Burrell and Fitzpatrick 1989, 176–177)

How Tannen's gay men wound up as heterosexuals in Burrell and Fitzpatrick's book is not entirely clear, but their transformation offers an illuminating example of how sexual identity is often disregarded within a two-cultures model of language and gender. What interests me is how the authors reformulate the excerpt as a conversation between "the independent spouse" Bob and the "traditional wife" Joanne. "Throughout this admittedly trivial interaction," the authors explain, "the independent spouse, Bob, saw his wife as becoming increasingly more demanding, whereas the traditional wife Joanne, perceived her husband as becoming more hypersensitive and temperamental" (1989, 177). That an excerpt between two gay men is so easily recast into a heterosexual discussion of "The Psychological Reality of Marital Conflict" betrays a much larger theoretical problem in the language and gender literature of the 1970s and 1980s: namely, the persistent assumption that sexual identity is really about gender.

When gays and lesbians do receive mention in the two-cultures model, they tend not to be subjects of study in their own right, but tangential characters who provide extreme evidence for a dichotomous view of gendered behavior. Tannen, for instance, in her subsequent bestseller *You Just Don't Understand* (1990), refers to Philip Blumstein and Pepper Schwartz's (1984) popular finding that "lesbians have sex less often than gay men and heterosexual couples" as support for her argument that men tend to be initiators and women respondents: "But among lesbians, they found, often neither feels comfortable taking the role of initiator, because neither wants to be perceived as making demands" (Tannen 1990, 147–148). Here, lesbians come to serve as a test-case for Tannen's theory, providing an archetypal female–female example of the behaviors she identifies for women speakers more generally. Tannen reads the purported lesbian hesitancy to initiate sex as a gendered trait, and offers it as evidence for a more general theory regarding women's discomfort with self-assertion. Lesbians, as same-sex partners, are discussed as a kind of "grown-up" version of the childhood all-girl playgroups so instrumental to two-cultures theorizing. Tannen's occasional comparisons of lesbians with gay men, as in a later chapter of the book when she contrasts lesbian and gay understandings of the relationship between money and independence (1990, 292), are intended not as discussions of sexual identity, but as paradigmatic examples of difference between women and men.

6. Queers and the Rest of Us

What is exceptional about Tannen's lesbians and gay men, however, is precisely that they are not exceptional; that is, their interactive behaviors are viewed not as deviant, but as entirely in line with the interactive behaviors of heterosexual women and men. While some scholars may fault her work for failing to consider the potential influences of sexual identity on conversational exchange (see Jacobs 1996), her refusal to portray lesbians and gay men as peculiarly deviant, in the manner of former generations of researchers, is better understood as progressive for the linguistic scholarship of the time. Her work might even be said to reflect a transitional point in the academic treatment of sexual identity, when identities previously viewed as deviant or non-normative began to be brought into the mainstream of scholarly discussion. I want to argue here that three theoretical moves in the language and gender research of the early to mid-1990s precipitated this transition: first, the introduction of the notion of *communities of practice* (Eckert and McConnell-Ginet 1992); second, the more sophisticated development of *ideological* approaches to the study of language and gender (e.g., Bucholtz and Hall 1995; Bucholtz, Liang, and Sutton 1999; Gal 1991); and finally, the birth of *queer linguistics* (Livia and Hall 1997), a field that activates, albeit critically, the philosophical notion of performativity. All of these moves were formulated within, and influenced by, larger theoretical moves in the academy. Most notable in this respect is multicultural feminism, which encouraged the intellectual embracement of heretofore understudied identities in a postmodern drive to diversify the academic canon. The linguistic reflexes of this drive, accordingly, share a focus on more localized organizations of language, gender, and sexuality. The two-norm approach of the previous generation gave way to a paradigm that reframes the normative as ideologically produced within specific practice-based communities. Norms of feminine and masculine speech, although always constrained and influenced by dominant ideologies of language and gender, become potentially infinite in local articulation, particularly as gendered ideologies are produced only in interaction with localized understandings of race, class, sexuality, and age.

The concept of gender performativity, as developed within queer linguistics and more generally in sociolinguistics, is closely allied with ideological and practice-based approaches to the study of language and gender, although this fact has been little discussed in the literature. As Anna Livia and I argue in our introduction to *Queerly Phrased* (Livia and Hall 1997), the concept is much needed in the field as a way out of the circular research paradigm encouraged by the theoretical tenets of social constructionism. The feminist distinction between *sex* and *gender*, with the first term being used for the biological and the second for the social, was a politically necessary one, as it threw a decisive wrench in essentialist arguments that limited social agency to biological predisposition. But this distinction also had a compromising effect on ethnographic research, leading language and gender scholars, for example, to seek out the sociolinguistic reflexes of a prediscursive biological sex. Working from the assumption that the social maps onto the biological (a perspective criticized by Nicholson 1994 as a "coat-rack model" of sex and gender; see McElhinny 2002; Chapter 2 in this volume), researchers pre-identified their subjects as "male" and "female" and then isolated the conversational strategies that distinguished these groupings from one another. Sexual identity, as a subjective designation not easily related to biology, remains invisible within this paradigm.

But the performativity of gender, as formulated by Judith Butler (1990) via a Derridean reworking of J. L. Austin's (1962) notion of the "performative utterance," disallows sociolinguistic approaches to identity that view the way we talk as directly indexing a prediscursive self. To a poststructuralist like Butler, there is no prediscursive identity, as even our understanding of biological sex is produced through cultural understandings of social gender. This kind of thinking puts much more weight on the speech event itself, requiring us to examine how speakers manage ideologies of feminine and masculine speech in the ongoing production of gendered selves. It also gives us a nonessentialist understanding of personhood, as what becomes important is not how speakers affirm or resist a pregiven biological designation, but how they activate various identity positions within particular conversations and localized contexts. Rusty Barrett's (1999) work on the "polyphonous identity" displays of African American drag queens in a Texas gay bar is an exemplary model of how such research might proceed, as he illustrates the ways in which speakers make use of linguistic variables with indexical associations to a variety of social categories.

Yet Butler's theory also has its limits for ethnographic sociolinguistic research. Most pressing in this regard is the restricted agency awarded the subject in a poststructuralist focus on discursive determinism, together with the undertheorization of the local in a philosophical text concerned with universal explanations for how gender works. Here is where the field would do well to remember how Austin's performative was taken up by linguistic anthropologists such as Dell Hymes, Charles Briggs, and Richard Bauman in the early ethnography of speaking. While Butler focuses almost exclusively on the rigid regulatory frames that make femininity and masculinity intelligible (in Austinian terms, the "conventional procedures" that make a performative utterance felicitous), these authors focus also on the emergent properties of specific speech events (see Hall 1999).

Hymes's (1975) repeated call to "understand structure as emergent in action" is critical here, as he and other scholars of performance, most notably Bauman and Briggs (1990), led us away from the analysis of ritual as mere reiteration. What moves into focus with their work is not Derridean iterability but "the total speech act," as they uncover not just the cultural conventions that make performance, ritual, and even everyday conversation felicitous, but also the creative aspects that govern any speech event. Butler's limitation of creativity to resignification – as, for instance, when a drag queen performs the "wrong" gender and thereby exposes the constructed nature of gender perceived as natural – is impoverished in ethnographic terms, since it reduces drag queen performance to an appropriation of a dominant ideology of femininity. This is, indeed, the assumption behind Butler's argument that drag is a kind of "double mimesis," that is, men acting like women acting like women. But as Barrett so cogently demonstrates in his linguistic research, drag queens are not acting like *women*; they are acting like *drag queens*. Their interwoven appropriations of African American Vernacular English, the "Standard" English phonology associated with "white woman style," and lexical items indexical of gay male speech suggest that gender identity is a multivocal phenomenon that depends on interaction with other social identities for its articulation. Because drag queen identity is always localized and produced through a variety of conflicting cultural scripts (race, class, sexuality, and gender among them), it would be ethnographically reductive to discuss their performances purely as a subversion of a nonlocalizable "femininity."

This brings me to the crux of an argument about how Butler's theory of gender performativity must be reworked, or at least acquire new focus, in the sociolinguistic study of language, gender, and sexuality. The only way identities previously regarded as non-normative can be brought into the mainstream of scholarship is if we localize what constitutes "felicitous" and "infelicitous" performances of gender and sexual identity within the language ideologies circulating in specific communities of practice. To discuss drag queen performance as the infelicitous enactment of dominant conventions of gender, as Butler does in her focus on drag as subversion, assumes a kind of singularity to drag queen identity, one that becomes interesting only in its potential to denaturalize heterosexual normativity. Queer linguistics, in contrast, invites us to discuss the conversational practices of all sexual identities – whether marginal or central to organizations of heterosexual kinship – as potentially felicitous on a more localized level. While much of the early research in the field has focused on the language practices of understudied sexual identities (just as much of the early research in language and gender focused on the language practices of women), its boundaries also embrace the findings of such scholars as Penelope Eckert (2002; Chapter 27 in this volume), whose ethnographic work on "the heterosexual marketplace" illustrates how heterosexual identity structures the adolescent social order in an American elementary school. Like queer theory, queer linguistics is necessarily concerned with how heterosexual normativity is produced, perpetuated, and resisted, but it seeks to localize these productions within specific communities of practice. (See Milani, Chapter 13 in this volume, for a discussion of this dimension of queer theory.)

In the last decade, the field of queer linguistics has come under fire from Don Kulick (2000; Chapter 3 in this volume), who argues that the language practices of gays and lesbians must be "unique to gays and lesbians" (2000, 259) if they are to be of interest to sociolinguists. Kulick takes difference to be the necessary starting point for scholarship on language and sexuality, arguing that because linguistic differences across sexual identities have not been satisfactorily demonstrated, the field is not viable. Yet an insistence on difference not only requires linguistic deviance as a prerequisite for sociolinguistic research; it also recalls the much criticized difference model of language and gender (see Bucholtz and Hall 2004 for a fuller discussion). This approach, as noted earlier, has been extensively problematized for its tendency to emphasize cross-gender variation at the expense of potentially more significant intragender variation and cross-gender similarity. The practice-based and ideological models of language and gender that developed in response to these critiques, such as queer linguistics, seek not to describe how women's language use differs from men's, or how homosexuals' language use differs from heterosexuals', but to document the diverse range of women's and men's linguistic repertoires as developed within particular contexts. In these models, gender is seen as materializing only in interaction with other sociological discourses, including historical, national, ethnic, racial, age-related, and sexual ones. This, I would argue, is the direction that research on language and sexual identity must continue to take if the exceptional speakers of previous generations are to move squarely out of the footnotes.

Acknowledgments

This chapter is an abbreviated version of a longer article that appeared in the 2003 edition of the *Handbook*. I would like to express my thanks to editors Miriam

Meyerhoff, Janet Holmes, and Susan Ehrlich for several careful readings of this chapter, and to Joshua Raclaw, Lal Zimman, and Chad Nilep, who provided excellent suggestions on ways to revise this chapter for the second edition.

REFERENCES

Austin, John L. 1962. *How to Do Things with Words*. Cambridge, MA: Harvard University Press.

Barrett, Rusty. 1999. "Indexing Polyphonous Identity in the Speech of African American Drag Queens." In Mary Bucholtz, Anita C. Liang, and Laurel A. Sutton (eds.), *Reinventing Identities: The Gendered Self in Discourse*, 313–331. New York: Oxford University Press.

Bauman, Richard, and Charles L. Briggs. 1990. "Poetics and Performance as Critical Perspectives on Language and Social Life." *Annual Review of Anthropology*, 19: 59–88.

Blumstein, Philip, and Pepper Schwartz. 1984. *American Couples: Money, Work, Sex*. New York: William Morrow.

Bogoras, Waldemar. 1922. "Chukchee." In Franz Boas (ed.), *Handbook of American Indian Languages* 2. Bureau of American Ethnology Bulletin 40, 631–903. Washington, DC: Smithsonian Institution.

Bucholtz, Mary, and Kira Hall. 1995. "Twenty Years after *Language and Woman's Place*." In Kira Hall and Mary Bucholtz (eds.), *Gender Articulated: Language and the Socially Constructed Self*, 1–22. New York: Routledge.

Bucholtz, Mary, and Kira Hall. 2004. "Theorizing Identity in Language and Sexuality Research." *Language in Society*, 33(4): 501–547.

Bucholtz, Mary, Anita C. Liang, and Laurel A. Sutton, eds. 1999. *Reinventing Identities: The Gendered Self in Discourse*. New York: Oxford University Press.

Burrell, Nancy, and Mary Anne Fitzpatrick. 1989. "The Psychological Reality of Marital Conflict." In Dudley D. Cahn (ed.), *Intimates in Conflict: A Communication Perspective*, 167–186. Hillsdale, NJ: Lawrence Erlbaum.

Burris, Barbara. 1973. "Fourth World Manifesto." In Anne Koedt, Ellen Levine, and Anita Rapone (eds.), *Radical Feminism*, 322–357. New York: Quadrangle Books.

Butler, Judith. 1990. *Gender Trouble: Feminism and the Subversion of Identity*. New York: Routledge.

Chamberlain, Alexander F. 1912. "Women's Languages." *American Anthropologist*, 14: 579–581.

Crosby, Faye, and Linda Nyquist. 1977. "The Female Register: An Empirical Study of Lakoff's Hypotheses." *Language in Society*, 6: 313–322.

Dubois, Betty Lou, and Isabel Crouch. 1975. "The Question of Tag Questions in Women's Speech: They Don't Really Use More of Them, Do They?" *Language in Society*, 4: 289–294.

Dunbar, Roxanne. 1970. "Female Liberation as the Basis for Social Revolution." In Robin Morgan (ed.), *Sisterhood is Powerful*, 477–492. New York: Random House.

Eckert, Penelope. 2002. "Demystifying Sexuality and Desire." In Kathryn Campbell-Kibler, Robert J. Podesva, Sarah J. Roberts, and Andrew Wong (eds.), *Language and Sexuality: Contesting Meaning in Theory and Practice*, 99–110. Stanford: CSLI Publications.

Eckert, Penelope, and Sally McConnell-Ginet. 1992. "Think Practically and Look Locally: Language and Gender as Community-Based Practice." *Annual Review of Anthropology*, 21: 461–490.

Flannery, Regina. 1946. "Men's and Women's Speech in Gros Ventre." *International Journal of American Linguistics*, 12: 133–135.

Furfey, Paul Hanly. 1944. "Men's and Women's Language." *American Catholic Sociological Review*, 5: 218–223.

Gal, Susan. 1991. "Between Speech and Silence: The Problematics of Research on Language and Gender." In Micaela di Leonardo (eds.), *Gender at the Crossroads of Knowledge: Feminist Anthropology in the Modern Era*, 175–203. Berkeley: University of California Press.

Gatschet, Albert S. 1884. *Hitchiti: A Migration Legend of the Creek Indians*. Philadelphia: Brinton.

Greenough, James Bradstreet, and George Lyman Kittredge. 1901. *Words and Their Ways in English Speech*. New York: Macmillan.

Gumperz, John J., ed. 1982. *Language and Social Identity*. Cambridge: Cambridge University Press.

Haas, Mary R. 1964 [1944]. "Men's and Women's Speech in Koasati." *Language*, 20: 142–149. Repr. in Dell Hymes (ed.), *Language in Culture and Society*, 228–233. New York: Harper & Row.

Hall, Kira. 1999. Performativity. *Journal of Linguistic Anthropology*, 9(1–2): 184–187.

Hymes, Dell. 1975. "Breakthrough into Performance." In Dan Ben-Amos and Kenneth S. Goldstein (eds.), *Folklore: Performance and Communication*, 11–74. The Hague: Mouton.

Jacobs, Greg. 1996. "Lesbian and Gay Male Language Use: A Critical Review of the Literature." *American Speech*, 71(1): 49–71.

Jespersen, Otto. 1990 [1922]. "The Woman." In *Language: Its Nature, Development, and Origin*. London: Allen & Unwin. Repr. in Deborah Cameron (ed.), *The Feminist Critique of Language: A Reader*, 201–220. New York: Routledge.

Keenan (Ochs), Elinor. 1996 [1974]. "Norm-Makers, Norm-Breakers: Uses of Speech by Men and Women in a Malagasy Community." Repr. in Donald Brenneis and Ronald K. S. Macaulay (eds.), *The Matrix of Language: Contemporary Linguistic Anthropology*, 99–115. Boulder, CO: Westview Press.

Kulick, Don. 2000. "Gay and Lesbian Language." *Annual Review of Anthropology*, 29: 243–285.

Lakoff, Robin. 1975. *Language and Woman's Place*. New York: Harper & Row.

Lasch, Richard. 1907. "Über Sondersprachen und ihre Entstehung." *Mitteilungen der Anthropologischen Gesellschaft in Wien*, 37: 89–101.

Livia, Anna, and Kira Hall. 1997. " 'It's a Girl!' Bringing Performativity Back to Linguistics." In Anna Livia and Kira Hall (eds.), *Queerly Phrased: Language, Gender, and Sexuality*, 1–18. New York: Oxford University Press.

Maccoby, Eleanor E. 1998. *The Two Sexes: Growing Up Apart, Coming Together*. Cambridge, MA: Harvard University Press.

Maltz, Daniel N., and Ruth A. Borker. 1982. "A Cultural Approach to Male–Female Miscommunication." In John J. Gumperz (ed.), *Language and Social Identity*, 196–216. Cambridge: Cambridge University Press.

McElhinny, Bonnie. 2002. "Language, Sexuality, and Political Economy." In Kathryn Campbell-Kibler, Robert J. Podesva, Sarah J. Roberts, and Andrew Wong (eds.), *Language and Sexuality: Contesting Meaning in Theory and Practice*, 111–134. Stanford: CSLI Publications.

Nicholson, Linda. 1994. "Interpreting Gender." *Signs*, 20(1): 79–105.

O'Barr, William M., and Bowman K. Atkins. 1980. " 'Women's Language' or 'Powerless Language'?" In Sally McConnell-Ginet, Ruth Borker, and Nelly Furman (eds.), *Women and Language in Literature and Society*, 93–109. New York: Praeger.

Sapir, Edward. 1949 [1915]. "Abnormal Types of Speech in Nootka." Reprinted in David Mandelbaum (ed.), *Selected Writings of Edward Sapir*, 179–196. Berkeley: University of California Press.

Sapir, Edward. 1949 [1929]. "Male and Female Forms of Speech in Yana." Repr. in David Mandelbaum (ed.), *Selected Writings of Edward Sapir*, 206–212. Berkeley: University of California Press.

Tannen, Deborah. 1986. *That's Not What I Meant! How Conversational Style Makes or Breaks Relationships*. New York: Ballantine.

Tannen, Deborah. 1990. *You Just Don't Understand: Women and Men in Conversation*. New York: Ballantine Books.

Thorne, Barrie. 1993. *Gender Play: Girls and Boys in School*. New Brunswick, NJ: Rutgers University Press.

Trechter, Sara. 1999. "Contextualizing the Exotic Few." In Mary Bucholtz, Anita C. Liang, and Laurel A. Sutton (eds.), *Reinventing Identities: The Gendered Self in Discourse*, 101–122. New York: Oxford University Press.

Wolf, Arthur. 1995. *Sexual Attraction and Childhood Association: A Chinese Brief for Edward Westermarck*. Stanford: Stanford University Press.

12 Language and Masculinity

BETHAN BENWELL

1. Introduction

A chapter entitled "Language and Masculinity" in a *Handbook of Language, Gender, and Sexuality* is not unproblematically descriptive, but embeds within it certain assumptions, some of which I hope to problematize in what follows. One reading is that, with no companion chapter on "Language and Femininity," it offers a kind of performative judgment on how we have historically viewed the study of gender as synonymous with the study of the (oppressed) condition of femininity or women. So what does it mean to isolate masculinity from broader considerations of gender in this way? In her insightful overview of the field of language and masculinity, Johnson argues that by exposing the hitherto neglected topic of masculinity to analytical scrutiny we offer a corrective to the view that the female/feminine is the problematic or "marked" sex/gender in the gender order (Johnson 1997, 12–13), and we challenge the status of masculinity as an unmarked and thus "invisible" category (Black and Coward 1998, 118; Benwell 2003, 155). An explicit (rather than implicit) (Johnson 1997, 13) study of masculinity, particularly as a relational, and power-based phenomenon, facilitates a clearer feminist understanding of the operations of male power and the perpetuation of the gender order. Such a project is not without contention, however: a common feminist critique of the "exposure" and topicalization of masculinity is that it is an ideologically mobile and appropriable politics which has fueled the antifeminist, reactionary strand of men's studies (see Ashe 2007 for a useful overview) as much as it has facilitated a critical deconstruction of the operations of masculine power and privilege. As Sally Robinson argues in *Marked Men: White Masculinity in Crisis*, "there is much symbolic power to be reaped from occupying the social and discursive position of the subject-in-crisis" (2000, 19).

Apart from these political objections, theoretical and ontological arguments are also presented in response to a contemplation of masculinity as an object of study. Recent ethnomethodologically inspired accounts of gender, particularly within the approaches of discursive psychology and conversation analysis (CA), have tended to problematize a conceptualization of masculinity and femininity as a

The Handbook of Language, Gender, and Sexuality, Second Edition.
Edited by Susan Ehrlich, Miriam Meyerhoff, and Janet Holmes.
© 2014 John Wiley & Sons, Inc. Published 2017 by John Wiley & Sons, Inc.

priori *analyst's* categories and argue that to topicalize "masculinity" (unless it is revealed as a participant's concern) in some senses is to reify it as a phenomenon. The increasing influence of scholarship in this area has led to a growing preoccupation with a notion of "warrants" and "gender relevance" (e.g., Kitzinger 2000; McIlvenny 2002a; Schegloff 1997; Speer 2001a; 2005; Speer and Stokoe 2011; Stokoe and Attenborough, Chapter 8 in this volume; Stokoe and Smithson 2002; Swann 2002; 2009; Weatherall 2000; Wilkinson and Kitzinger, Chapter 7 in this volume), which in turn is related to issues of context and indexicality (Ochs 1992), and the contested notion of gender "omnirelevance" (Fitzgerald, Housley, and Butler 2009; Garfinkel 1967; Weatherall 2000). Such a perspective raises vital questions such as: Does masculinity exist prior to the discourse contexts we study? What does it mean to *look* for it? What is *it*? And, crucially, what does it mean to talk about a relationship between language and masculinity? In the discussion that follows I engage with a number of approaches which, in research spanning four decades, have adopted a range of (sometimes conflicting) responses to these questions and whose articulations of the relationship between language and masculinity reflect different methodological, theoretical, and political assumptions. These include:

- how men talk;
- how men talk in the service of "doing being a man" or performing masculinity;
- how men talk/are represented in culturally identified, "exclusively male" communities of practice (e.g., fraternity societies, men's magazines);
- a discursive manifestation of power/relational position within the gender order;
- a set of culturally heightened discourses that are intersubjectively agreed to represent the experience/behavior/ideology/traits/orientations and character of masculinities (e.g., heteronormativity, "macho," "laddish," or "heroic" masculinity and associated attributes such as objectifying women, promiscuity, physical endurance, aggression);
- a series of performative alignments, identifications with/to/against these discourses in talk-in-interaction or written texts;
- a series of explicit verbal or textual orientations to mentions of maleness, male subjects/categories of masculinity.

Most of these articulations, except the first, are broadly (and to greater or lesser degrees) oriented to what we might term "constructionist" or "performative" accounts of gender, which conceive of masculinity as antiessential, emergent, discursive productions. In the first edition of this *Handbook*, Holmes and Meyerhoff argue that "the field has moved well beyond descriptions of (perceived or actual) differences between men's and women's speech" (2003, 8), and yet the desire to fall back on the sexed categories of "men" and "women" often proves ineluctable and comfortingly familiar in language and gender research, even for those of us making an explicit commitment to a constructionist or performative approach.

Objections notwithstanding, the project of making masculinity and language a valid area of investigation, arguably inaugurated by Johnson and Meinhof's important edited collection, *Language and Masculinity* (1997), has come to fruition, with their call to "[put] the study of male speech behaviour more firmly on the linguist's … agenda" heeded by numerous researchers in the past decade (Meinhof and Johnson 1997, 1). In Bucholtz, Liang, and Sutton's collection *Reinventing Identities: The Gendered Self in Discourse* (1999), there are no chapters devoted to masculinity. By contrast, a decade later, Pichler and Eppler's collection *Gender and Spoken Interaction* (2009) has three chapters looking exclusively at male settings/speakers or masculine language, and only two exploring feminine identities and female settings.[1] Indeed, Cameron (2009, 13) suggests that the pendulum has swung so far, there is now "more theoretical discussion of masculinity" than femininity as an object of study. This trend is perhaps indicative of the tacit assumption that masculinity is more socially "problematic" than femininity (evidenced in much of the sociological and psychological literature).

In what follows I outline the development of a field and a series of key studies that represent a range of different theoretical and methodological perspectives on language and masculinity. My overview deliberately excludes a discussion of the relationship between masculinity and sexuality, and specifically queer masculinities, since this is dealt with in Milani's contribution to this collection (Chapter 13). I will conclude by presenting a short case study from my own research in which I offer an analysis of a particular "discourse" culturally associated with masculinity – that of "gross out," partly as a way of exploring an approach to the vexed issue of "context" that figures in contemporary accounts of the relationship between language and gender. I will begin by presenting an overview of key theoretical ideas in masculinity studies, many of which are sociological in orientation.

2. Theorizing Masculinity

The emergence of masculinity theory, particularly in "men's studies," has been argued to be a political response to second-wave feminism (Ashe 2007, 78), and an attempt to shed light on the experiences and subjectivities of "being a man." However, as outlined in the introduction, this work has not occurred without contention and inhabits a sometimes uneasy ("both antagonistic and interdependent": Gardiner 2002, 6) relationship with feminism. The influence of certain conservative, essentialist, and antifeminist strands of men's studies (e.g., Bly 1990) has led to charges that men's studies are "perpetuating rather than interrogating the reproduction of male dominance" (Thomas 2002, 61). Even ostensibly "profeminist" (to use the term commonly employed in men's or masculinity studies) scholars, such as Victor Seidler, focus on the ground lost by men to social and political changes, wrought by, among other things, the feminist movement (Seidler 1989, 209). The profileration of "crisis" accounts of masculinity in the field is rooted in the claim that the social, economic, and political conditions of late capitalist societies have "exerted pressure on men's traditional roles and identities" (Ashe 2007, 1). However, some have argued that a notion of "crisis" is merely a means of recouping or protecting power, "a discursive strategy circulated by men in order to reoccupy centre stage and reclaim patriarchal privilege" (Walsh 2010, 7).

In attempting to locate and define "masculinity" as a term in masculinity studies, we find an often contradictory set of accounts. The more embodied conceptualizations of masculinity associated with "what it means to be a man" have tended to dominate sociological accounts of the "conditions" of manhood. Both Raewyn Connell and Jeff Hearn focus on definitions of masculinity as an effect of power. Hearn uses the term "gender class" to describe the "effects of the ... relationship of power between men and women" (Ashe 2007, 125) while Connell developed the hugely influential concept of "hegemonic masculinity" to articulate the forms and practices of domination by some men over women/other men. However, despite the relativist and discursive connotations of this definition, both Hearn and Connell invoke an embodied masculinity by grounding their research in the experiences and examples of "men."

The term "hegemonic masculinity" was first developed by Connell in her 1995 text *Masculinities* in order to account for both a thesis of plural masculinities and "a gender politics within masculinity" (1995, 37). The concept emerged out of the recognition that some configurations of masculinity and femininity are more "culturally exalted" (77) than others. Connell argued that the phenomenon of hegemonic masculinity gives rise to certain advantages for *all* men, regardless of whether, or to what extent, they embody the stereotypical attributes of the dominant male, and termed this the "patriarchal dividend." Connell theorizes hegemonic masculinity as a cultural ideal of masculinity – mobile in space and time – that can strategically and ambiguously incorporate other ideologies (even incongruous ones such as feminism) as a way of maintaining its stability and power (Connell and Messerschmidt 2005, 838), an observation taken up by a number of researchers examining discursive realizations or constructions of masculinity (e.g., Benwell 2002; Korobov and Bamberg 2004; Riley 2001; Talbot 1997), and one that will be explored later in the chapter. The thesis of hegemonic masculinity entails that masculine identity is broadly conceived as plural or multiple. Attention to "Muslim masculinity" (Archer 2001a), "gay masculinity" (Baker 2005), "working class masculinity" (Archer 2001b), "young masculinities" (Frosh, Phoenix, and Pattman 2002), as well as "subordinated masculinities" generally, has been amply attended to in a range of related disciplines. The plurality thesis does, however, tend to invoke the sexed body (rather than simply discursive productions), which perhaps suggests that masculinity remains stubbornly intertwined with, and invested in the embodied male.[2]

Poststructuralist theories of gender, such as Butler's (1990; 1993) theory of performativity, which theorize gender as an *effect* of discourse, creating an illusion of a seamless integrity between the sexed body and cultural gender, have been slow to make an impression on masculinity studies. Wiegman discusses the need for masculinity studies to "de-emphasis[e] the normative relationship between men and masculinity" (2002, 51), and in a thoughtful engagement with Butler's ideas which echoes Robinson's (2000) skepticism about the political uses to which "crisis" accounts have been put, Walsh theorizes "crisis" as a strategic "performative" where "ostensible disorder does not simply signal the radical dissolution of form, but rather its reorganization" (Walsh 2010, 1). Adopting an obviously Butlerian perspective, Reeser argues that "we cannot understand the male sex outside the realm of language" (2010, 75), and Halberstam, working with Butler's ideas of both gender stylization and a radical sex/gender split, proposes a theory of "female masculinity" which "disrupts contemporary cultural studies accounts of masculinity within which masculinity always boils down to the social, cultural and political effects of male embodiment and male privilege" (2002, 345).

Few theoretical accounts of masculinity have, however, engaged with detailed discursive or linguistic analyses of identity. Connell (2001), though sympathetic to the usefulness of combining large-scale analysis of the political, historical, and social processes of masculinity with a more microscopic focus on discursive analysis, warns against the "limitations" of discursive work (Connell and Messerschmidt 2005, 842). Yet the significance of looking at *language* in conjunction with masculinity is that it helps to give substance to arguably the most compelling account of gender in theoretical circulation – that of gender as a *discursive effect*. And from a third-wave feminist perspective of gender, such work is a crucial stage in the political project of dismantling or deconstructing norms and binaries of both sexuality and gender.

3. Implicit and Explicit Approaches: When Did Masculinity Become "Marked" in Language and Gender Studies?

Studies at the inception of language and gender as a field (in the 1970s and 1980s) tended not to theorize or mark masculinity explicitly, but nonetheless it was an implicit topic through both the Marxist-inspired critique of male interactional power (particularly in mixed-sex conversation) (e.g., Fishman 1978; Zimmerman and West 1975) and androcentrism in language (e.g., Spender 1980). Alongside this explicitly political work, other linguistic studies made men a social variable with which to correlate occurrences of regular speech behavior patterns or linguistic variables. An approach whereby gender is used to explain variation in linguistic phenomena has been critiqued both in terms of the assumptions it makes about the "normative" status of men's language (Cameron and Coates 1988; Spender 1980) and, more recently, in terms of the deterministic assumptions it makes about the relationship between sex and gender, particularly in the light of third-wave discursive accounts of gender (e.g., Cameron 1998; Stokoe and Smithson 2002). Masculinity as a topic in language and gender studies was arguably most visibly marked by the publication of Johnson and Meinhof's *Language and Masculinity* in 1997, and a flurry of research looking specifically at masculinity ensued (e.g., Benwell 2003; Coates 2003; Edley and Wetherell 1997; Gough 1998; Hall 2009; Holmes 2009; Kiesling 1997; 2005; Milani 2011; Preece 2009; Sidnell 2003; 2011; Speer 2005; 2005; Wetherell and Edley 1999).

Coates's *Men Talk* (2003) was the first monograph study of language and masculinity, but specifically focused on genres of storytelling/narrative. Based on a substantial corpus (203 stories), it combined a sex-difference focus, for example, "what is men's talk like" (1) and reference to "authentic men's talk" (2) with a more constructionist perspective: "men and women are actively engaged in constructing and maintaining masculinity and femininity in their storytelling" (37). The empirical basis of this work enables Coates to identify features of men's narratives that are common across her compellingly large sample – for example, avoidance of the personal; focus on male protagonists, narrator-as-hero; use of taboo language; and a stance of "emotional restraint." She also identifies the regular occurrence of "telling stories in sequence" (cf. Sacks's (1992) second stories) which she argues are a means of displaying "mutual understanding" and doing friendship without appearing "feminine" or "gay" (Coates 2003, 104). In this observation, Coates identifies a phenomenon that occurs repeatedly across language and masculinity studies: the "dilemma" occasioned by the potential clash of two conflicting systems of value (here homosociality and heterosexuality). The value of Coates's work lies in its empirical richness; however, the problem of focusing on talk that emerges from groups who happen to be male and assuming that it indexes masculinity is that it risks "reif[ying] stereotypes" (Kiesling 2004, 609). The limitations of a sex-based approach to analyzing gender identity has become an increasingly familiar critique, and other scholars examining the relationship between language and masculinity have attempted to engage variously with the vexed question of "gender relevance."

4. Communities of Practice and Ethnographic Methods

Kiesling's focus is also on men as a group (an American college fraternity) and their actions (e.g., Kiesling 1997; 2005), but his orientation to a "community of practice" (Lave and Wenger 1991) frame, and methods of participant observation and ethnography (Kiesling was a former member of the group he studied), enable him to identify performances and discourses of "hegemonic masculinity" (e.g., "fuck stories": Kiesling 2002) with more analytical authority. Kiesling articulates his research in broadly poststructuralist terms whereby masculinity is defined in terms of orientations through talk to cultural discourses that represent key tenets of masculinity (Kiesling (2005) identifies four key discourses: gender difference; heterosexism; dominance; male solidarity). As Coates also observed, however, some of these discourses are inherently contradictory (e.g., male solidarity may clash with heterosexuality), and these kinds of dilemmas (or the "male homosocial double bind": Kiesling 2005, 711) will often shape and determine the patterns of these male speakers' interactions. So Kiesling asks, for instance: "How do men use language to 'do friendship' in a heterosexist atmosphere?" (2005, 695) and goes on to argue that men in these fraternity situations use indirectness to create and display desire (see also Walsh 2010, 176).[3]

Hall (2009, 142) also suggests that we can assess gender relevance through methods of ethnography. Her anthropological study of symbolic, code-switching uses of Hindi by male-identified lesbians (or "boys") attending a support group promoting awareness about sexual health and diversity thus illuminates "the ways in which the links between language and masculinity emerge over time as a product of localised discursive exchange." By her understanding of the "cultural context that informs its interpretation" (145), Hall is able to conclude that Hindi is "a resource for the expression of an authentic masculinity" (145).

Like Kiesling and Hall, Sidnell (2003) acknowledges the role of ethnography in enabling him to identify gender as a feature of the social setting in his study of men's talk in a Guyanese rumshop. However, he also explicitly topicalizes (rather than merely taking for granted) the phenomenon of "male exclusivity," showing, using CA methods, that it is *produced and managed* by speakers within the talk itself. Sidnell's work thus emphasizes the value of "not treating the facts of the 'context' as pre-established" (2003, 327), arguing that characterizing a setting as "male only" without clear warrants to do so, partially predetermines the analysis of it. These debates around the issue of "warrants" for claiming gender relevance in studies of men's talk will be taken up again later in the chapter.

5. Hegemonic Masculinity, Performativity, and Other Poststructuralist Accounts

Kiesling's work is one of a number of language and gender studies to draw substantially on the sociological concept of hegemonic masculinity. One of the first papers to make this explicit connection between concepts of hegemonic masculinity and interaction-based analysis was Cameron's 1997 chapter "Performing Gender Identity: Young Men's Talk and the Construction of Heterosexual Masculinity." Cameron's analysis of the informal talk of a group of American students gossiping in homophobic terms about a number of classmates who represented, in their terms, the "antithesis" of normative or ideal gender, marked a shift in orientation from formal features as an index of gender (e.g., the idea that a collaborative floor was a feature of "women's talk") to a focus on explicit orientations to topics of masculinity and male sexuality. Like Kiesling's frat boys, Cameron's students were accomplishing homosociality through their talk, but in order to avoid "compromising the heterosexual masculinity they are so anxious to display" could only "legitimately talk amongst themselves in such intimate terms" about the despised gay "other" (Cameron 1997, 61).

The concept of "hegemonic masculinity" was taken up more critically by Edley and Wetherell (Edley and Wetherell 1997; Wetherell and Edley 1999). Their main contention with Connell's concept of "hegemonic masculinity" was its analytical vagueness and inability to provide a proper account of the "social psychological reproduction of male identities" (Wetherell and Edley 1999, 335). Conducting a number of interviews with groups of males of different ages and occupational backgrounds, they used a critical discursive psychology methodology, whereby they combined top-down and bottom-up approaches, acknowledging the existence of a "historically given set of discourses or interpretative repertoires," but simultaneously observing the "ways in which these cultural resources are manipulated and exploited within particular rhetorical or micro-political contexts" (Edley and Wetherell 1997, 206). One of Edley and Wetherell's key findings was how the men they interviewed frequently constructed alternative or counter-hegemonic identities for themselves often in explicit opposition to some form of "hegemonic" or exalted masculinity, while simultaneously making "subtle claims to key elements of those very masculinities" (1997, 210), recalling the "patriarchal dividend" key to Connell's original concept.

A key theme dominating much of this discursive work – and which seems to find echoes in the discourses of "crisis," "ambivalence," and "trouble" that inhabit more sociological accounts of masculinity – is that of ideological/interactional dilemmas and troubled subject positions, often realized by the way participants discursively attempt to manage dual concerns or "conflicting demands for accountability" (Speer 2005, 111) in their presentation of themselves. Korobov and Bamberg (2004, 473) for instance, in work on adolescent males negotiating "physical attraction" in group talk, observe the employment of discursive strategies to resist the "appearance of complicity with 'hegemonic masculinity.'" In Wetherell and Edley's (1999) interview-based study of men's formulations of their own masculinities, a dilemma arises for Martin in terms of presenting himself as neither stereotypically "masculine" nor lacking in masculinity, which results in an apparently contradictory account of the self:

```
Nigel:   OK (.) do you see yourselves as masculine men then?
Martin:  No (.) not by that description no
Nigel:   So (.) what do you think you are (.) do you think you are
         unmasculine?
Martin:  No (.) not unmasculine (.) no
```

(Wetherell and Edley 1999, 345)

In an analysis of the "management of heterosexist talk," Speer and Potter (2002) identify an interactional dilemma for the male interviewee (Ben) following a question of whether he found the man who chatted him up attractive. Speer and Potter demonstrate that Ben carefully manages this dilemma to avoid being seen as either gay (by answering "yes") or homophobic (by answering "no"):

```
1  Sue:  Was he attractive?
2        (0.6)
3  Ben:  Phh. (1.8) I s'pose he was reasonably well looking, ↑Yeah.
4        (1.6)
5        But you know it doesn't interest me,
6        (.)
7        I'm definitely (0.8) not interest(h)ed(h) in(h) men(h).
```

(Speer and Potter 2002, 168)

Ben constructs his response carefully to present himself as someone who has never given such a question much thought by using markers of hesitation ("Phh."), mitigation ("I s'pose"), and vague descriptions ("reasonably well looking"). Sue's pause at line 4 arguably prompts a more "upgraded" specificity of response which establishes that he is not gay. However, the more emphatic denial is suffused with laughter, which orients to the utterance being potentially "delicate" (Speer 2005, 113).

In an analysis of male readers' responses to men's magazines, Benwell (2005) identifies a point at which a reader's description of his engagement with the arguably feminized realm of "beauty treatments" is couched in a series of accounts which mitigate a clear investment in such activities or identities:

```
1   J:   I remember doing a Nivea thing that I bought Nivea after reading
         it years ago like y'know how they have like articles
2   I:   an article rather than an advert
3   J:   yeah it was like a sponsored article-
4   M:   (laughing) Lucky this is anonymous!
         (laughter from all)
```

(Benwell 2005, 163)

In this extract, J describes his consumption of a "beauty" product in ways which suggest he is already aware of its problematic gender status. "A Nivea thing" is a strategically vague formulation implying it was an experience not significant or memorable enough to be characterized in precise terms. The vagueness is supported by the information that this experience occurred "years ago," which implicitly invokes a different, younger self. The resultant laughter from the rest of the group, and reference to the desirable state of anonymity, tells us that J has breached some sort of normative code. The occurrence of such "gender trouble" in men's accounting practices is strikingly reproduced across a range of studies.

A related phenomenon in interview-based studies of men's talk is "new sexism," a term coined in discourse studies to describe utterances that are likely to be heard as sexist being accounted for by a range of rhetorical means.[4] Gough (1998, 39) observed how men employ discursive strategies to deflect potential accusations of prejudice. Riley (2001, 55) argues that "'New Sexism' discourses are defined as accounts that function to maintain male privileges but in ways that reduce the 'hearability' of sexism, presenting the speaker as egalitarian." "New sexism" is closely related to the theory that hegemonic masculinity is able to strategically accommodate often incongruous ideologies (Connell and Messerschmidt 2005, 845), discussed earlier, but while it is arguably prompted by the same clash of discourses that mobilize "troubled subject positions," it is more obviously invested in preserving the power that accompanies the masculine position.

6. Methodological Debates, Gender Relevance, and the Limits of Context

In the range of work so far surveyed we have seen a variety of means of conceiving of and locating masculinity, with earlier sex-difference approaches to studying language and masculinity challenged for their reifying, essentializing tendencies and assumptions that masculinity is "an attribute wholly of men" (McIlvenny 2002b, 11). McIlvenny goes on to comment that "[r]ecently ... even approaches to 'doing' gender have tended to reify stereotypes of gender ... in accounts of how men 'do' masculinity by 'doing' masculine things" (McIlvenny 2002b, 6; see also Stokoe and Attenborough, Chapter 8 in this volume; Stokoe and Smithson 2002). Other attempts to situate gender more clearly as an antifoundationalist, emergent phenomenon can be found in the work of discursive psychologists and conversation analysts. In such debates, a series of related questions linked to notions of context, gender (omni)relevance, and "warrants" (Swann 2002; 2009) for identifying the relevance of gender are never far from the surface. As McElhinny asks, "If part of the strategy ... for studying gender is not assuming that gender is always relevant, do we need some method for determining and demonstrating when and how gender is relevant?" (2003, 33).

In a published exchange, Speer and Edley debate the relative methods of CA-inspired discursive psychology and critical discursive psychology (which draws on poststructuralist theories of identity formation) for analyzing the social "doing" of masculinity in interactional terms (Edley 2001; Speer 2001a; 2001b). While Edley stresses the value of drawing on historical and cultural resources for a richer and more nuanced understanding of how masculinity is being accomplished in the data, Speer (2005, 149) rejects the necessity of this attention to the "extradiscursive" including the engagement with abstractions such as "hegemonic masculinity," which are *analysts'* rather than *members'* phenomena, arguing that CA's concern with "how members build, orient to, and reproduce those recognizable patterns, structures and norms within their talk" is a more robust means of validating claims about gender. CA's "demand" for warrants isn't just motivated by an epistemological purism, but can be seen as a form of political action: the avoidance of colluding in the perpetuation of gender stereotypes. On the other hand, abstractions (such as "hegemonic masculinity") have been argued by some to be a crucial part of intellectual inquiry, a means of reaching a particular understanding of the world which is not necessarily revealed by studying "members' methods" alone (Billig 1999, 550; Edley 2001, 137).

This discussion about the most appropriate ways for analyzing masculinity is just one reflection of an ongoing debate within language and gender studies, broadly between poststructuralist ideas about gender and discourse (including performativity theory and elements of critical discourse analysis) and conversation analytical/discursive psychology approaches to the study of social life. While Edley and Speer's debate evidences some of the incommensurate elements of the respective traditions, there have been productive attempts to engage with a possible confluence between the two. McIlvenny's 2002 collection *Talking Gender and Sexuality* is still the best example of an exploration of the potential mapping between the turn to performativity and conversation analytical methods. Any such consonance between the two approaches is likely to be found in the ways in which gender discourses are "locally operative in situated performances of talk" (McIlvenny 2002b, 17), but such work is still subject to the CA critique that the identification of "normative ideologies" and "gender discourses" are an extradiscursive matter lacking analytical specificity (Speer 2005, 67). Nonetheless, there are ways in which analytical specificity can be brought to bear on such discourses when they are endogenously produced, for instance by an examination of accounting practices which show collaborative orientations to established moral positions. Speer (2005, 135) herself has used the methods of CA in order to "explore the way masculinity(ies) are rhetorically constructed and deployed by participants in the management of certain interactional dilemmas." In this sense, Speer captures the point also made by Pichler and Eppler (discussing Swann's chapter in their collection): that in invoking gender, speakers are often not "doing gender" but "doing something with gender … gender is done to particular interactional effect" (Pichler and Eppler 2009, xiv). Speer demonstrates how her speakers construct a range of meanings for masculinity (masculinity as "extreme," as "inauthentic," etc.) in order to "invoke or manage a particular identity" (148). Sidnell (2011) shows – similarly through members' own orientations – that they invoke a "subcultural model of gender" in their talk. In "D'you Understand That, Honey?" he looks at this utterance as a means of invoking the relevance of the recipient's sex, but also to index that the kind of talk referred to by *that* is designed for an exclusively male audience.

An important strand of CA work that can coax "normative" cultural under-standings about gender out of the situated talk of members is that of membership categorization analysis (MCA). Stokoe has demonstrated convincingly that MCA's analysis of the production of social categories and their associated activities can illuminate how routine and taken-for-granted knowledge about gender is actively accomplished in talk (e.g., Stokoe 2003). (See also Stokoe and Attenborough, Chapter 8 in this volume.) More specifically, Stokoe (2012, 231) has analyzed how speakers routinely formulate idiomatic-style phrases that "package" cultural knowledge (e.g., "that's lads for you") revealing "what counts" as gendered behavior. In my own data (male readers discussing men's magazines) I found, for instance, the following formulation: "a normal kind of lad who'd be like 'oh I'm not going to go and have a facial' or something." Such utterances index not only this particular speaker's view of "normal masculinity" (in relation to the "feminized" realm of beauty treatments), but also an *inter-subjective* notion of "typicality" regardless of the ontology or "out-thereness" of such discourses. In these common and repeated formulations, an appeal to intertexuality, history, and context is embedded within the talk itself, and such expressions can be linked to a notion of performativity and repetition: "staging gender in a way that exposes its discursive as opposed to essential character" (Speer 2005, 64).

But do these possibilities within the ethnomethodological tradition offer a sufficiently rich version of context by which to capture a properly performative version of masculinity? Speer (2005, 102) claims that contexts invoked in more Foucauldian-inspired analyses "seem to float free outside talk, and as such they remain mysterious and elusive." However, we could argue that CA approaches are not equal to (or uninterested in) capturing the repeated and citational qualities of performative utterances by their lack of attention to intertextual, ethnographic, or diachronic resources: Butler (1990, 271) argues that gender scripts have to accumulate and congeal *over time*. There is perhaps an ambiguity about the term "extra discursive": even abstractions are still mediated discursively, and, by the examination of intertextual resources, it is possible to examine them *as they occur in discourse*. In the final section of this chapter I continue an exploration of a possible interface between conversation analytical approaches to gender identity, and poststructuralist notions of "regulatory discourses" through which masculine subjectivity emerges, by an exploration of a particular popular discourse – that of "gross out." In so doing, I will pay analytical attention to various inter-texts across which discourses and meanings coalesce, circulate, become reified, and are shared, and in which gross out becomes a discourse inflected with masculine meaning.

7. "Gross Out": A "Masculine" Discourse?

"Gross out" is a phenomenon (either discursive or visual) that aims to shock its audience by its graphic, scatological/violent qualities, and is a prominent feature of men's lifestyle magazines often explicitly labeled as such ("Gross-Out Special," *FHM*, March 2003). An Internet search for items involving gross out (calling up over 10 million hits on Google) reveals that one of its most common contexts is the genre of the anarchic "gross-out comedy," such as *American Pie*, *Animal House*, and the TV cartoon *South Park*, featuring sight gags usually involving bodily fluids and/or nudity. Another common context is commercial sites aimed at children such as Halloween confectionary and practical joke props, suggesting that gross out has immature connotations, chiming with critical and media commentary about the regressive, infantile culture of "lad" magazines (Edwards 1997; Whelehan 2000). A pattern emerged in this search linking *males* to gross-out culture (e.g., "gross-out books for boys," "juvenile male humor"), an observation supported by the performance of gross-out stunts (often involving humiliation and/or self-harm) exclusively by men for other men, (e.g., *Jackass*, *Dirty Sanchez*, and various amateur video spin-offs posted on YouTube) and its presence as a regular feature of men's magazines involving visual displays of deformities, injuries, or variously gory or insect- or rodent-related incidents, presented for the apparent entertainment of readers. Men's magazines as a location for such features provide a kind of virtual (and explicitly gendered) "community of practice" and a quasi-prescriptive "manual" on masculinity, which furnish our analysis with a potential ethnographic or anthropological framing.

Such speculative interpretations of the gendered connotations of gross out can, however, be supplemented by closer attention to the content of the texts in which it occurs. The graphic photographs, often of body parts deformed by accident or disease, in men's magazines are invariably accompanied by jokey, vernacular commentary which makes light of the condition, for example, "After a 48-hour drinking session, Simon still has no idea how he came to have a blackened sack. 'At first I thought I'd ripped an arse muscle' chortles the Middlesex lad 'But after closer inspection I realized I'd have to call work and explain I'd somehow hammered my cobblers'" (*FHM*, December 2001, 44).[5] In these features, where readers are often the subject of the afflicted body part, they are both feted ("brave Steve Towers") and mocked: "We'll sling you £20 for every one of your bodily disfigurements that we print … and we might even have a laugh at your misfortune in the process" (*FHM*, December 1999, 37) in a homosocial performance that combines camaraderie and male banter. Even images depicting more serious damage or death are presented without any indexing of real horror, but merely an understated disconcertion, for example, "not a pretty sight, but we'll all look like this one day" about an image of a decomposing body (*Ice*, April 2003, 130). The implication is that the magazine enacts a kind of performative "endurance" of gross out, and by extension, challenges the readers to do the same by their consumption of such images. In an analysis of the "jackassification" of male culture (referencing *Jackass*, an American TV show, targeted at and watched predominantly by a male audience and referenced frequently in men's magazines) Walsh (2010, 162) argues that "in their endurance and survival of [such risk-taking, "laddish" acts], the relationship between corporeal resistance … and an … inviolable male core is reinforced." The ability to "deal" with such images, in this reading, might therefore be a measure of one's masculine credentials.

We can also turn, for evidence of its "gendered" meanings, to naturally occurring data in which gross-out preoccupations are invoked as a resource to perform social actions and assert particular social relations. In *Men Talk* (2003), Coates includes a gross-out sequence where a male speaker relates an anecdote about eating maggots to two female friends. Coates suggests that this sequence is "designed to maintain gender boundaries" (Coates 2003, 143) whereby the female speakers display explicit disgust (by uttering "eugghh!") and a lack of "endurance" in the face of such anecdotes, while the male speaker's insouciant and matter-of-fact presentation of the information is reminiscent of the tone adopted in men's magazines to relate gross-out features. By supplementing such isolated readings with similar interpretations of naturally occurring data and quantitative corpus evidence[6] we start to build up a more persuasive warrant for reading deployments of gross out as a masculine performance.

These observations can finally be compared to an analysis of how magazine readers *themselves* frame their responses to such images. In a series of unstructured interviews with a male researcher, two groups of male readers were asked about their interpretations of the "gross-out feature" and looked at a particular example involving images of violent deaths in *Ice* magazine. What is interesting about the data is how alignments to the values of gross out shift rapidly within and between turns, reminding us of the shifting footings in relation to categories and attributes of masculinity observed in a number of studies of men's talk in interaction.

Extract 1: 17-year-olds

```
1   I:  ↑what do you think of this kind of article (.) this
2       um (.) 'Death by any other name'
3   A:  (.) extreme whoever thought of this
4   M:  it is actually it's more like [**]
5   M:  (2.0) mm
6   I:  I mean (0.2) how do you fee:l about these [in the magazines
7   M:                                            [y'see I c'n I c'n
8       look at it but I'm thinking that (.) it might just be
9       a little too extreme (0.5) for a magazine
```

The use of "extreme" by the 17-year-old readers indicates that there is a tacitly agreed "reasonable" threshold of violence or gore which this feature has breached, and the repeated mention of "extreme" by both speakers suggests that they are adopting a gatekeeping role legitimized by their status as knowledgeable and otherwise affiliated members of the community of "men's magazine readers." The speakers do not reject gross out as a discourse outright, but reject the excessive form it adopts. The reformulation by the interviewer of "what do you think" to "how do you feel" prompts a more positive alignment to the values of gross out whereby speaker M states "I c'n … look at it" (lines 7–8). In this statement, M embeds knowledge that such features are *difficult* and require courage to look at, while simultaneously claiming that courage for himself – a kind of performative, "claim-staking" function which is the voyeuristic equivalent of the "corporeal resistance" (Walsh 2010, 162) displayed by those who carry out self-harming activities. This reading is supported by our knowledge from the content of gross-out features in men's magazines that such insouciant acts of "courage" are culturally associated with masculinity, and might be situated, theoretically, as an example of the kinds of *regulatory* discourses discussed by Butler. The next extract involves the 21-year-old readers who have been asked to comment on gross-out features as a phenomenon:

Extract 2: 21-year-olds

```
1    I:  what do you thi:nk is the appeal of them because
2        they're quite popular in these magazines
3        (2.0)
4    G:  I think it's the whole "Jackass" syndrome as well
5        though (.)
6    M:  yeah
7    G:  a little bit
8    M:  people like to see stupid things happening to
9        them
10   I:  yeah indeed
11   G:  it's ↑laughing at other people's misfortunes
```

In line 4, G references an intertext, *Jackass* (discussed earlier), demonstrating that gross-out discourses have a provenance and set of shared meanings (partly indexing masculinity) circulating beyond and informing each local articulation.

The *shared* frame of reference is further indexed by the formulaic and elliptical expression "the whole 'Jackass' syndrome." The observation that such features are "laughing at other people's misfortunes" (line 11) recalls the displays of mockery seen earlier in relation to the gross-out content of men's magazines. Later, after being introduced to the specific article, "Death by Any Other Name," the 21-year-olds produce markedly different responses:

```
12   M:   ↑↑are these real dead people?
13   I:   ye:ah these are real dead people
14   C:   Go::d
15   I:   now wha[t..
16   M:        [↑↑↑eurrggh! (2.0) is that somebody's he:ad!
17   I:   yep
18   M:   dear oh dear (3.0)
19   J:   y'see I wouldn't buy that (1.0) there's a
20        curiosity thing(0.5)you have to look at it
```

The detachment displayed in the first part of this sequence is starkly contrasted with the appalled and incredulous reactions provoked by these images ("Go:d," line 14; "eurrggh," line 16; "dear oh dear," line 18). Interestingly, these spontaneous reactions echo Coates's speakers' "feminine" responses to gross-out discourse. If being able to withstand these images is a badge of masculinity, these informants signally fail to inhabit a traditional gender role at this point, and it can be contrasted with the disclaiming protestation of M in extract 1 ("I c'n look at it"). At 19, J upgrades the more emotional utterances of M and C to an explicit moral stance ("y'see I wouldn't buy that"), but then tempers this account by acknowledging a possible appeal for other readers ("there's a curiosity thing," line 20), and thus partially realigns to the value of gross out. M later consolidates this realignment further and perhaps with it, his orientation to the masculine values of the magazine, by a familiar strategy of defense: that the magazine is not to be taken too seriously ("well you can kind of justify that in a *men*'s magazine" (my emphasis)). Such (dis)alignments to the values of gross out (and by extension the magazine) are arguably performing gender identity work across these interactions. When set alongside the more censorious orientations to gross out (possibly prompted by existing critical discourses that it is "crass" and "puerile"), it informs us that participants are managing, through their talk, a series of often *competing* discourses.

While gross out is rarely indexed in this talk as gendered, there are useful insights to be afforded from noting similarities between some of the details of the readers' talk (e.g., that engaging with gross out on the magazines' terms involves insouciance and courage) with existing critical accounts which posit a more obviously gendered reading (Gardiner 2000; Gill 2003; Walsh 2010), as well as the various intertexts that form the context for this talk. Through the combination of evidence from a larger, more impressionistic corpus and the insights afforded by this more fine-grained, participant-oriented analysis, we begin to build warrants for interpreting gross-out discourse as a gender-inflected phenomenon.

8. Conclusion

In this review I have identified theoretical issues that attach to an explicit study of the relationship between language and masculinity, including its political objective of rendering masculinity visible as a category. I have surveyed some of the key sociological ideas informing the study of masculinity (e.g., "crisis" accounts, hegemonic masculinity; the "male homosocial bind") and explored how such theories have been persuasively and empirically contextualized by the situated and fine-grained discursive work occurring in the field of language and gender. In considering how language scholars variously engage with masculinity as a phenomenon, its location in or beyond discourse, and its precise relationship to language, we are able to explore key methodological debates about the ontology of masculinity.

The case study analysis of gross out offers a provisional way of rethinking the vexed issue of securing warrants for ascribing gender while attending to some of the valid criticisms of CA. In doing so, we sift out the value of discussing the relationship between language and masculinity without falling back on essentialist ideas about "how men talk." A combination of attention to the endogenous productions of masculinity in the details of talk, and a more ethnographically inflected (though still evidence-based, text- or interaction-bound) attention to the intertexts circulating and informing such talk, means that we don't prematurely foreclose any potential avenues for exploring the relevance of gender in the broader understanding of our data.

NOTES

1   See also two important special issues devoted to the relationship between discourse and masculinity: "Men and Masculinities: Discursive Approaches," *Feminism & Psychology* 11(1) (2001); and "Re-casting Language and Masculinities," *Gender and Language* 5(2) (2011).

2   Connell and Messerschmidt's (2005) re-evaluation of the concept of hegemonic masculinity makes the point that its realist critics (e.g., Seidler 2006) see it as overly abstract and divorced from actual practices, while a poststructuralist perspective identifies an overemphasis on the essentialist connection with male bodies (e.g., Wiegman 2002) and inadequate attention to the discursive construction of identity (Wetherell and Edley 1999).

3   The relationship between language, masculinity and desire is also explored in a collection of essays (Milani 2011) engaging with Cameron and Kulick's (2003) psychoanalytically inspired account of discourse and sexuality.

4   The idea draws on an earlier formulation of "new racism" (Barker 1981) – a series of rhetorical strategies which anticipate the view that beliefs (about, e.g., immigration, inequality) are likely to be heard as racist, and which thus sets out to deny this, explicitly or implicitly.

5   The colloquial word "sack" in this case refers to a man's scrotum. "Cobblers" is used informally here to refer more generally to a man's testicles.

6   A WordbankOnline search of the verb "gross-out" reveals a preponderance of female subjects associated with the state of "being grossed-out" (75% compared to 25% of male subjects) in examples where the sex of the subject was identified.

REFERENCES

Archer, Louise. 2001a. " 'Muslim Brothers, Black Lads, Traditional Asians': British Muslim Young Men's Constructions of Race, Religion and Masculinity." *Feminism & Psychology*, 11(1): 79–105.

Archer, Louise. 2001b. "Working Class Men's Constructions of Masculinity and Negotiations of (Non)Participation in Higher Education." *Gender and Education*, 13(4): 431–449.

Ashe, Fidelma. 2007. *The New Politics of Masculinity*. London: Routledge.

Baker, Paul. 2005. *Public Discourses of Gay Men*. London: Routledge.

Barker, Martin. 1981. *The New Racism: Conservatives and the Ideology of the Tribe*. London: Junction Books.

Benwell, Bethan. 2002. "Is There Anything 'New' about These Lads? The Construction of Masculinity in Men's Magazines." In Lia Litosseliti and Jane Sunderland (eds.), *Discourse Analysis and Gender Identity*, 149–174. Amsterdam: Benjamins.

Benwell, Bethan. 2003. "Ambiguous Masculinities: Heroism and Anti-Heroism in the Men's Lifestyle Magazine." In Bethan Benwell (ed.), *Masculinity and Men's Lifestyle Magazines*, 151–168. Oxford: Blackwell.

Benwell, Bethan. 2005. " 'Lucky This is Anonymous!' Men's Magazines and Ethnographies of Reading: A Textual Culture Approach." *Discourse and Society*, 16(2): 147–172.

Billig, Michael. 1999. "Whose Terms? Whose Ordinariness? Rhetoric and Ideology in Conversation Analysis." *Discourse and Society*, 10(4): 543–558.

Black, Maria, and Rosalind Coward. 1998. "Linguistic, Social and Sexual Relations: A Review of Dale Spender's *Man Made Language*." In Deborah Cameron (ed.), *The Feminist Critique of Language: A Reader*, 100–118. London: Routledge.

Bly, Robert. 1990. *Iron John: A Book about Men*. London: Addison-Wesley.

Bucholtz, Mary, A. C. Liang, and Laurel Sutton. 1999. *Reinventing Identities: The Gendered Self in Discourse*. New York: Oxford University Press.

Butler, Judith. 1990. *Gender Trouble: Feminism and the Subversion of Identity*. New York: Routledge.

Butler, Judith. 1993. *Bodies that Matter: On the Discursive Limits of Sex*. New York: Routledge.

Cameron, Deborah. 1997. "Performing Gender Identity: Young Men's Talk and the Construction of Heterosexual Masculinity." In Sally Johnson and Ulrike H. Meinhof (eds.), *Language and Masculinity*, 47–64. Oxford: Blackwell.

Cameron, Deborah. 1998. "Gender, Language, and Discourse: A Review Essay." *Signs*, 23(4): 945–973.

Cameron, Deborah. 2009. "Theoretical Issues for the Study of Gender and Spoken Interaction." In Pia Pichler and Eva Eppler (eds.), *Gender and Spoken Interaction*, 1–17. Basingstoke: Palgrave Macmillan.

Cameron, Deborah, and Jennifer Coates, eds. 1988. *Women in Their Speech Communities*. London: Longman.

Cameron, Deborah, and Don Kulick. 2003. *Language and Sexuality*. Cambridge: Cambridge University Press

Coates, Jennifer. 2003. *Men Talk: Stories in the Making of Masculinities*. Oxford: Blackwell.

Connell, R. W. 1995. *Masculinities*. Cambridge: Polity.

Connell, R. W. 2001. "Introduction and Overview." *Feminism & Psychology* (special issue: "Men and Masculinities: Discursive Approaches"), 11(1): 5–9.

Connell, R. W., and James W. Messerschmidt. 2005. "Hegemonic Masculinity: Rethinking the Concept." *Gender and Society*, 19(6): 829–859.

Edley, Nigel. 2001. "Conversation Analysis, Discursive Psychology and the Study of Ideology: A Response to Susan Speer." *Feminism & Psychology*, 11(1): 136–140.

Edley, Nigel, and Margaret Wetherell. 1997. "Jockeying for Position: The Construction of Masculine Identities." *Discourse and Society*, 8(2): 203–217.

Edwards, Tim. 1997. *Men in the Mirror: Men's Fashion, Masculinity and Consumer Fashion*. London: Cassell.

Fishman, Pamela. 1978. "Interaction: The Work Women Do." *Social Problems*, 25: 397–406.

Fitzgerald, Richard, William Housley, and Carly Butler. 2009. "Omni-Relevance and Interactional Context." Cardiff School of Social Sciences Working Paper 109.

Frosh, Stephen, Ann Phoenix, and Robert Pattman. 2002. *Young Masculinities: Understanding Boys in Contemporary Society*. Basingstoke: Palgrave Macmillan.

Gardiner, Judith Kegan. 2000. "*South Park*, Blue Men, Anality, and Market Masculinity." *Men and Masculinities*, 2(3): 251–271.

Gardiner, Judith Kegan. 2002. "Introduction." In Judith Kegan Gardiner (ed.), *Masculinity Studies and Feminist Theory: New Directions*, 1–30. New York: Columbia University Press.

Garfinkel, Harold. 1967. *Studies in Ethnomethodology*. London: Prentice Hall.

Gill, Rosalind. 2003. "Power and the Production of Subjects: A Genealogy of the New Man and the New Lad." In Bethan Benwell (ed.), *Masculinity and Men's Lifestyle Magazines*, 34–56. Oxford: Blackwell.

Gough, Brendan. 1998. "Men and the Discursive Reproduction of Sexism: Repertoires of Difference and Equality." *Feminism & Psychology*, 8(1): 25–49.

Halberstam, Judith. 2002. "The Good, the Bad and the Ugly: Men, Women and Masculinity." In Judith Kegan Gardiner (ed.), *Masculinity Studies and Feminist Theory: New Directions*, 344–368. New York: Columbia University Press.

Hall, Kira. 2009. "Boys' Talk: Hindi, Moustaches and Masculinity in New Delhi." In Pia Pichler and Eva Eppler (eds.), *Gender and Spoken Interaction*, 139–162. Basingstoke: Palgrave Macmillan.

Holmes, Janet. 2009. "Men, Masculinities and Leadership: Different Discourse Styles at Work." In Pia Pichler and Eva Eppler (eds.), *Gender and Spoken Interaction*, 186–210. Basingstoke: Palgrave Macmillan.

Holmes, Janet, and Miriam Meyerhoff. 2003. "Different Voices, Different Views: An Introduction to Current Research in Language and Gender." In Janet Holmes and Miriam Meyerhoff (eds.), *The Handbook of Language and Gender*, 1–17. Oxford: Blackwell.

Johnson, Sally. 1997. "Theorizing Language and Masculinity: A Feminist Perspective." In Sally Johnson and Ulrike H. Meinhof (eds.), *Language and Masculinity*, 8–26. Oxford: Blackwell.

Johnson, Sally, and Ulrike H. Meinhof, eds. 1997. *Language and Masculinity*. Oxford: Blackwell.

Kiesling, Scott. 1997. "Power and the Language of Men." In Sally Johnson and Ulrike H. Meinhof (eds.), *Language and Masculinity*, 65–85. Oxford: Blackwell.

Kiesling, Scott. 2002. "Playing the Straight Man: Displaying and Maintaining Male Heterosexuality in Discourse." In Kathryn Campbell-Kibler, Robert Podesva, Sarah Roberts, and Andrew Wong (eds.), *Language and Sexuality: Contesting Meaning in Theory and Practice*, 249–266. Stanford: CSLI Publications.

Kiesling, Scott. 2004. "Review of *Men Talk: Stories in the Making of Masculinities* by Jennifer Coates." *Language in Society*, 33: 609–612.

Kiesling, Scott. 2005. "Homosocial Desire in Men's Talk: Balancing and Recreating Cultural Discourses of Masculinity." *Language in Society*, 34(5): 695–727.

Kitzinger, Celia. 2000. "Doing Feminist Conversation Analysis." *Feminism & Psychology*, 10(2): 163–193.

Korobov, Neil, and Michael Bamberg. 2004. "Positioning a 'Mature' Self in Interactive Practices: How Adolescent Males Negotiate 'Physical Attraction' in Group Talk." *British Journal of Developmental Psychology*, 22, 471–492.

Lave, Jean, and Etienne Wenger. 1991. *Situated Learning: Legitimate Peripheral*

Participation. Cambridge: Cambridge University Press.

McElhinny, Bonnie. 2003. "Theorizing Gender in Sociolinguistics and Linguistic Anthropology." In Janet Holmes and Miriam Meyerhoff (eds.), *The Handbook of Language and Gender*, 21–42. Oxford: Blackwell.

McIlvenny, Paul, ed. 2002a. *Talking Gender and Sexuality*. Amsterdam: Benjamins.

McIlvenny, Paul. 2002b. "Introduction: Researching Talk, Gender and Sexuality." In Paul McIlvenny (ed.), *Talking Gender and Sexuality*, 1–48. Amsterdam: Benjamins.

Meinhof, Ulrike H., and Sally Johnson. 1997. "Introduction." In In Sally Johnson and Ulrike H. Meinhof (eds.), *Language and Masculinity*, 1–7. Oxford: Blackwell.

Milani, Tommaso, ed. 2011. "Re-casting Language and Masculinities" (special issue). *Gender and Language*, 5(2): 175–301.

Ochs, Elinor. 1992. "Indexing Gender." In Alessandro Duranti and Charles Goodwin (eds.), *Rethinking Context: Language as an Interactive Phenomenon*, 335–358. Cambridge: Cambridge University Press.

Pichler, Pia and Eva Eppler, eds. 2009. *Gender and Spoken Interaction*. Basingstoke: Palgrave Macmillan.

Preece, Sian. 2009. " 'A Group of Lads Innit?' Performances of Laddish Masculinity in British Higher Education." In Pia Pichler and Eva Eppler (eds.), *Gender and Spoken Interaction*, 115–138. Basingstoke: Palgrave Macmillan.

Reeser, Todd. 2010. *Masculinities in Theory*. Oxford: Wiley-Blackwell.

Riley, Sarah. 2001. "Maintaining Power: Male Constructions of 'Feminists' and 'Feminist Values.' " *Feminism & Psychology*, 11(1): 55–78.

Robinson, Sally. 2000. *Marked Men: White Masculinity in Crisis*. New York: Columbia University Press.

Sacks, Harvey. 1992. *Lectures on Conversation*, 2 vols., ed. Gail Jefferson. Oxford: Blackwell.

Schegloff, Emmanuel A. 1997. "Whose Text? Whose Context?" *Discourse & Society*, 8: 165–187.

Seidler, Victor. 1989. *Rediscovering Masculinity: Reason, Language and Sexuality*. London: Routledge.

Seidler, Victor. 2006. *Young Men and Masculinities: Global Cultures and Intimate Lives*. London: Zed Books.

Sidnell, Jack. 2003. "Constructing and Managing Male Exclusivity in Talk-in-Interaction." In Janet Holmes and Miriam Meyerhoff (eds.), *The Handbook of Language and Gender*, 327–352. Oxford: Blackwell.

Sidnell, Jack. 2011. " 'D'you Understand That Honey': Gender and Participation in Conversation." In Elizabeth Stokoe and Susan Speer (eds.), *Conversation and Gender*, 183–209. Cambridge: Cambridge University Press.

Speer, Susan. 2001a. "Reconsidering the Concept of Hegemonic Masculinity." *Feminism and Psychology*, 11(1): 107–135.

Speer, Susan. 2001b. "Participants' Orientations, Ideology and the Ontological Status of Hegemonic Masculinity: A Rejoinder to Nigel Edley." *Feminism & Psychology*, 11(1): 141–144.

Speer, Susan. 2005. *Gender Talk: Feminism, Discourse and Conversation Analysis*. London: Routledge.

Speer, Susan, and Jonathan Potter. 2002. "From Performatives to Practices: Judith Butler, Discursive Psychology, and the Management of Heterosexist Talk." In Paul McIlvenny (ed.), *Talking Gender and Sexuality*, 151–180. Amsterdam: Benjamins.

Speer, Susan, and Elizabeth Stokoe. 2011. *Conversation and Gender*. Cambridge: Cambridge University Press.

Spender, Dale. 1980. *Man Made Language*. London: Routledge.

Stokoe, Elizabeth. 2003. "Mothers, Single Women and Sluts: Gender, Morality and Membership Categorization in Neighbour Disputes." *Feminism & Psychology*, 13(3): 317–344.

Stokoe, Elizabeth. 2012. " 'You Know How Men Are': Description, Categorization and the Anatomy of a Categorial Practice." *Gender and Language*, 6(1): 231–253.

Stokoe, Elizabeth H., and Janet Smithson. 2002. "Gender and Sexuality in

Talk-in-Interaction: Considering Conversation Analytic Perspectives." In Paul McIlvenny (ed.), *Talking Gender and Sexuality*, 79–109. Amsterdam: Benjamins.

Swann, Joan. 2002. "Yes, but Is It Gender?" In Lia Litosseliti and Jane Sunderland (eds.), *Gender Identity and Discourse Analysis*, 43–67. Amsterdam: Benjamins.

Swann, Joan. 2009. "Doing Gender against the Odds: A Sociolinguistic Analysis of Educational Discourse." In Pia Pichler and Eva Eppler (eds.), *Gender and Spoken Interaction*, 18–41. Basingstoke: Palgrave Macmillan.

Talbot, Mary. 1997. "Randy Fish Boss Branded a Stinker: Coherence and the Construction of Masculinities in a British Tabloid Newspaper." In Sally Johnson and Ulrike H. Meinhof (eds.), *Language and Masculinity*, 173–187. Oxford: Blackwell.

Thomas, Calvin. 2002. "Reenfleshing the Bright Boys; or, How Male Bodies Matter to Feminist Theory." In Judith Kegan Gardiner (ed.), *Masculinity Studies and Feminist Theory: New Directions*, 60–89. New York: Columbia University Press.

Walsh, Fintan. 2010. *Male Trouble: Masculinity and the Performance of Crisis*. Basingstoke: Palgrave Macmillan.

Weatherall, Ann. 2000. "Gender Relevance in Talk-in-Interaction and Discourse." *Discourse and Society*, 11(2): 286–288.

Wetherell, Margaret, and Nigel Edley. 1999. "Negotiating Hegemonic Masculinity: Imaginary Positions and Psycho-Discursive Practices." *Feminism and Psychology*, 9(3): 335–356.

Whelehan, Imelda. 2000. *Overloaded: Popular Culture and the Future of Feminism*. London: Women's Press.

Wiegman, Robyn. 2002. "Unmaking: Men and Masculinity in Feminist Theory." In Judith Kegan Gardiner (ed.), *Masculinity Studies and Feminist Theory: New Directions*, 31–59. New York: Columbia University Press.

Zimmerman, Don, and Candace West. 1975. "Sex Roles, Interruptions and Silences in Conversation." In Barrie Thorne and Nancy Henley (eds.), *Language and Sex: Difference and Dominance*, 105–129. Rowley, MA: Newbury House.

13 Queering Masculinities

TOMMASO M. MILANI

1. Introduction

"Queering masculinities" is a semantically ambiguous title. If "masculinities" is read as the agent of "queering," we are dealing with a *particular* type of masculinities, those that engender some kind of "queer" characteristic. But, if masculinities is understood instead as the patient, the act of "queering" points to a broader academic enterprise of bringing under a "queer" epistemological spotlight *all* forms of masculinities (see also Grosz 1995, 249) for a similar position, according to which it is not only the *objects* of sexual and gender inquiry but also the *knowledge* produced about them that can be queer). As will become clearer later in the chapter, it is this ambivalence between espousing a narrower and minoritizing understanding of "queer" on the one hand, and embracing a broader and more inclusive one on the other, that has characterized one of the most recent and perhaps most radical developments in the field of language, gender, and sexuality. Here, the scare quotes around the adjective "queer" and its derivates do not represent a desire to distance myself from it, but are rather a typographic tool highlighting the fact that the notion is slippery and multifaceted – a "floating signifier" (Hall 1997) – which needs handling with caution.

I will begin with an outline of the origins and development of queer as a theoretical construct; I then move on to provide an overview of the debates surrounding queer in language, gender, and sexuality research, focusing in particular on the topic of male masculinities. This is followed by an example of how a queer lens can be applied to a fictional instance of doctor–patient interaction taken from the TV miniseries *Angels in America*. The chapter concludes with a few reflections about the future of queering language and masculinities.

2. Queer: What is It and What is It Good For?

Originally employed as a synonym of homosexual or as a homophobic slur, the term queer underwent a threefold process of re-signification, reappropriation,

The Handbook of Language, Gender, and Sexuality, Second Edition.
Edited by Susan Ehrlich, Miriam Meyerhoff, and Janet Holmes.
© 2014 John Wiley & Sons, Inc. Published 2017 by John Wiley & Sons, Inc.

and politicization in the United States during the late 1980s and early 1990s, this being a period characterized by a huge dissatisfaction on the part of many American non-heterosexuals with the kind of identity politics that had under-pinned "gay liberation." It lies beyond the scope of this chapter to offer a nuanced exegesis of the historical conditions which underpinned the emergence of queer (see Jagose 1996). Suffice it to say, however, that the main critique raised from a queer standpoint was that gay liberation in the United States was an exclusionary political movement characterized by a racialized (= white), gendered (= male), and social class (= middle-class) bias, which ultimately policed and excluded other forms of non-heterosexual identification. As Jagose (1996) reminds us, however, the dissatisfaction with sexual identity politics that underpinned gay liberation was only *one* component in the emergence and success of queer, the other being the HIV/AIDS outbreak, which not only galvanized non-heterosexuals in an unprecedented way but also helped them to start questioning the homo/hetero dichotomy (see below for further discussion).

It is in this historical landscape of political and social activism that queer was incorporated into the realm of academia, and was joined to the more "respectable" word "theory" (Kulick 2005).[1] Like any other theoretical framework developed in "post-" or "late" conditions (i.e., poststructuralism, postmodernism, late modernity, etc.), queer theory is not a consistent, coherent, and all-encompassing conceptual apparatus. In short, there is no such a thing as a queer theory in the singular. Rather, queer theory consists of many, very different, slippery, and at times apparently incoherent approaches (see Sauntson 2008, 271). As Halperin (1995, 61–62) puts it, "[q]ueer is by definition whatever is at odds with the normal, the legitimate, the dominant. There is nothing in particular to which it necessarily refers. It is an identity without essence." To use Saussure's terminology, queer is a signifier without a signified. But if all we have is a name, then we might want to ask ourselves: What kind of "added value" does a queer lens offer that other approaches don't?

At the risk of falling into the trap of imposing a single definition on queer theory and thus curtailing its radical potential, I would argue in line with Jagose that the core feature of any queer enterprise is to take a critical stance that problematizes "*normative* consolidations of sex, gender and sexuality – and that, consequently, is critical of all those versions of identity, community and politics that are believed to evolve 'naturally' from such consolidations" (Jagose 1996, 99; emphasis added). Underpinning the skeptical view of gender or sexual identity which is a key feature of queer approaches are the assumptions that (1) gender and sexuality have been "casually entangled in knots that must be undone" (Butler 1998, 225–226), and (2) "identity categories tend to be instruments of regulatory regimes, whether as the normalizing categories of oppressive structures or as the rallying points for a liberatory contestation of that very oppression" (Butler 1991, 13–14).

Several remarks can be made on the basis of Jagose's and Butler's statements. First, despite acknowledging that sex, gender, and sexuality are separate cate-gories, queer theory highlights that these are constructs that have been socially entwined in such a way that they have developed a "unique relationship"

(Sauntson 2008, 274) with each other (see also Baker 2008). Hence, what a queer stance tries to draw attention to is not simply how biological sex (the dichotomy between males and females on the basis of organs of reproduction) is mapped onto gender (the opposition between men and women, masculinity and femininity), and how these dyads are in turn the foundations on which heterosexuality rests (see Butler 1999 [1990], 194). Rather, it also seeks to foreground how some of the ties between sex, gender, and sexuality are socially (re)produced as "normal" and "desirable" (typically, the attraction between two allegedly opposite and complementary sexes/genders that underpins heterosexuality) while others are devalued as "deviant" and "unwanted" (usually, same-sex desire).

Second, queer theorists emphasize that an understanding of the social construction of normality versus deviance cannot be limited to unearthing the social conditions that enable and uphold *heterornormativity*, that is, "those structures, institutions, relations and actions that promote and produce heterosexuality as natural, self-evident, desirable, privileged and necessary" (Cameron and Kulick 2003, 55). Instead, it would be more productive to think of queer as a more antagonistic form of dissent, which "rejects a minoritizing logic of toleration or simple political interest-representation in favor of a more thorough resistance to regimes of the normal" (M. Warner 1993, xxvi). According to such a view, a queer perspective should also shed light on the ways in which certain forms of same-sex desire can *themselves* become normalized and legitimized over time (e.g., monogamous, committed homosexual relationships) while others are (re)cast into the domain of abjection (see Bourdieu 1998) (e.g., sadomasochist, uncommitted, and multipartnered relationships).

Finally, because of the suspicious stance on *all* versions of identity, queer approaches are *not* coextensive with LGBT (lesbian, gay, bisexual, and transgender) studies, although there are of course synergies and intersections between the two. As we will see below, scholarship inflected by queer theory is likely to be as concerned with casting a critical gaze on heterosexuality as it would be with scrutinizing homosexuality, as well as examining the complex intersections between the two (Cameron and Kulick 2003, 149).

Quite predictably, the skepticism about identity categories has not remained unchallenged by supporters of a liberal LGBT politics. Queer theory, so the argument goes, is an elitist enterprise led by a bunch of privileged academics who, having gained rights thanks to identity politics, can now comfortably turn their backs on it, and downplay or even deny the importance of sexual identities for people in "real" life. From this, it follows that queer theory does not contribute to the ongoing political emancipation of sexual minorities. The problem embedded in such an argument is that queer theorists do not deny that "'homosexuals' exist; just as there is no doubt that women 'really' exist, or that men do. If anything, these identity categories are only *too* real" (D. N. Warner 2004, 324; emphasis original). What queer theorists do is raise a cautionary warning against too optimistic a reliance on sexual identities as the catalyst for social change. And, in my view, this is neither an indicator of snobbish political apathy nor a token of "post-rights" ingratitude. Rather, the point that queer theorists want to make is that a politics based on sexual identities can, in the best of cases, lead only to a temporary recalibration of power inequalities, but will ultimately leave the homosexual/heterosexual binary intact and unchallenged (see Yep 2003, 47). In order to achieve a deeper radical project of social transformation of the status quo, queer approaches argue instead for questioning the seemingly "normal" and widely accepted nature of the homosexual/heterosexual divide itself, and destabilizing the very truth of that normality.

3. Queer Troubles in Researching Language and Masculinities

Although queer theory has had a substantial impact on a variety of disciplines since its inception, it did not immediately gain momentum in sociolinguistic and linguistic anthropological work. In a groundbreaking collection entitled *Queerly Phrased*, Livia and Hall (1997) were pioneers in arguing for "bringing performativity back to linguistics." In this way, they encouraged scholars interested in the intersections between language and social processes to seriously engage with the work of one of the most well-known queer theorists, Judith Butler, and her reflections on gender performativity.

Five years later, in an edited collection on language and sexuality, Campbell-Kibler et al. (2002) showcased a heated academic debate on the future of "queer linguistics" (Barrett 2002; Eckert 2002; Kulick 2002; Leap 2002; McElhinny 2002; Queen 2002; see also Baker (2008) and Motschenbacher (2011) for discussions about this debate). Like any other debate, the discussion was polarized between those who were adamant in proposing the importance of queer theory to (socio)linguistics, and those who were more skeptical about the enterprise. These disagreements notwithstanding, what is most interesting to note here is a tension surrounding the definition of what counts as queer. As Queen summarizes it, "most of the work that gets placed under the label 'queer linguistics' is not specifically queer theoretical but rather based on data from queer subjects" (2002, 70), where by queer is meant LGBT individuals. While this can be taken as a testimony to the minoritizing trends in the definition of queer mentioned in the introduction above, Barrett rejects such a reductionist interpretation of queer, and argues that "queer linguistics ... *cannot* be limited by application to a particular identity category" (2002, 26; emphasis added).

In a similar vein, Kulick proposes that "queer linguistics" should "move beyond the study of the linguistic behavior of people we know to be, or suspect might be, gay, lesbian, bisexual, or transgendered" (2002, 68). Kulick's suggestion here forestalls the more extended argument which he (together with Deborah Cameron) develops in the later and not always uncontroversial book *Language and Sexuality* (Cameron and Kulick 2003; Kulick, Chapter 3 in this volume), namely that a queer approach to language and sexuality entails the much broader remit of (1) going beyond the study of "queer peers" (McElhinny 2002, 116–117), and (2) bringing under the spotlight the discursive construction of the boundaries between normality and deviance.

3.1   Heterosexual deviance

Very few studies have thus far attempted to take up and operationalize Cameron and Kulick's notions through actual data. As I will illustrate in the remainder of this section, it is in the field of (heterosexual) masculinities that scholars have begun to apply a queer lens – as understood by Cameron and Kulick – to sociolinguistic and discourse analytical data. In doing so, they show different examples of masculine performances which either (re)produce and uphold heteronormativity, or conversely do not conform and thus "disrupt, or have the potential to disrupt, traditional images of the hegemonic heterosexual masculine" (Heasley 2005, 310) in those contexts (see in particular Milani 2011).

Kulick (2005) himself investigates an interesting example of the ways in which a particular form of heterosexual masculinity in Sweden – men who buy sex from female prostitutes – is undergoing a process of becoming *unintelligible* and *deviant*. Since 1999 Sweden has criminalized only the *purchase* of sex. Put bluntly, it is only the "John" that commits an unlawful act, according to Swedish legislation. Employing a Foucauldian approach to a series of policy documents on prostitution, Kulick teases out the ways in which male sex-buyers are represented through a pathologizing discourse that construes them as psychologically disturbed individuals who distinguish between "sex" and "love." The interesting and, at the same time, problematic aspect of this discursive process is that what was previously considered a practice ("the act of purchasing sex"), is now congealing into something more stable, an identity with its own (pathological) characteristics ("the client"). As Kulick (2005, 221) explains, the emergence of this new identity category is the discursive manifestation of a "potentially far-reaching reorganization of sexuality" in Sweden, which is not unrelated to broader processes of nationalism. It is not accidental that, only a few years before the passing of the law on prostitution, the topic of prostitution featured heavily in the discourses of those who lobbied against Sweden's entry into the European Union. In their view, joining the European Union would entail the spread of a "liberal view of prostitution," which, in turn, would bring with it a "flood" "of tens of thousands of prostitutes clamoring at the gates" (221). The crucial element here is that a perceived threat coming from a "transnational" view on prostitution not only led to the overt thematization in the national arena of who the "bad" and the "ugly" is in the context of Swedish sexuality, namely the male sex-buyer; but the discourse on prostitution also implicitly reinstated what counts as "good," namely "the normative national sexuality, grounded in love, that all Swedes are exhorted to share" (225).

Also looking at non-normative heterosexual masculinities in the Swedish context, Tommaso Milani and Rickard Jonsson (2011) take as a case in point the linguistic practices among "immigrant young men." As the authors indicate, an overview of the literature on media representations of these practices illustrates that there is a dominant discourse circulating in Swedish society that seeks not only to stigmatize these linguistic practices as "bad," "deviant," "homophobic," and "sexist," but also to present them as a form of "incomprehensible" jabbering. Taking these media discourses as starting point, Milani and Jonsson have analyzed a series of school interactions involving a group of those "immigrant young men" that have been at the center of so much media concern. As Milani and Jonsson illustrate, the linguistic practices of these young men are indeed sexist and at times homophobic. However, unlike dominant media representations which depict them as *inherently* homophobic, the authors demonstrate that heteronormativity and homophobia do not "naturally" flow from the young men's ethnicity, but are part of the school as a whole, as well as key components in the teaching strategy of a Swedish teacher. Moreover, the study shows how ethnic insults, gay innuendo, and misogynistic talk are far from being unintelligible, but are deeply *meaningful*; they constitute a rich pool of interactional resources that allow the young men in the study to actively partake in the negotiation of a local order in which different heterosexual masculine positions are enacted and/or contested for the achievement of power and/or solidarity. As with Kulick (2005), the queer dimension of this study lies in the attempt to denaturalize the matrix of intelligibility (Butler 1999 [1990]) in Swedish society which promotes images of certain people and practices as normal and intelligible while devaluing others as deviant and incomprehensible.

3.2 Heterosexual normality

Kulick's (2005) as well as Milani and Jonsson's (2011) studies can be taken as empirical examples of queer deconstructions of the social processes through which certain masculine identities, bodies, and desires are made *incomprehensible* and *deviant* at the expense of others. Cameron and Kulick (2003, 149), however, have also emphasized that our attention should not be limited to "the cases in which bodies/relations/desires 'deviate' from the norm, but also those cases in which they do not." Such an argument is underpinned by the belief that a deeper transformative project of the social world can be initiated only by unraveling those processes through which certain bodies, identities, and desires (and not others) become *unmarked*, *normal*, and *normative* (see Trechter, Chapter 17, and Benwell, Chapter 12, in this volume). It is to such a discursive construction of normality that I now turn.

While not overtly endorsing a queer theoretical stance, Kiesling (2002) illustrates the everyday, mundane ways in which some young men in a university fraternity in the United States reproduce and uphold heterosexuality as the taken-for-granted norm (see also Coates 2007 for the United Kingdom). This study also shows how heterosexuality constitutes the *sine qua non* for these young men to be able to negotiate homo*social* desire, that is, the need to bond with other men as well as to compete for dominance in the peer group. But men's homosociality brings with it an inherent conundrum. Dominant discourses of masculinity dictate that heterosexual men should strive to build solidarity with one another, yet the more they pursue this bonding enterprise, the more they run the risk of being perceived as entering the realm of same-sex desire, which paradoxically undermines their performance of heterosexual masculinity (Kiesling 2005, 720). Kiesling shows inter alia how homosocial dominance is negotiated linguistically through the usage of the sexist slur *bitch* as well as the expression *honey, are you at home?* which, in the context of the United States, evokes the familiar image of a husband addressing his wife upon returning from work. Interestingly, however, neither of these linguistic resources is employed to refer to women in Kiesling's data; they are part of two different interactions among the men in the fraternity. He concludes that the men in his study "display *same-sex* dominance by metaphorically referring to other men as 'feminine,' thus drawing on the cultural model of the heterosexual couple to index homosocial inequality" (Kiesling 2002, 250).

Taking a more quantitative corpus-linguistic approach to the study of masculinities, Baker (2008) looks at the ways in which the male-gendered terms *bachelor* and *husband* occur in the British National Corpus, and what kind of discourses underpin their usage. The analysis of concordances shows a complex picture. On the one hand, *bachelor* (unlike its feminine counterpart *spinster*) is a carrier of strongly positive connotations, as manifested in the recurrent collocational pair *eligible bachelor*, which refers "to young (heterosexual men) who are either physically attractive or wealthy and therefore eligible for marriage" (Baker 2008, 204). On the other hand, bachelorhood is seen in a positive light as long as it is a temporary condition on the way towards a more settled existence ratified through the institution of marriage: "[t]he phrase 'may he enjoy happy bachelor days but not too many' ... summarizes a belief that a bachelor identity ought to be temporary rather than permanent" (Baker 2008, 207). "Confirmed," "lifelong," and "steadfast" bachelors are viewed as societal problems not simply because they are represented as lonely eccentrics and potential victims of crime, but also because they are said to be prone to have affairs with married women, thus unsettling the moral order established by marriage.

The discourses surrounding the term *husband* are no less clear-cut than those relating to *bachelor*. What is unambiguous, however, is that *husband* strongly collocates with *wife* as well as with financial and legal terms (*conveyance, debt, creditor, seller, mortgage, pension, solicitor*). According to Baker, such collocational patterns can be taken as linguistic traces "suggesting a discourse of marriage in terms of a partnership sanctioned by law" (Baker 2008, 208). In the same way as *bachelor* becomes increasingly problematic when threatening the institution of marriage, the masculine identity of *husband* gains negative connotations in contexts where the conjugal bed is put at risk by death, separation, or infidelity.

Overall, as Baker points out, the examples in the British National Corpus cannot be easily explained through a Manichaean dichotomy of *bachelor* as negative and *husband* as positive. In fact, both identity categories are simultaneously carriers of negative and positive connotations. But an analysis of these masculine identities has provided us with an insight into an ongoing process of *normalization* of monogamous (heterosexual) marriage. What emerges clearly is that marriage and monogamy are more or less covertly thought to be something a man should aspire to and respect in order to accomplish for himself a rewarding (heterosexual) masculine (self-)identification. It will be interesting to see whether, and if so, how such a process of normalization will be replicated or disrupted in the near future as a result of same-sex civil unions.

3.3 Fraught intersections: normality, deviance, and same-sex desire

For scholars of language, gender, and sexuality at the beginning of the twenty-first century, it might sound unsurprising that the construction of "normal" and "normative" heterosexual masculinities relies on homophobic behavior which either casts homosexuality into the domain of abjection (as in Milani and Jonsson's (2011) study) or is built on the complete erasure of the possibility of same-sex desire (as in Kiesling's (2002) fraternity or in the British National Corpus analyzed by Baker (2008)). In this respect, Connell (1995) argued that hegemonic masculinity – the most valued form of masculinity in a given context typically – goes hand in hand with the vilification of homosexual men and the subjugation of women (see Benwell, Chapter 12 in this volume). It is important to remember that hegemony cannot take place without the *collusion* of those who are being subordinated. Reasoning along similar lines, one could argue that the hegemony of normality can be upheld only with the complicity of deviance. This is not simply because the "deviant" – whatever or whoever this may be in different contexts – can be said to be, in Butler's words, the "constitutive outside" of the "symbolic universe" of normality, "defining [its] limit or exteriority, one which, were it imported into that universe, would destroy its integrity and coherence" (Butler 1997, 180); it is also because those who are viewed as "deviant" may themselves reproduce and valorize – even fetishize – characteristics typically associated with normality. Put simply, even conceding that the subjugation and devaluing of real, perceived, or presumed male homosexuality is a key prerequisite for hegemonic masculinity to exist (see Cameron 1997), men who desire other men should not be viewed a priori as victims or passive spectators because they may well be active agents in sustaining the workings of hegemonic masculinity.

Linguistically, such complicity has been evidenced in a compelling analysis of public discourses of gay men in the United Kingdom (Baker 2005; 2008; see also Milani (2013) for South Africa). Looking at a large corpus of gay men's personal advertisements, Baker argues for the existence of "hegemonic homosexuality" in his data, in the sense that "the most highly valued identity is traditional heterosexual hegemonic masculinity or an approximation to it" (Baker 2008, 176). Such "approximation" to a heterosexual masculine ideal is most patently realized in the adjective "straight-acting," a positively laden characteristic which is recurrent in the advertisers' self-characterizations as well as in the descriptions of their "objects of desire." Crucially, Phua highlights that "[s]traight acting means more than being masculine: it also means to be undetectable as a gay person" (2002, 186). From this, one could conclude that gay men who desire or identify as "straight-acting" men are "buying into" a heteronormative discourse that implicitly valorizes heterosexuality as the acceptable norm in the public space at the same time as it devalues homosexuality as an inappropriate identity not to be displayed.

As Baker warns us, however, the valorization of masculine traits, with the concomitant stigmatization of male femininity should not lead us to draw conclusions too easily about these gay men's collusion in the workings of hegemonic masculinity. Not only is the mobilization of the notion of "straight(-acting)" not always necessarily "for real" but it can be ironic or parodic (Milani 2013; Thorne and Coupland 1998); but, even when serious, the emphasis on "straightactingness" could also be read as a way through which gay men contest widespread societal discourses that stereotype them as effeminate. Moreover, the fetishization of masculine traits could be interpreted as a form of objectification that reduces hegemonic masculinity to a commodity to be "consumed" either virtually (just by reading the advert) or really (by having sex). Finally, the men whom the advertisers describe might not necessarily coincide with those with whom they actually have sex or engage in a long-lasting relationship. All in all, from a queer perspective, it may be concluded that "such adverts could therefore be read as both complicit *and* empowering" (Baker 2008, 177; emphasis original).

If all queer theory does is help us to unpack the social constructedness of deviance and normality as well as complexify our understanding of gender and sexuality, it is not unreasonable to doubt, as many do, its actual impact in terms of achieving a deeper social transformative project. At this juncture, it is worth reiterating that

> a (queer or otherwise) analysis of the construction of a sexual [and gender] identity should not a priori assume the emancipatory goals of legitimisation or legalisation … Indeed, a central tenet of queer theory is that identity categories are socially constructed, which is a very different goal from seeking acceptance. (Baker 2008, 222)

I will exemplify this principle in the next section by bringing under a queer spotlight a fictional case of patient–doctor interaction.

4. "Roy Cohn is a Heterosexual Man who Fucks Around with Guys": Queer Positions and Dominant Discourses

Angels in America: A Gay Fantasia on National Themes was originally written by Tony Kushner as a play in two acts. After its premiere in San Francisco in 1991, it went on to achieve international acclaim on stage and in film.

Set in New York City in the mid-1980s, *Angels in America* could best be described as a form of political magic realism. It offers snippets of apparently "real" everyday tragedies during the outbreak of the AIDS epidemic, couched within a "magic," supernatural frame in which angels descend to earth to find their prophet. The magic and the real are marshaled together for political purposes, turning scrutiny on the national context of the United States at a particular historical turning point. The political undertone of the play emerges in the inclusion of a few historical characters who played a controversial role in North American politics. One of these is Roy Cohn, a much feared lawyer who, during the communist witch hunt of the McCarthy era, became famous for his involvement in the Rosenberg trial. Cohn was suspected of having intimate relationships with other men, and ultimately died from AIDS in 1986.

The following extracts are taken from the scene in the TV miniseries where Roy Cohn, played by Al Pacino, has just been visited by his family doctor and been told that he has developed AIDS.

Extract 1

1 R: This disease
2 D: Syndrome
3 R: Whatever. It afflicts mostly homosexuals and drug addicts
4 D: Mostly. Hemophiliacs are also at risk.
5 R: Homosexuals and drug addicts. So why are you implying that I … What are you implying, Henry?
6 D: I don't think I was implying anything.
7 R: I'm not a drug addict.
8 D: Oh come on, Roy
9 R: What? What? Come on Roy what? You think I'm a junkie, Henry? Do you see tracks?
10 D: This is absurd.
11 R: So say it.
12 D: Say what?
13 R: Say Roy Cohn, you are a …
14 D: Roy
15 R: You are a … Go on. Not Roy Cohn you are a drug fiend. Roy Marcus Cohn, you are a … Go on, Henry, it starts with an H.
16 D: Oh I'm not gonna get into.
17 R: With an H and it isn't hemophiliac. Come on!
18 D: Why are you doing this, Roy?
19 R: No, I mean it, say it. Say, Roy Cohn, you are a homosexual and I will proceed systematically to destroy your reputation and your practice and your career in the state of New York, Henry, which you know I can do.
20 D: Roy, you have been seeing me since 1958. Apart from the face lifts, I have treated you for everything from syphilis
21 R: From a whore in Dallas
22 D: from syphilis to venereal warts in your rectum, which you may have gotten from a whore in Dallas but it wasn't a female whore.
23 R: So say it.
24 D: Roy Cohn, you are … you have had sex with men many many times, Roy, and one of those men or any number of them has made you very sick. You have AIDS.

There are many entry points from which this verbal exchange can be analyzed. To begin with, this interaction could be seen as an interesting instance of the ways in which power is engendered, negotiated, and contested in discourse. Here, I take a

Foucauldian approach that conceptualizes power as a "multiplicity of force relations," which "is everywhere; not because it embraces everything, but because it comes from everywhere" (Foucault 1976, 92–93). While such a view of power has often been criticized for its vagueness and lack of heuristic force, it is of key importance because it forces us to avoid reducing power to physical violence, social status, and the law. Instead, it allows us to foreground the more subtle and mundane ways in which power is woven into discourse. According to Michel Foucault (1980), these ways are always imbricated with the (re)production and contestation of knowledge.

In the light of this, it is my contention that the intersection between power and knowledge constitutes the pivotal element around which the interaction above revolves. At a linguistic level, such a discursive struggle manifests itself most visibly in the opening turn, where the doctor corrects the lay word "disease" with the more accurate medical term "syndrome." This correction, however, is countered by Cohn's abrupt usage of the interjection "whatever," which dismisses the doctor's correction as irrelevant. The competition for power/knowledge continues in the following turns, where Roy Cohn lists two so-called risk groups – "homosexuals and drug addicts." To this, the doctor adds a parenthetical clause, including "hemophiliacs." However, the doctor's qualifying statement is once again immediately dismissed by Roy Cohn who repeats the words "homosexuals" and "drug addicts" in a raised voice, but leaves out "hemophiliacs," pretending not to have heard the doctor. Significantly, the reference to "risk groups" also marks the start of a new phase in the verbal dueling between the two interlocutors, namely a contest about sexual identity categories ("homosexual"/"heterosexual") and their referents, which begins in the guise of a word guessing game (turns 13–19).

Any social label is inherently political; it encodes particular ideologies and carries with it specific histories and connotations (see Milani 2010). This is no less true of labels regarding sexuality. Foucault (1976) demonstrated that it was not until the mid nineteenth century that same-sex practices – a man having sex with another man – became the terrain on which an identity category, "homosexual," was created in Europe. In other words, at that specific nexus of time and space, what had been viewed as something a man *does* more or less often (in addition to or exclusive of other sexual practices) became something a man *is*. Most notably, the birth of the "homosexual," together with its dyadic counterpart, the "heterosexual," was not a trivial incident of terminological novelty, but represented a key historical moment which would have far-reaching epistemological consequences insofar as it marked the origin of a particular understanding that conflates – equates even – particular sexual practices with a particular sexual identity. Put simply, according to the matrix of intelligibility (Butler 1999 [1990]), a man is *essentially* and *necessarily* homosexual, or gay, if he desires or has sex with other men. And while it is not impossible to question this logic, any such attempt will not be without consequences, but will ultimately result in the risk of becoming unintelligible, incoherent, and meaningless (see Butler 1999 [1990]; D. N. Warner 2004). Against this backdrop, what Roy Cohn is performing in the extract below, in my view, is an endeavor to queer the matrix of intelligibility around sexual identity.

Extract 2

25 R: AIDS? You know, your problem, Henry, is that you are hung up on words, on labels, that you believe they mean what they seem to mean. AIDS, homosexual, gay, lesbian. You think these are names that tell you who someone sleeps with? They don't tell you that.

26 D: No?

27 R: No. Like all labels, they tell you one thing and one thing only, where does an individual so identified fit in the food chain, in the pecking order. Not ideology or sexual taste but something much simpler clout. Not who I fuck or who fucks me but who will pick up the phone when I call, who owes me favors. This is what a label refers to. Now, to someone who does not understand this, homosexual is what I am because I have sex with men. But really, this is wrong. Homosexuals are not men who sleep with other men. Homosexuals are men who, in fifteen years of trying, cannot pass a pissant antidiscrimination bill through City Council. Homosexuals are men who know nobody and who nobody knows, who have zero clout. Does this sound like me, Henry?

28 D: No.

29 R: No. I have clout. Lots. I pick up this phone, I punch fifteen numbers, you know who's on the other end? In under five minutes, Henry.

30 D: The President.

31 R: Better, Henry. His wife.

32 D: I'm impressed.

33 R: I don't want you to be impressed. I want you to understand. This is not sophistry and this is not hypocrisy. This is reality. I have sex with men but unlike nearly every other man of whom this is true I bring the guy I'm screwing to the White House and President Reagan smiles at us and shakes his hand because what I am is entirely defined by who I am. Roy Cohn is not a homosexual. Roy Cohn is a heterosexual man, Henry, who fucks around with guys.

What Roy Cohn is stating here is that the fact that a man desires and has sex with another man does not make him necessarily homosexual. Admittedly, one could counterargue that Cohn was a "closeted gay." By this interpretation, his ranting against being pigeon-holed into the category "homosexual" is nothing but a strategic rhetorical maneuver through which he attempts to persuade the doctor to write a diagnosis of liver cancer instead of AIDS. The necessity of this rhetorical move can be understood if we consider that, since its inception, AIDS had been culturally scripted as the "gay plague" (see Sontag 1989). A diagnosis of AIDS, then, would have translated into a public reinforcement of the suspicions on the part of many of Cohn's detractors about his proclivity for men. This would have been politically fatal in the conservative political circles of which Cohn was part. In brief, according to this logic, the questioning of the category "homosexual" is nothing but a conscious tactic through which Cohn is aiming to safeguard his personal and political interests.

In arguing that Roy Cohn is, instead, queering hegemonic discourses about sexual identity, I would like to propose an alternative and more radical reading – one which relies rather less on positioning a priori Roy Cohn in alignment with an existing matrix of intelligibility (through the category "closeted gay") than on unveiling the ambiguous, conflicting, and often incoherent positions that he embodies in discourse. This is ultimately with a political view to shaking the grounds on which the matrix of intelligibility rests.

First of all, it is important to observe that Cohn does not opt out of identity categories altogether; rather, he invokes and thus reproduces the dyad homosexuality–heterosexuality by pitting these two categories one against the other. However, the meaning of what counts as homosexual or heterosexual is slippery and unstable in this context. What is highlighted most prominently is the power differential between their referents. This appears clearly in the claim that "homosexuals are men with zero clout," which evidently entails that their binary counterpart, heterosexuals (including Cohn himself), *do* have power. This power imbalance, however, is not employed as the springboard for a call for the enhancement of the social status of sexual minorities in New York City. On the contrary, Cohn is openly dismissive of the gay identity politics of the time, scornfully blaming homosexual New Yorkers for their political inability to lobby for a "pissant anti-discrimination law." Note in particular the masculinist discourse through which Cohn seems to make homosexuality a male-only precinct, thus erasing lesbianism.

Undeniably, it is an anthropological axiom that "ways of talking about the 'Other' are ways of talking about ourselves" (Woolard 1989, 276), and vice versa. This means that the negative representation of the "Other" – the "homosexual" – as powerless and politically inept could be interpreted as a discursive strategy through which Cohn aims to achieve a positive self-presentation (see van Dijk 1993) as powerful and politically skilled. That said, what is most interesting and most contentious in Cohn's argument is the semantic redeployment of the dyad "homosexual"–"heterosexual." The meaning of these categories is ambiguous in this context, not least because they seem to have less to do with sexual practices than with social status. Or, as Cohn puts it, "Homosexuals are not men who sleep with other men … Homosexuals are men who know nobody and who nobody knows, who have zero clout." Such twisting of the meaning of sexual identity categories reaches its climax at the end of the interaction, where Cohn baldly rejects the identity of "homosexual," and instead claims for himself the rather contentious subject position of "a heterosexual man … who fucks around with guys."

At a first glance, such an argument might sound paradoxical in the sense that "two apparently contradictory notions or views are held simultaneously" (Harvey 2000, 244). The paradox lies in the juxtaposition of two elements that are mutually exclusive according to the matrix of intelligibility: (1) a "heterosexual man" as someone who has sex with women; and (2) the sexual practice contained in the relative clause ("who fucks around with guys"), which is the key signifying element of homosexuality. However, Oscar Wilde has taught us that paradox can be an important rhetorical weapon of sociopolitical criticism. This is insofar as paradox allows the speaker/writer to occupy a liminal standpoint at the intersections between rationality and incoherence, a position from which to critique and unsettle established moral and social conventions. Similarly, paradox enables Cohn to inhabit a complex subject position, albeit a short-lived one, in which he treads the razor-thin verge between intelligibility and absurdity. Such a stance could be defined as queer because it disturbs "natural" assumptions about sexuality. More specifically, the troubling element here lies in two discursive moves: (1) the uncoupling of the identity "homosexual" from its signifying core, the practices ("fucks around with guys"), and, related to this, (2) the semantic twisting through which the sexual element in the categories "heterosexual" and "homosexual" is backgrounded while the power dimension is foregrounded, thus making these categories synonymous with "powerful" and "powerless," respectively.

In sum, Roy Cohn is indeed reproducing hegemonic discourses about sexuality in that he reinforces and legitimizes the power imbalances between the two. However, I would argue that, through paradox, he is also bringing into being a fleeting moment of queerness by temporarily "misperforming in such a way that 'natural' assumptions are called into question; mixing and matching in ways that are not allowed and not called for" (D. N. Warner 2004, 325). In saying this, I concur with Butler (1997, 157) that "it is precisely the *expropriability* of the dominant, 'authorized' discourse that constitutes one potential site of its subversive resignification." In the example above, it is through semantic resignification and creative juxtaposition of sexual categories and practices that Roy Cohn can both reproduce and contest dominant discourses.

One might wonder to what extent these isolated instances of fictional or real local practice can ultimately challenge hegemonic epistemologies of sexuality. While it lies outside the scope of this chapter to answer this question, I want to reiterate a point that has often been made in linguistic anthropological work, that politics, in the sense of the dynamic interplay between power and agency, "'happens' when one may be led to least expect it – in the nooks and crannies of everyday life, outside of institutionalized contexts that one ordinarily associates with politics" (Besnier 2009, 11; see also Butler 1999 [1990]). Not only should we not be blind to the "everyday life of politics" (Besnier 2009), but we also shouldn't downplay its subversive potential.

5. Imagining Queer Futures?

Virginia Woolf (2003, 350) wrote in a diary entry that "we live without a future. That's what's queer." Of course, this has nothing to do with queer theory and masculinities, but a similar sense of insecurity about the future, in this case, regarding the shapes and directions queer theory will or should take, is what has cropped up repeatedly in many queer theoretical writings (Butler 1993; Jagose 1996; O'Rourke 2011) – an uncertainty, I should add, that is not viewed as negative, but as the *sine qua non* for queer not to be domesticated, and thereby uphold its radical potential. Against this backdrop, it would be paradoxical if I began to indicate – dictate, even – the directions toward which the queering of masculinities should head in the field of language, gender, and sexuality. What I will do instead is outline what kind of "queer futures" I can imagine for my own research trajectory.

To begin with, *dislocating masculinities* (see Cornwall and Lindisfarne 1994) from men is something that warrants closer investigation. There is no doubt that research on language and gender has undergone a major epistemological shift as a result of poststructuralist theories, showing us how individuals *do* gender in different ways by creatively deploying linguistic means which allow them to orient themselves to available images or models of masculinity and femininity in specific sociocultural contexts. Yet it strikes me as odd that the largest portion of scholarship on language and masculinities has focused on male participants (and, not unsurprisingly, research on femininities on females). In a sense, one could argue then that the so-called "coat-rack model" of sex and gender so heavily criticized by Linda Nicholson (1994) nearly 20 years ago still seems to be the "normal" modus operandi of language and gender research. Queering such an epistemological normality will entail mapping more carefully the ways in which women – irrespective of sexual orientation – as well as transgendered and intersex individuals also do masculinities in their daily lives (see, however, Jones 2012; King 2011; Koller 2009; Zimman 2011 for notable exceptions).

The dislocation of cultural features (= masculinities) from biological attributes (= having a penis), however, should not make us blind to another aspect that has been largely unexplored in language, gender, and sexuality research, namely *corporeality*, the materiality of the body. In order to clarify this point, let us consider the real-life story of Brandon Teena, made famous by Kimberly Peirce in the well-known film *Boys Don't Cry*. Although biologically female, Brandon success-fully "passes" as a man, thus providing a living example of Butler's argument that "[g]ender is a kind of imitation for which there is no original" (1991, 21). Crucially, however, no sooner is his biological identity revealed than those male acquaintances who had so happily bonded with him now turn against him, rape, and ultimately kill him. This dreadful story shows that (biological) bodies *do* mat-ter; they matter to the point that "flouting" through culture what one has not been "naturally" endowed with by biology may lead to tragic consequences. Precisely because of this, I believe that the queering of masculinities cannot limit itself to the domains of discourse and representation surrounding those experiences of fear and violence linked to gender and sexual "deviance." Giving primacy to discourse as the object of investigation is not necessarily tantamount to the naive denial of the existence of materiality. Rather, the issue here is that the relationship between individuals and the world is never unmediated: material "stuff" can acquire meaning only in and through some kind of signifying system. But can the experiences of "corrective rape" and transphobia such as those depicted in *Boys Don't Cry* be fully captured only through an analysis of the discourses surrounding these phenomena?

Gunther Kress has recently argued that

> Many signs we encounter are in three-dimensional form ... We engage with [them] ... not only through the modes of image, writing, colour, but also in actual or imagined "inner" mimesis through touch and feel, scent and smell, in action – imagined or real ... *all engage more of our body in their materiality than sparser notions of "representation" might usually suggest.* (Kress 2010, 77; emphasis added)

In the same way that other strands of sociolinguistics and linguistic anthropology have over the last few years been moving toward the acknowledgment of the "material" (see in particular Stroud and Mpendukana 2009), I would like to seek to "immanentize queer theory" (O'Rourke 2011, 105) in the study of masculinities, taking into account the materiality of the body as a site of desire, identity, violence, and struggle (see Grosz 1995; O'Rourke 2011). Whether this is methodologically feasible with the tools offered by (socio)linguistics and semiotics, or whether new "promiscuous" methodologies (see O'Rourke 2011) should be devised remains to be seen. However, this uncertainty, together with its inherent potential, is after all the very spirit of what counts as "queer."

Acknowledgments

I would like to acknowledge the generous Promotion Grant offered by the Faculty of Humanities at the University of the Witwatersrand, Johannesburg, which allowed me to conduct the research on which this article is based. Some of the arguments made in this chapter have been elaborated in previous publications (Milani 2012; 2013; in press).

NOTE

1 Supposedly, the first public usage of the expression "queer theory" was as part of the title of a conference organized in 1990 by Teresa de Lauretis at the University of California, Santa Cruz (see de Lauretis 1991; Halperin 2003).

REFERENCES

Baker, Paul. 2005. *Public Discourses of Gay Men*. London: Routledge.

Baker, Paul. 2008. *Sexed Texts: Language, Gender and Sexuality*. London: Equinox.

Barrett, Rusty. 2002. "Is Queer Theory Important for Sociolinguistic Theory?" In Kathryn Campbell-Kibler, Robert J. Podesva, Sarah J. Roberts, and Andrew

Wong (eds.), *Language and Sexuality: Contesting Meaning in Theory and Practice*, 25–43. Stanford: CSLI Publications.

Besnier, Niko. 2009. *Gossip and the Everyday Production of Politics*. Honolulu: University of Hawai'i Press.

Bourdieu, Pierre. 1998. *Practical Reason*. Cambridge: Polity.

Butler, Judith. 1991. "Imitation and Gender Insubordination." In Diana Fuss (ed.), *Inside/Out: Lesbian Theories, Gay Theories*, 13–31. New York: Routledge.

Butler, Judith. 1993. *Bodies that Matter: On the Discursive Limits of Sex*. New York: Routledge.

Butler, Judith. 1997. *Excitable Speech: A Politics of the Performative*. New York: Routledge.

Butler, Judith. 1998. "Afterword." In Sally R. Munt (ed.), *Butch/Femme: Inside Lesbian Gender*, 225–230. London: Cassell.

Butler, Judith. 1999 [1990]. *Gender Trouble: Feminism and the Subversion of Identity*. New York: Routledge.

Cameron, Deborah. 1997. "Performing Gender Identity: Young Men's Talk and the Construction of Heterosexual Masculinity." In Sally Johnson and Ulrike H. Meinhof (eds.), *Language and Masculinity*, 47–64. Oxford: Blackwell.

Cameron, Deborah, and Don Kulick. 2003. *Language and Sexuality*. Cambridge: Cambridge University Press.

Campbell-Kibler, Kathryn, Robert J. Podesva, Sarah J. Roberts, and Andrew Wong, eds. 2002. *Language and Sexuality: Contesting Meaning in Theory and Practice*. Stanford: CSLI Publications.

Coates, Jennifer. 2007. " 'Everyone was Convinced that We Were Closet Fags': The Role of Heterosexuality in the Construction of Hegemonic Masculinity." In Helen Sauntson and Sakis Kyratzis (eds.), *Language, Sexualities and Desires*, 41–67. Basingstoke: Palgrave Macmillan.

Connell, Robert, 1995. *Masculinities*. Cambridge: Polity.

Cornwall, Andrea, and Nancy Lindisfarne, eds. 1994. *Dislocating Masculinity: Comparative Ethnographies*. London: Routledge.

de Lauretis, Teresa, ed. 1991. "Queer Theory: Lesbian and Gay Sexualities" (special issue). *Differences: A Journal of Feminist Cultural Studies* 3.

Eckert, Penelope. 2002. "Demystifying Sexuality and Desire." In Kathryn Campbell-Kibler, Robert J. Podesva, Sarah J. Roberts, and Andrew Wong (eds.), *Language and Sexuality: Contesting Meaning in Theory and Practice*, 99–110. Stanford: CSLI Publications.

Foucault, Michel. 1976. *The History of Sexuality*, vol. 2. Harmondsworth: Penguin.

Foucault, Michel. 1980. *Power/Knowledge*. New York: Pantheon.

Grosz, Elizabeth. 1995. *Space, Time, and Perversion: Essays on the Politics of Bodies*. New York: Routledge.

Hall, Stuart. 1997. *Race: The Floating Signifier* (film), dir. Sut Jally. Media Education Foundation.

Halperin, David M. 1995. *Saint Foucault: Towards a Gay Hagiography*. New York: Oxford University Press.

Halperin, David M. 2003. "The Normalization of Queer Theory." *Journal of Homosexuality*, 45: 339–343.

Harvey, Keith. 2000. "Describing Camp Talk: Language/Pragmatics/Politics." *Language and Literature*, 9: 240–260.

Heasley, Robert. 2005. "Queer Masculinities of Straight Men: A Typology." *Men and Masculinities*, 7: 310–320.

Jagose, Annamarie. 1996. *Queer Theory: An Introduction*. New York: NYU Press.

Jones, Lucy. 2012. *Dyke/Girl: Language and Identities in a Lesbian Group*. Basingstoke: Palgrave Macmillan.

Kiesling, Scott F. 2002. "Playing the Straight Man: Displaying and Maintaining Male Heterosexuality in Discourse." In Kathryn Campbell-Kibler, Robert J. Podesva, Sarah J. Roberts, and Andrew Wong (eds.), *Language and Sexuality: Contesting Meaning in Theory and Practice*, 249–266. Stanford: CSLI Publications.

Kiesling Scott F. 2005. "Homosocial Desire in Men's Talk: Balancing and Recreating Cultural Discourses of Masculinity." *Language in Society*, 34: 695–727.

King, Brian W. 2011. "Language, Agency and Sexuality in a Secondary-School Sexuality Education Programme." Unpublished PhD dissertation, Victoria University of Wellington.

Koller, Veronika. 2009. "Butch Camp: On the Discursive Construction of a Queer Identity Position." *Gender and Language*, 3: 249–274.

Kress, Gunther. 2010. *Multimodality: A Social Semiotic Approach to Contemporary Communication*. London: Routledge.

Kulick, Don. 2002. "Queer Linguistics?" In Kathryn Campbell-Kibler, Robert J. Podesva, Sarah J. Roberts, and Andrew Wong (eds.), *Language and Sexuality: Contesting Meaning in Theory and Practice*, 65–68. Stanford: CSLI Publications.

Kulick, Don. 2005. "Four Hundred Thousands Swedish Perverts." *GLQ: A Journal of Gay and Lesbian Studies*, 11: 205–235.

Leap, William L. 2002. "Not Entirely in Support of a Queer Linguistics." In Kathryn Campbell-Kibler, Robert J. Podesva, Sarah J. Roberts, and Andrew Wong (eds.), *Language and Sexuality: Contesting Meaning in Theory and Practice*, 45–63. Stanford: CSLI Publications.

Livia, Anna, and Kira Hall, eds. 1997. *Queerly Phrased: Language, Gender, and Sexuality*. Oxford: Oxford University Press.

McElhinny, Bonnie. 2002. "Language, Sexuality and Political Economy." In Kathryn Campbell-Kibler, Robert J. Podesva, Sarah J. Roberts, and Andrew Wong (eds.), *Language and Sexuality: Contesting Meaning in Theory and Practice*, 111–134. Stanford: CSLI Publications.

Milani, Tommaso M. 2010. "What's in a Name? Language Ideology and Social Differentiation in a Print-Mediated Swedish Language Debate." *Journal of Sociolinguistics*, 14: 116–142.

Milani, Tommaso M., ed. 2011. "Re-casting Language and Masculinities" (special issue). *Gender and Language*, 5(2).

Milani, Tommaso M. 2012. "Queering the Matrix? Language and Identity Troubles in HIV/AIDS Discourse." *SPIL Plus*, 41: 59–75.

Milani, Tommaso M. 2013. "Are 'Queers' Really 'Queer'? Language, Identity and Same-Sex Desire in a South African Online Community." *Discourse & Society*, 24(5): 615–633.

Milani, Tommaso M. In press. "Sexed Signs – Queering the Scenery." *International Journal of the Sociology of Language*.

Milani, Tommaso M., and Rickard Jonsson. 2011. "Incomprehensible Language? Language, Ethnicity and Heterosexual Masculinity in a Swedish School." *Gender and Language*, 5: 239–266.

Motschenbacher, Heiko. 2011. "Taking Queer Linguistics Further: Sociolinguistics and Critical Heteronormativity Research." *International Journal of the Sociology of Language*, 212: 149–179.

Nicholson, Linda. 1994. "Interpreting Gender." *Signs*, 20: 79–105.

O'Rourke, Michael. 2011. "The Afterlives of Queer Theory." *Continent*, 1: 102–116.

Phua, Voon Chin. 2002. "Sex and Sexuality in Men's Personal Advertisements." *Men and Masculinities*, 5: 178–191.

Queen, Robin. 2002. "A Matter of Interpretation: The 'Future' of 'Queer Linguistics.'" In Kathryn Campbell-Kibler, Robert J. Podesva, Sarah J. Roberts, and Andrew Wong (eds.), *Language and Sexuality: Contesting Meaning in Theory and Practice*, 69–86. Stanford: CSLI Publications.

Sauntson, Helen. 2008. "The Contributions of Queer Theory to Gender and Language Research." In Kate Harrington, Lia Litosseliti, Helen Sauntson, and Jane Sunderland (eds.), *Gender and Language Research Methodologies*, 271–282. Basingstoke: Palgrave Macmillan.

Sontag, Susan. 1989. *AIDS and Its Metaphors*. New York: Picador.

Stroud, Christopher, and Sibonile Mpendukana. 2009. "Towards a Material Ethnography of Linguistic Landscape: Multilingualism, Mobility and Space in a South African Township." *Journal of Sociolinguistics*, 13: 363–386.

Thorne, Adrian, and Justine Coupland. 1998. "Articulations of Same-Sex Desire: Lesbian and Gay Male Dating Advertisements." *Journal of Sociolinguistics*, 2: 233–257.

van Dijk, Teun A. 1993. *Elite Discourse and Racism*. Newbury Park, CA: Sage.

Warner, Daniel N. 2004. "Towards a Queer Research Methodology." *Qualitative Research in Psychology*, 1: 321–337.

Warner, Michael. 1993. "Introduction." In Michael Warner (ed.), *Fear of a Queer Planet*, vii–xliv. Minneapolis: University of Minnesota Press.

Woolard, Kathryn A. 1989. "Sentences in the Language Prison: The Rhetorical Structuring of an American Language Policy Debate." *American Ethnologist*, 16: 268–278.

Woolf, Virginia. 2003. *A Writer's Diary*. New York: Mariner Books.

Yep, Gust A. 2003. "The Violence of Heteronormativity in Communication Studies: Notes on Injury, Healing and Queer World Making." *Journal of Homosexuality*, 45: 11–59.

Zimman, Lal. 2011. "The Discursive Construction of Sex: Remaking and Reclaiming the Gendered Body in Talk about Genitals among Trans Men." At http://www.stanford.edu/~eckert/PDF/Zimman.pdf, accessed October 22, 2013.

Part IV Ideologies

14 Gender and Language Ideologies

DEBORAH CAMERON

1. Introduction

The term "language ideologies" (see, e.g., Schieffelin, Woolard, and Kroskrity 1998) is used to refer to the representations through which language is imbued with cultural meaning. Cultures may tell stories which explain the origins of language, or how a particular language came to be spoken by a particular group of people. Nations may represent their national languages as embodying certain qualities or virtues (e.g., French is said to be clear and logical, English pragmatic and flexible). In modern socially stratified societies, what Milroy and Milroy (1999) call the "ideology of standardization," a representation of the standard language as superior to nonstandard dialects, is prevalent; in multicultural societies, minority languages are frequently represented as a threat to the survival or the purity of the dominant language. And it is also common for communities to generate the kinds of language ideologies which are the subject of this chapter: representations of language as a gendered phenomenon, used differently by male and female speakers.

It might be asked why scholars define language ideologies as *representations* of language rather than, say, *beliefs* about it. One answer is that they are trying to avoid the narrow interpretation of *ideology* to mean a codified political belief system (e.g., "communism" or "fascism"). Focusing on representations allows a broader range of phenomena to be considered. It also challenges the tendency to distinguish "ideological" propositions from "scientific" facts. Most readers of this *Handbook*, for instance, will probably regard the ideology of standardization mentioned above as unscientific by comparison with the linguist's axiom that "all varieties are equal." But even if we believe that one is a folk prejudice and the other an objective scientific truth, they are both representations, and as such may be considered (competing) language ideologies.

Another difference between "belief" and "representation" is that "belief" suggests something located in the individual mind, whereas the study of language

The Handbook of Language, Gender, and Sexuality, Second Edition.
Edited by Susan Ehrlich, Miriam Meyerhoff, and Janet Holmes.
© 2014 John Wiley & Sons, Inc. Published 2017 by John Wiley & Sons, Inc.

ideologies is more concerned with the social production of meaning. It involves examining the texts and practices in which language is publicly represented – not just spoken or written, but spoken and written *about*. It is from these representations that language users learn how linguistic phenomena are conventionally understood in their culture. That need not imply that the conventional understandings are internalized as fixed beliefs by all members of the culture. Cultural representations of language change over time, and at any given moment they are likely to be contested.

Feminism is one of many social and political movements which have sought to challenge the understandings embedded in representations of language, and to produce their own alternatives. Ideas about how men and women use language, and how they ought ideally to use it, have been a recurring theme in discourse about language produced by many societies in many historical periods: this has been an issue for feminists because mainstream representations so often serve the purpose of justifying women's subordinate status. In the nineteenth century, for instance, "first-wave" feminists who campaigned for women's political rights felt impelled to contest the then common representation of female public speech as unnatural and indecent. This ideology placed severe limits on women's participation in the political process, and as such it became an explicit target for feminist opposition. Clearly, those who opposed it understood something which has since been articulated in more theoretical terms by scholars: that representations of language are seldom *only* representations of language. As Susan Gal notes (1995, 171), they are "systematically related to other areas of cultural discourse such as the nature of persons, of power, and of a desirable moral order." Most representations of male and female linguistic behavior are interpretable as symbolic statements about the nature of male and female persons, and about the social relationships which should properly obtain between them.

Consider, for instance, Otto Jespersen's assertion, made originally in 1922, that "women exercise a great and universal influence on linguistic development through their instinctive shrinking from coarse and vulgar expressions and their preference for refined ... veiled and indirect expressions" (1990 [1922], 210). On the surface this appears to be a descriptive generalization about women's linguistic behavior, but at a deeper level it is an assertion about the nature of women: their avoidance of vulgar language is described as "instinctive," which suggests it is viewed as an inherent female characteristic. In the text where this statement appears (a chapter called "The Woman" in a general book about language), Jespersen proposes that both "masculine" and "feminine" tendencies play a role in linguistic development. The natural inclinations of men give languages "variety and vigour," while those of women keep them within the bounds of propriety and civility. In language, as in early twentieth-century European society more generally, men are supposed to be the actors and innovators, women the civilizing influence that places limits on masculine excess. Jespersen thus offers exactly what Gal describes: a representation of language which is also a commentary on "the nature of persons, of power and of a desirable moral order."

2. Representing Language and Gender: Diversity and Change

"The Woman" is one instance of what is probably the most general, most cross-culturally widespread, and most historically persistent of all language ideologies pertaining to gender: that there are clear-cut, stable differences in the way language is used by women and men. In many versions of this ideology the differences are represented as "natural" (that is, not just the contingent product of social arrangements, but an expression of fundamental male and female characteristics); often they are also represented as desirable, precisely because they are part of the natural order. Beyond that, however, representations of gendered linguistic behavior are variable across cultures and through time.

The ethnographer Joel Sherzer (1987) has suggested that in any community, the normal linguistic behavior of men and women will be represented in ways that are congruent with the community's more general understanding of the natures of men and women. If women are said to be "naturally" modest and refined, their speech will also be represented as modest and refined. In observed reality there may be little evidence to support such statements, or the evidence may be contradictory. Or it may be that women generally do behave in the manner described, not because it is their "nature" to do so, but because the representation of their speech as modest and refined has acquired the force of a social norm. Women may make active efforts to conform to the prevailing ideal, or their behavior may be policed to ensure a high degree of conformity.

But as Sherzer also notes, there is cross-cultural variation in what qualities women's nature, and therefore women's language, is thought to exhibit. Jespersen's assertion that women instinctively avoid coarse or vulgar language might surprise the people of Gapun on the Sepik river in Papua New Guinea, where the anthropologist Don Kulick (1993) has described a local speech genre called a *kros* (Tok Pisin for "angry"), in which an individual villager ventilates a grievance against someone by delivering a long, abusive, and typically obscene monologue which is intended to be heard by the entire village. Almost without exception, the speaker in a *kros* is female. In Gapun, abusiveness and verbal aggression are understood as female characteristics – signs of the *hed* (roughly, "willfulness") which dominates women's makeup, whereas men are more able to subordinate *hed* to *save* ("judgment" or "sense"). Another group who do not share the modern Western view of women as indirect and unassertive speakers are the Malagasy speakers described by Elinor Keenan (Ochs) (1974). This community associates direct speech with women rather than men: only men master the traditional speech style known as *kabary*, which is characterized by a very high degree of indirectness, and also has high cultural prestige.

Even in a single community, representations of gendered speech are liable to change over time. The feminine ideal most often criticized by twentieth-century Western feminists – that of the modest, deferential, and publicly silent woman – is often presented as if it had prevailed throughout recorded history. This, however, is a considerable oversimplification. In a discussion of the conduct literature which instructed readers in socially acceptable behavior from the Middle Ages onward, Ann Rosalind Jones (1987) points out that texts intended for upper-class women in the royal courts of Renaissance Europe were far from exhorting them to be silent. On the contrary, the court lady was expected to hold her own in verbal duels and witty exchanges which took place in public, and often in mixed company. The ideal of the silent and deferential woman, Jones says, was essentially a product of the rise of the bourgeoisie. Especially where they espoused Puritan religious beliefs, the bourgeois class had different notions from the aristocracy of the proper relationship between the sexes: conduct literature written for a bourgeois audience emphasized the subordination of wives to husbands, and the confinement of women to the domestic sphere. The linguistic implications were set out in texts like *A Godly Forme of Household Gouernmente* (1614), which explicitly contrasted the verbal behavior of the ideal husband and the ideal wife. Whereas he would "deal with many men," she would "talk with few," and whereas he would "be skillfull in talk," she would "boast of silence" (quoted in Armstrong and Tennenhouse 1987, 8). This strict sexual division of linguistic labor symbolized the moral uprightness of the bourgeois household, implicitly contrasting it with the decadence of the aristocracy.

Over time, it was the gender norms of the bourgeoisie which triumphed, and which were adopted as ideals for women of all social classes to aspire to. In later eras, the reticent middle-class woman would be favorably contrasted not with the immoral court lady, but with the garrulous, vulgar, and vituperative working-class woman. Even today in British English, someone who wants to criticize a woman for displaying these qualities can label her a "fishwife" – a now archaic occupational term for the women who did the hard, low-status work of cleaning and selling fish. This illustrates another important point about ideologies of language and gender: they represent not only differences *between* men and women, but also differences *among* men and *among* women. This internal differentiation does significant ideological work.

The "fishwife" stereotype, for instance, is a gender-specific version of the more general representation of low-status speech as unrefined and vulgar. The effect of the interaction between class and gender representations is to define lower-status women as "unfeminine" by contrast with higher-status ones. In the case of men the same interaction has the opposite effect: the rough and uncultivated speech of working-class men is considered "more masculine" than the speech of their middle-class counterparts. Among other things, this perception produces the covert prestige of nonstandard forms for middle-class men noted long ago by Peter Trudgill (1972). A similar analysis could be made of the interaction between representations of gendered and ethnic styles of speaking. For instance, it is common for East Asian women to be represented as more reticent and polite than Western women speakers, and this gives rise to a stereotype of Asian women as "hyperfeminine." Conversely there are minority ethnic groups, such as African American women in the United States and African Caribbean women in the

United Kingdom, who are often represented as more direct and assertive in their speech than either white or East Asian women, and therefore as "less feminine." In general, the work done by such contrasting representations is to establish a norm of desirable femininity which is identified with a particular subset of women – usually those of the dominant social group (in the cases just discussed, the norm is Western, white, and middle class). The way "other" women are represented foregrounds the idea that they are different or deviant from the norm, just as women in general are typically represented as different from the human norm, that is, from men.

Ideologies of language and gender, then, are specific to their time and place: they vary across cultures and communities, and they are inflected by representations of other social characteristics such as ethnicity and social class. What is constant is only the insistence that in any identifiable social group, women and men are *different*. Their differences are frequently represented as complementarities – whatever men's language is, women's is not, or is the opposite. But as the examples already given illustrate, there may be great variation in the actual substance of claims about how male and female language-users differ from or complement each other.

Whatever their substance, though, these representations may be analyzed as part of a society's apparatus for maintaining gender distinctions and hierarchies. At the most basic level, they help to naturalize the notion of the sexes as "opposite," with differing natures and social roles or responsibilities. Often, too, they naturalize the social inequalities which are associated with gender difference. Commentators like Jespersen may praise women's "refinement," but such feminine qualities are readily invoked to explain and justify the exclusion or marginalization of women in powerful or public roles, while at the same time reinforcing the idea of their natural suitability for other, more menial, tasks. In Gapun or among the Malagasy, by contrast, it is women's alleged lack of refinement, reflected in their supposed inability to master prestigious forms of oratory or to refrain from socially disruptive behavior, which is used to justify their subordinate status.

Ideological representations do not in and of themselves accomplish the subordination of women. Their contribution is rather to justify inequality, making the relationship of women and men in a particular society appear natural and legitimate rather than arbitrary and unfair. Conversely, criticism of the way women are represented does not by itself produce changes in their real social position. Rather, it helps to undermine the legitimacy of the prevailing order, and so creates a climate in which practical demands for change become harder to resist. Western women's entry into numerous activities and institutions from which they were previously excluded has undoubtedly been facilitated by the success of feminists in challenging perceptions of women as unsuited by nature to public roles. And in many cases, the arguments feminists successfully challenged included arguments specifically about women's language: their verbal abilities, the qualities of their voices, and their styles of speaking or writing. No one today would entertain the propositions (all advanced quite seriously at some time in the past two centuries) that public speaking causes female infertility, that women's butterfly minds make them incapable of constructing complex sentences, or that female voices are unsuitable for broadcasting on serious topics.[1] To that extent, it may be said that mainstream Western ideologies of language and gender have become less overtly sexist over time. However, the core component of all mainstream ideologies of language and gender – the representation of men and women as distinct categories of language-users – has not become any less entrenched.

3. Shifting Ideological Landscapes: The Rise of Men and the Return of Biologism

In a review of Dale Spender's *Man Made Language* (1980), Maria Black and Rosalind Coward (1981) argued that one of the privileges accorded to men in patriarchal societies was not having to think of themselves, or see themselves represented, as gendered beings. Representations of gender focused obsessively on femininity: the effect was to make masculinity culturally invisible, so that men's behavior largely escaped the kind of ideological policing to which women's was constantly subjected. At the time, this argument was certainly applicable to representations of gendered linguistic behavior: the main preoccupation for both feminist and non- or anti-feminist commentators was describing and explaining the distinctive qualities of "women's language." But the early 1990s saw the emergence of what I have elsewhere called "the myth of Mars and Venus" (Cameron 2007), an allusion to the title of the bestselling self-help book *Men are from Mars, Women are from Venus* (Gray 1992). This book, along with numerous others, presents the problems endemic to male–female relationships as consequences of the two sexes' differing approaches to verbal communication. Since the logic of that argument requires both sexes, not just women, to be represented as gendered language-users, one effect of its popularity has been to create, or at least to codify, a new stereotype of "men's language." The hedging here is because the "Martian" stereotype was not without antecedents in earlier discourse. But the Mars and Venus genre made it more elaborate, more coherent, and far more culturally salient than it had been before.

One striking feature of the "Martian" stereotype is its reliance on a "deficit model" of men's language – that is, one which defines it largely in terms of what it allegedly lacks (e.g., articulacy, fluency, sensitivity, emotional expressiveness, and semantic nuance). In the past, the deficit approach has been more typical of discourse on women's language, which has been described by commentators over the centuries as lacking continence, logic, honesty, vigor, creativity, seriousness, directness, and authority. The myth of Mars and Venus departs from that tradition: though its ostensible message is that the two sexes' preferred communication styles should be considered "different but equal," its actual presentation of those styles implicitly suggests that when it comes to communication men are not women's equals. At best they are verbally unsophisticated, while at worst they are downright inept.

It should not be thought, however, that this is an ideological victory for feminism. If one considers the myth of Mars and Venus at the deeper symbolic level of what it says about "the nature of persons, of power and of a desirable moral order," it is soon revealed as the product of an extremely conservative ideology of gender. That it has nothing to do with feminism is further underlined by one of the most noticeable developments of the past 10–15 years: the incorporation of the popular myth into a new and apparently more "scientific" account in which the linguistic behavior of men and women is said to reflect more fundamental differences in their biological makeup.

In "The Woman," Jespersen describes a study in which women were found to be quicker readers than men, and offers the following comment:

> But … this rapidity was no proof of intellectual power, and some of the slowest readers were highly distinguished men … With the quick reader it is as though every statement were admitted immediately and without inspection to fill the vacant chambers of the mind, while with the slow reader every statement undergoes an instinctive process of cross-examination. (1990 [1922], 215)

To most contemporary readers this interpretation will seem obviously biased – a case of someone going to extraordinary lengths to make the evidence compatible with his axiomatic belief in men's intellectual superiority to women. But before we congratulate ourselves on having transcended such absurdities, we should pause to consider how the preconceptions of the present might be influencing our judgment of what was thought and said in the past. What makes Jespersen's comments on the reading study unconvincing to us is not only his assumption that women are stupider than men. His interpretation also conflicts with a more specific proposition which many people in our own time treat as axiomatic – the proposition that females are endowed by nature with superior verbal abilities.

This view has been around for several decades, particularly among psychologists and education professionals, but recently a particular version of it has become ubiquitous in both expert and popular discourse. Since approximately 2000, there has been a proliferation of representations which portray the female of the human species as biologically predisposed (or in the now familiar jargon, "hard-wired") to talk more than the male, and to perform better on measures of verbal skill. Below I reproduce a selection of examples, with the sources from which they are quoted:

(1) Men's brains are built for action and women's for talking: men do, women communicate. (Moir and Moir 1999)

(2) In females, it [the corpus callosum] is up to 20% larger than in males … Because of this difference in size, females have better verbal abilities and rely heavily on verbal communication; males tend to rely heavily on nonverbal communication and are less likely to verbalize feelings. (Hodgins 2003)

(3) Men do have trouble hearing women: research.
Men who are accused of never listening by women now have an excuse – women's voices are more difficult for men to listen to than other men's. Reports say researchers at Sheffield University in northern England have discovered startling differences in the way the brain responds to male and female sounds. The

research shows men decipher female voices using the auditory part of the brain that processes music, while male voices engage a simpler mechanism. (ABC News 2005)

(4)   Male brains are simply less versatile when it comes to language ... Much of this versatility has to do with the way the two cerebral hemispheres are organized for language storage and retrieval in men and women. MRI studies show that males have most language functions organized in one hemisphere. Meanwhile, most females use both hemispheres for language. Female brains might be proportionally smaller than male brains, but they are more networked for language. (Susan Pinker 2008, 46)

(5)   Q: What do women do three times more than men? A: Talk! ("Fun fact" printed on a shampoo bottle bought in 2010)

These examples (reproduced here in date order) come from a range of popular sources. Two of them (1 and 4) are taken from popular science books about sex differences: Moir and Moir (1999) represents the "down-market" end of this genre – the quote is from the back cover of a TV spin-off book entitled *Why Men Don't Iron* – while Susan Pinker's *The Sexual Paradox* (2008) belongs to the "up-market" end where the authors are reputable scientists and clinicians. The second example comes from a piece written by Dan Hodgins, an early childhood educator and activist in the current US movement for single-sex education, which argues that schools should respond to the discovery of "hard-wired" sex differences in the brain by separating boys and girls and teaching them in different ways. Example 3 is a news report about the findings of an academic study published in a scientific journal. Example 5, found on a bottle of shampoo purchased by a colleague's husband, recycles as a "fun fact" a claim that first appeared in a popular book called *The Female Brain* (Brizendine 2006): the author asserted that men on average utter 7,000 words per day, whereas for women the average is 20,000 words (i.e., about three times as many). These figures caught the attention of the news media and were widely reported. Their repackaging as a "fun fact" on shampoo bottles has given the claim renewed currency – though it is now several years since a study undertaken to investigate it (Mehl et al. 2007) found no empirical support for it at all.

As it happens, most of the factual assertions made in these examples are either clearly false or disputed among scientists.[2] But in the context of a discussion of language ideologies, the truth or falsity of a representation is not the main focus of interest. The key question, rather, is how and why representations of a particular kind achieve wide currency and influence at a particular historical moment, displacing or superseding the alternative representations. In this case, for instance, it is evident that stories which explain the characteristics of male and female language use in biological terms, and especially in terms of brain structure and organization, have come to occupy a place in popular consciousness which they did not occupy 20 years ago. In a relatively short time-period, these "brain sex" accounts have become so ubiquitous, it might not be unreasonable to describe them as constituting the dominant ideology of language and gender for the societies in which they circulate. What does the dominance of such accounts have to tell us about contemporary understandings of language, gender, and the relationship between them?

The idea that male–female differences have their roots in biology (a line of argument which I will refer to generically as "biologism") is not, of course, a recent invention. But it has not always taken the same form, or made the same substantive claims. To judge by his comments on the reading study, quoted above, Jespersen, writing in the 1920s, was influenced by the view that Charles Darwin had set out in *The Descent of Man, and Selection in Relation to Sex*, first published in 1871:

> The chief distinction in the intellectual powers of the two sexes is shewn by man attaining to a higher eminence, in whatever he takes up, than woman can attain … It is, indeed, fortunate that the law of the equal transmission of characters to both sexes has commonly prevailed throughout the whole class of mammals; otherwise it is probable that man would have become as superior in mental endowment to woman, as the peacock is in ornamental plumage to the peahen. (Darwin 2008 [1871], 304)

Today the orthodox view is that the two sexes do not differ with respect to their general intelligence. However, many researchers have claimed that they do differ with respect to more specific cognitive abilities: males are said on average to have superior spatial and mathematical skills, whereas females have more advanced linguistic skills. The newer scientific orthodoxy has made possible, among other things, the Mars and Venus stereotype of the articulate, fluent female who runs verbal rings around her inexpressive mate. This linguistically mismatched couple may seem always to have been with us, but in fact the language ideology that produced them is only a few decades old.

Though biologism has always been one strand in discourse on male–female differences, in relation to language it has not always been the dominant strand. Between the late 1960s and the early 1990s, when feminism and other progressive social movements were in the ascendant, popular as well as expert interest focused more on accounts which treated gender as a social and political construct. The representations that gained wide currency during the 1970s and 1980s exemplified what is now labeled the "dominance approach" (e.g., Lakoff 1975; Spender 1980), explaining "women's language" as a result of the way women were socialized and treated in male-dominated societies. The "difference" approach, which emerged in academic discourse during the 1980s, and entered popular consciousness through Deborah Tannen's bestselling *You Just Don't Understand* (1990), placed less emphasis on male dominance, but continued to locate the origins of difference in cultural socialization (specifically, the habits acquired by young children playing in single-sex groups) rather than biology. John Gray's *Men are from Mars, Women are from Venus* (1992) neatly sidestepped the whole question of where male–female differences came from with his whimsical tale about the two sexes originally migrating to earth from different planets.

At the time there were good commercial reasons why neither an academic popularizer like Tannen nor a mass-market writer like Gray might have wanted to be seen as taking nature's side in the perennial nature versus nurture debate. In the early 1990s you did not have to be a militant feminist to regard biologism as old-fashioned, scientifically dubious, and politically reactionary. Two decades later, however, it is far more mainstream. The popular science sections in book-stores are full of "brain sex" titles, while over in the self-help section, established figures like John Gray face competition from writers like Allan and Barbara Pease, whose formula involves applying the supposed insights of neuroscience to the sta-ple problems of the self-help genre (one of their books is titled *Why Men Don't Listen and Women Can't Read Maps* (2001) – the answer boils down to "it's the way their brains are wired"). Gray himself has tacitly acknowledged this trend, incorporat-ing references to hormones and brain wiring into his most recent Mars and Venus titles. Biologism, in short, has enjoyed a spectacular resurgence since the 1990s: but what larger cultural shifts have motivated its return to favor?

According to such heavyweight academic popularizers as Steven Pinker (2002) and Simon Baron-Cohen (2003), what has motivated the return of biologism is a recognition that recent scientific advances render the previous consensus untenable – an argument which implicitly invokes the distinction between "ideol-ogy" and "science," and suggests that what we are currently seeing is the belated but welcome victory of the latter over the former. But from the perspective adopted here that explanation is insufficient – even if you agree that biologism gives a truer account of male–female differences than the alternatives – because it does not address the issue of representation. Not all scientific truths are enthusiastically taken up in popular representations; if this one has achieved a cultural salience which many others have not, that is itself a datum in need of explanation. Part of the explanation may be that recent achievements, such as the decoding of the human genome and the development of brain-imaging technologies, have generated interest beyond the scientific community: in a secular and scientific age, stories about human evolution, the workings of our genes and our brains, undoubtedly offer a powerful way of understanding ourselves. But that does not explain why we are particularly receptive to stories which apply new scientific theories and methods, specifically, to the question of sexual difference.

Another reason to suspect that something else is going on here besides the onward march of science is the striking resemblance between the new "scientific" representations and those found in the nonscientific sources which preceded them. The examples reproduced above show how heavily "brain sex" writing, which claims to draw on the latest scientific research, depends on the anecdotal folk wisdom of self-help. Each of the examples takes a familiar Mars and Venus generalization (men don't like to talk, aren't good with words, don't verbalize their feelings, don't listen, etc.), and simply grafts a biological, "brain sex" explanation onto it. The text which inspired example 5 above, Brizendine's *The Female Brain* (2006), is a particularly dramatic illustration of science borrowing from folklore, since even the figures Brizendine cited to support the "women talk three times as much as men" claim turned out on investigation to have been taken directly from a self-help book. And in fact this indebtedness to popular mythology is not confined to mass-market "brain sex" books. Even in scientific journals one finds writers taking some well-worn folk representation of gendered linguistic behavior (often without citing any research evidence which attests to the reality of the behavior in question) and then arguing that it is best explained in terms of "hard-wired" sex differences.

A scholarly article by Rhawn Joseph (2000), for example, explains why women talk so much with reference to their roles in prehistoric society: their everyday activities, such as foraging and caring for infants, permitted them to engage in constant verbal interaction, whereas men, as hunters, were obliged to spend long periods in silence to avoid scaring off their prey. This division of labor developed early human women's verbal skills (and the parts of the brain responsible for those skills) while placing limits on the analogous development of men's. Joseph's proposal illustrates the contribution made to contemporary ideologies of language and gender by a scientific field other than neuroscience, namely evolutionary psychology (EP). Sometimes described as a new "science of human nature," EP argues that contemporary male–female differences arise from the evolutionary mechanism of natural selection acting on early humans who had to survive and reproduce in particular environmental and social conditions. We modern humans inherit our genes from the ancestors who were most successful in that endeavor; and one of the things that was advantageous to our ancestors was for males and females to develop the abilities and personality traits which were demanded by their differing roles. Joseph assumes that the persistence of the difference he discusses among modern humans, few of whom are still nomadic hunter-gatherers, can be explained by positing that characteristics which were favored by natural selection because of the advantages they conferred on ancestral humans eventually became "hard-wired," part of the genetic blueprint for the species. However much their roles change, therefore, there will always be differences in men's and women's ways of thinking, feeling, and behaving.

This evolutionary story about language and the sexes complements the "brain sex" account by explaining how, why, and indeed when, male and female brains came to be so different. But in this instance the story has a fatal flaw: there is no compelling evidence for the existence, let alone the timeless universality, of the sex difference it purports to explain. We will never know if a propensity for females to talk more than males existed among our prehistoric ancestors, since their conversations have left no traces for us to study. But no such propensity has been revealed by most empirical studies of modern humans (e.g., most recently, Mehl et al. 2007). If scientists like Joseph think that women talk more than men, that conviction cannot be based on any thorough review of the scientific literature; rather it must reflect the influence of the popular representations which place great emphasis on the loquacity of women.

It seems then that the new wave of biologism is not so much a seismic shift in representations of language and gender as a case of old wine in new bottles – taking the same facts which were presented in the preceding wave of self-help literature, but offering different and apparently more "scientific" explanations for them. For students of language ideologies, this might prompt the question: if the facts themselves have not changed, why have the preferred explanations changed so markedly? What has happened to make accounts invoking neuroscience or EP seem more compelling than the alternatives?

One possible answer relates to the cultural prestige of the fields in question. In societies which accord high value to science and technology, many people may tend to think that a "hard" biological explanation (especially when backed up by the kind of visible proof that something like an fMRI scan seems to offer[3]) must always trump a "soft" social explanation for the same phenomenon. But the resurgence of biologism may also reflect shifts which are ideological in the more narrowly political sense of the term. Historically, biologism has often been a weapon for antifeminists, enabling them to argue that women's status as second-class citizens is imposed by the law of nature rather than the laws of male-dominated society. "Anatomy is destiny" may be a quaintly old-fashioned slogan, but is "brain sex" the new anatomy?

Some prominent advocates of the new biologism, like Steven Pinker (2002), dismiss that suggestion as ignorant and paranoid. Pinker argues that acknowledging the existence of biologically based sex differences is not incompatible with a political commitment to gender equality – these are separate issues which ought not to be conflated. But many people do conflate them: it remains a common view that if male–female differences are part of our biological makeup, then the associated social arrangements are beyond criticism and the possibility of change. In popular books, that argument is sometimes made explicitly. Moir and Moir (1999), for instance, assert that feminist attempts to eliminate differences have been damaging to both sexes (though this seems a rather self-contradictory argument, since according to these authors' own theory of irreducible "hard-wired" difference, the actions of feminists should have had no effect whatever). Baron-Cohen (2003) and Susan Pinker (2008) suggest that gender equality has not been achieved because it is finally against the grain of human nature. Both argue, for instance, that the continued concentration of women in traditional female occupations and low-status positions is not the result of discrimination in the workplace or of unequal divisions of labor at home; it is simply the consequence of women (and men) following their natural aptitudes and preferences.

The popularity of arguments such as these could be seen as an expression of "postfeminism" – that is, the kind of cultural sensibility which emerges during the period immediately following a wave of militant feminist activity. (See also Lazar, Chapter 9 in this volume, for a discussion of postfeminism.) In postfeminist cultures there remains a strong consciousness of feminism as a significant influence in the recent past, but there is also ambivalence about it: it is something people feel they must position themselves in relation to, but in many cases the position they take involves repudiating or distancing themselves from it. This simultaneously fosters a continuing preoccupation with the questions feminism broached about sex/gender, and a heightened receptiveness to ideas which stand in opposition to the answers feminism gave – propitious conditions for a resurgence of interest in biologism.

Since the people who show that interest were socialized in a post- rather than a pre-feminist culture, however, it is probably important that the "new," twenty-first-century biologism avoids the crude sexism of older versions. The straightforward assertions of female inferiority found in the passages quoted above from Darwin and Jespersen would be neither convincing nor appealing to most present-day readers; they are more comfortable with the new biologism's insistence that the sexes are "different but equal," and that each is better than the other at certain things. Some women may be flattered, or consoled, by the idea that they excel in verbal communication, while for some men the idea that they are naturally poor communicators may serve as a convenient excuse for insensitive behavior.

But the most important thing I believe the new biologism offers is more abstract: a narrative about gender which addresses postfeminist anxieties about recent social change. In the West during the past half-century there has been a steady erosion of traditional gender distinctions. Whether one considers educational attainments, career aspirations, family roles, or sexual attitudes and freedoms, contemporary Western men and women, especially in the most privileged social strata, are less different (and less constrained by their reproductive biology), than people have ever been before in human history. In my view, one of the ideological functions of the new biologism is to reassure the many people for whom this is a source of anxiety that gender distinctions have not been, and cannot be, erased. However similar we may seem on the surface, deep in our essential natures we are and always will be different. Language use, a form of behavior which has always been perceived as closely connected with the "deeper" workings of our minds, is a privileged symbol of this difference. (See also Freed, Chapter 32 in this volume, for discussion.)

4. Representations and Realities

As I have already noted, representations of language and gender are part of the social apparatus which legitimizes and so helps to maintain gender distinctions and hierarchies. They do not have to be accurate descriptions to fulfill that ideological function – a point stressed by many commentators on language ideologies, who distinguish between *ideology* (the representation of language) and *practice* (the observed reality of language use). Feminists seeking to challenge sexist stereotypes have also emphasized that representations of linguistic behavior often do not correspond to the real-world facts – though there is also a feminist argument that stereotypes need to be challenged precisely because of their potential to shape behavior.

Sociolinguists, too, are interested in the possibility that language ideologies might influence linguistic practice. If language is seen in the way many sociolinguists now see it, as a resource for the performance of identity, then one might expect speakers making choices about how to perform gender to draw on culturally meaningful representations of constructs like "men's language" and "woman's language." And, indeed, there is evidence that they do draw on those representations.

Momoko Nakamura (2006; Chapter 19 in this volume) offers a striking historical example: the way the speech of young Japanese women in the late nineteenth century seems to have been influenced by fictional (and male-authored) representations of schoolgirls' speech, produced before actual schoolgirls, who at the time were a novel social category in Japan, had established any distinctive way of speaking. Similarly, some recent research has found that the currently popular "Martian" stereotype, which figures men as linguistically and emotionally inept, is being actively embraced by some men and boys as part of their own performances of masculinity. In their study of Australian boys' attitudes to foreign-language learning, Carr and Pauwels (2006) found boys well versed in the popular "brain sex" discourse which says that males are biologically predisposed to do poorly in linguistic subjects; the conclusion some boys drew was that they had little to gain by working at foreign languages, since if their efforts proved successful their peers would question their masculinity.

Today, questioning a boy's masculinity often takes the form of identifying him as (in English) "gay" or "a homo." In a longitudinal study of boys' same-sex friendships, the US psychologist Niobe Way (2011) observed how powerfully this discourse of sex/gender deviance affects young men's behavior, and how strongly ideologies of "men's language" are implicated in it. Way found that until late adolescence, boys make the same emotional investment as girls in same-sex friendships. At 14 or 15 her informants described what they felt for their closest male friends unequivocally as "love," defining a "close" friend as someone you could talk to about anything in the knowledge that they would listen, understand, and support you. But at around 17, boys began to tell Way that their ways of interacting with friends had changed. One explained: "we're like real manly around each other ... there's no room for like mushy talk." Another noted that "talking about feelings is gay, so we don't talk about feelings." Way also observed that the phrase *no homo* (glossed by UrbanDictionary.com as "a slang phrase used after one inadvertently says something that sounds gay") was used frequently by these informants after any reference to their feelings for or intimacy with another boy. It is surely not a coincidence that the norm these young men placed so much emphasis on – "men don't talk about feelings" – is one of the most salient components of the "Martian" stereotype discussed above.

Above I described men like these as "embracing" a particular representation, but Way's interview transcripts suggest that many experienced it as something imposed upon them: to grow up, they had to "man up." Sociolinguists in recent years have tended to emphasize speakers' agency in using linguistic resources to construct identities, but we should not forget that their choices are constrained by the nature of the available resources, including the representations which give gendered meanings to certain ways of speaking. Representations of gender are powerful because they shape our understanding of what is "normal" in some of the most basic areas of human experience – our physicality, sexuality, emotions, and intimate relationships. Psychologically as well as socially, the price of non-normality can be high. Representations of gendered language are part of that picture: recently, indeed, they have featured very prominently in it. That is why the study of language ideologies has always been, and will continue to be, a significant area of language and gender scholarship.

NOTES

1   The claim that public speaking made women infertile (as well as reducing them to the status of prostitutes) was influentially aired in a letter written to the press in 1837 by a group of US Congregational ministers (see Bean 2006); the assertion that women struggle to construct complex sentences (i.e., to use subordinate clauses rather than simple parataxis) appeared in Jespersen's "The Woman" (1990 [1922]); a spokesman for the BBC explained in 1937 that women's voices lacked the authority to present serious topics on the radio.

2   Claim (1) is too general to be tested empirically; in (2) the claim about the corpus callosum has been rejected by most scientists as simply mistaken; (3) reports a real (though apparently isolated) finding, but the claim that "men now have an excuse" for not listening to women is the journalist's own invention; in (4) what is said about sex differences in lateralization for language remains disputed; and (5) is refuted by Mehl et al. (2007).

3   In fact the evidence from neuroimaging studies is complex and difficult to interpret: many of the general claims based on it are highly problematic (for one accessible critical account see Fine 2010).

REFERENCES

ABC News. 2005. "Men Do Have Trouble Hearing Women: Research." At http://www.abc.net.au/news/2005-08-07/men-do-have-trouble-hearing-women-research/2075194, accessed October 22, 2013.

Armstrong, Nancy, and Leonard Tennenhouse, eds. 1987. *The Ideology of Conduct*. New York: Methuen.

Baron-Cohen, Simon. 2003. *The Essential Difference: Men, Women and the Extreme Male Brain*. London: Allen Lane.

Bean, Judith M. 2006. "Gaining a Public Voice: A Historical Perspective on American Women's Public Speaking." In Judith Baxter (ed.), *Speaking Out: The Female Voice in Public Contexts*, 21–39. Basingstoke: Palgrave Macmillan.

Black, Maria, and Rosalind Coward. 1981. "Linguistic, Social and Sexual Relations: A Review of Dale Spender's *Man Made Language*." *Screen Education*, 39: 69–85.

Brizendine, Louann. 2006. *The Female Brain*. New York: Morgan Road.

Cameron, Deborah. 2007. *The Myth of Mars and Venus: Do Men and Women Really Speak Different Languages?* Oxford: Oxford University Press.

Carr, Jo, and Anne Pauwels. 2006. *Boys and Foreign Language Learning: Real Boys Don't Do Languages*. Basingstoke: Palgrave Macmillan.

Darwin, Charles. 2008 [1871]. *The Descent of Man, and Selection in Relation to Sex*. Repr. in *Evolutionary Writings*, ed. John Secord, 233–333. Oxford: Oxford University Press

Fine, Cordelia. 2010. *Delusions of Gender: The Real Science behind Sex Differences*. London: Icon Books.

Gal, Susan. 1995. "Language, Gender and Power: An Anthropological Review." In Kira Hall and Mary Bucholtz (eds.), *Gender Articulated: Language and the Socially Constructed Self*, 169–182. London: Routledge.

Gray, John. 1992. *Men are from Mars, Women are from Venus*. New York: HarperCollins.

Hodgins, Dan. 2003. "Male and Female Differences." Accessed October 21 2011. http://www.docstoc.com/docs/41296831/Male-and-Female-Differences-Dan-Hodgins-Coordinator-Early-Childhood, accessed October 22, 2013.

Jespersen, Otto. 1990 [1922]. "The Woman." Repr. In Deborah Cameron (ed.), *The*

Feminist Critique of Language, 201–220. London: Routledge.

Jones, Ann Rosalind. 1987. "Nets and Bridles: Early Modern Conduct Books and Sixteenth Century Women's Lyrics." In Nancy Armstrong and Leonard Tennenhouse (eds.), *The Ideology of Conduct*, 39–72. New York: Methuen.

Joseph, Rhawn. 2000. "The Evolution of Sex Differences in Language, Sexuality and Visual-Spatial Skills." *Archives of Sexual Behavior*, 29(1): 35–66.

Keenan (Ochs), Elinor. 1974. "Norm-Makers, Norm-Breakers: Uses of Speech by Men and Women in a Malagasy Community." In Richard Bauman and Joel Sherzer (eds.), *Explorations in the Ethnography of Speaking*, 125–143. Cambridge: Cambridge University Press.

Kulick, Don. 1993. "Speaking as a Woman: Structure and Gender in Domestic Arguments in a New Guinea Village." *Cultural Anthropology*, 8(4): 510–541.

Lakoff, Robin. 1975. *Language and Woman's Place*. New York: Harper & Row.

Mehl, Mathias R., Simine Vazire, Nairán Ramírez-Esparza, Richard B. Slatcher, and James W. Pennebaker. 2007. "Are Women Really More Talkative than Men?" *Science*, July 6: 82.

Milroy, James, and Lesley Milroy. 1999. *Authority in Language*, 3rd edn. London: Routledge.

Moir, Ann, and Bill Moir. 1999. *Why Men Don't Iron: The Fascinating and Unalterable Differences between the Sexes*. New York: Citadel.

Nakamura, Momoko. 2006. "Creating Indexicality: Schoolgirl Speech in Meiji Japan." In Deborah Cameron and Don Kulick (eds.), *The Language and Sexuality Reader*, 270–284. London: Routledge.

Pease, Allan, and Barbara Pease. 2001. *Why Men Don't Listen and Women Can't Read Maps*. London: Orion.

Pinker, Steven. 2002. *The Blank Slate: The Modern Denial of Human Nature*. London: Allen Lane.

Pinker, Susan. 2008. *The Sexual Paradox: Troubled Boys, Gifted Girls and the Real Differences between the Sexes*. London: Atlantic Books.

Schieffelin, Bambi, Kathryn Woolard, and Paul Kroskrity, eds. 1998. *Language Ideologies: Practice and Theory*. New York: Oxford University Press.

Sherzer, Joel. 1987. "A Diversity of Voices: Men's and Women's Speech in Ethnographic Perspective." In Susan Philips, Susan Steele, and Christine Tanz (eds.), *Language, Gender and Sex in Comparative Perspective*, 95–120. Cambridge: Cambridge University Press.

Spender, Dale. 1980. *Man Made Language*. London: Routledge & Kegan Paul.

Tannen, Deborah. 1990. *You Just Don't Understand: Men and Women in Conversation*. New York: William Morrow.

Trudgill, Peter. 1972. "Sex, Covert Prestige and Linguistic Change in the Urban British English of Norwich." *Language in Society*, 1: 179–195.

Way, Niobe. 2011. *Deep Secrets: Boys' Friendships and the Crisis of Connection*. Cambridge, MA: Harvard University Press.

15   The Power of Gender Ideologies In Discourse

SUSAN U. PHILIPS

Shortly after I began my second period of fieldwork in Tonga in 1987, my Tongan research assistant, Amalia, a young woman from the village where I was living, invited me to a memorial gathering for her grandmother. "A memorial gathering?" Siale, the head of my own Tongan household was puzzled. He had never heard of such a thing. Perhaps it was a new Mormon invention, certainly not something the Free Wesleyan Church ever sponsored. I knew huge resources were being poured into the event in terms of money for food and labor for the food preparation. I wondered, was it egocentric for me to fear that my own pumping of cash into the local economy through my assistant's wages, in a context in which cash was not easy to come by, was altering cultural practices? When I got to the home where the event was being held, I was hooked up with a friend of the family who I was told would translate for me during the speeches as one person after another got up and tremulously remembered the woman being honored by this event.

The testimony with the greatest impact on me was that of the deceased woman's husband. He tearfully recalled how much love she showed for her family. She cooked for them; she washed clothes for them by hand, since they had no washing machine; and she always made sure none of her children left the house for school unless they were wearing immaculately clean clothing, freshly ironed without a wrinkle. I was startled by this testimony. It sounded as if the man's marriage came right out of a 1950s American family television program. What did it mean?

When I got home that night, following the feast that concluded the event, Siale asked me how things had gone: what was the memorial about? "Oh, they talked about what they remembered about her – people like her husband, her children, and friends of the family." He seemed slightly offended. "We remember things about the people we loved too," he said, "but we don't have to talk about it in public." I knew the "we" had to do with Mormons versus Free Wesleyans. But I was also aware that he had lost his own wife of 40 years only a short time before, too, like the husband of the woman remembered at the memorial. So I was not surprised when he then went on to say, "When my wife was alive, she always made

The Handbook of Language, Gender, and Sexuality, Second Edition.
Edited by Susan Ehrlich, Miriam Meyerhoff, and Janet Holmes.
© 2014 John Wiley & Sons, Inc. Published 2017 by John Wiley & Sons, Inc.

sure that any of us who left the house had on clean ironed clothes with no holes." He laughed, but he misted over a little as he laughed. I felt a little misty myself that this "Old Testament kind of a guy," as one American described him, or any man for that matter, still had tender feelings for a wife after so many years together.

At the same time, inside I registered a small astonishment. Siale had talked about his wife in exactly the same terms as the man remembering his wife in the memorial event! And it was not because I told him the specifics of what had been said at the memorial, because I had been careful not to. Regardless of where these ideas had come from (how Tongan, how European), I felt I was witnessing a conventionalized Tongan representation of the wifely role that had appeared in a formal public event, but that was now appearing in an everyday private conversation.

In truth, the American feminist in me was mildly appalled. Was *this* what a woman was valued for? Ironing? I could hardly think of an activity I valued less myself. I had certainly systematically organized my life to avoid ironing as much as possible. And here it seemed young Tongan women like my research assistant were being exposed to the same kind of gender ideology in discourse.

Clearly I had brought feminist concerns about the nature and impact of gender ideologies into the field with me, but this was just the beginning of my effort to take what I learned about gender ideologies in Tonga and relate that knowledge to broader issues in feminist anthropology.

My purpose in this chapter is show how an interest in the power of gender ideologies in discourse developed in linguistic anthropology and to locate what I went on to learn about gender ideologies in Tonga within that tradition. I first take up how gender ideologies emerged as a factor in men's domination of women in the political theory of the women's movement of the late sixties and early seventies. Then I discuss how feminist anthropologists took up the topic in cross-cultural research. This work emphasized men's control over the public sphere and women's exclusion from the public sphere as an exercise of power that was bolstered and justified by negative gender ideologies about women. Cultural and linguistic anthropologists documented women's resistance to this domination in specific ideologically laden genres of discourse. Awareness of such opposition in turn encouraged more general documentation of diversity in gender ideologies and of the way these were ordered into relations of domination and subordination. The final major section of the paper focuses on the need to relocate relations of ideological domination and subordination not just in discourse, but in the institutional contexts in which discourse occurs. Such a situating is desirable in part because of the *practical* need to better understand which ideologies are more powerful and why so that we can enhance their positive effects for women and ameliorate their negative effects.

1. The Political Roots of the Interest in Gender Ideology

The women's liberation movement of the late 1960s and 1970s, which started in the United States and then spread to Europe and other parts of the world, was an important stimulus for cross-cultural research on gender ideologies, and the politics of the movement significantly influenced this research as it emerged in the early 1970s. The most general political position of the women's liberation movement that shaped the study of gender ideologies was the view that women are not equal to men in American society. They do not have the same control over their own lives and the lives of others that men have.

This domination, it was argued, is bolstered by patriarchal gender ideologies that provided justification for men's domination of women. The term "patriarchal" was used to refer to ideologies that either assumed or asserted that men should dominate women, have authority over them, and tell them what to do. The use of the term "ideology" in this context had Marxist connotations. It suggested that the dominant view was one that served male interests in keeping women subordinated, without women necessarily recognizing that this was the case. And, just as Marx had argued that an ideological critique of bourgeois ideology was needed to help the working class recognize that the present order was not necessarily in their interest and that they should resist it, so too feminists argued for the need for ideological critique of patriarchal ideology. In replacing class with gender, feminists deeply undermined the privileging of class as the primary relation of domination and subordination of interest to the social sciences, and made power central to the study of women and gender.

The American patriarchal ideology that received the greatest attention in the women's movement was the view that women are biologically inferior to men. But this was and is not the only patriarchal gender ideology in the United States or elsewhere. Biological differences between women and men are not always involved. Nor is women's inferiority always asserted. What is necessary is that there be a cultural understanding that men should have some form of power and authority over women that women should not have over themselves or men. And some would argue that the more implicit and taken for granted this assumption is, the more powerful it is.

The role of language in expressing gender ideologies and in maintaining ideological domination over women was also articulated in the women's liberation movement from its inception, and awareness of that role rapidly moved from women's consciousness-raising groups into the university along with the interest in gender ideology – in linguistics this was marked by Lakoff's (1973) work, while a separate tradition focusing on gender ideology in discourse emerged in anthropology, which is our concern here.

2. Gender Ideology in Anthropology

Anthropology's response to these ideas emerged in the early 1970s at a time when ideas were passing rapidly across the boundary between grassroots political activity and the university. I will focus on several papers that can be viewed as both pivotal and representative of these ideas. Central here is Sherry Ortner's (1974) paper, "Is Female to Male as Nature is to Culture?" In this very Levi-Straussian structuralist analysis, Ortner argued that in all cultures women are seen as closer to nature than men by virtue of their involvement in the biological reproduction of the species, while men are seen as closer to culture. Culture, in turn, is more highly valued by humans in their efforts to distinguish themselves from the rest of the animal world. This provides a basis for the assertion of male superiority over women. Ortner's view was quickly taken up, empirically examined in a range of cultures, and found to have a basis in many societies (e.g., MacCormack and Strathern 1980; Ortner and Whitehead 1981). But it was also quickly criticized by others, most obviously on the grounds that not all gender ideologies are of this sort. Even within American society, while men may have controlled arts and sciences historically, they are also symbolically associated with an animal-like aggressiveness.

The influence of this Ortner article was bolstered by the even more influential "Introduction" to the volume it was in by Michelle Rosaldo (1974), who incorporated Ortner's views into her own. Rosaldo argued that cross-culturally, and apparently in all times and social orders, both women and men have authority in the domestic sphere, but overwhelmingly men have authority in the public sphere. Like Ortner, Rosaldo saw this asymmetry as based in women's reproductive roles, which kept their activities tied to the domestic sphere. And she argued that this arrangement was also bolstered by the kind of gender ideology Ortner described, which associated women with nature and men with culture, an association that gave men superiority over women and justified their control over the public sphere.

Almost simultaneously, in a paper titled "Men and Women in the South of France: Public and Private Domains," Rayna Reiter (1975) similarly argued that men have power by virtue of participation in the public domain that women lack in being limited to the private sphere. On the one hand, Reiter carefully documented what she meant by this in the context of a French Alps village, describing in detail the social geographies that segregated the sexes. The public sphere meant public institutions such as government and church, as well as the world of cafes where men socialized. And she also noted exceptions to her own generalizations. For example, it was predominantly women who went to church, even though men controlled the church, and women went to shops during hours when men were scarcely seen in public. On another level, Reiter limited her generalizations about the greater power of men by virtue of their control of the public sphere to societies in which state formation had taken place.

Close to this same time, in a paper many see as the beginning of the contemporary study of gender and language in linguistic anthropology, Elinor Keenan (Ochs) (1974) similarly focused on the ways that women's language use was different from men's. Like Ortner and Rosaldo, Keenan (Ochs) had gender ideology squarely in the center of her argument. She talked about how the ideal norm for socially appropriate speech among the Malagasy was one of indirectness. Men were seen as approximating that norm, while women were seen as woefully direct in their speech. For this reason, men controlled *kabary*, the ritual speech appropriate to intervillage events like funerals. Women did not have access to *kabary*, but rather were limited to the everyday speech of *resa*, which was appropriate to talk within the village and which men, of course, also controlled. Once again gender ideology, and in this case gender ideology about language use, was given a central place in justifying an allocation of roles that looked familiar, like the greater power of men by virtue of their control of public talk. This is true even though Keenan (Ochs) did not frame her ethnographic example in terms of a public/private dichotomy.

The group whose views on public and private I have been discussing really meant rather different things by the distinction. Rosaldo wasn't that specific about what she meant, but the others were ethnographically concrete. Reiter's concept of the public/private distinction was similar to that of sociologists working in Western European societies. In this concept there were links between local manifestations of public institutions like churches and schools, and their larger institutional complexes that encompassed the local scene. But in the 1970s and even 1980s, many anthropologists treated non-European societies as if nothing in the way of social organization existed above the village level. This entailed a setting aside of histories of colonialism and nationalism and their penetration to the village level that is no longer accepted in anthropology. At the village level, any social gathering that involved people of the village coming together could qualify as a public gathering – a rather different idea from what Reiter had in mind.

This male/female public/private dichotomy which gave power to men, bolstered by gender ideology that found women lacking in whatever was required for public participation, has been very important in feminist theory in the social sciences. Yet as soon as the idea was put forth, it was attacked. Among the key critiques launched against this view were the following. First, it is simply not true that women are not in the public sphere. They work outside the home in many societies, and in the ways public and private spheres were defined this would put them in the public sphere. In the early twentieth century in the United States, middle-class women played a major role in social reform – in the temperance movement, in the development of child labor laws, and in the emergence of state-sponsored social welfare programs. Second, there is no basis for claiming any universality for the public/private dichotomy. It is a Western concept, which has been reified in law by the establishment of the limits of state penetration into the privacy of the home. Third, it is too simple to say that the power in the public sphere is greater and of a different order than that in the private or domestic sphere. Power, influence, and ideas move across the boundaries between private and public, as does the influence of women.

These critiques of the public/private distinction have had consequences for the later treatment of gender ideologies. Some, though not all (e.g., McElhinny 1997), feminist scholars dealing with Western societies regrettably drifted away from the use of this very important distinction. But many linguistic and cultural anthropologists continued to use a predominantly village-level concept of public and private in talking about gender ideology and language use (e.g., Brown 1979; Lederman 1980; Philips, Steele, and Tanz 1987). And for good reason. It simply was and still is true that men dominate public talk, and not just in village-level politics, and not just in non-Western societies. It is true that the particular idea of public versus private which is most salient in the United States is not universal, but in all societies there is some conceptual differentiation of social domains that is closely related to the public/private distinction.

Accordingly, it is not surprising that the distinction as applied to the local level persisted in the linguistic anthropological research looking at the relationship between gender ideology and gendered patterns of language use. Sherzer (1987) suggested a number of cross-cultural similarities in the relations between gender, patterns of language use, and language ideology. The strongest or most unqualified pattern he described was one in which gender ideologies and gendered speaking patterns were closely related:

> First, differences in men's and women's speech are probably universal. Second, these differences are evaluated by members of the society as symbolic reflections of what men and women are like ... [S]pecific, recognized features distinguishing men's and women's speech are interpreted and reacted to by members of a society as valued or disvalued, positive or negative, according to the norms, values and power relationships of the society, in particular of course those concerning men and women. (Sherzer 1987, 116–119)

Note that this is a quite different position from Ortner's, in that it allows for significant variation cross-culturally in both gender ideologies and the status of women.

Even so, for the cultural group that Sherzer was working with, the Kuna Indians of Panama, he still noted that women's most public contributions to the life of language were lullabies and tuneful weeping, a type of lament, one genre near the beginning and one near the end of the life cycle. He suggested that these were genres in which women were commonly involved cross-culturally, and argued that this was due to women's intimate connection to the reproductive process. He also noted that lament sometimes entailed protest, a point to which we will return.

Note the strong tendency for gender differences in language use to be conceptualized in terms of speech events and genres, from Keenan (Ochs)'s aforementioned paper up to the present (Kulick 1998). Using a distinction between modern and traditional societies of which anthropologists have recently become more critical, Sherzer (1987) suggested that gender in modern societies that are less gender-segregated is expressed through stylistic differences, while gender in traditional societies is constituted more through gendered verbal speaking roles and discourse genres.

As the linguistic anthropologists became caught up in efforts to identify broad cross-cultural patterns of gendered language use in the 1980s, mainstream feminist scholarship in the United States in the social sciences and humanities had already developed a critique of universalist claims. Such work was said to essentialize women, by which it was meant that women were not only being written about as if they were everywhere the same, but also in a way that implied that this was their natural condition and could not be changed. Universalizing was also labeled as racist and classist, as coming out of a very middle-class women's movement that had failed to either embrace women of other backgrounds or address their concerns. These criticisms led to studies in which women were carefully and explicitly conceptualized as intersections of gender, race, ethnicity, class, and sexual orientation, some of which I will discuss in the following section. In this process, so-called third world women were often grouped with and conceptualized as analogous to women of ethnic minority background in the United States.

In the discussion so far, I have tried to carefully represent the seminal and foundational works that gave a place to the role of gender ideologies and language use in the effort to characterize and understand the power of men over women. To me these papers come across as a constant tracking back and forth between ethnographic particularities and general theoretical frameworks rather than as an unexceptioned universalizing (see also Holmes 1993 on gender and language universals). To my mind there was a careless and in some ways deliberate misunderstanding and misrepresentation of what the first generation of feminist cultural and linguistic anthropologists were doing. They were trying to demonstrate how very general and cross-cultural the problem of male power over women was and is. While a great deal was gained by the new feminist conceptualizing of women as intersections of various aspects of social identity, a great deal was lost too. The rhetorical force of the focus on the universal key problem of a very broad men's power over women, rather than the particularities of problems like domestic violence and rape, was obscured, and really has not regained center-stage in feminist writing since.

3. Diversity in Gender Ideology

Generally speaking, the early work on gender ideologies was written as if there was only one gender ideology for each society. This was a problem, because the actual existence of multiple gender ideologies in all societies made it easy to counter claims of any one such position. Moreover, while there was some documentation of the content of gender ideologies, neither the substance of gender ideologies, nor the linguistic expression of gender ideologies in discourse was given much attention by linguistic anthropologists (though see Sherzer 1987).

In this section, we see how work on gender ideologies took up the issue of ideological diversity. As earlier, the concept of speech genre continues to be of importance. Now more pointedly in some of this work, we begin to see that the actual content of gender ideologies is different in different discourse genres within a single society. Speech genres can be thought of as *containers* of gender ideology. They are named forms of talk with recognizable routinized sequential structures of content–form relations, sometimes referred to as scripts. Laments and lullabies are examples. Speech genres are experienced and represented as bounded, as having recognizable beginnings and ends, and as continuous within those boundaries. It is this boundedness that gives them a container-like quality, so that it becomes possible to speak of one speech genre or one instance of a speech genre as entailing a gender ideology that another speech genre or instance of a speech genre does not.

In the discussion to follow I will talk about two general ideas concerning gender and ideological diversity and their variants. The first idea is that women and men have different ideologies, or different ways of looking at the world generally. The second idea is that within a given society there is diversity in gender ideologies, a diversity that need not be conceptualized as organized along gender lines, but may be so conceptualized.

3.1 The idea that women and men have different ideologies

The idea that women and men think differently is certainly not new. But central to the women's movement was the idea that women's views are not heard and therefore cannot have an influence. Women are silenced (Ardener (1978) is credited with bringing this idea into anthropology).

Now why did feminists think this silencing mattered? It mattered for the simple injustice of it from within a broadly liberal political perspective that values people being able to have their say. It also mattered because of a disvaluing of women's words that could be harmful to their sense of self-worth. But whether implicitly or explicitly, it also mattered that women were shut down because what women had to contribute to social or cultural discourse in their point of view was different from that of men. This was one reason why anthropologists were thought to be missing a great deal of the culture of a group of people if they were only talking to men and not to women (e.g., Keesing 1985). Women's words stood for women's consciousness, and men's words for men's consciousness. Whether women are literally silenced or not, with an ideological valuing of men's words over women's, men are able to make others accept and enact their representation of the world and women are for all practical purposes silenced (Gal 1991; see also Lakoff 1995).

It is important to note that the point of this line of thinking is that women have a different perspective, and *whatever* that view is, its impact is not felt in society in the way men's view is. Now there are some scholars who have also tried to characterize the specifics of how women's culture or women's worldview is different from men's. But I think it has always been easier to put forth the general idea of a difference in perspective than to characterize that perspective, without falling into unsatisfactory statements, as, for example, in the views that women are more nurturing, and more concerned about interpersonal relationships than men.

Some scholars have offered explanations for differences in perspective between women and men. The most common explanations refer to the gender-segregated nature of early childhood (Maltz and Borker 1982; Tannen 1998) and to gender segregation in adult life (Harding 1975; Reiter 1975). However, male domination in itself is seen as a causal factor in interpretive differences too, so that the things women think about and the way they think about them is affected by their subordinated position (Gal 1991).

Scholars who posited general ideological differences between women and men, and men as ideologically dominant, have increasingly also documented women's ideological resistance against male ideological domination. The idea of women's ideological resistance has been present from early on in feminist academic writing (e.g., Reiter 1975). This should not be surprising, given the fundamental concern in the women's movement with the need for women to resist patriarchal ideological domination in a manner analogous to the Marxist concept of a need for the working class to ideologically resist ruling-class ideological as well as material domination.

Analytical reliance on some notion of speech genre has been important in discussion of resistance. Lila Abu-Lughod's (1986) *Veiled Sentiments* focuses on a genre of poetry performed by Bedouin women in private contexts. In this genre, feelings of strong emotion and suffering are expressed that run counter to dominant public Bedouin values of honor, autonomy, and emotional restraint. When the words of songs can be connected to a woman's individual circumstances, they can be understood as her protest, however veiled, against those circumstances.

Other documented forms of women's protest encoded in recognizable bounded genres have this similar quality of intense emotion in the context of personal suffering. Both Feld (1982) and Briggs (1992) have documented situations in which women have used their own public laments in the context of funeral mourning for the dead as opportunities for political critique of activities going on in their communities. Briggs makes it clear that Warao women regularly use one of their few rare opportunities for performance in the public sphere to raise their voices in opposition to dominant community practices or policies. Hirsch similarly characterizes women's rare opportunity to "tell their story" in Muslim courts in southern Africa (1998) as an opportunity to raise their voices against men.

The logic of recognizing gender-based ideological differences has also given rise to discussion of ideological contrasts *among* women, as well as between women and men. One study in which bounded instances of a genre are used to tease out such differences is Shula Marks's (1988) *Not Either an Experimental Doll*. Here Marks uses letters written by three different women in early twentieth-century South Africa. These letters, particularly those by and concerning the fate of a young black African girl, reveal gendered power dynamics of this racially segregated society that were very specific to their time.

An important development in the study of gender and ideological diversity, then, was diversity conceptualized primarily in terms of a dualistic gender system of males and females. In this development, it did not matter so much *how* they thought differently, but rather that in the context of male ideological domination, women were argued to have resisted that domination in specific genres of language use. Ultimately, then, we have a picture of ideological diversity that is organized into oppositional relations, yet seemingly in an undeniably static arrangement. Thus while one might expect that the idea of resistance could be inspiring, and its availability a comfort in the face of a vision of ideological domination, this was in some respects cold comfort indeed because the kinds of resistance described did not lead to any transformation of women's situations.

3.2   *The idea of intrasocietal diversity in gender ideology*

As interest in ideological diversity within societies emerged in the 1980s, a second important theme was the idea that there is more than one gender ideology within a given society. The earliest expressions of this idea typically did not ground or locate the diversity in gender ideologies within society. And when the view that some gender ideologies are dominant over others was expressed, the dominant and the subordinate were likewise not necessarily conceptualized as socially contextualized (e.g., Fineman 1988; Kennedy and Davis 1993; Schlegel 1990).

Indeed, it is common, I think, both in American and in other societies, to experience gender ideologies, and other kinds of ideologies as well, as floating free. However, sometimes we *can* locate them socially, and the literature on gender ideologies does also abound with examples of ideologies that belong to or are about people in specifiable social categories. It is in this work that we again find genres of discourse in which specific gender ideologies can be located. And here, in addition to socially occurring genres, by which I mean those who would be performed whether or not a researcher was present, I will also include analysis based on interviews.

There is less work delineating how men's gender ideologies differ from those of women than one might expect, possibly because gender ideologies are thought to be widely shared within societies. However, Emily Martin's (1987) book *The Woman in the Body* describes how medical books that represent women's reproductive processes treat the body metaphorically as if it were a machine, and she does view such a representation as male and patriarchal. Then in interviews with American women from both middle- and working-class backgrounds, she shows how middle-class women embrace this same medical textual rhetoric, but women from working-class backgrounds, both black and white, do not. There is definitely the sense in this that the medical images have become dominant, while the other representations are subordinated and resistant.

A second very useful and insightful example of differences between men and women's gender ideologies comes from Holly Mathews's (1992) work on different tellings of the popular Mexican folktale "La Llorona," which glosses as "weeping woman." La Llorona is a ghost often seen along river banks who is thought to try to lure men to their death by drowning in rivers. Mathews shows how men and women in a Mexican village tell the story behind this ghostly figure differently. In the men's version, La Llorona violated marital expectations. She neglected her children, gossiped, and was out on the street. Her husband turns her out of the house, so she commits suicide. In the women's version of "La Llorona" the man violates the expectations of marriage. He is unfaithful, he stays away from home, and he spends all their money. In her distress over her inability to feed her children, La Llorona commits suicide. Here we begin to see where there is commonality culturally and where there is difference in male and female ideas about gender roles. But clearly women hold men responsible for marital failure, while men hold women responsible. Limon (1986) suggests that the male view is the dominant view, so that women's marital failings are more imprinted on the public consciousness than those of men.

Both Mathews and Hirsch, discussed in the last section, tape-recorded men and women producing exactly the same genre, and then identified the ways in which the male perspective is different from the female's. Hirsch too found women dwelling on men's failings while men dwelt on women's, but again the difference was that men's voices tended to dominate the public consciousness, and women's voices were rarely heard in public in the way that they were in court. Mathews also makes the important point that a great deal of gender ideology is organized in terms of gender dyads, a point to which I will return.

The climate of the 1980s, and to some extent the 1990s, has been influenced, as noted earlier, by the critique of feminist writing that it was "essentializing" women, treating them as if they were in all times and places the same. This led to a good deal of writing that compared women in different social positions within a given society, usually American society, and this trend has included documentation of variation in women's gender ideologies in comparable forms of discourse (Kennedy and Davis 1993; Luker 1984; Silberstein 1988; Yanagisako 1987).

Finally, there are also many fine individual works on diverse gender ideologies tied to variation in gender identities and produced in highly specific ethnographic and/or historical circumstances and forms of talk. For example, Lata Mani (1998) has examined specifically positioned variation in gender ideologies constituted in written discourse genres from the colonial era on whether or not to ban widow-burning in India. Other fine examples include Krause (1999), Kray (1990), and Besnier (1997).

Discourse analysis made important contributions to work of these kinds on ideological diversity. Specific discourse genres were shown to be associated with specific ideological positions, displaying the way in which discourse genres can function to create boundaries and framings for interpretive perspectives. While we have done reasonably well in connecting ideological stances with particular gendered social identities, our sense of other ways in which culture and social structure contribute to the social ordering of dominant and subordinate gender ideologies is relatively underdeveloped. The lack of development of the early ideas about the power of the ideologies in the public sphere as opposed to the private sphere has created a situation where theoretically we do not have a well-developed sense of institutional complexes, and of how these potentiate and constrain gender ideologies in discourse (but see Hirsch 1998; McElhinny 1997).

There has also been a loss of a broader practical political perspective. While feminist concerns with women's subordination are typically still present in all of the works that have been discussed, they are often implicit rather than explicit. And while inspiring, visions of resistance against domination that have been documented seem meant more to raise the idea of resistance than anything else, because the examples of resistance are often themselves pre-political, individual, or routinized in a way that does not appear to be transformative. Then, too, the meanings of the terms "domination," "subordination," and "resistance" have not been closely interrogated or theoretically examined.

4. Institutional Contexts for Gender Ideologies in Discourse

We see, then, that the content of gender ideologies is different in different discourse genres within a given society. And different gender ideologies are perpetuated by women and men, and by women in different social positions and with different gender identities. Male power and authority are such that men achieve ideological domination over women through this gendered organization of ideology, which women resist through their production in and of specific genres of language use. With the multiplicity of gender ideologies and their discourse manifestations, then, comes ideological conflict, opposition, and struggle.

What is most apparently lacking in this way of thinking about gender ideology in discourse is some broader concept of social organization within which gender identity systems can be located and grounded. Anthropological research on gender ideology did begin with the ideas that societies are organized into public and private domains and that the ideological support for male control of the public domain sustains men's power over women. But as I noted earlier, the conceptual vision of society as ordered into public and private domains was severely criticized by feminists in a way that seems to have led to the fading rather than the transformation of this broad vision of societal organization.

In recent years an important domain distinction that has emerged in the language and gender literature is that between home and work (e.g., Tannen, Chapter 25, and Holmes, Chapter 22 in this volume). This is quite fitting, because as at least middle-class American women experience the social world, the home/work distinction is probably the most salient domain distinction, as at least middle-class women struggle in their own minds with how to have both in their lives in satisfactory ways. In actuality research in this area has focused more on work situations than on a home–work contrast (but cf. Kendall 2003). And an important theme of the writing on women in the workplace has been how much both women and men vary in their deployment of interactional strategies that feminists have long argued were gendered in power-laden ways. Gender ideologies have not been in the foreground in this work as such until recently.

However, there are recent promising developments. Holmes (Chapter 22 in this volume) discusses the concept of "masculine" and "feminine" workplaces, as this is experienced in New Zealand. McElhinny (1995) analyzes the ways policewomen developing identities as police officers must address the hypermasculinity of police departments in their work (see also Ostermann 2003). Both of their approaches resonate with the relatively recent emergence in the social sciences and humanities of the idea that we can speak of the "gendering" of massively complex sociocultural processes such as the military (Enloe 1989), the state (Philips 1994), the nation (Delaney 1995), and international relations (Peterson 1992). "Gendering" is to my mind a concept similar to gender ideology, but it has stronger connotations of an implicitness and diffuseness of widely shared meaning than the concept of gender ideology.

Another promising approach that grounds diversity in practice and diversity in ideology in some concept of social organization is the recent feminist linguistic interest in communities of practice (Eckert and McConnell-Ginet 2003). These are groups that engage in interaction and share interpretive orientations. People of different genders, ages, and class positions will predictably participate in different communities of practice. One can expect to find gender ideologies that are specific to specific communities of practice and that are manifest in their discourse practices.

But I still do think that we need to work with a concept of institutions in the sociological and anthropological sense, so that one can speak of gender ideologies in religion, education, law, and family, and in their prototypical public scenes of the church, school, court, and household. (See the chapters by Holmes (22), Ehrlich (23), Menard-Warwick, Mori, and Williams (24), and Tannen (25) in this volume.)

Institutions are by definition linked, interdependent, and creating of some whole. Contexts of interaction participate in broader ideological and behavioral systems that we call institutions. Thinking in terms of institutions allows us to ask the following useful questions: How are gender ideologies in different institutional settings similar and different? How are these gender ideologies shaped by their institutional contexts? Are some institutional complexes more ideologically powerful, influential, and/or hegemonic in shaping gender ideologies than others? From a Gramscian (1971) perspective, one would argue that state institutions (e.g., law, education) are the most powerful and are hegemonic and dominant in ideological struggles with civil institutions such as churches and political parties. At the same time, a Gramscian vision of state–civil articulation would also recognize that state institutions derive their hegemony in part from their ideological articulation with popular cultural ideologies in civil society.

Thinking about contemporary nations (and the whole world is organized into nations) as ideologically organized in terms of a state–civil articulation has some advantages. It sidesteps the private/public dichotomy, without precluding the recognition of a range of kinds of public spheres (Hanson 1993). It recognizes the interconnectedness and interpenetration of different institutional contexts, allowing for the flow, or replication, of ideological representations across domain boundaries (McElhinny 1997). And a Gramscian approach still allows for recognition of such lower-level organizations as villages as social units within which ideologies flow.

In the final discussion to follow I will try to show how the accumulated traditions for the study of gender ideologies in discourse have contributed to my thinking about gender ideologies in Tonga, taking into consideration the issues I have just raised.

In Tonga, which is a small country in the South Pacific, with one of the largest Polynesian populations, the most salient gender ideologies are encoded in three rather general gender dyads: the sister–brother relationship, the husband–wife relationship, and the sweetheart–sweetheart relationship. Mathews (1992) has argued that gender dyads are an important form of cultural model for the transmission of cultural gender systems. In saying that these three dyads and not others are key, I am saying that other kinds of dyads which might be more familiar to Americans, such as the mother–son dyad, or the father–daughter dyad, are much less often talked about and depicted, if at all. Meanwhile, the sister–brother relationship, which Americans do not elaborate, as "in story and song," is talked about and depicted all the time. Furthermore, as we will see, these dyads are depicted differently in Tongan than in American culture. This does not mean that *individual* figures are not also represented as models for women, like the Virgin is in Mexico. For example, Queen Sālote, who ruled Tonga for over 40 years in the twentieth century, is a revered figure. But the dyads are more pervasive.

For each of these three dyadic representations, the concept of dominance has relevance in more than one sense. The sister–brother relationship should be considered the culturally dominant image of gender relationships in Tonga. Verbal representations of this relationship abound, and they are often highly stereotyped, but also specialized and differentiated. They are also prominent in the public sphere (Philips 1994; 2000). This relationship is one in which the sister is represented as dominant, in the sense that her brother should subordinate himself to her, particularly through semiotic expressions of respect, but also through submission to her will, particularly the will of the eldest sister.

The husband–wife relationship, in contrast, is much less often depicted and talked about. It is a more private relationship. When it is talked about, the emphasis is not so much on the dyad itself, that is on marriage, and the relationship between husband and wife, as it is in the United States. Instead the emphasis is on the role of the woman in relationship to her husband and children. The role of the wife is to take care of the family as a whole, much as this is said of husbands in American culture. Recall the Tongan wife being remembered fondly for her ironing in the example of gender ideology at the beginning of the chapter. A woman's ironing in that example is a conventionalized sign of the way she takes care of her whole family. The idea that she should take care of them is more important, enduring, and pervasive than any particular sign of that care. It is also the wife's job to facilitate the relationship between children and their father, to make sure they get along. In loving and ideal depictions that focus on the wife, she is neither exhorted to obey her husband, nor praised for doing so, in the way that brothers are exhorted to subordinate themselves to their sisters. However, the wife's normative subordination to her husband is understood to be part of the relationship in some sense. Her ordering around of him is depicted in humorous representations of marriage, and his beating of her can be justified on the basis of her failing to do what he thinks she should do (Kavapalu 1993; Philips 1995).

Representations of the sweetheart–sweetheart relationship, like those of the other two dyads, also involve images of domination and subordination, but here who is dominated and who is dominating seems to flip-flop. Love songs are canonically written for and to women by men, but there are examples of high-status women who compose songs known to be to and about men. The songs themselves are composed in such an allusive way that many if not most can be "heard" to be from the point of view of either a man or a woman, and they are sung by both women and men. This gender dyad is the one of the three that is most stereotypically represented in public discourse. It is dominant in the sense that it is the dyad evoked in the most pervasively performed and heard genres in the country, love songs (Philips 2007).

Each dyad is very widespread in its representations. Each can appear or be talked about in formal, routinized, institutionalized contexts, both Western and Tongan in origin. Each can also appear in everyday forms of talk. Each appears in structured bounded discourse genres and in less predictable conversation. At the same time, each dyad can be said to have a distinct configuration ecologically.

Sister–brother representations are part of official nation-state governmental representations. The king's daughter and *her* daughter are the most ritually prominent women in the country because she is ritually superior to her brothers, one of whom will some day be king. The fact that one of the brothers will be king and not the sister shows the real limits of sisterly power, yet the sister's authority cannot be dismissed. If she had no brothers, she could be queen, like her grandmother, the earlier-mentioned Queen Sālote. The sister–brother relationship is held up as the model for cross-gendered relationships in court cases involving women taking men to court (Philips 2000). In one of the best-known traditional stories a brother kills his sister over his jealousy of her preferred treatment in the family, but her supernatural powers enable her to be brought back to life (Fānua n.d.). In everyday life, the treatment of sisters to brothers and brothers to sisters is constantly an issue.

As I have already noted, the husband–wife relationship is much less publicly visible in gender dyad representations than the other two. But it too appears in a range of kinds of contexts and genres. In Queen Sālote College, the best-known private girls' high school in the country, a play written and directed by its former principal Manu Faupula (1972) and performed by generations of girls in the twentieth century, instructed them in the proper role of the wife in caring for husband and children. In court cases, the husband's right to beat his wife is affirmed, though barely (Philips 1995). In a Tongatapu Hihifo District World Food Day song competition, presided over by a noble of the area, the song that won the competition and was later played on the radio, depicted a husband and wife. The husband would not go out to cultivate food for the family, and his wife repeatedly exhorted him to get food for them, a depiction people found hilarious because of its violation of the norms for appropriate husband and wife behavior. Schools, courts, World Food Day, the radio – these are all state-directed and state-sponsored organizational contexts in which gender representations are fostered. In a more traditional setting, speeches that are part of the *kava* ceremony in a traditional Tongan wedding invoke gendered stereotypes of proper husbandly and wifely qualities.

The sweetheart relationship as represented in love songs is within hearing day and night because of the prevalence of love songs on the radio all day long. They are sung in men's evening social gatherings throughout the country. They are also sung by women in work parties where bark cloth and mats are produced (Philips 2007). Anywhere where brothers and sisters are not co-present, humorous joking and teasing about romantic relationships is widespread in all adult age groups. In court, there are also silences about the sweetheart relationship. Physical and verbal aggression against women resulting in men being taken to court also occurs in the sweetheart relationship. But here the nature of the relationship will not be explicitly oriented to as an aspect of the case in the way it would be if the man and woman were husband and wife, if it is acknowledged at all. This is apparently because sexual relations between unmarried people that cannot be acknowledged in public are often thought to be involved in such cases. A young woman who has sexual relations before marriage is vulnerable to mistreatment and is unprotected in a way women in other social categories are not (Philips 2000).

These three dyadic gender ideologies are in a complementary relationship to one another. They define each other. One can't really fully comprehend any one of the dyads alone – we see the physical vulnerability of the wife and the sweetheart in a different light, knowing how protected the sister is.

These gender ideologies are shared by women and men and are not overtly opposed. However, clearly women are best off in the sister–brother relationship, when we consider whether women's subordination is countenanced in Tongan gender ideologies.

For all three dyads, there are Gramscian state–civil institutional ideological connections. In other words, for all three, state-funded institutions promulgate the gender ideologies in a way that penetrates people's lives on a day-to-day basis across institutional boundaries, resonating with views of the same kind that people already have. But it is the sister–brother dyad that has received greatest state sponsorship, elaboration, and proliferation. It is accordingly appropriate to speak of Tongan brother–sister gender ideology as hegemonic for Tonga.

In a context where there are multiple gender ideologies, one strategy that is available for transforming women's situation is to enhance, elaborate, and build on the gender ideologies that are most enabling of women. This is what happens in Tonga. There the high status of the sister has in a sense been used by women to enhance the status of the role of wife. In this regard Queen Sālote, the revered former queen of Tonga has been an important example for other Tongan women. As Ellem (1999) has insightfully documented, Queen Sālote interpreted her relationship to her husband, the prince consort, as one of brother and sister, as a way of creating a model of her partnership with him for ruling the country that would be familiar and acceptable to her subjects. In a similar way, Faupula (1972), in her dramaturgical representation of the ideal woman for the edification of the girls of Queen Sālote College, blends the roles of wife and sister. In this way, with a little help from specific state-linked institutional contexts, the sister in a woman empowers her as a wife, and there are many powerful Tongan women in partnership-like relations with their husbands.

5. Implications

Gender ideologies play a powerful role in shaping women's lives. They are used to interpret and motivate behavior and are enacted in socially meaningful behavior. But there is no such thing as a clear one-to-one relation between one gender ideology and one society. Instead there are multiple gender ideologies in all societies. Their nature is and should be of intrinsic interest to social scientists because of the fundamental importance of gender in human life. But beyond that it is of concern to feminists to identify patriarchal gender ideologies in order to ameliorate them and to enhance the development of gender ideologies that offer and encourage positive experiences for women.

The production of gender ideology in discourse is located in sociocultural systems and is socially organized through those systems. People and the genres they produce are organized into relations of domination and subordination that determine which gender ideologies are powerful and where ideological conflict and struggle are. Ideologies in institutions through which the state articulates with the population it governs are particularly powerful.

There are important roles for discourse analysis of gender ideology in both the general study of gender ideology and in political critique with policy implications. Discourse analysis allows for empirical documentation of the production of gender ideologies, and can reveal in detail how these ideologies are grounded and ordered in discourse.

REFERENCES

Abu-Lughod, Lila. 1986. *Veiled Sentiments*. Berkeley: University of California Press.

Ardener, Shirley. 1978. "Introduction." In Shirley Ardener (ed.), *Perceiving Women*, vii–xxiii. London: Malaby.

Besnier, Niko. 1997. "Sluts and Superwomen: The Politics of Gender Liminality in Urban Tonga." *Ethnos*, 62(1–2): 5–31.

Briggs, Charles. 1992. " 'Since I am a Woman, I Will Chastise My Relatives': Gender, Reported Speech, and the (Re)Production of Social Relations in Warao Ritual Wailing." *American Ethnologist*, 19(2): 337–361.

Brown, Penny. 1979. "Language, Interaction and Sex Roles in a Mayan Community: A Study of Politeness and the Position of Women." Unpublished PhD dissertation, University of California, Berkeley.

Delaney, Carol. 1995. "Father State, Motherland, and the Birth of Modern Turkey." In Sylvia Yanagisako and Carol Delaney (eds.), *Naturalizing Power: Essays in Feminist Cultural Analysis*, 177–199. New York: Routledge.

Eckert, Penelope, and Sally McConnell-Ginet. 2003. *Language and Gender*. Cambridge: Cambridge University Press.

Ellem, Elizabeth Wood. 1999. *Queen Sālote of Tonga: The Story of an Era, 1900–1965*. Auckland: Auckland University Press.

Enloe, Cynthia. 1989. *Bananas, Beaches and Bases: Making Feminist Sense of International Politics*. Berkeley: University of California Press.

Fānua Tupou Posesi.xxxx n.d. "Kuku mo Kuku/The Jealous Brother." In *Pō Fananga: Folk Tales of Tonga*, 35–39. Nuku'alofa, Tonga: Taulua Press.

Faupula, Manu. 1972. *Mafoa E Ata (Dawn of the Light)* (mimeograph copy). Nuku'alofa, Tonga: Queen Salote College.

Feld, Steve. 1982. *Sound and Sentiment: Birds, Weeping, Poetics, and Song in Kaluli Expression*. Philadelphia: University of Pennsylvania Press.

Fineman, Martha. 1988. "Dominant Discourse, Professional Language, and Legal Change in Child Custody Decision Making." *Harvard Law Review*, 101: 727–774.

Gal, Susan. 1991. "Between Speech and Silence: The Problematics of Research on Language and Gender." In Micaela di Leonardo (ed.), *Gender at the Crossroads of Knowledge: Feminist Anthropology in the Postmodern Era*, 175–203. Berkeley: University of California Press.

Gramsci, Antonio. 1971. *Selections from the Prison Notebooks*. New York: International Publishers.

Hanson, Miriam. 1993. "Foreword." In Oskar Negt and Alexander Kluge (eds.), *The Public Sphere and Experience*, ix–xli. Minneapolis: University of Minnesota Press.

Harding, Susan. 1975. "Women and Words in a Spanish Village." In Rayna R. Reiter (ed.), *Toward an Anthropology of Women*, 283–308. New York: Monthly Review Press.

Hirsch, Susan F. 1998. *Pronouncing and Persevering: Gender and the Discourses of Disputing in an African Islamic Court*. Chicago: University of Chicago Press.

Holmes, Janet. 1993. "Women's Talk: The Question of Sociolinguistic Universals." *Australian Journal of Communication*, 20(3): 125–149.

Kavapalu, Helen Morton. 1993. "Dealing with the Dark Side in the Ethnography of Childhood: Child Punishment in Tonga." *Oceania*, 63(4): 313–329.

Keenan (Ochs), Elinor. 1974. "Norm-Makers, Norm-Breakers: Uses of Speech by Men and Women in a Malagasy Community." In Richard Bauman and Joel Sherzer (eds.), *Explorations in the Ethnography of Speaking*, 125–143. Cambridge: Cambridge University Press.

Keesing, Roger. 1985. "Kwaio Women Speak: The Micropolitics of Autobiography in a Solomon Island Society." *American Anthropologist*, 87(1): 27–39.

Kendall, Shari. 2003. "Creating Gendered Demeanors of Authority at Work and at Home." In Janet Holmes and Miriam Meyerhoff (eds.), *The Handbook of Language and Gender*, 600–623. Oxford: Blackwell.

Kennedy, Elizabeth, and Madeleine Davis. 1993. *Boots of Leather, Slippers of Gold: The Story of a Lesbian Community*. New York: Routledge.

Krause, Elizabeth. 1999. "Natalism and Nationalism: The Political Economy of Love, Labor, and Low Fertility in Central Italy." Unpublished PhD dissertation, University of Arizona.

Kray, Susan. 1990. "Never Cry Bull Moose: Of Mooses and Men, The Case of the Scheming Gene." *Women and Language*, 13(1): 31–37.

Kulick, Don. 1998. "Anger, Gender, Language Shift and the Politics of Revelation in a Papua New Guinean Village." In Bambi B. Schieffelin, Kathryn A. Woolard, and Paul V. Kroskrity (eds.), *Language Ideologies:*

Practice and Theory, 87–102. New York: Oxford University Press.

Lakoff, Robin. 1973. "Language and Women's Place." *Language in Society*, 2: 45–80.

Lakoff, Robin. 1995. "Cries and Whispers: The Shattering of the Silence." In Kira Hall and Mary Bucholtz (eds.), *Gender Articulated: Language and the Socially Constructed Self*, 25–50. New York: Routledge.

Lederman, Rena. 1980. "Who Speaks Here: Formality and the Politics of Gender in Mendi, Highland Papua New Guinea." *Journal of the Polynesian Society*, 89: 479–498.

Limon, Jose. 1986. "La Llorona, the Third Legend of Greater Mexico: Cultural Symbols, Women and the Political Unconscious." Renato Rosaldo Lecture Series Monograph, 2: 59–93.

Luker, Kristin. 1984. "World View of the Activists." In *Abortion and the Politics of Motherhood*, 158–191. Berkeley: University of California Press.

MacCormack, Carol, and Marilyn Strathern, eds. 1980. *Nature, Culture and Gender*. Cambridge: Cambridge University Press.

Maltz, Daniel N., and Ruth A. Borker. 1982. "A Cultural Approach to Male–Female Miscommunication." In John J. Gumperz (ed.), *Language and Social Identity*, 196–216. Cambridge: Cambridge University Press.

Mani, Lata. 1998. *Contentious Traditions: The Debate on Sati in Colonial India*. Berkeley: University of California Press.

Marks, Shula. 1988. *Not Either an Experimental Doll*. Bloomington: Indiana University Press.

Martin, Emily. 1987. *The Woman in the Body: A Cultural Analysis of Reproduction*. Boston: Beacon.

Mathews, Holly. 1992. "The Directive Force of Morality Tales in a Mexican Community." In Roy D'Andrade and Claudia Strauss (eds.), *Human Motives and Cultural Models*, 127–161. Cambridge: Cambridge University Press.

McElhinny, Bonnie. 1995. "Challenging Hegemonic Masculinities: Female and Male Police Officers Handling Domestic Violence." In Kira Hall and Mary Bucholtz (eds.), *Gender Articulated: Language and the Socially Constructed Self*, 217–244. New York: Routledge.

McElhinny, Bonnie. 1997. "Ideologies of Public and Private Language in Sociolinguistics." In Ruth Wodak (ed.), *Gender and Discourse*, 106–139. London: Sage.

Ortner, Sherry. 1974. "Is Female to Male as Nature is to Culture?" In Michelle Rosaldo and Louise Lamphere (eds.), *Woman, Culture and Society*, 67–88. Stanford: Stanford University Press.

Ortner, Sherry, and Harriet Whitehead, eds. 1981. *Sexual Meanings: The Cultural Construction of Gender and Sexuality*. Cambridge: Cambridge University Press.

Ostermann, Ana Cristina. 2003. "Communities of Practice at Work: Gender, Facework and the Power of Habitus at an All-Female Police Station and a Feminist Crisis Intervention Center in Brazil." *Discourse & Society*, 14: 473–505.

Peterson, V. Spike. 1992. *Gendered States: Feminist (Re)Visions of International Relations Theory*. Boulder, CO: Lynne Rienner.

Philips, Susan U. 1994. "Local Legal Hegemony in the Tongan Magistrate's Court: How Sisters Fare Better than Wives." In Susan Hirsch and Mindy Lazarus-Black (eds.), *Contested States*, 59–88. London: Routledge.

Philips, Susan U. 1995. "Dominant and Subordinate Gender Ideologies in Tongan Courtroom Discourse." In Mary Bucholtz, A. C. Liang, Laurel Sutton, and Caitlin Hines (eds.), *Cultural Performances: Proceedings of the Third Berkeley Women and Language Conference*, 593–604. Berkeley: Berkeley Women and Language Group.

Philips, Susan U. 2000. "Constructing a Tongan Nation State through Language Ideology in the Courtroom." In Paul Kroskrity (ed.), *Regimes of Language*, 229–257. Santa Fe, NM: School of American Research Press.

Philips, Susan U. 2007. "Symbolically Central and Materially Marginal: Women's Talk in a Tongan Work Group." In Bonnie S. McElhinny (ed.), *Words, Worlds, and Material Girls: Language, Gender,*

Globalization, 41–75. New York: Mouton de Gruyter.

Philips, Susan U., Susan Steele, and Christine Tanz, eds. 1987. *Language, Gender, and Sex in Comparative Perspective*. Cambridge: Cambridge University Press.

Reiter, Rayna R. 1975. "Men and Women in the South of France: Public and Private Domains." In Rayna R. Reiter (ed.), *Toward an Anthropology of Women*, 252–282. New York: Monthly Review Press.

Rosaldo, Michelle. 1974. "Woman, Culture and Society: A Theoretical Overview." In Michelle Rosaldo and Louise Lamphere (eds.), *Woman, Culture, and Society*, 17–42. Stanford: Stanford University Press.

Schlegel, Alice. 1990. "Gender Meanings: General and Specific." In Peggy Reeves Sanday and Ruth Gallagher Goodenough (eds.), *Beyond the Second Sex: New Directions in the Anthropology of Gender*, 21–42. Philadelphia: University of Pennsylvania Press.

Sherzer, Joel. 1987. "A Diversity of Voices: Men's and Women's Speech in Ethnographic Perspective." In Susan Philips, Susan Steele, and Christine Tanz (eds.), *Language, Gender, and Sex in Comparative Perspective*, 95–120. Cambridge: Cambridge University Press.

Silberstein, Sandra. 1988. "Ideology as Process: Gender Ideology in Courtship Narratives." In Alexandra Todd and Sue Fisher (eds.), *Gender and Discourse: The Power of Talk*, 125–149. Norwood, NJ: Ablex.

Tannen, Deborah. 1994. *Talking from 9 to 5: How Women's and Men's Conversational Styles Affect Who Gets Ahead, Who Gets Credit, and What Gets Done at Work*. New York: William Morrow.

Tannen, Deborah. 1998. *The Argument Culture: Stopping America's War of Words*. New York: Ballantine Books.

Yanagisako, Sylvia. 1987. "Mixed Metaphors: Native and Anthropological Models of Gender and Kinship Domain." In Jane Collier and Sylvia Yanagisako (eds.), *Gender and Kinship: Essays toward a Unified Analysis*, 86–118. Stanford: Stanford University Press.

16   Meaning-Making and Ideologies of Gender and Sexuality

SALLY MCCONNELL-GINET

This chapter highlights some of the ways in which work on language, gender, and sexuality has drawn on standard ideas in linguistic semantics and pragmatics to illumine ideological dimensions of meaning-making that have been unnoticed and seem surprising in standard linguistic inquiry. Feminist and queer theorizing about language also, as illustrated by examples in this chapter, challenges the individualist and utterance-level focus of standard accounts of meaning, prompting us to develop more social and discourse-oriented approaches to enrich the study of linguistically communicated meaning. Both hearers and history matter more than we might have thought. Change and variation – indeed conflict – in meaning-making become centrally important when we look at how language can both help and hinder social reform. Language can help challenge dominant ideologies while at the same time channeling those same ideologies even in the mouths of those who no longer consciously endorse them. And "mouths" are not the only channel of communication, of course: writing was once a new technology and now computer-mediated communication of various kinds also helps shape and shift the ideologically loaded linguistic landscape.

1. Semantics/Pragmatics Overview

Given my background in philosophy of language and mathematics, it is unsurprising that I fell in love with formal semantics as soon as I encountered it, which happened as I was pursuing my PhD in linguistics in the early 1970s. Introduced in print to linguists by Barbara Hall Partee (1975), formal semantics uses tools from mathematical logic and related areas to model meaning in natural languages. As my coauthor Gennaro Chierchia and I try to convey in our introductory formal

The Handbook of Language, Gender, and Sexuality, Second Edition.
Edited by Susan Ehrlich, Miriam Meyerhoff, and Janet Holmes.
© 2014 John Wiley & Sons, Inc. Published 2017 by John Wiley & Sons, Inc.

semantics textbook (Chierchia and McConnell-Ginet 2000), logical and other mathematical resources can give significant insight into compositional meaning, how words combine systematically to make meaningful phrases and ultimately sentences. Formal semantics has also had considerable success in illuminating many other of the more abstract components of linguistic meaning – the meanings of quantifying expressions like *some* and *every* and of plurality, of tense and aspectual markers, of conjunction and negation, of modal expressions like *must* and *can*, of constructions like conditionals ("if she comes, I'm leaving") and comparatives ("Joan is taller than Jan"), even of interrogatives ("is she coming?" or "who is that?") and imperatives ("don't leave" or "have another beer").

Early on, however, most people working in formal semantics realized that it would not tell us everything about meaning. Indeed, even before linguists adopted formal methods for exploring meaning, work in the 1950s and 1960s by philosophers H. Paul Grice (1989) and J. L. Austin (1962) laid the foundations for the field that is now called pragmatics, which most semanticists recognize as an essential complement to their own work in any account of linguistic communication and meaning. Grice's notion of *conversational implicature* (often, just "implicature") arose in trying to show how someone might mean something more or different in using words like *some* or *and* than the literal meanings logical analyses suggest for them. Linguistically triggered *presupposition* such as that differentiating *but* from *and* Grice called *conventional implicature*. Both (conversational) implicatures and presuppositions figure prominently in conveying ideologies of gender and sexuality, and I will give a few examples later in this chapter.

Austin's focus was on what we *do* with the words we utter and how we do it. In addition to representational content, the primary focus of formal semantic theories, Austin proposed that utterances have *illocutionary force*. In saying things we not only represent or describe real or imagined states of affairs but we also do things like command, promise, implore, apologize, brag, hire, and fire (with access to the required institutional authority). Ideologies of gender and sexuality affect not only which speech or illocutionary acts people try to perform (and are institutionally situated to perform) but also their ability to bring them off successfully (examples appear later in this chapter). Betty J. Birner (2013) offers an excellent survey of the field of pragmatics, which has developed significantly over the past 50 years. She particularly emphasizes its connections to formal semantics, these two areas now generally being seen as intimately interconnected.

Formal semantics not only needs supplementation from pragmatics, which emphasizes inferences speakers count on hearers drawing to figure out what speakers and their utterances mean. It is also pretty thin on the ground in what nonsemanticists often think of as central to semantic inquiry – namely, systematic elucidation of the meaning of content words like *marry*, *mother*, or *maiden*. Content lexical items, I have suggested (e.g., in McConnell-Ginet 2006; 2008; 2011 [2002]) are rather like the constant expressions in formal linguistic systems. They are assigned different values on different occasions of use. What is underappreciated is that different values accomplish different things, contribute differently to socially organized thinking and action. This is why it is so important that lexical items, like constant expressions in formal linguistic systems, can be reinterpreted. In the case of natural language content words, their discourse histories constrain the values assignable to them: people use words in the expectation that others will be able to figure out what they are doing with them. There are also linguistic practices constraining interpretations of words in particular discourses or kinds of discourses, defining and analyzing terms for purposes of intellectual inquiry being prime examples. (The next section of this chapter illustrates defining and analysis practices.)

Furthermore, natural language content words often acquire what I've elsewhere dubbed "conceptual baggage" (McConnell-Ginet 2008 and below) as they are deployed in various kinds of discourse. Conceptual baggage is part of the significance attached to words, though it is not part of what those words or the speakers using them mean. An example discussed below is the assumption that a surgeon is male: maleness is not part of the meaning of *surgeon* nor of what speakers mean when they use *surgeon* but it is nonetheless frequently inferred by hearers when speakers utter *surgeon* to talk about someone. Thus conceptual baggage does enter into meaning-making in an extended sense, sometimes reinforcing ideological biases through its often unnoticed and unintended activating of stereotypes, stereotypes that in other ways are losing currency.

The focus of feminist inquiry into linguistic meaning has shifted from particular words and expressions, though these remain important (and fascinating), to meaning as it emerges in *discourse*, often transformed. I will sometimes use *discourse meaning* to cover not only the content conveyed over the course of an exchange (a "thread" in computer-mediated communication, or CMC) but also the *effects* that discourse participants have on the shape of the subsequent discourse and (to some extent) on one another's thoughts and actions. Discourse meaning includes both representations and also certain nonlinguistic causal effects those representations produce. Language, of course, is never all of what produces discourse meaning: there can be gestures, facial expressions, music, and much more adding to (or sometimes fighting against) the job done by language (see, e.g., Jones 2009a for contributions of digital pictures, including video). But my focus in this chapter is on the linguistic components of discourse meaning, both content and effects.

Meaning-making from this discourse perspective becomes *dynamic* – work is done each time words are used, fed by past discursive history and feeding the future, reshaping meaning-making possibilities. Content word meanings in particular are somewhat fluid and less than fully determinate: their meanings are fleshed out when they are used in discourse, often affecting their future uses. Meaning-making also becomes fundamentally *social* – semantic success depends on the active work of those who process words and is not simply up to the producer of the words, who may be handicapped by gender or sexual positioning or other factors. Meaning-making is less like walking or dancing solo than like ballroom or circle dancing. And even when ideologies are not what the discourse is about, meaning-making is *ideologically loaded*, not neutral. This chapter illustrates some of the ways that ideologies of gender and sexuality feed and are fed by meaning-making.

It also illustrates that what we learn about language depends in part on the ideologies that guide our investigation. This does not mean that how meanings are made is a matter of how we wish they were made or how we think they are made on the basis of casual observation or our own personal biases. Inquiry into meaning-making, like all empirical inquiry, builds on theories and methods developed over a considerable period, and is answerable to scholarly standards of various kinds. At the same time, political commitments and their ideological foundations can lead analysts to notice certain phenomena otherwise overlooked or to pursue lines of inquiry that had not been thought likely to be as fruitful as they prove. Feminist and queer scholarship on language does not by any means eschew mainstream linguistic frameworks, but it has often, as examples in this chapter illustrate, expanded and enriched our view of meaning-making.

2. Terminological Preliminaries

The rest of this chapter will develop and illustrate these ideas a bit more, but before talking about meaning-making specifically I will briefly sketch what I have in mind by *gender*, by *sexuality*, and by *ideology*. And along the way I will talk about other words in this area as well – for example, labels for what is called sexual orientation. In other words, I invite readers to engage with me in some preliminary meaning-making so we will be better able to engage with our topic.

Gender and sexuality are intimately intertwined. Cross-culturally, gender builds on (1) sexual categorization of people, with genital, chromosomal, and hormonal criteria sorting into female and male; (2) sexual encounters, especially potentially reproductive ones; (3) sexual reproduction, which creates infant humans; (4) subsequent rearing of the children produced. Gender involves the complex array of social arrangements and institutions, cultural practices and values, connected to these four matters, and gender varies greatly over time and space. Some cultures have wide-ranging divisions of labor for the sexes, some do not. Some strongly proscribe adolescent sexual activity, others promote it. We could continue with a long list of cross-cultural differences in gender.

Even the four apparently "biological" building blocks with which I begin show variation. Sexual categorization, for example, is not so straightforward or neatly dichotomizing as we often think. Our forebears could look at a baby's genitalia and (usually) thereby assign the baby to a sex class but they could not determine chromosomal makeup (which is not exhausted by the standard XX "female" and XY "male" patterns) or hormone levels. For one reason or another, some 1–2 percent of healthy babies fall outside the neat binary split into female and male. How cultures deal with such "recalcitrant" bodies varies. A recent movement in North America and elsewhere promotes acceptance of "intersex" people, not insisting on a strict sexual binarism. Note also that although a person may be assigned to one gender class quite readily at birth, they may not feel themselves to "belong" to that class. Gender identity as experienced internally may diverge from that ascribed by others, leading in some cases to sex reassignment in adulthood (or, in recent years, even earlier). Sex reassignment typically draws on technological developments such as hormone therapy to help produce a body that better fits the internally experienced gender identity than the body that developed without such interventions. Reproductive technologies have also changed the gender/sexual landscape. Only very recently, for example, did it become possible for an egg to be fertilized by a sperm without sexual contact between the individuals providing those resources, or for fertilization to occur in test tubes, or for a fertilized egg to be implanted in the uterus/womb of a different woman than the one from whom the egg came. Such new possibilities create a potential distinction between the gestational mother, the one whose body nurtures the developing fetus and finally gives birth to the resulting baby, and the genetic mother, the one whose body produced the egg. Or consider the nurturing of newborn infants and older children. At one time babies had to be fed by lactating females (though not necessarily the mother); formulas and bottles changed that. Washing machines and disposable diapers transformed the kind of work involved in dealing with infants' and young children's excretory processes. And so on. Biology is not as immutable as we have often thought, although prevalent ideologies of gender and sexuality still standardly take the biological as a given, impervious to cultural developments.

Sex and sexual reproduction, complex and variable as they may be, are still at the heart of gender, but it is also important to think about sexuality on its own terms. We speak of a person's "sexual orientation," by which is usually meant whether that person is disposed to be sexually attracted to those of the same sex (gay men and lesbians), of the other sex (heterosexuals), or of both sexes (bisexuals or, somewhat more broadly, pansexuals, a category that does not assume that two sexes exhaust the possibilities). Some analysts, though few ordinary folk, also include a category of those not disposed to sexual attraction at all, the "asexual."

Transgender people have found the homosexual/heterosexual split problematic since the match or mismatch between the sex of those to whom they are attracted and their own sex varies, depending on how their own sex is ascribed. So, for example, a trans man who is attracted to men is often dubbed homosexual (see, e.g., Coleman and Bockting 1989) and so, upon occasion, is a trans man attracted to women; in neither case is the categorization straightforward. The terms *gynecophilia* and *androphilia* designate attraction to women and attraction to men respectively, and thus the issue of gender assignment for the person whose orientation is being described does not arise. But even with this terminology not only may the gender ascribed to those who excite the person erotically not always be straightforward but gender is still being offered as a dichotomous binary criterion, as all that really matters in matters of sexual desire. And yet some people direct their desire to fat folks, others to those with mocha-colored skin, others to the very hairy, others to the very young. Although nongender features that can condition attraction are sometimes explicitly recognized (note, e.g., labels like *potato queen* or *rice queen* used by some gay men to signal Western or Asian ethnicity of the object of desire: see, e.g., Jones 2009b), the gender of desired sexual partners is overwhelmingly taken as centrally important. "Sexual identity" typically suggests that a person's sexual orientation is central to their sense of who they are and also to others' sense of what they are like and often also that they identify with others of the same orientation. The very idea of sexual identity, of sexual inclinations and desires as definitive of kinds of people and their connections to one another, is relatively recent. And notice that neither sexual orientation nor sexual identity – all part of sexuality – need determine sexual activity or sexual practices.

This brief discussion of gender and sexuality and some of the language used in speaking of them demonstrates the interplay of language and ideology. Stereotypes and common assumptions abound; most of us still ignore, for example, possible divergence between genetic and gestational motherhood, often using terms like *biological mother*, which doesn't distinguish these different "biological" components of motherhood. And of course being a *social mother* – rearing a child – does not depend on any kind of biological connections. Categorizing systems, which include labeling, incorporate systematic ideas of gender and of sexuality. So, for example, the expression *Lee's mother* is assumed, unlike *Lee's sister*, to pick out a single individual. Ideologies of gender and sexuality also include normative expectations (Lee's mother is likely, for example, to be held responsible for Lee's care in the first few years and censured if Lee is thought to have been neglected) and other value systems as well as hierarchies of prestige and power.

I speak of ideolog*ies* rather than ideolog*y*: not only do gender and sexual ideologies show considerable variation cross-culturally and historically, but at any time and location there are almost certainly competing gender and sexual ideologies with contests particularly obvious at certain times and places. Furthermore there are almost always some internal tensions in the gender and sexual ideological commitments for any particular individual person, especially at times of social change when ambivalence becomes more pronounced. In discourse, unnoticed stereotypical or normative assumptions may emerge that are completely at odds with positions individuals engaged in the discourse sincerely avow when focusing their attention on them.

3. Speakers Implicitly Exploiting (or Unwittingly Endorsing) Ideologies

Discourse content breaks down roughly into two large categories: what speakers *convey*, at least potentially, and what hearers *infer*, again potentially. What speakers convey includes (1) what is explicitly *said*, the conventional meaning of the expression uttered, fleshed out contextually as needed, and (2) what is implicitly conveyed by producing that expression in the particular context, which includes what philosopher H. Paul Grice (1989) called the speaker's meaning or *implicature*, as well as *presupposition* or what an utterance standardly takes for granted, what its being produced – again, in that particular context – must assume. I use "convey" because all of this content, both explicit and implicit, can in some sense be attributed to the speaker, the one who produced an utterance.

Even what is explicitly said, I have argued elsewhere, is not always completely determined by linguistic conventions or the "rules" of a language, even at a given point in its history. Linguistic conventions do indeed set limits on interpretation. In spite of what Humpty Dumpty said to Alice in Lewis Carroll's *Through the Looking Glass*, *glory* cannot (currently) mean what *knock-down argument* means, nor does *glory* (currently) refer to some kind of fruit as do English words like *apple* and *grape*. At the same time, many (perhaps most) content expressions are at least partially "empty," their content not completely fixed.

It is a commonplace that context is needed to fill in the value of familiar indexical expressions like English *I, you, here,* and *now*. What is less widely recognized (and indeed sometimes disputed) is that context also helps determine the content of such apparently already content-ful expressions as *marriage, have sex,* and *flirt*. Do same-sex unions count as *marriage*? Does fellatio get labeled as *having sex*? Is *flirting* applicable in situations involving continued attentions that are not reciprocated or welcomed? Such words are given their content in part contextually. In the case of expressions like these, these contents are often contested as part of ideological struggles over gender and sexuality. To account for this contextual and ideologically loaded fleshing out of what is said, however, it is useful to consider first the other aspects of discourse meaning, both implicit conveyed content and hearer-oriented dimensions of meaning. At the end of this chapter I will give brief pointers to what filling out "explicit" meaning might involve by discussing some Chinese research on how computer games transform understanding of marriage and the labels for it.[1] This section takes what is said more or less for granted and focuses on implicitly conveyed messages, which include implicature and presupposition.

An example can illustrate the contrast between what is implicated and what is said. A woman who is dating another woman and does not want to be "out" as not exclusively heterosexual can exploit familiar gender and sexual ideologies to answer questions like that asked by one concerned mother, "Are you dating again, sweetie, since you broke off with Michael?" The young woman may answer, "I'm OK, mom, but I'm not dating any man at the moment." Her answer literally only says that she is not dating a man at present. What she *says* is true in these circumstances, but it undoubtedly can be used to *implicate*, falsely, that she is not dating at all. She can count on her mother's failing to consider the possibility that she is now dating a woman. After all, heterosexual presumptions are still widespread, especially among older people. The daughter in this scenario is quite conscious of the false implication, even though she might point to the literal truth of what she said if her mother later finds out that the daughter misled her. And as A. C. Liang (1999) noted in the discussion that inspires this example, the very same words can be used to "come out" to someone who is, unlike our hypothetical mother, attuned to same-sex desire, perhaps someone the daughter thinks is overhearing the conversation with her mother and whom the daughter thinks may herself be lesbian. With different ideologies, different implicatures are possible. Grice did couch his account of implicatures and, more generally, of the speaker's meaning in terms of the effects a speaker intends to produce in a particular hearer, but Liang's observation of the possibility of conflicting implicatures conveyed by a single utterance to different hearers sheds light on social complexities Grice (and most subsequent pragmatic analysts) ignored.

On Grice's account, implicatures are indeed part of the speaker's intended message (of course, the hearer may draw inferences the speaker did not intend, but we'll consider such inferences later), the "speaker's meaning." Presupposition, in contrast, is often not noticed by the speaker and certainly often not consciously intended. Unnoticed background assumptions can, however, be brought to the speaker's attention, who must then either embrace them or reformulate the communication. If a young mother says to her daughter, "When you get married, your husband … ," she conveys implicitly and perhaps quite unwittingly the assumption that the little girl will indeed marry and that she will marry a man. Of course she could say something like "Suppose you get married to a man someday. Then your husband … " Hearing the *when you get married* formulation and similar utterances over the years may make it a bit more difficult for the daughter to seriously consider a future without heterosexual marriage. Her mother could well fail to notice that such assumptions are being made and might regret having activated them if they are pointed out to her. Many of us have had the experience of recognizing with some shock and dismay our own conveying of presuppositions that we then want to disavow. I suspect I said things like "When you get married, your husband … " to my own daughter when she was a child even though if asked I would have (sincerely) denied assuming she would marry or that she would necessarily have a long-term male rather than female partner (I don't think the possibility of anyone actually marrying a same-sex partner was in my consciousness at that point.) Importantly, speakers are in some fundamental way "responsible" for presuppositions like these, even for those they do not notice and might wish to disavow.[2] Though empirical studies of their impact are virtually nonexistent, being very hard to design and implement, such subterranean messages are almost certainly important in transmitting ideologies.

4. Hearers Inferring: Ideologically Driven or Ideology-Reinforcing

Now that we have sketched the broad contours of the speaker's side of meaning, let's turn to the hearer-oriented side, which I have sometimes called "hearer's meaning" to emphasize the contrast with Grice's speaker's meaning. In general, successful communication results in the hearer inferring what has been explicitly *and* implicitly conveyed, so that the rest of the discourse includes this conveyed content. The example of "I'm not dating any other man" shows that hearers' ideological commitments can determine what they take the speaker to be implying. But we also just saw in the example of the mother's talking of *when you get married* that presuppositions often go unnoticed by those relying on them in shaping their utterances. Such unnoticed presuppositions may also not be explicitly inferred, perhaps already being presumed by the hearer, who might well only infer at a conscious level what is presupposed when the assumption is not already read-ily accessible and therefore needs to be "accommodated" for discourse to proceed smoothly. With children we don't know, but there is some evidence that everyday presumptions do in part get conveyed in this subterranean way.

It's a commonplace that hearers have to recognize what speakers are up to, what their utterances convey. What I want to highlight now in this hearer-oriented component of discursive meaning is the *other* content that hearers can and often do infer, which is not conveyed but rendered accessible or *activated*: both what I've called *conceptual baggage* (CB) and content activated by hearer's experience with *nonparallelisms* contrast between what is and is not said in similar discourse contexts. Inferring CB is typically driven by ideologies, by existing assumptions, whereas observing nonparallelisms may shape ideologies, prompting hearers to infer certain assumptions of the discourse communities in which such nonparal-lelisms are found.

To illustrate the notion of conceptual baggage, consider this anecdote, versions of which were often told by American feminists in the early 1970s to illustrate lin-guistic sexism.

> A man and his son were driving along in torrential rains on a winding mountain road when they came to a very slippery stretch. The car swerved and went off the road, killing the man and badly injuring his son. Not long after, rescuers arrived and rushed the son to a nearby hospital, alerting the surgeon on duty to begin washing up. The surgeon, carefully scrubbing, turns when the patient is wheeled into the operating room and exclaims "I can't operate – that's my son."

Many who heard the story, including me on my first encounter with it, were puz-zled. After all, the boy's father had been killed – how could the boy be the surgeon's son? They/we were attaching maleness to *surgeon*, drawing on a stereotype of surgeons as men, a stereotype less robust now than it then was but by no means dead. When searching for pictures for a PowerPoint presentation of this anecdote, I found nothing labeled *surgeon* that was clearly female (though there were some labeled *woman surgeon* or *female surgeon*) but many pictures labeled just *surgeon* clearly showed males.

Some who originally presented the anecdote said it showed that *surgeon* was semantically male, but that seemed wrong to most linguists – after all, it is and was even back then quite possible to say of a woman *She's a surgeon*. My diagnosis is that maleness is part of the conceptual baggage activated by the word *surgeon* – we could see such activation at work if my friend told me she'd just seen the surgeon who was going to operate on her tomorrow and I responded, "Did he say anything about whether you can eat breakfast?" without knowing anything about the sur-geon's sex. (It is important to remember that in English the pronoun *he* in reference to a specific individual presumes maleness of that individual: *he* can not be sex-neutral in such uses.) My assumption that the surgeon is a man would proba-bly pass unnoticed by my friend and me unless indeed the surgeon were a woman, thus in some small way strengthening the stereotype of surgeons as men and not women.

Only recently did I notice the conceptual baggage in this story activated by the word *father*. I never heard anyone back in the 1970s speak of the possibility that the boy might have more than one father – two gay fathers, an adoptive and a biological father, and so on.[3] The standard assumption in the United States then was one father, one mother – the standard heterosexual family. Whether TV shows like *My Two Dads*, which I have not seen but which was very popular in the United States recently, have dislodged such presumptions among their viewers I don't know, though they may have at least weakened them, especially among younger people. I suspect, however, that most contemporary Americans who hear "his father died" would even now automatically infer that he has no living father, whereas "his brother died" would not trigger the same inference nearly so strongly.

It was Celia Kitzinger's (2005) fascinating study of the use of kin terminology in calls to doctors that led me to formulate the idea of conceptual baggage in the first place. Kitzinger found that when a caller used *my husband* to refer to the ill person on whose behalf she was phoning, it was overwhelmingly more likely that further discourse would show the hearer had inferred that the caller knew the patient's medical history, was willing to drive him in for an appointment or to pick up medicine for him, and so on than if the caller had used a nonkin term like *my boyfriend* or *my housemate*. Gender and sexual ideologies of family relations clearly attached considerable CB to the kin terminology in Kitzinger's data, and family ideologies clearly affect the way hearers interpret *father* in the car accident anecdote.

And indeed the *when you get married* example illustrates not only the presupposition introduced by *when* that marriage will indeed occur, but also shows conceptual baggage attached to *marriage*. Most processing the mother's message probably immediately inferred that the future marriage being assumed would be to a man, licensing her use of *your husband*. As many readers will know, there have been considerable debate in the United States (and elsewhere) about same-sex marriage for more than a decade and many attempts to define the word *marriage* so as to rule out marriage between two women or two men. Gender and sexual ideologies centered on the institutions of marriage and family are central to these debates, and the opponents of same-sex marriages are helped by the sometimes problematic conceptual baggage evoked by talk of marriage. The point I want to emphasize here is that the words *marriage* and *marry* activate certain heterosexist ideological assumptions about marriage even in those who may at a conscious level strongly support same-sex marriage. They also activate other much more positive pieces of conceptual baggage, like notions of socially recognized commitment and of connecting generations and families. Similarly, many of us unthinkingly assumed the maleness of the surgeon even though we knew that some surgeons are female and also strongly supported the increased visibility of women in surgery and other traditionally male-dominated occupations. CB associated with particular expressions can be very very difficult to shed.

I treat CB as hearer-oriented because the inferences drawn need have no relation to the speaker's own assumptions, even their tacit ones. A speaker may indeed rely on the CB they expect the hearer to have attached to a word in order to convey something: for example, someone might report to a friend, "I met a very good look-ing and smart surgeon at the party last night," and intend for the friend to infer that the new acquaintance is male. But the word *surgeon* may readily be used when a speaker neither wants nor expects such an inference. Furthermore, it would be odd indeed to utter "My sister is studying to be a surgeon" to convey that one's female sibling is not only entering the medical profession but is also transitioning to male gender status. And yet CB can attach itself so firmly to words that speakers find it hard to block hearers' inferences, which is one reason people think of it as part of word meaning. This is part of why, for example, Monique Wittig famously pro-claimed "a lesbian is not a woman." Assumptions of women's economic and erotic dependence on men are so firmly attached to *woman* (more accurately its French equivalent, *femme*) that hearers inferring such dependence for anyone so labeled is nearly inevitable.

The other component of hearer-oriented meaning is what I'm calling here *non-parallelisms* (and have discussed in McConnell-Ginet 2012a and 2012b under the rubric *meaningful discourse patterns*). What I mean by this are inferences that the hearer can draw not just from a single utterance but from *contrasts* with what is or is not said in other apparently parallel situations. As with all hearer-oriented meaning, inferences are only potential. For this component of discourse mean-ing, the potentiality is particularly important as the significance arises not from any situated particular exchange considered on its own but from contrasts across a wide range of similar situations. The content "added" to discourse by nonparal-lelism is clearly not added by single utterances but arises from comparing different exchanges. Content generated by nonparallelisms may well remain tacit, below the level of conscious attention.

Students of the interaction of language with gender and sexuality have long paid attention to nonparallelisms as ideologically significant. At the word level, Robin Lakoff (1973) noted the nonparallel use of *lady* and *gentleman*; affluent Americans often employ *cleaning ladies* but there are no **garbage gentlemen* picking up their rubbish. And statistical studies, for example, that contrast descriptions of men and women in news articles or that look at male and female referents in subject versus object position in children's stories emphasize nonparallelism. (For an exploration of nonparallelisms in syntax text examples, see Macaulay and Brice 1997; Baker 2010 compares corpora from four different periods, the most recent being 2006, on various dimensions of how they represent women and men, including frequency of mention, descriptive adjectives, pronouns, social titles, and more.) But such phe-nomena don't fit neatly in standard theories of semantics and pragmatics, much as socially significant variations in pronunciation don't fit neatly in standard phono-logical and phonetic theories. What I want to do here is suggest that nonparallelism does contribute to discourse content, although it does so not primarily via what expressions or the speakers who produce them mean, the standard focus of seman-tics and pragmatics, but, like conceptual baggage, via the inferences hearers may draw on the basis of their processing of their linguistic experiences.

Again, it is Celia Kitzinger's work that made me start thinking about this phenomenon as contributing to discourse meaning. Kitzinger (2002) reports that on arriving at the dining room of the hotel at which they were staying, she and her female partner were asked "Will anyone else be joining you?" The question itself might seem routine but Kitzinger stationed herself and observed numerous mixed-sex couples entering who were not asked the same question. That mixed-sex pairs were seen as complete social units whereas the same-sex pair was seen as needing augmentation is clear only by contrasting what was said to the same-sex pair with what was – or was not, in this case – said to mixed-sex pairs. It is not the single utterance but the nonparallelism in discourse pattern that activates the very common presumption that women need the company of men. (The guy in the bar approaches a table with two women and asks: "Are you ladies alone?" The women respond: "No we're together.")

5. Discourse Effects: Ideologies and Getting Things Done with Words

I have just scratched the surface of the ideological saturation of discourse content, but I want to move now to discuss the ideological shaping of discourse effects. Illocutionary effects, which are supposed to be brought off just *in* saying what one says, are essentially semantic and include what I call *uptake*, getting basic comprehension of what speech act(s) the speaker is trying to perform, and also *update*, getting recognition of that performance as having occurred in the discourse – that is, having one's claim treated as "on the floor," needing to be considered, even if it might ultimately be rejected. Perlocutionary effects, accomplished *by* saying what one says, can be very *basic*, tied almost as directly to the speech act (or acts) performed as the illocutionary effects – for example, getting others to believe one's claim or obey one's directive. Indeed, Grice spoke of aiming at these effects as part of a speaker's basic speech act, and, tenuous though they are, such basic effects as being believed do seem to be fundamental to why people bother speaking at all. Less basic but nonetheless very important are what I call *expanded* effects, which have much looser connections to the speech act as such – frightening someone, impressing others, elevating one's status among discourse participants. It is the basic effects, however, that are of special interest.

   Perlocutionary effects of the expanded sort have always been recognized as depending on the hearer's responding in ways the speaker may well not control, and I'm not going to discuss the expanded effects in any detail. But feminist inquiry into language use has helped us see much more clearly the deeply social character of illocutionary effects and of the basic perlocutionary effects. Uptake or basic understanding is often taken to require only shared knowledge of linguistic conventions and of readily assessed features of shared communicative context (of course online communication and offline communication via writing complicate this, but we can ignore those complications for now). When the hearer does not recognize the speaker's attempted illocutionary act, it is common to speak of "miscommunication" and to blame the lack of success on the speaker and the hearer having different communicative systems, different standard ways of doing things with words. Though not always putting it in quite these terms, a number of feminist analysts have shown that hearers sometimes do not so much "misunderstand" as actively resist "understanding" or uptake.

Deborah Cameron's wonderful paper, "'Is There Any Ketchup, Vera?' Gender, Power, and Pragmatics" (2006 [1998]) stresses the importance of gender ideologies to speakers' success in producing the illocutionary results they intend, and, importantly, the role of conflicting gender ideologies in apparent "misunderstandings." "Is there any ketchup, Vera?" when uttered by husband to wife in a traditional English family several decades ago was taken not as an inquiry about the existence or even location of ketchup in the house but as an indication that the husband wanted ketchup and expected Vera, the wife, to get it. Shared ideology promoted comprehension (and also further perlocutionary responsiveness – in this case, Vera's not only taking the utterance as a request but actually getting up from the table to fetch the ketchup). Cameron used the example to show that, contrary to what was often suggested by analysts focused on gender differences in speech styles, indirect requests can be and often are used by men to women whose service they consider their due. Indeed the person from whom Cameron heard this anecdote presented this use of indirection as quintessentially "masculine" – "Isn't that so like a man?" she commented in recounting the pattern she remembered from her childhood family. And, Cameron observed, there are many contexts in which parallel uses are unavailable to the woman – Vera, for example, did not use such indirect requests to her husband when seated at the dinner table. This heterosexual married couple (and many others) operated with the shared understanding that she was the one charged with such domestic service to him, not vice versa. The daughter reported that when she said, "Is there any ketchup, Mum," the response was something like "Yes, it's in the pantry" but not her mother's rising to get the ketchup for her. Husbands but not daughters were empowered to achieve such ends as getting the ketchup indirectly.

Cameron contrasted this case with the advice to women to avoid indirect requests to men in the workplace, advice commonly encountered in the American popular press after the publication of Deborah Tannen's (1990) influential book on supposed gender differences in communicative style. Why were women told to cast their instructions in direct form? Advisers claimed that men do not fully "understand" the genuinely directive force of such indirect forms. Not only were these advisers forgetting the *Is there any ketchup, Vera?* kind of scenario, one that was still operative at many late twentieth-century dinner tables in America as well as in England (and probably operates to some extent even in the early twenty-first century). They were also not adequately analyzing why men working under women might complain about such indirectly phrased requests in workplace contexts. Few men would *actually* fail to recognize that from a manager to her assistant, *Would you like to finish this report today?* does not inquire after the subordinate's preferences but directs him to get the report done now. This scenario is reminiscent of my habit many years ago of directing my children by saying things like "Would you like to set the table?" – trying to avoid flaunting my authority while still very clearly directing the children (who often called my bluff by replying "No, but I will"). It seems highly unlikely that a male employee would not understand the manager as directing him. What is much more likely going on, as Cameron astutely notes, is conflict, a power struggle. There are, I suggest, conflicting ideologies in play. The male employee is committed to a view of gender hierarchy that leads him to *resist* according full authority to his female supervisor: he is trying to make his sex trump her managerial title. She, in contrast, endorses a newer and competing ideology that sees women as fully legitimate occupants of workplace positions that might give them authority over men. He calculates, probably correctly, that he can opt not to get to work right away on the report and yet "protect" himself from her anger by pointing to the indirect form of her message. Advice to women to avoid using indirection in such cases is really advice not to speak authoritatively because their male subordinates do not like it. It is advice to act instead as if one could not rely on one's institutionally endorsed authority so as not to threaten gender hierarchies, not to remind male subordinates of their lower position. Of course, such advice helps undermine women's institutionally licensed authority and helps support male privilege – it allows the male employee, even if he does get working on the report, to complain about his female boss's "not saying what she means" or "being afraid to tell me what to do."

Among the most problematic cases where gender ideology results in communicative failure are those in which women's explicit refusals of men's sexual overtures do not get uptake – or at least comprehension is not acknowledged. Bolstered by views of women as standardly "playing hard to get," as saying *no* but meaning "please keep on trying," some men persist in sexual activity, while at least claiming not to have understood the *no*s produced by the women under assault as illocutionary acts of denial or refusal.[4] A number of feminist philosophers have addressed this way in which ideologies curtail some women's illocutionary capacities. Rae Langton and Jennifer Hornsby (1998) argue that certain kinds of pornography actively promote the "women play hard to get" ideology and that by doing so they wrongly limit the freedom of speech of women who are trying to resist unwanted sexual overtures from men. Such pornography, they propose, wrongly infringes on women's right to freedom of speech. Thus they conclude that it is quite legitimate for the state to legislate against such pornography. Although some porn does indeed present rape as welcomed by women and also similar offensive and dangerous scenarios endorsing "women *like* being forced into sex" ideologies, it is very difficult to legislate against precisely that kind of porn while allowing for sexually explicit material of other kinds. Because anti-porn laws are often used to harass those involved in minority sexual practices, I cannot endorse such proposals. And, of course, porn is far from the only source of these "*no* means *yes*" ideologies. Arguably, it is not even the most important. Indeed, ideologies that counsel against women's displaying their own sexual desire openly, some of which come from quite conservative sources who would happily join in supporting anti-porn legislation, also discourage some women from saying *yes* when they really would welcome sexual contact, and further encourage some women to say *no* when what they really do mean is *yes*. Such practices then put other women at greater risk of being disbelieved when they actually do say and mean *no*.

There is also an issue of what counts as "consent" to sexual activity. Arguably, consent should require active assent, not just the absence of dissent (whether actually absent because someone is afraid openly to dissent or viewed as absent because the initiator insists on taking the overt refusal as some kind of implicit assent). Notice that cybersex raises similar problems, some women reporting great difficulty in getting their *no*s understood as just that by online sexual aggressors, who often try to interpret those *no*s as *yes*es.

6. Return to Content Word Meanings: Ideological Struggles and Changing Contexts

Earlier in this chapter there was some discussion of terminology, including the meanings of some content words. In discussing the overall picture of discourse meaning, however, I postponed further consideration of how explicit meaning gets attached to words until after the discussion of implicit speaker's meaning, of hearer-oriented dimensions of meaning, and of discourse effects. Now we will briefly revisit the topic of contested and changing word meanings, starting by considering the talk and debate about word meanings often in the air when refusal of sexual activity is at issue. For example, is it *rape* if the *no* was "misunderstood" or if there was no overt consent but also what the assailant (and perhaps others judging him) took as lack of adequately strong and repeated resistance? Can a husband rape his wife? And so on.

Discourse analyst Susan Ehrlich's work on this general topic (see, e.g., Ehrlich 2001; 2007; Chapter 23 in this volume) is very illuminating, showing how gender and sexual ideologies infuse what content people attach to *rape*. Indeed, just as women can find it difficult to get uptake on their *no* as meaning "no," there has been significant resistance to extending the coverage of *rape* to include husbands or boyfriends as potential rapists or to allow that, for example, mutually enjoyed flirtation does not make subsequent rape impossible. There has been change here. For example, on December 6, 2011, an FBI advisory board voted overwhelmingly to expand the definition of *rape* from "carnal knowledge of a female forcibly and against her will" to "penetration, no matter how slight, of the vagina or anus with any body part or object, or oral penetration by a sex organ of another person, without the consent of the victim" (Terkel 2011). The new definition does not require the use of force (which led to the requirement that victims of rape needed to show resistance to the force) nor is it limited to female victims, an important difference from how it was generally understood some decades earlier. The recommended change in understanding *rape* was accepted by both the Director of the FBI and the Attorney General of the United States. This official recognition does not, of course, guarantee jurors, judges, or just plain folks will understand *rape* in the "authorized" way. Nor does the codification settle all questions of applicability of that label. For example, there is still that difficult question of what counts as *consent*.

In my own work I have explored debates in the United States over "defining" the word *marriage* (see, e.g., McConnell-Ginet 2006). There was even federal legislation "defining" marriage as a union between one woman and one man although that law was being contested at the time of writing this chapter and was indeed overturned before this book was published. By the end of 2013 19 states, including New York, where I live, had legalized same-sex marriage, and a number of other countries had also done so. Now neither China nor any of the other Chinese-speaking nations has gone down this route but marriage is certainly being reconceptualized in these areas and the relevant Chinese words are much discussed. Among the central changes in social life, including gender and sexual arrangements and ideologies, are the very recent and very rapid changes in social interactions that new communicative technologies have created. I will close this chapter by briefly considering a couple of accounts of online marriage in China (Wu et al. 2007 and McLaren 2007).

Online marriage includes some liaisons that are arranged or ceremonialized online but connect people who may have met or will eventually meet offline. Sometimes these are intended to be essentially the same as more conventional marriage; other times they are like a more or less grown-up version of "playing house," involving some pretense. Even further from traditional marriage are marriages incorporated into MMORPGs (massively multiplayer online role-playing games), which unite not the players but their avatars, the fictional characters whom they manipulate. Both studies of Chinese online marriage cited above interviewed players and found interesting accounts of why they engaged in these activities. "To have fun" was an important reason, but at the same time online marriage was also seen as a good substitute for an offline relationship – less expensive, easier to arrange, and so on – and was sometimes contracted between avatars of players with offline connections. Wu et al. emphasize the heteronormativity of these games, not only so far as marriage is concerned but as reflected in the general distrust of male players with female avatars, called *renyao*, even though such players often imbued their female avatars with much more conventional femininity than female players did.

Many critics of such games (*wanghun* or *xuni hunyin*) claim that they lead to the devaluation of traditional offline marriage. Both McLaren and Wu et al. argue, however, that the games may be helping Chinese youth reshape offline social relations and institutions, and may ultimately affect what kinds of relations will be labeled *hunyin* (or *marriage* in English). Blurring the lines, a Japanese man attracted considerable media attention in 2009 when he "married" and "honeymooned" with Nene Anagasaki, not a person but an avatar, a character in a popular Nintendo game (Lah 2009). Presumably, this was mainly a publicity stunt, but it does suggest how engagement in fantasies can have real life consequences.

How will institutions like marriage and family and the words that designate them change in the coming years? Will they continue to be sites for ideological and also definitional conflict. New technologies spawn new social and linguistic practices, which can in turn lead to new gender and sexual practices and ideologies. And linguistic practices are always part of the mix.

It is often the case that, statistically, women and men will advance different interpretations of particular words. So, for example, *flirt* is often treated by women as potentially nonsexual, playful, whereas men often see *flirt* as applied to women as evincing their sexual interest (see Dougherty et al. 2009). And it is also the case that one's sexual orientation can be statistically significant for interpretation, for example, whether oral–genital contact counts as "having sex" (see, e.g., Sanders and Reinisch 1999). But talk of gender-based or sexuality-based "meaning divergence" or "miscommunication" obscures struggles over gender and sexual ideologies and the practices they sustain.

Conflicts over word meaning are always embedded in larger discourse developments and in the wider world of social arrangements and cultural ideologies. Matters of gender and sexuality are not by any means the only areas where meanings are contested but work in feminist and queer studies has brought out especially clearly the fundamentally social and dynamic nature of meaning-making.

NOTES

1 Somewhat more detail on the ideological loading of explicit content can be found in McConnell-Ginet (2006; 2008) and in such earlier papers as McConnell-Ginet (2011 [2002]).
2 As an astute referee notes, this fact challenges a view of meaning as fully "intentional."
3 A referee reports having told the story to students who came up with the two-father possibility before entertaining the idea of the surgeon being the boy's mother, which would seem to show the great power of the gender assumptions about surgeons overriding assumptions about the uniqueness of fathers.
4 As a referee reminds me, saying *no* is very complex, as brought out in Kulick (2003).

REFERENCES

Austin, J. L. 1962. *How to Do Things with Words*. Cambridge, MA: Harvard University Press.

Baker, Paul. 2010. "Will *Ms* Ever Be as Frequent as *Mr*: A Corpus-Based Comparison of Gendered Terms across Four Diachronic Corpora of British English." *Gender and Language*, 4(1): 125–249.

Birner, Betty J. 2013. *Introduction to Pragmatics*. Oxford: Wiley-Blackwell.

Cameron, Deborah. 2006 [1998]. "'Is There Any Ketchup, Vera?' Gender, Power, and Pragmatics." *Discourse & Society*, 9:

437–455. Repr. in Deborah Cameron, *On Language and Sexual Politics*, 75–92. London: Routledge.

Chierchia, Gennaro, and Sally McConnell-Ginet. 2000. *Meaning and Grammar: An Introduction to Formal Semantics*, 2nd edn. Cambridge, MA: MIT Press.

Coleman, Eli, and Walter O. Bockting. 1989. "'Heterosexual' Prior to Sex Reassignment – 'Homosexual' Afterwards: A Case Study of a Female-to-Male Transsexual." *Journal of Psychology and Human Sexuality*, 1(2): 69–82.

Dougherty, Debbie S., Michael W. Kramer, Stephanie R. Klatzke, and Teddy K. K. Rogers. 2009. "Language Convergence and Meaning Divergence: A Meaning Centered Communication Theory." *Communication Monographs*, 78(1): 20–46.

Ehrlich, Susan. 2001. *Representing Rape: Language and Sexual Consent*. London: Routledge.

Ehrlich, Susan. 2007. "Legal Discourse and the Cultural Intelligibility of Gendered Meanings." *Journal of Sociolinguistics*, 11(4): 452–477.

Grice, H. Paul. 1989. *The Ways of Words*. Cambridge, MA: Harvard University Press.

Jones, Rodney H. 2009a. "Dancing, Skating and Sex: Action and Text in the Digital Age." *Journal of Applied Linguistics*, 6(3): 283–302.

Jones, Rodney H. 2009b. " 'Potato Seeking Rice': Language, Culture, and Identity in Gay Personal Ads in Hong Kong." *International Journal of the Sociology of Language*, 143(1): 33–62.

Kitzinger, Celia. 2002. "Doing Feminist Conversation Analysis." In Paul McIlvenny (ed.), *Talking Gender and Sexuality*, 49–110. Amsterdam: Benjamins.

Kitzinger, Celia. 2005. "Heteronormativity in Action: Reproducing the Heterosexual Nuclear Family in After-Hours Medical Calls." *Social Problems*, 52: 477–498.

Kulick, Don. 2003. "No." *Language and Communication*, 23(2): 139–151.

Lah, Kyung. 2009. "Tokyo Man Marries Video Game Character." *CNN*, December 17. At http://edition.cnn.com/2009/WORLD /asiapcf/12/16/japan.virtual.wedding /index.html?_s=PM:WORLD, accessed October 23, 2013.

Lakoff, Robin. 1973. *Language and Woman's Place*. New York: Harper & Row.

Langton, Rae, and Jennifer Hornsby. 1998. "Free Speech and Illocution." *Journal of Legal Theory*, 4: 21–37.

Liang, A. C. 1999. "Conversationally Implicating Lesbian and Gay Identity." In Mary Bucholtz, A. C. Liang, and Laurel A. Sutton (eds.), *Reinventing Identities: The Gendered Self in Discourse*, 293–310. New York: Oxford University Press.

Macaulay, Monica, and Colleen Brice. 1997. "Don't Touch My Projectile: Gender Bias and Stereotyping in Syntactic Examples." *Language*, 73: 798–825.

McConnell-Ginet, Sally. 2006. "Why Defining is Seldom 'Just Semantics': Marriage, 'Marriage,' and Other Minefields." In Betty Birner and Gregory Ward (eds.), *Drawing the Boundaries of Meaning: Neo-Gricean Studies in Pragmatics and Semantics in Honor of Laurence R. Horn*, 223–246. Amsterdam: Benjamins. Repr. in abridged form in Deborah Cameron and Don Kulick (eds.), *The Language and Sexuality Reader*, 227–240. London: Routledge.

McConnell-Ginet, Sally. 2008. "Words in the World: How and Why Meanings Can Matter." *Language*, 84(3): 497–527.

McConnell-Ginet, Sally. 2011 [2002]. " 'Queering' Semantics: Definitional Struggles." In Kathryn Campbell-Kibler, Robert Podesva, Sarah Roberts, and Andrew Wong (eds.), *Language and Sexuality: Contesting Meaning in Theory and Practice*, 137–160. Stanford: CSLI Publications. Repr. in *Gender, Sexuality, and Meaning: Linguistic Practice and Politics*, 237–259. New York: Oxford University Press.

McConnell-Ginet, Sally. 2012a. "Linguistics and Gender Studies." In Ruth Kempson, Tim Fernando, and Nicholas Asher (eds.), *Handbook of the Philosophy of Linguistics*, 503–530. Amsterdam: Elsevier.

McConnell-Ginet, Sally. 2012b. "Language, Gender, and Sexuality." In Gillian Russell and Delia Graff Fara (eds.), *The Routledge Companion to Philosophy of Language*, 741–752. London: Routledge.

McLaren, Anne E. 2007. "Online Intimacy in a Chinese Setting." *Asian Studies Review*, 31: 409–422.

Partee, Barbara Hall. 1975. "Montague Grammar and Transformational Grammar." *Linguistic Inquiry*, 6(2): 203–300.

Sanders, Stephanie A., and June M. Reinisch. 1999. "Would You Say You 'Had Sex' If … ?" *Journal of the American Medical Association*, 281: 275–277.

Tannen, Deborah. 1990. *You Just Don't Understand: Women and Men in Conversation.* New York: William Morrow.

Terkel, Amanda. 2011. "FBI Takes Major Step toward Updating Narrow Definition of Rape." *Huffington Post*, December 6. At http://www.huffingtonpost.com/2011 /12/06/fbi-definition-of-rape_n_1132913 .html, accessed October 23, 2013.

Wu, Weihua, Steve Fore, Xiying Wang, and Petula Sik Ying Ho. 2007. "Beyond Virtual Carnival and Masquerade: In-Game Marriage on the Chinese Internet." *Game and Culture*, 2: 59–79.

17 A Marked Man
The Contexts of Gender and Ethnicity

1. Introduction

As many chapters in this volume illustrate, the field of language and gender
has expanded significantly in recent years to consider the relevance of ethnicity,
masculinity, the debated place of sexual identity, and to a lesser extent class, the
construction of spoken and signed gendered identities (Bucholtz and Hall 2004;
Bucholtz, Liang, and Sutton 1999; Cameron and Kulick 2003; Livia and Hall 1997).
In studies from the not so distant past, the ethnic background of research participants was without question assumed because it was "unmarked" – White – and
conclusions about gender and language based on research participants from
this single ethnic background were often generalized to reflect on women and
men as a whole. Because of groundbreaking work critiquing the lack of ethnic
voices in relation to matrix languages and dialects and a growing body of work in
languages outside the Euro-American context, this situation has begun to change.

Nevertheless, if one glances at the titles of work in gender and language, it is
still common for studies considering ethnicity and gender to prominently feature
the nonmatrix language name or a non-White ethnic label in their title ("Good
Guys and 'Bad' Girls: Identity Construction by Latina and Latino Student Writers";
"No Woman No Cry: Claiming African American Women's Place"). Ethnicity is
foregrounded most often when it is non-White. Imagine changing some titles that
just specify "women" to what they truly consider – White women, such as "White
Women's Identities at Work." The field of gender and language still treats ethnicity
as "marked" through the construction of oppositional pairs that oppose non-White
to White, dialect to standard, non-English gendered constructs to English, and
nonmatrix language speakers to matrix within a society. Thus, we might suppose
that any contribution on gender and ethnicity will discuss research on each of the
marked members of these oppositions and how they have added to a more highly
diversified field of data, much as research in gender variation has taken us beyond
essentialist definitions of "male" and "female."

The Handbook of Language, Gender, and Sexuality, Second Edition.
Edited by Susan Ehrlich, Miriam Meyerhoff, and Janet Holmes.
© 2014 John Wiley & Sons, Inc. Published 2017 by John Wiley & Sons, Inc.

However, these two aspects of language and gender research have not developed apace. Researchers have for some time complicated the notion of binary gender by pointing out the interactional and contextually constructed nature (see Bergvall, Bing, and Freed 1996; Eckert and McConnell-Ginet 1992), interconnectedness, and ideological associations of sexual preference and identity (Livia and Hall 1997), and its indexical rather than isomorphic nature (Ochs 1992). Except for some recent exceptions, there has not been pervasive engagement with redefining linguistic ethnicity in the field of language and gender. This may partly be because there is still a great deal to do to make the field of language and gender more attentive to issues of ethnicity and to the diverse gendered voices before the constructional nature of ethnicity can be dealt with in detail. Important past contributions to gender and ethnicity research have examined how gender is constructed intra-ethnically and interactionally within an ingroup (Morgan 1999). A focus on interactional sequences in single-sex or cross-sex interactions has emphasized both the strategies for gendering that are available and interactive differences between men and women (Goodwin 1999; Goodwin & Kyratzis, Chapter 26 in this volume). Yet in such ethnic studies, there is some risk in assuming the gender (or ethnic) identity of participants as obvious or given as we look to their interactional strategies and available cultural ideology in constructing such identities (Kulick 2000; Chapter 3 in this volume; Urciuoli 1995). The available data on gender, language, and ethnicity has moved at a slower rate than our attempts to theorize it. In practice, the mutually constructive properties of gendered/ethnic identity are complex and difficult to balance within any one study, especially when constrained by markedness relations with society's matrix language. As a focus, this chapter balances the importance of studies that demonstrate the role of ethnicity in the construction of linguistically gendered identities with those that emphasize the ways ethnicity itself becomes gendered in both practice and ideology.

Much gender and ethnicity research has addressed past stereotyping and attempted to create a more complete picture of ethnically gendered language in groups that have been neglected in mainstream research. The first section of this chapter considers how such work has changed the field of our inquiry. Without the continuation of these efforts, gender and language research will continue with a rather skewed focus, where the unmarked focus will be women who just happen to be Anglo and middle class. Insofar as sociolinguistic research is in constant danger of losing the complexity of either gender or ethnicity when demonstrating the relevance of one to a specific interactional context, the second focus of this chapter examines recent work that addresses two central questions: (1) how gender and ethnicity mutually construct each other in negotiated discourse, and (2) how some features of gender or ethnicity become iconic – ideologically easily recognizable and interpretable community features that are then taken as natural. Finally, a central theme of this chapter is that even when gender and language research does not address ethnicity (i.e., it is assumed), the ethnicity of both the researched and the researcher should become highly marked in every reader's uptake. In fact, it is quite likely already salient in the interpretation of those readers whose ethnicity is often deemed worthy of comment in the academy. Thus, the conclusion of this chapter is a proposal, re-emphasizing the gender and language researcher's responsibilities toward changing the field of research rather than merely plowing in new directions.

Rather than assuming that our work theorizes and describes the lamentable nature of inequality, we as researchers both effect and reflect that nature, and therefore have obligations to advocate for and empower others in our work. To the extent that gender and ethnicity research reflects and promulgates dominant social norms, activist researchers could, without inordinate self-indulgence, continue to direct such reflections productively.

2. Revealing Ethnic Gender

The evolution of the field of language and gender has a great deal in common with language, gender, and ethnicity in that critical approaches in both have responded to the refusal to "see" the complexity or sometimes even the presence of the other. Cameron (1985), for instance, critiques the variationist work of Labov and Trudgill for predefining their core social and socioeconomic world through the male gaze. In defining the social world in terms of sex, rather than in terms of interaction, community contact, and gendered social action, nuanced behaviors that were outside of the centrally defined prototype were lost. In a similar vein, Foster (1995) and Morgan (1999) call for a renewal in the field of African American Vernacular English (AAVE) that recognizes the voices and interactions of women as central, and the work of African American women scholars in this field as valid. Morgan proposes that sociolinguistic work that types competitive genres in AAVE such as "playing the dozens" as particular to juvenile, male, culture obscures the gender complexity of the field by ignoring women's voices and genres (Labov 1972). Also excluded were other "deviant" genders such as boys who were considered "lame" because of their sexual preference or nonstereotypical behaviors. Morgan instead highlights examples of men and women's "reading," an extended public performance denouncing the actions and attitudes of the addressee. Because both the dozens and reading challenge the ability of the addressee to save face and be publicly cool, the inclusion of reading provides a more explanatory and socially grounded account. Along with Goodwin's (1990; 1999) analysis of AAVE-speaking girls' and boys' games and *he-said-she-said* interactions in Philadelphia, these analyses stress the importance of maintaining public face, confronting what others may have said behind one's back, and preserving public cool. Without the additions of the interactional resources and how these are taken up by women, or with an analysis of these genres as only competitive boy talk, the complex connections between these genres and historical oppression of African Americans, as well as construction of community values, would be lost.

Likewise, Galindo and Gonzales (1999, 4) demonstrate that there has been no far-reaching insider account of Chicana language, and though outsider accounts are important, they cannot recount the experience of women who live with both ethnic and gendered border crossings. Women in ethnic communities are often the mediators between traditional culture and language, preserving older forms, and the matrix language culture. Gonzales (1999) describes such women in New Mexico who cross between the local community and the larger Chicano- and English-speaking community as cultural and linguistic innovators. They maintain their Spanish through strong local networks, but switch codes to accommodate. The role of ethnic women as "cultural brokers" is often related to their economic role in the community. For instance, Hill (1987) argues that older Mexicano-speaking women were not as likely to speak Spanish but to maintain their Mexicano, and this correlates with their employment. Where men were more likely to leave and work in a Spanish-speaking urban center, women's cottage industry production affected their language choices. Even though women's ways of speaking were often devalued by the community at large, they were also envied by young men who had shifted to Spanish. Conversely, young Gullah women from the Sea Islands of the eastern US coast were more likely to speak a dialect nearer to Standard English because of their service work in the mainland industry (Nichols 1983). Finally, Medicine (1987) argues that Lakhota-speaking women maintain the language through their role as socializers of children, but are cultural brokers because of their bilingual skills (see also Goldstein 1995). (See Meek, Chapter 28 in this volume, for a consideration of gender in relation to language revitalization efforts.)

Women's borderland linguistic fluency does not only apply to language mediation; it also concerns gender borders. Much of the work on Latinas in the gender and language literature has purposefully sought to debunk gender stereotypes of Latinas as submissive followers (Orellana 1999). Galindo (1999), in particular, argues that Chicanas are often stereotyped from within their culture and by outsiders who regard Chicanas as pure, chaste, and conservative speakers. Slang vocabularies such as *pachuco* or *caló* in this tradition are associated with big-city male gang members, the lower classes, or prison inmates. Galindo offers examples of Texas women who choose to use such "rough" vocabulary and pronunciation to defy gender stereotypes and traditional gender expectations for Chicanas. Likewise, Zentella (1998, 641) examines an ideology constructing a distinction between "the Spanish/poor/non-White female identity … subordinate to an English/rich/White male identity," and the conflict between this ideology and the Madonna ideology which equates Spanish with country and motherhood. To the extent that Puertorriqueñas are responsible for passing on their *mother* language, while insuring their own advancement and their children's success in English-speaking schools in America, they are in a double bind. Zentella maintains that they are switching to English at phenomenal rates. Finally, Bucholtz (2004) demonstrates that in constructing diverse Asian American English linguistic styles, two Laotian teenagers draw off of dominant White and African American Vernacular English stereotypes to style and align themselves differently within the culture of one high school.

Such work demonstrates the need for more studies that explore the linguistic behavior and choices of ethnic women, especially in how they view their linguistic choices as constructing a powerful, gendered, ethnic voice for themselves despite expectations from the matrix culture and gender expectations within their own community. Inasmuch as heritage language and ideologies equating heritage language with ethnic membership are connected to women's available linguistic choices, studies which demonstrate women's place in the maintenance, evolution, or abandonment of heritage language, and how this gendered expectation comes into being, are vital to understanding how a linguistic gendered ethnicity is constructed within a "predefined" community.

3. Conflicting Styles

Although such representations allude to the multiple pressures of borderland gender, they do so primarily at the level of an overarching community ideology, simultaneously demonstrating that the ideologies of gender and ethnicity and the accompanying interactional behavior are not straightforward or necessarily standardized within such a "community." Drawing more heavily on the methodologies of conversation analysis and ethnography, Goodwin (1999; Goodwin and Kyratzis, Chapter 26 in this volume) consequently sees identities and, in particular, moral development as continually emerging from interactional contexts such as complex games rather than as static, predefined positions from which language emerges. Although the girls in her studies are both "markedly" gendered and ethnic – primarily Mexican and Central American children in Los Angeles, who speak Spanish, her work primarily demonstrates how different aspects of identity emerge in situations of play and conflict. Ethnicities and genders are consequently performative acts brought into being within particular contexts, rather than contained in traditional binaries of male/not male and White/non-White. In such a complex field of performance, it is not simple to pinpoint exactly how gender and ethnicity are mutually constructed or even that a particular linguistic behavior is necessarily "ethnic." The values of particular linguistic behaviors are multiple: in performance and uptake, they transform throughout an interchange. Goodwin consequently (1999, 402) notes: "Much more work is required to sort out the effects of ethnicity, age, and social class on norms of speaking." Nevertheless, by paying close attention to performative data, the linguistic detail of how "community" membership is regulated emerges in the face of different personal styles.

Mendoza-Denton (1999; 2008) provides further nuances to our understanding of Latina intragroup ethnicity. It is complicated by both class and urban versus rural associations, and the fact that linguistic actions contain multiple meanings. In high school girl intragroup conversations about class and ethnic affiliations, the stances that participants take do not always involve neat correlations of discourse markers with conversational effect; the same discourse marker may show oppositional co-construction or a collaborative denial. By utilizing conversations in which the teenagers argue about and explore their allegiance to different identities, Mendoza-Denton (1999) is able to compare the girls' stances concerning their own ethnic affiliations, while exploring the concomitant linguistic behaviors that serve to include or exclude.

That participants within any given community of practice will not always have similar styles, especially as they cross back and forth between borders displaying multiple allegiances, is central to the study of how ethnicity and gender are mutually constructed. As people use different voices to perform multiple identities, they may both invoke and challenge the prototypical categories associated with those identities. Hall (1995) and Barrett (1999) investigate such switching between voices as people utilize their performance for linguistic and material capital. The sex workers in Hall (1995) invent and "call on" the voices of ethnic (White Southern, Latino/a, African American) gender stereotypes, often catering to their clients' desires. African American Texas drag queens engage in abrupt shifts into and out of White women's "speech" (Barrett 1999); this is middle class, and "refined," exhibiting many of the stereotypic vocabulary and pronunciation characteristics of "women's speech," such as empty adjectives like "adorable" or "marvelous," hypercorrect pronunciation, and "dynamic" intonation. In crossing such borders, the drag queens inadvertently make the connections between stereotypic gender and ethnicity more explicit. To be really "woman-like," the drag queens invoke a voice that is "White." As people create different identities in such overt performances, the question remains whether the voices that such performers use are their "real" identities – those which form a stable sense of self. Of course, such a question could be asked for any performance – if participants are bringing different voices to bear, then to what extent does the performance necessarily construct gender and ethnic identity? If identity is interactionally constructed, for instance in children's games (Goodwin and Kyratzis, Chapter 26 in this volume) or in the workplace, then the validity of heritage ethnic categorizations such as African American, Latino/a, White, Punjabi, is questionable.

This latter question has been addressed in some detail by Walters (1996) as well as Anzaldúa (1991, 250), who defend identity categories against a perceived onslaught of performative umbrella analyses of identity. In effect, they argue that the practice of focusing on "performance" or interactional construction of identity prematurely effaces social categorization and a politically motivated conception of community. With the erasure of ethnicity, the non-White voice is assimilated into White, and the lesbian female voice is subsumed into a queer, unmarked, therefore male, perspective. The very social categorization that enables discrimination may ultimately be the political rallying point for the formation of a community of practice to resist historically rooted dominance. To the extent that performative analyses deal with individuals' use of multiple voices, gender and ethnicity researchers are in a double bind. The work summarized above both emphasizes the need to address a lack of ethnic (i.e., non-White) women's voices in gender and language research, and also seeks to reveal the complexity of voices within an established category. Researchers who have focused on the interactional construction of identity also feel obligated to address the lack of diversity in the gender and language tradition by categorizing participants first by gender and ethnic background. Work that addresses a lack of women's or ethnic voices in the gender and language literature assumes a priori both the gendered and ethnic identity of its subject by asking the question, "How do women and girls who identify as X speak or sign?" And if identity is not defined a priori through a common social construct such as Chicana, African American, Jew, or White, it may be through a particular kind of linguistic performance: those who speak Spanish, those who signify, and so on. This kind of definition is tautological: linguists simultaneously try to define the practices of a linguistic community while maintaining that the community as an entity is defined by its practice (Kulick 2000; Chapter 3 in this volume; Trechter 2000; Urciuoli 1995).

An approach which focuses on the emergent identity of participant(s) in a community of practice need not be in conflict with one that recognizes historically enforced social categories as sites of resistance and identity formation, nor should we be forced to abandon any study of linguistic communities or the social aspects of semiosis because participants in interactions draw on multiple voices. The relationship between gender and ethnicity *should* emphasize different definitions of linguistic communities as they come into prominence, especially considering the specific political goals of the researched and researcher. Recognizing that ethnic, community, and gender identities are fluid social constructs in practice, which index and draw on semiotic resources while simultaneously creatively constructing new resources through contextual interaction, is difficult to capture. Yet both historically grounded and performative meanings of community as well as linguistic judgments about such constructions explain why gender and ethnicity are neither static nor singular. Different definitions of "community" (identity-based, interaction-based, community-based) are also highlighted as they emerge from interaction.

4. Use and Construction of Models

Given an available repertoire and some notion of what choices of expression are associated with a particular projection of identity in a given context, a speaker can project multiple gender and ethnic affiliations. Myers-Scotton (1998) proposes a markedness model in which participants in speech events perform as rational actors who have in mind specific sets of rights and obligations (RO), providing a heuristic for how participants might choose possible moves within an interaction. For a specific interaction type, a speaker would often be aware of the language, dialect, or genre that indexes an unmarked RO set. Speakers usually choose an unmarked move, but may sometimes opt to build a new interactional norm by choosing a marked feature. For instance, the African American drag queen performances may shift from indexing stereotypic White woman speech to that of an African American man for shock humor in a performance as a marked shift (Barrett 1998).

Rampton (1991; 1995) examines how switches between unmarked norms for speech events operate in interethnic language crossing among urban youth. He focuses primarily on the ideology behind the unmarked uses of SAE (Stylized

Asian English) – used to disrespect; Caribbean Creole – used to demonstrate urban vitality and dissent; and Punjabi – associated with local networks. In particular, agonistic Punjabi words were especially prevalent in interethnic interactions among younger boys and were highly associated with the activity of tag games. Punjabi was thus an unmarked choice for agonistic boys' play. As the boys grew older, however, Punjabi use decreased in interethnic interactions, and White girls were not often recorded using Punjabi words unless they were discussing *bhangra* (a popular music extending beyond the local interaction networks) or had Punjabi boyfriends. Such crossing between urban ethnic linguistic varieties dissociates one variety from a natural marker of ethnicity so that ethnicity is interactionally negotiated.

Research that traces interethnic crossing demonstrates more than how speakers make choices about which variety to use for an appropriate context. It demonstrates the performative change or historical development of an ethnic variety as a preferential gender variety for the playful expression of conflict or teasing, as well as its association with age-related and historically sedimented genres. The political and social resistance associated with Caribbean Creole or African American dialects, Rampton theorizes, springs from political and social resistance movements of the 1960s and therefore is more likely to be adapted to function in the cool urban youth culture as a less local language of dissent. Thus, for gender or ethnic "crossing" to be possible, interactional participants draw on, as well as create, gendered and ethnic interactional norms. Gender crossing is consequently sometimes ethnic, as in White women's speech being the most "female," and ethnic crossing is often gendered, as researchers associate it primarily, though not always, with male behaviors (Bucholtz 1999; Chun 2001; Kiesling 2001).

Because the interaction obviously draws on and creates new historical linguistic norms, how such notions become naturalized or denaturalized (e.g., Rampton's new ethnicities) becomes of primary importance, especially if our desire is to disrupt and resist such processes. Obviously, research calling attention to the socially constructive nature of ethnicity and gender is not new to the social sciences. However, Irvine and Gal (2000) theorize how *linguistic* differentiation gets constructed as a typical semiotic process in culture. They identify three semiotic processes through which people create ideologies of *linguistic* difference: *iconization, fractal recursivity*, and *erasure*. *Iconization* is a process by which linguistic features that normally index stances, genres, or dialect become so strongly associated with a social group that they are thought to be inherent or essential characteristics of that group. Even group members who do not frequently use such linguistic features become associated with them by default. Through *fractal recursivity*, the linguistic relationship between form and social meaning that is salient in one context is projected into new areas or levels of discourse as speakers draw on salient resources to create shifting "identities" or communities. In other words, form(s) including pronunciation, word choice, phrases, dialect, or even a particular language associated iconically with one group may be utilized by both in- and out-group members, sometimes projecting new meanings. Such projection can have the effect of further stabilizing the iconic connection between linguistic form and social group identity through repetition and expansion of the form into multiple contexts, despite some potential of destabilizing the original iconic form.[1] Finally, the ideological process of *erasure* effectually removes some groups and social behaviors from vision and sight. They become subsumed under the totalizing and dominant ideology. In effect, they become *unmarked* (see Bucholtz and Hall 2004 and Trechter and Bucholtz 2001 for theoretical development regarding performative identity). Erasure may be perpetuated on a number of different levels both within the interactional norms of a community and as that community is viewed by outsiders. Together such ideological processes serve to equate social identity with linguistic form.

Multiple-level erasure often occurs in accounting for gender in several Native American languages. Lakhota, a Siouan language, spoken by about 11,000 people in the northern Middle West of the United States, for instance, is described by linguists and native speakers as possessing a set of sentence-final particles that indicate illocutionary force and gender of the speaker. Native speakers typically cite one or two iconic forms: men say *lo* and women say *le*; men say *yo*, and women say *ye*. It is difficult to tell how much native speakers have been influenced by academic researchers in creating such a neat complementary distribution. Researches have taken this iconization and the erasure of women's voices to new levels (see Trechter 2000 for a detailed discussion). Table 17.1 is an amalgam of Rood and Taylor (1997) and native speaker representations of their language from my own fieldwork.[2]

By examining a variety of Lakhota speech acts, genres, and conversations, I have found that, of course, this neat table of "separate but equal" behavior for men and women breaks down. This is partly because discourse genres/styles of speaking were gendered, some of the same particles are used more often than others, and some forms are dying out (Trechter 2000). Women tend to use *kʃto* more often, and men use *wã* more often than women. However, there are three forms that are used almost exclusively by men (*lo*, *yo*, and *hũwo*) and two that are used exclusively by women (*na*, *mã*). By "exclusive" use here, I mean that such forms give a clearly gendered flavor to one's voice. Thus, men using the exclusively women's particles are considered to be acting in a womanly manner or maternally, and women

Table 17.1. Lakhota clitics, by gender and speech act

Illocutionary/affective force	Man	Woman
Formal question	hũwo	hũwe (obsolete)
Imperative	yo	ye$_a$
Opinion/emphasis	lo	le (archaic), ye$_a$
Emphatic statement		kʃto
Entreaty	ye$_e$	na
Surprise/opinion	wã	mã

who use the men's particles are "tomboys." The particles *lo* and *yo* have in fact become highly salient to speakers, and it is only in contradistinction to these that the "women's" forms are defined as appropriate to women's use at all. It is considered "natural" or an essential quality for men to use *lo* and *yo*, and though some speakers acknowledge that some boys in situations of limited linguistic access have difficulty nowadays acquiring the male forms, others have told me that boys do this naturally without correction. In this sense, certain of the gender deictics in Lakhota that point to the gender of the speaker have gone beyond indexical relationships and become *iconic*.

Iconization of these forms, as Irvine and Gal (2000) assert, seems to have come from their repeated association with certain speech events. As these markers became an increasingly salient part of such events, speakers were considered to "naturally" speak this way. In fact, in a vast collection of multigenred text collected by Native speaker and linguist Ella Deloria in the 1920s and 1930s and in the conversational data of my own fieldwork, *lo* "m. assertion" as a gender and assertion particle is considerably higher in frequency than any other gender particle. It occurred thousands of times. Its supposed female counterpart, *le* "f. assertion," was very rare, and it is now obsolescent, and *kʃto* "emphatic," often associated with women and especially the genre of gossip, was used only 40 times. The largest concentration of men using male assertion particles is found in the conversations of men speaking publicly.

In a speech transcribed by Ella Deloria in the 1930s (example 1), a group of male acquaintances are jokingly and agonistically talking about political speeches. There are nine uses of *lo* in a text that is only 11 lines long. I reproduce the text in full because it illustrates the good humor but polite distancing evoked with the use of *lo*, its association with public speaking and its assertion of opinion in public. Men here end their turn with an assertion particle after they make their point. The interactions between B and C (an insistent and slightly critical participant) contain more masculine assertions as the two men negotiate the proper length of a good political speech and whether the role of the old guard has changed. Potentially, every sentence could end with *lo*, but there is an especial increase of use in line 9 as the younger man (speaker B) reflects personally and gives his opinion on broader issues. When speaker C authoritatively continues this reflection, combining personal and public matters, he also ends his opinions with *lo*.[3]

1   Comments around the inauguration

1 A: hūhū hi! Tʰakoʒa, ʃicaya ukoyakix'āpe **ló!!**
2 B: Tókʰel hé?
3 A: óx, le pcelyéla ūkóyakaksãu kī he wakʰé kī. Tuwá wóyute wãʒí otʰá cʰāke cʰa cʰiʃká ogná iyáta iyéyī nã yawáʃteʃte yatʰī nã iyókʰpiyexcī napcī nã akʰé ocápa yūkʰã cʰūʃká-inūpa kī akhé wóyute-waʃte ū hé etãhã ogná él aúpi nã kákʰel ihá icáxtake kī hécʰegna kícigluzãu kī iyécʰel ūkókyakix'āpe **ló!**
4 B: Hã, éyaʃ tʰūkaʃila, cʰī waná líla tʰéhã-yākʰapi cʰãké hécʰamū?. Tʰiyókʰatī nã oyāk-ʃice éyaʃ líla wótlakau kī ótapi ecʰíyatãhã oʃílya?. Niyéʃ wanáx'ū yāke kī tʰawát'elcʰicʰiyapiʃni nã hécʰamū we **ló!**

5 A: Hũhí, niʃnálaʃ onáx'ũ-awaʃtecʰilake ũ. ímnayexcī iyáyīkte séce ũ!

6 B: Wã, tʰūkaʃila, tkʰáʃ henála slolwáya cʰa epʰé séca **wã!**

7 A: ox, tuwá akʰákʃá!

8 C: Kʰola, kahãskeyala s'e iyáyeʃni, ehãni. Takúku mahétuya ilúkcã nã yuhá ináyaʔ3ĩ-iteke ʃã owehãhãpi ecé ecʰánu nã ílotake **ló.**

9 B: Hã, Wã, itéʃniyã oíyokʃice?. Táku éyaʃ iyúha oíhãke yukʰã keyápi k'ũ wicákʰape **ló.** Lé ãpét ukī Lakʰóta wicʰaxca wakícʰũza-ũpi k'ũ wicʰákicigluzapi nã kʰoʃkálaka wicʰák'upi yũkʰ ãkítãla s'e iyõmayake **ló.** Heũ ehãʃ áwicakʰeya-iwayīkte kī omáyatʰake **ló.**

10 C: Tó, eyá cʰĩ hécʰetu?. Waná Lakʰólwichoxʼã-tʰanila k'ũ hécʰeyá-ina3ĩ s'elél. éyaʃ hãkéyela ecʰél ehé **ló,** tʰako3a, hé wicʰákicigluzapi ehé k'u hé hécʰetuʃni?. Iyecʰpka xeyáp iná3īpe **ló.**

11 B: Hã, hãk'u. icʰe?

1 A: Well, of all things! Grandson, that was no way to treat us **m**!

2 B: What do you mean by that?

3 A: What you did to us was exactly like what happens to a man who has taken a spoonful of the best tasting food, and chewed it with ecstasy, and then swallowed it most agreeably, and again opened his mouth for more; but this time, the second spoonful of the same fine food is brought to his lips, and the instant it touches his lips, it is immediately withdrawn, leaving him wanting more **m**.

4 B: Yes, perhaps, grandfather, but you know the audience had already been sitting there quite a while. The room was warm, and the seats uncomfortable, but there were so many speakers which made it bad. It was only out of consideration for you listeners that I did as I did **m**.

5 A: Oh, and you are the only one I really like to hear, too. I thought you would talk so satisfyingly!

6 B: But grandfather, there's just a chance that that was all I knew to say **m.surprise**!

7 A: Impossible!

8 C: My friend, why didn't you speak a little longer? It was obvious you had various worthwhile ideas which you had thought up and kept in mind, but all you did was "wise-crack" and then you sat down **m**.

9 B: Yes, I guess so; but really, don't you know, it was a sorrowful occasion. They are right who say that everything must end sometime **m**. On this day, the leadership of the Dakota has been taken away from the old men and given over to the young, and it affected my spirit, the very least bit **m**. On that account, I couldn't talk really seriously. It stuck in my throat **m**.

10 C: Of course, well, you are right. It seems that the old Dakota ways are really and truly at an end. But grandchild, you got only part of it right **m**. To say the leadership was wrested from the old men is not to put it accurately. Of their own accord, the old men have stepped aside **m**.

11 B: Yes, really; isn't it so?

(Deloria 1937?, 212–220)

Authoritative male opinions often contain the use of *lo* in other contexts, but I argue that the frequency of *lo* in public speaking makes this particular genre a prototype for its use. Women who must make speeches and offer public opinions tell me they use *lo*, but that this in no way should create the impression they are gay. They know the iconic use means they would be expected to act like men (have desire for women), but they are merely using the particle in its authoritative context (Trechter 1999).

Fractal recursivity occurs when this gender indicator is used in other contexts. Even though *lo* suggests an authoritative stance, when males are not acting authoritatively they may feel obligated to use it. Deloria (*c*.1937, 306) notes such an instance as a man (example 2) speaks to her of his experiences in *Wokiksikuye K'eya* ("Some Memories").

> When the ending *lo* is used simply as a closing to a statement by a man who isn't trying to be authoritative, he sometimes "swallows" it instead of accenting it for emphasis. This informant does so constantly, except where he is quoting.

Unlike the speakers in example 1, this particular man was relating stories about himself where he was truly frightened but kept his calm, or where he appeared weak or silly to himself and others, but ultimately proved his strength of character. In the introduction and conclusion to his story, his use of *lo* reflects a narrative frame of a differently authoritative self as it is "swallowed."

2   Introduction to "Some Memories"

Oglálata tʰoká wahí k'ūhā wóixa wãʒígʒi awákʰipʰa k'éyaʃ iyúhaxcī wóixaʃni. Woyuʃ'iyaye nakū slolwáye **lo**. Yūkʰā wãʒi lecʰetū.

"When I first came among the Oglala, laughable experiences were mine but not everything was funny. I also knew fear **m**. And one such time was as follows."

(Deloria *c*.1937, 306)

3   Conclusion to "Some Memories"

maya-apʰaʒeʒe ekawīgapi kī lecʰel wicʰūt'etaha wakpapte **lo**.

"I had just come through, escaping death just as one might turn about just at the very rim of a cliff **m**."

(Deloria *c*.1937, 309)

This man's constrained use of *lo* in his introduction and the conclusion illustrates that he is under some pressure to display masculinity. Not all men do this. Because men are now constrained to use *lo* in a variety of discourse contexts, even when not speaking authoritatively or publicly, iconization and recursion for this form is rampant. Although the original meanings of authority and public opinion are still apparent through a thorough examination of discourse contexts, it has become an indicator of maleness rather than only one of stance, affect, or discourse context.

Erasure in the context of gendered discourse particles in Lakhota is now obvious. *Le*, the phonologically similar and iconically female assertive counterpart of *lo*, has become obsolescent. *Le* as a form was associated both with opinion and also with maternal caregiving. Although I have heard males use the form in a childcare context, it has not been refracted in numerous contexts. The form *kʃto* "emphatic" which is currently becoming the iconic counterpart of *lo* (see Rood and Taylor 1997) also does not seem to be a good candidate for broad recursive spread because it is usually associated with the genre of gossip. It is perhaps the negative associations of some forms that marks them for a type of erasure even in cultures where balance between men's and women's cultural activities and semiotic resources is highly emphasized ("men say X; women say Y").

5. Conclusion

A model of linguistic and semiotic differentiation is important to the treatment of language, gender, and ethnicity for three reasons: (1) it demonstrates how iconization can establish categories of ethnic and gendered linguistic forms, (2)how and why gender and ethnicity are often mutual constructions as people draw on multiple voices for self and other representation; and (3) why certain populations, behaviors, genders, and ethnicities are effaced. The academic study of language and gender is also a type of cultural community. As a community of practice, we are potentially susceptible to the same constructive ideological processes we examine: iconization, recursivity, and erasure. Interestingly, the process of erasure has permeated not just the folk conceptualizations of language, gender, and ethnicity, but in reviewing this chapter, it is apparent that such erasure continues to be present in gender and ethnicity research. Recognizing previous erasure among academics of ethnic women's voices and styles – even those which are iconic within ethnic communities, Morgan, Galindo and Gonzales, and others make them more audible. Focusing on interaction, Goodwin and Mendoza-Denton draw our attention to hitherto unobserved competitiveness and stylistic differences in intragroup interactions among girls of different ethnicities, whereas Anzaldúa notes the possible erasure of ethnicity through over emphasis on performative theory. Though much research attends to the iconization of ethnic and gender language and subsequent recursivity through double-voiced uses, there is still some danger of promulgating the practice of erasure. For example, in the border crossings among urban and White youth with the consequent creation of "new ethnicities" (Rampton 1995) or the appropriation of ethnic language in fraternities (Kiesling 2001), Morgan's critique of Labov's (1972) work on ethnic vernacular springs to mind. With the exception of Bucholtz (2004), appropriation of ethnic varieties is constructed as a male practice. By unconsciously focusing attention on boys and young men's appropriations, through repetition, the presence and practice of women is in danger of erasure.

Language and gender researchers have sought to examine the connections between interactional work and the formation of ideology about gender and ethnicity while working to include greater diversity of gender and ethnic voices. Yet the complex semiotic processes associated with erasure cannot be addressed by only emphasizing alternative practices and voices that hitherto have been ignored. Early on Black and Coward (1990 [1981]) encouraged turning the tables. Rather than focusing on "women's language" to counteract men's historical hegemony, they encouraged men's recognition of themselves as also living within gendered subjectivities (see Johnson and Meinhof 1997; Preece 2009). Similar challenges have been put forth by researchers in Whiteness studies (Dyer 1997; Ignatiev and Garvey 1996), arguing that the objective of these is ultimately to eradicate the privileged category through the realization of its hegemonic nature.

Although there are already many studies of White folk in gender and language, very few engage the topic by considering participants' ethnicity or consider *Whiteness* to be part of their linguistic gender construction, leaving it an unmarked norm. A shift toward recognizing or marking White ethnicity in gender and language studies is not only important for complicating our view of ethnicity in the political realm; it is also a responsible research move – for Whiteness is not always the unmarked norm, though that may be how it is approached by our academic community. For instance, Hartigan (1999), Modan (2001), and Trechter (2001) argue that in many locales – Detroit, Washington, DC, Pine Ridge Indian reservation, respectively – "Whiteness" is clearly marked. Hillbillies living in predominantly African American neighborhoods in Detroit, for example, are ethnically marked in their local network because of their Whiteness, and also in the larger American context because of their obviously deviant non-middle-class White ethnicity. Bucholtz (2001, 96) argues that nerd speech, as a hyperstandard White variety, "undermines the racial project of Whiteness as a normative and unmarked construct." In effect, focusing the lens of gender and ethnicity in one direction only leads us to miss how the ideological and interactional processes of linguistic differentiation, erasure, and discrimination operate. Similarly, they do not recognize how Whiteness is discursively appropriated and regimented among non-White communities of practice (see Touré 2011).

Because sociolinguistic variables of gender and ethnicity are not consistently regarded in the same light within a community, "authentic" indicators, though salient, do not always become iconic representations for a community. Moreover, gender and ethnicity are often constructed in terms of each other, enabling erasure along the axis of either. For instance, "authentic" male ethnic language may be quite different from women's, but both are not always treated as equally ethnic by researchers or within a community. Schilling-Estes (1998) notes that speakers of Ocracoke English considered the most authentic ethnic speech (though it is not referenced in racial terms) to be that of White men who have historical connections to maritime occupations and who "play poker." These men had exaggeratedly raised /ay/ and did not actually possess another typical feature of Ocracoke Island speech (fronted /aw/) to the degree of many other speakers, yet they were most often mentioned as "real" examples of the dialect by people on the island. She concludes that women and gay Ocracokan men who use fronted /aw/ and a less exaggerated pronunciation of /ay/ also have a strong sense of Ocracoke (ethnic) identity. *Erasure* takes place along a gendered axis within this community – the speech of the poker players is held up as authentic and the other common pronunciation feature is not recognized. Ethnicity becomes de facto male as it is indexed by a poker-playing maritime community of practice. Another common kind of erasure takes place at the level of language and gender research. As the focus in Schilling-Estes's study is the gendering of language and how community membership is linguistically and ideologically realized through gender, the construction of presumably White ethnicity is largely obscured.

The linguistic study of gender and ethnicity has come a long way since the early 1970s, with more work on a greater diversity of voices and as notions of gender and ethnicity have been rooted in interaction and ideological promulgation. One objective in reflecting on the processes of linguistic differentiation in culture is to destabilize the process and to effectively counteract the hegemonic force of erasure. Increased attention to how such erasure is accomplished at different levels of construction, both folk and in the academy, is now possible. There is still much to be done in providing adequate data from a variety of languages, dialects, and ethnic perspectives.

Acknowledgment

I am grateful to the American Philosophical Society for access to and permission to publish excerpts from Ella Deloria, "Dakota Ethnographic and Conversational Texts," MS 30 (x8a.7), and "Dakota Autobiographies," Boas Collection, MS 30 (x8a.6).

NOTES

1   This "double effect" of recursivity has been one of the recurrent criticisms of drag queen speech – drawing on stereotypic "women's" language, it fails to destabilize the connection between the stereotype and actual women, and in some interpretations it actually reinforces it.
2   Ye_a and ye_e are pronounced the same, but trigger different morphophonemic processes. They are different homophonous morphemes.
3   For reasons of length, I only provide a running translation with gender particles highlighted and translated with "m." (male assertion), "m. surprise," etc. Lakhota transcription is in the International Phonetic Alphabet, with /c/ indicating an alveopalatal affricate.

REFERENCES

Anzaldúa, Gloria. 1991. "To(o) Queer the Writer – Loca, Excritora y Chicana." In Betsy Warland (ed.), *Writings by Dykes, Queers, and Lesbians*, 249–263. Vancouver: Press Gang.

Barrett, Rusty. 1998. "Markedness and Styleswitching in Performances by African American Drag Queens." In Carol Myers-Scotton (ed.), *Codes and Consequences: Choosing Linguistic Varieties*, 139–161. New York: Oxford University Press.

Barrett, Rusty. 1999. "Indexing Polyphonous Identity in the Speech of African American Drag Queens." In Mary Bucholtz, Anita Liang, and Laurel Sutton (eds.), *Reinventing Identities: The Gendered Self in Discourse*, 313–331. New York: Oxford University Press.

Bergvall, Victoria, Janet Bing, and Alice Freed, eds. 1996. *Rethinking Language and Gender Research*. New York: Longman.

Black, Maria, and Rosalind Coward. 1990 [1981]. "Linguistic, Social and Sexual

350   *Ideologies*

Relations: A Review of Dale Spender's *Man Made Language*." Repr. in Deborah Cameron (ed.), *The Feminist Critique of Language, 113–133*. London: Routledge.

Bucholtz, Mary. 1999. "You da Man: Narrating the Racial Other in the Production of White Masculinity." *Journal of Sociolinguistics*, 3: 443–460.

Bucholtz, Mary. 2001. "The Whiteness of Nerds: Superstandard English and Racial Markedness." *Journal of Linguistic Anthropology*, 11: 84–100.

Bucholtz, Mary. 2004. "Styles and Stereotypes: The Linguistic Negotiation of Identity among Laotian American Youth." *Pragmatics*, 14: 127–147.

Bucholtz, Mary, and Kira Hall. 2004. "Language and Identity." In Alessandro Duranti (ed.), *A Companion to Linguistic Anthropology*, 369–394. Oxford: Blackwell.

Bucholtz, Mary, A. C. Liang, and Laurel Sutton, eds. 1999. *Reinventing Identities: The Gendered Self in Discourse*. New York: Oxford University Press.

Cameron, Deborah. 1985. *Feminism and Linguistic Theory*. London: Macmillan.

Cameron, Deborah, and Don Kulick. 2003. *Language and Sexuality*. Cambridge: Cambridge University Press.

Chun, Elaine. 2001. "The Construction of White, Black, and Korean American Identities through African American Vernacular English." *Journal of Linguistic Anthropology*, 11: 52–64.

Deloria, Ella. 1937? "Dakota Ethnographic and Conversational Texts." MS 30 (x8a.7). Philadelphia: American Philosophical Society.

Deloria, Ella. c.1937. "Dakota Autobiographies." Boas Collection, MS 30 (x8a.6). Philadelphia: American Philosophical Society.

Dyer, Richard. 1997. *White*. New York: Routledge.

Eckert, Penelope, and Sally McConnell-Ginet. 1992. "Think Practically and Look Locally: Language and Gender as Community-Based Practice." *Annual Review of Anthropology*, 21: 461–490.

Foster, Michèle. 1995. "Are You With Me? Power and Solidarity in the Discourse of African American Women." In Kira Hall and Mary Bucholtz (eds.), *Gender Articulated: Language and the Socially Constructed Self*, 329–350. New York: Routledge.

Galindo, Letticia. 1999. "Caló and Taboo Language Use among Chicanas: A Description of Linguistic Appropriation and Innovation." In Letticia Galindo and María Gonzales (eds.), *Speaking Chicana: Voice, Power and Identity*, 175–193. Tucson: University of Arizona Press.

Galindo, D. Letticia, and María Gonzales, eds. 1999. *Speaking Chicana: Voice, Power and Identity*. Tucson: University of Arizona Press.

Goldstein, Tara. 1995. " 'Nobody is Talking Bad': Creating Community and Claiming Power on the Production Lines." In Kira Hall and Mary Bucholtz (eds.), *Gender Articulated: Language and the Socially Constructed Self*, 374–400. New York: Routledge.

Gonzales, María. 1999. "Crossing Social and Cultural Borders: The Road to Language Hybridity." In Letticia Galindo and María Gonzales (eds.), *Speaking Chicana: Voice, Power and Identity*, 13–38. Tucson: University of Arizona Press.

Goodwin, Marjorie Harness. 1990. *He-Said-She-Said: Talk as Social Organization among Black Children*. Bloomington: Indiana University Press.

Goodwin, Marjorie Harness. 1999. "Constructing Opposition within Girls' Games." In Mary Bucholtz, Anita C. Liang, and Laurel A. Sutton (eds.), *Reinventing Identities: The Gendered Self in Discourse*, 388–409. New York: Oxford University Press.

Hall, Kira. 1995. "Lip Service on the Fantasy Lines." In Kira Hall and Mary Bucholtz (eds.), *Gender Articulated: Language and the Socially Constructed Self*, 184–216. New York: Routledge.

Hartigan, John. 1999. *Racial Situations: Class Predicaments of Whiteness in Detroit*. Princeton: Princeton University Press.

Hill, Jane. 1987. "Women's Speech in Modern Mexicano." In Susan Philips, Susan Steele, and Christine Tanz (eds.), *Language, Gender,* and *Sex in Comparative Perspective*, 121–160. Cambridge: Cambridge University Press.

Ignatiev, Noel, and John Garvey, eds. 1996. *Race Traitor*. New York: Routledge.

Irvine, Judith, and Susan Gal. 2000. "Language Ideology and Linguistic Differentiation." In Paul Kroskrity (ed.), *Regimes of Language: Ideologies, Polities, and Identities*, 35–84. Santa Fe, NM: School of American Research Press.

Johnson, Sally, and Ulrike Meinhof, eds. 1997. *Language and Masculinity*. Oxford: Blackwell.

Kiesling, Scott. 2001. "Stances of Whiteness and Hegemony in Fraternity Men's Discourse." *Journal of Linguistic Anthropology*, 11: 101–115.

Kulick, Don. 2000. "Gay and Lesbian Language." *Annual Review of Anthropology*, 29: 243–285.

Labov, William. 1972. *Language in the Inner City: Studies in the Black English Vernacular*. Philadelphia: University of Pennsylvania Press.

Livia, Anna, and Kira Hall, eds. 1997. *Queerly Phrased: Language, Gender, and Sexuality*. New York: Oxford University Press.

Medicine, Beatrice. 1987. "The Role of American Indian Women in Cultural Continuity and Transition." In Joyce Penfield (ed.), *Women and Language in Transition*, 159–165. New York: SUNY Press.

Mendoza-Denton, Norma. 1999. "Turn Initial *No*: Collaborative Opposition among Latina Adolescents." In Mary Bucholtz, Anita C. Liang, and Laurel A. Sutton (eds.), *Reinventing Identities: The Gendered Self in Discourse*, 273–292. New York: Oxford University Press.

Mendoza-Denton, Norma. 2008. *Home Girls: Language and Cultural Practice among Latina Youth Gangs*. Oxford: Blackwell.

Modan, Gabriella. 2001. "White, Whole Wheat, Rye: Jews and Ethnic Construction in Washington, D.C." *Journal of Linguistic Anthropology*, 11: 116–130.

Morgan, Marcyliena. 1999. "No Woman No Cry: Claiming African American Women's Place." In Mary Bucholtz, Anita C. Liang, and Laurel A. Sutton (eds.), *Reinventing*

Identities: The Gendered Self in Discourse, 27–45. New York: Oxford University Press.

Myers-Scotton, Carol. 1998. "A Theoretical Introduction to the Markedness Model." In Carol Myers-Scotton (ed.), *Codes and Consequences: Choosing Linguistic Varieties*, 18–39. New York: Oxford University Press.

Nichols, Patricia. 1983. "Linguistic Options and Choices for Black Women in the Rural South." In Barrie Thorne, Cheris Kramarae, and Nancy Henley (eds.), *Language, Gender and Society*, 54–68. Rowley, MA: Newbury House.

Ochs, Elinor. 1992. "Indexing Gender." In Alessandro Duranti and Charles Goodwin (eds.), *Rethinking Context: Language as an Interactive Phenomenon*, 335–358. Cambridge: Cambridge University Press.

Orellana, Marjorie. 1999. "Good Guys and Bad Girls: Identity Construction by Latina and Latino Student Writers." In Mary Bucholtz, A. C. Liang, and Laurel Sutton (eds.), *Reinventing Identities: The Gendered Self in Discourse*, 64–82. New York: Oxford University Press.

Preece, Sian. 2009. "'A Group of Lads, Innit': Performance of Laddish Masculinity in British Higher Education." In Pia Pichler and Eva Eppler (eds.), *Gender and Spoken Interaction*, 115–138. Basingstone: Palgrave Macmillan.

Rampton, Ben. 1991. "Interracial Panjabi in a British Adolescent Peer Group." *Language in Society*, 20: 391–422.

Rampton, Ben. 1995. *Crossing: Language and Identity among Adolescents*. London: Longman.

Rood, David, and Alan Taylor. 1997. "A Lakhota Sketch." In William Sturtevant and Ives Goddard (eds.), *Handbook of North American Indians*, vol. 17, 440–482. Washington, DC: Smithsonian Institution.

Schilling-Estes, Natalie. 1998. "Reshaping Economies, Reshaping Identities: Gender-Based Patterns of Language Variation in Ocracoke English." In Suzanne Wertheim, Ashlee C. Bailey, and Monica Corston-Oliver (eds.), *Engendering Communication: Proceedings of the Fifth Berkeley Women and Language Conference*, 509–520. Berkeley: Berkeley Women and Language Group.

Touré . 2011. *Who's Afraid of Post-Blackness?* New York: Free Press.

Trechter, Sara. 1999. "Contextualizing the Exotic Few: Gender Oppositions in Lakhota." In Mary Bucholtz, Anita C. Liang, and Laurel A. Sutton (eds.), *Reinventing Identities: The Gendered Self in Discourse*, 101–122. New York: Oxford University Press.

Trechter, Sara. 2000. "Review of *Queerly Phrased*." *Language*, 76: 444–446.

Trechter, Sara. 2001. "White between the Lines: Ethnic Positioning in Lakhota Discourse." *Journal of Linguistic Anthropology*, 11: 22–35.

Trechter, Sara, and Mary Bucholtz. 2001. "White Noise: Bringing Language into Whiteness Studies." *Journal of Linguistic Anthropology*, 11: 3–21.

Urciuoli, Bonnie. 1995. "Language and Borders." *Annual Review of Anthropology*, 23: 55–82.

Walters, Suzanna. 1996. "From Here to Queer: Radical Feminism, Postmodernism, and the Lesbian Menace." *Signs*, 21: 831–869.

Zentella, Ana Celia. 1998. "Spanish Madonnas: U.S. Latinas and Language Loyalty." In Suzanne Wertheim, Ashlee Bailey, and Monica Corston-Oliver (eds.), *Engendering Communication: Proceedings from the Fifth Berkeley Women and Language Conference*, 637–652. Berkeley: Berkeley Women and Language Group, University of California.

Part V Global and Cross-Cultural Perspectives

18 Language and Gender Research in Poland
An Overview

AGNIESZKA KIEŁKIEWICZ-JANOWIAK
AND JOANNA PAWELCZYK

1. Historical Background: Gender Roles in Poland

Researchers have observed an ongoing change in sociocultural perceptions of gender in Polish culture. For example, Titkow (2011) analyzed Poles' perception of their own masculinity and femininity in 1998 and 2002, using the Psychological Gender Inventory (adapted for the Polish context by Kuczyńska 1992 from Bem's 1974 Sex Role Inventory). Her results pointed to relative stability of gender types; however, a significant increase of women's educational status correlates with their self-perception as androgynistic. For men as well as women, combining masculine and feminine features seems to increase their social capital (see Bourdieu 1977), making it possible for them to be effective in the public and the private sphere. Women thus aim at winning public careers and men want to gain social skills in order to establish rapport. Both are dedicated to implementing the ethics of care. Titkow pointed out how her data showed a striking similarity between women and men in 2002 in defining cultural femininity and masculinity, thus indicating that the symbolic constructs of femininity and masculinity in the Polish context have remained largely unchanged even as women's and men's orientation to these constructs may have changed.

Gender roles in Poland have been shaped by a number of historical and cultural factors. In the late eighteenth century, Poland was partitioned between its three powerful neighbors (the Russian empire, the kingdom of Prussia, and Habsburg Austria), and it ceased to exist for the next 123 years. The time of partitions (1795–1918) had a significant impact on the social position of Polish women. The loss of Poland's independence made the issue of children's upbringing a political matter and the family, understood to be the domain of women, took on a new

The Handbook of Language, Gender, and Sexuality, Second Edition.
Edited by Susan Ehrlich, Miriam Meyerhoff, and Janet Holmes.
© 2014 John Wiley & Sons, Inc. Published 2017 by John Wiley & Sons, Inc.

significance: it was made responsible for preserving cultural identity, particularly in the context of the partitioning powers' active policies for political and cultural domination (i.e., Russification, Germanization).

Under the strong influence of Roman Catholicism, Polish society glorified the role of the woman. During the time of the partitions, effectively under prolonged occupation, a powerful identity, the "Polish mother"[1] (P. *matka Polka*), emerged: patriotic and caring, dedicated to the national cause and ready to sacrifice her own ambitions for the well-being of her country and to support its men in the fight for independence (Siwik 2011, 25).

Poland's loss of independence resulted in the creation of a newly defined social model of a woman – one that persists to this day – as a person who is able to cope with the most difficult demands imposed by an adverse social reality (Titkow 2007, 52). However, this established a double bind: on the one hand, a Polish woman had to be more self-reliant and independent but, on the other, her own plans, needs, and aspirations had to be set aside. Thus she was a winner and a loser at the same time (Siwik 2011, 25).

This period also significantly circumscribed the women's movement in Poland. From early on, Polish women were on a "patriotic mission" in the family as well as in the public sphere, for instance by supporting the fight for the maintenance of the Polish language at schools. This led to a blurring of private and professional activities (Żarnowska and Szwarc 2008, 25–26). The patriotic mission created female activists who defined themselves as social activists rather than feminist ones. They were always facing the dilemma between the fight for the country's independence and the fight for women's emancipation. It can be observed that patriotic duty tended to win over the struggle for gender equality and consequently contributed to the strengthening of the woman-patriot stereotype (Siwik 2011, 28).

Poland regained independence in 1918 to enjoy it rather briefly until the outbreak of World War II in 1939. Understandably, during wartime the nation faced extreme danger and distress, the challenges being significantly different for men and women; men were cast in a struggle for the nation while women's role was to care for the men and the family. Once again in Polish history, the survival of the family and the endurance of the nation and its culture was a responsibility imposed upon women, who, in accepting this role, legitimized the model.

After World War II, both the communist regime and the authority of the Roman Catholic Church preserved traditional gender roles. Even though communist ideology and laws affirmed gender equality, women's rights were relegated to a mere propaganda slogan (Siwik 2011, 35), though one that still positively affected women's self-identity and shaped their own beliefs about their equal status in society.

In the second half of the twentieth century, the period of "state socialism" cemented women's already strong identification with the private sphere (home, family, religion) as a safe haven from the communist-oppressed public sphere (Graff 2003). Again, they received social recognition: they were appreciated as brave and resourceful in the face of everyday economic hardships. The official propaganda also praised their dedication to both domestic and professional work, and encouraged them to take up every challenge, emphasizing the availability of many career options.

Nevertheless, the heroic Polish woman, who was able to combine a professional career with family life, when challenged, chose the family as her priority. Titkow (2007, 65) refers to this model as the "matriarchy model," a common characteristic of communist and postcommunist countries. The official recognition a woman received from the state mitigated the effects of her being overworked, improved her self-esteem, and legitimized her vital role in the family (Siwik 2011, 36). Whether, after 1989, the self-sacrificing Polish woman has given way to the self-investing professional remains to be seen (Marody and Giza-Poleszczuk 2000). The feminist movement did not attract much interest and support until much later – unlike the emancipation movement of a hundred years earlier, which had been particularly actively supported by Polish female writers (see Handke 2008, 137–139) and concluded with the introduction of women's suffrage in 1918.

The overturn of communism stimulated a social transformation that involved a redefinition of gender roles. This process was closely related to the rapid development of feminist thinking. However, for women this was a difficult transition, as – for many women – rejecting communist ideology implied returning to Catholicism in defining gender roles, in particular preserving the traditional, symbolic, Polish Mother persona (Kowalska 2011).[2]

2. Terminology

In sociology (where gender studies has primarily been conducted since the 1990s) and linguistics, the complex link between gender-based social issues and language use has been largely neglected in Polish research. One aspect of how the social and the linguistic intertwine is reflected in the terminological complexities.

The Polish noun *płeć* must be postmodified – *płeć (biologiczna)* (E. "sex") and *płeć społeczno-kulturowa* (E. "gender") – to make the distinction between the biological and the sociocultural aspects of their characteristics that relate to their being women and men. Due to the inconvenience of *płeć społeczno-kulturowa*, a borrowing from English, "gender," is relatively common and the adjective *genderowy* is increasingly in frequent use.[3]

Unlike in English, where *(sociocultural) gender* is homophonous with *(grammatical) gender*, the term *płeć (społeczno-kulturowa)* is homophonous with the equivalent of the English "sex." Therefore, the terms relating to biology, culture, and grammar are differently linked (by being homophonous with one another) in Polish and in English. The following table shows the terminology in Polish and English.

Table 18.1. Sex/gender terms in Polish and English

	English	*Polish*
biological	sex	**płeć** *(biologiczna)*
sociocultural	**gender**	**płeć** *społeczno-kulturowa*
grammatical	(grammatical) **gender**	*rodzaj (gramatyczny)*

3. Major Themes in Language and Gender Research in Poland

One of the main themes in language and gender research in Poland is the relationship between grammatical gender and the sex of the (animate) referent.

The Polish language has a grammatical gender system, which is partly semantically motivated (for animate referents). Polish has five gender classes in the singular (masculine personal, masculine animate, masculine inanimate, neuter, and feminine). In the plural, with respect to syntactic concord, a gender distinction is made between masculine personal (P. *męskoosobowy*) and nonmasculine personal (P. *niemęskoosobowy*), which includes female human, animate nonhuman, and nonanimate referents.[4] Gender is marked throughout the noun phrase and many verb phrases.

The relationship between grammatical gender and the sex of the referent is symmetrical in the singular, where most animate female referents are marked for feminine gender and male referents for masculine gender. For example, in (1) the pronoun, noun, adjective, and verb (past tense) are all marked for feminine gender.

(1)   *ta*   *mała*   *dziewczynka*   *czytała*
      this   little   girl   was reading

However, in the plural, the nonmasculine personal includes nouns whose animate referents are female as well as nouns referring to nonanimate referents.

(2)   *dziewczynki*   *poszły*   *do*   *szkoły*
      the.girls   went.NONMASC.PERS.   to   school

The sex–gender relation is asymmetrical when the masculine personal gender is used not only for male personal referents but also for coordinate noun phrases referring to people of both sexes – one male referent noun triggers masculine personal verbal agreement:

(3)   *dziewczynki*   *i*   *chłopiec poszli*   *do*   *szkoły*
      the girls   and   the boy went.MASC.PERS.   to   school

The masculine noun determines the masculine personal verb agreement even if the referent of one of the coordinate nouns is not a person (Handke 2008, 150):

(4)   *dziewczynka i*   *pies*   *patrzyli*   *sobie*   *w oczy*
      the.girl   and the.dog were.   each other   in the eyes
                                   looking.PAST.MASC.PERS.

The very existence in the Polish grammatical system of the distinction between masculine personal and nonmasculine personal has been described as sexist (e.g., Herbert and Nykiel-Herbert 1986) and the option of reassigning male nouns with a derogatory implicature (see Rothstein 1993) may be seen as particularly sexist. However, Trudgill (1999, 146) questions this interpretation, suggesting that the homophony between categories of nouns signifying human females, animals, and nonanimates may not have any cognitive effect on the speakers and may be "a relatively minor and derivative sociolinguistic function" (140).

4. Is the Linguistic Gender System "Sexist"?

One of the earliest internationally renowned Polish publications to take up language and gender issues was Jaworski (1989). In an earlier study, Jaworski (1986) found that there was a significant tendency for the masculine generic noun *człowiek* (E. "man") to be associated with masculine co-referents and male imagery. The noun *osoba* (f.) (E. "person"), one of the few feminine generics, showed a weak tendency to be co-referential with feminine nouns (Jaworski 1986, 44).

The norm is to use masculine generics even in contexts that are sex-specific. The Polish law on higher education consistently uses a masculine generic noun phrase *nauczyciel* (m.) *akademicki* (m.) (E. "university lecturer"), even when specifying the rights of a university teacher who is pregnant (Law on Higher Education of July 27, 2005, art. 131.3.).[5]

Although one of the primary functions of (natural) gender is to indicate the sex of the (animate) referent (Trudgill 1999, 138), actual usage suggests that sociopolitical considerations influence linguistic practice. Common usage in the Polish public sphere testifies to speakers' need to mark the femaleness of the referent, particularly in contexts where maleness is culturally unmarked. The following three examples show three ways in which the femaleness of Angela Merkel was marked in political commentaries on the radio.

(5) (a) *Angela Merkel i Sarkozy*
     (b) *pani Merkel i Nicolas Sarkozy*
     (c) *Merklowa*

In 5(a) her first name is given, in 5(b) her name is modified by the feminine polite pronoun *pani*, in 5(c), the most informal usage, a feminine suffix *-owa* (marking "the wife of") is added to her family name.[6]

5. "Feminist" Language Reform?

After conducting a number of experiments, designed to determine the semantic value of masculine nouns and pronouns used in generic contexts, Jaworski concluded that "nouns referring to adult males occupy a unique and somehow privileged position in the structure of Polish" (1989, 84; see also Koniuszaniec and Błaszkowska 2003).[7]

More recently, experiments have been conducted to find out the referential value of the Polish noun *człowiek* (E. "man, human being"). For example, Karwatowska and Szpyra-Kozłowska (2005) asked schoolchildren to draw pictures of *człowiek pierwotny* (E. "caveman"). Eighty two out of 90 drawings represented a male. However, we agree with Łaziński (2006, 201–204) who questions the credibility of experiments testing the impact of the linguistic system on (gender) stereotyping on the grounds that it is impossible to eliminate numerous and uncontrolled extralinguistic factors which influence the results. For example, participants' personal social experience and interdiscursive factors will interfere with how the grammatical gender system mediates their perception of males and females.

Polish proponents of feminist language reform (e.g., Koniuszaniec and Błaszkowska 2003), who believe that implementing language change will promote social equality, have opted for a feminization strategy that aims to make women more visible in the public space, particularly in the workforce.

The derivational system of Polish is highly asymmetrical with respect to gender. The functional range of masculine forms is wider than the range of feminine counterparts in that the masculine forms are (1) primary in derivation and (2) semantically generic.[8] For example:

(6) *lekarz* (m).*/lekarka* (f.) "doctor"
(7) *nauczyciel* (m.)*/nauczycielka* (f.) "teacher"

Moreover, numerous lexical gaps reflect the historical under-representation of women in many occupations and professions. For instance, the feminine derivative of *leśnik* (E. "forester") is hardly ever used, and the name of a female *marynarz/pilot* (E. "seaman"/"air-pilot") is not *marynarka/pilotka*, as this derivative is already reserved for another meaning ("a jacket"/"a kind of cap worn by pilots"). Many names of prestigious professions exist only in the masculine form, while the feminine equivalents are formed by descriptive means, for instance by adding the feminine address noun (*pani*) or periphrastically:

(8) *adwokat* (m.)*/pani* (f.) *adwokat*, E. "attorney"/"Ms attorney"
(9) *kierowca* (m.)*/kobieta kierująca pojazdem*, E. "driver"/"woman driving the vehicle"[9]

Apart from nouns that describe female practitioners, suffixes are still used to create names of women who are wives and daughters of male professionals or men of rank (e.g., *prezydentowa*, E. "president's wife"; *prezydentówna*, E. "president's daughter").[10] Some of these seem to have shifted in meaning; for example, *szefowa* commonly, though informally, refers to a female boss, rather than the wife of the boss.

Professional and occupational terms are another example: many prestigious jobs have no counterpart names denoting female practitioners, despite these being derivationally possible. The women's emancipation movement in Poland hardly involved a plea for a language reform, until post-transition times. The current language reform, instigated by feminist ideologies, includes a tendency toward avoiding androcentric "generics."[11]

In some languages, including English, striving for a balanced representation of the sexes in language involves eliminating gender-specific terms (gender neutralization). In Polish, as in other languages with grammatical gender, the reform endorses symmetrical gender marking (gender specification), which requires the use of existing feminine forms (e.g., *aktorka* (f.), E. "actress") and creating new ones that are missing in the lexicon (e.g., *minister* (m.), E. "male minister"/*ministra* (f.), E. "female minister"). This is a choice that promotes female visibility with a view to achieving linguistic and social equality.

In fact, there are two ways to implement gender specification in Polish: synthetic and analytic. The synthetic approach creates feminine forms via suffixation (e.g., *rzecznik* (m.), E. "spokesman"/*rzeczniczka* (f.), E. "spokeswoman").[12] The analytic method marks feminine gender by premodifying a masculine noun by the quasi-pronoun "pani" (e.g., *pani rzecznik*, E. "lady spokesman") or by having the masculine noun agree with a feminine verb (e.g. *rzecznik* (m.) *powiedziała* (past tense, f.), E. "spokesman said") or a feminine adjective (e.g. *nowa* (f.) *rzecznik* (m.), E. "new (f.) spokesman").

Which of the two strategies is more common at different points in history has been unpredictable (Łaziński 2006, 228). For example, in December 1922 the University of Poznań awarded an honorary doctorate to the outstanding Polish chemist, Maria Skłodowska-Curie, and the University Senate document referred to this act as "udzielenie stopnia *doktorki* w dziedzinie nauk lekarskich honoris causa" (E. "awarding an honorary doctor's (f.) degree in medical sciences").[13] Feminine derivatives of academic titles, such as *doktorka* and *docentka*, were popular in the 1920s and 1930s. By the latter part of the twentieth century, however, such constructions had lost currency, and had become stylistically marked as jocular (see below). According to Łaziński (2006, 248), the "analytic" strategy has been the dominant one from the mid twentieth century onward. The grammar books published around mid-century acknowledged the use of masculine (or feminine) occupational terms as upgrading (or downgrading) the status of the (female) referents.

Apparently, nowadays, both male and female speakers of Polish, perhaps for different reasons, still often choose to use masculine generic terms. The preference for masculine generics is sometimes observable even when feminine derivatives do exist. The feminine forms are less prestigious (e.g., *lekarka*, E. "female doctor") and/or semantically narrower (e.g., *dyrektorka*, E. "headmistress") or even semantically different (e.g., *sekretarka*, E. "office assistant") from their masculine derivational bases.

Additionally, the derivation of feminine forms may be blocked by nonlinguistic factors, such as the perception that feminized forms sound trivial, funny, or ugly. These perceptions are reproduced in the normative publications about Polish (which many Poles very much look up to). The feminine derivatives *socjolożka* (E. "female sociologist") and *architektka* (E. "female architect"), for example, illustrate the point. The opinions of both dictionary editors and ordinary language users are divided, which puts the aesthetic criterion into question and suggests that change is in progress. Łaziński (2006, 268) claims that the probability of the formation and spread of feminine derivatives is directly related to the probability of their use in the referential context.

No conclusive studies (or evaluations) of the impact of the proposed reform have yet been published. There are very few accounts of the ongoing change, which has perhaps been inspired by the reform. Most reports have been based on researchers' introspection and speakers' self-report data (e.g., Handke 2008). One of the few studies that relied on a sound methodology is that of Nowosad-Bakalarczyk (2009), who analyzed three kinds of data – grammar books and dictionaries, questionnaire responses, and press texts – with the aim of describing norms, attitudes, and usage.

Perhaps the most important effect of the language reform has been its power to provoke a public debate on its assumptions and the direction of the proposed change. Much of the debate is conducted in the media, especially online. The feminist-reformed language is considered by many as "newspeak," and some commentators even suggest that Poles are in principle against any kind of newspeak. In a heated (political) debate, they claim that introducing feminized language forms is counterproductive for the much needed social changes, and works to the detriment of the egalitarian ideology. One way to resolve the debate over the directions and goals of language reform is to empirically examine strongly stereotyped forms that raise sex-specific imagery.

Łaziński (2006) conducted a questionnaire study asking respondents to describe the way they would address a representative of an occupation or profession, for example, "How would you address a shop assistant?" The survey included five different versions of the question, using five different forms of referring to the practitioner of the occupation/profession, including a split form (analogous to *actor/actress*), and periphrastic forms with the words *człowiek* (m.) (E. "man") and *osoba* (f.) (E. "person"). Łaziński wondered whether the form used in the question would prime the address form in the answer. He claims that the results of the experiment suggest that introducing split forms is of questionable value because the use of masculines in the plural does not seem to trigger a male bias.

With the ongoing emotion-laden debate over whether and how implementing language reform could impact speakers' perceptions of gender identities and relations, it is difficult to say if actual language change will tend toward gender neutralization or specification (i.e., feminization).

Warchoł-Schlottmann (2007) suggests that part of the problem is having too many options to mark the feminine form of profession and/or function. According to her, the wide range of choice of linguistic forms makes potential users uncertain as to which form constitutes the best option in the specific context. Even the proponents of the reform admit that sometimes the new derivations have unwanted connotations of trivialization because the most common feminine derivational suffixes are identical to diminutives.

However, the real problem, we believe, is the lack of a clear language policy regarding the feminist language reform as formulated and upheld by the guardians of Polish language norms, that is, linguists. While the Council for the Polish Language (*Rada Języka Polskiego*), an institution responsible for sanctioning language use in Poland, recognizes the use of feminine professional terms as linguistically correct and permissible, it also adds that these forms are regarded by the majority of Poles as artificial and clumsy. It is striking that the Council does not acknowledge its crucial role in educating Polish society about the importance of incorporating these forms into the linguistic repertoire of Poles, and dismisses its own role in the reform process by claiming that "nothing can be imposed on the language system."[14] We agree with Koniuszaniec and Błaszkowska (2003) that the use of the feminine forms in official contexts would lead to their gradual acceptance and eventually their full integration and unmarkedness in the Polish language.

In fact, according to Karwatowska and Szpyra-Kozłowska (2005, 269), the issue of nonsexist language reform tends to be approached negatively by many Polish linguists who regard it as "unnecessary, artificial, complicated and unjustified." Despite the little support for the reform from linguists, language changes anyway through "formulating the norm by setting example" (Łaziński 2006, 278), for instance, when journalists report on major female public figures with the use of feminine derivatives. Łaziński observes a decrease in the use of feminine derivatives for much of the mid twentieth century and their expansion from the 1990s, mainly in press articles and readers' letters. For instance, *Wysokie Obcasy* (a women's weekly supplement to the daily newspaper *Gazeta Wyborcza*) launched a campaign entitled "Precz z męską końcówką!" (E. "Away with the masculine ending!") in 2005 aimed at encouraging women to use the feminine forms.

Some (more liberal) Polish media (e.g., *Gazeta Wyborcza*, *Radio Tok*) actively implement feminist language reform. We can often hear guests on various radio programs self-correct (or being corrected) when they use a masculine job title when referring to a female professional. Such an involved and consistent endorsement of feminine forms stirs up a very heated debate among both Polish women and men. Consider two examples:

- A male viewer of a TV program upon hearing the proposed feminine form of the title "minister" (P. *ministra*), voiced the following comment: "the feminine endings are ridiculous and there is no point in using them" (*Wysokie Obcasy*, March 21, 2012).
- In *Gazeta Wyborcza* (April 26, 2012), a letter was published from an educated Polish female reader who stated that the "pseudo-feminist tendency to utilize the feminine names of the professions, so common nowadays, drives [her] mad."

These two comments are representative of the general social climate on feminist language reform. Yet, change is still very much in progress and its results remain to be seen. The change has been, since the beginning of the 1990s, advocated by feminist circles. At the moment, feminine occupational terms are commonly used in texts produced in feminist contexts.

Internet forums constitute interesting data sites for considering Poles' attitudes to and potential uptake of the new feminine names of professions. Although some

Table 18.2.   Two variants of analytic future tense construction in Polish

Infinitive variant	Participle variant
Ania będzie czytać	*Ania będzie czytała* (f.)
E. "Anne will be reading"	
Janek będzie czytać	*Janek będzie czytał* (m.)
E. "John will be reading"	

mass media clearly subscribe to reformed use, it seems that Poles typically distance themselves from the marked forms of a feminine profession. That means these forms are still unstable and quite unusual. On these forums, the feminine names of professions are regarded as instances of newspeak and construed as discrediting the feminist movement. Thus, to use them means to make a political statement but also to risk being ostracized or even ridiculed.

Studies have pointed to an interplay between considerations of the (extralinguistic) context and the grammatical system (see Warchoł-Schlottmann 2007). For example, the movement toward the feminization of professional and occupational terms currently seems very robust. It is strongly supported by vocal social organizations and media, and just as vigorously opposed by others who widely publicize their views through social media forums. On the other hand, however, Łaziński (2006) points out tendencies toward neutralization, for example, the decline of feminine markers on family names (*-owa*, *-ówna*) and the preference for occupational terms without feminine gender marking. Both may be manifestations of an ongoing change whose progress and direction is yet to be researched.

An interesting case of gendered distribution of grammatical variants is the analytic future tense construction, in which the future form of the auxiliary "be" (P. *być*) combines with either (1) the infinitive of the imperfective verb or (2) the past participle form of the verb (marked for gender), as shown in Table 18.2. Both variants of the construction are currently accepted (though the latter construction is archaic), yet linguists have long observed its gendered distribution. Subjects referring to women co-occur with the infinitive construction more often than subjects referring to men (Grzegorczykowa, Laskowski, and Wróbel 1998 [1984], 238). This pattern was more recently corroborated by Łaziński's (2006, 318–320) analysis of corpus data. Especially in self-reference, women use the gender-unmarked variant with the infinitive much more often than men.

Łaziński (2006, 320) further sought to verify the corpus results by means of a questionnaire. The (admittedly small) sample of respondents created a roughly comparable variant distribution, except in first-person singular utterances, where men's preference for the variant with the participle showed an even greater contrast to that of women's (see Table 18.3.). In contexts when a woman is the speaker and the implied subject (Polish is a pro-drop language)

Table 18.3.   Use of analytic future tense with imperfective verbs in the first-person singular (infinitive or participle construction) in the National Corpus of Polish (3.7 million words demo version) (adapted from Łaziński 2006, 319)

"I will be dreaming"

Women		Men	
Infinitive variant	Participle variant	Infinitive variant	Participle variant
będę (1st p.) *marzyć*	*będę* (1st p.) *marzyła* (f.)	*będę* (1st p.) *marzyć*	*będę* (1st p.) *marzył* (m.)
49	122	16	206

is marked as feminine elsewhere in the clause, female respondents definitely opted for the (gender-unmarked) infinitive construction. This finding should be further verified. Łaziński (2006, 321) highlights the possibility that women prefer non-sex-identifying variants. This hypothesis should be seriously considered in view of the relatively slow adoption of feminine variants of occupation names and other nouns referring to women.

6. Gendered Interactional Styles

A more recent motif in Polish language and gender research has been the exploration of how women and men use language in various types of discourses. A variety of texts have been analyzed, for instance news texts and small ads in the press (Nowosad-Bakalarczyk 2009), abstracts of academic articles (Łyda and Warchał 2010), matrimonial ads (Karwatowska 2010), and private and formal letters (Ziębka 2010). In most of these studies, authors described aspects of gendered self-representation through language. The focus has, however, shifted from self-construction to social construction: the cultural texts have been understood as constructing gendered images, which are further imposed on women (and men) as part of the socialization process (Stawiak-Ososińska 2009).

Yet the research on the construction of femininities and masculinities in discourse and interaction in the context of the Polish language remains far from conclusive. This is due to two main reasons. First, the few existing studies (e.g., Dąbrowska 2007) are based on very small samples of respondents while making claims about the whole population ("gender differences appear more striking with regard to the users of English rather than the users of Polish": Dąbrowska 2007, 57). Second, the methods selected for data collection do not allow observation of how women and men draw on the available linguistic and discursive resources to perform (gendered) identities in their communities of practice.

For example, Karwatowska and Szpyra-Kozłowska (2005) rely on questionnaires and interviews to describe men's and women's linguistic performances, despite the evident limitations of these tools in capturing *actual* linguistic performance. Consequently, the precepts of social constructionism (e.g., such concepts as the community of practice, *doing* gender, the continuum of gender experience) commonly applied in the current language and gender research in the larger field do not feature in the Polish studies.

Handke (1990; 1995; 2008) lists the features of *feminine style* for the Polish language, yet, to a large extent, these reflect normative expectations and stereotypical assumptions about a Polish woman's (but not man's) linguistic performance, rather than the findings of actual empirical analyses of usage. Thus we are offered "representations of gendered language" (Cameron 2006, 15), and the feminine style functions as a symbolic construct (Litosseliti 2006), not an empirical category (Cameron 2006). Symbolic constructs reflect the dominant or socially idealized discourses. Nevertheless, probing social expectations and stereotypes is vital as "they are resources for the *active* process of self-fashioning which is now understood by most feminists to have a significant role in the construction of gendered identity" (Cameron 2006, 15; emphasis added). Moreover, Cameron (2009) argues that stereotypes are of immense importance in view of the emergence of the "new biologism" in social science.

Before discussing the features of the feminine style in the Polish context, let us briefly present the local cultural images of femininity and masculinity as these are interwoven with the gendered stereotypes about language use. Kuczyńska (1992) – on the basis of the Bem Sex-Role Inventory (1974) – described the cultural stereotypes of femininity and masculinity for the local Polish context. She describes the feminine cultural stereotype as:

> sensitive, caring, other-centered, soft, coquettish, caring for the appearance, thrifty, with a sense of aesthetics, grumbling, tender, emotional, sensitive to the needs of others, able to sacrifice, delicate, naïve.

The masculine cultural stereotype is described as:

> dominating, independent, competitive, success-oriented, forcing one's way through, a quick decision-taker, arrogant, fit, with a sense of humor, with an ability to convince others, self-confident, self-sufficient, open to the external events, experimental in sex life, cunning. (Titkow 2011, 44)

These strong cultural stereotypes are clearly manifested in the expectations that the Polish people have about the language use of men and women. In Kiełkiewicz-Janowiak and Pawelczyk's study (2006), 120 respondents were divided into four groups by age and sex. The study, whose results are shown in Table 18.4, revealed a consistent picture of gendered expectations of the language use and communicative strategies of women and men.

The Polish woman is expected to be emotional and talkative, while men are believed to be more fact-oriented, matter-of-fact, and brief. This picture of gendered language behavior is consonant with widespread social stereotypes of

Table 18.4.   Beliefs about gendered language use (Kiełkiewicz-Janowiak and Pawelczyk 2006, 360)

Women (in comparison to men)	Men (in comparison to women)
Often talk only for the sake of talking	Are more fact-oriented
Use diminutives more often than men	Are more matter-of-fact
Speak more emotionally	Are more authoritative
Talk more	Are more categorical
Ask more questions because they are nosy	Are more brief
Use vulgar and offensive words less often	Tend not to use diminutives
Introduce new topics into conversation more often	Use vulgar words more often
Are able to "read between the lines"	Tend to stick to one topic in conversation
Use more adjectives to make their descriptions more vivid	Like to show off
Often talk simultaneously with other speakers	
Are more oriented toward details	
Show more understanding toward their listener	

women's communality and men's agency (see Eagly, Beall, and Sternberg 2004). The study also demonstrated that gender stereotypes held by men and women are very similar, with both giving more emphasis to what women are or should be like. It is interesting that no social change was indicated in an intergenerational comparison, strongly implying that these stereotypes are stable and immune to change (Kiełkiewicz-Janowiak and Pawelczyk 2006, 370). A study in which high school students were asked to comment on Polish sexist proverbs and fixed phrases offers similar findings. Students' comments elaborated on the notion that women talk too much (often nonsensically), gossip, and complain. Men's talk, by contrast, is viewed as more to the point, brief, matter-of-fact, impersonal, and clear (Karwatowska and Szpyra-Kozłowska 2005, 181–182). These stereotypes correspond directly to findings for speakers of English (see Holmes 1998; Kramer 1977; Talbot 2003). However, two important points of divergence must be singled out:

- Polish studies have not found that either women or men are believed to be (linguistically) more polite or use prestigious variants more frequently.
- There were no strong claims in the Polish studies about either sex being dominant or competitive in communication. (Kiełkiewicz-Janowiak and Pawelczyk 2006, 368)

Stereotypes about gendered language use function as ideological discourses with a clear prescriptive power. They provide language users with the tools to judge each other's behavior in terms of whether they subscribe to or breach normative gendered expectations (see Aries 1996). Breaches obviously carry a risk of high social cost (see Mullany 2007).

The gendered expectations of women's talk are reflected in Handke's (1994; 2008) concept of the *feminine style* in Polish. Handke (2008) refers to the emergence of the feminine style (after World War II) as a consequence of the changes in the political system and the *alleged* emancipation of women in Poland which enabled them to participate in the professional and social spheres. She claims that the feminine style characterizes the speech of urban women with high school education but that its selected features can also be found in the language used by women with university degrees, particularly in the speech of women who are journalists, medical doctors, and nurses (Handke 2008, 163).

Handke (2008, 163–166) observes the following features of the feminine style:

- expressing *positive emotions* (linked to women's traditional role and position) by means of: diminutives, hypocoristics, interjections, synonyms, augmentative forms, neologisms;
- expressing *negative emotions* (which Handke claims functions as the most representative feature of the feminine style and is used by all women) by means of: augmentative forms, interjections, interruptions, swear words, diminutives in the negative use, back-formations, neologisms.

The feminine style consists of often quite contradictory tendencies. For example, it strives for tenderness and gentleness in its expression but, at the same time, it can be relatively vulgar. It also evinces women's rejection of the traditional role of the guardian of correct and elegant style, and underlines their (new) independent and emancipated status. The feminine style is described as being variable and non-uniform, open to absorbing the features of other styles and varieties. Handke claims that the feminine style can be found in family interactions as well as in professional and social settings; hence it does not index particular contexts but characterizes the way women talk in general (2008, 164) – regrettably, she refers to women's mental and psychological attributes as factors in the communication process.

Handke's attempt at describing a Polish feminine style resembles Lakoff's (1975) classic in the field in its data shortcomings: Handke, too, relied primarily on her own observations and introspection. Similarly, the concept of the Polish feminine style relates to normative expectations toward the linguistic performance of women. Still, the Polish feminine style stresses women's emotional expressivity (both positive and negative) as its most salient aspect (see Holmes's (1998) gendered sociolinguistic universals).

Kiełkiewicz-Janowiak and Pawelczyk (2008) examined gendered interactional styles by looking at the context of a global institution in the local context, in this case Polish call centers, to find out whether a combination of Polish stereotypical feminine features and stereotypical masculine features (Kiełkiewicz-Janowiak and Pawelczyk 2006) overlap with global prescriptions for call center communication

(Cameron 2000a; 2000b). The analysis revealed two styles. Style 1 was predominantly masculine, that is, it overlapped with the stereotypically masculine features of matter-of-factness and of being categorical/authoritative, brief, unemotional, institutional. Style 2 involved both masculine and feminine features as reflected by the following characteristics: informational, fact-oriented, empathic, caring, involved. The styles were exemplified by a number of linguistic and discursive strategies used by the call center operators.

The study showed that the preferred communicative style in the context of a call center can be best described as a "both ... and" style. Thus an ideal call center worker possesses a mixture of communicative features stereotyped in Poland as feminine and masculine. Importantly, feminine and masculine features become salient depending on the type of task to be tackled (one focuses on providing information or making transactions, while the other is relational and therapeutic) and the personality of the customer (Kiełkiewicz-Janowiak and Pawelczyk 2008, 77). The study also exemplified how the symbolic concepts of linguistic femininity and masculinity function as professional tools in the hands of a call center operator regardless of his/her sex.

The extant research into the gendered interactional styles offers robust findings as to what is linguistically *expected* of the Polish woman and less so of the Polish man. Despite the evident methodological limitations of the existing studies, new paradigms, sources of data, and research proposals are gradually emerging. For instance, the National Corpus of Polish (*National Corpus of Polish* 2008–2011; Górski et al. 2009) provides opportunities for contextualized and empirically sound explorations of the way Polish women and men use language, while new analytical tools (e.g., E-Prime 2.0) are capable of verifying the results of investigations relying on respondents' conscious and declared beliefs and attitudes. A semantic priming experiment, for example, can uncover implicit gender-based language stereotypes (Rojczyk 2012).

7. Ambivalent Sexism

The double status of Polish women mirrored in their social/professional and family roles, which carries over onto their language and discursive choices, is also reflected in the ambivalent sexism characterizing gender relations in Poland. The ambivalence lies in both the hostile and benevolent aspects of social prejudice (see Glick and Fiske 1996). Glick et al. (2000, 763) state that "hostile sexism is evidenced by an adversarial view of gender relations in which women are perceived as seeking to control men, whether through sexuality or feminist ideology," while benevolent sexism refers to "subjectively positive attitudes that put women on a pedestal but reinforce their subordination." These ideologies reflect and effectively promote gender inequality. Kiełkiewicz-Janowiak and Pawelczyk (2010a; 2010b) looked into Polish women's and men's awareness of and attitudes toward ambivalent sexist discourse. It has been assumed that both types of sexism are marked at the level of language and that ambivalent attitudes feed on the dominant values of Polish culture and society. It was claimed that the benevolent form of sexism in particular is very well established in Poland, and deeply rooted in the Polish culture (see also Forbes et al. 2004). Thus, in a clear manifestation of ambivalent sexism, women in Poland are disadvantaged and idealized at the same time.

Both studies relied on the method of semi-structured interviews in which triggers prompted women and men to produce personal narratives concerning a set of common sayings which are a part of traditional local "gender lore." The narration of the personal experiences revealed important aspects of the local gender order, in particular speakers' either identifying with or distancing themselves from the dominant ideology. The selected sayings encoded both benevolent (Table 18.5) and hostile (Table 18.6) sexism.

The participants of the studies were able to contextualize the trigger phrases (see Tables 18.5. and 18.6.), explain their meaning as well as assess their social significance, specifically their potential hostile and/or benevolent stance toward women. The first study revealed young Polish women's relatively high awareness of sexism as a social problem and of gender issues in general. Young Polish women in their narratives evidenced their awareness of the stereotypical assumptions about the role of women (as encoded in the trigger sayings) and their conscious distancing from such thinking and perception (Kiełkiewicz-Janowiak and Pawelczyk 2010a, 141). Significantly, in the second study, the respondents' comments and narratives often revealed their *ambivalent* perceptions and attitudes as encoded in their use of such linguistic markers as: "but" (P. *ale*), "only" (P. *tylko*), "it depends" (P. *to zależy*), "although" (P. *aczkolwiek*) (Kiełkiewicz-Janowiak and Pawelczyk 2010b).

The participants' comments and opinions on the trigger sayings were categorized into four main response patterns (Kiełkiewicz-Janowiak and Pawelczyk 2010b):

- contextualization – pointing to culture-embeddedness;
- recognition and evaluation of ideologies – pointing to ambivalence;
- personal attitude expression – pointing to detachment;
- recontextualization – achieved through self-reflection.

Table 18.5.   Trigger sayings: benevolent (Kiełkiewicz-Janowiak and Pawelczyk 2010b, 177–178)

Panie mają pierwszeństwo.

Ladies first.

Kobiety nie wolno uderzyć nawet kwiatkiem.

You're not supposed to hit a woman even with a flower.

Zdrowie pięknych pań!

To beautiful women! [a toast]

Rączki całuję!

I welcome you humbly! (lit. I kiss your hands) [a greeting]

Table 18.6.   Trigger sayings: hostile (Kiełkiewicz-Janowiak and Pawelczyk 2010b, 178)

Baba z wozu, koniom lżej.

If a woman falls off the wagon, it's a load off for the horses.

Kobieta ma włos długi, a rozum krótki.

A woman has long hair but a small brain.

Gdzie diabeł nie może, tam babę pośle.

Where the devil can't manage, he sends a woman.

Jak się baby nie bije to jej wątroba gnije.

If you don't beat a woman, her liver will rot.

This study did not reveal a clear generational or gender difference. Both generations under investigation (Polish women and men aged 21–25 and 45+) showed an ambivalent attitude, namely a reserved reverence for the cultural values encoded in the trigger sayings. They were aware of the sayings' datedness, yet did not reject them as completely outdated (Kiełkiewicz-Janowiak and Pawelczyk 2010b).

Both studies on ambivalent sexism (2010a; 2010b) used the discourse-oriented qualitative approach. Unlike the quantitative methods typically adopted for measuring hostile and benevolent sexism, a qualitative approach exposed how respondents' views evolved or were modified in the process of narration. It allowed the complexities of gender ideologies to be revealed in the responses and narratives of the respondents. It also uncovered the process by which the respondents arrived at their opinions through self-reflection and recontextualization (Kiełkiewicz-Janowiak and Pawelczyk 2010b). This is very much in line with Chouliaraki and Fairclough's (1999, 110) view that recontextualizing social practices from their original discourse orders to other discourse orders occurs through an individual's reflection upon his/her personal experience.

In their study of sexist attitudes in 19 different countries, Glick et al. (2000) showed that "both hostile and benevolent sexism were at their highest levels in societies in which the degrees of gender equality and female empowerment were lowest" (Jost and Kay 2005, 499, referring to Glick et al. 2000). Kiełkiewicz-Janowiak and Pawelczyk's (2010a; 2010b) qualitative discourse-oriented studies suggest that Polish society is a case in point. Furthermore, the language encoding benevolent attitudes to women is particularly devious in that it camouflages the social damage caused by sexism. Its victims often do not have the perception of being victimized.

8. Conclusion

Polish language and gender research has for centuries been defined by the country's sociohistorical context which shaped the peculiar gender roles. Specifically, women held the roles of leaders of family life and guardians of cultural heritage during the partitions of Poland, that is, the long period of the country's political dependence and social foreignization. Their patriotic mission continued during World War II and, importantly, through communist times. For over four decades in the latter part of the twentieth century society was encouraged to believe that the egalitarian ideal had already been attained rather than that it was still to be striven for.

For decades, the dominant topic in Polish language and gender research has been the untangling of the complex relationship between the grammatical category of gender and its semantic reference. This relationship, described as asymmetrical, has largely been discussed without interpreting it in terms of social equality and/or with reference to sexist attitudes encoded in the language system.

The women's emancipation movement hardly ever problematized language as reflecting and perpetuating social inequality. It was only after the sociopolitical transformation of the later 1980s that feminists raised the issue of women's visibility in the Polish language. The implementation of language reform with a view to achieving a more balanced representation of women and men in language use and in society is now central in the Polish context. Feminist language reform is currently very much in progress, yet at this point it is impossible to tell whether the feminine inclusive forms will be accepted as legitimate linguistic forms by the majority of Polish society.

Over the years, hardly any quantitative studies have been conducted to verify the direction of the ongoing change. Today, with the availability of the National Corpus of Polish, current trends in usage can be traced. Future studies examining actual language use are called for, as well as interpretations of the mutual impact between language and society.

Acknowledgments

We would like to thank an anonymous reviewer as well as several colleagues – Professor Marek Łaziński, Kevin Hagarty, and Dr Anne White – whose comments helped us to improve the final version of this chapter.

NOTES

1   Translations of Polish terms, quotations, and titles are the authors'.
2   While this volume was in production (winter 2013/14) a political debate on gender issues was being conducted in the Polish public sphere. The debate, however acrimonious, also raised public awareness of "gender:" as a concept, a social problem, and a research perspective.
3   Arabski and Ziębka (2010) note that in Poland the research and study of problems relating to gender (e.g., at universities) is labeled in English – as "gender studies," for lack of a Polish term. However, a web search again reveals a robust ongoing change with 9,000 hits for

studia genderowe (see also *teoria genderu*, E. "gender theory," defined in Wikipedia). The form borrowed from English seems quite well adapted. A National Corpus of Polish search (based on 1,800 million words) gave six results for the adjective *genderowy*, while a Google search revealed 8,120 hits. Prominent on the Google list of results was the title of a recently published academic book entitled *Kalejdoskop genderowy* (Slany, Kowalska, and Ślusarczyk 2011).

4 Unlike in the masculine personal paradigm, the nominative and the accusative are identical in nonmasculine personal.

5 Łaziński (2006, 269) pointed out this usage in the Act of Law on Higher Education of September 12, 1990. The most recent amendment to the Act (March 18, 2011) has not changed the phrasing.

6 This last usage also occurs in Internet discussion posts, for example, *To Merklowa nacisnela Holendrow,* … " (E. "It was Merkel who pressed the Dutch … ") (http://fakty.interia.pl/new -york-times/news/koniec-z-wakacjami-na-haju,1783943, accessed October 23, 2013).

7 Researchers often phrase the relationship in terms of language performing a social act, for example, "the way language treats gender" (P. *"traktowanie płci przez język"*: Handke 2008, 149), that is, blurring the structure and use distinction (see also Jaworski 1989, 83).

8 Exceptions are rare: *wdowa* (f.) (E. "widow")/*wdowiec* (m.) (E. "widower"); *położna* (f.) (E. "midwife")/*położnik* (m.) (E. "obstetrician") (note the status difference involved in the latter pair).

9 The feminine derivative of *kierowca* (m.) (E. "driver") does not exist, even though the derivation would be a simple analogy to *sprzedawca* (m.) (E. "salesman")/*sprzedawczyni* (f.) (E. "saleswoman").

10 Females' surnames are likewise denoted: women's names are typically their father's and the suffix marks – in adjectival names – the sex (e.g., *Jankowski* m./*Jankowska* f.) or – in surnames with the form of nouns – both the female sex and the woman's marital status (e.g., *Nowakowa* ("wife of Nowak")/*Nowakówna* ("daughter of Nowak")). The suffixes have been going out of use since the end of the nineteenth century. Admittedly, Polish legislation is very liberal in allowing people to choose the husband's or the wife's surname, or a combination, as the family name. Yet, the social practice still prefers the husband's name as the family name, despite the example set over a century ago by Maria Skłodowska-Curie, the world-famous Polish physicist and chemist.

11 The Polish language is grammatically complex enough (gender-wise) that solutions used in other Europeans languages cannot be so easily adopted. For instance, *autor/ka* (E. "author/ ess") allows orthographic "splitting" but not all of the nine types of feminine personal suffixes (Łazinski 2006, 207) lend themselves readily to this.

12 There are some constraints that block derivation of a feminine form (e.g., *szpieg*, E. "spy"), but these constraints can be overridden whenever extralinguistic needs arise that override the dictates of the system (e.g., *Norweg* (m.), E. "male Norwegian"/*Norweżka* (f.), E. "female Norwegian") (Łaziński 2006, 267).

13 University Senate Minutes 15/S/3, Adam Mickiewicz University Archive, Poznań.

14 See "Rada Języka Polskiego: forma 'ministra' jest niezręczna," at http://wiadomosci.wp.pl /kat,1342,title,Rada-Jezyka-Polskiego-forma-ministra-jest-niezreczna,wid,14370795, wiadomosc.html, accessed October 24, 2013.

REFERENCES

Arabski Janusz, and Justyna Ziębka, eds. 2010. *Płeć języka – Język płci* [Gender of Language – Language of Gender]. Katowice: Wyższa Szkoła Zarządzania Marketingowego i Języków Obcych.

Aries, Elizabeth. 1996. *Men and Women in Interaction: Reconsidering the Differences.* New York: Oxford University Press.

Bem, Sandra. 1974. "The Measurement of Psychological Androgyny." *Journal of Consulting and Clinical Psychology*, 42: 155–162.

Bourdieu, Pierre. 1977. *Outline of a Theory of Practice.* Cambridge: Cambridge University Press.

Cameron, Deborah. 2000a. "Styling the Worker: Gender and the Commodification of Language in the Globalized Service Economy." *Journal of Sociolinguistics*, 4(3): 323–347.

Cameron, Deborah. 2000b. *Good to Talk? Living and Working in a Communication Culture.* London: Sage.

Cameron, Deborah. 2006. "Theorizing the Female Voice in Public Contexts." In Judith Baxter (ed.), *Speaking Out: The Female Voice in Public Context*, 3–20. Basingstoke: Palgrave Macmillan.

Cameron, Deborah. 2009. "Sex/Gender, Language and the New Biologism." *Applied Linguistics*, 31(2): 173–192.

Chouliaraki, Lilie, and Norman Fairclough. 1999. *Discourse in Late Modernity.* Edinburgh: Edinburgh University Press.

Dąbrowska, Marta. 2007. "Are Genderlects Universal?" *Studia Linguistica Universitatis Jagellonicae Cracoviensis*, 124: 49–58.

Eagly, Alice, Anne Beall, and Robert Sternberg. 2004. *The Psychology of Gender.* New York: Guilford Press.

Forbes, Gordon B., Krystyna Doroszewicz, Kristin Card, and Leah Adams-Curtis. 2004. "Association of the Thin Body Ideal, Ambivalent Sexism, and Self-Esteem with Body Acceptance and the Preferred Body Size of College Women in Poland and the United States." *Sex Roles*, 50(5–6): 331–345.

Glick, Peter, and Susan T. Fiske. 1996. "The Ambivalent Sexism Inventory: Differentiating Hostile and Benevolent Sexism." *Journal of Personality and Social Psychology*, 70: 491–512.

Glick, Peter, et al. 2000. "Beyond Prejudice as Simple Antipathy: Hostile and Benevolent Sexism across Cultures." *Journal of Personality and Social Psychology*, 79: 763–775.

Górski, Rafał L., Adam Przepiórkowski, Marek Łaziński, and Barbara Lewandowska-Tomaszczyk. 2009. "A Corpus of Polish." *Academia: The Magazine of the Polish Academy of Sciences*, 4–7. At http://nkjp.pl/settings /papers/NKJP_ACADEMIA2009_pl.pdf, accessed October 23, 2013.

Graff, Agnieszka. 2003. "Lost between the Waves? The Paradoxes of Feminist Chronology and Activism in Contemporary Poland." *Journal of International Women's Studies*, 4(2): 100–116.

Grzegorczykowa, Renata, Roman Laskowski, and Henryk Wróbel, eds. 1998 [1984]. *Gramatyka współczesnego języka polskiego: Morfologia* [Grammar of Contemporary Polish Language: Morphology]. Warsaw: Wydawnictwo Naukowe PWN.

Handke, Kwiryna. 1990. "Wpływ emancypacji na język kobie" [The Impact of Emancipation on Women's Language]. In Barbara Jedynak (ed.), *Kobieta w kulturze i społeczeństwie* [Woman in Culture and Society], 156–170. Lublin: Wydawnictwo UMCS.

Handke, Kwiryna. 1994. "Język a determinanty płci" [Language and Gender]. In Janusz Anusiewicz (ed.), *Język a kultura 9: Płeć w języku i kulturze* [Language and Culture: Gender in Language and Culture], 15–29. Wrocław: Wiedza o Kulturze.

Handke, Kwiryna. 1995. *Polski język familijny* [Polish Language of the Family]. Warsaw: Polska Akademia Nauk.

Handke, Kwiryna. 2008. "Język kobiet i mężczyzn" [Language of Women and Men]. In Kwiryna Handke, *Socjologia języka* [The Sociology of Language], 134–219. Warsaw: Wydawnictwo Naukowe PWN.

Herbert, Robert K., and Barbara Nykiel-Herbert. 1986. "Explorations in Linguistic Sexism: A Contrastive Sketch." *Papers and Studies in Contrastive Linguistics*, 21: 47–85.

Holmes, Janet. 1998. "Women's Talk: The Question of Sociolinguistic Universals." In Jennifer Coates (ed.), *Language and Gender: A Reader*, 461–483. Oxford: Blackwell.

Jaworski, Adam. 1986. *A Linguistic Picture of Women's Position in Society: A*

Polish–English Contrastive Study. Frankfurt: Peter Lang.

Jaworski, Adam. 1989. "On Gender and Sex in Polish." *International Journal of the Sociology of Language*, 78: 83–92.

Jost, John T., and Aaron C. Kay. 2005. "Exposure to Benevolent Sexism and Complementary Gender Stereotypes: Consequences for Specific and Diffuse Forms of System Justification." *Journal of Personality and Social Psychology*, 88(3): 498–509.

Karwatowska, Małgorzata. 2010. "Twardy i niezależny czy nieśmiały i uczuciowy? Wizerunek mężczyzny w tekstach ogłoszeń towarzysko-matrymonialnych" [Tough and Independent or Shy and Emotional? The Image of Men in Social and Matrimonial Ads]. In Janusz Arabski and Justyna Ziębka (eds.), *Płeć Języka – Język Płci* [Gender of Language – Language of Gender], 127–140. Katowice: Wyższa Szkola Zarządzania Marketingowego i Języków Obcych.

Karwatowska, Małgorzata, and Jolanta Szpyra-Kozłowska. 2005. *Lingwistyka płci: On i ona w języku polskim* [The Linguistics of Gender: Him and Her in the Polish Language]. Lublin: Wydawnictwo Uniwersytetu Marii Curie-Skłodowskiej.

Kiełkiewicz-Janowiak, Agnieszka, and Joanna Pawelczyk. 2006. "Gender Stereotypes in Language Use: Polish and English." In Katarzyna Dziubalska-Kołaczyk (ed.), *IFAtuation: A Life in IFA: A Festschrift for Professor Jacek Fisiak on the Occasion of His 70th Birthday*, 349–383. Poznań: Wydawnictwo Naukowe UAM.

Kiełkiewicz-Janowiak, Agnieszka, and Joanna Pawelczyk. 2008. "Gender Stereotypes and Globalised Customer Service Communication in Poland." In José Santaemilia and Patricia Bou (eds.), *Gender and Sexual Identities in Transition: International Perspectives*, 76–100. Newcastle upon Tyne: Cambridge Scholars Publishing.

Kiełkiewicz-Janowiak, Agnieszka, and Joanna Pawelczyk. 2010a. "*Ladies First* ('Panie mają pierwszeństwo'): Polish Women's Responses to Ambivalent Sexism in Language." In Ana Antón-Pacheco and Isabel Durán (eds.), *Estudios de Mujeres* [Women's Studies Collection], vol. 7, *Diferencia, (des)Igualdad y Justicia* [Differences, (In)Equality and Justice], ed. Carmen Méndez, Joanne Neff, and Ana Laura Rodríguez, 133–148. Madrid: Editorial Fundamentos.

Kiełkiewicz-Janowiak, Agnieszka, and Joanna Pawelczyk. 2010b. "Deconstructing Ambivalent Sexism in Discourse: A Cross-Generational Study of Polish Men's and Women's Attitudes." In Claire Maree and Kyoko Satoh (eds.), *Proceedings of the 6th Biennial International Gender and Language Association Conference IGALA6* (CD edition), 176–185. Tokyo: Tsuda College.

Koniuszaniec, Gabriela, and Hanka Błaszkowska. 2003. "Language and Gender in Polish." In Marlis Hellinger and Hadumod Bußmann (eds.), *Gender across Languages: The Linguistic Representation of Women and Men*, 259–285. Amsterdam: Benjamins.

Kowalska, Beata. 2011. "Socjologia krytyczna a rozwój gender studies" [Critical Sociology and the Development of Gender Studies]. In Krystyna Slany, Justyna Struzik, and Katarzyna Wojnicka (eds.), *Gender w społeczeństwie polskim* [Gender in Polish Society], 57–69. Cracow: Nomos.

Kramer, Chris. 1977. "Perceptions of Male and Female Speech." *Journal of Language and Speech*, 20: 151–161.

Kuczyńska, Alicja. 1992. *Inwentarz do oceny płci psychologicznej* [Psychological Gender Inventory]. Warsaw: Pracownia Testów Psychologicznych PTP.

Lakoff, Robin. 1975. *Language and Woman's Place*. New York: Harper & Row.

Łaziński, Marek. 2006. *O paniach i panach: Polskie rzeczowniki tytularne i ich asymetria rodzajowo-płciowa* [On Ladies and Gentlemen: Polish Address Nouns and the Gender–Sex Asymmetry]. Warsaw: Wydawnictwo Naukowe PWN.

Litosseliti, Lia. 2006. "Constructing Gender in Public Arguments: The Female Voice as Emotional Voice." In Judith Baxter (ed.), *Speaking Out: The Female Voice in Public*

Context, 40–58. Basingstoke: Palgrave Macmillan.

Łyda, Andrzej, and Krystyna Warchał. 2010. "Jak akademicki jest dyskurs akademicki – płeć a leksyka w abstraktach artykułów naukowych" [How Academic is Academic Discourse? Gender and Lexicon in Abstracts of Scholarly Articles]. In Janusz Arabski and Justyna Ziębka (eds.), *Płeć języka – Język płci* [Gender of Language – Language of Gender], 85–105. Katowice: Wyższa Szkola Zarządzania Marketingowego i Języków Obcych.

Marody, Mirosława, and Anna Giza-Poleszczuk. 2000. "Być kobietą, być mężczyzną – czyli o przemianach tożsamości związanej z płcią we współczesnej Polsce" [Being a Woman, Being a Man, or about Gender Identity Changes in Contemporary Poland]. In Mirosława Marody (ed.), *Między rynkiem a etatem: Społeczne negocjowanie rzeczywistości* [Between the Market and Employment: Social Negotiation of Reality], 44–74. Warsaw: Scholar.

Mullany, Louise. 2007. *Gendered Discourse in the Professional Workplace*. Basingstoke: Palgrave Macmillan.

National Corpus of Polish. 2008–2011 At http://nkjp.pl/index.php?page=0&lang=1, accessed October 23, 2013.

Nowosad-Bakalarczyk, Marta. 2009. *Płeć a rodzaj gramatyczny we współczesnej polszczyźnie* [Sex and Grammatical Gender in Contemporary Polish]. Lublin: Wydawnictwo UMCS.

Rojczyk, Arkadiusz. 2012. "Stereotypy dotyczące płci w badaniu primingowym" [Gender Stereotypes in a Priming Study]. In Małgorzata Karwatowska and Jolanta Szpyra-Kozłowska (eds.), *Oblicza płci: Język – kultura – edukacja* [Images of Gender: Language – Culture – Education], 105–115. Lublin: Wydawnictwo UMCS.

Rothstein, Robert. 1993. "Polish." In Bernard Comrie and Greville G. Corbett (eds.), *The Slavonic Languages*, 686–758. London: Routledge.

Siwik, Anna. 2011. "Kobieta w Historii Polski" [Women in Polish History]. In Krystyna Slany, Beata Kowalska, and

Magdalena Ślusarczyk (eds.), *Kalejdoskop genderowy: W drodze do poznania płci społeczno-kulturowej w Polsce* [Gender Kaleidoscope: Toward Understanding Gender in Poland], 17–41. Cracow: Wydawnictwo Uniwersytetu Jagiellońskiego.

Slany, Krystyna, Beata Kowalska, and Magdalena Ślusarczyk, eds. 2011. *Kalejdoskop genderowy: w drodze do poznania płci społeczno-kulturowej w Polsce* [Gender Kaleidoscope: Toward Understanding Gender in Poland]. Cracow: Wydawnictwo Uniwersytetu Jagiellońskiego.

Stawiak-Ososińska, Agnieszka. 2009. *Ponętna, uległa, akuratna: Ideał i wizerunek kobiety polskiej pierwszej połowy XIX wieku (w świetle ówczesnych poradników)* [Alluring, Submissive, Scrupulous: The Ideal and the Image/Representation of the Polish Woman of the First Half of the 20th Century (Based on Advice Books)]. Cracow: Oficyna Wydawnicza Impuls.

Talbot, Mary. 2003. "Gender Stereotypes: Reproduction and Challenge." In Janet Holmes and Miriam Meyerhoff (eds.), *The Handbook of Language and Gender*, 468–486. Oxford: Blackwell.

Titkow, Anna. 2007. *Tożsamość polskich kobiet: Ciągłość, zmiana, konteksty* [Polish Women's Identity: Continuity, Change, Contexts]. Warsaw: Wydawnictwo, IFiS PAN.

Titkow, Anna. 2011. "Kategoria płci kulturowej jako instrumentarium badawcze i zródło wiedzy o społeczeństwie" [Gender as a Research Tool and Source of Knowledge of Polish Society]. In Krystyna Slany, Justyna Struzik, and Katarzyna Wojnicka (eds.), *Gender w społeczeństwie polskim* [Gender in Polish Society], 36–56. Cracow: Nomos.

Trudgill. Peter. 1999. "Language Contact and the Function of Linguistic Gender." *Poznań Studies in Contemporary Linguistics*, 35: 9–28.

Warchoł-Schlottmann, Małgorzata. 2007. "Aktualne problemy z feminizacją nazewnictwa w języku polskim" [Current Problems with the Feminization of Professional Names in Polish]. In Grzegorz Szpila (ed.), *Język polski XXI wieku: Analizy, oceny, perspektywy* [The Polish Language of the 21st Century: Analyses, Evaluations, Prospects], 237–248. Cracow: Tertium.

Żarnowska, Anna, and Andrzej Szwarc. 2008. "Ruch emancypacyjny i stowarzyszenia kobiece na ziemiach polskich przed odzyskaniem niepodległości – Dylematy i ograniczenia" [The Emancipation Movement and Women's Organizations in Polish Territories Before the Regaining of Independence: Dilemmas and Restrictions]. In Agnieszka Janiak-Jasińska, Katarzyna Sierakowska, and Andrzej Szwarc (eds.), *Działaczki społeczne, feministki, obywatelki … Samoorganizowanie się kobiet na ziemiach polskich do 1918 roku (na tle porównawczym)* [Female Social Activists, Feminists, Citizens … Women's Self-organization in Poland Before 1918], 14–28. Warsaw: Neriton.

Ziębka, Justyna. 2010. "Język płci – Dyskurs – Wartościowanie, czyli jacy jesteśmy prywatnie i służbowo" [Gendered Language – Discourse – Valuation, or What We Are Like at Home and at Work]. In Janusz Arabski and Justyna Ziębka (eds.), *Płeć Języka – Język Płci* [Gender of Language – Language of Gender], 141–157. Katowice: Wyższa Szkoła Zarządzania Marketingowego i Języków Obcych.

19 Historical Discourse Approach to Japanese Women's Language

Ideology, Indexicality, and Metalanguage

MOMOKO NAKAMURA

1. Introduction

Japanese women's language is a hegemonic ideological construct. Most Japanese language dictionaries include at least one of the terms *onna kotoba*, *josei go*, or *fujin go*, which all indicate women's language. Most Japanese have knowledge of what phonological, morphological, syntactic, and paralinguistic features are indexically associated with gender and are able to give typical contrastive examples of women's and men's languages, such as *Atashi onaka suita wa* and *Ore hara hetta zo* (both mean "I am hungry"), in which the first-person pronouns *atashi/ore*, the expressions for "hungry" *onaka suita/hara hetta*, and the sentence-final particles *wa/zo* are clearly gendered. Moreover, the polite, indirect, and soft ways of speaking are established as normative ways of expressing the speaker's femininity, high class, and/or elegance. Furthermore, women's language is assigned meanings and value other than gender alone. It is widely believed that women's language has a long history peculiar to the Japanese language, resulting in many people having a strong affection for women's language (Nakamura, in press).

Because of its hegemonic, normative status and rich meaning, Japanese women's language has provided one of the most interesting data sets for an ideological approach to language and gender studies. This chapter introduces historical discourse studies exploring the genealogy of Japanese women's language. The first section discusses problems with the previous approach. The second section describes the framework of a historical discourse approach. The third section demonstrates the contributions of the approach to language and gender studies. My choice of topic for this chapter is intended not to deny the importance of studies on local interactions but to inform readers of controversies emerging specific to the studies of Japanese language, attempting to frame them within a general discussion of language and gender. I hope that readers will integrate those contributions into the general theories of language and gender without falling into linguistic orientalism.

2. Japanese Women's Language: Problems

What constitutes women's language has been one of the major questions in language and gender studies. Women's language is the very site where gender, language, and power intersect in a complex manner. As any research is based on a specific conceptualization of the research objective, how women's language is conceptualized strongly affects the framework, research method, and interpretation of the data.

Previous studies on Japanese women's language have been carried out in precisely that way. The concept of women's language in previous studies had three major characteristics. First, it has been assumed that women's language naturally evolved from women's actual speech, because Japanese women spoke differently from men. Women's linguistic practice, therefore, is directly related to the notion of women's language. Second, such a view of gender differences is easily connected to the essentialist view that they are "rooted in women's common sensitivity based on their physiological nature" (Horii 1993, 101). Women's speech is claimed to reflect their feminine nature. Third, as women's linguistic practice is directly related to the notion of women's language, gender differences in language are considered to be derived from observable facts about women's linguistic practice. Numerous studies have been conducted to discover gender differences in local linguistic interactions, based on the assumption that the accumulation of gender differences ultimately delineates the whole picture of women's language. I refer to this approach as the essentialist-evolutionary approach. Many language and gender studies in Japan are still conducted based on that approach (see Yukawa and Saito 2004 for a review). Some scholars have pointed out, however, that such an approach cannot account for the crucial aspects of women's language. I will mention four major problems.

2.1   Women's heterogeneous practices

The first problem is the heterogeneity of women's linguistic practices. Studies of local interactions in Japanese have revealed that women's speech constantly changes and varies, according to age (Okamoto 1995), family relation and generation (M. Kobayashi 1993), education and occupation (Takasaki 1993), differences in everyday experience (Takano 2000), and region of residence (Sunaoshi 2004). They have demonstrated that women's linguistic practices are far too diverse to naturally form a single category of women's language, explicitly refuting the assumption that women's language has directly evolved from women's practice. Studies on queer-identified speakers (Abe 2010) and the ideological connection between politeness and women (Okamoto 2004) have also shown that the dominant values and functions of linguistic features, norms, and categories, including those associated with women's language, can be articulated in numerous forms in specific local interactions.

These findings indicate that homogeneous "linguistic gender differences" cannot be extracted from heterogeneous linguistic practice. Rather, linguistic gender differences are the products of past language and gender studies. It is impossible to assume that the diverse practices of women naturally form a single category of women's language. Women's language is not the style in which women speak. It is the category of women's language itself that presents heterogeneous women's linguistic practices as if they have something in common.

2.2   Women's language as the norm

Second, the essentialist-evolutionary approach cannot capture the normative aspect of women's language. In Japan, polite, indirect, and soft women's language functions as the strong norm of feminine speech. Parents scold young girls who use the vulgar speech of boys, in a common pattern of discipline. The norms of women's language are so naturalized as common sense that etiquette books of feminine speech are constantly on the list of bestsellers. The following is the result of searching books on amazon.com by *josei* (woman) and *hanashi kata* (way of speaking) in June 2008. Though 73 books are listed, I translate the titles of the first seven books:

(1) *Josei wa hanashi kata de kyuu wari kawaru*
   Women Can Change 90 percent by Changing Their Way of Speaking
(2) *Zettai Shiawase ni nareru hanashi kata no himitsu: Anata o kaeru "kotoba no purezento"*
   The Secrets of Speech that Bring Absolute Happiness: "Gifts of Language" that Change You
(3) *Josei no utsukushii hanashi kata to kaiwa jutsu: Kookan o motareru kotoba no manaa*
   Woman's Beautiful Way of Speaking and Conversation Techniques: Language Manners that Make a Favorable Impression
(4) *Soomei na josei no hanashi kata*
   How a Wise Woman Should Speak
(5) *"Hinkaku aru otona" ni naru tameno aisareru Nihongo*
   Japanese Language to Be Loved: How to Become "an Elegant Adult"
(6) *Ereganto na manaa to hanashi kata: Miryokuteki na josei ni naru 77 no ressun*
   An Elegant Manner and Way of Speaking: 77 Lessons to Become a Charming Woman
(7) *Bijin no hanashi kata: Sono hitokoto de anata wa aisareru*
   How a Beauty Speaks: Just One Word, Then You Will Be Loved

They all emphasize that a woman can improve her attractiveness by changing her way of speaking, and by speaking feminine women's language she can be elegant, wise, beautiful, happy, and loved. A woman's value and femininity are strongly connected to her way of speaking. At the same time, these books testify that feminine speech is a norm women need to read about and to learn consciously.

Why does women's language function as the norm? One reason is a long history of etiquette books telling women the norms of speech. These appeared as early as the fourteenth century, with the name of *jokunsho* (women's disciplinary books). In the seventeenth century, they were used as writing textbooks at *terakoya* (private temple schools) and, in the modern period, their lessons were incorporated in the moral textbooks used at schools (Nakamura 2003). The major lesson of these disciplinary books was that women should not speak:

(8) *Jokun sho* (Women's Disciplinary Excerpts) (1642).
  Do not praise others too much nor speak ill of others. Do not speak too much.

(Ishikawa 1973, 75).

(9) *Wazoku dooshi kun* (Lessons for Japanese Children) (1710).
  Too many words mean speaking too much… An ancient proverb says: "A woman's long tongue is the origin of trouble." It means that women's talk brings trouble to the country.

(Ishikawa 1977, 14)

This tradition of disciplinary books has continued through to today's etiquette books. The long history of etiquette books has made women's speech the object of control and regulation. The content of the norms, of course, has changed. No how-to-talk book today tells women not to speak. However, women's speech has remained the object of norms, control, and regulation over several centuries. Women's language is defined as polite, soft, and indirect, not because women have actually spoken politely, softly, and indirectly, but because numerous etiquette books have been telling women to speak politely, softly, and indirectly for hundreds of years. The control of women's speech is naturalized and legitimated as a way for women to achieve elegance, intelligence, beauty, happiness and love. That is why parents are supposed to scold their daughters for not speaking in a feminine manner.

The norms of feminine speech still restrict women's free expression today, in that women's speech can always be evaluated based on how she speaks rather than what she says. In November 2009, a government committee started screening ministries' budget requests. An Upper House female member of the committee, Renho, had several fierce, face-to-face battles with bureaucrats and gained public attention. On the last day of the committee's deliberation, a 70-year-old male rock musician Yuya Uchida appeared in the screening room. People were surprised to find him in this most unexpected place. Why did he come? His answer to a newspaper reporter was:

"The screening itself really shows democracy in action, but watching Renho on TV, I got angry at her rude way of speaking. That's why I came here today." [But, when asked about Renho on that very day, he said,] "Today, she was feminine. Her voice got hoarse and I felt pity for her." (*Asahi Shimbun*, November 28, 2009)

The rock musician decided to come to the screening because he was angry at her way of speaking, not at what she said. And he felt pity for her on the day he came to the screening, not because she stopped attacking bureaucrats, but because her way of speaking sounded feminine. This indicates that women's speech is often evaluated based on the norms of feminine speech – whether she sounds polite, soft, or indirect. At the same time, this example shows that the norms become a resource that women draw upon to become elegant, pleasant ladies. It is very possible that Renho learned there was some criticism about her way of speaking on previous days and that she changed it to a more feminine style on the last day of the committee's deliberations, when the rock musician visited. But as long as we directly relate women's language to women's practice, as the essentialist-evolutionary approach claims we should, we cannot ascertain how the norms of feminine speech simultaneously restrict and enable women's practice.

2.3   Values assigned to women's language

Third, the essentialist-evolutionary approach cannot explain why the notion of women's language is assigned more meanings and value than gender alone. It is widely believed, for instance, that women's language is a "beautiful" tradition of Japanese language. Women's language is a tradition, it is claimed, because it is the style in which women have spoken since ancient times. This belief is supported by another belief that women in the past used feminine language. Whenever I have argued that women's actual practices were too diverse to form a single notion of women's language, many people have responded, "Yes, women today do not speak women's language anymore, but women in the past did use feminine language and their speech became women's language."

Throughout history, however, we find documents criticizing certain women for not speaking in a feminine manner. This indirectly proves that there were always some women who did not use language in a feminine manner in any period. In the world's oldest novel, *The Tale of Genji*, there is a scene where young men discuss the daughter of a learned scholar who uses many Chinese words in her speech, and they say, "Where could you find such a woman? Better to have a quiet evening with a witch" (Murasaki 1976 [1003–1008], 36). At the time, the use of Chinese words was considered the ultimate in unfeminine behavior, but some women did use them. C. Kobayashi (1996, 298) documents that in a traditional *Kyoogen* play in the fourteenth century, entitled *Renjaku*, a female merchant says *Oryara shimasu* (I am), using the most polite and elegant women's language, when she introduces herself to the audience, but yells *Yai, kokonamono. Sokonoke* (Hey you! Move) at the man who has taken her place in the market. Even a woman in the fourteenth century used vulgar speech when necessary.

What, then, maintains the belief that women in the past used a feminine women's language? One of the factors constructing this belief is readers' letters to newspapers. Many Japanese newspapers have a readers' column and one of the most popular topics is the corruption of the Japanese language. Readers complain that the Japanese language is being destroyed, often citing women's use of nonfeminine language as an example. One peculiar characteristic of these letters, furthermore, is that they present women's use of nonfeminine language as a recent change. Thus almost all these letters start with the word, "recently." A 22-year-old student writes: "*Recently*, it seems noteworthy that the speech of young women, including mine, has gotten worse" (*Asahi Shimbun*, March 11, 1999; emphasis added). Interestingly, such criticism of recent corruption in women's speech can be found since the early modern period, as shown in the following discourses by two influential linguists in the early modern period and around World War II:

> (10) It is disgusting to hear a phrase **recently** popular among female students, such as *yokutte yo* (all right). Before the Meiji Restoration, the wives of *shogun*, feudal lords, and Tokugawa retainers all used elegant language. As a lady's language shows her dignity, women should watch their language. (Otsuki 1905, 17; emphasis added)
>
> (11) **Recently** in our country, the language of young men and women has declined dramatically. (Hoshina 1936, 231; emphasis added)

Japanese people have complained about the "recent" corruption of women's speech for over 100 years. Yet it is impossible that a recent change can have occurred for 100 years. Moreover, if complaining about women's unfeminine speech has not corrected their speech for 100 years, one might reasonably conclude that it is no use writing such letters to newspapers. Nevertheless, talking about the recent corruption of women's speech has another important function: to create the myth that women in the past indeed spoke feminine women's language. Implicit in the criticism that "recent" women's speech is unfeminine is the claim that, though recent women speak in an unfeminine manner, women in the past did indeed use feminine language. These letters thus play an important role in maintaining the myth that women in the past used feminine language and, also, the belief that such past feminine speech constituted a tradition of women's language.

2.4   Women's language as knowledge

Fourth, the essentialist-evolutionary approach ignores the fact that most Japanese learn about women's language from fictional conversations in the media. Most people in Japan speak their regional varieties in their everyday interactions. Women's language, however, is a standard variety. This means that most Japanese do not have the opportunity to hear standard women's language spoken by the women around them. This indicates that we acquire knowledge of women's language by listening to and reading female characters' speech in the media, such as TV dramas, films, comics, and novels. We learn what linguistic and stylistic features can be used to construct particular feminine identities from those fictional conversations. Women's language is not a style of speech used by actual women, as the essentialist-evolutionary approach claims, but knowledge we acquire by listening to the conversations of fictional characters in the media. As the use of particular features by female characters in fiction is repeatedly reproduced and widely consumed by a large audience, those features become associated with particular feminine identities.

The construction of indexicality through the language use of fictional characters is not confined to women's language. Most Japanese know, for instance, how aliens talk and what they say when they come to Earth. They are supposed to say *Wareware wa uchuu-jin da* ("We are aliens from outer space") with a flat intonation in a shrill, mechanical voice. They speak in Japanese. Japanese people know this not because their alien friends repeatedly say it, but because they have heard alien characters in fiction repeatedly talking like this in Japanese. We have the knowledge of how a particular group uses language, even if no group embodying that association actually exists, because we often acquire the knowledge from fictional conversations in the media. Accordingly, I argue that most Japanese take their knowledge of women's language from the media.

Such women's language is most typically demonstrated in the translation of non-Japanese literary works (Nakamura 2011). The following is the Japanese translation of Hermione Granger when she first appears in *Harry Potter and the Philosopher's Stone*:

(12)   "Maa, anmari umaku ikanakatta**wane**. Watashi mo renshuu no tsumori de kantan na jumon o tameshite mita koto ga aru**kedo**, minna umaku itta**wa**. Watashi no kazoku ni mahoozoku wa daremo inai**no**. Dakara, tegami o moratta toki, odoroita**wa**." (Rowling 1999 [1997], 158; emphasis added)
"Well, it's not very good, is it? I've tried a few simple spells just for practice and it's all worked for me. Nobody in my family's magic at all, it was ever such a surprise when I got my letter." (Rowling 1997, 117)

Her speech is translated into typical women's language with feminine final particles such as *wane*, *no*, and *wa*. Hermione, at this time, is 11 years old. I don't know any Japanese 11-year-old girl who talks like this. This is very feminine women's language which we rarely hear from Japanese women, especially from girls. Hermione's speech is translated into typical women's language that most Japanese girls of her age do not use.

This practice is not confined to literary works. In an interview with a Japanese newspaper, Angelina Jolie uses women's language in the Japanese translation, with the prototypically feminine final forms *wa* and *yo*.

(13)   Eiga o mita Braddo ga, "okaa-san ni niteru ne," to itte kureta nowa ureshikatta**wa**.
(I was happy when Brad [Pitt], on seeing the film, said, "You look like your mother.")
Mama-gyoo ni tenshoku **yo**.
(I'm switching to motherhood.)
(Asahi Shimbun, February 20, 2009; emphasis added)

The article emphasizes that overall, despite hardships and scandal in her past, Jolie's strong will to pursue what she believes in makes her shine like nobody else. This description of her independent character, however, is at odds with her use of women's language.

These mismatches happen precisely because the belief that women speak women's language causes the translator to draw on her knowledge of women's language in the translation process. A well-known translator, Kaori Oshima, confesses that:

> I sometimes translate even the same words differently depending on whether they are spoken by a man or a woman. Although I do not think that my translation is controlled by the so-called women's language, I realize that I restrict my own choice of words since I am unconsciously influenced by the norms of women's language internalized in myself. (Oshima 1990, 43)

From Scarlett O'Hara in *Gone with the Wind* to Hermione Granger in *Harry Potter* and Angelina Jolie in her interview with a Japanese newspaper, the speech of non-Japanese heroines has been translated into feminine women's language. Paradoxically, it is the translated speech of non-Japanese women that helps preserve the tradition of Japanese women's language. This leads us to the crucial question of who the authentic speaker of Japanese women's language is, requiring a translingual, global perspective to analyze the relationships between language and gender (Nakamura, 2013).

3. Historical Discourse Approach to Women's Language

How should we capture these norms, beliefs, and knowledge of women's language? Poststructural conception of gender performativity in the 1990s have precipitated not only studies of local interaction but also ideological approaches to language and gender studies (Hall 2003, 372). The diversity and differences observed in women's practices motivate redefining women's language as an ideological construct of preferred feminine speech patterns. As Gal (1995, 171) points out, "the categories of women's speech, men's speech, and prestigious or powerful speech are not just indexically derived from the identities of speakers ... [but are] culturally constructed within social groups." Gal's argument enables us to see the category of women's language not just as the sum total of linguistic features whose frequency of use distinguishes women from men, but as "an 'ideological-symbolic' construct which is potentially constitutive of those identities" (Cameron 1997, 28). The uses of women's language by "fantasy-line workers working for telephone sex lines (Hall 1995) and by drag queens on stage (Barrett 1999) testify that women's language serves as a symbolic resource anyone can draw on in constructing an identity. The ideological concept of women's language has instigated historical discourse studies exploring the development of Japanese women's language (Endo 1997; Inoue 2006; Nakamura 2007a; Okamoto and Smith 2004). The historical discourse approach to women's language is characterized by three major perspectives.

3.1 Women's language as language ideology

First, the historical discourse approach claims to distinguish practice from ideology, that is, to distinguish women's speech from the notion of women's language, and it proposes to examine women's language as a language ideology (see, e.g., Schieffelin, Woolard, and Kroskrity 1998; Cameron, Chapter 14 in this volume). One of the definitions of language ideologies is: "the cultural system of ideas about social and linguistic relationships, together with their loading of moral and political interests" (Irvine 1989, 255). This definition contains four assertions concerning the notion. First, language ideologies are not actual speech but ideas (including norms, beliefs, and knowledge) concerning language use. Second, language ideologies constitute a system. The boundaries and values of Japanese women's language are assigned in relation to other language ideologies, such as a Japanese national language and men's language, and the ideology of women's language should be examined in relation to the other language ideologies. Third, they are culturally constructed, and the system of language ideologies differs and varies according to the different political, economic, and academic situations that obtain at different times and places. Fourth, they form relationships that are hierarchically ordered by moral and political values, such as good/bad and correct/incorrect.

Language ideologies have been mainly identified on four linguistic levels. The most abstract level is ideologies of language itself, such as "language is a tool to express one's thoughts." Second, some languages are given ideological values, such as "the Japanese language is ambiguous." Third, within a particular language, linguistic categories, such as standard/nonstandard varieties, are distinguished by different values, of which women's language is one example. Finally, linguistic features, often through linguistic categories, are given different ideological values.

To study women's language as a language ideology, then, is to redefine it as the norms operating as a powerful hegemonic construct of preferred feminine speech patterns; as the belief that women's language is a Japanese language tradition that many Japanese women have used based on their natural femininity; and as knowledge about the indexical associations between particular styles and linguistic features with a particular kind of feminine identity.

3.2 Metalinguistic comments and fictional conversation as data

Second, the historical discourse approach assumes that the ideology of women's language has been historically constructed through discourse rather than through repeated use by women. We have already seen that etiquette books of feminine speech play a major role in producing and maintaining the norms of women's language. Readers' letters to newspapers are similarly pivotal in preserving the belief that women in the past used feminine language. Conversations in fiction and translated works effectively reproduce knowledge of women's language. These etiquette books, readers' letters, and fictional conversations constitute what I call "discourse." Following Foucault's (1981 [1972], 49) definition of discourse as "practices that systematically form the objects of which they speak," it becomes possible to consider women's language as constructed by these discourses. While the essentialist-evolutionary approach treats women's local practices as the discourses which formed the notion of women's language, the historical discourse approach considers that discourses such as etiquette books, readers' letters to newspapers, and fictional conversations have constructed women's language.

Etiquette books and readers' letters to newspapers constitute what are called "metalinguistic practices," talk about local practices. Recent work on language ideologies has been concerned with the ways our understanding of language is shaped by metalinguistic practice. Talk about local practice has been variously termed metapragmatics (Silverstein 1979), metadiscursive practices (Bauman and Briggs 2000), metalanguage (Jaworski, Coupland, and Galasinski, 2004), or metadiscourse (Hyland 2005), depending on which aspect of the process the researcher wants to emphasize. I use the term "metalinguistic practices" to emphasize the importance of locating them in a specific political process. Although the term "(linguistic) practice" commonly refers to the use of language in interactional contexts, it can also apply to metadiscursive practice, that is "discourse to represent and regulate other discourses" (Bauman and Briggs 2000, 142). Grammar books, for instance, are usually perceived to offer descriptions of the way language is spoken. Most grammar books, however, mainly delineate one variety as a standard and play a crucial role in giving it some kind of normative value, and privileging those who speak it. The analysis of grammar books as practice highlights who undertakes these practices, in what political context, and why. It relocates academic publications in what Silverstein (1998, 136) has called ideological sites, that is "institutional sites of social practice as both object and modality of ideological expression."

Metalinguistic practices, as a crucial site in constructing language ideologies, have been divided into two types, explicit metapragmatics, explicit talk about language, and implicit metapragmatics, the "linguistic signaling that is part of the stream of language use in process and that simultaneously indicates how to interpret that language-in-use," through interpretive guides such as contextualization cues (Woolard 1998, 9). The historical discourse approach argues, however, that the distinction between local practice and fictional practice is also crucial in analyzing the ideology of women's language, since it refutes the view that only women's local practices have constructed the ideology of women's language. Although I do not deny that people's attitudes toward women's language can be traced in part to women's local practices, conversation in fiction is repeatedly reproduced and widely consumed by a much larger audience over a longer time than face-to-face local practices are, and it has enormous influence on local practice. To deny the essentialist ideology that women's local practice directly constructs women's language, it is vital to strictly distinguish local practice from fictional practice. More attention to fictional conversation is necessary to study women's language as a language ideology, that is, as knowledge that we learn from conversation in media, as distinct from the heterogeneously creative local practices of women.

The historical discourse approach, therefore, mainly analyzes two types of discourse as data: metalinguistic discourse, that is, explicit commentary on women's speech, and language usage in fiction. The former type of discourse includes etiquette books, readers' letters to newspapers, school textbooks, dictionaries, grammar books, and commentaries by intellectuals. By evaluating, criticizing, and giving norms for women's speech, they construct women's speech as a socially important topic and they categorize the heterogeneity of actual women's speech into a homogeneous women's language. The latter type of discourse includes conversations in novels, movies, TV dramas, comics, TV games, advertisements, and folktales, and Japanese translation of these media.

3.3   Historical perspective

Third, the historical discourse approach emphasizes the importance of a historical perspective. A historical perspective does not simply entail analyzing diachronic changes in women's practice. Rather, a historical perspective is insightful because it makes explicit why a particular discourse became possible, acceptable, and meaningful in what political, economic, and academic context, while other discourses were excluded. As Inoue (2006, 16) has emphasized, what is important is not so much the content of what is said about women's speech, "but the sheer fact that it is said, or can be said in certain contexts by certain agents, and the fact that what is said is intelligibly repeatable in other domains of the society." The location of discourse in a historical context enables us to examine both metalinguistic discourse and fictional conversation as practices undertaken by a particular agent engaged in a particular sociopolitical process.

4. Theoretical Implications of the Historical Discourse Approach

This section describes four major theoretical contributions of the historical discourse approach to language and gender studies, citing the results of some major studies. For the details of analyses, see the studies cited in the References at the end of the chapter.

4.1   Construction of indexicality

The conception of language as a resource of identity construction urges us to ask how and why the indexical association between particular linguistic features and a particular identity is constructed, because people face problems not only in occupying existing identity categories, but, more often, by the fact that existing identity categories are already asymmetrically distributed. Nakamura (2007b), for instance, argues that Japanese gendered first-person pronouns function so as to force children to construct a heterosexual identity, maintaining and legitimating heteronormativity. In Japan, young children, both girls and boys, often call themselves by their first names, as that is how their family members address them. Once they are old enough to get into school, teachers and parents tell them to refer to themselves by gendered pronouns, *watashi* for girls and *boku* for boys, because the use of the pronoun rather than the first name is considered to be the common sense, standard way for a Japanese grown-up speaker to self-refer. Some homosexual and transgendered speakers have, in retrospective essays, expressed the difficulty and confusion they experienced both in referring to themselves by the gendered pronouns and in stating, or even understanding, their unwillingness to follow alleged mere linguistic custom. Their confusion increased as they faced further interventions from teachers and parents, and a sense of being different from their peer groups who seemed to have no difficulty changing to the use of pronouns. This problem resides not in occupying the heterosexual identity categories provided by the gendered pronouns, but in that the Japanese pronoun system allows only binary gendered identities.

In many of the linguistic approaches, however, identity categories are often taken for granted. The well-known debate between conversation analysis and critical discourse analysis discusses whether and how much social information, including gendered identity categories, we should consider in interpreting conversation data. Membership categorization analysis takes subject positions as given and examines how subject positions are occupied by speakers. Ochs's (1992) refined theorization of indexicality as the process in which some linguistic features directly index affective meanings, through which they are indirectly associated with social identities, also presupposes that indexical association already exists. The process by which indexicality is constructed has not become a major research objective because many assume that indexicality is constructed by repeated use by a particular group. In fact, the very term "indexicality" has been adopted from one of the Peircean signs, indices, which is the semiotic operation of juxtaposition. For example, the repeated co-occurrence of smoke and fire makes smoke an index of fire. Accordingly, the repeated use of particular linguistic features by a particular group is presumed to construct the indexical association between the features and the identity of the group. In discussing women's language or gay speech, therefore, whether the speakers so identified, and only those speakers, actually use specific features became one of the controversies (see criticisms of Lakoff 1975 and Kulick 2000). Nevertheless, as we have seen in the case of alien speech, Japanese language provides ample examples of indexicality, where there is no group embodying that association. In such a case, it is meaningless to discuss whether or not aliens, and only aliens, say, "We are aliens from outer space." Moreover, if we assume that indexicality is constructed by repeated use, we should conclude that women's language is also constructed by the repeated local practices of women, since the indexicality between feminine identities and particular linguistic features constitutes the notion of women's language. The logic of indexicality formation by repeated use contradicts the argument that women's language is not directly formed by the repeated local practices of women.

Rather, it is necessary to take into consideration the ideological mediation of indexicality construction. Woolard (1998, 18) points out that "simply using language in particular ways is not what forms social groups, identities, or relations … ; rather, ideological interpretations of such uses of language always mediate these effects." Gal and Irvine (1995) argue that three semiotic processes, iconization, fractal recursivity, and erasure, are at work in creating boundaries between languages and linguistic varieties.

The most elaborated study of indexicality construction is the historical discourse analysis of the construction of schoolgirl speech in Japan's early modern period from the late nineteenth to the early twentieth century. The process by which schoolgirl speech was formed provides an insightful case in point because the linguistic features of schoolgirl speech are assumed to constitute what we now call Japanese women's language. The historical discourse approach has demonstrated that metalinguistic discourse, that is, talk about women's speech, and fictional conversation have constructed schoolgirl speech. Briefly summarizing the studies on schoolgirl speech (Inoue 2006; Nakamura 2006; 2007a), metalinguistic discourse such as the commentaries of academics and politicians, by evaluating, criticizing, and giving norms for the speech of female students, drew people's attention to a new style of speech that had been innovated by a proportion of female students. This was named *teyo-dawa* speech, from its use of sentence-final forms *teyo* and *dawa*. The novel writers selected *teyo-dawa* speech out of the heterogeneous speech styles of female students and let their fictional student characters use it in conversation. As student characters in novels began to be described as sexual objects, *teyo-dawa* speech came to be recognized as schoolgirl speech. The sexualization of female students created a new identity category of schoolgirl by associating it with schoolgirl speech.

The construction process of schoolgirl speech explicitly demonstrates that the formation of a linguistic indexicality itself constructed the identity category of schoolgirl. When the Japanese government established the school system in 1872 and young women officially became students for the first time, there was no identity of "female student" as distinct from "male student." The schoolgirl identity did not exist before schoolgirl speech; instead, it was created by being associated with the use of a particular style. Indexicality construction is therefore not simply a process associating linguistic features with the identity of people that already exist, but a political process by which both social identity and language ideology are simultaneously constructed.

4.2   *Historical account of indexicality construction*

The historical discourse studies of schoolgirl speech also account for why the discourses which constructed the sexual identity of schoolgirl became possible, meaningful, and acceptable in the early modern period. One of the reasons is that

Japan's modernization in the late nineteenth century was pursued in conjunction with a gendered nationalization process that ascribed to male citizens the roles of worker and soldier and to female citizens those of wife and mother. In this project, the emergence of young educated women was deemed a threat to the nationalization of women. Thus it was urgent to distinguish students as schoolgirls and schoolboys, as sex objects and prosperous future citizens. The construction of schoolgirls transformed female students from dangerous women, who might attempt to become citizens equal to men, into sexual objects for men. Sexualization is always an effective means of genderization. This accounts for why intellectuals' metalinguistic discourses that paid critical attention to the *teyo-dawa* speech of female students and the use of the speech in novels became possible, meaningful, and acceptable. The explanatory power of the historical perspective gives a way out of a circular research paradigm, what Cameron (1990, 85) has called the "correlational fallacy," whereby merely establishing correlations between certain linguistic variables and a speaker's gender suffices but there is no explanation of why such correlations occur. By situating metalinguistic discourse and fictional conversation as practices in the specific political and economic processes of a particular historical juncture, the historical discourse approach allows us to account for why a particular indexicality has been constructed, that is, why a particular distinction between people was required.

4.3 Temporality of subversive practice

Third, the historical discourse approach gives an insight into the question of subversiveness. The poststructural notion of gender as performative has made it possible to imagine the transformation of gender asymmetry by subversive practices. Some researchers thus interpret the uses of women's language by queer-identified speakers as resisting and contesting, and as subversive performances showing the possibility of transforming the existing power order. However, researchers have also questioned why subversive performances often remain ephemeral, leaving the prevailing power order largely untouched (Kotthoff and Wodak 1997, xi). Philips (2003, 263) contends that "[t]he kinds of resistance described did not lead to any transformation of women's situations." (See also Philips, Chapter 15 in this volume.)

A historical discourse analysis of schoolgirl speech reveals that metalinguistic discourse transformed a resisting style (*teyo-dawa* speech), created by female students to express their own identity, into schoolgirl speech, a symbol of sexuality. Female students began using *teyo-dawa* speech to signify a nonchalant resistance to the Confucian-based policy of women's schools to educate girls to become good wives and wise mothers, which required them to use polite language (Honda 1990, 134). However, the gendered nationalization project exploited *teyo-dawa* speech in a broader context to transform female students into schoolgirls. No matter how many female students used it, *teyo-dawa* speech could not index the identity of the intellectual young woman. Simply using innovative language does not guarantee the creation of new identities because metalinguistic practices backed up by dominant ideologies are privileged in defining, characterizing, and determining the value and function of local practices. This denies the argument that we can actively construct our identities by using language. Moreover, the process of constructing schoolgirl speech shows that creative, innovative, and resistant local practice is often exploited to reinforce and complete the formation of dominant language ideologies. The novel writers selected one conspicuous style (*teyo-dawa* speech) out of the heterogeneous speech of female students to fuel the ideology of women's language. Nakamura (2003) similarly demonstrates how the speech of court women created by women working in the imperial court in the fourteenth century was exploited to reinforce the norms of feminine speech in the discourses of disciplinary books from the seventeenth to the nineteenth centuries.

Women's linguistic creativity and resistance have often been co-opted to support language ideologies consistent with dominant ideologies. More attention is needed on how dominant ideologies enable the metalinguistic practices of certain speakers to define the value of other speakers' local practices.

4.4   *Values of linguistic varieties*

Fourth, the historical discourse approach deconstructs and denaturalizes the value and affect assigned to linguistic varieties by describing the exact historical process of how values are assigned. As mentioned at the beginning of this chapter, it is widely believed in Japan that, because Japanese women have spoken women's language since ancient times, women's language is a tradition of the Japanese language. Nakamura (2004) has demonstrated, however, that women's language was invented as a Japanese tradition during the war period (1914–1945), when Japan was colonizing East Asia by forcing the colonized people to speak the Japanese language. To reinforce the superiority of the Japanese language and to legitimate Japan's linguistic invasions, the discourses which praised women's language as tradition suddenly became meaningful and prevalent. Mitchell (2009, 214), in analyzing the shifting emotional values attached to the Telugu language in south India, concludes that "emotional attachments to language, far from being naturally inherent in speakers' relationships to the words that they use, are historically situated."

5.   Conclusion

In analyzing discourse about Japanese women's speech, I was overwhelmed by a large amount of discourse criticizing, praising, referring, citing, and talking about women's speech throughout history. Women's relationship to language has certainly played a major role in constructing the gender order in Japan. Nevertheless, women's own voices and their changing, creative linguistic practices are absent from the discourse. The historical discourse approach makes it explicit that the complex ways women manage, negotiate, and manipulate language to express their own identities and experiences have yet to be explored. We have come a long way since Nichols's early contention (1983, 54) that "'[w]omen's language' is as much a myth as 'private language.'"

The historical discourse approach to women's language opens new interdisciplinary perspectives to language and gender studies. First, it enables us to deconstruct and denaturalize the essentialized relationship between language, gender, and sexuality by exploring the historical formation as well as the political and economic function of not only women's language but also men's language, gay speech, and other language ideologies related to gender and sexuality. Whose and what metalinguistic discourses have constructed these language ideologies, and what political and economic conditions enabled those discourses to be meaningful and acceptable in a specific time and place? (See also Cameron, Chapter 14 in this volume, for discussion.) It expands the data of language and gender studies from face-to-face local interactions to metalinguistic comments, fictional conversation, and their translations. Second, by redefining the norms, beliefs, and knowledge of women's language as a linguistic resource anybody can use, this approach makes it possible to examine the relationship between a language ideology and both fictional and local practices. How do the norms, beliefs, and knowledge of a language ideology simultaneously enable and restrict fictional and local practices? When and how do the norms, beliefs, and knowledge of a gender-related language ideology become relevant or irrelevant to a specific local interaction? And how do the fictional and local practices reproduce and transform a language ideology under what political and economic conditions?

REFERENCES

Abe, Hideko. 2010. *Queer Japanese: Gender and Sexual Identities through Linguistic Practices.* New York: Palgrave Macmillan.

Barrett, Rusty. 1999. "Indexing Polyphonous Identity in the Speech of African American Drag Queens." In Mary Bucholtz, A. C. Liang, and Laurel A. Sutton (eds.), *Reinventing Identities: The Gendered Self in Discourse*, 313–331. New York: Oxford University Press.

Bauman, Richard, and Charles L. Briggs. 2000. "Language Philosophy as Language Ideology: John Locke and Johann Gottfried Herder." In Paul V. Kroskrity (ed.), *Regimes of Language: Ideologies, Polities, and Identities*, 139–204. Santa Fe, NM: School of American Research Press.

Cameron, Deborah. 1990. "Demythologizing Sociolinguistics: Why Language Does Not Reflect Society." In John E. Joseph and Talbot J. Taylor (eds.), *Ideologies of Language*, 79–93. London: Routledge.

Cameron, Deborah. 1997. "Theoretical Debates in Feminist Linguistics: Questions of Sex and Gender." In Ruth Wodak (ed.), *Gender and Discourse*, 21–36. London: Sage.

Endo, Orie. 1997. *Onna no Kotoba no Bunka Shi* [The Cultural History of Women's Language]. Tokyo: Gakuyoo Shobo.

Foucault, Michel. 1981 [1972]. The Archaeology of Knowledge, trans. A. M. Sheridan Smith. New York: Pantheon.

Gal, Susan. 1995. "Language, Gender, and Power: An Anthropological Review." In Kira Hall and Mary Bucholtz (eds.), *Gender Articulated: Language and the Socially Constructed Self*, 169–182. New York: Routledge.

Gal, Susan, and Judith T. Irvine. 1995. "The Boundaries of Language and Disciplines: How Ideologies Construct Difference." *Social Research*, 62(4): 967–1001.

Hall, Kira. 1995. "Lip Service on the Fantasy Lines." In Kira Hall and Mary Bucholtz (eds.), *Gender Articulated: Language and the Socially Constructed Self*, 183–216. New York: Routledge.

Hall, Kira. 2003. "Exceptional Speakers: Contested and Problematized Gender Identities." In Janet Holmes and Miriam Meyerhoff (eds.), *The Handbook of Language and Gender*, 353–380. Oxford: Blackwell.

Honda, Masuko. 1990. *Jogakusei no Keifu: Saishiki sareru Meiji* [The Genealogy of Schoolgirl: Painted *Meiji*]. Tokyo: Seido Sha.

Horii, Reichi. 1993. "Joseigo no Seiritsu" [The Formation of Women's Language]. *Nihongo Gaku*, 12: 100–108.

Hoshina, Kooichi. 1936. *Kokugo to Nihon Seishin* [National Language and Japanese Spirit]. Tokyo: Jitsugyoo no Nihon Sha.

Hyland, Ken. 2005. *Metadiscourse: Exploring Interaction in Writing*. London: Continuum.

Inoue, Miyako. 2006. *Vicarious Language: Gender and Linguistic Modernity in Japan*. Berkeley: University of California Press.

Irvine, Judith T. 1989. "When Talk isn't Cheap: Language and Political Economy." *American Ethnologist*, 16(2): 248–267.

Ishikawa, Matsutaro, ed. 1973. *Nihon Kyookasho Taikei Oorai Hen 15: Joshi Yoo* [A Great Collection of School Textbooks in Japan, Letters 15: For Women]. Tokyo: Koodan Sha.

Ishikawa, Matsutaro, ed. 1977. *Onna Daigaku Shuu* [A Collection of Women's Studies]. Tokyo: Heibon Sha.

Jaworski, Adam, Nikolas Coupland, and Dariusz Galasinski, eds. 2004. *Metalanguage: Social and Ideological Perspectives*. Berlin: Mouton de Gruyter.

Kobayashi, Chigusa. 1996. "Josei no Ishiki to Joseigo no Keisei: Nyooboo Kotoba o Chuushin ni" [Women's Consciousness and the Construction of Women's Language: Centering on Court-Women Speech]. In Haruko Okano (ed.), *Onna to Otoko no Jikuu: Nihon Joseishi Saikoo 3 Onna to Otoko no Ran Chuusei* [The Space-Time of Women and Men: The Reconsideration of Japanese Women's History 3: The War of Women and Men, the Middle Ages], 293–336. Tokyo: Fujiwara Shoten.

Kobayashi, Mieko. 1993. "Sedai to Joseigo: Wakai Sedai no Kotoba no 'Chuuseika" ni Tsuite'" [Generations and Women's Language: On "Gender Neutralization" of Young Generations]. *Nihongo Gaku*, 12(6): 181–192.

Kotthoff, Helga, and Ruth Wodak. 1997. "Preface." In Helga Kotthoff and Ruth Wodak (eds.), *Communicating Gender in Context*, vi–xxv. Amsterdam: Benjamins.

Kulick, Don. 2000. "Gay and Lesbian Language." *Annual Review of Anthropology*, 29: 243–285.

Lakoff, Robin. 1975. *Language and Woman's Place*. New York: Harper & Row.

Mitchell, Lisa. 2009. *Language, Emotion, and Politics in South India: The Making of a Mother Tongue*. Bloomington: Indiana University Press.

Murasaki, Shikibu. 1976 [1003–1008]. *The Tale of Genji*, trans. Edward G. Seidensticker. New York: Knopf.

Nakamura, Momoko. 2003. "Discursive Construction of the Ideology of 'Women's Language': From *Kamakura, Muromachi* to *Edo* Periods (1180–1867)." *Nature–People–Society*, 34: 21–64.

Nakamura, Momoko. 2004. "Discursive Construction of the Ideology of 'Women's Language': The Impact of War (1914–1945)." *Nature–People–Society*, 37: 1–39.

Nakamura, Momoko. 2006. "Creating Indexicality: Schoolgirl Speech in Meiji Japan." In Deborah Cameron and Don Kulick (eds.), *The Language and Sexuality Reader*, 270–284. London: Routledge.

Nakamura, Momoko. 2007a. *Onna Kotoba wa Tsukurareru* [Constructing Women's Language]. Tokyo: Hitsuji Shobo.

Nakamura, Momoko. 2007b. *Sei to Nihongo: Kotoba ga Tsukuru Onna to Otoko* [Sex and Japanese: Woman and Man Constructed by Language]. Tokyo: Nihon Hosoo Shuppan Kyokai.

Nakamura, Momoko. 2011. "Translation: Inter-lingual Construction of Indexicality." *Nature–People–Society*, 50: 25–50.

Nakamura, Momoko. 2013. *Honyaku ga Tsukuru Nihongo: Hiroin wa Onna Kotoba o Hanashi Tsuzukeru* [Japanese Language Constructed by Translation: Heroines Speak Women's Language]. Tokyo: Hakutaku Sha.

Nakamura, Momoko. In press. "Affective Attachments to Japanese Women's Language: Language, Gender, and Emotion in Colonialism." In Jie Yang (ed.), *The Political Economy of Affect and Emotion in East Asia*. New York: Routledge.

Nichols, Patricia C. 1983. "Linguistic Options and Choices for Black Women in the Rural South." In Barrie Thorne, Cheris Kramarae, and Nancy Henley (eds.), *Language, Gender and Society*, 54–68. Rowley, MA: Newbury House.

Ochs, Elinor. 1992. "Indexing Gender." In Alessandro Duranti and Charles Goodwin (eds.), *Rethinking Context: Language as an Interactive Phenomenon*, 335–358. Cambridge: Cambridge University Press.

Okamoto, Shigeko. 1995. "'Tasteless' Japanese: Less 'Feminine' Speech among Young Japanese Women." In Kira Hall and Mary Bucholtz (eds.), *Gender Articulated: Language and the Socially Constructed Self*, 287–325. New York: Routledge.

Okamoto, Shigeko. 2004. "Ideology in Linguistic Practice and Analysis: Gender and Politeness in Japanese Revisited." In Shigeko Okamoto and Janet S. Shibamoto Smith (eds.), *Japanese Language, Gender, and Ideology: Cultural Models and Real People*, 38–56. Oxford: Oxford University Press.

Okamoto, Shigeko, and Janet S. Shibamoto Smith, eds. 2004. *Japanese Language, Gender, and Ideology: Cultural Models and Real People*. Oxford: Oxford University Press.

Oshima, Kaori. 1990. "Onna ga Onna o Yakusu Toki" [A Woman Translating a Woman]. *Honyaku no Sekai*, 15(11): 42–45.

Otsuki, Fumihiko. 1905. "Nihon Hoogen no Bunpu Kuiki" [The Distribution of Japanese Dialects]. *Fuuzoku Gahoo*, 318: 12–17.

Philips, Susan U. 2003. "The Power of Gender Ideologies in Discourse." In Janet Holmes and Miriam Meyerhoff (eds.), *The Handbook of Language and Gender*, 252–276. Oxford: Blackwell.

Rowling, J. K. 1997a. *Harry Potter and the Philosopher's Stone*. London: Bloomsbury.

Rowling, J. K. 1999 [1997b]. *Harii Pottaa to Kenja no Ishi* [Harry Potter and the Philosopher's Stone], trans. Yuko Matsuoka. Tokyo: Seizan Sha.

Schieffelin, Bambi B., Kathryn A. Woolard, and Paul V. Kroskrity, eds. 1998. *Language Ideologies: Practice and Theory*. New York: Oxford University Press.

Silverstein, Michael. 1979. "Language Structure and Linguistic Ideology." In Paul R. Clyne, William Hanks, and Carol L. Hofbauer (eds.), *The Elements: A Parasession on Linguistic Units and Levels*, 193–247. Chicago: Chicago Linguistic Society.

Silverstein, Michael. 1998. "The Uses and Utility of Ideology: A Commentary." In Bambi Schieffelin, Kathryn A. Woolard, and Paul V. Kroskrity (eds.), *Language Ideologies: Practice and Theory*, 123–145. New York: Oxford University Press.

Sunaoshi, Yukako. 2004. "Farm Women's Professional Discourse in Ibaraki." In Shigeko Okamoto and Janet S. Shibamoto Smith (eds.), *Japanese Language, Gender, and Ideology: Cultural Models and Real People*, 187–204. Oxford: Oxford University Press.

Takano, Shoji. 2000. "The Myth of a Homogeneous Speech Community: A Sociolinguistic Study of the Speech of Japanese Women in Diverse Gender Roles." *International Journal of the Sociology of Language*, 146: 43–85.

Takasaki, Midori. 1993. "Josei no Kotoba to Kaisoo" [Women's Language and Classes]. *Nihongo Gaku*, 12(6): 169–180.

Woolard, Kathryn A. 1998. "Language Ideology as a Field of Inquiry." In Bambi B. Schieffelin, Kathryn A. Woolard, and Paul V. Kroskrity (eds.), *Language Ideologies: Practice and Theory*, 3–47. New York: Oxford University Press.

Yukawa, Sumiyuki, and Masami Saito. 2004. "Cultural Ideologies in Japanese Language and Gender Studies: A Theoretical Review." In Shigeko Okamoto and Janet S. Shibamoto Smith (eds.), *Japanese Language, Gender, and Ideology: Cultural Models and Real People*, 23–37. Oxford: Oxford University Press.

20 Language and Gender in the Middle East and North Africa

ENAM AL-WER

1. Introduction

This chapter aims to review the most prominent results and interpretations emanating from research on the interaction between language and gender in the Arabic-speaking countries.[1] The vast majority of research on Arabic in this field follows the variationist sociolinguistic paradigm. (See Meyerhoff, Chapter 4 in this volume, for an overview of the treatment of gender within variationist sociolinguistics.) The early findings from Arabic appeared to contravene the general pattern of gender differentiation found elsewhere in sociolinguistic research by suggesting that Arab women use standard forms less frequently than Arab men. This apparent divergence from the pattern thought to be common forced scholars in the field to consider the case of Arabic as some sort of an anomaly. For instance, Labov (2001, 270) considered it "a widespread reversal of the positions of men and women predicted by Principle 2." By way of interpretation, the Arabic results were attributed to Arab women playing a less prominent role in public life, a domain that was presumed to require the use of standard linguistic features. Some scholars have also suggested that the pattern found in Arabic can be explained with reference to Arab women having less opportunity for access to standard linguistic features since a functional knowledge of the Standard variety is accessible only through formal education, and illiteracy levels are generally higher among female adults in many parts of Arabic-speaking communities. However, it is now widely accepted that the early findings from Arabic were misinterpreted. An alternative and more realistic interpretation was first put forward in Ibrahim's seminal article of 1986. Ibrahim's framework was consolidated by the findings and interpretation of gender-differentiated patterns in Haeri's Cairo study (1987), and by Al-Wer (1997), where findings from a range of Arabic speech communities are cited.

The Handbook of Language, Gender, and Sexuality, Second Edition.
Edited by Susan Ehrlich, Miriam Meyerhoff, and Janet Holmes.
© 2014 John Wiley & Sons, Inc. Published 2017 by John Wiley & Sons, Inc.

The reinterpretation of gender-differentiated patterns in Arabic has led to a critical review of the traditional ways of analyzing variation in Arabic altogether, and to fundamental changes in the methods and analytical framework adopted in current research on Arabic (see Al-Wer, 2013). The bulk of this chapter will be dedicated to these issues, which will at the same time provide a review of the major works on gender differentiation in Arabic as well as future directions in the field. We begin with some necessary background information about Arabic and Arab societies.

2. Arabic and Its Milieu

Arabic is spoken as a native language by some 250 million people in 22 separate countries collectively known as the "Arab world," which stretch from the Arabian (or Persian) Gulf in the east to the Atlantic Ocean in the west. Arabic is also spoken as a minority language in a number of neighboring locations, for example, Iran (Khuzestan), Uzbekistan, and Cyprus.[2]

Throughout the Arab world, the linguistic situation can be described as diglossic. Classical Arabic is the official Standard language (henceforth SA), used or required for use in the formal domains of the media and education and for all written purposes, while the dialects are used in informal domains and for everyday purposes. Typical of such situations is that the formal Standard language, here Classical Arabic, is not the mother tongue of anybody and while the spoken vernaculars, the mother tongues of Arabs, are extremely diverse, SA is almost uniform throughout the Arab world.[3]

Notwithstanding the apparent similarity in the linguistic situation as described above, it is important to emphasize that the countries of the Arab world are diverse in the ethnic composition of their populations, in social and political history, economic resources, and means of production. Literacy rates and gender parity in literacy and participation in the labor force vary tremendously. In some regions the literacy rate of the adult population of both sexes is similar to that of the developed world, whereas in other regions, the female literacy rate is as low as 28 percent. Typical of the countries of the Arab world, as of developing countries in general, is a relatively wide gap between the city and the countryside in development and access to resources and services. These sharp differences across countries and within communities have parallel social, cultural, and socioeconomic differences that influence the daily pursuits and future prospects of individuals. Therefore, global generalizations with respect to language and gender issues in Arabic as a whole remain superficial unless the analysis begins at the level of the local dialect and is situated in the local social context.

Analyses of gender as a social construct and its dynamics in Arab societies are still in the early stages of development, although important contributions have been made, especially over the past two decades, by intellectuals, social scientists, and feminist writers whose primary concern is gender inequality and questions of women's rights.[4] The lagging behind of Arab societies in this area is closely connected with underdevelopment in the political systems of the Arab countries as a whole. Issues of gender politics are often treated as nationalist issues, which are tied up with the political history of the region in various ways. While the general paucity of sophisticated analyses of gender in Arab societies has adversely affected the ways in which Arabic data have been interpreted, more acutely the problem can be described as a lack of integration into sociolinguistic interpretations of the advances that have been made in other disciplines, particularly in sociology, political theory and anthropology. It is fair to say that while there has been a marked improvement in research methodologies and more generally of the quality of the data obtained from sociolinguistic research, the interpretation of gender-differentiated patterns in Arabic continues to rely on a stereotyped understanding of gender, with a few shining exceptions that will be pointed out in the course of this review.

With this background in mind, I now turn to reviewing the major findings from sociolinguistic research. I begin with the studies and analyses that deal with gender differentiation in some aspect of "discourse" and "code choice.'

3. Research on Language Use and Code Choice

As mentioned above, the bulk of research on gender differentiation in Arabic is variationist in approach, dealing with variables at the level of the word for the most part and covering structural features in phonology, morphology, and morphosyntax. Research on gender differentiation in language use in Arabic, of the type that investigated the use of some of the features mentioned by Lakoff (1975), for example, "tag questions," "hedges," "interruptions," and so on, or research that deals with conversational/discourse strategies in Arabic is rather thin on the ground, and most such research focuses on explaining the behavior of women.

In the field of "code choice," and focusing in particular on Morocco, an important analysis is Fatima Sadiqi (2003).[5] Sadiqi presents a view of the interaction between the Arabic language and gender from the perspective of "sites of power" in the Arab Islamic World, namely religion, politics, the law, and literacy, such that the domination of men in these arenas and the exclusion of women from them has created an association between the use of SA and male speech, thus establishing what Sadiqi calls "sociolinguistic androcentricity" paralleling the social and cultural patriarchy of Arab Islamic societies which is based on "space dichotomy": men are associated with the public space and women with the private space. There are thus two components to this analysis: (1) SA is associated with the public space while vernacular Arabic is associated with the private space; the exercise of real power takes place in the public space. (2) In the public space, men are dominant while women are marginalized (see Philips, Chapter 15 in this volume.) In religion, she suggests that the language of the Quran, SA, is both more accessible to and more significant for men than for women. This is because although Arab Muslim women may express strong belonging to their religion, and, by association, to SA as the medium through which the religion is practiced (e.g., prayer and religious sermons), *public* religious practices are largely confined to men. In cases where women venture to express views on religious matters in public they are often severely rebuked and their views are seen to lack authority. For instance, Sadiqi draws attention to the hostile reactions of some sectors in Arab societies across the Arab world against the well-known thinker Nawal El Saadawi who often speaks out on controversial religious matters. Sadiqi further suggests that the confinement of women's "religious space" also leads to women having less exposure to, and hence less proficiency in, SA. In politics, Sadiqi's second site of power where SA rules supreme, women's public space, is just as marginalized, which is clearly reflected in Arab women's modest participation in political activity overall, although there are significant variations across different countries in this sphere. In literacy, women's marginalization can be seen in the gender disparity in literacy. Where gender disparity exists, it is always the women who lag behind. Since a functional knowledge of SA is closely connected with formal schooling, the relatively high rates of illiteracy among women in some parts of the Arab world denies them an important tool of competition in the public space. Literate and highly educated women can also be marginalized in this sphere; women writers, for instance, are relatively scarce. Sadiqi makes the interesting observation that "knowledge" in general is seen to threaten women's femininity, a highly valued attribute that women are expected to possess. The marginalization of women in the law can be connected with illiteracy. In this case, illiterate individuals are less likely to understand the language of the law and hence are often ignorant of their rights. The advances that have been achieved by women in the public sphere in some countries of the Arab world are recognized by Sadiqi to have linguistic consequences. Interestingly, not only is there an increase in the use of SA by women in public debates in Morocco, as a means to gain legitimacy and to compete on equal grounds with men in the public space, but there also seems to be an increase in the use of the vernacular in the media, a domain in which SA is predominant; the implication being that the increase in women's visibility in the public space has widened the domains in which the vernacular is used. This is an interesting hypothesis, although there is as yet no empirical data to establish a direct link between the increase in the use of the vernacular in the media and women's involvement. Arab women's success in gaining some recognition in the public space may be seen as a development toward recognition of the rights of marginalized groups in general, and thus the inclusion in the public domain of the vernacular, a marginalized code that is accessible to all rather than being the monopoly of an elite, may be considered as a concomitant development.

Within the same area of inquiry, code choice, Reem Bassiouney (2010) investigated gender differentiation in the use of SA and the Egyptian vernacular by educated men and women in talk shows, factoring in the intended audience and topic of discussion, in addition to the educational background and expertise of the participants in the topic of discussion. Her results overall show no differences in the frequency of usage of SA and Egyptian vernacular features between the women and the men participants, and in some cases the women in fact used SA features more frequently than the men. The significant factor that showed positive correlation with the frequency of switches to SA features in this study was expertise in the topic of discussion rather than the sex of the speaker. Bassiouney interprets this finding as a projection of "identity." For instance, when the topic of discussion was poverty and street children, the woman participant who was a director of a nongovernmental organization that cares for street children interrupted a male journalist participant and switched to SA, thus displaying her expertise knowledge on the subject. Another extract shows a female judge switching to SA when the topic of discussion fell within her area of expertise. In this example the use of SA can be further interpreted in terms of "indexicality"; SA is associated with authority in the courtroom, and the speaker appropriates this association to give her statements an authoritative tone. Similarly, in an extract from a male member of parliament addressing the Egyptian assembly on the matter of sanctions on Iraq the speaker uses SA, rather than a mixture of SA and the Egyptian vernacular as often happens in the Egyptian parliament. Bassiouney interprets the use of SA in this example as indexing both authority and a pan-Arab identity (rather than a narrower Egyptian identity). Both the female and male participants in this research were found to appropriate the values associated with the use of SA and the Egyptian vernacular in a meaningful way.

In another study, Bassiouney (2009) investigated the language of commercials on Egyptian television in relation to the target audience. Her findings confirm a popular perception of a link between women and vernacular speech on the one hand and between SA, men, and professionals (of both sexes) on the other. For example, in an advertisement for ghee (purified cooking butter) targeting housewives the language used by the female character is purely vernacular Egyptian. In a commercial advertising baby food targeting professional women a mixture of both codes is used. Interestingly, the code used when advertisers targeted housewives in the ghee advert is the same code used in an advert employing talking cockroach cartoon characters to advertise a brand of insecticide.

In a unique study of its kind on Arabic, Barontini and Ziamari (2009) analyzed the discourses of a middle-aged peasant woman (M) who worked in a male-dominated rough environment and six young urban women aged 17–20 from Meknes, Morocco. The analysis revealed a tendency in all women informants to adopt features of speech and strategies that are widely recognized as representing "masculine talk." In the case of M, learning to talk like a man is a survival strategy in the harsh chauvinistic environment of the workplace. It is a way to gain some respect. Talking like a man involves learning how to take control when confronted with verbal abuse and harassment, to be witty, and to return abuse tenfold. So, when a male colleague refers to a woman (not present) as a "whore," M responds by calling him a "jackass son of donkeys" (159); and if a man "curses the religion of her God" she responds by "cursing his mother's religion" and threatens to "shred his face and knock him senseless" (160) – in this way "she gains respect" (162) and "they do not come anywhere near her again" (163). M says "the women who do not respond to abuse are abused further" – "it takes guts, a scared woman will not respond" (161).

In the case of young urban women, "masculine talk" involves using specific linguistic features. These include terms of address like "my friend," "my brother" (both used with masculine grammatical endings); using masculine grammatical inflections and endings on verbs, adjectives, and participles; phonetic features widely recognized as being characteristic of male speech, for example palatalization of /t/ as /tʃ/ rather than /tˢ/ which is characteristic of women's speech; lexical features such as the use of obscenities and insults. For the young women, integrating features of male speech into their discourse is a way of self-representation, a rebellious act to free themselves from the prescribed social rules about how women should behave. In this network, this way of talking was used also as a symbol of "bonding" and "fitting in" among the network members; it is a "fun game" that breaks normative rules (164–165).

4. Variation in Vernacular Arabic and Gender Differentiation

Interest in vernacular Arabic began with research in Arabic dialectology, which goes back to the late nineteenth century, that is, around the same time that studies on the dialect geography of European languages were being developed.[6] Early work in Arabic dialectology, and to some extent sociolinguistics, suffered methodological drawbacks similar to those found in the early dialectological research in Europe, in terms of the predominance of male researchers and the under-representation or absence of female and younger informants, in addition to focusing on rural/tribal dialects. Naturally, in this type of research it is rare to find data dealing with gender differentiation. A rather unique study in this field is Roux (1925), which investigated the Muslim dialect of Meknes, Morocco, in particular his report concerning the use of three innovative phonetic features exclusively by the women of Meknes.[7] These features are: fronting of /ʃ/ and /ʒ/ to [s] and [z] respectively, and a uvular [ʁ] pronunciation of /r/. Although Roux's claim regarding "exclusive usage" of the innovative sounds by the women of Meknes cannot be verified (and may well be exaggerated), his findings can be taken to indicate sound changes in progress, especially since the sounds considered to be innovations in Roux's research are now known to be widespread in various dialects of the Maghreb (e.g., in Jewish Algerian and in Fes in Morocco). In other words, what Roux's study seems to have captured may have been early stages of sound change which was led by female speakers.

While sociolinguistic research in North America and the United Kingdom from the start anchored its findings on dialectological descriptions where available, regrettably for Arabic sociolinguistics it is rare to find references to dialectological research in studies of variation in spoken Arabic. In this sense, Arabic sociolinguistics has remained disconnected from Arabic dialectology, although this situation is beginning to improve. A fundamental problem that may have contributed to this disconnection is a top-down approach to the analysis of Arabic data, which begins with "diglossia" as the framework of analysis, thus presenting variation in spoken Arabic as a case of opposition between standard and nonstandard features/ varieties.[8] Since the norms of SA are strictly prescribed throughout the Arab world, this framework of analysis is tantamount to assuming that the structure of variation and the course of language change in Arabic are invariant, which is of course incorrect. In Arabic, as in all other languages, linguistic variation and change is structured by an interaction between linguistic and social variables, and both types of constraints are peculiar to each dialect and each community. Importantly, the linguistic constraints on variation are dictated by the respective native Arabic dialects of each community, not by structures or features found in the Standard variety (see below). The failure to account for these basic facts in the analysis in some of the research on Arabic has led to all sorts of misleading conclusions, including conclusions about gender differentiation.[9]

One such conclusion regarding gender differentiation in Arabic, made on the basis of research findings from the 1970s and 1980s that analyzed variation in spoken Arabic as a case of approximation to or divergence from the Standard variety, claimed that Arab women contradicted the pattern found elsewhere by *not* using "standard prestigious features" as frequently as Arab men.[10] This was found to be a misconstrued generalization by Muhammad H. Ibrahim (1986). He pointed out a number of problems in the interpretation of Arabic data in general, which stem from what he identified as confusing the notions of "standard variety" with "prestigious variety." He suggested making a distinction between the status of the Standard variety as a transnational norm, and the status of the spoken dialects, which have their own hierarchy of prestige at the local and regional levels. On the basis of her data from Cairo, Niloofar Haeri (1987) also refuted the claim that gender-differentiated patterns in spoken Arabic were anomalous in any way. I have argued (Al-Wer 1997; 2013) that while Standard Arabic clearly has a function in Arabic-speaking societies, as the norm used in formal written and spoken domains, and it undoubtedly also has a psychological claim on native speakers of Arabic, it does not play a role nor does it have a normative effect on the structure of variation in spoken Arabic in the core domains of phonology, morphology, and syntax (nor on the direction of language change in the vernacular).[11] Its involvement in studies of variation in spoken Arabic seems to be based on ideological considerations rather than on empirical data.

A related problem in the interpretation of data from Arabic concerns the use of labels such as "prestige" and "stigma" without prior analysis of the factors that may have given rise to such values, and in some cases in contradiction to the empirical evidence. The controversy surrounding the notion of "prestige" is widely recognized in sociolinguistic research in general but while the problems associated with the use of the term largely arise at the level of data interpretation in the case of English, in the Arabic case the problems extend to the analytical framework, yielding contradictions between the empirical findings and the interpretation of these findings. For instance, in many cases of change in progress a "standard" feature is abandoned in favor of a "nonstandard" feature and in all such cases the leaders of the change are the most educated and the most upwardly mobile members of the community. To illustrate this point, consider the case of the interdental variable (θ) in Jordan which has two variants: the variant [θ] is characteristic of the traditional Jordanian dialects and at the same time is a standard feature; the variant [t] is characteristic of the new city dialects and is the variant found in all of the urban and dominant varieties in the region as a whole. The results from five studies in Jordan[12] found that a change is in progress led by young and highly educated speakers from the local (and standard) feature [θ] towards the new supralocal (and nonstandard) feature [t]. Clearly, the standard feature is not the target in this change. At the same time, it would be inaccurate to interpret this result as an abandonment of a standard feature; rather, the departing feature just *happens* to be identical to the feature found in the Standard variety. The data available so far suggest that the Standard variety is simply irrelevant in the processes of variation and change in vernacular Arabic.

Data from research on Arabic are not always presented in such a way as to make it possible to test them against generalizations in the field, in addition to the fact that the research available so far covers only very few communities relative to the size of the population of native speakers of Arabic. Put as closely as possible in the terms of the two generalizations about gender-differentiated patterns (Labov 1990), data from Arabic seem to confirm both generalizations. Other things being equal, the female speakers use features which are "rated favorably" or have positive connotations of various sorts and for various reasons more consistently than men. The notions of localized versus supralocal features (Milroy et al. 1994) aptly describe the results from Arabic. In these terms, women favor supralocal forms whereas men tend to use localized forms more consistently. In cases of change in progress, the available evidence suggests that women are ahead of men.[13] In the data available, women are sometimes ahead of men by a whole generation. For example in Al-Wer's (1991) investigation of the use of four phonological variables in three towns in Jordan, the men were found not to participate in the variation between the local and nonlocal features at all. In a follow-up study in one of these towns 10 years later, the young men were beginning to participate in the variation that involved three sounds /θ/, /ð/ and /dʒ/. In the dialect of Amman, the female speakers were found to lead in all cases of divergence from the traditional features.[14] A counterexample to these findings is reported by Atiqa Hachimi (2011) in Casablanca with reference to the behavior of male and female speakers from a Fessi background, that is, descendants of families who originally came from the city of Fez, Morocco. One of the features that distinguish between the dialects of Fez and Casablanca is the phonetic quality of /r/. The traditional Fessi dialect has a postalveolar approximant [ɹ] while Casablanca has alveolar trill [r]. Hachimi found that among this migrant group in Casablanca the Fessi men lead the Fessi women in adopting the Casablancan trill pronunciation of /r/.[15]

A very interesting pattern of variation is reported by Aziza Al-Essa's research (2008; 2009) of dialect contact in the city of Jeddah, Saudi Arabia. Overall, she found that among the oldest generation, the women were considerably more conservative with respect to the traditional (Najdi dialect) features, which is explained with reference to "social segregation" and thus lack of contact with and access to the target (Hijazi dialect). The Najdi community in Jeddah impose strict rules against mixing with members of the majority community (Hijazi), and this prohibition is stronger on the women. However, as the social restrictions were eased off in successive generations, the women outscored the men overall in adopting new features that were characteristic of the dialect spoken by the wider city community. In this study, the effect of frequency of exposure to the target features and social restrictions on socialization is demonstrated quite dramatically in the case of the morphophonemic variable -*ik*, the second-person singular feminine suffix. Tokens of this variable can occur *only* in the context of a female addressee. Because interaction between women and men outside the family is heavily restricted, the men end up having less frequent encounter with the target variant -*ik*. The findings show that while in the oldest generation the men use a higher proportion of the target feature than women, in the middle age group the women score 100 percent success in adopting the target feature. Walters (1991) reports a similar finding in Korba, Tunisia, where due to isolation the old women maintain the usage of stigmatized raised variants of /ɛ:/. Jabeur (1987) found a similar pattern regarding the use of diphthongs versus monophthongs in Rades, Tunisia.

In the world's oldest city, Damascus, Hanadi Ismail (2007; 2009) investigated variation and change in the use of two linguistic variables, one of which turned out to be in stable variation and the other in change in progress. Ismail's analysis of the community's history in relation to the socioeconomic changes in Damascus showed that as a result of the physical expansion of the city, which began in the early 1970s, new dimensions of linguistic variation emerged which related to two aspects of life in Damascus, namely residence in a traditional inner city district (Shaghoor) versus in a new satellite suburb (Dummar). These in turn broadly correlated with two different "life modes" (Højrup 2003), self-employed versus professional, respectively. She found very little variation across age and gender groups with respect to the stable variable. The second variable, (r), is a new variable that concerns lenition of /r/. Four types of variants were identified: trills (the traditional variant), retroflex, fricative, and approximant. In all, 4,763 tokens were coded for five phonetic environments. The results of the GoldVarb analysis showing the most advanced (innovative) nontrill variant are displayed below.

Statistically all correlations were found to be significant and the variable of age was found to have the most significant effect, indicating a change in progress toward an approximant type of /r/. The results also show that the locus of the change is the suburb (Dummar), where the new pronunciation appears in significant proportions also in the speeches of the middle and old age groups. The gender effect is particularly interesting: here we notice that while in the suburb the young female speakers have a clear lead, in the inner city locality of Shaghoor it is the young male speakers who lead the change. This finding is explained in relation to the employment situation. At the time of research, all except one of the women in Shaghoor were unemployed and all of the men were employed in the retail sector, which brought them into direct and regular contact with customers from all walks of life and from all parts of the city.

Table 20.1. Distribution of (r) by age groups and gender in Dummar and Shaghoor (based on Ismail 2007, 207)

		Male	*Female*
Shaghoor	Y	29% (406)	23% (407)
	M	4% (294)	5% (449)
	O	1% (380)	3% (393)
Dummar	Y	19% (422)	27% (499)
	M	21% (414)	10% (393)
	O	4% (379)	20% (427)

Atiqa Hachimi's research in Casablanca (mentioned earlier; also see Hachimi 2007; 2012) is the first study in Arabic to use the "communities of practice" methods. It focused on style and dialect leveling; in particular it investigated the linguistic and social outcomes of contact between the Fessi (from Fez) and Casablancan dialects in the speech of a group of women in the city. She shows how growth and increasing heterogeneity in the city's population have disrupted the old rural/urban dichotomy, the once dominant characteristic of Moroccan city dialects and identities. In Casablanca, mass migration has created a new linguistic urban model. Fessi is a well-established old urban dialect but Casablancan in contrast is a newly formed koine. Among the linguistic variables investigated, two are phonological, (r) and (q). These variables distinguish between the Fessi dialect, an old urban dialect that enjoys considerable prestige, and Casablancan, a fairly new urban dialect. The results overall show that the speakers use the linguistic forms as a resource in the construction of identities and different styles that are directly related to their lives and daily pursuits in the city. In addition to the old identities, such as "pure Fessi," and their linguistic correlates (maintenance of the heritage variants), the speakers construct hybrid identities, which correlate with hybrid linguistic behavior. For instance, for a Fessi to become Casablancan, the heritage Fessi variants [ʔ] and [q] are selectively filtered in favor of [g] in [ga:l], and the Casablancan trilled /r/ is adopted instead of the Fessi approximant [ɹ]. Importantly, in addition to denoting the status of "becoming Casablancan," this combination of features, [g] and trilled [r], is central to becoming "tough," "street smart," and "independent." Sounding "tough" is valued positively by the Fessi women in Casablanca as a criterion that distinguishes them from the Fessis from Fez. The stylistic shifts in the informants' speech is not dictated by the diglossic situation or by the shifting of task or topic, but by a dynamic that is directly related to the everyday realities which inhabitants of a heterogeneous city have to negotiate on daily basis. The studies by Hachimi and by Barontini and Ziamari (see above) clearly demonstrate the inadequacy of a stereotyped understanding of gender differentiation in Arabic. In both studies, female groups behave in a manner that contradicts popular perceptions of "feminine" linguistic behavior.

A recent analysis of "the lifecycle" of the variable (q) in Jordan traces all stages of development in the progression of the change from [g] to [ʔ] in the dialect of Amman, the capital city of Jordan (Al-Wer and Herin 2011). The analysis is based on nearly 90 hours of recorded material, collected intermittently over the past 25 years. The Amman community is made up of two Arabic-speaking ethnic groups: a Jordanian group and a Palestinian group. Variation in (q) involves Jordanian [g] and (urban) Palestinian [ʔ]. The urban Palestinian variant [ʔ] is also found in all major city dialects in the Levant region as a whole, such as the dialects of Damascus, Beirut, Aleppo, and Jerusalem. In this sense, [ʔ] can be considered a supralocal variant. On the other hand, the variant [g] is characteristic of less dominant and more provincial dialects, although it can be found in all of the dialects in southern Syria as well as all of the indigenous Jordanian dialects. In the Levant region, [g] can be considered a localized feature. Amman is an ancient location whose long history goes back to the eighth century BCE, but it was established as an Arabic-speaking city only in 1921. Therefore, it has no traditional dialect and only three generations of native inhabitants.

Regarding the variable (q), the results from Amman show that across the three generations, gender has a consistent effect, although it interacts with other social variables differently in different generations. In the first generation, there is a high degree of maintenance of the respective heritage variants. However, two groups of speakers diverged from this pattern. The Palestinian men, whose heritage variant is the glottal stop, used a few tokens of Jordanian [g] (7/52 tokens); the other group that showed divergence from the heritage dialect was the Jordanian women. They used a few tokens of the glottal stop (5/48 tokens). The remaining subgroups, the Palestinian women and the Jordanian men, consistently used their respective heritage variants and thus showed no variation. The divergences by the Palestinian men and the Jordanian women of this generation, although relatively low in frequency, are the first signs of some of the trends that became established in successive generations. In the second generation, there is no change to the patterns found among the most conservative groups, the Jordanian men and the Palestinian women. On the other hand, the divergence we saw in the first generation on the part of the Jordanian women and the Palestinian men increases considerably. In this generation, the Jordanian women use [ʔ] predominantly (65/74 tokens) and the Palestinian men use the Jordanian variant [g] in nearly 50 percent of the total number of tokens (59 tokens). In this generation gender differentiation emerges as an important variable, and the significance of ethnicity (or dialectal background) is blurred since speakers from both backgrounds use both variants.

In the third generation, there are two important developments. First, in addition to gender and ethnic affiliation, context and interlocutor emerge as further constraints on the choice of (q) variants for the men. Second, gender emerges as the *major* organizing category while ethnic affiliation assumes a subsidiary role in influencing the speakers' choices. In this generation, the female speakers simply advance the pattern that was set out by their mothers' and, to some extent, their grandmothers' generations. They use the glottal stop consistently (regardless of their ethnic origin). On the other hand, the men's choices are constrained by three variables: *dialectal background, gender* and *context*. The expansion in the use of the glottal stop can be taken to indicate a change in progress since all of the young female speakers, regardless of their origins, use this variant consistently. Furthermore, regional koineization clearly plays a role in advancing the glottal stop.

This example from Amman is particularly interesting because it is not often that one comes across cases where it is the male speakers who do more work, so to speak, in shifting their speech in social interaction. In particular, the finding that the male speakers (especially those from a [g]-speaking background) also use the glottal stop, a sound that is widely described as "feminine" and "soft" in the literature on Arabic, is significant. The expansion in the use of the glottal stop among the young men can be explained in relation to the creation of new job opportunities in the private sector, especially in the financial sector and tourism, which have created new types of employment for the younger generation in particular. Importantly, the new types of employment have expanded the linguistic market of the glottal stop as a variant that symbolizes supralocalism and a transnational and cosmopolitan character. These attributes have become precious commodities to acquire, especially for the mobile, outward- and forward-looking younger generations (of both sexes). The glottal stop has therefore acquired a new set of social meanings (in addition to the old meanings), which are relevant to the daily pursuits of the young man as well as the young woman in various arenas. This expansion in the value of the glottal stop has not been achieved at the expense of the value of the local variant [g], but has proceeded alongside it. The variant [g] continues to be a valuable commodity, especially for the male speakers, and the old associations with male power and influence continue to exist and are functionalized when required by the context. For instance, it is normal for a young man in Amman to use [g] when interacting with male friends and to switch to [ʔ] when addressing a young woman in the same group; or to use [g] when running an errand in a government office and to switch to [ʔ] if he answers his phone in the same place. We can thus see that it is not an issue of one variant being prestigious while the other variant is stigmatized. Rather, both variants are valuable commodities to have, and the sociolinguistically competent speakers know how to appropriate variability in social interaction.[16]

Finally, there has been a marked and much needed increase in the number of variation studies on various Arabic-speaking communities, especially from the early 1990s or so, and many of the new generation of studies include "gender" as a variable. A notable development, also seen in studies on English, is the tendency to focus on smaller communities and to provide more sophisticated analyses. A much welcome development for the future would be more consistent integration into sociolinguistic research of findings and analyses from related social sciences.

Acknowledgments

I am grateful to my friends and colleagues Ángeles Vicente, Catherine Miller, and Uri Horesh for responding to my queries and for supplying material; and to Atiqa Hachimi for casting her critical eye over, as well as reading and commenting on, an earlier version of this chapter. I thank Miriam and Susan for their friendliness and patience; and the anonymous reviewers for their comments. Any remaining errors are my own.

NOTES

1   The bulk of the material presented in this chapter comes from work published in English.
2   In dialectological terms, Arabic dialects are classified into two major types: (1) the Eastern type (*Mashreqi*), which includes the dialects of the Arabian Peninsula, the Levant (Syria, Jordan, Lebanon, and Palestine), Egypt, and the Sudan; (2) the Western type (*Maghrebi*), which includes most of the dialects of North Africa. The isogloss between the two types runs through western Egypt. Egyptian dialects can thus be considered the "bridge dialects." Despite Egypt's geographical location in North Africa, most of its dialects, including Cairo, are classified as Eastern dialects.
3   The term "diglossia" is used here in accordance with the definition in Ferguson (1959). Classical Arabic, the High code, was codified during the eighth century. Whether Classical Arabic was a single variety or an amalgam of varieties is subject to debate among Arabists. The language of the holy book of Islam, the Quran, and pre-Islamic poetry are examples of Classical Arabic. A modern version of this variety is called Modern Standard Arabic, which it although preserves the essential syntactic structure and morphological paradigms of Classical Arabic contains some innovations, especially in the lexicon. Modern Standard Arabic is the language used in newspapers, and generally in the written media.
4   Contributors in this field include the famous thinker and novelist Nawal El Saadawi, the sociologist Fatema Mernissi, and the anthropologist Lila Abu-Lughod.
5   A synthesis of her multifaceted contributions can also be found in Sadiqi (2007).
6   A succinct history and review of the early work in Arabic dialectology can be found in Behnstedt and Woidich (2005).
7   The findings of Roux (1925) regarding some male/female phonetic differences are presented in an article by Harry Stroomer (2004). All of the details cited here from Roux (1925) are derived from Stroomer's article.
8   The problem discussed here is not concerned with research that specifically aimed to investigate the ways in which Arabic speakers sometimes resort to the use of SA as a stylistic resource in specific domains, but with research that assumes that diglossia is the key to understanding variation in Arabic altogether.
9   For a detailed critique of this approach, see Al-Wer (2013).
10   Among the early studies, and which have been widely quoted in the sociolinguistics literature, are those by Abdel-Jawad (1981), Bakir (1986), Kojak (1983), and Schmidt (1974), which investigated variation in the use of a few phonological variables in Jordan, Iraq, Syria, and Egypt, respectively.
11   This conclusion is backed up by a large body of empirical evidence covering a wide range of communities throughout the Arab world.

12 Abdel-Jawad and Awwad 1989; Al-Khatib 1988; Al-Tamimi 2001; Al-Wer 1991; El Salman 2003a.
13 See the findings in Abdel-Jawad 1981; Al-Essa 2009; Al-Khatib 1988; Al-Shehri 1993; Al-Tamimi 2001; El Salman 2003a; 2003b; Haeri 1996; Ismail 2009.
14 See Al-Wer 2002; 2003; 2007.
15 Hachimi's analysis of the social meanings associated with the use of these variants reveals that the approximant (Fessi) feature or lack of trilling of /r/ has come to be associated with "erectile dysfunction and homosexuality."
16 A comprehensive interpretation of these data can be found in Al-Wer and Herin (2011).

REFERENCES

Abdel-Jawad, Hassan. 1981. "Lexical and Phonological Variation in Spoken Arabic of Amman." Unpublished PhD dissertation, University of Pennsylvania.

Abdel-Jawad, Hassan, and Mohammad Awwad. 1989. "Reflexes of Classical Arabic Interdentals: A Study in Historical Sociolinguistics." *Linguistische Berichte*, 122: 259–282.

Al-Essa, Aziza. 2008. "Najdi Speakers in Hijaz: A Sociolinguistic Investigation of Dialect Contact in Jeddah." Unpublished PhD dissertation, University of Essex.

Al-Essa, Aziza. 2009. "When Najd Meets Hijaz: Dialect Contact in Jeddah." In Enam Al-Wer and Rudolf de Jong (eds.), *Arabic Dialectology*, 203–222. Amsterdam: Brill.

Al-Khatib, Mahmoud. 1988. "Sociolinguistic Change in an Expanding Urban Context." Unpublished PhD dissertation, University of Durham.

Al-Shehri, Abdullah. 1993. "Urbanization and Linguistic Variation and Change: A Sociolinguistic Study of the Impact of Urbanization on the Linguistic Behaviour of Urbanized Rural Immigrants in Hijaz, Saudi Arabia." Unpublished PhD dissertation, University of Essex.

Al-Tamimi, Fida. 2001. "Phonetic and Phonological Variation in the Speech of Rural Migrants in a Jordanian City." Unpublished PhD dissertation, University of Leeds.

Al-Wer, Enam. 1991. "Phonological Variation in the Speech of Women from Three Urban Areas in Jordan." Unpublished PhD dissertation, University of Essex.

Al-Wer, Enam. 1997. "Arabic between Reality and Ideology." *International Journal of Applied Linguistics*, 7(2): 251–265.

Al-Wer, Enam. 2002. "Jordanian and Palestinian Dialects in Contact: Vowel Raising in Amman." In Mari Jones and Edith Esch (eds.), *Language Change: The Interplay of Internal, External and Extra-linguistic Factors*, 63–79. Berlin: Mouton de Gruyter.

Al-Wer, Enam. 2003. "New Dialect Formation: The Focusing of -kum in Amman." In David Britain and Jenny Cheshire (eds.), *Social Dialectology: In Honour of Peter Trudgill*, 59–67. Amsterdam: Benjamins.

Al-Wer, Enam. 2007. "The Formation of the Dialect of Amman." In Catherine Miller, Enam Al-Wer, Dominique Caubet, and Janet Watson (eds.), *Arabic in the City: Issues in Dialect Contact and Language Variation*, 55–76. New York: Routledge.

Al-Wer, Enam. 2013. "Sociolinguistics." In Jonathan Owens (ed.), *Handbook of Arabic Linguistics*, 241–263. Oxford: Oxford University Press.

Al-Wer, Enam, and Bruno Herin. 2011. "The Lifecycle of Qaf in Jordan." *Langage & Société*, 138: 59–76.

Bakir, Murtadha. 1986. "Sex Differences in Approximation to Standard Arabic: A Case Study." *Anthropological Linguistics*, 28(1): 3–9.

Barontini, Alexandrine, and Karima Ziamari. 2009. "Comment des (jeunes) femmes Marocaines parlent 'masculine': tentative de definition sociolinguistique." In

Ángeles Vicente (ed.), *Women's World – Women's Word: Female Life as Reflected in the Arabic Dialects*, 153–172. Estudios de Dialectología Norteafricana y Andalusí (EDNA) 13. Zaragoza: Instituto de Estudios Islámicos y del Oriente Proximo.

Bassiouney, Reem. 2009. "The Variety of Houswives and Cockroaches: Examining Code-Choice in Advertisements in Egypt." In Enam Al-Wer and Rudolf de Jong (eds.), *Arabic Dialectology*, 273–285. Amsterdam: Brill.

Bassiouney, Reem. 2010. "Identity and Code-Choice in the Speech of Educated Women and Men in Egypt: Evidence from Talk Shows." In Reem Bassiouney (ed.), *Arabic and the Media*, 97–123. Leiden: Brill.

Behnstedt, Peter, and Manfred Woidich. 2005. *Arabische Dialektgeographie*. Leiden: Brill.

El Salman, Mahmoud. 2003a. "Phonological and Morphological Variation in the Speech of Fallahis in Karak (Jordan)." Unpublished PhD dissertation, University of Durham.

El Salman, Mahmoud. 2003b. "The Use of the /q/ Variants in the Arabic Dialect of Tirat Haifa." *Anthropological Linguistics*, 45(4): 413–426.

Ferguson, Charles. 1959. "Diglossia." *Word*, 15: 325–340.

Hachimi, Atiqa. 2007. "Becoming Casablancan: Fessis in Casablanca as a Case Study." In Catherine Miller, Enam Al-Wer, Dominique Caubet, and Janet Watson (eds.), *Arabic in the City: Issues in Language Variation and Change*, 97–122. London: Routledge.

Hachimi, Atiqa. 2011. "Réinterprétation sociale d'un vieux parler citadin maghrébin à Casablanca." *Langage et Société*, 138: 21–42.

Hachimi, Atiqa. 2012. "The Urban and the Urbane: Identities, Language Ideologies and Arabic Dialects in Morocco." *Language in Society*, 41(3): 321–341.

Haeri, Niloofar. 1987. "Male/Female Differences in Speech: an Alternative Interpretation." In Keith M. Denning, Sharon Inkelas, John R. Rickford, and Faye McNair-Knox (eds.), *Variation in Language:*

NWAV-XV at Stanford: Proceedings of the Fifteenth Annual Conference on New Ways of Analyzing Variation, 173–183. Stanford: Stanford University Press.

Haeri, Niloofar. 1996. *The Sociolinguistic Market in Cairo: Gender, Class, and Education*. London: Kegan Paul International.

Højrup, Thomas. 2003. *State, Culture and Life-Modes*. Aldershot: Ashgate.

Ibrahim, Muhammad H. 1986. "Standard and Prestige Language: A Problem in Arabic Sociolinguistics." *Anthropological Linguistics*, 28: 115–126.

Ismail, Hanadi. 2007. "The Urban and Suburban Modes: Patterns of Linguistic Variation and Change in Damascus." In Catherine Miller, Enam Al-Wer, Dominique Caubet, and Janet Watson (eds.), *Arabic in the City: Issues in Dialect Contact and Language Variation*, 188–213. London: Routledge.

Ismail, Hanadi. 2009. "The Variable (h) in Damascus: Analysis of a Stable Variable." In Enam Al-Wer and Rudolf de Jong (eds.), *Arabic Dialectology*, 249–272. Amsterdam: Brill.

Jabeur, Mohamed. 1987. "A Sociolinguistic Study in Rades: Tunisia." Unpublished PhD dissertation, University of Reading.

Kojak, Wafa. 1983. "Language and Sex: A Case Study of a Group of Educated Syrian Speakers of Arabic." Unpublished MA thesis, University of Lancaster.

Labov, William. 1990. "The Intersection of Sex and Social Class in the Course of Linguistic Change." *Language Variation and Change*, 2: 205–254.

Labov, William. 2001. *Principles of Linguistic Change: Social Factors*. Oxford: Blackwell.

Lakoff, Robin. 1975. *Language and Woman's Place*. New York: Harper & Row.

Milroy, James, Lesley Milroy, Sue Hartley, and David Walshaw. 1994. "Glottal Stops and Tyneside Glottalization: Competing Patterns of Variation and Change in British English." *Language Variation and Change*, 6: 327–357.

Roux, Arsène. 1925. *Le parler arabe de Meknès* [The Dialect of Meknes]. Unpublished doctoral thesis.

Sadiqi, Fatima. 2003. *Women, Gender and Language in Morocco*. Leiden: Brill.

Sadiqi, Fatima. 2007. "Language and Gender." In Kees Versteegh (ed.), *Encyclopedia of Arabic Language and Linguistics*, 642–650. Leiden: Brill.

Schmidt, Richard. 1974. "Sociolinguistic Variation on Spoken Egyptian Arabic: A Re-examination of the Concept of Diglossia." Unpublished PhD dissertation, Brown University.

Stroomer, Harry. 2004. "The Arabic Dialect of Women in Meknès (Morocco): Gender Linked Sound Changes?" In Martine Haak, Rudolf de Jong, and Kees Versteegh (eds.), *Approaches to Arabic Dialects: A Collection of Articles Presented to Manfred Woidich on the Occasion of His Sixtieth Birthday*, 291–307. Leiden: Brill.

Walters, Keith. 1991. "Women, Men and Linguistic Variation in the Arab World." In Bernard Comrie and Mushira Eid (eds.), *Perspectives on Arabic Linguistics III*, 199–229. Amsterdam: Benjamins.

21 Language and Gender Research in Brazil

An Overview

ANA CRISTINA OSTERMANN AND LUIZ PAULO MOITA-LOPES

1. Introduction

The first studies on language and gender in Brazil date from the mid-1980s with quantitative sociolinguistic research (e.g., Callou 1984), which has a very strong research tradition in Brazil, and in which sex/gender is very often one of the variables studied. However, most of the research in the field of language and gender has concentrated on discourse/interaction-oriented investigation in the field of discourse analysis and applied linguistics. In this tradition, the earliest publications were Judith Hoffnagel and Elizabeth Marcuschi (1992) on what they call "feminine speech style," and Carmen Rosa Caldas-Coulthard (1993) on the representation of women and women's voices in newspapers. Whereas the investigation of naturalistic spoken interaction has been slow to take off in the Brazilian context, studies on language and gender in the media – especially in the print media – have increased exponentially (e.g., Ferreira 2009; Funck and Widholzer 2005; Heberle, Ostermann, and Figueiredo 2006), largely due to the continuing and influential work of Caldas-Coulthard, which has been paramount in drawing attention to this area of research and has attracted a large number of researchers to this field in Brazil.

Since the early 1980s, however, much has changed in language studies in Brazil, particularly in regard to the great developments in the areas of discourse analysis and applied linguistics, which have attracted many students to the subject. Nevertheless, there are relatively few investigations on topics related to gender and sexuality in the broad field of quantitative sociolinguistics, discourse studies, and applied linguistics, even though the number of younger researchers in the field has continued to grow.[1] This may be explained, at least in part, by the role that Marxist-influenced theorizing has played in the academic world,

The Handbook of Language, Gender, and Sexuality, Second Edition.
Edited by Susan Ehrlich, Miriam Meyerhoff, and Janet Holmes.
© 2014 John Wiley & Sons, Inc. Published 2017 by John Wiley & Sons, Inc.

in a country which until recently was ruled by a right-wing military dictatorial regime (1964–1985). In such a context, Marxist logic has been a powerful theoretical weapon which cut across the academic world as a way of opposing the political regime.

As a consequence, a large number of studies are oriented toward Marxist theory, and social class issues continue to motivate most researchers. This is not to suggest that Marxist philosophy is irrelevant or that social class is not a crucial aspect of our lives. Social class is particularly relevant in a developing country which continues to face all kinds of difficulties relating to poverty. However, this myopic perspective ignores the important fact that no one is only either poor or rich. Social class is intertwined with gender, sexuality, race, ethnicity, nationality, and other factors to make us who we are continually becoming. Nevertheless, despite the relatively limited concern with gender and sexuality in language studies, social movements – feminist, LGBTT (lesbian, gay, bisexual, transvestis, transsexual), and racial movements – have gone beyond social class differences to raise issues of social inequality for a long time in Brazil. In the field of language studies this places social movements ahead of the academic context. One could perhaps say that the academic world was actually driven toward issues of language, gender, and sexuality by the social movements, which have also been an influence in other Brazilian humanities and social science fields, and perhaps elsewhere too.

2. Methodological and Organizational Notes

In order to review studies on language and gender in the Brazilian context, we took two steps: (1) we contacted researchers who we knew were involved in studies in the field; and (2) we searched the national database Plataforma Lattes,[2] which includes the curricula vitae of all researchers in the country, looking for other publications. In addition, we also used bibliographical branching and referrals from other researchers. We reviewed only research that was published in peer-reviewed journals or in the format of books and book chapters. We certainly do not claim to have included every article or chapter on gender and language ever published by Brazilian scholars, but we believe we covered a faithful representation of the major publications and authors in the field.

In this review, therefore, we restrict our scope to published research on quantitative sociolinguistics and language as discourse/interaction which investigates gender and sexuality. (See Meyerhoff, Chapter 4 in this volume, for an overview of the treatment of gender within variationist sociolinguistics.) The first section reports on quantitative sociolinguistics and the second on discourse/interaction. The latter is the larger and is subdivided into media discourse, the area most of the studies concentrate on; investigation into educational contexts and how gender and sexuality are constructed; and research on diverse contexts, from spontaneous conversations to highly institutionalized settings. Finally, the last section reflects on the development of the field so far, and puts forward a proposal for the direction in which we believe research should now move.

3. Variationist Studies in Brazil: Moving Out of Understanding Sex and Gender as Interchangeable and Essentialized Concepts

In an attempt to compile and to systematize the quantitative sociolinguistic studies in Brazilian Portuguese (BP) that deal with, among other variables, "sex/gender," Maria Paiva (2003) revisits a number of papers published by Brazilian scholars (e.g., Omena 1996; Paredes da Silva 1996; Scherre 1996). Aware of the lack of distinction in most sociolinguistic studies on BP between gender and sex – studies commonly use the two terms interchangeably, or simply replace "sex" with "gender," without necessarily changing their ways of theorizing and analyzing data – Paiva shows that a vast majority of women use the standard variants at higher rates than men, thus demonstrating their preference for the most socially prestigious linguistic variants. This is true, for instance, for agreement particles, as in the case of plural forms (Scherre 1996), and of second-person conjugation (Paredes da Silva 1996). In relation to linguistic change, as with the case for the forms *nós e a gente* (both used to signify first-person plural, with the variant *a gente* being the innovative one), women have been found to be leading the innovation process (Omena 1996).

Overall, Paiva (2003) demonstrates that, according to the studies, women are more "sensitive" to the social prestige attributed by the community to certain linguistic varieties. She argues that this difference is most accentuated in the middle class, and that women tend to be more conservative or more oriented to prestigious variants in some communities, perhaps as a consequence of a different socialization process between males and females and the dynamics of social mobility that characterize each community. Paiva believes that the greater awareness among women of the social status of some linguistic variants may be a result of women taking up the more professional roles in society and of women's social position being less secure than that of men. Above all, Paiva calls for care to be taken in defining the variable "sex/gender," which should be studied in the individual context of the social organization of each community and of the social changes in women's and men's roles in those communities.

In their analysis of both the progressive and the conservative roles of women in BP, especially in the variants of the second-person singular *tu* and *você* in BP, Maria Scherre and Lilian Yacovenco (2011) – in addition to agreeing with Paiva (2003) that sociolinguistic studies of BP that aim to understand the role of the variable gender must investigate gender as situated within specific communities of practice – also claim that they should take into consideration Givón's markedness principle.

By also taking sex and gender as interchangeable concepts, Ronald Mendes (2012) shows that in the Portuguese spoken in the city of São Paulo there is a strong correlation between sex/gender and the uses of diminutives. He analyzes a corpus of 104 sociolinguistic interviews, separated into two samples. The first (consisting of 84 interviews with 42 men and 42 women) is quantitatively analyzed. The analyses reveal that women use diminutives 1.70 times more than men.

The second sample (20 interviews), qualitatively and quantitatively analyzed, shows that the average frequency in the use of diminutives for heterosexual men is 0.28, for lesbians 1.20, for heterosexual women 2.97, and for gay men 2.53. The conclusion is that in the São Paulo Portuguese there is a strong correlation between sex / gender and the use of diminutives.

In another study, in attempt to bring in sexuality (and linguistic perception) as a factor in quantitative sociolinguistic studies in Brazil, Mendes (2011) investigates how people in the city of São Paulo perceive male linguistic performance as gay. The author interviewed 107 persons (men and women) of different ages, sexual orientations, and educational levels by having them listen to a text previously recorded by five self-identified gay men. Participants were asked to grade each man on a 1–5 scale, 5 being the speech most strongly identified as "gay." The results show that nearly all the participants agreed on which readings sounded most "gay." They identified the following linguistic features as factors for their conclusions: lengthening of tonic vowels, pitch dynamism, and carefully pronounced words. Mendes argues that these perceptions were derived from sociolinguistic evaluations that interviewees brought from their life experiences. Masculinity and sexuality are nevertheless essentialized in the study.

Although Paiva (2003) in her review of the field of quantitative sociolinguistics in Brazil shows awareness of the need to theorize gender and sex separately and within specific communities of practice, one still wonders how quantitative sociolinguistic research in Brazil can be more responsive to a world which is increasingly contingent and mobile, and in which what is happening here and now – in situated practices – is what needs to be focused on in research.

4. Discourse/Interaction Studies in Brazil: Moving Out of the Disciplinary Bounds in the Understanding of Language and Gender

4.1 *Media*

As a result of the strong influence of the media in our hyper-semiotized societies, and of the heated debates in academia about whether it contributes to the construction of who we are in our social lives, media discourse has received a lot of attention as a research topic in studies of language and gender in Brazil. In addition, the Department of English and Applied Linguistics at the Federal University of Santa Catarina, where most of the initial studies in this area were carried out because of its emphasis on research on English-language data, triggered a number of research projects on written media, as that type of data was more readily accessible. Norman Fairclough's early work on critical discourse analysis of the press was very influential in several departments in Brazil, and formed the theoretical and methodological basis of most studies reviewed in this section. (See Talbot, Chapter 31 in this volume, for an overview of language, gender, and media studies in anglophone contexts.)

As mentioned earlier, the first study on media was that by Caldas-Coulthard (1993), which examines the ways in which newspaper reporters represent oral interaction in the news. An investigation of "hard news" narratives in quality British newspapers demonstrates that women are denied the role of speakers in the news, and are relegated to less powerful roles. Caldas-Coulthard (1993) claims that such representation does more than reflect the asymmetrical relationships in society; it also reinforces and naturalizes them. Similar asymmetry is found by Susana Funck (2007) in her investigation of Brazilian newspapers. The author looks at how women and men are portrayed (graphically and textually) in different news sections, and finds that women are represented as "being" (including being passive) or as "having" (including having physical attributes), while men are represented as "doing," as agents in society.

Dina Ferreira (2006; 2009) also investigates news articles, specifically in relation to the 2002 Brazilian presidential elections, which brought to power several women politicians. Ferreira refers to how symbolic nominations are used to designate women, and shows that they are either constructed as politicians or as companions of male politicians. These women fit what Ferreira refers to as the "feminility" category (according to a patriarchal view of women) or the "feminilitude" category (more contemporary women who manage their own world).

Adopting the view of masculinity and narrative as performance, Luiz Paulo Moita-Lopes (2009b) analyzes the narrative performance of hegemonic masculinity of the Brazilian soccer player Ronaldo in a news article, and the positioning of two men and the researcher in a focus-group interview about this text. The results show how the positionings of the readers iconicize those who appear in the newspaper, by supporting common sense views of hegemonic masculinity. Moita-Lopes (2009b) argues that, because the media aims to sell news to a particular social niche, it is society that acts on the media – in an oblique or indirect manner – and not only the other way around, as is traditionally thought.

Another set of media texts that have been analyzed in Brazil are magazines addressed to adult and young women. For instance, Ana Cristina Ostermann's study (1994) on the contradictory discourses in teenage girls' magazines shows that while they encourage girls to be more assertive, independent, and self-confident, these magazines also work hard to reinforce and maintain traditional norms of femininity in young females within a society which is essentially consumerist. In order to accomplish that, Ostermann finds, feelings of inadequacy and low self-confidence are triggered, even though they may be conveyed in fun and entertaining ways. Similar results are found by Viviane Heberle (1999) when looking at how women are addressed in editors' letters in Brazilian and British women's magazines: with a high degree of informality and personalization. The magazines' editors take up a "conversational" type of discourse and an assumed intimate relationship with the readers so as to convey certain norms of gendered behavior.

Some of the studies on magazines focus on their disciplinary agenda. By specifically analyzing the quizzes in teenage girls magazines, Ostermann and Deborah Keller-Cohen (1998) show that, in addition to encouraging young females toward self-scrutiny over their behavior and attitudes, quizzes work as "disciplinary instruments" (Foucault 1977), that is, the informality and playful appearance of quizzes mask an important agenda: to discipline girls to be "good." Similar results are shown by Débora Figueiredo (2008; 2009) in examining "body control" in texts about the body in women's magazines. Figueiredo indicates that they play a disciplinary role in body control, commending women who practice self-discipline, and pointing out the risks to those who are not able to resist the pleasures of "gluttony."

Caldas-Coulthard (1996) examines first-person narratives that describe women's experiences with sex. The analysis reveals that women's magazines reaffirm traditional views of the role of women in society, helping to construct a paradoxical ideology of femininity and sexuality which is defined through consumerism, that is, sex is sold as a commodity, from a perspective against which feminism has argued.

Some of the studies on the media have also adopted a social semiotics perspective (e.g., Funck 2004; Magalhães 2005). In looking at Brazilian home decoration magazines, Susana Funck (2004) investigates how the gender identities of children and adolescents are represented. Both the language and images are informed by social and cultural differences, naturalized in essentialist ways, which see the female identity as docile, private, and self-contained, and the masculine identity as public and agentive. Izabel Magalhães's semiotic investigation (2005) of gender identities and power relations in ads in news magazines shows that both women and men are represented in heterogeneous ways and that traditional gender identities coexist with new representations of women and men (e.g., even when women are presented as professionals, they are associated with dependence on men).

In another study of ads – free "personal ads" published by homosexuals on a website – Leandro Prado and Désirée Motta-Roth (2006) investigate the use of descriptors chosen to describe both themselves and their targets. The language used to represent their identities reveals that physical appearance is the most valued characteristic in the description of an announcer, whereas personality is the most valued aspect in the target. Prado and Motta-Roth interpret such a contrast as a commodification process, that is, the announcer offers certain physical attributes in exchange for particular personality features.

Marluce Silva and Carmen Moura's (2008) paper constitutes the only Brazilian study on language and gender in the media that intersects with the issue of race, which is at the forefront of the discussion. Based on a Foucauldian approach to discourse, the study discusses the notions of masturbation, anomaly, and confession practices, and their relationship with female subjectivities presented by the media. The "testimony-confession" TV genre is analyzed whereby a member of the public is invited to report on how she/he has overcome some difficulty in life. The particular confession analyzed by Silva and Moura is that of a Brazilian 68-year-old poor black woman who reports on the first moment of self-eroticism, having never experienced sexual pleasure before. The article discusses how the genre of confession, a new trend in the media, presents and constitutes new forms of subjectivities, approximating the private to the public domain and making what was once invisible now visible and normalized.

Moita-Lopes (2006c) undertakes a multimodal critical discourse analysis of an article published in a Rio de Janeiro daily about gay men who complain about the scarcity of active sexual partners – that is, "real" men as sexual partners are in demand by men themselves. The study shows how the media discursive order constructs a particular view of hegemonic masculinity, inscribing the reader in specific discursive positionings through which men are naturalized. Moita-Lopes contends that particular kinds of media texts help to organize and crystallize specific discourses, probably as a fundamentalist response to a series of destabilizing discourses subjects continually faced in contemporary life.

Fabrício and Moita-Lopes (2008) argue that the public emergence of gay identity and culture has given rise to an intense debate about sexualities in the media. Their concern with the production of innovative meanings makes them look into media discursive practices through the articulation of positive actions in discourse analysis, positioning theory, and interactional sociolinguistics, by focusing on a Brazilian national daily article about "gay sheep." The analysis shows that, by giving space to several voices and different perspectives, the article is ambiguous in relation to the traditional biological paradigm, and therefore allows for the questioning of a reductionist view and the inauguration of innovative meanings of sexuality.

Theorizing the so-called new digital literacies as sociocultural practices, Moita-Lopes (2010) argues that such practices have become contemporary spaces for political activism and for the construction of transgressive meanings about public and private life. He also argues that social life in such literacies is theorized as typical of web 2.0 in the sense that it questions authorship, since they are collaborative and participative, positioning us amid an unquantifiable number of people and their unexpected discourses. Finally, two spaces of affinity (LGBTT and feminist) are analyzed through the characterization of the interactional moves (highlighting asymmetries and symmetries) in such social practices and through the ways they expose us to different discourses.

4.2   *Educational contexts*

Most of the research on language and gender in educational contexts in Brazil is of an ethnographic nature, although some are also interventionist-collaborative. Schools are crucial arenas for language and gender studies because they are usually the first institution children go to outside their families, and where they are exposed to different discourses. In addition, peers at school may confront children with a sense of group membership which is crucial in gender construction. (See also Menard-Warwick, Mori, and Williams, Chapter 24 in this volume, for a description of other research investigating language and gender in educational contexts.)

One could say that Brazilian research that focuses on how students learn to do gender and sexuality at school has been concentrated in two universities: the Federal University of Rio Grande do Sul (Almeida 2009a; Jung and Garcez 2007; Semechechem and Jung 2008) and the Federal University of Rio de Janeiro (Fabrício and Moita-Lopes 2010; Moita-Lopes 2002; 2003; 2006a; 2006b; 2009a; Santos and Fabrício 2006). Both groups analyze interaction but using different theoretical frameworks. The first group relies on talk-in-interaction from a conversational analysis perspective; the second focuses on what talk about texts in literacy contexts does to students. Discourse in the second group is taken as action through which participants in literacy contexts are doing things to one another through interaction by embedding narratives, for example, while they are being discursively (re)constructed. Both groups are involved with ethnographic research, the main difference being that, as ethnomethodologists, the first group believes that the micro analysis of the interaction indexes macro social issues, whereas the second understands that contextual macro social analysis has to coexist with interactional analysis. Both groups come to similar conclusions: what goes on in classrooms reinforces or helps construct common sense views of what men or women are like in the world outside school.

Almeida (2009a) and Moita-Lopes (2002; 2003; 2006a; 2006b; 2009a) have both focused on masculinities. Almeida's findings about elementary classrooms indicate that participants orient to one another by indexing gender common sense knowledge in interactional sequences. Such an order is guided by heteronormative principles which operate, on the one hand, in the construction of hegemonic masculinities, and, on the other, in the rejection of whatever differs from them. Almeida argues that his research shows how heteronormativity is locally and continually constructed through the collaborative work of identity categorization.

In Moita-Lopes's research the same heterosexual matrix is identified. In his book *Identidades Fragmentadas* (2002), he is basically concerned with the politics of difference in a fifth grade classroom. Three chapters in the book focus on gender and sexuality. One of them shows how the female teacher refuses to accept homosexuality as an interactional topic suggested by one of the students whereas, in focus-group interviews, the students compete for turns of talk to gossip about a particular classmate. The analysis draws attention to how homophobia is constitutive of the limits between gender and sexuality. In another chapter, the analysis centers on nonelicited narratives told by the students (boys and girls), both in the classroom and in focus-group interviews, in their efforts to make sense of masculinities. The narratives echo a common sense system of coherence of what men do and are – powerful, sexually incontinent, heterosexual, and so on. These characteristics are mainly expressed through discursive strategies of "adequate" and natural causality. Some of the issues discussed in these two chapters also appear, in slightly modified versions, in Moita-Lopes (2003). In view of these findings, the last chapter of the book puts forward a way of deconstructing essentialist views of gender and sexuality by appealing to a particular pedagogical view of critical discourse analysis to which teachers have recourse in classrooms. This proposal is further developed from the perspective of queer theory in Moita-Lopes (2006a), where the author argues for an ethical need for queering literacy teaching, with the incorporation of gay, lesbian, and other than heterosexual themes in classrooms.

Moita-Lopes (2006b; 2009a) focuses on the interactional positionings a particular boy takes up in narrative telling in the same literacy classroom scenario described in Moita-Lopes (2002). The study shows that this participant hegemonically positions himself (and is actually positioned by other participants) as male, white, and heterosexual in three different stories. The study is particularly interesting, for it analyzes gender, sexuality, and race simultaneously – an analytical perspective not often found in the Brazilian literature. In this research, a white heterosexual boy is objectified so as to draw attention to his discursive construction in the interactional positionings he takes up, and which are indexically marked. The three stories could be considered as a single narrative about the boy's efforts to interactionally position himself as hegemonic.

Jakeline Semechechem and Neiva Jung (2008) work from an ethnomethodological perspective in bringing ethnic issues to the analysis of classroom discourse. They argue that students' and teachers' institutional identities compete with other identities from the ethnic communities to which the participants belong. Semechechem and Jung's research on an elementary school in southern Brazil shows how gender and German ethnolinguistic identities in a multilingual community are intricately related since men and women follow different social patterns in relation to urban life. However, in a different way from the studies reviewed above, this study shows that schools reinforce the hegemonic prestigious role that women (and not men!) occupy outside school. On the other hand, some boys maintain the identity features followed by the men in the community (they must learn German and work in agriculture) at the same time as they learn to negotiate the hegemonic features of women. This actually provides men with prestige at school. Semechechem and Jung's investigation also draws attention to the relevance of gender as a social identity in an English as a foreign language (EFL) classroom with reference to how male students participate in the class. It is argued that their participation is due to the fact that the teacher allows more opportunities for the boys to self-select themselves in turn-taking. Some of Semechechem and Jung's arguments and findings are further developed in Jung and Pedro Garcez (2007).

Other relevant research in school contexts is of an interventionist nature, aiming at contributing to change the existing heteronormative and male-oriented pattern within which Brazilian schools traditionally operate. Denise Santos and Fabrício (2006) report on their ethnographic research in an EFL classroom in a Brazilian language school. Their objective was both to develop critical thinking and at the same time to involve students in the denaturalization of gender dualism. Both authors, as teacher-researchers, reconfigured their English-language teaching classroom as a multicultural site in which essentialized meanings were challenged, and altered the typical interactional participation structures from teacher- to student-centered interactions. Their results show how these innovative classroom participation structures enabled students to relativize stereotypical gender roles.

Fabrício and Moita-Lopes (2010) report on their ethnographic collaborative-inteventionist research study about gender and sexuality repositionings in school literacy practices with fifth graders. They argue that the implementation in classrooms of an approach which focuses on the discursive nature of genders and sexualities, following a view of literacies as social practices and the principles of a multimodal critical discourse analysis and of queer theory, may help to generate less crystallized meanings about sexualities, by showing desire to be a continually changing process. Classroom interactional data show discursive micro move-ments, which indicate students' attempts to question the heteronormative logic.

4.3 Other contexts

The analysis of spoken interaction in studies of language and gender in other contexts in Brazil has taken diverse methodological approaches that vary between interactional analysis and pragmatics, narratives and life stories, and, more recently, conversation analysis and membership categorization analysis. In contrast to other places in the world, in Brazil studies that look at male–female differences in spoken interaction have been scarce. As mentioned earlier, the first study on the rela-tionship between gender and spoken language in Brazilian Portuguese, that of Hoffnagel and Marcuschi (1992), was dedicated to the study of what the authors named a "feminine style of speech." By taking a theoretical perspective that sees interaction as a site of the construction and reproduction of inequalities, Hoffnagel and Marcuschi investigated topic management and the use of conversational mark-ers in recorded interactions that involved participants in different arrangements: females–females, males–males, and females–males. The investigation points out the existence of a "feminine interactional style" that shows women to be, in gen-eral, more collaborative than men in conversation. Similar results are shown on a later study, carried out by Hoffnagel (2010), with the same participant arrange-ments, but by looking at a different interactional phenomenon, "other-repetition." By understanding that other-repetitions function as cooperative devices in inter-action, Hoffnagel (2010) asserts that, overall, women are more cooperative, except when their interlocutors are males, when they are less cooperative.

Liliana Bastos (2003) and Maria das Graças Pereira (2006) also find similar results in their studies on the differences between male and female interactional speech styles. Bastos (2003) analyzes 40 recorded interactions at a call center (20 carried out by a male operator and 20 by a female operator) with the objective of investigating how corporate image, trained behavior, and technology interact with patterns of gender identity. The results show that the female operator tends to be more author-itative, more directive, less sensitive, and less patient toward the interlocutor's needs, and takes up a more "corporate speech style," whereas the male operator does more "emotional labor," is more cooperative and patient with callers, and is less oriented to a corporate style. In analyzing discursive strategies used by a female former boss in a professional meeting in which a new male boss partici-pates, Pereira (2006) shows that the female boss makes use of bold directives, and positions herself as someone who is in control, whereas the new male boss shows more involvement and solidarity with his subordinates.

In a shift away from the analysis of female versus male interaction styles, in different studies and with different analytical purposes, Ostermann (2003a; 2003b; 2008; 2011) investigates discursive practices and their relations to gender and the workplace in two all-female institutions that address violence against women in Brazil. With the aim of understanding intragender differences, Ostermann analyzes recorded interactions with victims of domestic violence at an all-female police station and at a feminist activist crisis intervention center. In particular, Ostermann (2003a; reprinted, with modifications, 2008 and 2011) investigates the types of responses the professionals in each setting provide to victims. The results reveal that police officers provide minimal feedback when the victims report their problems, and are four times more likely than feminists to provide no responses to the victims' turns, as well as four times more likely to change topics in their responses to the victims' turns. Ostermann (2003a; 2008; 2011) explains the differences based on the Bourdieuian concept of habitus, by claiming that it is the situated communities of practice in which groups mutually engage that give rise to a particular set of socially shared linguistic and nonlinguistic practices. In another analysis of the same data (Ostermann 2003b) she finds similar results, but of a different linguistic and interactional phenomenon – pronoun selection and pronoun shifting. The analysis demonstrates that the female police officers' alignment is of an institutional character, as the speakers tend to switch to the more formal, distancing pronoun, *a senhora* (V pronoun), whereas the feminists manipulate the pronoun system, by shifting toward the less formal choice, *você* (T pronoun). According to Ostermann, it becomes clear from both studies (2003a; 2003b) that the interactional styles studied cannot be collapsed within a single category called "female speech," and that gender alone cannot predict interactional patterns; instead they are best understood as reflecting the gendered communities of practice from which the professionals are drawn.

Another group of studies of spoken language and gender in Brazil focuses on issues of identity construction in narratives and life stories. Bastos and Maria Tereza Dantas (2003) investigate the process of identity construction of a female psychiatric patient by means of interviews. Their analysis shows that the patient's narrative is simultaneously oriented by both masculine and feminine stereotyped behaviors. While she shows strong emotional involvement with the interviewer, in what the authors call a "typical feminine self disclosure process" (Bastos and Dantas 2003, 23), she also talks about how rational, independent, and successful she is, attributes traditionally seen as masculine. Similar results are presented by Maria do Carmo Oliveira, Bastos, and Elizabeth Lima (2006) in looking at how gender emerges in the life story of a female Portuguese immigrant in Brazil. The results reveal that gender, immigrant, and entrepreneurial identities relate to one another in very complex ways, but that the entrepreneur's identity, in particular, is oriented to and is understood as traditionally masculine patterns of behavior.

By also drawing on narratives by means of recorded interviews, Rodrigo Borba and Ostermann (2007) investigate Brazilian *travestis*' manipulation of gender identity through the manipulation of the Portuguese grammatical gender system. According to the authors, even though most of the time the *travestis* use the feminine grammatical gender for self-referral, ideological and bodily tensions seem to impel them to use masculine forms in certain discursive contexts, such as in narratives about the time before their body changes took place. Borba and Ostermann argue that the embodiment of feminine features in biologically male bodies enables *travestis* to wander through a number of ideologies about masculinity and femininity and to incorporate these ideologies in their linguistic construction of identity. Borba (2011) also investigates how the *travestis* occupy transmasculinity interactional positionings when specifically reporting on their sexual encounters with partners. This transmasculinity comes about as semantic effects of positionings which are in common sense identified as male performances.

In a related study, but using a conversational methodological approach, Borba (2009) investigates interactions between sex professional *travestis* and female safer-sex outreach nongovernmental organization (NGO) workers during the event called "intervention" – when the NGO representatives engage with disseminating information and with distributing free condoms. By analyzing "tactics of intersubjectivity," Borba shows that the repertoire of identities of the safer-sex workers is affected by the *travestis* as much as the identities constructed by the *travestis* are affected by those of the safer-sex workers, thus producing interactional dynamics over which the identity borders might be crossed.

The study conducted by Mariléia Sell and Ostermann (2009) represents the first in the Brazilian literature to employ membership categorization analysis (MCA), combined with conversation analysis, in the study of recorded interactions. (See Stokoe and Attenborough, Chapter 8, and Wilkinson and Kitzinger, Chapter 7, in this volume, for descriptions of membership categorization analysis and conversation analysis, respectively.) The authors analyze how gender identities are negotiated in interactions between a psychologist and candidates for vasectomy surgery. Sell and Ostermann (2009) show the workings of the normative gender understandings that operate on macro social levels and how those are brought into the interactional micro sphere, by demonstrating the laborious ways by which candidates for the vasectomy procedure categorize themselves within some type of homogeneous and naturalized masculine identity.

In studies of written language and its relationship with gender in other contexts, just as in the study of media, most of the work developed in Brazil takes up a critical discourse analysis perspective. An important area of interface is the law, with studies such as those conducted by Débora Figueiredo (2002a; 2002b: 2004) which investigated reported appellate decisions on cases of rape. In analyzing lexical choices in British law reports, for instance, Figueiredo (2002a; 2002b) reveals that while the judicial discourse condemns violence against women, the official rhetoric of the reported appellate decisions reinforces sexual and gender discrimination. Figueiredo (2002a) argues that such a unidimensional understanding of rape constructs it as an isolated crime, motivated by uncontrolled sexual desire or emotional distress, without any links to sociocultural issues such as gendered violence, unequal gender relations, and the high degree of tolerance of violence against women. Figueiredo (2002b) demonstrates that rape trials also involve punishment and discipline of female victims, who end up being judged on possibly "inappropriate" behavior. In her analysis of Brazilian decision appeals on cases of violence and sexual abuse against women in which the perpetrators were absolved, Figueiredo (2004) shows that, among other strategies, the judicial system privileges men's power and rights while presenting male violence and sexual abuse of females as secondary themes. According to Figueiredo, the judicial discourse on rape might even increase the power unbalance between genders, such as with the trivialization of domestic violence. (See also Ehrlich, Chapter 23 in this volume, for a discussion of language and violence against women in the legal system.)

By also drawing on critical discourse analysis, Lúcia Freitas and Veralúcia Pinheiro (2010) and Freitas (2011) examine roles, processes, and circumstances in narratives of gendered violence in the home sphere in a document called *termos de declaração*, which is part of the police investigation and which constitutes the first judicial document in the investigation for penal infractions and their authorship. Freitas and Pinheiro look at how the actors involved in an episode of violence (i.e., husband and wife) report on the violent event. The analysis reveals that whereas the woman describes herself as a passive victim of her husband's physical attacks, the man attributes agency to his wife's actions, impregnating them with aggression.

5. And What Now? Looking Back and Forward at Studies on Language and Gender in Brazil

From this review, it is clear that studies on language and gender in the Brazilian context have developed historically in a similar way to other places around the world. That is, they evolved from an understanding of sex and gender as interchangeable concepts, and from dualist and essentialist views of gender and sexuality, to a very complex and intertwined view of the relationships between biological sex, gender, sexuality, and language. In addition, the studies have evolved from an interest largely centered on media representation/construction (especially in the print media) to the investigation of more complex settings of performativity where everyday life takes place, such as educational and other institutional contexts. To our understanding, however, the expansion of context has not been large and encompassing enough, and it is one of the challenges we would like to put forward: the expansion of the scope of the studies so as to involve more diverse discursive contexts, more ethnography, more fieldwork.

It is also evident that most of the studies on language and gender in Brazil, despite some attempts to interact with other fields of expertise, are still largely restricted to the fields of linguistics and applied linguistics. There have been few moves to work across different disciplinary fields, and this situation creates another challenge for the advancement of the field in Brazil. In contrast to some other places, where sociologists, psychologists, anthropologists, and educators work closely with (applied) linguists in conducting research on language, gender, and sexuality, such interdisciplinary studies are, with a few exceptions, still scarce in the country.

This may be partly explained by the fact that many academic departments hire scholars with a degree in that department's specialization rather than according to their research needs, as Alessandro Duranti (2001) reports. A few academics have made efforts to work across disciplines or to cross the threshold into other departments, but such endeavors are still looked upon with suspicion in many circles. However, we consider such efforts essential to foster research development in the field. If, for no other reason, interdisciplinarity will improve the ways we have been theorizing gender, sexuality, and language. In a world where languages, texts, discourses, and people are increasingly understood as in flux or in movement, such retheorization is crucial.

Moreover, while race, ethnicity, embodiment, nationality, and age have been taken into consideration by a few researchers, we propose that it is of paramount importance that, together with a movement toward interdisciplinary studies, these issues be brought into the discussion of gender, sexuality, and language in Brazil. Perhaps this segregation of categories was necessary in the establishment of the field, but it does not make sense any more on the basis of what we now know about what gender and sexuality mean when racialized, embodied, nationalized, and so on.

Finally, since research in the humanities and social sciences constitutes a type of discourse about the social world, and since we are constructed by the performances we enact, we need to imagine ways of doing research which may collaborate with the reinvention of social life in the field of language and gender studies. First, it is necessary to go beyond the level of description of common sense ways of doing gender and sexuality, and to favor emerging performances as research topics. Such topics may draw attention to alternative ways of experiencing social life. Second, we need to imagine other ways of doing research (interventionist-collaborative and so on) which may help inaugurate new meanings about who we are or who we can become. In Foucault's often quoted words, we believe that what matters is not who we are, but who we can become.

NOTES

1   See, e.g., Alexandre Almeida (2009b), whose PhD dissertation won the 2009 Best Dissertation Award of the Brazilian Association of Graduate Programs and Research in Literature and Linguistics Studies.
2   The Lattes Platform currently has around 1.62 million curricula (http://lattes.cnpq.br/).

REFERENCES

Almeida, Alexandre. 2009a. "A Noção de Relevância Sequencial: Construindo Identidades Masculinas na Sala de Aula" [The Notion of Sequential Relevance: The Construction of Masculine Identities in the Classroom]. In Letícia Loder and Neiva Jung (eds.), *Análises de Fala-em-Interação Institucional* [Analyses of Institutional Talk], 45–70. São Paulo: Mercado de Letras.

Almeida, Alexandre. 2009b. "A Construção de Masculinidades na Fala-em-interação em Cenários Escolares" [The Construction of Masculinities in Interaction in School Settings]. Unpublished PhD dissertation, Federal University of Rio Grande do Sul.

Bastos, Liliana C. 2003. "Fala Treinada, Tecnologia e Identidade de Gênero em Atendimentos Telefônicos" [Trained Talk, Technology and Gender Identity in Telephone Services]. *Crop*, 9: 31–53.

Bastos, Liliana C., and Maria Dantas. 2003. "Construções Identitárias de Gênero na Fala de uma Paciente Psiquiátrica/Artesã: Em Busca da Cura pelo Trabalho" [Gender Identity Constructions in the Talk of a Psychiatric Patient/Handcrafter: Searching for the Cure through Work]. *Trabalhos em Linguística Aplicada*, 41: 23–37.

Borba, Rodrigo. 2009. "Discurso e (Trans)Identidades: Interação, Intersubjetividade e Acesso à Prevenção de DST/AIDS entre Travestis" [Discourse and (Trans)Identities: Interaction, Intersubjectivity and Access to STDs/AIDS Prevention among Travestis]. *Revista Brasileira de Linguística Aplicada*, 9: 441–473.

Borba, Rodrigo. 2011. "Travestis, (Trans)Masculinidade e Narrativas Orais: Reconstruções da Travestividade" [Travestis, (Trans)Masculinities and Oral Narratives: Reconstructions of Travestivity]. *Bagoas*, 6: 181–210.

Borba, Rodrigo, and Ana C. Ostermann. 2007. "Do Bodies Matter? Travestis' Embodiment of (Trans)Gender Identity through the Manipulation of the Brazilian Portuguese Grammatical Gender System." *Gender and Language*, 1: 131–147.

Caldas-Coulthard, Carmen R. 1993. "From Discourse Analysis to Critical Discourse Analysis: The Differential Re-representation of Women and Men Speaking in Written News." In John Sinclair, Michael Hoey, and Gwyneth Fox (eds.), *Techniques of Description: Spoken and Written Discourse*, 196–208. London: Routledge.

Caldas-Coulthard, Carmen R. 1996. "'Women who Pay for Sex. And Enjoy It': Transgression versus Morality in Women's Magazines." In Carmen Caldas-Coulthard and Malcolm Coulthard (eds.), *Texts and Practices*, 248–268. London: Routledge.

Callou, Dinah M. 1984. "A Variável Sexo na Fala Urbana Culta no Rio de Janeiro" [The Variable Sex in Standard Urban Talk in Rio de Janeiro]. *Anais II Congresso de Sócio-e-Etnolinguística*, 5: 146–148.

Duranti, Alessandro. 2001. "Linguistic Anthropology: History, Ideas, and Issues." In Alessandro Duranti (ed.), *Linguistic Anthropology: A Reader*, 1–38. Oxford: Blackwell.

Fabrício, Branca, and Luiz P. Moita-Lopes. 2008. "'A Guerra dos Carneiros Gays': A (Re)Construção Discursiva do Fantasma da Eugenia Sexual" ["The War between Gay Sheep": The Discursive (Re-)Construction of the Phantasm of Sexual Eugeny]. *Matraga*, 15: 64–84.

Fabrício, Branca, and Luiz P. Moita-Lopes. 2010. "A Dinâmica dos (Re)Posicionamentos de Sexualidade em Práticas de Letramento Escolar" [The Dynamics of Sexuality (Re)Positionings in School Literacy Practices]. In Luiz P. Moita-Lopes and Liliana Bastos (eds.), *Para Além da Identidade: Fluxos, Movimentos e Trânsitos* [Beyond Identities: Fluxes, Movements and Transits], 283–314. Belo Horizonte: UFMG.

Ferreira, Dina. 2006. "Identidade Feminina no Espaço Político: Percurso Simbólico na Ecologia da Linguagem" [Female Identity in the Political Arena: Symbolic Trajectory in the Ecology of Language]. In Dina Ferreira and Kanavillil Rajagopalan (eds.), *Políticas em Linguagem* [Language Policies], 277–298. São Paulo: Ed. Mackenzie.

Ferreira, Dina. 2009. *Discurso Feminino e Identidade Social* [Female Discourse and Social Identity]. São Paulo: Annablume/FAFESP.

Figueiredo, Débora C. 2002a. "Vítimas e Vilãs, Monstros e Desesperados: Como o Discurso Judicial Representa os Participantes de um Crime de Estupro" [Victims and Villains: How the Judicial Discourse Represents the Participants of a Rape Crime]. *Linguagem em (Dis)curso*, 3: 135–156.

Figueiredo, Débora C. 2002b. "Decisões Legais em Casos de Estupro como Parte de uma Pedagogia do Comportamento"

[Legal Decisions on Rape Trials as Part of a Pedagogy of Behavior]. *Linguagem em (Dis)curso*, 2: 133–153.

Figueiredo, Débora C. 2004. "Violência Sexual e Controle Legal: Uma Análise Crítica de Três Extratos de Sentenças em Casos de Violência Contra a Mulher" [Sexual Violence and Legal Control: A Critical View of Three Sentence Extracts on Cases of Violence against Women]. *Linguagem em (Dis)curso*, 4: 61–84.

Figueiredo, Débora C. 2008. "Como Você se Relaciona com a Comida? A Construção da Identidade Feminina no Discurso Midiático sobre o Emagrecimento" [How Do You Relate to Food? The Construction of Female Identity in Media Discourse about Weight Loss]. *Matraga*, 22: 171–188.

Figueiredo, Débora C. 2009. "Narrative and Identity Formation: An Analysis of Media Personal Accounts from Patients of Cosmetic Plastic Surgery." In Charles Bazerman, Adair Bonini, and Débora Figueiredo (eds.), *Genre in a Changing World*, 255–276. Fort Collins, CO: WAC Clearinghouse.

Foucault, Michel. 1977. *Vigiar e Punir: Nascimento da Prisão* [Discipline and Punish: The Birth of the Prison]. Petrópolis: Vozes.

Freitas, Lúcia. 2011. "Representações de Papeis de Gênero na Violência Conjugal em Inquéritos Policiais" [Representations of Gender Roles in Marital Violence in Police Investigations]. *Cadernos de Linguagem e Sociedade*, 12: 128–152.

Freitas, Lúcia, and Veralúcia Pinheiro. 2010. "Atores da Violência de Gênero: Suas Narrativas no Inquérito Policial" [Social Actors in Gendered Violence: Their Narratives in Policy Inquiry]. In Sonia Zyngier and Vander Viana (eds.), *Avaliações e Perspectivas* [Assessments and Perspectives], 223–243. Rio de Janeiro: UFRJ.

Funck, Susana B. 2004. "Anjos e Feras no Espaço Doméstico: Decoração para Meninas e Meninos" [Angels and Beasts in the Domestic Context: Decoration for Girls and Boys]. In Claudia Costa and Simone Schmidt (eds.), *Poéticas e Políticas Feministas* [Feminist Poetics and Policies], 157–163. Florianópolis: Mulheres.

Funck, Susana B. 2007. "A (In)Visibilidade da Mulher na Mídia Impressa: Uma Análise Discursiva" [The (In)Visibility of Women in the Printed Media: A Discursive Analysis]. *Comunicação & Inovação*, 8: 15–22.

Funck, Susana B., and Nara Widholzer, eds. 2005. *Gênero em Discursos na Mídia* [Gender in Media Discourse]. Florianópolis: EDUNISC/Mulheres.

Heberle, Viviane. 1999. "A Representação das Experiências Femininas em Editoriais de Revistas para Mulheres" [Female Experience Representation in Editorials in Women's Magazines]. *Revista Iberoamericana de Discurso & Sociedad*, 1: 73–86.

Heberle, Viviane, Ana C. Ostermann, and Débora Figueiredo, eds. 2006. *Linguagem e Gênero no Trabalho, na Mídia e em Outros Contextos* [Language and Gender at Work, in the Media and in Other Contexts]. Florianópolis: UFSC.

Hoffnagel, Judith C. 2010. "Hesitação e Variações na Interação Homem–Mulher: O Caso da Repetição" [Hesitation and Variations in Male–Female Interaction: The Case of Repetition]. In Judith Hoffnagel (ed.), *Temas em Antropologia Linguística* [Themes in Linguistic Anthropology], 193–206. Recife: Bagaço.

Hoffnagel, Judith C., and Elizabeth Marcuschi. 1992. "O Estilo Feminino na Interação Verbal" [Female Style in Verbal Interaction]. In Albertina Costa and Cristina Bruschini (eds.), *Entre a Virtude e o Pecado* [Between Virtue and Sin], 118–146. São Paulo: Rosa dos Tempos.

Jung, Neiva M., and Pedro Garcez. 2007. "Além do Repertório Linguístico: Aspectos Simbólicos Diversos na Construção da Identidade Étnico-Linguística Alemã na Escola de Comunidade Rural Multilíngue" [Beyond Linguistic Repertoire: Symbolic Aspects in the Construction of German Ethnic-Linguistic Identity in a Multilingual Rural Community School]. In Marilda Cavalcanti and Stela Bortoni-Ricardo (eds.), *Transculturalidade, Linguagem e*

Educação [Cross-Culturality, Language and Education], 97–122. Campinas: Mercado de Letras.

Magalhães, Izabel. 2005. "Critical Discourse Analysis and the Semiotic Construction of Gender Identities." *DELTA*, 21: 179–205.

Mendes, Ronald. 2011. "Gênero/Sexo, Variação Linguística e Intolerância" [Gender/Sex, Linguistic Variation and Intolerance]. In Diana Luz Pessoa de Barros (ed.), *Preconceito e Intolerância: Reflexões Linguístico-Discursivas* [Prejudice and Intolerance: Linguistic and Discursive Reflexions], 99–116. São Paulo: Mackenzie.

Mendes, Ronald. 2012. "Diminutivos como Marcadores de Sexo/Gênero" [Diminutives as Sex/Gender Markers]. *Revista Linguística*, 8: 113–124.

Moita-Lopes, Luiz P. 2002. *Identidades Fragmentadas* [Fragmented Identities]. Campinas: Mercado de Letras.

Moita-Lopes, Luiz P. 2003. "Storytelling as Action: Constructing Masculinities in a School Context." *Pedagogy, Culture & Society*, 11: 31–47.

Moita-Lopes, Luiz P. 2006a. "Queering Literacy Teaching: Analyzing Gay-Themed Discourses in a Fifth Grade Class in Brazil." *Journal of Language, Identity & Education*, 5: 31–50.

Moita-Lopes, Luiz P. 2006b. "On Being White, Heterosexual and Male in a Brazilian School: Multiple Positionings in Oral Narratives." In Anna de Finna, Deborah Schiffrin, and Michael Bamberg (eds.), *Discourse and Identity*, 288–313. Cambridge: Cambridge University Press.

Moita-Lopes, Luiz P. 2006c. "'Falta Homem até para Homem': A Construção da Masculinidade Hegemônica no Discurso Mediático" ["Men are in Demand for Men Themselves": The Construction of Hegemonic Masculinity in Media Discourse]. In Viviane Heberle, Ana C. Ostermann, and Débora Figueiredo (eds.), *Linguagem e Gênero no Trabalho, na Mídia e em Outros Contextos* [Language and Gender at Work, in the Media and in Other Contexts], 131–157. Florianópolis: UFSC.

Moita-Lopes, Luiz P. 2009a. "Acerca de ser Blanco, Heterosexual y Masculino en una Escuela Brasileña: Múltiples Posturas en Narrativas Orales" [On Being White, Heterosexual and Male in a Brazilian School: Multiple Positionings in Oral Narratives]. In Carmen Curcó and Maite Ezcurdia (eds.), *Discurso, Identidad y Cultura: Perspectivas Filosóficas y Discursivas* [Discourse, Identity and Culture: Philosophical and Discursive Perspectives], 287–323. Mexico City: Universidad Nacional Autónoma de México.

Moita-Lopes, Luiz P. 2009b. "A Performance Narrativa do Jogador Ronaldo como Fenômeno Sexual em um Jornal Carioca: Multimodalidade, Posicionameneto e Iconicidade" [The Narrative Performance of the Footballer Ronaldo as a Sex Phenomenon in a Rio de Janeiro Daily: Multimodality, Positioning and Iconicity]. *Revista da Anpoll*, 27: 128–157.

Moita-Lopes, Luiz P. 2010. "Os Novos Letramentos Digitais como Lugares de Construção de Ativismo Político sobre Sexualidade e Gênero" [The New Digital Literacies as Sites for the Construction of Political Activism about Sexuality and Gender]. *Trabalhos em Linguística Aplicada*, 49: 393–417.

Oliveira, Maria do C., Liliana Bastos, and Elizabeth Lima. 2006. "Imigração e Trabalho: Revendo Estereótipos de Gênero" [Immigration and Work: Revisiting Gender Stereotypes]. In Viviane Heberle, Ana C. Ostermann, and Débora Figueiredo (eds.), *Linguagem e Gênero no Trabalho, na Mídia e em Outros Contextos* [Language and Gender at Work, in the Media and in Other Contexts], 49–68. Florianópolis: UFSC.

Omena, Nelize. 1996. "A Referência à Primeira Pessoa no Plural" [First-Person Plural Reference]. In Giselle Silva and Maria Scherre (eds.), *Padrões Sociolinguísticos* [Sociolinguistic Standards], 311–323. Rio de Janeiro: Tempo Brasileiro.

Ostermann, Ana C. 1994. "'Bonita de Doer': Análise Crítica do Discurso em Revistas para Meninas Adolescentes" ["Dying to Look Good": Critical Discourse Analysis of Teenage Girls' Magazines]. *ESPecialist*, 15: 151–162.

Ostermann, Ana C. 2003a. "Communities of Practice at Work: Gender, Facework and the Power of Habitus at an All-Female Police Station and a Feminist Crisis Intervention Center in Brazil." *Discourse & Society*, 14: 473–505.

Ostermann, Ana C. 2003b. "Localizing Power and Solidarity: Pronoun Alternation at an All-Female Police Station and a Feminist Crisis Intervention Center in Brazil." *Language in Society*, 32: 351–381.

Ostermann, Ana C. 2008. "Communities of Practice at Work: Gender, Facework and the Power of Habitus at an All-Female Police Station and a Feminist Crisis Intervention Center in Brazil." In Susan Ehrlich (ed.), *Language and Gender: Major Themes in English Studies*, 132–167. London: Routledge.

Ostermann, Ana Cristina. 2011. "Communities of Practice at Work: Gender, Facework and the Power of Habitus at an All-Female Police Station and a Feminist Crisis Intervention Center in Brazil." In Jennifer Coates and Pia Pichler (eds.), *Language and Gender: A Reader*, 2nd edn, 332–355. Oxford: Wiley-Blackwell.

Ostermann, Ana C., and Deborah Keller-Cohen. 1998. "'Good Girls Go to Heaven; Bad Girls ... ' Learn to be Good: Quizzes in American and Brazilian Teenage Girls' Magazines." *Discourse & Society*, 9: 531–558.

Paiva, Maria C. de. 2003. "A Variável Gênero/Sexo" [The Sex/Gender Variable]. In Maria Mollica and Maria Braga (eds.), *Introdução à Sociolinguística: O Tratamento da Variação* [Introduction to Sociolinguistics: Variation Treatment], 33–42. São Paulo: Contexto.

Paredes da Silva, Vera. 1996. "Quando Escrita e Fala se Aproximam: Pronomes de Terceira Pessoa em Cartas Pessoais" [When Writing and Speech Meet: Third-Person Pronouns in Personal Letters]. In Alzira Macedo, Claudia Roncarati, and Maria Mollica (eds.), *Variação e Discurso* [Variation and Discourse], 63–74. Rio de Janeiro: Tempo Brasileiro.

Pereira, Maria das G. 2006. "Estratégias de Manutenção de Poder de uma Ex-Chefe em uma Reunião Empresarial: Indiretividade e Diretividade em Atos de Comando" [Power-Holding Strategies of a Former Female Boss in a Business Meeting: Indirectivity and Directivity in Commanding Acts]. In Viviane Heberle, Ana C. Ostermann, and Débora Figueiredo (eds.), *Linguagem e Gênero no Trabalho, na Mídia e em Outros Contextos* [Language and Gender at Work, in the Media and in Other Contexts], 93–128. Florianópolis: UFSC.

Prado, Leandro, and Désirée Motta-Roth. 2006. "Comodificação e Homoerotismo" [Commodification and Homoeroticism]. In Viviane Heberle, Ana C. Ostermann, and Débora Figueiredo (eds.), *Linguagem e Gênero no Trabalho, na Mídia e em Outros Contextos* [Language and Gender at Work, in the Media and in Other Contexts], 159–176. Florianópolis: UFSC.

Santos, Denise, and Branca B. Fabrício. 2006. "The English Lesson as a Site for the Development of Critical Thinking." *Teaching English as a Second or Foreign Language*, 10: 1–23.

Scherre, Maria. 1996. "Sobre a Influência de Variáveis Sociais na Concordância Nominal em Português" [On the Influence of Social Variables on Noun Agreement in Portuguese]. In Giselle de Oliveira e Silva and Maria Scherre (eds.), *Padrões Sociolinguísticos* [Sociolinguistic Patterns], 239–264. Rio de Janeiro: Tempo Brasileiro.

Scherre, Maria, and Lilian Yacovenco. 2011. "A Variação Linguística e o Papel dos Fatores Sociais: o Gênero do Falante em Foco" [Linguistic Variation and the Role of Social Factors: Focusing on the Gender of the Speaker]. *Revista da ABRALIN*, 14: 121–146.

Semechechem, Jakeline, and Neiva Jung. 2008. "A Co-construção de Identidades Sociais em Sala de Aula" [The Co-construction of Social Identities in the Classroom]. *Uniletras*, 30: 9–31.

Sell, Mariléia, and Ana C. Ostermann. 2009. "Análise de Categorias de Pertença (ACP) em Estudos de Linguagem e Gênero: A (des)Construção Discursiva do Homogêneo Masculino" [Membership Categorization Analysis (MCA) in Studies of Language and Gender: The Discursive (De)Construction of Homogeneous Masculinity]. *Alfa*, 53: 11–34.

Silva, Marluce P., and Carmen Moura. 2008. "Mídia e a Figura do Anormal na Mira do Sinóptico: A Constituição Discursiva de Subjetividades Femininas" [The Media and the Abnormal Figure from the Perspective of the Synoptic: The Discursive Constitution of Feminine Subjectivity]. *Revista Estudos Feministas*, 16: 841–855.

Part VI Domains and Institutions

22 Language and Gender in the Workplace

JANET HOLMES

1. Introduction

Workplace discourse has become an important source of insight in language and gender research over the last couple of decades. This chapter reviews research which demonstrates the value of the workplace as a research site for examining gender performances, and discusses some of the range of approaches and findings which have emerged from research examining the relationship between gender and workplace discourse. This research demonstrates that gender is an indisputable influence on workplace behavior, including workplace talk, and an inescapable lens through which workplace performances are viewed. As Cameron (1997, 30) points out, we cannot deny "the materiality of gender and power relations," just as we cannot ignore the relevance of "the institutional contexts and the power relations within which gender is being enacted."

The interaction between gender and workplace discourse has been analyzed from many different perspectives, using a range of different methodological approaches. While early researchers tended to adopt a difference approach (e.g., Coates 1996; Tannen 1990) or a dominance framework (e.g., Eakins and Eakins 1979; Edelsky 1981),[1] postmodern (e.g., Baxter 2003; Mills 2003) or social constructionist perspectives (e.g., Holmes 2006; Mullany 2007) tend to characterize more recent research.[2] In terms of methodology, workplace discourse researchers have used both quantitative and qualitative data collection methods, as I will illustrate below, and analysis has been undertaken using a wide range of approaches from conversation analysis (e.g., Stokoe 2009) through interactional sociolinguistics (e.g., Schnurr 2009), to critical discourse analysis (e.g., Wodak 1995; 2003). The focus adopted by different researchers has included different occupations, different types of workplace interaction, different workplace roles and identities, and different workplace contexts. Research on gendered workplace discourse has also focused predominantly on spoken discourse. So while there is considerable

The Handbook of Language, Gender, and Sexuality, Second Edition.
Edited by Susan Ehrlich, Miriam Meyerhoff, and Janet Holmes.
© 2014 John Wiley & Sons, Inc. Published 2017 by John Wiley & Sons, Inc.

research on written communication in the workplace, including valuable discourse analyses of reports, emails, letters, and notes (e.g., Bargiela-Chiappini, Nickerson, and Planken 2007; Gunnarsson 2009), very few researchers have paid attention to the gendered features of written discourse (but see Koller 2004, discussed below). Consequently this chapter, illustrating mainly social constructionist approaches, concentrates on spoken workplace discourse. I have selected three themes which facilitate the discussion of a range of research in this area: first, research which examines the relevance of gender in different *types of workplace interaction*; second, research which examines the relevance of gender in the construction of *workplace identity*; and, third, research illustrating the concept of *the gendered workplace*.

Before proceeding, it will be useful to briefly outline my own position on the relationship between gender and language. As indicated above, I believe that gender is potentially relevant in every social interaction, a "pervasive social category" (Weatherall 2000, 287), and an ever present influence on how we behave, and how others perceive our behavior. While our level of awareness of gender varies from one interaction to another, and from moment to moment within an interaction, it is nevertheless a latent, omnipresent influence in every communicative encounter, with the potential to move into the foreground at any moment, to creep into our talk in subtle and not so subtle ways (Kitzinger 2002). As Eckert and McConnell-Ginet (2003, 87) point out, we orient to gender norms "as a kind of organizing device in society, an ideological map, setting out the range of the possible within which we place ourselves and assess others." In other words, we bring to every interaction our familiarity with societal gender stereotypes, behavioral constraints, and the gendered norms to which women and men are expected to conform. And these constraints are nowhere more apparent than in workplace interaction, as this chapter will demonstrate.

2. Types of Workplace Interaction

Language and gender researchers have examined a range of types of workplace discourse, from job interviews (e.g., Buzzanell and Meisenbach 2006), through commercial transactions (e.g., Ayoola 2009; Cameron 2000) and on-the-job encounters with clients, patients, and the general public (e.g., McElhinny 1992; Ostermann 2003; West 1990), through to workplace meetings of all sizes and kinds. Analyses tend to focus on different kinds of gendered behavior (e.g., flirtation, flattery, ribald banter, swearing), or ways in which gender identity is constructed in different types of interaction (see the next section for further discussion of this issue). Swearing, like verbal sexual harassment, for instance, is characterized as normatively masculine verbal behavior with negative consequences for women in some workplaces. Examining gendered discourses in Kenyan workplaces, Yieke (2004) focuses on the fine line between positively oriented teasing and sexual harassment. Workplace humor can provide effective cover for harassment which places women in a double bind, unable to respond without loss of respect, yet risking condemnation or punishment if they do. There is a good deal of research on such gendered discourse in different types of workplace interaction.

Meetings are by far the most widely studied type of workplace interaction, and they will serve here to illustrate more fully some of the diverse evidence of gendered behavior in workplace interaction. Quantitative analyses of workplace meeting discourse have identified a tendency for men to dominate meeting talking time (e.g., Eakins and Eakins 1979; Edelsky 1981; Gunnarsson 2001; James and Drakich 1993), and to interrupt more than women (e.g., Case 1988; Eakins and Eakins 1979; Tannen 1994a). In relation to styles of interaction, as Kendall and Tannen (1997, 87) note, compared to men in equivalent roles, women professionals appeared to "speak in ways which minimize status differences and downplay their own authority." These findings have proved remarkably robust, reflecting the continued numerical dominance of men, and the pervasiveness of masculinist (Baxter 2003; 2010) norms in many workplaces (Koenig et al. 2011).

Our New Zealand research also suggests the benefit of more detailed analysis, indicating that gender may sometimes be confounded with organizational role and status. Even in workplaces with higher proportions of women, positions of power are often held by men, and this is typically the most significant influence on who talks most in meetings. So, for example, the proportion of the total talking time taken by female chairs and male chairs in our study was remarkably similar (ranging from 37% to 53%) with no significant variation along gender lines (Holmes 2000). In another quantitative study, we analyzed the amount of humor contributed by women and men in 22 workplace meetings (Holmes, Marra, and Burns 2001). Examining 396 instances of humor, our data challenged the negative stereotype of women at work as humorless creatures: the women produced more humor than the men in these meetings – the average ratio for women was 25 instances per 100 minutes compared to the men's ratio of 14 instances per 100 minutes. Moreover, the very presence of women tended to be associated with higher levels of humor: as the proportion of female participants in a meeting increased, so did the amount of humor.

Earlier research on interaction in meetings also describes features of gendered styles of meeting talk, reporting that a more facilitative interactional style tends to be associated with women in group discussion, while men tend to adopt a more assertive and authoritative style (e.g., Case 1988; Hanak 1998), an analysis supported by the observations of Tannen (1994b) in large corporations, and Holmes (1995) in a range of mixed-sex interaction contexts. Initially identified in extensive scholarly research in the 1980s and 1990s, these features have been widely cited in popular "self-help" texts ever since (e.g., Gray 1992). Holmes and Stubbe (2003, 574) provide a table summarizing some of the most widely cited features of "feminine" and "masculine" interactional styles, a table which has itself been well cited.

More recent research on interaction in meetings has focused on how both women and men make use of linguistic, pragmatic, and discursive resources to construct femininity and masculinity in different workplace contexts (Baxter 2006; Holmes 2006; McConnell-Ginet 2011; Mullany 2007). This research demonstrates, for example, the wide range of affiliative or relational strategies used by women and men in different communities of practice to establish rapport and construct solidarity, strategies which include small talk, supportive humor and narratives, expressions of approval, and compliments, all of which are associated with normatively feminine styles of interaction (Holmes 2006; Holmes and Stubbe 2003). This change in orientation reflects the important insight that linguistic features and ways of speaking do not directly encode social meanings such as gender and ethnicity, but rather do so indirectly through their associations with particular roles, activities, traits, and stances (Ochs 1992). Since this approach encourages attention to the situational context in which meanings are produced, it tends to be associated with more detailed qualitative analysis of discourse in context. Much of this research has focused on the construction of professional identity in workplace contexts, a theme which is discussed below. In the next section, I briefly discuss just one normatively gendered aspect of meeting behavior, namely small talk.

3. Small Talk at Work

Small talk, like gossip, is widely culturally coded as feminine, and stereotypically associated with female activities and domains (Holmes 2006; Holmes and Stubbe 2003; Mullany 2007). Earlier research on small talk provides some support for this association: Coupland book (2000), for example, a collection devoted to small talk, but without gender as an explicit focus, is dominated by data from stereotypically feminine contexts (e.g., hairdressing, supermarket, travel agency, call center, women's healthcare). The reasons for the association of small talk with femininity are obvious on the basis of such research. However, the reality is that both women and men engage in small talk, although the topics are often gendered.

In our New Zealand workplace data, small talk appears to be obligatory at the beginning of meetings. Variations relate to its length and preferred topics, and this tends to reflect workplace culture or community-of-practice norms rather than gender per se (Holmes 2000; 2006). In some workplaces, typically those with a majority of women or Maori participants, social activities and family matters were common small talk currency. In other, mainly non-Maori workplaces, where males dominated, sport, outdoor activities, or electronic equipment dominated the small talk before the meeting.

In general, people seem well aware of the stereotype that small talk is women's talk, and that typical topics involve clothes, hair, and social activities. This is parodied in example 1 where Rob's failure to engage in small talk, the standard opening steps of a meeting, is noticeable to the participants and provides a source of humor.[3]

Example 1

Context: NZ Productions: Jaeson, the general manager, is having a catch up meeting with another senior manager, Rob. This is the very start of the interaction.[4]

```
1 Jaeson: yeah I'm talking to Rob Bellinger
2 Rob:    I broke it down [coughs] to
3         what I thought was the most logical
4 Jaeson: what happened to the small talk?
5 Rob:    [laughs] I love the col-
6         I love what you're doing with your hair these days
7 Jaeson: [laughs] oh you're just so straight into it you know [laughs]
8 Rob:    [laughs] um when we talked about the style of operation
```

The interaction begins with "verbal labeling" for the benefit of the researchers (line 1), a practice we encourage to help us understand who is interacting with whom when there is no associated video recording. Rob then plunges straight into the first topic on their agenda (lines 2–3). These two men usually discuss their shared sailing interests at the start of a meeting and so Jaeson's parodic metadiscoursal comment about the lack of small talk, albeit humorous (line 4), highlights the marked character of a meeting which skips this obligatory initial component, a point underlined later when he comments that Rob is "just so straight into it" (line 7). Rob quickly plays along with the humor, and introduces a stereotypical, and noticeably gendered, topic for small talk, a compliment about Jaeson's hair. However, the interchange indicates that, if small talk is totally missing, even between men with a busy schedule, this is a noticeable and unacceptable absence.

The material we collected from more masculine or "masculinist" workplaces suggests the issue of gendered small talk topics merits further research (Baxter 2003).[5] In at least three such workplaces, we found that the topics of the pre-meeting and post-meeting talk, though unrelated to the agenda of the meeting ahead, were much more work-related than in other workplaces. In these workplaces, there was relatively little conventional small talk focused on personal or social topics. Rather the participants used the times around the edges of the meeting to catch up on work-related topics that were typically unrelated to the meeting's ratified business. In six meetings of one team, for instance, there is scarcely a single topic of pre-meeting talk that is not related to some aspect of the team's work, although none related to items on the meeting agenda. Despite the work focus of the topics, this talk seems to serve as a kind of social glue for the members of these teams, and can be regarded as an alternative kind of small talk used to maintain collegial relations.[6]

This section has suggested some of the ways in which women and men use gendered resources in workplace meetings. In the next section I consider how people negotiate their gender identities alongside their professional identities at work, illustrating in particular how participants use different discursive resources to accomplish the integration of different workplace demands.

4. Gender and Workplace Identity

Research on professional identity and its intersection with gender has mushroomed since the beginning of the twenty-first century, with a great deal of attention being paid to the relatively new phenomenon of women in leadership roles (e.g., Baxter 2006; 2010; 2011; Eagly 2005; Mullany 2007; Olsson 2006; Schnurr 2009; Sinclair 1998). As Adler (1993, 289) points out, "the single most uncontroversial, incontrovertible statement to make about women in management is that there are very few of them." Speculation about the reasons for this phenomenon abound, including considerations of the "glass ceiling effect" (Holmes 2005; McConnell-Ginet 2011) but one undoubtedly relevant reason is the widespread perception in many countries that effective leaders are typically male. Early researchers in leadership studies noted that "what counts as leadership, the means of gaining legitimacy, and so on, are male dominated in most organizations" (Hearn and Parkin 1989, 27), with the result that women leaders are perceived as deviant exceptions to the male norm. Eagly (2005, 463) notes, "when leadership is defined in masculine terms, the leaders who emerge are disproportionately men, regardless of the sex composition of the community." This refrain is repeated in Eagly's most recent work (Koenig et al. 2011), although, hearteningly, with some evidence that this masculine construal of leadership is weaker than it was. In other words, leadership is a gendered concept (Holmes 2006; Ladegaard 2011), and this presents women leaders with a double bind, as summarized neatly by Jones (2000, 196): "If she talks like a manager she is transgressing the boundaries of femininity: if she talks like a woman she no longer represents herself as a manager."

Work by sociolinguists at the micro-level of workplace interaction has tended to confirm this perception in the leadership literature. Until recently, the prevailing stereotypes of a leader, chief executive officer, and even senior manager have been decidedly masculine, and the female voice in public contexts has often been silenced or at least muted (Baxter 2006). Many of the articles in Baxter (2006) provide evidence that, as a public rather than a private domain, the workplace is typically male-dominated, and until the last few years, what have been considered appropriate interactional styles, even in professional white collar interactions, could be characterized as distinctly "masculine." This evidence finds further support in McRae's (2009) analysis of interactions in 11 commercial companies, Baxter's (2003) research on management meetings in a dot-com company, and Mullany's (2007) detailed study of meetings in a retail and a manufacturing company.

There is, however, some evidence that the shape of the gendered concept of leadership is gradually being modified to accommodate attributes regarded as normatively feminine as well as those regarded as stereotypically masculine. In the area of business studies, Kram and Hampton (2003, 211) argue that "practitioners and scholars alike are recognizing that organizations struggling to survive in an increasingly complex and changing environment need leadership that is transformational, collaborative, and relationship-oriented." Ladegaard (2011, 5) makes the point that if this were true, we would expect normatively feminine styles to be sought after. Both male and female leaders tended to prefer an indirect, normatively feminine management style, with male leaders more likely to use a wide verbal repertoire style, drawing on elements in their speech that are both normatively male and normatively female. However, worryingly, the perceptions of employees seemed unaffected by this change. In particular, Ladegaard notes that the authority of male leaders was never questioned, while female leaders were often challenged by their male colleagues. In the European context, Wodak (2003) identifies the diverse strategies used by women members of the European Union parliament to present and promote themselves, and to guarantee that they are taken seriously, while Wagner and Wodak (2006) provide evidence that senior women may subtly subvert dominant male norms. Their analysis shows how women working in male-dominated fields avoid using localized male patterns for constructing success, but rather construct their own success stories using cooperating, nonantagonistic positioning strategies. On the other hand, Mullany (2008) describes how women in a manufacturing company draw on stereotypically masculine behaviors (i.e., impoliteness) as a resource in meetings for being assertive and gaining power over men who are their equals in the managerial hierarchy.

Our New Zealand research (Holmes 2006) supports the view that effective managers, female and male, make use of a range of gendered resources to achieve their transactional and relational goals. Constructing oneself as powerful and "leader-like" generally entails using discourse strategies which encode authority and decisiveness, traits normatively associated with masculinity. So, for example, leaders issue directives and give instructions, they open and close meetings, and manage the discussion in between, assigning turns at talk, managing topics, and confirming decisions. These are social acts which are generally considered constitutive of the professional identity of a manager (Harris 2003; Holmes 2006). Early research in this area indicated that men in managerial positions tended to use, or report that they would use, forms which maintained or maximized status differences, while women superiors more often minimized status differences (Tannen 1994b; Tracy and Eisenberg 1990–1991). However, our research indicates that in contexts where they need to assert authority and bolster perceptions of themselves as effective leaders, both women and men make use of more direct ways of speaking, adopting features which typically index masculinity. So, when they judge that they need to enact decisive leadership, both female and male managers tend to use linguistic forms such as *need* statements and imperatives when giving instructions or getting someone to do something: for example, "I need that file by 10"; "you need to get that to me soon"; "make some notes"; "ring the applicants today"; "get him to make the changes." Equally, however, both women and men make use of more facilitative and negotiative strategies when these are deemed to be more effective means of accomplishing their workplace objectives (Holmes 2006).

Detailed ethnographic sociolinguistic research using an interactional sociolinguistic framework thus provides a more nuanced picture of workplace interaction, qualifying the rather unmitigatedly masculine representation of the decisive authoritarian leader which dominated earlier leadership research.[7] Baxter (2011) provides yet further support for this analysis in her examination of the discourse of female leaders in British male-dominated organizations. She uses the term "double-voiced discourse" (Bakhtin 1994) to describe the ways in which these women use language consciously and strategically to compensate for their marginalized status in large male-dominated organizations. In sum, a leader's linguistic choices depend for their effect on where, when, and to whom they are uttered, as well as what has preceded them in the discourse. Typically, effective leaders make use of a wide range of linguistic forms and discourse strategies, skillfully negotiating their choices according to contextual factors.

To illustrate a little of this complexity, I provide just two examples from our New Zealand research. Suzanne is a senior manager in NZ Consultations, a white collar professional organization with a clear hierarchy of power and responsibility. Within this context Suzanne has developed a distinctive leadership style, indicative of a model which we observed as widespread in her organization. Rather than presenting herself as a "hero" (see Holmes 2009; Olsson 2006), a visionary and authoritative autocrat, Suzanne enacts responsible and consultative leadership. She describes herself as "a guide and a mentor," coaching people "to the stage where they can do tasks themselves." While she states that she can be challenging in dealing with difficult people in complex negotiations, she also indicates that her preferred style is encouraging and supportive, a style consistent with the norms and expectations of "the gender order" (Eckert and McConnell-Ginet 2003). These comments from her interview are strongly supported in the extensive recordings of Suzanne's interactions with her colleagues. Throughout our notes on the transcripts of these recordings, in large team meetings as well as small-group consultations, the words "consultative" and "collaborative" constantly recur. Example 2 illustrates some of the features of Suzanne's consultative interactional style.

Example 2

Context: Suzanne, Senior Manager, NZ Consultations, senior team meeting

```
 1 Suzanne: I just thought a couple more points I'd raise
 2          is um or one other matter really the budget approval
 3          for [Company] we'll need to follow that up...
 4          but um perhaps if we start with the training of juniors
 5          this is probably the thing that can be put off most
 6          during the next three weeks but um I wondered
 7          whether I should actually go ahead and tee up [name]
 8          to do you know those two seminars...
 9          so I wonder if we can sort of pick that
10          that's an o- ongoing issue that we just need to monitor
```

Suzanne here provides clear direction but she is consistently collaborative, consultative, and approving throughout this short but typical excerpt. She uses the inclusive pronoun "we" rather than "I" at several key points (lines 3, 4, 9, 10), indexing a consultative stance when indicating what she wants to happen. And she also uses many mitigating devices and attenuating phrases to soften the impact of the directives she is giving: "I just thought" (line 1), "um perhaps if" (line 4), "probably" (line 5), "um I wondered" (line 6), "I wonder if we can sort of" (line 9), "just" (line 10). These are linguistic features which index a deferential and consultative stance associated with a normatively feminine identity. And it is clear from our analysis that it is extremely effective and appropriate in the very consultative community of practice in which she works.

Overall, then, Suzanne presents an alternative construction of leadership to the global hero leader model. She is decisive and authoritative when required, but her preferred interactional style is consultative and negotiative, a style which treats the views of others with respect. If, as Philips (2003) proposes, feminist linguists should build on ways of doing things which benefit women,[8] then Suzanne offers a plausible model. Our analyses demonstrate that she skillfully integrates features of a normatively masculine leadership style with positive aspects of normatively feminine talk, to construct a leadership style which is appropriate to and greatly valued in her organization.

My second example is Daniel, a Maori leader working in a white collar professional organization (pseudonymed Kiwi Consultations), with a formal hierarchical structure and in the same organizational sector as Suzanne's organization. The difference is that Kiwi Consultations can be described as an ethnicized community of practice (Holmes, Marra, and Vine 2011; Schnurr, Marra, and Holmes 2007), an organization with a majority of employees who identify as Maori, and with an explicit commitment to achieving good outcomes for Maori, and an all-encompassing awareness of the Maori values underpinning every workplace interaction. Daniel's discourse indexes a range of stances some of which express social meanings associated with a relatively conventional leadership identity, but some of which instantiates a new hybridized model, introducing some unconventional features into his leadership performance.[9] In interview, for example, Daniel constructs himself as a decisive, hard-nosed leader, and also as an expert in contemporary leadership theories. He describes how he "reshaped the reporting lines," for example, and reports, "we had a few casualties, they don't work here anymore." His decisive, unsentimental stance indexes the authoritative leadership identity of someone familiar with current Western conceptions of management theory.

Interacting with his staff in a formal planning meeting, Daniel's discourse provides convincing performative support for this self-construction as an authoritative, decisive, and even visionary leader. Example 3 is an excerpt from a full staff meeting where he outlines plans for the next phase of planned changes to the company's processes.

Example 3

Context: Kiwi Consultations: Meeting of all staff

```
1 Daniel: if you think back a couple of meetings
2         I said that er I was trying to turn turn our minds
3         to the process management issues in front of us
4         because we've er got a pretty good handle on allocation
5         and we've got to start turning our mind towards the things
6         we're gonna be doing in the long term
```

Here Daniel clearly identifies the direction in which he thinks the organization should be moving, and the importance of looking beyond the immediate goals to the bigger picture. He reminds people that he has signaled earlier that they would need to start paying attention to the issue of how to manage the new process, and indicates that he wants to develop a longer-term view: "we've got to start turning our mind towards the things we're gonna be doing in the long term" (lines 5–6). He presents the big picture view, the classic responsibility of a visionary leader. This is delivered in direct clear language, with no hedging or attenuation. Moreover, Daniel skillfully moves from his role as visionary leader indexed through "I" (line 2) to the inclusive "our" (line 2), "us" (line 3), and "we" (lines 4, 5, 6) indexing a much more collaborative stance. His workplace performance demonstrates a skillful integration of the transactional and relational skills which extensive research has demonstrated is generally evident in effective leadership performances (Baxter 2010; Holmes, Marra, and Vine 2011; Mullany 2007; Schnurr 2009).

There is also, however, at least one other important dimension of Daniel's complex leadership performance, which relates to his Maori ethnicity. In his interactions with the staff of Kiwi Consultations, Daniel behaves in ways which are quite consistent with Maori values and beliefs. He regularly opens staff meetings with a formal Maori ritual *karakia*, for instance.[10] He also demonstrates sensitivity to the important Maori cultural value of *whakaiti*, the requirement for Maori leaders to be humble and modest. Daniel's main interactional strategy for managing the tension between the need to appear authoritative and leader-like on the one hand, and the Maori cultural requirement to behave in an unpretentious way on the other, is to adopt a distinctly informal leadership style. He manages even the most formal meetings with a light hand and uses many different linguistic devices to emphasize the lack of formality. In particular, as illustrated in example 4, he makes extensive use of the New Zealand pragmatic tag *eh*, a feature associated with both informality and Maori ethnicity.

Example 4

Context: Daniel is talking to his Human Resources Manager, Caleb, in a regular weekly meeting.

```
1 Daniel: but it also an indication
2         that you don't have to wear ties here any more eh
3         you don't have to but don't wear rags [laughs]
4         [laughs] you know
5         here are what you can wear eh...
6         I don't wear ties any more
7         I'm hōhā ["fed up"] with it eh um
8         and so nobody else feels they have to wear them
9         either eh
```

In this excerpt, Daniel expresses his preference for a more casual style of dress, and emphasizes this attitude by his frequent use of the casual tag *eh* (lines 2, 5, 7, 9) as well as the informal Maori word *hōhā*. Similarly, the following comment on a politician, recorded in another meeting, not only illustrates his use of *eh* but also indicates his distaste for people who play up their status and "put on side": "he's just an imperialist eh he's gotta a very er high opinion of his worth eh." The pragmatic particle *eh* indexes an informal, matey stance, emphasizing the content of this example, as well as being strongly associated with Maori identity (Meyerhoff 1994). Daniel thus uses a range of different discursive devices to accomplish a "hybridised" identity (Lemke 2008, 33), an identity which represents "a compromise by the individual among the pressures and forces of multiple cultures and institutions which are seeking to control [their] identities" (2008, 33).

And just as Suzanne's skilled exploitation of a range of discourse strategies illustrates how she negotiates the gender order, and especially the double bind facing women leaders, so Daniel demonstrates in his discourse how he manages the conflict between conventional, Pakeha leadership expectations and those consistent with his Maori cultural values and norms.

These brief examples can only hint at the complexities of the performances of current leaders in professional organizations. While males in our data often, like Daniel, told "hero stories" (Holmes, Marra, and Vine 2011), especially in interview with a leadership expert, the reality of their leadership performances was far more nuanced and variegated (reinforcing our commitment to observing what people do rather than relying like so many leadership studies on self-report data). Similarly, female leaders were often described by their staff, and described themselves, as taking a "motherly" role (Holmes 2005; Mullany 2007), but the reality of their daily workplace interactions displayed a much more complex leadership performance characterized by components of normatively masculine as well as feminine interactional style.[11] Moreover, as illustrated by Daniel, ethnicity frequently added another interesting component to the mix with both female and male leaders integrating appropriate cultural features into their leadership performances, especially in "ethnicised communities of practice" (e.g., Holmes, Marra, and Vine 2011; Schnurr, Marra, and Holmes 2007).

Thus gender is always relevant, though the way it is enacted is sensitive to the specific workplace context in which individuals operate. And, as detailed analyses of workplace discourse have demonstrated, particular patterns of linguistic choices can accumulate over time to contribute to the construction of relatively feminine or relatively masculine styles of discourse, and to the subtle gendering of the workplace environment in ways inimical to some women's (and some men's) comfort levels, a point explored in the next section.

5. Gendered Workplaces

The notion of the "gendered" workplace is a well-recognized if controversial concept which has proved useful in analyzing workplace interaction in a variety of different countries and social contexts. (See Philips, Chapter 15 in this volume, for discussion.) As discussed by Holmes and Stubbe (2003), it is a concept which has arisen regularly during our research on workplace discourse in New Zealand. While some scholars have challenged the value of analyses which reinforce gender dichotomies, both those participating in our research and members of the wider New Zealand community are very willing to identify some workplaces as particularly "feminine" and others as very "masculine," and there is a growing body of research which supports the view that these terms usefully identify poles on a continuum of perception. This section discusses some characteristics of workplaces perceived as differently gendered, and briefly illustrates how effective leaders may exploit these perceptions to achieve their transactional goals.

What exactly do people mean when they refer to a "feminine" or a "masculine" workplace? While nonlinguistic characteristics such as the gender composition of the workforce and the nature of the organization's work (e.g., McElhinny 1992; Nielsen 2008) are undoubtedly components of the picture, it is also clear that specific communicative patterns are equally important. A number of researchers have examined ways in which workplaces can be experienced as gendered through the use of workplace discourse which alienates women in particular (e.g., Baxter 2003; Baxter and Wallace 2009; Beck 1999; Holmes 2006; Mullany 2007). Baxter and Wallace (2009), for example, demonstrate how, through their on-the-job talk, UK builders construct building sites as masculine workplaces. They note that "there is almost no reference to women" (2009, 411). Indeed, women are viewed as so unthreatening to male domination of the building industry that they don't even seem to qualify for "othering."

In the same vein, Koller (2004) explicitly links the use of war metaphors to describe both businesswomen and businessmen in business magazines to ideologies of hegemonic masculinity. She argues that such metaphors help to "masculinise both that discourse and related social practices" (Koller 2004, 5) Similarly, Baxter (2010, 159) notes the negative impact of sexist language, as well as the preponderance of war and sport metaphors in the workplace, arguing that such language marginalizes femininity and "positions women as an 'out-group' in business." In an African context, as mentioned above, Yieke analyzes verbal sexual harassment (2004) and toilet graffiti (2006) as examples of discriminatory workplace practices suffered by women. She points out that toilet graffiti is one means for otherwise muted individuals to share their concerns with others, protest, and "sensitise the general public to their plight" (2006, 49). Thus metaphor and graffiti are two examples of the ways in which workplaces can be experienced as gendered (in these cases as masculine).

As discussed above, the normative characteristics of feminine and masculine talk are now very familiar. These stereotypical features clearly contribute to employees' perceptions that some workplaces are more masculine, while others are more feminine. For example, Nielsen (2008, 173) describes Danish bakeries as "masculine workplaces," characterized by "masculine discourse" (2008, 185), which is perceived by the women as "really rough and unpleasant. The tone is aggressive and can be nasty" (2008, 185). Similarly, Plester and Sayers (2007) explore the use of aggressive humor in Internet technology (IT) companies, identifying a style of humor which they characterize as banter or "taking the piss." This style involved jocular abuse, aggressive barbs, and potentially hurtful teasing (Plester and Sayers 2007, 158–159) – all features generally associated with "masculinist" discourse (Baxter 2003).

By contrast, more feminine workplaces and communities of practice have been described as characterized by more collaborative and supportive humor, a greater amount of personal small talk, and, in general, greater attention to participants' face needs in interaction (Holmes 2006; Holmes and Stubbe 2003). Operators in UK call centers, for example, are required to use speech patterns which match Lakoff's (1973) description of "women's language" (Cameron 2000). Similarly, women managers often feel under pressure to adopt a "feminine" style of interaction: as one female manager commented, "I'm supposed to nurture and encourage them. I see that as my role" (Mullany 2007, 170). Supporting this gendered perspective, the men interviewed by Mullany judged assertive women colleagues very negatively. All this research illustrates how gender is "produced and reproduced in differential forms of participation in particular CoPs [communities of practice]" (Eckert and McConnell-Ginet 1995, 491). Gender seems to be institutionalized, or embedded within the institutional structure of the workplace.

As indicated above, like Mullany (2007) and Baxter (2010), we have consistently demonstrated that effective leaders, both female and male, draw on a wide range of different styles in enacting leadership. The concept of the gendered workplace thus interacts with these leadership performances in interesting ways. In a stereotypically feminine workplace, with consultation as its main business, Suzanne's concern for her colleagues' face needs and her negotiative interactional style (illustrated above) is unmarked and normative (Holmes, Marra, and Vine 2011; see also Leila's leadership performance in Holmes and Stubbe 2003). Similarly, an aggressive and challenging interactional style is regarded as normal and appropriate for a leader in a more masculine workplace oriented to producing goods under pressure to meet deadlines, as illustrated by Seamus. In example 5, Seamus sets out a course of action in a very decisive way.

Example 5

Context: Seamus is discussing how to handle a new client with his management team.

```
 1 Seamus:   I'll ring this guy up I'll make a decision...
 2 Jaeson:   make sure you make him sweat though eh
 3           and then we wanna hear the story afterwards +
 4 Seamus:   I'll make him sweat...
 5           I'll ring him /+ make a decision\
 6 Jaeson:   /alright keep us informed\
 7           be interest- be interesting to see how /you get on\
 8 Chrissie: /well I\ I wanna know what he says yeah [laughs]
 9           are you so you're gonna ring Bruce too?
10 Seamus:   I'll ring Bruce Ford I'll ring him now
```

This is very direct, decisive, and authoritative language. Holmes, Marra, and Vine (2011) provide further examples of the ways in which Seamus questions and challenges his managers on even small points of detail.

But, as noted, effective leaders exploit a diversity of styles to achieve their interactional goals. And gendered workplace contexts provide skilled leaders with an additional means of making an impact with their discourse. Thus in a relatively masculine workplace, when the manager softens her typically aggressive performance with humor the effect is particularly marked, as the appreciative response of her colleagues indicates. The discourse of Ginette, for example, a tough factory supervisor, is characterized by imperatives, swearing, and criticism (Holmes and Stubbe 2003); hence when she uses humor to soften a complaint, or hedge a criticism, the effect is marked and appreciated. Similarly, Angelina, a senior manager in NZ Consultations, generally uses a very consultative and collaborative style in her relatively feminine workplace (Holmes, Marra, and Vine 2011, ch. 6). Consequently, when she adopts a direct and assertive approach on a particular issue, the effect on her colleagues is very clear. They are extremely attentive, and their responses are succinct and focused.

Finally it is worth noting the potential implications of gendered workplace discourse. Over 20 years ago, McElhinny pointed to the restrictive consequences of gendered blinkers in the workplace: "Workplaces are gendered both by the numerical predominance of one sex within them and by the cultural interpretation of given types of work which, in conjunction with cultural norms and interpretations of gender, dictate who is understood as best suited for different types of employment (McElhinny 1992, 386). Beck provides a specific example in her research on gendered discourse in an Australian bank, noting that women managers found themselves "forced to strategically adopt a masculinised managerial discourse for their organisational survival" (1999, 207). Similarly, Nielsen notes that the rough and masculine discourse of the Danish bakery he researched resulted in female apprentices learning "to marginalize themselves" (2008, 185). He describes how female apprentices found themselves disadvantaged in a myriad of ways in this gendered workplace, including being powerless to fully and freely participate in workplace interaction. The very few women who attempted to participate found they could only do so by conforming to the dominant male discourse norms.

In conclusion, it has been widely documented that women who use contestive and challenging discourse features, especially in a normatively feminine occupational sphere, or a normatively feminine workplace, run the risk of negative evaluation (e.g., Baxter 2006; Sinclair 1998; Walsh 2001). Similarly men who use features of normatively feminine speech styles in more masculine workplaces expose themselves to the risk of ridicule (Holmes 2006). Thus perceptions of gendered workplaces deserve consideration as one important contextual factor which interacts with the performance of the individual's professional identity in the workplace.

6. Conclusion

Gender is a pervasive influence on how we perform our social identity and how we perceive the behavior of others in all types of workplace interactions and in all kinds of different workplaces. We view people through social spectacles and gender is one very important and unavoidable component of the lens.

While there is continuing evidence of gendered patterns of interaction which shore up the stereotypes of cooperative female and contestive male discourses, there is also a growing body of research indicating that effective communicators, both female and male, typically draw from a very wide and varied discursive repertoire, ranging from normatively "feminine" to normatively "masculine" ways of talking, and that they skillfully select their discursive strategies in response to particular interactional contexts. Indeed, their effectiveness derives precisely from this discursive flexibility and contextual sensitivity (Holmes 2006).

Nonetheless, as illustrated in the final section, in particular, it is important to be aware that many workplaces continue to be predominantly masculine domains with masculine discourse norms and norms of interaction. Consequently, women often find themselves disadvantaged in such contexts. The growing body of research evidence that stylistic diversity and sensitivity to context are features of the ways in which effective women and men interact at work may help to counter negative stereotypes and undermine the prejudice that affects women in particular in many workplaces. Similarly, there is some evidence that, as more women move into senior positions and take on managerial responsibility, traditional stereotypes of the normatively masculine leader are beginning to erode.

Acknowledgements

I would like to record my appreciation for the sterling assistance provided by Brian King in identifying relevant recent literature. I would also like to express my gratitude to Bernadette Vine and Meredith Marra who assisted with finding relevant excerpts and references.

NOTES

1   See Kendall and Tannen (1997) for a comprehensive overview of earlier research in this area.
2   But note that Baxter (2010) uses both difference and dominance approaches in her recent analysis of the position of women in different types of corporations.
3   See Holmes, Marra, and Vine (2011) for further discussion of this example.
4   All names are pseudonyms. Transcription conventions:

[laughs]	Square brackets indicate paralinguistic features and other information
+	Pause of up to one second
.../......\...	Simultaneous speech
?	Rising or question intonation
-	Incomplete or cut-off utterance
...	Some words omitted
hōhā ["fed up"]	Maori words in italics; gloss provided in square brackets

5   This section draws on Holmes (2006).
6   Drawing on data from a car factory, a hospital, and an administrative context to compare women's and men's relational strategies, Eggins and Slade (1997) make a similar point about teasing between Australian men at work.
7   For further examples of this more complex and nuanced picture of the components which contribute to effective leadership, see Kendall (2003) and Schnurr (2009). And for a study of the interaction between the complex form of directives (including metaphorical style shifts to maintain control) and contextual factors, see Takano's (2005) research with women managers in nine workplaces in three cities in Japan.

8   Philips argues that we should "enhance, elaborate, and build on the gender ideologies that are most enabling of women" (2003, 271–272).
9   For more details on Daniel's complex style see Holmes, Marra, and Vine (2011, ch. 8).
10 The *karakia* is typically a recitation, or formal greeting in the form of a prayer, used to open Maori events. It is a significant component of the opening of a Maori meeting. See Holmes, Marra, and Vine (2011, ch. 4) for further discussion of meeting openings in Maori workplaces.
11 See also Kendall (2003) on this issue.

REFERENCES

Adler, Nancy. 1993. "An International Perspective on the Barriers to the Advancement of Women Managers." *Applied Psychology*, 42(4): 289–300.

Ayoola, Kehinde A. 2009. "Haggling Exchanges at Meat Stalls in Some Markets in Lagos, Nigeria." *Discourse Studies*, 11(4): 387–400.

Bakhtin, Mikhail. 1994. "Double-Voiced Discourse in Dostoevsky." In *The Bakhtin Reader: Selected Writings*, ed. Pam Morris, 102–111. London: Edward Arnold.

Bargiela-Chiappini, Francesca, Catherine Nickerson, and Brigitte Planken. 2007. *Business Discourse*. Basingstoke: Palgrave Macmillan.

Baxter, Judith. 2003. *Positioning Gender in Discourse: A Feminist Methodology*. Basingstoke: Palgrave Macmillan.

Baxter, Judith, ed. 2006. *Speaking Out: The Female Voice in Public Contexts*. Basingstoke: Palgrave Macmillan.

Baxter, Judith. 2010. *The Language of Female Leadership*. Basingstoke: Palgrave Macmillan.

Baxter, Judith. 2011. "Survival or Success? A Critical Exploration of the Use of 'Double-Voiced Discourse' by Women Business Leaders in the UK." *Discourse & Communication*, 5(3): 231–245.

Baxter, Judith, and Kieran Wallace. 2009. "Outside In-group and Out-group Identities? Constructing Male Solidarity and Female Exclusion in UK Builders' Talk." *Discourse & Society*, 20(4): 411–429.

Beck, Dominique M. 1999. "*Managing Discourse, Self and Others: Women in Senior Management Positions.*" Unpublished PhD dissertation, University of Western Sydney.

Buzzanell, Patrice M., and Rebecca Meisenbach. 2006. "Gendered Performance and Communication in the Employment Interview." In Mary Barrett and Marilyn J. Davidson (eds.), *Gender and Communication at Work*, 19–37. Aldershot: Ashgate.

Cameron, Deborah. 1997. "Theoretical Debates in Feminist Linguistics: Questions of Sex and Gender." In Ruth Wodak (ed.), *Gender and Discourse*, 21–36. London: Sage.

Cameron, Deborah. 2000. "Styling the Worker: Gender and the Commodification of Language in the Globalized Service Economy." *Journal of Sociolinguistics*, 4(3): 323–347.

Case, Susan S. 1988 "Cultural Differences, Not Deficiencies: An Analysis of Managerial Women's Language." In Suzanna Rose and Laurie Larwood (eds.), *Women's Careers: Pathways and Pitfalls*, 41–63. New York: Praeger.

Coates, Jennifer. 1996. *Women Talk*. Oxford: Blackwell.

Coupland, Justine, ed. 2000. *Small Talk*. London: Longman.

Eagly, Alice H. 2005. "Achieving Relational Authenticity in Leadership: Does Gender Matter?" *Leadership Quarterly*, 16(3): 459–474.

Eakins, Barbara W., and Gene Eakins. 1979. "Verbal Turn-Taking and Exchanges in Faculty Dialogue." In Betty Lou Dubois and Isobel Crouch (eds.), *The Sociology of the Languages of American Women*, 53–62. San Antonio, TX: Trinity University Press.

Eckert, Penelope, and Sally McConnell-Ginet. 1995. "Constructing Meaning, Constructing Selves: Snapshots of Language, Gender, and Class from Belten

High." In Kira Hall and Mary Bucholtz (eds.), *Gender Articulated: Language and the Socially Constructed Self*, 469–507. London: Routledge.

Eckert, Penelope, and Sally McConnell-Ginet. 2003. *Language and Gender*. Cambridge: Cambridge University Press.

Edelsky, Carol. 1981. "Who's Got the Floor?" *Language in Society*, 10: 383–421.

Eggins, Susan, and Diana Slade. 1997. *Analysing Casual Conversation*. London: Continuum.

Gray, John. 1992. *Men are from Mars, Women are from Venus*. New York: HarperCollins.

Gunnarsson, Britt-Louise. 2001. "Academic Women in the Male University Field: Communicative Practices at Postgraduate Seminars." In Bettina Baron and Helga Kotthoff (eds.), *Gender in Interaction*, 247–281. Amsterdam: Benjamins.

Gunnarsson, Britt-Louise. 2009. *Professional Discourse*. London: Continuum.

Hanak, Irmi. 1998. "Chairing Meetings: Turn and Topic Control in Development Communication in Rural Zanzibar." *Discourse & Society*, 9(1): 33–56.

Harris, Sandra J. 2003. "Politeness and Power: Making and Responding to 'Requests' in Institutional Settings." *Text*, 21(1): 27–52.

Hearn, Jeff, and Wendy P. Parkin. 1989. "Women, Men, and Leadership: A Critical Review of Assumptions, Practices, and Change in the Industrialized Nations." In Nancy Adler and Dalna Izraeli (eds.), *Women in Management Worldwide*, 17–40. London: M. E. Sharpe.

Holmes, Janet. 1995. *Women, Men and Politeness*. London: Longman.

Holmes, Janet. 2000. "Women at Work: Analysing Women's Talk in New Zealand Workplaces." *Australian Review of Applied Linguistics*, 22(2): 1–17.

Holmes, Janet. 2005. "The Glass Ceiling – Does Talk Contribute? Gendered Discourse in the New Zealand Workplace." In Colleen Mills and Donald Matheson (eds.), *Communication at Work: Showcasing Communication Scholarship*. Christchurch: Australian and New Zealand Communication Association. At

http://pandora.nla.gov.au/pan/31914/20070320-0000/www.mang.canterbury.ac.nz/ANZCA/FullPapers/JANET%20HOLMES%20KEYNOTE.pdf, accessed November 4, 2013.

Holmes, Janet. 2006. *Gendered Talk at Work*. Oxford: Blackwell.

Holmes, Janet. 2009. "Men, Masculinities and Leadership: Different Discourse Styles at Work." In Pia Pichler and Eve M. Eppler (eds.), *Gender and Spoken Interaction*, 186–210. Basingstoke: Palgrave Macmillan.

Holmes, Janet, Meredith Marra, and Louise Burns. 2001. "Women's Humour in the Workplace: A Quantitative Analysis." *Australian Journal of Communication*, 28(1): 83–108.

Holmes, Janet, Meredith Marra, and Bernadette Vine. 2011. *Leadership, Discourse, and Ethnicity*. Oxford: Oxford University Press.

Holmes, Janet, and Maria Stubbe. 2003. "'Feminine' Workplaces: Stereotypes and Reality." In Janet Holmes and Miriam Meyerhoff (eds.), *The Handbook of Language and Gender*, 573–599. Oxford: Blackwell.

James, Deborah, and Janice Drakich. 1993 "Understanding Gender Differences in Amount of Talk." In Deborah Tannen (ed.), *Gender and Conversational Interaction*, 281–312. Oxford: Oxford University Press.

Jones, Deborah. 2000. "Gender Trouble in the Workplace: 'Language and Gender' Meets 'Feminist Organizational Communication.'" In Janet Holmes (ed.), *Gendered Speech in Social Context: Perspectives from Gown to Town*, 192–210. Wellington, New Zealand: Victoria University Press.

Kendall, Shari. 2003. "Creating Gendered Demeanours of Authority at Work and at Home." In Janet Holmes and Miriam Meyerhoff (eds.), *The Handbook of Language and Gender*, 600–623. Oxford: Blackwell.

Kendall, Shari, and Deborah Tannen. 1997. "Gender and Language in the Workplace." In Ruth Wodak (ed.), *Gender and Discourse*, 81–105. London: Sage.

Kitzinger, Celia. 2002. "Doing Feminist Conversational Analysis." In Paul McIlvenny (ed.), *Talking Gender and Sexuality*, 163–193. Amsterdam: Benjamins.

Koenig, Anne M., Alice H. Eagly, Abigail A. Mitchell, and Tiina Ristikari. 2011. "Are Leader Stereotypes Masculine? A Meta-analysis of Three Research Paradigms." *Psychological Bulletin*, 137(4): 616–642.

Koller, Veronika. 2004. "Businesswomen and War Metaphors: 'Possessive, Jealous and Pugnacious'?" *Journal of Sociolinguistics*, 8(1): 3–22.

Kram, Kathy E., and Marion McCollom Hampton. 2003. "When Women Lead: The Visibility–Vulnerability Spiral." In Robin J. Ely, Erica Gabrielle Foldy, and Maureen A. Scully (eds.), *Reader in Gender, Work, and Organization*, 211–223. Oxford: Blackwell.

Ladegaard, Hans. 2011. "'Doing Power' at Work: Responding to Male and Female Management Styles in a Global Business Corporation." *Journal of Pragmatics*, 43: 4–19.

Lakoff, Robin. 1973. "Language and Woman's Place." *Language in Society*, 2(1): 45–80.

Lemke, Jan L. 2008. "Identity, Development and Desire: Critical Questions." In Carmen R. Caldas-Coulthard and Rick Iedema (eds.), *Identity Trouble: Critical Discourse and Contested Identities*, 17–42. London: Palgrave Macmillan.

McConnell-Ginet, Sally. 2011 "Breaking through the 'Glass Ceiling': Can Linguistic Awareness Help?" In *Gender, Sexuality, and Meaning*, 263–282. Oxford: Oxford University Press.

McElhinny, Bonnie S. 1992. "'I Don't Smile Much Anymore': Affect, Gender and the Discourse of Pittsburgh Police Officers." In *Locating Power: Proceedings of the Second Berkeley Women and Language Conference*, 386–403. Berkeley: Berkeley Women and Language Group.

McRae, Sue. 2009. "It's a Blokes' Thing: Gender, Occupational Roles and Talk in the Workplace." In Pia Pichler and Eve M. Eppler (eds.), *Gender and Spoken Interaction*, 163–185. Basingstoke: Palgrave Macmillan.

Meyerhoff, Miriam. 1994. "Sounds Pretty Ethnic eh? A Pragmatic Particle in New Zealand English." *Language in Society*, 23(3): 367–388.

Mills, Sarah. 2003. *Gender and Politeness*. Cambridge: Cambridge University Press.

Mullany, Louise. 2007. *Gendered Discourse in the Professional Workplace*. Basingstoke: Palgrave Macmillan.

Mullany, Louise. 2008. "'Stop Hassling Me': Impoliteness, Power and Gender Identity in the Professional Workplace." In Derek Bousfield and Miriam A. Locher (eds.), *Impoliteness in Language*, 231–251. Berlin: Mouton de Gruyter.

Nielsen, Klaus. 2008. "Gender, Learning and Social Practice: Gendered Discourses in the Bakery." *Vocations and Learning: Studies in Vocational and Professional Education*, 1(3): 175–190.

Ochs, Elinor. 1992. "Indexing Gender." In Alessandro Duranti and Charles Goodwin (eds.), *Rethinking Context: Language as an Interactive Phenomenon*, 335–358. Cambridge: Cambridge University Press.

Olsson, Sue. 2006. "'We Don't Need Another Hero!' Organizational Storytelling as a Vehicle for Communicating a Female Archetype." In Mary Barrett and Marilyn J. Davidson (eds.), *Gender and Communication at Work*, 195–210. Aldershot: Ashgate.

Ostermann, Ana. C. 2003. "Communities of Practice at Work: Gender, Facework and the Power of Habitus at an All-Female Police Station and a Feminist Crisis Intervention Center in Brazil." *Discourse & Society*, 14(4): 473–505.

Philips, Susan U. 2003. "The Power of Gender Ideologies in Discourse." In Janet Holmes and Miriam Meyerhoff (eds.), *The Handbook of Language and Gender*, 252–276. Oxford: Blackwell.

Plester, Barbara A., and Janet Sayers. 2007. "'Taking the Piss': The Use of Banter in the IT Industry." *Humor*, 20(2): 157–187.

Schnurr, Stephanie. 2009. *Leadership Discourse at Work: Interactions of Humour, Gender and Workplace Culture*. Basingstoke: Palgrave Macmillan.

Schnurr, Stephanie, Meredith Marra, and Janet Holmes. 2007. "Being (Im)Polite in New Zealand Workplaces: Māori and Pākehā Leaders." *Journal of Pragmatics*, 39(4): 712–729.

Sinclair, Adrienne. 1998. *Doing Leadership Differently: Gender, Power and Sexuality in a Changing Business Culture*. Melbourne: Melbourne University Press.

Stokoe, Elizabeth. 2009. "'I've Got a Girlfriend': Police Officers Doing 'Self-Disclosure' in Their Interrogations of Suspects." *Narrative Inquiry*, 19(1): 154–182.

Takano, Shoji. 2005. "Re-examining Linguistic Power: Strategic Uses of Directives by Professional Japanese Women in Positions of Authority and Leadership." *Journal of Pragmatics*, 37: 633–666.

Tannen, Deborah. 1990. *You Just Don't Understand: Women and Men in Conversation*. New York: William Morrow.

Tannen, Deborah. 1994a. *Gender and Discourse*. Oxford: Oxford University Press.

Tannen, Deborah. 1994b. *Talking from 9 to 5*. London: Virago.

Tracy, Karen, and Eric M. Eisenberg. 1990–1991. "Giving Criticism: A Multiple Goals Case Study." *Research on Language and Social Interaction*, 24: 37–70.

Wagner, Ina, and Ruth Wodak. 2006. "Performing Success: Identifying Strategies of Self-Presentation in Women's Biographical Narratives." *Discourse & Society*, 17(3): 385–411.

Walsh, Claire. 2001. *Gender and Discourse: Language and Power in Politics, the Church and Organizations*. Harlow: Longman.

Weatherall, Ann. 2000. "Gender Relevance in Talk-in-Interaction and Discourse." *Discourse & Society*, 11: 290–292.

West, Candice. 1990. "Not Just 'Doctors' Orders': Directive–Response Sequences in Patients' Visits to Women and Men Physicians." *Discourse & Society*, 1(1): 85–112.

Wodak, Ruth. 1995. "Power, Discourse and Styles of Female Leadership in School Committee Meetings." In David Corson (ed.), *Discourse and Power in Educational Organizations*, 31–54. Cresskill, NJ: Hampton Press.

Wodak, Ruth. 2003. "Multiple Identities: The Roles of Female Parliamentarians in the EU Parliament." In Janet Holmes and Miriam Meyerhoff (eds.), *The Handbook of Language and Gender*, 671–698. Oxford: Blackwell.

Yieke, Felicia. 2004. "Sexual Harassment in the Workplace: A Case for Linguistic and Sexual Politics?" *Journal of Cultural Studies*, 6(2): 175–196.

Yieke, Felicia. 2006. "Graffiti: Communication Avenues for Women at the Workplace?" In Colin Creighton and Felicia Yieke (eds.), *Gender Inequalities in Kenya*, 49–60. Paris: UNESCO.

23   Language, Gender, and Sexual Violence

Legal Perspectives

SUSAN EHRLICH

1. Introduction

Recent formulations of the relationship between language and gender, following Butler (1990), have emphasized the performative aspect of gender. Under this account, language is one important means by which gender – an ongoing accomplishment – is enacted or constituted; gender is something that individuals *do*, in part through linguistic practices, as opposed to something that individuals *are* or *have* (West and Zimmerman 1987). While the theorizing of gender as "performative" has encouraged language and gender researchers to focus on the agency of social actors in the constitution of a diverse range of gendered identities (Cameron 2005), according to Butler performances of gender are always subject to regulation and constraint. That is, they are produced within what Butler calls a "highly rigid regulatory frame" (1990, 32) which "operates as a condition of cultural intelligibility" (2004, 52). This means that certain enactments of gender are rendered appropriate and intelligible as a result of the "frame" while others – those that depart from cultural norms – are rendered unintelligible and run the risk of sanctions and/or penalties. Thus, in investigating the linguistic dimensions of gendered identities within the legal system, in this chapter I am interested not only in the situated details of participants' talk and texts, but also in the ways that this talk and text is facilitated and constrained by legal structures. In keeping with Butler's notion of the "frame," I attempt to elucidate the force of gendered ideologies and institutional practices in the legal system, specifically, how they both regulate the kinds of gendered identities participants can take up and create the lens through which such identities are assessed and evaluated. Given that the vast majority of scholarship adopting a linguistic approach to these kinds of questions has centered on the law and violence against women, this is also the focus of this chapter.

The Handbook of Language, Gender, and Sexuality, Second Edition.
Edited by Susan Ehrlich, Miriam Meyerhoff, and Janet Holmes.
© 2014 John Wiley & Sons, Inc. Published 2017 by John Wiley & Sons, Inc.

The impetus for much work in sociolinguistics and linguistic anthropology on the interrelationship of language, gender, and the law has been Conley and O'Barr's 1998 book, *Just Words: Law, Language, and Power*. Conley and O'Barr come from a tradition of "critical" legal scholarship and, thus, are interested in how the law works *in practice*, that is, how it departs from its statutory ideals and how social power may be implicated in the inconsistent and selective application of laws. According to Conley and O'Barr, however, critical legal scholars (or sociolegal scholars) have not been terribly successful at identifying "the actual mechanisms through which the legal system fails to deliver justice" (Eades 2008, 7) because they have not attended to the details of legal discourse. In order to understand how the law's power "is realized, exercised, reproduced, and occasionally challenged and subverted", Conley and O'Barr argue, scholars need to pay attention to the details of linguistic interactions (1998, 129). Like Conley and O'Barr, and in some cases as a result of their work, a number of feminists interested in the law have turned to examining legal *discourse* in order to make sense of the often large gap that exists between legal statutes and policies, on the one hand, and their implementation, on the other hand. This gap is perhaps most evident in the areas of sexual assault and domestic violence where feminist lobbying in countries such as Canada, the United States, and the United Kingdom has led to substantial legal reform; yet much of this reform has gone unrealized in practice (e.g., Caringella 2009; Comack 1999; Gregory and Lees 1999). As Schulhofer (1998, 17) says about the failure of rape law reform in the United States, "social attitudes are tenacious, and they can easily nullify the theories and doctrines found in the law books. The story of failed reforms is in part a story about the overriding importance of culture, about the seeming irrelevance of law."

Thus, in what follows my emphasis is not so much on feminist-inspired statutory reform, but rather on the gendered dimensions of some of the legal practices and processes associated with sexual assault and domestic violence that seem to "nullify" that reform. I begin by examining scholarship that has investigated trial discourse and then move on to consider research that has traced the "movement" of talk from trials or pre-trial interviews to other sites in the legal system, such as appellate decisions and affidavits. (See Andrus 2011 for a comparable investigation of violence against women in relation to a rule of evidence in the legal system.) In both cases, I am interested in the way that ideologies and legal conventions can shape and constrain gendered identities.

2. Tracking Gendered Ideologies in Trial Discourse

The adversarial nature of the Anglo-American common law system means that various versions of events will emerge within the context of a trial as the prosecution and the defense each attempt to put forward an account of the events that will support their own clients' interests. The trial, therefore, provides a good illustration of the role of language in constructing and constituting different kinds of social realities. Put somewhat differently, lawyers and witnesses do not simply describe events in a transparent and straightforward way; they are actively involved in shaping and "building the character" of those events (Hutchby and Wooffitt 1998, 228). Duranti elaborates on this view of language as constitutive of social realities:

> Reality is routinely negotiated by participants in an interaction and "facts" are constituted differently according to the points of view of the actors involved, the norms evoked, and the processes activated within specific institutional settings (e.g., legal, medical, educational). This view does not imply that there is no reality outside of talk or that all interpretations are equally acceptable, but rather it holds that in institutional as well as in mundane settings various versions of reality are proposed, sustained or challenged precisely by the language that describes or sustains them and that such negotiations are not irrelevant linguistic games but potentially important social acts. (1994, 4–5)

Duranti's observations about the *social* importance of linguistic negotiations in institutional settings are particularly well illustrated in the investigations of trial discourse discussed in this section. Not only do they show lawyers and witnesses employing various kinds of linguistic resources to construct "facts" in ways that will support their or their clients' interests, these "facts" are also often strategically designed to trigger gendered ideologies that serve their side's version of the events. As Matoesian (2013, 715) points out, a key issue for scholars interested in the relationship between law, language, and power (what he terms *the language and power school of legal anthropology*) is the question of how the constitution of "facts" in the courtroom "relate[s] to sociolegal power and sociocultural inferences."

2.1   O. J. Simpson trial: opening statements

Cotterill's (2003) analysis of the O. J. Simpson trial provides a particularly good example of how lexical items can be used by lawyers to index gendered frameworks. Cotterill (2003, 67) analyzes the "connotational and collocational properties of the lexical items selected" by the prosecution and the defense in the opening statements of this trial, arguing that lawyers exploit these features of lexical items in order to create for the jury "a particular conceptualization of the trial events and personalities." Indeed, the prosecution in the O. J. Simpson case "conceptualized" O. J. Simpson as a violent and aggressive husband, whose long history of abuse of Nicole Brown Simpson "culminated in the double murder of Nicole Brown and Ron Goldman in a jealous rage killing" (68). According to Cotterill, this portrayal of O. J. Simpson resulted from a series of "significant lexical choices" in the prosecution's opening statement. First, the word *control* was used 66 times in the opening statement, with O. J. Simpson as its agent and Nicole Brown Smith as its recipient. An examination of the collocational profile of the word *control* (i.e., a profile of words that typically co-occur with *control*) shows that the sorts of people who are typically agents of the verb are those with some official authority to control. And, the kinds of entities that are typically the recipients of the verb are "things that represent a danger or a negative influence of some kind" (72). Because

O. J. Simpson was not in an official position to control Nicole Brown Simpson (i.e., husbands are no longer thought to be the masters of their household) and because Nicole Brown Simpson did not "represent a danger" to Simpson, Cotterill argues that the prosecution used *control* in an *atypical* way (i.e., its collocations were atypical) and that this atypical use represented Simpson's controlling behavior as "unjustified and unreasonable" (73). In keeping with this kind of representation of Simpson was a second term used by the prosecution – the violence perpetrated by Simpson was characterized as *a cycle of violence*. Cotterill's examination of the collocational profile of *cycle of violence* showed that it was typically associated with violence that "increase[d] in severity over a long period of time" (77). Thus, by representing the events that led up to Nicole Brown Simpson's murder as a long series of increasingly brutal acts of violence perpetrated by an overcontrolling husband, the prosecution was able to construct the murder as the logical outcome of an escalating cycle of violence.

In response to the prosecution's representation of O. J. Simpson, the defense, according to Cotterill, used lexical items that challenged both the systemic and the physical nature of Simpson's violence. For example, the lexical item *incident* was used throughout the defense's opening argument to refer to acts of violence committed by Simpson against Nicole Brown Simpson. Cotterill shows that a collocational profile of the word *incident* reveals its association with random and unrelated events. Unlike the prosecution, then, the defense represented Simpson's acts of violence as sporadic events that were unconnected to one another as opposed to repeated events that constituted a pattern of abuse. In addition, "the theme of verbal debate rather than physical violence ... was developed by [Johnny] Cochran through the use of verbal process nominalizations – *dispute*, *discussion* and *conversation*" (Cotterill 2003, 83). A striking example of this kind of lexical strategy was evident when Cochran employed the lexical item *discussion* to refer to Simpson's shouting of expletives during one of Nicole Brown Simpson's 911 calls. As Cotterill points out, terms such as *discussion* and *conversation* do not "involve any degree of violence or aggression" (87), and thereby contributed to the defense's construction of the Simpson marriage as fundamentally nonviolent.

The work of Bakhtin has been notable in elucidating the "socially charged life" of words and expressions; that is, according to Bakhtin (1981, 293), all words have "contextual overtones" – they have "the 'taste' of a profession, a genre, a tendency, a party, a particular work, a particular person, a generation, an age group, the day and hour." Reinforcing the "connotational and collocational properties" of an expression such as *cycle of violence*, then, is the fact that this term has its origins in the domestic violence literature. In particular, Lenore Walker (1979) in the 1970s developed the idea of a "battered women's syndrome" based on her finding that women who had been physically, sexually, or psychologically abused typically showed the same pattern of symptoms, one of which involved a cycle of violence vis-à-vis their abusive partners. Thus, in Bakhtin's terms, the expression *cycle of violence* has the "taste" of a particular theory of violence against women, and, as such, when the prosecution repeatedly deployed such a term in the O. J. Simpson trial, it no doubt evoked an image of Nicole Brown Simpson as a *battered* woman – a characterization that the defense resisted with their own set of socially significant lexical items.

2.2   *Question–answer sequences in rape trials*

While Cotterill's analysis was based on the opening statements of lawyers, there is much linguistically oriented work on courtroom discourse that has focused on the question–answer sequences of lawyers and witnesses. Atkinson and Drew (1979) have called the turn-taking system characteristic of the courtroom, and of other kinds of institutional settings more generally, *turn-type preallocation*, in recognition of the fact that the types of turns participants can take, or typically take, are predetermined by their institutional roles. In courtrooms, for example, lawyers have the right to initiate and allocate turns by asking questions of witnesses, but the reverse is not generally true: witnesses are obligated to answer questions or run the risk of being sanctioned by the court. And, this question–answer *interactional asymmetry has been shown to have significant implications for whose formulations of events dominate in these kinds of settings.* Drew and Heritage (1992, 49), for example, note that answerers, frequently laypersons, are afforded little opportunity to initiate talk and thus the institutional representatives as questioners are allowed to "gain a measure of control over the introduction of topics and hence of the 'agenda' for the occasion." Referring to legal settings specifically, Holt and Johnson (2010, 21) say that "lay interactants are largely controlled by and at the mercy of questions from professionals in dyadic legal encounters: a caller to a 999 or 911 number; an interviewee in a police interview; a witness in a trial." Given the important role of questions in controlling and shaping the talk of laypersons in legal contexts, it is perhaps not surprising that they have been of interest to scholars investigating the way that language and discourse can be implicated in social inequalities. In keeping with the discussion above, if lawyers control, through their questioning, the way that "facts" come to be constituted in the courtroom, then they also control the (gendered) ideological frameworks and the "sociocultural inferences" (Matoesian 2013, 715) generated by such frameworks.

In spite of widespread reform to sexual assault and rape statutes over the last four decades in Canada and the United States, cultural mythologies surrounding rape continue to inform the adjudication of rape trials (e.g., Coates, Bavelas, and Gibson 1994; Coates and Wade 2004; Ehrlich 2007; Tiersma 2007). Tiersma (2007, 93), for example, makes the point that within the context of rape law, juries and judges must often draw inferences in determining whether or not a woman has consented to sex and these inferences may be based "on questionable or offensive (some would say: patriarchal) assumptions." Indeed, both Ehrlich (2001) and Matoesian (2001) demonstrate the way that defense lawyers in rape trials can strategically activate these kinds of "questionable or offensive … assumptions" through their questioning, thereby undermining the credibility of complainants. Ehrlich (2001), for instance, argues that the utmost resistance standard – an outdated statutory rule that required a rape victim's "utmost resistance" in order for rape to have occurred – is invoked below (and more generally in this trial) when a defense lawyer questions a complainant, MB, about her efforts to end the sexual aggression of the accused, Matt.

Example 1

```
 1 MB: And then we got back into bed and Matt immediately started
 2     again and then I said to Bob, "Bob where do you get these
 3     persistent friends?"
 4 Q:  Why did you even say that? You wanted to get Bob's attention?
 5 MB: I assumed that Bob talked to Matt in the hallway and told him
 6     to knock it off.
 7 Q:  You assumed?
 8 MB: He was talking to him and came back in and said everything was
 9     all right.
10 Q:  Bob said that?
11 MB: Yes.
12 Q:  But when you made that comment, you wanted someone to know, you
13     wanted Bob to know that this was a signal that Matt was doing
14     it again?
15 MB: Yes.
16 Q:  A mixed signal, ma'am, I suggest?
17 MB: To whom?
18 Q:  What would you have meant by, "Where do you get these
19     persistent friends?"
20 MB: Meaning Bob he's doing it again, please help me.
21 Q:  Why didn't you say, "Bob, he was doing it again, please help
22     me?"
23 MB: Because I was afraid Matt would get mad.
```

(Ehrlich 2001, 82)

In this example, MB recounts one of several incidents in which she attempted to elicit the help of Bob, a friend of the accused, in order to curtail the accused's advances. In lines 2 and 3, we see that MB reports saying "Bob where do you get these persistent friends." Not only is this utterance characterized as a "mixed signal" (line 16) by the defense lawyer; it is also problematized when the lawyer poses the question "Why didn't you say 'Bob, he was doing it again, please help me?'" That is, the question asked in lines 21 and 22 is a negative interrogative, a type of interrogative that Heritage (2002, 1432) argues is often used to "frame negative or critical propositions." This means that the defense lawyer is communicating a negative and/or critical attitude toward the fact that MB did not produce the utterance "He [Matt] is doing it again, please help me" and, in a more general way, is suggesting that MB has not expressed her resistance directly and forcefully enough. What is problematic about the resistance standard invoked by the defense lawyer's questioning in example 1 is the fact that it downplays and obscures the unequal power dynamics that often characterize male–female sexual relations. For example, in line 23, MB explains that her seemingly indirect utterance was motivated by her fear that a more direct approach would have provoked Matt's anger. Thus, while MB's act of resistance could have been framed as an intelligent and thoughtful response to a man's escalating sexual violence, it was instead characterized as an inadequate act of resistance. This characterization, in turn, has the effect of generating inferences (for the benefit of the judge and/or jury) that the complainant has not resisted "to the utmost" and, correspondingly, that rape has not occurred. In other words, there is an inconsistency between the complainant's allegations of sexual assault and her behavior, which is framed in the defense lawyer's questioning as lacking in appropriate resistance.

The interactional means by which inconsistency is created in witness testimony is a major theme of Matoesian's (2001) analysis of the William Kennedy Smith rape trial.[1] In Part I of his book, Matoesian focuses on some of the inconsistencies in "logic" imputed to the testimonies of the complainant, Patricia Bowman, and her primary witness, Ann Mercer, during their cross-examination by the defense attorney, Roy Black. While Matoesian notes that the exposing of inconsistencies in witness testimony is a *generic* trial practice designed to undermine the credibility of witnesses, in this particular case he argues that the "logical" standard against which the two women's testimonies were measured – and rendered inconsistent – was not a gender-neutral standard, but rather a male standard of sexuality, what he terms "the patriarchal logic of sexual rationality" (Matoesian 2001, 41). In other words, the defense lawyer, Roy Black, activated (patriarchal) cultural frames in his questioning that, like the utmost resistance standard discussed by Ehrlich, called into question the complainant's, Patricia Bowman's, charge that William Kennedy Smith had raped her. Consider example 2 below:

Example 2

```
 1 RB: And you were interested in him as a person.
       (0.9)
 2 PB: He seemed like a nice person.
       (0.5)
 3 RB: Interested enough that tuh- (0.5) to give him a ride home.
       (0.9)
 4 PB: I saw no-(.) no problem with giving him a ride home as I stated
 5     because it was up the street it wasn't out of my way (.)
 6     he hadn't tou::ched me (.) I felt no threats from him and I
 7     assumed that there would be security at the home.
       (0.5)
 8 RB: You were interested enough (.) that you were ho:::ping that he
 9     would ask for your pho::ne number.
       (0.7)
10 PB: That was later.
       (0.7)
11 RB: Interested enough (.) tha:t when he said to come into the
12     hou::se you went into the hou::se with him.
       (1.6)
13 PB: I (woul-) it wasn't necessarily an interest with William (.) it
14     was an interest in the house.
       (0.6)
15 RB: Interested enough that uh:: at sometime during that period
16     of time you took off your panty hose?
       (1.2)
17 PB: I still don't know how my panty hose came off.
```

(Matoesian 2001, 62–63)

In this excerpt, Roy Black's questions make available to the jury a number of propositions that are confirmed by Patricia Bowman: that she gave the defendant a ride home, that she went into the house with him, and that she hoped he would ask for her telephone number. (Note that while Bowman acknowledges that her panty hose came off, she doesn't confirm the proposition that she was the one to take them off.) However, it is not just Bowman's acknowledgment of these events that is of interest to Matoesian; of more importance, Matoesian argues, is the semantic connection created between these events through the defense lawyer's use of syntactic parallelism. The defense attorney, Roy Black, had impressive oratorical skills and, according to Matoesian, employed these skills to amplify and intensify the "inconsistencies" in the complainant's testimony. In example 2, for example, an element of the main clause of line 1 – "interested" – is incorporated into the syntactic frame, "interested enough" plus complementizer, and then this syntactic frame is repeated four times (in lines 3, 8–9, 11–12, and 15–16) each time with a different complement clause. In this way, a semantic link is created between the referential content of the complement clauses that are embedded within the syntactic frame, "interested enough" plus complementizer. As Matoesian (2001, 57) says, "incremental repetition … unifies and organizes otherwise disparate particulars of evidence into a coherent, gestalt-like pattern of persuasive parallelism." That is, the syntactic repetition in example 2 functions to create a link between a series of events that might not otherwise appear connected; and, crucially, the fact that these events seem more compatible with consensual sex than with the crime of rape intensifies the "inconsistency" in Patricia Bowman's testimony. Although acquaintance rape, of the type that Kennedy Smith was charged with, is much more common than stranger rape (Russell 1982; 1984), Estrich (1987) has argued that the American legal system, and the culture at large, treat sexual violence committed by strangers in singular, random acts much more seriously than sexual violence committed by men women know, men women meet in a bar, and/or men women are intimate with. Put somewhat differently, Estrich's work seems to suggest that a "culturally intelligible" rape victim is a woman raped by a stranger, not a woman who expresses interest in a man. Thus, Patricia Bowman's acknowledgment, under the influence of Roy Black's questioning, that she had a sexual interest in Kennedy Smith contradicts her claim of rape, according to this logic; exhibiting sexual interest in a man is more consistent with consensual sex.

Taken together, the work of Ehrlich and Matoesian demonstrates how defense lawyers in rape trials can strategically exploit cultural ideologies about what constitutes a "legitimate" rape victim and, in so doing, undermine the credibility of complainants who do not appear to conform to these ideas (e.g., victims who do not resist their perpetrators "forcefully enough" or who show an interest in their perpetrators prior to the sexual aggression). And, ultimately, in undermining the credibility of complainants, defense lawyers cast doubt on and call into question the allegations, or narratives, of the complainants – that they have been victims of sexual violence. Anderson and Doherty (2008, 13) have said that "a decision to report a rape incident may … ultimately rest on whether the victim believes that they conform to the culturally defined 'ideal' or 'genuine' victim type." The work of Ehrlich and Matoesian provides evidence, based on the linguistic details of rape trials, that such decisions may be completely justified.

The adversarial nature of the Anglo-American common law system means that the narratives and cultural frames mobilized by one side in a courtroom contest can be challenged and resisted by the opposing side. (This was demonstrated in Cotterill's analysis of the O. J. Simpson trial.) Drew (1992) provides an example of this kind of resistance in a rape trial where he focuses on the rape victim's answers to a cross-examining lawyer's questions. While answerers in courtroom contexts have generally been viewed as lacking in interactional control, Drew's analysis shows how the complainant (i.e., the rape survivor) in this particular trial often produced "alternative descriptions" in her answers – descriptions that contested the cross-examining lawyer's version of events. That is, rather than providing "yes" or "no" answers to the cross-examining lawyer's yes-no questions (what Raymond (2003) calls type-conforming answers to questions), the complainant provided competing descriptions that transformed the lawyer's damaging characterizations into more benign ones. In example 3 below, for example, the cross-examining lawyer, through the use of declarative questions, attempts to represent the events that preceded the alleged rape as precursors to a consensual sexual interaction. (This is similar to the strategy adopted by Roy Black in example 2.)

Example 3

```
 1 A: Well yuh had some uh (p) (.) uh fairly lengthy
 2    conversations with the defendant uh: did'n you?
 3    (0.7)
 4 A: On that evening uv February fourteenth?
 5    (1.0)
 6 W: We:ll we were all talkin.
 7    (0.8)
 8 A: Well you kne:w, at that ti:me. that the
 9    defendant was. in:terested (.) in you (.)
10    did'n you?
11    (1.3)
12 W: He: asked me how I'(d) bin: en
13    (1.1)
14 W: J- just stuff like that
```

(Drew 1992, 501)

Although the lawyer's questions in lines 1–2 and 8–10 suggest that there was a closeness or intimacy developing between the defendant and the complainant, Drew argues that the complainant provides answers that depict a lack of intimacy between the complainant and the defendant, that is, a scene in which there were a number of people who "were all talkin" and in which the defendant issued a greeting that was more friendly than intimate. But, why, as Matoesian (2013, 711) says, does the rape victim dispute the lawyer's characterization of the events with her alternative descriptions? In keeping with the findings of Estrich discussed above, the complainant seems to be rejecting the suggestion that there was any intimacy developing between the two because to do so would be to portray herself as a less than ideal victim of rape.

2.3   Determining the "official story"

Given the presence of competing and contradictory "facts" within the courtroom, Cotterill (2003, 25) has argued that "the name often given to the jury in adversarial trial procedure, that of the 'factfinder,' is actually something of a misnomer." For Cotterill, juries do not determine the facts, rather they "adjudicate between more and less plausible narrative accounts." Capps and Ochs make similar observations about adjudicators in trials:

> On the basis of divergent versions of events, jury members construct a narrative that is plausible and coherent in their eyes, but the truth is beyond their reach. In this sense, rendering a verdict is analogous not to ascertaining the facts but to determining an official story. (Capps and Ochs 1995, 21)

So, if the truth and the facts are "beyond the reach" of juries, and adjudicators more generally, what kind of criteria are used in determining "official stories"? Capps and Ochs (1995, 20) suggest that, while the internal consistency and external corroboration of stories told in the courtroom are important to their believability,[2] of equal importance is the "rhetorical prowess" of the witnesses and lawyers who tell the stories. Matoesian's (2001) analysis of Roy Black's "rhetorical prowess" in the William Kennedy Smith trial certainly supports this idea. (Recall that the jury in this trial acquitted Smith of his rape charges.) According to Matoesian (2001, 31), the testimonies of Patricia Bowman and Ann Mercer were not "that inconsistent"; rather, "Black knew how to *create* inconsistency through powerful and affective forms of language, much more so than prosecutor Lasch" (emphasis original). But Black's success was not solely the result of his impressive oratorical skills. Matoesian (2001, 31) argues that "persuasive forms of language" and ideology worked together to create an interpretive lens "through which jurors evaluate[d] legal issues such as consent, coercion, and violence." In particular, when Black successfully created inconsistencies in the testimony of Patricia Bowman and Ann Mercer, Bowman's witness, he did so by measuring their behavior against "the expectations of patriarchal ideology governing victim identity." For example, as noted above, through the lens of "patriarchal ideology," the characterization of Patricia Bowman as (initially) sexually interested in William Kennedy Smith (represented in example 2) was inconsistent with her claim that she was a survivor of rape. Put somewhat differently, Black managed to "tap into" the jury's "questionable or offensive (some would say: patriarchal) assumptions" (Tiersma 2007, 93) about sexual violence and consent and Bowman's behavior was then assessed in relation to such cultural assumptions.

The idea that gendered ideologies are at play when adjudicators decide between conflicting stories in the courtroom is also evident in the work of Ehrlich (2007).

Ehrlich (2007) analyzes both the trial proceedings and the judicial opinions of a Canadian rape trial where two lower courts acquitted the accused of sexual assault, after which the Supreme Court of Canada overturned this acquittal and convicted the accused. The two lower courts acquitted the accused because they claimed that the complainant "implied consent" through her behavior or what they termed her "conduct." Significant about the lower courts' rulings was the fact that both courts found the complainant credible; in particular, they found her expressions of fear vis-à-vis the accused to be genuine. In spite of finding these expressions of fear credible, however, both courts also commented in their decisions that she did not communicate her fear to the accused. As the trial judge (i.e., the lowest court) said in his ruling, for example, the complainant "was 'frozen' by a fear of force" and "successfully kept all her thoughts, emotions, and speculations deep within herself" (Ehrlich 2007, 469). Ehrlich points out that the picture emerging from these descriptions of the complainant is one of passivity and, consequently, that the two lower courts seemed to consider passive behavior or "conduct" on the part of the complainant to be "implying consent." But what kind of cultural sense-making framework equates passivity with consent? Ehrlich (2007) argues that the trial judge and the Alberta Court of Appeal judges seemed to view sexual passivity as appropriately feminine and, as a result, what the complainant described as submitting to sex out of fear became intelligible to these courts as consenting to sex, or at the least, implying consent to the perpetrator. (See McConnell-Ginet, Chapter 16 in this volume, for a discussion of how dominant ideologies can invest linguistic forms with meaning.) While the Supreme Court of Canada ultimately overturned the decisions of the two lower courts, arguing that submission on the part of the complainant did not constitute consent, the kind of "logic" employed by the lower courts is not unusual in the judicial opinions of sexual assault cases more generally (see, e.g., Coates, Bavelas, and Gibson 1994; Coates and Wade 2004; Tiersma 2007) and is revealing of the problematic cultural assumptions that can underlie such opinions. Moreover, as we have seen in the preceding discussion, the power of such cultural mythologies is not lost on defense lawyers who routinely invoke them in their questioning (and in opening and closing statements), using a variety of linguistic resources.

3. Tracing Meaning Transformations in Women's Accounts of Violence

A recurring theme in the work of critical legal scholars, including those who focus on the language of the law (e.g., Conley and O'Barr 1990; 1998), has been the way that lay litigants' voices are altered and/or rendered unrecognizable once they enter the legal system. For example, as we have seen in the previous section, lawyers' questions in trials – especially in cross-examination – can (re)shape and (re)structure witness testimony so as to activate gendered ideologies that undermine the credibility of that testimony. But the interactional work performed by lawyers is not the only means through which witness narratives can be altered. Once extracted from the original sites in which they were produced, the testimonies of witnesses can be reinserted into written documents, quoted, and/or summarized by participants not involved in the original speech events, and, in the process, can undergo significant transformations in meaning, "often deeply different from the ones performed in the initial act of communication" (Blommaert 2005, 76). It is these kinds of meaning transformations that the following section takes up.

3.1   *From oral narratives to affidavits*

The first example of this kind of transformation comes from Trinch's (2003) work on the process by which women obtain protective orders (i.e., restraining orders) that will prohibit their violent partners from making contact with them. In order to secure these protective orders, the US Latina women that were the focus of Trinch's study had to be interviewed about their abuse (i.e., the abuse inflicted upon them by their domestic partners) by paralegals who would then produce affidavits for the court. Of interest to Trinch were the discrepancies between the oral narratives of abuse produced by the survivors and the written reports of abuse (i.e., affidavits) produced by the legal authorities, the paralegals. That is, as the survivors' narratives traveled in the legal system and were transplanted into written affidavits, Trinch found that their meanings shifted in ways that transformed the representations of the domestic abuse. In particular, Trinch shows how the cyclical, habitual, and repetitive nature of domestic violence was lost as the survivors' experiences were shaped and molded in order to conform to the structure of the affidavit. For example, the survivors of domestic violence often relayed their experiences in present-tense generic narrative types, which, according to Trinch (2003, 111), "broaden[ed] the scope of their [the survivors'] narration ... in order to relate abuse and events in terms of constant and consistent behavior." By contrast, in keeping with the requirements of the protective order affidavits, the types of narratives that the paralegals attempted to elicit from their clients and ultimately produced in the affidavits were ones that recounted "unique past events, that is, ... events that happen once, and will seldom, if ever be repeated" (Trinch 2003, 111). Consider the excerpt from an interaction between a paralegal and client, as seen in example 4, and the way it is re-presented in the corresponding affidavit, as seen in example 5.

Example 4

```
P: Did he make any threats this morning?
C: Um, yeah. He keeps telling me that he's gonna take the kids. That if,
   if he finds out that I'm doing anything, he just said, any little
   thing that I do, then he's gonna go over and he's gonna take the
   kids, he's not gonna let me see them. He, he calls like, ten times
   a day.
P: And he calls every day?
C: Yeah.
```

Example 5

```
On or about ((date)) ((Abuser's name)) called me at home and threatened
to take the kids and not let me see them. He called over ten times that
day.
```

(Trinch 2003, 195)

In example 4, we see the client representing her partner's actions as ongoing and repetitive (e.g., "He keeps telling me … , he's gonna take the kids, he's not gonna let me see them. He, he calls like ten times a day") through the use of present tense denoting habitual events; by contrast, the affidavit reproduces the partner's actions in a Labovian-type narrative where the simple past tense is used to mark the narrative events (e.g., "[He] called me at home and threatened to take the kids … He called over ten times that day"). As a result, in the affidavit the partner's actions are understood as discrete events that occurred on a single occasion. And, as Trinch argues, linear narratives representing violence as single, discrete occurrences are inadequate to capture the recurring and cyclical character of domestic violence. But what accounts for the various types of omissions and distortions that the survivors' narratives underwent? In part, the reformulation of survivors' narratives produced reports that conformed to legally relevant categories and were "'maximally interpretable' for its [the story's] subsequent recipients" (Briggs and Bauman 1992, quoted in Trinch 2003, 188). That is, the narratives were constrained by the structure of the affidavit, which required the listing of specific discrete incidents of abuse that occurred on specific dates, and such constraints, according to Trinch (2003, 188), enabled the district attorney and judge to assess easily and quickly how the elements of the abuse conformed (or not) to the relevant laws.

However, Trinch provides a further explanation for the distortion of survivors' narratives in the process of institutionalization. While the transformation of the abuse into legally recognizable categories "facilitate[d] the short-term goal of getting women injunctions" (Trinch 2003, 155), Trinch argues that it also kept intact an understanding of violence against women that is intelligible within the existing system. Specifically, by representing domestic violence "as singular, unconnected incidents" (Trinch 2003, 274), the paralegals and the affidavits authorized a definition of violence against women that is more consistent with stranger violence than with intimate partner violence. In other words, the transformations in meaning that Trinch documents did nothing to challenge prevailing notions of violence against women. Recall Estrich's work discussed above, which shows that even though violence committed by men women know and are intimate with is much more frequent than that committed by strangers, it is sexual violence committed by strangers in singular random acts that the law takes seriously.

3.2   *From trial testimony to appellate decisions*

Like Trinch's work, the next example also shows how women's accounts of violence can be recast and reframed once they move beyond the context of their "original" telling to other sites in the legal system. This transformation in meaning occurred once the 2004 American rape case, *Maouloud Baby* vs. *State of Maryland* (analyzed in Ehrlich 2012; 2013), moved from its trial phase to its appellate decisions. In particular, the case became known as a post-penetration rape case in the appellate decisions, even though it was not framed in these terms in the context of the trial. Post-penetration rape is defined as a situation in which both parties initially consent to sexual intercourse, but at some time during the act of intercourse, one party, typically the woman, withdraws her consent; after this withdrawal of consent, the other party, typically the man, forces the woman to continue intercourse against her will (Davis 2005, 732–733). While this was the characterization of events that became the "official story" of this case, it did not correspond with what transpired during the trial. That is, during the trial, the prosecution in the case argued that the complainant, Jewel Lankford, never consented to the sexual acts initiated by the accused, Maouloud Baby, while the defense argued that she did consent to these acts. Crucially, neither the prosecution nor the defense invoked the categories of pre- versus post-penetration consent or withdrawal of consent. In fact, the defense argued that the accused was unable to penetrate the complainant. In other words, for the prosecution, there was never consent and, for the defense, there was never penetration.

Given that the appellate courts' post-penetration framing of this case was predicated on the assumption that the complainant at some point consented to sex with the accused, one of the questions that Ehrlich addresses was the means by which the complainant's behavior became construed as consent under this framing. The testimony of the complainant, in both direct and cross-examination, revealed that she attempted to resist the accused and his friend, Mike, multiple times, said "no" and "it hurts" multiple times, but finally allowed the accused "to take his turn" as long as he stopped when she told him to and allowed her to go home. Yet, it was this "agreement" that came to be understood as the initial consent issued by the complainant – and then withdrawn – once the case became recontextualized as a post-penetration rape case. Ehrlich argues that both gendered and linguistic ideologies were at play in the recasting of the complainant's submission to sex (i.e., letting the accused "take his turn") as consensual sex. Research on violence against women has demonstrated that women's submission to sex can, in many circumstances, be a better strategy for surviving violence than physical resistance, given that physical resistance has the potential to escalate and intensify men's violence (Dobash and Dobash 1992). For example, work conducted on rape victim impact statements in the United Kingdom (Woodhams 2008) has shown women to deploy what Woodhams (2008) refers to as "offender management strategies" in order to resist their assailants. Such strategies involve women negotiating with their perpetrators in order to minimize the harm inflicted upon them: women may agree to submit to "lesser" forms of sexual assault in exchange for being let go. At the point in the Baby case when the complainant allowed the accused "to take his turn," she had already endured much nonconsensual sexual activity from the accused and his friend and indicated that the accused could take his turn as long as he stopped when she told him to and allowed her to go home. In other words, the complainant could be understood as negotiating with the accused in order to avoid further and more intense sexual violence. But, if the complainant's agreement to have sex with the accused was not in fact a signal of consent, but rather a strategy of compliance or submission designed to end the sexual violence sooner rather than later, why was it not understood in this way as the case moved out of its trial phase into the appellate decisions?[3]

Ehrlich locates the problem in metalevel understandings of language, what linguistic anthropologists have termed linguistic ideologies (Schieffelin, Woolard, and Kroskrity 1998). (See Cameron, Chapter 14 in this volume, for a discussion of gender and linguistic ideologies.) Indeed, a powerful ideology surrounding the interpretation of texts in the West is what has been called a "referentialist" or "textualist" ideology (Collins 1996) – a belief in stable, denotational, and context-free meaning. According to this idea, meaning resides exclusively in linguistic forms and, as a result, words, phrases, or sentences can be extracted from their original interactional and social context and moved to other contexts without any change in meaning. The relevance of this linguistic ideology to the interpretation of the complainant's apparent consent should be clear: her one instance of "agreement" (i.e., allowing the accused "to take his turn") was removed from its context – the series of nonconsensual sexual acts that preceded it – and, once decontextualized in this way, it lost its meaning as a strategy of resistance and instead became interpreted as consent.

Interestingly, while the jury found the accused guilty of rape and some other sexually related charges, it was also the jury members who first introduced the notion of post-penetration rape into the case via a question they posed to the judge during their deliberations: "If a female consents to sex initially and, during the course of the sex act to which she consented, for whatever reason, she changes her mind and the man continues until climax, does the result constitute rape?" (*State of Maryland* vs. *Maouloud Baby*, Court of Appeals of Maryland, 2007). Although the judge did not answer this question and instead directed the jurors to answer it for themselves (based on the legal definitions of rape and of consent provided during jury instructions), this question suggests that at least some of the jurors believed that the complainant's allowing the accused to "take his turn" *was* consent. What ultimately led the jury to find the accused guilty is not known; however, once the notion of post-penetration rape (and the *presupposition* of consent on the part of the complainant) was introduced into the case via the jurors' question, this question then became the basis for the defense's appeal and, by extension, for the transformation of the case into a post-penetration rape case. Appellate courts can only address issues in their opinions that are invoked during appeals; as Mertz (2007, 62) says, "the semiotic frame imposed by … litigants as they [choose] particular issues to appeal" constrains "the issues to which an appellate court may speak." In the Baby case, then, what began as an investigation of whether consent was given in the first place evolved, in part because of institutional constraints, into one in which consent was presupposed and the question at issue for the courts was the legal status of post-penetration rape. Put somewhat differently, as the complainant's testimony was recontextualized in various kinds of settings within the legal system, it underwent a fairly radical transformation: a strategy for resisting more extreme and prolonged instances of sexual violence became reconstructed as consensual sex.

4. Conclusion

I began this chapter by reflecting on Butler's notion of the "rigid regulatory frame" – the idea that cultural norms specify a range of practices and behaviors that are intelligible as gendered. Identities are produced within this frame and to depart from the range of norms regarded as culturally appropriate is to run the risk of social and physical penalties and sanctions, be they ostracism, ridicule, shame, or loss of rights and freedoms. This chapter has attempted to show how the legal system exhibits such regulatory power, particularly in relation to violence against women. Within rape trials, for example, the range of acceptable subject positions for women who claim to be survivors of rape is extremely limited: if women seem to show interest in their perpetrators or remain seemingly passive during a rape, they garner little credibility in the courtroom. As shown above, complainants' claims of rape can be called into question through the triggering of gendered ideologies that privilege stranger rape over acquaintance rape. And, just as subject positions are restricted by the law, so too is the type of violence that the legal system will authorize. Trinch (2003) and Ehrlich (2012; 2013) demonstrate that, as women's narratives of violence move beyond their original contexts of productions into other sites within the legal system, they are modified so that they conform to institutionally privileged genres and categories that are intelligible to the legal system. In Trinch's 2003 work, for example, survivors of domestic violence benefitted from the legal system in securing temporary restraining orders against their abusive partners but only once their representations of violence were transformed into singular, bounded events (see also Trinch 2006). And, while the ultimate judicial decision in the post-penetration case that Ehrlich describes deemed post-penetration rape a legal possibility (presumably a positive result), such a decision relied upon an understanding of consent that ignored the gendered and unequal power relations that shape women's responses to escalating sexual violence. The telling of stories in legal contexts has sometimes been viewed as an important act of resistance (Lazarus-Black and Hirsch 1994), yet the findings reviewed in this chapter do not unequivocally support such a position. As Merry (1994, 54) has argued, the law may allow protest and resistance but "such resistance must be framed in the terms of the law itself." Indeed, Merry's assertion is in keeping with the more general argument put forward in this chapter. In order to understand the meanings that come to be attached to lay litigants' testimonies and narratives in the legal system, it is essential to attend to the structures in which they are produced – structures that are informed and inflected by gendered and linguistic ideologies and the processes and categories of the law.

Acknowledgment

I thank Shonna Trinch for extremely valuable comments on a previous version of this chapter. All remaining shortcomings are, of course, my own.

NOTES

1   William Kennedy Smith (the nephew of the late President John Kennedy, Senator Robert Kennedy, and Senator Edward Kennedy) was charged with, and subsequently acquitted of, simple battery (unwanted touching) and second-degree sexual battery (rape without the use of a weapon) in the state of Florida in 1991.
2   Early work on this issue (i.e., Bennett and Feldman 1981) concluded that a well-constructed story may be more important to jurors' assessments of plausibility than the existence of evidence.
3   It should be noted that Ehrlich's analysis of the complainant's behavior as compliance or submission, rather than consent, is consistent with the state of Maryland's definition of consent. More specifically, the definition of consent provided by the judge (and reiterated in the judge's answer to the jurors' questions) stipulated that agreement to sex be freely given: that is, consent was defined as "actually agreeing to the sexual act rather than merely submitting as a result of force or threat of force" (*Maouloud Baby* vs. *State of Maryland*, Court of Special Appeals of Maryland, 2005).

REFERENCES

Anderson, Irina, and Kathy Doherty. 2008. *Accounting for Rape: Psychology, Feminism and Discourse Analysis in the Study of Sexual Violence.* London: Routledge.

Andrus, Jennifer. 2011. "Beyond Texts in Context: Recontextualization and the Co-production of Texts and Contexts in the Legal Discourse, Excited Utterance Exception to Hearsay." *Discourse & Society*, 22: 115–136.

Atkinson, J. Maxwell, and Paul Drew. 1979. *Order in Court.* Atlantic Highlands, NJ: Humanities Press.

Bakhtin, M. M. 1981. "Discourse in the Novel." In *The Dialogic Imagination: Four Essays*, ed. Michael Holquist, 259–422. Austin: University of Texas Press.

Bennett, Walter, and Martha Feldman. 1981. *Reconstructing Reality in the Courtroom.* London: Tavistock.

Blommaert, Jan. 2005. *Discourse.* Cambridge: Cambridge University Press.

Briggs, Charles, and Richard Bauman. 1992. "Genre, Intertextuality and Social Power." *Journal of Linguistic Anthropology*, 2: 131–172.

Butler, Judith. 1990. *Gender Trouble: Feminism and the Subversion of Identity.* New York: Routledge.

Butler, Judith. 2004. *Undoing Gender.* New York: Routledge.

Cameron, Deborah. 2005. "Language, Gender and Sexuality: Current Issues and New Directions." *Applied Linguistics*, 26: 482–502.

Capps, Lisa, and Elinor Ochs. 1995. *Constructing Panic: The Discourse of Agoraphobia.* Cambridge, MA: Harvard University Press.

Caringella, Susan. 2009. *Addressing Rape Reform in Law and Practice.* New York: Columbia University Press.

Coates, Linda, Janet Bavelas, and James Gibson. 1994. "Anomalous Language in Sexual Assault Trial Judgements." *Discourse & Society*, 5: 189–206.

Coates, Linda, and Allan Wade. 2004. "Telling It Like It Isn't: Obscuring Perpetrator Responsibility for Violent Crime." *Discourse & Society*, 15: 499–526.

Collins, James. 1996. "Socialization to Text: Structure and Contradiction in Schooled Literacy." In Michael Silverstein and Greg Urban (eds.), *Natural Histories of Discourse*, 203–228. Chicago: University of Chicago Press.

Comack, Elizabeth. 1999. "Theoretical Excursions." In Elizabeth Comack (ed.), *Locating Law: Race/Class/Gender Connections*, 19–68. Halifax, NS: Fernwood Publishing.

Conley, John M., and William M. O'Barr. 1990. *Rules versus Relationships.* Chicago: University of Chicago Press.

Conley, John M., and William M. O'Barr. 1998. *Just Words: Law, Language, and Power.* Chicago: University of Chicago Press.

Cotterill, Janet. 2003. *Language and Power in Court: A Linguistic Analysis of the O. J. Simpson Trial.* Basingstoke: Palgrave Macmillan.

Davis, Amanda. 2005. "Clarifying the Issue of Consent: The Evolution of Post-Penetration Rape Law." *Stetson Law Review*, 34: 729–766.

Dobash, R. Emerson, and Russell P. Dobash. 1992. *Women, Violence and Social Change.* London: Routledge.

Drew, Paul. 1992. "Contested Evidence in Courtroom Examination: The Case of a Trial for Rape." In Paul Drew and John Heritage (eds.), *Talk at Work: Interaction in Institutional Settings*, 470–520. Cambridge: Cambridge University Press.

Drew, Paul, and John Heritage. 1992. "Analyzing Talk at Work: An Introduction." In Paul Drew and John Heritage (eds.), *Talk at Work: Interaction in Institutional Settings*, 3–65. Cambridge: Cambridge University Press.

Duranti, Alessandro. 1994. *From Grammar to Politics: Linguistic Anthropology in a Western Samoan Village.* Berkeley: University of California Press.

Eades, Diana. 2008. *Courtroom Talk and Neocolonial Control.* Berlin: Mouton de Gruyter.

Ehrlich, Susan. 2001. *Representing Rape: Language and Sexual Consent.* London: Routledge.

Ehrlich, Susan. 2007. "Legal Discourse and the Cultural Intelligibility of Gendered Meanings." *Journal of Sociolinguistics*, 11: 452–477.

Ehrlich, Susan. 2012. "Text Trajectories, Legal Discourse and Gendered Inequalities." *Applied Linguistics Review*, 3: 47–73.

Ehrlich, Susan. 2013. "Post-Penetration Rape and the Decontextualization of Witness Testimony." In Chris Heffer, Frances Rock, and John Conley (eds.), *Legal-Lay Communication: Textual Travels in the Legal System*, 189–205. Oxford: Oxford University Press.

Estrich, Susan. 1987. *Real Rape.* Cambridge, MA: Harvard University Press.

Gregory, Jeanne, and Sue Lees. 1999. *Policing Sexual Assault.* London: Routledge.

Heritage, John. 2002. "The Limits of Questioning: Negative Interrogatives and Hostile Question Content." *Journal of Pragmatics*, 34: 1427–1446.

Holt, Elizabeth, and Alison Johnson. 2010. "Socio-Pragmatics of Legal Talk: Police Interviews and Trial Discourse." In Malcolm Coulthard and Alison Johnson (eds.), *The Routledge Handbook of Forensic Linguistics*, 21–36. London: Routledge.

Hutchby, Ian, and Robin Wooffitt. 1998. *Conversation Analysis.* Cambridge: Polity.

Lazarus-Black, Mindie, and Susan Hirsch. 1994. *Contested States: Law, Hegemony and Resistance.* New York: Routledge.

Mertz, Elizabeth. 2007. *The Language of Law School: Learning to "Think like a Lawyer."* New York: Oxford University Press.

Matoesian, Greg. 2001. *Law and the Language of Identity: Discourse in the William Kennedy Rape Trial.* New York: Oxford University Press.

Matoesian, Greg. 2013. "Language and Law." In Robert Bailey and Richard Cameron (eds.), *The Oxford Handbook of Sociolinguistics*, 701–719. New York: Oxford University Press.

Merry, Sally. 1994. "Courts as Performances: Domestic Violence Hearings in a Hawaii Family Court." In Mindie Lazarus-Black and Susan Hirsch (eds.), *Contested States: Law, Hegemony and Resistance*, 35–59. New York: Routledge.

Raymond, Geoffrey. 2003. "Grammar and Social Organization: Yes/No Type Interrogatives and the Structure of Responding." *American Sociological Review*, 68: 939–966.

Russell, Diana. 1982. *Rape in Marriage.* New York: Macmillan.

Russell, Diana. 1984. *Sexual Exploitation: Rape, Child Sexual Abuse, and Workplace Harassment.* Beverly Hills, CA: Sage.

Schieffelin, Bambi, Kathryn Woolard, and Paul V. Kroskrity, eds. 1998. *Language Ideologies: Practice and Theory.* Oxford: Oxford University Press.

Schulhofer, Stephen J. 1998. *Unwanted Sex: The Culture of Intimidation and the Failure of Law.* Cambridge, MA: Harvard University Press.

Tiersma, Peter. 2007. "The Language of Consent in Rape Law." In Janet Cotterill (ed.), *The Language of Sexual Crime*, 83–103. Basingstoke: Palgrave Macmillan.

Trinch, Shonna. 2003. *Latinas' Narratives of Domestic Abuse: Discrepant Versions of Violence.* Amsterdam: Benjamins.

Trinch, Shonna. 2006. "Bilingualism and Representation: Locating Spanish–English Contact in Legal Institutional Memory." *Language in Society*, 35: 559–593.

Walker, Lenore. 1979. *The Battered Woman.* New York: Harper & Row.

West, Candace, and Don Zimmerman. 1987. "Doing Gender." *Gender in Society*, 1: 125–151.

Woodhams, Jessica. 2008. "How Victims Behave during Stranger Sexual Assaults." Unpublished manuscript.

CASES CITED

Maouloud Baby vs. State of Maryland, Court of Special Appeals of Maryland, 2005. 172 Md. App. 588, 916 A.2d 410; 2007 Md. App. LEXIS 60.

State of Maryland vs. Maouloud Baby, Court of Appeals of Maryland, 2007. 404 Md.220, 946 A.2d 463; 2008 Md. LEXIS 190.

24 Language and Gender in Educational Contexts

JULIA MENARD-WARWICK, MIKI MORI,
AND SERENA WILLIAMS

The central concern of educational research is necessarily *learning*, which is often operationalized as *achievement*, the measurement of learning outcomes in specific populations of students.[1] Since the 1970s, cyclical controversies have erupted over relative gender advantage in educational achievement; at times girls are seen as disadvantaged, and at other times boys (Davies 2003). Hopes arise that educators can someday "get it right," balance competing gender needs, and achieve equity for all. Such hopes spawn research, and since so much of education, and so much of identity development, is mediated through language, a great deal of the educational research on gender examines linguistic practices. Although this research has not demonstrated that gendered linguistic practices stand in relevant relationship to educational (dis)advantage in all contexts, Sunderland (2000, 170) cautions researchers to remain "equally open to the *possibility* of (this) relationship" as they are "to the possibility that a given set of gender tendencies ... may not straight-forwardly equate with disadvantage" (emphasis original).

In this chapter we explore these complexities and related issues, reviewing research on language and gender in recent decades in educational settings, from preschools to workplace literacy classes, attempting to include an array of national and ethnic contexts. Aware of the diversity of educational settings around the world, and aware that gender is always performed against a sociocultural backdrop, we also recognize diverse ideas about how to make sense of language and gender. Such was the case in 2005 when Cameron noted that "a paradigm organized around the concept of binary gender *difference*" as well as "the 1970s style '*dominance* approach'" had shifted to a research perspective "concerned with the *diversity* of gender identities and gendered practices" (Cameron 2005, 482, 490, 482). The theoretical shift does not mean that researchers posit a worldwide decline in the effect of sexist practices on learning; rather, scholars have refocused their efforts to understand how aspects of identity such as ethnicity, class, or sexuality intersect with gender to create or limit learning opportunities.

The Handbook of Language, Gender, and Sexuality, Second Edition.
Edited by Susan Ehrlich, Miriam Meyerhoff, and Janet Holmes.
© 2014 John Wiley & Sons, Inc. Published 2017 by John Wiley & Sons, Inc.

Like Cameron, Eckert and McConnell-Ginet (2003) introduce language and gender studies by arguing that earlier "dominance" and "difference" approaches have been superseded by the *discourse turn* in language studies and the *performance turn* in gender studies: theoretical approaches that view gender as continually reshaped in fluid relationship with linguistic practices in specific social contexts. They argue that gendered trends are perhaps best analyzed in terms of "communities of practice" (Eckert and McConnell-Ginet 1992; Lave and Wenger 1991) which construct *local* gendered norms in specific social contexts (e.g., Bucholtz 1999). Likewise, Sunderland's (2000) discussion of issues in gender and language classroom research includes a reanalysis and retheorization of some classroom data that she had originally employed to show differences between male and female students; in her new analysis she illustrates variation in gendered performances within groups, noting that one boy in particular (not all boys in general) had monopolized the teacher's attention during the observed lesson.

As scholars, we agree that an explicit theorization of gender diversity is crucial for making sense of language and identity construction across social fields, and we are likewise convinced that attention to social context is crucial. However, in reviewing studies on language and gender in education, and in attempting to accurately represent trends around the world, we find ourselves unable to argue that this research has progressed smoothly in the way argued by language and gender theorists, from earlier research based on dominance and difference paradigms to contemporary research that examines gender diversity (Cameron 2005; Eckert and McConnell-Ginet 2003). We find, rather, that educational research on language and gender in various geographical regions has not followed particular theoretical models uniformly, or even always theorized findings using an explicit framework. In discussing the range of research on this topic over the last few decades, we find *dominance*, *difference*, and *diversity* a useful heuristic for classifying studies and understanding trends in this field, and so we draw upon these terms for this purpose in this chapter. At the same time, we recognize that in actual research these categorizations often overlap, and the boundaries blur. As we note below, all three tendencies may appear within a single study (e.g., Bogoch 1999). Nevertheless, this categorization facilitates our comprehension of educational research trends.

To further facilitate understanding, we have organized this chapter into sections, based on what we view as the most salient topics in the research literature: classroom interaction, literacy, and language learning. Interaction, through which education at every level occurs, is a tool both for social life and for making meaning in and out of the classroom. Literacy is also integral to education, as teaching and learning is organized around textbooks, worksheets, websites, and other textually based cultural genres; studies in this section include those that focus on canonical notions of literacy as learning to read and write, along with more current approaches to literacy as social practices (Street 2003). Finally, language learning encompasses both interaction and literacy as learners navigate how to engage with other speakers and with texts; in our review we discuss both second-language settings (e.g., Mexican immigrants in the United States learning English) and foreign-language settings (e.g., Australian high school students studying Japanese). A prominent subtopic is the analysis of texts and materials used in educational settings in relation to language and gender. Studies focusing on materials analysis fall under both the literacy and language learning categories and will be briefly discussed in each of the two sections. In each of the three sections, in order to address a wide range of language and gender research, we highlight one study that addresses issues of male dominance, another study that focuses on gender differences, and finally a study that provides a good illustration of gender diversity. For reasons of space, we do not discuss the extensive and very interesting research into the construction of gendered practices and ideologies in adolescent friendship groups (e.g., Bucholtz 1999).

1. Classroom Interaction Research

Classroom studies demonstrate how interactional differences can be detrimental to particular groups of students such as girls, document gender differences in student conversations with other students or teachers, and explore multiple teacher and student identities in educational interactions. We outline studies addressing these issues before highlighting representative studies from the literature.

David Sadker and Myra Sadker dedicated their educational research careers to documenting gender bias in American K-12 schools (e.g., Sadker and Sadker 1994). Several linguistic studies have mirrored Sadker and Sadker's efforts, documenting differences between boys and girls in classroom discourse (e.g., Julé 2004; Pavlidou 2003), usually focusing not on what was said, but on who spoke and how. At times, these studies attempt to explain why differences exist (or not), and often connect differences to relative disadvantages. For example, among US third grade children, Latina girls were seen to adopt a brokering role in group work in contrast to their competitive male classmates (Cook-Gumperz and Szymanski 2001), while among adults attending college bilingual women were observed choosing silence (Losey 1995), thus undermining their learning opportunities. Cooperative and competitive styles were also found in Swedish graduate seminars, in which male professors dominated and female professors facilitated discussion (Gunnarsson 1995), whereas Wodak (1997) noted that Austrian headmistresses were unable to maintain authority when using more cooperative speech styles. Bergvall and Remlinger (1996) found that though US undergraduate females spoke as often as males, women's control of discussion was often derided by off-task asides. Not all studies, however, reveal conclusive differences between men and women or boys and girls in classroom interaction. Instructors directing talk to students in Taiwanese college classes did not favor either men or women (Lee 2001), and in US college contexts tutors were not found to change strategies when speaking to male or female students (Thonus 1999).

To account for such complexity, socialization studies detail the production of identities in school contexts (Eckert and McConnell-Ginet 2003), and how local factors intersect to create complicated gender dynamics. For example, Burdelski and Mitsuhashi (2010) explore the Japanese preschool use of *kawaii*, an adjective referring to cute, delicate, and immature objects, which teachers use to socialize children into affective and gendered relationships. Fordham (1993) writes about black women silenced by their desire to avoid stereotypes that equate blackness with loudness, while Ek (2009) shows how Anglo and Hispanic classmates of a Guatemalan high school student influenced her to be both more American and more Mexican in gendered practices. In Ghanaian universities students used personal names, descriptive phrases, and titles in interactions to express and resist gender identities (Afful 2010), and in Canada a Japanese exchange student found his classroom participation limited both by the roles ascribed to him and by his own identity construction (Morita 2009). However, whether such practices affected educational outcomes for the participants is not a focus of these gender identity studies.

In examining this research, it is important to keep in mind the agency and also the resistance of local participants without losing sight of how disadvantages occur (Sunderland 2000) or how stereotypes influence expectations (DeFrancisco 1992). These themes arise again as we examine Davies's (2003) article on gendered discourse in small-group discussions.

1.1   *"Gendered group dynamics" in northern England (Davies 2003)*

As Davies explains in her introduction, 1980s gender research suggested that girls were educationally disadvantaged compared to boys, while 1990s research suggested that boys were suffering. Observing 14-year-old adolescents in northern England, Davies complicates this picture by illustrating how boys' discourse styles can undermine their learning while girls' linguistic practices may contribute to their achievement. Davies points out how traditionally gendered behavior leads to inequity – but in this case contends that boys create their own disadvantage.

Davies observed interaction among single-sex groups across three tasks: recalling early school experiences, role-playing as teachers, and analyzing poetry. Here girls discuss imagery in the *The Lady of Shalott*, a nineteenth-century poem by Alfred Tennyson:

```
Jo:  So she's weaving a magic web with colours gay/
Liz: And it's like weaving her feelings into it/
Kit: It's her way of expressing her feelings [...]
Sal: There isn't a way of expressing in words/her way is through
     colour/
```

(Davies 2003, 124)

In contrast, when one member of a boys' group attempted a similar discussion, "using such words as 'dazzling,' 'gorgeous,' 'yellow gold' and 'golden galaxy,'... he was harangued repeatedly [by his male classmates]... eventually being called 'stupid,' 'queer' and told to 'shut up'" (127).

In Davies's analysis "the girls created a sense of unity through their language, creating texts in which individuals formed learning allegiances" (128), while boys used "verbally articulated displays of seeming homophobia (to) … set the mood of an anti-school, anti-female culture … (which) often restricted their freedom to experiment with words and ideas" (129). Her findings suggest that if girls tend to be more successful in English classes at British secondary schools, this is because boys actively sabotage their male classmates' participation, with the worst effects of male dominance falling upon boys "who have problems conforming to a macho stereotype" (129). Davies suggests that teachers keep in mind the "impact of gendered group dynamics" (130) and accommodate their teaching methods to create learning opportunities for both boys and girls, but she offers few suggestions for overcoming the negative dynamics she describes.

1.2   Boys' and girls' conversational participation in Norwegian classrooms (Aukrust 2008)

While Davies offers close analysis of British adolescents' gendered language in group discussions, Aukrust more broadly examines differences between boys and girls in Norwegian schools across multiple grade levels and types of talk, focusing on conversational strategies (giving, waiting for, and taking the floor) and roles (teacher to student, student to teacher). The study draws little on gender theory; the intention was to investigate boys' and girls' interaction at various ages and to compare the Scandinavian situation to US and UK studies that found girls to be educationally disadvantaged. The researcher examined variation in taking or being given the floor, as well as strategies used by boys and by girls to take the floor.

In 26 classrooms in 20 schools (grades 1, 3, 6, and 9), a research team observed lessons in which students expressed opinions. Participation frequency, turn allocations, and off-task comments were quantified. Data analysis showed both boys and girls "participat(ing) broadly in conversations" (242), but boys spoke more than girls at each grade level, and this difference was more pronounced in higher grades and with male teachers. Teachers allocated turns nearly equally to boys and girls, but boys took the floor more often than girls in most classrooms. However, this was an inefficient strategy for keeping the floor since teachers often ignored unsolicited comments, as in the following exchange (244):

```
Teacher: hvilket land var det som hadde fasismen...? (which country
         had fascism...?)
Boy:     Italia (Italy).
Teacher: Ellen?
Ellen:   Italia (Italy).
Teacher: Italia (Italy).
```

Boys overlapped teachers' comments more frequently than girls, and spoke off task on more occasions (often in the form of jokes). Since girls' achievement in these classrooms was equal to or higher than boys', the author does not suggest that the observed interaction patterns put either girls or boys at an educational disadvantage. Nevertheless, Aukrust notes that girls "seemed less permitted to challenge conversational rules and expectations, which may have impacted the repertoire of the conversational strategies they acquired" (249). This study is an example of research focusing on the structure of student talk with the assumption that linguistic acts such as overlapping and taking the floor have a generally fixed meaning of domination or hierarchy; Aukrust's analysis shows that not all recent work in language, gender, and education has taken the "discourse turn" (Eckert and McConnell-Ginet 2003, 4) in which the relationship between (gendered) identity, context, culture, and power is investigated closely to determine how linguistic resources function in situated uses.

1.3   Social positioning and classroom discourse among US Latina immigrants (Menard-Warwick 2008)

Whereas Aukrust examined overall differences between boys and girls, Menard-Warwick showed how women in the same classroom may respond differently to gendered curricular materials. Her research explored how Latina immigrants in a Californian adult English as a second language (ESL) class positioned themselves and were positioned in gendered social interactions. This positioning differed between students within one classroom.

In an interaction between a Peruvian immigrant and her teacher during a unit on employment, the student was positioned as a homemaker by the teacher through a job skills worksheet which included options for students to check such as *cut hair*, *clean house*, and *cook*. The student challenged being positioned as a homemaker, claiming skills from her previous work in buying and selling chemical products, and indicating these in a blank on the bottom of the worksheet. However, due to the student's limited English, her teacher misunderstood the nature of her career in the Peruvian pharmaceutical industry, remarking later in an interview that all her students would say, "I can't do anything except clean my house and take care of kids and cook or sew" (267). Therefore, the student was unable to position herself in the interaction as a former businesswoman, nor learn the English skills necessary to describe her job skills effectively.

This first example is contrasted with a second interaction, in which a Salvadoran immigrant successfully negotiated disagreement during a worksheet activity on employment categories. Drawing on her experience as a homemaker, this student prevailed in her argument that housework is more boring than factory work. Agreeing with her, a female classmate summed up the repetitive nature of domestic chores: "Make the beds. Clean the bathroom … Pass the vacuum. Clean the mirrors … Everyday the same thing, that's why the work is boring" (283). Positioning themselves as knowledgeable about types of employment and also as skilled bilingual speakers, these women effectively silenced a male student who disagreed with them.

These two situations demonstrate how interlocutors can take different social positions within a context, affecting classroom interaction and thus learning outcomes. In discussing the class's curricular emphasis on how household skills connect to employability, Menard-Warwick concludes that "these women were being interactively positioned and thus socialized into their teacher's (and society's) notions of realistic career goals for Latina immigrants" (285). Similar gendered dynamics can be found in the literacy studies that we survey next.

2. Literacy

Studies that address differences between boys and girls or men and women in literacy practices and education mostly involve quantitative methods and have looked broadly at writing (Beard and Burrell 2010) and reading (Moss 1999), with the general concern that boys perform more poorly than girls.

Many studies examine attitudes and learning strategies. In the United States, McKenna, Kear, and Ellsworth (1995) found that elementary school boys had more negative attitudes toward reading, both recreational and academic, though the attitudes of all students tended to become more negative the longer they attended school. However, school children in grades 3–5 had equally positive attitudes about a newspaper-reading literacy implementation (Sargent, Mwavita, and Smith 2009), and reading strategies among ESL college students were not found to differ between men and women (Poole 2005).

Other research on literacy has tended to differ by setting, with US and other Anglo research being done on materials analysis and issues of identity, while research in non-Anglo settings has tended to focus on issues of equality and empowerment. A large amount of US research starting in the mid-1990s and continuing into the 2010s has focused on gender representations in texts and selection of materials (Millard 1997). Textbooks and curricular materials are a popular site for inquiry because they are the mainstay of education and can have a great impact on students and society at large. The abundance of studies on this topic may also stem from practical reasons, such as the relative ease with which a researcher can access a text versus the interactions of a classroom. Research on school readers has shown males in the protagonist roles (Foley and Boulware 1996; Witt 1997), and also noted portrayals of masculinity as aggressive and argumentative (Evans and Davies 2000). To overcome bias, more recent researchers suggest attention to diversity, arguing for the representation of a range of gendered identities, and more variety in sexualities and ethnicities presented in texts (Boston and Baxley 2007; Wickens 2007). However, since texts may be used in various ways by teachers and students, it is perhaps more important to see how teachers and students engage texts (Sunderland 2000), as in Martínez-Roldán's (2005) study of Latino children (discussed below).

International studies since the early 2000s have examined how literacy education furthers feminine empowerment and quality of life. In Turkey, adult literacy classes were observed to improve women's ability to participate in public social spheres (Kagitcibasi, Goksen, and Gulgoz 2005). Similarly, in Nigeria, Olateju (2007) demonstrated that providing girls with "reading kiosks" helped them develop societal life skills as well as a relationship with texts. Research in South African high school classrooms showed that critical literacy activities can raise awareness about attitudes toward women (Ralfe 2009).

Another group of studies, particularly from the United States, elucidate connections between literacies and identities. For example, Dutro (2003) showed how African American elementary school boys performed masculinity through public choices of reading material, becoming more open to novels with female protagonists once a few dominant boys engaged the texts. Blackburn (2002–2003) chronicled the literacy development of a teenager who both performed and challenged African American lesbian identity through journal writing and video production at a youth center. Whereas Blackburn and Dutro examined new literacies, Menard-Warwick (2011) explored how immigrant women drew on first-language literacies tied to valued identities to make sense of ESL classroom materials and their new lives in California.

2.1   *Workplace literacy and empowerment of African American women (Gowen and Bartlett 1997)*

In another adult literacy study, Gowen and Bartlett conducted an ethnography of African American women in a program for blue collar workers at a university. The researchers, who were also the instructors and course designers, found that the women's experiences of sexual abuse and domestic violence directly affected the structure of the class.

Over time, the literacies some women developed helped them begin to heal and also take steps to leave abusive situations. One woman used mathematics skills developed in the literacy program to assess her finances and purchase a condominium; this allowed her to separate from her husband. Another woman learned to set goals for herself through journal writing about her relationships with her abusive stepfather and unsupportive mother. As she remarked to one of the teachers: "Before I didn't have any goals. The secret took up all my space for goals. Now I don't have a secret and I have goals" (147). A third woman explored in her journal her husband's disapproval of the literacy classes, and ended up filing for divorce. For these women, literacy development increased opportunities to exercise agency in life choices.

Such transformations did not occur without struggle. The instructors had designed the curriculum around a "learner-centered model" (143), based on their review of the adult pedagogical literature. However, "critical literacy" practices such as group work and goal-setting discussions in fact alienated the women from the class and resulted in their silence. Attempts to get students to "use literacy to improve their working conditions" were met with distrust (145). Instructors had to rethink classroom practices, allowing women to work alone and write in journals rather than requiring them to share ideas and experiences.

Literacies developed in the program were tools that students used to change their lives. According to the authors, isolation and silence are common characteristics of abuse survivors, and creating language to express traumas is essential for recovery (148). In addition, financial literacy is key to independence. Adult literacy instruction must take into account gender and life histories; as the authors write, "if a woman is a victim of domestic violence, then her reasons for enrolling in a literacy class and the changes that occur in her life as a result of becoming more literate are fundamentally different" compared with other women (149). Thus, Gowen and Bartlett's research on gender and literacy suggests how inequities can be challenged through education. In contrast, the next study shows how literacy practices may reinforce gendered inequalities in traditional communities.

2.2   *Differing literacies between boys and girls in Israeli schools (Bogoch 1999)*

Examining education in Haredi (ultra-Orthodox) primary and secondary schools in Israel, Bogoch found a variety of differences between the experiences of boys and girls, which she explains but does not theorize. Nevertheless, the article clarifies that gender differences in this community are religiously constructed and vigilantly maintained. Haredi schools are separated according to sex, and approaches to literacy and language instruction differ. While boys tend to receive lessons in Yiddish, girls have typically been instructed in Hebrew, though this varies between schools. Opposite linguistic choices are made for literacy instruction: boys learn to read and write in Hebrew, while girls typically read and write in Yiddish.

There has been a shift, however, toward teaching girls in Yiddish as a result of shifting perceptions of a woman's role in Haredi society, which has traditionally considered religious scholarship the "valued occupation for men" (130). While women have long been expected to support their husbands' religious studies, in recent years the need has grown to educate girls for paid employment to meet these family obligations. However, as education for girls expands,

> there is fear that too much secular education will lead to laxity in religious matters and unwanted outside influences. Even too much religious education for girls is considered dangerous, because it is felt that women can't really understand the complexities of the text and may misinterpret the meanings. (133)

Thus, literacy education for girls is connected to their underlying difference from boys in their future roles as Haredi wives and mothers, community members, and preservers of religious and cultural traditions. Boys' literacy practices are clearly understood by the community, as they focus on religious scholarship, but educators are divided as to how girls should use literacy – whether to learn about their Jewish heritage, gain employment, or instruct their children. As literacy education evolves in the Haredi community, controversies about women's role in the community, empowerment, and secularism are bound to continue. Bogoch's research shows that even studies primarily detailing differences in the educational experiences of boys and girls cannot avoid issues of hierarchy and patriarchy, and also illustrates how studies of gender difference inflected by ethnic and religious context contribute to a more nuanced understanding.

2.3　Contested gender ideologies during literature discussion of US Latino children (Martínez-Roldán 2005)

Whereas Bogoch shows individuals constrained by traditional gender roles and literacy practices, Martínez-Roldán's ethnography of bilingual Latino children in a second grade classroom depicts young students' active engagement in negotiating gender during literacy events. With a strong base in gender theory, the article portrays children voicing varied gender ideologies during their discussion of a storybook about a boy ridiculed for enjoying stereotypically feminine pastimes, such as dancing and picking flowers.

While one boy early in the conversation insisted on a rigid, dichotomous view of gender, in which there are "boy games and girl games" (166), other students, both boys and girls, took a more fluid view, contesting the idea of strictly gendered games and stating that the character should be able to do what he wanted because "it's his life" (168). One girl went a step further by applying this to her own life: "If you want, pretend I was always dressing like a boy, and I always wanted to be like a boy, nobody needed to tell me what I did because it's not their life, it's my life" (169). However, other children insisted that she could not become a boy but had to be born one, and that people would not like her if she became a boy.

In pursuing her question, the girl showed awareness not only of stereotypical and atypical gender roles but also of male dominance. She expressed frustration with her own gendered options, voicing desires to play soccer and to pursue a career as a soldier, as well as her belief that she would not be allowed to do so. When discussing her perceived inability to be president, one boy first said that she could be the "president's wife," but then stated "if women want to do a man's job, they have the rights to do a man's job" (172), revealing shifting and contradictory values regarding gender.

Developing literacy through participation in a literature discussion group, students explored their understandings of gender – what is and what should or can be. They thoughtfully questioned the gendered world around them and in books. As one boy remarked toward the end, "I'm still wondering about that boy and girl thingy; if they should do whatever they want" (173). Martínez-Roldán's findings point to children's nonlinear, complex, and conflicting understanding of gender, as well as suggesting a resourceful way to explore such understandings in classrooms. Indeed, this study shows how literacy learning and gender development may go hand in hand.

3.　Second- and Foreign-Language Learning

As with literacy studies, gender rarely stands alone in research on second-language (L2) and foreign-language (FL) education but rather connects with other research topics, such as attitudes toward L2 learning or the connected but more contested topic of language learning motivation (Norton 2000). In a typical motivation and gender study, Kobayashi (2002) found that Japanese high school girls had more positive attitudes toward English than their male classmates. In contrast, during Spanish-language instruction in same-sex classes of Canadian high school students, pre and post questionnaires revealed higher motivation for boys than for girls (Kissau, Quach (Kolano), and Wang 2009). In interviews, boys expressed lower anxiety in same-sex groups, whereas the girls' class saw their motivation affected by poor discipline and "clashing female personalities" (73). On the other hand, 12-year-old boys and girls in England reported more confidence in same-sex French and German classes (Chambers 2005).

With some exceptions, attitude and motivation research for both mixed- and same-sex language instruction confirms the common notion that girls are more likely to study foreign languages, and more likely to make an effort to succeed. However, in many studies, gender differences turn out to be minor (e.g., Kissau, Kolano, and Wang 2010; Lai 2007). Moreover, greater effort does not necessarily translate to progress in language learning, as shown in Green and Oxford's (1995) study comparing the use of learning strategies by male and female college-age Puerto Rican students. Indeed, achievement research overall offers a mixed picture. In Russia, male study-abroad students showed greater gains than female students (see discussion of Polanyi (1995), below); while in Turkey, Kurdish high school girls displayed more native-like accents in Turkish than their male counterparts (Polat and Mahalingappa 2010); in a US elementary school, an ESL intervention program served Spanish-speaking boys and girls equally well (Tong et al. 2010). In the absence of clear contextual descriptions, it is not clear how observing gender differences and similarities can translate to educational improvement.

As with research on gender and literacy, a principal means for investigating sexism in L2 education is content analysis of textbooks. Such analyses, which demonstrate that male characters preponderate in L2 textbooks, especially in active professional roles, began in the 1970s in English-speaking countries and continued for decades (e.g., Porreca 1984; Poulou 1997). They have appeared more recently in other national contexts, for example, Brazil (Oliveira 2008) and Iran (Ghorbani 2009). In order to counter sexist materials and traditional gender ideologies, some authors advocate feminist pedagogies (McMahill 2001), such as Ó'Móchain's use of local "queer narratives" in a Japanese English college classroom (2006).

Additionally, some ethnographic studies have demonstrated the negative effect of sexism on women's L2 learning in ESL contexts (e.g., Rockhill 1993) and study abroad (e.g., Talburt and Stewart 1999). Other ethnographies offer a contextualized exploration of the role of gender in linguistic lives, as in Norton's (2000) study of immigrant women in Canada, or Ibrahim's (1999) research on African refugee youth learning English through hip-hop and rap music. Menard-Warwick's (2009) ethnography contrasts two Latina immigrants in California, one of whom began studying English at home to protect her children from urban perils – while the other encountered English in the workplace after a battle with her husband who believed her place was in the home. The one male immigrant she interviewed was able to study English only after a back injury prevented him from working. In a very different study of male learners, King (2008) found that according to his Korean informants, "being gay guy, that is advantage." In traveling and living abroad, their sexual identities provided them with access to English-speaking gay social networks, allowing them to learn the language informally and effectively in a way that was impossible for their heterosexual counterparts. In Piller and Takahashi's research (2006), Japanese female exchange students in Australia were often disappointed in their hope of finding a white monolingual Australian boyfriend who would help them perfect their English.

3.1   *Effects of male dominance on L2 achievement of US students in Russia (Polanyi 1995)*

Learning a language informally was perhaps even more challenging for college-age American women studying abroad in Russia in the early 1990s. A large study conducted on students in the program showed a clear advantage for males on oral proficiency post-testing, despite students having begun with similar pre-test scores and despite the widespread observation that girls tend to be more avid L2 learners.

Polanyi conducted narrative analysis on student journals to examine the different experiences of men and women in the study-abroad context. She found that female students "[went] to class as frequently as their male counterparts; they (were) out of the dorm and on the town as often as male colleagues" (288). However, their experiences "on the town" were qualitatively different: in their journals girls wrote about exerting great linguistic effort to fend off sexual advances from male acquaintances; boys did not report similar experiences. One unpleasant encounter occurred between an American girl and her Russian suitor in church on Easter Sunday:

> It was just the two of us hanging around in front of these icons and me kind of trying to put space between us in an impossible situation … I mean, I didn't want to insult him, he kept saying, "Oh, well, I know why you don't like me, it's because I'm Russian and you think that we're all these stalking bears." (282)

A contrasting report from an American boy described an evening that "went wonderfully. We discussed music, art, economics, and film, along with politics … I could even crack an occasional joke … Marina doubled up with laughter" (281).

As a result of such experiences, Polanyi argues, young men and women developed different linguistic skills. One girl reported, "I learned a few words like 'pressure' … having to do with being fed up with something … feeling caged in and feeling you don't know what to do, and those are really useful vocabulary words in this country" (285). As Polanyi notes, such hard-won proficiencies of female language learners do not appear on language tests. Thus, for this particular context, Polanyi demonstrates the effects of male dominance on feminine language learning: the ubiquity of sexual harassment, the linguistic strategies used to cope with that harassment, and the inefficacy of these strategies in responding to examination questions.

3.2   Australian boys' disengagement from L2 learning (Carr and Pauwels 2006)

Whereas Polanyi explored the effects of male dominance on language learning in Russia, a decade later at secondary schools in Australia, Carr and Pauwels were attempting to account for the differences in girls' and boys' engagements with foreign-language study. Boys tended to stop taking languages as soon as possible; in compulsory classes, most boys misbehaved and learned little. Language learning was widely regarded as a feminine domain. To investigate these phenomena, Carr and Pauwels conducted interviews with more than 200 boys over a two-year period, as well as some teachers and female classmates.

Although many of Carr and Pauwels's informants offered biological explanations for boys' disengagement, the authors reject simplistic gender binaries. Writing about observed differences between boys and girls, they draw on contemporary gender theory to examine the ideologies that construct and maintain these gender binaries. They also contextualized these ideologies, noting that masculine monolingualism is less an option in non-English-speaking countries, such as Korea or Switzerland. They additionally note the role played by social class in constructing boys' language attitudes, observing that young men who foresee careers in international business perceive more utility in language study. Thus, Carr and Pauwels draw significantly on the diversity approach of language and gender studies, even while focusing on differences between boys and girls in their research context.

The authors found boys well able to articulate the ideologies that prevented commitment to L2 learning, even when this fit with their career goals, and even when they enjoyed the classes. Especially for younger boys in working-class schools, it was essential to avoid "being seen to work and therefore being identified as a nerd … 'boys muck up because they want to be cool'" (63), one boy explained. In contrast, girls were viewed as innately able to sit still, pay attention, and do their homework: as one boy phrased this common sentiment, "girls are smarter, they work harder" (64). Girls and teachers interviewed for the study made similar remarks. In Carr and Pauwels's analysis, "the wordings of these comments … indicate the non-negotiability of the account" (68). Even upper-class boys with strong career aspirations argued the innate suitability of girls for language study. As Carr and Pauwels point out, there are boys who resist these ideologies, but they face social sanctions (see Davies 2003, above).

In this way, Carr and Pauwels demonstrate that, yes, there can be significant differences in how males and females approach foreign languages – however, rather than attribute these differences to immutable biological or cultural characteristics, they note the ways that difference is constructed in language and social practice.

3.3   English-learning and the cultural identities of exiled Tibetan nuns (Macpherson 2005)

Whereas both Polanyi and Carr and Pauwels investigate the role of hierarchies and gender construction in language learning, Macpherson's research with Tibetan nuns in India provides varied case studies of how gendered cultural identities interacted with English learning in this setting, as individual nuns decided how to live out their religious practice and political aspirations in exile. To illustrate the complexity, Macpherson opens with a narrative of herself as a novice English teacher presenting the sentence "a nun is a woman and a monk is a man." One student argued, in very limited English, that nuns and monks were more similar to each other than to ordinary men and women. This nun soon rejected English study as religiously and culturally problematic.

However, other nuns saw English as a tool in their struggle against Chinese dominance of their homeland. They constructed nontraditional gender identities as political activists in communication with the English-speaking world. Some nuns saw modernity (and thus English) as liberating in contrast to Tibetan tradition. One activist at the monastery argued that Tibet before the Chinese invasion was "dominated by monks ... [who] failed to adequately protect the interests of Tibetan people" (595). Meanwhile, other nuns whose "modern" aspirations for education and political progress led them to study English nevertheless continued to strongly value Tibetan education and religious practice. As Macpherson describes one such woman: "Each of the two languages and cultures prepared her for different socially significant roles in her community, both as Tibetan refugee woman defending the traditions of her culture, and as modern English-speaking woman serving her community as mediator, translator, and healthcare worker" (600). And sadly, one nun profiled in the article was unable to cope with memories of torture in her homeland, left the monastery, and fell into poverty. As Macpherson notes, English may have little utility for the marginalized and alienated.

As these cases demonstrate, individuals with similar gender roles from traditional societies can respond to cultural and political changes in strikingly different ways, and these contrasting responses can profoundly influence their L2 learning trajectories and gendered identity development. Although, unlike Carr and Pauwels, she does not cite gender theory, Macpherson's study illuminates the possibility of varied L2 learning results within one small community.

4. Conclusion

In this chapter we have reviewed language and gender research since the early 1980s in the areas of classroom interaction, literacy, and second-language learning, and have found a number of common trends in the issues examined: attitude, motivation, silence, strategies, texts, identity, achievement, empowerment. However, our analysis of this research shows few clear-cut gender tendencies but rather variation across contexts. While it is often easy to find differences between the sexes in particular research sites, manifestations of gender intertwine with power, ethnicity, and culture, so that gendered practices and ideologies differ significantly from one place to another, as well as varying between individuals of the same gender within a single classroom. Male dominance is common across many settings, but shows no inevitable effect on learning outcomes.

We should also emphasize that although the quest for generalizable gender differences is considered passé by many researchers in the language and gender field, studies comparing male and female students continue to be published regularly in educational journals, often relying on quantifiable measures such as surveys. Indeed, quantitative methodology seems ascendant in education, due to the pressure in planning and policy for unequivocal, numbers-driven research that is convincing to contemporary funding agencies (Tong et al. 2010). While quantitative research can lead to the understanding of large societal phenomena, observing solely how males and females use language differently offers a restricted view of gender in education. It is insufficient to examine binaries because without context they reveal little and can hardly lead to the useful implementation of educational practices.

Rather, to account for the complex relationships between gendered practices and educational achievement (Sunderland 2000), research into discourse has become important, with scholars examining *what* is said in addition to *who* says something and *how* it is said, and attending to the context in which the utterances are made. The community of practice framework (Eckert and McConnell-Ginet 1992; Lave and Wenger 1991) is useful for examining the social backdrop upon which gendered identities are enacted. As Toohey (2000) illustrates, in some cases, a single classroom could be considered a community of practice, a domain in which individuals engage in similar activities, work toward a common goal, and make meaning of their identity performances. While Burdelski and Mitsuhashi (2010) do not draw on community of practice theory, the Japanese preschool they describe might easily be considered such a community. We recommend further research in this area.

Research that fully accounts for context can offer plausible reasons why men and women (or boys and girls) act the way they do. Such studies showcase not only the varied ways of performing gender and learning language but also the interconnections with other factors such as class and ethnicity. Although it has been argued that local context-specific studies are difficult to generalize, our literature review suggests that the few sweeping generalizations available ("girls are more motivated") are not universal, and in any case offer little promise for educational improvement. The best practice for research on these issues is to thoroughly contextualize any differences and findings, so that there is room to discuss the larger factors that construct gendered practices and ideologies. Moreover, it may be wise to incorporate a range of methods, quantitative and qualitative, to insure that research examines gender from multiple perspectives. In any case, it is important for researchers to be explicit about the theories they are drawing on, and to justify their methods on the basis of their assumptions about gender.

Beyond the necessity for greater clarity in theory and methodology, there is a need for more wide-ranging research on the topic of gender in education. First, we caution against the trend in the last decade to assume that male dominance is a thing of the past, and we call for renewed attention to gender inequities in educational research. Second, although a few studies in literacy and L2 learning have examined issues of sexuality, there is a lack of research in this field, especially in regard to classroom interaction. This includes discussion of sexualities and sexualization, as well as specifically how students' sexualities come into play in learning environments. Because educational institutions tend to be heteronormative, looking at sexualities is as important as examining ethnicity and class. From romantic activities in L2 classrooms to games in physical education, schools are a site of struggle for those whose sexuality is not mainstream. These struggles need to be more closely documented, using a variety of methods.

Moreover, it is difficult to draw firm conclusions about the effects of gender on education when we still know so little about how gender affects the achievement of students in societies worldwide. While a growing number of studies are conducted in non-English-dominant contexts, many still occur in North America, the United Kingdom, and Australia. Industrialized countries such as Korea, China, and Japan are the main locations for language and gender research in Asia, while studies done in Africa are mainly from South Africa, or West African nations such as Nigeria and Ghana. Some Middle Eastern and European nations are represented, including Israel, Turkey, Scandinavia, Austria, and Greece, but studies based in Latin America or the Pacific are more difficult to find. More research in non-Anglo settings is essential.

What we need is not some new grand generalization about language and gender that can be applied across educational settings, but rather renewed ways of theorizing gender and relating these theories to local contexts in ways accessible to educational practitioners who wish to make a difference in their own classrooms. The work we survey offers some promising paths toward this end. For example, Martínez-Roldán (2005) demonstrates how literature discussions can inspire sophisticated gender theorizing among second graders; Gowen and Bartlett (1997) explain how they adapted adult learning theory to the needs of domestic violence survivors; Carr and Pauwels (2006) chronicle a few teachers' successful efforts to engage boy learners with drama activities and Internet technology. While not all inquiry into classroom practices will yield robust pedagogical implications, it is a concern that some research in classroom settings provides no new implications for educators. This is not to say that practitioners should be "told" what to do; what is needed is a stronger link between research findings and classroom practices, as well as better dialogue between researchers and practitioners. That being said, the work reviewed in this chapter illuminates the complex connections between language and gender in diverse educational settings. Taking these factors into account offers educators greater potential to facilitate the learning of all students.

NOTE

1   The authors' names are given in alphabetical order.

REFERENCES

Afful, Joseph B. A. 2010. "Address Forms among University Students in Ghana: A Case of Gendered Identities?" *Journal of Multilingual and Multicultural Development*, 31: 443–456.

Aukrust, Vibeke G. 2008. "Boys' and Girls' Conversational Participation across Four Grade Levels in Norwegian Classrooms: Taking the Floor or Being Given the Floor?" *Gender and Education*, 20: 237–252.

Beard, Roger, and Andrew Burrell. 2010. "Writing Attainment in 9- to 11-Year-Olds: Some Differences between Girls and Boys in Two Genres." *Language and Education*, 24: 495–515.

Bergvall, Victoria L., and Kathryn A. Remlinger. 1996. "Reproduction, Resistance and Gender in Educational Discourse: The Role of Critical Discourse Analysis." *Discourse & Society*, 7: 453–479.

Blackburn, Mollie V. 2002–2003. "Disrupting the (Hetero)Normative: Exploring Literacy Performances and Identity Work with Queer Youth." *Journal of Adolescent & Adult Literacy*, 45: 312–324.

Bogoch, Bryna. 1999. "Gender, Literacy, and Religiosity: Dimensions of Yiddish Education in Israeli Government-Supported Schools." *International Journal of the Sociology of Language*, 138: 123–160.

Boston, Genyne H., and Traci Baxley. 2007. "Living the Literature: Race, Gender Construction, and Black Female Adolescents." *Urban Education*, 42: 560–581.

Bucholtz, Mary. 1999. "'Why Be Normal?' Language and Identity Practices in a Community of Nerd Girls." *Language in Society*, 28: 203–224.

Burdelski, Matthew, and Koji Mitsuhashi. 2010. "'She Thinks You're Kawaii': Socializing Affect, Gender, and Relationships in a Japanese Preschool." *Language in Society*, 39: 65–93.

Cameron, Deborah. 2005. "Language, Gender, and Sexuality: Current Issues and New Directions." *Applied Linguistics*, 26: 482–502.

Carr, Jo, and Anne Pauwels. 2006. *Boys and Foreign Language Learning: Real Boys Don't Do Languages*. New York: Palgrave Macmillan.

Chambers, Gary. 2005. "Teaching Modern Foreign Languages in Single-Sex Classes in a Co-educational Context: Review of a Project in a North Yorkshire Comprehensive School." *Language Learning Journal*, 32: 45–54

Cook-Gumperz, Jenny, and Margaret Szymanski. 2001. "Interactional Styles in a Bilingual Classroom." *Research on Language and Social Interaction*, 34: 107–130.

Davies, Julia. 2003. "Expressions of Gender: An Analysis of Pupils' Gendered Discourse Styles in Small Group Classroom Discussions." *Discourse & Society*, 14: 115–132.

DeFrancisco, Victoria L. 1992. "Ethnography and Gender: Learning to Talk Like Girls and Boys." *Topics in Language Disorders*, 12: 40–53.

Dutro, Elizabeth. 2003. "'Us Boys Like to Read Football and Boy Stuff': Reading Masculinities, Performing Boyhood." *Journal of Literacy Research*, 34: 465–500.

Eckert, Penelope, and Sally McConnell-Ginet. 1992. "Think Practically and Look Locally: Language and Gender as Community-Based Practice." *Annual Review of Anthropology*, 21: 461–490.

Eckert, Penelope, and Sally McConnell-Ginet. 2003. *Language and Gender*. New York: Cambridge University Press.

Ek, Lucila D. 2009. "'It's Different Lives': A Guatemalan American Adolescent's Construction of Ethnic and Gender Identities across Educational Contexts." *Anthropology & Education Quarterly*, 40: 405–420.

Evans, Lorraine, and Kimberly Davies. 2000. "No Sissy Boys Here: A Content Analysis of the Representation of Masculinity in Elementary School Reading Textbooks." *Sex Roles: A Journal of Research*, 42: 255–270.

Foley, Christy L., and Beverly J. Boulware. 1996. "Gender Equity in 1990 Middle School Basal Readers." *Reading Improvement*, 33: 220–223.

Fordham, Signithia. 1993. "'Those Loud Black Girls': (Black) Women, Silence, and Gender 'Passing' in the Academy." *Anthropology & Education Quarterly*, 24: 3–32.

Ghorbani, Laya. 2009. *An Investigation of the Manifestation of Sexism in EFL/ESL Textbooks*. Institute of Education Sciences. ERIC Accession Number: ED505434. At http://files.eric.ed.gov/fulltext/ED505434.pdf, accessed October 29, 2013.

Gowen, Sheryl G., and Carol Bartlett. 1997. "'Friends in the Kitchen': Lessons from Survivors." In Glynda A. Hull (ed.), *Changing Work, Changing Workers: Critical Perspectives on Language, Literacy, and Skills*, 141–458. Albany: SUNY Press.

Green, John M., and Rebecca Oxford. 1995. "A Closer Look at Learning Strategies, L2 Proficiency, and Gender." *TESOL Quarterly*, 29: 261–297.

Gunnarsson, Britt-Louise. 1995. "Academic Leadership and Gender: The Case of the Seminar Chair." *Nordlyd*, 23: 174–193.

Ibrahim, Awad. 1999. "Becoming Black: Rap and Hip-Hop, Race, Gender, Identity and the Politics of ESL Learning." *TESOL Quarterly*, 33: 349–369.

Julé, Allyson. 2004. *Gender, Participation and Silence in the Language Classroom: Sh-shushing the Girls*. New York: Palgrave Macmillan.

Kagitcibasi, Cigdem, Fatos Goksen, and Sami Gulgoz. 2005. "Functional Adult Literacy and Empowerment of Women: Impact of a Functional Literacy Program in Turkey." *Journal of Adolescent & Adult Literacy*, 48: 472–489.

King, Brian W. 2008. "'Being Gay Guy, That is the Advantage': Queer Korean Language Learning and Identity Construction." *Journal of Language, Identity & Education*, 7: 230–252.

Kissau, Scott P., Lan Quach (Kolano), and Chuang Wang. 2009. "Impact of Single-Sex Instruction on Student Motivation to Learn Spanish." *Canadian Journal of Applied Linguistics*, 12: 54–78.

Kissau, Scott P., Lan Quach Kolano, and Chuang Wang. 2010. "Perceptions of Gender Differences in High School Students' Motivation to Learn Spanish." *Foreign Language Annals*, 43: 703–721.

Kobayashi, Yoko. 2002. "The Role of Gender in Foreign Language Learning Attitudes: Japanese Female Students' Attitudes towards English Learning." *Gender and Education*, 14: 181–197.

Lai, Mee-Ling. 2007. "Gender and Language Attitudes: A Case of Postcolonial Hong Kong." *International Journal of Multilingualism*, 4: 83–116.

Lave, Jean, and Etienne Wenger. 1991. *Situated Learning: Legitimate Peripheral Participation*. Cambridge: Cambridge University Press.

Lee, Shujung M. 2001. "Gender Bias in Taiwan's EFL Classrooms: A Classroom Observation Study." Unpublished PhD dissertation, University of Mississippi. At http://search.proquest.com/docview/275609947/13BAC117C5614ACE5F8/1?accountid=14505, accessed January 16, 2013.

Losey, Kay M. 1995. "Gender and Ethnicity as Factors in the Development of Verbal Skills in Bilingual Mexican American Women." *TESOL Quarterly*, 29: 635–661.

McKenna, Michael C., Dennis J. Kear, and Randolph A. Ellsworth. 1995. "Children's Attitudes toward Readings: A National Survey." *Reading Research Quarterly*, 30: 934–956.

McMahill, Cheiron. 2001. "Self-Expression, Gender, and Community: A Japanese Feminist English Class." In Aneta Pavlenko, Adrian Blackledge, Ingrid Piller, and Marya Teutsch-Dwyer (eds.), *Multilingualism, Second Language Learning, and Gender*, 307–344. Berlin: De Gruyter.

MacPherson, Seonaigh. 2005. "Negotiating Language Contact and Identity Change in Developing Tibetan–English Bilingualism." *TESOL Quarterly*, 39: 585–607.

Martínez-Roldán, Carmen M. 2005. "Examining Bilingual Children's Gender Ideologies through Critical Discourse Analysis." *Critical Inquiry in Language Studies*, 2: 157–178.

Menard-Warwick, Julia. 2008. "'Because She Made Beds. Every Day': Social Positioning, Classroom Discourse, and Language Learning." *Applied Linguistics*, 29: 267–289.

Menard-Warwick, Julia. 2009. *Gendered Identities and Immigrant Language Learning*. Clevedon: Multilingual Matters.

Menard-Warwick, Julia. 2011. "L1 and L2 Reading Practices in the Lives of Latina Immigrant Women Studying English." In Christina Higgins (ed.), *Identity Formation in Globalizing Contexts*, 99–118. Berlin: Mouton de Gruyter.

Millard, Elaine. 1997. *Differently Literate: Boys, Girls and the Schooling of Literacy*. London: Falmer Press.

Morita, Naoko. 2009. "Language, Culture, Gender, and Academic Socialization." *Language and Education*, 23: 443–460.

Moss, Gemma. 1999. "Texts in Context: Mapping Out the Gender Differentiation of the Reading Curriculum." *Pedagogy, Culture & Society*, 7: 507–522.

Norton, Bonny. 2000. *Identity and Language Learning: Gender, Ethnicity and Educational Change*. Harlow: Pearson.

Olateju, Moji A. 2007. "Reading Kiosks: Literacy Empowerment for the Girl-Child." *Language, Culture and Curriculum*, 20: 155–163.

Oliveira, Sara. 2008. "Visual Text, Gender Stereotypes and Foreign Language Textbooks." *Trabalhos em Linguistica Aplicada*, 47: 91–117.

Ó'Móchain, Robert. 2006. "Discussing Gender and Sexuality in a Context-Appropriate Way: Queer Narratives in an EFL College Classroom in Japan." *Journal of Language, Identity, and Education*, 5: 51–66.

Pavlidou, Theodossia-Soula. 2003. "Patterns of Participation in Classroom Interaction: Girls' and Boys' Non-Compliance in a Greek High School." *Linguistics and Education*, 14: 123–141.

Piller, Ingrid, and Kimie Takahashi. 2006. "A Passion for English: Desire and the Language Market." In Aneta Pavlenko (ed.), *Bilingual Minds: Emotional Experience, Expression, and Representation*, 59–83. Clevedon: Multilingual Matters.

Polanyi, Livia. 1995. "Language Learning and Living Abroad." In Barbara Freed (ed.), *Second Language Acquisition in a Study Abroad Context*, 271–291. Amsterdam: Benjamins.

Polat, Nihat, and Laura J. Mahalingappa. 2010. "Gender Differences in Identity and Acculturation Patterns and L2 Accent Attainment." *Journal of Language, Identity, and Education*, 9: 17 35.

Poole, Alexander. 2005. "Gender Differences in Reading Strategy Use among ESL College Students." *Journal of College Reading and Learning*, 36: 7–20.

Porreca, Karen L. 1984. "Sexism in Current ESL Textbooks." *TESOL Quarterly*, 18: 705–724.

Poulou, Sophia. 1997. "Sexism and the Discourse Roles of Textbook Dialogues." *Language Learning Journal*, 15: 68–73.

Ralfe, Elizabeth. 2009. "Policy: Powerful or Pointless? An Exploration of the Role of Critical Literacy in Challenging and Changing Gender Stereotypes." *Language Learning Journal*, 37: 305–321.

Rockhill, Kathleen. 1993. "Gender, Language and the Politics of Literacy." In Brian Street (ed.), *Cross-Cultural Approaches to Literacy,*

156–175. Cambridge: Cambridge University Press.

Sadker, David M., and Myra Sadker. 1994. *Failing at Fairness: How Our Schools Cheat Girls*. New York: Macmillan.

Sargent, Stephan, Mwarumba Mwavita, and Melinda Smith. 2009. "Newspapers for Boys? Newspapers for Girls? Newspapers for Everyone!" *Reading Improvement*, 46: 227–237.

Street, Brian. 2003. "What's 'New' in New Literacy Studies? Critical Approaches to Literacy in Theory and Practice." *Current Issues in Comparative Education*, 5: 77–91.

Sunderland, Jane. 2000. "New Understandings of Gender and Language Classroom Research: Texts, Teacher Talk and Student Talk." *Language Teaching Research*, 4: 149–173.

Talburt, Susan, and Melissa A. Stewart. 1999. "What's the Subject of Study Abroad? Race, Gender, and 'Living Culture.'" *Modern Language Journal*, 83: 163–175.

Thonus, Terese. 1999. "Dominance in Academic Writing Tutorials: Gender, Language Proficiency, and the Offering of Suggestions." *Discourse & Society*, 10: 225–248.

Tong, Fuhui, Beverly J. Irby, Rafael Lara-Alecio, Myeongsun Yoon, and Patricia G. Mathes. 2010. "Hispanic English Learners' Responses to Longitudinal English Instructional Intervention and the Effect of Gender: A Multilevel Analysis." *Elementary School Journal*, 110: 542–566.

Toohey, Kelleen. 2000. *Learning English at School: Identity, Social Relations and Classroom Practice*. Clevedon: Multilingual Matters.

Wickens, Corrine M. 2007. "Queering Young Adult Literature: Examining Sexual Minorities in Contemporary Realistic Fiction between 2000–2005." Unpublished PhD dissertation, Texas A&M University. At http://search.proquest.com/docview/304727560?accountid=14505, accessed January 16, 2013.

Witt, Susan D. 1997. "Boys Will Be Boys, and Girls Will Be … Hard to Find: Gender Representation in Third Grade Basal Readers." *Education and Society*, 15: 47–57.

Wodak, Ruth. 1997. "'I Know, We Won't Revolutionize the World with It, but …': Styles of Female Leadership in Institutions." In Helga Kotthoff and Ruth Wodak (eds.), *Communicating Gender in Context*, 335–370. Amsterdam: Benjamins.

25 Gender and Family Interaction

DEBORAH TANNEN

1. Introduction

In the quarter-century after the field was launched by the publication of Robin Lakoff's *Language and Woman's Place* (1975) and Mary Ritchie Key's *Male/Female Language* (1975), a mountain of research on gender and language arose – research well documented in the present volume. During the same years, discourse analysts began undertaking studies of language in the context of family interaction. For the most part, however, the twain didn't meet: few scholars writing in the area of language and gender focused on family interaction, and few researchers concerned with family discourse focused on gender. This gap has been addressed by the Georgetown Work–Family Project, in which both parents in four dual-career couples with children living at home self-recorded all their interactions for a week. In this chapter, I cite examples from this study, which I co-directed with Shari Kendall, as well as a brief excerpt from a naturally occurring conversation taken from a public television documentary, to demonstrate: (1) how gender-related patterns of interaction influence and illuminate family interaction, and (2) how this insight sheds light on the ideology of language in the family as well as on theoretical approaches to discourse. In particular, I question the prevailing inclination to approach family interaction as exclusively, or primarily, a struggle for power. I argue – and, I hope, demonstrate – that power is inseparable from connection. Therefore, in exploring how family interaction is mediated by gender-related patterns of discourse, I also suggest that gender identity is negotiated along the dual, paradoxically related, dimensions of power and connection.

2. Power and Connection in the Family: Prior Research

Researchers routinely interpret family interaction through an ideology of the family as the locus of a struggle for power. In my view, this ideology needs to

The Handbook of Language, Gender, and Sexuality, Second Edition.
Edited by Susan Ehrlich, Miriam Meyerhoff, and Janet Holmes.
© 2014 John Wiley & Sons, Inc. Published 2017 by John Wiley & Sons, Inc.

be reframed. Power is inextricably intertwined with connection. Discourse in the family can be seen as a struggle for power, yes, but it is also – and equally – a struggle for connection. Indeed, the family is a prime example – perhaps *the* prime example – of the nexus of power and connection in human relationships. Thus, a study of gender and family interaction becomes a means not only to understand gender and language more deeply but also to reveal, contest, and reframe the ideology of the family and of power in discourse.

Early research on discourse in family interaction focused on power. The earliest, Richard Watts's *Power in Family Discourse* (1991), was unique in analyzing conversations involving adult siblings and their spouses rather than the nuclear family of parents and young children living in a single household. For Watts, as his title suggests, power is the force defining familial relations. A year later, Hervé Varenne's *Ambiguous Harmony* (1992) examined a conversation that took place on a single evening in the living room of a blended family: mother, father, and two children – a teenage son from the mother's previous marriage and a younger child born to this couple. Varenne (1992, 76), too, saw power as the central dynamic, explaining: "The power we are interested in here is the power of the catalyst who, with a minimal amount of its own energy, gets other entities to spend large amounts of their own."

Shoshana Blum-Kulka's *Dinner Talk* (1997) indirectly addressed the interrelationship of power and connection in the family. Comparing dinner conversations in three cultural contexts – Americans of east European Jewish background, Israelis of east European Jewish background, and Israeli families in which the parents were born and raised in the United States – she examined the parents' dual and sometimes conflicting needs both to socialize their children in the sense of teaching them how to behave properly (hence, power), and at the same time to socialize with them in the sense of enjoying their company (hence, connection).

Millar, Rogers, and Bavelas (1984, 232) write of "control maneuvers" and note that in interpersonal relationships, conflict takes place "within the power dimension of relationships." I neither deny nor question this assumption, but I would complexify it by emphasizing that power and solidarity are in paradoxical and mutually constitutive relationship to each other. Thus family interaction (including conflict) also takes place within the intimacy dimension, and we can also speak of "connection maneuvers." My goal in this chapter is to explicate how what researchers would typically regard as control (that is, power) maneuvers can also be seen as connection maneuvers, in part because connection and control are bought with the same linguistic currency.

3. The Ambiguity and Polysemy of Hierarchy and Connection

Elsewhere (Tannen 1994), I explore and argue for the ambiguity and polysemy of power and solidarity – or, in different terms, of hierarchy and connection. Here I briefly recap the analysis developed in that and other essays.

In conventional wisdom, as well as in research tracing back to Brown and Gilman's (1960) classic study of power and solidarity, Americans have tended to conceptualize the relationship between hierarchy (or power) and connection (or solidarity) as unidimensional and mutually exclusive. In this view, family relationships are seen as prototypically close, so Americans frequently use the terms "sisters," "brothers," and "family" to indicate "close and equal." If someone says "We are like sisters," "He is like a brother to me," or "They're like family," the implication is, "We are close, and we are comfortable together – no status games, no one-upping." The prototypical hierarchical relationship, in this schema, is also distant: boss and underling.

In contrast, for members of many other cultures, such as Japanese, Chinese, and Javanese, the archetypal hierarchical relationship is the parent–child constellation: extremely hierarchical but also extremely close. By the same token, sibling relationships may or may not be close but their relative ages always affect their relationships. In reality, then, power (or hierarchy) and solidarity (or connection) do not fall on a single continuum with hierarchy and distance at one end and equality and connection at the other. Instead, they must be conceptualized as a grid with two axes: a vertical axis with hierarchy at one end and equality at the other, and a horizontal axis running between the poles of closeness and distance. Conversations, and relationships, can be positioned anywhere on the grid, resulting in complex combinations of hierarchy and connection.

Understanding how language functions to negotiate hierarchy and connection in interaction must begin with the awareness that these two dynamics are ambiguous and polysemous. They are ambiguous because an utterance can express one or the other; they are polysemous because an utterance can express both at once. Here is a brief, quotidian example. On a chilly fall day, I was walking with a colleague, a woman, when we spotted an older colleague walking toward us. My companion greeted him and asked, cheerily, "Where's your coat?" He replied, "Thanks, Mom." She was taken aback by his remark, since she had intended her greeting in the spirit of connection. But her question "Where's your coat?" was ambiguous: in addition to being a friendly greeting, it could also be a mother's protective reminder to a child. In this case, it was also polysemous: it functioned as a friendly greeting, thereby positioning the two colleagues toward the closeness end of the closeness–distance axis, but it simultaneously reminded her addressee of a mother's warning to a child, thereby positioning the interlocutors closer to the hierarchical end of the hierarchy–equality axis. I doubt it was a coincidence that the speaker who was focused on the connection level of her remark was a woman, while the one who focused on the hierarchy level was a man, but I cite the exchange here only to illustrate my notion of ambiguity and polysemy.

4. Mother: A Paradigm of the Ambiguity and Polysemy of Power and Connection

It is no coincidence, moreover, that the coatless professor in the preceding example perceived a hierarchical positioning in terms of a family constellation, specifically a mother–child relationship. The family is a key locus for understanding the complex and inextricable relationship between power (negotiations along the hierarchy–equality axis) and connection (negotiations along the closeness–distance axis). And nowhere does this relationship become clearer than in the role of a key family member, the mother. For example, Hildred Geertz (1989 [1961], 20) writes that there are, in Javanese, "two major levels of language, respect and familiarity." She observes that children use the familiar register when speaking with their parents and siblings until about age 10 or 12, when they gradually shift to respect in adulthood. However, she adds, "Most people continue to speak to the mother in the same way as they did as children; a few shift to respect in adulthood" (22). This leaves open the question whether mothers are addressed in the familiar register because they receive less respect than fathers, or because their children feel closer to them. I suspect it is both at once, and that trying to pick these motivations apart may be futile.

Although the linguistic encoding of respect and familiarity as morphologically distinct registers is a phenomenon not found in English, nonetheless there are phenomena in English that parallel those described by Geertz. Ervin-Tripp, O'Connor, and Rosenberg (1984) looked at "control acts" in families in order to gauge power in that context. They found that "effective power and esteem were related to age" (134). Again, however, "the mothers in our sample were an important exception to the pattern" (135). "In their role as caregivers," the authors note, mothers "received nondeferent orders, suggesting that the children expected compliance and believed their desires to be justification enough." As with Javanese, one could ask whether children use more bald imperatives when speaking to their mothers because they have less respect for them, or because they feel closer to them, or (as I suspect) both.

Recent research has seen an increase in interest in the discourse of mothers, especially in interaction with daughters (Dills 1998; Gordon 2002; 2007; Kendall 2008; Schiffrin 2000; 2002; Tannen 2006). Though far less attention has focused on the discourse of fathers (but see Gordon, Tannen, and Sacknovitz 2007; Marinova 2007), comparisons of mothers' and fathers' discourse have emerged not only from the Georgetown Work–Family Project (Tannen, Kendall, and Gordon 2007) but also from a larger study, led by Elinor Ochs at the UCLA Center on the Everyday Lives of Families (Ochs and Kremer-Sadlik 2013). Many of the papers that examine mothers' or fathers' discourse, or compare the two, directly or indirectly examine the interrelationship of power and connection. For example, Ochs and Campos (2013) observed that when parents returned home from work, their children frequently failed to greet them because they were distracted by screen media. The authors note that when a parent's greeting (a connection maneuver) is not reciprocated, the elder is showing respect to the younger, a reversal of the expected hierarchy-related exchange.

5. Power Lines – or Connection Lines – in Telling Your Day

A great deal of the research on family discourse has focused on talk produced in the context of dinner table conversation. The dinner table is a favorite site, no doubt, both because dinner is a prime time that family members typically come together and exchange talk, and also because it is a bounded event for which speakers gather around a table and which is therefore relatively easy to record. Both Blum-Kulka (1997) and Elinor Ochs and her students (e.g., Ochs and Taylor 1992) identify a ritual that typifies American dinner table conversation in many families: a ritual that Blum-Kulka dubs "telling your day." When the family includes a mother and father (as the families recorded in both these studies did), mothers typically encourage children to tell their fathers about events experienced during the day.

Ochs and Taylor (1992, 310) give the examples of a mother who urges, "Tell Dad what you thought about gymnastics and what you did," and another who prompts, "Chuck did you tell Daddy what happened at karate when you came in your new uniform? What did Daisy do for you?" The authors note that in a majority of the instances recorded in this study, fathers responded to the resultant stories by passing judgment, assessing the rightness of their children's actions and feelings, and thereby setting up a constellation the researchers call "father knows best."

In the families Ochs and her students observed, mothers usually knew what the children had to say. This was true even of mothers who worked full-time, because generally they had arrived home from work earlier than the father, and they had asked the children about their day during the time they had with them before Daddy came home. (Later research by Ochs and her colleagues supported this pattern with a larger sample; Ochs and Campos (2013) note that among the 32 families studied, fathers came home on average two hours later than mothers; during weekdays, mothers were the first to make contact with children more than three-quarters of the time, fathers less than one-quarter.) At the dinner table, Father could have asked "How was your day?" just as Mother did before dinner. But in these families, he usually didn't.

Ochs and Taylor (1992) identify the roles in these narrative exchanges as "problematizer" and "problematizee." The problematizer reacts to a family member's account of an experience in a way that is critical of how the speaker handled the situation. For example, when an eight-year-old child, Josh, who has been doing homework, announced, "I'm done," his father asked in a "disbelieving tone," "Already Josh? Read me what you wrote." Thus the father questioned whether Josh really was finished or not (313). In Ochs and Taylor's terms, he "problematized" Josh's announcement "I'm done."

The family power structure, Ochs and Taylor observe, is established in these storytelling dynamics. Just as Mother typically prompted a child to tell Daddy what happened, older siblings were much more likely to urge younger ones to tell about something that happened than the other way around. In this sense, older siblings were treating their younger siblings more or less the way parents treat children (a pattern that I observed in my own research on siblings (Tannen 2009) and that, I also observed, younger siblings often perceive and resent).

Ochs and Taylor found that children were most often problematizees – the ones whose behavior was judged by others. Rarely were they problematizers – the ones who questioned others' behavior as problematic. This puts children firmly at the bottom of the hierarchy. Fathers were the most frequent problematizers and rarely were problematizees: rarely was their behavior held up to the scrutiny and judgment of others. This puts them firmly at the top of the hierarchy. Mothers, however, were not up there, as parents, along with fathers. Instead, mothers found themselves in the position of problematizee (the one whose behavior was held up for judgment) as often as they were problematizer (the one who was judging others). Thus fathers judged their wives' actions in addition to their children's, but mothers judged only their children's behavior, not their husbands'. The storytelling dynamic placed mothers in the middle of the family hierarchy – over the children, but under the father.

The authors also observe that mothers often problematized their own actions. For example, a woman named Marie owned and ran a day care center. At dinner, she told of a client who was taking her child out of the center, and paid her last bill. The client handed over more money than was needed to cover the time her child had spent in day care, so Marie returned the excess. But she later wondered whether she had made a mistake. After all, her policy required clients to give two weeks' notice before withdrawing a child, and this mother had not given notice. So perhaps the client had intended the overpayment to cover those two weeks, and Marie should have kept it, enforcing her policy. The father made clear that he endorsed this view: "When I say something I stick to it unless she brings it up … I do not change it" (Ochs and Taylor 1992, 312). Marie was the problematizee because her action was called into question. She had problematized herself by raising the issue of whether she had handled the situation in the best way; her husband then further problematized her by letting her know that he thought she had not. Ochs and Taylor found that this pattern was common: if mothers questioned their own actions, fathers often "dumped on" them by reinforcing the conclusion that the mothers had not acted properly. In contrast, the authors found that in the rare instances when fathers problematized themselves, mothers did not further problematize them.

Ochs and Taylor thus identify a crucial dynamic in middle-class American families by which the family is a power structure with the father at the top. They further show that mothers play a crucial role in setting up this dynamic: "Father as problematizer," they argue, is "facilitated … by the active role of mothers who sometimes (perhaps inadvertently) set fathers up as potential problematizers – by introducing the stories and reports of children and mothers in the first place and orienting them towards fathers as primary recipients" (1992, 329). For me, the most important word in this excerpt is "inadvertently." I would argue that the "father knows best" dynamic results from gender differences in assumptions about the place of talk in a relationship, and that it reflects the ambiguity and polysemy of hierarchy and connection. When a mother asks her children what they did during the day, she is creating closeness by exchanging details of daily life, a verbal ritual frequently observed to characterize women's friendships (see, e.g., Coates 1996; Tannen 1990) and family relationships (Tannen 2006; 2009). In this sense, it is a connection maneuver. If the father does not ask "How was your day?" it does not mean that he is not interested in his family, or does not feel – or wish to be – close to them. It may only mean that he does not assume that closeness is created by the verbal ritual of telling the details of one's day.

When Mother prods a child, "Tell Daddy what you did in karate today," she is, it is true, initiating a dynamic by which the father will assess the child's actions and thus be installed as the family judge. But I would bet that her goal is to *involve* the father in the family, bring him into the circle of intimacy she feels is established by such talk. From this point of view, the "father knows best" dynamic is as much a misfire as is the common source of frustration between women and men that I have described elsewhere (Tannen 1990): a woman tells a man about a frustrating experience she had that day, performing a ritual common among women friends that Gail Jefferson (1988) dubs "troubles talk." Since troubles talk is not a ritual common among men friends, he thinks he is being asked to solve the problem, which he proceeds to do – to her frustration. She protests, which frustrates him. Similarly, the mother who prods her children to tell their father what they did that day, or who talks about her own day, is trying to create connection. But the father, not recognizing the ritual nature of her comment, thinks he is being asked to judge.

In this view, it is not the mothers' initiation of the "telling your day" routine in itself that sets fathers up as family judge. Instead, the "father knows best" dynamic is created by the interaction of gender-related patterns. Fathers take the role of judge of actions recounted in stories because they presume that's why they are being told the stories. Fathers are less likely to talk about their own work problems because they don't want advice about how to solve problems there, so they see no reason to talk about them. Many men feel that rehashing what upset them at work forces them to relive it and get upset all over again, when they'd rather put it out of their minds and enjoy the oasis of home. They may also resist telling about problems precisely to avoid being placed in the one-down position of receiving advice or of being told that they did not handle the situation in the best way. On the few occasions that Ochs and Taylor found fathers problematizing themselves, it is no surprise that mothers did not further dump on them – not necessarily because mothers felt they had no right to judge, but more likely because they took these revelations in the spirit of troubles talk rather than as invitations to pass judgment. These clashing rituals result in mothers finding themselves one-down in the family hierarchy without knowing how they got there.

Wagner (2010) applies Ochs and Taylor's framework to the discourse of seven lesbian families, replacing the term "problematizing" with the term "evaluating" to further distinguish between positive and negative responses. She found that in five of the seven families, one parent evaluated the other's speech and actions more often than the reverse, and in all but one of these cases, negative evaluations accounted for the imbalance, whereas positive evaluations were equally distributed or nearly so. (Of the other two families, one was evenly balanced, and one had almost no evaluations at all.) This suggests that gender is not the only factor influencing the "telling your day" family ritual, though another of Wagner's (2010, 33) findings is suggestive of another frequently observed gender-related conversational pattern: she found "a high incidence of joint elicitation and narration by the parents, and an active attempt to include children in conversations."

I have discussed the Ochs and Taylor example at length to demonstrate how gender-related patterns of discourse can explain a phenomenon observed in family interaction in prior research, and how what has been accurately identified as a matter of negotiating power is also simultaneously and inextricably a matter of negotiating connection. This analysis supports my contentions that (1) power and connection are inextricably intertwined; (2) the relationship between power and connection is fundamental to an understanding of gender and language; and (3) the relationship between gender and language is fundamental to an understanding of family interaction.

6. Self-Revelation: A Gender-Specific Conversational Ritual

The "telling your day" ritual, for many women, is just one way that connection is created and maintained through talk. Another way is exchanging information about personal relationships and emotions. Here, too, conversations that take place in families reflect the divergent expectations of family members of different genders.

One way that many women create and maintain closeness is by keeping tabs on each other's lives, including (perhaps especially) romantic relationships. When male and female family members interact, gender differences in expectations regarding the use of talk to create closeness can lead to unbalanced interchanges. The following example, which comes from the Georgetown Work–Family Project, illustrates just such a conversation. In this example, one of the project participants recorded a conversation with her unmarried brother. The sister (a woman in her thirties) is asking her brother (who is a few years younger) about his girlfriend, Kerry. Clearly the sister is looking for a kind of interchange that her brother is not providing:

Sister:	So how's things with Kerry?
Brother:	Cool.
Sister:	Cool. Does that mean very good?
Brother:	Yeah.
Sister:	True love?
Brother:	Pretty much.
Sister:	PRETTY much? When you say PRETTY much, what do you mean?
Brother:	I mean it's all good.

The conversation takes on an almost comic character, as the sister becomes more and more probing in reaction to her brother's minimal responses. Evident in the example is a process I call, adapting a term that Gregory Bateson (1972) applied to larger cultural processes, complementary schismogenesis. By this process, each person's verbal behavior drives the other to more and more exaggerated forms of an opposing behavior. In this example, the sister asks repeated and increasingly probing questions *because* her brother's responses are minimal, and his responses may well become more guarded *because* her questions become increasingly insistent. Indeed, she starts to sound a bit like an inquisitor.

Moreover, this conversation between sister and brother sounds rather like a mother talking to a teenage child. (Recall that the sister is older.) It is strikingly similar to the conversation represented in the next example, which took place between a mother and her 12-year-old daughter. This conversational excerpt was identified and analyzed by Alla Tovares in connection with a seminar I taught on family interaction. The excerpt comes from a documentary made by filmmaker Jennifer Fox entitled *An American Love Story*. The documentary aired in five two-hour segments on the United States' Public Broadcasting System in September 1999. In preparing the documentary, Fox followed the family of Karen Wilson, Bill Sims, and their two daughters, in Queens, New York, over two years beginning in 1992. In this episode, the younger daughter, Chaney, was anticipating her first "date" – a daytime walk – with a boy, despite her parents' misgivings. The boy (who was 13) failed to appear on the appointed day. After the entire family spent several hours waiting for him, Chaney got a telephone call explaining that his grandmother had refused permission for him to go. Karen tries to discuss this development with Chaney, who responds minimally:

Karen:	That's too bad. Aren't you mad?
Chaney:	No.
Karen:	I mean just in general.
Chaney:	What do you mean?
Karen:	Not at him, just in general.
Chaney:	No, not that much.
Karen:	Disappointed?
Chaney:	No, not that much.
Karen:	Relieved?
Chaney:	No. [*laughs*]
Karen:	What- [*also laughing*]
	Give us a feeling here, Chaney!

Through her questions and comments, Karen is showing her daughter the kind of conversation she expects to have – one in which Chaney tells how she felt about what happened. I doubt that Chaney is unable to hold such conversations; I would bet she has them frequently with her best friend, Nelly. But, like many teenagers, she seems reluctant to divulge her feelings to her mother.

On a later day, the boy shows up unexpectedly, and Chaney goes out for a walk with him. When she returns, a similar conversation ensues. The trouble starts immediately, as Chaney heads for her room:

Karen:	Come sit and tell us all about it.
Chaney:	I have to call Nelly.
Karen:	Come, tell us all about it first.
	I am your first priority here.

Chaney complies by sitting down, but she volunteers nothing. She offers only cryptic and minimally informative answers to her mother's questions. Throughout the conversation, Chaney laughs or chuckles.

Karen: Did he hold your hand?
Chaney: Yeah. [*laughs*]
Karen: How did that feel?
Chaney: His hands were cold.
Karen: Did you kiss?
Chaney: Yeah.
Karen: Where?
Chaney: Where do you think? [*chuckling*]
Karen: On your lip?
Chaney: Just a short one.
Karen: [*whispering*] Oh my god!
                [*normal voice*] Where. At our door?
Chaney: Yeah.
Karen: What did you think?
Chaney: Nothing.
Karen: Did you have any feelings about it?
Chaney: Yeah.
Karen: A good one or a bad one, or a stupid one?
Chaney: Good.
Karen: Wh- When are you going to see him?
Chaney: Mmm, probably in June.
Karen: Mm, that's nice and safe.
Chaney: [*laughing and trying to get up*] Bye!
Karen: So are you happy to see him?
Chaney: Yeah.
Karen: Is he the same you thought he would be?
Chaney: He's just the same.

At this point, Chaney rises and retreats to her room. To learn how she felt about her date, we would have to listen in on her conversation with Nelly. And that must be a source of frustration to Karen as it would be to most mothers of teenagers. Although Chaney answered her mother's questions, the interchange, like the exchange between brother and sister in the preceding example, feels more like an interrogation than a conversation.

Why is the mother in this example and the sister in the earlier one so intent on getting a family member to divulge feelings? I have argued elsewhere (Tannen 1990), drawing on a large body of language and gender research, that women and girls typically define their relationships with friends along the connection axis: best friends tell each other "everything." (See Eckert, Chapter 27, and Goodwin and Kyratzis, Chapter 26, in this volume, for a somewhat different view on girls' linguistic practices.) This includes not only large and small life events but also how they feel about those events. They define and evaluate family relationships the same way: a good relationship is a "close" one, and that means a relationship in which one tells the other what is happening in one's life, and how one *feels* about it. When children are small, the confidences go one way: mothers want to know what their children are experiencing and feeling, though they typically do not confide their own feelings to their small children. When daughters become adults, however, as noted by Henwood (1993) and as I found in my own research (Tannen 2006), both daughters and mothers typically evaluate their relationship in terms of how "close" they are – and this is gauged by relative mutual revelation about feelings. I found a similar pattern among adult sisters (Tannen 2008; 2009): complaints often focused on a sister's failure to reveal personal information and/or feelings about them.

7. Balancing Power and Connection in a Family Argument

In this section, I examine several examples from the family discourse recorded by another of the couples in the Georgetown Work–Family project. In each of the following examples, the mother and father use complex verbal strategies to balance the needs to negotiate both power and connection as they go about the tasks required to maintain the daily life of their young family. In addition, their discourse strategies simultaneously create gender-related parental identities.

The couple, Kathy and Sam, have a two-year-old daughter, Kira. Both parents work outside the home, Sam full-time and Kathy a reduced schedule of 30 hours per week. Each regularly takes off one day a week to spend with Kira, who attends day care only three days a week. One day, Kathy and Sam are both at home, Kathy in the kitchen by herself and Sam taking care of Kira in another room, when he calls out:

> Sam: Kathy! Kath! Let's switch.
>   You take care of her.
>   I'll do whatever you're doing.

Kathy responds from the kitchen, "I'm making popcorn," then adds, "You always burn it."

Clearly what is at stake, and what ensues, can be understood as a series of control maneuvers. Sam wants to switch roles with Kathy, so she will take over childcare and he will take over popcorn preparation. Kathy resists this switch. In a direct confrontation over power, she might simply refuse: "No, I don't want to switch." Instead, by saying "You always burn it," she resists relinquishing her task by appealing to the good of the family rather than her personal preference. Insofar as she resists doing what Sam wants her to do, her statement is a control maneuver. But to the extent that she appeals to the family good, it is a connection maneuver. At the same time, however, by impugning Sam's popcorn-making ability, she is putting him down, a hierarchy-inflected move.

Because Kathy has based her resistance on her husband's putative deficiency, he responds on this level:

> Sam: No I don't!
>   I never burn it.
>   I make it perfect.

Although they continue to exchange accusations, self-defense, and counterac-cusations about popcorn-making skills, Sam and Kathy execute the switch: Sam takes over in the kitchen, and Kathy takes charge of Kira. However, she continues to try to engineer her return to the kitchen. In this endeavor, she addresses the two-year-old:

Kathy: You wanna help Mommy make popcorn?
Kira: Okay.
Kathy: Let's not let Daddy do it.
Kira: Okay.
Kathy: Okay, come on.

Here, again, Kathy's utterances are a blend of power and connection. Insofar as she is trying to get her way and regain control of the popcorn preparation Kathy is engaged in control maneuvers. But by suggesting that Kira "help Mommy make popcorn," she is proposing to satisfy both herself and her husband: she would thereby return to the kitchen, yes, but she would also fulfill Sam's request, "You take care of her." Moreover, by involving Kira in the plan, Kathy is involving the child in the interaction. Furthermore, her linguistic choices ("Let's not let Daddy do it") align herself with her daughter: "Let's" merges mother and daughter; "not let" includes the child in the mother's perspective as someone who has authority over Sam's actions; and "Daddy" adopts the child's point of view in referring to her husband. All these are connection maneuvers, though they create connection to Kira rather than Sam.

From the kitchen, Sam overhears this conversation and resists in turn. While Kathy continues to urge their daughter to accompany her, Sam follows a strategy of "the best defense is a good offense":

Sam: I know how to make popcorn!
Kathy: Let's hurry up so Daddy doesn't ...
Sam: I can make popcorn better than you can!

The argument between Kathy and Sam continues, as Sam retains the role of chef and maintains that his performance in this role is successful, while Kathy becomes increasingly apprehensive of impending failure:

Kathy: Just heat it! Heat it!
        No, I don't want you ...
Sam: It's going, it's going. Hear it?
Kathy: It's too slow.
        It's all soaking in.
        You hear that little ...
Sam: It's not soaking in, it's fine.
Kathy: It's just a few kernels.
Sam: All the popcorn is being popped!

Soon Kathy tries another strategy to regain control of the kitchen, or to salvage the popcorn, or both:

> Kathy: You gotta take the trash outside.
> Sam: I can't, I'm doing the popcorn.
> Kathy: I'll DO it, I'll watch it.
> You take the trash out
> and come back in a few minutes and –

Again, Kathy proposes to reclaim the popcorn preparation, but she phrases her proposal in a way that seems to benefit him rather than her: she'll help Sam do his job of taking out the trash. This reframes the meaning of her taking over popcorn-making as temporarily spelling Sam while he fulfills another obligation.

In the end, Sam keeps control of the popcorn – and it burns. This result lends credence to Kathy's reluctance to accede to his request to do it. What is interesting for my purposes here, however, is how Kathy's attempts to prevent this outcome are a blend of control and connection maneuvers.

Another aspect of this example that intrigues me is Kathy's use of Kira as addressee in her negotiation with Sam over popcorn-making. When Kathy said "Let's not let Daddy do it," she communicates her wishes to her husband by addressing their child. By involving a third party, her attempt to get her way (a control maneuver) becomes less directly confrontational (the power play is mitigated) and also entails aligning herself with Kira (a connection maneuver).

In the next example, Kathy is at home with Kira when she hears Sam's car approaching the house. (Kendall's (2006) study of dinnertime homecomings includes analysis of this exchange.) Kathy prepares Kira for her father's arrival in a way that seems designed to inspire excitement and anticipation, encouraging involvement between the child and her father in much the same way that mothers do when they encourage children to tell their fathers about their day.

> Kathy: Daddy's home.
> Kira: Da da.
> Kathy: Daddy's gonna be home in a minute.
> Kira: Da da pop.
> Da da pop.
> Da da pop.
> Kathy: You gonna give Da da a pop?
> Kira: Yes. Shoes. Shoes. ahh.
> Kathy: You gonna tell Daddy to take his shoes off?

In this interchange, Kathy is negotiating connection by orienting Kira toward integrating the father into the family circle. Kira's minimal utterances, "Da da pop" and "Shoes," could be interpreted in many different ways. The expansions Kathy supplies ("You gonna give Da da a [fruit] pop?" and "You gonna tell Daddy to take his shoes off?") frame Kira's words as plans to involve her father in interaction. This too negotiates connection.

When Sam enters the house, however, he is tired, hungry, and out of sorts. As he sits at the table trying to eat something, Kira tries to climb on him, and he has a momentary eruption of irritation:

Sam: No! I'm eating! [*very irritated*]
         Daddy eats. [*conciliatory*]
Kira: [*cries*]
Kathy: O::h. [*sympathetic tone*]
Sam: Da da eats. [*more conciliatory*]
Kira: [*cries louder*]
Sam: Wanna come up?

In a sense, Sam's first three statements are control maneuvers: he wants to prevent Kira from doing what she wants to do – climb into his lap. But the progression of modifications to his linguistic strategies evince a subtle negotiation of closeness. When Kira begins to wail, Sam retreats from his refusal and ends up inviting her to climb on him ("Wanna come up?"). In building up to that invitation, he repeats the reason for his initial resistance three times: that he is eating. But each time he repeats this proposition, the way he words it and the tone in which he speaks bring him closer to his daughter.

The first iteration, "I'm eating!" is spoken in a very irritated tone and is preceded by the harsh injunction "No!" Furthermore, in using the first-person pronoun "I," Sam describes what he is doing from his own point of view. This contrasts with the perspective of his next iteration, "Daddy eats." Not only is this statement spoken in a more conciliatory tone, as if he is trying to make amends for the harshness of his previous burst of annoyance, but he also shifts to Kira's perspective when he says "Daddy eats." "Daddy" identifies him from his daughter's point of view, not his own. The third repetition, "Da da eats," moves even closer to the child's perspective, since "Da da" is what she calls him. These linguistic forms bring the father progressively closer to the child's perspective, even as he is softening in his resistance to her attempt to climb on him, and moving toward offering her what she wanted (but no longer wants now that he has made her cry). Sam's responses to Kira, then, in these few brief lines, are a subtle negotiation of power and connection.

At this point, Kathy joins the interaction in a way that blends power and connection in particularly complex and intriguing ways. She explains to Sam why Kira is crying, indirectly chastising him for causing this reaction. At the same time, she explains Kira's own feelings to her and suggests how she might, when she learns to talk, use words rather than tears to express those feelings and get her way. Because Kathy does all this by talking through Kira, she is connecting the three of them as a family unit:

Kathy: She got her feelings hurt.
         ...
         I think she just wanted
         some Daddy's attention.

> You were missing Daddy today, weren't you?
> You were missing Daddy, weren't you?
> Can you say,
> "I was just missing you Daddy
> that was all?"

Kira: [*cries*] Nnno.
Kathy: And I don't really feel too good.
Kira: [*cries*] No.
Kathy: No, she doesn't feel too good either.

Just as Sam moved progressively closer to Kira's point of view as he repeated his explanation that he was eating, in this example Kathy's repeated explanations of why Kira is crying follow the same progression. In the first line ("She got her feelings hurt"), Kathy speaks of Kira in the third person, so mother and daughter are linguistically distinct. She next addresses Kira directly ("You were missing Daddy, weren't you?"), bringing her into alignment with the child. She then models for Kira what the child might say to articulate her own feelings ("Can you say, 'I was just missing you, Daddy, that was all?'"). By animating Kira's feelings from the child's point of view ("And I don't really feel too good"), Kathy linguistically merges with her daughter. Finally, she mitigates her alignment with Kira and reorients to Sam by addressing him and referring to Kira rather than animating her ("No, she doesn't feel too good either").

Kathy's explanation of why Kira is crying ("She got her feelings hurt") is an indirect criticism because it implies that Sam should not hurt his daughter's feelings. After a short amount of intervening talk, she makes this injunction more explicit:

Kathy: Why are you so edgy?
Sam: Cause I haven't eaten yet.
Kathy: Why didn't you get a *snack*
         on the way home or something?
         Save your family a little stress.
Kira: Mm mm
Kathy: Yeah give us a break, Daddy.
         We just miss you.
         We try to get your attention
         and then you come home
         and you go ROW ROW ROW ROW.
Kira: Row Row!

This last example is especially fascinating as an instance of what I call ventriloquizing – communicating to a second party by animating the voice of a third. Whereas Sam speaks only for himself ("I haven't eaten yet"), Kathy speaks for (and as) Kira when she says "We just miss you. We try to get your attention … " Then, still speaking as Kira, she mimics how Sam comes across from Kira's point of view: "you go ROW ROW ROW ROW." In this utterance, Kathy is animating Kira animating Sam. So the linguistic strategy by which Kathy tells

Sam that he should alter his behavior (a control maneuver) also linguistically merges the three of them (a connection maneuver).

8. Gender and Family Interaction: Coda

In all these examples, I have tried to show that whereas family interaction is, as researchers have assumed and shown, an ongoing power struggle, it is also simultaneously an ongoing struggle for connection. Furthermore, family interaction is a continuing negotiation of gender identities and roles. In analyses of the interactions tape-recorded by this family as well as others in the study, Kendall (2007) has shown that whereas both mothers and fathers espouse an ideology of equal co-parenting and wage-earning, in their ways of speaking the mothers frequently position themselves as primary childcare providers and their husbands as breadwinners. Alexandra Johnston (2007), the research team member who spent time with Kathy and Sam and transcribed their conversations, observed that one way Kathy positions herself as primary caretaker is by frequently correcting Sam's parenting, whereas Sam rarely corrects hers. This, indeed, is what Kathy is doing in the last example by implicitly criticizing Sam for hurting Kira's feelings and by suggesting that he "save [his] family a little stress" by getting a snack on the way home.

In this way, the final example, like all those preceding it, illustrates that we need to understand family interaction – like all human interaction – not only as negotiations for power but also as negotiations for connection. Given the ambiguity and polysemy of power and connection, linguistic strategies that can be identified as control maneuvers must also be examined as connection maneuvers. Power and connection are the dimensions along which human relationships are negotiated, and they are inextricably intertwined with the way gender identity is negotiated. Thus an appreciation of the interplay of power and connection, and of the ways power and connection underlie gender identity and gender performance, is necessary to understand family interaction as well as the relationship between gender and language.

Acknowledgments

The project by which four families tape-recorded their own conversations for a week each was supported by an initial grant from the Alfred P. Sloan Foundation to me and Shari Kendall and a subsequent grant to me, Kendall, and Cynthia Gordon. For this support I am deeply grateful to the Sloan Foundation and to project officer Kathleen Christensen. I also thank project members Alexandra Johnston and Cynthia Gordon, the research team members who worked with the families whose talk I have cited here, and who transcribed and identified the examples that I cite. My discussion of the Ochs and Taylor example is adapted from my discussion of the same example in my book *I Only Say This Because I Love You* © 2001 by Deborah

Tannen, reprinted by permission of Random House, an imprint of The Random House Publishing Group, a division of Random House LLC.

REFERENCES

Bateson, Gregory. 1972. "A Theory of Play and Fantasy." In *Steps to an Ecology of Mind*, 177–193. New York: Ballantine Books.

Blum-Kulka, Shoshana. 1997. *Dinner Talk: Cultural Patterns of Sociability and Socialization in Family Discourse*. Mahwah, NJ: Lawrence Erlbaum.

Brown, Roger, and Albert Gilman. 1960. "The Pronouns of Power and Solidarity." In Thomas Sebeok (ed.), *Style in Language*, 253–276. Cambridge, MA: MIT Press.

Coates, Jennifer. 1996. *Women Talk*. Oxford: Blackwell.

Dills, Vivian Lee. 1998. "Transferring and Transforming Cultural Norms: A Mother–Daughter Lifestory in Progress." *Narrative Inquiry*, 8(1): 213–222.

Ervin-Tripp, Susan, Mary Catherine O'Connor, and Jarrett Rosenberg. 1984. "Language and Power in the Family." In Cheris Kramarae, Muriel Schultz, and William M. O'Barr (eds.), *Language and Power*, 116–135. New York: Sage.

Geertz, Hildred. 1989 [1961]. *The Javanese Family: A Study of Kinship and Socialization*. Prospect Heights, IL: Waveland Press.

Gordon, Cynthia. 2002. "'I'm Mommy and You're Natalie': Role-Reversal and Embedded Frames in Mother–Child Discourse." *Language in Society*, 31(5): 679–720.

Gordon, Cynthia. 2007. "'I Just Feel Horribly Embarrassed When She Does That': Constituting a Mother's Identity." In Deborah Tannen, Shari Kendall, and Cynthia Gordon (eds.), *Family Talk: Discourse and Identity in Four American Families*, 71–101. New York: Oxford University Press.

Gordon, Cynthia, Deborah Tannen, and Aliza Sacknovitz. 2007. "A Working Father: One Man's Talk about Parenting at Work." In Deborah Tannen, Shari Kendall, and Cynthia Gordon (eds.), *Family Talk: Discourse and Identity in Four American Families*, 195–230. New York: Oxford University Press.

Henwood, Karen L. 1993. "Women and Later Life: The Discursive Construction of Identities within Family Relationships." *Journal of Aging Studies*, 7(3): 303–319.

Jefferson, Gail. 1988. "On the Sequential Organization of Troubles-Talk in Ordinary Conversation." *Social Problems*, 35(4): 418–441.

Johnston, Alexandra. 2007. "Gatekeeping in the Family: How Family Members Position One Another as Decision Makers." In Deborah Tannen, Shari Kendall, and Cynthia Gordon (eds.), *Family Talk: Discourse and Identity in Four American Families*, 165–193. New York: Oxford University Press.

Kendall, Shari. 2006. "'Honey, I'm Home!' Framing in Family Dinnertime Homecomings." *Text & Talk*, 26(4–5): 411–441.

Kendall, Shari. 2007. "Father as Breadwinner, Mother as Worker: Gendered Positions in Feminist and Traditional Discourses of Work and Family." In Deborah Tannen, Shari Kendall, and Cynthia Gordon (eds.), *Family Talk: Discourse and Identity in Four American Families*, 123–163. New York: Oxford University Press.

Kendall, Shari. 2008. "The Balancing Act: Framing Gendered Parental Identities at Dinnertime." *Language in Society*, 37(4): 539–568.

Key, Mary Ritchie. 1975. *Male/Female Language: With a Comprehensive Bibliography*. Metuchen, NJ: Scarecrow Press.

Lakoff, Robin. 1975. *Language and Woman's Place*. New York: Harper & Row.

Marinova, Diana. 2007. "Finding the Right Balance between Connection and Control: A Father's Identity Construction in Conversation with his College-Age Daughter." In Deborah Tannen, Shari Kendall, and Cynthia Gordon (eds.), *Family Talk: Discourse and Identity in Four American Families*, 103–120. New York: Oxford University Press.

Millar, Frank E., Edna L. Rogers, and Janet Beavin Bavelas. 1984. "Identifying Patterns of Verbal Conflict in Interpersonal Dynamics." *Western Journal of Speech Communication*, 48: 231–246.

Ochs, Elinor, and Belinda Campos. 2013. "Coming Home." In Elinor Ochs and Tamar Kremer-Sadlik (eds.), *Fast Forward Family: Home, Work, and Relationships in Middle Class America*, 13–26. Berkeley: University of California Press.

Ochs, Elinor, and Tamar Kremer-Sadlik, eds. 2013. *Fast Forward Family: Home, Work, and Relationships in Middle Class America*. Berkeley: University of California Press.

Ochs, Elinor, and Carolyn Taylor. 1992. "Family Narrative as Political Activity." *Discourse & Society*, 3(3): 301–340.

Schiffrin, Deborah. 2000. "Mother/Daughter Discourse in a Holocaust Survivor Oral History: 'Because Then You Admit that You're Guilty.'" *Narrative Inquiry*, 10(1): 1–44.

Schiffrin, Deborah. 2002. "Mother and Friends in a Holocaust Life Story." *Language in Society*, 31(3): 309–353.

Tannen, Deborah. 1990. *You Just Don't Understand: Women and Men in Conversation*. New York: William Morrow.

Tannen, Deborah. 1994. "The Relativity of Linguistic Strategies: Rethinking Power and Solidarity in Gender and Dominance." In *Gender and Discourse*, 19–52. Oxford: Oxford University Press.

Tannen, Deborah. 2001. *I Only Say This Because I Love You*. New York: Random House.

Tannen, Deborah. 2006. *You're Wearing That? Understanding Mothers and Daughters in Conversation*. New York: Ballantine Books.

Tannen, Deborah. 2008. "'We've Never Been Close, We're Very Different': Three Narrative Types in Sister Discourse." *Narrative Inquiry*, 18(2): 206–229.

Tannen, Deborah. 2009. *You Were Always Mom's Favorite! Sisters in Conversation throughout Their Lives*. New York: Random House.

Tannen, Deborah, Shari Kendall, and Cynthia Gordon, eds. 2007. *Family Talk: Discourse and Identity in Four American Families*. New York: Oxford University Press.

Varenne, Hervé. 1992. *Ambiguous Harmony: Family Talk in America*. Norwood, NJ: Ablex.

Wagner, Sarah. 2010. "Bringing Sexuality to the Table: Language, Gender and Power in Seven Lesbian Families." *Gender and Language*, 4(1): 33–72.

Watts, Richard J. 1991. *Power in Family Discourse*. Berlin: Mouton de Gruyter.

26   Language and Gender in Peer Interactions among Children and Youth

MARJORIE HARNESS GOODWIN AND AMY KYRATZIS

1. Introduction

This chapter explores an array of different paradigms that motivate research on language and gender in children's and youths' peer groups. Anthropologists and sociolinguists have for some time recognized that the peer group is an important institution for learning language as well as culture. According to Malinowski (1959, 283):

> In many communities we find that the child passes through a period of almost complete detachment from home: running around, playing about, and engaging in early activities with his playmates and contemporaries. In such activities strict teaching in tribal law is enforced more directly and poignantly than in the parental home.

Labov (1970, 34), writing about linguistic change, comments that the peer group has more influence than the family in shaping how children speak: "it is the local group of their children's peers which determines this generation's speech patterns." With respect to larger discourse patterns Ervin-Tripp and Mitchell-Kernan (1977, 7) found that "many of the speech events in which children engage typically occur among children apart from adults, and they are explicitly taught, in many cases, by children." Margaret Mead (1933, 1, 15) argued that anthropologists should include children in their studies, noting that "children's allegiances" and "child behavior" were as patterned as adult interaction. Mead noted that while there were studies of parent–child interaction, studies of peer group interaction were uncommon. As noted by Scheper-Hughes and Sargent (1998, 13–14), "children's voices are conspicuously absent in most ethnographic writing": "By and large, children appear in ethnographic texts the way cattle make their appearance in

The Handbook of Language, Gender, and Sexuality, Second Edition.
Edited by Susan Ehrlich, Miriam Meyerhoff, and Janet Holmes.
© 2014 John Wiley & Sons, Inc. Published 2017 by John Wiley & Sons, Inc.

Evans-Pritchard's classic, *The Nuer* – as forming an essential backdrop to everyday life, but mute and unable to teach us anything significant about society and culture." Only recently have anthropologists and sociologists (e.g., Corsaro 1997; Eder 1995; Thorne 1993) studied children as subjects, actors, and creators of culture.

In this chapter we discuss how various approaches to gendered language in peer groups have changed with shifting paradigms and notions about the appropriate unit of study as well as methodology. Cameron (2005, 81) argues that since the early 1990s language and gender research has shifted from a concern with binary differences to diversity of gendered identities and gendered practices. Similarly Mills (2004, 1) has stated that third-wave feminism challenges the idea of the homogeneity of women as a group, preferring studies that are "locally oriented," where gender is viewed as constrained by class, ethnicity, and context. With the postmodern turn in gender and language studies there is a switch from essentialist perceptions of gender and notions of fixed and natural categories to viewing gender as a locally managed practical accomplishment (Garfinkel 1967) or an emergent performance (J. Butler 1990). As argued by Baxter (2003, 28):

> While modernist feminism supports a liberal-humanist belief in a unified notion of woman as an authentic being, post-structuralist feminism has posited that being recognized as female is but one effect of the multiple ways in which individual identities are constituted through discourse.

We begin by reviewing the more traditional approach to studies of gender construction in children's interactions, the separate worlds hypothesis – what Cameron (2005) refers to as the "modern" feminist approach to language and gender – and then move to a discussion of the challenges that came from perspectives on language and gender that view identity as fluid, situated, and localized within communities of practice (Bucholtz 2000; Bucholtz and Hall 2004). We then review studies of children's moral and identity work in peer group interactions and synthesize these studies to see what can be concluded about the relevance of gender in children's peer interactions.

2. Binary Views of Gender

The dichotomous views of male and female personality put forward by Maccoby and Jacklin (1974) in the 1970s were revitalized in anthropologists Maltz and Borker's (1982) separate worlds hypothesis (for a review see Kyratzis 2001a). Maltz and Borker proposed that the gender segregation girls and boys experience results not only in differing activities becoming the focus of their worlds, but also alternative ways of speaking. Girls' collaborative talk contrasts with boys' competitive talk (see also Tannen 2001; Chapter 25 in this volume). Maltz and Borker's hypothesis was based on selective readings of fieldwork done by other researchers, including Goodwin's (1980) work on African American children's interactive patterns and Harding's (1975) studies of gender role segregation in the Near East and the Mediterranean. Henley's (1995, 361) observation that "much writing on the topic of language and gender is founded on the assumptions of White/Anglo (upper) middle-class experience" is relevant when considering the paradigm that generated research on language and gender for more than two decades.

2.1   *Separate worlds hypothesis*

Cross-cultural work by psychological anthropologists Whiting and Edwards (1988, 81) posited that "the emergence of same-sex preferences in childhood is a cross cultural universal and robust phenomenon." Such a perspective resonates with the work of Maccoby who has consistently argued that "segregated play groups constitute powerful socialization environments in which children acquire distinctive interaction skills that are adapted to same-sex partners" (1990, 516). Psychologist Campbell Leaper (1994, 68), in a review article on gender segregation, further elaborated that "to the extent that girls and boys emphasize different patterns of social interaction and activities in their respective peer groups, different norms for social behavior may be expected to emerge." Leaper maintains that girls' sex-typed activities help to foster nurturance and affection, as well as forms of social sensitivity, whereas boys' physically aggressive forms of play emphasize overt competition and dominance.

Ethnographically based research on language in interaction has challenged the gendered stereotypes of the separate worlds hypothesis with respect to (1) the universality of gender segregation, and (2) polarizations of gendered norms of social interaction and communication. Specifically, a number of researchers have analyzed how considerations of ethnicity, social class, power, and context are critical in the examination of gendered talk-in-interaction among children.

2.2   *Gender segregation*

Forms of gender segregation affecting norms of interaction have been described for preschool children in Japan (Nakamura 2001), Norway (Berentzen 1984), Sweden (Evaldsson and Tellgren 2009), Australia (Danby and Baker 1998), Wales (Bateman 2010), Italy (Loyd 2012), the Peruvian Aymara (Smith 2010), and the United States (Best 1983; Kyratzis and Guo 1996; Sheldon 1993). Bateman (2010, 164–177) discusses how reference to gender-segregated locations (the girls' toilet, a boys' hut) provides a way of doing gender categorization; such practices provide ways of avoiding threatening situations with the opposite gender and for affirming exclusive friendship affiliations. However, Thorne (1993), Goodwin (1990), Cook-Gumperz and Szymanski (2001), Kyratzis and Guo (2001), and Streeck (1986) caution that boys and girls are not always segregated. In a study of interaction on school playgrounds in the American Midwest and California among largely white working-class fourth and fifth graders, Thorne (1986) found that boys and girls established "with-then-apart" social arrangements. Gender boundaries could become heightened during team handball when boys made the game competitive, through slamming the ball hard; however, at other points (e.g., while eating) boundaries between the gender groups were not salient. Goodwin (1990) found that working-class African American girls ages 4 to 13 in a Philadelphia neighborhood would exclude boys during more serious *he-said-she-said* disputes, when girls were ostracizing members of their group. Generally, however, girls and boys were frequently in each other's co-presence and engaged in playful cross-sex verbal disputes. Joking and teasing between girls and boys was also common among the working-class white Midwestern middle school adolescents Eder (1995) studied, as well as among 10-year-old Greek children and minority Turkish-speaking children of Roma heritage in a multilingual, multicultural, and multiethnic peer group studied by Lytra (2007). Gender segregation in white middle-class groups (Best 1983; Schofield 1981), by way of contrast, prevents the development of friendships where playful conflictual types of exchanges might occur, perhaps due to "boys' and girls' notions of each other as possible romantic and sexual partners" (Schofield 1981, 72). In general, white upper middle-class children in America experience more gender segregation than African American or Italian children, regardless of age. Indeed Corsaro (1997, 150) found age to be an important variable when considering gender segregation. More gender segregation occurs among children five to six than among children three to five years of age.

3. Challenges to Separate Worlds Considering Class, Contextual Variation, and Power in Girls' Groups

3.1 Influences of social class

The universality of the separate worlds hypothesis has been challenged by numerous studies that consider the variability of language practices across different groups of girls and across contexts. Goodwin's study of African American working-class children (Goodwin 1985, 1990), bilingual Spanish and English speakers, and children of diverse ethnicities at a progressive school (Goodwin 2006) refute the notion that females are noncompetitive or passive in comparison to boys (Adler, Kless, and Adler 1992). In contrast to adult polite talk in which disagreement is dispreferred, often delayed, and minimized through various features of turn design, in adversarial talk during children's games, girls' "out" calls occur without doubt or delay.

Fighting back and "being able to take it" (Evaldsson 2005) are noted as commonplace in everyday masculine experience (Danby and Baker 1998; Eder 1995; Morgan 2002; Thorne 1993), promoting "toughness" (Smith 2010) and competition (Evaldsson 2002; Willis 1981). While ritual insult is generally associated with African American males (Kochman 1972; Labov 1972), Eder's (1990) study of white girls, Goodwin's (1990) work with African American girls, Mendoza-Denton's (2008, 186) study of Latina gang girls' clowning, and Tetreault's (2009; 2010), analysis of name calling of French adolescents of Algerian descent, have found that working-class girls participate in ritual insult, and develop competitive and self-defense skills. According to Eder (1990, 82), "insulting skills would not only allow these females to assert and defend their rights, but might also contribute to an impression of greater intelligence and wit, since quick and clever responses are often viewed as an indicator of general cleverness and intelligence." When girls enjoyed humorous teasing bouts with boys they mocked the traditional gender role stereotypes of middle-class white girls who are routinely "educated in romance" (Holland and Eisenhart 1990). Eder suggests that ritual insult may be more likely to occur among groups of girls where "toughness" is valued. In her study of girls in inner city Naples Loyd (2012) finds that, faced with adverse economic conditions and social marginalization from mainstream society, they learn and deploy communicative strategies or what she terms "rhetorical practices of appiccecarse [argumentation]" to cope with the risk inherent in their environment; they display virtuosity in assuming oppositional stances in both same- and cross-sex interaction.

3.2   Power asymmetries and exclusion in girls' groups

Beyond the ability to defend positions, both working-class and middle-class girls from the preschool years through young adulthood have shown a strong concern with building asymmetrical relationships and exclusion in their peer group interactions in a number of ethnographic studies (e.g., Berentzen 1984; Eder 1995; Evaldsson 2007; Evaldsson and Svahn 2012; Flores Nájera 2009; Goodwin 1990; 2006; Griswold 2007; Kyratzis 2007; Kyratzis, Marx, and Wade 2001; Sheldon 1996; Svahn 2012; Svahn and Evaldsson 2011). Longitudinal observation allows the full range of forms of social organization that are possible for the group to become evident. For example, Goodwin (1990, 127–129) shows how a peer group of African American working-class girls enacted asymmetry through directives in games of "house" over sequences of turns. Observing same-sex groups of middle-class four-year-olds, Kyratzis, Marx, and Wade (2001) found that in both girls' and boys' groups power asymmetries were created. One child would project a leadership role by issuing directives and challenging others' directives; the other group members would ratify the right of the leader to issue orders by making permission and information requests. In her study of six- to nine-year-old Russian girls from middle- and working-class families Griswold (2007) found that both directive forms (requests for permission, information, and assistance), as well as crouched bodily positions, were employed by girls to enact their own subordinate positions vis-à-vis a girl they constructed as leader (someone who issued role assignments and offers of help and information). Among a triad of middle-class preschool girls engaged in news reporter play (Kyratzis 2007), one girl assuming the role of the main reporter/lead announcer projected the right to determine transition points of the activity by using in-role directives, which other group members ratified by complying and asking questions. A group of preadolescent girls of diverse ethnicities at a progressive school practiced forms of social exclusion such as sanctioning members for putting themselves above others; they also built power asymmetries through comparing one another in terms of possessions and pursuits of the upper class (Goodwin 2006).

Bolonyai (2005, 4), studying bilingual Hungarian American preadolescent girls playing school in the presence of a Hungarian parent examines how girls "manage power asymmetries in everyday talk." Girls spoke more Hungarian while negotiating what to play, mediated through the mother's authority and preferred language (Hungarian). While playing school and engaging in conflict in an unmitigated style among one another, the girls code switch to English, as this provides the language for "sounding competent" and maintaining the floor. Flores Nájera (2009), following a sibling-kin group of bilingual Nahuatl and Spanish-speaking children in Tlaxcala, Mexico observed that in a pretend game of *dueñas y criadas* (masters and maids), girls code switched from Nahuatl to Spanish to intensify exclusion of group members and from Spanish to Nahuatl to intensify negative evaluation of inappropriate behavior. Oppositional stances were enacted through response cries, grammatical intensifiers, reduplication that registered negative assessment, and by glances displaying annoyance. O'Malley (2011) observed power asymmetries being constructed among triads of young women at a sorority through comparison sequences and assessments.

3.3   *Contextual influences*

Contextual variation is critical to studies of gender and language (Ervin-Tripp 2001). Goodwin's (2001) study of girls' and boys' uses of directives during the game of jump rope at a progressive elementary school attended by children of mixed ethnicities and social classes shows that the grammatical form of directives varies with levels of expertise in the activity of jumping rather than gender. Investigating role play in 48 peer dyads among Swedish preschool (age 6) and elementary school (age 8) children, Aronsson and Thorell (1999) found that both boys and girls made use of aggravated actions, though the "fathers" were more direct than the "mothers" (more often the compromisers and mitigators).

Kyratzis and Guo (1996; 2001) studied cross-cultural differences in the language behavior of preschoolers in mainland China and the United States. They found that during same-sex interaction in the United States boys are more assertive than girls; the reverse is true in China. Context is important in examining who is more assertive in cross-sex conflict; while US girls dominate contexts dealing with courtship, boys are dominant in contexts where work is the theme. Guo (2007) argues that both the boys and the girls he studied in a university-affiliated preschool in Beijing can become engaged in very direct verbal conflict. What differs are the types of thematic domains in which arguments occur. Guo found that five-year-old Mandarin-speaking girls order boys around when issues of social status or morality are at stake, making use of aggravated actions, while boys by comparison are submissive. However, with respect to exchanges involving technical, problem-solving issues girls assume a subordinate position, seeking assistance from others. The studies of Guo (2002) and Streeck (1986) have important implications for the organization of small groups in classrooms, as they demonstrate that within task-specific settings boys may dominate and not allow girls full participation in the activity.

Children make use of a repertoire of voices. Kyratzis (2001b) found that a friendship group of preschool middle-class boys made references to physical acts of aggression ("smash this girl!"), while the characters that a group of girls at the same preschool enacted suggested their value of qualities of lovingness and graciousness. These displays of emotion, however, were heavily influenced by the group makeup and other contextual factors. Kyratzis and Tarım (2010) found that members of a friendship group of middle-class preschool Turkish girls used forms of directives (tag questions, joint directives) that did not differentiate participants when engaged in pretend play or task activities with one another. These same girls, however, used bald imperatives when they enacted the role of mothers (e.g., *Stop! I did not give you the money, come here!* to a child in the father role) or engaged in task activities with boys.

Nakamura (2001) shows that while Japanese girls use language to create and maintain positions of closeness and equality, they can also use language to make assertive moves – negotiating roles, establishing the physical setting, and defining appropriate role behavior. Nakamura's depiction of male and female roles in a Japanese preschool has several parallels with Farris's (1991; 2000) descriptions of language use among Taiwanese preschoolers. Farris (1991, 204) argues that boys "create a childish masculine ethos that centers on action, competition, and aggression, and that is organized and expressed discursively through loud, terse, direct forms of speech." By way of contrast, Taiwanese girls attempt to maintain an ethos of "quasi-familial social relations ... organized and expressed discursively through coy, affected, and indirect forms of speech." In comparison to Japanese female preschoolers, however, Taiwanese girls can be quite assertive; they talk pejoratively about other people in the third person *in the presence of the target*, making use of a particular style (*sajiao*), which involves gross body movements, pouting, ambiguous lexical items, and expressive particles (Farris 1991, 208).

The notion of "quasi-familial social relations" discussed by Farris (1991) for Taiwanese children has parallels with the structuring of social roles among peers in a California third grade bilingual classroom described by Cook-Gumperz and Szymanski (2001). An organization of groups in terms of families was initiated by the teacher, and children themselves oriented toward ideas of quasi-family. Girls took the lead in orchestrating group activities, such as coordinating the activity of correcting answers for the group, or playing the role of "big sisters." They acted as "cultural brokers" who were responsible for "organizing and translating the needs and requirements of family to and from the outside world" (Cook-Gumperz and Szymanski 2001, 127). Children moved fluidly in and out of familial-based and gender-based groups; their social organization resembled the pattern of "with-then-apart" described by Thorne (1986) rather than the gender-segregated groups described by the separate worlds hypothesis.

4. Practices for Negotiating the Social Order in Children's Groups

Two approaches, one focusing on practice and performance in communities of practice, and one based on conversation analysis (CA) and focusing on gender as a practical accomplishment that is locally managed (Garfinkel 1967), make possible a more dynamic view of gender among peers. As the former approach is reviewed by Eckert (Chapter 27 in this volume), we will focus our attention on work which takes conversation analysis as a point of departure. (See Wilkinson and Kitzinger, Chapter 7 in this volume, for a description of conversation analysis.) The focus is on the interactional unfolding of social relations "within the interactive contingencies of the situated moment" (Rampton 2003, 51), rather than in interview contexts. Researchers who adopt a somewhat strict CA approach attempt to show how the parties embody for one another the relevancies of a particular interaction and thereby produce the social structure (Schegloff 1991, 51). Identity is a locally managed accomplishment (Benwell and Stokoe 2006).

Recent work integrating CA, ethnomethodology, and feminist discursive psychology (C. Butler and Weatherall 2006; Speer and Stokoe 2011) analyzes how participants elaborate membership categorizations (Sacks 1995) and "make concerns of identity relevant for their business at hand in the interaction" (Deppermann 2007, 275). (See Stokoe and Attenborough, Chapter 8 in this volume, for a description of membership categorization analysis.) Through participation in activities such as disputes, gossip, assessments, pretend play games, and storytelling, children continuously define and redefine the social situation and hold one another accountable to it as they negotiate how they stand vis-à-vis one another in the local peer group interaction (Goodwin 1990; 2006; Goodwin and Kyratzis 2007; 2012). By taking up stances with respect to a target and making others accountable for interactional acts children locate and reference the peer group's notion of culturally appropriate moral behavior (Svahn 2012).

4.1   *Assessments and ritual insult in children's interactions*

In the midst of talk, peers actively police the local social landscape and make evaluative commentary to one another regarding the valued signs in their larger social universe – ones that are linked to social status (Eder 1995; Goodwin 2006). Among boys of working-class or immigrant background in multiethnic elementary school groups in Sweden, negative person descriptors include being poor, having limited Swedish language proficiency, dressing like a girl, and being labeled a "Gypsy" (rather than the in-group label "Romany" commonly used in school) (Evaldsson 2005, 771). Boys create multiparty consensus (Evaldsson 2002) through upgrades, laughter, recycles, repetitions, and evaluations. Among multiethnic girls negative category-bound activities including fighting, blaming, exploiting others, lying, and talking behind people's backs were associated with the category "bad friend" (Evaldsson 2007). By way of contrast, boys' gossip concerns "anxieties about being excluded, associated with physical vulnerability, emotional weakness, and cowardice such as crying, sulking, wetting one's pants, or calling for a teacher's intervention" (Evaldsson 2002, 199).

Assessment adjectives, pejorative person descriptors, and negative categorizations of activities and actors all point to implicit cultural values that children invoke and orient to as they position themselves vis-à-vis one another. Svahn and Evaldsson (2011) examine the invocation of the social category of "snitch" among fifth graders (11-year-olds) in the midst of a gossip trajectory at a low-income multiethnic Swedish school. Subtle practices of social exclusion studied by Svahn and Evaldsson (2011) include bodily alignments and disalignments, word play, repeated summons and non-replies, and ritualized forms entailed in "indirect bullying."

Sophocleous and Themistocleous (2011) examine how eight 16-year-old Greek Cypriot female bidialectal speakers project and reshape their identity during in-class secret written interactions during note passing over a four month period. They find that the same interactants make use of a range of assessments (about hygienic practices, behavior, and friends) and nicknames. On the basis of a two-year study with German adolescent girls during their leisure activities, Spreckels (2009) discusses how important music is in the culture of German adolescents (and hence in identity construction). Knowledge of musical style (e.g., *ganschta* and *hip hopper*) is used to index those who are hip from those who are not. Such framings as "he thinks he's doing X" are often used to project the category of someone who is a "wannabe" and cannot appropriately occupy the category.

Deppermann (2007) discusses forms of entertaining and competitive forms of negative assessment activities caricaturing outgroup members performed by adolescent German males in a small town. Boys police the social order by talking about the behavior of outgroup members who violate local norms ("bean eaters," "trash sluts," "canyon shitters," "buffaloes" (Turkish or Arabic speaking adolescents from southern Europe). Making use of jokes, gossip, ritual insults, puns, and bragging, they strengthen ingroup bonds in the process.

4.2   *Play and performance in children's interactions*

As Bauman and Briggs (1990, 63) argue "play frames not only alter the performative force of utterances but provide settings in which speech and society can be questioned and transformed." When children "recontextualize in play different kinds of texts" (Reynolds 2007, 440), for example, enacting character "voices," "animating" peers' and adults' talk (Goffman 1981), or playfully performing greetings, song games, or genres of verbal competition for an audience of peers, they create intertextual relations between current utterances and prior discourse and genres (Bakhtin 1986). By invoking genres, speakers "creat[e] indexical connections that extend far beyond the present setting of production or reception, thereby linking a particular act to other times, places, and persons" (Briggs and

Bauman 1992, 147–148). Consequently, children's playful renderings provide them with resources for taking stances and negotiating subjectivities and local social order, as well as for exploring relations between, and evaluating, different social roles, speakers, settings, and discourses with other group members (Minks 2006; 2008; 2013; Reynolds 2007; 2010).

Tetreault (2007) examines how peer groups of adolescent girls of Algerian descent living in a French *cité* ("subsidized housing project") socialize one another to adopting a tough masculine communicative style, performing genres of verbal competition such as playful bragging and ritualized insults about clothing and brand names. Later in their adolescence, they abandon these practices, conforming to the local community's moral discourses of "'le respect' in observance of Arab-Muslim cultural models for young women's sexual and social modesty" (Tetreault 2007, 4).

According to Tetreault (2008, 158), the younger girls' language practices "valorize 'la racaille' [male street toughs] as part of crafting a tough, transgressive identity for themselves" and in response to racializing discourses of the dominant French society, which construct the practices of immigrant youth, particularly male immigrant youth, as stigmatized or illicit. Shankar (2008, 270) examines how middle-class Desi (South Asian American) teens respond to monolingual school ideologies and differentiate themselves from upper middle-class Desi teens at a Silicon Valley high school, who "appear more model." Middle-class Desi males "construct heteroglossic 'FOB' styles" (Shankar 2008, 268), which draw on Punjabi, viewed as "nonnormative linguistic practice" (Shankar 2008, 282) by the monolingual school ideology, as well as on Desi Accented English and other linguistic resources. They also use profanity and expressions linked to heightened masculinity. Because Silicon Valley Desi community norms value maintaining a good reputation for girls, middle-class Desi girls make less use of these stylistic practices. Rhetorical practices of *appiccecarse* (argumentation), used by girls in inner city Naples in Loyd's (2012) study, were adopted in response to stigmatization by the dominant Italian society of the girls' Neopolitan dialect, poverty, and other life circumstances.

Several other studies followed girls' identity and language in diaspora communities. Keim (2007) interviewed Turkish "Powergirls" in Mannheim, Germany and observed them in leisure interactions at a youth center. Girls aged 12–15 used German–Turkish code switching and a "coarse" communicative style. Powergirls expressed their opposition to the image of the "'traditional Turkish woman'" by using aggressive features taken from "'male worlds' of the migrant 'ghetto'" and displayed their "opposition to German teachers of the higher educational institutions … by the extensive use of elaborated Turkish–German mixings" (Keim 2007, 178).

García-Sánchez (2010) examines how members of a neighborhood peer group of Moroccan immigrant girls in Spain used hybrid linguistic practices during play with their dolls. The doll characters, voiced in Spanish, "create an idealized Spanish high society life style" (2010, 542). García-Sánchez's (2010, 523) analysis illustrates how the girls' play explorations and hybrid (Spanish and Moroccan Arabic) language practices are "imbued with moral tensions." The practices constitute their way of reconciling constraints imposed by both the Moroccan immigrant community, which closely monitors girls' actions and imposes social restrictions on them, as well as the dominant Spanish society, which marginalizes the Moroccan community. Kyratzis (2010) analyzes language practices used during an extended episode of birthday party play among a peer group of Spanish- and English-speaking preschoolers of primarily Mexican descent in a bilingual California preschool. The preschoolers inscribed a regimentation of the codes, associating "English practices with … events of U.S. consumer culture … and Spanish practices with traditional activities of preparing and serving food" (Kyratzis 2010, 580). They also sometimes challenged this regimentation through using heteroglossic forms across the two frames.

Members of boys' groups growing up in communities characterized by multi-lingualism and linguistic variability (e.g., diaspora communities in transnational societies, indigenous communities in postcolonial societies) may come to associate one of the codes (e.g., the native language or dialect of their local group, or the wider form of communication designated by the group in power in the society for use in the government and schools) with adult masculine activities and identities (Garrett 2007; Shankar 2008). Garrett (2007, 249), studying a peer group of older boys in St Lucia, observed them using Kwéyòl phrases in unsupervised peer contexts to index adult masculinity while, in adult-supervised contexts, they were pressured to use English. Paugh (2012) found that Patwa- and English-speaking children in Dominica in the West Indies used Patwa in imaginary play to depict predominantly male authoritative working-class occupations related to the banana field, road, or bush, while English was used to enact school or official activities. Paugh and Garrett argue that such practices have the potential to influence and counter processes of language shift. Smith (2010) examines how notions of "man-liness" are interactionally negotiated and performed among Aymara boys in the Peruvian Andes during marbles play.

Minks (2008; 2013) studied performances of Spanish song games among peer and sibling-kin groups of Miskitu-, Spanish-, and Creole English-speaking children on Corn Island, Nicaragua. In the face of the Corn Island Miskitu community's "anxious discussions about women's and girls' affective and sexual stances and behaviors," the Spanish song games provided highly "kinetic forms" which Miskitu children used to "play out" "tensions between gendered desires and … anxious discourses about women and girls" (Minks 2008, 41, 37, 43). Reynolds (2007) followed a sibling-kin network of children in a Kaqchikel–Spanish bilingual Mayan community in Guatemala and analyzes the children's "entextualization" (Bauman and Briggs 1990) of one specific politeness genre, the greeting *Buenos días*, which they "laminate" on top of another, a military salute, using it as an "improvised insult" (Reynolds 2007, 446) in conflict moves with one another. Reynolds observed the children inserting pejorative nicknames indexing broader cultural stereotypes of gender and race into the improvised greeting. Fuller (2007) illustrates the ways in which four Mexican American fourth grade school children, followed ethnographically, make use of multiple languages to construct gender-differentiated forms of identities in a fourth to sixth grade bilingual Spanish–English classroom in southern Illinois. The two girls engaged in code switching to formulate identities of bilingual "best friends." In so doing, they constructed hybrid identities showing affiliation with both Mexican and US culture. In contrast, the two boys used code switching to perform an identity of "good student" in a US classroom. These patterns go against many studies that associate language choice only with ethnicity by considering a range of other social dimensions important to children, such as gender, school achievement, and friendship. Along similar lines, Pujolar (2001, 22) studied the language practices of two cliques of youth in Barcelona, which he called the "Rambleros" and the "Trepas." The youth were from working-class neighborhoods associated with a "particularly bad reputation in Barcelona." While gender was salient, members of both groups made use of a diversity of divisions (e.g., gender, social class, language ideologies with respect to Spanish and Catalan) to differentiate group identity. Although both groups worked to create "a transgressive ethos" subverting "middle and upper-class cultural forms," the Rambleros used stylized Spanish as part of their efforts to sustain a "'simple truth'" version of masculinity, while the Trepas "rejected simplified versions of masculinity," defining "peer group practices in emancipatory terms" (Pujolar 2001, 308, 302, 302).

The studies just reviewed demonstrate how children and teens play with and lay claim to social spaces, discourses, and subjectivities in ways that alternatively resist and reproduce both dominant societal discourses that marginalize their local communities (e.g., diaspora communities in transnational societies; indigenous communities in postcolonial societies) and construct the local vernaculars spoken within those communities as non-normative or deficient, as well as parental discourses that construct different norms for girls and boys (e.g., discourses of "traditional" femininity). They also demonstrate how peer group members hold other members accountable to these discourses through their language practices (assessment adjectives, ritualized insults, pejorative person descriptors, and negative categorizations of activities). Gender was one resource or identity category that was drawn upon by children and youth in negotiating local peer group hierarchies in the transnational, postcolonial, and multilingual settings studied, but was not the only identity category (e.g., Fuller 2007; Keim 2007; Pujolar 2001).

In other studies of peer groups, gender does not so clearly come into play. Children have a range of semiotic and linguistic resources available to draw upon in negotiating local identities. There have been several studies conducted within the language socialization paradigm (Ochs and Schieffelin 2012) which have been concerned with language contact phenomena and language ideologies (e.g., Woolard 1998), documenting how, through their language practices, child speakers respond to, reproduce, and challenge "more broadly held ideologies about the relationship and meanings of the two languages" (Schieffelin 2003, 158; see also Garrett and Baquedano-López 2002; Paugh 2012). In particular, when children and youth use hybrid and "heteroglossic" (Bakhtin 1981) language practices (Bailey 2007; Kyratzis, Reynolds, and Evaldsson 2010; Minks 2010; Zentella 1997), these practices can be revealing of how speakers express "tensions between the multiplicities of language varieties within a national language, which are drawing it towards a standard central version, and those that are moving away from national standards through hybrid linguistic forms of official and unofficial languages" (Kyratzis, Reynolds, and Evaldsson 2010, 457).

As noted by Minks (2010), when children use heteroglossic and hybrid communicative practices, as did a group of Miskitu-, Spanish-, and Creole English-speaking sibling-kin whom she followed on Corn Island off the Caribbean coast of Nicaragua, these forms are "expressing the[ir] experiences of moving between languages and cultures" (Minks 2010, 516). Heteroglossic and hybrid communicative practices of children and youth, as well as their transformations of associations for the languages in peer play and performance (Garrett 2007; Paugh 2012), enable them to explore possible subjectivities (Minks 2008; 2013), including bilingual subjectivities (de León 2011; Keim 2007; Minks 2010; 2013), as well as enabling them to assert "interethnic" peer group communities (Rampton 1995) and resist dominant (e.g., monolingual) institutional or societal discourses that marginalize speakers of "unofficial" languages (see also Bailey 2007; Cekaite and Evaldsson 2008; Chun 2009; Lytra 2007; Paugh 2012; Tarım and Kyratzis 2012; Shankar 2008; Zentella 1997). However, other practices, such as "exaggerated use of stylized 'beginner language'" or stylized immigrant mocking can reproduce the dominant discourses and hierarchies (e.g., Cekaite and Evaldsson 2008, 182; Chun 2009).

5. Conclusion

In the transnational and postcolonial societies in which the majority of the world's children grow up today, it is essential to study the language practices of children and youth in peer and sibling-kin groups, to shed light on how the peers and sibling-kin socialize one another (Goodwin and Kyratzis 2007; 2012), that is, how the children locate and reference the peer group's notion of culturally appropriate moral behavior, as they negotiate their alignments to one another and position one another in the local social group. All of the studies reviewed in the previous two sections demonstrate how children and teens in everyday peer and sibling-kin group interactions play with and lay claim to social spaces, discourses, and subjectivities in ways that alternatively resist and reproduce dominant discourses that marginalize their local communities (e.g., diaspora communities in transnational societies, indigenous communities in postcolonial societies) and construct the native languages or dialects spoken by members of those communities as deficient. They also demonstrate how the children and teens resist and reproduce parental discourses that construct different norms for girls and boys. Children and teens across a range of ages, from preschool to young adulthood, engage in these practices; the only differences are that teens and young adults may use a broader range of genres to explore identities (e.g., teasing, storytelling), while younger children may have less of a sense of named group belonging and may explore identities and perform voices within a more restricted range of genres (e.g., song games and pretend play.) A large number of these studies show children and youth taking their own stances on parental discourses that construct different norms for girls and boys. The children invoke category terms and assessments, and engage in performances that create "a sanctioned space for imagining and experimenting with gendered and sexual identities" (Minks 2008, 54), identities that may be transgressive with respect to parental discourses (e.g., discourses of "traditional" femininity) of the local community.

Early ethnographic studies of children's and teens' peer groups, done predominantly with white children in the United States (Adler, Kless, and Adler 1992; Eder 1995) and European settings (Berentzen 1984), found that gender divisions were a major division to which children and youth oriented (although see Eckert 1987 for an exception) in negotiating peer group asymmetries and claiming social spaces on school grounds. Not only is there tremendous linguistic heterogeneity both within and across girls' and boys' groups, but, as noted by Thorne (1993) some time ago, gender categories are not the only social categories that children can draw upon in negotiating power asymmetries and identities in the local peer group interaction. The children in the transnational and postcolonial settings reviewed here also drew upon categories of race, language, social class (Eckert 1987; Pujolar 2001; Rampton 2006; Shankar 2008), and ethnicity, as well as other social categories. Several of the studies demonstrated how children and teens play with and lay claim to social spaces, discourses, and subjectivities in ways that alternatively resist and reproduce dominant societal discourses that marginalize their local communities and construct the local vernaculars spoken by members of those communities as deficient, especially through using heteroglossic (Bailey 2007; Kyratzis, Reynolds, and Evaldsson 2010; Minks 2010; Zentella 1997) and hybrid communicative practices, or by refusing to use them (e.g., Mendoza-Denton 2008). These practices are drawn upon as part and parcel of the ways in which children and youth negotiate local hierarchies, create distinctive ways of speaking (Eckert 2005), and lay claim to social spaces, positioning themselves in relation to other children and youth in their schools, neighborhoods, and compounds (e.g., Shankar 2008). Ethnographic fieldwork and analysis of talk-in-interaction are both essential if researchers are to understand how children and youth draw upon a range of social dimensions that are important to them, including but not limited to gender, ethnicity, language, social class, age, and friendship, in everyday practices of play, assessment, and performance, as they render commentary and negotiate how they are aligned with one another moment to moment in the local interaction.

REFERENCES

Adler, Patricia A., Steven J. Kless, and Peter Adler. 1992. "Socialization to Gender Roles: Popularity among Elementary School Boys and Girls." *Sociology of Education*, 65(3): 169–187.

Aronsson, Karin, and Mia Thorell. 1999. "Family Politics in Children's Play Directives." *Journal of Pragmatics*, 31: 25–47.

Bailey, Benjamin. 2007. "Heteroglossia and Boundaries." In Monica Heller (ed.),

Bilingualism: A Social Approach, 257–274. Basingstoke: Palgrave Macmillan.

Bakhtin, Mikhail M. 1981. *The Dialogic Imagination: Four Essays*, ed. Michael Holquist, trans. Caryl Emerson and Michael Holquist. Austin: University of Texas Press.

Bakhtin, Mikhail M. 1986. *Speech Genres and Other Late Essays*, ed. Michael Holquist and Caryl Emerson. Austin: University of Texas Press.

Bateman, Amanda. 2010. "Children's Co-construction of Context: Prosocial and Antisocial Behaviour Revisited." Unpublished PhD dissertation, Swansea University.

Bauman, Richard, and Charles L. Briggs. 1990. "Poetics and Performance as Critical Perspectives on Language and Social Life." *Annual Review of Anthropology*, 19: 59–88.

Baxter, Judith. 2003. *Positioning Gender in Discourse: A Feminist Methodology*. New York: Palgrave Macmillan.

Benwell, Bethan, and Elizabeth H. Stokoe. 2006. *Discourse and Identity*. Edinburgh: Edinburgh University Press.

Berentzen, Sigurd. 1984. Children Constructing Their Social World: An Analysis of Gender Contrast in Children's Interaction in a Nursery School. Bergen Occasional Papers in Social Anthropology, no. 36. Bergen: Department of Social Anthropology, University of Bergen.

Best, Raphaela. 1983. *We've All Got Scars*. Bloomington: Indiana University Press.

Bolonyai, Agnes. 2005. "'Who Was the Best?' Power, Knowledge and Rationality in Bilingual Girls' Code Choices." *Journal of Sociolinguistics*, 9(1): 3–27.

Briggs, Charles L., and Richard Bauman. 1992. "Genre, Intertextuality, and Social Power." *Journal of Linguistic Anthropology*, 2(2): 131–172.

Bucholtz, Mary. 2000. "Gender." *Journal of Linguistic Anthropology*, 9: 80–83.

Bucholtz, Mary, and Kira Hall. 2004. "Language and Identity." In Alessandro Duranti (ed.), *A Companion to Linguistic Anthropology*, 369–394. Oxford: Blackwell.

Butler, Carly, and Ann Weatherall. 2006. "'No, We're Not Playing Families':

Membership Categorization in Children's Play." *Research on Language and Social Interaction*, 39(4): 441–470.

Butler, Judith. 1990. *Gender Trouble: Feminism and the Subversion of Identity*. New York: Routledge.

Cameron, Deborah. 2005. "Language, Gender, and Sexuality: Current Issues and New Directions." *Applied Linguistics*, 26(4): 482–502.

Cekaite, Asta, and Ann-Carita Evaldsson. 2008. "Staging Linguistic Identities and Negotiating Monolingual Norms in Multiethnic School Settings." *International Journal of Multilingualism*, 5(3): 177–196.

Chun, Elaine. 2009. "Speaking Like Asian Immigrants: Intersections of Accommodation and Mocking at a U.S. High School." *Pragmatics*, 19(1): 17–38.

Cook-Gumperz, Jenny, and Margaret Szymanski. 2001. "Classroom 'Families': Cooperating or Competing – Girls' and Boys' Interactional Styles in a Bilingual Classroom." *Research on Language and Social Interaction*, 34(1): 107–130.

Corsaro, William A. 1997. *The Sociology of Childhood*. Thousand Oaks, CA: Pine Forge Press.

Danby, Susan, and Carolyn Baker. 1998. "How to be Masculine in the Block Area." *Childhood*, 5(2): 151–175.

de León, Lourdes. 2011. "Emergent Bilingual Performances: Parallelism and Intertextuality in Tzotzil-Spanish Siblings' Play." Paper presented at the American Anthropological Association Annual Meeting, Montreal, November 15.

Deppermann, Arnulf. 2007. "Using the Other for Oneself: Conversational Practices of Representing Out-Group Members among Adolescents." In Michael Bamberg, Anna De Fina, and Deborah Schiffrin (eds.), *Selves and Identities in Narrative and Discourse*, 273–301. Amsterdam: Benjamins.

Eckert, Penelope. 1987. *Jocks and Burnouts: Social Categories and Identity in the High School*. New York: Teachers College Press.

Eckert, Penelope. 2005. "Slang and Swearing as Markers of Inclusion and Exclusion in Adolescence." In Angie Williams and

Crispin Thurlow (eds.), *Talking Adolescence: Perspectives on Communication in the Teenage Years*, 111–128. New York: Peter Lang.

Eder, Donna. 1990. "Serious and Playful Disputes: Variation in Conflict Talk among Female Adolescents." In Allen D. Grimshaw (ed.), *Conflict Talk: Sociolinguistic Investigations of Arguments in Conversations*, 67–84. Cambridge: Cambridge University Press.

Eder, Donna. 1995. *School Talk: Gender and Adolescent Culture*. New Brunswick, NJ: Rutgers University Press.

Ervin-Tripp, Susan M. 2001. "The Place of Gender in Developmental Pragmatics: Cultural Factors." *Research on Language in Social Interaction*, 34(1): 131–147.

Ervin-Tripp, Susan M., and Claudia Mitchell-Kernan. 1977. "Introduction." In Susan Ervin-Tripp and Claudia Mitchell-Kernan (eds.), *Child Discourse*, 1–26. New York: Academic Press.

Evaldsson, Ann-Carita. 2002. "Boys' Gossip Telling: Staging Identities and Indexing (Unacceptable) Masculine Behavior." *Text*, 22(2): 199–225.

Evaldsson, Ann-Carita. 2005. "Staging Insults and Mobilizing Categorizations in a Multiethnic Peer Group." *Discourse and Society*, 16(6): 763–786.

Evaldsson, Ann-Carita. 2007. "Accounting for Friendship: Moral Ordering and Category Membership in Preadolescent Girls' Relational Talk." *Research on Language and Social Interaction*, 40(4): 377–404.

Evaldsson, Ann-Carita, and Johanna Svahn. 2012. "School Bullying and the Micro-Politics of Girls' Gossip Disputes." In Susan Danby and Maryanne Theobald (eds.), *Disputes in Everyday Life: Social and Moral Orders of Children and Young People*, 297–323. Bingley: American Sociological Association's Studies of Children and Youth/Emerald Group.

Evaldsson, Ann-Carita, and Britt Tellgren. 2009. "'Don't Enter – It's Dangerous': Negotiations for Power and Exclusion in Preschool Girls' Play Interactions." *Educational and Child Psychology*, 26(2): 9–18.

Farris, Catherine. 1991. "The Gender of Child Discourse: Same-Sex Peer Socialization through Language Use in a Taiwanese Preschool." *Journal of Linguistic Anthropology*, 1: 198–224.

Farris, Catherine E. P. 2000. "Cross-Sex Peer Conflict and the Discursive Production of Gender in a Chinese Preschool in Taiwan." *Journal of Pragmatics*, 32: 539–568.

Flores Nájera, Lucero. 2009. "Los Directivos en la Organización Social del Grupo de Pares de Niños Bilingues de San Isidro Buensuceso, Tlaxcala: Un Enfoque Interactivo, Maestria en Linguistica Indoamericana" [Directives in the Social Organization of Peer Groups of Bilingual Children in San Isidro Buensuceso, Tlaxcala: An Interactive Approach]. Unpublished master's thesis, Centro de Investigaciones y Estudios Superiores en Antropologia Social (CIESAS), Mexico City.

Fuller, Janet M. 2007. "Language Choice as a Means of Shaping Identity." *Journal of Linguistic Anthropology*, 17(1): 105–129.

García-Sánchez, Inmaculada. 2010. "Serious Games: Code-Switching and Gendered Identities in Moroccan Immigrant Girls' Pretend Play." *Pragmatics*, 20(4): 523–555.

Garfinkel, Harold. 1967. *Studies in Ethnomethodology*. Englewood Cliffs, NJ: Prentice Hall.

Garrett, Paul. 2007. "Language Socialization and the (Re)production of Bilingual Subjectivities." In Monica Heller (ed.), *Bilingualism: A Social Approach*, 233–256. New York: Palgrave Macmillan.

Garrett, Paul, and Patricia Baquedano-López. 2002. "Language Socialization: Reproduction and Continuity, Transformation and Change." *Annual Review of Anthropology*, 31: 339–361.

Goffman, Erving. 1981. "Footing." In *Forms of Talk*, 124–159. Philadelphia: University of Pennsylvania Press.

Goodwin, Marjorie Harness. 1980. "'He-Said-She-Said': Formal Cultural Procedures for the Construction of a Gossip Dispute Activity." *American Ethnologist*, 7: 674–695.

Goodwin, Marjorie Harness. 1985. "The Serious Side of Jump Rope: Conversational Practices and Social Organization in the Frame of Play." *Journal of American Folklore*, 98: 315–330.

Goodwin, Marjorie Harness. 1990. *He-Said-She-Said: Talk as Social Organization among Black Children.* Bloomington: Indiana University Press.

Goodwin, Marjorie Harness. 2001. "Organizing Participation in Cross-Sex Jump Rope: Situating Gender Differences within Longitudinal Studies of Activities." *Research on Language and Social Interaction*, Special issue entitled "Gender Construction in Children's Interactions: A Cultural Perspective" 34(1): 75–106.

Goodwin, Marjorie Harness. 2006. *The Hidden Life of Girls: Games of Stance, Status, and Exclusion.* Oxford: Blackwell.

Goodwin, Marjorie Harness, and Amy Kyratzis. 2007. "Introduction." *Research on Language and Social Interaction* (special issue: "Children Socializing Children: Practices for Negotiating the Social and Moral Order among Peers"), 40(4): 279–289.

Goodwin, Marjorie Harness, and Amy Kyratzis. 2012. "Peer Language Socialization." In Alessandro Duranti, Elinor Ochs, and Bambi B. Schieffelin (ed.), *The Handbook of Language Socialization*, 391–419. Oxford: Wiley-Blackwell.

Griswold, Olga. 2007. "Achieving Authority: Discursive Practices in Russian Girls' Pretend Play." *Research on Language and Social Interaction*, 40(4): 291–320.

Guo, Jiansheng. 2002. When Do Chinese Girls Order Boys Around? Culture and Context in Gender Differences in Communicative Strategies by 5-year Old Mandarin-Speaking Children. *Journal of Asian Pacific Communication*, 12(2): 185–216.

Guo, Jiansheng. 2007. "Multiple Selves and Thematic Domains in Gender Identity: Perspectives from Chinese Children's Conflict Management Styles." In Michael Bamberg, Anna De Fina, and Deborah Schiffrin (eds.), *Selves and Identities in Narrative and Discourse*, 181–227. Amsterdam: Benjamins.

Harding, Susan. 1975. "Women and Words in a Spanish Village." In Rayna R. Reiter (ed.), *Towards an Anthropology of Women*, 283–308. New York: Monthly Review Press.

Henley, Nancy M. 1995. "Ethnicity and Gender Issues in Language." In Hope Landrine (ed.), *Bringing Cultural Diversity to Feminist Psychology: Theory, Research, and Practice*, 361–396. Washington, DC: American Psychological Association.

Holland, Dorothy C., and Margaret A. Eisenhart. 1990. *Educated in Romance: Women, Achievement, and College Culture.* Chicago: University of Chicago Press.

Keim, Inken. 2007. "Socio-cultural Identity, Communicative Style, and Their Change over Time: A Case Study of a Group of German-Turkish Girls in Mannheim/ Germany." In Peter Auer (ed.), *Style and Social Identities: Alternative Approaches to Linguistic Heterogeneity*, 155–185. Berlin: Mouton de Gruyter.

Kochman, Thomas. 1972. "Toward an Ethnography of Black American Speech Behavior." In Thomas Kochman (ed.), *Rappin' and Stylin' Out: Communication in Urban Black America*, 241–264. Chicago: University of Illinois Press.

Kyratzis, Amy. 2001a. "Children's Gender Indexing in Language: From the Separate Worlds Hypothesis to Considerations of Culture, Context, and Power." *Research on Language and Social Interaction*, 34(1): 1–13.

Kyratzis, Amy. 2001b. "Emotion Talk in Preschool Same-Sex Friendship Groups: Fluidity over Time and Context." *Early Education and Development*, 12: 359–391.

Kyratzis, Amy. 2007. "Using the Social Organizational Affordances of Pretend Play in American Preschool Girls' Interactions." *Research on Language and Social Interaction*, 40(4): 321–352.

Kyratzis, Amy. 2010. "Latina Girls' Peer Play Interactions in a Bilingual Spanish-English U.S. Preschool: Heteroglossia, Frame-Shifting, and Language Ideology." *Pragmatics*, 20(4): 557–586.

Kyratzis, Amy, and Jiansheng Guo. 1996. "'Separate Worlds for Girls and Boys?' Views from U.S. and Chinese Mixed-Sex Friendship Groups." In Dan Slobin, Julie

Gerhardt, Amy Kyratzis, and Jiansheng Guo (eds.), *Social Interaction, Social Context, and Language, Essays in Honor of Susan Ervin-Tripp*, 555–578. Mahwah, NJ: Lawrence Erlbaum.

Kyratzis, Amy, and Jiansheng Guo. 2001. "Preschool Girls' and Boys' Verbal Conflict Strategies in the U.S. and China: Cross-Cultural and Contextual Considerations." *Research on Language and Social Interaction* (special issue: "Gender Construction in Children's Interactions: A Cultural Perspective"), 34: 45–74.

Kyratzis, Amy, Traci Marx, and Evelyn R. Wade. 2001. "Preschoolers' Communicative Competence: Register Shift in the Marking of Power in Different Contexts of Friendship Group Talk." *First Language*, 21: 387–431.

Kyratzis, Amy, Jennifer F. Reynolds, and Ann-Carita Evaldsson. 2010. "Introduction: Heteroglossia and Language Ideologies in Children's Peer Play Interactions." *Pragmatics* (special issue: "Heteroglossia and Language Ideologies in Children's Peer Play Interactions"), 20(4): 457–466.

Kyratzis, Amy, and Şeyda D. Tarım. 2010. "Using Directives to Construct Egalitarian or Hierarchical Relationships: Turkish Middle-Class Preschool Girls' Socialization about Gender, Affect, and Context in Peer Conversations." *First Language*, 30(3–4): 473–492.

Labov, William. 1970. *The Study of Nonstandard English*. Champaign, IL: National Council of Teachers.

Labov, William. 1972. "Rules for Ritual Insults." In *Language in the Inner City: Studies in the Black English Vernacular*, 297–353. Philadelphia: University of Pennsylvania Press.

Leaper, Campbell. 1994. "Exploring the Consequences of Gender Segregation on Social Relationships." *New Directions for Child Development*, 65 (Fall): 67–86.

Loyd, Heather. 2012. "The Logic of Conflict: Practices of Social Control among Inner City Neapolitan Girls." In Susan Danby and Maryanne Theobald (eds.), *Disputes in Everyday Life: Social and Moral Orders of Children and Young People*, 325–353. Bingley: Emerald Group.

Lytra, Vally. 2007. "Teasing in Contact Encounters: Frames, Participant Positions and Responses." *Multilingual Journal of Crosscultural and Interlanguage Communication*, 26: 381–408.

Maccoby, Eleanor E. 1990. "Gender and Relationships: A Developmental Account." *American Psychologist*, 45(4): 513–520.

Maccoby, Eleanor Emmons, and Carol Nagy Jacklin. 1974. *The Psychology of Sex Differences*. Stanford: Stanford University Press.

Malinowski, Bronisław. 1959 [1923]. "The Problem of Meaning in Primitive Languages." In Charles K. Ogden and Ivor A. Richards (eds.), *The Meaning of Meaning*, 296–336. New York: Harcourt, Brace & World.

Maltz, Daniel N., and Ruth A. Borker. 1982. "A Cultural Approach to Male–Female Miscommunication." In John J. Gumperz (ed.), *Language and Social Identity*, 196–216. Cambridge: Cambridge University Press.

Mead, Margaret. 1933. "More Comprehensive Field Methods." *American Anthropologist*, 35: 1–15.

Mendoza-Denton, Norma. 2008. *Homegirls: Symbolic Practices in the Making of Latina Youth Styles*. Oxford: Blackwell.

Mills, Sara. 2004. "Third Wave Feminist Linguistics and the Analysis of Sexism." *Discourse Analysis Online*. At http://extra.shu.ac.uk/daol/articles/open/2003/001/mills2003001-t.html, accessed October 30, 2013.

Minks, Amanda. 2006. "Mediated Intertextuality in Pretend Play among Nicaraguan Miskitu Children." *Texas Linguistic Forum (SALSA)*, 49: 117–127.

Minks, Amanda. 2008. "Performing Gender in Song Games among Nicaraguan Miskitu Children." *Language & Communication*, 28: 36–56.

Minks, Amanda. 2010. "Socializing Heteroglossia among Miskitu Children on the Caribbean Coast of Nicaragua." *Pragmatics*, 20(4): 495–522.

Minks, Amanda. 2013. *Voices of Play: Miskitu Children's Speech and Song on the Atlantic Coast of Nicaragua*. Tucson: University of Arizona Press.

Morgan, Marcyliena. 2002. *Language, Discourse, and Power in African American Culture*. Cambridge: Cambridge University Press.

Nakamura, Keiko. 2001. "Gender and Language Use in Japanese Preschool Children." *Research on Language and Social Interaction*, 34(1): 15–44.

Ochs, Elinor, and Bambi B. Schieffelin. 2012. "The Theory of Language Socialization." In Alessandro Duranti, Elinor Ochs, and Bambi B. Schieffelin (eds.), *The Handbook of Language Socialization*, 1–20. Oxford: Wiley-Blackwell.

O'Malley, Margaret Whitney. 2011. "Learning to Be Greek: A Social and Negotiated Process." Unpublished MA thesis, University of California, Santa Barbara.

Paugh, Amy L. 2012. *Playing with Languages: Children and Change in a Caribbean Village*. New York: Berghahn.

Pujolar, Joan. 2001. *Gender, Heteroglossia and Power: A Sociolinguistic Study of Youth Culture*. Berlin: Mouton de Gruyter.

Rampton, Ben. 1995. *Crossing: Language and Ethnicity among Adolescents*. London: Longman.

Rampton, Ben. 2003. "Hegemony, Social Class, and Stylisation." *Pragmatics*, 13(1): 49–84.

Rampton, Ben. 2006. *Language in Late Modernity. Interaction in an Urban School*. Cambridge: Cambridge University Press.

Reynolds, Jennifer F. 2007. "'Buenos Días/((Military Salute))': The Natural History of a Coined Insult." *Research on Language and Social Interaction*, 40(4): 437–465.

Reynolds, Jennifer F. 2010. "Enregistering the Voices of Discursive Figures of Authority in Antonero Children's Socio-dramatic Play." *Pragmatics*, 20(4): 467–493.

Sacks, Harvey. 1995. *Lectures on Conversation*, vols. 1 and 2, ed. Gail Jefferson, intro. Emanuel A. Schegloff. Oxford: Blackwell.

Schegloff, Emanuel A. 1991. "Reflections on Talk and Social Structure." In Deirdre Boden and Don H. Zimmerman (eds.), *Talk and Social Structure*, 44–70. Berkeley: University of California Press.

Scheper-Hughes, Nancy, and Carolyn Sargent. 1998. "Introduction: The Cultural Politics of Childhood." In Nancy Scheper-Hughes and Carolyn Sargent (eds.), *Small Wars: The Cultural Politics of Childhood*, 1–34. Berkeley: University of California Press.

Schieffelin, Bambi B. 2003. "Language and Place in Children's Worlds." *Texas Linguistics Forum (SALSA)*, 45: 152–166.

Schofield, Janet Ward. 1981. "Complementary and Conflicting Identities: Images and Interaction in an Interracial School." In Steven R. Asher and John M. Gottman (eds.), *The Development of Children's Friendships*, 53–90. Cambridge: Cambridge University Press.

Shankar, Shalini. 2008. "Speaking Like a Model Minority: 'FOB' Styles, Gender, and Racial Meanings among Desi Teens in Silicon Valley." *Journal of Linguistic Anthropology*, 18(2): 268–289.

Sheldon, Amy. 1993. "Pickle Fights: Gendered Talk in Preschool Disputes." In Deborah Tannen (ed.), *Gender and Conversational Interaction*, 83–109. Oxford: Oxford University Press.

Sheldon, Amy. 1996. "You Can Be the Baby Brother, but You Aren't Born Yet: Preschool Girls' Negotiation for Power and Access in Pretend Play." *Research on Language and Social Interaction*, 29(1): 57–80.

Smith, Benjamin. 2010. "Of Marbles and (Little) Men: Bad Luck and Masculine Identification in Aymara Boyhood." *Journal of Linguistic Anthropology*, 20(1): 225–239.

Sophocleous, Andry, and Christiana Themistocleous. 2011. "Ingroup Allegiances and Outgroup Antipathies: Positioning Self and Other in Female Bidialectal Written Interactions." Paper presented at the Sixth International Conference on Youth Language, University of Freiburg, Hermann Paul Center for Linguistics.

Speer, Susan A., and Elizabeth H. Stokoe. 2011. *Conversation and Gender*. Cambridge: Cambridge University Press.

Spreckels, Janet. 2009. "'Now He Thinks He's Listening to Rock Music': Identity

Construction among German Teenage Girls." In Anna-Brita Strenstroem and Annette M. Jorgensen (eds.), *Youngspeak in a Multilingual Perspective*, 31–53. Amsterdam: Benjamins.

Streeck, Jürgen. 1986. "Towards Reciprocity: Politics, Rank and Gender in the Interaction of a Group of Schoolchildren." In Jenny Cook-Gumperz, William A. Corsaro, and Jurgen Streeck (eds.), *Children's Worlds and Children's Language*, 295–326. Berlin: Mouton de Gruyter.

Svahn, Johanna. 2012. *The Everyday Practice of School Bullying: Children's Participation in Peer Group Activities and School-Based Anti-Bullying Initiatives*. Uppsala Studies in Education, no. 129. Uppsala: Department of Education, Uppsala University.

Svahn, Johanna, and Ann-Carita Evaldsson. 2011. "You Could Just Ignore Me: Situating Peer Exclusion within the Contingencies of Girls' Everyday Interactional Practices." *Childhood*, 18(4): 155–171.

Tannen, Deborah. 2001. *He Said, She Said: Gender, Language, and Communication* (video). Los Angeles: Into the Classroom Media.

Tarım, Şeyda D., and Amy Kyratzis. 2012. "Challenging and Orienting to Monolingual School Norms in Turkish American Children's Peer Disputes and Classroom Negotiations at a U.S. Turkish Saturday School." In Susan Danby and Maryanne Theobald (eds.), *Disputes in Everyday Life: Social and Moral Orders of Children and Young People*, 193–220. Bingley: Emerald Group.

Tetreault, Chantal. 2007. "Peer Group Communication at the Onset of Adulthood: Algerian Youth in France." *Texas Linguistic Forum (SALSA XIV)*, 50: 1–8.

Tetreault, Chantal. 2008. "*La Racaille*: Figuring Gender, Generation, and Stigmatized Space in a French *Cité*." *Gender and Language*, 2(2): 141–170.

Tetreault, Chantal. 2009. "Reflecting Respect: Transcultural Communicative Practices of Muslim French Youth." *Pragmatics*, 19(1): 65–84.

Tetreault, Chantal. 2010. "Collaborative Conflicts: Teens Performing Aggression and Intimacy in a French *Cité*." *Journal of Linguistic Anthropology*, 20(1): 72–86.

Thorne, Barrie. 1986. "Girls and Boys Together … But Mostly Apart: Gender Arrangements in Elementary School." In William W. Hartup and Zick Rubin (eds.), *Relationships and Development*, 167–184. Hillsdale, NJ: Lawrence Erlbaum.

Thorne, Barrie. 1993. *Gender Play: Girls and Boys in School*. New Brunswick, NJ: Rutgers University Press.

Whiting, Beatrice Blyth, and Carolyn Pope Edwards. 1988. *Children of Different Worlds: The Formation of Social Behavior*. Cambridge, MA: Harvard University Press.

Willis, Paul. 1981. *Learning to Labor: How Working Class Kids Get Working Class Jobs*. New York: Columbia University Press.

Woolard, Kathryn A. 1998. "Introduction: Language Ideology as a Field of Inquiry." In Bambi B. Schieffelin, Kathryn A. Woolard, and Paul V. Kroskrity (eds.), *Language Ideologies: Practice and Theory*, 3–49. Oxford: Oxford University Press.

Zentella, Ana Celia. 1997. *Growing up Bilingual: Puerto Rican Children in New York*. Oxford: Blackwell.

27 Language and Gender in Adolescence

PENELOPE ECKERT

1. Adolescence as Ideology

Like gender, adolescence is an ideological construct. It is an outgrowth of industrialization – of the shift to institutionalized preparation for work, and the need to keep the young out of the workforce. And like gender, adolescence is subjected to biologizing discourses. But while there are physiological changes that coincide to some extent with the entrance into adolescence, to attribute "adolescent behavior" to "raging hormones" is to ignore the obvious: that, above all, adolescence is an age- and generation-based location in the political economy.

Adolescents in postindustrial society are not simply left to develop into adults, but spend much of their time in institutions that isolate them from adults. In the United States particularly, where secondary schools are close to total institutions (Goffman 1961), school produces a social hothouse, in which a social order emerges that solidifies the gender hierarchy as well as class, racial, and ethnic hierarchies. Adolescence slows time for the age group as, rather than focusing on getting to adulthood, adolescents enter into a kind of cultural sink in which adolescence is not something to pass through, but something to achieve. And in the process, people become not more adult, but more adolescent. "Adolescent culture," in other words, is very much the product of the place given to adolescents in our society. If we want to consider gender in adolescence (and beyond), we need to consider how our adolescent institutions constrain the construction of gender (see, e.g., Connell et al. 1982; Thorne 1993).

If adolescents and women share a naturalizing discourse, they also share stigma and trivialization of their activities and concerns. Discourses of gender, and of race and class, are built on discourses of age – discourses of responsibility, maturity, control, emotionality, intellectual capacity, and rationality. The ultimate legitimate person in the social order, the white upper middle-class male,[1] is slated to be unemotional, rational, focused on "business," and endowed with global and

The Handbook of Language, Gender, and Sexuality, Second Edition.
Edited by Susan Ehrlich, Miriam Meyerhoff, and Janet Holmes.
© 2014 John Wiley & Sons, Inc. Published 2017 by John Wiley & Sons, Inc.

objective knowledge. Women and adolescents, on the other hand, are viewed as emotional, changeable, irrational, trivial, and unobjective. Adults can always get a sigh, a groan, or a laugh of commiseration just by announcing that they have adolescent offspring. People joke with those of us who work with adolescents about our bravery and forbearance. At a campus celebration of books published by Stanford faculty in 2000, I was awarded a tongue-in-cheek prize for "work above and beyond the call of duty" for the ethnographic research involved in my book on adolescent linguistic and social practice (Eckert 2000).

In other words, life stage and gender are intertwining constructions, and the examination of one calls for the examination of the other. Adolescence is a particularly rich life stage for the study of the interplay between the construction of language and the construction of social identity because while it is eminently transitional, it is also highly reified and experienced as static (by many as painfully so).

2. School as Site for the Construction of Adolescence

As the official transition from childhood to adulthood, adolescence is the time when the age cohort moves from their parents' and families' social sphere to one that they construct for themselves – one that is transitional from the social order of their childhood to the social order of their adulthood. Because adolescence is defined by secondary education, this takes place primarily in reference to schools. Even for those who are not in school, or who don't spend much time there, the very fact of their relation to the school is central to their place in society as *dropouts* or *truants*. And within the school, those who choose to minimize their institutional participation are labeled *antisocial*. In other words, participation in the secondary school institution defines legitimate adolescence.

The dominant adult view of adolescence is of an "unfinished" population – a population in which judgment has not quite caught up with desire. This attribution constructs the age group as not yet responsible but harmless, their antics relatively predictable. And it defines adolescents as a special leisure class – without family and financial responsibilities, living out of danger and with comfortable adult caretakers, and content to participate in the school institution until it's "time" to join the adult world. The many people in their teens who for whatever reason do not fit this description are cast as anti-adolescents. For them, adolescence and adulthood are blurred, both in day-to-day experience and in treatment by the institutions of society – schools, social services, the courts. Any focus on adolescence as a life stage locates struggle between adolescents and adults, erasing the ways in which adult-built institutions have set up a struggle among adolescents – a struggle that will endure into the cohort's own adulthood.

2.1   *Accomplishing heterosociability*

To understand gender in adolescence, we need to begin with the stage at which the adolescent social order emerges. As an age cohort approaches adolescence (in my work in the United States, this is in late elementary school), there is a gradual appropriation of power and authority from adults into the cohort, the development of an integrated social order, and the reorganization of normative relations within the cohort from asexual to heterosexual. By the time the cohort moves into secondary school, it has accomplished the social changes that move it into a heterosexual and hierarchical social order. And as the official locus of adolescence, the US high school brings with it an institutionalization of traditional gender arrangements, heterosexuality, and romance. Heterosexuality and romance are also publicly constructed in high school through dances and prom kings and queens, in the relation between dating and social status, and in the careful following of the antics of the "famous couples" of each graduating class.

Achieving adolescence is a goal for younger children – the move to adolescence is not an individual experience – it is an age cohort's *prise de conscience*. The initial stages of this process involve a transcendence of the teacher-dominated classroom, developing a social order that spans the age cohort, moving toward age-group autonomy. This transcendence is accomplished through the emergence of a heterosexual market (Eckert 2011; Thorne 1993), dominated by a *crowd* – a socially heterosexual community of practice that comes to dominate attention and space, and comes to be known as the "popular crowd." In the crowd, heterosexual pairing takes place as a group endeavor, providing support and encouragement for individuals as they experiment, on behalf of the rest of the cohort, with unfamiliar and face-threatening practices. As the visible locus of emerging social heterosexuality, the crowd dominates attention through its fast-paced new activity, as couples form and break up at a dizzying rate. The rapid negotiation of alliances creates a market, constructing desirability and worth in heterosexual terms. Within this enterprise arises a new gender differentiation and division of labor. Boys come to dominate certain arenas of recognized accomplishment – most notably sports and overt competition of many kinds. They begin to accomplish masculinity – to expand themselves physically, developing sports moves and postures that maximize the appearance of contained volume and strength, and engaging in aggressive, competitive talk about "masculine" subjects. And as girls become marginalized in these activities, they establish and dominate new spheres of activity and accomplishment. They engage with the technology of beauty and personality, experimenting with cosmetics, clothing, hairstyles, and the development of cute or clever personalities. And more importantly, they engage in *social engineering*. The entire heterosexual enterprise at this point is about alignments within the cohort rather than about individual boy–girl relationships. The pairs are brokered by members of the crowd, and the individual couples generally do not spend time together except in a few cases for very brief ritual appearances. And it is the girls who do the brokering. Girls control the heterosexual market – they decide who will go with whom, they arrange meetings and alliances, and they negotiate desirability.

As part of their role as brokers in the market, girls take up new forms of verbal activity. In the fifth grade playground, boys come to dominate the large games that take up the central area – to become *athletes* rather than *boys playing*. And girls, one by one and group by group, move away from some of their old playground activities, and take to standing, sitting, or walking around the periphery, watching the boys, heckling them, or talking intensely together. The practice of walking around has in itself symbolic significance. Moving away from the crowd and walking around slowly, intensely engaged in conversation, draws attention to those who do it. It stands in stark contrast to the fast movements of their peers, to play, to the larger groups engaged in games, and to the louder tone of children's talk and shouting. This walking, furthermore, is a visible occasion on which girls engage in intense negotiation of heterosexual pairings and realignment of friendships.

One might be inclined to attribute girls' engagement in negotiating relationships as evidence of the kind of connection orientation that is commonly attributed to girls and women (Belenky et al. 1986; Gilligan, Lyons, and Hanmer 1990). If this is so, then *connection* has a different meaning than is commonly assumed. The focus on connection in the literature portrays girls as benign and positive in their relationships, in spite of the fact that any observer of adolescents during this period knows that girls can get quite mean and their friendships volatile, while boys' relationships tend to remain on a fairly even keel. A major activity among girls during this period is the development of cliques, ganging up on each other, shunning individuals, changing friends – a development of social toughness comparable to boys' development of physical or athletic toughness. Marjorie Harness Goodwin has chronicled this kind of activity in a variety of venues, and what is particularly striking about her findings is the elaborateness of girls' verbal activity in the accomplishment of exclusivity and the termination of relationships. The drawn-out nature of *he-said-she-said*, as girls police and sanction each other's behavior (Goodwin 1990), and the cleverness of girls' insults as they shun undesirables (Goodwin 2000), all show an engagement in mean articulateness. It may be that a certain amount of this nastiness comes from the feeling of subordination and exclusion in the new gender order, but the fact is that girls are not sugar and spice. (See also Goodwin & Kyratzis, Chapter 26 in this volume.)

This emerging social order brings with it – indeed depends on – an increase in peer-based social control and negotiation. Much of the linguistic activity observed as "adolescent" is part of the means of construction and maintenance of the social order. Certain kinds of speech acts gain particular prominence in the search for social control, and in the monitoring, particularly, of individuals' and groups' conformity to new gender norms. With the new heterosexual social order comes an intensification of pressure on boys to be aggressively masculine and heterosexual. Teasing is one of the more important and obvious verbal forms of social control that is certainly common in childhood, but continues in later elementary school and junior high school in highly focused encounters (Eder 1991). Much of this pressure comes from other boys, but Eder, Evans, and Parker (1995) found in their research in a junior high school that girls participate in sexual and homophobic verbal teasing and aggression as well. The use of labels such as *fag* to refer to any male who does not match up to masculine norms, or of *gay* to refer more generally to someone who also does not match up to norms, brings together the heterosexual and the masculine imperatives. And the gender asymmetry of terms like *slut* and *stud* create gender-asymmetrical categorizations based on sexual behavior – or in fact, at this stage, on behavior only remotely related, but nonetheless linked, to sexuality. The meaning of *slut* in early adolescence, and even to some extent in adolescence, is closer to the meaning of *hussy* – a female who oversteps general bounds of propriety, whether a girl who dates too many boys, or who is loud, or who does what she pleases.

Just as "talking" emerges with the heterosexual market, so does another speech activity often taken as indicative of females' connection orientation. Perhaps the most interesting verbal means by which girls monitor progress in the accomplishment of new feminine norms of behavior and adornment is the use of compliments. As the heterosexual market takes off, one can see girls learning to do compliments, and indeed complimenting becomes a heightened verbal activity. As in the adult population (Holmes 1995), compliments are overwhelmingly addressed to females, and focus on appearance. Like the pairing of couples on the heterosexual market, complimenting is intense and almost compulsive among girls engaged in the market. And like trade on the market, it serves to establish norms of behavior and appearance. Girls accomplish this work through both sincere and sarcastic complimenting. Sincere compliments to players in the market add value to the receiver as evidence of her quality, and to the giver as evidence of her possession and exercise of cultural knowledge. The practice of offering obviously false compliments to stigmatized girls is a major means of pointing out infractions of the new norms, but more important, of establishing and enforcing social hierarchies and boundaries. As with the more direct forms of social engineering, this use of compliments might lead us to reconsider the source of behaviors commonly viewed as reflecting girls' greater "connection" orientation (see Tannen, Chapter 25 in this volume).

Gender differences begin to appear in data on phonological and grammatical variation at around the time that the adolescent social order begins to emerge in elementary school. Several authors have found boys leading girls in the use of nonstandard variants at about the age of 10 (Biondi 1975; Macaulay 1977; Romaine 1984). Macaulay shows gender differences setting in between the earlier age in his sample (age 10) and the later age (age 14). It is certainly a general pattern that at least where clear nonstandardisms (particularly grammatical) are concerned, from early adolescence on, males in general use more of them than females. The use of vernacular language – language that is discouraged by adults, particularly teachers – is one means to establish one's independence, one's toughness, and one's right to "make the rules." And closely related to the use of vernacular language, for many, is the use of expletives and sexual references (de Klerk 1997; Eder, Evans, and Parker 1995; Kiesling 1997). Inasmuch as this is an important goal for boys as they try to achieve hegemonic masculinity, one might expect boys to make greater use of vernacular variants. This attitudinal gender difference is what Trudgill (1972) invokes in his discussion of *covert prestige*. And this may well explain the pattern that John Fischer (1958) found in his study of elementary school children, as boys reduced more occurrences of *-ng* than girls, and "typical" boys reduced more than "model" boys. Cheshire's (1982) study of an adolescent social network as defined by the use of a playground in Reading showed correlations between linguistic variables and participation in "vernacular" culture, which Cheshire defined primarily in terms of "toughness" (carrying weapons, engaging in criminal activity, demonstrating skill at fighting, swearing) – which, in turn, was strongly related to male gender. In her work with adolescents in Sydney, Edina Eisikovits (1987) found boys increasing their use of vernacular variables in their interviews with her, apparently as a show of defiance in the face of an authority figure. But we need to be careful not to automatically equate the search for autonomy and toughness with male gender, however much societal norms may lean in this direction. For, however compelling this view of gender may be, it breaks down in part when we take a closer look at general patterns, as becomes particularly clear in the data on adolescent speakers.

2.2   Constructing adolescent social categories

The arrival in secondary school marks the official beginning of adolescence, and with heterosociability firmly in place in the cohort, there is increased attention to other forms of diversity. In most places, primary schools feed into larger secondary schools, where there is often greater class, racial, and ethnic diversity – and sufficient numbers to form crowds based in these categories. Thrown together in a close environment for the better part of the week, students engage in identity politics, vying for space, visibility, social resources, legitimation. Space is exploited in such a way that the school layout becomes a highly charged social map, providing a variety of stages from which people can mount cultural performances. The semiotic activity that constitutes social categories within and beyond the school permeates just about every aspect of people's day-to-day practice. Styles emerge laden with social significance, mapping out the ideological terrain of the age cohort within an adult-defined environment. Differences in class, race, religion, and ethnicity, and positioning in relation to adult institutions (not only the school but government, police, courts, the media), to adult control, and to adolescence itself, create a highly charged atmosphere for the creation of distinction (Irvine 2001). These categories, in turn, are saturated with gender. Categories may be constructed around different gender practices, for example, with more or less gender segregation, more or less gender hierarchy, more or less consensuality – and these within different kinds of activities. The degree of hostility and/or segregation of categories may differ among males and among females, as may the need to exercise difference. It is the magnitude of this complexity that can make generalizations about gender problematic.

Labeling is an important means of producing and maintaining social distinctions. The simple existence of a term for a social type creates a category, allowing it to enter into everyday discourse. At the same time, the potential for labeling can serve as a strong means of social control. Labels arise in real use, and in relation to real people in real situations (Bucholtz 2011; Eckert and McConnell-Ginet 1995). We make social meaning by labeling as we chat. It is in speech activities such as making observations and judgments about people, pointing people out to others, describing absent people, that we endow labels with meaning. And in thus endowing labels with meaning, we create categorizations. In this way, the day-to-day use and reuse of labels brings about the continual ebb and flow of meaning and social change. This goes for the use of *fag, gay, slut,* and *stud* mentioned above, as well as for the huge range of category names that constitute an important part of the lexicon in any high school. In every school, a proliferation of labels maps out the local social terrain, the margins of respectability, and the terms of evaluation (T. Labov 1992). These labels connect to those in other schools, but always with either small differences in meaning or with strikingly different inventories – depending on the nature of the local social order. And these terms are used differentially by gender. Eckert and McConnell-Ginet (1995) have noted that the hegemonic categories (such as *jock* and *burnout*) tend to be primarily defined in terms of males, and female participants in these categories need to work harder to emphasize their category status. On the other hand, certain categories may be specifically male or female (such as *nerd* or *ditz*), while others may be used differently when referring to males and females. At any rate, the practice of labeling is a powerful means of co-constructing gender and other social categorizations, and of controlling social meaning within the community.

The volatility of these labels attests to – indeed is an agent of – social change. Mary Bucholtz's (1996; 2011) account of a group of girls claiming status as *nerds* – a status normally reserved for males – is a striking example of the process of change through the contestation of categories, the regendering of categories, and the reclaiming of epithets. These girls, in appropriating an aggressively intellectual and independent style, are making a claim about their ability not only to be smart but, like boys, to "make the rules." They lay this claim by constructing an entire style of speech that includes specialized names, lexicon, and phonological variables signaling articulateness (e.g., the hyper-articulation of stops). Thus as labels serve to produce and reproduce categories in discourse, speech style joins with other aspects of style (e.g., dress and other adornment, substance use, musical taste, territory, activities, movement) to make claims about one's own relation to those labels. Norma Mendoza-Denton's (1996; 2008) study of Mexican American girls in northern California shows how gang girls use a wide range of semiotic means, from language choice and variation to make-up and dress, to lay claim to gang identity and practice that has been traditionally reserved for males. Specific features of this style (e.g., the span of black eyeliner) are iconic of toughness, simultaneously signaling ethnic identity to non-Latinos, claiming access to the male prerogative of toughness, and setting themselves off from tamer girls.

Adolescent styles are viewed as ever changing, but trivialized as stylistic activity for its own sake. This attitude toward stylistic activity is part of the construction of hegemony by which style is an add-on for people who are not sufficient in their "natural state." The business suit and the man who wears it are "styleless" – and this stylelessness goes with seriousness of purpose, the important work of the world. Women in high heels and makeup, teeny-boppers, goths, and hip-hoppers, on the other hand, are frivolous: their stylistic activity a bid to be noticed or to rebel, and their activities just noise in the world. The opposition between the real and the styled is repeated across society in many ways. Most crucial to this discussion is the recursiveness of this opposition (Gal and Irvine 1995), as it distinguishes the middle from the working class, male from female, adult from adolescent, white from nonwhite.

In his study of white middle-class Parisian adolescents, Steve Albert (2000) noted how they distinguish themselves from adolescents who are "into" youth styles (*à fond dedans*). For these teenagers, knowledge of youth styles – of dress, of music, and so on – is crucial to being cosmopolitan, but so also is a lack of engagement in conscious stylistic activity, and an avoidance of specific youth styles. In this way, they lay claim to naturalness by claiming to choose what they like, what's comfortable, and, presumably, what's objectively good. Being *à fond dedans* ("into") styles, for them, signals a lack of the self-control and perspective that come with maturity – and with class. Unmarked, they are *hors style* – needing no explanation, packaging, or self-presentation.

At the same time, the situated appropriation of elements of these styles allows "mainstream" adolescents to lay temporary claim to bits of meaning. The use of Latino and African American Vernacular English (AAVE) features by white Anglo teenagers in the United States signals coolness, toughness, attitude. And while these acts of identity may indicate admiration, the admiration is for a specific set of attributes, and as such, as argued by scholars such as Mary Bucholtz (1999), Cecilia Cutler (1999), and Jane Hill (1993), it preserves the racial hierarchy. Based on her work in Rio de Janeiro, Jennifer Roth-Gordon (2001) argues that middle-class Brazilian adolescents engage in just enough slang use to establish their connection to youth culture. But the youth culture that they're connected to is a kind of imagined community in which youth are aligned in their up-to-dateness in opposition to their out-of-date parents. Originating in the tough poor *favelas*, urban slang represents youthful autonomy, but it is also linked to crime, race, and poverty. In their selective use of *favela* slang, middle-class adolescents assert that they are the upcoming generation, but signal restraint. And their ability to dispassionately appropriate *favela* youth resources constitutes, in their and their parents' view, legitimate adolescence, and an anticipation of legitimate adulthood. In other words, they construct their age group as aligned with their parents' class position. The *favela* youth, on the other hand, engage in slang "for real," and are expected to carry their slang into adulthood – an adulthood that will not differ significantly from youth.

3. Adolescents as Leaders in Linguistic Change

There is every reason to believe that linguistic change is propelled – or accelerated – by social upheaval. Historical linguists have noted that languages tend to change more rapidly during historical periods of unrest, and we have seen major linguistic developments at specific times of social change (Clermont and Cedergren 1979; Zhang 2005). One might consider that very similar dynamics are at work during the adolescent life stage. The cohort is undergoing rapid social change, with changing alliances, and ever emerging new forms of identity.

It is in, and by virtue of, this process that adolescents act as major agents of linguistic change.

By virtue of their transitional place in the life course, adolescents are in a particularly strong position to respond to change in the conditions of life, and in so doing bring about lasting social change. It is particularly apparent in communities undergoing rapid change that adolescents are society's transition teams, reinterpreting the world, resolving the old with the new, substrate with superstrate, culture with culture, local with transnational. In her study of Piniq, a Yup'ik community in southeastern Alaska, Leisy Wyman (2012) found that gender among adolescents is deeply intertwined with the loss of traditional culture, and she shows how gender mediates language and cultural shift (see also Meek, Chapter 28 in this volume). While young men continue to ice-fish and hunt seals, they do it now for sport rather than for survival, and women's traditional role in processing the products of the hunt has disappeared along with the survival needs. Young men have greater access to Yup'ik, since the male elders with whom they hunt use Yup'ik terminology and issue directives in Yup'ik, and there are Yup'ik prayers associated with hunting (such as a short prayer offered when returning a seal's head to the water). While young women participate in few situations that call for the use of Yup'ik, young men continue to use Yup'ik as they hunt, emerging in their generation as the leading speakers of the language as well as maintainers of the culture.

Chantal Tetrault (2000) describes the multilingual punning of French adolescents of North African descent. In *hachek*, a competitive word duel played by two participants, rhyming play between Arabic and French allows these teenagers to play with cultural meaning as they construct a new cultural space, or as she puts it, create "cultural crossroads from which to speak." Norma Mendoza-Denton's (2008) examination of the raising of /ɪ/ and (th)-stopping in the speech of Latino adolescents shows the importation of Spanish phonology into English, transforming English into a language that can construct Latino identities. In particular, the heightened use of this particular phonological feature in a highlighted discourse use of *and everything* relates it directly to the US life of these adolescents. Teenagers in immigrant communities are simultaneously mediating cultures, and they can do it not simply because they are a transitional generation, but precisely because of their life stage. As youth, they are expected to mess with meaning. By virtue of their location in time and social and cultural space, they have special knowledge, and in working with this knowledge – in making new meanings – they are constructing authenticity of a new kind. They are not just resolving ethnicity, gender, class, and race for today, but constructing permanent meanings that they will carry into adulthood, to be worked on in turn by the next generation.

Work in phonological and grammatical variation has shown adolescents interrupting what might otherwise be smooth age grading, leading all other age groups – younger and older – in sound change and in the use of vernacular forms. Adolescents are producing linguistic patterns that no longer reflect their family of origin, but that reflect their own search for a place in the peer social order.

As a cohort moves into adolescence, this use of variation in the aid of adolescent practice increases. Walt Wolfram's data (1969) on African American English in Detroit and Ronald Macaulay's data (1977) from Glasgow show better correlations of language use with parents' socioeconomic class for preadolescents than for adolescents. My own Detroit suburban study (Eckert 2000), which included only adolescents, saw parents' socioeconomic class give way as a significant correlate with variation in favor of the age-specific social categories that mediate social class for the adolescent age group. Potentially more striking evidence of the role of adolescent social practice on language change is Sarah Roberts's (2000; 2005) powerful argument, on the basis of historical Hawaiian data, that creolization in the case of Hawaiian Creole was effected not by children learning pidgin as their first language, but by older children and adolescents in peer-based communities of practice as they mutually constructed local-based identities.

This use of variation to construct a peer-based social order begins in preadolescence. In ethnographic studies of two elementary schools, Eckert (2008; 2011) found that the emerging popular crowd advanced sound changes as they engaged in heightened stylistic activity in their claim on the lead in adolescent practice. This work, for example, shows girls leading boys in the fronting of /ow/ and /uw/, and the girls in the popular crowd leading everyone. A hint at the relation between this phonological variability and social practice emerges in the close-up patterns of one mover and shaker in the popular crowd, as she fronts /ow/ significantly more in quotative uses of *go* than in other uses of the verb *go*. Direct quotation, particularly with innovative quotatives, is used above all in relating peers' actions, often judgmentally in the negotiation of norms that is a prime activity among girls in the crowd.

The more detailed data on variation in adolescence shows gender as a crucial aspect of the development of phonological distinctions among emerging social categories. In Ronald Macaulay's (1977) data, for example, the relation between boys' and girls' speech interacts strikingly with class. The middle-class boys use, fairly consistently, more vernacular variants than the middle-class girls, but the difference decreases as one moves through the lower middle class and upper working class, and disappears or reverses in the lower working class. The only consistent class stratification pattern across all five variables is among the 15-year-old girls; this suggests that this population is the most sensitive to the use of language to construct whatever social differences are embedded in class. William Labov (1991) has found this crossover pattern among adults as well (see also Meyerhoff, Chapter 4 in this volume).

A similar pattern emerges among Detroit suburban adolescents (Eckert 1989; 2000), which intensifies as one breaks down social categories and focuses on the social practices that constitute those categories. The polar school-based categories, the *jocks* and the *burnouts*, constitute middle-class and working-class cultures in the high school. The burnouts lead in the use of vernacular variants, including urban sound changes spreading outward from the urban periphery. The jocks show a considerable gender difference, with the boys generally using more vernacular forms, while the gender difference is small among the burnouts. Put otherwise, the social category difference is greater among the girls. Furthermore, the most vernacular speakers in the school – dramatically leading all other speakers – are a group of girls known to be the "wildest" burnouts, while the most conservative speakers are the "corporate" jock boys – leaders in student government. If there is a consistent gender pattern in all these data, it is girls' greater overall indexical use of linguistic variability.

4. Policing Adolescent Language

An important part of the verbal culture of adolescence is produced not by the adolescents but by the media they engage with. It is continually observed that adolescence provides a crucial market for consumer goods and services, and that the media are poised to exploit that market. The media target preadolescent audiences with adolescent-oriented consumerism, marketing adolescence itself. An examination of magazines aimed at adolescents shows an overwhelming gender ideology, with magazines aimed at boys focusing on activities (skateboarding, sports) and magazines aimed at girls focusing on romance and the production of the self.[2] The encouragement of a preoccupation with the self as object is an important means of building a market (Chanda 1991), and it is well known that the media target adolescents with sexually oriented consumerism, and girls in particular with the technology of physical and spiritual perfection. These magazines do not simply put forth ideas – they set up a gendered discourse for adolescents to participate in, engaging them in imagined communities that are formed to a great extent by linguistic practice. Mary Talbot (1992) examines the discourse of a British teen magazine, *Jackie*, showing how the writers engage girls in a "synthetic sisterhood." Through the use of such things as emotive punctuation, first- and second-person pronouns, response-demanding utterances, and through setting up shared presuppositions, the writers engage the reader in imaginary dialogue – all the while constraining the reader's part in the dialogue (see Talbot, Chapter 31 in this volume). Many of these magazines also introduce readers to the writing and editorial staff, showing photographs and portraying their speech as cool, perky, and "teenage," and inviting them into friendship. In the process, the young adult writers recycle a form of discourse that they view as adolescent. In this way, the readers are engaged in an adolescent discourse invented by adults. This is reminiscent of the role of the media in the late Meiji era in constructing Japanese "women's language" (Inoue 2006).

Adolescent language is also directly policed – in school, in after-school programs, and even in colleges. The "mallspeak" frenzy in the early part of the twenty-first century in the United States was a particularly dramatic illustration of the convergence of the stigmatization of the language of adolescents and females. In 1999 Smith and Mount Holyoke Colleges (private colleges in Massachusetts) created a big media splash by introducing programs in speaking across the curriculum. Aimed at training students to be articulate public speakers, a reasonable goal in itself, this initiative was unfortunately couched in a discourse of verbal hygiene (Cameron 1995 and Chapter 14 in this volume), locating the problem not in the need to learn an academic register, but in the need to eradicate "mallspeak." In an article in the *Seattle Times*, Elizabeth Mehren (1999, A4) characterized mallspeak thus:

> A product of both the urban street scene and the consumer cathedrals of the San Fernando Valley in Los Angeles, Mallspeak is the speech form that gave forth the dreaded phrase "gag me with a spoon" and made "like" the first word to be a verb, adjective, adverb and conjunction – all at once. "Minimalist," "repetitive," "imprecise," and "inarticulate" are some of the words Smith College President Ruth Simmons uses to describe Mallspeak, adding, "It drives me crazy."

This packaged gender stereotype based on "valley girls" has endured, and, interestingly, features that haven't necessarily originated in California are reliably added to the package. Considerable attention was paid at one point to the use of *like* as a discourse marker, and to the use of rising intonation on declaratives (dubbed "uptalk"). Both were attributed to adolescents, and particularly to adolescent girls, and both were interpreted as hedges and taken to signal the speakers' lack of concern with precision, or unwillingness to take responsibility for their statements. And when they are discussed specifically with respect to girls, they are taken to indicate insecurity and an unwillingness to state a forceful opinion. There is some evidence that young people, and females, make greater use of both of these than older and male people. What is problematic is the situated nature of the evidence and the interpretation of this use. Suzanne Romaine and Deborah Lange (1991) note that in an informally gathered corpus of quotative uses of *like*, the vast majority were used by women and girls. They do not claim, however, that girls are more likely to use *like* more as a quotative, but that they actually use more of the kind of constructed dialogue that calls for the use of *like*.

Women and adolescents also appear to lead in the use of rising intonation on declaratives. In Australia, this feature is used most frequently by working-class speakers, teenagers, and women, and in description and narrative (Guy et al. 1986). Cynthia McLemore (1992), in a study of sorority speech, found that this intonational contour is part of "sorority" style, and that within the sorority it carries authority. Nonetheless, it is regularly targeted as a threat to a woman's professional success. A class project observed 300 people ordering drinks at a Stanford University juice stand during parents' weekend. As part of the ordering process, the female undergraduate server asked the customer to give his or her name. The demographic group that overwhelmingly used rising intonation the most in stating their names were middle-aged men. How many analysts would be ready to label this as an expression of insecurity? Mark Liberman has written a series of blogs[3] debunking the popular interpretation of rising intonation, including a discussion of its use in the construction of power and threat.

More recently, creak or "vocal fry" has achieved center stage in the media's never-ending search for things wrong with young women's speech (Freed, Chapter 32 in this volume). As yet they have reached no consensus about its "meaning," but only point to it as remarkable and annoying. What little quantitative research has been done on the topic (Wolk, Abdelli-Beruh, and Slavin 2012;

Yuasa 2010) has only shown that young women do use creak when they lower their pitch at the ends of phrases, but has not compared young women with older women or with men. While it does appear that creak is used increasingly in the speech of young people, and while we certainly notice it more in the speech of young women, speculation about some global function is bound to be wrong. It may be, for example, that some younger women are lowering their pitch ranges, which brings on creak – and perhaps in some cases this is an authoritative move. But creak is used stylistically in myriad ways – to index nonchalance, sexual interest, fatigue, boredom. Norma Mendoza-Denton (2011) emphasizes this multiplicity of functions, and shows how creak emerges in the construction of a "hardcore Chicano gangster," which can be gendered both male and female. (See also Podesva and Kajino, Chapter 5 in this volume.)

Marginalized, delegitimized youth are singled out for their own kind of verbal hygiene. Cathryn Houghton (1992, 282) chronicles the practice of group therapy in an institutional setting, which aims at socializing a group made up largely of poor Latina adolescents into "productive and independently functioning adults." Key to this socialization is the imposition of a discourse style that constructs the speaker as autonomous (i.e., referring to the self rather than the group). It is worth noting that the kind of group-oriented language that is being problematized in this therapy group is precisely the kind of language that is commonly celebrated in discussions of "women's language." While I am not endorsing the view of women's language as particularly collaborative, I do note that it is apparently all right for some women and girls to conform to the maternalistic construction of female speech, but not for others.

5. Conclusion

My purpose in this chapter has been twofold: to consider the interactions between language, gender, and other aspects of identity in adolescence, and to consider the status of adolescence as a site for the study of language and social identity. It should be clear that I believe that age-related ideology is inseparable from gender ideology, as well as from ideologies of class, race, and ethnicity. The study of language and gender, therefore, needs to move into the study of the life span, and the gendering of life stages.

As the move into and through adolescence is a particularly important cross-roads for gender, it is one place to look to examine some of our most deeply ingrained beliefs about gender. Work on girls moving toward adolescence, for example, clearly calls into question any view that girls' language use reflects any more of a "connection" orientation than boys' (e.g., Cameron 1997). A focus on other life stages may well provide a new way of looking at other aspects of gender. Consider, for example, the view of women as nurturant. This, I would argue, is one of those essentialist ideals built on something that is in fact specific to a particular life stage. Nurturing is an activity, which can become a long-term characteristic of those who identify with nurturing activity in a long-term way.

Just as competitiveness is required of any athlete and studiousness of any scholar, nurturing is required of any caretaker of small children, including mothers. And being an athlete, a scholar, or a caretaker of small children may be a temporary phase in one's life. I would argue that there is nothing particularly nurturant about girls. Children who have strong attachments to young pets may feel nurturant toward them, and girls may be more encouraged than boys to nurture their pets, but this nurturance does not carry over into other relationships. Gender norms constrain many women to develop a nurturing persona as they seek to qualify as potential (wives and) mothers, and while gender norms may also lead women to maintain this persona after it has served its purpose, many older women are impatient and eager to move away from nurturing activity. Serious thought about life stages, therefore, may be an important aspect of the study of gender, and of its manifestations in language. This exploration of language and gender in adolescence should, I hope, encourage people to explore language and gender in young adulthood, old age, and any other stages that may or may not have names, and that emerge as relevant in people's lives.

NOTES

1   I have argued elsewhere (Eckert 1997, 151–167) that the study of language and age (or anything else and age) has been dominated by the middle-aged bias of those who do most of the research, and those who "manage" the age groups other than their own. Indeed, one might argue that the study of the life stage of middle age could be analogous to the study of whiteness.
2   I subscribed to a set of boys' magazines and a set of girls' magazines under two different names for several years. The two names found their ways onto quite different sets of mailing lists. My girls' magazine name received invitations to enter beauty contests, while my boys' magazine name received offers of credit cards.
3   See, e.g., http://itre.cis.upenn.edu/~myl/languagelog/archives/002708.html, accessed October 30, 2013.

REFERENCES

Albert, Steve J. 2000. "The Language of Authenticity: French Adolescents Talk about Personality, Style, and the Individual." Paper presented at the Annual Meeting of the American Anthropological Association, San Francisco.

Belenky, Mary F., Blythe. M. Clinchy, Nancy R. Goldberger, and Jill M. Tarule. 1986. *Women's Ways of Knowing*. New York: Basic Books.

Biondi, Lawrence. 1975. *The Italian-American Child: His Sociolinguistic Acculturation*. Washington, DC: Georgetown University Press.

Bucholtz, Mary. 1996. "Geek the Girl: Language, Femininity and Female Nerds." In Natasha Warner, Jocelyn Ahlers, Leela Bilmes, Monica Oliver, Suzanne Wertheim, and Melinda Chen (eds.), *Gender and Belief Systems*, 119–131. Berkeley: Berkeley Women and Language Group.

Bucholtz, Mary. 1999. "You da Man: Narrating the Racial Other in the Production of White Masculinity." *Journal of Sociolinguistics*, 3: 443–460.

Bucholtz, Mary. 2011. *White Kids: Language, Race, and Styles of Youth Identity.* Cambridge: Cambridge University Press.

Cameron, Deborah. 1995. *Verbal Hygiene.* London: Routledge.

Cameron, Deborah. 1997. "Performing Gender Identity: Young Men's Talk and the Construction of Heterosexual Masculinity." In Sally Johnson and Ulrike Hanna Meinhof (eds.), *Language and Masculinity*, 47–64. Oxford: Blackwell.

Chanda, P. Sita. 1991. "Birthing Terrible Beauties: Feminisms and 'Women's Magazines.'" *Economic and Political Weekly*, 26(43) (October 26): WS 67–70.

Cheshire, Jenny. 1982. *Variation in an English Dialect*. Cambridge: Cambridge University Press.

Clermont, Jacques, and Henrietta Cedergren. 1979. "Les 'R' de Ma Mère Sont Perdus dans l'Air." In Pierrette Thibault (ed.), *Le Français Parlé: etudes sociolinguistiques*, 13–28. Edmonton: Linguistic Research.

Connell, Robert W., Dean J. Ashenden, Sandra Kessler, and Gary W. Dowsett. 1982. *Making the Difference: Schools, Families and Social Division.* Sydney: George Allen & Unwin.

Cutler, Cecilia A. 1999. "Yorkville Crossing: White Teens, Hip Hop and African American English." *Journal of Sociolinguistics*, 3: 428–441.

de Klerk, Vivian. 1997. "The Role of Expletives in the Construction of Masculinity." In Sally Johnson and Ulrike Hanna Meinhof (eds.), *Language and Masculinity*, 144–158. Oxford: Blackwell.

Eckert, Penelope. 1989. *Jocks and Burnouts: Social Categories and Identity in the High School*. New York: Teachers College Press.

Eckert, Penelope. 1997. "Age as a Sociolinguistic Variable." In Florian Coulmas (ed.), *The Handbook of Sociolinguistics*, 151–167. Oxford: Blackwell.

Eckert, Penelope. 2000. *Linguistic Variation as Social Practice.* Oxford: Blackwell.

Eckert, Penelope. 2008. "Where do Ethnolects Stop?" *International Journal of Bilingualism*, 12: 25–42.

Eckert, Penelope. 2011. "Language and Power in the Preadolescent Heterosexual Market." *American Speech*, 86: 85–97.

Eckert, Penelope, and Sally McConnell-Ginet. 1995. "Constructing Meaning, Constructing Selves: Snapshots of Language, Gender and Class from Belten High." In Mary Bucholtz and Kira Hall (eds.), *Gender Articulated: Language and the Culturally Constructed Self*, 469–507. London: Routledge.

Eder, Donna. 1991. "The Role of Teasing in Adolescent Peer Group Culture." In Spencer Cahill (ed.), *Social Studies of Child Development*, 181–197. Greenwich, CT: JAI Press.

Eder, Donna, Catherine Colleen Evans, and Stephen Parker. 1995. *School Talk: Gender and Adolescent Culture*. New Brunswick, NJ: Rutgers University Press.

Eisikovits, Edina. 1987. "Sex Differences in Inter- and Intra-Group Interaction among Adolescents." In Anne Pauwels (ed.), *Women and Language in Australian and New Zealand Society*, 45–58. Sydney: Australian Professional Publications.

Fischer, John L. 1958. "Social Influences on the Choice of a Linguistic Variant." *Word*, 14: 47–56.

Gal, Susan, and Judith T. Irvine. 1995. "The Boundaries of Languages and Disciplines: How Ideologies Construct Difference." *Social Research*, 62: 967–1001.

Gilligan, Carol, Nona P. Lyons, and Trudy J. Hanmer, eds. 1990. *Making Connections: The Relational Worlds of Adolescent Girls at Emma Willard School*. Cambridge, MA: Harvard University Press.

Goffman, Erving. 1961. *Asylums: Essays on the Social Situation of Mental Patients and Other Inmates*. New York: Anchor.

Goodwin, Marjorie Harness. 1990. *He-Said-She-Said: Talk as Social Organization among Black Children*. Bloomington: Indiana University Press.

Goodwin, Marjorie Harness. 2000. "Constituting the Moral Order in Girls' Social Organization: Language Practices in the Construction of Social Exclusion."

Paper presented at the International Gender and Language Association conference (IGALA 2), Stanford.

Guy, Gregory, Barbara Horvath, Julia Vonwiller, Elaine Daisley, and Inge Rogers. 1986. "An Intonational Change in Progress in Australian English." *Language in Society*, 15: 23–52.

Hill, Jane H. 1993. "Hasta la Vista, Baby: Anglo Spanish in the American Southwest." *Critique of Anthropology*, 13: 145–176.

Holmes, Janet. 1995. *Women, Men and Politeness*. London: Longman.

Houghton, Cathryn. 1992. "'Talking It Out' or Talking It In: An Ethnography of Power and Language in Psychotherapeutic Practice." In Kira Hall, Mary Bucholtz, and Birch Moonwomon (eds.), *Locating Power: Proceedings of the Second Berkeley Women and Language Conference*, 272–285. Berkeley: Berkeley Women and Language Group.

Inoue, Miyako. 2006. *Vicarious Language: Gender and Linguistic Modernity in Japan*. Berkeley: University of California Press.

Irvine, Judith. 2001. "'Style' as Distinctiveness: The Culture and Ideology of Linguistic Differentiation." In Penelope Eckert and John Rickford (eds.), *Stylistic Variation in Language*, 21–43. Cambridge: Cambridge University Press.

Kiesling, Scott. 1997. "Power and the Language of Men." In Sally Johnson and Ulrike Hanna Meinhof (eds.), *Language and Masculinity*, 65–85. Oxford: Blackwell.

Labov, William. 1991. "The Intersection of Sex and Social Class in the Course of Linguistic Change." *Language Variation and Change*, 2: 205–251.

Labov, Theresa. 1992. "Social and Language Boundaries among Adolescents." *American Speech*, 67: 339–366.

Macaulay, Ronald K. S. 1977. *Language, Social Class and Education: A Glasgow Study*. Edinburgh: Edinburgh University Press.

McLemore, Cynthia. 1992. "The Interpretation of L*H in English." *Texas Linguistic Forum*, 32: 127–147.

Mehren, Elizabeth. 1999. "Like, Y'know, They Learn to Speak More Effectively." *Seattle Times*, March 25: A4. At http://community.seattletimes.nwsource.com/archive/?date=19990325&slug=2951471, accessed October 30, 2013.

Mendoza-Denton, Norma. 1996. "'Muy Macha': Gender and Ideology in Gang Girls' Discourse about Makeup." *Ethnos*, 61(1–2): 47–63.

Mendoza-Denton, Norma. 2008. *Homegirls: Symbolic Practices in the Making of Latina Youth Styles*. Oxford: Blackwell.

Mendoza-Denton, Norma. 2011. "The Semiotic Hitchhiker's Guide to Creaky Voice: Circulation and Gendered Hardcore in a Chicana/o Gang Persona." *Journal of Linguistic Anthropology*, 21: 261–280.

Roberts, Sarah. 2000. "Nativization and the Genesis of Hawaiian Creole." In John H. McWhorter (ed.), *Language Change and Language Contact in Pidgins and Creoles*, 257–300. Amsterdam: Benjamins.

Roberts, Sarah. 2005. "The Emergence of Hawai'i Creole English in the Early Twentieth Century: The Sociohistorical Context of Creole Genesis." Unpublished doctoral dissertation, Stanford University.

Romaine, Suzanne. 1984. *The Language of Children and Adolescents*. Oxford: Blackwell.

Romaine, Suzanne, and Deborah Lange. 1991. "The Use of *Like* as a Marker of Reported Speech and Thought: A Case of Grammaticalization in Progress." *American Speech*, 66: 227–279.

Roth-Gordon, Jennifer. 2001. "Slang and the Struggle over Meaning: Race, Language, and Power in Brazil." Unpublished PhD dissertation, Department of Cultural and Social Anthropology, Stanford University.

Talbot, Mary. 1992. "A Synthetic Sisterhood: False Friends in a Teenage Magazine." In Kira Hall, Mary Bucholtz, and Birch Moonwomon (eds.), *Locating Power: Proceedings of the Second Berkeley Women and Language Conference*, 573–580. Berkeley: Berkeley Women and Language Group.

Tetrault, Chantal. 2000. "Adolescents' Multilingual Punning and Identity Play in a French *Cité*." Paper presented at the Annual Meeting of the American Anthropological Association, San Francisco.

Thorne, Barrie. 1993. *Gender Play*. New Brunswick, NJ: Rutgers University Press.

Trudgill, Peter. 1972. "Sex, Covert Prestige and Linguistic Change in the Urban British English of Norwich." *Language in Society*, 1: 179–195.

Wolfram, Walt. 1969. *A Sociolinguistic Description of Detroit Negro Speech*. Washington, DC: Center for Applied Linguistics.

Wolk, Lesley, Nassima B. Abdelli-Beruh, and Dianne Slavin. 2012. "Habitual Use of Vocal Fry in Young Adult Female Speakers." *Journal of Voice*, 26: 111–116.

Wyman, Leisy. 2012. *Youth Culture and Linguistic Survivance*. Clevedon: Multilingual Matters.

Yuasa, Ikuko. 2010. "Creaky Voice: A New Feminine Voice Quality for Young Urban-oriented Upwardly Mobile American Women?" *American Speech*, 85: 315–337.

Zhang, Qing. 2005. "A Chinese Yuppie in Beijing: Phonological Variation and the Construction of a New Professional Identity." *Language in Society*, 34: 431–466.

Part VII Engagement and Application

28 Gender, Endangered Languages, and Revitalization

BARBRA A. MEEK

Representations of language as gendered (and gender as languaged) cover the gamut of theorization, from the ideational (ideas at the intersection of conceptualizing language and conceptualizing gender) to the ideological (the constitution, and contestation, of power and authority in relation to practices and theories of language and gender). In the late twentieth century, Judith Butler's emphasis on performance engaged the fields of linguistic anthropology and sociolinguistics, demanding not only analytic attention to bodily hexis, often read as identity, but an attention to a more general semiosis involving the transience of speech and its regimentation through practice, in context, in relation to the imagining, emergence, and management of social character and sociality (Cameron 2003; Holmes and Meyerhoff 2003; McElhinny 2003; Trechter 1999). This chapter attends to such transience and regimentation in relation to language endangerment and revitalization. However, the concern is not so much with the impending transience of the grammatical elements of endangered languages that have been claimed to index gender (see Trechter 1999 and Chapter 17 in this volume for discussion), but with the emerging regimentation of such languages through discourses and practices of revitalization and through institutions and individuals sanctioned to legitimate these languages. Attending more generally to the relationship between linguistic practices and institutions, Susan Gal and Kathryn Woolard (2001, 3–4) claim that "images of linguistic phenomena gain credibility when they create ties with other arguments about aspects of aesthetic or moral life … [R]epresentations of language phenomena gain social authority … from the institutional locations from which their proponents speak." This quote suggests that the social meaningfulness of what we might call gender and endangered languages becomes significant and interpretable (and evaluable) only in relation to the web of practice and ideology that attempts to conserve and to reconstitute "dying" languages. The reconstitution

The Handbook of Language, Gender, and Sexuality, Second Edition.
Edited by Susan Ehrlich, Miriam Meyerhoff, and Janet Holmes.
© 2014 John Wiley & Sons, Inc. Published 2017 by John Wiley & Sons, Inc.

of linguistic form, the documentation of structure, the entextualization of narrative, and the invention of orthography "gain credibility" through the institutional sites, the institutionalized authors, and the instituted aesthetics of typified practices resulting in conventions of (re)presentation, and of participation.

Of course institutional regimentations do not necessarily progress in a top-down fashion such that individuals (in this case, endangered language speakers and users) merely accept their fates without participation in or contestation over the discourses and practices so mandated. Some of these contestations and innovations have been documented and discussed, especially in relation to the creation of orthographies (e.g., Bender 2008), texts (e.g., Frawley, Hill, and Munro 2002), and indigenous language education (e.g., McCarty 2002; 2005). Complicating this directionality further, Susan Philips (2003, 272) has pointed out on several occasions that "[i]deologies in institutions through which the state articulates with the population it governs are particularly powerful." For endangered languages undergoing revitalization, institutional power, especially as authority, becomes magnified when institutional ideas about language converge or seemingly harmonize with ideas about language in circulation on the ground. Thus, the linguistic representations that result from such institutionally sanctioned endeavors acquire an authoritative weight that other similar projects do not (e.g., Meek and Messing 2007; Will 2012).[1]

Furthermore, not only do "images of linguistic phenomena" acquire legitimacy and authority as they articulate with different aspects of the evaluative sphere, but the individuals participating in these linguistic investments also affect and are affected by this evaluative environment ("aesthetic or moral life"); they "create the ties" and in so doing, become "tied" themselves to this "moral" sphere which is pervaded by judgments of accuracy, authenticity, and adequacy. For example, aboriginal language revitalization projects in the Yukon Territory frequently cast women participants in caregiving-type roles, such as preschool teachers and language instructors at the elementary school level (or as teachers generally). They have not usually been the spokespeople for the cause nor have they been the principal investigator on a project or the chief director of aboriginal language programming. They have, however, been responsible for heritage language maintenance, "as conservers of language" (Cotter 1999, 271; cf. Labov 1990). Thus, in keeping with the well-recognized public/private dichotomy in gender studies (see Philips 2003 and Chapter 15 in this volume), the value of women's practices in language revitalization and endangerment remains tied to the private spaces of linguistic practice, if not directly in the home, then at least in complementary, home-like, atmospheres of socialization (as with preschool immersion programs like Maori "language nests," Aboriginal Head Start, and Master-Apprentice approaches; see Hinton and Hale 2001). Certainly the pervasive discourse of orality,[2] being a discourse of "tradition," locates the learning of an endangered language within the home and other more intimate contexts, and between family members and relatives rather than amid some nameless mass public and in some "modern" institutional domain. This pattern, though, does not necessarily place the future of endangered languages and the success of language revitalization on the shoulders, or in the mouths, of women. That is, though women may be the primary vehicles for transmission, and in this way carry primary responsibility for the state of an endangered language, they are not necessarily granted equivalent authority over these languages or their programming. In this way, women might be discursively "tied" to the "home" and socializing practices while men might be "tied" to "institutions" and bureaucratic measures, women's authority remaining circumscribed by men's. I will return to this later in the chapter.

In contrast to these private, gendered "ties," Cotter (1999) provides a wonderful example of "tying" where women who speak Irish have become licit interviewers and interviewees on Irish-language radio. As she reveals the innovativeness of this move (of women into a hitherto male domain of practice), she also reveals a shift in the aesthetic moral sphere where women's participation "in a language-revitalization project … modernizes the role both of the Irish language and of Irish women in contemporary society" (Cotter 1999, 371). She points out as well that the linguistic devices used by these women during the interview promoted neither a gendering nor an anglicizing of their speech, but rather provided evidence of their social competence and fluency within a genre and medium of talk. Such linguistic flourishes point to opportunities for negotiating women's roles and authority in endangered language contexts through processes of language revitalization.

Thus, the authority of participants becomes negotiable and negotiated in relation to the various sites of their participation and the layering of institutional authorization and status. Given that women actively participate in indigenous language renewal, endangered language research, and revitalization and that they are the primary teachers of these languages (Hinton 1993; Kroskrity 2009), we might hypothesize that women have become the social authorities on/of endangered indigenous languages and practices of revitalization, and thus conclude that a gendering of practice has emerged. But is this in fact the case? Through their active participation in language revitalization, have women become the predominant authorities on the processes of language revitalization and the endangered languages they're revitalizing?

The rest of this chapter will consider this question in relation to three dimensions of language revitalization: communal socialization norms, institutional instruction, and language politics. Because language endangerment and revitalization are social phenomena, the latter entailing the former, the following questions will frame this discussion: What social roles have become relevant to the project of language revitalization, and how are they valenced (gender, age, ethnicity, status, etc.)? In what ways do ideologies of gender and language become enmeshed in the everyday practices of revitalization? And, most generally, how is gender relevant to language endangerment and revitalization? To address these questions, I begin with the latter and a brief discussion of some of the work that has attended to this question.

1. Why Gender?

Across the language endangerment and revitalization literature, research pertaining to gender falls into four general categories: grammatical gender (masculine/feminine) and speech (e.g., Haas 1944; Hill 1987; Hinton 1994; Kroskrity 1983; Sapir 1951 [1929]; Taylor 1982; Trechter 1999 and Chapter 17 in this volume); discourses about gender and identity (e.g., Adkins and Davis 2012; Ahlers 2012; Bilaniuk 2003; Chernela 2004; Echeverria 2003; Trechter 2003); the role of women in language shift (e.g., Cameron 2003; Gal 1978; Hill 1987; Kulick 1992a; 1992b; see also Labov 1972; 1990); and the politics of gender in language endangerment and revitalization (e.g., Bull 1992; Cotter 1999; Chernela 2004; Feliciano-Santos 2011; Hill and Zepeda 1992; Kroskrity 1998; 2009; Leonard 2012; Wertheim 2012).[3] These categories are not mutually exclusive, but rather indicate a scholarly orientation – as linguistically descriptive, sociolinguistic, and anthropological. They also reflect the kind of scholarly attention devoted to women's practices in relation to language change such that women are seen either as upwardly mobile antagonists or socially disabled protagonists (Aikio 1992, 43–44). This sociolinguistic attention has frequently been negative, with language shift and obsolescence being attributed to women because of their failure as caregivers to socialize children into the endangered language or dialect (cf. Cameron 2003). With some exceptions (e.g., Altman 2011; Cotter 1999; Dick and McCarty 1997; Kroskrity 2009), scholarship – and media in general – has underacknowledged women's *contributions* to endangered language research and language revitalization successes despite their overrepresentation on the ground, in action (cf. Echeverria 2003).

This observation alone might be enough to motivate a focus on gender and women in particular. However, two other pervasive perspectives, one pertaining to American Indian women's roles as leaders in their communities and the other to women's roles as caregivers, suggest we turn our gaze toward women's work and to discourses by and about women in order to understand more completely their role(s) in and impact on processes of language endangerment and revitalization. I focus on American Indian women in particular because of the case from my own research which I discuss below.

Much of the scholarship on American Indian beliefs and practices has argued that men's and women's roles are complementary to each other, and that there is an equality of the sexes rather than a subordination of and discrimination toward women (Knack 2004). For example, Roger Spielmann (1998) has argued that Ojibwe is a nonsexist language because there are no gendered third-person pronouns. His argument suggests that languages that do mark gender grammatically or pragmatically are sexist. Linguists have shown that for some Native American languages, gender corresponds with certain grammatical elements (Haas 1944; Hill 1987; Hinton 1994; Taylor 1982; Trechter 1999). While it has been argued that some of these subtle discursive flourishes index a dichotomy of public/private, formal/informal, or prestigious/quotidian rather than male/female, such linguistic indices certainly suggest the presence of a sociocultural distinction. That the overt marking of gender difference signals practices of gender discrimination cannot be assumed. As Jane Hill and Ofelia Zepeda (1992, 223) have cautioned, "much of linguistic structure itself may be ideologically quite neutral: we must consider the possibility that ideologies … are founded, not upon what is intrinsic in linguistic structure, but upon what our cultures invite us to notice in it." What is clear is that for those languages that have grammatically gendered elements or discourse markers, gender may be more readily available for convergence with cultural practices of conceptualization, evaluation, and typification. This does not exclude "nonsexist" language speakers from also demarcating difference along gendered lines. In such cases, those distinctions will arise in relation to other practices and observations. What this means more generally is that such distinctions and the gendering of practice will vary. For the case below, such distinctions emerge at the intersection of institutional roles, cultural discourses, and everyday practice.

For American Indian communities, Rebecca Tsosie has highlighted a gendering of leadership, arguing that women serve an important function in their role as leaders in their communities. Women's leadership, she contends, is "an ethics of survival, of connection to the past generations, of responsiveness to needs of this and future generations … That spirit is what sustains Native peoples, what inspires us and gives us hope for the future" (Tsosie 2010, 29). As leaders, American Indian women become key players in the rehabilitation of their communities, the maintenance of past and present traditions, and the future of Native America. Leadership, however, has many guises. For American Indian women involved in language revitalization, it would seem that this role often plays out behind the scenes.[4]

Assuming that women are leaders in language revitalization, it would be unsurprising to find that American Indian men are subsequently less active in revitalization projects. On the one hand, discourses of gender in American Indian communities may promote this division of labor. Tsosie (2010, 32) notes that "[i]n most tribes, gender roles were perceived as complementary and not dichotomous," distinct yet equal,[5] as with an expectation that women raise the children (in the home), and men provide wage-earning labor (outside the home).[6] On the other hand, employment practices in North American societies continue to undervalue women's work, especially women of color (see recent article by Brodkin, Morgen, and Hutchinson (2011) on women of color in anthropology). This pattern suggests that employment opportunities for women will be less lucrative and marginalized (see Hill 1987, for example). So, if language revitalization appears as "women's work," we might predict that men – either for investment reasons or gender complementarity – will tend to place their efforts elsewhere. Michelle Jacob (2013) has documented the role of women in the revitalization, or rehabilitation, of Yakama traditions of dance, language, and subsistence. While a few men participate in and support these activities, Jacob reveals a discourse that identifies women as the critical actors in these endeavors, yet these women also bemoan the minimal participation of men. Thus, women's leadership in projects of revitalization/rehabilitation – women who often donate their labor for free to these enterprises – may not be as authoritative, or as empowering and sustaining, as men's.

The other arena considered to be dominated by women, and thusly gendered, is childrearing. As Deborah Cameron (2003, 188) has observed, "Since women and girls in most societies are primary carers for young children, researchers have paid attention to their role in promoting shift – and, conversely, in maintaining ancestral languages or revitalizing those which have become endangered." A popular ethnographic example is Don Kulick's earlier work (1992a; 1992b) in Papua New Guinea on language socialization and shift. In this case, children were perceived as shifting from speaking the indigenous language, Taiap, to the lingua franca, Tok Pisin. Within an ideological framework that already distinguished men's and women's speech, the shift itself became mapped onto these gendered speech norms and practices, resulting in Taiap being associated with women and Tok Pisin with men. Children were assumed, or were encouraged, to prefer Tok Pisin to Taiap because of these ideological associations. Responsibility for the shift, however, fell on the children who "refused" to speak Taiap.

More recent scholarship has focused on the responsibility of women for maintaining a certain sociolinguistic environment. Chernela (2004) elaborates on the role of women in a Tukanoan-speaking community. In this Amazonian case, women speak a different variety (language) from their husbands. Upon marriage, a woman moves to her husband's village. While this may be the village of her own mother, it results in a kind of linguistic isolation that is further reinforced by the prohibition on children from speaking their mother's language. Chernela (2004, 20) shows that women, the mothers, maintain this linguistic patrilineality because "it is the work of women to construct the shared meanings that constitute the Tukanoan social and cultural universe." Women are thus responsible for teaching their own children the father's language and for discouraging the acquisition of their own language. Bilaniuk (2003) examines a similar scenario of linguistic responsibility where women are charged with preserving the Ukrainian language. Through surveys and matched guise tasks, she reveals the discursive terrain surrounding the use and maintenance of Ukrainian and its association with women. This ideology is vividly captured by the following quotation: "I am often asked where I got my language. I got my language from my mother's nipple. That is the inexhaustible well of language. Take notice of this, mothers, and your children will never need to be Ukrainianized" (Bilaniuk 2003, 54). Ideologically, then, women appear to hold the key to linguistic salvation, or at least its responsibility, but do not necessarily have the authority to do so.

To examine this responsibility–authority nexus as it intersects with language revitalization and gender more closely, the next section presents excerpts from my own research and fieldwork experience working with First Nations in the Yukon Territory, Canada, on various language preservation and revitalization projects. All aboriginal languages associated with the Yukon Territory and/or officially recognized by the Yukon Territorial Government are endangered. This status is fully acknowledged by the territorial and federal governments, such that a range of measures have been taken either to prevent further loss or to reverse loss, depending on the sociolinguistic situation. The following sections will discuss some of these measures in relation to discourses of gender and the potential gendering of these projects.

2. The Blurriness of Gender among the Kaska (Athabaskans)

In the Yukon, the majority of aboriginal languages are Athabaskan, with the exception of Tlingit. Grammatically, none of these languages mark gender in the masculine/feminine sense. According to an Alaskan educational website,

> Some languages ascribe gender (male, female, and neuter) to certain parts of speech. Many European languages classify all nouns in this way. English has gender only in the third person singular pronouns, he/him/his, she/her/hers, and it/its. Athabaskan languages do not distinguish gender in their pronouns. For example, the Deg Hit'an word itrix can mean either "he is crying," "she is crying," or "it is crying." (Eskimo languages too lack gender distinctions.) This may be the reason speakers of Athabaskan-influenced English sometimes confuse genders, saying for instance, "I called my mother and he answered." (Alaskool, n.d.)

For Athabaskan languages like Kaska, gender is more or less a morphologically unmarked category or characteristic. At the level of the noun word, terms exist across types of fauna that distinguish the male from the female, as with *keda* ("moose") and *keda ma* ("female moose or cow") or *destl'ede* ("squirrel") and *destl'ede ma* ("female squirrel"). And certainly gender is a salient semantic feature in kinship terms that distinguishes men from women. In addition to distinguishing types by gender, other terms within these categories delineate types by age and/or lifespan. At the level of discourse, gender inflects ethnographic descriptions, the narratives people tell, and the socializing commentary of elders because gender is considered a relevant feature of social organization.

Twentieth-century anthropologists often described the Kaska people in relation to gender, noting that women typically did X and men did Y. Honigmann (1954, 120) observed that such "sex typing" did not become overt until "late childhood [when a] youth of 12 began accompanying his father hunting and so learned to track, ambush, and butcher game and became familiar with the habits of animals. A girl continued to spend much time with her mother, who encouraged feminine pursuits." In a collection of reflections on women's roles and practices by Angela Wheelock and Patrick Moore (1997), the Kaska women they interviewed reiterated this tenet, describing their own practices in implicit juxtaposition to men's and focusing much of their attention on practices and taboos surrounding menses, childbirth, and raising children. Some contributors even directly stated that men should socialize boys and women girls. In a recording session I conducted in 1999, the elder had agreed to the recording because she feared that young women and girls were no longer learning behaviors appropriate to their gender and age, and as a result were endangering themselves and others (Meek 2010, 36–37). Similar commentary appears in statements about aboriginal language instruction and language revitalization (see below).

On the other hand, a rigid gendered division of labor was not practiced. As Goulet (1997, 58–59) points out:

> among the Kaska, male and female were not the dichotomized categories found in Western culture. The ideal person in Kaska culture, whether male or female, is the autonomous and independent individual. In a society in which women routinely "learn many of the duties of the opposite sex" and whose dress styles are not marked in opposition to men's, gender differences tend to be blurred.

Occupational opportunity accompanied such semiotic vagueness. Women I knew held positions on tribal council, ran their own organizations, went hunting and fishing, sought university degrees, worked as accountants, and participated in any occupation or pastime they desired. Their husbands often were the primary care-givers for their children and grandchildren. One type of labor, though, that none of these women or their daughters sought certification or training for was work in mines; that was left to the men. Women, however, did and do dominate the employ-ment opportunities involving aboriginal language (Meek 2010, ch. 1). They were hired as the language instructors and teacher's assistants in public schools and preschools, they served as translators in courts and at other public meetings, they worked as the First Nations' language coordinators, and they were key consultants on many, if not all, aboriginal language projects. Women's prevailing presence in these institutional roles implies a possible gendering of aboriginal language revi-talization in the Yukon, and if so, how and why? Might they not simply be better speakers than men? And even if they are, does that mean women are controlling the direction of aboriginal language revitalization in the Yukon, or have they merely been charged with the responsibility for its survival and the shouldering of respon-sibility for its (possible) failure?

3. First Nations' Politics and Aboriginal Language Planning in the Yukon

Language planning is about imposing an order, whether derived from (local or real-time) practice, mandated by institutional bodies, or a blend of the two. As Tove Bull (1992, 165) remarked, reflecting on the history and politics of language planning in Norway:

> to establish a linguistic order is to establish a social order. Language constitutes social life, just as language is constituted by social life. Language planning may thus be regarded as a kind of ruling technique. To replace older prestigious linguistic forms by colloquial forms is a way of reducing the power of groups who by heritage and tradition are the possessors of political and social power in society.

In her case, the role of women in language planning and policy had been severely hampered, if not entirely erased, by the practices of the committees and govern-ments determined to manage the sociolinguistic landscape within institutions, and ultimately beyond their walls. Aboriginal language planning in the Yukon attended to women's voices but also proceeded to manage and compartmentalize them in relation to a discourse of practice and education, where women maintain the family (and children) and men head the family.

This subtle gendering emerges discursively in tandem with First Nations' attempts to reclaim control over their lands, their languages, and their lives. In the Yukon in the 1970s, First Nations began to advocate for the need to institutionalize their heritage languages as part of an overall petition for a (re)valuing of Indian cultures and peoples and for an implicit recognition of the continuing decline of aboriginal language use as a result of previous government practices. The emphasis on language coincided with a general concern for the welfare and future of First Nations peoples. Elaborated in the now historic document, *Together Today for Our Children Tomorrow*, the then Yukon Native Brotherhood (now the Council for Yukon First Nations) went to Ottawa to advocate on behalf of the territory's First Nations,

> presenting to the Government of Canada this Statement of our Grievances, and our suggestion about a Settlement on behalf of the Yukon Indian People. At the same time we want the Government to know that we feel that this is a big responsibility for us. Our people have many deep feelings about our land and about the future of our children. (Council for Yukon Indians 1977)

In this document, the Yukon Indian Brotherhood, in tandem with similar proclamations asserted by the national organization Assembly of First Nations (AFN), implied that should the government and its institutions fail to intervene on their behalf, then the disappearance of these languages and cultures would be at the hands of these Canadian governments and their institutions. Reproduced in Appendix 1 of this document is the Yukon First Nations' 1972 statement regarding public education provided by the Territory:

> We believe that our children should be educated in public schools, but we also believe consideration should be given to the special problems, *the preservation of the language*, and the factual representation of the culture of a group comprising nearly one-third of the Yukon's population ... Education of Indians has been characterized by a policy of cultural replacement under which the textbooks, the schools, the philosophy of *education has been designed to make White men out of Indians. Little attention has been paid to Indian culture, history and language*. (CYI 1977, 50, 52; emphases added)

The sentiment expressed a commitment to public education yet demanded a revision of policy and practice. In that vein, the following recommendations were made and later implemented:

> *Recommendation Four*: That education programs be changed to allow for revival and re-establishment of Indian languages and for a true picture of Indian history, culture, and contribution to the modern world ... *Recommendation Five*: That the necessary encouragement and assistance be extended to ensure employment of native people as teachers, counselors, temporary teaching aides and kindergarten instructors. (CYI 1977, 55–56)

Education, language, and heritage became a cornerstone of the eventual settlement, entitled "The Umbrella Final Agreement," which set the stage for land claims in the Yukon and for aboriginal language programming. However, in these passages responsibility for aboriginal languages and employment strategies are not gendered.

Elsewhere in this same document, this changes. A brief history of practice and interaction with "Whitemen" states that

> the Indian People had no books. Our way of life was handed down by word of mouth ... Our Family was the centre of "The Indian Way." The man was head of the family and was the provider of food, clothing, housing and protection. The Mother was the centre of the family and the children took her name ... Education was handled by our parents and was done by children watching and copying what they saw. It was the method of learning by doing. (CYI 1977, 9)

This passage provides a subtle indication of the ideological positioning of a gendered figure in social life. A more direct articulation of such gendering appears in later language planning documentation. For example, at the 1991 territorial language planning conference, elder Stanley Jonathan (Northern Tutchone) recommended:

> You know I think the best way to teach ... we all take bunch of boys out, out in the bush for month, just talk Indian to them, how to do work, cut wood, bring wood, bring water, all sit down there Indian way, but that the only way they gonna catch on fast. (Aboriginal Language Services 1991, 17)

Similarly, women elders emphasized the need for young girls to learn certain skills alongside the acquisition of their heritage language (see Meek 2010, ch. 3). Most discourse about the necessity of heritage language maintenance and revival attended to the cultural and spiritual dimensions of language rather than the sociological (see Meek 2009). They also emphasized both generic and specific links with "identity" in public pronouncements of need and significance (Meek 2009; 2010, ch. 5). Furthermore, most gendered elements remained tacit and linked with language only through other social experiences or gendered expectations. The most salient dimension of gendering in aboriginal language revitalization in the Yukon appears in the actual implementation of these policies and plans rather than in the rhetoric of their establishment.

4. Institutions and Axes of Regimentation

As Philips (2003; Chapter 15 in this volume) and Gal and Woolard (2001) among others have argued, the ideologies stemming from institutions that a governing body uses to interact with its governed populace are especially "powerful" as are the representations they produce. They mediate moral investments and aesthetic preferences; they inflect people's evaluations and attitudes; they permeate the sentimental realm of interaction. For language endangerment and revitalization, these mediations exist along a number of axes of practice; in legislation (political), in rhetoric (discursive), in documentation/entextualization (material), in pedagogy (educational), in employment (economic), in interaction (social) (see Meek 2010). This section focuses on two areas of practice – materials produced and employment – with an eye toward the moral-aesthetic imagery surrounding and emanating from these regimentations. In both cases, women are "tied" to dominant institutional domains, as teachers and participants in the production of the language texts, yet in the actual images used in the language texts they remain peripheral to the linguistic enterprise.

The most apparent pattern corresponding to gender in language revitalization appears in the involvement and employment of women. Echeverria (2003) has shown how women were at the forefront of Basque-language education and revitalization, but were erased from public representations and formal acknowledgments of efforts to sustain the language. Similarly, First Nations personnel recruited into government-funded positions have tended to be predominantly aboriginal women, while the planners and institutional management have tended to be otherwise (men and nonaboriginal women). In 1986 the first group of aboriginal language instructors graduated from the Yukon College teacher training course. Of the 12 graduates, only one individual was male, Mr Patrick Carlick (Tlen 1986, 76). This pattern has continued; the current Kaska language instructors are women, and a similar pattern can be found across the other First Nations. Some men whom I interviewed mentioned having considered seeking a teaching certificate so that they could work in the schools, but they often hedged this by claiming that their "language wasn't that good." However, most of these men were raised by parents or grandparents who spoke Kaska with each other and to their children and grandchildren. Some of these men worked with me on transcription and translation and also served as test subjects for tasks I developed to probe individuals' comprehension of Kaska. They aced these tasks. Linguistic competence was not the issue.

In contrast, women have been quite vocal and public in their advocacy of aboriginal languages. From the former International Yukon Storytelling Festival to local CHON FM radio broadcasts, both women and men have been front and center at events celebrating and promoting aboriginal languages. Mrs Mida Donnessey has performed as a storyteller at the festival, sharing Kaska narratives. Mrs Leda Jules regularly reports the news in Kaska on the radio. Mrs Agnes Washpan, Mrs Evelyn Skookum, and Mrs Ann Ranigler spearheaded efforts to produce traditional Northern Tutchone tales as plays, including hiring a well-known British Columbian playwright to write a script. Mrs Washpan also directed the play and performed some of the key parts (see Carr and Meek 2013). Locally, Kaska women have occupied program director positions for language and education within the First Nations' government. They coordinated the first language workshops and continue to seek funding for future projects. Perhaps the one unfortunate side effect of this pattern has been the minimal regular participation of men.

On the other hand, men were present at the inception of this move to regiment aboriginal languages. Daniel Tlen, a Southern Tutchone educator and linguist, wrote some of the earliest reports petitioning the Yukon and federal governments to support aboriginal language education (Tlen 1986). Elijah Smith, the first chair of the Council for Yukon Indians, used his political clout to influence both nonaboriginal politicians and First Nations communities convincing them of the importance of aboriginal languages and the need to fund aboriginal language initiatives, including public education (ALS 1991; Tlen 1986). Former premier of Yukon Tony Penikett, former prime minister Pierre Trudeau, and then minister of Indian and Eskimo affairs and former prime minister Jean Chretién were all instrumental in securing resources and support for the Yukon's aboriginal languages. The support and resources became reality in part through and as the Yukon Native Language Centre (YNLC). Established originally as a program and housed by Yukon College, the YNLC, under Mr John Ritter's direction, runs the aboriginal language teacher training program and literacy workshops, creates instructional materials, and documents and archives innumerable records of the territory's aboriginal languages. The Centre manages and authorizes aboriginal language representations throughout the Yukon.

The materials produced by the YNLC for teaching and learning aboriginal languages emphasize orality alongside literacy and allow for individual creativity. The teacher's guidebook serves primarily as a template, encouraging individual instructors to elaborate on provided topics as desired. The language lesson booklets reflect this topical orientation, but are for individuals interested in learning one of the many dialects. Across dialects, the formatting and topic organization remain consistent and reflect a degree of sensitivity to First Nations' norms and values. While there is some variation by language and dialect, lessons maintain identical phrases, terms, and illustrations. Given that the grammar of the language does not mark masculine/feminine gender, my focus here is on the representation of gender differences through text illustrations. In the 55 pages of lesson text, there are 41 illustrations. Of these, 15 are of people and of those two are definitively women. Under "relatives," an image of a female elder is depicted and under "tanning hides," a woman is portrayed scraping a hide, indicated by style of dress. Other gendered imagery are associated with the following actions and activities: an image of a male elder accompanies the lesson on "speaking Native language"; an image of a young boy crying accompanies a lesson on "body parts" and "activities";[7] an image of a man carrying a gun accompanies the lesson on hunting; and in one lesson book there's an image of a man fishing, though in other books the gender of the person portrayed is ambiguous. In all other images of individuals, the gender is also relatively ambiguous. Unlike the Basque situation or the Ukrainian one mentioned above, aboriginal languages in the Yukon do not appear to be remarkably gendered representationally.[8]

The overall (re)valuation of aboriginal languages in the Yukon gained traction through the initial efforts of men in strategic political positions, and this continues to be the case for the most part today. Additionally, the institutional regimentation of these languages has been greatly impacted by one individual, the Euro-American director of the YNLC. Orthographic conventions and spelling norms are created and regulated by the Centre. Thus, the moral aesthetics of Native language representation reside there. As a result, this institutional governance of linguistic form also impacts linguistic function. During my fieldwork, First Nations members and aboriginal language employees sometimes expressed a fearfulness and hesitancy to document and write aboriginal languages, often in relation to this critical regimenting of practice. My own efforts have been "corrected" by the YNLC, as have the efforts of my colleagues. While one approach to standardization is as a process intimately related to individual habits and aesthetic preferences that emerge through use and sociality, many First Nations people with whom I've worked consider the writing norms and spelling conventions for these languages to be already established. Orthographic conventions have certainly been institutionalized, but whether or not they are the standard remains to be seen. While many consultants and friends may accept the representational conventions devised by the YNLC, the avoidance of use by consultants and friends suggests a negative acceptance or conformity rather than a positive evaluation. Standardization is a complicated process, but its demand is simple – conformity. While such conformity seems to have been achieved in the Yukon, it is a costly agreement that may eventually contribute to the demise of linguistic practice rather than its flourishing. It is an agreement based on an institutional authority derived from a colonial legacy of "Whiteman" dominion.

5. Norms, the Normative, and the Normal: Practical Intersections

Graphic representations and employment patterns are only two axes through which norms and expectations about language use emerge. The influence of such norms and expectations inflect evaluations of appropriateness, adequacy, and authority. However, as Woolard (1989, 21) has pointed out, "[a]uthority is established and inculcated most thoroughly not in schools and other formal institutions, but in personal relations [and] face-to-face encounters." Returning to the social-interactional axis, this section examines the intricate web of ideology, interaction, and norms that intersect situations of language revitalization.

The trajectory of my research in the Yukon Territory gained direction through local ideologies of gender and language. For example, I was discouraged from working with men, especially older men, while at the same time being encouraged to work with women (and children). Given that my original project focused on the socialization and acquisition of language by children, part of this guidance resulted from people's understandings of this endeavor despite the fact that fathers were just as likely to be raising their children as mothers. This guidance also conformed to a more general discourse of socialization and acquisition. Women elders often emphasized the need for young girls to learn certain skills alongside the acquisition of their heritage language. The women I spoke with and interviewed brought this up directly and indirectly when speaking about the importance of the Kaska language, tradition, and history for today's youth. While teaching Kaska at the Aboriginal Head Start, women elders lectured children about appropriate behaviors and their own childhood experiences and expectations. They often mentioned monitoring young children and helping their mothers (Meek 2010, 64–65). On other occasions, these elders expressed grave concern for the lack of knowledge about respect that young women showed (or failed to show), from knowing that they should wash their clothes in a separate tub from boys' to realizing that they should avoid stepping over other people's belongings, especially men's and boys' (Meek 2010, 34–35). These elders also bemoaned the fact that young women no longer practiced appropriate puberty rituals, learned to snare and trap from their mothers, or disposed of personal items properly (Meek 2010, 36–37). All of this socializing discourse transpired in contexts of Kaska language revitalization. Thus, a critical component of language endangerment was and is the endangerment of such discourse, that is, knowing the gendered expectations of behavior (whether expressed in Kaska, English, or Tagalog, for example).

Norms of appropriateness and respect also extended to spoken language (see Meek 2007 on respect). For language, however, the sanctioning of practice pertained to the dialect or variety being spoken rather than grammatical acuity, pragmatics of politeness, or lexical acumen. Recall that for Athabaskan Nations in the Yukon "[t]he Mother was the centre of the family and the children took her name" (CYI 1977, 9). For the Kaska community, novices were expected to speak the dialect of their mother and other maternal relatives (Meek 2007, 27). A person acquired her or his linguistic variety in ways that paralleled other forms of inheritance, such as clan affiliation and property distribution; it was reckoned matrilineally.

The challenge this indexical link poses for endangered languages arises prominently in events of learning and revitalization. One of the frequent criticisms adults launched against school-based aboriginal language programs in the Yukon was related to the instructor's own language variety, and the lack of language choice afforded students. Even though schools are incapable of accommodating such diversity, parents and grandparents hoped that their children and grandchildren would learn their (home) dialect and not the dialect of a nonmatrilineally reckoned relative. Another unintended consequence of such linguistic diversity is the privileging of one dialect or variety over another. Again, several families raised this as an issue in the education of their children. Such concerns also call into question the recognition or configuration of authority. The ways in which authority, as a type of power, might be indexed or deployed in the use or misuse of these linguistic elements could signal a gendering of roles. In the case of the Kaska language, and in the Yukon more generally, I have shown that while women have taken on the burden of responsibility for the future of aboriginal languages, their authority remains circumscribed by gendered domains of practice, from dominant institutional organizations authorizing aboriginal language education and politics to communal norms of inheritance and acquisition.

6. Conclusion

While other research on endangered languages has shown a more striking gendering, the situation in the Yukon Territory reveals a more subtle inflection where sociolinguistic norms associated with matrilineal descent, alongside dominant institutional domains of regimentation, affect expectations and evaluations of linguistic performance. If gender is a relevant variable to understanding language endangerment and revitalization, its salience and effect will clearly vary from situation to situation. On the other hand, given that the predominant institutional framing for language endangerment and revitalization is "Western" (or elite "white" rhetoric; cf. Hill 2002), we might expect a "Western" gendering of these axes of practice, that the moral-aesthetic enfigurement of gender in dominant realms will infuse these "endangered" realms. For Kaska this seems to be the case. Thus, an enduring question that underlies this research is to what extent dominant ideologies of gender have influenced local conceptualizations and practices, and/or how they have converged. It is the point(s) of convergence – of ideas and their subtle undulations into practice, and vice versa – that will have the greatest consequence for language endangerment and revitalization, and alas on women's participation and authority.

NOTES

1 These examples illustrate individuals' preferences for state-funded publications over locally produced texts used by indigenous or minority language educators. Of course not everyone shares these preferences, nor does everyone support literacy projects, but enough people do in these cases that their textual authority is maintained.
2 The discourse goes something like this: because our languages were learned orally in the past, they should be learned that way now. This has been the guiding philosophy for some indigenous language programs, such as the Yukon Territory's approach to aboriginal language teaching (see Carr and Meek 2013) and the Pueblos' long-standing commitment against literacy (Brandt 1982; Debenport 2011; Sims 2001).
3 For this chapter, "gender" is understood to mean "the embodied social and cultural ideologies of how biological sex should be [or are assumed to be] manifested" (Bilaniuk 2003, 48).
4 Wertheim (2012) has made a similar observation for men's and women's roles in Tatar language activism.
5 Equal can mean that women "held decision-making power over their own lives and activities to the same extent that men did over theirs" (Leacock 1978, 247, quoted in Knack 2004, 53). In this context, equal means of mutual investment rather than mutual control.
6 This is an intentional oversimplification. In my own research and personal experience, the reverse pattern is the more robust one. See Knack (2004) for a more nuanced discussion of women and men in American Indian societies.
7 In one case the image is of a baby crying.
8 It is remarkable that the image accompanying "speaking" an aboriginal language is that of an elderly man while the image accompanying "relatives" and family is an elderly woman.

REFERENCES

Aboriginal Language Services (ALS). 1991. *Voices of the Talking Circle: Yukon Aboriginal Languages Conference 1991.* Whitehorse, YT: Yukon Executive Council Office.

Adkins, Madeleine, and Jenny Davis. 2012. "The Naïf, the Sophisticate, and the Party Girl: Regional and Gender Stereotypes in Breton Language Web Videos." *Gender and Language,* 6(2): 291–308.

Ahlers, Jocelyn. 2012. "Language Revitalization and the (re)Constituting of Gender: Silence and Women in Native California Language Revitalization." *Gender and Language,* 6(2): 309–338.

Aikio, Marjut. 1992. "Are Women Innovators in the Shift to a Second Language? A Case Study of Reindeer Sámi Women and Men." *International Journal of the Sociology of Language,* 94: 43–61.

Alaskool . n.d. "Linguistic Characteristics of Athabaskan and English." At http://www .alaskool.org/language/athabaskan /linguistic.htm, accessed October 30, 2013.

Altman, Heidi M. 2011. "Intersections: History, Language, and Globalization in the North Carolina Cherokee Communities." In Tania Granadillo and Heidi Orcutt-Gachiri (eds.), *Ethnographic Contributions to the Study of Endangered Languages,* 177–188. Tucson: University of Arizona Press.

Bender, Margaret. 2008. "Indexicality, Voice, and Context in the Distribution of Cherokee Scripts." *International Journal of the Sociology of Language,* 192: 91–103.

Bilaniuk, Laada. 2003. "Gender, Language Attitudes, and Language Status in Ukraine." *Language in Society,* 32(1): 47–78.

Brandt, Elizabeth. 1982. "Native American Attitudes toward Literacy and Recording in the Southwest." *Journal of the Linguistic Association of the Southwest,* 4(2): 185–195.

Brodkin, Karen, Sandra Morgen, and Janis Hutchinson. 2011. "Anthropology as White Public Space?" *American Anthropologist,* 113(4): 545–556.

Bull, Tove. 1992. "Male Power and Language Planning: The Role of Women in Norwegian Language Policy." *International Journal of the Sociology of Language,* 94: 155–172.

Cameron, Deborah. 2003. "Gender Issues in Language Change." *Annual Review of Applied Linguistics,* 23: 187–201.

Carr, Gerald L., and Barbra A. Meek. 2013. "The Poetics of Language Revitalization: Text, Performance, and Change." *Journal of Folklore Research,* 50(1–3): 191–216.

Chernela, Janet M. 2004. "The Politics of Language Acquisition: Language Learning as Social Modeling in the Northwest Amazon." *Women & Language,* 27(1): 13–21.

Cotter, Colleen. 1999. "From Folklore to 'News at 6': Maintaining Language and Reframing Identity through the Media." In Mary Bucholtz, A. C. Liang, and Laurel A. Sutton (eds.), *Reinventing Identities: The Gendered Self in Discourse,* 369–387. Oxford: Oxford University Press.

Council for Yukon Indians (CYI). 1977. *Together Today for Our Children Tomorrow.* Brampton, ON: Charters Publishing.

Debenport, Erin. 2011. "As the Rez Turns: Anomalies Within and Beyond the Boundaries of a Pueblo Community." *American Indian Culture and Research Journal,* 35(2): 87–110.

Dick, Galena Sells, and Teresa L. McCarty. 1997. "Reclaiming Navajo: Language Renewal in an American Indian Community School." In Nancy H. Hornberger (ed.), *Indigenous Literacies in the Americas: Language Planning from the Bottom Up,* 69–94. Berlin: Mouton de Gruyter.

Echeverria, Begoña. 2003. "Language Ideologies and Practices in (En)Gendering the Basque Nation." *Language in Society,* 32(3): 383–413.

Feliciano-Santos, Sherina. 2011. "An Inconceivable Indigeneity: Historical, Cultural, and Interactional Dimensions of Puerto Rican Taíno Activism." Unpublished PhD dissertation, University of Michigan.

Frawley, William, Kenneth C. Hill, and Pamela Munro. 2002. *Making Dictionaries: Preserving Indigenous Languages of the Americas.* Berkeley: University of California Press.

Gal, Susan. 1978. "Peasant Men Can't Get Wives: Language Change and Sex Roles in a Bilingual Community." *Language in Society*, 7(1): 1–16.

Gal, Susan, and Kathryn Woolard. 2001. "Introduction." In *Languages and Publics: The Making of Authority*, 1–12. Manchester: St Jerome Publishing.

Goulet, Jean Guy. 1997. "The Northern Athabaskan 'Berdache' Reconsidered: On Reading More Than There is in the Ethnographic Record." In Sue-Ellen Jacobs, Wesley Thomas, and Sabine Lang (eds.), *Two-Spirit People: Native American Gender Identity, Sexuality, and Spirituality*, 45–68. Urbana: University of Illinois Press.

Haas, Mary R. 1944. "Men's and Women's Speech in Koasati." *Language*, 20(3): 142–149.

Hill, Jane H. 1987. "Women's Speech in Modern Mexicano." In Susan U. Philips, Susan Steele, and Christine Tanz (eds.), *Language, Gender, and Sex in Comparative Perspective*, 121–160. Cambridge: Cambridge University Press.

Hill, Jane H. 2002. " 'Expert Rhetorics' in Advocacy for Endangered Languages: Who is Listening, and What Do They Hear?" *Journal of Linguistic Anthropology*, 12(2): 119–133.

Hill, Jane H., and Ofelia Zepeda. 1992. "Mrs. Patricio's Trouble: The Distribution of Responsibility in an Account of Personal Experience." In Jane H. Hill and Judith T. Irvine (eds.), *Responsibility and Evidence in Oral Discourse*, 197–225. Cambridge: Cambridge University Press.

Hinton, Leanne. 1993. "Awakening Tongues: Elders, Youth, and Educators Embark on Language Renaissance." *News from Native California*, 7(3): 13–16.

Hinton, Leanne. 1994. *Flutes of Fire.* Berkeley: Heyday Books.

Hinton, Leanne, and Ken Hale. 2001. *The Green Book of Language Revitalization in Practice.* San Diego: Academic Press.

Holmes, Janet, and Miriam Meyerhoff. 2003. "Different Voices, Different Views: An Introduction to Current Research in Language and Gender." In Janet Holmes and Miriam Meyerhoff (eds.), *The Handbook of Language and Gender*, 1–17. Oxford: Blackwell.

Honigmann, John J. 1954. *The Kaska Indians: An Ethnographic Reconstruction.* New Haven: Yale University Press.

Jacob, Michelle. 2013. *Yakama Rising.* Tucson: University of Arizona Press.

Knack, Martha C. 2004. "Women and Men." In Thomas Biolsi (eds.), *A Companion to the Anthropology of American Indians*, 51–68. Oxford: Blackwell.

Kroskrity, Paul V. 1983. "On Male and Female Speech in the Pueblo Southwest." *International Journal of American Linguistics*, 49(1): 88–91.

Kroskrity, Paul V. 1998. "Arizona Tewa Kiva Speech as a Manifestation of a Dominant Language Ideology." In Bambi Schieffelin, Kathryn A. Woolard, and Paul V. Kroskrity (eds.), *Language Ideologies*, 103–122. Oxford: Oxford University Press.

Kroskrity, Paul V. 2009. "Embodying the Reversal of Language Shift." In Paul V. Kroskrity and Margaret C. Field (eds.), *Native American Language Ideologies*, 190–210. Tucson: University of Arizona Press.

Kulick, Don. 1992a. "Anger, Gender, Language Shift and the Politics of Revelation in a Papua New Guinea Village." *Pragmatics*, 2(3): 281–296.

Kulick, Don. 1992b. *Language Shift and Cultural Reproduction: Socialization, Self, and Syncretism in a Papua New Guinean Village.* New York: Cambridge University Press.

Labov, William. 1972. *Sociolinguistic Patterns.* Philadelphia: University of Pennsylvania Press.

Labov, William. 1990. "The Intersection of Sex and Social Class in the Course of Linguistic Change." *Language Variation and Change*, 2: 205–254.

Leacock, Eleanor. 1978. "Women's Status in Egalitarian Society: Implications for Social Evolution." *Current Anthropology*, 19: 247–275.

Leonard, Wesley. 2012. "Reframing Language Reclamation Programmes for Everybody's Empowerment." *Gender and Language*, 6(2): 339–367.

McCarty, Teresa. 2002. *A Place to Be Navajo: Rough Rock and the Struggle for Self-Determination in Indigenous Schooling*. Mahwah, NJ: Lawrence Erlbaum.

McCarty, Teresa, ed. 2005. *Language, Literacy, and Power in Schooling*. Mahwah, NJ: Lawrence Erlbaum.

McElhinny, Bonnie. 2003. "Theorizing Gender in Sociolinguistics and Linguistic Anthropology." In Janet Holmes and Miriam Meyerhoff (eds.), *The Handbook of Language and Gender*, 21–42. Oxford: Blackwell.

Meek, Barbra A. 2007. "Respecting the Language of Elders: Ideological Shift and Linguistic Discontinuity in a Northern Athapascan Community." *Journal of Linguistic Anthropology*, 17(1): 23–43.

Meek, Barbra A. 2009. "Language Ideology and Aboriginal Language Revitalization in Yukon, Canada." In Paul Kroskrity and Margaret Field (eds.), *Native American Language Ideologies: Beliefs, Practices, and Struggles in Indian Country*, 151–171. Tucson: University of Arizona Press.

Meek, Barbra A. 2010. *We Are Our Language: An Ethnography of Language Revitalization in a Northern Athabaskan Community*. Tucson: University of Arizona Press.

Meek, Barbra A., and Jacqueline Messing. 2007. "Framing Indigenous Language as Secondary to Matrix Languages." *Anthropology and Education Quarterly*, 38(2): 99–118.

Philips, Susan. 2003. "The Power of Gender Ideologies in Discourse." In Janet Holmes and Miriam Meyerhoff (eds.), *The Handbook of Language and Gender*, 252–276. Oxford: Blackwell.

Sapir, Edward. 1951 [1929]. "Male and Female Forms of Speech in Yana." In David G. Mandelbaum (eds.), *Selected Writings of Edward Sapir*, 206–212. Berkeley: University of California Press.

Sims, Christine. 2001. "Native Language Planning: A Pilot Process in the Acoma Pueblo Community." In Leanne Hinton and Ken Hale (eds.), *The Green Book of Language Revitalization*, 63–73. New York: Academic Press.

Spielmann, Roger W. 1998. *You're So Fat: Exploring Ojibwe Discourse*. Toronto: University of Toronto Press.

Taylor, Allan R. 1982. " 'Male' and 'Female' Speech in Gros Ventre." *Anthropological Linguistics*, 24(3): 301–307.

Tlen, Daniel. 1986. *Speaking Out: Consultations and Survey of Yukon Native Languages: Planning, Visibility, and Growth*. Whitehorse, YT: Yukon Native Language Centre.

Trechter, Sara. 1999. "Contextualizing the Exotic Few: Gender Dichotomies in Lakhota." In Mary Bucholtz, A. C. Liang, and Laurel A. Sutton (eds.), *Reinventing Identities: The Gendered Self in Discourse*, 101–119. Oxford: Oxford University Press.

Trechter, Sara. 2003. "A Marked Man: The Contexts of Gender and Ethnicity." In Janet Holmes and Miriam Meyerhoff (eds.), *The Handbook of Language and Gender*, 423–443. Oxford: Blackwell.

Tsosie, Rebecca. 2010. "Native Women and Leadership: An Ethics of Culture and Relationship." In Cheryl Suzack, Shari M. Huhndorf, Jeanne Perreault, and Jean Barman (eds.), *Indigenous Women and Feminism: Politics, Activism, Culture*, 29–42. Vancouver: University of British Columbia Press.

Wertheim, Suzanne. 2012. "Gender, Nationalism, and the Attempted Reconfiguration of Sociolinguistic Norms." *Gender and Language*, 6(2): 261–290.

Wheelock, Angela, and Patrick Moore. 1997. *(Dene) Gédéni: Traditional Lifestyles of Kaska Women*. Ross River, YT: Ross River Dena Council.

Will, Vanessa. 2012. *"Why Kenny Can't Can: Language Socialization Experiences of Gaelic-Medium Educated Children in Scotland."* Unpublished PhD dissertation, University of Michigan.

Woolard, Kathryn. 1989. *Double Talk: Bilingualism and the Politics of Ethnicity in Catalonia*. Stanford: Stanford University Press.

29 Gender and (A)nonymity in Computer-Mediated Communication

SUSAN C. HERRING AND SHARON STOERGER

1. Introduction

Computer-mediated communication (CMC) has been claimed to be inherently democratic, leveling traditional distinctions of social status and creating opportunities for less powerful individuals and groups to participate on a par with members of more powerful groups. Specifically, this form of Internet-based interaction has been claimed to lead to greater gender equality, with women, as the socially, politically, and economically less powerful gender, especially likely to reap its benefits (e.g., Graddol and Swann 1989). The argument goes as follows:

> Text-based CMC, lacking physical and auditory cues, possesses a degree of anonymity that makes the gender of online communicators irrelevant or invisible. This allows women and men to participate (and be recognized for their contributions) equally, in contrast with patterns of male dominance traditionally observed in face-to-face communication.

Of course, men too stand to benefit from anonymous online communication; the difference is that for women, the technological environment purportedly removes barriers to participation in domains where barriers do not exist – or do not exist to the same extent – for men.

Some 30 years after the introduction of CMC, we may ask whether this potential has been realized. Extrapolating from the properties of a technology to its social effects – a paradigm known as "technological determinism" (Markus 1994) – tends to overlook the fact that the development and uses of any technology are themselves embedded in a social context and are shaped by that context (Kling, McKim, and King 2003). Does CMC alter deeply rooted cultural patterns of gender

The Handbook of Language, Gender, and Sexuality, Second Edition.
Edited by Susan Ehrlich, Miriam Meyerhoff, and Janet Holmes.
© 2014 John Wiley & Sons, Inc. Published 2017 by John Wiley & Sons, Inc.

inequality, or do those patterns carry over into online communication? What role does anonymity play in either outcome?

This chapter surveys research on gender and CMC published between 1989, when gender issues first began to be raised in print, and the time of this writing (2013). During that time, Internet access – a prerequisite for online communication – reached parity for males and females in the United States. However, the body of evidence taken as a whole runs counter to the claim that gender is invisible or irrelevant in CMC, or that CMC equalizes gender-based power and status differentials.

The chapter is organized into seven sections. The following section considers gender in relation to issues of Internet *access and use*. Evidence, both early and recent, is then presented that bears on claims of gender equality in interactive *textual CMC*. The fourth section discusses gender behavior and representation in *multimodal CMC*, including via graphical avatars and photographs, and in video and audio chat, followed by a fifth section on *mobile CMC* via smartphones. In the *discussion*, the notion of anonymity is critiqued, and the question of difference versus disparity is addressed. The *conclusion* looks toward the future of gender and CMC and identifies topics in need of research.

2. Access and Use

CMC is as old as the Internet itself. In the early days of the Arpanet – the predecessor of the Internet – in the 1970s, online access, largely via email, was restricted to the US Defense Department personnel and computer scientists (almost entirely male) who designed and developed computer networking (Hafner and Lyon 1996). The Internet, so called since around 1983, expanded geographically in the 1980s to include more universities, especially faculty and students in computing-related departments (mostly male), and other asynchronous CMC modes such as discussion forums. The trend by the late 1980s of increased diffusion to academicians in other disciplines and employees in a growing number of workplaces became a full-fledged sweep toward popular access in the 1990s, with the rise of Internet service providers (ISPs) which enabled people to connect and communicate from their homes, including via synchronous chat. The percentage of female users increased along with this expansion, as did public knowledge about the Internet and individual access to it.

Nonetheless, computer use remained a stumbling block for gender equity throughout much of the 1990s. Women were initially more reticent about using computers, less willing to invest time and effort in learning to use the Internet, and less likely to be employed in workplaces with Internet access (Balka 1993). In the early 1990s, an estimated 5 percent of Internet users were women (Sproull 1992, cited in Ebben and Kramarae 1993). When they did log on, women were less likely to participate in online discussion forums and more likely than men to be alienated by the often contentious culture they encountered there (Herring 1992; 1993). Even women-only CMC environments were regularly targeted by disruptive males (Collins-Jarvis 1997; Herring, Johnson, and DiBenedetto, 1995), in keeping with the anything-goes, free-speech ethic that pervaded the Internet at the time (Brail 1996; Sutton 1994).

The introduction of the world wide web in the early 1990s brought with it ubiquity, easy-to-use graphical interfaces, and mainstream content (e.g., news, online shopping), making the Internet a "safer," more familiar-seeming place. Women flocked online: by 2000, slightly more than 50 percent of web users in the United States were female (Pastore 2000). The gender demographics of web users now mirrors that of the broader US population, although women are still somewhat under-represented online in the rest of the world (Abraham, Morn, and Vollman 2010).

Recently, women have come to outnumber men in some social media domains. They use social network sites such as Facebook more often and more actively than men (Brenner 2012), and female users predominate on the microblogging site Twitter, the consumer review site Yelp, and the online pinboard Pinterest. More males, in contrast, frequent music-sharing sites such as last.fm, as well as Reddit, a social news website known for its sometimes misogynistic content (HuffPost Women 2012; Williams 2012); contributors to Wikipedia are also overwhelmingly male (Lam et al. 2011). Moreover, the professional social network site LinkedIn has attracted almost twice as many males as females. LinkedIn representatives claim that this is because men are better at professional networking than women, at least in some industries (Berkow 2011), whereas women have traditionally focused on maintaining relationships (Fallows 2005; cf. Tannen 1990). Women's greater concerns about privacy and identity disclosure on social network sites (Fogel and Nehmad 2009) may also predispose them to interact with individuals they already know and trust (Muscanell and Guadagno 2012), which Facebook and other social network sites facilitate through features such as "friending."

Crocco, Cramer, and Meier (2008) argue that the move toward web-based computing has had an equalizing effect on gendered technology use. If equality is defined as equal in principle access, women in the United States have caught up with men. At the same time, the web is becoming increasingly specialized by gender. Although many sites are male-dominated, women today have more choices of online environments than they did in the past, including social media sites in which they can exercise a degree of control over who reads and comments on their contributions. As discussed further below, users of these social media sites tend to be less anonymous than in earlier text-based forums.

3. Textual CMC

3.1 Early studies

CMC comprises a variety of interactive sociotechnical modes including email, discussion lists, web forums, chat, MUDs (multi-user dimensions) and MOOs (MUDs, object oriented), IM (instant messaging), text messaging (SMS), weblogs (blogs), and microblogs. These modes are primarily textual, involving typed words that are read on digital screens.

Early CMC research did not typically discuss gender or control for it in experimental studies. As more women began to venture online in the early 1990s, however, studies of gender and CMC started appearing with greater frequency. In contrast to the optimism of Graddol and Swann (1989), the findings of these studies problematized claims of gender-free equality in cyberspace. In an early article documenting the results of an academic discussion group's self-directed experiment with anonymity, Selfe and Meyer (1991) found that males and high-status participants in the group dominated the interaction, both under normal conditions and under conditions of anonymity. Other research reported the use of aggressive tactics by men in online discussions, sometimes explicitly targeted at female participants (Dibbell 1993; Herring 1992; 1993; 1999; Herring, Johnson, and DiBenedetto 1995; Kramarae and Taylor 1993; Sutton 1994). Women and participants suspected of being female also received a disproportionate amount of (unwelcome) sexual attention (Bruckman 1993; Herring 1998; 1999; Rodino 1997). These findings raised an apparent paradox: how can gender disparity persist in an anonymous medium that allegedly renders gender invisible?

Part of the answer to this paradox is that gender is often visible in CMC on the basis of features of a participant's discourse style – features that the individual may not be consciously aware of or be able to change easily. The linguistic features that signal gender in CMC are stereotypically sex-linked and similar to those that have been described previously for face-to-face interaction. They include verbosity, assertiveness, use of profanity, (im)politeness, typed representations of smiling and laughter, and degree of interactive engagement (cf. Coates 1993; Tannen 1990).

In asynchronous CMC in discussion lists and newsgroups, researchers found that males were more likely to post longer messages, begin and close discussions in mixed-sex groups, assert opinions strongly as "facts," challenge others, use crude language (including insults and profanity), and in general adopt an adversarial stance toward their interlocutors (Herring 1992; 1993; 1994; 1996a; 1996b; 1999; Kramarae and Taylor 1993; Savicki, Lingenfelter, and Kelley 1996; Sutton 1994). In contrast, females tended to post relatively short messages, and they were more likely to qualify and justify their assertions, apologize, express appreciation, support others, and in general, adopt an "aligned" stance toward their interlocutors (Hall 1996; Herring 1993; 1994; 1996a; 1996b; Savicki, Lingenfelter, and Kelley 1996). Females also used more emoticons and other representations of smiles (Witmer and Katzman 1997; Wolf 2000). Moreover, Herring (1996b) observed a majority-gender effect: women tend to be more aggressive in male-dominated groups than among other women, and men tend to be more aligned in female-dominated groups than in groups dominated by men.

Analogous behaviors were observed in synchronous ("real-time") CMC. Cherny (1994) reported that female-presenting characters in a social MUD used mostly neutral and affectionate "action verbs" (such as "hugs" and "whuggles"), while male characters used more violent verbs (such as "kills"), especially in actions directed toward other males. Herring (1998) found that females on Internet Relay Chat (IRC) typed three times as many representations of smiling and laughter as males did, while the gender ratio was reversed for challenging and insulting speech acts. Males also produced overwhelmingly more profanity and sexual references. Rodino (1997) concluded a case study of an IRC interaction by noting that "despite multiple and conflicting gender performances [by one participant], the binary gender system is alive and well in IRC."

Gender-based harassment and the contentious tone of many online forums have tended to discourage participation by women (Herring 1992; 1999). In mixed-sex public forums, females post fewer messages (Herring 1993; 1996a), and chat rooms are typically frequented by fewer females than males (Herring 1998). Women are also less likely to persist in posting when their messages receive no response (Broadhurst 1993; Herring 2010). Even when they persist, their messages receive fewer responses, including from other women (Herring 1993; 2010). Moreover, they typically do not control the topic or the terms of the discussion except in groups where women make up a clear majority of participants (Herring 1996b; 2010; Herring, Johnson, and DiBenedetto 1992; 1995; Hert 1997). The lesser influence exercised by women in mixed-sex group interactions accounts in part for the existence of women-centered and women-only online groups (Balka 1993; Camp 1996), whereas explicitly designated men-only online environments are rare.

Online chat environments often encourage users to take on pseudonyms. For Danet (1998), these pseudonyms function as masks that invite experimentation with gender identities in playful, "carnivalesque" ways, liberating users from restrictive gender binaries. The literature contains anecdotal reports of play with gender identity, including gender switching sustained over periods of weeks or months, in chat environments (e.g., Bruckman 1993; McRae 1996). Bruckman (1993) interviewed MOO participants and found that females tended to assume gender-neutral pseudonyms in order to avoid sexual attention, while males assumed female-sounding names in order to attract it, as well as to experience virtually what it is like to be a different gender.

Empirical observation of synchronous CMC users suggests that gender switching is actually rather infrequent, however. After years of observation, LambdaMOO founder Pavel Curtis (1992) concluded that because of the effort involved in trying to be something one is not, most participants interact as themselves, regardless of the name or character description they choose. Herring (1998) found that 89 percent of all gendered behavior in six IRC channels indexed maleness and femaleness in traditional, even stereotyped, ways; instances of gender switching constituted less than half of the remaining 11 percent. In theory, it is possible that gender switching takes place more often but is so successful that it goes undetected. In practice, the longer someone participates, the more likely it is that they will produce cues that reveal their actual gender (Herring 1998). Thus researchers concluded that gender differences – and gender asymmetry – were evident in textual CMC, despite the use of pseudonyms.[1]

3.2   Recent studies

Since female Internet users achieved numerical parity in 2000 (Pastore 2000), it has popularly been assumed that gender differences in CMC have leveled out as well. This is supported by reports that, overall, women's participation now equals or exceeds that of men in environments such as blogs and social network sites (Herring et al. 2004; HuffPost Women 2012).

As regards language, however, the research results are mixed. Some of this research focuses on variables that are not a priori stereotyped by sex. In a study of adolescent blogs, Huffaker and Calvert (2005) found no significant gender differences in frequencies of words expressing cooperation and passivity, although males used more resolute and active language. Herring and Paolillo (2006) found that gender differences in grammatical word frequency disappeared when they controlled for blog genre – personal diary versus "filter" blogs commenting on events external to the blogger – although females produce more of the former and males more of the latter genre. Guiller and Durndell (2007) also found few gender differences in lower-level linguistic features in their study of computer-mediated student discussion groups, although stylistic differences were found. In a multilevel study of teen chat, Kapidzic and Herring (2011) discovered that gender differences were most evident in discourse style, somewhat evident at the level of speech acts, and least evident in word choice. However, not all Internet users exhibit gendered discourse styles: female computing professionals on the technology news website Slashdot adopt both aligned and adversarial stances (Bucholtz 2002), and Subrahmanyam, Smahel, and Greenfield (2006) observed that girls were quite sexually assertive in the two teen chatrooms they studied – although the girls used more sexually implicit communication, whereas the boys were sexually explicit. These findings complicate and refine the body of CMC and gender scholarship.

Other studies directly echo earlier findings. Koch et al. (2005) found that men were more dominant and assertive in computer chat, even under conditions of anonymity, similar to the findings of Selfe and Meyer (1991). Thomson and Murachver (2001) found that subjects could identify a partner's gender accurately based on features of the gendered styles described by Herring (1993; 1996a; 1996b). Gendered discourse styles continue to be used in forums on the social network site MySpace (Fullwood, Morris, and Evans 2011; Thelwall, Wilkinson, and Uppal 2010). In addition to using more emoticons (e.g., Baron and Ling 2007; Tossell et al. 2012) and exclamation points (Waseleski 2006), the latest female communication trend is the inclusion of *xo* ("a kiss and a hug") in tweets, IM, and email (Bennet and Simons 2012).

Alongside difference, disparity also persists. On Twitter, men's tweets are retweeted more often, especially by men, even though women post more tweets overall (Mashable 2012). Blogs by men are linked to and reported on in the mass media more than women's blogs (Herring et al. 2004). Moreover, women are still disproportionately the targets of online verbal violence and harassment, as attested by the case of technology blogger Kathy Sierra, who in 2007 received sexualized death threats on her blog from well-known male bloggers for, as Harding (2007) put it, the crime of publicly "Writing While Female." Recent incidents of threatening communication directed toward women "speaking up" on social media continue to deter women's participation in online environments (e.g., Marwick 2013).

4. Multimodal CMC

The world wide web, more than any other Internet application, was responsible for bringing women online in large numbers in the mid-1990s. The main property of the web that sets it apart from text-based CMC is that it is multimodal, encompassing text, graphics, video, and audio. Moreover, CMC itself is increasingly multimodal on web 2.0 sites such as blogs, social network sites, media-sharing sites, and multiplayer online games.

Along with these technological changes, there has been a shift in the ways people represent themselves online. In early text-only environments, individuals could construct creative self-representations through user names and textual self-descriptions (Danet 1998; McRae 1996). In the graphical chat environments that followed, users were represented by cartoon-like avatars (Kolko 1999; Scheidt 2004). In recent years, however, the combination of increased bandwidth and the rise in popularity of social network sites has led many Internet users to post photographs of themselves, which show them, in principle, "as they really are."[2] Accompanying this is a trend for people to make their personal information openly accessible. Thus, there has been a shift from (relative) anonymity toward "nonymity" (Zhao, Grasmuck, and Martin 2008). At the same time, one is free to select any image to represent oneself, since the actual physical appearance of the user remains hidden, as in text-based CMC. Unfortunately, little research as yet relates multimodal representations to verbal language. The focus of the following discussion is on how multimodality affects gender and online communication more broadly, although language is mentioned where research findings are available.

The first studies to address this question were of graphical avatars. Subjects in experiments conducted by Nowak and Rauh (2005) reported preferring graphical avatars that portrayed them realistically. However, other research found that avatars in chat and 3-D environments exaggerated secondary sex characteristics, especially of females, not only in environments designed by (male) professionals (Kolko 1999; McDonough 1999) but also in self-chosen and self-designed avatars (Scheidt 2004). Moreover, avatar gender switching has been reported in online games: men sometimes play as female avatars in order to get more help from other players, and women sometimes play as male avatars in order to be taken more seriously by male players and/or avoid harassment (Hussain and Griffiths 2008; Lehdonvirta et al. 2012).

There is evidence that the gender of one's avatar reflects and influences one's communication style. In experiments by Palomares and Lee (2010), women were more apologetic and tentative when using a female avatar, whereas gender-mismatched avatars encouraged the use of countertypical language. In contrast, Herring and Martinson (2004) found that players of a textual online gender identity game largely preserved the discourse style associated with their offline gender.

The earliest studies of photographic self-representations were of personal homepages. Blair and Takayoshi (1999) found that some women's homepage pictures were sexualized, showing the subjects in provocative clothing and/or postures. This practice has since become the norm on social media sites (e.g., Kapidzic and Herring 2011; Wang 2011), arguably due to the ubiquity of pornography online, leading to what Paasonen (2011) calls "self-commodification." On one photo-sharing site, Willem et al. (2012) found that even girls who did not initially post sexualized pictures moved toward that photographic style over time.

Blair and Takayoshi (1999) critique the practice of sexualized self-representation, pointing out that even when girls and women consider displaying their images online as an act of self-empowerment, the reception and use of those images can objectify them. For example, an infamous site from the mid-1990s, *Babes on the Web*, linked to photographs on women's homepages without their permission and rated them in offensively sexist terms (Spertus 1996). In that case, women were objectified independently of the "provocativeness" of their images. More recently, a 2012 Facebook page titled "12-Year-Old Slut Meme's" [*sic*] reposted photographs of young girls so that others could comment on their sluttiness; in this case, the girls self-sexualized in their original images. Chemaly (2012) concludes that "use of photography (especially without the subject's consent) intensifies harassment, abuse and violence against women."

Self-sexualization online appears to be spreading to young males. The young men Manago et al. (2008) interviewed felt pressure to present themselves in an attractive manner and reported representing themselves as "playboys" on MySpace. Relatedly, 15 percent of profile photographs of males on a popular teen chat site showed the subject with a nude upper body; this was more often the case for white than for black boys (Kapidzic and Herring 2011; 2013). In contrast to the cases involving females reported above, there is no evidence so far that males who post self-sexualized images are publicly demeaned.

One type of multimodal content that has been associated more with men is video. Following the meteoric rise in popularity of the video-sharing site YouTube, a number of studies reported that males were uploading more video content and using more video-sharing applications than females (e.g., Chen 2007). In a study of YouTube video bloggers ("vloggers"), Molyneaux et al. (2008) found that almost twice as many men as women posted vlogs, and many more men than women reported visiting YouTube on a daily basis. Further, only 13 percent of female respondents had ever posted comments on videos or uploaded videos, compared to 50 percent of males. Biel and Gatica-Perez (2009) also found more men (73%) than women (27%) in their study of YouTube use. However, the women accumulated more subscribers, had more subscriptions, and had double the numbers of friends that men had, leading the authors to conclude that "women, overall, have a more social-driven behavior in YouTube" (Biel and Gatica-Perez 2009, 835).

Moreover, recent numbers indicate that female teens today are more likely than teen males to video chat and to create and share videos (Lenhart 2012; Lenhart et al. 2010), suggesting that video communication patterns may be shifting.

Research on representations of males and females in online videos is lacking. One might posit that because of gender role schemas and the trend toward self-sexualization, some women would represent themselves in online videos in sexualized ways. Anecdotal evidence in support of this is the phenomenon of "reply girls," young women who seek to garner views by posting video replies on YouTube with the camera focused on their cleavage. Because of its manipulative nature, this practice is generally condemned by both male and female YouTube users (Eördögh 2012).

Gender identity is more difficult to disguise in video than in textual CMC. The same is true in audio chat, which has become popular in multiplayer online games, despite the concerns of some players that it will make playing with an avatar of a different gender more difficult and that it will open the door for discrimination against and harassment of female players (Wadley, Gibbs, and Benda 2007). However, in a study of second-language learners communicating online via voice, Jepsen (2005, 84) noted that although "the gender of the participant was often identifiable due to the sound quality of the participant's voice…, the participant's gender could not be verified simply by voice quality." Issues of gender identification aside, there is a need for research into gender and communication style in audio CMC, including in dyadic interactions using popular applications such as Skype.

5. Mobile CMC

Another recent trend is the growth of CMC via mobile phones. "Smartphones" enable one to send text messages (SMS), access the Internet, record video, and take and share photos (Duggan and Rainie 2012). Smartphones differ from previous CMC technologies in supporting mostly private communication between known interlocutors, and both men and women use them actively (in the United States 46% and 45%, respectively: Brenner 2012).

They tend to use them in different ways, however. Female teens and college students around the globe typically use their mobile phones for socializing (including expressing affection and support), whereas males use theirs for information seeking and planning (e.g., Israel: Lemish and Cohen 2005; Hong Kong: Lin 2005; Japan: Okuyama 2009; Taiwan: Wei and Lo 2006). Similar patterns have been found in the United States (Lenhart et al. 2010), Australia (Horstmanshof and Power 2005), and the United Kingdom (Barnett 2012). Moreover, girls and women tend to send longer and more frequent SMS texts than men and boys (Baron and Campbell 2012; Herring and Zelenkauskaite 2009; Lenhart et al. 2010; Ling 2005).

Texting via mobile phones and "textspeak" are stereotypically associated with young females in the mass media, the latest manifestation of "the convergence of telephony and teenage girlhood in [American] popular culture" (Kearney 2005,

571, quoted in Jones and Schieffelin 2009, 1054). A few studies have empirically analyzed the language of text messaging in relation to gender. Tossell et al. (2012) found that females had a higher emoticons-to-words ratio in their messages than males, although the emoticon vocabulary in male messages was more varied. However, emoticons were found in only 4 percent of the SMS texts they examined. In a study of SMS texts posted to an interactive television program in Italy, Herring and Zelenkauskaite (2009) also found that emoticons were rare, although women used significantly more nonstandard typography and orthography than men. This contrasts with previous variationist sociolinguistic findings that women use more standard language in speech (cf. Labov 1990); the researchers interpreted the nonstandard usage as gendered social capital, with females earning value in the virtual marketplace by appearing playful, sociable, and friendly.

Finally, mobile phones themselves are social and cultural artifacts that participate in the presentation of self. Men tend to display their phones as symbols of their status and wealth, especially in groups of men and in mixed-sex groups with more males than females (Lycett and Dunbar 2000). Females physically decorate their phones more than males do, and females are also more likely to feign talking on their mobile phone to avoid harassment by potential predators (Baron and Ling 2007).

6. Discussion

6.1 Anonymity

Anonymity is a major theme that runs through gender and CMC research, where it (or its close relative, pseudonymity) is often claimed to promote gender equality. Yet this claim is problematic for several reasons. While some research suggests that anonymous forms of online communication are more comfortable for and encourage participation by women (e.g., Koch et al. 2005; Selfe and Meyer 1991), anonymity also reduces social accountability, making it easier for harassers to engage in hostile, aggressive acts. On sites such as the image discussion board 4Chan, which encourages absolute anonymity as a way to promote the posting of open and uninhibited content, the discourse is notoriously profane and sexist (Bernstein et al. 2011). Further, the literal meaning of "anonymous" is "not identified by name"; however, most participants use their real names in asynchronous CMC (Herring 1993), and those names often indicate the bearer's gender. In addition, communicators give off cues through their interactional style and message content, making it possible sometimes to identify their gender even when they use pseudonyms (Donath 1999; Herring 1996a; 1996b).

To this can be added the technologically driven trend toward increased "nonymity" online (Zhao, Grasmuck, and Martin 2008), in keeping with the evolution of CMC technologies toward multimodal systems rich in visual and auditory cues. This trend is encouraged by anonymity policies implemented by technology companies such as Google (Osborne 2012), as well as by proposed legislation, such as the Internet Protection Act in New York, that would ban anonymous criticism (Sandoval 2012). The intent of these rules is to protect individuals from false claims and cyberbullying[3] by making Internet communicators more accountable. Using real names instead of pseudonyms also makes individuals "3-dimensional" and more "authentic," according to Sheryl Sandberg, the chief operating officer of Facebook (*Economist* 2012). However, as the cases of Kathy Sierra and the "12-Year-Old-Slut Meme's" [*sic*] show, online harassment occurs even when harassers use their real names, and women still tend to receive fewer responses and retweets in nonymous CMC (Herring 1993; Mashable 2012).

The increasing popularity of mobile CMC can be seen as a parallel, related shift from public communication with strangers to private communication with individuals of one's choosing. Communicators also know who their audience is in social network sites where they can choose their friends, such as Facebook, although Facebook's "walled garden" model has been eroded recently by changes to the site that make more user information public by default (Bankston 2009). The enthusiastic embrace of these more controlled environments by female users can be seen as a reverse reflection of the problematic nature of less controlled public environments, where anonymity is insufficient to insure females equal access to the conversational floor or protection from harassment.

6.2 Difference and disparity

The Internet was predicted to lead to gender equality by rendering gender differences in communication invisible or irrelevant. This prediction clearly has not been supported; many traditional gender differences carry over into CMC. Males and females "like" different products, services, and entertainers on Facebook, consistent with traditional gender stereotypes (Glenn 2013). Moreover, they tend to communicate online about different topics, in different contexts, for different purposes, and often (albeit not always) in different ways. These differences have remained relatively stable over the past 20 years, suggesting that gendered identities are socially facilitative – for example, when engaging in heteronormative activities such as flirting (Kapidzic and Herring 2011). That many girls and women choose to reveal their gender in textual CMC and produce gendered (including self-sexualized) images supports this view. More generally, social capital can be accrued by engaging in gender-appropriate behavior online (Herring and Zelenkauskaite 2009).

Internet users also orient to stereotypes of gender differences. In their study of an online gender identity game, Herring and Martinson (2004) found that players guessed gender based on stereotypes about male and female behavior. Relatedly, Thompson (2006) found that online discussions about gender-stereotypical topics triggered use of gender-preferential language by both men and women.

Disparity is evident, as well, as described in the preceding sections. Public CMC is often contentious, favoring assertive male over supportive female discourse styles. The perception that a participant is female can lead to discursive discrimination (e.g., lack of turn uptake) and harassment. Females self-commodify and are commodified and sexually demeaned by males online. More broadly, while the gender digital divide has been bridged in terms of who logs on, at least in the United States, women and men still do not have equal access to the creation and control of what takes place on the Internet. Roles that require technical expertise, such as network administrator, are disproportionately filled by men, consistent with the traditional association of technology with masculinity (Wajcman 1991). Women, given their lower numbers in fields such as computer science,[4] are less likely to have the necessary qualifications to take on these roles. In these respects, the Internet and CMC reproduce the larger societal gender status quo.

7. Conclusion

The reality of gender and online communication may fall short of the early projections because the projections were unrealistic in the first place – for example, because they were based on the problematic assumption of technological determinism. Computer networks do not guarantee gender-free, equal-opportunity interaction any more than any previous communication technology has done. Still, the current status quo represents a gain over the recent past, in which the Internet was limited to a predominantly male elite; it has now caught up with – and reflects – the larger society in which it is embedded.

Moreover, the interplay of a popular technology such as the Internet with social and cultural forces over time may yet lead to change, just as technologies such as the typewriter and the telephone have altered patterns of sociability and business practice, and affected women's lives, in particular, in significant ways (Davies 1988; Martin 1991). A desirable future outcome would be that as more and more women go online globally the Internet will become a truly egalitarian environment. An increasing number of women would control web content and distribution, and more women would become computer network designers and administrators, giving them real influence – both numerical and technical – to shape the nature and uses of the Internet. The likelihood of this coming about depends crucially on a critical mass of women entering information technology professions. It may also depend on policies being implemented that increase user accountability and CMC environments being designed that give users control over who and what is included in their online spaces.

The coverage in this chapter is limited by the lack of research in some (especially emerging technology) domains. Topics in need of research include gender and sexuality and gender and race in online communication, language use in video and audio CMC, and user responses to multimodal representations. Some studies have addressed the latter topics by analyzing user comments on language use in multilingual YouTube videos (e.g., Chun and Walters 2011), but gender has not been their focus. The trend toward Internet multimodality, in particular, opens up new vistas for CMC research and raises particular challenges for language and gender research as textual, oral, and nonverbal communication increasingly converge.

NOTES

1   Gender is often visible in recreational public chat, even aside from discourse style. Chatters frequently ask other participants about their biological sex, along with their age and location (abbreviated "asl"). Moreover, they display their gender through their message content and use of third-person pronouns to describe their own actions (Herring 1998).
2   Photographic images may be modified as well. Zhao, Grasmuck, and Martin (2008, 1827) report that in social network sites, users of both genders enhance their representations in ways that may be viewed as more socially desirable and "anti-nerd."
3   Anonymity can also be abused by females. Some studies (e.g., Hinduja and Patchin 2010) investigating the online behaviors of young people age 10–18 suggest that females are more likely to be cyberbullying victims *and* offenders. According to this research, young girls are more likely to spread rumors online about others, whereas young boys are more likely to post mean/hurtful pictures or videos.
4   Recent reports contend that women continue to be severely underrepresented in technology-related fields. Only 14% of undergraduate computer science degree earners at major US research institutions in 2010 were women, and in 2011 women made up only 25% of the computing workforce (NCWIT 2012).

REFERENCES

Abraham, Linda B., Marie P. Morn, and A. Vollman. 2010. "Women on the Web: How Women are Shaping the Internet." *ComScore* (June). At http://www.researchfindr.com/women-web-how-women-are-shaping-internet, accessed November 5, 2013.

Balka, Ellen. 1993. "Women's Access to Online Discussions about Feminism." *Electronic Journal of Communication*, 3(1). At http://www.cios.org/EJCPUBLIC/003/1/00311.HTML, accessed October 30, 2013.

Bankston, Kevin. 2009. "Facebook's New Privacy Changes: The Good, the Bad, and the Ugly." *Electronic Frontier Foundation*, December 9. At https://www.eff.org/deeplinks/2009/12/facebooks-new-privacy-changes-good-bad-and-ugly, accessed October 30, 2013.

Barnett, Emma. 2012. "Women More Likely to Text 'I Love You.'" *Telegraph*, July 18. At http://www.telegraph.co.uk/technology/mobile-phones/9407824/Women-more-likely-to-text-I-love-you.html, accessed October 30, 2013.

Baron, Naomi S., and Elise M. Campbell. 2012. "Gender and Mobile Phones in Cross-National Context." *Language Sciences*, 34: 13–27.

Baron, Naomi S., and Rich Ling. 2007. "Emerging Patterns of American Mobile Phone Use: Electronically-Mediated Communication in Transition." In Gerard Goggin and Larissa Hjorth (eds.), *Mobile Media 2007: Proceedings of an International Conference*, University of Sydney, *July 2–4, 2007*. At http://www.american.edu/cas/lfs/faculty-docs/upload/Emerging-Patterns-of-American-Mobile-Phone-Use-3.pdf, accessed October 30, 2013.

Bennett, Jessica, and Rachel Simons. 2012. "Kisses and Hugs in the Office." *Atlantic*, December. At http://www.theatlantic.com/magazine/archive/2012/12/the-xo-factor/309174/, accessed October 30, 2013.

Berkow, Jameson. 2011. "LinkedIn Declares Men Better than Women at Professional Online Networking." *FP Tech Desk*. At http://business.financialpost.com/2011/06/22/linkedin-declares-men-better-than

-women-at-professional-online
-networking/, accessed October 30, 2013.

Bernstein, Michael Scott, Andrés
Monroy–Hernández, Drew Harry, Paul
André, Katrina Panovich, and Greg
Vargas. 2011. "4chan and /b/: An Analysis
of Anonymity and Ephemerality in a
Large Online Community." In *Proceedings
of the Fifth International Conference on
Weblogs and Social Media*, 50–57. Menlo
Park, CA: AAAI Press. At http://projects
.csail.mit.edu/chanthropology/4chan.pdf,
accessed October 30, 2013.

Biel, Joan-Isaac, and Daniel Gatica-Perez.
2009. "Wearing a YouTube Hat: Directors,
Comedians, Gurus, and User Aggregated
Behavior." In *MM '09: Proceedings of the
17th ACM International Conference on
Multimedia*, 833–836. New York:
Association for Computing Machinery.

Blair, Kristine, and Pamela Takayoshi. 1999.
"Mapping the Terrain of Feminist
Cyberscapes." In Kristine Blair and Pamela
Takayoshi (eds.), *Feminist Cyberscapes:
Mapping Gendered Academic Spaces*, 1–18.
Stamford, CT: Ablex.

Brail, Stephanie. 1996. "The Price of
Admission: Harassment and Free Speech
in the Wild, Wild West." In Lynn Cherny
and Elizabeth R. Weise (eds.), *Wired
Women*, 141–157. Seattle: Seal Press.

Brenner, Joanna. 2012. "Pew Internet: Social
Networking (Full Detail)." *Pew Internet and
American Life Project*. At http://
pewinternet.org/Commentary/2012
/March/Pew-Internet-Social-Networking
-full-detail.aspx, accessed October 30, 2013.

Broadhurst, Judith. 1993. "Lurkers and
Flamers." *Online Access*, 8(3): 48–51.

Bruckman, Amy S. 1993. "Gender Swapping
on the Internet." In *Proceedings of INET '93*.
Reston, VA: Internet Society. At
http://mith.umd.edu//WomensStudies
/Computing/Articles+ResearchPapers
/gender-swapping, accessed October 30,
2013.

Bucholtz, Mary. 2002. "Geek Feminism." In
Sarah Benor, Mary Rose, Devyani Sharma,
Julie Sweetland, and Qing Zhang (eds.),
Gendered Practices in Language, 277–307.
Stanford: CSLI Publications.

Camp, L. Jean. 1996. "We are Geeks, and We
are Not Guys: The Systers Mailing List." In
Lynn Cherny and Elizabeth R. Weise (eds.),
Wired Women, 114–125. Seattle: Seal Press.

Chemaly, Soraya. 2012. "The 12-Year-Old Slut
Meme and Facebook's Misogyny
Problem." *HuffPost Media*, September 26.
At http://www.huffingtonpost.com
/soraya-chemaly/12-year-old-slut-meme
-and_b_1911056.html, accessed October 30,
2013.

Chen, Hsuan-Ting. 2007. "Sharing,
Connection, and Creation in the Web 2.0
Era: Profiling the Adopters of
Video-Sharing and Social-Networking
Sites." Paper presented at the Association
for Education in Journalism and Mass
Communication (AEJMC) Annual
Conference, Washington, DC.

Cherny, Lynn. 1994. "Gender Differences in
Text-Based Virtual Reality." In Mary
Bucholtz, Anita C. Liang, Laurel A. Sutton,
and Caitlin Hines (eds.), *Cultural
Performances: Proceedings of the Third
Berkeley Women and Language Conference*,
102–115. Berkeley: Berkeley Women and
Language Group.

Chun, Elaine, and Keith Walters. 2011.
"Orienting to Arab Orientalisms:
Language, Race and Humour in a YouTube
Video." In Crispin Thurlow and Kristine
Mroczek (eds.), *Digital Discourse: Language
in the New Media*, 251–270. New York:
Oxford University Press.

Coates, Jennifer. 1993. *Women, Men and
Language*, 2nd edn. London: Longman.

Collins-Jarvis, Lori. 1997. "Discriminatory
Messages and Gendered Power Relations
in On-line Discussion Groups." Paper
presented at the Annual Meeting of the
National Communication Association,
Chicago.

Crocco, Margaret S., Judith Cramer, and Ellen
B. Meier. 2008. "(Never) Mind the Gap!
Gender Equity in Social Studies Research
on Technology in the Twenty-First
Century." *Multicultural Education &
Technology Journal*, 2(1): 19–36.

Curtis, Pavel. 1992. "Mudding: Social
Phenomena in Text-Based Virtual
Realities." In Douglas Schuler (ed.),
Directions and Implications of Advanced

Computing: Proceedings from the DIAC '92 Conference. Palo Alto, CA: Computer Professionals for Social Responsibility. At http://w2.eff.org/Net_culture/MOO_MUD_IRC/curtis_mudding.article, accessed October 30, 2013.

Danet, Brenda. 1998. "Text as Mask: Gender and Identity on the Internet." In Steve Jones (ed.), *Cybersociety 2.0*, 129–158. Thousand Oaks, CA: Sage.

Davies, Margery W. 1988. "Women Clerical Workers and the Typewriter: The Writing Machine." In Cheris Kramarae (ed.), *Technology and Women's Voices: Keeping in Touch*, 29–40. New York: Routledge.

Dibbell, Julian. 1993. "A Rape in Cyberspace, or How an Evil Clown, a Haitian Trickster Spirit, Two Wizards, and a Cast of Dozens Turned a Database Into a Society." *Village Voice*, December 23: 36–42.

Donath, Judith. 1999. "Identity and Deception in the Virtual Community." In Marc A. Smith and Peter Kollock (eds.), *Communities in Cyberspace*, 29–59. New York: Routledge.

Duggan, Maeve, and Lee Rainie. 2012. "Cell Phone Activities 2012." *Pew Internet and American Life Project*, November 25. At http://www.pewinternet.org/Reports/2012/Cell-Activities.aspx, accessed October 30, 2013.

Ebben, Maureen, and Cheris Kramarae. 1993. "Women and Information Technologies: Creating a Cyberspace of Our Own." In H. Jeanie Taylor, Cheris Kramarae, and Maureen Ebben (eds.), *Women, Information Technology, and Scholarship*, 15–27. Urbana, IL: Center for Advanced Study.

Economist. 2011. "Sharing to the Power of 2012." November 17. At http://www.economist.com/node/21537000, accessed October 30, 2013.

Eördögh, Fruzsina. 2012. "YouTube or Boob Tube: Replay Girl Scandal Rocks Video World." *Daily Dot*, February 25. At http://www.dailydot.com/entertainment/reply-girls-yogscast-meganspeaks/, accessed October 30, 2013.

Fallows, Deborah. 2005. "How Women and Men Use the Internet." *Pew Internet and American Life Project*, December 28. At http://www.pewinternet.org/Reports/2005/How-Women-and-Men-Use-the-Internet.aspx, accessed October 30, 2013.

Fogel, Joshua, and Elham Nehmad. 2009. "Internet Social Network Communities: Risk Taking, Trust, and Privacy Concerns." *Computers in Human Behavior*, 25: 153–160.

Fullwood, Chris, Neil Morris, and Libby Evans. 2011. "Linguistic Androgyny on MySpace." *Journal of Language and Social Psychology*, 30(1): 114–124.

Glenn, Devon. 2013. "Facebook Likes Confirm Stereotypes for Men and Women." *Social Times*, May 7. At http://socialtimes.com/facebook-likes-confirm-stereotypes-for-men-and-women-infographic_b126245, accessed October 30, 2013.

Graddol, David, and Joan Swann. 1989. *Gender Voices*. Oxford: Blackwell.

Guiller, Jane, and Allan Durndell. 2007. "Students' Linguistic Behavior in Online Discussion Groups: Does Gender Matter?" *Computers in Human Behavior*, 23(5): 2240–2255.

Hafner, Katie, and Lyon Matthew. 1996. *Where Wizards Stay up Late: The Origins of the Internet*. New York: Simon & Schuster.

Hall, Kira. 1996. "Cyberfeminism." In Susan C. Herring (ed.), *Computer-Mediated Communication: Linguistic, Social, and Cross-Cultural Perspectives*, 147–170. Amsterdam: Benjamins.

Harding, Kate. 2007. "On Being a No-Name Blogger Using Her Real Name." *Shapely Prose*, April 14. At http://kateharding.net/2007/04/14/on-being-a-no-name-blogger-using-her-real-name/, accessed October 30, 2013.

Herring, Susan C. 1992. *Gender and Participation in Computer-Mediated Linguistic Discourse*. Washington, DC: ERIC Clearinghouse on Languages and Linguistics, Document no. ED345552.

Herring, Susan C. 1993. "Gender and Democracy in Computer-Mediated Communication." *Electronic Journal of Communication*, 3(2). At http://www.cios.org/EJCPUBLIC/003/2/00328.HTML, accessed October 30, 2013.

Herring, Susan C. 1994. "Politeness in
    Computer Culture: Why Women Thank
    and Men Flame." In Mary Bucholtz, Anita
    C. Liang, Laurel A. Sutton, and Caitlin
    Hines (eds.), *Cultural Performances:
    Proceedings of the Third Berkeley Women and
    Language Conference*, 278–294. Berkeley:
    Berkeley Women and Language Group.
Herring, Susan C. 1996a. "Posting in a
    Different Voice: Gender and Ethics in
    Computer-Mediated Communication." In
    Charles Ess (ed.), *Philosophical Perspectives
    on Computer-Mediated Communication*,
    115–145. Albany, NY: SUNY Press.
Herring, Susan C. 1996b. "Two Variants of an
    Electronic Message Schema." In Susan C.
    Herring (ed.), *Computer-Mediated
    Communication: Linguistic, Social, and
    Cross-cultural Perspectives*, 81–106.
    Amsterdam: Benjamins.
Herring, Susan C. 1998. "Virtual Gender
    Performances." Talk presented at Texas
    A&M University, September 25.
Herring, Susan C. 1999. "The Rhetorical
    Dynamics of Gender Harassment Online."
    The Information Society, 15(3): 151–167.
Herring, Susan C. 2010. "Who's Got the Floor
    in Computer-Mediated Conversation?
    Edelsky's Gender Patterns Revisited."
    Language@Internet 7, article 8. At http://
    www.languageatinternet.org/articles
    /2010/2857, accessed October 30, 2013.
Herring, Susan C., Deborah Johnson, and
    Tamra DiBenedetto. 1992. "Participation in
    Electronic Discourse in a 'Feminist' Field."
    In Kira Hall, Mary Bucholtz, and Birch
    Moonwomon (ed.), *Locating Power:
    Proceedings of the Second Berkeley Women
    and Language Conference*, 250–262.
    Berkeley: Berkeley Women and Language
    Group.
Herring, Susan C., Deborah Johnson, and
    Tamra DiBenedetto. 1995. " 'This
    Discussion is Going Too Far!' Male
    Resistance to Female Participation on the
    Internet." In Kira Hall and Mary Bucholtz
    (ed.), *Gender Articulated: Language and the
    Socially Constructed Self*, 67–96. New York:
    Routledge.
Herring, Susan C., and Anna Martinson.
    2004. "Assessing Gender Authenticity in

Computer-Mediated Language Use:
    Evidence from an Identity Game." *Journal
    of Language and Social Psychology*, 23(4):
    424–446.
Herring, Susan C., and John C. Paolillo. 2006.
    "Gender and Genre Variation in Weblogs."
    Journal of Sociolinguistics, 10: 439–459.
Herring, Susan C., and Asta Zelenkauskaite.
    2009. "Symbolic Capital in a Virtual
    Heterosexual Market: Abbreviation and
    Insertion in Italian iTV SMS." *Written
    Communication*, 26(1): 5–31.
Herring, Susan C., Inna Kouper, Lois Ann
    Scheidt, and Elijah L. Wright. 2004.
    "Women and Children Last: The
    Discursive Construction of Weblogs." In
    Laura Gurak, Smiljana Antonijevic, Laurie
    Johnson, Clancy Ratliff, and Jessica
    Reyman (eds.), *Into the Blogosphere:
    Rhetoric, Community, and Culture of Weblogs*
    (online). At http://blog.lib.umn.edu
    /blogosphere/women_and_children.html,
    accessed October 30, 2013.
Hert, Philippe. 1997. "Social Dynamics of an
    Online Scholarly Debate." *The Information
    Society*, 13: 329–360.
Hinduja, Sameer, and Justin W. Patchin. 2010.
    "Cyberbullying Offending." At
    http://www.cyberbullying.us/2010
    _charts/cyberbullying_gender_2010.jpg,
    accessed October 30, 2013.
Horstmanshof, Louise, and Mary R. Power.
    2005. "Mobile Phones, SMS, and
    Relationships." *Australian Journal of
    Communication*, 32(1): 33–61.
Huffaker, David A., and Sandra L. Calvert.
    2005. "Gender, Identity, and Language Use
    in Teenage Blogs." *Journal of
    Computer-Mediated Communication*, 10(2):
    article 1. At http://onlinelibrary.wiley
    .com/doi/10.1111/j.1083-6101.2005
    .tb00238.x/full, accessed November 11,
    2013.
HuffPost Women. 2012. "Social Media by
    Gender: Women Dominate Pinterest,
    Twitter, Men Dominate Reddit, YouTube."
    Huffington Post, June 21. At http://www
    .huffingtonpost.com/2012/06/20/social
    -media-by-gender-women-pinterest-men
    -reddit-infographic_n_1613812.html,
    accessed October 30, 2013.

Hussain, Zaheer, and Mark D. Griffiths. 2008. "Gender Swapping and Socializing in Cyberspace: An Exploratory Study." *Cyberpsychology & Behavior*, 11(1): 47–53.

Jepsen, Kevin. 2005, "Conversations – and Negotiated Interaction – in Text and Voice Chat Rooms." *Language Learning & Technology*, 9(3): 79–98.

Jones, Graham M., and Bambi Schieffelin. 2009. "Talking Text and Talking Back: 'My BFF Jill' from Boob Tube to YouTube." *Journal of Computer-Mediated Communication*, 14: 1050–1079.

Kapidzic, Sanja, and Susan C. Herring. 2011. "Gender, Communication, and Self-Presentation in Teen Chatrooms Revisited: Have Patterns Changed?" *Journal of Computer-Mediated Communication*, 17(1): 39–59.

Kapidzic, Sanja, and Susan C. Herring. 2013. "Race, Gender, and Self-Presentation in Teen Profile Photographs." Unpublished paper.

Kearney, M. 2005. "Birds on the Wire: Troping Teenage Girlhood through Telephony in Mid-Twentieth Century US Media Culture." *Cultural Studies*, 19: 568–601.

Kling, Rob, Geoff McKim, and Adam King. 2003. "A Bit More to IT: Scholarly Communication Forums as Socio-technical Interaction Networks." *Journal of the American Society for Information Science and Technology*, 54(1): 47–67.

Koch, Sabine C., Barbara Mueller, Lenelis Kruse, and Joerg Zumbach. 2005. "Constructing Gender in Chat Groups." *Sex Roles*, 53(1–2): 29–41.

Kolko, Beth. 1999. "Representing Bodies in Virtual Space: The Rhetoric of Avatar Design." *The Information Society*, 15: 177–186.

Kramarae, Cheris, and H. Jeanie Taylor. 1993. "Women and Men on Electronic Networks: A Conversation or a Monologue?" In H. Jeanie Taylor, Cheris Kramarae, and Maureen Ebben (eds.), *Women, Information Technology, and Scholarship*, 52–61. Urbana, IL: Center for Advanced Study.

Labov, William. 1990. "The Intersection of Sex and Social Class in the Course of Linguistic Change." *Language Variation and Change*, 2(2): 205–254.

Lam, Shyong K., Anuradha Uduwage, Zhenhua Dong, Shilad Sen, David R. Musicant, et al. 2011. "WP:Clubhouse? An Exploration of Wikipedia's Gender Imbalance." *WikiSym 2011*. At http://grouplens.org/system/files/wp-gender-wikisym2011.pdf, accessed October 30, 2013.

Lehdonvirta, Mika, Yosuke Nagashima, Vili Lehdonvirta, and Akira Baba. 2012. "The Stoic Male: How Avatar Gender Affects Help-Seeking Behavior in an Online Game." *Games and Culture*, 7(1): 29–47.

Lemish, Dafna, and Akiba A. Cohen. 2005. "On the Gendered Nature of Mobile Phone Culture in Israel." *Sex Roles*, 52(7–8): 511–521.

Lenhart, Amanda. 2012. "Teens and Video: Shooting, Sharing, Streaming and Chatting." *Pew Internet and American Life Project*, May 3. At http://pewinternet.org/Reports/2012/Teens-and-online-video/Findings.aspx?view=all, accessed October 30, 2013.

Lenhart, Amanda, Rich Ling, Scott Campbell, and Kristin Purcell. 2010. "Teens and Mobile Phones." *Pew Internet and American Life Project*, April 20. At http://www.pewinternet.org/Reports/2010/Teens-and-Mobile-Phones.aspx, accessed October 30, 2013.

Lin, Angel. 2005. "Gendered, Bilingual Communication Practices: Mobile Text-Messaging among Hong Kong College Students." *Fibreculture Journal*, 6. At http://fibreculturejournal.org/?s=Gendered%2C+Bilingual+Communication+Practices%3A+Mobile+Text-Messaging+among+Hong+Kong+College+Students, accessed October 30, 2013.

Ling, Rich. 2005. "The Socio-linguistics of SMS: An Analysis of SMS Use by a Random Sample of Norwegians." In Rich Ling and Per E. Pedersen (eds.), *Mobile Communications: Renegotiation of the Social Sphere*, 335–349. London: Springer.

Lycett, John E., and Robin I. M. Dunbar. 2000. "Mobile Phones as Lekking Devices among Human Males." *Human Nature*, 11(1): 93–104.

Manago, Adriana M., Michael B. Graham, Patricia M. Greenfield, and Goldie Salimkhan. 2008. "Self-Presentation and Gender on MySpace." *Journal of Applied Developmental Psychology*, 29: 446–458.

Markus, M. Lynne. 1994. "Finding a Happy Medium: Explaining the Negative Effects of Electronic Communication on Social Life at Work." *ACM Transactions on Information Systems*, 12(2): 119–149.

Martin, Michèle. 1991. "The Making of the Perfect Operator." In *"Hello, Central?" Gender, Technology and the Re-formation of Telephone Systems*, 50–81. Montreal: McGill-Queen's University Press.

Marwick, Alice. 2013. "Donglegate: Why the Tech Community Hates Feminists." *Wired*, March 29. At http://www.wired.com /opinion/2013/03/richards-affair-and -misogyny-in-tech/, accessed October 30, 2013.

Mashable. 2012. "63% of Retweets are of Male Users." *Mashable Social Media*, July 30. At http://mashable.com/2012/07/30 /men-dominate-retweets/, accessed October 30, 2013.

McDonough, Jerome P. 1999. "Designer Selves: Construction of Technologically Mediated Identity Within." *Journal of the American Society for Information Science*, 50(10): 855–869.

McRae, Shannon. 1996. "Coming Apart at the Seams: Sex, Text and the Virtual Body." In Lynn Cherny and Elizabeth R. Weise (eds.), *Wired Women*, 242–263. Seattle: Seal Press.

Molyneaux, Heather, Susan O'Donnell, Karrie Gibson, and Janice Singer. 2008. "Exploring the Gender Divide on YouTube: An Analysis of the Creation and Reception of Vlogs." *American Communication Journal*, 10(2). At http://www.it.uu.se/edu/course /homepage/avint/vt09/1.pdf, accessed October 30, 2013.

Muscanell, Nicole L., and Rosanna E. Guadagno. 2012. "Make New Friends or Keep the Old: Gender and Personality in Social Networking Use." *Computers in Human Behavior*, 28: 107–112.

NCWIT. 2012. "Women and Information Technology: By the Numbers." *National Center for Women & Information Technology*.

At http://www.ncwit.org/sites/default /files/resources/2012bythenumbers _web.pdf, accessed October 30, 2013.

Nowak, Kristine L., and Christian Rauh. 2005. "The Influence of the Avatar on Online Perceptions of Anthropomorphism, Androgyny, Credibility, Homophily, and Attraction." *Journal of Computer-Mediated Communication*, 11(1): article 8. At http:// onlinelibrary.wiley.com/doi/10.1111 /j.1083-6101.2006.tb00308.x/full, accessed November 11, 2013.

Okuyama, Yoshiko. 2009. "Keetai Meeru: Younger People's Mobile Written Communication in Japan." *Electronic Journal of Contemporary Japanese Studies*. At http://www.japanesestudies.org.uk /articles/2009/Okuyama.html, accessed October 30, 2013.

Osborne, Charlie. 2012. "Google Play Bids Adieu to Anonymous Reviews." *CNET*. At http://news.cnet.com/8301-1023_3 -57554621-93/google-play-bids-adieu -to-anonymous-reviews/, accessed October 30, 2013.

Paasonen, Susanna. 2011. "Online Pornography: Ubiquitous and Effaced." In Mia Consalvo and Charles Ess (eds.), *The Handbook of Internet Research*, 424–439. Oxford: Blackwell.

Palomares, Nicholas A., and Eun-Ju Lee. 2010. "Virtual Gender Identity: The Linguistic Assimilation to Gendered Avatars in Computer-Mediated Communication." *Journal of Language and Social Psychology*, 29(1): 5–23.

Pastore, M. (2000). "Women Surpass Men as US Web Users." *Clickz*. At http://www .clickz.com/clickz/news/1706714 /women-surpass-men-us-web-users, accessed November 5, 2013.

Rodino, Michelle. 1997, "Breaking Out of Binaries: Reconceptualizing Gender and Its Relationship to Language in Computer-Mediated Communication." *Journal of Computer-Mediated Communication*, 3(3). At http://onlinelibrary.wiley.com/doi/10.1111 /j.1083-6101.1997.tb00074.x/full, accessed October 30, 2013.

Sandoval, Greg. 2012. "Proposed NY Ban on Anonymous Posts Comes under Fire." *CNET*. At http://news.cnet.com/8301

-1009_3-57440152-83/proposed-ny-ban
-on-anonymous-posts-comes-under-fire/,
accessed October 30, 2013.

Savicki, Victor, Dawn Lingenfelter, and Merle
Kelley. 1996. "Gender Language Style and
Group Composition in Internet Discussion
Groups." *Journal of Computer-Mediated
Communication*, 2(3). At http://
onlinelibrary.wiley.com/doi/10.1111
/j.1083-6101.1996.tb00191.x/full, accessed
October 30, 2013.

Scheidt, Lois A. 2004. "Buxom Girls and Boys
in Baseball Hats: Adolescent Avatars in
Graphical Chat Spaces." Paper presented
at the 54th Annual Conference of the
International Communication Association,
New Orleans. At http://www.academia
.edu/214175/Buxom_girls_and_boys_in
_baseball_hats_Adolescent_avatars_in
_graphical_chat_spaces, accessed October
30, 2013.

Selfe, Cynthia L., and Paul R. Meyer. 1991.
"Testing Claims for Online Conferences."
Written Communication, 8(2): 163–192.

Spertus, Ellen. 1996. "Social and Technical
Means for Fighting Online Harassment."
At http://people.mills.edu/spertus
/Gender/glc/glc.html, accessed October
30, 2013.

Sproull, Lee. 1992. "Women and the
Networked Organization." Paper
presented at the Women, Information
Technology, and Scholarship Colloquium,
University of Illinois, Center for Advanced
Study, February 12.

Subrahmanyam, Kaveri, David Smahel, and
Patricia M. Greenfield. 2006. "Connecting
Developmental Constructions to the
Internet: Identity Presentation and Sexual
Exploration in Online Teen Chat Rooms."
Developmental Psychology, 42(3): 395–406.

Sutton, Laurel. 1994. "Using USENET:
Gender, Power, and Silence in Electronic
Discourse." In Susanne Gahl, Andy
Dolbey and Christopher Johnson (eds.),
*Proceedings of the Twentieth Annual Meeting
of the Berkeley Linguistics Society*, 506–520.
Berkeley: Berkeley Linguistics Society.

Tannen, Deborah. 1990. *You Just Don't
Understand: Women and Men in
Conversation*. New York: William Morrow.

Thelwall, Mike, David Wilkinson, and
Sukhvinder Uppal. 2010. "Data Mining
Emotion in Social Network
Communication: Gender Differences in
MySpace." *Journal of the American Society
for Information Science and Technology*, 61(1):
190–199.

Thompson, Rob. 2006. "The Effect of Topic of
Discussion on Gendered Language in
Computer-Mediated Communication
Discussion." *Journal of Language and Social
Psychology*, 25: 167–178.

Thomson, Rob, and Tamar Murachver. 2001.
"Predicting Gender from Electronic
Discourse." *British Journal of Social
Psychology*, 40: 193–208.

Tossell, Chad C., Phillip Kortum, Clayton
Shepard, Laura H. Barg-Walkow, Ahmad
Rahmati, and Lin Zhong. 2012. "A
Longitudinal Study of Emoticon Use in
Text Messaging from Smartphones."
Computers in Human Behavior, 28: 659–663.

Wadley, Greg, Martin Gibbs, and Peter
Benda. 2007. "Speaking in Character:
Using Voice-over-IP to Communicate
within MMORPGs." In Martin Gibbs,
Larissa Hjorth, Esther Milne, and Yusuf
Pisan (eds.), *Proceedings of the 4th
Australasian Conference on Interactive
Entertainment*, article 24. Melbourne:
School of Creative Media, RMIT
University.

Wajcman, Judith. 1991. *Feminism Confronts
Technology*. University Park: Pennsylvania
State University Press.

Wang, Yin-Han. 2011. "Teenage Girls' Views
and Practices of 'Sexy' Self-Portraits in a
Taiwanese Social Networking Site."
*Interactions: Studies in Communication &
Culture*, 2(3): 209–224.

Waseleski, Carol. 2006. "Gender and the Use
of Exclamation Points in
Computer-Mediated Communication: An
Analysis of Exclamations Posted to Two
Electronic Discussion Lists." *Journal of
Computer-Mediated Communication*, 11(4):
article 6. At http://onlinelibrary.wiley
.com/doi/10.1111/j.1083-6101.2006.00305
.x/full, accessed October 30, 2013.

Wei, Ran, and Ven-Hwei Lo. 2006. "Staying
Connected While on the Move: Cell Phone

Use and Social Connectedness." *New Media & Society*, 8(1): 53–72.

Willem, Cilia, Núria Araüna, Lucrezia Crescenzi, and Iolanda Tortajada. 2012. "Girls on Fotolog: Reproduction of Gender Stereotypes or Identity Play?" *Interactions: Studies in Communication & Culture*, 2(3): 225–242.

Williams, Mary Elizabeth. 2012. "The War on 12-Year-Old Girls." *Salon*, October 19. At http://www.salon.com/2012/10/19 /the_war_on_12_year_old_girls/, accessed October 30, 2013.

Witmer, Diane, and Sandra L. Katzman. 1997. "On-line Smiles: Does Gender Make a Difference in the Use of Graphic Accents?" *Journal of Computer-Mediated Communication*, 2(4). At http:// onlinelibrary.wiley.com/doi/10.1111 /j.1083-6101.1997.tb00192.x/full, accessed October 30, 2013.

Wolf, Alecia. 2000. "Emotional Expression Online: Gender Differences in Emoticon Use." *CyberPsychology & Behavior*, 3: 827–833.

Zhao, Shanyang, Sherri Grasmuck, and Jason Martin. 2008. "Identity Construction on Facebook: Digital Empowerment in Anchored Relationships." *Computers in Human Behavior*, 24: 1816–1836.

30 "One Man in Two is a Woman"

Linguistic Approaches to Gender in Literary Texts

ANNA LIVIA

1. Introduction

The question of gender in literary texts has been approached by linguists in two different ways. The first involves a comparison of the fiction created by male and female authors and is typified by the search for "the female sentence" or a specifically female style of writing. The second involves a study of the uses to which the linguistic gender system of different languages has been put in literary works. In the former, gender is seen as a cultural property of the author, in the latter, a morphological property of the text. A third perspective on language and gender in literary texts is provided by translators and translation theorists. Translation theorists typically view a text as expressive of a particular time and place as well as being expressed in a particular language. The differences between source and target language may be accompanied by differences in culture and period; thus translators often work with both morphological gender and cultural gender. In this chapter, I will discuss men's and women's style in literature as well as literary uses of linguistic gender. I will also survey material on translation theory and what it offers to students of gender.

2. Male and Female Literary Styles

The most prominent modern thinker to discuss the differences between male and female literary styles is Virginia Woolf, writing at the beginning of the twentieth century. In a review of Dorothy Richardson's novel *Revolving Lights* (1923), she

The Handbook of Language, Gender, and Sexuality, Second Edition.
Edited by Susan Ehrlich, Miriam Meyerhoff, and Janet Holmes.
© 2014 John Wiley & Sons, Inc. Published 2017 by John Wiley & Sons, Inc.

describes the female sentence as "of a more elastic fibre than the old, capable of stretching to the extreme, of suspending the frailest particles, of enveloping the vaguest shapes" (Woolf 1990 [1919], 72). Assuming the traditional literary sentence to be masculine, she argues that it simply does not fit women, who need something less pompous and more elastic which they can bend in different ways to suit their purpose. However, descriptions such as "more elastic," "too loose, too heavy, too pompous" are annoyingly vague and impossible to quantify.

Woolf comes closest to giving a more specific evaluation of the female sentence in a review of Dorothy Richardson's *The Tunnel* (1919). Here she quotes a passage of interior monologue as triumphantly escaping "the him and her" and embedding the reader in the consciousness of the character: "It is like dropping everything and walking backward to something you know is there. However far you go out, you come back. I am back now" (Woolf 1990 [1919], 71). The exact relationship between the pronouns "you" and "I" in this passage is unclear. They seem to refer to the same person, the self, but also to include the reader. Because we do not know who "I" is, we have no referent for the temporal or spatial indicators "now" or "come back" either. This slipperiness of the referent seems to be what Woolf means by "elasticity."

It is significant that Woolf chose the writings of Dorothy Richardson to illustrate the female sentence, and specifically a passage of interior monologue. Interior monologue has the property of breaking down the boundaries between character and narrator, so that the angle of focalization (who sees the action) coincides with the narration of that action (who tells about the action). More traditional methods of storytelling present a narrator who recounts, but is separate from the character whose point of view is related. It was one of the projects of modernism (and both Richardson and Woolf are considered modernist) to render the depths of modern experience in an appropriate form, which meant breaking away from what they considered a smug, self-satisfied Edwardian frame of social realism and an omniscient narrator. Although we cannot speak of a "modernist sentence" as such, nevertheless, the other authors usually included in the modernist canon, such as T. S. Eliot, James Joyce, D. H. Lawrence, Ezra Pound, as well as Woolf and Richardson, have all experimented with sentence fragments, elimination of predicates, meandering syntax with many clauses in apposition. These are the very elements which tend also to typify interior monologue.

We would do best, therefore, to take Woolf's description of the female sentence as a literary rather than a linguistic commentary. As the stuffy Edwardian era gave way to greater freedom for women, especially in the interwar period, so women novelists felt freer to express themselves in new ways. The literary movement of modernism coincided with (and was also itself a product of) the new social developments consequent upon the horror and paradoxical liberty of the post-World War I period. Woolf's unremitting self-consciousness was shared by her contemporaries. Indeed her precursor Henry James writes of his own awareness of a fragmented consciousness in a discussion of his novel *Portrait of a Lady* (quoted in Millett 1951, v): "'Place the centre of the subject in the woman's own consciousness,' I said to myself, 'and you get as interesting and as beautiful a difficulty as you could wish.'" The challenge of this "beautiful difficulty" may be taken up by men or women authors.

Although Woolf's discussion of feminine style is impressionistic and essentialist, modern theorists have looked at more subtle differences in men's and women's writing. Sara Mills (1995) examines features such as descriptions of characters and self-descriptions in personal ads. In an analysis of a romance novel by best-selling author Barbara Taylor Bradford, Mills (1995, 147–149) demonstrates that the actions performed by the female character are of a different quality from those performed by the male. Parts of the woman's body move without her volition and she is represented as the passive recipient of the male's actions. The male acts while the female feels.

That male and female characters in fiction receive very different treatment is not particularly controversial, but the claim that women's writing differs in some essential way from that of men is more tendentious. Quoting Woolf's categorization of the female sentence as loose and accretive, Mills proceeds to look at some concrete examples to see what proof there may be of these differences. She concludes that the concept of a female-authored sentence stems from overgeneralization on the part of the literary critic rather than from any inherent quality in the writing, but she demonstrates that a female (or male) affiliation may be a motivating factor in certain texts (Mills 1995, 47–48). Comparing descriptions of a landscape taken from two well-known novels, Anita Brookner's *Hotel du Lac* and Malcolm Lowry's *Under the Volcano*, she shows that the first is conventionally feminine while the second is conventionally masculine (58–60). The features which mark the first as feminine include: abundant use of epistemic modality ("it was supposed," "it could be seen"); grammatically complex, meandering sentences with many clauses in apposition; and an impressionistic, subjective vocabulary such as "stiffish," "skimming," and "area of grey." In contrast, the second landscape is masculine in style, featuring the absence of an obvious authorial voice; an impersonal, objective tone; the description of amenities rather than people: "Overlooking one of these valleys, which is dominated by two volcanoes, lies, six thousand feet above sea-level, the town of Quauhnahuac" (60).

Female affiliation, or a distinctly feminist style, is a third possibility, in which the tone may be ironic or detached; female characters are presented as assertive and self-confident, and the reader is addressed directly and drawn into the text to share the narrator's point of view. Mills (1995, 60–61) quotes a passage from Ellen Galford's *Moll Cutpurse* to illustrate her point: "She had a voice like a bellowing ox and a laugh like a love-sick lion." This heroine is clearly very different from the passive female, mere object of the male's attention. The oxymoronic (apparently contradictory) quality of the comparison between Moll and a "love-sick lion" demonstrates the playful, almost parodic nature of the description. A lion is usually a symbol of masculine strength, but this lion is in love and therefore emotional. Moll thus combines a traditionally masculine quality (strength) with a traditionally feminine quality (deep feeling).

For contemporary critics, it is possible to identify certain features such as complex sentences with many subordinate clauses and a vocabulary that is vague and impressionistic as typifying the "female sentence," but there is no essential link between the fact of being a woman and this type of writing. It is a style which may be deliberately chosen by either sex. Indeed, if one considers Marcel Proust's sometimes page-length sentences, and his deliberations about the exact quality of colors and smells, one is obliged to classify his style as distinctly feminine:

> Jamais je ne m'étais avisé qu'elle pouvait avoir une figure rouge, une cravate mauve comme Mme Sazerat, et l'ovale de ses joues me fit tellement souvenir de personnes que j'avais vues à la maison que le soupçon m'effleura, pour se dissiper aussitôt, que cette dame, en son principe générateur, en toutes ses molécules n'était peut-être pas substantiellement la duchesse de Guermantes, mais que son corps, ignorant du nom qu'on lui appliquait, appartenait à un certain type féminin qui comprenait aussi des femmes de médecins et de commerçants.
>
> (I had never imagined that she could have a red face, a mauve scarf like Madame Sazerat, and her oval cheeks reminded me so much of people I had seen at home that I had the fleeting suspicion, a suspicion which evaporated immediately afterwards, that this lady, in her generative principle, in each one of her molecules was perhaps not in substance the Duchess of Guermantes but that her body, ignorant of the name she had been given, belonged to a certain feminine type which also included the wives of doctors and tradespeople.)
>
> (Proust 1954, 209–210)

Proust's sentence in the above extract is indisputably long, complex and meandering, convoluted, and concerned with female apparel and appearance – all traits which have been classified as "feminine."

It is equally possible for a woman author to deliberately flout this convention and write in a recognizably feminist style, or indeed a traditionally masculine one. The writer James Tiptree Junior was declared by the science fiction author Robert Silverberg to be a man in the introduction to one of her short story collections:

> For me there is something ineluctably masculine about Tiptree's writing. I don't think that a woman could have written the short stories of Hemingway, just as I don't think a man could have written the novels of Jane Austen, and in this way I think that Tiptree is male. (Silverberg 1975, xii)

Tiptree was invited to participate in a symposium organized by the science fiction magazine *Khatru*, the ensuing discussion being published in issues 3 and 4, but "his" style was felt to be so rebarbative that "he" was asked to withdraw (Lefanu 1988, 105–106). At this point "he" revealed that "he" was none other than Alice Sheldon, a renowned and definitely female author. The ensuing discussion of each participant's perceptions and misconceptions turned out to be the most fruitful part of the forum.

Novels may be identified as the work of a woman purely because of their content. The British feminist publishing company Virago was about to publish a novel by a young Indian woman, when they learned that the book had in fact been written by a middle-aged English vicar. Upon hearing this, Virago stopped publication.

As a company that was set up specifically to publish books by women, they were angry at being hoodwinked into accepting a manuscript written by a man. Critics of Virago's actions argued that it was the submissive, downtrodden status of the heroine which had at first convinced the editors that the novel was written by an Indian woman. This, they said, was a form of racism as the editors assumed that a victim status was typical of Asian women. Dinty Moore, a male author, was assumed to be female when he published a short story in an anthology of reminiscences of a Catholic girls' school. This also caused hot debate, though the anthology was not withdrawn (Rubin 1975).

In a study on the micro-level of text-making (looking at the immediate linguistic environment rather than the whole novel), Susan Ehrlich (1990, 101–103) has analyzed the use of reported speech and thought in canonical texts, particularly the novels of Virginia Woolf. She compares Woolf's style with that of Henry James and Ernest Hemingway with regard to the types of cohesive devices each uses. James depends heavily on what is known as grammatical cohesion, or anaphora. This means he introduces a character, and as soon as the reader has had the chance to form a mental image of this character, he replaces the character's name with a pronoun (this is, of course, a very traditional strategy). Hemingway relies instead on lexical cohesion, or a simple repetition of the character's name. Woolf, in contrast, uses a much greater variety of cohesive devices including grammatical and lexical cohesion as well as semantic connectors, temporal linking, and progressive aspect. A semantic connector tells the reader explicitly to connect two pieces of information in a particular way: *at the same time; in this way; in addition*. Temporal linking gives two clauses the same time reference and is a feature that often involves hypothetical clauses which have no time reference of their own: *Edith would be sure to know; I would have arrived before the others*. Progressive aspect also links two propositions where one clause provides an anchor for the other.

The advantage of research like Ehrlich's is that it provides a concrete set of criteria by which to distinguish different literary styles. We cannot assume that all women will write like Woolf and all men like James or Hemingway, but if we know that a researcher has based his or her claims entirely on a study of canonical texts by male authors, we can predict that certain types of data will be missing.

Studies of gender in literary texts have not been confined to stylistic analysis but also include investigations into the representation of men and women and what these literary models can tell us about conversational expectations in the real world. In an insightful analysis of the preferred conversational strategies of a husband and wife at loggerheads with each other, Robin Lakoff and Deborah Tannen (1994) propose a new methodology for interpreting communication between the sexes. They analyze the contrasting conversational strategies of Johan and Marianne in Ingmar Bergman's film *Scenes from a Marriage*.

In this study, they introduce the concepts of pragmatic identity, pragmatic synonymy, and pragmatic homonymy, which, as they demonstrate, replicate the semantic relations of synonymy (having the same meaning but a different form), homonymy (having the same form but a different meaning), and identity (having the same form and the same meaning) (Lakoff and Tannen 1994, 148–149). The analysis shows that the two partners often use similar strategies to very different ends and – an even more significant finding – that they also achieve the same end (avoiding conflict) by very different strategies: excessive verbiage on Marianne's part and pompous pontification on Johan's. Marianne prattles: "Here already! You weren't coming until tomorrow. What a lovely surprise. Are you hungry? And me with my hair in curlers" (152); Johann drones, "I'd been out all day at the institute with the zombie from the ministry. You wonder sometimes who those idiots are who sit on the state moneybags" (154–155). Marianne's contribution is characterized by short sentences, abrupt changes of topic, and a homely, domestic tone. Johan's style is more cohesive and elaborate; it concerns the world of work and is distanced from the current situation. Although their styles are very different, they share the same goal: each is trying to avoid a confrontation about their deteriorating marriage.

Justifying their choice of the constructed, nonspontaneous dialogue of a film script, Lakoff and Tannen (1994, 137) explain that "artificial dialog may represent an internalized model … for the production of conversation – a competence model that speakers have access to." They later define this type of competence as "the knowledge a speaker has at his/her disposal to determine what s/he is reasonably expected to contribute, in terms of the implicitly internalized assumptions made in her/his speech community" (139). Although this type of analysis has not been widely imitated, it demonstrates the utility of looking at constructed dialogue precisely because such pre-planned scripts allow us to see what pragmatic roles have been internalized and what expectations speakers have of patterns of speech appropriate for each sex.

In the French tradition, the *écriture féminine* school, made famous by writers like Hélène Cixous, Chantal Chawaf, and Annie Leclerc in the 1970s, defines women's writing as corporeal, tied to the workings of the body, and at the same time multivalent and polysemic, defying syntactic norms. Chawaf (1976) challenges the reader with the rhetorical question *"l'aboutissement de l'écriture n'est-il pas de prononcer le corps?"* (is not the aim of writing to articulate the body?), while Cixous and Clément (1975, 40, 48) exhort, *"Ecris! L'Écriture est pour toi, tu es pour toi, ton corps est toi, prends-le … Les femmes sont corps. Plus corps donc plus écriture"* ("Write! Writing is for you, you are for you, your body is yours, take it … Women are bodies. More body so more writing"). The assertion that women are bodies is a little puzzling. Are women, according to Cixous, more corporeal than men? How can writing be corporeal except in a pen and ink sense?

Écriture féminine came out of the women's liberation movement as a response to the complaint that men's writing was increasingly abstract and distanced from material concerns. Where the prevailing ideology, which dominates most text forms from highbrow novels to the language of advertising, tended to see the female body as dirty, messy, shameful, and generally problematic, *écriture féminine* set out to celebrate this body in all its wet, bloody, sticky functions and by-products from menarche to pregnancy and childbirth to menopause. Where the subliminal message of mainstream, misogynist discourse was that women were mired in their own physicality and therefore constitutionally unable to produce great works of fiction, *écriture féminine* saw men as cut off from their own bodies, decentered, and more interested in the play of signifiers than in their real-world referents.

When we encounter sentences like the following from Cixous and Clément's *La Jeune née* (*The Newly Born Woman*) "Alors elle, immobile et apparemment passive, livrée aux regards, qu'elle appelle, qu'elle prend" ("Then she, immobile and apparently passive, prey to glances, that she calls, that she takes") (1975, 237) which has no main verb and two subordinate clauses, we may feel lost, confused, or simply impatient. In order to appreciate the innovatory quality of this style, which provides no object for usually transitive verbs (who does she call? what does she take?) we need to feel the weight of the well-formed French sentence and the desire of the feminist writer to wriggle out from under it at all costs. For the French, their language is "la langue de Molière" (the language of Molière), while English is "la langue de Shakespeare" (the language of Shakespeare). The apex of literary achievement was apparently achieved many centuries ago, and perfected by male writers. *Écriture féminine* is a reaction to this assumption of perfection and its attribution to men.

3. Literary Uses of Linguistic Gender

In my own work on the literary uses of linguistic gender (Livia 2000), I have examined the role of gender concord in the creation of particular stylistic effects like focalization (or point of view), empathy, and textual cohesion (what makes everything fit together). Insofar as gender concord may be considered a choice in a given language, and not a morphological or syntactic necessity, it can be used as a stylistic device to express some aspect of character or personality. While Judith Butler's research on the performativity of gender emphasizes the iterative and citational aspects of speech, greatly reducing the role of speaker agency, my own work on the gender performances of characters such as drag queens, transsexuals and hermaphrodites, and those whose gender is never given, demonstrates that observing (or ignoring) the requirements of gender concord allows authors to express a wide range of positions.

In her pioneering work *Gender Trouble*, Judith Butler (1990, 145) argues that speakers, or in her words "culturally intelligible subjects" are the results, rather than the creators, "of a rule-bound discourse that inserts itself into the pervasive and mundane signifying acts of linguistic life." Although her prose is a little dense, what this means in simple terms is that she sees individual speakers as being formed by the discourse they use. This discourse is "performative" because it is by uttering (or performing) it that speakers, obligatorily, gender themselves. They are compelled by the syntactic structure and vocabulary available to position themselves only in certain restricted ways with regard to gender, that is, the traditional roles of "men" and "women." They are not free to take up any gender stance they like, for this would not be "culturally intelligible." Although she does suggest three linguistic strategies by which a speaker can undermine the system (parody, subversion, and fragmentation), on the whole Butler sees agency as severely curtailed, limited merely to "variations on repetition." For her, it is the gender norms themselves which provide the lynchpins keeping "man" and "woman" in their place. She argues that "the loss of gender norms would have the effect of proliferating gender configurations, destabilizing substantive identity, depriving the naturalizing narratives of compulsory heterosexuality of their cultural protagonists" (Butler 1990, 146). Once these stabilizing norms have been lost, other possibilities become available, moving beyond the heteronormative lynchpins "man" and "woman."

This view of gender as performative has become a key tenet of queer theory, which investigates and analyzes "the naturalizing narratives of compulsory heterosexuality" (Butler 1990: 200) and the various sexually liminal figures that do not fit into this traditional framework. Arguing against the linguistic determinism of Butler's stance, I refute the claim that gender, and particularly linguistic gender, is rigidly confining and explore the different messages it can convey. My research on a corpus of literary texts in both English and French, presented in *Pronoun Envy* (Livia 2000) shows that the realm of what is "culturally intelligible" is much wider and more diverse than queer theorists have supposed and that the traditional gender norms are often used as a foil against which more experimental positions are understood.

Anne Garréta, writing in French, and Maureen Duffy, Sarah Caudwell, and Jeanette Winterson, writing in English, have each created characters without gender in at least one of their works. Nowhere in these novels is there any grammatical clue as to whether the main protagonists are male or female. In French, this is a particularly difficult feat, for gender is usually conveyed not only by the third-person pronouns *il/elle* and *ils/elles* (like the English *he/she* and unlike the English *they*) but also in adjectives and past participles. Thus in a sentence of five words like *la vieille femme est assise* ("the old woman sat down"), the gender of the person sitting is conveyed four times: in the definite determiner *la*, in the form of the adjective *vieille*, in the lexical item *femme*, and in the form of the adjective *assise*. In English, the difficulty is decreased by the fact that morphological (or linguistic) gender is limited to the distinction between *he/she*, *his/her*, *his/hers*.

Garréta's novel *Sphinx* (1986) features both a genderless narrator and his or her genderless beloved. The novel is written in the first person singular *je* ("I"), which is gender-neutral. Thus when the narrator describes his or her own actions, the author can avoid giving gender information by using only gender-neutral adjectives and tenses, like the *passé simple* rather than the *passé composé*. However, gender-neutral adjectives and expressions tend to be less frequently used than those which agree with the gender of the noun: The use of the *passé simple* rather than the more common *passé composé* also introduces a literary, almost anachronistic element to the text. Since the novel recounts how a white Parisian theology student becomes a disc jockey in a seedy bar and falls in love with a black American disco dancer, the use of markedly literary tenses and descriptive expressions seems somewhat out of place. It is as though the theology student never really left the seminary.

When the narrator describes the actions and attributes of the beloved, the situation becomes even more complex and the language somewhat convoluted, for here the use of pronouns must be avoided as well. The beloved can never simply be refered to as *il* (he) or *elle* (she) and various techniques are introduced to avoid this. Often the proper name, A***, is repeated. This repetition makes it appear that a new character is being introduced, so that A*** (already confined to an initial and a string of asterisks) never becomes a familiar figure, but always seems a little strange and distant.

Another technique used by the author to avoid conveying A***'s gender, is to describe A***'s body parts rather than the person himself/herself. Instead of the more straightforward *Elle avait les hanches musculeuses, les cheveux rasés et le visage ainsi rendu à sa pure nudité* ("she had muscular hips, a shaven head and her face was thus returned to its pure, bare state"), for example, the author is obliged to avoid mention of gender by describing A***'s body in the following far more distanced and depersonalized way: *Le modelé musculeux de ses hanches ... ses cheveux rasés ... le visage ainsi rendu à sa pure nudité* ("the muscular moulding of her/his hips ... her/his shaven hair ... the face thus restored to its naked purity") (Garréta 1986, 27). Because A*** is systematically referred to by a proper name, or in terms of parts of the body rather than the whole, this character seems fragmented and static.

Clearly, a text which avoids gender agreement produces a very different effect from one which follows a more orthodox pattern of reference. But it is perfectly possible to create a whole novel on this basis, as Garréta's achievement has shown. One could argue that the style of *Sphinx*, whether or not it was initially imposed by the decision to avoid gender, suits the plot of the novel admirably. Given the different worlds the narrator and the beloved inhabited prior to their meeting, and the enormous social distance between them, one a white Parisian intellectual, the other a black dancer from Harlem, the presentation of A*** as strange, constantly unfamiliar, and composed of a series of bodily fragments, creates an exoticism which well suits the story of infatuation, incomprehension, and loss.

Maureen Duffy's novel *Love Child* (1994 [1971]) tells the story of the adolescent Kit and his/her murderous jealousy for Ajax, his/her father's secretary whom he/she believes to be his/her mother's lover. (In the third person, gender-neutral pronominal reference can become extremely clumsy.) While the mother and father are clearly gendered, Duffy gives no clue as to Kit's or Ajax's gender. The effect of this is rather different for each character since Kit, as first-person narrator, can use the pronoun *I*, while Ajax is never referred to by pronoun. In this *Love Child* resembles *Sphinx*. A character referred to without pronouns is simultaneously less empathic and less of a coherent whole. Empathy for a character may be gauged by the types of reference used for that character. Repetition of the proper name and the use of different lexical items such as "my father's secretary" or "my mother's lover" create the least empathy, while pronouns and ellipses create the most. Use of pronouns and ellipses presuppose that the reader is already familiar with the referent and can readily access it, given minimal or zero prompts. In a similar pattern, the linguistic device which creates the strongest cohesive link is ellipsis followed by pronominalization. If the proper name is simply repeated, there is no necessary link forged between each of its appearances. In contrast, in the following sentence –: "Ajax spieled, pattered, manipulated unseen puppets, drew scenes and characters" (1994 [1971], 50) in order to understand that Ajax is the subject not only of "spieled," but also of "pattered," "manipulated," and "drew," the reader must connect the four verbs, and this connection creates a strongly cohesive text.

While Kit comes across as a lonely, angry, jealous teenager who causes the death of his/her mother's lover, Ajax (like A***) seems not quite real, a mere collection of qualities and attributes, not someone who acts on his/her own behalf. We never find out if Kit is an adolescent girl witnessing a lesbian affair, a boy jealous of his mother's male suitor, a boy watching his mother flirt with another woman, or a girl who is aware of her mother's heterosexual conquests. Each interpretation gives very different readings to the text. Nevertheless, Kit is a character for whom the reader can feel some emotional connection while Ajax is not. It is the presence or absence of pronouns which creates this contrast, not information about gender, since neither character is gendered.

Jeanette Winterson's *Written on the Body* (1993) and Sarah Caudwell's mysteries (1981; 1984; 1989) revolve around a genderless narrator but all third-person characters are assigned traditional gender markers; these novels do not, therefore, offer the same degree of complexity as Duffy's or Garréta's.

Science fiction authors, like Ursula Le Guin and Marge Piercy, have used the possibilities offered by new worlds and new biologies to invent imaginary communities whose gender positions are very different from those of twentieth-century Earth. In *The Left Hand of Darkness* (1973 [1969]), Le Guin introduces the ambisexual Gethenians whose gender status changes at different phases of their life cycle. During most of the year their bodies are asexual, but when they enter their mating phase (called *kemmer*) they develop either male or female reproductive organs. They never know in advance which organs will develop and their gender may change from one period of *kemmer* to another. For her part, Piercy has experimented with utopian worlds in which gender is so insignificant that it is no longer encoded in the grammar. In the futuristic community of Mattapoisett, described in *Woman on the Edge of Time* (1976), people are anatomically male or female, but this distinction is almost entirely irrelevant in determining their social roles. To demonstrate the effect this egalitarianism has on the language they speak, Piercy has invented the pronouns *person* and *per* in place of *he/she* and *his/her/hers*. These neologisms are used to describe the futuristic characters, in contrast with the twentieth century characters.

Monique Wittig, writing in French, has experimented with a different aspect of the linguistic gender system in each one of her works. In her first novel, *L'Opoponax* (1964), she uses *on* as the voice of the narrator, recounting the daily lives and relationships among a group of young school children in a small village in eastern France. Traditional literary texts in French are narrated either in the first-person *je* or in the third-person *il* or *elle*. *On* is grammatically a third-person singular pronoun which, unlike *il/elle*, is not marked for gender. Furthermore, it may be used with the meaning of "I," "we" (inclusive, i.e., *I* and *you*, or exclusive, i.e., *I* and a third party), "you" (singular or plural), "he," "she," or "they" (masculine or feminine). This means that *on* is both remarkably flexible to manipulate and remarkably slippery in meaning. Wittig chose it because it did not encode gender information, but its effect is to neutralize other oppositions as well.

On refers most often to the narrator, a little girl called Catherine Legrand, but it is not always clear from the immediate context when it refers exclusively to Catherine, when it also refers to the other children who are all participating in the same actions and share the narrator's thoughts and feelings, and when it includes not only other children but adults as well. In one particularly memorable scene, a new child arrives at school and is instantly separated from the other children, sitting on a bench by herself. Subsequently, in a sequence of increasing violence, she is searched for lice, then beaten on the head by hand and then with rulers. Who performs each of these acts? It must be the teacher who seats the girl apart from the others, but does she also participate in, or even instigate, searching for lice? Wittig states that she uses *on* to "universalize" a very specific and somewhat unusual point of view: that of a group of young children. In fact *on* does far more than this. Because of its many possible meanings, it forces the reader to pay close attention not only to assumptions about gender, but also to assumptions about age appropriateness and common sense.

In *Les Guérillères* (1969), Wittig uses the feminine plural *elles* to tell the story of a group of women warriors who live a separatist lifestyle away from men. This feminine plural is less common than the feminine singular *elle*, the masculine plural *ils*, and the masculine singular *il*, for the following grammatical reasons. *Il* can refer either to an animate entity like a person (*Eric arrive, il aime le chocolat*, "Eric is coming, **he** likes chocolate"); to an inanimate object (*le clou m'a griffe, il m'a fait de la peine*, "the nail scratched me, **it** hurt me"); or an abstract idea (*le théorème est trop abstrait, il est mal expliqué*, "the theorem is too abstract, **it** is ill-explained"). *Il* is also used as a "dummy morpheme" or verb marker in meteorological and modal expressions such as *il faut venir* ("**it** is necessary to come," i.e., you must come; *il pleut* ("**it** is raining"). *Elle*, in contrast, refers to a person, an inanimate object, or an abstract idea, but is never used in modal or meteorological expressions. The plural *ils* refers to people, inanimate objects, abstract ideas, or a combination of these, as does *elles*. However, *ils* is also used for a combination of grammatically masculine and feminine items, while *elles* is restricted to feminine items only.

As well as these grammatical reasons for the more limited use of *elles*, the French psychoanalyst Luce Irigaray (1987) has found that people talk more rarely about groups of women than about men, mixed groups, or singular subjects. When asked to finish sample sentences, her respondents were far more likely to speak of singular, masculine referents than of anyone else. Although *il/elle* and *ils/elles* appear to have contrasting but equal functions in the pronominal system, their frequency of use is actually steeply graded from *il* to *ils* to *elle* to *elles*. A novel in which the least favored pronoun among the third-person set, *elles*, is used as the main reference point of narration is a radical innovation.

For the narrator of *Le Corps lesbien* (*The Lesbian Body*, 1973/1975), Wittig has invented the pronoun *j/e*, a divided *I* who describes and interacts with another woman. This "barred" spelling is repeated throughout the first-person possessive paradigm: *me* is spelled *m/e*, *ma m/a*, *mon m/on*, and *moi m/oi*. Although, as we have seen, *je* is nongendered, it is clear in *The Lesbian Body* that the narrator is a woman since there are frequent lyrical descriptions of specifically female body parts such as clitoris, labia, vagina.

As for exactly what this divided *j/e* represents, Wittig herself has provided two rather different explanations. In the "Author's Note" to the English translation of 1975, Wittig states that *je*, as a feminine subject, is obliged to force her way into language since what is human is, grammatically, masculine as *elle* and *elles* are sub-sumed under *il* and *ils*. The female writer must use a language which is structured to erase her (as *elle* is erased in *il*). Wittig explains that the bar through the *j/e* is intended as a visual reminder of women's alienation from (by and within) language. Ten years later, however, Wittig claims "the bar in the *j/e* of *The Lesbian Body* is a sign of excess. A sign that helps to imagine an excess of *I*, an *I* exalted" (71). This new explanation suggests that, far from signaling the difficulty for women of taking up the subject position in a linguistic structure in which the masculine is both the unmarked and the universal term, the bar through the *j/e* has the positive value of an exuberance so powerful it is "like a lava flow that nothing can stop" (71). Within 10 years, *j/e* has evolved from a mark of alienation to a mark of exuberance.

Members of liminal communities like hermaphrodites, transsexuals, drag queens, and drag kings, who do not fit easily into the existing bipartite gender positions, often use the linguistic gender system to rather different effect than its traditional function. Drag queens (gay men who wear stereotypically feminine clothing and use hyper-feminine mannerisms) and drag kings (lesbians who wear stereotypically masculine clothing and use hyper-masculine mannerisms) often cross-express, using the pronouns which traditionally refer to the opposite sex. Thus a drag queen might refer to another drag queen as *her* and speak about getting her periods, engaging in a catfight, or putting on her makeup. A drag king might speak about *his* butch brothers, getting an erection, or going home to *his* wife.

In a study I carried out on the use of linguistic gender by male-to-female trans-sexuals writing in French, I found that although all the authors stated that they had always felt they were women, in fact they alternated between masculine and feminine grammatical agreement throughout their autobiographies (Livia 2000, 168–176). Masculine agreement could indicate variously a sense of belonging with other males, the gender other people ascribed to them, or a feeling of power and superiority. Feminine agreement indicated the gender they felt most comfortable in, isolation and alienation, or a triumphant affirmation. There was no simple, one-to-one alignment of masculine pronouns with the rejected gender and feminine pronouns with the desired gender.

When we turn to the descriptions of hermaphrodites in literary texts, we find that the situation is even more complex. Possessing the sexual organs of both sexes, hermaphrodites tend to vary in self-presentation far more than the transsexuals I studied. Feelings of solidarity, isolation, alienation, success, failure are all encoded in switches from one gender to another. Indeed, the switch may be made from one sentence to another with no attempt to naturalize it, or it may be presented as a positive sign of the fluidity of gender.

4. Gender and Translation

Where the two types of analysis come together (discussion of writing styles and discussion of uses of linguistic gender) is in investigations of gender and translation, a field in which both morphological gender and cultural gender are highly relevant. Translators work both as interpreters of the original text and, often, as guides to the culture which produced the text. If the social expectations of gender in the target culture are very different from those of the source culture, they need to deal with this anomaly. Similarly, if the languages encode gender in very different ways, they need to devise a system to encompass the differences. In their dual role as linguistic interpreters and cultural guides, translators must decide what to naturalize, what to explain, and what to exoticize.

Studying the role gender plays in translation, Sherry Simon (1996, 10–11) observes that since as early as the seventeenth century translations themselves have been seen as *belles infidèles* (beautiful but unfaithful) because, like women, they can be either beautiful or faithful, but not both. Many of the metaphors for the act or process of translation are highly sexed, and indeed heterosexed. One dominant model views translation as a power struggle between author and translator (both male) over the text (female). In this model, the translator must wrest the text away from the original author, like a son growing up to rival his father. George Steiner (1975), himself a prominent translator, describes the translator as penetrating and capturing the text in a manner very similar to erotic possession. Lori Chamberlain (1992, 61–62), another translation theorist, quotes Thomas Drant, the sixteenth-century translator of Horace, who claims: "[I have] done as the people of God were commanded to do with their captive women: I have shaved off his hair and pared off his nails." For Drant, the original text must be utterly enslaved and deprived of its foreignness, or, in his own words, "Englished." In another model, the original author becomes the translator's mistress whose hidden charms must be revealed and whose blemishes must be improved. In yet another view, the translator is a submissive, subjugated female, alienated, absorbed, ravished, and dispossessed, entirely taken over by the author (Chamberlain 1992, 57–66). Although the imagined relationships that prevail among author, text, and translator vary widely, at the core is the sense that translation is a sexual act.

Given this intense gendering of the process itself, it is hardly surprising that when it comes to linguistic gender in the original text, the problems posed are complex and sometimes unanswerable. The novels and poetry of French Canadian feminist writers such as Nicole Brossard and Louky Bersianik are characterized by rich alliteration, plays on words, and the creation of portmanteau words. The title of Brossard's (1977) novel *L'Amèr*, for example, is a portmanteau word containing three others: *la mer* ("the sea"), *la mère* ("the mother"), and *amère* ("bitter"). *Amer* is the masculine form of the adjective, while *amère* with a grave accent and a terminal *-e* is the feminine form. In itself *amèr* is a neologism invented by Brossard. Since the English words *sea*, *mother*, and *bitter* do not contain the same phonemes as the French words, the neatness of the alliteration is necessarily lost. The gender play is also lost in English since the adjective *bitter* has only one form. Brossard's translator, Barbara Godard, decided to use a very elaborate graphic representation for the translated title, composed of three distinct phrases: The Sea Our Mother, Sea (S)mothers, and (S)our Mothers, all twined around a large *S*. The English title can therefore read either *These Our Mothers* or *These Sour Mothers* (Simon 1996, 14). This is an elegant rendition of the original French, but it does not address the practical problem of how librarians and book catalogues are to refer to the novel.

In my own translation of Lucie Delarue-Mardrus's *L'Ange et les Pervers* (*The Angel and the Perverts*: Livia 1995), I had to tackle the question of how to refer to the central character who is a hermaphrodite. Here both linguistic and cultural gender are at issue. Delarue-Mardrus describes Mario (or Marion, in her female persona), the main protagonist, as alternately masculine and feminine. The changes in gender concord in the original French are intended to produce a sense of shock, requiring the reader to work out how the grammatical system relates to Mario/n's personality and mental state. The first chapter introduces us to the young boy and his childhood in a glacial chateau in Normandy. Here masculine pronouns and concord are used: *Il avait toujours été seul au monde* ("he had always been alone in the world": Delarue-Mardrus 1930, 19). The second chapter begins in the bedroom of a rich society woman in an upper middle-class suburb of Paris. In this section, Marion is described in the feminine: *Elle n'aime rien ni personne* ("She loves nothing and no-one": Delarue-Mardrus 1930, 21). There is no obvious connection between the *il* of the first chapter and the *elle* of the second. Furthermore, both place and social setting have changed, from Normandy to Paris, and from an old, lonely castle to a gossipy boudoir. By withholding any explicit link, Delarue-Mardrus forces readers to make the connection themselves between Mario(n)'s male and female personae. In this way, they are also implicated in his/her change of gender.

Occasionally, Delarue-Mardrus shocks the reader by referring to Mario/n in the masculine and then immediately afterward in the feminine, without providing any intervening material or a change of context to make this seem more natural. The River Seine provides a geographical divide between Mario's bachelor garret and Marion's more luxurious rooms. In one scene we watch as Mario/n crosses the river and moves from one personality to the other: *La voilà chez elle. Le voilà chez lui.* ("She was home. He was home": Delarue-Mardrus 1930, 38). For a translator the lack of gender concord in English poses a problem. While the pronouns *la* and *le* may easily and effectively be translated as "she" and "he," their grammatical connection to the expressions *chez elle* ("at her house") and *chez lui* ("at his house"), are harder to convey. "There she was at her house" and "there he was at his house" are more faithful translations than "she was home," "he was home," and they retain the naturalizing effect of grammatical necessity. They sound rather stilted in English, however.

In the memoirs of a nineteenth-century hermaphrodite, Herculine Barbin, recently rediscovered and annotated by Michel Foucault (1980), the narrator's unusual gender status is conveyed to the reader on the first page. Barbin begins her self-description in the masculine *soucieux et rêveur* ("anxious and dreamy"), but ends in the feminine *j'étais froide timide* ("I was cold, shy": Barbin 1978 [1868], 9). By this movement from masculine concord in the adjective *soucieux* to feminine concord in the adjective *froide* in the next sentence, Barbin gets immediately to the crux of the matter. In contrast, in the English translation it is not until page 58 that reference is made to the grammatical ambiguity of Herculine's identity: "She took pleasure in using masculine qualifiers for me, qualifiers which would later suit my official status." The expression "using masculine qualifiers" is strangely formal, even learned, and stands out in this plaintive, simply stated autobiography.

5. Implications

We have seen that although many prominent writers have set out to discover the differences between men's and women's sentences, following in the footsteps of Virginia Woolf at the beginning of the century, no convincing linguistic evidence has yet been provided to indicate the stylistic characteristics of each. Instead, we have found that there are conventions of masculine and feminine style which any sophisticated writer, whether male or female, can follow.

When we turned to look at linguistic gender, we saw that, far from being a tyrannical system which forces speakers to follow a rigid dualistic structure, it actually provides means by which speakers may create alternative, oppositional, or conventional identities. In the realm of science fiction, authors have created neologistic, nongendered pronouns to speak of egalitarian utopias, supplementing the existing system, which is retained for more traditional worlds. Authors have experimented with nongendered protagonists in both the first and the third person. Although these literary experiments have an effect on our reading of the novel, it is the lack of pronominal reference, not the lack of gender markers per se, which causes disturbance.

Finally, in our discussion of the role of the translator and the metaphors used for the process of translation, we observed that while many different metaphors exist for the act itself, the dominant metaphors place the translator in a sexual role in relation to the text and the author. Frequently, when translating from a language in which there are many linguistic gender markers into a language which has fewer, either gender information is lost or it is overstated, overtly asserted where in the original it is more subtly presupposed.

This research on linguistic approaches to gender in literature demonstrates the utility for students of gender in society at large to investigate the uses to which gender may be put in the unspontaneous, carefully planned discourse of fiction. It reveals not what native speakers naturally do but what they are able to understand, and the inventions and models that influence their understanding.

REFERENCES

Barbin, Herculine. 1978 [1868]. "Mes Souvenirs." In Michel Foucault (ed.), *Herculine Barbin dite Alexina B*, 9–128. Paris: Gallimard.

Brossard, Nicole. 1977. *L'Amèr ou le Chaptire Effrité*. Montreal: l'Hexagone. Published in English as *These Our Mothers, or The Disintegrating Chapter*, trans.

Barbara Godard. Toronto: Coach House Quebec Translations, 1983.

Butler, Judith. 1990. *Gender Trouble*. New York: Routledge.

Caudwell, Sarah. 1981. *Thus Was Adonis Murdered*. London: Penguin.

Caudwell, Sarah. 1984. *The Shortest Way to Hades*. New York: Scribner.

Caudwell, Sarah. 1989. *The Sirens Sang of Murder*. New York: Bantam Doubleday Dell.

Chamberlain, Lori. 1992. "Gender and the Metaphorics of Translation." In Lawrence Venuti (ed.), *Rethinking Translation: Discourse, Subjectivity, Ideology*, 57–74. London: Routledge.

Chawaf, Chantal. 1976. "La Chair linguistique." *Nouvelles Littéraires*, May 26: 18.

Cixous, Hélène, and Catherine Clément. 1975. *La Jeune Née*. Paris: Union Générale d'Éditions. Published in English as *The Newly Born Woman*. Manchester: Manchester University Press, 1986.

Delarue-Mardrus, Lucie. 1930. *L'Ange et les Pervers*. Paris: Ferenczi.

Duffy, Maureen. 1994 [1971]. *Love Child*. London: Virago.

Ehrlich, Susan. 1990. *Point of View: A Linguistic Analysis of Literary Style*. London: Routledge.

Foucault, Michel. 1980. *Herculine Barbin*, trans. Richard MacDougall. New York: Random House.

Garréta, Anne. 1986. *Sphinx*. Paris: Grasset.

Irigaray, Luce. 1987. "L'Ordre sexuel du discours." *Langages: Le Sexe Linguistique*, 85: 81–123.

Lakoff, Robin, and Deborah Tannen. 1994. "Conversational Strategy and Metastrategy in a Pragmatic Theory: The Example of *Scenes from a Marriage*." In Deborah Tannen (ed.), *Gender and Discourse*, 137–173. New York: Oxford University Press.

Lefanu, Sarah. 1988. *In the Chinks of the World Machine: Feminism and Science Fiction*. London: Women's Press.

Le Guin, Ursula. 1973 [1969]. *The Left Hand of Darkness*. St Albans: Granada.

Livia, Anna. 1995. "Introduction: Lucie Delarue-Mardrus and the Phrenetic Harlequinade." In Lucie Delarue-Mardrus, *The Angel and the Perverts*, trans. Anna Livia, 1–60. New York: NYU Press.

Livia, Anna. 2000. *Pronoun Envy: Literary Uses of Linguistic Gender*. New York: Oxford University Press.

Millett, Fred. 1951. "Introduction." In Henry James, *The Portrait of a Lady*, v–xxxv. New York: Random House.

Mills, Sara. 1995. *Feminist Stylistics*. London: Routledge.

Piercy, Marge. 1976. *Woman on the Edge of Time*. New York: Ballantine Books.

Proust, Marcel. 1954 [1913]. *Du côté de chez Swann*. Paris: Gallimard.

Richardson, Dorothy. 1919. *The Tunnel*. London: Duckworth.

Richardson, Dorothy. 1923. *Revolving Lights*. London: Duckworth

Rubin, Gayle. 1975. "The Traffic in Women: Notes on the 'Political Economy' of Sex." In Rayna Reiter (ed.), *Toward an Anthropology of Women*, 157–210. New York: Monthly Review Press.

Silverberg, Robert. 1975. "Introduction." In James Tiptree, *Warm Worlds and Otherwise*. New York: Ballantine Books.

Simon, Sherry. 1996. *Gender in Translation*. New York: Routledge.

Steiner, George. 1975. *After Babel*. London: Oxford University Press.

Winterson, Jeannette. 1993. *Written on the Body*. London: Jonathan Cape.

Wittig, Monique. 1964. *L'Opoponax*. Paris: Éditions de Minuit. Published in English as *The Opoponax*, trans. Helen Weaver. London: Peter Owen, 1966.

Wittig, Monique. 1969. *Les Guérillères*. Paris: Éditions de Minuit. Published in English as *Les Guérillères*, trans. David Le Vay. New York: Avon, 1971.

Wittig, Monique. 1973. *Le Corps lesbien*. Paris: Éditions de Minuit. Published in English as *The Lesbian Body*, trans. David Le Vay. New York: Avon, 1975.

Wittig, Monique. 1985. "The Mark of Gender." In Nancy K. Miller (ed.), *The Poetics of Gender*, 63–73. New York: Columbia University Press.

Woolf, Virginia. 1990 [1919]. "Dorothy Richardson and the Women's Sentence." In Deborah Cameron (ed.), *The Feminist Critique of Language: A Reader*, 70–74. London: Routledge.

31 Language, Gender, and Popular Culture

MARY TALBOT

1. Introduction: Popular Culture

Popular culture is a crucial site for the study of language and gender. It exists in a symbiotic relationship with both the mass media and consumerism, without being reducible to either. After all, a person can sketch a cartoon or break into song without being involved in either mass media or commodity consumption directly. Popular culture is embodied in lived social relations in communities. It impinges on the everyday lives of ordinary people everywhere; it permeates the mass media; it is intricately bound up with consumer culture. Such ubiquity makes it a potentially huge influence on the formation of views and attitudes toward both gender and language.

From a Gramscian standpoint on the relationship between popular culture and hegemony, popular cultural forms are involved in securing consent to particular understandings of gender and sexuality (Roman and Christian-Smith 1988, 3). As Stuart Hall (1981, 239) puts it:

> Popular culture is one of the sites where this struggle for and against a culture of the powerful is engaged: it is also the stake to be won or lost in that struggle. It is the arena of consent and resistance. It is partly where hegemony arises, and where it is secured ... That is why "popular culture" matters.

The concept is not without problems of definition. The term "popular" is sometimes used pejoratively, in elitist dismissal of "inferior" cultural forms as superficial or trivial. A slightly less unsatisfactory contrast is with "high culture," understood to refer to classical music, literature (with a capital L) and so on. However, this more quantitative definition is also problematic; the converse of "high" is, after all, "low." Moreover, high culture is often popularized; TV adaptations of Jane Austen's novels and comic-book versions of Shakespeare's

The Handbook of Language, Gender, and Sexuality, Second Edition.
Edited by Susan Ehrlich, Miriam Meyerhoff, and Janet Holmes.
© 2014 John Wiley & Sons, Inc. Published 2017 by John Wiley & Sons, Inc.

plays, for example, straddle the boundaries between the categories of "high" and "popular." The distinction appears to be a hazy one. It often depends on who uses the form and what prestige it has, as in the case of romance fiction (contrast Jane Austen's *Pride and Prejudice* with Diane Hamilton's *No Guarantees*, published by Harlequin Mills & Boon). People would be unlikely to hesitate in identifying comics in general as popular culture, but if presented with a comic in the relatively expensive, book-length format of the graphic novel they might be less certain.[1]

There is an abundance of literature in media and cultural studies devoted explicitly to gender and popular culture, yet very little of it addresses language directly. Fortunately, however, within the emerging field of language and gender studies there is equally abundant research on specific popular cultural forms. This research covers a wide range of genres: from printed material such as advertisements, tabloid news articles, genre fiction, and magazine features for women and men, to forms of broadcast talk including shopping channels, lifestyle television programming, and talk radio.

In cultural studies, cultural practices are understood to circulate continuously within a circuit of culture. They may be investigated at each point in that circuit, which includes production, regulation and consumption, representation, and identity construction (for discussion, see Hall 1997). The methods of discourse analysis little used in cultural studies but familiar to many linguists offer a nuanced approach to investigations of cultural practices in circulation. In this chapter, I present a sample of explorations of language and gender both in and through popular cultural forms. Given limitations of space, attention to a wide range of these forms would be unmanageable, so for detailed discussion I have chosen a small selection of critical analyses that attend to participation in media discourse at different points in the cultural circuit. Addressing a range of print and broadcast media forms, sections cover magazines and their offers of friendship and community, gendered style and professional identity in a radio production team, and audience engagement with television talk. The selected studies have been chosen to illustrate some central concerns in work on language, gender, and popular culture: the consumption of texts and audience engagement on the one hand, and, on the other, critical engagement with representations and with oppressive behavior. A final section then turns from academic critique of popular culture, from outside it, to critical engagement within popular culture itself. While gender stereotypes, sexist attitudes and oppressive patterns of behavior circulate abundantly in popular culture, popular media themselves can also be used to engage with these things critically. The final section presents some nonacademic texts which do just that: cartoons and comics.

2. Magazines, Friendship, and Community

This section outlines some research on magazines. It discusses textual representations in magazines and what they offer their addressee, then turns to interviews with magazine readers.

I will begin with an investigation of the mass media's contribution to the construction of a kind of femininity based on consumption. Focusing on a two-page consumer feature from a British magazine for teenagers called *Jackie* (which ceased publication in 1993), this study outlines the notion of women's magazines as a "synthetic sisterhood" (Talbot 1992; 1995; 2010). Talbot (1995) concentrates specifically on one aspect of how this imaginary community is established: the simulation of a friendly relationship. By means of such devices as expressive punctuation and lexis, first- and second-person pronouns, response-demanding utterances, the setting up of shared presuppositions, and a range of positive politeness strategies, the anonymous writers of this feature engage the target reader in an imaginary dialogue. In one section, the writer assumes shared preoccupation with historical details about "breeds" of women, kinds of "look," fashion changes, choice and ownership of lipstick, details relating to lipstick as a commodity that is subject to fashion change, and so on. In another, two-way discourse is simulated in a set of testimonials, giving the impression of overhearing gossip. They were accompanied by snapshots of the testimonial givers:

Margaret (15)

"I wear it all the time, because I always wear make-up. My favourite shade's a sort of brown-and-red mixture I usually buy Boots 17 or Max Factor lipstick. I got my first one when I was 10, for Xmas it was a sort of pink colour, I think it was just for me to play with."

Emily (12)

"Usually I just wear lipstick when I'm going out, but sometimes for school. I like pinks, oranges and plain glosses. I was about 7 when my mum gave me a bright red lipstick to experiment with I think I've worn it ever since!"

Clara (wouldn't tell us her age!)

"I always wear red dark red and usually from Mary Quant or Estee Lauder. I don't know if I can remember my first lipstick wait! Yes I can! It was called "Choosy Cherry" by Mary Quant everyone used to ask me if I was ill when I was wearing it!"

Rhona (18)

"I like pinks and deep reds. I don't wear it all that often. My first lipstick? I stole it from my sister's drawer I was about 12 dying to look grown-up even then!"

To make any sense of these statements at all we need to postulate a set of questions or first pair-parts that were asked by an interviewer but that do not appear on the page. They are interviewee responses to three reconstructable questions: "How often do you wear lipstick?" "What's your favorite shade?" "When did you get your first lipstick?" Notice the echoing repetition of the question in the fourth testimonial.

Interestingly, although the whole consumer feature establishes a friendly relationship between apparently like-minded people, it is particularly in these testimonials that we see positive politeness strategies of the kind used in women's face-to-face interaction. The high proportion of hedges ("sort of," "I think," "about") contrasts sharply with the authority of the editorial voice in the other sections. The editorial voice is that of the expert with special knowledge. The interviewees do not always use the modality of categorical certainty, as the editorial voice does; in fact, the only things they are *not* tentative about are their color preferences. But, of course, the interviewees' supposed "own words" have been structured by the interests of the editor as interviewer (present only as the shadow cast by her questions), who has set the agenda and constructed these interviews with "ordinary" people. The hedging presumably contributes to the simulation of informal speech.

The *Jackie* advertorial text is now somewhat dated, but the aim of achieving an active and "intimate" relationship with a remote readership is even older. Indeed, it was explicit editorial policy as far back as 1910, in the first issue of *Women's Weekly* (Talbot 1995; White 1970). A more recent publication is the "lad mag," projecting a youthful masculine community: not a synthetic sisterhood but a "fallacious fraternity" (or perhaps a "phallacious fraternity" (Talbot 2007, 51)). Simulations of a close relationship between writers and their readership continue to be very common in these magazines. Reciprocal discourse is simulated on the printed page by means of response-demanding utterances (especially commands and questions), adjacency pairs, and interpolations. For example, a consumer feature in *FHM* called "Double vision!" uses an interactive style in the question and command in the subheading: "Watching telly from a chair too strenuous? Try this!" This feature (about a bed with its own built-in widescreen TV) also supplies examples of the establishment of common ground: shared preoccupations and traits (in this case, idleness, squalor, TV watching, porn, and gadgets).

While, at first glance, men's magazines seem far from "polite," as with the girls' magazines, there is an abundance of positive politeness strategies signaling friendship. Common strategies for positive politeness in recent men's magazines are aggressively friendly banter and other humor. The establishment of like-mindedness and sharing of common ground is notable in the numerous reader contribution sections in *FHM*. For example, there are regular readers' letter columns devoted to sharing scorn at the ignorance of outgroups: such as female faux pas ("Out of the mouths of babes") and the linguistic ignorance of foreigners ("Funny foreigners"). The establishment of common ground is clear in the distancing from women and from foreigners, but also in the overall catalogue of things-worth-knowing-about. Gossip contributes to the establishment of a community with shared values. It reinforces the values of a group. Below is an example from *Loaded* magazine. In fact, the term "bitching" would be more precise, since the article's writer indulges in pejorative talk about absent others (Guendouzi 2001):

> Many a funny bone was tickled recently when it came out that two strapping Welsh guardsmen had been well and truly hung out to dry by three slightly built women during a late night brawl in a West London 7-Eleven. In the course of what appears to have been a merry old dust-up, Private Dean Morgan suffered a gashed head, while Private Vincent Jones was reduced to seeking refuge in a nearby bakery after suffering a broken nose and bruised jaw. Conclusive proof, some might say, that all Welshmen are as soft as a limp chip. (*Loaded*, 1997, quoted in Benwell 2001, 22)

As a piece of bitching gossip, it displays third-person focus, involving polarization of "us" and "them," and negative evaluation, here in terms of national identity. The guardsmen's departure from normality (perceived cowardice, vulnerability) is used as a "hook to hang the pejorative evaluation on" (Benwell 2001, 23). The two Welsh army privates simply don't "fit."

Both these sets of studies dwell on the way the magazine writers approximate the supposed language habits of their respective target readerships. Benwell (2005) shifts the focus of interest in magazines from the moment of representation to the moment of consumption (or rather, to magazine readers' reflections on it). That is, it goes on to investigate interview talk with actual readers. The study examined two unstructured interviews with six readers of men's magazines altogether: two 17-year-olds in one interview and four 21-year-olds in the other. Benwell identifies implicit categories of kinds of reader that emerge – "invested" and "uninvested" readers – and notes that the older group have frequent recollections of the activities of their "former invested reading self" (Benwell 2005, 157). Interestingly, the distance of these "uninvested" readers is contradicted by the way they ventriloquize magazine discourse and by the shared common sense cultural knowledge referenced throughout interviews (161). Benwell points to the readers' articulation of discourses that she had previously identified in the magazines, for example, observing that the interview talk among the 21-year-olds "mirrors the teasing, joshing register of the magazines themselves" (160). This observation produces a rather intriguing mirror image of my own, above, about the magazines approximating their readers' language habits. It would be a mistake, however, to try to prioritize one site of articulation over another. The "ventriloquism" goes both ways. As one of the interviewees remarks about the magazines' style of humor:

> M: It's the same kind of humour as when you're out with your pals and one of your pals falls over and you laugh at him (.) it's laughing at rather than with (1.0) asking the kinds of questions likely to embarrass them (.) looking for a rise

(Benwell 2005, 160)

This "joshing" manner circulates across different communicative contexts.

As data, the interviews with readers are not treated as transparent records of their views. Instead, Benwell investigates them as emergent accounts with the potential to reveal attitudes and opinions indirectly and even in contradiction to explicitly stated views. For instance, among the topics of discussion were "grooming" products; the discussion generated is interesting for norms of masculinity that are implied rather than outright statements. A question about attention to product advertising elicits the following:

> M: I don't (.) at all but that's because I'm a bit
>   of a scab
> G: You moisturize!
>   [laughter]

(Benwell 2005, 160)

Mike's self-disparagement positions him at a distance from the feminized identity potentially attributable to users of grooming products. Gordon mockingly challenges this position: "Mike *is* invested in his appearance after all-a familiar put-down in masculine culture, and one invoking the spectre of femininity" (160). Benwell argues that drawing inferences from such sequences of interview talk is more revealing about attitudes than direct questioning would have been. Both in this extract and the one below, the general laughter suggests group policing of others' accounts and hints at implicit norms. In this next extract, Jonathan "confesses" his former self as an "invested" reader:

```
J:    I remember doing a Nivea thing that I bought Nivea after reading
      it (.) years ago like y'know how they have like articles
                                                              [
I:                                             An article
      rather than an advert
                        [
J:                        Yeah it was like a sponsored article
M:    L(h)ucky this is anonymous
      [laughter]
```

(Benwell 2005, 163)

In terms of understanding the consumption or reception of magazine texts, the study indicates that the interviewee readers are both critically distant and complicit: "The concomitant critical distance and complicity via a 'lived' or ventriloquized internalization of the magazine values points to a complexity and sophistication of reading practices and an easy ability to accommodate contradiction in the reading experience" (Benwell 2005, 167). (See also Benwell, Chapter 12 in this volume.)

In this section we have seen how magazines contribute to the construction of gender identities and shared community based on consumption. We have also seen that actual readers can be both critically distant and complicit in the identities and community on offer. In conclusion, for fruitful engagement with media discourse it is not particularly helpful to isolate either text or audience as the object of study, since clearly we need to focus on both (Talbot 2007). Another study of magazines combining both perspectives can be found in McLoughlin (2008). This study examines some controversial "sex specials" appearing in two publications for teenage girls, *Bliss* and *Sugar*. McLoughlin combines textual analysis with focus-group work to challenge claims to emancipatory potential made by the magazine producers at the height of the "moral panic" surrounding them.

3. Broadcast Talk, Gendered Styles, and Professional Identities

Focusing on prime-time radio, this section switches attention to gendered style and professional broadcasting identity in an on-air production team. Interest in women's participation in the public sphere of broadcasting has led to a few studies of gendered styles. Though these include broadcast genres that would probably not be designated as popular culture (for instance, studies of interviewing style in current affairs (Talbot 2009; Walsh 2006; Winter 1992)), popular cultural broadcast texts have received some attention. The performance of heterosexual masculinity on *Top Gear* (a prime-time British TV show about cars) is the subject of Smith (2008), while a recent study of D-J-hosted radio (BBC's *Radio 1 Breakfast Show*) also examines a masculine style and suggests that women's on-air participation is heavily restricted (Talbot 2012). Both these studies draw parallels with the "lad mag" genre in publishing.

In contrast with 50 years ago, female media professionals on air are now highly visible and audible. In "zoo format" media, however, the discursive space available to women appears to be limited. This format involves the regular and deliberate breaching of the professional broadcasting procedures that keep behind-the-scenes talk out of a broadcast. It indicates authenticity, spontaneity, and lack of pretension, generating what Richardson and Meinhof (1999) have called an aesthetic of "liveness" (more detail on "zoo" can be found in Talbot 2007 or Tolson 2006). *Radio 1 Breakfast*, hosted by Chris Moyles,[2] has this broadcast format. With consistently high ratings, it is one of the most popular shows on British radio; by Moyles's own account, it is popular with children (Jeffries 2010). As it has a short track list, it is predominantly talk. An impression of pub banter is projected, with a soundscape of overlapping dialogue and topics ranging from the previous night's television, to football, Formula One racing, boxing, boozing, scatological jokes, and, not least, an aggressive kind of ritualized abuse known as "slagging." This kind of verbal intimidation has been observed in male-dominated workplaces, such as building sites (Watts 2007) and oil rigs (Faulkner 2008), but a study of violence among girls will furnish a definition: "an umbrella term covering a range of different types of verbal intimidation, including gossip, threats, ridicule, harassment" (Alder and Worrall 2004, 193).

"Wind-up scenarios" in DJ discourse can be viewed as a form of slagging. They are a component of Chris Moyles's repertoire. I have selected one of these "wind-up scenarios" from a single broadcast for close attention here (taken from Talbot 2012). The extract begins about five minutes before the eight o'clock news and contains a little episode where Chris Moyles tricks the sports newsreader, Tina Daheley, into singing along on air:

```
[MCFLY'S "EVERYBODY KNOWS" IS PLAYING]
 1  Chris:  [singing] "Everybody Knows" it
            c'mo:n (.) McFly On McFlyday
 2          Will you sing along Tina?
 3  Tina:   I er- b- er Yeah
 4  Chris:  You've got a good voice
 5  Tina:   No you said I've got a better scream than I have a
 6          singing voice
 7  Dave:   I thought you nailed it
 8  Chris:  Shall we have a little sing-along?
 9  Tina:   Not on my own
```

```
10   Chris:   Together
11   Tina:    We go "ooh ooh"?
12   Chris:   Yeah (We'll have to) get the timing right though
13   CHRIS CUTS MUSIC
14   Tina:    [singing slightly off-key] ooh ooh ooh ooh ugh (.)
15            [with echo effect] you're supposed to join in
16   MUSIC RESUMES
```

Chris Moyles does not join in with Tina Daheley, as he implicitly promises (lines 10 and 12). Instead he records her singing (in line 14). A good deal of mockery ensues, including some from listeners, whose texted remarks are read out by the "comedy content assistant," Dave Vitty:

```
17   Chris:       Beautiful [mimicking, wailing as if in pain] uuh
18                uuh uuh uuh
19   Dave:        sounded like a chimpanzee
20   Chris/Dave:              [intermittent wailing]
21   Dave:        someone's texted in "are you in pain?"
       [30 SECONDS OF WAILING AND LAUGHTER. OMITTED]
```

Chris is evidently pleased with the sound artifact he has created at Tina's expense and invites the audience to join in:

```
22   Chris:   If you enjoyed Tina's singing please text
23            "Tina amazing" (eight double one double nine)
24            that's eight double one double nine
             [
25   Tina:    Why would anyone do that?=
26   Chris:                          =because it's funny
       [4 MINS OF NEWS AND SPORT. OMITTED]
```

Between lines 26 and 27 most of the news and sport bulletin has been omitted from the transcription. These segments of the broadcast were relatively formal, highly conventional in delivery, in fluent and articulate professional newsreader voices. I take up transcription again at the point Tina performs two self-repairs (lines 26 and 27):

```
27   Tina:    and Alan Argreaves (.) Hargreaves even (.) will
28            make a football r- return to football after
29            eighteen months (xxxxxx) injured
                                  [
30   Chris:   [wailing]       Alan Argreaves
31   TINA'S OFF-KEY SINGING REPLAYED
```

After Tina's second self-repair, Chris cuts in. He does this initially with mimicry of her singing, then with mocking repetition of her pronunciation error (both in line 30), then a replay of her singing (line 31). These incursions disrupt the professional delivery and undermine Tina's newsreader identity. Her complaint (line 32) elicits more of the same:

```
32  Tina:   Oh stop it (.) I can't (.) listen to it again
33  SINGING REPLAYED AGAIN
34  Chris:  [wailing]
35  Tina:   [short laugh] Hargreaves played forty-five
36          minutes...
[TINA COMPLETES THE SPORTS NEWS. OMITTED]
```

The sports news completed, the main newsreader, Dominic Byrne, acknowledges her with a receipt token (line 37), as he performs a conventionally professional takeover of the floor. As soon as he finishes the weather report, the mockery resumes:

```
37  Dom:    Tina, thanks.
    [DOMINIC PRESENTS THE WEATHER FORECAST. OMITTED]
38  Chris:  [wailing]
39  SINGING REPLAYED FIVE MORE TIMES
40  Chris:  It's that cracked bit at the end
41  Tina:   It's because you didn't join in
42  Chris:  Tina sounds like the wookie off of Star Wars
43  SINGING REPLAYED
44  [Laughter]
```

From line 45, Dave Vitty joins in the teasing with enthusiasm. The ridicule of long-suffering Tina develops as a co-production:

```
45  Dave:   Can you imagine- Can you imagine karaoke with Tina?
46  Chris:  Oh it'd be brilliant (.) Two hours
47  Tina:   [Sigh]
48  Dave:   Don't take any lessons, don't change who you are
49  Tina:   No (I want) singing lessons
50  Dave:   Don't change who you are
51  Tina:   Charming
52  Chris:  You are rubbish
53  Tina:   (alright then teach) me to sing
54  Chris:  Twelve quid an hour
55          No it's lovely
56  SINGING REPLAYED EIGHT MORE TIMES
57  Dave:   Tina Tuner
58  Chris:  Tina Tuner
59  [Laughter]
60  Chris:  All right I'll stop
61  SINGING REPLAYED
62  Tina:   (I'm never gonna get a) boyfriend
63  Chris:  What?
64  Tina:   I'm never gonna get a boyfriend if you keep playing
65          that
66  Chris:  But it's part of your personality Nobody's gonna
67          care if you can singin tune or not (.) Never
68          gonna get one anyway You're too high maintenance
```

At this point, Chris inserts a pre-recorded voice, some promotional material for the show:

```
69   Prerecorded voice:  [gravelly movie-trailer delivery]
70                        Leonardo da Vinci (.) Donatello (.) Rafael (.) Sir
71                        Isaac Newton (.) and Chris Moyles (.) The world has
72                        always loved great artists and this one is here
73                        every weekday morning
```

(*Radio 1 Breakfast Show*, March 19, 2010)

This extract introduces another component of the star's verbal repertoire: boasting. While there is no bragging from him directly in the "wind-up" sample, there is a great deal built into the same show on his behalf, as in lines 69–73. The exaggeration makes the boasting ludicrous in the extreme, but an implication is that the teasing of Tina is a prime example of Chris Moyles's work as a "great artist." The bragging may be absurd but it is relentless. Every program listing is a fanfare: "The award-winning Chris Moyles Show with the award-winning Chris Moyles." His website profile hails him as the "saviour of Radio One." On the morning after an annual awards ceremony in March, his boasting throughout the show became overwhelming.

In the "wind-up scenario" extract above, there is a great deal of laughter. Unsurprisingly, much of the laughter comes, not from Tina, but from the two who gang up on her in their co-production of ridicule. Chris Moyles returns to this episode repeatedly throughout the broadcast. Moreover, a segment of the wind-up is used later in the day as a trailer for the breakfast show. Consisting of lines 1–15 ("Will you sing along Tina?" etc.) plus some of the wailing and laughter I omitted between lines 21–22, this trailer is broadcast in the afternoon. From its use in this way, it is clear that it is being used to represent the spirit of the show, what the show is all about.

There is a conversational division of labor in these broadcasts that is probably not apparent on normal listening. The host initiates first-person narratives, boasting, teasing and ridicule, pranks and practical jokes; the others, his "sidekicks," perform reaction work (laughter and so on) and other support work (particularly endorsements). The jointly produced live broadcast talk is casual, unscripted chatter, but it is broadcast for the purpose of entertaining a national audience. As in the lad mags we looked at in the previous section, the bantering humor is a positive politeness strategy that contributes to establishing friendship and shared community identity with listeners. The show projects a "laddish" community that listeners are invited to join.

In this section, I have focused on a 20-minute segment from a single radio broadcast, in which a woman reading sports news is the butt of humor. This sample of zoo media suggests that, despite the major inroads that women have made into professional media environments, in this particular format the discursive space women occupy is severely limited, at least on air. Tina may have achieved the position of sports newsreader but she is routinely positioned as the butt of humor, as a foil for the host's wit. Her participation contributes to the aggrandizement, or valorization, of the host's masculine broadcasting identity.

The focus of this section has been the moment of production. On the basis of the broadcast text and the interaction it contains I have been able to explore the gendering of a specific professional media environment. As an account of the point of production on the cultural circuit it is partial. I have not gone beyond the broadcast text to the broader in-studio social space in which it was produced. Nor could I do so, except to note the production team details provided elsewhere; including the information, incidentally, that the overall producer is a woman. In this regard, an Australian study of aggressive masculine authority in a radio phone-in offers an interesting suggestion. It contrasts the discursively constructed male control on air with women's control of the studio: "the daily elaboration of a myth of outwardly-directed male agency over the reality of in-studio female control" (Cook 2000, 72).

4. Talking with the Television

Focusing on daytime television, this section shifts attention to women watching talk shows at home. Shopping channel broadcasts with women viewers as phone-in participants have been the subject of a number of studies (Bucholtz 1999; 2000; Talbot 2007). Helen Wood (2007; 2009) looks at audiences at home, in a study of what she calls the "mediated conversational floor." She engages with TV viewers' participation in mediated quasi-interaction (Talbot 2007; Thompson 1995). Wood visited 12 women in their homes, where she watched talk shows with them. As a reviewer observes: "What is new here is that Wood focuses upon the interaction between the viewer and programme as it happens, simultaneously recording text and viewer in order to interrogate the 'act' of television viewing" (Sadler 2010, 180). Wood recorded the talk from the television and the living room. She distinguishes various levels of participation in the mediated conversational floor. The most basic is identifiable by the presence of second-person pronouns, use of minimal responses, and turn completion, all directed to a speaker on the television. For example, while watching a section on *Vanessa* on "jealousy," Eve produces a response-demanding utterance, addressing the speaker as "you":

```
     Studio                                    Home
1    Woman:   I just wanna say one
2             thing it takes two
3             to play tonsil tennis
4             it's not just the
5             woman's fault
6             he's doin it as well.        Eve:  Oh shut up
7                                                you:::
```

                                                        (Wood 2007, 14)

As Wood notes, she obviously does not expect a response, but she makes the remark as if she does. Wood reports similar expressions of involvement from all the women in the study. All use minimal responses, of which these are two examples:

```
    Studio                              Home
1   Woman:   No matter how old they
2            are if the father lets
3            them down if the fa:ther
4            has a problem- children
5            make up their own
6            minds      "              Bette:   Mhm

    Studio                              Home
1   Caller:  erm right I've got
2            a problem with my
3            polystyrene coving
4            erm I've                   Jenny:   Ooo::h [sarcastically]
5            bought it and I haven't
6            a clue how I'm going to
7            cut it to size
```

(Wood 2007, 15)

Wood relates such use of minimal responses to Jennifer Coates's study of shared "collaborative floor" in women's friendly conversation, arguing that they signal "I am here, this is my floor too, and I am participating in the shared construction of talk" (Coates 1996, 143, quoted in Wood 2007, 16). The sarcasm she evidently hears in Jenny's voice also suggests an element of hostile "double voicing," using the caller's words against her will (Bakhtin 1973; Talbot 2007); the "Ooo::h" in line 4 suggests some unspecified "rude" interpretation of "I've got a problem with my polystyrene coving." Wood presents the next extract to further illustrate collaborative aspects of the "mediated floor":

```
    Studio                              Home
1   Woman:   What I'd like to say very
2            briefly is if the reward
3            for a ca::ring daughter
4            who sacrifices marriage
5            and career is to find
6            herself on the streets
7            that's                     Alice:   Homeless
8            no encouragement for
9            anybody [...]
```

(Wood 2007, 21)

In this example of joint turn construction, Alice chips in with the woman in the studio, as if helping her to get her point across by rewording "on the streets" (line 6) as "homeless" (line 7). That is Wood's analysis, at least; it may instead be offering sentence completion; following "that's" with "homeless."

The viewers also signal active participation by engaging with adjacency pairs in the broadcast talk. They *always* respond to questions, for instance; sometimes in simple disagreement, but often with more sustained engagement in debate, as in this example:

```
    Studio                                      Home
1   Kilroy:    Jonathan, ar::e the
2              police racist?
3   Jonathan:  I think in some
4              cases the police are
5              very racist butlike     Cathy:    I: think so
6              in other cases it all             I don't think
7              sortof depends how                they're all racist
8              you sort of ta::lk to             but I think some
9              to the police I think if          of them are
10             you talk to police with [...]
```

(Wood 2007, 19)

Wood points to the clear operation of "double articulation" in this sample, as the addressees in the studio and at home both respond to the question simultaneously. In my view, it also points to an audience double articulation.

The viewers also participated in the mediated floor more actively, interrogating the broadcast talk. In a *Vanessa* segment on "women bouncers," Bev is a bouncer and Maggie is her disapproving sister:

```
    Studio                                      Home
1   Maggie:  You've gotta think of your
2            kids you're letting your
3            kids down you go home you
4            can go home and you can't
5            work ever again=
6   Bev:     =but you do a job to make
7            a better li::fe for your
8            kids
9   Maggie:  yeh but there's other      Jana:  So basically we
10           ways of supporting you             shouldn't have
11           kids than (x) come                 female police women
12           home injured                       we shouldn't have
13                                              female-
```

(Wood 2007, 26)

Jana engages critically with the broadcast discussion, using an uncooperative formulation to pull out an equal opportunities issue (lines 9–13). This is one of several extracts that Wood uses to argue that, over the duration of the broadcast, Jana challenges the talk show's representation of sociopolitical issues as personal psychological ones (Wood 2007, 27). Elsewhere, viewers' disagreement with the discussants triggered substantial argumentative engagements with broadcasts and, as Wood notes, they were not constrained by the face needs of the participants. Here is one fairly simple example, with relatively short interjections into a phone-in discussion on *This Morning* from a viewer who thinks she knows better:

```
       Studio                                Home
 1   Caller:   Hello
 2   Richard:  Hello now how long have
 3             you been               Angela:  you've told us
 4             trying to get pregnant?          now
 5   Caller:   erm about eighteen months
 6             now erm
 7   Richard:  Right go on            Angela:  ( xxx )
 8   Caller:   I don't have regular
 9             periods so I erm
10             obviously don't know when
11             I'm about to ovulate-
12   Richard:  arrh
13   Caller:   erm I see my doctor
14             but he says to give it
15             two years before he's
16             willing to go any
17             fur- [any further      Angela:  t- .hh it should
                                               be a year hh
18   Richard:       [so-
19   Judy:          [so- so another six
20             months basically
21   Richard:  so you and your partner
22             have had not specific
23             tests at all then
24             I mean he hasn't had his
25             sperm count checked or
26             anything like that
27   Caller:   no
28   Richard:  so you're just
29             trying=                Angela:  Blame him
30   Caller:      =I mean my partner does       heh heh heh
31             smoke and I don't know if
32             that has anything to do
33             with it but the main thing
34             is that I am-
35   Richard:  irregular
36   Caller:   I have irregular periods
```

(Wood 2007, 30)

In the context of face-to-face interaction, Angela's comments would be barracking. At a point in the broadcast discussion when all three participants are talking at once (lines 17–19), she chips in as well with a challenge to the advice given by the caller's doctor (line 17). Later, her directive "Blame him!" seems to be implied criticism of Richard's line of questioning (line 29).

It is possible that the women's vocal challenges to the talk shows' representation of issues were for the researcher's benefit. Wood acknowledges that her presence as a researcher is highly likely to have prompted the viewers to talk. But viewing in groups is commonplace, so that her presence does not compromise the validity of her findings. It is true that, as a researcher, her expert status may well have prompted displays of critical sophistication for her benefit, but she was simply present as a viewing companion. The mediated conversational floor that she describes has a double articulation, in that the speaking audience addresses both the studio and the home. Wood's findings are an effective corrective to naive assumptions about "media effects." Like the magazine readers earlier, these viewers of daytime talk shows are not simply soaking up the attitudes and beliefs they encounter in their engagement with popular culture. Popular culture is crucial in the formation of views and attitudes, to be sure, but its consumers are not dupes or passive sponges – a conception perhaps particularly attributed to female magazine readers and viewers of daytime television.

5. Creative Engagement: Putting Gender on the Agenda

This final section turns from academic scholarship to a different form of critical engagement: from within popular culture itself. In the early decades of the twentieth century, the now forgotten Suffrage Atelier produced posters and postcards that were strident and clever. A postcard in 1912, for example, contrasts "What a Woman may be and yet not have the Vote" (depicting women as mayor, nurse, mother, doctor, teacher, and factory hand) with "What a Man may have been & yet not lose the Vote" (convict, lunatic, drunkard, etc.). Perhaps surprisingly, Donald McGill (best known for his "saucy" seaside postcards) sometimes expressed protofeminist sentiments in his cartoons too. On a 1919 postcard, for example, a woman sits contentedly in her armchair and asks: "Why should I want a husband? I've got a parrot that swears, a dog that growls, a lamp that smokes and a cat that stops out all night!"

Cartoons can be clear and economical, vivid and engaging. Outside the academic world, these qualities make their combination of word and image ideal for contesting the status quo. They can be useful in teaching about language and gender too; they can succinctly draw attention to double standards about women and men's behavior, for example, as shown in Figures 31.1 and 31.2.

A British cartoonist, Posy Simmonds, has been using her creative abilities to engage with sexist attitudes and assumptions for decades. "Join the Professionals" (1977) parodies the army recruitment campaigns of the period, which included advertisements that presented the British Army as heroic "Professionals" and promised rewarding work and the chance to travel. Opening her

Figure 31.1. Assertive and arrogant stances

Figure 31.2. Single-minded and stubborn stances

spoof advertisement with a call for "volunteer (or willing conscript) mothers," Simmonds goes on:

> A mother provides a **vital service** to the country, which often goes **unrecognised and unrewarded**. Motherhood costs spare time and the chance of travel. But it does bring much in return: the chance to develop skills & resourcefulness. Above all, it is a **challenge** and a chance to **serve** the country in a worthwhile way. (Posy Simmonds, *Guardian*, 1977)

In producing this recruitment ad for mothers, Simmonds is of course making the point that bringing up children is valuable work, as challenging as paid employment and every bit as worthwhile as military service. Workplace sexism is the subject of one of her most well-known strip cartoons, "The World Turned Upside Down" (Posy Simmonds, *Guardian*, 1987). It presents a female secretary's daydream of role reversal: her male boss is transformed into her secretary (**"Hallo Ronnie! Ooh**, we're looking **gorgeous** as per usual!"); he creeps past a building site with his head down, subject to the unwanted attention of the women lounging around there ("Smile! It may never happen! "Not **bad**"; "Hello, Ballsy!") on his way to the local pub on an errand ("Ooh make way for the **little gentleman**, Denise!"). In her role reversal daydream, for once it is him, not her, on the receiving end of leering comments and patronizing terms of address.[3]

The subject of gender politics is also taken up in novel-length sequential art. A graphic novel, *Dotter of Her Father's Eyes* (Talbot and Talbot 2012), winner of the 2012 Costa Biography Award, explores shifting views about the proper sphere of girls and women through two coming-of-age stories (the author's, that is, my own and that of Lucia Joyce, daughter of the modernist writer James Joyce). Set at different points in the twentieth century, it follows their fortunes through childhood, adolescence, and early adulthood. One of the themes of the book is the differentiation of girls and boys in the institutions of education and the family. The significance of schooling in the imposition of gender difference is the subject of the pages reproduced in Figures 31.3 and 31.4.

At this school (the Catholic school I attended from 1958 to 1965), difference is quite literally inscribed in stone, as the girl learns when she starts to attend. The older girls and boys must play separately; the boys are given space to roam that is not allowed to the girls, who are squeezed in with the younger children in the smaller playground. Their play activities are different. But this gender segregation is not simply imposed from above, by the designers of the building itself and the teachers who staff it. The children themselves also enforce it, particularly the older boys, who stand to benefit most from this arrangement.

Narrative explorations of gender issues reach a different, and wider, audience from academic investigations. The kind of work they do is different too. While they do not often engage with theories as such, they can readily provide examples with which to illuminate them. The scenes in Figures 31.3 and 31.4 present a narrative illustration of the fact that gender differences are not simply "natural" but constructed, and indeed enforced (in fact, it's a visualization of an autobiographical account that I have presented in seminars for years, to make precisely that point).

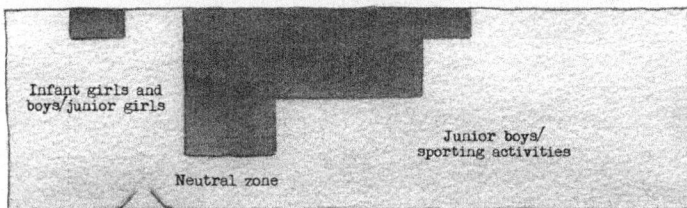

Figure 31.3. A page from *Dotter of Her Father's Eyes* (Talbot and Talbot 2012, 17)

As I said at the outset, sexist attitudes and oppressive patterns of behavior circulate abundantly in popular culture, but popular media can also be used to engage with these things critically. It's unlikely that we have seen the end of cartoons that reproduce negative stereotypes of over-talkative women and their henpecked husbands. Popular culture, more broadly, will no doubt continue to circulate such folk linguistic beliefs about the language practices of women and men for a long time

Figure 31.4.　These two panels from *Dotter of Her Father's Eyes* (Talbot and Talbot 2012, 18) follow the page in Figure 31.3

yet. It's up to feminists working with popular cultural forms to insure that a wealth of alternatives also remain in circulation.

6. Concluding Remarks

Popular culture has a potentially huge influence on the formation of views and attitudes toward gender and language. Critical engagements with popular culture in the media tend to focus on representations in print or broadcast texts. By attending to participation in media discourse at different points on the cultural circuit, this chapter has indicated the need for awareness of the broader communicative complex in which such representations are produced and consumed. Investigations of representation such as the study of magazines and their offer of a "synthetic sisterhood" based on consumption are undoubtedly valuable, but they can make no claim about influence on actual audiences. Similar limitations apply to investigations of broadcast production that hang solely on the interaction in the broadcast text itself, such as the study of the "laddish" social space of a zoo format broadcast.

NOTES

1　For a full discussion of six definitions of popular culture, see Storey (2006).
2　Chris Moyles left BBC Radio 1 in September 2012, after eight years on the *Breakfast Show*.
3　The strip cartoons and postcards referred to above are all reproduced in Atkinson (1997).

REFERENCES

Alder, Christine, and Anne Worrall, eds. 2004. *Girls' Violence: Myths and Realities*. New York: SUNY Press.

Atkinson, Diane. 1997. *Funny Girls: Cartooning for Equality*. Harmondsworth: Penguin.

Bakhtin, Mikhail. 1973. *Problems of Dostoevsky's Poetics*, trans. Caryl Emerson. New York: Ardis.

Benwell, Bethan. 2001. " 'Have a Go if You Think You're Hard Enough': Male Gossip and Language Play in the Letters Pages of Men's Lifestyle Magazines." *Journal of Popular Culture*, 35: 19–33.

Benwell, Bethan. 2005. " 'Lucky This is Anonymous': Ethnographies of Reception in Men's Magazines: A 'Textual Culture' Approach." *Discourse & Society*, 16: 147–172.

Bucholtz, Mary. 1999. "Purchasing Power: The Gender and Class Imaginary on the Shopping Channel." In Mary Bucholtz, A. C. Liang, and Laurel A. Sutton (eds.), *Reinventing Identities: The Gendered Self in Discourse*, 348–368. New York: Oxford University Press.

Bucholtz, Mary. 2000. " 'Thanks for Stopping By': Gender and Virtual Intimacy in American Shop-By-Television Discourse." In Maggie Andrews and Mary M. Talbot (eds.), *"All the World and Her Husband": Women in Twentieth-Century Consumer Culture*, 193–209. London: Cassell.

Coates, Jennifer. 1996. *Women Talk*. Oxford: Blackwell.

Cook, Jackie. 2000. "Dangerously Radioactive: The Plural Vocalities of Radio Talk." In Alison Lee and Cate Poynton (eds.), *Culture and Text: Discourse and Methodology in Social Research and Cultural Studies*, 59–80. Oxford: Rowman & Littlefield.

Faulkner, Wendy. 2008. "Doing Gender in Engineering Workplace Cultures. I. Observations from the Field." *Engineering Studies*, 1(1): 3–18.

Guendouzi, Jackie. 2001. " 'You'll Think We're Always Bitching': The Function of Cooperativity and Competition in Women's Gossip." *Discourse & Society*, 3: 29–51.

Hall, Stuart. 1981. "Notes on Deconstructing 'the Popular.'" In Raphael Samuel (ed.), *People's History and Socialist Theory*, 227–241. London: Routledge & Kegan Paul.

Hall, Stuart. 1997. *Representation: Cultural Representations and Signifying Practices*. London: Sage.

Jeffries, Mark. 2010. "Moyles Says Kids Love Me, Not Evans." *Mirror Online*, May 14. At http://www.thefreelibrary.com/Moyles+says+kids+love+me,+not+Evans%3B+RADIO+1.-a0226326244, accessed November 6, 2013.

McLoughlin, Linda. 2008. "The Construction of Female Sexuality in the 'Sex Special': Transgression or Containment in Magazines' Information on Sexuality for Girls?" *Gender and Language*, 2: 171–195.

Richardson, Kay, and Ulrike Meinhof. 1999. *Worlds in Common? Television Discourse in a Changing Europe*. London: Routledge.

Roman, Leslie G., and Linda K. Christian-Smith. 1988. "Introduction." In Leslie G. Roman and Linda K. Christian-Smith (eds.), *Becoming Feminine: The Politics of Popular Culture*, 1–34. London: Falmer Press.

Sadler, Barbara. 2010. "Review: Wood, Helen, 2009, *Talking with Television: Women, Talk Shows and Modern Self-Reflexivity*." *Participations: Journal of Audience & Reception Studies*, 7: 180–182.

Smith, Angela. 2008. "*Top Gear* as a Bastion of Heterosexual Masculinity." In Karen Ross and Paul Allen (eds.), *Popular Media and Communication: Essays on Publics, Practices and Processes*, 83–102. Newcastle upon Tyne: Cambridge Scholars Publishing.

Storey, John. 2006. *Cultural Theory and Popular Culture*. London: Pearson Education.

Talbot, Bryan, and Mary Talbot. 2012. *Dotter of Her Father's Eyes*. London: Jonathan Cape.

Talbot, Mary. 1992. "The Construction of Gender in a Teenage Magazine." In Norman Fairclough (ed.), *Critical Language Awareness*, 174–199. London: Longman.

Talbot, Mary. 1995. "Synthetic Sisterhood: False Friends in a Teenage Magazine." In Kira Hall and Mary Bucholtz (eds.), *Gender Articulated: Language and the Socially Constructed Self*, 143–165. New York: Routledge.

Talbot, Mary. 2007. *Media Discourse: Representation and Interaction*. Edinburgh: Edinburgh University Press.

Talbot, Mary. 2009. "The Valorisation of a Discursive Style on the BBC's *Westminster Hour*." In Ken Turner and Bruce Fraser (eds.), *Language in a Life, and a Life in Languages: Jacob Mey: A Festschrift*, 381–388. Bingley: Emerald Group.

Talbot, Mary. 2010. *Language, Intertextuality and Subjectivity: Voices in the Construction of Consumer Femininity*. Berlin: Lambert Academic.

Talbot, Mary. 2012. "'Will You Sing Along, Tina?' Zoo Format and Women's Place on Radio One." *Culture, Society and Masculinities*, 4(2): 155–166.

Thompson, John. 1995. *The Media and Modernity: A Social Theory of the Media*. Cambridge: Polity.

Tolson, Andrew. 2006. *Media Talk: Spoken Discourse on TV and Radio*. Edinburgh: Edinburgh University Press.

Walsh, Clare. 2006. "Gender and the Genre of the Broadcast Political Interview." In Judith Baxter (ed.), *Speaking Out: The Female Voice in Public Contexts*, 121–138. Basingstoke: Palgrave Macmillan.

Watts, Janice. 2007. "Can't Take a Joke? Humour as Resistance, Refuge and Exclusion in a Highly Gendered Workplace." *Feminism & Psychology*, 17(2): 259–266.

White, Cynthia. 1970. *Women's Magazines 1693–1968*. London: Michael Joseph.

Winter, Joanne. 1992. "Gender and the Political Interview in an Australian Context." *Journal of Pragmatics*, 20: 117–139.

Wood, Helen. 2007. "The Mediated Conversational Floor: An Interactive Approach to Audience Reception Analysis." *Media, Culture & Society*, 29: 75–103.

Wood, Helen. 2009. *Talking with Television: Women, Talk Shows and Modern Self-Reflexivity*. Urbana: University of Illinois Press.

32 The Public View of Language and Gender

Still Wrong After All These Years

ALICE F. FREED

In the 2003 edition of *The Handbook of Language and Gender*, I reported on the significant discrepancy that existed between public representations and popular perceptions of how women and men speak (and how they are expected to speak) and the empirically verifiable character of the language that people use (Freed 2003). At the time, the magnitude of this inconsistency seemed to underscore the vitality of deeply engrained stereotypes about sex and gender and the weight and influence of societal efforts to maintain the impression that, simply put, women and men are different. The data reviewed for the current chapter lead to the dismaying conclusion that this phenomenon is as firmly entrenched in 2013 as it was a decade ago. The public representation of the way women and men speak continues to be at odds with the realities of peoples' relationship to language, and bears a disturbing similarity to the characterization provided when the field of language and gender was in its infancy 50 years ago (Lakoff 1973). In general, stereotypes about women and men, ideas that we might call folk linguistic beliefs, remain strong. Moreover, the lines being drawn to differentiate people along gender and sexual lines are even more disturbing than in past years because of the inclusion in the discussions of so-called scientific evidence from controversial brain science research, what Deborah Cameron (2009) calls the new "biologism." Questionable and limited findings about the human brain, used in conjunction with sweeping theoretical assertions that include claims about the way women and men use language, are increasingly incorporated into public debates about male–female difference. (For a critique of this research, see Cameron 2007; 2009; Chapter 14 in this volume; Fine 2010; Jordan-Young 2010.)

As I did in 2003, I reviewed news articles and online sources, and searched a variety of databases for evidence that the public is continuing to be exposed to an avalanche of information about sex and gender difference, augmented, as indicated above, by preliminary and highly inconsistent brain research and a resurgence

The Handbook of Language, Gender, and Sexuality, Second Edition.
Edited by Susan Ehrlich, Miriam Meyerhoff, and Janet Holmes.
© 2014 John Wiley & Sons, Inc. Published 2017 by John Wiley & Sons, Inc.

Figure 32.1.   Zits, by Jerry Scott and Jim Borgman, *Zits* (www.zitscomics.com), August 17, 2008. © 2008 Hearst Holdings/King Features Syndicate Inc.

of interest in evolutionary biology.[1] More specifically, I traced the evolution from scholarly research to media coverage of several language and gender stories and examined the attention given in the English-language press to the broad topics "gender" and "gender difference," this time adding "brain studies" and "brain and gender." As was the case in 2003, my analysis reveals that there is considerable public interest in these topics, demonstrated by the enormous amount of press they receive. Yet, while the reporting of stories related to sex and gender difference has multiplied (and more recently stories about gender and the brain have increased), neither the reliability nor the quality of the content of these reports has improved. We learn that one of the most persistent social narratives of our time, repeated in newspapers, Internet blogs, television, radio, and cartoons continues to be one that tells us that boys (or men) and girls (or women) are essentially different and that they constitute separate groups.[2] We are explicitly told that despite our cherished connections with mothers and fathers, sisters and brothers, and friends and lovers of the same or "opposite" sex, women and men are not the same. A barrage of media examples showcases how women and men contrast physically, socially, sexually, and emotionally. The script, as popular as ever and still selling books, movies, and newspapers, includes a cast of characters who are portrayed as having a fixed nature, differentiated by sex, gender, and sexuality.

In many other areas of contemporary life, people are turning to science for enlightenment and guidance. Indeed, in the first dozen years of the twenty-first century, we have made groundbreaking advances in medical research, in Internet technology, and we have witnessed the unraveling and identification of the human genome. Yet, brain science researchers and cognitive scientists interested in sex and gender[3] seem to be seeking scientific evidence to support the concepts and constructs about human behavior and sexuality that they consider well established and self-evident (Jordan-Young 2010, 58) rather than exploring what they don't yet understand or know. In her detailed study of the "flaws in the science of sex differences," Rebecca Jordan-Young (2010, 109) describes that in her "interviews with the top scientists conducting brain organization research," they continually reported that "masculine and feminine sexuality are simply 'commonsense' ideas." Their purpose is to use new scientific technologies to establish the physiological foundation for notions that they take as given: not only that men and women "look" different, but that they behave differently, have different interests, and that they learn and use language in different ways.

According to "brain organization theory," explains Jordan-Young (2010, xi), "prenatal hormone exposures create permanent masculine or feminine patterns of desire, personality, temperament, and cognition." While it is somewhat uncontroversial that these hormones create genital differentiation, Jordan-Young's exhaustive investigation of the research documents that there is little consistent evidence that these same hormones shape human brains. Nonetheless, the public narrative that proclaims that men and women comprise two distinct groups permeates brain science research and is taken as the starting point in well-funded studies carried out by highly respected scientists. In other words, the brain research that is having an effect on the public view of gender has itself been co-opted by stereotyped views of men and women. Jordan-Young (2010, 291) writes:

> When research starts to look too much like an "infomercial" for cherished beliefs, it is no longer science. Brain organization theory is little more than an elaboration of long-standing folk tales about antagonistic male and female essences and how they connect to antagonistic male and female natures. As a folktale, it's a pat answer, a curiosity killer. And the data don't fit into the tidy male–female brain patterns anyway … Why keep trying to fit the data into a story about sex? … The theory of sexual organization of the brain is getting in the way of the science of human development.

1. Language and Gender, 1973 to the Present

Relatively little of the innovative scholarly work on language, gender, and sexuality that has been carried out in the past dozen years is reflected in public discussions of language and gender. Vast quantities of naturally occurring language drawn from a wide range of contexts have now been analyzed; these analyses have failed to expose any consistent correlation between language use and either sex or gender.[4] This accumulation of analyzed data demonstrates in vivid detail that speakers use language in creative and divergent ways depending on a wide range of factors. Setting and context, type of activity engaged in, group and/or personal identity, topic of conversation, channel of communication, community of practice, and language repertoires of various sorts contribute to the way we speak. Economic and symbolic resources, political purpose, symbolic and actual resistance to various forms of oppression, relative rank, audience, and nature of relationship to addressee all affect how we talk.

There is a broad consensus in the community of language and gender scholars that: (1) a greater amount of language variation (i.e., heterogeneity) is found across groups of women and across groups of men than between men and women who are members of the same community of speakers (Ahearn 2012, 197; Goodwin 2006; Hyde 2005); and (2) the minor differences that have sometimes been identified in the way girls and boys (women and men) use language (and, according to Jordan-Young (2010, 54) the small differences that are found in male and female brains) are smaller and less well established than are the large social differences in the expectations and beliefs attached to being female or male (Eckert and McConnell-Ginet 2003); these minor variations do not – and cannot – account for the public view and emphasis on gender difference.

Overall, linguists examining the relationship of language to sex, gender, and sexuality, increasingly object to using male–female "difference" as a starting point and question research on gender and sexuality that begins with other fixed categories of people (Cameron 2005; 2007; Cameron and Kulick 2003; Ehrlich 2007b; Stokoe 2005; Talbot 2010). The "paradigm organized around the concept of binary gender *difference* has been superseded … by one that is concerned with the *diversity* of gender identities and gendered practices" (Cameron 2005, 482). It is unclear whether the change in the field is a product of the large quantities of empirical data that have been examined or whether the shift followed new questions and perspectives that were considered about the interaction of language and gender (see Bing and Bergvall 1996). Regardless, the scholarly understanding of the interaction between language and our gendered lives is dramatically different in 2013 than it was in 1973 (Lakoff 1973).

Studying categories of speakers who are "biologically" women and simply comparing them to people who are "anatomically" men is understood to be flawed in two significant ways. Not only does this approach mistakenly assume the naturalness of these as social categories (or, for that matter, biological classifications) but it also assumes that we can succeed in learning anything useful about gender by starting with these predetermined groups. Susan Ehrlich (2007a, 453) reminds us, following Stokoe (2005), of the methodological issues that develop when researchers "pre-categorize groups of people as women and men and then investigate how women 'do femininity' and men 'do masculinity.' Such pre-categorization means that analysts begin their research already knowing the identities" of, and making assumptions about, the people who are being studied. (See also Stokoe and Attenborough, Chapter 8 in this volume.)

"The challenge now," writes Mary Talbot (2010, 112), "is how to conceptualize gender without polarization." She cautions against studying how women and men comprise two distinct groups of people not only because there is no valid reason for starting with that assumption but also because this practice assumes that the biological sex of individuals is naturally manifested as corresponding gendered behavior. If we are interested in "investigating the way that linguistic resources contribute to the constitution of individuals as gendered" (Ehrlich 2007a, 453), then we need to avoid assumptions about the people we are studying.

However, as Elizabeth Stokoe (2005, 125) argues, there exists "an underlying tension … in so far as many researchers advance anti-essentialist, theoretical conceptions of gender … but at the same time employ the very same categories in their analysis." Jordan-Young (2010) makes a similar point about most contemporary brain research where "commonsensical" assumptions about male and female sexuality are the starting point and basis for studies of sex difference. Admittedly, it can be difficult to navigate the space between an empirical study of gender (or gender identities) that avoids these predetermined categories and the reality of the norms and stereotypes that societies impose in our everyday lives – stereotypes reinforced by the media and public discussions of gender. As a practical way forward, while allowing that most societies typically "divide" populations into binary groups (male and female, gay and straight), and while acknowledging the assumptions that inhere in these categories (i.e., the societal norms for masculinities and femininities), our investigations of how people talk and how they construct their gendered selves need to look beyond the public groupings. Our focus should be on understanding what people actually do with language and how they present themselves relative to these gendered norms. For example, rather than merely observing and attempting to explain the stereotypes that society dictates, we might focus on how men "do" what is traditionally labeled femininity or how women do masculinity.

Studying groups of people whose identities or characteristics are pre-categorized, and then concluding that what these individuals say or do can be accurately attributed to the very category to which they were assigned, "can easily give rise to a circular argument": "If you believe that 'women's language' somehow inheres in or arises from a speaker's identity as a woman, why look at anyone else?" (Cameron and Kulick 2003, 93). Early "research on gay or lesbian language was [also] based on [these sorts of] circular assumptions … : anything a gay or lesbian person said was taken to be characteristic of gay or lesbian language" (93). As Sally McConnell-Ginet (2011, 14) reasons, "'women's language' becomes an empty notion if anything any woman says is included under that rubric." What do we do, ask Deborah Cameron and Don Kulick (2003), with the information that not all gays or lesbians, or women and men, use the features of language attributed to them? What do we do with the people within these groups who do not speak or behave as expected? As will be demonstrated in what follows, the media does not seem to raise or consider such questions.

2. Media Trends: When Scholarly Work Goes Public

In recent years, monumental changes have taken place in how people get news and information and how they communicate with one another. Consider that in 1973, when Robin Lakoff's pioneering article "Language and Women's Place" first appeared and ushered in what became a burgeoning field of study, only three major television networks existed in the United States: ABC, CBS, and NBC.

Fox Broadcasting Company wasn't established until 1986. The earliest hand-held analog mobile telephones were made commercially available in 1978; digital cellular networks were not developed until the 1990s. According to data from the Pew Internet and American Life project, "As of December 2012, 87% of American adults have a cell phone, and 45% have a smartphone," up from 73% cellphone ownership in 2006 (Pew Internet 2013). Text messaging first appeared in 1989 but wasn't widely used until after 2000. As of April 2012, "some 79% of cell phone owners say they use text messaging on their cells" (Brenner 2013). Google search began in 1998. Facebook was launched in 2004 and Twitter was created in 2006. By 2004, there were 14,000 radio stations in the United States. By 2012, television news was being broadcast by hundreds of cable and nationally syndicated channels. In the context of this immeasurable volume of media and interactive communication, the prominence of one relatively fixed public image of women and men, along with the persistence of long-standing stereotypes about how women and men talk – despite scholarly work that refutes them – is all the more remarkable.

Other linguists have also addressed the public interpretation of scholarly research about women's and men's language. For example, Penelope Eckert (2003) discusses a series of popular media accounts of how adolescent girls speak and relates these to the details of her own research on adolescents and gender. She considers the press "fervor about 'Mallspeak' in the USA" to be "a particularly dramatic illustration of the convergence and stigmatization of the language of adolescents and females" (Eckert 2003, 393). The media's treatment of "Mallspeak" in the 1990s emphasized that the use by teenage girls of *like, you know,* and *I mean* was a sign of being "inarticulate." Although both boys and girls use these forms, when the press discusses their occurrence "specifically with respect to girls, they are taken to indicate insecurity, and an unwillingness to state a forceful opinion" (Eckert 203, 394), thereby perpetuating a negative view of teenage girls.

Cameron's 2007 book *The Myth of Mars and Venus* similarly tackles the discrepancy between public beliefs about language and gender and the findings of linguistic research. She characterizes public discourse on language and gender as "mythological" and refers to media accounts of male–female language difference as the "literature of Mars and Venus." She reminds us that "popular sources are selective in the use they make of research evidence. On the one hand they ignore some very consistent research findings, while on the other, some of their claims are not supported by evidence at all" (Cameron 2007, 13). Cameron argues that because most people learn about scientific research from summaries in the popular press; they are exposed to whatever it is that publishers believe the public will find most interesting. And even when research is reported in approximately accurate terms, the conclusions drawn for the public are often quite different from the conclusions arrived at by the researchers themselves (17–19).

A case in point is the stir about women and "vocal fry" that appeared on the Internet, then radio, TV, and in major US newspapers after a study appeared in the online edition of the *Journal of Voice* in September 2011.[5] As the result of a single study (Wolk, Abdelli-Beruh, and Slavin 2012), "vocal fry" (long described by linguists as "creaky voice") became the latest sensation in a world that seems determined to make exaggerated claims about the "peculiarities" of female speech. The headlines of a few of the articles about "vocal fry" illustrate how they are pitched to suggest that all young women (and by implication, no men) use this supposedly new form of vocalization.

"'Vocal Fry' Sweeping Young Women's Speech Patterns, Study Suggests" (Dillard 2011).

"They're, Like, Way Ahead of the Linguistic Currrrve" (Quenqua 2012).

"Everyone Totes Copying How Young Women, Like, Talk and Stuff" (Ryan 2012).

"The Art of the Fry: Female Vocal Trends and Linguistics" (League 2012).

The published work in the *Journal of Voice* (Wolk, Abdelli-Beruh, and Slavin 2012) is quite limited in scope, consisting as it did of a study of 34 college-age female students who attended the C. W. Post campus of Long Island University. The research, experimental in design, consisted of an analysis of recorded utterances of single isolated vowels and six sentences read by the speakers. The stated goal of the research was "(1) to quantify the prevalence of vocal fry in a population of young female SAE college students, and (2) to describe the acoustic characteristics of vocal fry in these speakers using phonetically balanced material" (Wolk, Abdelli-Beruh, and Slavin 2012, 111). A secondary goal was to consider whether "vocal fry usage in college students" has "long-term consequences for vocal health" (115). The authors found that "vocal fry was used in sentence reading (but not in the isolated vowels) by more than two-thirds [27] of this population of [34] female college students" (114). The data included no conversational speech at all. Unlike the media reports, the authors made no attempt to generalize their findings beyond the phonetic conditions examined or the population studied. Additionally, they make no comparison between these female speakers and male speakers except in a suggestion that "empirical studies comparing males and females may also be valuable in drawing epidemiological conclusions" (115). The authors call for future studies that compare their results to the use of vocal fry in naturally occurring conversation, but there is nothing in the publication that informs us about how people talk in everyday settings.

Despite the narrow claims made by the researchers themselves, the representation of this work in the media consists of sweeping statements about young women and the widespread use of vocal fry, explicitly comparing the results to the lack of vocal fry in the speech of men. Furthermore, the stories poke fun at women's way of talking. In a *Scientific American* podcast, author Christie Nicholson (2011) remarks, "What used to be thought of as a symptom of a speech disorder might now be a hot trend in vocal style among rock stars and young women." She goes on to claim (without providing documentation) that the researchers also tested men but found no evidence of vocal fry in male speech. Nassima B. Abdelli-Beruh, one of the authors of the original 2011 study, (which appeared as Wolk, Abdelli-Beruh, and Slavin 2012), informed me (in an email exchange from June 2012) that they had not been asked to review the *Scientific American* blog before it was published.

But she confirmed that she and a different group of researchers had, in fact, subsequently conducted a parallel study of 34 male students from the same university (Abdelli-Beruh et al. 2011). The results of this second study were presented as a poster (unpublished at the time of this writing) at the American Speech–Language–Hearing Association Convention in San Diego in November 2011. In this follow-up research, two listeners judged that vocal fry occurred in 18 percent (6) of the 34 male college students' reading of sentences, in comparison to 81 percent (27) of the 34 female students previously tested.[6] Surprisingly, despite the absence of conversational data in either study, this time, one of the researchers' preliminary conclusions was that "[v]ocal fry can be used by speakers as a gender identifier in languages and dialects" (Abdelli-Beruh et al. 2011, 10). For her part, Nicholson, the *Scientific American* blogger, uses these two very limited experimental studies to emphasize gender "difference" in everyday speech.

In comments again characteristic of the derision often included in descriptions of young women's speech, Nicholson concludes, "At least this is a bit more bearable and sexy than other vocal trends like the uptick at the end of sentences." Even in the February 27, 2012 *New York Times* article "They're, Like, Way Ahead of the Linguistic Currrrve," a fairly sophisticated and well-balanced article that makes good use of relevant comments by linguists Penelope Eckert and Mark Liberman, we find girl-talk and girl-culture referred to as a "curiosity": "The latest linguistic curiosity to emerge from the petri dish of girl culture gained a burst of public recognition in December, when researchers from Long Island University published a paper about it in the *Journal of Voice*" (Quenqua 2012). And although the *New York Times* author tries to correct misimpressions about the "mindlessness" often associated with young women's speech, he doesn't hesitate to remind the reading public of the usual beliefs: "Whether it be uptalk (pronouncing statements as if they were questions? Like this?), creating slang words like 'bitchin'' and 'ridic,' or the incessant use of 'like' as a conversation filler, vocal trends associated with young women are often seen as markers of immaturity or even stupidity" (Quenqua 2012).

Most disturbing, however, are the completely inaccurate statements that find their way into otherwise smart reporting. In a December 15, 2011 interview on NBC's *The Today Show*,[7] host Matt Lauer interviewed chief medical editor Nancy Snyderman about the "new trend called vocal fry." While the segment includes a clip of linguist Janet Pierrehumbert describing the phonetic nature of creaky voice/vocal fry, Snyderman states categorically that vocal fry is a speech characteristic that women use that "does not occur" in the speech of young men. At the end of the exchange, Lauer repeats an earlier question, "Is there *anything* equivalent in men?" and Nancy Snyderman replies, "No, there isn't … it's almost a women's affectation of sort of wanting to be in … girls will pick it up because it makes them feel part of a macro-culture." Not only do these examples demonstrate the sorts of distortions that occur in moving from the scholarly to the popular press and the kinds of overgeneralizations that result, but we also discover that details critical to the accuracy of the information are absent. Nowhere in these press reports do we learn that the results pertain to only 27 female undergraduates whose language was studied in an experimental setting; nowhere do we read about linguists' past observations and analyses of vocal fry (creaky voice) in men's natural speech. The public doesn't learn, for example, that Dwight Bolinger, writing in 1989, described creaky voice as a "macho style" that men often adopt, sometimes to convey authority, nor do they hear about the other specific studies of male use of creaky voice cited by Bolinger (1989, 22; see also Mendoza-Denton 2011; Podesva 2007; Podesva and Kajino, Chapter 5 in this volume).

Public reports about young women and vocal fry are only one of the most recent examples of media excitement and subsequent misrepresentations about male and female speech. A more damaging stereotype than the rash of articles about the supposed peculiarities of young female vocal fry are the relentless assertions, based on an age-old sexist adage, that women talk more than men. A number of studies published in both the scholarly and popular press provide solid evidence that should put these claims to rest but the stereotype persists. Mark Liberman (2006a) and Matthias Mehl et al. (2007) have each conducted detailed analyses that refute the assertion about talkative women but neither piece of research has loosened the public hold on this popular misconception about women.[8] The claim has even found its way into "scientific" trade books. In an article in the *Boston Globe* in 2006, "Sex on the Brain," Liberman (2006a) explains:

> The most recent to join the chorus [about women's talkativeness] is Dr. Louann Brizendine, clinical professor of psychiatry at the University of California, San Francisco. In her current best-seller [2006], "The Female Brain" … Brizendine tells us that "A woman uses about 20,000 words per day while a man uses about 7,000."

Liberman describes Brizendine's failure to cite specific studies and the complete absence of research to back up her numbers.

"On the basis of available empirical evidence," concludes Mehl et al. (2007, 82) "the widespread and highly publicized stereotype about female talkativeness is unfounded."[9] And still, linguist Deborah Tannen (2007), writing in the *Washington Post* in response to this research, explains that she wasn't surprised by the results of Mehl's study. She suggests that measuring talk time in experimental or public settings is of little overall use because, she asserts, those are the settings in which men are comfortable talking. (She offers no empirical data to support this.) She adds that women's "rapport-talk probably explains why people think women talk more" – even if they don't. Thus, Tannen, best known outside of the academic community for her trade book on women's and men's conversation (Tannen 1990), does little to discourage the inaccurate portrayal of women as "talkers." Instead she repeats her widely publicized view that men (all men, she suggests) use language for status and independence while women (again, all women) use language for rapport and connection.

Radio news is still another source of stereotypes and distortions about language use. In the fall of 2011, while listening to an all-news radio station, I heard a short report that started with the headline, "Funny study. Men are funnier than women."

The reporter proceeded to describe a study carried out at the University of San Diego (i.e., the University of California at San Diego) in which 16 men and 16 women were asked to write captions for 20 blank *New Yorker* cartoons, resulting in 640 captions. When the captions were rated, the men's average "funny" score was only 0.11 higher than the women's, a statistically insignificant number. What happened as this study traveled from an academic journal to the public airwaves is a valuable example of the chain of events that can lead to the media's misrepresentation of male and female difference. At each step in the process from research to reporting, some key element of the research was omitted or skewed, resulting in an incorrect portrayal of the content and intent of the original research. Consider the transcript of the radio report:

> Funny study. Men are funnier than women. That's according to researchers at the University of San Diego who did a study asking 16 men and 16 women to fill out blank *New Yorker* cartoons and then have other men and women rating which ones were funnier. Yes, the men did better but the difference was minuscule getting an average score that was only zero-point-eleven higher than the women. (WCBS 880 Radio, New York City, October 24, 2011)

Why had the news writers chosen to start the story with the stereotype only to finish by contradicting the opening line? I wrote to Tim Scheld, director of News and Programming at WCBS 888 radio in New York, first asking for the transcript. He sent the transcript and the report that they had used as the basis for their report (Kiderra 2011). Having confirmed what I thought I had heard, I wrote again asking why WCBS 880 had led the story with the stereotype about men's being funnier than women when the study had failed to confirm it; Scheld agreed with my observation and said that he would pass the question on. But there is more.

The abstract for the original study about men and humor (Mickes et al. 2012) states that the researchers were interested in both the source of the stereotype that men are funnier than women and the role that "memory" plays in attributing humor to one party or another. They concluded that "false" memories were often at play. "We explored two possible explanations for [the view that men are funnier] ... , first testing whether men, when instructed to be as funny as possible, write funnier cartoon captions than do women, and second examining whether there is a tendency to falsely remember funny things as having been produced by men" (Mickes et al. 2012, 108). The conclusion of the study hedges about whether their results do or do not confirm that men are funnier, suggesting that men might be funnier in certain contexts. "Men, at least under the conditions and constraints of the present experimental situation, were funnier. In addition, funny captions were preferentially attributed to male authors, a bias that was present in both men and women" (Mickes et al. 2012, 112).[10]

The University of California press release presents a good summary of the research but focuses only on the first part of the work, the source of the stereotype, and fails to mention anything about the authors' interest in assessing the role that memory plays in perpetuating the stereotype. Furthermore, in the press release,

Mickes, the lead author of the study, is reported as saying, "The differences we find between men's and women's ability to be funny are so small that they can't account for the strength of the belief in the stereotype," but this point is never stated in the published article. For their part, WCBS radio, working from the press release, commented only on the comparison between women's and men's humor and ran with the stereotyped headline. Perhaps the writers at WCBS radio were doing what Sally McConnell-Ginet (2011, 29) refers to in quoting social psychologist Virginia Valian: "People tend to notice phenomena that confirm stereotypes and ideologies and to ignore or downplay those that might threaten them." In and of themselves, neither vocal fry nor humor associated with *New Yorker* cartoon captions is a topic with any serious consequences and I suspect there is an element of fun intended in all of this reporting. But they do add to the patterns of overgeneralization, misrepresentation, and perpetuation of stereotypes about male–female language difference. Complex or nuanced stories about gender and language appear to be incompatible with the modern English-language media.

As a final example of the exaggerated claims about male–female difference found online and in the popular press, consider an article from the *Minneapolis Examiner* (April 2012) entitled, "Gender differences arise in social media use" (Carranza 2012). The discussion centers on a study, conducted by uSamp, a "premier provider of technology and survey respondents to obtain consumer and business insights" of 600 adult men and women between the ages of 18 and 50 (age range is the only information provided about the people surveyed). The participants were asked what social media sites they used most frequently and what kind of information they shared online. The differences found between the male and female responses pertained to privacy issues: more men than women were willing to share their location and their email addresses. More women than men expressed concerns about privacy. Of interest for the current discussion is that the online version of the article not only supplies a link to the full uSamp study (Isozio 2012) but the author also refers readers to a website about brain differences between women and men. Under "Takeaways of gender practices in social media," Carranza writes: "The differences have always existed between men and women long before this discussion of gender gap began in social media. According to the Mastersofhealthcare.com there are 10 differences between men's and women's brains." When we follow the Masters of Healthcare link (Hensley 2009), not surprisingly, there is an entry for language. Under each of the 10 items listed, the reader is invited to explore additional links that investigate male–female difference in ever greater detail.

3. Quantitative Media Data

As a complement to an account of the qualitative public rendering of scholarly work on language and gender, I explored three data sources (the Corpus of Contemporary American English (COCA), Google Trends, and LexisNexis Academic) to examine the degree of press coverage given to the topics "gender" and "the

Table 32.1. Keyword "Gender" in the Corpus of Contemporary American English

	Spoken	Fiction	Magazine	Newspaper	Academic	1990–4	1995–9	2000–4	2005–9	2010–11
Frequency	1,170	626	2,187	1,499	17,757	3,986	5,143	5,649	7,364	1,097
Per million words	12.99	7.37	24.22	17.30	206.98	38.33	49.72	54.88	72.18	43.24

Table 32.2. Keyword "Gender Difference" in the Corpus of Contemporary American English

	Spoken	Fiction	Magazine	Newspaper	Academic	1990–4	1995–9	2000–4	2005–9	2010–11
Frequency	12	3	10	3	241	38	49	81	91	10
Per million words	0.13	0.04	0.11	0.03	2.81	0.37	0.47	0.79	0.89	0.39

brain." I started with the Corpus of Contemporary American English, an online corpus of 425 million words (Davis 2012). A search of the database for the terms "gender" and "gender difference" revealed an overall increase in the use of these terms in spoken language, fiction, magazine, newspaper and academic prose for each of the five-year intervals considered from 1990 to 2009. Tables 32.1 and 32.2 display the raw numbers as well as the results normalized per million words; the normalized numbers reveal a steady increase in the occurrence of both "gender" and "gender difference" without regard for the type or number of sources considered. (Note that the last column is for the single year 2010–2011. We learn that the normalized totals for the occurrence of the terms "gender" and "gender difference" were greater in the one year, 2010–2011, than in the five- year period 1990–1994.)

I turned next to Google Trends, a tool provided by Google, arguably today's most powerful and widely used search engine. Google Trends shows "how often [a topic has] been searched on Google over time. [It] also shows how frequently … topics have appeared in Google News stories."[11] The time-line begins in 2004 and continues through the first half of 2012. All results are normalized to account for differences in regional interest in topics. As seen in Figures 32.2 to 32.5, Google Trends presents two types of information, represented by two vacillating horizontal lines: the top line displays the volume of search frequency; the bottom line shows how often the topic/ term appeared in Google news stories. (Zero on the graph indicates insufficient search volume for the purpose of graphing. The capital letters shown on the graphs refer to sample articles which have been omitted in this discussion.) I explored the frequency of searches related to gender and to the brain. By comparing Figures 32.2 and 32.3 ("gender studies" and "brain studies") and Figures 32.4 and 32.5 ("gender difference" and "brain difference"), we learn that in each case, searches for "gender" predate

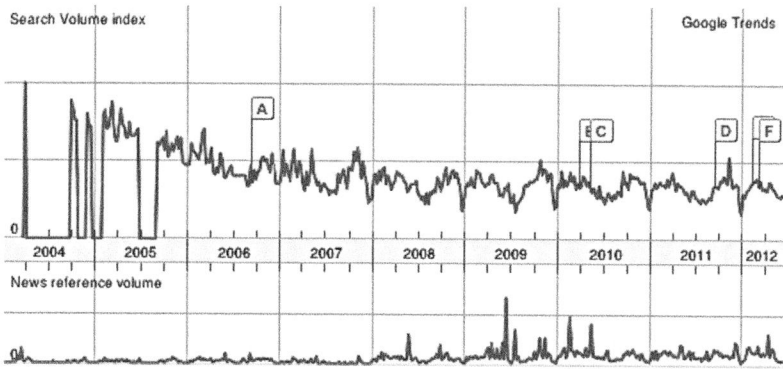

Figure 32.2. Google Trends: search term "gender studies" (Google and the Google logo are registered trademarks of Google Inc., used with permission)

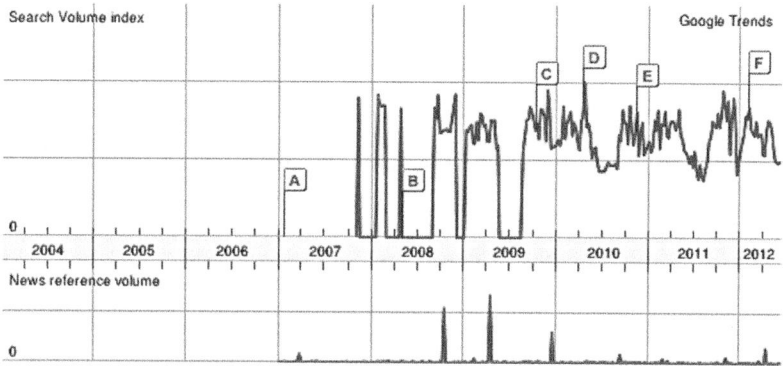

Figure 32.3. Google Trends: search term "brain studies" (Google and the Google logo are registered trademarks of Google Inc., used with permission)

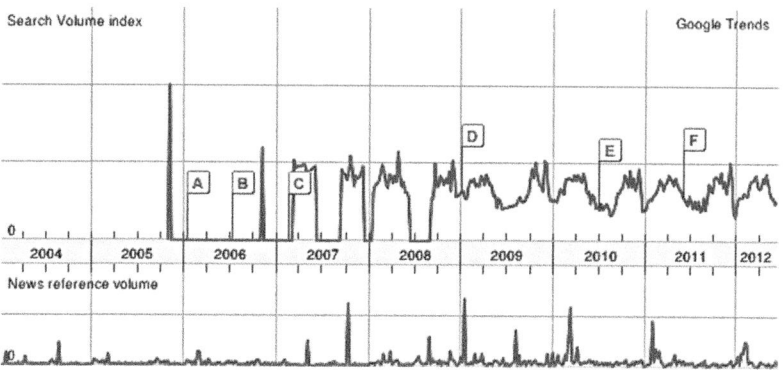

Figure 32.4. Google Trends: search term "gender difference" (Google and the Google logo are registered trademarks of Google Inc., used with permission)

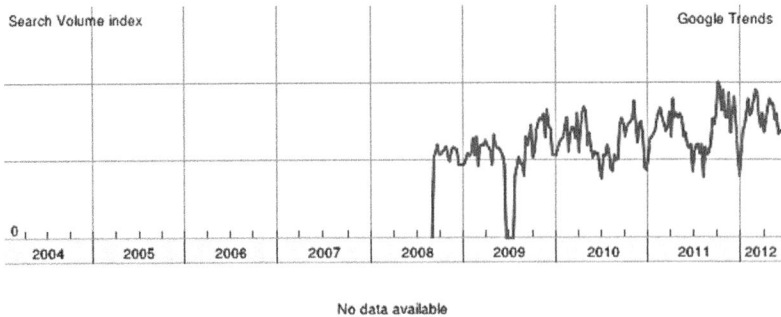

Figure 32.5.   Google Trends: search terms "brain difference" (Google and the Google logo are registered trademarks of Google Inc., used with permission)

those for topics related to the "brain." The numbers for searches related to the brain first appeared at the end of 2007 and the beginning of 2008. Although these trends show neither the content of the searches nor the details of the news stories associated with them, what we discover is that, relative to each other, since 2007 searches for information about the brain have been equal to or have surpassed searches related to gender.

A third search, using the database LexisNexis Academic[12] for "All News" (English-language news), provided still more evidence of the trend of increased media attention in the past three decades to "sex differences," "gender differences," "brain studies," and "brain and gender differences." "All News" considers sources from traditional and nontraditional (web-based) publications, blog posts, the Internet, and so on. The search turned up an unambiguous pattern of growing public exposure to news stories that include reference to sex, gender, brain studies, and/or male–female difference. These patterns are displayed in Figures 32.6 and 32.7. LexisNexis does not specify the size of their database at different periods of time; concerned that the changing size of the database could skew the results, I also searched for the same set of terms by decades in one newspaper at a time. I examined six individual newspapers, four American and two British papers that span the political spectrum from "progressive" to "conservative." Three periods of time were considered for each search: 1980–1990; 1990–2000; 2000–2010. The terms considered were: "gender difference," "sex difference," "brain difference," "brain and gender and language," "language and brain," "brain studies," "gender studies," and "brain and gender."

In all eight searches, the overall occurrence of news items that mention sex, gender, and/or the brain increased in each of the decades considered, from 1980 to 2010. Figure 32.6 exhibits the results for the whole database "English Language News." (The highest number displayed is 3,000; LexisNexis interrupts a search when there are more than 3,000 results returned.) Figure 32.7 presents the same series of searched terms as they appeared in the *New York Times*. While the increase shown is less dramatic for this single news source, the pattern of rising attention to these topics is revealed for all but one ("sex difference") of the items considered.

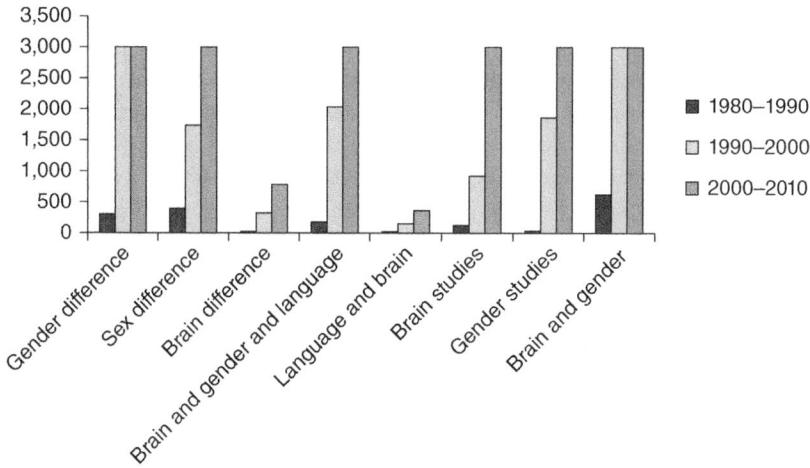

Figure 32.6. LexisNexis Academic: All-English News

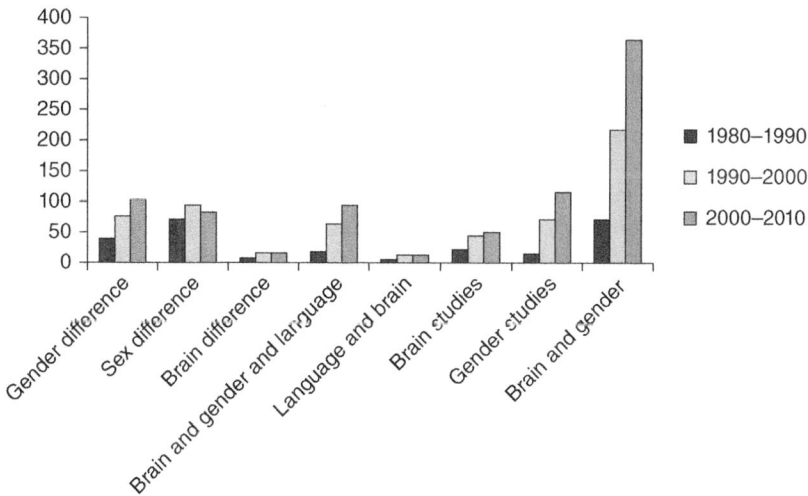

Figure 32.7. LexisNexis Academic: *New York Times*

The pattern of increased media coverage shown for "All English Language News" for the decades 1980–1990, 1990–2000, and 2000–2010 was also confirmed in the other five sources examined.

4. Conclusion

Despite the enormous social changes that have taken place since 2003, little has shifted in the media's depiction of how women and men behave and how they talk.

Popular representations of women and men rarely suggest that the boundaries between the sexes are becoming fuzzier – even if they are – or that the edges of the two-gender system are softening. The public continues to be exposed to verbal and pictorial renderings of men and women that conform to traditional assumptions and common misperceptions about sex and gender. Beliefs and generalizations about language use that have been successfully refuted by careful linguistic analysis remain unchanged in the public sphere. Popular culture still instructs us that "boys will be boys," that heterosexuality is the sexual imperative for humans, and that the battle between the sexes rages on. In sum, the flood of published and broadcast reports about differences between women and men has continued unabated since I reported on this in 2003. What was commonplace in print and broadcast news before 2000 is now supplemented by a deluge of Internet news, cable TV channels, and personal and private Internet blogs. These undocumented and distorted media reports about sex and gender difference may partially explain the persistent and continuing discrepancy between public perceptions of how we speak and the empirical findings of our field, but something else seems to be fueling this significant disparity.

In the past I argued that this trend might be a response to an unexpressed fear that the distinction between the sexes was breaking down, and that social changes taking place were arousing public resistance to variability in patterns of gendered behavior. I suggested, as Cameron (1995, 202) argues, that alarm about gender instability was inspiring an emphasis on difference; "It is striking," she reminds us, "that popular discourse on gender, though seemingly prompted by the increasing complexity and fuzziness of gender boundaries, continues to be organized around a simple binary opposition." It seemed then, as now, that the attention being conferred on male and female difference is due in part to the gradual realization that things are not entirely what they seem. Perhaps as Cameron (1997) suggests, the insistence on gendered behavior is part of the mechanism not only for creating but also for attempting to maintain gendered behavior. The real threat to the two-gender system may be that people are beginning to experience first hand the constructed nature of gender and are grasping the degree to which gender is "performed" and variable. Perhaps people are increasingly aware that we are able to create and recreate ourselves in part through the enormous flexibility of human language. (See also Cameron, Chapter 14 in this volume, for discussion.)

The signs of gender destabilization that we began to witness in the last quarter of the twentieth century are indeed proliferating, and conceptualizations about sexual and gendered behavior are in flux. The website Care2 Make a Difference (www.care2.com) reported in January 2012 that gay or lesbian public officials were serving openly in 48 of the 50 states in the United States. According to the Victory Fund (Keen 2012), the national election in the United States in November 2012 saw an unprecedented increase in the success of openly gay and lesbian candidates, with contests in 37 states and an overall success rate of 77 percent compared to a 65 percent victory rate in 2010.

J. C. Penney, one of the 50 largest US retailers, engaged Ellen DeGeneres, an openly gay entertainer, as its public commercial spokesperson above the objections of the antigay group, One Million Moms (a division of the American Family Association), which wanted her fired because she is a lesbian. J. C. Penney CEO Ron Johnson countered, "we stand squarely behind Ellen as our spokesperson … [b]ecause she shares the same values that we do in our company" (*Huffpost Gay Voices* 2012). The American primary presidential elections of 2008 saw the first nearly successful candidacy of a female candidate when Hillary Clinton ran neck and neck against Barack Obama for the Democratic presidential nomination. The US military policy that prevented gays and lesbians from serving openly ("Don't Ask, Don't Tell") was repealed in September 2011. In February 2011 President Barak Obama ordered the United States Justice Department to abandon its support of the Defense of Marriage Act, a federal law in the United States that defines marriage as the legal union of one man and one woman. Same-sex marriage gained dramatic favor among the general population in the United States, moving from 33 percent supporting it in 2004 to 51 percent in favor, according to polling in early 2013 (Silver 2013). Arguments in favor of the legalization of same-sex marriage were heard before the United States Supreme Court in March 2013.

What remains mysterious, then, is why the strength of our research findings has not enabled us to make inroads into changing or at least adjusting the public discourse on language and the sexes. The relative stability over the past 10 years of the two-sex, two-gendered worldview is all the more disheartening because, during this same period of time, the academic field of language and gender has largely moved away from a difference model, thus making the mismatch between the public and the scholarly view of language and gender even more stark. We might ask how we can move the public to a conceptualization of gender that abandons a strict ideology of male–female "difference" for one that emphasizes human "diversity." "If one challenge for the future is to engage seriously with the revival of biological essentialism, then another must be to find ways of telling more complicated stories in ways a wider audience will find compelling" (Cameron 2005, 500). Or, as Janet Hyde concludes in "The Gender Similarities Hypothesis":

> It is time to consider the costs of overinflated claims of gender differences. Arguably, they cause harm in numerous realms, including women's opportunities in the workplace, couple conflict and communication, and analyses of self esteem problems among adolescents. Most important, these claims are not consistent with the scientific data. (Hyde 2005, 590)

Our struggle is to change public discourse about language and gender to a realistic view that recognizes the role that language plays in our lives. We need to educate the public that language itself can be instrumental in "creating and sustaining (and sometimes challenging and changing) all the varied kinds of beliefs and practices that inform gender and sexual identities, relations, practices and ideologies" (McConnell-Ginet 2011, 15).

5. Postscript

When I was making the final edits to this chapter, an article appeared in the Sunday *New York Times* (April 21, 2013) that addresses some of the issues that I discuss above about the popular press. In "The Tangle of the Sexes," authors Bobbi Carothers (a data analyst) and Harry Reisapril (a psychologist) argue against categorical sex difference and explain how their own research shows how similar men and women are:

> Across analyses spanning 122 attributes from more than 13,000 individuals, one conclusion stood out: instead of dividing into two groups, men and women overlapped considerably on attributes like the frequency of science-related activities, interest in casual sex, or the allure of a potential mate's virginity … Even stereotypical traits, like assertiveness or valuing close friendships, fell along a continuum. In other words, we found little or no evidence of categorical distinctions based on sex. (Carothers and Reisapril 2013)

Maybe there is hope after all.

NOTES

1 A striking example of evolutionary biology's take on language is John Locke's *Duels and Duets: Why Men and Women Talk So Differently* (2011). What Locke writes is quite similar to what Deborah Tannen wrote in 1990 in *You Just Don't Understand*, but Locke argues that what characterizes women's and men's speech comes from our evolutionary past and not from cultural norms.

2 An off-shoot of the narrative is that gay men and lesbians are "different" from heterosexuals and that they, too, constitute distinct social groups. The irony of this view is that it reveals (but this is never stated) that the public actually does not think that all women and all men are "the same."

3 Some of the most influential books on "brain research" are Simon Baron-Cohen's *The Essential Difference: The Truth about the Male and Female Brain* (2003); Louanne Brizendine's *The Female Brain* (2006); and Steven Pinker's *The Blank Slate: The Modern Denial of Human Nature* (2002) and *The Sexual Paradox: Men, Women, and the Real Gender Gap* (2008). New York: Scribner. These are not otherwise cited in this chapter.

4 Among studies, textbooks, collections, and reviews published since 2000 that are useful for an overview of the past decade are Cameron 2005; Cameron and Kulick 2003; Eckert and McConnell-Ginet 2003; Ehrlich 2007a; Goodwin, 2006; Inoue 2006; McConnell-Ginet 2011; Stokoe 2005; Sunderland 2006; Talbot 2010; and Stokoe and Weatherall 2002.

5 The online version was published on September 15, 2011. The printed version didn't appear until May 2012, long after the public discussion of the study had taken place.

6 The relative pitch of the male and female participants' voices was not taken into account.

7 At http://today.msnbc.msn.com/id/26184891/vp/45681253#45681253, accessed November 4, 2013.

8 See also *Language Log*, an online language blog maintained by University of Pennsylvania phonetician Mark Liberman at http://languagelog.ldc.upenn.edu/nll/. Specific to the topic of "talkativeness" is Liberman (2006b).

9   For an earlier comparison of studies related to "talkativeness" see James and Drakich (1993).
10   There is a large literature on gender and humor. See, among others, Norrick and Chiaro 2009; Schnurr 2009.
11   At http://itools.com/tool/google-trends-topic-popularity, accessed November 12, 2013.
12   At http://www.lexisnexis.com/en-us/products/lexisnexis-academic.page, accessed November 13, 2013.

REFERENCES

Abdelli-Beruh, Nassima B., Lesley Wolk, Dianne Slavin, and Ellen James. 2011. "Gender Differences in the Prevalence of Vocal Fry in Young Adult English Speakers." Paper presented at the American Speech–Language–Hearing Association (ASHA) Convention, San Diego, November 17–20, 2011.

Ahearn, Laura M. 2012. "Language and Gender." In *Living Language: An Introduction to Linguistic Anthropology*, 187–213. Oxford: Wiley-Blackwell.

Baron-Cohen, Simon. 2003. *The Essential Difference: The Truth about the Male and Female Brain*. New York: Basic Books.

Bing, Janet, and Victoria Bergvall. 1996. "The Question of Questions: Beyond Binary Thinking." In Victoria Bergvall, Janet Bing, and Alice F. Freed (eds.), *Rethinking Language and Gender Research: Theory and Practice*, 1–30. London: Longman.

Bolinger, Dwight. 1989. *Intonation and Its Uses: Melody in Grammar and Discourse*. Stanford: Stanford University Press.

Brenner, Joanna. 2013. "Pew Internet: Mobile." *Pew Internet and American Life Project*. At http://pewinternet.org/Commentary/2012/February/Pew-Internet-Mobile.aspx, accessed November 4, 2013.

Brizendine, Louanne. 2006. *The Female Brain*. New York: Morgan Road Books.

Cameron, Deborah. 1995. *Verbal Hygiene*. London: Routledge.

Cameron, Deborah. 1997. "Performing Gender Identity: Young Men's Talk and the Construction of Heterosexual Masculinity." In Sally Johnson and Ulrike Hanna Meinhof (eds.), *Language and Masculinity*, 47–64. Oxford: Blackwell.

Cameron, Deborah. 2005. "Language, Gender, and Sexuality: Current Issues and New Directions." *Applied Linguistics*, 26(4): 482–502.

Cameron, Deborah. 2007. *The Myth of Mars and Venus*. New York: Oxford University Press.

Cameron, Deborah. 2009. "Sex/Gender, Language and the New Biologism." *Applied Linguistics*, 31(2): 173–192.

Cameron, Deborah, and Don Kulick. 2003. *Language and Sexuality*. Cambridge: Cambridge University Press.

Carothers, Bobbi, and Harry Reisapril. 2013. "The Tangle of the Sexes." *New York Times*, April 20, 2013. At http://www.nytimes.com/2013/04/21/opinion/sunday/the-tangle-of-the-sexes.html?ref=opinion&_r=0, accessed November 4, 2013.

Carranza, Anthony. 2012. "Gender Differences Arise in Social Media Use." *Minneapolis Examiner*, April 14, 2012. At http://www.examiner.com/article/gender-differences-arise-social-media-use, accessed November 4, 2013.

Davis, Mark. 2012. "Corpus of Contemporary American English." At http://corpus.byu.edu/coca/, accessed November 13, 2013.

Dillard, Mechele R. 2011. "'Vocal Fry' Sweeping Young Women's Speech Patterns, Study Suggests." *HULIQ*, December 15. At http://www.huliq.com/10473/vocal-fry-sweeping-young-womens-speech-patterns-study-suggests-video, accessed November 4, 2013.

Eckert, Penelope. 2003. "Language and Gender in Adolescence. In Janet Holmes and Miriam Meyerhoff (eds.), *The

Handbook of Language and Gender, 381–400.
Oxford: Blackwell.

Eckert, Penelope, and Sally McConnell-Ginet.
2003. *Language and Gender*. New York:
Cambridge University Press.

Ehrlich, Susan, ed. 2007a. *Language and
Gender*, 4 vols. New York: Routledge.

Ehrlich, Susan. 2007b. "Legal Discourse and
the Cultural Intelligiblity of Gendered
Meanings." *Journal of Sociolinguistics*, 11(4):
452–477.

Fine, Cordelia. 2010. *Delusions of Gender: How
Our Minds, Society, and Neurosexism Create
Difference*. New York: W. W. Norton.

Freed, Alice F. 2003. "Epilogue: Reflections on
Language and Gender Research." In Janet
Holmes and Miriam Meyerhoff (eds.), *The
Handbook on Language and Gender*, 699–721.
Oxford: Blackwell.

Goodwin, Marjorie Harness. 2006. *The Hidden
Life of Girls: Games of Stance, Status and
Exclusion*. Oxford: Blackwell.

Hensley, Amber. 2009. "10 Big Differences
between Men's and Women's Brains."
Masters of Healthcare, June 16. At http://
www.mastersofhealthcare.com/blog/,
accessed November 4, 2013.

Huffpost Gay Voices. 2012. "Ellen DeGeneres'
JCPenney Partnership Defended by
Company CEO Ron Johnson" (video).
February 9. At http://www.huffingtonpost
.com/2012/02/09/ellen-degeneres
-jcpenney-ron-johnson_n_1265833.html,
accessed November 4, 2013.

Hyde, Janet Shibley. 2005. "The Gender
Similarities Hypothesis." *American
Psychologist*, 60(6): 581–592.

Inoue, Miyako. 2006. *Vicarious Language:
Gender and Linguistic Modernity in Japan*.
Berkeley: University of California Press.

Isozio. 2012. "Infographic: uSamp Datapoint
Study Finds Gender Gap over Social
Media Privacy." *uSamp*, January 30. At
http://blog.usamp.com/blog/2012/01/30
/infographic-usamp-datapoint-study-finds
-gender-gap-over-social-media-privacy/,
accessed November 4, 2013.

James, Deborah, and Drakich, Janice. 1993.
"Understanding Gender Differences in
Amount of Talk: A Critical Review of
Research." In Deborah Tannen (ed.),

Gender and Conversational Interaction,
281–312. Oxford: Oxford University Press.

Jordan-Young, Rebecca M. 2010. *Brain Storm:
The Flaws in the Science of Sex Differences*.
Cambridge, MA: Harvard University
Press.

Keen, Lisa. 2012. "LGBT Candidates Score
Long List of Firsts." *Keen News Service*,
November 15. At http://www.keennews
service.com/2012/11/15/lgbt-candidates
-score-long-list-of-firsts/, accessed
November 4, 2013.

Kiderra, Inga. 2011. "Funny Finding: Men
Win Humor Test (by a Hair)." *UC San
Diego News Center*, October 19. At
http://ucsdnews.ucsd.edu/archive
/newsrel/soc/20111019HumorTest.asp,
accessed November 4, 2013.

Lakoff, Robin. 1973. "Language and Woman's
Place." *Language in Society*, 2(1): 45–80.

League, Levo. 2012. "The Art of the Fry:
Female Vocal Trends and Linguistics."
Forbes, February 28. At http://www.forbes
.com/sites/levoleague/2012/02/28/the
-art-of-the-fry-female-vocal-trends-and
-linguistics/, accessed November 4, 2013.

Liberman, Mark. 2006a. "Sex on the Brain."
Boston Globe, September 24, 2006. At
http://www.boston.com/news/globe
/ideas/articles/2006/09/24/sex_on_the
_brain/, accessed November 4, 2013.

Liberman, Mark. 2006b. "Gabby Guys: The
Effect Size." Language Log, September 23.
At http://itre.cis.upenn.edu/~myl
/languagelog/archives/003607.html,
accessed November 4, 2013.

Locke, John. 2011. *Duels and Duets: Why Men
and Women Talk So Differently*. New York:
Cambridge University Press.

McConnell-Ginet, Sally. 2011. "Gender,
Sexuality, and Meaning: An Overview." In
*Gender, Sexuality, and Meaning: Linguistic
Practice and Politics*, 5–31. New York:
Oxford University Press.

Mehl, Matthias R., Simine Vazire, Nairán
Ramírez-Esparza, Richard B. Slatcher, and
James W. Pennebaker. 2007. "Are Women
Really More Talkative Than Men?" *Science*,
317(5834): 82.

Mendoza-Denton, Norma. 2011. "The
Semiotic Hitchhiker's Guide to Creaky
Voice: Circulation and Gendered Hardcore

in a Chicana/o Gang Persona." *Journal of Linguistic Anthropology*, 21(2): 261–280.

Mickes, Laura, Drew E. Walker, Julian L. Parris, Robert Mankoff, and Nicholas J. S. Christenfeld. 2012. "Who's Funny: Gender Stereotypes, Humor Production, and Memory Bias." *Psychonomic Bulletin & Review*, 19(1): 108–112.

Nicholson, Christie. 2011. "A Quirk of Speech May Become a New Vocal Style." Scientific American, December 17. At http://www .scientificamerican.com/podcast/episode .cfm?id=a-quirk-of-speech-may-become-a -new-11-12-17, accessed November 4, 2013.

Norrick, Neal R., and Delia Chiaro, eds. 2009. *Humor in Interaction*. Amsterdam: Benjamins.

Pew Internet. 2013. "Trend Data (Adults)." *Pew Internet and American Life Project*. At http://www.pewinternet.org/Trend-Data -(Adults)/Device-Ownership.aspx, accessed November 4, 2013.

Pinker, Steven. 2002. *The Blank Slate: The Modern Denial of Human Nature*. New York: Viking.

Pinker, Steven. 2008. *The Sexual Paradox: Men, Women, and the Real Gender Gap*. New York: Scribner.

Podesva, Robert. 2007. "Phonation Type as a Stylistic Variable: The Use of Falsetto in Constructing a Persona." *Journal of Sociolinguistics*, 11(4): 478–504.

Quenqua, Douglas. 2012. "They're, Like, Way Ahead of the Linguistic Currrrve." *New York Times*, February 27. At http://www .nytimes.com/2012/02/28/science/young -women-often-trendsetters-in-vocal -patterns.html?pagewanted=all, accessed November 4, 2013.

Ryan, Erin Gloria. 2012. "Everyone Totes Copying How Young Women, Like, Talk and Stuff." *Jezebel*, February 27. At http://jezebel.com/5888758/everyone -totes-copying-how-young-women-like -talk-and-stuff, accessed November 4, 2013.

Schnurr, Stephanie, 2009. *Leadership Discourse at Work: Interactions of Humour, Gender and Workplace Culture* (electronic resource). Basingstoke: Palgrave Macmillan.

Silver, Nate. 2013. "How Opinion on Same-Sex Marriage is Changing, and What It Means." *New York Times*, March 26. At http://fivethirtyeight.blogs.nytimes.com /2013/03/26/how-opinion-on-same-sex -marriage-is-changing-and-what-it-means/, accessed November 4, 2013.

Stokoe, Elizabeth H. 2005. "Analysing Gender and Language." *Journal of Sociolinguistics*, 9: 118–133.

Stokoe, Elizabeth, and Ann Weatherall, eds. 2002. "Guest Editorial: Gender, Language, Conversation Analysis and Feminism." *Discourse & Society* (special issue), 13(6): 707–713.

Sunderland, Jane. 2006. *Gender and Language: An Advanced Resourcebook*. London: Routledge.

Tannen, Deborah. 1990. *You Just Don't Understand: Women and Men in Conversation*. New York: William Morrow.

Tannen, Deborah. 2007. "Who Does the Talking Here?" *Washington Post*, July 15, 2007. At http://www.washingtonpost.com /wp-dyn/content/article/2007/07/13 /AR2007071301815.html, accessed November 4, 2013.

Talbot, Mary. 2010. *Language and Gender*, 2nd edn. Cambridge: Polity.

Wolk, Lesley, Nassima B. Abdelli-Beruh, and Dianne Slavin. 2012. "Habitual Use of Vocal Fry in Young Adult Female Speakers." *Journal of Voice*, 26(3): 111–116.

Index

Page numbers in *italics* refer to figures; those in **bold** refer to tables.

The Handbook of Language, Gender, and Sexuality, Second Edition.
Edited by Susan Ehrlich, Miriam Meyerhoff, and Janet Holmes.
© 2014 John Wiley & Sons, Inc. Published 2017 by John Wiley & Sons, Inc.

Printed and bound by CPI Group (UK) Ltd, Croydon, CR0 4YY
26/08/2021
03080587-0001